HISTORIC DOCUMENTS OF 1987

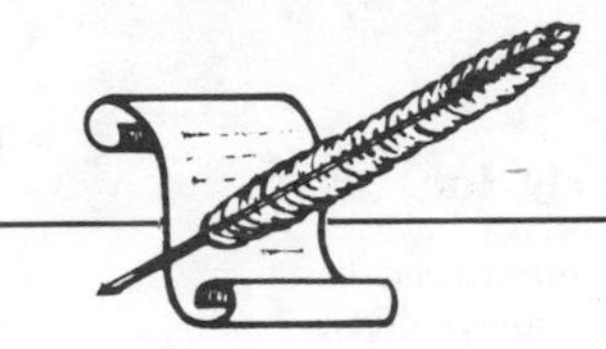

HISTORIC DOCUMENTS OF 1987

Cumulative Index, 1983-1987

Congressional Quarterly Inc.

Printed in the United States of America

Congressional Quarterly Inc.
1414 22nd St. N.W., Washington, D.C. 20037

The Library of Congress cataloged the first issue of this title as follows:

Historic documents. 1972—
Washington. Congressional Quarterly Inc.

1. United States — Politics and government — 1945— —Yearbooks. 2. World politics — 1945— —Yearbooks. I. Congressional Quarterly Inc.

E839.5H57 917.3'03'9205 72-97888

ISBN 0-87187-445-8

ISSN 0892-080X

Historic Documents of 1987

Editor: Carolyn McGovern
Assistant Editors: Jane S. Gilligan, Amy S. Meyers
Contributors: Noelle Beatty, Bryan de Boinville, Catherine Buckley, Linda Busetti, Kimberly A. Davis, Charles Dervarics, Daniel C. Diller, Carolyn Goldinger, James R. Ingram, Richard Karno, Marc Leepson, Sara Lowen, Mary L. McNeil, Jodean Marks, Richard Marshall, Dirk Olin, Patricia Pine, Michael Pleasants, Susan Santo, Elizabeth H. Summers, Park Teter, Margaret C. Thompson, Pat Towell, Jane S. Wilson
Indexer: Victoria Agee

Congressional Quarterly Inc.

Eugene Patterson *Chairman*
Andrew Barnes *President*
Wayne P. Kelley *Publisher*
Neil Skene *Executive Editor*
John J. Coyle *General Manager, Electronic Information Services*
Robert E. Cuthriell *Director of Development, Electronic Information Services*
Jonathan C. Angier *Business Manager*
Robert C. Hur *General Counsel*

Book Division

Robert C. Hur *Director*

Book Editorial

David R. Tarr *Director, Book Department*
John L. Moore *Assistant Director*
Joanne D. Daniels *Director, CQ Press*
Mary W. Cohn *Associate Editor*
Nancy A. Lammers *Managing Editor*
Carolyn Goldinger *Senior Editor*
Margaret Seawell Benjaminson *Project Editor*
Ann Pelham Cullen *Project Editor*
Ann Davies *Project Editor*
Carolyn McGovern *Project Editor*
Colleen McGuiness *Project Editor*
Jane S. Gilligan *Production Editor*
Kerry V. Kern *Production Editor*
Kimberly A. Davis *Editorial Assistant*
Richard Karno *Editorial Assistant*
Noell H. Sottile *Editorial Assistant*
Linda White *Secretary*

Book Marketing

Kathryn C. Suárez *Director, Book Marketing*
Jacqueline A. Davey *Sales Promotion Coordinator*
Ellen Kresky *College Services Coordinator*

Production

I. D. Fuller *Production Manager*
Maceo Mayo *Assistant Production Manager*

PREFACE

Publication of *Historic Documents of 1987* carries through a sixteenth year the project Congressional Quarterly launched with *Historic Documents of 1972*. The purpose of this series is to give students, scholars, librarians, journalists, and citizens convenient access to documents of basic importance in the broad range of public affairs.

To place the documents in perspective, each entry is preceded by a brief introduction explaining the historical background, the main points, reactions to the document, and in some cases subsequent developments. We believe these introductions will prove increasingly useful in the future, when the events and issues are no longer in the public eye and the documents are more difficult to locate.

Historic Documents of 1987 contains official statements, Supreme Court decisions, reports, special studies, communiqués, treaties, and speeches related to events of national and international significance and, in our judgment, of lasting interest. Where space limitations prevent reproduction of a full text, we have chosen excerpts that provide essential details and preserve the flavor of the whole.

The documents that appear in the 1987 volume reflect the power of foreign affairs to drive domestic events. The Tower commission and the congressional investigating committees laid to rest some of the nation's questions about the Iran-contra affair, but the Middle East and Central America continued to preoccupy Americans.

The Iran-Iraq war was a major topic of discussions at the Venice Economic Summit of the seven largest industrialized democracies, at the Arab Summit in Amman, Jordan, and in the UN Security Council. We include documents from all three. The Reagan administration responded to heightened tensions in the Persian Gulf by reflagging and escorting Kuwaiti oil tankers in the area. Two U.S. Navy reports on the Iraqi attack on the USS *Stark* appear in this volume.

President Oscar Arias Sánchez of Costa Rica succeeded in bringing together five Central American presidents to sign a regional peace plan, dramatically changing the nature of the contra aid debate in the U.S. Congress. Both the text of the agreement and Arias's Nobel Peace Prize acceptance speech are included in *Historic Documents*.

General Secretary Mikhail S. Gorbachev consolidated his power in the Soviet Union, announced personnel reforms in the Communist party, reexamined Soviet historical figures such as Stalin and Khrushchev, and came to Washington to meet with President Ronald Reagan and sign the INF treaty. Other significant developments included South Korea's first presidential election in forty years, and Corazon Aquino's feisty survival, in the face of coup attempts and a strong insurgency, as president of the Philippines. Haiti was not so fortunate; presidential elections ended in a shambles in November, prompting the United States to halt its aid.

Health and medicine continued to be primary concerns in 1987. There were breakthroughs: new information about Alzheimer's disease and Food and Drug Administration approval of drugs to combat heart attacks and AIDS. And there was controversy, as American institutions struggled with the complexities of the AIDS crisis: how to fund AIDS research in a time of burgeoning deficits, how to present educational material, how to care for the afflicted, and how to deal with testing and discrimination. The religious and legal implications of biotechnology were examined in 1987. Congress's Office of Technology Assessment studied the question of ownership of human tissue. The Vatican denounced the new reproductive technologies, just as a New Jersey judge determined the validity of a contract with a surrogate mother.

The historic events of 1987 have impacts beyond the calendar year and will influence the issues discussed in years to come. The stock market crash inspired numerous reassessments of how the market works and how it is regulated. The FCC's ruling on the fairness doctrine in broadcasting will affect the 1988 presidential election campaign. The debate on the ABM treaty interpretation will fuel controversies over SDI development and the treaty ratification process. *Historic Documents* will continue to chronicle these and other significant events.

Carolyn McGovern, Editor

How to Use This Book

The documents are arranged in chronological order. If you know the approximate date of the report, speech, statement, court decision, or other document you are looking for, glance through the titles for that month in the table of contents.

If the table of contents does not lead you directly to the document you want, turn to the index at the end of the book. There you may find references not only to the particular document you seek but also to other entries on the same or a related subject. The index in this volume is a five-year cumulative index of *Historic Documents* covering the years 1983-1987.

The introduction to each document is printed in italic type. The document itself, printed in roman type, follows the spelling, capitalization, and punctuation of the original or official copy. Where the full text is not given, omissions of material are indicated by the customary ellipsis points.

CONTENTS

January

February

March

April

May

June

July

August

September

October

November

December

January

PRESIDENT'S BUDGET MESSAGE

January 5, 1987

President Ronald Reagan submitted his budget requests for fiscal 1988 to Congress January 5, proposing outlays of about $1.024 trillion against revenues of about $916.6 billion. The resulting deficit of approximately $107.8 billion was within the $108-billion deficit-reduction target established by the Balanced Budget and Emergency Deficit Control Act of 1985 (PL 99-177), known as Gramm-Rudman-Hollings after its original sponsors. (Historic Documents of 1985, p. 803)

It was the first time any president had sent a trillion-dollar budget to Congress and the second time that Reagan had submitted a budget under the deficit-reduction legislation. Although Reagan's fiscal 1987 budget had set expenditures at $994 billion, the administration projected early in 1987 that spending would reach $1.016 trillion in that year. (Historic Documents of 1986, p. 49)

Many members of Congress, Republicans as well as Democrats, were quick to criticize Reagan's fiscal 1988 budget, some calling it "dead on arrival" at the Capitol. Some legislators said that the president had achieved the deficit-cutting target only with a combination of roseate economic assumptions, tax increases disguised as user fees (federal taxes paid directly or indirectly by those who benefit from a product or service, such as the gasoline tax), and one-shot savings produced by the proposed sale of federal assets. Indeed, it was manifestly evident that the president's budget embodied old proposals that had been soundly rejected by Congress in the past and new ones that had little chance for enactment.

However, James C. Miller III, director of the Office of Management and Budget (OMB), January 4 defended the budget and said that Reagan would "hang tough" in the face of expected moves by Congress to alter budget priorities. Miller said, "He's not going along with a tax increase, and he's not going along with a big cut in defense. He's not going to touch Social Security, and he wants to get the deficit down."

Deficit Reduction

The president's fiscal 1988 budget failed to reach the targets set by the Gramm-Rudman-Hollings act in every year through 1991 except 1988. In fact, the budget projected a deficit of $21 billion in 1991 when that year's budget, according to the legislation, should be balanced.

Many observers believed that time had run out on Reagan's efforts to reduce the federal debt, which had grown enormously during his years in office. They pointed to Reagan's weakened political posture as a result of Democratic control of the Senate and the unfolding Iran-contra affair.

Whether Reagan's fiscal 1988 budget would produce a deficit of less than the mandated $108 billion was widely doubted. The Congressional Budget Office (CBO) released a preliminary estimate January 20 that projected a fiscal 1988 deficit of between $135 billion and $140 billion. Sen. Lawton Chiles, D-Fla., chairman of the Senate Budget Committee, remarked, "What we have here is a tacit admission that the deficit can't be erased with spending cuts alone."

Budget Proposals

Reagan's fiscal 1988 budget proposed substantial cuts in such major domestic programs as food stamps, school lunches, and student loans. Also among the budget reductions were cuts of $7.7 billion in major federal medical programs. Reductions of $4.7 billion in the Medicare program would be made largely in payments to hospitals and physicians.

On the other hand, the budget request for the nation's defense included increases for the MX and Minuteman intercontinental missile programs and for the Strategic Defense Initiative (SDI) program. Funding for SDI would grow from $3.6 billion in fiscal 1987 to $5.9 billion in fiscal 1988. The national defense spending level was designed to provide 3 percent growth after inflation. That level would be achieved with a total fiscal 1988 defense request of $297.6 billion. Yet the increase, Reagan administration officials said, was still too small to fund adequately the rearmament program pushed during the Reagan years in the White House.

In addition to program cuts, the president's budget provided additional revenues from the sale of such federal assets as Amtrak's "Northeast corridor" and five power-marketing administrations. The budget estimated that the sale of such properties together with the sale of government loans would produce more than $10 billion.

Congressional Reaction

Rep. William H. Gray III, D-Pa., chairman of the House Budget Committee, commented January 5 that the budget "raised fairness questions that Congress will be asking." Gray also pointed to "hidden taxes" contained in the budget, some of them in the form of new or increased user fees.

Sen. Pete V. Domenici, R-N.M., the ranking Republican member of the Senate Budget Committee, said the budget underestimated the size of the deficit and the amount of "savings" needed to meet the Gramm-Rudman-Hollings target. Sen. John Glenn, D-Ohio, declared that the president had presented "the most consistently unrealistic budget in the history of our country." According to Sen. Mark Hatfield, R-Ore., the fiscal 1988 budget represented the "utter and complete failure of the administration to meet the problem of the deficit."

Economic Assumptions

The predictions of revenues and expenditures in the president's budget were based on a collection of economic assumptions. Differences in forecasts of how the U.S. economy would perform in coming years could result in substantial differences in estimates of revenue and spending. Many congressional leaders and economists criticized a number of the assumptions of the fiscal 1988 budget as overly optimistic.

The fiscal 1988 budget assumed that the gross national product (GNP) would increase from $4,218 billion in 1986 to $4,493 billion in 1987 and to $6,214 billion in 1992. The budget also projected a 3.3 percent inflation rate in 1987, rising slightly to 3.5 percent in 1988. It forecast that the unemployment rate would be 6.7 percent in 1987 and would drop to 6.3 percent in 1988. Finally, it predicted that the "short" interest rate would fall from 6 percent in 1986 to 5.4 percent in 1987, rising again to 5.6 percent in 1988.

Following is the text of President Ronald Reagan's January 5, 1987, budget message to Congress:

To the Speaker of the House of Representatives and the President of the Senate:

The current economic expansion, now in its 50th month, is already one of the longest of the postwar era and shows promise of continuing to record length. This has not been due simply to chance—it is the result of successful policies adopted during the past 6 years. Disposable personal income is at an all-time high and is still rising; total production and living standards are both increasing; employment gains have been excellent. Inflation, which raged at double-digit rates in 1980, has been reduced dramatically. Defense capabilities, which had been dangerously weakened during the 1970's, have been substantially rebuilt, restoring a more adequate level of national security. An insupportable growth in tax burdens and Federal regulations has been halted, an intolerably complex and inequitable income tax structure has been radically reformed, and the largest management improvement program ever attempted is in full swing in all major Federal agencies. It has been a good 6 years.

Now in its 5th year, the current expansion already has exceeded 5 of the 7 previous postwar expansions in duration, and leading economic indicators point to continued growth ahead. Our policies have worked. Let me mention a few highlights of the current economic expansion:

- In the past 4 years 12.4 million new jobs have been created, while the total unemployment rate has fallen by 3.7 percentage points. By comparison, jobs in other developed countries have not grown significantly, and unemployment rates have remained high.
- Inflation, which averaged 10.3 percent a year during the 4 years before I came to office, has averaged less than a third of that during the last 4 years—3.0 percent; inflation in 1986, at about 1 percent, was at its lowest rate in over two decades.
- The prime rate of interest, and other key interest rates, are less than half what they were in 1981.
- Between 1981 and 1986, numerous changes in the tax code, including a complete overhaul last year, have simplified reporting, made the tax law more equitable, and significantly lowered tax rates for individuals and corporations. Six million low-income taxpayers are being removed from the income tax rolls. The inhibitive effect of our tax code on individual initiative has been reduced dramatically. Real after-tax personal income has risen 15 percent during the last 4 years, increasing our overall standard of living.
- Our defense capabilities have been strengthened with modernized equipment and successful recruiting and retention of higher caliber personnel; the readiness, training, and morale of our troops has been improved.
- After years of unsustainably rapid growth, Federal spending for domestic programs other than entitlements has been held essentially flat over the last 4 years.
- Since 1981, the amount of time spent by the public filling out forms required by the Federal Government has been cut by over 600 million hours, and the number of pages published annually in the *Federal Register* has been reduced by over 45 percent.
- Our continuing fight against waste, fraud, and abuse in Government programs has paid off, as the President's Council on Integrity and Efficiency has saved $84 billion in funds that have been put to more efficient use.
- Finally, Federal agencies have instituted the largest management improvement program ever attempted to bring a more business-like approach to Government.

The dramatic improvement in the performance of our economy stemmed from steadfast adherence to the four fundamental principles of the economic program I presented in February 1981:

- limiting the growth of Federal spending;
- reducing tax burdens;
- relieving the economy of excessive regulation and paperwork; and
- supporting a sound and stable monetary policy.

Need for Deficit Reduction

The foundation has been laid for a sustained era of national prosperity. But a major threat to our future prosperity remains: the Federal deficit. If this deficit is not brought under control by limiting Government spending, we put in jeopardy all we have achieved. Deficits brought on by continued high spending threaten the lower tax rates incorporated in tax reform and inhibit progress in our balance of trade.

We cannot permit this to happen. Therefore, one of the major objectives of this budget is to assure a steady reduction in the deficit until a balanced budget is reached.

This budget meets the $108 billion deficit target for 1988 set out in the Balanced Budget and Emergency Deficit Control Act, commonly known for its principal sponsors as Gramm-Rudman-Hollings. Gramm-Rudman-Hollings committed both the President and Congress to a fixed schedule of progress toward reducing the deficit. In submitting this budget, I am keeping my part of the bargain—and on schedule. I ask Congress to do the same. If the deficit reduction goals were to be abandoned, we could see unparalleled spending growth that this Nation cannot afford.

This budget shows that eliminating the deficit over time is possible *without* raising taxes, *without* sacrificing our defense preparedness, and *without* cutting into legitimate programs for the poor and the elderly, while at the same time providing needed additional resources for other high priority programs.

Deficit Reduction in 1988

Although the deficit has equalled or exceeded 5 percent of the gross national product (GNP) in each of the past 4 years, each year I have proposed a path to lower deficits—involving primarily the curtailment of unnecessary domestic spending. Congress, however, has rejected most of these proposals; hence, our progress toward reducing the deficit has been much more modest than it could have been.

This year there appears to be a major turn for the better. The 1987 deficit is estimated to be about $48 billion less than in 1986 and should decline to less than 4 percent of GNP. As the economy expands, Federal receipts will rise faster than the increase in outlays Congress enacted for the year.

However, there is no firm guarantee that progress toward a steadily smaller deficit and eventual budget balance will continue. On a current services basis the deficit will continue to decline over the next 5 years, but this decline is gradual and vulnerable to potential fiscally irresponsible congressional action on a multitude of spending programs. It is also threatened by the possibility of a less robust economic performance than is projected, for that projection is based on the assumption that the necessary spending cuts will be made.

This 1988 budget can deal the deficit a crucial blow. If the proposals in this budget are adopted and if the economy performs according to the budget assumptions for growth and inflation, then for the second consecutive year the deficit should shrink substantially, by $65 billion, and thus decline to less than 2½ percent of GNP. Reducing the deficit this far would bring it within the range of our previous peacetime experience and bring our goal of a balanced budget much closer to realization.

Moreover, if Congress adopts the proposals contained in this budget, it will ensure additional deficit reductions in future years, because in many cases the savings from a given action, although small in 1988, would mount in later years. Given the good start made in 1987, Congress has an opportunity this year—by enacting this budget—to put the worst of the deficit problem behind us.

Adopting the spending reductions and other reforms proposed in this budget would reduce the Federal deficit an average $54 billion annually for the next 3 years. This represents $220 each year for every individual American and about $600 for every household. I believe this is the appropriate way to deal with the deficit: cutting excessive Federal spending rather than attacking the family budget by increasing taxes, weakening our national security, breaking faith with the poor and the elderly, or ignoring the requirements for additional resources for other high priority programs.

A More Competitive, Productive America

The task of deficit reduction is a formidable one—but it can and should be achieved with serious attention to the effects on America's economy, businesses, State and local governments, social organizations, and individual citizens. Reducing the deficit will reduce the burden the Federal Government places on private credit markets. The specific deficit reduction measures proposed in this budget would also help make our economy more competitive—and more productive. These objectives have been major considerations in the formulation of this budget.

High priority programs must be funded adequately. Despite the very tight overall fiscal environment, this budget provides adequate funds for maintaining and, in selected cases, expanding high priority programs in key areas of national interest. For example:

- essential services and income support for the aged and needy are expanded;
- the prevention, treatment, and research efforts begun in my 1987 drug abuse initiative are continued, while resources devoted to drug law enforcement have tripled since my administration began;
- the budget allocates $85 million to more intensive health care for those with the highest incidence of infant mortality;
- over half a billion dollars is provided for AIDS research and education in 1988—a 28 percent increase above the 1987 level and more than double our 1986 effort (an additional $100 million is provided for AIDS treatment and blood screening by the Veterans Administration and the Department of Defense);
- building upon the Nation's preeminence in basic biomedical research, the budget seeks funding for the full multiyear costs of biomedical research grants made by the National Institutes of Health;
- a $200 million increase over the 1987 level is proposed for compensatory education for educationally disadvantaged children;
- current ineffective programs intended to assist dislocated workers are replaced by an expanded billion-dollar program carefully designed to help those displaced from their jobs move quickly into new careers;
- a 68 percent increase in funding is provided to permit the Federal Aviation Administration to modernize the Nation's air traffic control system; this includes the procurement of doppler radars capable of detecting severe downdrafts that imperil landings and takeoffs at airports where this is a hazard;
- for 1988, $400 million is provided to carry out newly enacted immigration reform legislation;
- substantial increases in funding for clean coal technology demonstrations, as well as research on acid rain formation and environmental effects, are provided to address the acid rain problem; and
- a new civil space technology initiative, together with previously planned increases to construct a space station, develop a national aerospace plane, and foster the commercial development of space, are provided in this budget.

Restoring our national security also has been one of my highest priorities over the past 6 years due to the serious weakness arising from severe underfunding during the middle and late 1970's. Nonetheless, defense and international programs have not escaped the effects of fiscal stringency. The defense budget actually has declined in real terms in each of the past 2 years. This trend cannot be allowed to continue. I am proposing in this budget a 3 percent real increase over last year's appropriated level. This request—some $8 billion less than last year's—is the minimum level consistent with maintaining an adequate defense of our Nation.

Likewise, my request for our international affairs programs is also crucial to our effort to maintain our national security. I urge Congress not to repeat last year's damaging cuts, but rather to fund these programs fully.

The incentive structure for other Federal programs should be changed to promote efficiency and competitiveness. One of the problems with many Federal programs is that they provide payments without encouraging performance or efficiency. They are perceived to be "free" and, therefore, there is potentially unlimited demand. This has to be changed—and this budget proposes creating needed incentives in critical areas.

Our farm price support programs, under the Food Security Act of 1985, are proving much too costly—half again as costly as estimated when the bill was enacted just one year ago. The $25 billion being spent on farm subsidies in 1987 is 14 percent of our total Federal deficit and equivalent to taking $415 of each nonfarm family's taxes to support farmers' incomes—over and above the amount that price supports add to their grocery bills. Some of the provisions of the Act encourage farmers to overproduce just to receive Federal benefits. Other provisions give the greatest benefits to our largest and most efficient agricultural producers instead of to those family farmers most in need of help. My administration will propose amendments to the Food Security Act to focus its benefits on the full-time family farmer by placing effective limitations on the amount paid to large producers and removing the incentive for farmers to overproduce solely to receive Federal payments.

Reform of the medicare physician payment system is also proposed. Under the proposals, medicare would pay for radiology, anesthesiology, and pathology (RAP) services based on average area costs instead of inflationary fee-for-service reimbursements. The current fee-for-service payment distorts incentives and induces inappropriate billing for unneeded services. This initiative would remove the distortions caused by medicare's current reimbursement rules, eliminating a key barrier preventing the restoration of traditional arrangements between RAP physicians and hospital staffs.

The budget proposes continued increases in federally supported basic research that will lead to longer term improvements in the Nation's productivity and global competitiveness. For example, the budget projects a doubling within 5 years of the National Science Foundation's support for academic research. I also propose to increase support for training future scientists and engineers, and to foster greater technology transfer from Government to industry.

Another way of attaching a "value" to Government-provided services—and an incentive to use them only as needed—is to charge user fees where appropriate. Those who receive special Federal services—not the general taxpayer—should bear a greater share of the costs of those services. Accordingly, this budget imposes fees for Federal lending activities, for meat and poultry inspection, for National park and forest facilities, for Coast Guard services, for Customs inspections, and for many other services.

The Government should stop competing with the private sector. The Federal Government interferes with the productivity of the private sector in many ways. One is through borrowing from the credit markets to finance programs that are no longer needed—as in the case of the rural housing insurance fund, direct student financial assistance, urban mass transit discretionary grants, vocational education grants, the Federal Crop Insurance Corporation fund, sewage plant construction grants, justice assistance grants, the Legal Services Corporation, and rural electrification loans. I am proposing in this budget that we terminate these programs and rely instead on private or State and local government provision of these services.

The budget also proposes that a number of programs that have real utility be transferred back to the private sector, through public offerings or outright sales. Following our successful effort to authorize sale of Conrail, I am now proposing the sale of the Naval Petroleum Reserves, AMTRAK, the Alaska Power Administration, the helium program, and excess real property. In addition, I am proposing legislation to authorize study of a possible divestiture of the Southeastern Power Administration. These "privatization" efforts continue to be a high priority of my administration and, I believe, will result in increased productivity and lower total costs of providing these services. The Federal Government needs to provide essential services that are truly public in nature and national in scope. It has no business providing services to individuals that private markets or their State or local governments can provide just as well or better.

The Federal Government should depend more on the private sector to provide ancillary and support services for activities that remain in Federal hands. The budget proposes that the work associated with over 40,000 Federal positions be contracted out to the private sector as yet another way to increase productivity, reduce costs, and improve services.

Federal credit programs should operate through the private markets and reveal their true costs. The Federal Government provides credit for housing, agriculture, small business, education, and many other purposes. Currently, over a trillion dollars of Federal or federally assisted loans are outstanding. Including lending of Government-sponsored enterprises, federally assisted lending amounted to 14 percent of all lending in U.S. credit markets in 1985.

Under current treatment, loan guarantees appear to be "free"; they do not affect the budget until and unless borrowers default. Direct loans are counted as outlays when they are made, but as "negative outlays" when they are repaid; thus, direct loans seem "free" too, inasmuch as it is presumed they will be repaid. But neither direct loans nor loan guarantees are free. Besides the better terms and conditions a borrower gets from the Government, there is the matter of default. When a borrower does not repay a direct loan, the negative outlay does not occur, and this is a subsidy implicit in the original loan transaction. When a borrower defaults on a guaranteed loan, the Government has to make good on repayment—also a program subsidy.

Since these effects are poorly understood and lead to grave inefficiencies in our credit programs, we will ask Congress to enact legislation whereby the true cost to the economy of Federal credit programs would be counted in the budget. By selling a substantial portion of newly made loans to the private sector and reinsuring some newly made guarantees, the implicit subsidy in the current practice will become explicit. This reform will revolutionize the way Federal credit activities are conducted.

The private sector will also be increasingly involved in the management of our huge portfolio of outstanding loans and loan guarantees. Delinquent Federal borrowers will be reported to private credit bureaus, and private loan collection agencies will be used to help in our collection efforts. The Internal Revenue Service (IRS) will expand its "offsetting" of refunds to pay off delinquent Federal debts, and Federal employees who have not paid back Federal loans will have their wages garnished.

Increased role for State and local governments. Over the past 6 years I have sought to return various Federal services to State and local governments—which are in a much better position to respond effectively to the needs of the recipients of these services. To me, this is a question of reorganizing responsibilities within our Federal system in a manner that will result in more productive delivery of the services that we all agree should be provided. Thus, this budget phases out inappropriate Federal Government involvement in local law enforcement, sewage treatment, public schools, and community and regional development. Transportation programs will be consolidated or States will be given greater flexibility in the use of Federal funds for highways, mass transit, and airports.

Federal regulations must be reduced even further to improve productivity. My administration will continue the deregulation and regulatory relief efforts that were begun in 1981. The Task Force on Regulatory Relief, headed by the Vice President, has been reinstated. In the past, excessive Federal regulations and related paperwork have stifled American productivity and individual freedom. We must continue our efforts to streamline the regulatory process and to strike the proper balance between necessary regulation and associated paperwork on the one hand, and the costs of these requirements on the other.

Federal activities should be better managed. The American people deserve the best managed Federal Government possible. Last year, I initiated the Federal Government Productivity Program, with the goal of improving productivity in selected areas by 20 percent by 1992. A substantial portion of total direct Federal employment falls within the program, including such activities as the Department of Agriculture meat and poultry inspection, Navy aircraft maintenance and repair, social security claims processing, National Park maintenance, operation of

Federal prisons, and IRS processing of tax returns.

Credit reform, privatization, productivity improvement, and other proposals will be described in more detail in the *Management Report* to be issued this month. It will also identify further measures to reduce waste, fraud, and abuse; to improve management of the Government's $1.7 trillion cashflow; to institute compatible financial management systems across all Federal agencies; and other initiatives to improve the management of Government operations. These ambitious management reform undertakings, called "Reform '88," constitute the largest management reform effort ever attempted.

The budget also proposes a new approach to paying Federal employees who increase their productivity. I ask that Congress approve a new plan to transform the current system of virtually automatic "within-grade" salary increases for the roughly 40 percent of employees eligible each year for these 3 percent hidden pay raises to one that is "performance-oriented." This will give Federal employees stronger incentives to improve service delivery.

I include with this budget my recommendations for increases in executive level pay for the executive, legislative, and judicial branches of the Federal Government. The Quadrennial Commission report submitted to me on December 15, 1986 documented both the substantial erosion in the real level of Federal executive pay that has occurred since 1969 and the recruitment and retention problems that have resulted, especially for the Federal judiciary. The Commission is to be commended for its diligent and conscientious effort to address the complicated and complex problems associated with Federal pay levels.

Every one of the Quadrennial Commissions that have met over the past 18 years has recognized that a pay increase for key Federal officials was necessary. Each Commission concluded that pay for senior Government officials fell far behind that of their counterparts in the private sector. They also understood that we cannot afford a Government composed primarily of those who are wealthy enough to serve. Unfortunately, the last major Quadrennial Commission pay adjustment was in 1977—a decade ago.

However, I recognize that we are under mandated efforts to reduce the Federal deficit and hold down the costs of Government to the absolute minimum level. In this environment, I do not believe it would be appropriate to implement fully the Quadrennial Commission recommendations.

Accordingly, I have decided to propose a pay increase, but have cut substantially the recommendations made by the Quadrennial Commissioners in their report to me last month. Moreover, I have decided to establish a Career Manager Pay Commission to review and report to me by next August on appropriate pay scales for our elite corps of career Government managers. The pay increases I am proposing to Congress, plus the results of this new Commission, should place Government compensation on a fairer and more comparable footing.

Peace Through Strength

I have become convinced that the only way we can bring our adversaries to the bargaining table for arms reduction is to give them a reason to negotiate—while, at the same time, fulfilling our responsibility to our citizens and allies to provide an environment safe and secure from aggression.

We have built our defense capabilities back toward levels more in accord with today's requirements for security. Modest and sustained growth in defense funding will be required to consolidate the real gains we have made. Because of severe fiscal constraints, we are proceeding at a slower pace than I originally planned, and the budget I propose provides the minimum necessary to ensure an adequate defense.

I am also submitting, for the first time, a two-year budget for National Defense. This will permit greater stability in providing resources for our defense efforts and should lead to greater economy in using these resources.

Budget Process Reform

The current budget process has failed to provide a disciplined and responsible mechanism for consideration of the Federal budget. Budget procedures are cumbersome, complex, and convoluted. They permit and encourage a process that results in evasion of our duty to the American people to budget their public resources responsibly. Last year Congress did not complete action on a budget for 8 months and 2 weeks—2 weeks past the statutory deadline. Except for the initial report of the Senate Budget Committee, Congress missed every deadline it had set for itself just 9 months earlier. In the end, Congress passed a year-long, 389-page omnibus appropriations bill full of excessive and wasteful spending. Because Congress had not completed action on the annual appropriations bills, at one point I was compelled by law to initiate a shutdown of Federal Government activities. Such abrogation of a responsible budget process not only discourages careful, prudent legislation—it encourages excessive spending and waste.

Furthermore, since I, as President, do not have a line-item veto, I had to ignore the many objectionable features of the omnibus appropriations legislation and sign it to avoid a Federal funding crisis. I am sure that many Members of Congress do not approve of this method of budgeting the Federal Government.

Last Fall's funding crisis and its slap-dash resolution are only one of the most obvious manifestations of the flaws in the system. Congress passes budget resolutions (without the concurrence of the President) based on functions; it considers 13 separate, but related, appropriations bills based on agencies, not functions; it develops a reconciliation bill; it passes authorizing legislation, sometimes annually; and it enacts limits on the public debt. The words alone are obscure and confusing; the process behind it is chaotic. The process must be streamlined and made more accountable.

Shortly, I will outline specific reforms designed to make the process more efficient and increase accountability, so that we can give the American people what they deserve from us: a budget that is fiscally responsible and on time.

Conclusion

Looking back over the past 6 years, we can feel a sense of pride and satisfaction in our accomplishments. Inflation has been brought under control. Growth and investment are up, while interest rates, tax rates, and unemployment rates have all come down substantially. A foundation for sustained economic expansion is now in place. Our national security has been restored to more adequate levels. The proliferation of unnecessary and burdensome Federal regulations has been halted. A significant beginning has been made toward curbing the excessive growth of domestic spending. Management of the Government is being improved, with special emphasis on productivity.

Important tasks, however, still remain to be accomplished. The large and stubbornly persistent budget deficit has been a major source of frustration. It threatens our prosperity and our hopes for continued economic growth.

Last year, the legislative and executive branches of Government responded to this threat by mandating gradual, orderly progress toward a balanced budget over the next 4 years. The proposals outlined here achieve the 1988 target while preserving legitimate programs for the aged and needy, providing for adequate national security, devoting more resources to other high-priority activities, and doing this without raising taxes.

This budget presents hard choices which must be faced squarely. Congress must not abandon the statutory deficit targets of Gramm-Rudman-Hollings. Honoring the provisions and promises of this legislation offers the best opportunity for us to escape the chronic pattern of deficit spending that has plagued us for the past half century. We must realize that the deficit problem is also an opportunity of a different kind—an opportunity to construct a new, leaner, better focused, and better managed Federal structure supporting a more productive and more competitive America.

COURT ON MATERNITY LEAVE

January 13, 1987

The Supreme Court affirmed, 6-3, laws requiring employers to grant unpaid pregnancy leave to female employees, saying such measures do not conflict with federal civil rights laws. In California Federal Savings and Loan v. Guerra *the Court upheld a California law requiring disability leave and job reinstatement rights for pregnancy and childbirth even at businesses that have no leave policy for other disabilities. The decision was viewed as a significant advancement for supporters of parental leave legislation on both the state and federal level.*

Justice Thurgood Marshall delivered the opinion of the Court and was joined by Justices William J. Brennan, Jr., Harry A. Blackmun, and Sandra Day O'Connor. Justices John Paul Stevens and Antonin Scalia concurred in the ruling. Justice Byron R. White, joined by Chief Justice William H. Rehnquist and Justice Lewis F. Powell, Jr., dissented.

Background

According to the Bureau of Labor Statistics, between 1965 and 1985 the number of mothers in the U.S. workforce almost doubled, and nearly half of new mothers in 1985 returned to work before their babies were one year old. Although 117 other industrialized nations had national pregnancy or maternity leave policies, the United States relied instead on a patchwork of state laws.

Title VII of the 1964 Civil Rights Act prohibited employment discrimination on a number of grounds, including sex. The Supreme Court had ruled in General Electric Co. v. Gilbert *(1976) that an employee health plan that omitted pregnancy from its list of covered illnesses and accidents was not sexually discriminatory. In reaction, Congress in October 1978 passed the Pregnancy Discrimination Act (PDA), which specifically included pregnancy in the sex discrimination category. One month earlier California had amended its Fair Employment and Housing Act (FEHA) to require employers to provide the pregnant employee up to four months of unpaid leave and reinstatement to the job she held before becoming pregnant. If the previously held position was no longer available, the employer was required to attempt to place the employee in a similar job.*

In January 1982 Lillian Garland, a receptionist for a Los Angeles office of California Federal Savings and Loan, took an unpaid pregnancy disability leave. When Garland notified the company in April that she was able to return to work, she was told her job had been filled and no similar positions were available. Although company policy was to try to provide a similar position for any employee following unpaid leave, California Federal did not guarantee reinstatement. Garland filed a complaint with the state's Department of Fair Employment and Housing, charging the bank with violation of California law.

California Federal claimed the state law conflicted with the PDA, which, the bank argued, required employers to treat pregnancy in a completely neutral manner, thereby prohibiting preferential treatment of pregnant women. A federal district judge agreed with California Federal, but the U.S. Court of Appeals for the Ninth Circuit reversed the decision, arguing that the lower court's interpretation "defies common sense, misinterprets case law, and flouts Title VII and the PDA." The Supreme Court affirmed the decision of the Court of Appeals.

Interpreting Congressional Intent

The majority found that Congress did not intend the PDA to limit the benefits available to pregnant women or to prohibit preferential treatment such as that provided by the California statute. The Court agreed with the Court of Appeals' interpretation that the PDA was meant to be "a floor beneath which pregnancy disability benefits may not drop—not a ceiling above which they may not rise."

The Court rejected arguments that California violated Title VII by discriminating in favor of pregnant women, saying instead that the federal and state statutes shared a common goal—"to achieve equality of employment opportunities." The California law would be discriminatory, the decision noted, if it were founded on "archaic or stereotypical" notions about pregnant women's ability to work; but that was not the case.

The majority emphasized the limits of the California statute, noting that it covered only the "period of actual physical disability *on account of pregnancy, childbirth or related medical conditions." The law "does not compel California employers to treat pregnant workers* better *than other disabled employees; it merely establishes benefits that employers must, at a minimum, provide to pregnant workers." Companies could provide the same benefits to other disabled employees and the benefit mandated by the law was "only . . . a qualified right to reinstatement."*

Justice White's dissent argued that the California law directly conflicted with the PDA. The wording of the federal law "mandates that pregnant employees 'shall be treated the same for all employment-related purposes' as nonpregnant employees. . . . This language leaves no room for preferential treatment of pregnant workers." The dissent contended that Congress did not design the PDA to allow preferential treatment. Rather, "Congress intended employers . . . to provide any level of disability benefits they wished—or none at all—as long as pregnancy was not a factor in allocating such benefits."

Reaction

Employer groups who had opposed the California law, led by the U.S. Chamber of Commerce, reacted with dismay, but supporters of broad-based legislation defining childbirth and parental leave rights were encouraged. Chamber of Commerce attorney Paula Connelly said the ruling seemed to "leave no limit on what the states can do . . . in terms of favorable treatment. Preferential leave and reinstatement and even paid leave" could be legislated.

Rep. Patricia Schroeder, D-Colo., who was preparing to introduce a bill requiring unpaid parental leave with job reinstatement rights, said the Court's ruling had "opened the doors" for her bill. Eleanor Smeal, president of the National Organization for Women, hailed the ruling as a "clear win" for women, although her organization had argued against the law. Joining with the American Civil Liberties Union, the feminist group had been concerned that preferential treatment for pregnant employees might make employers reluctant to hire women of childbearing age and had argued for uniform job reinstatement rights for all disabled workers.

Following are excerpts from the Supreme Court's January 13, 1987, decision in California Federal Savings and Loan v. Guerra, *ruling that laws requiring employers to grant unpaid pregnancy leave to female employees are not discriminatory, and from the dissenting opinion of Justice Byron R. White:*

No. 85-494

California Federal Savings and Loan Association, et al., Petitioners *v.* Mark Guerra, Director, Department of Fair Employment and Housing, et al.	On writ of certiorari to the United States Court of Appeals for the Ninth Circuit

[January 13, 1987]

JUSTICE MARSHALL delivered the opinion of the Court.

The question presented is whether Title VII of the Civil Rights Act of 1964, as amended by the Pregnancy Discrimination Act of 1978, pre-empts a state statute that requires employers to provide leave and reinstatement to employees disabled by pregnancy.

I

California's Fair Employment and Housing Act (FEHA), Cal. Gov't Code Ann. § 12900 *et seq.*, is a comprehensive statute that prohibits discrimination in employment and housing. In September 1978, California amended the FEHA to proscribe certain forms of employment discrimination on the basis of pregnancy. See Cal. Labor Code Ann. § 1420.35, 1978 Cal Stats. ch. 1321, § 1, p. 4320-4322, now codified at Cal. Gov't Code Ann. § 12945(b)(2). Subdivision (b)(2)—the provision at issue here—is the only portion of the statute that applies to employers subject to Title VII. It requires these employers to provide female employees an unpaid pregnancy disability leave of up to four months. Respondent Fair Employment and Housing Commission, the state agency authorized to interpret the FEHA, has construed § 12945(b)(2) to require California employers to reinstate an employee returning from such pregnancy leave to the job she previously held, unless it is no longer available due to business necessity. In the latter case, the employer must make a reasonable, good faith effort to place the employee in a substantially similar job. The statute does not compel employers to provide *paid* leave to pregnant employees. Accordingly, the only benefit pregnant workers actually derive from § 12945(b)(2) is a qualified right to reinstatement.

Title VII of the Civil Rights Act of 1964, 42 U.S.C. § 2000e *et seq.*, also prohibits various forms of employment discrimination, including discrimination on the basis of sex. However, in *General Electric Co.* v. *Gilbert* (1976) this Court ruled that discrimination on the basis of pregnancy was not sex discrimination under Title VII. In response to the *Gilbert* decision, Congress passed the Pregnancy Discrimination Act of 1978 (PDA), 42 U.S.C. § 2000e(k). The PDA specifies that sex discrimination includes discrimination on the basis of pregnancy. . . .

[Part II omitted]

III

A

In determining whether a state statute is pre-empted by federal law and therefore invalid under the Supremacy Clause of the Constitution, our sole task is to ascertain the intent of Congress. See *Shaw* v. *Delta Air Lines, Inc.* (1983); *Malone* v. *White Motor Corp.* (1978). Federal law may supersede state law in several different ways. First, when acting within constitutional limits, Congress is empowered to pre-empt state law by so stating in express terms. *E.g., Jones* v. *Rath Packing Co.* (1977). Second, congressional intent to pre-empt state law in a particular area may be inferred where the scheme of federal regulation is sufficiently comprehensive to make reasonable the inference that Congress "left no room" for supplementary state regulation. *Rice* v. *Santa Fe Elevator Corp.* (1947). Neither of these bases for pre-emption exists in this case. Congress has explicitly disclaimed any intent categorically to pre-empt state law or to "occupy the field" of employment discrimination law.

As a third alternative, in those areas where Congress has not completely displaced state regulation, federal law may nonetheless pre-empt state law to the extent it actually conflicts with federal law. Such a conflict occurs either because "compliance with both federal and state regulations is a physical impossibility," *Florida Lime & Avocado Growers, Inc.* v. *Paul* (1963), or because the state law stands "as an obstacle to the accomplishment and execution of the full purposes and objectives of Congress." *Hines* v. *Davidowitz* (1941). See *Michigan Canners & Freezers Assn., Inc.* v. *Agricultural Marketing and Bargaining Bd.* (1984); *Fidelity Federal Savings & Loan Assn.* v. *De la Cuesta* (1982). Nevertheless, pre-emption is not to be lightly presumed. See *Maryland* v. *Louisiana* (1981).

This third basis for pre-emption is at issue in this case. In two sections of the 1964 Civil Rights Act, §§ 708 and 1104, Congress has indicated that state laws will be pre-empted only if they actually conflict with federal law. . . . Accordingly, there is no need to infer congressional intent to pre-empt state laws from the substantive provisions of Title VII; these two sections provide a "reliable indicium of congressional intent with respect to state authority" to regulate employment practice. *Malone* v. *White Motor Corp., supra.*

Sections 708 and 1104 severely limit Title VII's pre-emptive effect. Instead of pre-empting state fair employment laws, § 708 " 'simply left them where they were before the enactment of title VII.' " *Shaw* v. *Delta Air Lines, Inc., supra.* Similarly, § 1104 was intended primarily to "assert the intention of Congress to preserve existing civil rights laws." 110 Cong. Rec. 2788 (1964) (remarks of Rep. Meader). The narrow scope of pre-emption available under §§ 708 and 1104 reflects the importance Congress attached to state antidiscrimination laws in achieving Title VII's goal of equal employment opportunity. . . . The legislative history of the PDA also supports a narrow interpretation of these provisions, as does our opinion in *Shaw* v. *Delta Airlines, Inc.*[1]

In order to decide whether the California statute requires or permits employers to violate Title VII, as amended by the PDA, or is inconsistent with the purposes of the statute, we must determine whether the PDA prohibits the States from requiring employers to provide reinstatement to pregnant workers, regardless of their policy for disabled workers generally.

B

Petitioners argue that the language of the federal statute itself unambiguously rejects California's "special treatment" approach to pregnancy discrimination, thus rendering any resort to the legislative history unnecessary. They contend that the second clause of the PDA forbids an employer to treat pregnant employees any differently than other disabled employees. Because "[t]he purpose of Congress is the ultimate touchstone" of the pre-emption inquiry, *Malone* v. *White Motor Corp.* (quoting *Retail Clerks* v. *Schermerhorn* (1963)), however, we must examine the PDA's language against the background of its legislative history and historical context. As to the language of the PDA, "[i]t is a 'familiar rule, that a thing may be within the letter of the statute and yet not within the statute, because not within its spirit, nor within the intention of its makers.' " *Steelworkers* v. *Weber* (1979) (quoting *Church of the Holy Trinity* v. *United States* (1892)).

It is well established that the PDA was passed in reaction to this Court's decision in *General Electric Co.* v. *Gilbert* (1976). "When Congress amended Title VII in 1978, it unambiguously expressed its disapproval of both the holding and the reasoning of the Court in the *Gilbert* decision." *Newport News Shipbuilding & Dry Dock Co.* v. *EEOC* [1983]. By adding pregnancy to the definition of sex discrimination prohibited by Title VII, the first clause of the PDA reflects Congress' disapproval of the reasoning in *Gilbert*. *Newport News*. Rather than imposing a limitation on the remedial purpose of the PDA, we believe that the second clause was intended to overrule the holding in *Gilbert* and to illustrate how discrimination against pregnancy is to be remedied. . . . Accordingly, subject to certain limitations,[2] we agree with the Court of Appeals' conclusion that Congress intended the PDA to be "a floor beneath which pregnancy disability benefits may not drop—not a ceiling above which they may not rise."

The context in which Congress considered the issue of pregnancy discrimination supports this view of the PDA. Congress had before it

[1] In *Shaw* v. *Delta Air Lines, Inc.*, 463 U.S. 85, 100-104 (1983), we concluded that Title VII did not pre-empt a New York statute which proscribed discrimination on the basis of pregnancy as sex discrimination at a time when Title VII did not equate the two.

[2] For example, a State could not mandate special treatment of pregnant workers based on stereotypes or generalizations about their needs and abilities.

extensive evidence of discrimination *against* pregnancy, particularly in disability and health insurance programs like those challenged in *Gilbert* and *Nashville Gas Co.* v. *Satty* (1977). The reports, debates, and hearings make abundantly clear that Congress intended the PDA to provide relief for working women and to end discrimination against pregnant workers. In contrast to the thorough account of discrimination against pregnant workers, the legislative history is devoid of any discussion of preferential treatment of pregnancy, beyond acknowledgments of the existence of state statutes providing for such preferential treatment. Opposition to the PDA came from those concerned with the cost of including pregnancy in health and disability benefit plans and the application of the bill to abortion, not from those who favored special accommodation of pregnancy.

In support of their argument that the PDA prohibits employment practices that favor pregnant women, petitioners and several *amici* cite statements in the legislative history to the effect that the PDA does not *require* employers to extend any benefits to pregnant women that they do not already provide to other disabled employees. . . . We do not interpret these references to support petitioners' construction of the statute. On the contrary, if Congress had intended to *prohibit* preferential treatment, it would have been the height of understatement to say only that the legislation would not *require* such conduct. It is hardly conceivable that Congress would have extensively discussed only its intent not to require preferential treatment if in fact it had intended to prohibit such treatment.

We also find it significant that Congress was aware of state laws similar to California's but apparently did not consider them inconsistent with the PDA. In the debates and reports on the bill, Congress repeatedly acknowledged the existence of state antidiscrimination laws that prohibit sex discrimination on the basis of pregnancy. Two of the States mentioned then required employers to provide reasonable leave to pregnant workers.[3] After citing these state laws, Congress failed to evince the requisite "clear and manifest purpose" to supersede them. See *Pacific Gas & Electric Co.* v. *State Energy Resources Conservation and Development Comm'n* (1983). To the contrary, both the House and Senate Reports suggest that these laws would continue to have effect under the PDA.

---

[3] See, *e.g.*, Conn. Gen. Stat. § 31-126(g) (1977), now codified at § 46a-60(a)(7) (1985); Mont. Rev. Codes § 41-2602, now codified at Mont. Code Ann. §§ 49-2-310 and 49-2-311 (1986). The Connecticut statute provided, in relevant part: "It shall be an unfair employment practice. . . . "(g) For an employer . . . (ii) to refuse to grant to [a pregnant] employee a reasonable leave of absence for disability resulting from such pregnancy. . . . (iii) Upon signifying her intent to return, such employee shall be reinstated to her original job or to an equivalent position with equivalent pay and accumulated seniority, retirement, fringe benefits and other service credits unless, in the case of a private employer, the employer's circumstances have so changed as to make it impossible or unreasonable to do so." Conn. Gen. Stat. § 31-126(g) (1977).

The Montana statute in effect in 1977 was virtually identical. Both have been recodified in current statutory compilations, but the leave and reinstatement requirements are unchanged. . . .

Title VII, as amended by the PDA, and California's pregnancy disability leave statute share a common goal. The purpose of Title VII is "to achieve equality of employment opportunities and remove barriers that have operated in the past to favor an identifiable group of ... employees over other employees." *Griggs* v. *Duke Power Co.* (1971). See *Hishon* v. *King & Spalding* (1984); *Franks* v. *Bowman Transportation Co.* (1976); *Alexander* v. *Gardner-Denver Co.* (1974); *McDonnell Douglas Corp.* v. *Green* (1973). Rather than limiting existing Title VII principles and objectives, the PDA extends them to cover pregnancy.[4] As Senator Williams, a sponsor of the Act, stated: "The entire thrust ... behind this legislation is to guarantee women the basic right to participate fully and equally in the workforce, without denying them the fundamental right to full participation in family life." 123 Cong. Rec. 29658 (1977).

Section 12945(b)(2) also promotes equal employment opportunity. By requiring employers to reinstate women after a reasonable pregnancy disability leave, § 12945(b)(2) ensures that they will not lose their jobs on account of pregnancy disability. California's approach is consistent with the dissenting opinion of JUSTICE BRENNAN in *General Electric Co.* v. *Gilbert,* which Congress adopted in enacting the PDA. Referring to *Lau* v. *Nichols* (1974), a Title VI decision, JUSTICE BRENNAN stated:

> "[D]iscrimination is a social phenomenon encased in a social context and, therefore, unavoidably takes its meaning from the desired end products of the relevant legislative enactment, end products that may demand due consideration of the uniqueness of the 'disadvantaged' individuals. A realistic understanding of conditions found in today's labor environment warrants taking pregnancy into account in fashioning disability policies."

By "taking pregnancy into account," California's pregnancy disability leave statute allows women, as well as men, to have families without losing their jobs.

We emphasize the limited nature of the benefits § 12945(b)(2) provides. The statute is narrowly drawn to cover only the period of *actual physical disability* on account of pregnancy, childbirth, or related medical conditions. Accordingly, unlike the protective labor legislation prevalent earlier in this century, § 12945(b)(2) does not reflect archaic or stereotypical notions about pregnancy and the abilities of pregnant workers. A statute based on such stereotypical assumptions would, of course, be inconsistent with Title VII's goal of equal employment opportunity. See, *e.g., Los Angeles Dept. of Water and Power* v. *Manhart* (1978); *Phillips* v. *Martin Marietta Corp.* (1971).

C

Moreover, even if we agreed with petitioners' construction of the PDA,

---

[4] "Proponents of the bill repeatedly emphasized that the Supreme Court had erroneously interpreted congressional intent and that the amending legislation was necessary to reestablish the principles of Title VII law as they had been understood prior to the *Gilbert* decision." *Newport News Shipbuilding & Dry Dock Co.* v. *EEOC* [1983].

we would nonetheless reject their argument that the California statute requires employers to violate Title VII. Section 12945(b)(2) does not prevent employers from complying with both the federal law (as petitioners construe it) and the state law. This is not a case where "compliance with both federal and state regulations is a physical impossibility," *Florida Lime & Avocado Growers, Inc.* v. *Paul* (1963), or where there is an "inevitable collision between the two schemes of regulation." Section 12945(b)(2) does not compel California employers to treat pregnant workers *better* than other disabled employees; it merely establishes benefits that employers must, at a minimum, provide to pregnant workers. Employers are free to give comparable benefits to other disabled employees, thereby treating "women affected by pregnancy" no better than "other persons not so affected but similar in their ability or inability to work." Indeed, at oral argument, petitioners conceded that compliance with both statutes "is theoretically possible."

Petitioners argue that "extension" of the state statute to cover other employees would be inappropriate in the absence of a clear indication that this is what the California Legislature intended.... This argument is beside the point. Extension is a remedial option to be exercised by a court once a statute is found to be invalid. See, *e.g., Califano* v. *Wescott* (1979) (quoting *Welsh* v. *United States* (1970)).

IV

Thus, petitioners' facial challenge to § 12945(b)(2) fails. The statute is not pre-empted by Title VII, as amended by the PDA, because it is not inconsistent with the purposes of the federal statute, nor does it require the doing of an act which is unlawful under Title VII.

The judgment of the Court of Appeals is

Affirmed.

JUSTICE WHITE, with whom THE CHIEF JUSTICE and JUSTICE POWELL join, dissenting.

I disagree with the Court that Cal. Gov't Code Ann. § 12945(b)(2) is not pre-empted by the Pregnancy Discrimination Act of 1978 (PDA), 92 Stat. 2076, codified at 42 U.S.C. § 2000e(k), and § 708 of Title VII. Section 703(a) of Title VII forbids discrimination in the terms of employment on the basis of race, color, religion, sex, or national origin. The PDA gave added meaning to discrimination on the basis of sex:

> "The terms 'because of sex' or 'on the basis of sex' [in section 703(a) of this title] include, but are not limited to, because of or on the basis of pregnancy, childbirth or related medical conditions; and women affected by pregnancy, childbirth, or related medical conditions shall be treated the same for all employment-related purposes, including receipt of benefits under fringe benefit programs, as other persons not so affected but similar in their ability or inability to work...." § 2000e(k).

The second clause quoted above could not be clearer: it mandates that pregnant employees "shall be treated the same for all employment-related purposes" as nonpregnant employees similarly situated with respect to their ability or inability to work. This language leaves no room for preferential treatment of pregnant workers....

Contrary to the mandate of the PDA, California law requires every employer to have a disability leave policy for pregnancy even if it has none for any other disability. An employer complies with California law if it has a leave policy for pregnancy but denies it for every other disability. On its face, § 12945(b)(2) is in square conflict with the PDA and is therefore pre-empted. Because the California law permits employers to single out pregnancy for preferential treatment and therefore to violate Title VII, it is not saved by § 708 which limits pre-emption of state laws to those that require or permit an employer to commit an unfair employment practice.

The majority nevertheless would save the California law on two grounds. First, it holds that the PDA does not require disability from pregnancy to be treated the same as other disabilities; instead, it forbids less favorable, but permits more favorable, benefits for pregnancy disability. The express command of the PDA is unambiguously to the contrary, and the legislative history casts no doubt on that mandate.

The legislative materials reveal Congress' plain intent not to put pregnancy in a class by itself within Title VII, as the majority does with its "floor ... not a ceiling" approach....

The majority correctly reports that Congress focused on discrimination against, rather than preferential treatment of, pregnant workers. There is only one direct reference in the legislative history to preferential treatment. Senator Brooke stated during the Senate debate: "I would emphasize most strongly that S. 995 in no way provides special disability benefits for working women. They have not demanded, nor asked, for such benefits. They have asked only to be treated with fairness, to be accorded the same employment rights as men." Given the evidence before Congress of the widespread discrimination against pregnant workers, it is probable that most Congresspersons did not seriously consider the possibility that someone would want to afford preferential treatment to pregnant workers. The parties and their *amici* argued vigorously to this Court the policy implications of preferential treatment of pregnant workers. In favor of preferential treatment it was urged with conviction that preferential treatment merely enables women, like men, to have children without losing their jobs. In opposition to preferential treatment it was urged with equal conviction that preferential treatment represents a resurgence of the 19th century protective legislation which perpetuated sex-role stereotypes and which impeded women in their efforts to take their rightful place in the workplace.... It is not the place of this Court, however, to resolve this policy dispute. Our task is to interpret Congress' intent in enacting the PDA. Congress' silence in its consideration of the PDA with respect to preferential treatment of pregnant workers cannot fairly be interpreted to abrogate the plain statements in the legislative history, not to mention the language of the statute, that equality of treatment was to be the guiding principle of the PDA.

Congress' acknowledgement of state antidiscrimination laws does not support a contrary inference. . . . Indeed, the state statues were considered, not in the context of pre-emption, but in the context of a discussion of health insurance costs. The House Report expressly stated that "[t]he significance of this State coverage" is that "many employers are *already* under a State law obligation to provide benefits to pregnant disabled workers. Passage of the bill thus has little or no economic impact on such employers.

Nor does anything in the legislative history from the Senate side indicate that it carefully considered the state statutes . . . and expressly endorsed their provisions. . . . Passing reference to state statutes without express recognition of their content and without express endorsement is insufficient . . . to override the PDA's clear equal-treatment mandate. . . .

The Court's second, and equally strange, ground is that even if the PDA does prohibit special benefits for pregnant women, an employer may still comply with both the California law and the PDA: it can adopt the specified leave policies for pregnancy and at the same time afford similar benefits for all other disabilities. This is untenable. California surely had no intent to require employers to provide general disability leave benefits. It intended to prefer pregnancy and went no farther. Extension of these benefits to the entire work force would be a dramatic increase in the scope of the state law and would impose a significantly greater burden on California employers. That is the province of the California Legislature. See *Wengler* v. *Druggists Mutual Insurance Co.* (1980); *Caban* v. *Mohammed* (1979); *Craig* v. *Boren* (1976). Nor can § 12945(b)(2) be saved by applying Title VII in tandem with it, such that employers would be required to afford reinstatement rights to pregnant workers as a matter of state law but would be required to afford the same rights to all other workers as a matter of federal law. . . . It is clear from the legislative history that Congress did not intend for the PDA to impose such burdens on employers. As recognized by the majority, opposition to the PDA came from those concerned with the cost of including pregnancy in health and disability benefit plans. The House Report acknowledged these concerns and explained that the bill "in no way requires the institution of any new programs where none currently exist." The Senate Report gave a similar assurance. In addition, legislator after legislator stated during the floor debates that the PDA would not require an employer to institute a disability benefits program if it did not already have one in effect. Congress intended employers to be free to provide any level of disability benefits they wished—or none at all—as long as pregnancy was not a factor in allocating such benefits. . . .

. . . [P]referential treatment of pregnant workers is prohibited by Title VII, as amended by the PDA. Section 12945(b)(2) of the California Gov't Code, which extends preferential benefits for pregnancy, is therefore pre-empted. It is not saved by § 708 because it purports to authorize employers to commit an unfair employment practice forbidden by Title VII.

[illegible]

[illegible] proposal [illegible] contrary influence [illegible] the [illegible] insurance [illegible] this State [illegible] State [illegible] employment.

[illegible] that it [illegible] the [illegible]

[illegible] any purpose [illegible] the same [illegible] Congress did not intend [illegible] the [illegible] explained that the [illegible]

[illegible]

NATIONAL SECURITY EXPORT CONTROLS

January 14, 1987

A panel of the National Academy of Sciences (NAS) January 14 urged revision of U.S. export controls designed to impede Soviet bloc access to technology of potential military use. Pointing to "a dramatically altered economic and technological environment," the panel recommended that export control decisions give greater weight to maintaining U.S. technological strength, economic vitality, and allied unity.

The panel focused on "dual use technology," technology that has both commercial and military applications, and its findings reflected growing concern over U.S. competitiveness in high technology. American producers, who had to secure licenses to export restricted technology to any country (usually excepting Canada), often found themselves at a disadvantage with other free world competitors. U.S. export controls were more extensive than those of other countries, involved bureaucratic delays, created customer uncertainties, and restricted reexport to third countries. In a survey by the panel of U.S. exporters of high technology, 52 percent reported lost sales primarily as a consequence of export controls, and more than half expected the number of such occurrences to increase over the next two years.

To simplify export controls and eliminate the disadvantages to U.S. exporters, the panel suggested strengthening the mechanism of the Coordinating Committee on Multilateral Export Controls (CoCom), an informal, nontreaty organization composed of Japan and all members of the North Atlantic Treaty Organization (NATO) except Iceland. The report said the United States should, with rare exceptions, control only the export of CoCom proscribed items, and then only when they are destined for a proscribed country or a free world country that has not agreed to control such exports.

Balancing Security, Commercial Needs

Chaired by Lew Allen, Jr., a former Air Force chief of staff, the panel also included former defense secretary Melvin Laird and former CIA deputy director Bobby Ray Inman, as well as prominent business executives, scientists, and economists. Although six of the twenty-one members were former defense or intelligence officials, Assistant Secretary of Defense Richard N. Perle complained that it was "predominantly representative of the outlook of the business community." Perle, quoted in the Washington Post, *described the report as "comments by a group of largely interested parties about public policy that affects their financial interests."*

The report's emphasis on economic concerns was in part a reaction to stricter controls on high technology exports that followed Inman's release in 1982 of a CIA report that found a "hemorrhage" of U.S. technology to the Soviet bloc. Erosion of U.S. leadership in high technology trade led to the appointment in 1984 of the NAS panel to examine the effect of export controls on the vigor of the U.S. high technology industry. Funding for the study was provided by the Defense, Energy, and State departments, the National Aeronautics and Space Administration, the National Science Foundation, and fifteen private organizations representing industry and science.

The title of the report, Balancing the National Interest, *reflected a tension within the Reagan administration, which was committed both to vigorous pursuit of the cold war and to the competitiveness of American business. Despite the difficulty of this balancing act, the panel adopted the report unanimously. A similar NAS panel in 1982 weighed the competing claims of scientific communication and national security.* (Historic Documents of 1982, pp. 813-819).

Evolution of Controls

Government control of exports that might prove militarily useful to potential enemies began in 1940, on the brink of U.S. entry into World War II. Temporary legislation was renewed periodically until enactment in 1949 of the Export Control Act, aimed at cold war adversaries. This legislation, continued in the Export Administration Act of 1979, controlled dual-use products and technologies and was implemented by the Department of Commerce. Export of military weaponry and services was governed by the Arms Control Act of 1976, implemented by the State Department. The Defense Department provided advice on the strategic significance of both commercial and military exports.

During the cold war the Western allies shifted from World War II reliance on outproducing the enemy to NATO dependence on superior technology to offset Soviet numerical advantages. In recent years technologies of widespread commercial use—such as computers—assumed a larger role in the military, and innovation advanced more rapidly in the commercial sector than in the military. But efforts to restrict Soviet access to dual-use technologies were made difficult by their wide diffusion, the NAS panel observed, and had to be balanced against the need to keep U.S. producers competitive.

> *Following are excerpts from the executive summary of* Balancing the National Interest: U.S. National Security Export Controls and Global Economic Competition, *released by the National Academy of Sciences January 14, 1987:*

Introduction

The vigor of science and technology in the Western democracies [including Japan] and the greater economic vitality of these nations in comparison to the Soviet bloc are sources of strength for the West in its continuing effort to maintain its military security. The Soviet Union lacks these advantages; it seeks to compensate for them by directing a substantial portion of its gross national product to the development and production of military equipment and by making aggressive attempts to acquire and apply Western technology to its military programs. Although the prime targets of the Soviet acquisition program are military hardware and technology related directly to military systems, dual use products and technology available for sale in international markets also constitute major targets. The importance of dual use technology to Western economic vitality poses a policy dilemma for the West in turn: The open communication and free markets that are fundamental to the Western advantage in technology also facilitate the Soviet acquisition effort. Given what is known about the scope and extent of these Soviet activities, the West must pursue a dual strategy of continuing to maintain its technological leadership over potential adversaries while also denying—or at least impeding—their access to militarily significant Western technology.

This study had a twofold objective: (1) to examine the current system of laws, regulations, international agreements, and organizations—defined collectively as the national security export control regime—that control the international transfer of technology through industrial channels; and (2) where appropriate, to recommend new approaches to achieve the interrelated national policy objectives of military security, scientific and technological advance, and economic vitality.

To achieve this objective the panel and its professional staff undertook a broad agenda of research and briefings.

- Pertinent public literature was analyzed as well as restricted documents from the various federal agencies involved in export control policy formulation. . . .

• Representatives of these agencies briefed the panel, as did the Intelligence Community in classified session.

• The panel also heard the views of industry (including a broad range of sectors and firm sizes) and held a series of discussions with individuals well-versed in aspects of the national security export control regime.

• Delegations of the panel traveled to six European countries (Austria, Belgium, France, Great Britain, Sweden, and West Germany) and five Asian countries (Japan, Hong Kong, Malaysia, Singapore, and South Korea) for frank and confidential meetings with government officials, industry leaders, and other informed observers on export control matters.

• The panel commissioned a series of research reports, prepared both by outside consultants and by the panel's professional staff. Some of these studies developed and analyzed new primary data; others reexamined existing problems from new perspectives.

From these efforts has come a set of general principles and specific prescriptions for developing a more balanced and effective national security export control regime. The panel's findings and recommendations are set forth in the concluding sections of this summary. The three general principles that underlie the panel's analysis propose that *it should be the policy of the United States*

• to promote the economic vitality of Free World countries,

• to maintain and invigorate the domestic technological base, and

• to cooperate with its allies to impede the Soviet Union and other Warsaw Pact countries in their efforts to acquire Western technology that can be used directly or indirectly to enhance their military capability.

As a general policy, the United States should strive to achieve clarity, simplicity, and consistency in its national security export control procedures, as well as in the multilateral CoCom [Coordinating Committee on Multilateral Export Controls] export control structure, and broader consensus on the need for national security export controls among the Free World nations that use and produce dual use technology. To achieve these ends the United States should develop policies and procedures that emphasize efficiency and effectiveness rather than total comprehensiveness.

The Technology Transfer Problem

Intelligence information reviewed by the panel—including some at high levels of classification—indicates that the Soviet technology acquisition effort is massive, well financed, and frequently effective. Militarily significant Western technology has flowed to Warsaw Pact countries in recent years through three primary channels:

• *espionage*—the theft of classified information or items of relevance to military systems;

• *diversion*—shipment of militarily significant dual use products and technology to unapproved end users, either directly through the export of controlled products without a license (i.e., smuggling), or indirectly through transshipment using a complex chain of increasingly untraceable reexports (i.e., legal transshipment of products or components by firms operating in countries that do not impose controls); and

- *legal sales*—direct trade with the Soviet bloc, usually after receipt of a license. Such trade also may include some reexports.

As in other areas of intelligence, data on Soviet acquisition of militarily sensitive technology are incomplete and fragmentary and often become available relatively late in the development of national security export control policy. Nevertheless, available evidence—including the so-called "Farewell" papers, which are actual Soviet documents obtained by French intelligence services in 1981 detailing the plans, organization, and financing for technology acquisition efforts in the West—indicates that, by the Soviets' own estimates, approximately 70 percent of the items they target and eventually acquire in the West are subject to some form of national security export control. There is also growing concern in the Intelligence Community about the extent to which the Soviet Union and other Warsaw Pact countries have been or may be able to obtain controlled technology in Free World countries that do not cooperate in national security export controls. This concern applies both to the industrialized neutral countries of Europe and to some of the more advanced newly industrializing countries (such as India, Singapore, and Brazil).

It is only on rare occasions—for instance, when isolated examples of specific Western components, or copies of them, appear in Soviet military equipment—that the Intelligence Community can declare without reservation that the application of Western technology has contributed substantially to Soviet military developments. As a result, assessing the impacts of technology acquired by the Soviets is subject to considerable uncertainty. In general, it appears that the loss of a few items does not raise significant risks. Although the Soviets may attempt to reverse-engineer a technology (i.e., use an item obtained in the West as a basis for producing the technology themselves for their military systems), the panel has come to believe that this process is generally unproductive for many types of items (for example, high-density semiconductor devices).

Nevertheless, certain key items of process control or manufacturing hardware (known as keystone equipment) *can* provide the Soviets with substantial leverage—even if only a few are obtained—because these items facilitate the production of quantities of other hardware. Consequently, a prevalent judgment in the United States is that the emphasis of national security export control policy properly should be on constraining the flow of manufacturing equipment ... rather than on the end products of the manufacturing process.

Although there are some cases in which different conclusions can be drawn, on the basis of available information the panel has determined that for most types of dual use technology the Soviet Union is approximately 5 to 10 years behind the West and does not appear to be closing the gap. The situation is different for military technology. Although the West remains generally ahead in the most advanced systems, the Soviets' great emphasis (relative to that of the United States) on the development and production of military hardware results in fielded equipment that in specific cases is as modern as that deployed in the West. However, as indicated in the 1986 Packard commission report *A Quest for Excellence: Final Report to the President,* it is important to understand that this fact may reflect delays in the U.S. procurement process rather than a failure of export controls.

Despite years of effort, then, the Soviets continue to lag [behind] the West technologically, and this gap may actually be widening due to Soviet dependence on generally outdated Western equipment and technology (particularly in the field of computer science). Although it would be foolhardy for the United States or other CoCom nations to facilitate Soviet access to militarily critical technology, the panel considers it unlikely that an influx of Western technology will enable the Soviet bloc to reduce the current gap substantially—as long as the West continues its own rapid pace of innovation.

There are other facets of the technology transfer problem that also warrant attention. Intelligence evidence on the extent of unwanted West-East technology transfer must be juxtaposed against the fact that the United States is now confronted with a dramatically altered economic and technological environment—an environment substantially different from that existing for most of the post-World War II period. The panel reviewed in this regard the implications of the following five major developments.

1. *The character of the international marketplace is evolving in such a way that diffusion of technology is rapid and global in scope.* Factors promoting this diffusion include the tendency among multinational corporations to locate research, development, and production facilities around the world and the existence of indigenous capability in many developing countries. Massive amounts of information must be transferred by such companies as they attempt to control and coordinate their international efforts.

2. *There is a growing global market for dual use products, most of which embody advanced technology.* The high-technology sector demands heavy investment in research and development. The rapid technological advances promoted by this investment are tending to push commercial development of technology ahead of military development—a reversal of the pattern established after World War II. Acceleration of commercial development, coupled with a lengthening of the U.S. military procurement cycle, has resulted in the increased availability of dual use products embodying technology more sophisticated than that deployed by the military.

3. *Because trade is a steadily growing part of U.S economic activity, policies that affect it are increasingly important to the overall U.S. economy.* The United States is the single largest international trader, reporting exports of $360 billion in 1985. U.S. exports to CoCom countries

represented over 60 percent of that total in 1985; in contrast, exports to Soviet bloc countries represented less than 1 percent of U.S. exports for that year. Trade policies that might diminish West-West trade thus have greater potential to damage the U.S. economy than do those that might reduce exports to the Eastern bloc. Although export controls are not a leading cause of the recent decline in U.S. high-technology performance, they may contribute to lost sales and to an environment that discourages export activities by U.S. firms.

4. *U.S. dominance over advanced technology is declining.* The United States now faces stiff competition in almost every high-technology sector from companies in both developed and developing countries with non-U.S.-source technology. The growing technical sophistication of such countries is the result of long-term efforts to develop and enhance indigenous technical capability.... The newly industrializing countries currently do not possess sufficient indigenous high-technology capability to compete at the cutting edge of most industries, but many are beginning to make great strides toward this goal.... Thus, the United States cannot succeed in its efforts to block Soviet acquisition of militarily sensitive Western technology unless it has the full cooperation of the (increasing number of) other technologically advanced countries that may represent alternative sources of supply.

5. *Maintaining the vitality of all the Western economies has assumed greater importance for the national security of the United States.* To the extent that technological and economic leadership is now shared with the other principal CoCom countries—namely, Japan, the United Kingdom, France, and the Federal Republic of Germany—it is essential to the national security interests of the United States, for both military and trade reasons, that the economies of these countries remain strong....

Findings and Key Judgments of the Panel

Based on the research initiatives and deliberations undertaken in pursuit of its charge, the panel reached unanimous agreement on a series of principal findings and key judgments listed below.

I. The Practical Basis for National Security Export Controls

The fundamental objective of the national security export control regime maintained by CoCom is to deny—or at least to delay—the Soviet Union and its Warsaw Pact allies access to state-of-the-art Western technology that would permit them to narrow the existing gap in military systems. Yet there are no well-defined criteria that can be used to determine whether a given technology will enhance significantly Soviet military capability. Moreover, the precise definition and implementation of such criteria will depend to a large extent on the world view of the decision maker. For an export control system to be operationally effective, however, such distinctions must be drawn. This difficulty can be surmounted in practice by establishing a definition that permits effective, practical implementation of controls with our allies, which means restricting controls to technologies that are easily identified with military uses.

II. Considerations Influencing National Policy

1. Technology lead is vital to Western security and must be maintained.

Western security depends on the maintenance of technology lead over potential adversaries. This lead can only be sustained through a dual policy of promoting a vigorous domestic technological base and impeding the outward flow of technologies useful to the Warsaw Pact in military systems.

2. Export competitiveness is essential to the health of the U.S. domestic economy.

In some industrial sectors, especially high-technology enterprises, firms now must remain competitive in the world market to maintain a share of the U.S. domestic market, due to necessary economies of scale and the increased importance of R&D from foreign sources. The new realities of global competition are not yet fully reflected in the policies underlying current U.S. national security export controls.

3. The scope of current U.S. national security export controls undermines their effectiveness.

U.S. national security export controls are not generally perceived as rational, credible, and predictable by many of the nations and commercial interests whose active cooperation is required for an effective system. In their view the scope of current U.S. controls encompasses too many products and technologies to be administratively feasible. The panel concurs with this judgment.

4. U.S. national security export controls impede the export sales of U.S. companies.

There is limited but specific evidence that export sales have been lost or foregone because of uncertainty or delays in the licensing process and because of concern about future license approvals, availability of spare parts and components, and possible reexport constraints. Once changes in buying preferences occur, they may require large investments of time and effort to reverse.

5. Pragmatic control lists must be technically sound, narrowly focused, and coordinated multilaterally.

Although the control criteria developed in 1976 as part of the report of the Defense Science Board task force *(An Analysis of Export Control of U.S. Technology—A DoD Perspective)*, also known as the Bucy report, are theoretically sound, they have not always proven useful to the implementation of national security export controls. The preparation of control lists must be a dynamic process that is both informed by advice from technical advisory groups and constrained by the need to be clear, to focus control efforts more narrowly on fewer items, and to coordinate U.S. action more closely with that of our CoCom allies.

6. The extraterritorial aspects of U.S. controls engender mistrust and weaken allied unity.

Several elements of U.S. national security export controls, especially the requirement for reexport authorization, are having an increasingly corrosive effect on relations with many NATO countries and on other close bilateral relationships. They signal U.S. mistrust of the will and capacity of allies to control the flow of sensitive technology to the Soviet bloc.

III. Soviet Technology Acquisition Efforts in the West

1. Available evidence on Soviet technology acquisition efforts reinforces the need for effective multilateral export controls.

The panel has reviewed a substantial body of evidence—both classified and unclassified—that reveals a large and aggressive Soviet effort to target and acquire Western dual use technology through espionage, diversions, and to a lesser degree legitimate trade. There is limited but specific evidence both on the means by which Soviet acquisitions are accomplished and on their important role in upgrading or modernizing Soviet military systems. Although internationally cooordinated efforts are necessary to counter the use of diversions or legitimate trade for such purposes, export controls are not a means for controlling espionage, which alone accounts for a high proportion of successful Soviet acquisition activities.

2. Despite systemic difficulties, Soviet technical capabilities have successfully supported the military objectives of the USSR.

Because the Soviet system does not enjoy the benefits of a robust commercial sector, it is at a fundamental disadvantage in terms of the promotion of technological innovation. Nevertheless, the Soviets have demonstrated an effective technical capability to meet their military objectives.

IV. Diffusion and Transfer of Technical Capability

1. Wide global diffusion of advanced technology necessitates a fully multilateral approach to controls.

Because advanced technology has now diffused so widely, national security export controls cannot succeed without the following: (1) an effective CoCom process by which the other major CoCom countries accept responsibility for regulating exports and reexports from their territory of CoCom-controlled technology to non-CoCom Free World countries; and (2) the adoption by the more advanced newly industrializing countries of CoCom-like standards for their own indigenous technology.

2. Controls on the employment of foreign nationals in the U.S. R&D infrastructure must be used selectively and sparingly.

Foreign nationals now play a significant role in U.S. domestic R&D activities as well as in the laboratories of U.S. foreign subsidiaries. Such individuals contribute significantly to U.S. technological innovation and hence promote the national interest. Sparing use should therefore be made of existing legislative authority to restrict technical exchanges or to limit full participation of foreign citizens in the U.S. R&D community. It is particularly important to distinguish, as appropriate, between citizens of nations to whom exports are proscribed and citizens of all other nations.

V. Foreign Availability and Foreign Control of Technology

1. The congressional mandate for decontrol of items based on foreign availability is not being fulfilled.

The lack of action on foreign availability is inconsistent with the intent of Congress as expressed most recently in the Export Administration Amendments Act of 1985. In those cases in which there is foreign availability of U.S.-controlled items, U.S. industry is unfairly placed at a competitive disadvantage with respect to firms from other countries that are not similarly constrained. This disadvantage can lead to the erosion of competitive market advantages previously enjoyed by U.S. industry and in some cases to the permanent loss of U.S. markets.

2. Control of "technological commodities" is impractical.

The control of goods for which the volume of manufacture is so large and the scope of marketing and usage so wide that they have become "technological commodities" (e.g., some classes of personal computers or memory chips) is not practical. Decontrol of such goods to all Free World destinations is, in some cases, the only appropriate solution.

3. Bilateral agreements with Free World non-CoCom countries must protect all CoCom-origin technology and must control similar indigenously produced goods.

Over the short term, bilateral agreements that restrict only the reexport of U.S.-origin technology unfairly disadvantage U.S. companies in international trade. Over the long term, these agreements with non-CoCom countries will not promote the effectiveness of the CoCom export control system unless they restrict the reexport of technology from all CoCom sources as well as technology produced indigenously.

4. Other CoCom countries must be more vigilant in preventing diversions of both CoCom-origin and indigenously produced technology.

Some members of CoCom could substantially improve their efforts to prevent diversions of CoCom-origin products and technology being exported to third countries. Since compliance with U.S. reexport controls is not likely to become politically acceptable in most CoCom countries, some compromise solution must be reached.

5. The extraterritorial reach of U.S. controls damages allied relations and disadvantages U.S. exporters.

The extraterritorial reach of U.S. reexport controls is anathema to most U.S. trading partners. Moreover, many foreign governments do not agree that the United States has jurisdiction over the actions of their citizens outside U.S. territory. The extraterritorial extension of U.S. controls is viewed by these governments as a direct challenge to national sovereignty and a clear violation of international law. It is seen as additional evidence of mistrust by the United States of the capacity of these governments to further the West's common interest in preventing the diversion of militarily important goods and technologies.

VI. Effectiveness of the Multilateral Process

1. The United States must clearly distinguish foreign policy export controls from national security export controls.

There is much less consensus among the CoCom allies on the use of trade restrictions for foreign policy reasons than on controls in the interests of national security. Thus, to the extent that the United States fails to distinguish clearly between the two, allied cooperation in support of consensual national security objectives is undermined.

2. The impact of controls on advantageous scientific communication and transfer within the Western alliance must be minimized.

Because open scientific communication and trade within the West are as important to maintaining Western technology lead as is controlling the flow of technology to the Soviet bloc, U.S. policy should lend equal emphasis to both objectives.

3. The CoCom countries should take specific steps to bolster the efficiency and effectiveness of multilateral controls.

Among the most important issues now facing CoCom are: (a) reduction in the overall scope of the list, (b) modification of the procedures for decontrolling items from the International List of dual use items, and (c) provision of greater transparency in CoCom decision making.

4. The CoCom process woud benefit if all country delegations had balanced economic and defense representation.

The U.S. delegation to CoCom, unlike those of other member nations, includes a significant contingent of defense officials. A balance of economic and defense representation on all CoCom delegations would enhance CoCom unity and the usefulness of the CoCom process, in part by helping to resolve conflicts between competing economic and military objectives.

5. Foreign perceptions of U.S. commercial advantage derived from export controls impede multilateral cooperation.

There is a widely held view in Europe and the Far East that the United States uses its national security export controls to afford commercial advantage to U.S. companies. Although the panel found no substantive evidence to support this view, the existence of these perceptions makes it difficult to gain effective multilateral cooperation.

6. Unilateral controls are of limited efficacy and may undermine allied cooperation.

The imposition by the United States of unilateral national security export controls for dual use items can be justified only as a stopgap measure pending negotiations for the imposition of multilateral controls or in rare cases in which critical national security concerns are at stake requiring unilateral restrictions. It must be recognized that, except when used as a temporary measure, the application of unilateral controls undermines the incentive of the allies to develop a sound basis for multilateral restriction.

VII. Administration of U.S. National Security Export Control Policies and Procedures

1. The lack of high-level oversight and direction degrades the effectiveness of U.S. controls.

The administrative structures established by the executive branch have not proven effective in resolving the frequent policy differences among the three principal line agencies (the Departments of State, Defense, and Commerce). The White House has intervened only intermittently and then primarily to contain interagency conflict rather than to provide adequate policy direction. The lack of higher-level oversight and direction results in duplication of effort, uncertain lines of authority, serious delays in decision making, and underutilization of information-sharing capacity.

2. Unequal effort by and resources of the three principal line agencies have led to conflict, confusion, and unbalanced policy.

DoD's determined efforts to reinvigorate the national security export control regime have been useful in raising the general level of awareness in the United States and in other CoCom countries. But this increasingly active DoD role also has led to an imbalance in the distribution of government effort and resources. Although DoD has created a new dedicated agency for technology security, neither the Department of Commerce nor the Department of State has been able to implement equally effective measures. The result is a lack of balance in the interagency policy formulation process and an inefficient licensing process.

3. Shifts in responsibility within the line agencies may preclude broadly informed and balanced policy judgments.

Reorganization initiatives in a number of the principal line agencies tasked with managing export controls have resulted in a shift of responsibility away from organizations with expertise in technology development and international trade and toward those whose principal and often only concern is technology control. Although there have been positive effects of this shift in responsibility, there has been a loss of sustained technical input into the policy process for national security export controls.

4. Current licensing requirements, classification procedures, and proprietary controls for technical data are both appropriate and adequate.

Although technical data that are not publicly available require a validated license for export to the Soviet bloc, data exports to other destinations for the most part are eligible for a general license. The need for the unhindered exchange of large volumes of data in international commerce and research indicates that a strict system of control is neither feasible nor desirable. Existing licensing requirements, classification procedures, and proprietary controls offer sufficient protection.

5. Controls on unclassified DoD technical data have a chilling effect on the U.S. R&D community and should be imposed sparingly.

The Department of Defense Authorization Act (DAA) of 1984 permits DoD to impose restrictions on domestic dissemination or export of DoD-funded or DoD-generated technical data whose export would otherwise require a validated license under EAR or ITAR. Such restrictions have the effect of creating de facto a new category of unclassified but restricted information. These new, more comprehensive technical data restrictions have had a chilling effect on some professional scientific and engineering societies that have elected voluntarily to close certain sessions. It is the panel's judgment that imposing controls on technical data that are broader than those now in effect is not warranted by the demonstrable national security benefits.

6. The congressional mandate for integrating the Militarily Critical Technologies List (MCTL) into the Commerce Department Control List practically cannot be accomplished.

The MCTL has been used inappropriately as a control list, and its annual revision has resulted in a voluminous itemization of many important technologies without apparent prioritization. Because the Departments of Defense and Commerce maintain fundamentally different objectives in their list development exercises, the congressionally mandated task of integrating the MCTL into the Commerce Department's control list practically cannot be accomplished.

7. The complexity of U.S. export controls discourages compliance.

The complexity of U.S. controls discourages compliance, especially by foreign firms and small- to medium-sized U.S. companies. For example, the Export Administration Regulations constitute nearly 600 pages of rules and procedures. These could be reduced and simplified substantially—and made more "user friendly."

8. There is a need for high-level industry input in the formulation of national security export control policy.

There is a need for an effective mechanism within the government to provide meaningful input from the private sector on the formulation of a coordinated national security export control policy. Such a group must be constituted at sufficiently high corporate levels to reflect major industry concerns, and it must be able to have an impact on the actual policy process.

9. Voluntary cooperation from industry is important to the enforcement of export controls.

Voluntary cooperation by U.S. industry—particularly companies with overseas subsidiaries—is important to export control enforcement, especially in the identification of violations. Companies frequently have knowledge otherwise unavailable to the government of possible violations by other firms.

10. Adequate information to evaluate the impact of national security export controls is not maintained by the U.S. government.

This study has revealed serious shortcomings in both the quality and quantity of information maintained and analyzed by the U.S. government on the coverage, operation, and domestic and global impacts of national security export controls. In the absence of better information, it will continue to be difficult for policymakers to arrive at more informed and balanced judgments as to the advisability of controls.

11. A comprehensive cost/benefit analysis of controls currently is infeasible.

Despite some preliminary efforts to assess the competitive effects of national security export controls, a *comprehensive* empirical analysis of the costs and benefits is precluded by the lack of data, by the complexity of the system, and by a variety of qualitative judgments that must enter into any evaluation.

There is little doubt that, without the heightened attention to these issues initiated in the early years of the current administration by DoD, the problem of Western technology diversion to the Soviet Union would by now be considerably worse. But the panel is concerned that this policy "correction"—useful and necessary as it was—should not now overshoot the mark. The panel wishes to reiterate therefore its concern about the continuing lack of balance within the policy process for national security export controls regarding the representation of technical, national security, economic, and domestic and international political interests. This balance should be developed and maintained within each agency, among agencies of the U.S. government, and among countries participating in CoCom.

URBAN LEAGUE REPORT ON BLACK AMERICA

January 14, 1987

The National Urban League's The State of Black America 1987, *its twelfth annual report, offered a gloomy picture of conditions for black Americans and placed much of the blame for the bleak outlook on the Reagan administration. Urban League president John E. Jacob, releasing the report January 14, stated that black Americans entered 1987 "besieged by the resurgence of raw racism, persistent economic depression, and the continued erosion of past gains."*

Jacob's overview touched on some of the major problems confronting blacks: the Justice Department's "war on affirmative action," high unemployment, a rise in poverty, and an increase in the number of homeless people. Lambasting the Reagan administration, Jacob wrote: "It tried to win tax exemptions for segregated schools, fought extension of civil rights laws, undermined affirmative action, destroyed the U.S. Civil Rights Commission, stacked the judiciary with right-wingers, and refused to budge from its support for South Africa's apartheid government."

Twelve chapters by leading scholars followed Jacob's introduction. These studies, focusing on a range of legal, educational, economic, and social issues, constituted the league's strongest attack on the Reagan administration to date.

Retreat from Civil Rights

The chapter entitled "The Law and Black Americans: Retreat From Civil Rights" came down hard on the Justice Department for its vigorous efforts to halt civil rights progress and reverse past gains in a number of areas. The writer, civil rights lawyer Julius L. Chambers, criticized the administration's actions in the areas of school desegregation, voting rights, and equal employment opportunity. Chambers also discussed racial discrimination in sentencing and jury selection and documented the administration's efforts to appoint to the federal bench judges who typically were young, white, and conservative. Of the 289 federal district and appellate court judges appointed during Reagan's term, Chambers noted, all but five were white.

Another chapter blamed the Reagan administration for the grim economic status of blacks. According to the report, the income gap between blacks and whites and the poverty rate for both groups increased under Reagan. Unemployment for blacks generally was higher during the Reagan years, and the labor market position of blacks had deteriorated, the writer, economist David Swinton, maintained.

In a chapter on budget and tax reform, Howard University professor Lenneal J. Henderson stated that a benefit of the tax reform bill enacted in 1986 would be the removal of 6 million low-income persons from the federal tax rolls. He predicted, however, that 1985 enactment of the Gramm-Rudman-Hollings balanced budget bill and the tax reform measure would have a largely negative effect on the black community by reducing or eliminating social, economic, and political resources.

Social Concerns and Recommendations

The report devoted two chapters to the educational problems of black Americans and the future of school desegregation. A large number of student dropouts, a dramatic increase in teen pregnancies, and an inadequate number of black teachers and administrators were among the problems noted, and the league advocated community-based efforts to tackle these issues. In addition, the report urged more blacks to become members of local school boards and community "decision-making bodies" to ensure continued school desegregation efforts.

Social welfare reform, the state of the black family, the black underclass, drug use, and the impact of AIDS (acquired immune deficiency syndrome) also received attention. The authors noted the need for increased employment opportunities, restoration of spiritual values, promotion of family stability, and educational and research programs on drug use and on AIDS.

In a concluding chapter, the league called for repudiation of racism; continued support for affirmative action and civil rights enforcement; social welfare reform linked to employment and training; and improvements in education, health, and housing.

Jacob wrote in his opening chapter that "the tide may yet turn," and Chambers noted that with a new Democrat-controlled Senate, administration efforts to halt civil rights gains should prove more difficult. In line with these observations, the Senate Labor and Human Resources Committee in late May easily approved legislation restoring the full reach of four civil rights laws limited by a 1984 Supreme Court decision. The Senate Judiciary Committee in May readied a bill to provide faster and more effective remedies for victims of housing discrimination. At the end of 1987 both bills were pending.

Following are excerpts from the National Urban League's annual report, The State of Black America 1987, *released January 14, 1987:*

Black America, 1986: An Overview

1986 will go down in history as the year the nation staggered between the twin scandals of what have been called "Irangate" and "Boeskygate."

The first involved secret arms sales to Iran, illegal transfers of funds to the Nicaraguan Contras, and possibly illegal acts by high government officials. The second involved illegal financial manipulation of the stock market. Both have serious implications for the American political order and economic life, and both shed light on aspects of the black situation in ways most Americans have not considered....

The mushrooming scandal [of "Irangate"] ... dealt a heavy blow to the administration's credibility, especially in the context of the other incidents that demonstrated the primacy of public relations over substantive policy.

The general picture was that of a government contemptuous of the laws of the land and of public opinion, obsessed by appearances, and devoted to "spin control," or shaping public perceptions rather than providing the public with the information it needs to make informed choices about policies.

What went virtually unnoticed in the public uproar over these foreign policy misadventures was the fact that they carried over into foreign policy patterns of behavior that have long typified the administration's domestic policies, and especially its policies directly or indirectly affecting black citizens.

What columnist David Broder called the "fatal blend of ignorance and arrogance" also describes the administration's civil rights policies. It tried to win tax exemptions for segregated schools, fought extension of civil rights laws, undermined affirmative action, destroyed the U.S. Civil Rights Commission, stacked the judiciary with right-wingers, and refused to budge from its support for South Africa's apartheid government—all the while implementing a public relations policy designed to convince Americans that we are now a color-blind, racially neutral society.

At the same time, it ignored mounting black poverty. In place of substantive domestic policy, it substituted demonstrably false statements designed to convince the public that unemployment was no longer a problem, that the poor don't want to work, and that social programs simply compound social problems instead of helping resolve them.

What our government did to all of its citizens in foreign policy it first did to black citizens in its domestic policies. The persistent disinformation campaigns and factual distortions characteristic of the administration's public relations thrust on domestic matters were simply translated to foreign policy. It is hard to determine which is more shameful—that the administration did all this, or that the public let it get away with it for so long.

The second major scandal, involving insider trading and financial manipulation, reflects the failure of a laissez-faire philosophy that encouraged greed, weakened our economy, and undermined public faith in the economic system, just as "Irangate" weakened public faith in government.

Some of the biggest names on Wall Street were implicated in the scandal. Financier Ivan Boesky was fined $100 million, young investment bankers earning six- and seven-figure incomes were guilty of criminal acts, and formerly respected financial organizations fell under a cloud of suspicion.

The scandal focused attention on the way sheer greed had become the prevailing creed of Ronald Reagan's America, and it shone a spotlight on the way short-term financial considerations have come to dominate American business, at the expense of long-term policies that increase productive capacity and create jobs.

As the prominent investment banker, Felix Rohatyn, stated in an address to the Urban League of Greater New York in December:

"Greed and corruption are the cancer of a free society. They are a cancer because they erode our value system.... I have been in business for almost forty years and I cannot recall a period in which greed and corruption appeared as prevalent as they are today."

And Rohatyn went on to point out that insider-trading scandals go beyond a handful of bankers, brokers, and lawyers engaged in criminal behavior to undermine the integrity of the financial system and its institutions.

The scandal also focused attention on the wave of mergers and acquisitions that have been so widespread in recent years. The dominance of financial considerations, leading companies to stress short-term financial results in an effort to ward off mergers, may have undermined industry's ability to compete in world markets where our competitors implement long-term strategies to increase market shares.

The ideal image of corporations as socially responsible institutions mandated to produce goods and services the public wants and to create the jobs society needs was dealt a severe blow. The wave of asset-shifting, liquidations, plant-closings, and loss of markets to foreign competitors shook public confidence in the prevailing laissez-faire philosophy.

Liberal critics called for more and tighter regulation; conservative critics like Deputy Treasury Secretary Richard G. Darman issued populist calls for reordering corporate structures, and many business leaders criticized the way greed and the rush to get rich in a hurry have siphoned top talent away from creating products to creating deals.

So the twin scandals of "Irangate" and "Boeskygate" are not just politically titillating events—90-day wonders that produce headlines, gossip, and bad jokes. They are seismatic tremors running through our political and economic systems that call into question the values and practices adopted over the past half-dozen years.

Nor can they be seen as excesses that mar otherwise satisfactory systems, for they are symptomatic of serious disorders that plague our society—disorders that stem from ideologies contemptuous of democratic processes and humane social considerations.

Black Americans have lived with those societal disorders and felt their effects in ways most white Americans have not, for disproportionate black disadvantage means blacks suffer most from undemocratic processes and from public and private policies that devalue human mandates.

Typical of the moral blinders donned by the nation in recent years is its indifference to the continued existence of racism and racial disadvantage that permeate our society and degrade national life and aspirations.

Racism continues to live on despite the pious pronouncements that we are now a color-blind society. It can be seen in the daily drumfire of local reports about racially inspired outrages that show old forms of racism thriving alongside the more subtle forms of discrimination that have become more popular.

Several incidents that made national news toward the end of the year suffice to demonstrate this. In one, the police chief of a New Orleans suburb announced that police officers would routinely stop blacks seen in white neighborhoods. This "anti-crime" measure was rescinded after protests, but similar policies prevail in other communities without benefit of formal announcements.

A second incident involved The Citadel, the South's historic military academy. White cadets in Klan dress invaded the room of a black cadet. Had they been using drugs, they would have been expelled. But racist violence is apparently considered a schoolboy prank by the institution's administrators, and the offenders' punishment stopped far short of suspension. The black victim resigned from the school in protest against continued harassment, and a persistent pattern of racist harassment of black cadets was revealed in subsequent reports.

Finally, a lynch mob in the Howard Beach section of Queens, New York, assaulted three black men for the "crime" of being in their neighborhood. One died after the attack, which followed similar incidents in recent years.

In addition, housing discrimination is commonplace, as has been documented time and again. Discrimination in other aspects of life is also documented in incidents ranging from blacks passed over for jobs and promotions to blacks discriminated against in voting procedures.

It is hard to avoid the conclusion that the continuation of illegal discrimination and the resurgence of racist feelings are fostered by the administration's refusal to admit that racism may still be a problem.

The Justice Department's war on affirmative action and the powerful disinformation campaign it wages to convince the public that affirmative action is actually reverse discrimination cannot but prejudice public attitudes and encourage hostility toward black citizens.

The department persists in narrow interpretations of the law that emasculate key protections, such as its insistence that it will not object to certain voting changes that have a discriminatory result despite the clear Congressional mandate requiring it to do so.

Its philosophy, as enunciated by the Attorney General in a highly publicized address at Tulane University, remains uncomfortably close to the states' rights philosophy of the old-line segregationists who held that public officials may defy Supreme Court rulings they disagree with.

The department which also spearheaded a year-long attempt to get the President to rescind a 20-year-old Executive Order promoting federal minority employment is laggard in enforcing civil rights laws, expends its energies in fighting civil rights goals, and demonstrates its attitudes toward blacks by not having a single black person among the department's top officers.

Conservative spokesmen are fond of pointing out that the real problems facing black Americans are those that may not be ameliorated by more aggressive civil rights policies—problems like unemployment, inadequate education, teenage pregnancy, and others. It is unconscionable to use these tragic circumstances as an excuse to avoid necessary civil rights strategies while at the same time refusing to implement policies that deal positively with black disadvantage.

The fourth consecutive year of economic prosperity found unemployment remaining at an unacceptably high seven percent level. What used to be labelled "recession-level unemployment" is now described as "full employment." For black workers, unemployment remained stuck at Depression-level rates of 15 percent, with rates for inner-city teenagers above the 50 percent mark.

The highly vaunted American "job machine" was widely praised for creating some three million jobs over the course of the year, but less noted was the growth in part-time positions and the destruction of high-paying manufacturing jobs and their replacement by low-paying retail and service industry jobs. A study prepared for the Joint Economic Committee of Congress found that of the eight million new jobs created between 1979 and 1984, more than half paid less than $7,000 per year, indicating that the bulk of job growth has been in part-time and low-wage positions.

The U.S. Bureau of Labor Statistics estimates that nearly four million part-time workers want to work full-time, and almost 1.2 million discouraged workers have given up searching for jobs, an extraordinarily high figure for this stage of an economic recovery.

The Census Bureau reports that over 33 million people were poor in 1985—a rise of four million since 1980. More than one of every five American children are poor; for blacks, about half are poor. The rise in poverty has been accompanied by a widening gap between rich and poor. The Center for Budget and Policy Priorities states:

"The Census data show that from 1980 to 1985, the typical (or median) family in the poorest 40 percent of the population saw its income decline by $236, after adjusting for inflation. During the same five-year period, the typical family in the top 40 percent of the population saw its income rise $2,195, while the typical family in the richest 10 percent saw its income increase by $7,130."

Alongside the income gap is the wealth gap: the Census Bureau reports that the typical white family had a net worth twelve times as great as the net worth of the typical black family. Almost a third of all black families had no assets at all.

The growing gap between the rich and the poor cuts across racial lines, although it is most pronounced in white-black comparisons. . . .

Growing disparities in income and wealth are not accidental; they are the result of policies that encourage higher unemployment and lower levels of social spending and investment. Estimates of the cumulative effects of federal social spending cuts range from $114 billion to well over that figure, depending on the programs included. The most severe budget cuts have been in programs that invest in providing individuals with skills and opportunities, such as job training programs, which are a third smaller than they would have been had the 1981 law been kept in effect. Survival programs such as welfare and food stamps were also cut heavily, accounting for part of the rise in poverty and the added pressures burdening the poor.

The failure of current social welfare policies is most strongly dramatized by the plight of the homeless, now numbering some 3.5 million, according to the National Coalition for the Homeless. Despite the myth that the homeless are mentally disturbed individuals, the bulk of the homeless are individuals and families too poor to afford available housing. The administration has slashed federal funds for subsidized housing by 78 percent since 1980, and the gentrification of many urban areas coupled with the abandonment and destruction of low-income housing and the increased demand for such housing is primarily responsible for the shameful existence of widespread homelessness. . . .

In lieu of broad-based national programs, however, the administration's task force on welfare recommended localization of social welfare programs and warned against sweeping reform. Its disgracefully shallow report betrayed ignorance about the poor, the causes of poverty, and the potential of federal policies to encourage independence. While many states have implemented interesting experimental programs, including programs that place primary stress on providing education and training opportunities for welfare recipients, poverty is a national problem demanding national solutions, and a further withdrawal by the federal government can only worsen the situation.

While 1986 was yet another year of trial and tribulation for Black

America, there were some signs that the tide may yet turn, and that the cause of black and poor citizens, invisible for so long, may return to the nation's consciousness and its conscience. The brief national fling with policies encouraging personal greed at the expense of the public good cannot obscure the powerful vein of idealism lying just beneath the surface. As historian Arthur Schlesinger, Jr., put it: "The political cycle is due to turn at the end of the 1980s, and private interest is scheduled to give way to public purpose as the guiding principle of our politics."

There is nothing mechanistic or deterministic about this process, however. National policies will change because the present ones demonstrably harm the national interest, and because they go against the grain of traditional American concepts of morality and fair play.

Such considerations were behind the startling reversal of the nation's South Africa policy—the result of grass-roots sentiment that rejected South Africa's racism and direct and indirect American complicity in the apartheid system. Americans saw that it was in their best interests to withdraw from even minimal interaction with the present South African regime, and their will was embodied by Congress and by the leaders of many corporations, who ended their business relations there.

A similar outcome will result from the feeling spreading among Americans that social and economic policies are encouraging a dangerous gap between the affluent and the poor, harming our economy and crippling our cities. The election results indicated that such a shift in national opinion is now under way. Despite the President's popularity in November 1986—before "Irangate" broke—voters rejected candidates that shared his ideology, and expressed their concerns about an economic recovery that excludes millions of Americans. The deterioration we have noted in jobs and incomes will spur a reconsideration of government's role as a creator of opportunities for all, and not just for a limited number of financial speculators. There is also widespread concern about the ability of our economy to compete in the global marketplace, and the realization that America's future depends on national investment in human resources—in education and training that tap the potential of millions of disadvantaged people now excluded from full participation in our economy.

While white Americans remain largely ignorant of—or indifferent to—the plight of black citizens, there is a convergence of opinion among the races on some key issues. A national poll by the Gallup Organization conducted for the Joint Center for Political Studies found surprising agreement between blacks and whites on the major problems confronting the nation. Although white Americans continued to believe that civil rights was not a major problem, respondents of both races identified unemployment, drug abuse, and the high cost of living as the three most important issues, and both ranked crime, health care, and the quality of public education among the top ten. This suggests the possibility of increased interracial cooperation on issues that disproportionately affect the black population.

Another positive sign in 1986 was the final approval of the pastoral letter, "Economic Justice for All," by the National Conference of Catholic Bishops. "That so many people are poor in a nation as rich as ours is a social and moral scandal that we cannot ignore," the Bishops stated. They recommended an agenda similar to that supported by the National Urban League . . . including full employment policies, expanded job-training programs in the private sector, alternatives to welfare, job creation for the long-term unemployed, and others.

Perhaps the most positive development in 1986 was the intensification of the black community's effort to deal with such serious problems as crime, drugs, teenage pregnancy, family breakup, and public education. The National Urban League launched its nationwide Education Initiative in September to get the schools back on track, to motivate our young people, and to involve our communities in making the schools work better. It is a results-oriented program with a five-year time frame and concrete, achievable goals to improve the school performance of disadvantaged youngsters.

Each Urban League will mobilize the community to define key issues, maximize use of existing resources, build coalitions and support for change, and implement concrete action designed to target at-risk children and to have measurable results. Some of our affiliates have already developed action plans with five-year time frames designed to increase the number of black students in college-track classes and math and science courses. Others have programs to engage black adults and students in activities that have a positive impact on educational achievement, such as mentoring and guidance projects.

Other national and local community-based organizations are deeply involved in similar programs directly tackling internal community problems. The wave of community activism will counter the powerlessness that has impeded resolution of our problems, and will harness the tremendous resources and energies of black citizens to create brighter prospects for all black people.

So the black community enters 1987 in a hopeful mood, convinced it has weathered the worst and prepared to play its part in assuring a more hopeful future. . . .

The Law and Black Americans: Retreat from Civil Rights

The Federal Judiciary

A grave threat to established gains—one that will affect all of us far into the future—is the administration's effort to appoint to the federal bench judges who have views that show a lack of sympathy for the plight of blacks and other disadvantaged groups. To date, the administration has appointed 289 of the authorized total of 648 federal district and appellate court judges. All but five are white. Typically, they are young as well as conservative; many will be sitting for the next three or four decades.

Recently the Senate has begun to resist some of the administration's nominees. The Senate Judiciary Committee refused to send the nomination of Jefferson B. Sessions 3d from Alabama to the full Senate. Opponents had provided ample evidence of Sessions' gross insensitivity to issues of concern to black Americans.

Moreover, the selection and appointment of federal judges, under the Reagan administration, has changed profoundly from what it was during the Carter administration. The number of blacks, Hispanics and women who were Federal judges at the time the Congress passed the Omnibus Judgeship Act in 1978 was appallingly low. Out of 399 district court judges, less than 20 were black; of the 97 appeals courts judges, five were black. The bill created 152 additional federal judgeships, 117 for the district courts and 35 for the appeals courts, thereby expanding the judiciary by approximately 29 percent.

After passage of the bill, the Carter administration set in motion procedures to open up the selection process in order to increase the numbers of qualified minorities and women appointed to the federal bench, including selection commissions with members drawn from different backgrounds and racial groups as well as some non-lawyers. Civil rights groups were invited to recommend persons for appointment to the commissions, as well as to suggest potential nominees for the newly created vacancies.

Not surprisingly, the names of many qualified blacks, Hispanics, and women began to appear among the nominees, with the result that by the time Mr. Carter left office, his record in appointing blacks, other minorities, and women to the bench was singular and exemplary. Mr. Carter appointed a total of 258 federal judges. Among a total of 202 appointed to district courts, 29 were women, 28 were black, and 14 were Hispanic; of the 56 appeals courts appointments, 11 were women, nine were black, and two, Hispanic.

All of this changed when the Reagan administration took office. The innovative and successful experiment in "democratizing" the nomination and confirmation process came to an abrupt end, and the process once more became a closed one. Moreover, the administration still has more than 50 vacancies to fill—*not including* additional vacancies bound to occur through attrition, resignation, death, and retirement. By the end of his term, according to estimates by the Department of Justice, the President will have appointed to lifetime positions more than 45 percent of the entire federal judiciary....

Blacks, Budgets, and Taxes

Anticipated Impacts of Fiscal Reform on the Black Political Economy

Both GRH [Gramm-Rudman-Hollings] and Tax Reform will have significant effects on the distribution and redistribution of economic and political resources among blacks and between blacks and other Americans.

As these impacts are assessed, it is important to keep in mind both the criteria for good fiscal policies and their compatibility with the economic and political goals of blacks. Fiscal policies should maintain the principles of *productivity, equity,* and *elasticity.* Both budget and tax policies should adhere to these principles.

A productive fiscal policy generates sufficient revenues to meet governmental needs on the tax side and makes investments in human needs, economic development, and defense on the spending side. If tax policies fail to generate adequate revenue, more public monies must be spent on borrowing with a subsequent effect on interest rates and economic growth.

An equitable fiscal policy is fair to both taxpayers and to specific public constituencies benefiting from public expenditures. In tax policy, economists refer to two kinds of equity—*horizontal* and *vertical.* Horizontal equity means that taxpayers who have the same amounts of income should be taxed at the same rate. Vertical equity implies that wealthier people should pay more taxes than poorer people. A related principle is that tax policies should be *progressive.* Taxes increase as income increases. *Proportional* principles of taxation increase tax in exact and direct proportion to increases in income. *Regressive* taxes impose greater burdens on taxpayers less able to pay or taxes increase as income decreases.

Although applied traditionally to taxes, notions of progressivity, proportionality, and regressivity also have a budgetary counterpart. Fiscal policies that tend to benefit the least needy and deprive the most needy are budgetarily regressive. Generally, GRH is regressive in its impacts on blacks because it utilizes budget bases that were already retrenched before 1985 as baselines for GRH-mandated cuts. Even exempted programs will not experience significant increases in expenditure. On the other hand, the Tax Reform Act is generally progressive in that it seeks to eliminate the working poor from the tax rolls, to impose greater taxes on those able to pay, and to shift tax burden to income-generating corporations.

Finally, the principle of *elasticity* suggests that the fiscal system be flexible enough to address its revenue and spending needs regardless of macroeconomic changes in economic conditions. Taxes and spending make a contribution to the stabilization of the economy. An additional principle, somewhat at odds with the elasticity principle, is that taxes be *neutral.* Neutrality suggests that tax laws should not affect taxpayers' spending, saving, investment, and other financial decisions. Not all experts agree that this is a realistic or desirable policy.

As we review the anticipated impacts of GRH and the Tax Reform Act on blacks, these fiscal principles are essential. Generally, they are compatible with black economic and political aspirations, particularly with regard to the need to have more affluent and able taxpayers pay their share of the tax burden; to promote fiscal policies that encourage economic development and, hence, employment; to support human services and education; . . . and to foster successful minority business development. . . .

. . . Many of the benefits to black households and individuals from tax reform are likely to be overshadowed by the economic impacts of GRH. Since blacks depend more upon direct government support than whites, their income and occupational status are particularly sensitive to reductions in government spending, even in defense. Raises in the income tax threshold may shift more tax burden to middle- and upper-income groups, but the offsetting effects of deficit-reduction measures should also be considered in calculating net benefits from the new tax provisions.

Tax reform is particularly beneficial for middle-income Americans, including blacks. Increasing the standard deduction and personal exemptions, and across-the-board reduction in income tax are identified as major aspects of tax relief to this group. The retention of deductions most relevant to middle-income working families in the black community is another. These deductions include the exclusion of employer-provided health benefits and other fringe benefits, deductibility of state and local taxes, and the continued deduction for home mortgage interest.

But, returning to the budget side, much of these benefits depends upon continued levels of employment in middle-income families and households, particularly since a disproportionate number of middle-income blacks works in government-related or government-sponsored occupations and institutions affected by GRH. Federal government support for agencies with substantial black employment—the Postal Service; the Labor Department; the Departments of Health and Human Services, Housing and Urban Development, and Education—and for state and local government has been and will continue to be directly affected by GRH and other efforts to control the deficit....

A key concern for black individuals and households is housing. As indicated earlier, discouragement of real estate investments, curtailment of capital gains, and stricter rules on income losses for rental property tend to discourage the development of low-income housing in the black community, just as GRH reductions in the housing and Community Development Block Grants under GRH are occurring. Since blacks tend to occupy rental housing to a much greater extent than whites, it is not likely that tax credits for investors in low-income housing can offset disincentives combined with steadily increasing operating costs. Moreover, the National Association of Home Builders predicts a rent increase of 28 percent in new developments as a result of tax reform. Whether for new or existing housing, it is not clear that the combination of GRH and Tax Reform will encourage rapid development of low-income housing and, consequently, accommodation to the needs of urban blacks....

Macroeconomic Impacts on the Black Community

The combination of GRH reductions and both progressive and regressive impacts of tax reform on black individuals/households and black institutions constitutes a macroeconomic impact on the black community, which is largely negative. Coming back to the Ilchman-Uphoff model, marginal declines in income resulting from budget retrenchment, tax and expenditure limitations at the state and local level, and the new tax reform legislation pose serious challenges to the cultivation of social, economic, and political resources in the black political economy. Early indications are that federal budget reductions are likely to continue while the realities of tax reform are realized.

When budget and tax impacts are considered together, the minimal benefits of tax reform for some black household and institutional taxpayers are likely to be canceled both by negative impacts of tax reform and deficit reduction. However, taxpayer adjustments to both deficit reduction and tax reform are still in progress. The consequences of these short-term and longer-term adjustments are, as yet, not fully discernible.

Recommended Strategies

Given the combined impact of GRH, other federal budget decisions, and tax reform, the following recommendations are proposed:

1. Tax reform legislation should be closely monitored as it is implemented to identify both anticipated and unanticipated impacts on the black community that are significant and should be addressed;
2. Serious review and analysis of the Congressional Black Caucus' Alternative Budget should be carried out in every major black institution and among black elected officials and managers. It is the most thoughtful and systematic analysis and statement of budgetary priorities for all U.S. citizens now available.
3. Black business needs support in both the federal budget and in tax reform legislation. Continued support for the Small Business Administration's management of the 8(a) program, Small Business Development Centers, and technical assistance programs to black businesses are needed. Far from being abolished, the SBA should be strengthened to support small and minority businesses during this turbulent period of fiscal transition. Moreover, small and minority businesses should be exempted from repeal of the investment tax credit when their expenditures on such equipment equal or exceed five percent of their net worth. In this time of shrinking manufacturing activity in the U.S., no tax or budget policy should frustrate investments in capital equipment, new technology, and retrofitting of old plants and tools.
4. A national fiscal hotline should be developed to monitor the impacts of GRH and tax legislation on charitable, education, and community institutions. This hotline would document the impact of such measures on blacks and would coordinate efforts to lobby for modification of fiscal policy when needed.

AIDS: A Special Report

...Black Americans suffer from AIDS at an alarmingly high incidence and prevalence rate. From June 1, 1981, to September 8, 1986, U.S. physicians and health departments notified the Centers for Disease

Control (CDC) of 24,576 patients meeting the AIDS case definition (positive antibody test for HIV, presence of HIV, and one opportunistic infection or malignancy). Of these 6,192 (25 percent) were blacks, whereas blacks represent only 12 percent of the U.S. population, according to the 1980 U.S. Census. The proportion of black cases has remained relatively constant, but the number of reported AIDS cases among persons of all racial and ethnic backgrounds continues to rise.

More black adults with AIDS than white adults with AIDS (62 percent and 33 percent, respectively) were likely to reside in New York, New Jersey, or Florida. Black men accounted for 23 percent of the 22,648 cases, and black women accounted for 51 percent of the 1,634 female cases (compared with whites at 28 percent of all AIDS cases).

The mode of transmission also differed among races. Homosexual or bisexual men who had AIDS and patients who acquired AIDS from blood or blood products were predominantly white. Patients with a history of intravenous drug abuse or heterosexual contact with persons of increased risk for acquiring AIDS and patients with no identified mode of transmission were predominantly black or Hispanic. The proportion of blacks with AIDS was high in all transmission categories with the exception of hemophilia.

The racial/ethnic distribution of homosexual/bisexual patients differed from that of heterosexual patients. Among homosexual/bisexual male AIDS patients, 16 percent were black, 11 percent Hispanic, and 73 percent white. Among heterosexual AIDS patients in other transmission categories, 50 percent were black, 25 percent for both Hispanic and white....

AIDS poses a definite challenge to the physical and psycho-emotional health of black women nationwide. As previously stated, black women account for 51 percent of the total diagnosed AIDS cases among women. Women make up seven percent, or 1,789 of the total number of Americans with AIDS. And of this number, 1,080 have died. The majority of these women are poor, single mothers, most of whom live in New York City. A devastating by-product of this is that, of the total U.S. pediatric AIDS cases, 82 percent, or 204 of the 250 babies, are born to black women....

Early in 1982, a significant number of AIDS cases was found among Haitians in the U.S. and Haiti. Also beginning in 1982, cases of AIDS were identified in Europe among Africans, and among Europeans of both sexes with histories of sexual contact with Africans in Europe or in Africa. Epidemiological studies conducted in central Africa by European, U.S., and African scientists revealed a high incidence of AIDS in Zaire and among west and east-central African countries. It is estimated that 50,000 people have died from the disease called "Slim" (AIDS) in central Africa since its confirmed appearances in the late 1970s. Privately some leading AIDS researchers say the death toll to date is several hundred thousand!...

Africans and Haitians are represented significantly in the populations of New York, Washington, Miami, Delray Beach, Los Angeles, Houston, and other cities. They are street merchants, taxicab drivers, students, diplomats, lawyers, doctors, etc., and are otherwise socially interactive with all segments of American society.

When blacks are viewed by the larger society, they are often perceived as one homogeneous mass indistinguishable from one another with reference to origin or cultural differences. To the nonsophisticate, a stigma for Haitians or Africans is a stigma for all black Americans. We all suffer equally the same prejudices, racial slurs, and maltreatment....

Another possible source of homosexual/bisexual and heterosexual transmission is the prisons. In January, 1986, the National Prison Project of the American Civil Liberties Union found that about 420 cases of AIDS had been diagnosed in state prisons across the country. Most of these inmates were intravenous drug abusers, and the majority of the cases were reported from the Middle Atlantic region: New York, New Jersey, Pennsylvania, and Washington, D.C., with all other parts of the United States contributing to much smaller percentages.

U.S. prisons have a disproportionate number of black inmates (60 percent) compared with our representation in the general population of 12 percent. In New York state, blacks constitute 70 percent of the inmate population. However, there is no available racial breakdown data of the reported 292 cases of AIDS presently in New York prisons.

At the time of the National Prison Project report, New York prisons were reported to have 245 AIDS cases and 153 deaths; 40 cases had been released and 52 cases remained incarcerated. As of this writing, New York state prisons report 292 AIDS cases, an increase of 47 cases in 10 months, for an average of about four diagnosed cases per month. If the CDC criteria were used to make the diagnosis, these new cases had to have contracted an opportunistic infection and were most likely very sick....

Rates for blacks [among military recruit applicants] are extremely alarming: the services are universally known to not accept homosexuals/bisexuals or intravenous drug users, and such persons should not apply. If one is to assume that these young, black people were from the general population, that almost 1/250 examined was infected with HIV, and that 10-30 percent of them will eventually develop AIDS, then *Black America is in an extremely precarious position.*

Fifty-eight percent of all persons dying of AIDS in New York City are black, an obviously disproportionate rate when compared with our 30 percent representation of the total New York City AIDS cases. Researchers attribute this high death rate to: very poor health prior to contracting the disease; delayed medical consultation; lack of available, sensitive health care providers; and outright denial of the problem....

Black gays, jointly with whites and in their own organizations, such as the National Coalition of Black Lesbians and Gays (NCBLG), have sponsored conferences and meetings all over the country to raise awareness in black communities about the problem of AIDS, its prevention, and how to get help and counseling. Their efforts have included all minorities

(Asians, Haitians, Latinos, Hispanics, Native Americans) and have been laudable despite a "brush off" from most black organizations, allegedly because of the organizations' fear of endorsing homosexual behavior....

What is needed is a massive and sustained prevention and education effort, culturally and ethnically focused to attract the attention of the community to those disproportionately affected by this fatal disease. Federal, state, municipal, and private funds must be allocated to support this effort. Physicians, ministers, politicians, and community leaders must be at the forefront of these efforts, in order to reduce the sensitivity that has spread in relationship to homophobia that negatively influences the degree of caring and support we give to both the afflicted and the worried well. Housing and hospices must be provided so that AIDS victims can die with dignity. Morticians must be alerted to be prepared for the 179,000 deaths predicted to occur in the U.S. by 1991. Twelve thousand of those dying will be black and from New York City where burial space is limited—crematories are not equipped to handle these numbers. What I perceive for Black America is a major catastrophe if we do not begin effective programs immediately....

Recommendations

1. Racism in any of its insidious forms, exacts a toll on those who practice it, those who tolerate it, and those who suffer from it. We call upon our national leadership, in both public and private domains, to repudiate racism as a tolerable element within our country's moral fiber and to condemn discriminatory acts and attitudes that serve to degrade our image as a land of freedom, justice and opportunity.

2. The Justice Department's failure to enforce the spirit as well as the letter of civil rights law collaborates in the perpetuation of injustices against blacks and other minorities. We call upon Congress to eliminate the loopholes evident in current civil rights laws and for increased civil rights enforcement by the Justice Department. We urge passing of the proposed Civil Rights Restoration Act of 1986 which would restore the broad coverage and protection embodied in Title VI of the Civil Rights Act of 1964, Title IX of the Education Amendments of 1972, Section 504 of the Rehabilitation Act of 1973 and the Age Discrimination Act of 1975.

3. Affirmative action policies and practices on the part of the government and private sector are still needed as a remedy for past and present racial discrimination. We therefore advocate continued support of consistent, results-oriented affirmative action policies and practices with no change in Executive Order 11246 as a remedy for past and present discrimination.

4. Joblessness has a devastating impact on unemployed people, in lowered self-esteem, higher levels of illness, mental strains, and family problems. Full employment is vital because it produces crucially important human and social benefits. We urge Congressional enactment of legislation establishing a full employment policy and a universal employment and

training system to ensure the availability of productive work for the unemployed and the skills training necessary to obtain and hold a job.

5. Social welfare reform must ensure a comprehensive, adequate, equitable, publicly acceptable, universal and dignified system of benefits. The welfare system should ideally be linked to both adult employment and youth training opportunities which provide a living wage. Reform of the welfare system should provide an income floor below which no child should fall. We encourage Congress to consider the recent legislation supported by the National Urban League, Inc. These legislative pieces, The Opportunities for Employment Preparation Act of 1986, (SB. 2578) and the Aid for Families and Employment Transition Act of 1986, (SB. 2579) were prepared to address long-term unemployed persons or AFDC recipients, thereby strengthening both one- and two-parent poor families. While incremental in nature, this legislation provides for the long-range view of full employment nationally, and other needed supportive services.

6. Almost 63 percent of black students attend predominantly minority schools. In an economy that is restructuring to emphasize highly-skilled jobs and technical know-how, students must have access to appropriate use of an educational technology. The U.S. Department of Education and related federal agencies must reassert their roles as keepers of the flame of educational equity by ensuring that predominantly minority schools have the resources to provide quality education. Targeted, categorical supplemental academic assistance needs to be increased. With supportive federal standards for equal educational access and opportunity for success, and by organizing community-wide coalitions for reform which demand changes in the schools and changed behavior in our own families, the black community can stem the further loss of our youngsters to the dropout syndrome, to crime, and to premature parenthood.

7. The nation's black community suffers from an unequal standard of health care due to a complexity of social problems: lack of financial support, resources, inadequate education, little job training or job opportunities. We therefore call for continued governmental and community-based efforts, imperative to combating teen pregnancy through the funding of Title X of the Public Health Services Act, Medicaid, the Maternal and Child Health Block Grant, and other related services; increasing government support of male involvement in family planning programs; education for parents and teens on the importance of examining and planning life options.

8. A lack of affordable housing is the crux of the nation's housing crisis. Congress and the administration must be committed to developing and funding a national affordable housing program with a primary emphasis on meeting the housing needs of low-income families. While shelters are effective as a temporary solution, their impact on family relationships can be damaging and far-reaching. Congress must support the Homeless Personal Survival Act as a major tool in providing comprehensive support services and permanent housing to the homeless. The Community Devel-

opment Block Grant Program has been an important component in sponsoring and stimulating housing and community development activities at the local level. The CDBG program in the current budget climate can achieve its most effective results if it is administered as a program targeted to aid the housing and community development needs of low-income families.

9. Attacks on "big government" too often focus on the problems experienced in the implementation of programs without enough attention and creativity devoted to solving the problems that government programs were developed to address. We strengthen our call for legislative actions to preserve and defend federal and state programs that encourage social and economic development as well as urban revitalization.

10. While government has an obligation to care for all of its citizens, we recognize and encourage the responsibility of Black America as active participants and leaders in the struggle for equality. We urge increased community and institutional activism, which addresses problems, offers solutions, demands accountability and commits its own resources—financial as well as moral—to make a world of difference for the black community as well as the whole of American society.

AID REPORT ON CAMEROON DISASTER

January 15, 1987

More than 1,700 people died August 21, 1986, in Cameroon, a country on the west coast of Africa, after a dense cloud of carbon dioxide at lethal concentrations erupted on Lake Nyos and swept through surrounding villages, displacing atmospheric air vital to human and animal life.

The U.S. Agency for International Development's (AID) Office of Foreign Disaster Assistance sent a group of scientists to Cameroon to determine the cause of the eruptions and the likelihood of similar events in the future. After three weeks of field studies beginning in late August, the team issued their final report January 15, 1987.

Rescue workers arriving after the eruption found people and animals lying dead as far as ten kilometers from Lake Nyos, a volcanic crater lake in Cameroon's northwest region. The United States, Israel, and Western European countries assisted with food, water, and shelter for more than 10,000 survivors of the disaster.

The incident was the second time in two years that gas escaping from a volcanic crater lake in Cameroon had taken human lives. In August 1984, thirty-seven people died after a gas eruption on Lake Monoun, ninety-five kilometers southeast of Lake Nyos.

Causes of Eruption

The researchers concluded that victims died from asphyxiation resulting from exposure to high concentrations of carbon dioxide. The gas was formed in magma, or molten rock, underlying the lake bed; it had seeped into the lake dissolved in groundwater. Apparently the level of carbon dioxide in the bottom strata of the lake water had built up until the water was supersaturated with the gas.

Although the AID report left unresolved the actual cause of the eruption, it stated that any slight disturbance could have released the gas from the supersaturated water. The report ruled out volcanic activity as the source of the eruption because of the lake's relatively cool temperature and low sulfur content, and the composition of its dissolved gases.

Precautionary Measures

A main concern of the AID study was whether gas eruptions were likely to occur again. The study concluded that all forty crater lakes in northwest Cameroon had the potential to release carbon dioxide and recommended several precautionary measures to reduce the chance of future gas eruptions. Among these suggestions were monitoring the volcanic crater lakes for high carbon dioxide levels and siphoning bottom waters to the top to reduce the levels of the gas. In addition, a spillway draining Lake Nyos could be redesigned to prevent flooding in the valleys below.

Another Explanation

Four months after the August 1986 eruption, Lake Nyos was again the scene of unusual activity. On December 30, 1986, two French scientists stationed at Lake Nyos heard rumbling noises on the lake and on nearby Lake Njupi. The following day they noticed on the surfaces of both lakes reddish spots that resembled the coloration of Lake Nyos after the August eruption.

AID scientists sent to the area determined that layers of cold water at the bottom of the lake had flip-flopped with warmer waters near the surface. This sudden "overturn" sent forth a burst of carbon dioxide from the deep waters. The researchers witnessed a rockfall and noticed evidence of other rockfalls from the sheer cliffs surrounding Lake Nyos. They concluded that rockfalls may have been responsible for the noise heard by the scientists and may have disturbed the deep water of the lake, producing the reddish stains. The researchers theorized that similar occurrences had set off the August 1986 eruption.

Following are excerpts from the January 15, 1987, final report of the scientific team sent to Cameroon by the U.S. Agency for International Development's Office of Foreign Disaster Assistance to investigate the August 1986 gas eruption and catastrophic loss of life:

Introduction

Cameroon is a country of about 8.5 million people located on the west coast of Africa. English and French are the official languages. In the northwest part of the country, there is a volcanic zone characterized by many craters filled with beautiful lakes. Lake Nyos is one such lake: located high in the mountains, normally deep blue in color, peaceful.

On Thursday evening, 21 August 1986, tragic events occurred at this idyllic lake that made it known throughout the world as a "killer lake." The early part of the evening began with heavy rains and thunderstorms typical of the rainy season. By 9:30 P.M., however, the weather was calm, the air temperature cool, and most people were engaged in their usual evening activities. This tranquil scene was suddenly disturbed by a series of rumbling sounds lasting perhaps 15-20 seconds. Many people in the immediate area of the lake came out of their homes, experienced a warm sensation, smelled rotten eggs or gunpowder, and rapidly lost consciousness. Other individuals either became unconscious without preliminary symptoms, or never awakened from their sleep. One observer, who was on high ground above Lake Nyos, reported hearing a bubbling sound. Walking to a better vantage point, he saw a white cloud rise from the lake, accompanied by a large water wave that washed up onto the southern shore. None of the survivors in the valley saw a visible cloud.

Survivors of the incident awakened 6 to 36 hours later, and many found that their oil lamps had gone out while still containing oil, their animals and members of their family were dead, and they themselves were weak and confused.

About 1,700 people and 3,000 cattle died near the lake and along drainages up to 10 km north of the lake. The pattern of death within this region was definitely not uniform. For example, in the Nyos area there was a pen with four of the five goats dead, and nearby a home where only four of the nine family members survived. Cattle in the lower lying areas perished, while those at the higher elevations were still grazing normally. Many small animals died, but many others were still alive. The bird and insect populations were significantly reduced for at least 48 hours, but the plant life remained essentially unaffected. As best as could be determined, however, the humans and animals that did not survive died very quickly with no signs of panic or discomfort.

On Friday morning, 22 August, people from the surrounding villages began to drift into the area and start the grim task of recovery and burial. It was not until Saturday morning that the rest of the world heard of the incident, after two helicopter pilots from Helimission (a Swiss missionary service) flew into the area and quickly reported their findings. The pilots and other people approaching the lake on Saturday or Sunday reported no general discomfort or problems related to breathing.

As best as could be ascertained, there were no premonitory changes in Lake Nyos that served to forewarn of the incident. Following the event, however, the water level was noted to have dropped about one meter, and there was vegetation damage showing that a large water surge had washed up on the southern lake shore to a height of about 25 m. A water surge 6 m in height had overflowed the spillway, and a fountain of water or froth had splashed over an 80 m high rock promontory on the southwestern side of the lake. On Saturday morning, a transient white chalky substance was noted covering the rocky cliffs on the west side of the lake, but this was not present when we arrived. We did find that the water was calm, but had turned a rusty-red color with mats of vegetation floating on the surface. The household goods in the homes surrounding the lakes were undisturbed, and rocks perched precariously on the cliffs at the edge of the lake had not been shifted. There was, however, one small area on the steep west side of the lake which showed evidence of a fresh landslide, that could have occurred either just before, during, or after the incident.

A similar catastrophic event occurred at Lake Monoun, about 95 km to the southeast in August 1984. In the Monoun disaster, 37 people died after walking into a visible cloud around the lake. An evaluation, done seven months after the incident, concluded that the causative agent was carbon dioxide (CO_2) released from the lake. According to local legends, there may have been at least three additional incidents where exploding lakes or mass deaths have occurred in this same area of Cameroon.

Because of the previous incident at Lake Monoun, . . . a more extensive and timely evaluation of the Lake Nyos event was immediately initiated, and a diversified, eleven-member scientific team consisting of forensic pathologists, geologists, water chemists, environmental engineers, a limnologist, and a clinical physician was organized and sent on short notice to Cameroon. The team arrived in Yaounde on Wednesday, 27 August 1986. The following report is a summation of its 3-week field evaluation of the area plus the results of later analytical studies.

Geology

Regional

A number of small, young basaltic volcanoes have formed cinder cones and lava flows in northwest Cameroon along part of the "Cameroon Volcanic Line," a northeast-southwest (NE-SW) trending zone of crustal weakness that extends 1,600 km from islands in the Atlantic ocean into northwestern Cameroon and northeastern Nigeria. Volcanic explosions have also formed numerous circular craters (maars), many of which are now occupied by deep crater lakes. . . .

The Lake Nyos Area

Lake Nyos, 310 km northwest of Yaounde, is a classic maar, formed in a coarse-grained biotite-quartz monzonite (granitic) terrain of uncertain, pre-Tertiary age (older than 65 million years). This rock is overlain by a deeply weathered, red-orange soil. The granitic terrain is cut by prominent faults which are marked by pronounced erosional lineaments, including the linear Nyos valley north of Lake Nyos. Many volcanoes are localized along these faults.

Lake Nyos is one of three eruptive features in the immediate area. The others are prominent basaltic cinder cones located 1 km to the NE and 2 km to the south. Although the Lake Nyos crater may be the oldest of these eruptive features, it is still very young. Judging by the unweathered and little-eroded ash deposits on the flanks of the Lake Nyos crater, it may be only a few hundred years old. The lake is 1,925 m in maximum length (elongated NW-SE), and 1,180 m in maximum width. It is shallow at the southern end, but drops off steeply to a large, flat plain at a depth of 208 m. This plain is formed of silt and mud of unknown thickness. Electron microprobe analysis of one sediment sample from the bottom indicated the presence of feldspar, quartz, biotite, and kaolinite; no fresh volcanic constituents were observed.

About two-thirds of the Lake Nyos crater is rimmed by quartz monzonite, and the rest by ash beds that were mainly erupted at the time of crater formation. These ash beds consist principally of pyroclastic surge deposits (deposits formed by violent explosions that accompanied crater formation). The irregularly bedded deposits are up to 30 m thick at the crater rim, but thin very rapidly and become finer-grained away from the crater. Maximum size of rock fragments (clasts) increases upwards in the deposit, suggesting increased violence later in the crater-forming event. Ultramafic fragments (fragments rich in Fe and Mg) are common in the upper third of the surge deposits, and are up to 25 cm in size. These fragments, carried to the surface from great depths, are composed mostly of the minerals olivine, orthopyroxene, clinopyroxene, and spinel. They contain abundant tiny fluid inclusions of CO_2 and H_2O). Many of the ultramafic clasts are mantled by olivine-plagioclase basalt (a dark, silica-poor volcanic rock), and angular basalt clasts are common throughout the surge deposits.

The ash beds are moderately well consolidated near the crater rim, but are poorly consolidated and easily erodable on the flanks. They form vertical cliffs along the NE rim, and are sufficiently durable to form the resistant bed of the stream draining Lake Nyos to the NW. This stream plunges over a 35- to 40-m-high waterfall after descending a few meters below lake level, leaving a 40-m wide septum or "spillway" to bound Lake Nyos on the north. The thickness of ash underlying the spillway is not known. The pyroclastic surge deposits were originally deposited around the entire circumference of the lake, but they are now exposed discontinuously around the southern end of the lake. This suggests that they may have been eroded away by waves generated by previous gas events.

Origin and Subsurface Structure of Lake Nyos

The formation of the present Lake Nyos crater was preceded by a short period of relatively quiescent eruptive activity, as indicated by fire-fountain volcanic deposits and a thin basalt flow exposed beneath pyroclastic ash beds on the northeast shore of the lake. The volume of the ejected pyroclastic material is considerably less than the volume of the present maar crater, indicating that the Lake Nyos crater was formed in part by collapse of adjoining rocks.

The Lake Nyos maar is undoubtedly underlain by a diatreme (a near-vertical pipe-like conduit consisting largely of fragmental, permeable ash). A schematic cross-section of this diatreme shows a complex pipe filled with fragmented rocks and ash, and intruded by volcanic material. The diatreme was formed above a dike (lava-filled crack) of ascending, volatile (gas)-rich basaltic magma (molten rock), whose source lay within the Earth's mantle as evidenced by the abundant ultramafic fragments. This rising basaltic magma explosively fragmented as it neared the Earth's surface, either by release of dissolved magmatic volatiles or by contact with meteoric (near-surface) water. The diatreme could extend to as much as 2-3 km depth, to a point where it becomes transitional to its feeder dike.

Gas Origin

There are three potential sources for the gas released on 21 August: *volcanic, magmatic, and biogenic.* Our distinctions between the terms *volcanic* and *magmatic* as used in this report are important. As used here, *volcanic* gas is associated with high-temperature, near-surface eruptive processes; *magmatic* gas is released from magma deep within the earth, is relatively cool by the time it reaches the surface, and has lost its reactive constituents such as sulfur and chlorine compounds and carbon monoxide. *Biogenic* gas is produced by decomposition of organic matter and has a low temperature.

Based on geophysical and geochemical evidence, it has been inferred that the mantle source region of basaltic Cameroon magmas lies at depths greater than about 90 km. In addition, the isotopic and trace-element geochemistry of Cameroon magmas suggest that they are derived from parent melts produced by very small degrees of partial melting of the mantle. These two critical observations help explain why Cameroon magmas tend to be rich in CO_2.

Specifically, the deep source region exists at pressures so great that any carbon at those depths is likely to exist as the carbonate mineral dolomite rather than in a fluid phase. Under these conditions, small degrees of partial melting of the mantle result in rapid breakdown of the carbonate mineral, which then enters the melt, making the melt very CO_2-rich. If such melts begin to ascend from the source region toward the lower pressure surface, they cannot retain high concentrations of CO_2 in solution, and will begin to degas some of their dissolved CO_2 at depths between 80 and 100 km.

Furthermore, crystallization of any magma that proceeds to advanced degrees within the crust will lead to saturation of H_2O or CO_2 in the residual melt, and a gas phase may begin to separate from the melt, creating bubbles. The bubbles have a strong tendency to ascend buoyantly, first through the melt and then up along grain boundaries in overlying crustal rocks. If such gases reach the surface by rising along crustal faults, they may simply escape to the atmosphere and safely dissipate. If, however, such gases are prevented from reaching the atmosphere, they may begin to accumulate. In Cameroon, potential accumulation sites include possible near-surface voids within the disrupted feeder conduits of old volcanic craters, ground water, or stratified crater lakes. Therefore, it is not necessary to invoke special geologic conditions in order to explain the accumulation of CO_2-rich gas in Lake Nyos and environs.

Distinctions Between High- and Low-Temperature Gas

Temperature profiles of Lake Nyos taken on 4 and 5 September indicate that the water was relatively cool and nearly isothermal after the event. The bottom temperatures in Lake Nyos were no higher than those in other tropical lakes at similar elevation and latitude. We could not substantiate a report by a few local villagers of hot water in the Lake Nyos outflow stream near Nyos village.

A volcanic injection of magma or gas into the lake would have been accompanied by an input of heat and an increase in water temperature. For example, during volcanic injection of lava and gas into the Soufriere crater lake (St. Vincent) water temperatures reached 82°C. On the basis of maximum cooling rates in tropical lakes, Lake Nyos could have dissipated only enough heat in the 12 days prior to our sampling to decrease the temperature at each depth by 0.5°C. Thus, the supposition of a significant heat input becomes untenable.

We sampled water from the maar Lakes Nyos, Barombi Mbo, Bambuluwe, Nyi, and Wum; one cold freshwater spring above Lake Nyos; local precipitation; and two soda springs approximately 40 km south of Lake Nyos.

Only the top 10 m of Lake Nyos contained measurable dissolved oxygen. Precipitation of ferric hydroxide in the oxygenated surface waters was responsible for the lake's reddish-brown color; below 10 m the water was clear.

. . . The composition of the bottom water before the event is unknown. The most noticeable change in surface-water chemistry after the event was an increase in the concentration of most elements. The concentrations of many solutes (dissolved substances) showed a definite increase with depth, implying either that the bottom water was more concentrated than the surface water prior to the event, or less likely, that there had been incomplete mixing of a recent input of solutes near the bottom.

Any large input of lava or volcanic gas into the lake would add sulfur and chlorine compounds. Again, an example of this is found in Soufriere crater lake, where large increases in concentrations of sulfur and chlorine compounds accompanied volcanic injection. Lake Nyos, however, shows no such enrichment of sulfur and chlorine compounds in either lake waters or sediments. Hydrogen fluoride is also a common volcanic gas, but its aqueous form was nearly absent from Lake Nyos.

Based on our field sampling, we estimate that one liter of hypolimnetic water in Lake Nyos contains one to five liters of dissolved gas. Carbon dioxide comprises 98-99 percent of the dissolved gas. The non-volcanic character of the gas is most apparent in the low concentrations of carbon monoxide, hydrogen, hydrogen sulfide, and sulfur dioxide compared to those in volcanic gas. Studies of volcanic emanations from magmas similar in composition to those erupted in Cameroon, notably those from Iceland and Hawaii, show that the relative proportions of CO_2 and sulfur in near-surface volcanic gases vary within certain limits. The weight ratio of CO_2 to sulfur in such volcanic gases is typically less than 100. In contrast, the ratio CO_2 to sulfur for Lake Nyos bottom waters is greater than 10^4. The water temperature, composition of dissolved gases, and the low sulfur content of Lake Nyos waters and sediments does not support a hypothesis of recent, direct injection of lava or volcanic gas.

Distinctions Between Low-Temperature Gases: Magmatic Versus Biogenic

This distinction is best made by examination of carbon-14 isotopes, which undergo constant decay, and thus can be used as a dating tool. Biogenic carbon, the carbon incorporated in organisms living in lakes, is enriched in recently produced carbon-14 and, therefore, has a young age. Carbon in magmatic gas has an infinitely old apparent age. A preliminary carbon-14 date of >35,000 BP (years before present) obtained from CO_2 gas dissolved in Lake Nyos strongly suggests that the carbon dioxide is mainly magmatic rather than biogenic. One could argue that this carbon-14 date is reflecting old organic carbon in the sediments or water. This argument, however, is not supportable since Lake Nyos is probably no more than a few hundred years old.

A ratio of helium-3 to helium-4 isotopes greater than 1 demonstrates the presence of significant amounts of magmatic gas.... The ratio of 6 in Lake Nyos clearly supports the conclusion that the gas is magmatic rather than biogenic. Our minimum estimate of helium-3 concentration in the lake of 2.9×10^{-7} mol L^{-1} is very much greater than any possible enrichment from tritium decay, which also produces helium-3.

The stable carbon isotope composition ($\delta^{13}C$) of CO_2 and methane in lakes may also distinguish between biogenic and magmatic sources. The average values of ($\delta^{13}C$) in the CO_2 and bicarbonate dissolved in Lake Nyos and the two soda springs we sampled range from -0.7 to -8.0 per mil (parts per thousand). These values are consistent with the hypothesis of a magmatic carbon source, but they ... fall in the range where biogenic and magmatic carbon values overlap.

There does appear to be some biogenic gas in Lake Nyos, although it is limited to very small amounts as evidenced by the carbon-14 data. The

$\delta^{13}C$ value of the methane (composing <0.3 percent of the dissolved gas), for instance, indicates production by a biogenic pathway (for comparison, see Whiticar and others, 1986; Deuser and others, 1973). Taken together, however, the carbon-14, He, and $\delta^{13}C$ data clearly indicate that almost all of the carbon dioxide in Lake Nyos is of magmatic origin.

Gas Accumulation

Numerous springs in Cameroon contain high concentrations of dissolved CO_2. We feel that the high concentrations in these springs could not be produced by biogenic processes. The relative proportions of ions found in one nearby soda spring are similar to the major-ion chemistry of Lake Nyos. Both the spring and Lake Nyos waters are significantly enriched in magnesium relative to the other lakes and springs in the area. This similarity suggests a common origin for the spring and lake water. This common ground-water source contains large amounts of CO_2 and could have provided a means by which dissolved CO_2 entered the lake and was stored in the bottom waters.

In order for the dissolved CO_2 to build up to high concentrations in the lake, the bottom waters cannot be brought to the surface where they would lose CO_2 to the atmosphere. Relatively little mixing of surface and bottom waters occurs in lakes that are stratified. This condition is produced by a layer of less dense water overlying a layer of more dense water. Stratification resulting from a large density difference may persist for long periods of time, allowing buildup of solutes and dissolved gases in the bottom waters. The observed vertical distribution of solutes in Lake Nyos suggests that the lake was stratified before the event. In addition, movement of dissolved iron from deep waters to the surface, where the iron combined with oxygen to form a reddish precipitate, indicates that some mixing of surface and bottom waters occurred during the event.

Oxygen and hydrogen isotopes are useful in studying the history and origin of waters. In order to test the hypothesis that CO_2 entered the lake dissolved in ground water, we examined the isotopic composition of the lake waters. The isotope data of all the lakes and springs . . . are similar to the trends produced by evaporative concentration or by mixing of groundwater and surface water. If evaporative concentration is the only process affecting the waters studied, both $\delta^{18}O$ and δD values should increase with increasing ionic strength. Our data show an inverse relationship, however, with Lake Monoun and Lake Nyos being intermediate between the springs and the waters of the remaining lakes. The isotope data and the vertical distribution of solutes are therefore consistent with the hypothesis that the CO_2 in Lake Nyos entered as dissolved in ground water and accumulated in the bottom waters.

Release of Gas from the Lake

The hypothesis of gas storage in the bottom waters requires that the amount of CO_2 released could have been dissolved in the lake. Our calculations show that Lake Nyos could hold 1.5 km^3 of CO_2 at full saturation. Preliminary reports indicate that the bottom waters of Lake Nyos are still 30 percent saturated with CO_2. Assuming pre-event saturation, the lake could have released about 1.0 km^3 of CO_2. Release of 1.0 km^3 would have caused lake level to drop approximately 90 cm, which is in accord with the observations of Helimission pilots and local villagers.

The gas cloud was produced by the rapid exsolution of large amounts of CO_2 from the lake. This gas rose, expanded, and pushed up overlying water. The effervescing gas made a considerable rumbling noise as it escaped from the lake, and then rose until its momentum was overcome by gravity. The burst of gas leaving the lake resulted in the formation of surface waves.

The distribution of dead cattle around the lake indicates that the gas cloud initially rose approximately 100 m above the crater rim. Because CO_2 is denser than ambient air the cloud tended to maintain its integrity (pure CO_2 is 1.54 times more dense than atmospheric air under similar conditions). As it emerged from the lake, the gas cloud filled the lake basin by displacing the ambient air, and then spilled over the crater rim into low-lying areas. Flow of CO_2 at lethal concentrations into topographic lows has been well documented in previous studies.

A characteristic, thick "head" would have formed along the front of the advancing cloud as it started to move down-gradient. The head of the flowing cloud probably maintained the highest concentrations of CO_2, because it would have been continually recharged from the faster flowing tail. This means that the head of the cloud would have remained lethal to greater distances than one might expect.

Because of imprecise time observations, it was not possible to determine how fast the head of the cloud advanced down the river valleys. We can infer, however, that there would be a tendency for the flow to become stretched out and slowed down due to friction on the cloud from trees and other obstacles in the flow path. This would result in dispersion and partial dissipation of gas behind the flow front, and would create areas of significant concentrations of CO_2 in topographic depressions, in areas of dense vegetation, and in enclosed spaces. These gas pockets could linger for long periods of time.

Analysis of the location of reported deaths has shown that the total surface area affected was about 29 km^2. When estimating the volume of CO_2 released from Lake Nyos, assumptions were made regarding the height of the gas cloud in given areas. These assumptions included an initial cloud height of 100 m; between Lake Nyos and the village of Nyos, the cloud height was assumed to have tapered from 100 to 50 m. The minimum volume estimate of a 100 percent CO_2 cloud that would fill the described area and account for all fatalities is 0.9 km^3, a value just less than our estimate of the maximum volume released during the event. This estimate is conservative because concentrations of CO_2 above 10 percent are lethal to humans.

Given that, before the event, the gas was probably dissolved in the bottom waters, we now examine the possible mechanisms for release. These mechanisms include an internal wave, a seismic shock, a landslide into the lake, or any disturbance of this metastable system. During our study in late August, we observed that water brought to the surface from a depth of 5 m effervesced. This suggests that nucleation sites in these lakes are not a limiting factor, and that bubble formation is spontaneous upon pressure reduction under supersaturated conditions. As a parcel of water is moved toward the surface, the total pressure decreases until saturation conditions are met and bubbles form. The distance moved is the *critical amplitude* of vertical water movement required to initiate degassing.

The Lake Nyos event could have been triggered by any disturbance that moved water vertically a distance greater than the critical amplitude. Internal wave movements that occur at the boundary between two layers of water at different densities are common in lakes. They are most often generated and intensified by wind stress or traveling pressure fields. It is not yet possible to estimate a likely internal wave amplitude in Lake Nyos because the fundamental fluid dynamics equations do not apply in a system where expanding gas is producing turbulence. However, measuring the actual amplitude of internal water movements and comparing them to the critical amplitude as calculated from the CO_2 saturation would provide a means of monitoring the stability of the lake.

Significant seismic activity during or preceding the event was not observed at the Kumba recording station 220 km southwest of Lake Nyos. Several large boulders still perched on topographic high points around the lake, and the neatly stacked household goods in many homes imply that the magnitude of any local shock was negligible. Anecdotal evidence ... also does not support the hypothesis of a seismic shock. There was a fresh landslide scar on the western cliffs of the lake, although we found no evidence of anomalies in sediment topography in the western basin.

If a reservoir of gas were contained below the lake sediments, then a sudden release of the gas would likely disrupt the bottom topography during its ascent through the sediments. A series of four depth-sounding profiles across the lake revealed no crater or disturbance on the lake bottom corresponding to a localized vent. Any release of gas through the sediments also would have dispersed particles of fine sediment up into the water. No suspended sediment particles were detected in any water sample taken below 5 m. Settling times of fine sediment would be very slow, and outflow rates are too small in Lake Nyos to account for removal of deep suspended sediment by flushing. The lack of evidence for bottom disruption and suspended sediment argues against the possibility that the gas released was stored beneath the lake.

Pathology

Based on survivor reports and initial surveys, definite similarities exist between the 1986 Lake Nyos disaster and the Lake Monoun disaster of

August 1984. No autopsies were performed on victims of the Lake Monoun disaster. In the Lake Nyos incident, although somewhere between 1,500 and 2,000 persons died, all bodies were rapidly buried. One victim, who survived for several days, was preserved for examination at the hospital in Wum. For these reasons, we were faced with a considerable problem in gathering medical information. The medical team's investigations at Lake Nyos were subsequently directed into four areas: (1) the interviewing, examination and photography of survivors hospitalized at Nkambe and Wum; (2) postmortem examination of human and animal fatalities; (3) site investigations at the Subum, Nyos, and Fulani villages, as well as at Lake Nyos itself, with an emphasis on biological observations; and (4) analysis of photographs and movies taken by Helimission missionary pilots who were some of the first outsiders in the area on 23 August 1986.

Survivors from Nyos, Subum, Cha, Fang, and Fungam were interviewed at the government hospitals in Wum and Nkambe. Based on their testimonies, there appeared to be a changing spectrum of perceptions and symptoms as a function of distance from the lake. Survivors from Nyos and surrounding Fulani settlements, localities within 3 km of the lake, described two different experiences. Fifty percent (20 of 40) of those interviewed described no unusual odor or taste. They did describe fatigue, light headedness, warmth, and confusion prior to collapsing and being unconscious for up to 36 hours. Upon awakening, they did not complain of eye irritation or pain, and at the hospital they did not exhibit any skin lesions. Their admitting hospital diagnoses related primarily to trauma from falls and included temporary paralysis and loss of feeling attributed to fractures, dislocations, or prolonged lying in fixed positions.

The other 50 percent of the Nyos area victims described an odor of rotten eggs, burning eyes, and difficulty in breathing, followed by collapse and varying periods of unconsciousness. These people showed local skin lesions, predominantly unilateral and overlying bony prominences, and occasionally showed skin lesions on the torso and legs. The skin lesions displayed sharply circumscribed borders and showed a central area of injured tissue. There was no reddening of the margins suggesting that the overall appearance was that of traumatic pressure sores rather than chemical burns. Frequently, these lesions were covered by an eschar, or crust. This group of survivors also complained of nausea, vomiting, and diarrhea, all of which are consistent with symptoms of carbon dioxide poisoning.

In contrast to the complaints of patients from the Nyos area, all survivors from Subum (approximately 10 km from Lake Nyos) described the odor of rotten eggs or gunpowder, associated with difficulty in breathing, hyperventilation, fatigue, confusion, and profound weakness prior to collapse. Periods of unconsciousness ranged from several hours to as long as 36 hours. All hospitalized survivors had discrete skin lesions limited to one side of the face or arms. Several had burns involving up to 15 to 25 percent of the body surface area. These people uniformly experienced nausea, vomiting, and diarrhea upon awakening, and many complained of burning eyes. The ocular complaints resolved within several days without specific treatment. Except for a 25-year-old female with pneumonia who had been successfully treated with intravenous antibiotics, no survivors had significant pulmonary complaints lasting more than 36 hours. All women and new-born infants confined in the second floor of the Subum maternity dispensary, which was the only two story structure in Subum, survived and showed minimal physical findings. Other people in the rest of Subum either died or were significantly affected.

Missionary pilots from Helimission who arrived Saturday morning, 23 August, described a spectrum of survivors and fatalities, including people, mammals, birds, amphibians, and reptiles. Most deaths appeared to the missionaries to have occurred quickly because there was little evidence of agonal struggle (such as furniture or personal belongings in disarray). Additionally, many victims were found in their beds still covered by bed clothing. Victims found outside appeared to have collapsed suddenly without substantial movement. Animals were described as "dead in their tracks" in herds rather than dispersed. The Helimission pilots described skin blisters and blood-tinged fluid flowing from the mouths and nostrils of the deceased as well as a bloated appearance of the faces. These observations were confirmed in the photographs taken at the time by the pilots, and are felt to be typical of early postmortem decomposition. The Helimission pilots also noted blistered lesions on the faces of some survivors which presumably were the same skin lesions observed in hospitalized patients on 29 and 30 August.

An autopsy was performed on a 30-year-old male from Nyos who died 2 days after admission to the hospital at Wum. The body had been embalmed as a means of preservation. The cause of death was pneumonia involving both lungs. There were no skin lesions. Another male victim was examined on site following exhumation at Subum. Postmortem decomposition was moderately advanced, but tissue specimens were obtained for analysis. Pulmonary congestion and edema were not evident. Additional material collected by Cameroonian physicians from a male victim on 27 August 1986 in Subum was also analyzed. Tissues obtained at autopsies conducted in the field showed decomposition, but no specific pathology. Toxicologic analyses on the specimens from the three autopsied human victims were negative for cyanide, carbon monoxide, and sulfur compounds. Small quantities of alcohol found in human material and not in animal material supports premortem alcohol consumption versus decomposition change.

It is the opinion of the forensic pathology evaluation team that the human and animal victims died of asphyxia secondary to exposure to the CO_2 gas cloud. The best medical and scientific evidence at this time indicates that carbon dioxide was the toxic agent. Asphyxia is, by definition, the deprivation of the body or its vital parts (viz., the brain) of oxygen. In this incident, asphyxia resulted from the displacement of the normal atmosphere (approximately 21 percent oxygen) by a cloud of carbon dioxide gas. Under such circumstances victims will literally "drop in their tracks" after taking a few breaths and experience no feeling of suffocation. The actual mechanism of death is believed to be a paralysis of the respiratory centers in the brain by the very high concentrations of carbon dioxide. Lethal levels of carbon dioxide are in the range of 8 to 10 percent. There is no toxicologic evidence implicating hydrogen cyanide, carbon monoxide, or hydrogen sulfide in the deaths. The description of the odor of "rotten eggs" or "gunpowder" by many survivors, although usually associated with sulfur gases, is also commonly described by individuals exposed to high concentrations of carbon dioxide. This phenomenon is termed an "olfactory hallucination." In addition to the sense of smell being impaired by high levels of carbon dioxide, other senses may be affected as well. The feeling of warmth may be a sensory hallucination because 60 percent of known cases exposed to an atmosphere containing 6 percent CO_2 experienced sweating. Additionally, fatigue, headaches, and nausea were relatively common in this group.

Reports of the 1984 Lake Monoun event describe fatalities with skin lesions, distended abdomens, and puffy faces as well as mucus and blood flowing from the nose and mouth. Our analysis of photographs of similar findings in victims of the 1986 Lake Nyos event leads us to believe that the lesions described at Lake Monoun were merely those of postmortem decomposition. Survivors of the Lake Monoun event also described feelings of nausea, dizziness, and generalized weakness when they approached the gas cloud, which was suspended 0-3 meters above the ground. One survivor from the Lake Monoun incident spent a week in the hospital being treated for gastrointestinal complaints. He had no skin lesions or difficulty in breathing, but he complained of body aches and joint pains. He described the smell of the gas as "sulfurous, like car battery liquid," as did other survivors.

We divide the skin lesions seen in the survivors of the Lake Nyos incident into three groups. The first and largest group of survivors had skin lesions which they attributed to exposure to the gas, but we recognized clinically as being other disease processes which clearly antedated 21 August 1986.

The second group of survivors had bed-sore-like areas usually on one side of the face overlying bony prominences. Such lesions were healing and were virtually identical to traumatic skin lesions previously described in survivors of drug-induced comas. In the drug patients ... these lesions were felt to result from localized pressure associated with prolonged lying in fixed positions while in a comatose state. Because many of the patients at Nyos gave a history of being comatose for up to 36 hours, and also complained of temporary paralysis caused by lying in fixed positions for long periods of time, the explanation of skin lesions caused by pressure is quite plausible.

The third group of survivors consisted of five to ten victims who exhibited thermal burns that may represent injuries that were incurred while the victims were lying in a comatose state near heat sources. For example, one elderly lady had collapsed with her right hand and forearm coming to rest in a cooking fire. Notably, there was no reflexive withdrawal from the painful stimulus. Upon awakening, her hand and forearm were so severely burned that amputation was required. Several elderly people and two children had extensive second degree burns on their chests and abdomens; these burns may also have resulted from prolonged exposure to heat sources.

We could find no references in the medical literature relating specific skin lesions to carbon dioxide exposure, and we therefore conclude that none of the skin lesions resulted directly from this type of gas exposure. We also do not feel that the skin lesions resulted from exposure to a blast of hot gas, because none of the victims exhibited singeing of the hair, flash burns, or damaged clothing.

Vegetation samples from the Lake Nyos area were examined for physical damage and chemically analyzed for traces of volcanic gas. None of the plants surrounding the lake showed visible signs of chemical burns or heat stress by either infrared photography or gross examination. Much of the grass near the northern and southern shores was flattened or uprooted by the passing water waves. Slight damage to lower leaf surfaces was evident in three samples when compared to controls collected from distant locations. Results from x-ray photoelectron spectroscopy, scanning electron microscopy, and energy dispersive x-ray analyses showed no significant differences in structural features or elemental composition between the Lake Nyos samples and the controls. Because stomates are closed at night in most plants, the uptake of any poisonous gas into the plant would be reduced. Some plant species may be more susceptable [*sic*] than others, and so we cannot exclude short term plant injury due to airborne gases.

Conclusions

Lake Nyos is a classic maar, formed in a coarse-grained biotite-quartz monzonite of uncertain, pre-Tertiary age. On the basis of the geochemical and geophysical characteristics of Cameroon magmas, it is not necessary to invoke special geologic conditions in order to explain the accumulation of CO_2-rich gas in Lake Nyos and environs.

The temperature, composition of dissolved gases, and the low sulfur content of lake waters and sediments do not support a hypothesis of recent, direct injection of lava or volcanic gas. Taken together, the carbon-14, helium, and ^{13}C (CO_2) data clearly indicate that almost all of the carbon dioxide in Lake Nyos is of deep-seated magmatic origin.

The similarity in relative proportions of solutes in Lake Nyos and a nearby soda spring suggests a common origin for the spring and lake water. This common source contains large amounts of CO_2; hydrogen and oxygen isotope data are consistent with the hypothesis that CO_2 entered the lake dissolved in groundwater. The lack of evidence for bottom disruption and suspended sediment argues against the possibility that the gas was stored in fissures beneath the lake and then explosively released. Lake stratification prior to the event is indicated by the present vertical distribution of solutes. If persistent, this stratification would allow CO_2 to accumulate in bottom waters. If saturated before the event, Lake Nyos could have released about 1 km^3 of CO_2, an amount slightly greater than the minimum volume estimate of a 100 percent CO_2 cloud that would fill the affected area and account for all fatalities. The trigger that released gas from the lake is unknown, although, if waters were supersaturated before the event, any small disturbance of the water column would initiate degassing.

Interviews with survivors and pathologic studies indicated that victims rapidly lost consciousness and that death was caused by asphyxiation. Carbon dioxide will produce these effects. At nonlethal levels, CO_2 acts like an anesthetic and can produce hallucinations, such that many people exposed to CO_2 will report the odor of sulfur compounds when none are present. Skin lesions found on survivors represent pressure sores, and in a few cases, exposure to a heat source such as cooking fires. There is no evidence of flash burns from exposure to hot gases. Finally, all other findings on the deceased can be explained by postmortem decomposition.

Remaining Hazards

Associated with Lake Nyos

The tragic gas release of 21 August was probably not the first such event at Lake Nyos, judging from geologic evidence, although such occurrences are uncommon. A large amount of CO_2 remains dissolved in the lake, and until it is removed, the lake cannot be regarded as being completely safe.

Another hazard associated with Lake Nyos involves the stability of the spillway which drains the lake to the north. The spillway is formed by relatively weak pyroclastic ash beds. If these ash beds were to fail, a catastrophic flood would move down stream valleys, destroying Nyos village, Subum, and other populated areas to the north. A rapid lowering of the Lake Nyos surface level could also cause depressurization of the water column, triggering another gas release event.

Other Areas of Northwest Cameroon

The deep maar lakes of northwest Cameroon must all be regarded as potentially capable of lethal gas release until proven safe. Much preliminary work to evaluate this hazard has already been done by George Kling.

The northwest Cameroon maar lakes all appear to be geologically young (of Quaternary age; some have doubtless formed within the past few hundred years). The formation of new maars in the future is quite likely and will be accompanied by catastrophic ash deposition that could be lethal to residents over areas as much as 10 km in diameter.

Recommendations

Required Field Investigations

We have concluded that slow "leakage" of carbon dioxide gas from magmatic sources beneath the Earth's surface was involved in setting the stage for the Lake Nyos tragedy. The rate at which the gas is being supplied to the lake system will be critical to determine the potential for, and timing of, future gas releases. This will require repeated sampling of the deep lake water in the future to determine if dangerous levels of dissolved CO_2 have built up within the lake. Saturation levels of gas can be calculated after collecting the water with a standard water sampler that has been modified to allow expanding gas to fill an attached bell jar instead of leaking out into the water as the sample is brought to the surface.

Nine of the approximately 40 crater lakes in Cameroon have not yet been sampled to determine if their bottom waters contain anomalously high levels of dissolved carbon dioxide. As dangerous lakes are identified, a profile of common characteristics (age, geographic position, geological and limnological features, etc.) should be compiled. This would facilitate identification of dangerous lakes in Cameroon, as well as suggesting potentially hazardous lakes in other countries.

Sediment cores should be collected from Lake Nyos and other lakes to evaluate the historical record of lake mixing and prior gas release events.

Anthropologists should conduct interviews with people living adjacent to northwest Cameroonian lakes to identify and evaluate any legends pertaining to the origin of the lakes or to accounts of mass deaths in this area.

The narrow spillway draining Lake Nyos should be studied in detail to evaluate its structure, stability, and potential for collapse.

Direct Risk Mitigation

The gas content of lakes found to contain dangerously high levels of dissolved CO_2 should be lowered. This could be accomplished by "controlled degassing." . . . Lake Nyos is an obvious candidate for development of this technology. If judged to be unsafe, the spillway draining Lake Nyos should be removed to eliminate the potential for catastrophic failure. This could be accomplished either by explosive demolition after lowering of the lake to safe levels, or by gradual "staged" excavation. Thorough pre-removal engineering studies would be required in either case.

GORBACHEV ON DEMOCRATIC REFORMS

January 27, 1987

Mikhail S. Gorbachev, the Soviet Communist party general secretary, opened the January 27 plenary session of the 307-member Central Committee with a speech in which he proposed startling democratic reforms. Gorbachev called for secret ballots and multiple-candidate slates in elections for party and government officials and factory managers, a change from the system in which candidates ran unopposed after they were approved by party officials at a higher level. Gorbachev hinted that "further democratization" could eventually be applied to the party's top leadership bodies. He also advocated increasing the opportunities for nonparty members to hold government positions.

Gorbachev's proposals did not represent a radical turn to open elections. The Communist party would still control the selection of candidates, and a multiparty political system remained unthinkable. Gorbachev emphasized, "The point at issue is, certainly, not any breakup of our political system." If the reforms were implemented they would be merely a first step toward political liberalization. But considering the Soviet Union's history of dictatorship and forced unanimity, the proposals were dramatic.

Gorbachev's call for greater democracy was another initiative in his campaign to revitalize the Soviet Union's leadership and stimulate its troubled economy. Since becoming general secretary in 1985, he had replaced leaders appointed under Leonid Brezhnev with younger officials; introduced measures to reduce alcoholism, worker absenteeism, and corruption; and fostered a new atmosphere of glasnost *(openness). Under* glasnost *artists and writers were given more creative freedom, public criticism of corruption and inefficiency was encouraged, and the Soviet leadership provided more information to its citizens. In addition to proposing his new reforms, Gorbachev delivered a harsh attack against the corruption and conservatism of the Brezhnev era. He called for a special party conference in 1988 to resolve issues relating to democratization and further the implementation of his economic and social reforms.* (Gorbachev speech to 27th party congress, Historic Documents of 1986, p. 145).

Gorbachev's Reform Strategy

Gorbachev had several reasons for proposing democratic reforms. First, he needed the support of Soviet intellectuals and young educated professionals who would play a crucial role in modernizing the Soviet economy. His call for a larger number of nonparty members in responsible posts was an obvious appeal to this group. Second, Gorbachev undoubtedly saw these reforms as a way to enhance the Soviet Union's improving image in the West. The prospects for foreign trade, joint economic ventures, and arms control, all of which would provide a boost to the Soviet economy, would be increased by Western perceptions of a more liberal, open, and trustworthy Soviet Union. Finally, Gorbachev appeared to believe that democratic reforms were necessary to foster a greater sense of involvement in the Soviet people and accountability among Soviet officials that would ultimately improve the nation's standard of living and ability to compete.

Gorbachev took a significant political risk. By thoroughly denouncing the mistakes of the Brezhnev regime and by asking to change the rules by which the Communist party chooses officials, he could further alienate the conservative elements of the party. Soviet party and government officials traditionally have opposed any significant change in the way the party operates, out of fear that they might lose their power and privileges. Many Soviet bureaucrats already felt threatened by Gorbachev's attempts to reduce the power of the central government by giving managers of state enterprises more autonomy.

Gorbachev's position appeared to be secure. If his policies were perceived as failing or diverging too far from Communist orthodoxy, however, his support could falter. Nikita Khrushchev's ouster in 1964 demonstrated that a Soviet leader could be toppled by an erosion of party support. Therefore, Gorbachev was expected to proceed slowly with democratic reforms while building a consensus in their favor.

Reaction and Resistance to Proposals

Gorbachev's speech was well received in the West; Western leaders generally applauded his calls for more democracy and openness but warned against the Soviet Union's growing military threat. The Kremlin continued its campaign to change its image in the West by releasing more than 150 imprisoned dissidents in February.

The speech had a more unsettling effect on East European leaders, who were wary of implementing any kind of political reform. The regimes in East Germany and Czechoslovakia avoided embracing glasnost, *because they feared the policy might stimulate the liberal elements of their societies to press for even greater reforms that could threaten Communist supremacy. Nevertheless, most East European leaders responded to Soviet pressure by giving a degree of rhetorical support to the Soviet domestic reforms. The relatively liberal Hungarian regime declared the Soviet policies an endorsement of their own economic and political experiments.*

Although Gorbachev expressed great confidence in his proposals and claimed to be speaking on behalf of the Politburo, the implementation of his reforms was uncertain. Gorbachev and his allies promoted many of their supporters at all levels of the party and government, but a substantial number of conservative, antireform officials, who were capable of frustrating Gorbachev's initiatives, remained entrenched.

The events of the plenum demonstrated the party leadership's resistance to Gorbachev and his plans. The resolution passed by the Central Committee at the end of the plenum endorsed the general idea of greater democracy, but was conspicuously vague on the subject compared with Gorbachev's speech. In addition, Gorbachev was not able to engineer the wave of high-level personnel changes that many Western analysts had predicted. For example, Anatolii Dobrynin, the former ambassador to the United States, whom Gorbachev had called back to Moscow to formulate foreign policy in the Secretariat, was not promoted to the Politburo. Gorbachev was able to control the general direction of the plenum, but he clearly was not able to impose his will upon it.

By the end of March, however, the Kremlin announced experimental elections in several locations. Voters were given a choice of candidates for district court judgeships and positions on local governing councils in elections held in June. The leadership also began implementing plans for more competitive elections of factory managers.

Following are excerpts from Mikhail S. Gorbachev's January 27, 1987, speech entitled "Reorganization and the Party's Personnel Policy," delivered to a plenary meeting of the Central Committee of the Communist Party of the Soviet Union:

Comrades,

The 27th Party Congress vested in us, the members of the Central Committee, an immense responsibility—to implement the strategic course of accelerating the socio-economic development of the country. The Political Bureau understands the situation and the role of the Central Committee at the current stage in the life of Soviet society precisely in this way.

Proceeding from this, the Plenary Meeting has put on its agenda a matter of paramount importance for the effective implementation of the political strategy drafted by the April 1985 Plenary Meeting of the Central Committee and the 27th CPSU Congress—the question of reorganization and the Party's personnel policy. We should consider it in a broad social and political context, with due regard for the lessons of the past, the nature of the current moment and the tasks of the future.

The April Plenary Meeting and the 27th Party Congress prepared the ground for an objective critical analysis of the situation in society and took decisions of historic importance for the country's future. We have begun reorganization and will not look back. The first steps on that road have been taken.

Drawing an overall political conclusion, we can say with confidence that major changes are taking place in the life of Soviet society and that positive tendencies are gaining momentum.

Before the Plenary Meeting, I myself and other Political Bureau members and Central Committee Secretaries had many meetings and conversations with members of the Central Committee, public figures, workers, collective farmers, intellectuals, veterans and young people. The overall tenor and meaning of what they had to say was unambiguous: the policies for renovating our society should be firmly pursued and efforts redoubled in every area....

The main evaluations of the state of society and the conclusions drawn from them by the Political Bureau have already been presented to the 27th Party Congress and Plenary Meetings of the Central Committee. They have been fully corroborated. But today we know more, that is why there is a need to examine once again and in detail the sources of the obtaining situation and to sort out the reasons for what took place in the country in the late 1970s and early 1980s.

This analysis is necessary to prevent mistakes from recurring and to fulfil the resolutions of the Congress on which the future of our people and the destiny of socialism depend. It is all the more important since there is still some misunderstanding in society and in the Party of the complexity of the situation in which the country has found itself. Perhaps, this also explains questions from some comrades about the measures that are being taken by the Political Bureau and the government in the course of reorganization. We are often asked if we are not taking too sharp a turn.

We need to be absolutely clear on all the vital issues, including this one. Only a deep understanding of the situation can enable us to find correct solutions to the complex tasks.

By and large, Comrades, there is an urgent need to return to an analysis of those problems which confronted the Party and Soviet society in the few years before the April 1985 Plenary Meeting of the CPSU Central Committee. The experience of the past 18 months has bolstered our resolve to deepen that analysis, to comprehend the causes of adverse processes and to work out measures to accelerate our progress, to keep us from repeating mistakes and to allow us only to advance, proving in practice socialism's organic ability to continuously renovate itself.

The Political Bureau believes that on the basis of this approach we should hold this Plenary Meeting.

Reorganization Is an Objective Necessity

Comrades,

Our Plenary Meeting is taking place in the year of the 70th anniversary of the Great October Socialist Revolution. Almost seven decades ago the Leninist Party raised over the country the victorious banner of socialist revolution, of struggle for socialism, freedom, equality, social justice and social progress and against oppression and exploitation, poverty and national discrimination. . . .

Our achievements are immense and indubitable and the Soviet people by right take pride in their successes. They constitute a firm base for the fulfilment of our current programmes and our plans for the future. But the Party must see life in its entirety and complexity. No accomplishments, even the most impressive ones, should obscure either contradictions in social development or our mistakes and failings.

We talked about all that and must repeat again today that at some point the country began to lose momentum, difficulties and unresolved problems started to pile up, and there appeared elements of stagnation and other phenomena alien to socialism. All that had a most adverse effect on the economy and social, cultural and intellectual life.

Of course, Comrades, the country did not cease to develop. Tens of millions of Soviet people were working honestly and many Party organizations and our personnel were working actively in the interests of the people. All that held back the intensification of negative processes but could not avert them altogether.

A need for change was ripening in the economy and other fields—but it did not materialize in the political and practical work of the Party and the state.

What was the reason for that complex and controversial situation?

The main cause—and the Political Bureau considers it necessary to say so with utmost frankness at the Plenary Meeting—was that the CPSU Central Committee and the leadership of the country failed, primarily for subjective reasons, to see in time and in full the need for change and the dangerous growth of crisis phenomena in society, and to formulate a clear-cut policy for overcoming them and making better use of the possibilities intrinsic to the socialist system.

A conservative outlook, inertia, a tendency to brush aside all that did not fit into conventional patterns, and an unwillingness to come to grips with outstanding socio-economic problems prevailed in policy-making and practical work.

Comrades, the leading bodies of the Party and the state bear responsibility for all this....

Lenin's ideas of socialism were interpreted simplistically and their theoretical depth and significance were often emaciated. This was true of such key problems as public ownership, relations between classes and nationalities, the measure of work and the measure of consumption, cooperation, methods of economic management, people's rule and self-government, struggle against bureaucratic abuses, the revolutionary transforming character of socialist ideology, the principles of education and upbringing, and guarantees for the healthy development of the Party and society....

Special mention should be made of socialist property. Control over those who managed it and how had slackened. Departmental and parochial attitudes eroded socialist property, it became "no one's," free, belonging to no real owner, and in many cases was used to derive unearned income.

There was an incorrect attitude to cooperative property, which was viewed as something "second-rate" and having no future. All this had grievous consequences for agrarian and social policies, bred management by injunction in relations with collective farms and resulted in the abolition of producer cooperatives. There were also grave misconceptions about personal subsidiary holdings and individual labour, which did much economic and social harm as well.

Serious discrepancies kept piling up in planning. The authority of the plan as the main tool of economic policy was being subverted by subjective approaches, imbalances, instability, the striving to embrace everything down to trifles, and a host of sectoral and regional decisions, taken in circumvention of the plan and often without due regard for real possibilities. Plans were often short of scientific substantiation, they did not aim at outlining national economic proportions, proper care for the development of the social sphere and the accomplishment of many strategic tasks.

As a consequence, the huge advantage offered by the socialist economic system, primarily its planned character, was used inefficiently. In this situation irresponsibility struck root, and diverse bureaucratic rules and instructions were devised. Day-to-day practical activity was supplanted with decree-making, a show of efficiency and mountains of paperwork.

Misconceptions about the role of monetary-commodity relations and the operation of the law of value, and sometimes their direct opposition to socialism as something alien to it, led to voluntarist attitudes in the economy, to an underestimation of profit and loss accountability and to wage levelling, and bred subjective approaches to price formation, imbalances in money circulation and disregard for the regulation of demand and supply.

Restrictions of the rights of enterprises and associations in the use of profit and loss accountability principles had especially grave consequences.

They undermined the foundations of material incentive, blocked the achievement of high end results, and led to a lowering of the people's labour and social activity and to a slackening of discipline and order.

In fact, a whole system that weakened the economic tools of government emerged and a mechanism that slowed socio-economic development and hindered the progressive transformations which make it possible to tap and use the advantages of socialism. That retarding process was rooted in serious shortcomings in the functioning of the institutions of socialist democracy, outdated political and theoretical concepts, which often did not correspond to reality, and in the conservative managerial mechanism.

All that, Comrades, adversely affected the development of many spheres in the life of society. Take material production. The growth rates of the national income in the past three five-year plan periods dropped by more than half. From the early 1970s most plan targets were not met. The economy as a whole became cumbersome and little responsive to innovation. The quality of a considerable part of the output no longer met the current requirements and imbalances in production were aggravated.

Attention to the development of engineering was slackened. Research and development work fell behind the needs of the national economy and did not meet the modernization demands. Purchases of equipment and many other commodities on the capitalist market were excessive and far from always justified.

Negative processes seriously affected the social sphere. The 27th Party Congress has already appraised its condition. The social goals of the economy in the past few five-year plan periods were obviously diluted and there emerged a sort of deafness to social issues. We see today what all this has led to. Having successfully resolved the employment question and provided basic social guarantees, we at the same time failed to fully realize the potential of socialism for improving housing, food supply, transport, health care and education, and for solving other vital problems.

There were violations of the most important principle of socialism, distribution according to work. Struggle against unearned income was not determined enough. The policy of providing material and moral incentives for efficient work was inconsistent. Large, unjustified bonuses and fringe benefits were paid and figure-padding for profit took place. Parasitic sentiments grew stronger and the mentality of wage levelling began to take hold. All that hit those workers who could and wanted to work better, while making life easier for the lazy ones.

Violation of the organic relationship between the measure of work and the measure of consumption not only warps the attitude to work, holding back the growth of productivity, but also leads to distortion of the principle of social justice—and that is a question of great political importance.

Elements of social corrosion that emerged in recent years have adversely affected society's morale and insidiously eroded the high moral values which have always been characteristic of our people and of which we are proud, namely, ideological conviction, labour enthusiasm and Soviet patriotism.

As an inevitable consequence of all this, interest in the affairs of society slackened, signs of amorality and scepticism appeared and the role of moral incentives in work declined. The section of people, including youth, whose ultimate goal in life was material well-being and gain by any means, grew wider. Their cynical stand acquired more and more aggressive forms, poisoned the mentality of those around them and triggered a wave of consumerism. The spread of alcohol and drug abuse and a rise in crime witnessed the decline of social mores.

Disregard for laws, report-padding, bribe-taking and encouragement of toadyism and adulation had a deleterious effect on the moral atmosphere in society. Real care for people, for the conditions of their life and work and for their social well-being was often supplanted with political flirtation—the mass distribution of awards, titles and prizes. An atmosphere of lenience was formed, and exactingness, discipline and responsibility declined.

Serious shortcomings in ideological and political education in many cases were disguised with ostentatious activities and campaigns and celebrations of numerous jubilees in the center and in the provinces. The world of day-to-day realities and that of make-believe well-being were increasingly parting ways. . . .

The state of the Party and its personnel also affected the socio-economic and political situation that took shape in the late 1970s and early 1980s. Leading Party bodies failed to timely and critically appraise the danger of the growing negative tendencies in society and in the conduct of some Communists, and to take decisions which life was imperatively demanding. . . .

We cannot overlook the just indignation of working people at the conduct of those senior officials, vested with trust and authority and called upon to stand guard over the interests of the state and citizens, who abused their authority, suppressed criticism, sought gain, and some of whom even became accomplices in, if not organizers of, criminal activities. . . .

The overwhelming majority of those who joined the Party are the best representatives of the working class, collective farmers and intelligentsia. They have been honestly and selflessly performing their Party duty. Yet we should admit that in those years there was no strong barrier put up to stop dishonest, pushing, self-seeking people who were intent on benefitting from their Party membership. We deviated to some extent from the rule that the main thing is not the number of new members but the quality of the Party ranks. This told on the combative spirit of our Party organizations. . . .

In this situation, Comrades, the question of accelerating the socio-economic development of the country, the question of reorganization was raised. The case in point is actually a radical turn and measures of a revolutionary character. As we talk about reorganization and associated processes of deep-going democratization of society, we mean truly revolutionary and comprehensive transformations in society.

We must make this decisive turn because there is no other choice. We must not retreat and there is no place to retreat to. We must consistently and unswervingly steer the course charted by the April Plenary Meeting of the Central Committee and the 27th Congress, go further and raise society to a qualitatively new development level. . . .

Today it is essential to say once again what we mean by reorganization.

Reorganization is a resolute overcoming of the processes of stagnation, destruction of the retarding mechanism, and the creation of dependable and efficient machinery for expediting the social and economic progress of Soviet society. The main purport of our strategy is to combine the achievements of the scientific and technological revolution with a plan-based economy and set the entire potential of socialism in motion.

Reorganization is reliance on the creative endeavour of the masses, an all-round extension of democracy and socialist self-government, the encouragement of initiative and self-organized activities, better discipline and order, greater openness, criticism and self-criticism in all fields of public life, and full and proper respect for the value and dignity of the individual. . . .

The final aim of reorganization is, I believe, clear: it is to effect thorough-going changes in all aspects of public life, to give socialism the most advanced form of social organization, and bring out to the utmost the humane nature of our system in all decisive aspects—economic, social, political and moral.

This is, Comrades, the job we have started. The reorganization is getting under way everywhere. It is acquiring a new quality, not only gaining in scope but also penetrating the deepest fibres of our life. . . .

We must clearly realize that we are only at the initial stage of the restructuring. The most important and complex work is yet to come. We must advance step by step, persistently and without wavering. We must soberly assess what has been done and not be afraid to rectify mistakes. We must search for and find new ways and means of solving tasks as they arise and definitely achieve progress towards the goals that have been set.

We should absolutely learn from the lesson of the past, that is, allowing no gap to form between decisions and the practical work for their implementation. There should be no conceit or self-complacency. I am saying this once again because we are still encountering this even now. We must act, act and act again—vigorously, boldly, creatively and competently.

The need to pose the question in this way is dictated by the fact that to this day in many economic, government, state and even Party bodies, and in the work collectives themselves far from everyone is marching in step with the demands being set by life. Many people are slow to cast off the burden of the past, are adopting a wait-and-see attitude and openly putting a spoke in the wheel, impeding the extensive development of the people's political, public and labour activity.

Not everyone has understood that working in the new way means to resolutely give up old habits and methods. In the long run, this depends on the civic stand of every person, on a conscientious attitude to one's job and duties, and we all have a responsibility for this towards the Party, the country and our own conscience.

Meetings and conversations with working people, with Party and economic personnel show that the reorganization is receiving ardent support. It can be said that the people are all for it. But what stands out is that many people, while supporting innovations, believe that the reorganization must take place somewhere higher up, that this has to be done by others—by Party, state and economic bodies, other sectors of the economy, allied enterprises, by others in the factory shop, on the farm or construction site. In short, that this must be done by everybody except themselves.

No, Comrades, while justly demanding reorganization at every level, each of us must begin with himself. All of us—workers, collective farmers, intellectuals, in short everybody, from those in work collectives to the Central Committee of the CPSU and the government must work in a new way—vigorously, creatively and, I repeat, conscientiously....

We must clearly realize that today a whole system of measures is needed. This includes the formulation of theoretical provisions based on the realities of our time and a deeply substantiated scientific forecast of the future, changes in social consciousness and consistent development of democratic institutions, the fostering of the political culture of the masses and reorganization of the mechanism of economic management, of organizational structures and, of course, the pursuance of a vigorous social policy.

This is the only way to remove the brake on progress and give the necessary scope to the forces of acceleration.

I think today's Plenary Meeting of the Central Committee should tell the Party and the people that a difficult struggle lies ahead, requiring of every Communist and every citizen a high degree of consciousness and organization, stamina and utmost selflessness.

Comrades, the analysis of the state our society was in on the eve of the April Plenary Meeting of the Central Committee and the experience of reorganization have raised an acute and most important question. Do we have guarantees that the process of transformations that we have started will be continued to the end, that the past mistakes will not be repeated, and we'll be able to ensure the comprehensive development of our society?

The Political Bureau answers these questions in the affirmative: yes, we have such guarantees.

These are the united will, the joint actions of the Party and people united by past experience, by awareness of their responsibility for the present and the future of the socialist homeland.

These are the all-round development of the democracy of the socialist system, the real and ever more active participation of the people in solving all questions of the country's life, full restoration of the Leninist principles of openness, public control, criticism and self-criticism, and sincerity in policy consisting in the unity of words and deeds.

Finally, these are the healthy development of the Party itself, its ability to critically analyze its own activity, to update the forms and methods of its work, to determine, on the basis of revolutionary theory, the prospects of society's development, and to work for accomplishing the new tasks life poses.

It is the promotion of socialist democracy, the creative endeavour of Soviet people, the vanguard role of Communists in practical deeds that will ensure both the success and the irreversibility of the revolutionary transformations charted by the 27th Congress.

To Promote Socialist Democracy and Develop the People's Self-Government

Comrades,

We now understand better than before the profundity of Lenin's thought about the vital, inner link between socialism and democracy. The entire historical experience of our country has convincingly demonstrated that the socialist system has in practice ensured citizens' political and socio-economic rights, their personal freedoms, revealed the advantages of Soviet democracy and given each person confidence in the morrow....

It is only through the consistent development of the democratic forms inherent in socialism and more extensive self-government that our progress in production, science and technology, literature, culture and the arts, in all areas of social life is possible. It is only this way that ensures conscientious discipline. The reorganization itself is possible only through democracy and due to democracy. It is only this way that it is possible to open broad vistas for socialism's most powerful creative force—free labour and free thought in a free country.

Therefore, the further democratization of Soviet society is becoming the Party's urgent task. This, in effect, is the essence of the course charted by the April Plenary Meeting and the 27th CPSU Congress for promoting people's socialist self-government. The point at issue is, certainly, not any breakup of our political system. We should use with maximum effectiveness all its potentialities, fill the work of the Party, the Soviets and the government bodies, public organizations and work collectives with deep democratic content, breathe new life into all cells of the social organism....

What ways does the Political Bureau see to further deepen democracy in Soviet society?

We will be able to boost people's initiative and creativity effectively if our democratic institutions have a strong and real influence on the state of things in every work collective, be it in terms of planning, labour organization, distribution of material and other benefits, or selection and promotion of the most respected and competent people to leading positions. It can be said with certainty that the sooner every Soviet citizen experiences these changes for himself, the more active his civic stance and participation in all public and state affairs will be.

Of paramount importance is the development of democracy in production and the consistent implementation of the principles of working people's self-management. The economy is the decisive area of society's life. Tens of millions of people are daily engaged in it. Therefore the development of democracy in production is the most important trend in deepening and broadening socialist democracy in general. This is the lever that will enable us to ensure the broad and active participation of the working people in all areas of social life and make it possible to avoid many errors and miscalculations. . . .

Life itself made the need for drawing up a fundamental legal act, such as the Law on the State Enterprise whose draft has already been issued to you, the order of the day. This law is designed to radically change the conditions and methods of management in the main section of the economy, to consolidate the combination of the principle of planning and full-scale profit and loss accountability, independence and responsibility in the activities of enterprises, and to give the new forms of self-administration, born of the creativity of the masses, a legal basis.

The Law is intended to put one of the most important directives of the Party Congress into practice, namely, the course towards a more effective use of direct democracy. Under the draft Law, the powers to be given to the general meetings and councils of work collectives in dealing with questions bearing on production, social and personnel affairs will be a major political measure towards, as V. I. Lenin put it, "genuine self-government by the people."

The consistent implementation of the Law on the State Enterprise in combination with the package of measures being implemented in the economic field will, we believe, create an altogether new situation in the economy, will accelerate economic development and lead to the qualitative improvement of many aspects of social life. Considering the tremendous significance of this Law, the Political Bureau proposes that it be submitted for nationwide discussion. I believe that the members of the Central Committee will support this proposal. . . .

It is necessary to concentrate on the question of the electivity of heads of enterprises, factories, workshops, departments, sectors, farms and teams, team leaders and foremen. The current stage in restructuring, the transition to new methods of economic management, profit and loss accountability, self-financing and self-repayment make that task a very practical one. This is an important and urgent measure, and it will undoubtedly have working people's approval.

We have embarked in a big way on the path of transferring enterprises to full-scale profit and loss accountability, self-financing and self-repayment; we have introduced state quality control. This means that the profits of enterprises, all forms of incentives for the members of the work collective, the degree to which social demands are met will totally depend on the end results of their work, the quality and quantity of the products made and the services rendered.

Under these circumstances workers and collective farmers will be far from indifferent as to who heads the enterprise, workshop, sector or team. Since the well-being of the collective is made dependent on the abilities of the managers, the working people should also have a real say in their appointment and control their activities. . . .

Comrades, to sum it up. From whatever angle we may approach this important matter, one conclusion begs of itself: the time has come for change, for democratizing the process of management selection at enterprises on the basis of all-round application of the electivity principle. This, as you understand, means a qualitatively new situation, a fundamentally different form of working people's participation in production management, an essential enhancement of the role and responsibility of the collective for the results of its activities.

All this should be taken into account in the course of the practical solution of that issue. However, I would like to convey one idea right now. The point at issue is one-man management. We think that electiveness, far from undermining, enhances the authority of the leader. He feels the support of the people who elected him. This enhances the feeling of responsibility for the matter on hand, and mutual exactingness in the collective.

The role of the Party and public organizations and economic management bodies should be comprehended in a new way. A great amount of work is to be carried out to inculcate in all our personnel a correct understanding of the fact that extension of democracy in production presupposes an organic combination of one-man management and collective effort, promotion of democratic centralism and development of self-government.

The Political Bureau considers the advancement of the Soviet electoral system to be one of the main avenues in democratizing our life. Corresponding proposals are being drafted on that issue on the instructions of the 27th Congress.

What can be said here? The existing electoral system ensures representation for all sections of the population in the elective bodies of power. The working class, collective farmers, intellectuals, men and women, veterans and young people, all nations and nationalities in the country are represented in the present Soviets at all levels. The elective bodies reflect the social, professional and national structure of Soviet society and the diversity of the interests of the entire population. This in itself is an immense achievement of socialist democracy.

However, just as all political, economic and social institutions, the electoral system cannot remain unchanged and away from the reorganization and the new processes developing in society.

What is the essence of proposals and wishes on these matters, which people are sending to the CPSU Central Committee, the Presidium of the USSR Supreme Soviet and to other central bodies and the mass media?

From the political point of view, it is a question of enhancing the democratic nature of the electoral system and of a more effective and real involvement of the electorate at all stages of the pre-election and election campaigns.

Concretely, most proposals suggest that voters at meetings in work collectives and at places of residence, as well as at election meetings, discuss, as a rule, several candidacies, that elections be held in larger constituencies, and that several deputies be elected from each of them. People believe that this would enable each citizen to express his attitude to a greater number of candidates and would enable Party and local government bodies to get to know better the sentiments and will of the population.

Responding to these wishes we should look anew at the way the elections themselves are organized and at the practice of nomination and discussion of candidacies for people's deputies. It is essential to rid the voting procedure of formalism and to see to it that the election campaign of even this year be held in an atmosphere of broader democracy with the interested participation of the people.

As far as a legislative act on introducing amendments to the electoral system is concerned, it would be useful to publish its draft for nationwide preliminary discussion.

The implementation of these proposals would be the first major step towards the further democratization of the process of forming the bodies of state power and of their functioning. But, obviously, it is also necessary to consider deeper changes and further steps in this direction. With due regard for the experience gained and the new tasks we must once again make a thorough and profound analysis of Lenin's legacy on matters of Soviet state development and draw on it in solving the tasks facing society today.

It is quite natural that questions of promoting inner-party democracy should be considered within the overall framework of the further democratization of Soviet society.

At the 27th Congress a number of important provisions strengthening the democratic principles of Party life were introduced in amending the CPSU Rules. This work should be continued. It appears advisable to confer together on improving the mechanism for forming leading Party bodies.

Many different proposals have come to the Central Committee in this connection. Allow me to report on the conclusions which have been made by summing up the proposals.

To begin with, the formation of elective bodies in the primary Party organization. The gist of most proposals on this score is to give full scope to the expression of the will of all Communists without exception during the election of secretaries, of Party bureaus and Party committees and to enhance their responsibility to those who elect them.

There is also a need to think of amending the procedure for the election of secretaries of district, area, city, regional and territorial Party committees, and the Central Committees of the Communist Parties of the Union republics. Here comrades suggest that secretaries, including first secretaries, could be elected by secret ballot at the plenary sessions of the respective Party committees. In such a case the members of the Party committee would have a right to enter any number of candidates in the voting list. Such a measure would greatly increase the responsibility of secretaries to the Party committees that elected them, giving them more confidence in their work and making it possible for them to determine more accurately the degree of their authority.

Of course, the principle of the Party Rules, under which the decisions of higher bodies are binding on all lower Party committees, including those on personnel matters, must remain immutable in the Party.

The Political Bureau's opinion is that further democratization should also apply to the formation of the central leading bodies of the Party. I think this is quite logical. It would seem logical to democratize the elections of leading bodies in other public organizations as well.

Comrades, I think you will agree that all these measures will strengthen the principles of democratic centralism in the Party's life and will promote greater unity and cohesion of the Party ranks, tougher discipline, responsibility, and activity of each Communist, all Party organizations, and the Party as a whole.

The following questions will possibly arise: shall we not be complicating the procedure of the formation of elective bodies of the Party, to what extent is all this justified, and how much will it help?

Ever since the April Plenary Meeting of the Central Committee we have been continuously emphasizing that the problems which have accumulated in society are connected to a considerable extent with the drawbacks in the activity of the Party itself and in its personnel policy. The Political Bureau believes that the further democratization of the process of forming elective bodies is one of the important conditions for boosting Party activities, for the infusion of fresh blood, the active work of Party organizations, and a safeguard against a repetition of the errors of the past.

Elections within the Party are not a formal act, and we should approach their preparation in a well-thought-out way, in a spirit of great responsibility, proceeding from the interests of the Party and society.

The democratization of society poses in a new way the question of control over the work of the Party, local government, and economic bodies and their personnel. As far as control "from above" is concerned, marked changes, as you know, have occurred in this respect of late. So-called "forbidden subjects" for criticism and control are becoming a thing of the past. The Political Bureau and the Secretariat of the Central Committee at their meetings regularly hear reports by the Central Committees of the Communist Parties of the Union republics, territorial and regional Party committees, and consider other fundamental questions of the life of the Party and society profoundly and comprehensively. The Council of Ministers of the USSR and its Presidium have become much more exacting to ministries and departments and to the Councils of Ministers of the Union republics.

Frankly speaking, the Political Bureau, the Secretariat of the Central Committee and the Government still have a lot to do in this respect. We still have to return to one and the same problem several times over and adopt additional measures to solve it. This has been vividly shown, in particular, by the discussion at the latest meeting of the Political Bureau on the course of implementing the resolutions of the Central Committee and the Council of Ministers of the USSR on accelerating the development of the engineering industry. We take the necessary decisions but, as before, we do not implement them to the full and on time. This happens also because many have not yet got rid of the burden of old habits and an irresponsible attitude to their duties. Discipline is lax. Far from all executives follow the principle of the unity of words and deeds, while others do more speaking than working. We must draw the most serious conclusions from this.

But with all the importance of control "from above," it is of fundamental importance in the conditions of the democratization of society to raise the level and effectiveness of control "from below" so that each executive and each official constantly feel their responsibility to and dependence on the electorate, on the work collectives, public organizations, on the Party and the people as a whole. The main thing in this respect is to create and strengthen all instruments and forms of real control by the working people.

What instruments and forms do I have in mind?

Accountability, first of all. The time has come to observe strictly the rules for systematic accountability of all elected and appointed officials before work collectives and the population. It is necessary that every such account be accompanied by lively and principled discussion, criticism and self-criticism and businesslike proposals, and end with an evaluation of the activities of the person giving an account of his work.

This would be the implementation of Lenin's demand that the work of elective bodies and executives be open to everyone and be done in sight of the people. It we achieve such control, there can be no doubt that many causes for complaints and appeals to higher organizations will disappear, and most questions raised in them will be solved at the local level. In the conditions of extended democracy, people themselves will put things in order in their work collective, town, or village....

While normalizing the atmosphere in society, it is essential to further encourage openness. This is a powerful lever for improving work in all sectors of our development and an effective form of control by the whole people. The experience which has been gained since the April Plenary

Meeting of the Central Committee is good proof of this.

Obviously, the time has come to begin elaborating legal acts guaranteeing openness. These should ensure maximum openness in the activities of state and public organizations and give the working people a real opportunity to express their opinions on any question of social life.

Criticism and self-criticism are a tested instrument of socialist democracy. There seems to be no open objection to this. However, in real life we encounter situations indicating that by no means everyone has become aware of the need to support critical-mindedness in society. Matters at times go so far that some officials regard even the slightest remarks as an encroachment upon their prestige and defend it in any way they can. Then there are those officials, the more experienced ones, who admit the justness of criticism and even thank you for it, but are in no hurry to eliminate drawbacks, expecting to get away with things as usual.

Such an attitude to criticism has nothing in common with our principles and ethics. At the present stage, when we are asserting new approaches in socio-political life, in the cultural and intellectual sphere, the importance of criticism and self-criticism grows immeasurably. People's attitude to criticism is an important criterion of their attitude to reorganization, to everything new that is taking place in our society.

And here I cannot but say regretfully that we continue to encounter not only cases of non-acceptance of criticism but also facts of persecution for it, of direct suppression of criticism. Not infrequently this assumes such proportions and takes such forms that the Central Committee has to intervene in order to reestablish the truth and justice and to support honest people who take the interests of work close to heart. I have already spoken of this matter, but things are improving only slowly. Take, for instance, the central press reports for January and you'll see that the persecution of people for criticism is far from a rare thing.

In this connection we must support the efforts of the mass media to develop criticism and self-criticism in our society. Their position in the struggle for reorganization has been appreciated by Soviet people.

The readership of central newspapers and magazines has increased by over 14 million and Central TV programmes on topical subjects are attracting audiences of many millions. People are impressed by the bold and profound treatment of urgent problems which are involved in the acceleration of the country's socio-economic development and which cover all aspects of life in our society. The Party believes that the programmes of the mass media will continue to be marked by depth and objectivity and a high degree of civic responsibility. . . .

A draft law has been prepared on the procedure for filing a complaint in court against illegal actions of officials infringing upon the rights of a citizen. This law is soon to be submitted for discussion. Additional steps are planned to improve the work of state arbitration and improve legal education of the population. . . .

One important aspect of the democratization of public life is promotion of non-Party comrades to leading positions. This is a matter of principle. One of the firm guarantees of the health and progress of a socialist society lies in the political and professional growth of the front-rank worker, farmer, engineer, researcher, doctor, teacher, and public services employee. We need to constantly push to the fore and promote talent from the thick of the people.

Sometimes we come across the opinion that promotion of non-Party people is outdated because the CPSU now has over 19 million members. I think it is erroneous. To believe so is to deform the Party's relations with the people. Moreover, coming straight to the point, this infringes on the constitutional rights of citizens and limits our opportunities as regards the employment of personnel.

We have had, and continue to have, quite a few remarkable examples of fruitful work by non-Party comrades who hold leading positions. They head mills and factories, collective and state farms, construction organizations, scientific and pedagogical collectives, engineering services and are actively involved in public activities.

Open selection of workers to be promoted—from among both Communists and non-Party people—will accord with the aims of democratization and will help involve large numbers of working people in management.

There is also the question of promoting more women to leading positions. There are many women holding Party and state posts and working successfully in science, health care, education, culture, the light industry, trade, and public services. In order to meet our country's needs today, we must more actively involve women in running the economy and culture on an all-Union or republican scale. We have such possibilities. All we have to do is trust and support women.

Comrades, there isn't one single fundamental issue that we could resolve, now as in the past, without taking into account the fact that we live in a multinational country. There is no need to prove the importance of socialist principles in the development of relations between the nationalities. It is socialism that did away with national oppression, inequality, and infringements upon the rights of people on grounds of nationality. It ensured the economic and cultural progress of all nationalities and ethnic groups. In short, the successes of our Party's nationalities policy are beyond any doubt and we can justly take pride in them.

But we must also see the real picture of the relations between nationalities and the prospects for their development. Now that democracy and self-government are expanding, that there is rapid growth of national awareness of all nationalities and ethnic groups, and the processes of internationalization are developing in depth, it is especially important to settle promptly and fairly outstanding questions in the only possible way—in the interest of the progress of each nationality and ethnic group, in the interest of their further drawing closer together, and in the interest of society as a whole.

In this connection it must be added that negative phenomena and deformities in our society, something we are combatting today, have also appeared in relations between nationalities. There have been manifestations of parochialism, ethnic isolation, and ethnic arrogance and even incidents similar to those which took place quite recently in Alma-Ata.

The events in Alma-Ata and what led up to them require a serious analysis and a principled assessment. This has not yet been thoroughly examined. It is clear today that what has occurred should compel not only Communists in Kazakhstan, but all Party organizations and their Committees to deal with the problems of further developing relations between nationalities, and enhancing internationalist education. It is especially important to protect our younger generation from the demoralizing effect of nationalism. . . .

Acting in the spirit of Leninist precepts, in the spirit of the directives of the 27th CPSU Congress, it is necessary to follow firmly the line of all nationalities and ethnic groups of the country being represented in Party, state and economic bodies, including at a countrywide level, so that the composition of the leading personnel fully reflects the country's national structure.

Naturally, the point at issue is not a mechanical assignment of jobs and posts according to the national principle—this would mean vulgarization of the very idea of internationalism. Political, professional and moral qualities is what determines in all instances the image of the worker. Besides, one should not disregard the particular delicacy of national aspects in one problem or another, folk traditions in the way of life, in people's psychology and behaviour. All this should be taken into account most carefully. . . .

It is in the traditions of Bolshevism to wage a principled struggle against any manifestations of national narrow-mindedness and snobbery, nationalism and chauvinism, parochialism, Zionism and anti-semitism—no matter what their forms might be. We should bear in mind that nationalism and proletarian internationalism are two opposite policies, two opposing world outlooks.

Proceeding from these positions we shall be firm and principled. People's national sentiments deserve respect, they cannot be ignored, but they should not be flirted with either. Let those who would like to play on nationalist or chauvinistic prejudices entertain no illusions and expect no leniency. . . .

Personnel Policy in Conditions of Reorganization

Comrades,

I think we clearly understand that success of the reorganization largely depends on how quickly and deeply our workers realize the need for changes and how creatively and purposefully they implement the Party's policy. What is necessary today is a personnel policy that matches the reorganization tasks and the need to accelerate social and economic development. When formulating its initial requirements, we ought to take into account both the lessons of the past and the new large-scale tasks life poses today.

The years of socialist construction in the USSR saw the formation of a powerful potential of highly skilled personnel, while the immeasurably improved level of education and culture of workers and peasants, of the entire people creates favourable conditions for its constant replenishment and renewal. Everything that we have accomplished, everything that we have attained, is the result of Soviet people's work and is due to our personnel's selfless effort.

At the same time, one should also mention at this Plenary Meeting mistakes in work with personnel, distortions in personnel policy that have occurred in recent years and resulted in major shortcomings in the activity of several links in the Party, state and economic apparatus, and in negative phenomena in society. Many errors could have been avoided if Party bodies had always consistently pursued a principled, effective personnel policy ensuring high efficiency of all links in Party leadership and economic management.

Of course, we should not confine ourselves today to the mere admission of mistakes. In order to avoid such mistakes in the future, we must benefit from lessons of the past.

What are these lessons?

The first is the need to resolve in good time the urgent personnel questions within the Party Central Committee, its Political Bureau—above all from the viewpoint of ensuring continuity in the leadership and the influx of fresh forces. At a certain stage, the violation of this natural process weakened the work-capacity of the Political Bureau, the Secretariat and the entire CPSU Central Committee and its apparatus, as well as the government.

Indeed, Comrades, following the April Plenary Meeting a large part of the Secretariat and heads of departments in the CPSU Central Committee have been replaced, along with practically all of the Presidium of the USSR Council of Ministers. This was a forced change since the composition of the Central Committee and the government was not changed or replenished with new members for a long time, as life demanded. All this ultimately affected policy and the practical work of the Party in guiding society.

This cannot and should not be repeated. In order to ensure continuity and prevent a break in the process of renewal, the CPSU Central Committee, the Political Bureau and the Secretariat of the Central Committee, the government, the top echelons of the Party and state leadership should be open to the influx of fresh forces from various spheres of activity. Doing this fully corresponds to the Leninist understanding of personnel policy, to the interests of the Party and the people....

The second lesson from past experience, Comrades, is that we should not underestimate political and theoretical training, the ideological and moral steeling of Party workers. Otherwise, very serious disruptions in the activity of Party committees as bodies of political leadership occur.

These criteria in the selection, placement and education of personnel were not always taken into account in recent years. Often, the greatest significance was attached to a worker's knowledge of the specifics of one or other branch of production, science, engineering or technology, or his strength of will. Undoubtedly, all that has importance, but such qualities in the managerial staff as ideological and theoretical outlook, political maturity, moral standards and the capacity to persuade and lead people should also not be ignored.

It should be directly and honestly admitted that the technocratic, "administrative pressure" style of work caused great damage to the Party cause, especially to work with people which is the main element of the Party's activity. By plunging into economic work and, in several instances, assuming functions out of their jurisdictions, many Party workers did not pay enough attention to political issues, to socially significant phenomena in the economy, and in social and cultural life. . . .

The third lesson we must learn is that two opposite tendencies paradoxically coexisted in the personnel policy in recent years. You may wonder what I mean, comrades.

The signs of stagnation have manifested themselves rather strongly in the personnel body. Secretaries of many Party committees and top executives of government and economic bodies at the local, republican and all-union levels often have not been replaced for decades and there has been no influx of new forces there.

Saying this, I do not want to cast the slightest aspersions on many hundreds and thousands of marvelous workers, particularly at the district and city levels, who have always devoted all their energies and knowledge to selflessly serving the Party and the people. . . . The CPSU and all the people highly appreciate their difficult work, their great services, and give them due credit for that.

I think that the well-known and well-assimilated truth that personnel stability is essential does not need additional proof. This should not be carried to extremes, to the point of absurdity, if you will.

We know all too well what this led to, what price is now being paid for artificial stability which has essentially turned into personnel stagnation.

On the other hand, there also existed another, no less disquieting, tendency in the work with personnel, particularly in the primary units of the national economy. It is excessive personnel rotation, a real reshuffling of managers of industrial enterprises, construction projects, collective and state farms and other organizations. . . .

Regrettably, there are also Party committees and secretaries who cover up their own blunders and, on occasion, failures with ostentatious exactingness towards personnel, by pseudo-adherence to principle without regard for either the essence of the matter or the fate of the people involved.

In this connection I want to mention yet another inadmissible quality: the intolerance of some executives of independent actions and thoughts of subordinates. It quite often happens that as soon as workers begin to express independent opinions which do not coincide with those of the secretary of a Party committee or the head of a ministry or department, enterprise, institution or organization, attempts are made to get rid of them under any pretext, at times even under outwardly plausible ones. It may appear to be better. But better for whom or for what? For the work? Nothing of the kind. It is always worse for the work....

The fourth lesson of our work with personnel is to enhance responsibility for the work assigned, to tighten discipline, and to create an atmosphere of mutual exactingness. How could it happen, comrades, that many leading positions at the district, city, regional, republican, and even all-union levels were held for decades by executives who could not cope with their duties, by undependable and undisciplined people? ...

Are not there regions, republics, cities and districts where production targets have not been met for years and where social matters have been neglected? Their leaders bore no responsibility for failures in work. They got away with it all....

Finally, one more lesson. It is natural to raise this question at our Plenary Meeting: why have all these problems that have piled up in the work with personnel remained for a long time unattended and unresolved? How could this happen? The question, as you well understand, is very serious.

The Political Bureau's opinion is that the main cause is the weakness of democratic principles in the work with personnel. I have already spoken of inner-Party democracy in a principled way as the chief guarantor of the implementation of the Party's strategic course and the tasks of reorganization. Proposals on such a cardinal question of democratization as the formation of elective bodies within the CPSU were made as well.

Now I would like to present the question of raising the role of all elective bodies. It must be frankly admitted that if they acted to the best of their abilities both in the Party and in the state, trade unions and other public organizations, many serious omissions in the work with personnel could have been avoided.

Let us look at life with open eyes, so to speak. An excessive growth of the role of executive bodies to the detriment of elective ones has occurred. At first glance everything proceeds as it should. Plenary meetings, sessions and sittings of other elective bodies are held regularly. But their work is often excessively formalized; secondary matters or those decided upon in advance are brought up for discussion. As a result, there is a lack of proper control over the activities of executive bodies and their leaders. Let's face it, some comrades began to view elective bodies as a nuisance which gives only headaches and creates the troubles. That's what we have come to.

That resulted in the decreased role of the deputies of the Soviets, of members of Party and other collective decision-making bodies in forming executive committees, selecting personnel, and controlling over their activities. Is not the same evidenced by the nature and style of relationships between the permanent staff and members of elective bodies? Quite often one comes across attempts by staff members to command members of Party committees, other public organizations and deputies to the Soviets. It turns out, in fact, that democratic mechanisms for the formation and functioning of the elective bodies are proclaimed but far from always work, and consequently, are not sufficiently effective. . . .

The necessary political and legal prerequisites should be created for the elective bodies to exercise effective control over the executive staff, its formation and activities. This will be a reliable safeguard against many errors, including those in the work with personnel. . . .

Organizational standards and discipline are assuming increasing importance. They are indispensable everywhere, but are especially vital in conditions of modern production with the extensive use of the latest technologies. In recent years, consequent upon things being set in order and carelessness being dealt with, there has been a noticeable increase in the economic growth rates.

Yet the task remains here. Poor discipline and negligence are too deeply rooted and are felt painfully to this day. It was criminal negligence and lack of responsibility that stood behind such tragedies as the accident at the Chernobyl nuclear power station, the wrecking of the *Admiral Nakhimov* and a number of air and railway accidents which claimed a toll of human lives.

An atmosphere ruling out any possibility of a repetition of such tragedies must be created everywhere. Discipline, promptness and efficiency should become the law for everybody.

And finally, the most important quality is the high moral standard of our personnel—honesty, incorruptibility, modesty. We now know, not only from the past, but also from our recent experience, that we would not be able to carry out the reorganization tasks without strengthening our society's moral health. It is therefore only logical that we have come to grips so uncompromisingly with negative phenomena precisely in the moral sphere. I mean the struggle to eradicate drunkenness, embezzlement, bribery, abuse of office and protectionism. . . .

I wish to repeat that without developing democracy, without the broad involvement of the working people we will not be able to cope with the tasks of reorganization. The Party committees and all workers should learn to operate in conditions of greater democracy and growing political and labour activity on the part of the people. . . .

Comrades, immense responsibility for putting into effect the strategic policy for accelerated social and economic development devolves on the managerial personnel. A changeover is currently under way across the country from administrative to cost-benefit methods of management and to a responsible and creative manner of running affairs.

Today, the work collectives of factories and amalgamations are being provided with vast financial, material and technical resources to modernize production and solve social problems. The managers are granted wide latitude, not only to make whatever tactical economic manoeuvres are expedient, but also to pursue long-term aims within the five-year plan period and beyond, in short, a new economic, social and political situation is developing, in which an energetic and competent executive can fully use his abilities.

Most executives welcome the far-reaching measures being implemented by the Party and the government to reform the system of management. They are becoming more active in their implementation. . . .

Changes in the work of ministries and departments are taking place, even though slowly and painfully. Headquarters of various branches of the economy are directly participating in drafting proposals for enterprises' operation in new economic conditions. They are giving more attention to questions of scientific and technological policy, the restructuring of enterprises and starting the production of goods meeting modern requirements.

We have reinforced some branches and their sub-divisions with capable people. As a rule, energetic specialists who want to run things in a new way and ensure the introduction of modern methods of work have been placed in key posts. This policy should be continued, the performance of ministries and departments actively improved and their staff replenished with highly-qualified personnel capable of initiative.

At the same time, there are still instances of red tape and irresponsibility in the work of ministries and departments which carry out the Party and government resolutions. The staff of ministries and departments appears to be a captive of old regulations and instructions, acts by inertia and refuses to give up its prerogatives.

It is not the first time, Comrades, that we have drawn the attention of the heads and staff members of ministries and departments to the need for a radical reorganization of their activity. In this way, everyone gets the opportunity to join in this work and master new approaches to the business at hand. But it is impermissible for a ministry or its staff to be idle or, even more so, to impede the restructuring process. . . .

Comrades, in conclusion I would like to speak briefly about the goals for 1987. This year, which marks the 70th anniversary of the October Revolution, holds special significance for us. The Soviet people are looking forward to the forthcoming anniversary as they thoroughly reorganize all aspects of public life. This year the Political Bureau believes it would be well to issue an Address to all Party members and all working people in the USSR.

The Central Committee calls on Communists and all Soviet people to display a still greater understanding and sense of responsibility for what is to be accomplished, for the destiny of the country and for the future image of socialism. We have achieved a lot in the decades of socialist construction. But time is putting new and ever greater demands on us. In these new changed conditions Soviet society is passing a test of dynamism, of the ability to climb the steps of progress rapidly.

Our economy is passing the test of high efficiency, of receptivity to advanced technologies, of ability to produce first-class goods and compete on the world markets. Our morality and the entire Soviet way of life are being put to test for an ability to develop steadily and enrich the values of socialist democracy, social justice and humanism. Our foreign policy is being tested for firmness and consistency in the defense of peace, for flexibility and self-possession in conditions of the frenzied arms race fuelled by imperialism and the international tension fanned by it. . . .

While orientating the personnel to tackling the current tasks and fulfilling the assignments of the 12th five-year plan period by all means, we must, as Lenin taught us, not lose sight of our perspective. We must specify and finalize ways of economic and social progress. The drafting of the plan for the 13th five-year plan period will begin shortly. It will be based on the new system of management making it possible to utilize socialism's potentialities and advantages to a greater extent.

Since the ongoing radical reform of economic management concerns fundamental questions of the functioning of the socialist economic system, as well as many aspects of political and social life and the style and methods of work, it would be expedient to examine the entire range of these problems at the Central Committee's next plenary meeting. . . .

It is possible to sum up what has been said as follows: we all, and everyone of us, should improve our work. The mobilizing role of our Party, of all its organizations and of all Communists should manifest itself with particular force in the new situation. It is important to continuously keep in touch with the pulse of life and to do everything for the projected plans to be implemented.

In this connection, I would like to take counsel on this fundamental issue. Perhaps, it is advisable to convene an all-Union Party conference next year on the eve of the report-and-election campaign within the Party, and to extensively review the course of the implementation of the decisions of the 27th CPSU Congress and sum up the results of the first half of the five-year plan period. It would also be in line for the conference to discuss ways to further democratize the life of the Party and society as a whole.

The discussion started at this conference could be continued at report-and-election Party meetings and conferences, at which the results of the restructuring work of each Party organization should be analyzed in an exacting way.

The very fact of convening an all-Union Party conference in accordance with the CPSU's Rules would be a serious step towards making our Party life more democratic in practice and developing Communists' activity.

Comrades, by formulating a personnel policy in the conditions of the reorganization and acceleration of the country's social and economic development, the Plenary Meeting of the Central Committee thereby determines the most important areas of our work for many years to come.

At the Plenary Meeting today we have repeatedly referred to Lenin, his thoughts and ideas. This is not just a tribute of great respect, not only an acknowledgement of Lenin's authority. This reflects the pressing desire to revive in modern conditions and to the fullest possible extent the spirit of Leninism, to assert in our life the Leninist demands on personnel. You will recall, Comrades, how passionately, how tirelessly Lenin taught us that the success of revolutionary struggle, the success of any cardinal restructuring of society is largely determined by the tone set by the Party.

We wish to turn our country into a model highly developed state, into a society with the most advanced economy, the broadest democracy, the most humane and lofty ethics, where the working man feels that he is real master, enjoys all the benefits of material and intellectual culture, where the future of his children is secure, where he has everything that is necessary for a full and interesting life. And even sceptics will be forced to say: yes, the Bolsheviks can accomplish anything. Yes, the truth is on their side. Yes, socialism is a system serving man, working for his benefit, in his social and economic interests, for his cultural elevation.

STATE OF THE UNION

January 27, 1987

President Ronald Reagan delivered his sixth State of the Union message to Congress and the nation January 27. The speech was as important for what it said about Reagan as for what it said about the United States. Reagan was fighting to revive his presidency after a series of events that had lowered his popularity and raised questions about his credibility and influence.

Three events had combined to weaken Reagan politically. First, the nation had been rocked by the unfolding story of the Iran-contra scandal. In ongoing congressional investigations, details surfaced regarding the administration's secret sale of arms to Iran and the alleged diversion of profits from the sale to the Nicaraguan contras. The State of the Union address provided Reagan an opportunity to defuse the controversy and clarify his position. (Historic Documents of 1986, p. 1049)

The second damaging event was the Republican loss of control of the Senate as a result of the November 1986 elections. For the first time in his presidency, Reagan faced Democratic majorities in both houses. This fact, combined with the historic tendency of presidents to lose influence in their last years in office, presented a challenge to Reagan's political clout.

Reagan needed a strong performance in the State of the Union address for a third reason. At age seventy-five, the president was recovering from prostate surgery. For the White House it was crucial that the president appear to be in good health and in command in his first major public appearance since the January 5 operation.

Iran-Contra Affair

Reagan commented briefly on the Iran-contra issue early in his message. He declared that his "one major regret" was that efforts to establish contacts with Iran and to free American hostages held by Middle East terrorists had failed. "Serious mistakes were made," Reagan acknowledged, adding, "We will get to the bottom of this, and I will take whatever action is called for."

His statement fell short of the apology that some congressional Republicans had urged him to make to Americans for conducting a secret policy that contradicted his public opposition to bargaining with terrorists. The president asserted his conviction that the goals of the plan were worthy. "I do not believe it was wrong to try to establish contacts with a country of strategic importance or to try to save lives," he said. He made no explicit mention of arms sales to Iran or diversion of their profits to Nicaraguan rebels.

Foreign Policy and Arms Control

Reagan focused more on foreign policy and defense than he had in previous State of the Union addresses. He used Soviet expansionism and the threat of a growing Soviet presence to justify support for both the Strategic Defense Initiative (SDI) and the Nicaraguan contras in their fight against the Sandinista government. The administration knew that both SDI and contra aid would face opposition in the 100th Congress.

Reagan reaffirmed his commitment to SDI, the antimissile space defense program, which he said the Soviets had "sought to cripple" during his October 1986 meeting with General Secretary Mikhail S. Gorbachev in Reykjavik, Iceland. Reagan also vowed continued support for the contras. "I will fight any effort," he warned, "to shut off their lifeblood and consign them to death, defeat or a life without freedom. There must be no Soviet beachhead in Central America." (Historic Documents of 1986, p. 875)

Economic Issues

The president touched briefly on U.S. trade policy, stating that he remained "opposed as ever to protectionism." Reagan did not address the growing U.S. trade deficit, but did promise comprehensive proposals to improve America's competitiveness in world markets and the quality of life in the United States. Members of Congress received an outline of these proposals in an accompanying written legislative message from the White House, titled "A Quest for Excellence."

Reagan termed the federal deficit "outrageous" and repeated his annual call for a constitutional amendment to balance the budget. Reagan also reiterated a request for the power to veto items within appropriations bills and emphasized his continued opposition to new taxes as a way to reduce the deficit.

Domestic Issues

Reagan touched on two domestic issues on which he had promised action in the 1986 address. He proposed revision of the welfare system, which he called an "outmoded dinosaur." Without offering details, he said his new welfare strategy would rely on "state-sponsored, community-based" projects. He also promised to submit legislation to "help free the elderly from the fear of catastrophic illness."

The president briefly reaffirmed his support for voluntary school prayer, the crusade against drugs, and the need for more rigorous educational requirements.

Reagan framed his speech with references to the U.S. Constitution, which celebrated its bicentennial in 1987. The Constitution's first three words, "We the people," are what makes it so exceptional, Reagan asserted. "In our Constitution, we the people tell the government what it can do and it can do only those things listed in that document and no others."

Reaction

A highly charged partisan atmosphere was evident throughout the president's address. Democrats groaned and withheld applause, giving Reagan his coolest reception in six years. Republicans, meanwhile, rallied behind him.

In the official Democratic response televised after Reagan's address, House speaker Jim Wright, D-Tex., and Senate majority leader Robert C. Byrd, D-W. Va., called for cooperation in addressing concerns about the budget, trade deficits, the farm crisis, education, and foreign policy. They also criticized Reagan's policies in each area. Byrd's remarks focused on the Iran-contra affair. "The sale of arms to Iran—in direct contradiction to our stated foreign policy—raises real doubts about competence," he declared.

Reaction to Reagan's address fell along sharply drawn party lines. Democrats criticized the lack of new legislative proposals; Republicans supported the president's style and general themes. The confrontational atmosphere in evidence on Capitol Hill forecast what one representative predicted would be "a bumpy two years ahead."

> *Following is the text of President Ronald Reagan's sixth nationally televised State of the Union address, delivered before a joint session of Congress January 27, 1987:*

Mr. Speaker, Mr. President, distinguished Members of Congress, honored guests and fellow citizens:

May I congratulate all of you who are members of this historic 100th Congress of the United States of America. In this 200th anniversary year of our Constitution, you and I stand on the shoulders of giants—men whose words and deeds put wind in the sails of freedom. However, we must always remember that our Constitution is to be celebrated not for being old, but for being young—young with the same energy, spirit, and promise that filled each eventful day in Philadelphia's statehouse. We will be guided tonight by their acts, and we will be guided forever by their words.

Now, forgive me, but I can't resist sharing a story from those historic days. Philadelphia was bursting with civic pride in the spring of 1787, and its newspapers began embellishing the arrival of the convention delegates with elaborate social classifications.

Governors of States were called Excellency. Justices and chancellors had reserved for them honorable with a capital "H." For Congressmen, it was honorable with a small "h." And all others were referred to as "the following respectable characters."

Well, for this 100th Congress, I invoke special executive powers to declare that each of you must never be titled less than honorable with a capital "H." Incidentally, I'm delighted you are celebrating the 100th birthday of the Congress. It's always a pleasure to congratulate someone with more birthdays than I've had.

Now, there's a new face at this place of honor tonight. And please join me in warm congratulations to the Speaker of the House, Jim Wright. Mr. Speaker, you might recall a similar situation in your very first session of Congress, 32 years ago. Then, as now, the speakership had changed hands and another great son of Texas, Sam Rayburn—"Mr. Sam"—sat in your chair. I cannot find better words than those used by President Eisenhower that evening. He said, "We shall have much to do together; I am sure that we will get it done and that we shall do it in harmony and goodwill."

Tonight, I renew that pledge. To you, Mr. Speaker, and to Senate Majority Leader Robert Byrd, who brings 34 years of distinguished service to the Congress, may I say: Though there are changes in the Congress, America's interests remain the same. And I am confident that, along with Republican leaders Bob Michel and Bob Dole, this Congress can make history.

Six years ago, I was here to ask the Congress to join me in America's new beginning. Well, the results are something of which we can all be proud. Our inflation rate is now the lowest in a quarter of a century. The prime interest rate has fallen from the 21½ percent the month before we took office to 7½ percent today. And those rates have triggered the most housing starts in 8 years.

The unemployment rate—still too high—is the lowest in nearly 7 years, and our people have created nearly 13 million new jobs. Over 61 percent of everyone over the age of 16, male and female, is employed—the highest percentage on record. Let's roll up our sleeves and go to work and put America's economic engine at full throttle.

We can also be heartened by our progress across the world. Most important, America is at peace tonight, and freedom is on the march. And we've done much these past years to restore our defenses, our alliances, and our leadership in the world. Our sons and daughters in the services once again wear their uniforms with pride.

But though we've made much progress, I have one major regret: I took a risk with regard to our action in Iran. It did not work, and for that I assume full responsibility. The goals were worthy. I do not believe it was wrong to try to establish contacts with a country of strategic importance or to try to save lives. And certainly it was not wrong to try to secure freedom for our citizens held in barbaric captivity. But we did not achieve what we wished, and serious mistakes were made in trying to do so. We will get to the bottom of this, and I will take whatever action is called for.

But in debating the past, we must not deny ourselves the successes of the future. Let it never be said of this generation of Americans that we became so obsessed with failure that we refused to take risks that could further the cause of peace and freedom in the world.

Much is at stake here, and the Nation and the world are watching to see if we go forward together in the national interest or if we let partisanship weaken us. And let there be no mistake about American policy: We will not sit idly by if our interests or our friends in the Middle East are threatened nor will we yield to terrorist blackmail.

And now, ladies and gentlemen of the Congress, why don't we get to work?

I am pleased to report that because of our efforts to rebuild the strength of America, the world is a safer place. Earlier this month I submitted a budget to defend America and maintain our momentum to make up for neglect in the last decade. Well, I ask you to vote out a defense and foreign affairs budget that says yes to protecting our country. While the world is safer, it is not safe.

Since 1970 the Soviets have invested $500 billion more on their military forces than we have. Even today, though nearly one in three Soviet families is without running hot water and the average family spends two hours a day shopping for the basic necessities of life, their government still found the resources to transfer $75 billion in weapons to client states in the past five years—clients like Syria, Vietnam, Cuba, Libya, Angola, Ethiopia, Afghanistan, and Nicaragua.

With 120,000 Soviet combat and military personnel and 15,000 military advisers in Asia, Africa, and Latin America, can anyone still doubt their single-minded determination to expand their power? Despite this, the Congress cut my request for critical U.S. security assistance to free nations by 21 percent this year, and cut defense requests by $85 billion in the last 3 years.

These assistance programs serve our national interests as well as mutual interests. And when the programs are devastated, American interests are harmed. My friends, it's my duty as President to say to you again tonight that there is no surer way to lose freedom than to lose our resolve.

Today the brave people of Afghanistan are showing that resolve. The Soviet Union says it wants a peaceful settlement in Afghanistan, yet it continues a brutal war and props up a regime whose days are clearly numbered. We are ready to support a political solution that guarantees the rapid withdrawal of all Soviet troops and genuine self-determination for the Afghan people. In Central America, too, the cause of freedom is being tested. And our resolve is being tested there as well. Here, especially, the world is watching to see how this nation responds.

Today over 90 percent of the people of Latin America live in democracy. Democracy is on the march in Central and South America. Communist Nicaragua is the odd man out—suppressing the church, the press, and democratic dissent and promoting subversion in the region. We support diplomatic efforts, but these efforts can never succeed if the Sandinistas win their war against the Nicaraguan people.

Our commitment to a Western Hemisphere safe from aggression did not occur by spontaneous generation on the day that we took office. It began with the Monroe Doctrine in 1823 and continues our historic bipartisan American policy. Franklin Roosevelt said we "are determined to do everything possible to maintain peace on this hemisphere." President Truman was very blunt: "International communism seeks to crush and undermine and destroy the independence of the Americans. We cannot let that happen here." And John F. Kennedy made clear that "Communist domination in this hemisphere can never be negotiated." Some in this Congress may choose to depart from this historic commitment, but I will not.

This year we celebrate the second century of our Constitution. The Sandinistas just signed theirs two weeks ago, and then suspended it. We won't know how my words tonight will be reported there for one simple reason: There is no free press in Nicaragua.

Nicaraguan freedom fighters have never asked us to wage their battle, but I will fight any effort to shut off their lifeblood and consign them to death, defeat, or a life without freedom. There must be no Soviet beachhead in Central America.

You know, we Americans have always preferred dialog to conflict, and so, we always remain open to more constructive relations with the Soviet Union. But more responsible Soviet conduct around the world is a key element of the U.S.-Soviet agenda. Progress is also required on the other items of our agenda as well—real respect for human rights and more open contacts between our societies and, of course, arms reduction.

In Iceland, last October, we had one moment of opportunity that the Soviets dashed because they sought to cripple our Strategic Defense Initiative, SDI. I wouldn't let them do it then; I won't let them do it now or in the future. This is the most positive and promising defense program we have undertaken. It's the path, for both sides, to a safer future—a system that defends human life instead of threatening it. SDI will go forward.

The United States has made serious, fair, and far-reaching proposals to the Soviet Union, and this is a moment of rare opportunity for arms reduction. But I will need, and American negotiators in Geneva will need, Congress' support. Enacting the Soviet negotiating position into American law would not be the way to win a good agreement. So, I must tell you in this Congress I will veto any effort that undercuts our national security and our negotiating leverage.

Now, today, we also find ourselves engaged in expanding peaceful commerce across the world. We will work to expand our opportunities in international markets through the Uruguay round of trade negotiations and to complete an historic free trade arrangement between the world's two largest trading partners, Canada and the United States.

Our basic trade policy remains the same: We remain opposed as ever to protectionism, because America's growth and future depend on trade. But we would insist on trade that is fair and free. We are always willing to be trade partners but never trade patsies.

Now, from foreign borders, let us return to our own, because America in the world is only as strong as America at home. This 100th Congress has high responsibilities. I begin with a gentle reminder that many of these are simply the incomplete obligations of the past. The American people deserve to be impatient, because we do not yet have the public house in order.

We've had great success in restoring our economic integrity, and we've rescued our nation from the worst economic mess since the Depression. But there's more to do. For starters, the federal deficit is outrageous. For years I've asked that we stop pushing onto our children the excesses of our government. And what the Congress finally needs to do is pass a constitutional amendment that mandates a balanced budget and forces government to live within its means. States, cities, and the families of America balance their budgets. Why can't we?

Next, the budget process is a sorry spectacle. The missing of deadlines and the nightmare of monstrous continuing resolutions packing hundreds of billions of dollars of spending into one bill must be stopped. We ask the Congress once again: Give us the same tool that 43 Governors have—a line-item veto so we can carve out the boondoggles and pork, those items that would never survive on their own. I will send the Congress broad recommendations on the budget, but first I'd like to see yours. Let's go to work and get this done together.

But now let's talk about this year's budget. Even though I have submitted it within the Gramm-Rudman-Hollings deficit-reduction target, I have seen suggestions that we might postpone that timetable. Well, I think the American people are tired of hearing the same old excuses. Together we made a commitment to balance the budget. Now, let's keep it.

As for those suggestions that the answer is higher taxes, the American people have repeatedly rejected that shopworn advice. They know that we don't have deficits because people are taxed too little. We have deficits because big government spends too much.

Now, next month I'll place two additional reforms before the Congress. We've created a welfare monster that is a shocking indictment of our sense of priorities. Our national welfare system consists of some 59 major programs and over 6,000 pages of federal laws and regulations on which more than $132 billion was spent in 1985. I will propose a new national welfare strategy, a program of welfare reform through State-sponsored, community-based demonstration projects. This is the time to reform this outmoded social dinosaur and finally break the poverty trap. Now, we will never abandon those who, through no fault of their own, must have our help. But let us work to see how many can be freed from the dependency of welfare and made self-supporting, which the great majority of welfare recipients want more than anything else.

Next, let us remove a financial specter facing our older Americans: the fear of an illness so expensive that it can result in having to make an intolerable choice between bankruptcy and death. I will submit legislation shortly to help free the elderly from the fear of catastrophic illness.

Now let's turn to the future. It's widely said that America is losing her competitive edge. Well, that won't happen if we act now. How well prepared are we to enter the 21st century? In my lifetime, America set the standard for the world. It is now time to determine that we should enter the next century having achieved a level of excellence unsurpassed in history.

We will achieve this, first, by guaranteeing that government does everything possible to promote America's ability to compete. Second, we must act as individuals in a quest for excellence that will not be measured by new proposals or billions in new funding. Rather, it involves an expenditure of American spirit and just plain American grit.

The Congress will soon receive my comprehensive proposals to enhance our competitiveness, including new science and technology centers and strong new funding for basic research. The bill will include legal and regulatory reforms and weapons to fight unfair trade practices. Competitiveness also means giving our farmers a shot at participating fairly and fully in a changing world market.

Preparing for the future must begin, as always, with our children. We need to set for them new and more rigorous goals. We must demand more of ourselves and our children by raising literacy levels dramatically by the year 2000. Our children should master the basic concepts of math and science, and let's insist that students not leave high school until they have studied and understood the basic documents of our national heritage.

There's one more thing we can't let up on: Let's redouble our personal efforts to provide for every child a safe and drug-free learning environment. If our crusade against drugs succeeds with our children, we will defeat that scourge all over the country.

Finally, let's stop suppressing the spiritual core of our national being. Our nation could not have been conceived without divine help. Why is it that we can build a nation with our prayers but we can't use a schoolroom for voluntary prayer? The 100th Congress of the United States should be remembered as the one that ended the expulsion of God from America's classrooms.

The quest for excellence into the 21st century begins in the schoolroom but must go next to the workplace. More than 20 million new jobs will be created before the new century unfolds, and by then, our economy should be able to provide a job for everyone who wants to work. We must also enable our workers to adapt to the rapidly changing nature of the workplace. And I will propose substantial, new Federal commitments keyed to retraining and job mobility.

Over the next few weeks, I'll be sending the Congress a complete series of these special messages—on budget reform, welfare reform, competitiveness, including education, trade, worker training and assistance, agriculture, and other subjects. The Congress can give us these tools, but to make these tools work, it really comes down to just being our best. And that is the core of American greatness.

The responsibility of freedom presses us towards higher knowledge and, I believe, moral and spiritual greatness. Through lower taxes and smaller government, government has its ways of freeing people's spirit. But only we, each of us, can let the spirit soar against our own individual standards. Excellence is what makes freedom ring. And isn't that what we do best?

We're entering our third century now, but it's wrong to judge our nation by its years. The calendar can't measure America because we were meant to be an endless experiment in freedom—with no limit to our reaches, no boundaries to what we can do, no end point to our hopes.

The United States Constitution is the impassioned and inspired vehicle by which we travel through history. It grew out of the most fundamental inspiration of our existence: that we are here to serve Him by living free—that living free releases in us the noblest of impulses and the best of our abilities; that we would use these gifts for good and generous purposes and would secure them not just for ourselves, and for our children, but for all mankind.

Over the years—I won't count if you don't—nothing has been so heartwarming to me as speaking to America's young, and the little ones especially, so fresh-faced and so eager to know. Well, from time to time I've been with them—they will ask about our Constitution. And I hope you Members of Congress will not deem this a breach of protocol if you'll permit me to share these thoughts again with the young people who might be listening or watching this evening.

I have read the constitutions of a number of countries—including the Soviet Union's. Now, some people are surprised to hear that they have a constitution, and it even supposedly grants a number of freedoms to its people. Many countries have written into their constitution provisions for freedom of speech and freedom of assembly. Well, if this is true, why is the Constitution of the United States so exceptional?

Well, the difference is so small that it almost escapes you, but it's so great it tells you the whole story in just three words: We the people. In those other constitutions, the Government tells the people of those countries what they're allowed to do. In our Constitution, we the people tell the Government what it can do, and it can do only those things listed in that document and no others.

Virtually every other revolution in history has just exchanged one set of rulers for another set of rulers. Our revolution is the first to say the people are the masters and government is their servant. And you young people out there, don't ever forget that. Someday you could be in this room, but wherever you are, America is depending on you to reach your highest and be your best—because here in America, we the people are in charge.

Just three words: We the people. Those are the kids on Christmas Day looking out from a frozen sentry post on the 38th Parallel in Korea or aboard an aircraft carrier in the Mediterranean. A million miles from home, but doing their duty.

We the people—those are the warm-hearted whose numbers we can't begin to count, who'll begin the day with a little prayer for hostages they will never know and MIA families they will never meet. Why? Because that's the way we are, this unique breed we call Americans.

We the people—they're farmers on tough times, but who never stop feeding a hungry world. They're the volunteers at the hospital choking back their tears for the hundredth time, caring for a baby struggling for life because of a mother who used drugs. And you'll forgive me a special memory—it's a million mothers like Nelle Reagan who never knew a stranger or turned a hungry person away from her kitchen door.

We the people—they refute last week's television commentary downgrading our optimism and our idealism. They are the entrepreneurs, the builders, the pioneers, and a lot of regular folks—the true heroes of our land who make up the most uncommon nation of doers in history. You know they're Americans because their spirit is as big as the universe and their hearts are bigger than their spirits.

We the people—starting the third century of a dream and standing up to some cynic who's trying to tell us we're not going to get any better. Are we at the end? Well, I can't tell it any better than the real thing—a story recorded by James Madison from the final moments of the Constitutional Convention, September 17th, 1787. As the last few members signed the document, Benjamin Franklin—the oldest delegate at 81 years and in frail health—looked over toward the chair where George Washington daily presided. At the back of the chair was painted the picture of a Sun on the horizon. And turning to those sitting next to him, Franklin observed that artists found it difficult in their painting to distinguish between a rising and a setting Sun.

Well, I know if we were there, we could see those delegates sitting around Franklin—leaning in to listen more closely to him. And then Dr. Franklin began to share his deepest hopes and fears about the outcome of their efforts, and this is what he said: "I have often looked at that picture behind the President without being able to tell whether it was a rising or setting sun: But now at length I have the happiness to know that it is a rising and not a setting sun."

Well, you can bet it's rising because, my fellow citizens, America isn't finished. Her best days have just begun.

Thank you, God bless you, and God bless America.

PRESIDENT'S ECONOMIC REPORT, ECONOMIC ADVISERS' REPORT

January 28, 1987

President Ronald Reagan January 28 presented Congress with an optimistic view of the U.S. economy. In his annual economic report, Reagan claimed credit for the "longest peacetime expansion of the postwar era." He said, "Our market-oriented policies have paid off." Sounding familiar themes, he urged Congress to restrain federal spending and called for a "limited role" for government in the nation's economy.

In a separate, 205-page report accompanying the president's message, the Council of Economic Advisers analyzed the problems that "remained," which were "primarily sectoral and structural." In their report the economists discussed the large U.S. trade deficit, the impact on the oil and gas industry of the sharp decline in world oil prices, the continued depression in agriculture, and what the president and the council considered "excessive and inappropriate" regulation.

The council disputed a number of ideas that appeared to be taking hold in the country. An example was the contention that the huge trade deficit was largely the result of declining international competitiveness of U.S. industry. The council instead traced the imbalance to the rising value of the dollar in the first half of the decade, to slow economic growth abroad, and to the high U.S. budget deficit.

Trade Deficit

The large U.S. trade deficit, representing the excess of imports over exports, was a source of growing political concern. According to Com-

merce Department figures, the deficit swelled from $148.5 billion in 1985 to $169.8 billion in 1986. The Council of Economic Advisers said the country's bilateral trade deficit with Japan soared from $19 billion in 1982 to more than $55 billion in 1986.

The president's economists called the "deterioration" of the trade balance a "disturbing feature" of the economic recovery. The deficit was a matter of concern, they said, because it adversely affected "many trade-sensitive industries" and encouraged "protectionist sentiment."

In his message, Reagan linked the trade deficit to the nation's large budget deficit. The trade deficit, he said, "reflects that . . . we have spent more than we have produced—and we have spent too much because of the profligacy of the Federal Government." But the Council of Economic Advisers provided a broader explanation of the imbalance. Calling the deficit a "macroeconomic phenomenon," the economists said that imports had grown strongly for three reasons: the "fall in U.S. price competitiveness" associated with the appreciation of the dollar in 1980-1985, developing countries' difficulties in managing external debts, and the strong growth of the U.S. economy.

Protectionism

Both President Reagan and the Council of Economic Advisers firmly rejected protectionist moves by the United States in reaction to the large trade deficit. Resorting to protectionism, the president said, would neither reduce the U.S. deficit nor make American firms more competitive. He characterized protectionism as "antigrowth."

The president's economists wrote that the argument in favor of free trade "is relatively simple yet compelling." They also said that however justified were American "claims of unfair trade practices" by other countries, the "massive" deterioration of the U.S. trade balance "clearly has not occurred primarily because foreign trade practices have become vastly more unfair."

Oil and Agriculture

The Council of Economic Advisers singled out the drop in world oil prices, which had resulted from the collapse of the Organization of Petroleum Exporting Countries (OPEC), as probably the most important "special factor" in the economic picture in 1986. The spot price of West Texas crude had fallen from $30.90 to $13.75 per barrel between November 1985 and April 1986.

But while the economists stressed the severe impact of the price collapse on the oil and gas industry, they also highlighted "important beneficial effects" for the rest of the economy. A result was the "first significant decline" in the consumer price index since 1954. That drop, they said, "contributed to strong gains in real disposable income that, in turn, fueled the strong growth of consumer spending, which was the mainstay of overall economic growth."

The president's economists attributed severe problems in U.S. agriculture to government policies in the United States and many other industrialized nations. Those policies, they said, had stimulated excess farm production, which led to depressed prices in world markets.

Some commentators, focusing on economic problems in the oil and gas, agriculture, and mining industries in the center of the country, had suggested that the United States was becoming a "bicoastal economy." But the council strongly rejected that notion, which suggested that the Midwest was in decline, calling it "highly exaggerated."

Economic Outlook

The president's economists predicted a strengthening of economic growth with continued moderate inflation in 1987. They forecast 3.2 percent growth in the gross national product (GNP) and a rise in inflation at a 3.6 percent annual rate (as measured by the GNP deflator), compared with a 2.2 percent rate of increase during 1986. They also predicted that unemployment, which had stood at 6.6 percent in 1986, would drop only slightly, to 6.5 percent, in 1987.

Over the next six years, they expected that real GNP would rise to 3.6 percent in 1989 and decline slowly to 3.4 percent in 1992. They envisioned that the consumer price index would be as high as 3.6 percent in 1988 and 1989 but would drop to 2.2 percent in 1992. The consumer price index had hit a low 1.1 percent in 1986, largely as a consequence of the sharp decline in oil prices.

Testifying about the report of the Council of Economic Advisers before the Joint Economic Committee of Congress, council chairman Beryl W. Sprinkel said the projections were based on the assumption that Congress would enact spending cuts to reduce the budget deficit and that Japan and West Germany would boost their own economic growth. He said that he expected the decline in the value of the dollar to reduce the trade deficit by about $30 billion in 1987.

Following are the text of the Economic Report of the President and excerpts from the Annual Report of the Council of Economic Advisers, both issued January 28, 1987:

ECONOMIC REPORT OF THE PRESIDENT

To the Congress of the United States:

For 6 years, my Administration has pursued policies to promote sustained, noninflationary growth and greater opportunity for all Americans.

We have put in place policies that are in the long-term best interest of the Nation, policies that rely on the inherent vigor of our economy and its ability to allocate resources efficiently and generate economic growth. Taming the Federal Government's propensity to overtax, overspend, and overregulate has been a major element of these policies.

The Current Expansion

Our market-oriented policies have paid off. The economic expansion is now in its fifth year, and the growth rate of the gross national product, adjusted for inflation, should accelerate to 3.2 percent in 1987. By October, the current expansion will become the longest peacetime expansion of the postwar era.

Since the beginning of this expansion, the economy has created more than 12 million new jobs. In each of the past 2 years, the percentage of the working-age population with jobs was the highest on record. Although I am encouraged by the fall in the overall unemployment rate to 6.6 percent in December 1986, I will not be satisfied until all Americans who want to work can find a job.

Our efforts to reduce taxes and inflation and to eliminate excessive regulation have created a favorable climate for investing in new plant and equipment. Business fixed investment set records as a share of real gross national product in 1984 and 1985, and remains high by historical standards.

Despite the economy's tremendous gains in employment and production, inflation has remained below or near 4 percent for the past 5 years and, in 1986, declined to its lowest rate in 25 years. Although last year's low inflation rate in part reflected the substantial decline in energy prices during 1986, we expect inflation in 1987 to continue at the moderate pace experienced during the first 3 years of the expansion. The financial markets have acknowledged our progress in reducing inflation from its double-digit levels, and interest rates declined during 1986, reaching their lowest levels in 9 years. To sustain these developments, the Federal Reserve should continue to pursue monetary and credit policies that serve the joint goals of growth and price stability.

In short, since 1982, we have avoided the economic problems that plagued our recent past—accelerating inflation, rising interest rates, and severe recessions. Production and employment have grown significantly, while inflation has remained low and interest rates have declined. This expansion already has achieved substantial progress toward our long-term goals of sustainable economic growth and price stability.

The Economic Role of Government

Government should play a limited role in the economy. The Federal Government should encourage a stable economy in which people can make informed decisions. It should not make those decisions for them, nor should it arbitrarily distort economic choices by the way it taxes or regulates productive activity. It should not and cannot continue to spend excessively, abuse its power to tax, and borrow to live beyond its means.

The Federal Government should provide certain goods and services, public in nature and national in scope, that private firms cannot effectively provide—but it should not try to provide public goods and services that State or local governments can provide more efficiently. When government removes decisions from individuals and private firms, incentives to produce become dulled and distorted; growth, productivity, and employment suffer. Therefore, to the greatest extent possible, the Federal Government should foster responsible individual action and should rely on the initiative of the private sector.

Tax Reform

My 1984 State of the Union Message set tax reform as a national priority. After more than 2 years of bipartisan effort, we achieved our goal last fall when I signed into law the Tax Reform Act of 1986. Tax reform broadens the personal and corporate income tax bases and substantially reduces tax rates. These changes benefit Americans in at least three ways.

First, by reducing marginal tax rates, tax reform enhances incentives to work, save, and invest. Second, by reducing disparities in tax rates on income from alternative capital investments, tax reform encourages more efficient deployment of investment funds. Investment decisions will now reflect the productive merits of an activity more than its tax consequences, leading to a more efficient allocation of resources, higher growth, and more jobs. Finally, tax reform makes the tax system more equitable. The simpler, lower rate structure will make compliance easier and tax avoidance less attractive. Americans will know that everyone is now paying his or her fair share and is not hiding income behind loopholes or in unproductive shelters. Tax reform will especially benefit millions of working poor by removing them from the Federal income tax rolls.

Remaining Challenges of Economic Policy

We have successfully reformed the tax code, controlled inflation, and reduced government intervention in the economy. The result has been an expansion of production and employment, now in its fifth year, which we fully expect will continue with greater strength in 1987. Although much has been accomplished, we must and will address the remaining challenges confronting the economy. We must continue to reduce the Federal budget deficit through spending restraint. We must reduce the trade deficit, while avoiding protectionism. We must strengthen America's productivity and competitiveness in the world economy. And we must reform our costly, inefficient, and unfair agricultural programs.

Control Federal Spending

For the first time since 1973, Federal spending in 1987 will fall in real terms. As a result, the Federal budget deficit will decline from its 1986 level by nearly $50 billion. My budget for 1988 continues this process by meeting the Gramm-Rudman-Hollings deficit target of $108 billion.

Deficit reduction must continue and must be achieved by restraining the growth of Federal spending—not by raising taxes, which would reduce growth and opportunity. Large and persistent Federal deficits shift the burden of paying for current government spending to future generations. Deficit reduction achieved through spending restraint is essential if we are to preserve the substantial benefits of tax rate reduction and tax code reform; it is also essential for reducing our international payments imbalances. Finally, spending on many programs exceeds the amounts necessary to provide essential Federal services in a cost-effective manner.

Besides exercising spending restraint, we must reform the budget process to build a check on the Federal Government's power to overtax and overspend. I support a constitutional amendment providing for a balanced peacetime budget, and I ask the Congress to give the President the same power that 43 Governors have—the power to veto individual line items in appropriations measures.

Maintain Free and Fair Trade

One of the principal challenges remaining for the U.S. economy is to reduce our trade deficit. However, we cannot accomplish this, or make American firms more competitive, by resorting to protectionism. Protectionism is antigrowth. It would make us less competitive, not more. It would not create jobs. It would hurt most Americans in the interest of helping a few. It would invite retaliation by our trading partners. In the long run, protectionism would trap us in those areas of our economy where we are relatively weak, instead of allowing growth in areas where we are relatively strong.

We cannot gain from protectionism. But we can gain by working steadfastly to eliminate unfair trading practices and to open markets around the world. This year, I will continue to press to open foreign markets and to oppose vigorously unfair trading practices wherever they may exist. In addition, I will ask the Congress to renew the President's negotiating authority for the Uruguay Round under the General Agreement on Tariffs and Trade. These talks offer an important and promising opportunity to liberalize trade in areas critical to the United States; trade in services, protection of intellectual property rights, fair rules governing international investment, and world trade in agricultural products.

More remains to be done to end our trade deficit. We must sustain world economic growth, increase productivity, and restrain government spending. For U.S. exports to grow, the economies of our trading partners must grow. Therefore, it is essential that our trading partners enact policies that will promote internally generated economic growth. At the Tokyo Economic Summit last year, the leaders of the seven largest industrial countries continued efforts, begun at the Versailles Economic Summit in 1982, to increase international coordination of economic policies. We must also continue to encourage developing countries to adopt policy reforms to promote growth and restore creditworthiness.

Here in the United States, we must restrain government spending. Our trade deficit in goods and services reflects that, over the past several years, we have spent more than we have produced—and we have spent too much because of the profligacy of the Federal Government. As the Congress reviews my proposed 1988 budget, it should remember that a vote for more government spending is a vote against correcting our trade deficit.

Strengthen Productivity and Competitiveness

We must work to improve our international competitiveness through greater productivity growth. The depreciation of the dollar since early 1985 has done much to restore our competitiveness. However, we do not want to rely on exchange-rate movements alone. Productivity growth provides the means by which we can strengthen our competitiveness while increasing income and opportunity. Since 1981, U.S. manufacturing productivity has grown at a rate 46 percent faster than the postwar average. This is a solid accomplishment, but still more remains to be done. We must encourage continued productivity growth in manufacturing and in other sectors of our economy.

One way to strengthen our global competitiveness is to free American producers from unnecessary regulation. My Administration has sought to deregulate industries in which increased competition will provide greater benefits to consumers and producers. It has also streamlined the Federal Government's regulatory structure. Americans have benefited significantly from the deregulation of airlines, financial services, railroads, and trucking. I will resist any attempt to reregulate these industries. Our economy will benefit further if we eliminate natural gas price controls, remaining trucking regulations, and unnecessary labor market restrictions. Also, without compromising the Nation's air quality, we should eliminate the bias that exists in current air pollution regulations against cleaner and more efficient new factories and power facilities. Where regulation is necessary, its costs should be balanced against its benefits to ensure that regulatory efforts are applied where they do the most good and to avoid placing American firms at a competitive disadvantage in the world marketplace.

Privatization shifts the production of goods and services from government ownership to the private sector. Privatization can also improve American competitiveness because private firms can produce better quality goods and services, and deliver them to consumers at lower cost, than can government. For these reasons, Americans benefit when government steps aside. Like deregulation and federalism, privatization embodies my Administration's belief that the Federal Government should minimize its interference in the marketplace and in local governance. We must return more government activities to the competitive marketplace by selling or transferring government-owned businesses. In 1986, the Congress authorized the Department of Transportation to sell Conrail in a public offering, which we hope will take place this year. Other businesses suitable for privatization include the Naval Petroleum Reserves, the Alaska Power Administration, and Amtrak.

Reform Agricultural Policies

Another high priority in 1987 must be to reform our agricultural programs. Besides costing taxpayers $34 billion this year alone, these programs divert land, labor, and other resources from their most productive uses. Most farm programs are costly and unfair because they give literally millions of dollars to relatively few individuals and corporations while many family farmers—who are those most often in need—receive little. In the process, farm programs raise the prices of many food items for all Americans, rich and poor.

Farm income support should not be linked to production through direct subsidies or propped-up prices for agricultural products. My Administration will seek a market-oriented reform package with two goals: gradually separating farm income support from farm production, and focusing that income support on those family farmers who need it most.

Conclusion

The economic policies of my Administration have created greater economic freedom and opportunity for men and women, private firms, and State and local governments to pursue their own interests and make their own decisions. These policies have produced a sustained economic expansion with low inflation, lower tax rates and a simpler tax code, the unshackling of industries from regulation, a surge in investment spending, and more than 12 million new jobs.

The American people demand a sound, productive, growing economy. Therefore, I shall continue to pursue policies to encourage growth, reduce the Federal budget deficit, correct the trade deficit, and strengthen the competitiveness of American producers. The American people will not tolerate a replay of the failed economic policies of the past. Therefore, I shall resist proposals to adopt any economic policy that abandons the accomplishments of tax reform, stymies growth, fuels inflation, perpetuates needless government interference in the marketplace, or fosters protectionism. With the help and cooperation of the Congress, we can sustain and strengthen the current economic expansion, and preserve and extend the economic achievements of the past 6 years.

THE ANNUAL REPORT OF THE COUNCIL OF ECONOMIC ADVISERS

Growth and Adjustment in the United States Economy

The United States economy is in the fifth year of the current expansion, and an acceleration of real growth with continued moderate inflation is projected for 1987 and beyond. While the pace of economic growth remained moderate in 1986, expansion proceeded on a broad front. Real gross national product (GNP) rose by 2.2 percent during the year, with output expanding in most sectors. Due in large part to a sharp decline in energy prices, inflation fell to the lowest rate in more than two decades. Rising real personal income and significantly lower interest rates contributed to strong growth of consumption and of residential investment. Despite a decline in business fixed investment and further deterioration of the trade balance, the unemployment rate fell to 6.6 percent and total employment grew by more than 2½ million persons. In each year of this expansion, more jobs were created in the United States than in the combined economies of the next six largest industrial democracies.

More than 4 years of economic expansion, with the inflation rate remaining near or below 4 percent and interest rates declining to their lowest levels in 9 years, have laid the foundation for sustainable real growth with moderate inflation. The problems that remain in the U.S. economy are primarily sectoral and structural: the Federal Government controls too much of the Nation's resources; a large trade deficit adversely affects many trade-sensitive industries and encourages protectionist sentiment; the domestic oil and gas industry and local areas heavily dependent on it are suffering the consequences of the decline in world oil prices; conditions remain depressed in much of American agriculture; and excessive and inappropriate regulation continues to burden business and consumers.

Overview of the Report

This *Report* analyzes the structural and sectoral problems that remain in the U.S. economy. It assesses policies to deal with these problems while maintaining a sustainable rate of overall growth and making continued progress in moderating inflation. This chapter begins with a summary of the *Report*. . . .

Fiscal Policy

Chapter 2 examines two elements of fiscal policy, budget control and tax reform, that influence both the sectoral and overall performance of the U.S. economy. Better control of the Federal budget is required to reduce the Federal deficit, primarily by reducing the share of Federal spending in GNP. Realization of the long-run benefits of the Tax Reform Act of 1986 is one of the many important reasons for pursuing this approach to deficit reduction. This Act improves overall incentives for economic activity and reduces disparities in rates of taxation on different forms of economic activity....

International Imbalances

Chapter 3 demonstrates that the large U.S. trade deficit is primarily a macroeconomic phenomenon. This phenomenon is fundamentally related to the rapid growth of domestic demand in the United States relative to the growth of U.S. output and relative to demand and output growth in the rest of the world. It is also related to the appreciation of the U.S. dollar between 1980 and 1985, which reduced the international competitiveness of U.S.-produced goods and services. And it is related to the deterioration of the U.S. national saving-investment balance, which reflects not abnormal behavior of the private saving-investment balance, but rather the persistence of a large Federal deficit late into the current expansion.

Stronger internally generated growth in other industrial countries, reduction of the Federal deficit through spending restraint, and policy reforms that encourage growth and restore credit worthiness in developing countries are critical elements in the global strategy to reduce international trade imbalances. Stronger internally generated growth in foreign countries is essential to maintain satisfactory rates of real growth in the world economy....

Free and Fair Trade

Protectionism is a false solution to the U.S. trade imbalance. However justified are the claims of unfair trade practices by other countries, the massive deterioration of the U.S. trade balance clearly has not occurred primarily because foreign trade practices have become vastly more unfair. Moreover, starting a world trade war by resorting to protectionism would be especially imprudent at a time when the improving competitiveness of U.S. industries appears likely to bring significant expansion of U.S. exports.

... [T]he Administration's policy of free and fair trade is to avoid protectionism at home while opening markets to U.S. products abroad....

Reform of Agricultural Policies

The problems of U.S. agriculture are the focus of Chapter 5. Government policies have directly or indirectly subsidized agricultural production in the United States and in many other industrial countries. These policies have stimulated excess production that has depressed agricultural product prices in world markets. Government intervention has wasted resources by encouraging farmers to incur costs in order to produce commodities for which only the government provides a market. Much of the money spent on agricultural support programs has been dissipated in outright waste or delivered to owners of large farms that invariably receive the largest subsidy payments.

The solution is to reform agricultural programs by gradually decoupling farm income support from farm production and linking it to financial need. . . .

Risk, Regulation, and Safety

. . . In some cases, regulations even work against their intended purposes. Rigid rules, such as some designed to reduce workplace hazards, can reduce production and employment opportunities without a corresponding gain in occupational safety. In this and other areas where government intervention may be indicated, the costs of regulations should be weighed against their likely benefits. Reliance on personal responsibility and market incentives often provides the best methods for reducing risk.

Women in the Labor Force

. . . Over the past decade, women have accounted for 62 percent of total labor force growth. Increasing labor force participation of women has not led to large increases in unemployment rates for either men or women, and has made an important contribution to growth of real per capita income. Because many women now plan longer careers and acquire the requisite education, experience and skills, wages of women relative to those of men have been rising in the 1980s. . . .

The U.S. Economy in 1986

Economic growth proceeded at a moderate pace in 1986, while significant declines were recorded in both the inflation rate and interest rates. Between the fourth quarter of 1985 and the fourth quarter of 1986 (preliminary estimate), real GNP rose by 2.2 percent. While the unemployment rate declined by only 0.3 of a percentage point during the year, and remained relatively high by postwar standards, the employment-population ratio for persons over 16 years of age reached a new postwar peak of 61.3 percent at the end of 1986. Given the impact of declining oil prices, the inflation rate, measured by the consumer price index (CPI), turned negative in the first quarter. Over the entire year, the CPI rose by only 1.1 percent, the lowest inflation rate in more than 20 years. Nominal interest rates fell sharply early in the year and by yearend were near their lowest levels for the year and since 1977. . . .

The Oil Price Decline

Probably the most important special factor affecting the U.S. economy in 1986 was the sharp drop in world oil prices, which was promptly reflected in domestic oil prices. Between November 1985 and April 1986, the spot price of West Texas Crude fell from $30.90 to $13.75 per barrel. A further $2.45 per barrel decline in domestic oil prices occurred between April and July, before prices recovered to $17.60 per barrel in December. The sharp decline in oil prices had pronounced adverse effects on the domestic oil and gas industry. Real investment in this industry declined by more than $10 billion in the first half of 1986, accounting for more than half of the decline in real business fixed investment. Employment in the domestic oil and gas industry fell by nearly 150,000, mainly in the first half. Further employment losses occurred in regions heavily dependent on the oil and gas industry.

For the rest of the economy, the decline in oil and gas prices had important beneficial effects. The CPI fell at an annual rate of 4.3 percent between January and April, the first significant decline in this index since 1954. The decline in consumer prices was clearly attributable to lower oil and gas prices, because the CPI excluding energy rose at an annual rate of 2.9 percent between January and April. The decline in consumer prices contributed to strong gains in real disposable personal income that, in turn, fueled the strong growth of consumer spending, which was the mainstay of overall economic growth.

The fall in oil prices, inflation, and inflationary expectations also played a critical role in the sharp decline in nominal interest rates. Interest rates on 10-year Treasury securities fell from 9.26 percent in December 1985 to 7.30 percent in April 1986, and declined a further 19 basis points by yearend. Interest rates on 91-day Treasury bills fell somewhat less, moving down from 7.10 percent in December 1985 to 6.06 percent by April 1986 and to 5.53 percent by yearend. The sharp decline of interest rates spread rapidly to mortgage interest rates.

Assuming no further substantial change in domestic oil prices, most of the negative effects of lower oil prices have probably been absorbed, while the beneficial effects are yet to be fully realized. Lower energy costs will contribute to lower production costs in many important domestic industries. Productivity growth may be enhanced in the long run as firms adopt more efficient energy-using technologies, partially reversing the adverse productivity effects of higher energy prices in the 1970s....

Regional Developments

While GNP data are not available on a regional basis, data on employment by State provide a reasonably good impression of the regional economic performance of nonagricultural business....

Widespread employment gains across most of the country do not imply an absence of economic problems in some industries and regions. Agriculture, mining, the oil and gas industry, and other trade-sensitive industries have experienced problems for some time, and particularly for the oil and gas industry, these problems have recently deepened. In areas heavily dependent on declining firms and industries, economic problems have spread to the support and service industries. However, assertions that the United States is becoming a "bicoastal economy" with broad areas of economic depression across the Nation's midsection, are greatly exaggerated. Economic progress has been widespread. Remaining economic problems tend to be concentrated in particular industries and in specific areas of the country....

Productivity Growth and Real Per Capita GNP

Prospects and Policies for Productivity Growth

Slower measured labor productivity growth since mid-1984, relative to that recorded earlier in this expansion, probably partly reflects the usual cyclical effect of slower output growth on productivity growth. If real output growth accelerates in accord with Administration projections (discussed in the next section), then productivity growth should increase. Thus, the macroeconomic developments and policies that underlie the Administration's forecast of moderately stronger real GNP growth are critical for near-term prospects for stronger productivity growth.

Four important developments also seem likely to contribute to stronger long-term productivity growth. First, as the labor force on the average grows older and more experienced over the next 15 years, labor productivity is likely to advance more rapidly. Second, the recent decline in energy prices should allow for some labor productivity improvement, especially in energy-intensive industries. Third, expenditures on research and development, which declined as a share of GNP in the 1970s, have been increasing since 1978 and should contribute to a higher rate of technological progress. Fourth, as is discussed in Chapter 2, tax reform may have a small negative effect on the long-run capital stock, which would tend to depress labor productivity. However, tax reform will also reduce distortions affecting the distribution of capital among productive activities. A more efficient distribution of capital should contribute to higher productivity.

Productivity can be promoted by avoiding policies that inhibit the efficient functioning of private businesses and competitive markets. For example, productivity is impeded by subsidies that keep unprofitable and inefficient firms in business, at the expense of more profitable and efficient firms that must ultimately face such subsidies. This applies not only to direct subsidies, but also to tax subsidies and to protectionist measures that provide subsidies by forcing consumers to pay higher prices. Particularly troublesome are protectionist measures applied to intermediate products. They increase production costs and diminish economic efficiency for industries that use these products, injuring their ability to compete with foreign firms. . . . Government can also contribute to stronger productivity growth by eliminating or reducing burdensome and inappropriate regulation. . . .

Economic Policies and Outlook

The future performance of the U.S. economy depends primarily on the productive activities of individuals and businesses. Government policies enhance economic performance by allowing the private enterprise system to function as freely as possible, by maintaining a stable macroeconomic environment, by providing essential public goods and services and support for the needy, and by correcting externalities, distortions, and deficiencies in the operation of the economic system. . . .

Economic Forecast for 1987

The Administration forecasts a strengthening of economic growth with continued moderate inflation in 1987. The impediments to economic growth that brought past expansions to a halt are not evident: inflation and interest rates remain low, inventory stocks are relatively lean, and resource constraints and production capacity pressures are absent.... The Administration's estimate of real GNP growth this year is 3.2 percent, measured fourth quarter to fourth quarter, compared with a growth rate of 2.2 percent in 1986. For 1987, strong growth in employment is forecast to continue and the total unemployment rate is predicted to be 6.5 percent in the fourth quarter. An improved balance of trade, an increase in inventory investment, and cessation of the economic deterioration caused by the drop in oil prices should contribute to stronger growth in 1987.

The inflation rate in 1987 is forecast to return to the 3.5 to 4 percent range of recent years, before the decline in oil prices temporarily depressed the inflation rate in 1986. Specifically, the GNP deflator is forecast to rise at a 3.6 percent annual rate during 1987, after a 2.2 percent rate of increase during 1986. During 1987, the CPI is expected to increase at a slightly faster rate than the GNP implicit price deflator, reversing the pattern in 1986. This is because the CPI embodies import prices more directly than does the GNP implicit price deflator, and import prices are expected to rise more rapidly than domestic prices because of the continuing effects of depreciation of the dollar.

The Administration's forecast embodies the following assessments for the four main components of GNP: consumption, investment, government spending, and net exports. First, growth of real consumption spending is forecast to slow from the 4.0 percent annual growth rate in 1986, but is still expected to make a substantial contribution to real GNP growth in 1987. As discussed earlier, a rapid increase and high level of real household net worth tend to raise consumption spending. However, the relatively low personal saving rate in 1986 suggests that households may wish to hold growth of consumption spending below that of disposable personal income in order to restore personal saving rates to more normal levels. Moreover, the boost to real disposable personal income, and hence to real consumption spending, from the sharp decline in oil prices in 1986, is unlikely to be repeated in 1987.

Second, real investment is expected to strengthen because of gains in nonresidential fixed investment and inventory investment, despite a substantial slowdown in residential investment growth. Real nonresidential fixed investment fell in 1986, partly because of the problems of the oil and gas industry and perhaps also because of some short-run adverse effects of the tax reform process. Lower interest rates, rising corporate profits, stronger economic growth, and (as previously explained) a high ratio of the market value of financial claims for ownership of business enterprises to the price of capital goods should contribute to some strengthening of real nonresidential fixed investment in 1987. Real residential investment, however, seems unlikely to repeat the strong growth performance of 1986. In particular, high vacancy rates and the effects of tax reform may inhibit growth of multifamily housing construction. Concerning inventory investment, it is noteworthy that manufacturing inventories have generally been falling for more than a year and a half and the inventory-sales ratio is currently low for other sectors as well. With continued growth of domestic sales and improvement in net exports, producers should begin accumulating inventories at a faster pace.

Third, given their relatively strong budget positions, continued modest growth of real spending by State and local governments seems probable. In contrast, the program to reduce the Federal fiscal deficit should lead to a modest reduction in real Federal purchases of goods and services in 1987.

Fourth, after deducting 0.7 percent from economic growth in 1986, real net exports are expected to contribute a similar amount to growth in 1987. The falling dollar appears finally to be influencing the prices of non-oil imports. The fixed-weighted price index for non-oil imports rose 9.4 percent during 1986 and further increases are expected in 1987. Higher relative prices for goods imported into the United States and lower relative prices of U.S. exports in foreign markets should improve U.S. net exports.

A special factor that should aid real GNP growth in 1987 is the end of the decline of production and investment in the domestic oil and gas industry. Following the oil price drop in early 1986, drilling operations for gas and oil plummeted, pulling down nonresidential fixed investment for most of the year. If oil prices remain near yearend levels, declining activity in the domestic oil and gas industry should not continue to detract from real GNP growth in 1987. While the direct effects of lower oil prices were largely completely absorbed by the economy in 1986, secondary benefits may still be forthcoming.

Economic Projections for 1988-92

The Administration's longer term economic projections represent expected trends and should not be interpreted as year-to-year forecasts. They reflect the long-run economic policy goals of the Administration and long-run trends in the economy. Specifically, it is assumed that the incentives for economic activity embodied in the reduced marginal tax rates contained in the Tax Reform Act of 1986 are preserved and that further gains are made in reducing government spending and the burden of government regulation. Also, the Federal Reserve is assumed to continue a policy that is both consistent with gradual achievement of the long-term goal of price stability and not so restrictive as to impair economic growth.

The Full Employment and Balanced Growth Act of 1978 requires the *Economic Report of the President,* together with the *Annual Report of the Council of Economic Advisers,* to include an Investment Policy Report and review progress in achieving goals specified in the Act. The projections for 1987 through 1992 . . . constitute the " . . . annual numerical goals for employment and unemployment, production, real income, productivity and prices...", prescribed by this Act. The projections go far in achieving the goals specified in the Act for unemployment and inflation, while achieving many other aims of the legislation such as balanced growth, reduced Federal spending, adequate productivity growth, an improved trade balance, and increased competitiveness of agriculture, business, and industry. Although the goal of 4 percent unemployment, specified in the legislation, is not attained by 1992, this does not indicate a lack of commitment to achieving full employment. On the contrary, the Administration is dedicated to bringing about full employment and stable prices by creating an environment conducive to healthy and sustained economic growth. There are no quick fixes to reach the legislation's stated goals; government best serves these goals by allowing private enterprise to flourish, thereby generating long-term growth and full utilization of resources in a noninflationary environment.

Specifically, the Administration's economic projections ... show real GNP growth rising to 3.6 percent in 1989 and declining slowly to 3.4 percent in 1992. Stronger real growth reflects the long-term benefits of tax reform, as well as factors that will improve growth in the current year and carry forward in later years. Further improvements in real net exports are expected, especially in 1988. Higher production will lift incomes and consumption, and business investment shold strengthen further in 1988 and beyond. Production is projected to grow sufficiently rapidly to lower the unemployment rate to 5.5 percent by 1992. Consistent with gradual achievement of the long-term goal of price stability, the inflation rate is projected to decline to 2.2 percent by 1991. Productivity growth is projected to improve from recent levels because of the normal cyclical effect of stronger output growth and because of expected improvements (discussed earlier) in the trend rate of growth of labor productivity. Coincident with this improvement in productivity growth, increases are expected in real compensation per hour.

These projections reflect the Administration's policies to promote long-term, noninflationary growth by encouraging investment in physical and human capital and improvements in productive technology. The Administration believes that creating an economic environment that provides strong incentives for work and production is the best policy for promoting investment and productivity growth. Reducing disparities in the rate of taxation on different economic activities contributes to this result by encouraging resources to be allocated to activities where they can be used most productively....

Conclusion

Although 1986 was not an outstanding year in terms of real GNP growth, the economic expansion proceeded on a broad front through its fourth year, and important progress was made in expanding employment and reducing inflation and interest rates. The problems that kept overall growth below expectations were largely sectoral: a decline in world oil prices that depressed employment and investment in the domestic oil and gas industry; continued difficulties in U.S. agriculture; and a further deterioration of the U.S. trade balance. Nowhere evident were the problems that usually portend the end of expansions. Rather, the economic developments of 1986 affirm that the destructive sequence of progressively rising inflation rates and interest rates, interrupted by severe recessions, has been broken....

Budget Control and Tax Reform

Government tax and expenditure policies strongly influence the economy's long-run performance. Government-provided goods and services improve economic performance if their value exceeds their cost, as measured by the value of the private goods and services they displace. The cost of government-provided goods and services, in turn, depends on the efficiency of the tax system. An efficient tax system entails low and unvarying marginal tax rates that have minimal effects on private investment and consumption choices.

The Administration is committed to a policy of restructuring Federal fiscal activities to serve the national interest more effectively. Tax reform, the Administration's number one domestic priority for the past several years, has been accomplished. The Tax Reform Act of 1986 significantly lowers tax rates and will decrease tax-induced distortions in private economic decisions. Progress has also been made in Federal spending restraint. The upward trend in Federal Government expenditures as a share of gross national product (GNP), which had persisted for most of two decades, was reversed in 1984. For the first time since 1973, real Federal Government expenditure is projected to fall in fiscal 1987. Further spending restraint, however, will be necessary to achieve the future deficit targets set in the Balanced Budget and Emergency Deficit Control Act of 1985 (popularly known as Gramm-Rudman-Hollings), targets to which the Administration is firmly committed....

Spending Restraint and Deficit Reduction

The current economic expansion marks the first occasion in the postwar period when Federal deficits have exceeded 5 percent of GNP, and when very large deficits have persisted into the third and fourth years of an expansion. At comparable periods during the expansions of the 1960s and 1970s, the Federal deficit as a share of GNP was generally less than one-half the level of 1985 and 1986. The underlying cause of the growing Federal deficit is illustrated in Chart 2-1. The share of Federal spending in GNP has continued on an upward trend, while the secular trend in the share of Federal revenues has remained virtually flat.

Under the provisions of Gramm-Rudman-Hollings, significant deficit reduction will occur in fiscal 1987. With moderately good economic performance and absent large new spending initiatives, the Office of

Management and Budget projects that the Federal deficit will decline by almost $50 billion between fiscal 1986 and fiscal 1987, equivalent to more than a full percentage point of GNP. The Administration's proposed budget for 1988 provides for another important step in the process of deficit reduction, to the target of $108 billion, along a path to reach a balanced Federal budget by 1991....

Tax Reform

This section assesses the economic effects of the Tax Reform Act of 1986. The purpose of this assessment is twofold: to forecast the effects that tax reform will have on future macroeconomic activity and, by demonstrating the substantial benefits of tax reform, to guard against possible future changes in the tax code that would undo the important progress that has been made.

Overview

The Tax Reform Act of 1986 fundamentally alters the structure of the Federal income tax. It broadens the personal and corporate income tax bases and substantially lowers tax rates. These changes will significantly alter private incentives and, accordingly, will influence the economy's performance through three principal channels:

- Lower marginal tax rates on personal income, in conjunction with a broader tax base, will increase labor effort and reduce the exploitation of tax loopholes.
- More uniform tax rates on income from alternative capital investments will induce a more efficient allocation of investment funds.
- A somewhat higher overall marginal tax rate on capital income will modestly reduce the economy's long-run capital intensity.

The analysis in this section indicates that tax reform will significantly improve the economy's long-run performance....

Summary

TRA will lead to substantial long-run increases in economic welfare. Relative to net national product, the approximate changes in economic welfare that have been quantified are 0.1 percent for a more efficient allocation of investment funds and 1.2 percent for changing long-run factor supplies. Additional welfare gains, which have not been quantified, will result from greater levels of human capital investment; from less tax bias toward corporate debt; from less excessive consumption of employee fringe benefits, consumer durables, and State and local government services; and from less tax evasion.

TRA will increase the long-run fairness of the income tax. All income classes receive a personal income tax cut and the percentage tax cut tends to be largest for low-income taxpayers. TRA also severely limits the opportunities for tax avoidance and will tend to equalize effective tax rates within income classes.

TRA will inflict some short-run costs on the economy as resources are reallocated to more highly valued uses. However, these transition costs will be minor relative to the permanent long-run gains. . . .

Growth, Competitiveness, and the Trade Deficit

The deterioration of the U.S. trade balance has been a disturbing feature of the current recovery. From a surplus equivalent to almost 1 percent of real gross national product (GNP) in 1982, U.S. real net exports of goods and services declined sharply to a deficit equivalent to more than 4 percent of real GNP in 1986, far larger than the deficit recorded in any postwar year before 1984. The growing U.S. trade deficit is often cited as a principal cause of the slowdown of real GNP growth since mid-1984 and of the problems of many trade-sensitive industries. This chapter assesses the causes and effects of the growing U.S. trade deficit and discusses policies adopted by the United States and other countries that will gradually reduce international trade imbalances in a manner consistent with sustainable growth in the world economy.

The increase in the U.S. trade deficit is a macroeconomic phenomenon. Imports have grown strongly and exports have stagnated primarily because of the strong growth of the U.S. economy (especially in terms of demand growth) relative to other countries, the difficulties faced by many developing countries in managing their external debts, and the fall in U.S. price competitiveness associated with the large appreciation of the dollar between 1980 and early 1985. Underlying these developments are several macroeconomic imbalances, including the deterioration in the U.S. saving-investment balance that has resulted from the failure of the Federal Government to bring its expenditures in line with revenues.

Initially, the deterioration of the U.S. trade balance was associated with developments that had favorable effects for the U.S. economy (reduced inflation because of dollar appreciation and reduced upward pressure on interest rates because of a capital inflow). It certainly had favorable effects for the rest of the world, which was suffering from sluggish economic growth. More recently, however, large trade and payments imbalances have been recognized to pose substantial problems for the world economy, including the stimulation of protectionist sentiments.

Important policy actions have been taken in the United States and other countries to reduce international trade and payments imbalances. Better convergence of performance and policies and efforts at policy coordination have brought about exchange-rate adjustments that improve the price competitiveness of U.S. industries. However, there is a lag in the effect of exchange-rate adjustments on trade flows. . . .

The Macroeconomic Character of the U.S. Payments Position

By any measure, the United States has experienced an unprecedented deterioration in its international payments position. The U.S. current account deficit—i.e., the excess of imports of goods and services over exports, plus net transfers made to foreign residents—widened from $9 billion in 1982 to an estimated $145 billion in 1986. Almost all of this change is attributable to the increase in the merchandise trade deficit, which rose to an estimated record $150 billion in 1986.

The deterioration of the U.S. trade balance has been across-the-board. Between 1982 and 1986, the U.S. merchandise trade balance (census basis) worsened in 9 of the 10 major product groups used to classify trade, including such disparate sectors as chemicals, food and live animals, and machinery and transport equipment. Among these major product groups, the U.S. merchandise trade balance improved only in the mineral fuels and lubricants sector. This exception, however, has clearly resulted from special factors, the most important being the decline in oil imports following the 1979-80 oil shock and the recent drop in petroleum prices.

Similarly, deteriorations in U.S. bilateral trade balances have been widespread. Between 1982 and 1986, the U.S. bilateral trade position worsened against all of the top 10 U.S. trading partners (based on total trade) and 19 of the top 20. The widening of the U.S. bilateral trade deficit with Japan from $19 billion in 1982 to more than $55 billion in 1986 has attracted the most public attention, but this deterioration is not unique. The change in the U.S. bilateral trade balance with Western Europe has been about as large, falling from a surplus of $5 billion to a deficit of more than $30 billion. Substantial deteriorations in U.S. bilateral trade positions have also been recorded with Latin America and the newly industrializing countries of East Asia, in each case exceeding $10 billion.

Special factors have undoubtedly influenced bilateral trading patterns and some markets are more open to U.S. exports than others. It is not correct, however, to place primary blame for the more than $100 billion increase in the U.S. trade deficit over the past 4 years on unfair trading practices by U.S. trading partners. The deterioration of the U.S. trade balance is too pervasive to be credibly explained ... on a product-by-product, country-by-country, basis. Rather, the great bulk of the widespread deterioration must be viewed as a product of general macroeconomic developments in the United States and the rest of the world....

Economic Growth and the Trade Deficit

A striking feature of the current expansion—and certainly one of the key factors in assessing world economic performance—is that the United States has enjoyed a strong expansion while the recovery of economic activity in most foreign countries has been weak. This difference in growth has been especially marked in total national spending, known as domestic demand.... [T]otal domestic demand grew much more rapidly in the United States than in other countries during the first six quarters of the expansion (through mid-1984). Since then, differentials between U.S. and foreign demand growth have narrowed considerably, but a large cumulative gap in domestic demand growth remains. This gap reflects the fact that the current recovery of U.S. domestic demand is one of the strongest of the postwar period. It also reflects the fact, however, that the recovery of domestic demand abroad has been one of the weakest....

Exchange Rates and Competitiveness

Exchange-rate changes are a direct channel through which international divergences in economic policy are transmitted to domestic economic performance. Exchange-rate movements that persistently exceed international inflation differentials—real exchange-rate movements—change the prices of a country's imports relative to domestically produced goods and alter the ability of its producers to compete in world markets....

Productivity and Competitiveness

Declining international competitiveness of the U.S. economy, especially manufacturing industries, is often cited as an important cause of the deterioration of the U.S. trade balance. Programs to revive supposedly sagging productivity growth are often recommended as a means of improving competitiveness and reducing the trade deficit.

In fact, as is discussed in Chapter 1, productivity growth in manufacturing during the current cycle has exceeded the postwar average and substantially exceeded the sluggish rate of productivity growth during the 1970s....

In sum, the deterioration of international cost competitiveness in U.S. manufacturing during the first half of this decade was the result of the real appreciation of the dollar, not sagging productivity growth or excessive wage increases. This fact does not imply, however, that the United States can or should rely solely on exchange-rate movements to improve further its international cost competitiveness. Exchange-rate depreciation can increase competitiveness in the intermediate run by making foreign-produced products more expensive, but at the cost of slower real income growth. By contrast, improving international cost competitiveness through greater productivity and economic efficiency increases real income growth. The United States should seek to strengthen international competitiveness by implementing policies that increase productivity....

Opening International Markets

One of the more remarkable features of the past 40 years has been the rapid increase in real income per capita in many parts of the world. This economic expansion has been fueled in large part by a tremendous growth in world trade. In turn, growth in world trade has resulted from a major effort led by the United States and other countries to reduce global barriers to international commerce.

These events stand in direct contrast with the decade preceding the start of World War II. Then, stagnation in the domestic economies of major nations was compounded by the spread of import barriers, export subsidies, trade wars, and a general emphasis on closing domestic markets to foreign competition....

The Case for Free Trade

Governments have long interfered with the exchange of goods across their boundaries. One purpose of their barriers was to collect revenues through tariffs or tolls. Local industry usually supported and benefited from the protective effect of these policies. Indeed, in many instances, pressure from domestic producers induced governments to shelter them from foreign competition with trade restrictions. Another purpose was to achieve trade surpluses through export subsidies and import restrictions. These policies, whose ostensible goal was to increase and preserve domestic wealth at the expense of other countries, became known as mercantilism.

For more than 200 years, many economists have argued against mercantilist policies and made the case for free trade. They generally believe that restrictions on commercial activity reduce wealth rather than increase it. Conversely, the argument for free trade is relatively simple yet compelling.

The case for free international trade is much the same as the case for free internal trade. Commerce between the United States and Japan benefits Americans as does commerce between New York and California. The exchange of goods, internally or internationally, arises as a natural outcome of specialization. Because of factors such as climate, natural resource endowments, or technology, different economic regions possess different abilities to produce certain goods. Individuals, firms, and industries within these regions tend to concentrate their efforts in the goods and services that they are best able to produce. Then their output is exchanged in the marketplace for that of other economic agents.

Specialization allows for a more efficient use of scarce resources and permits improved productivity of the economy. The larger the size of the market, the greater are the possibilities for specialization and for increasing the wealth of the community. The extent of specialization in international trade is related to the forces of international competition. As barriers between markets are lowered, some domestic producers will face increased competition from abroad. Other producers will exploit opportunities as accessible markets expand. Hence, production will tend to contract in industries where foreign goods are superior relative to domestic goods on a price and/or quality basis. In those industries where domestic goods are relatively superior to foreign, local output will expand. These latter industries are said to have a comparative advantage.

In essence, comparative advantage means that an industry will export if it is more efficient relative to other domestic industries. An industry's productivity relative to other industries within the same country determines its ability to command scarce resources within that economy and, thereby, to export to the rest of the world. Thus, a local industry's efficiency compared with that industry in foreign countries is not the main determinant of whether it exports or faces import competition.

Because comparative advantage refers to an internal ranking of productivity, a country may import goods even if the local producing industry is more efficient than its foreign rival. A country will tend to concentrate production in those industries in which it has the greatest comparative advantage. Standards of living rise as resources are put to their most productive uses. One sign of rising standards of living, of course, is a rise in real wages.

A common misconception about international trade is that it is unfair. For instance, some argue that because U.S. wages are high relative to wages in other countries, U.S. producers cannot compete. This argument is true for some industries, but not true in general. U.S. wages are high because American workers are in general more productive than their foreign counterparts. The relatively high U.S. productivity comes about from this Nation's enormous stock of physical and human capital. As U.S. productivity levels increase, so do wages paid to workers. This puts pressure on wages even in relatively inefficient sectors of the economy. But if wages rise and productivity does not keep pace, then American firms will have trouble competing. . . .

. . . [T]he benefits of free trade do not require that trade be balanced at any point in time. Indeed, overall trade balances and the associated international capital flows allow countries the mutual benefit of trading goods and services over time. Countries with overall trade deficits borrow from the rest of the world. Such borrowing can provide the requisite funds for financing investment expenditures crucial to economic growth. Countries with overall surpluses lend to the rest of the world. This lending raises the wealth of the country if it is allocated to projects that earn higher rates of return than would otherwise be possible. However, neither borrowing nor lending can go on indefinitely, and economic forces will work over time to ensure that imbalances are closed. Thus, trade in goods and services between any country and the rest of the world tends to be in balance over the long run.

On the other hand, trade between any two countries may never be in balance. For a variety of reasons, countries tend to amass surpluses with some countries and deficits with others. Unfortunately, interest in bilateral trade balances—essentially a mercantilist trait—remains great. In May 1986, the House of Representatives passed an omnibus trade bill, H.R. 4800, that called for the President to identify countries that have "excessive" trade surpluses with the United States and then to negotiate with or take actions against these countries, regardless of the underlying causes of the surpluses. The President labeled the bill "kamikaze legislation" and promised to veto the measure, but it died when the 99th Congress adjourned.

Despite the obvious benefits of a liberal trading order, various forms of protection abound and are proliferating at an alarming rate. Why do governments continue to pursue these policies? Various justifications have been put forward by governments to defend protectionist policies. Examples include government revenue, national defense, unfair foreign trade practices, preservation of certain ways of life, and short-term aid to revitalize industry.

Whatever the motive, protection in any form redistributes income and wealth. And because the redistributive effects are usually not readily apparent, special interest groups sometimes favor and governments often choose these methods over other more visible and much less costly forms of subsidy. Protection raises the price of imports and domestically produced import-competing products. But, consumers are seldom aware of the tax imposed upon them by protection because they rarely have the opportunity to observe the difference betweeen domestic and world prices. The cost of protection to consumers can be quite dramatic. For instance, the Council of Economic Advisers estimated that if Congress had been successful in its attempt to override the President's veto of the Textile and Apparel Trade Enforcement Act of 1985, Americans would have had to pay up to an additional $44 billion for textiles and apparel over the next 5 years....

[T]he Administration supports.... retraining for displaced workers, reforming antitrust laws, and strengthening property rights....

Toward Agricultural Policy Reform

U.S. agricultural programs have resulted in enormous budgetary costs, benefits that do not reach those most in need, huge surpluses of farm products, major trade disputes with other countries, and great harm to well-functioning international markets. Programs instituted at the Federal level have distorted economic incentives sufficiently to create serious long-term problems. Programs for some commodities have imposed substantial losses on consumers. Chronic surpluses of major commodities exist throughout the world, largely because of high U.S. government target prices and heavy subsidization of agricultural production by most other developed countries.

Despite the massive taxpayer and consumer costs of current programs, the U.S. agricultural sector faces its most severe economic crisis since the 1930s. Instability within the sector continues, with little improvement apparent in the financial condition of many family farms and rural banks. Soil erosion and the pollution of surface and groundwater with toxic waste continue with only moderate signs of relief.

Agricultural policies have become contentious issues of immense importance to all countries. The shift in U.S. agriculture from its prosperous state in the inflationary period of the 1970s to its unsettled existence in the 1980s is linked to events abroad and to the policies pursued in both the agricultural sector and the U.S. economy in general. For these reasons, this chapter focuses on the current state of U.S. and world agriculture, how the Nation arrived at this state, and what public policies would foster a healthy U.S. farm economy....

Reform of U.S. Agricultural Policy

The Food Security Act of 1985 and its predecessors have helped to create many new problems that afflict the U.S. agricultural sector, and have failed adequately to solve many old problems. The fundamental flaw is that Federal farm subsidy payments are linked directly to farm production. Because farmers are paid subsidies (explicit or implicit) that are proportional to their output, they are encouraged to produce even more. Excess production must either be stockpiled by the government, dumped on world markets, or restrained through inefficient land or production restrictions....

Supply Management Bias

The cornerstone of any comprehensive reform of agricultural policy is the elimination of incentives to produce for government programs rather than for the market. As long as such incentives exist, surpluses will be generated. As a consequence, the government will attempt to manage supply by acreage reduction programs, voluntary diversion, acreage set-asides, or production quotas.

Given the changes that have occurred within agriculture, the supply management bias of current programs is doomed to failure....

Conclusion

Today's highly complex patchwork of agricultural policies has become increasingly antiquated and unproductive. Agriculture and rural communities have become so vastly different in structure and in their relationships to the domestic and world economies that the premises underlying current policies are no longer valid. Besides costing taxpayers and consumers billions of dollars and representing a significant portion of the Federal deficit, agricultural policies divert land, labor, and other resources from more to less productive uses. The huge surpluses generated in the United States and throughout the world harm U.S. allies and less developed countries, while providing huge windfalls to powerful economic interest groups. These programs are unfair, with some individuals receiving millions of dollars from the government. The policy reforms outlined here would correct the major imbalances that exist within U.S. agriculture. Other reforms are also needed....

Risk and Responsibility

Risk is a fact of life. Every person balances risks of accident and injury against the attainment of other goals, and trades off some kinds of hazards against others. Whether to smoke, take a particular job, travel by automobile or airplane, use a safety belt while driving, or engage in a dangerous recreational activity are all decisions that involve risk. People are subject to hazards from the actions of other individuals as well. Determination of the proper role of government ... is a complex ... policy issue....

Protection Against Risk

. . . The institutional means for increasing safety and reducing risk are provided through three social arrangements—markets, the legal system, and government regulation. Markets create incentives for safe behavior and allow individual choice in decisions involving risk. Consumers can purchase reductions in risk directly by choosing safer products. . . . Companies that earn reputations for making unsafe products face retribution in the marketplace, just as if they charged excessive prices or offered shoddy goods. The market also promotes safety in the workplace. All other things equal, employers must pay higher wages for riskier jobs, which creates an incentive to reduce occupational hazards.

Private insurance enables individuals and firms to protect themselves against the costs of various risks. Consumers purchase insurance against losses from death, illness and accidents, and some kinds of natural disasters. Manufacturers insure against product liability lawsuits, and professional practitioners insure against liability for malpractice. By spreading the costs of risk, insurance can also undermine incentives for safe behavior; but where premiums are closely linked to the likelihood of events insured against, safety incentives are substantially preserved.

Markets cannot entirely protect an individual from being harmed by the actions of others. The legal system, specifically tort law, provides victims the opportunity to be compensated. By transferring to those who cause harm the costs they impose on others, tort law creates incentives for individuals to behave responsibly. . . .

The Tort System

. . . Tort law . . . serves to compensate persons injured by the negligent or wrongful conduct of others, and also to deter such conduct. . . .

Tort Reform

Many States have enacted or are considering reforms in tort law. The Administration has also supported legislation to address the factors that have led to the high price and scarcity of product liability insurance. This legislation would ensure that fault remains a basis for determining legal liability for injury caused by a defective product. . . . Another provision . . . would make joint and several liability inapplicable to product liability cases. . . . These proposals seek to ensure that fault and wrongdoing continue to be essential to determining liability for defective products. These reforms should lessen the unpredictability of product liability awards for manufacturers and insurers and, by emphasizing the importance of personal responsibility, reduce accidents. . . .

Conclusion

Government regulation can reduce some risks significantly, but can also reduce productivity, personal income, and individual choice. Risks ordinarily cannot be controlled without cost. The resources used to reduce them are not available for alternative improvements in safety or well-being. When government regulates, makes public expenditures, or requires private expenditures to reduce risk, the cost of these actions should be weighed against their likely benefits.

It is not possible to eliminate all hazards to safety and health, nor is it desirable for the government to attempt to reduce risks that could be controlled in less costly ways. In many cases, government control of risk is neither efficient nor effective. Markets accommodate individual preferences for avoiding risk and produce information that helps people make informed choices. Markets and the legal system provide powerful incentives for reducing personal hazards; government regulatory actions should avoid diminishing the incentives for safety that markets and tort law provide. Because many of the greatest risks are subject to personal control, government regulation can never replace the need for responsible individual action.

Women in the Labor Force

Women now constitute 44 percent of the U.S. labor force. They provide services that range from teaching, air traffic control, medicine, and legal advice to administrative and technical support. Women have always played a major productive role in American society. In this century, however, they have increasingly shifted thair productive activities from the home to the marketplace. This shift was accomplished through market processes, without the intervention of government in either job training or job placement activities.

In the early 20th century, about 20 percent of women worked outside the home, and those who did were typically single or widowed. By 1986, the majority of adult women (two-thirds of those between the ages of 25 and 54) worked outside the home and most were married. Female employment increased throughout the century, but the pace has accelerated since World War II. In the postwar period, the number of women working in the United States has risen from 16 million to 49 million. That this important structural change was accomplished in an environment of rising real wage rates underscores the flexibility and resilience of the U.S economy. . . .

Changes in the household and the market meant that the wages women could command outside the home rose relative to the value of time spent in the home. This growing market opportunity encouraged women to enter the labor force. Real earnings of men increased throughout the 1950s and 1960s, at a time when married women were rapidly entering the labor force, implying that family standards of living would have risen even without the earnings of the wife. Thus, while higher real incomes for male wage earners meant less financial need for their wives to work, the attraction of higher wages and less need for women to work at home drew women into the labor market. In some years in the 1970s, however, real wages for both men and women fell. Then, many married women probably did enter the labor market to maintain family incomes. The 1980s have brought increases in both women's real earnings and women's earnings relative to men's, changes that further encouraged work in the marketplace....

Conclusion

This chapter tells two stories. The first is about women and their shift from work in the home to work in the market. The number of women in the labor force has tripled, women's real earnings are rising, and women are increasingly entering higher paid occupations. Women have successfully integrated work in the market with work in the home, making important contributions to both their family's income and the Nation's output.

The second story, which underlies the story of women's economic achievements, is about the adaptability and flexibility of U.S. labor markets in accommodating such a major structural change. Not only has the economy created over 30 million additional jobs filled by women since World War II, but it has also created jobs that interest and attract women: in business and the professions, science and technology, and the service sector. The market produced these jobs while still providing rising real wages and incomes for both men and women.

The success of the responsive and flexible U.S. labor markets has not been confined to adapting to increasing numbers of women. Last year the Council of Economic Advisers chronicled the labor market success of immigrants. Since 1950, the United States has absorbed about 13 million legal immigrants. During the same time, 4 million workers left farming and found other jobs. The market provided non-farm jobs for those who left agriculture, as well as jobs for immigrants who often knew neither the English language nor American customs. It did this without major government programs to force accommodation.

The central conclusion that can be drawn from this chapter ... is clear. The success of the markets is reflected in their adaptability. In the labor market, as with all markets, it is important to retain this ability to respond to change. Regulations to mandate wages or benefits would, even if enacted with the best of intentions, restrict this flexibility and inhibit the ability of markets to adapt. In contrast, free and flexible labor markets provide employment opportunities for new workers, even in the face of enormous and rapid structural change.

As this *Report* demonstrates, the success of the U.S. economy in creating employment opportunities, increasing national income, and raising real living standards begins with reliance upon private enterprise and a competitive-market system. The incentives for individual effort and initiative generated by this system provide the essential stimulus for economic progress. By facilitating the operation of this system, government policy most effectively contributes to the goals specified 40 years ago in the Employment Act of 1946: "... maximum employment, production and purchasing power."

February

CHILDREN'S DEFENSE FUND ON INFANT MORTALITY

February 2, 1987

The Children's Defense Fund (CDF), in a report released February 2, criticized the inadequacy of U.S. efforts to reduce the number of infant deaths. The report found the U.S. infant mortality rate one of the highest in the industrialized world and noted that U.S. progress in reducing infant mortality had stagnated: between 1983 and 1984 the national infant mortality rate had decreased only 4 percent. Moreover, preliminary 1985 data showed no further reduction.

According to the CDF study, health care programs for pregnant women needed to be improved, requiring greater federal and local spending. Marian Wright Edelman, founder and president of the nonprofit child advocacy group, criticized what she said were paltry U.S. efforts to provide maternity care and family support services to poor women. "Many deaths occur because of a lack of very basic supports," she said. "This country is going to have to see that every mother and child gets access to basic preventive maternal care."

Background and Findings

In 1984, the last year for which government figures were available, there were 10.8 infant deaths for every 1,000 live births in the United States. The statistics further revealed that black infants were approximately twice as likely to die as white infants. If the 1984 black infant mortality rate had equaled the white rate, 5,309 fewer black infants would have died that year.

Health experts considered low birthweight the main medical reason for infant death. In the first year of life a low-birthweight baby was twenty times more likely to die than a normal weight baby. Low-birthweight infants also have a greater chance of being born with hearing impairments, learning disabilities, and autism. Between 1969 and 1984 the number of low-birthweight babies had not declined significantly. In 1969, 14 percent of black infants were underweight at birth—twice the rate of white infants. In 1984, 12.4 percent of black babies had low birthweights compared to 5.6 percent of white babies.

The higher incidence of black low-birthweight babies might account for the higher rate of infant mortality among blacks. A study conducted by the National Center for Health Statistics, released after the CDF report, found that younger, less educated, and poorer women were more likely to have low-birthweight babies. However, those factors together still did not explain the difference between the races. The wide difference in low-birthweight babies between black and white women could be found even among the college-educated and married.

Another 1987 study, published in the New England Journal of Medicine, *reported that one reason for the high rate of premature births and infant mortality among blacks was that anemia was more common among black women than white women. The low oxygen levels in the blood of black women were linked to premature births—almost undoubtedly to low birthweights—and so to the risk of infant death.*

The CDF study noted that another factor in the high U.S. infant mortality rate was the relatively high rate of teenage childbearing. Teenage pregnancy contributed greatly to low birthweights and to the stagnating progress in reducing infant mortality rates. Teenagers were considered physically and emotionally unready to have children; moreover, many did not have access to prenatal care. In 1984 only 53.7 percent of infants born to teens had mothers who began prenatal care early in pregnancy, compared to 76.5 percent of all infants.

Factors in America's Relative Decline

Among twenty industrialized countries surveyed by CDF, the United States tied with West Germany, East Germany, and Belgium for the highest rates of infant mortality. For the United States, this marked a dramatic decline from its 1950 ranking. The U.S. infant mortality rate had not increased; rather, the other nineteen industrialized countries (with the exception of Australia) had achieved greater rates of improvement. Other nations had reduced low birthweights and infant mortality by promoting lower rates of teenage childbearing. They also provided pregnant women and infants with maternity care and family supports. A Columbia University study conducted in 1980 found that the United States was the only nation among the twenty that had failed to provide certain basic medical and nutritional services, adequate income support, and generous parental leave policies.

The CDF study revealed significant regional and racial differences within the United States. Urban America showed particularly high rates of infant mortality. Rates rose in six of America's twenty-two largest cities between 1983 and 1984. The difference between black and white infant mortality rates in these cities, said the CDF, was "startling."

Some U.S. cities reported rates higher even than Third World countries. The District of Columbia had the worst rates of infant mortality of any state or any large city—twice the national average. In 1984, said the CDF, a black infant born in Washington, D.C., within ten miles of the White House was more likely to die in the first year of life than an infant born in Trinidad and Tobago.

This observation prompted Washington mayor Marion Barry to question the statistics-gathering techniques of CDF. "I've been to Trinidad. Babies are born in the hills, away from the towns; nobody even knows that they are there." Barry also questioned the extent of government's obligation. "The responsiblity for infant mortality rests with the parents. The mothers are the ones who bear children and mothers ought to take care of their bodies long before they get pregnant. Government does not get women pregnant, men do, and men have a responsibility to try to help the one they got pregnant to stay healthy, eat the right kind of food, to stop drinking alcohol, to stop taking drugs."

Goals Unmet, Spending Inadequate

The CDF also expressed concern that the United States was off course in its effort to meet the surgeon general's 1990 Infant Health Objectives, first issued in 1980. The CDF and the Health and Human Services Department predicted that the nation and the states at their current rates of progress would fail to meet nearly all of the objectives for reducing infant mortality among minorities and the poor, the number of low-birthweight births, and the number of women who received no prenatal care or received it too late.

The CDF predicted that between 1978 and 1990 more than 300,000 low-birthweight babies would be born. By that time, the CDF calculated, the United States would have spent $2.1 billion in first-year medical costs to care for them.

In addition, the report charged that cuts in federal programs, including Medicaid and Aid to Families with Dependent Children, had left many poor families without access to adequate prenatal and postnatal care. In a call for increased government action, the Children's Defense Fund concluded that the nation could more quickly reduce the incidence of low birthweights, disabilities, and infant mortality—and the financial drain that comes with them—if the $2.1 billion could be spent on maternity care, supplemental food programs, and pediatric care for low-income mothers.

Following are excerpts from "The Health of America's Children," a report issued by the Children's Defense Fund February 2, 1987:

National and International Findings

National Findings

A virtual stagnation in key maternal and infant health indicators in 1984 accompanied deeply entrenched childhood poverty and a major increase in the number of children without private health insurance. Stagnation in the U.S. infant mortality rate in the 1980s is the result of numerous factors, including: persistently high postneonatal mortality; the lack of an appreciable decline in the proportion of infants born at low birthweight (which is exacerbated by high rates of teenage childbearing); failure to increase the proportion of pregnant women who have access to early and continuous prenatal care; the ongoing erosion of major public health programs in the face of high poverty rates; and the more than one-third increase since 1978 in the number of Americans without health insurance, one-third of whom are children younger than 18.

Infant Mortality. Nearly 40,000 of the 3,669,141 children who were born in the United States in 1984 died before their first birthday, a rate of 10.8 infant deaths per 1,000 live births. This infant mortality rate represents a 4 percent decline compared to the 11.2 rate that prevailed in 1983. This is a modest improvement over the 3 percent annual rate of decline of the previous two years. Mortality rates among black and nonwhite infants also declined by 4 percent between 1983 and 1984 from rates of 19.2 and 16.8 to rates of 18.4 and 16.1, respectively. The infant mortality rate among whites declined by 3 percent, from 9.7 to 9.4.

Despite their declining infant mortality, black children remained nearly twice (1.96 times) as likely as white infants to die in the first year of life. Only three times since 1940 has the disparity in black and white infant mortality been as wide.

While modest gains were made in 1984, experts anticipate no similar improvements for 1985. According to the National Center for Health Statistics (NCHS), an examination of preliminary data indicates that "there was no statistically significant difference between the estimated infant mortality rate for 1985 of 10.6 deaths per 1,000 live births and the 1984 revised provisional estimate of 10.7. The absence of a statistically significant change in the provisional infant mortality rate between 1984 and 1985 is consistent with the slowing in the rate of decline in infant mortality since 1981, following two decades of sustained decline."

The slowing rate of decline can be seen by comparing the annual rate of decline during the 1981-1984 period (a 3.7 percent change) to the average annual rate of decline during the preceding ten years (a 4.5 percent change).

Neonatal Mortality. The 1984 national neonatal mortality rate (deaths from birth to twenty-eight days of life) was 7.0 deaths per 1,000 live births. This was 4.10 percent lower than the 1983 rate of 7.3.

Postneonatal Mortality. The 1984 national postneonatal mortality rate (deaths between twenty-eight days and one year of life) was 3.8 deaths per 1,000 live births. This represented only a 2.56 percent decline from the 1983 rate. This decline simply returned the nation's postneonatal mortality rate to its 1982 level, since in 1983 there was a nationwide increase in postneonatal mortality. Thus, the nation made no progress in reducing the rate of postneonatal mortality between 1982 and 1984.

Postneonatal mortality in the United States has remained persistently high, even during the great infant mortality decline that occurred between 1966 and 1979. Postneonatal mortality is particularly disturbing in a country as wealthy as the United States. While the neonatal mortality rate is largely a function of maternal health status and access to medical and supportive services during pregnancy and labor, postneonatal mortality is a more sensitive indicator of the basic environment in which an infant lives. During the postneonatal period, infants need decent housing, food, sanitation, and primary medical care, yet poor children frequently lack these supports. Experts estimate that 80 percent of all infants who die during the postneonatal period were born at normal birthweight.

Low Birthweight. The incidence of low birthweight in 1984 remained virtually unchanged from earlier years. Contributing to the national low birthweight problem is the high rate of teenage childbearing in the United States. In 1984, 13 percent of all births were to teens and these infants were 1.4 times more likely than all infants to be born at low birthweight. Even when births to only older women are considered, however, America has a serious low birthweight problem.

Between 1983 and 1984 the percentage of low-birthweight babies (weighing less than 5.5 pounds at birth) declined only .1 percentage point, from 6.8 percent to 6.7 percent. The wide disparity in low birthweight among racial groups also persisted. While 5.6 percent of white infants were born at low birthweight in 1984, the figures for black and nonwhite infants were 12.4 percent and 11.1 percent, respectively. Black infants in 1984 thus were 2.21 times more likely than white infants to be born at low birthweight. Only twice since 1970—in 1982 and 1983—has the disparity in black and white low birthweight percentages been as great.

Numerous studies have examined the persistent problem of low birthweight in this country. Several of these demonstrate a link between low birthweight and access to medical and nutritional services as well as environmental factors such as exposure to critical levels of lead during pregnancy. Yet in 1986, the Supplemental Food Program for Women, Infants, and Children (WIC) served only 40 percent of all financially eligible women, infants, and children nationally.

Similarly, in 1986 critical public health programs such as Community and Migrant Health Centers, the Title V Maternal and Child Health Block Grant, and the Federal Immunization Program suffered funding reductions as a result of the across-the-board cuts required by the Gramm-Rudman-Hollings provision of the Balanced Budget Act of 1985. Finally, contributing to the one-third increase in the number of uninsured Americans between 1978 and 1984, the Medicaid program in 1984 served 3.5 percent fewer children than were served in 1978.

Prematurity. In 1984, 9.4 percent of all births were premature (occurring prior to the thirty-seventh week of pregnancy). Infants born prematurely are more than three times more likely to be born at low birthweight than those born at full term. Prematurity can occur for many reasons, including poor maternal nutrition, inadequate prenatal care, and untreated maternal infections.

Prenatal Care. Between 1983 and 1984, the percentage of pregnant women receiving prenatal care early in pregnancy (during the first trimester) increased only .3 percentage point, from 76.2 percent to 76.5 percent. The percentage of women who received either no prenatal care or none until the seventh month or later did not decline at all from the 1983 figure of 5.6 percent. Indeed, 1984 was the fifth consecutive year during which the percentage of babies born to mothers who received late or no care worsened or failed to improve. By comparison, between 1969 and 1979 the percentage of pregnant women receiving late or no care in pregnancy improved by 37.03 percent.

Inadequate prenatal care can have serious implications for infant health. For example, between 1978 and 1985 the number of infants infected from birth by their mothers' syphilis rose by 150 percent nationally. According to the U.S. Centers for Disease Control (CDC), this increase in the rate of congenital syphilis resulted from, among other things, the lack of adequate prenatal care experienced by pregnant women, which could have detected and treated the disease. CDC estimates that, had adequate prenatal care been received, at least 60 percent of the cases could have been prevented.

International Findings

As a result of stagnating maternal and infant health indicators, *the United States' international ranking on infant mortality has deteriorated substantially during the past thirty years.*

Infant mortality in the United States has declined steadily since the turn of the century, as it has in other countries. Several factors have contributed to the decline both here and in other industrialized nations, including the introduction of public health sanitation measures, immunizations, improved access to basic health services (such as prenatal care and primary pediatric health care), and reduction in the incidence of low-birthweight births.

In this book we compare the rate of decline in U.S. infant mortality to that of nineteen other nations. We selected these other nations for three reasons. First, they have reliable vital statistics reporting systems. Second, they have comparable economic structures. Third, their standards of living are comparable to that of the United States.

During the 1950-1955 period, the United States ranked sixth best among twenty industrialized countries. By the 1980-1985 period, the nation had fallen to a tie for last place among the same countries. The U.S. position has deteriorated not because infant mortality rates in this country have worsened, but because the nation has failed to reduce infant mortality as rapidly as have these other countries.

Between the 1950-1955 and 1980-1985 time periods, the U.S. infant mortality rate declined by 61 percent. The other nineteen countries had greater rates of improvement during this period, with the sole exception of Australia. Even countries with 1950-1955 infant mortality rates substantially lower than ours (such as Iceland, Norway, Sweden, and the Netherlands), as well as countries with comparable rates (such as Denmark and the United Kingdom), improved more rapidly than the United States. Many of the nations that experienced more rapid improvements and have reached lower rates were substantially poorer than the United States.

Experts point to numerous factors that account for the United States' failure to reduce infant mortality as rapidly as other countries. The first is a relatively high incidence of low birthweight, which is exacerbated (but by no means caused solely) by our high rate of teenage childbearing. Other countries have managed to reduce both low birthweight and infant mortality. They have done so both by promoting much lower rates of teenage childbearing and by ensuring access by pregnant women and infants to maternity care and family supports.

The percentage of babies born at low birthweight in the United States has declined only slightly since 1950. Indeed, the U.S. Department of Health and Human Services recently reported that declines in low birthweight in the United States have been so slight that such reductions are responsible for only 10 percent of the decrease in infant mortality that has occurred since 1960. As a result, the incidence of low birthweight in the United States is substantially higher than in other industrialized countries.

A key major factor that distinguishes the United States from countries that have reduced infant mortality rates more rapidly is the provision of maternity services. Of all industrialized countries, the United States stands alone in its failure to assure pregnant women access to prenatal care *and* delivery services through either a public health service or universal health insurance. While 23.5 percent of all mothers, more than 20 percent of white mothers, and nearly 40 percent of all black mothers in the United States did not receive early prenatal care in 1980, fewer than 1 percent of all mothers in Sweden received inadequate care that year. In France, ensuring early and continuous prenatal care is regarded as so important that pregnant women are provided with cash payments as part of their prenatal care program in order to encourage their use of services and to ensure them an adequate standard of living.

The United States also has other social policies that affect infant mortality and differ significantly from those of countries with better records. A study of maternity policies for working women in seventy-five countries (including all industrialized countries and some developing nations) found that the United States was the only nation that failed to ensure provision of certain basic health services and social supports needed during pregnancy, childbirth, and infancy. Those services and supports include necessities such as medical and nutritional care, and some form of income support or protection (such as a family allowance or a parental leave policy).

The powerful influence that a nation's social policies can have on the health of infants is evident when one examines the experience of immigrants now living in Sweden who came from Southeastern European and other countries with heavily depressed economies and high rates of infant mortality. As in many countries, the immigrants (who came to Sweden in the late 1960s and early 1970s) generally had lower incomes than native Swedes and experienced lower standards of living. However, their mothers were provided with comprehensive health and social services. As a result, babies born to these immigrant mothers in recent years experienced slightly lower infant mortality rates than infants born to native Swedes, despite their higher social risk and relative economic disadvantage.

State and City Findings

National maternal and infant health problems, already serious when compared to those of other countries, mask particularly severe problems in many states and cities.

State Findings

Infant Mortality. Clear regional patterns in infant mortality rates can be discerned.

In 1984, the states with the highest rates of infant mortality tended to be concentrated in the South. With the exception of Illinois, the ten states with the highest 1984 overall infant mortality rates were all southern.

Southern states also exhibit the highest rates of neonatal mortality. With the exception of Illinois, the ten states with the highest overall neonatal mortality rates in 1984 were all in the South. In contrast, it is the western states that experienced the most serious postneonatal mortality problems in 1984. Of the ten states with the greatest overall postneonatal mortality rates in 1984, seven were western.

These region-specific neonatal and postneonatal mortality patterns may result in part from the fact that the South has a greater share of the nation's black births, and the western states have higher concentrations of Native American and Mexican-American births. These groups are desperately poor. Black infants tend to experience relatively high neonatal mortality because of their higher incidence of low birthweight. Native American and Mexican-American infants tend to have a lower incidence of low birthweight but relatively greater rates of postneonatal mortality.

While southern states had high overall infant mortality rates in 1984, five of the ten states with the highest 1984 black infant mortality rates were located ouside the South. The ten states were Connecticut, Delaware, Mississippi, Virginia, South Carolina, Washington State, Pennsylvania, Illinois, Michigan, and the District of Columbia.

Low Birthweight. Low birthweight is the single greatest cause of death during the neonatal period. Seven of the ten jurisdictions with the highest overall incidence of low birthweight in 1984 also were among the ten jurisdictions with the highest overall neonatal mortality rates that year. These seven were the District of Columbia, South Carolina, Mississippi, Louisiana, Georgia, Alabama, and North Carolina.

Prenatal Care. Of the ten states with the highest overall percentage of pregnant women who received late or no prenatal care in 1984, the percentage of such women actually increased between 1983 and 1984 in five of the states. These were Arkansas, Arizona, Florida, Texas, and New Mexico.

Wide Variations in State Indicators. In 1984 there continued to be enormous variations from state to state in infant mortality rates, the percentage of low-birthweight babies, and the proportion of infants born to women who had received early or late or no prenatal care.

For example, in 1984 a white infant born in Wyoming was nearly one and a half times more likely to die in the first year of life than a white infant born in North Dakota. A black infant born in the District of Columbia was 1.7 times more likely to die in the first year of life and more than two times more likely to die in the first twenty-eight days of life than a black infant born in Massachusetts. A black infant born in Illinois was nearly 1.6 times more likely than one born in Maryland to die during the postneonatal period.

An infant born to a black woman in New York in 1984 was more than three times more likely than one born to a black woman in Mississippi, and more than four times more likely than one born to a black woman in Massachusetts, to have a mother who received late or no prenatal care.

Among the states that accounted for 99 percent of all black births in 1984, one out of every four infants was born to a woman who failed to receive early prenatal care.

City Findings

Between 1983 and 1984, infant mortality rates rose in six of America's twenty-two largest cities. These were the District of Columbia, San Antonio, Cleveland, Boston, Detroit, and Milwaukee. The District experienced an alarming 8.8 percent increase in infant mortality between 1983 and 1984 alone.

Milwaukee, Wisconsin experienced a particularly notable 1984 infant mortality rate. Milwaukee's 1984 overall infant mortality rate of 14.2 deaths per 1,000 live births stood at the highest point in five years and was higher than the city's average infant mortality rate for the preceding four-year period.

In general, infant mortality in America's largest cities tends to be more serious than for the nation as a whole. Only five of America's twenty-two largest cities had 1984 infant mortality rates equal to or lower than the national average. These were Columbus, Phoenix, San Diego, San Francisco, and San Jose.

In 1984 there was a substantial disparity in infant mortality rates from city to city. Indianapolis, the city with the highest black infant mortality rate, had a rate that was 1.8 times higher than the black rate in Columbus and 1.6 times higher than the rate in Dallas. Similarly, the District of Columbia's 1984 nonwhite infant mortality rate, the highest among the twenty-two largest cities, was nearly three times greater than the nonwhite rate in San Francisco, the city with the lowest rate that year.

The disparity between black and white infant mortality rates in America's twenty-two largest cities in 1984 was startling. In seven cities, (Philadelphia, San Diego, Chicago, Cleveland, Indianapolis, Los Angeles, and Memphis) black infant mortality rates were more than twice as high as white rates. (The national black infant mortality rate is 1.96 times higher than the white rate.) The highest white infant mortality city rate among the cities in 1984 (13.8 deaths per 1,000 live births in Detroit) was nearly identical to the lowest black city rate that year (13.5 deaths per 1,000 births in Columbus).

A black infant born in Indianapolis or the District of Columbia in 1984 was more likely to die in the first year of life than an infant born in Trinidad and Tobago, a country much poorer than ours.

The infant mortality rates of certain cities stand out. For example, regardless of whether the District of Columbia is considered a state or city, its 1984 black infant mortality rate was shockingly high. In 1984, the District's black infant mortality rate ranked twenty-first worst out of twenty-two large American cities, and last among thirty-two states with a sufficient sample size of black live births.

Urban infant mortality rates can vary dramatically on an intrastate as well as interstate basis. For example, in 1984 there was a remarkable difference in infant mortality rates between Columbus, Ohio, and Cleveland, Ohio. A black infant born in Cleveland was 1.7 times more likely to die in the first year of life than one born in Columbus.

Findings on Births to Teens and Unmarried Women

Births to teens and unmarried women were nationwide problems in 1984.

Percent of 1984 Births That Occurred to Teens

Nationally in 1984, 13.1 percent of all births, and 23.6 percent of all black births, occurred to women younger than twenty. These figures varied dramatically from state to state. For example, the percentage of all births that occurred to mothers younger than twenty in Mississippi was three times higher than in Minnesota.

Low Birthweight Among Infants Born to Teens

Babies born to teen mothers are more likely to be born at low birthweight than those born to older mothers. In 1984, 9.4 percent of births to women younger than twenty were at low birthweight, compared to 6.7 percent of all births nationally.

There was wide variation from state to state in the incidence of low birthweight among infants born to teens in 1984. An infant born to a South Carolina teen was 2.5 times more likely to be born at low birthweight than one born to a North Dakota teen. Similar dramatic state-to-state variations can be seen when the incidence of low birthweight to teens is examined by race. For example, an infant born to a white teen in Wyoming was 1.9 times more likely to be low birthweight than one born in North Dakota. Finally, southern teens in general were more likely to have low birthweight infants than teens in other regions.

Prenatal Care Among Teens

Despite their greater need for prenatal care, pregnant teens are less likely than older women to begin care early in pregnancy and are more likely to receive either no care or none until the last trimester of pregnancy. In 1984, only 53.7 percent of infants born to teens had mothers who began care early in pregnancy, compared to 76.5 percent of all births. Similarly, 11.9 percent of infants born to teens had mothers who received no prenatal care or none until the last trimester, compared to 5.6 percent of all infants.

In some states, teens' lack of access to early prenatal care is particularly shocking. In 1984, for example, two out of every three black births to teens in New York, South Carolina, Florida, Oklahoma, and West Virginia occurred to mothers who had received no prenatal care early in pregnancy.

Births to Unmarried Teens and Older Women

Nationally in 1984, 56.3 percent of all births to teens, 42.0 percent of births to white teens, 89.5 percent of births to black teens, and 86.4 percent of births to nonwhite teens were to unmarried mothers. Since 1970, both teen birth rates and the percentage of all births that are to teen mothers have fallen significantly. But the percentage of births to teens that occur to unmarried women has climbed dramatically.

In the case of white infants, there was an enormous difference among the states in the percentage of births to teens that occurred to unmarried mothers. This was not the case with infants born to black teen mothers, however. In thirty-eight of forty-one states with sufficient data on black teen births, more than 80 percent of births to black teens occurred to unmarried mothers in 1984.

Births to unmarried white teens were less common in southern states than in other regions in 1984. However, this means only that a white teen was more likely to be married at the time of her baby's birth. Many of these pregnancies were conceived prior to the mother's marriage. Research indicates that, regardless of the timing of the marriage, many of the problems associated with teen pregnancy and parenthood remain, including ignorance about contraception and prenatal care, and inadequate parenting skills, as well as an increased risk of poverty. Teen marriages also are more likely to result in divorce. More than one-third of all divorces in 1984 occurred among women who had married while still in their teens. The greatest rate of divorce that year occurred among women who were younger than twenty.

While births to unmarried teens represent an extremely disturbing trend, births to unmarried teenage mothers in 1984 constituted a minority of all births to unmarried women that year. In 1984, teens accounted for only 35 percent of all births that occurred to unmarried mothers. This percentage was consistent across racial groups. These data suggest that the phenomenon of births to unmarried teens is part of a much larger childbearing pattern that persists well beyond adolescence.

Progress Toward Meeting the Surgeon General's 1990 Infant Health Objectives

In 1978, the Surgeon General of the United States established a set of 1990 Health Objectives for the Nation in the area of infant health. CDF has calculated the nation's and states' rates of progress in meeting these goals. In determining these rates we have included the years of greater progress (generally, 1978 to 1981) as well as those of slower progress (1982 to 1984). As a result, the bleak picture described below may be overly optimistic. If the slower rates of progress that generally prevailed in 1982, 1983, and 1984 continue throughout all, or most of, the rest of the decade (and provisional 1985 infant mortality rates suggest that this may well be the case), even fewer states and fewer subgroups than are described below will meet the Surgeon General's goals.

For example, based on the infant mortality rate of progress for the nation as a whole from 1978 to 1984, we project that the nation will meet this goal. Even this is questionable, however, if one projects on the basis of 1982 to 1984 trends. The Public Health Service of the U.S. Department of Health and Human Services itself reported to Congress in 1985 that the 1990 annual infant mortality goal would not be met based on 1982-1984 trends. In a more recent study, *The 1990 Health Objectives for the Nation: A Midcourse Review,* the U.S. Department of Health and Human Services concurred that at its current rate of progress, the United States will not meet the 1990 infant mortality goal.

Overall, it is clear that inadequate progress toward the Surgeon General's Objectives is being made. For some key measurements, a number of states actually are moving in the wrong direction.

Objective 1: Infant Mortality

Surgeon General's Objective. By 1990, the national infant mortality rate (deaths of children younger than one year old) should be reduced to no more than nine deaths per 1,000 live births, with no county and no racial or ethnic subgroup having an infant mortality rate in excess of twelve deaths per 1,000 live births.

Findings. Based on CDF's five-year trend calculations, we have concluded that the nation will meet the Surgeon General's overall 1990 infant mortality goal. However, CDF's calculations are more conservative than those performed by the Department of Health and Human Services and therefore have yielded a larger average annual rate of progress. The Department's recently published *Midcourse Review* of the Surgeon General's 1990 Health Objectives, discussed above, found that "based on progress to date, achievement of this objective (infant mortality) is questionable. Applying the 1983-85 rate of decline (9 percent) to the final 1983 figure yields a projected rate in 1990 of 9.2 per 1,000," which is above the 9.0 goal.

Both CDF and the Department have concluded that the goal will not be met for key racial and ethnic subgroups. First, the Surgeon General's Objective for infant mortality among racial and ethnic subgroups will not be met nationally for blacks.

Second, while the Department did not chart states' progress toward the 1990 goals, CDF's state trend analysis shows that twenty-two of the thirty four jurisdictions with measurable numbers of black infant deaths in 1984 will not meet the infant mortality objective for black infants. These are Alabama, Arizona, Colorado, Connecticut, Delaware, District of Columbia, Florida, Georgia, Illinois, Indiana, Kansas, Kentucky, Michigan, Minnesota, Mississippi, New Jersey, North Carolina, Ohio, Pennsylvania, South Carolina, Tennessee, and Virginia. Two additional states, Washington and Wisconsin, actually are moving in the wrong direction.

Third, seventeen of the thirty-one jurisdictions (thirty states and the District of Columbia) with measurable numbers of nonwhite infant deaths in 1984 will not meet the goal for nonwhite infants. These include: Alabama, Alaska, Connecticut, Delaware, District of Columbia, Florida, Georgia, Illinois, Indiana, Kentucky, Michigan, Mississippi, Ohio, Pennsylvania, South Carolina, Tennessee, and Virginia. A nineteenth state, Wisconsin, actually is moving in the wrong direction.

Thirteen jurisdictions (Alabama, Colorado, Connecticut, District of Columbia, Georgia, Indiana, Kentucky, Michigan, Mississippi, New Hampshire, South Carolina, Virginia, and Wyoming) will not meet the overall infant mortality goal. . . .

Objective 2: Neonatal Mortality

Surgeon General's Objective. By 1990, the neonatal mortality rate (deaths of infants younger than twenty-eight days of age) should be reduced to no more than six deaths per 1,000 live births.

Findings. Both CDF's and the Department's analyses show the nation will meet this 1990 Objective.

While states' progress generally has been adequate to assure that this objective is attained, five jurisdictions, (the District of Columbia, Georgia, Michigan, South Carolina, and Virginia), show inadequate annual rates of progress to meet the goal.

Objective 3: Postneonatal Mortality

Surgeon General's Objective. By 1990, the postneonatal mortality rate (deaths of infants age twenty-eight days to one year) should be reduced to no more than 2.5 deaths per 1,000 live births.

Findings. Both CDF and the Department project that the nation as a whole will not meet the Surgeon General's 1990 goal. In addition, forty-four jurisdictions with sufficient postneonatal deaths to compute progress will not meet the goal. These are Alabama, Alaska, Arizona, California, Colorado, Connecticut, Delaware, the District of Columbia, Florida, Georgia, Hawaii, Idaho, Illinois, Indiana, Kansas, Kentucky, Louisiana, Maryland, Massachusetts, Michigan, Minnesota, Mississippi, Missouri, Montana, Nebraska, Nevada, New Jersey, New York, North Carolina, North Dakota, Ohio, Oregon, Pennsylvania, Rhode Island, South Carolina, South Dakota, Tennessee, Texas, Utah, Virginia, Washington State, West Virginia, Wisconsin, and Wyoming.

Some of these states actually are moving in the wrong direction. These are Alaska, Colorado, Connecticut, Idaho, Kentucky, Maryland, Missouri, Montana, Nevada, Pennsylvania, South Dakota, Utah, Washington State, and Wisconsin.

Objective 4: Low-birthweight Babies

Surgeon General's Objective. By 1990, low-birthweight babies (those weighing 5.5 pounds or less at birth) should constitute no more than 5 percent of all live births, and in no county or racial or ethnic subgroup of the population should more than 9 percent of all live births be low birthweight.

Findings. Both CDF and the Department project that the nation will not meet the Surgeon General's overall objective for low birthweight and will not meet the goal for black infants.

CDF's analysis of state trends revealed that only ten states have met or will meet the objective for all races. These are Alaska, Idaho, Iowa, Minnesota, Nebraska, New Hampshire, North Dakota, South Dakota, Washington State, and Wisconsin. Six states (Arizona, Delaware, Hawaii, Maine, Oregon, and West Virginia), are moving in the wrong direction.

Only seventeen states will meet the low birthweight goal for white infants.

Only fifteen of the forty-two jurisdictions with sufficient numbers of black infant deaths to compute trends will reach the low birthweight goals. Ten states actually are moving in the wrong direction. These are Arizona, Illinois, Kansas, Louisiana, Michigan, North Carolina, Oregon, Pennsylvania, Virginia, and West Virginia.

Only twenty of the forty-eight jurisdictions with statistically significant numbers of nonwhite low-birthweight births will meet the objective for nonwhite infants. These include: Alaska, Arizona, California, Hawaii, Idaho, Iowa, Massachusetts, Minnesota, Montana, Nebraska, Nevada, New Mexico, North Dakota, Oklahoma, Oregon, Rhode Island, South Dakota, Utah, Washington State, and Wyoming. The other twenty-eight jurisdictions will not meet the goal.

Objective 5: Early Prenatal Care

Surgeon General's Objective. By 1990, 90 percent of all pregnant women should obtain prenatal care within the first three months of pregnancy.

Findings. Based on CDF's and the Department's analyses of recent trends, the nation will not meet the Surgeon General's goal.

No state will reach the goal at its current rate of progress. Ten jurisdictions are moving in the wrong direction. These are Connecticut, District of Columbia, Maryland, Massachusetts, Pennsylvania, Rhode Island, South Carolina, Texas, Virginia, and Washington State.

Health and Social Programs for Mothers and Children

Major public health and social programs are inadequate to meet the national need created by persistent and widespread maternal and child poverty and loss of private health insurance. Stagnation in the nation's rate of progress in improving infant health has occurred at a time of persistently high unemployment and poverty rates, as well as massive changes in the American employment structure. These changes have led to the loss of millions of jobs with decent fringe benefits (such as health insurance), and the rapid growth of low-paying jobs with no health insurance. Yet public health programs have not responded to these major trends.

Between 1978 and 1984, the number of uninsured Americans increased by more than one-third, from 26 million to 35 million. There are numerous causes of this phenomenon, and all have long-term implications. First, poverty increased substantially during this same time period (usually resulting from unemployment or under-employment)....

Second, eligibility for private health insurance among American families with children is closely related to their employment status.... [T]he persistently high unemployment pattern that has prevailed in the United States in the 1980s ... means greater loss of insurance among families.

Third, ... [m]ore than 75 percent of the Americans who have private insurance are covered through their employer. Over the past several years, ... [t]he nation has begun to move away from higher paying manufacturing jobs that furnish decent fringe benefits, including private health insurance, and toward low-paying jobs (often in the service sector) that carry few or no benefits. When this shift is added to other trends—more poverty, rising unemployment, higher number of female-headed families in which the primary wage earner tends to have a lower paying service-sector job, and an increase in part-time employment—the elements of significant private disinsurance are all present. The employer-based private health insurance system—the bedrock of the American approach to health care financing for the non-elderly—simply has disappeared for millions of Americans.

As dependents, children's access to private coverage depends on their parents' economic and employment status. And as that economic and employment picture has eroded for young families, so has children's health insurance status. By 1984:

- One-third of all uninsured Americans younger than sixty-five were children younger than eighteen, even though children in that age group represented only 25 percent of all Americans younger than sixty-five.
- One out of every three poor children and one out of every three women of childbearing age was uninsured.
- Three-quarters of uninsured children had a family income of less than 200 percent of the federal poverty level.
- The great majority of uninsured children were white, although black children were more likely to be uninsured.
- The lack of health insurance was greatest in the South, the region of the country with the highest infant mortality rates and the least generous public assistance programs. Nearly 55 percent of all uninsured Americans lived in the southern region of the nation.

Some public health programs have been improved modestly during the past several years, but not sufficiently to meet enormous maternal and child health needs. In some cases, particularly Medicaid, improvements occurred in one part of a program while funding reductions occurred in other portions of the same program. Still other health programs simply were reduced in funding, either in absolute terms or compared to medical care inflation.

Beginning in 1984, Congress enacted a series of Medicaid reforms for pregnant women and children. First, it mandated that states provide coverage to all pregnant women and all children younger than five whose family incomes fall below state AFDC eligibility levels.... Then it gave states a new option of covering all pregnant women and children younger than five whose family incomes fall below the federal poverty level but exceed the states' very low AFDC eligibility levels. . . . In addition, since 1982 between fifteen and twenty states on their own initiative have expanded the categories of pregnant women and children eligible for Medicaid. . . .

At the same time, however, there have been other serious and offsetting cuts in Medicaid eligibility. Many states have permitted their AFDC benefit levels to erode further. In 1986, thirty-two states maintained AFDC eligibility levels that were less than 50 percent of the federal poverty level. As a result, a shrinking percentage of poor pregnant women and children are eligible for benefits. Moreover, eligibility restrictions imposed on the AFDC program by Congress since 1981 have removed virtually all working poor families and many other families from the program. Because children's eligibility for Medicaid is tied closely to AFDC eligibility requirements, long-term erosion and cutbacks in AFDC have undermined the Medicaid expansions enacted by Congress and the states during the past few years.

Beginning in April 1987, states will have the option to set Medicaid eligibility levels for children younger than five and pregnant women higher than their AFDC levels. But past experience with states' response to Medicaid maternal and child health options suggests that it will be many years before such an option is fully implemented in all states.

Federal and state reforms enacted since 1982 thus have had only the slightest impact on the number of children and pregnant women enrolled in Medicaid. In Fiscal Year 1985, after the Deficit Reduction Act took effect and after many states had expanded the categories of children eligible for Medicaid additionally, the number of children receiving Medicaid benefits totalled 10,969,293—only 148,645 more than in Fiscal Year 1984. This small expansion failed to offset earlier cutbacks and the effects of program erosion. The total number of children receiving Medicaid in Fiscal Year 1985 was lower than the number who had received benefits in 1978.

By 1986, states' lifeline public health programs reached only a fraction of those who needed aid:

Medicaid. Thirty-two states maintained eligibility levels for families with no income other than AFDC that were less than 50 percent of the federal poverty levels.

The Supplemental Food Program for Women, Infants, and Children (WIC). In no state are all women and children who are eligible for WIC actually served. Nationally WIC reached only 40 percent of eligible women and children in 1986. In eleven states (Nebraska, Arkansas, South Dakota, Washington State, California, Utah, Arizona, Idaho, Arizona, Idaho, Alaska, New Mexico, and Hawaii) fewer than one-third of all eligible women and children were served.

The Cost of Infant Death and Disability

By the end of this decade, at its current rate of progress, the nation will have spent at least $2.1 billion in first-year costs alone to care for the excess numbers of low-birthweight infants who need extensive medical care and whose tragic situations could have been averted had the nation moved more rapidly to reduce the incidence of low birthweight.

On average, the nation's annual rate of progress between 1978 and 1984 in reducing low birthweight has been only 40 percent of what it needs to be if the 1990 goal is to be achieved. At the nation's average annual rate of progress, we will not meet the Surgeon General's 1990 low birthweight goal until the year 2044. Given our consistently slow rate of progress and the absence of any foreseeable, significant improvement in the rate of progress during the rest of the decade, it is evident that the nation will continue to experience an excessive number of low-birthweight births. We estimate that ... between 1978 and 1990 the nation will experience in excess of 300,701 low-birthweight births (including 57,133 very low-birthweight births) that could have been avoided had progress been sufficient to achieve the goal.

These excess low-birthweight births represent lost lives. Infants born at low birthweight are twenty times more likely than normal weight infants to die in the first year of life. Moreover, many of these infants become permanently disabled children who need a lifetime of medical care and supportive services. Low-birthweight infants are substantially more likely to be impaired for life by autism, retardation, cerebral palsy, epilepsy, learning disabilities, and vision and hearing disabilities.

The excess number of low-birthweight births also represents an enormous financial drain on the nation. Because low-birthweight infants need far greater levels of hospitalization, rehospitalization, and intensive medical care, we calculate that the *first year costs alone* that are involved in caring for the 300,701 excess low-birthweight babies born between 1978 and 1990 will amount to $2,103,830,500 by 1990. This expenditure does not take into account the long-term costs of specialized medical, educational, and social services that these infants may need, nor does it estimate the value of these children's lost productivity to the nation.

For the same money that we will spend over this time period to care for excessive numbers of low-birthweight infants, we could have:

- Provided 60,109,443 WIC monthly supplemental food packages;
- Provided comprehensive prenatal care to 3,187,000 women;
- Provided comprehensive maternity care (including delivery costs) to 701,277 women; or
- Provided comprehensive basic pediatric care to 4,207,661 additional infants and children.

By spending $2.1 billion on maternity care, WIC, or primary pediatric health care, we would have reduced infant low birthweight, disability, and mortality more rapidly and therefore could have achieved substantial long-term savings.

ABA ON TORT REFORM

February 17, 1987

The House of Delegates of the American Bar Association (ABA) adopted a report February 17 that opposed putting ceilings on civil damage awards but recommended substantial reforms to the way personal injury and product liability disputes are resolved. The action responded to the widespread perception that the court system was in serious trouble because of excessive verdicts in favor of civil plaintiffs. The report was prepared by the ABA's Action Commission to Improve the Tort Liability System.

No single event defined the tort liability crisis, but enormous civil verdicts had become commonplace. Juries regularly awarded millions to injured plaintiffs both as compensation for pain and suffering and as punishment to losing defendants. Premiums for liability insurance jumped nearly 60 percent between 1983 and 1986, but insurance companies still sustained underwriting losses. The upward spiral pushed the problem of providing fair compensation to those injured by the civil wrongs of others to the forefront of national attention.

By 1986 the problem had grown to such a magnitude that towns and small cities were finding it difficult or impossible to buy even minimum liability coverage, and large cities became self-insurers. Some doctors were forced to abandon their practices because of higher malpractice premiums. In several states doctors went on strike; in others they simply passed the new rates through to their patients. Nearly two-thirds of the profession had been sued for malpractice at one time or another, suggesting how pervasive the problem had become. Other professions and businesses of all sizes also suffered from premiums that went up 50 percent in a year, or doubled, or tripled.

State Law Reform

The collective response to the crisis was to urge reform to the common law tort system as it had evolved at the state level, but until the ABA action, the campaign had been without formal support from the bar. One tactic was to urge Congress to preempt state jurisdiction by establishing a federal compensation standard and to remove the provision that exempted the insurance industry from antitrust laws. Another was to press for state statutory reform of the common law procedures for determining civil liability. Under that system plaintiffs had a strong incentive to sue everyone in sight, but especially those with "deep pockets" who could actually pay the awarded damages. This resulted from the common law rule that once the defendants had been found jointly and severally liable, the plaintiff could look to any one of them to recover the full amount of the jury award. This meant that if one large, rich institution had been even nominally at fault, it could be forced to pay the full award.

A second problem was the size of the jury verdicts. While many cases involved serious damage to plaintiffs caused by the negligence of others, the process of deciding what value should be placed on the plaintiff's pain and suffering, or how much to punish a willfully reckless defendant, was necessarily subjective and depended greatly on the jurors' perceptions of fairness. Reaction to the size of awards was no less subjective, but insurers and the companies they insured believed that jurors often awarded verdicts grossly disproportionate to the actual injuries a plaintiff may have suffered. Horror stories abounded: the man who attempted suicide by throwing himself in front of a speeding subway train and then settled for $650,000, arguing the driver should have stopped sooner; the man who won $1,750,000 from Sears when he suffered a heart attack trying to start a lawn mower; the $115 million punitive damages charged to a businessman who dishonored stock conversion privileges; the $64 million awarded an oil-field worker who fell from a rig; the $37.5 million verdict against a bank when a farmer was forced into bankruptcy.

Headlines generated by sensational cases like these, however, were sometimes misleading. In many cases, the jury's verdict was reduced by the trial judge, a process known as remittitur, or a new trial was granted, putting pressure on plaintiffs to settle rather than try the case again, or the verdict was upset on appeal. Even so, the number of verdicts in excess of $1 million was more than four hundred in 1986, and many of the actual recoveries were very substantial.

A third problem was the process itself. Lawyers, who often take personal injury cases on a contingency basis, were accused of receiving as much as a third of a plaintiff's award for doing very little work. Given the size of jury awards, many defendants chose to settle out of court without trial, which some argued encouraged lawyers to bring even more actions. There was also the troubling question of what standard of care should be used in deciding what constitutes negligence. Did physicians guarantee that each of their patients would be cured? Or should doctors be held only to a standard that met the level of competence of other doctors in the region? Were juries qualified to make highly technical decisions where experts might well disagree?

Concerns of this type provoked many states to legislative action. Nine states acted to restrict contingency fees or to penalize lawyers who filed frivolous suits. Some states put limits on the amount of pain and suffering for which the plaintiff could be compensated. Others opted for the use of a comparative negligence standard to reduce the all-or-nothing nature of the trial result. By 1986 eight states had put caps on noneconomic damages, such as Colorado's limit of $250,000 in most cases. Sixteen states enacted protections to keep deep-pocket defendants like municipalities and major corporations from becoming responsible for the full liability when their responsibility was minimal. Approximately thirty more states were considering legislation to curb damages.

The Bar Weighs In

The recommendations offered by the ABA's commission proved highly controversial. Representatives from the insurance industry thought they did not go far enough to cap large jury awards, but trial lawyers were unhappy with discussion of damage limits and fee review. The drafters of the report agreed they did not have the resources to tackle the insurance industry, which lawyers often held responsible for many of the system's problems. But the commission made several recommendations for serious reform, including judicial review of fee agreements, greater judicial review of jury awards, less than unanimous jury verdicts to avoid hung juries and costly retrials, greater difficulty in recovering punitive damages, and modifications to the absolute nature of rules covering joint and several liability.

Not all lawyers felt comfortable with this approach. A dissenting commission member said, "These recommendations are all to take something away from the innocent injured party in favor of the person whose fault caused the injury and the insurer. . . . I don't think it's fair to continue to imply that the fault for what has gone wrong in the insurance system is attributable to juries or to judges or to lawyers." It remained an open question whether the recommendations responded to the full dimensions of the crisis, but for the first time in its history, the ABA took a position favoring important changes to the personal injury system.

Following are excerpts from the recommendations made by the Action Commission to Improve the Tort Liability Sys-

tem and approved on February 17, 1987, by the American Bar Association's House of Delegates, together with portions of the report discussing the key issues:

Recommendations

BE IT RESOLVED, that the American Bar Association adopts the following recommendations:

A. Insurance

1. The American Bar Association should establish a commission to study and recommend ways to improve the liability insurance system as it affects the tort system.

B. Pain and Suffering Damages

2. There should be no ceilings on pain and suffering damages, but instead trial and appellate courts should make greater use of the power of remittitur or additur with reference to verdicts which are either so excessive or inadequate as to be clearly disproportionate to community expectations by setting aside such verdicts unless the affected parties agree to the modification.

3. One or more tort award commissions should be established, which would be empowered to review tort awards during the preceding year, publish information on trends, and suggest guidelines for future trial court reference.

4. Options should be explored to provide more guidance to the jury on the appropriate range of damages to be awarded for pain and suffering in a particular case.

C. Punitive Damages

5. The scope of punitive damages in cases involving damage to person or property should be narrowed through the following measures:

a. *The standard of conduct.* Punitive damages should be allowed only in cases where the defendant's conduct indicates substantially greater indifference to the safety of others than ordinary negligence, such as intentional action or conduct in conscious disregard of the rights or safety of others.

b. *The standard of proof.* The standard of proof in awarding punitive damages should be higher than in awarding compensatory damages. The standard should be proof by "clear and convincing evidence."

c. *The process of decision.*

(1) Appropriate pre-trial procedures should be routinely utilized to weed out frivolous claims for punitive damages prior to trial, with a savings mechanism available for late discovery of misconduct meeting the standard of liability.

(2) Evidence of net worth and any other evidence relevant only to the question of punitive damages ordinarily should be introduced only

after the defendant's liability for compensatory damages and the amount of those damages have been determined.

d. *Multiple judgment torts.* While the total amount of any punitive damages awarded should be adequate to accomplish the purposes of punitive damages, appropriate safeguards should be put in force to prevent any defendant from being subjected to punitive damages that are excessive in the aggregate for the same wrongful act.

e. *To whom award should be paid.* After deducting costs and expenses, the court should determine what is a reasonable portion of the punitive damages award to compensate the plaintiff and counsel for bringing the action and prosecuting the punitive damages claim, with the balance of that award allocated to public purposes.

D. Joint-and-Several Liability

6. The doctrine of joint-and-several liability should be modified to recognize that defendants whose responsibility is substantially disproportionate to liability for the entire loss suffered by the plaintiff are to be held liable for only their equitable share of the plaintiff's non-economic loss, while remaining liable for the plaintiff's full economic loss. A defendant's responsibility should be regarded as "substantially disproportionate" when it is significantly less than any of the other defendants; for example, when one of two defendants is determined to be less than 25% responsible for the plaintiff's injury.

E. Attorneys' Fees

7. Fee arrangements with each party in tort cases should be set forth in a written agreement that clearly identifies the basis on which the fee is to be calculated. In addition, ... there should be a requirement that the contingency fee information form be given to each plaintiff a reasonable time before a contingency fee agreement is signed. The content of the information form should be specified in each jurisdiction and should include at least the maximum fee percentage, if any, in the jurisdiction, the option of using different fee percentages depending on the amount of work the attorney has done in obtaining a recovery, and the option of using fee percentages that decrease as the size of a recovery increases. The form should be written in plain English, and, where appropriate, other languages.

8. Courts should prohibit the practice of taking a percentage fee out of the gross amount of any judgment or settlement. Contingent fees should be based only on the net amount recovered after litigation disbursements such as filing fees, deposition costs, trial transcripts, travel, expert witness fees, and other expenses necessary to conduct the litigation.

9. Whenever judgment is entered in a tort case, fee arrangements with each party and the fee amount billed should be submitted *in camera* to the court, which should have the authority to disallow, after a hearing, any portion of a fee found to be "plainly excessive" in light of prevailing rates and practices.

F. Secrecy and Coercive Agreements

10. Where information obtained under secrecy agreements (a) indicates risk of hazards to other persons, or (b) reveals evidence relevant to claims based on such hazards, courts should ordinarily permit disclosure of such information, after hearing, to other plaintiffs or to government agencies who agree to be bound by appropriate agreements or court orders to protect the confidentiality of trade secrets and sensitive proprietary information.

11. No protective order should contain any provision that requires an attorney for a plaintiff in a tort action to destroy information or records furnished pursuant to such order, including the attorney's notes and other work product, unless the attorney for a plaintiff refuses to agree to be bound by the order after the case has been concluded. An attorney for plaintiff should only be required to return copies of documents obtained from the defendant on condition that defendant agrees not to destroy any such documents so that they will be available, under appropriate circumstances, to government agencies or to other litigants in future cases.

12. Any provision in a settlement or other agreement that prohibits an attorney from representing any other claimant in a similar action against the defendant should be void and of no effect. An attorney should not be permitted to sign such an agreement or request another attorney to do so.

G. Streamlining the Litigation Process: Frivolous Claims and Unnecessary Delay

13. A "fast track" system should be adopted for the trial of tort cases. In recommending such a system, we endorse a policy of active judicial management of the pre-trial phases of tort litigation. We anticipate a system that sets up a rigorous pre-trial schedule with a series of deadlines intended to ensure that tort cases are ready to be placed on the trial calendar within a specified time after filing and tried promptly thereafter. The courts should enforce a firm policy against continuances.

14. Steps should be taken by the courts of the various states to adopt procedures for the control and limitation of the scope and duration of discovery in tort cases. The courts should consider, among other initiatives:

a. At an early scheduling conference, limiting the number of interrogatories any party may serve, and establishing the number and time of depositions according to a firm schedule. Additional discovery could be allowed upon a showing of good cause.

b. When appropriate, sanctioning attorneys and other persons for abuse of discovery procedures.

15. Standards should be adopted substantially similar to those set forth in Rule 11 of the Federal Rules of Civil Procedure as a means of discouraging dilatory motions practice and frivolous claims and defenses.

16. Trial judges should carefully examine, on a case-by-case basis, whether liability and damage issues can or should be tried separately.

17. Non-unanimous jury verdicts should be permitted in tort cases, such

as verdicts by five of six or ten of twelve jurors.

18. Use of the various alternative dispute resolution mechanisms should be encouraged by federal and state legislatures, by federal and state courts, and by all parties who are likely to, or do become involved in tort disputes with others.

H. Injury Prevention/Reduction

19. Increased attention should be paid to the disciplining of licensed professionals through the following measures:

a. A commitment to impose discipline, where warranted, and a substantial increase in the funding of full-time staff for disciplinary authorities. Discipline should be lodged in the hands of a state body, and not controlled by the profession itself, although professionals should have a substantial role in the process.

b. In every case in which a claim of negligence is made against a licensed professional, and a judgment for the plaintiff is entered or a settlement paid to an injured person, the insurance carrier, or in the absence of a carrier, the plaintiff's attorney, should report the fact and the amount of payment to the licensing authority. Any agreement to withhold such information and/or to close the files from the disciplinary authorities should be unenforceable as contrary to public policy.

I. Mass Tort

20. The American Bar Association should establish a commission as soon as feasible, including members with expertise in tort law, insurance, environmental policy, civil procedure, and regulatory design, to undertake a comprehensive study of the mass tort problem with the goal of offering a set of concrete proposals for dealing in a fair and efficient manner with these cases.

J. Concluding Recommendation

21. After publication of the report, the ABA Action Commission to Improve the Tort Liability System should be discharged of its assignment.

Report

Introduction

In November 1984, the Special Committee on the Tort Liability System of the American Bar Association completed a broad-ranging, five-year study of the tort system, *Towards a Jurisprudence of Injury: The Continuing Creation of a System of Substantive Justice in American Tort Law* (the Bell Committee Report). The study examined the network of substantive and remedial tort rules, explored the underlying goals of the system, and analyzed its institutional structure. Although the Bell Committee Report included a chapter of recommendations, its principal purpose was to conduct a systematic review and evaluation of the existing tort system. As its sweeping mandate and expansive time-frame suggest, the Committee was not expected to focus primarily on the details of change in the existing system.

The present Action Commission to Improve the Tort Liability System, established in November, 1985, was set up by the ABA as a successor group to the earlier committee. Prompted both by a desire to build on the foundation established by the Bell Committee and to respond to current calls for tort reform, the ABA charged the Action Commission as follows:

1. Consider recommendations for improving methods and procedures for compensating persons injured as the result of the tortious conduct of other persons;

2. Recommend means of implementing at the earliest possible date those improvements that the Commission finds to be most desirable or necessary to serve the best interests of the public;

3. Recommend any further studies or actions by the American Bar Association that the Commission deems necessary or appropriate to improve methods and procedures for compensating persons injured as the result of the tortious conduct of other persons.

In our deliberations, the Commission has ranged widely over the principal areas of personal injury law, discussing current developments in the fields of medical malpractice, municipal liability, defective products, auto accidents and environmental harm. We have examined the basic goals of the tort system, the processes by which those goals are implemented, and the major recent proposals for tort reform. In addition, we have assessed the limited empirical data on the actual operation of the tort system. In short, we have taken the view that an action commission can fully discharge its responsibility to recommend changes in the present system only after it has conducted a broad examination of the strengths and weaknesses of the tort law in operation.

A truly comprehensive analysis of the tort system must, of necessity, range even beyond liability rules and the litigation process in tort cases. Since midcentury, there has been a dramatic growth in the influence of insurance on the tort system. In virtually every major area where personal injury occurs—in auto accidents, workplace injuries, products liability, medical malpractice, and municipal liability—liability insurance is the rule rather than the exception. As a consequence, the institution of insurance has had a pervasive impact on tort doctrine. Consider, as illustrative, the abolition of governmental, intrafamily and charitable immunity; the development of strict liability for defective products; the liberalization of medical malpractice doctrine (e.g. the abolition of the "same locality" rule); the expansion of landowners' liability; and the rejection of the absolute defense of contributory negligence. Although the dynamic growth of insurance coverage has not been the only factor contributing to these doctrinal developments, it has clearly been an important consideration.

Just as insurance has altered the landscape of liability rules, it has also affected the allocation of injury costs to insured parties. For the drug manufacturer or gynecologist, premium costs of insurance and policy limitations on coverage are frequently critical questions, along with the likelihood of legal liability. The availability and affordability of liability insurance, in other words, has become an important element in measuring the efficacy of the tort system for a considerable number of those most tangibly affected by personal injury law.

Nonetheless, it does not follow that fluctuations in the costs of liability insurance are a direct reflection of corresponding changes in the tort claims system. Other factors affect these trends. Insurers earn income on premium dollars through investment practices that are carried on separately from underwriting and claims activities, and that reflect different economic trends. Moreover, insurers' experience rating practices are influenced by internal administrative considerations which reflect other factors besides the risk-related performance of insured parties. And, to complicate matters still further, insurability in particular lines of activity is partially determined by a re-insurance market that operates, in part, outside the United States economy, subject to its own constraints.

In sum, analysis of the need for tort reform is complicated by the fact that the business practices of the liability insurance industry reflect a wide range of economic factors, in addition to the performance of the tort system. The analysis is made more difficult by the current atmosphere of heated debate about whether the problems of the tort liability system are attributable to the performance of the tort system, the insurance mechanism, or both. The debate has focused on the recent phenomenon of steeply rising insurance costs—indeed, in some cases the unavailability of insurance—faced by service providers such as doctors and daycare centers, manufacturers of a variety of products, and municipalities engaged in their traditional public functions. . . .

A threshold question remains, however, whether fairness and efficiency suggest the need for replacement rather than incremental efforts to improve the existing system of tort liability. Much of the recent academic criticism of tort law attacks the major foundations upon which the system is built; assigning liability through individualized determinations of fault or defect, tailoring compensation to the particularized losses of a specific injury victim, and relying upon the jury system for determinations of liability and damages.

In this century, two significant tort reform movements have developed in response to criticism of this fundamental kind. Shortly after the turn of the century, the workers' compensation movement, advocating replacement of the tort system in cases of industrial injury, swept the country and led to no-fault compensation schemes for workers' injuries in every state. In the 1960s, widespread dissatisfaction with tort litigation in auto accident cases triggered a reform movement which eventually led to some form of no-fault auto accident legislation in half the states. The question now arises whether such wholesale reform ought to be adopted either (1) system-wide, (2) in selected areas of high-risk activity, or (3) for a category of cases involving seriously disabled accident victims.

For two major reasons, the Commission reached an early decision to focus principally on reforms aimed at improving the present system, rather than allocating its energy to a comprehensive analysis of the case for universal social insurance or broad-ranging no-fault schemes replacing the tort system. In the first place, it was apparent to us that the Commission would be sharply divided on the wisdom of any proposal advocating substantial dismantling of the tort system. This Commission was consciously selected to represent a wide spectrum of views on the efficacy of tort law, and the members decided at the outset that such a diverse group could make a positive contribution to the current reassessment of the tort system only by an effort to find common ground among most of its members....

Discussion and Recommendations

B. Pain and Suffering Damages

From the earliest development of the fault system, compensation for intangible loss has been a fundamental tenet of damages. There has been a general understanding that serious injury results not only in out-of-pocket loss but in a measure of pain and suffering that is real despite its intangible character. Indeed, even prior to the Industrial Revolution, when redress for civil tortious wrong was simply a loosely connected set of actions in the form of trespass, assault, false imprisonment, and the like, the medieval common law courts recognized the legitimacy of claims for damage based on mental distress or personal outrage without requiring any attendant outlays for actual economic loss.

As the negligence system evolved, the common law of damages recognized an individualized form of redress in which the plaintiff presented evidence of the tangible and intangible loss suffered in the immediate case. Perhaps the clearest expression of this view is in the so-called "thin-skulled plaintiff" rule which has always been understood to mean that, once liability has been established, the defendant takes his victim as he finds him. The injured pedestrian who is so traumatized by the defendant's negligent driving that he suffers recurrent nightmares and neuroses after his body has mended can legitimately claim damages beyond that suffered by a less sensitive accident victim. More generally, the ordinary claims of an accident victim to recover for pain suffered during a period of rehabilitation—and in an appropriate case the estimated *continuing* pain and sense of humiliation associated with his injuries—is recompensed without any fixed limit. Tort law aims to make the victim whole.

Reservations about compensating for intangible loss are not new. There has been long-standing criticism about the seemingly insurmountable problem of translating suffering into dollar-and-cents terms. Moreover, pain and suffering is subjective in the added sense that it varies tremendously from one individual to another. Amputation of a limb, for example, may be psychologically devastating to one injury victim, while another quite successfully comes to terms with the handicap. These uncertainties of measurement carry a number of implications: (1) any figure, in a case of serious injury, may appear speculative; (2) damages may appear, to the outside observer at least, to have very little "compensatory" effect; and (3) awards inevitably vary greatly from case to case—raising questions about whether like cases are being treated in like fashion.

Traditionally, the response to these objections has been the intuitively appealing argument that no matter how arbitrary the precise dollar valuation of pain and suffering may appear in a particular case, there is clearly a real element of loss associated with serious injury, above and beyond the doctor's bills and lost income. If the costs of torts are to be properly measured, both from a compensation and a deterrence perspective, intangible loss must be taken into account. Moreover, the argument goes, there is good reason to think that money does have a salutary effect—that it addresses, to some extent, the victim's feelings of outrage and indignation, and that it provides the means of purchasing some material relief from sustained suffering.

Recently, the arguments for eliminating or controlling the amount of compensation for pain and suffering have taken a somewhat different form. To begin with, it is pointed out that no-fault systems for industrial injuries and auto accidents invariably involve a trade-off of reduced recovery, if any, for intangible loss, in return for widespread coverage of injury victims. While medical malpractice, products liability, and claims against municipalities have not been incorporated into no-fault schemes, the substantial doctrinal expansions of liability in these areas have led some critics to call for trade-offs in the form of limitations on noneconomic loss to maintain a lid on the overall costs of liability associated with these activities.

Another variant of this criticism relies on the recent empirical data on claims and costs of the tort system. As mentioned earlier, there is considerable evidence that the average size of tort awards (in contrast to the median size) has increased substantially in recent years—and reason to believe that this increase is due to a significant growth in the upper range of recoveries in serious injury cases. These data, the doctrinal extensions referred to above, and the claims experience of insurers have led some critics to argue that the tort system is out of control, and that runaway costs will be effectively checked only when limitations are placed on intangible damage recoveries.

The Commission has given careful consideration to the arguments and concluded that legislative caps on non-economic loss are unwarranted, but limited judicial controls are advisable. In the Commission's view, there are two major reasons for opposing any ceiling on non-economic loss. As a matter of principle, many members of the Commission believe that it is simply unjust to discriminate against the relatively small number of accident victims who suffer the most devastating physical and psychological injuries. Clearly, the lower the ceiling the more drastic is the discrimination against the most grievously injured accident victims.

The Commission's related objection is aimed at the setting of any particular cut-off point. The entire commission regards the setting of a cap on non-economic loss at $100,000 or $250,000 as unacceptably low, but even if a low cap seemed desirable the related question is how a rational choice could possibly be made between these figures. Correlatively, as one moves to the higher range of caps—in the $1 million neighborhood—where concern for the plight of the most seriously injured would be diminished, the question arises whether a cap any longer accomplishes significant gains that warrant its largely symbolic effect. In light of these considerations, there is substantial agreement on the Commission that the case has not been made for a ceiling on intangible loss without far better evidence that the occasional multimillion dollar verdict is creating havoc in the tort/insurance system.

Some Commission members would support a ceiling on non-economic loss if a compensation plan for catastrophic injury victims were adopted which featured universal coverage. In other words, if a social insurance scheme were put in place which assured *every* catastrophic injury victim full compensation for economic loss—and not just those who are fortunate enough to recover under the restrictive criteria of the tort system—then a moderate ceiling on recovery of non-economic loss might well be warranted. Those sharing this view would emphasize their concern that the most serious problem of accidental injury existing in our society today is the treatment and rehabilitation of the singularly unfortunate accident victim who has been totally or gravely disabled for life.

Even if a ceiling on pain and suffering is regarded as objectionable, it does not follow that there is no merit to the concerns about the rise in the size of tort awards in more serious cases and the lack of uniformity in redressing apparently similar injuries. The Commission believes, however, that these concerns can be addressed through the exercise of greater controls on the non-economic component of damage awards without altering the fundamental discretionary authority of juries in personal injury cases. If, however, credible evidence emerges in the future that the average size of verdicts is continuing to rise at an excessive rate and that relatively few large verdicts are consuming an increasingly large proportion of the total amount awarded in tort cases, some members of the Commission think that a case for ceilings might well be made out....

C. Punitive Damages

Since the main purpose of tort law is to provide compensation to injury victims rather than vindicate a public sense of indignation, punitive damages have always been somewhat of an anomaly in the tort system. Nonetheless, recourse to punitive damages has a long history in common law tort actions, associated for the most part with intentional wrongdoing.

In the classic cases of intentional harm, the justification for punitive damages is twofold: From the standpoint of tort theory, punitive damages express the full measure of societal outrage and assure the appropriate deterrent effect in cases where a defendant's conduct is outside the bounds of civilized behavior. Frequently in such cases, recovery limited to the plaintiff's actual harm—the indignity of being spat upon in the courtroom by a disappointed suitor, defamed by an adversary, or bloodied in combat by an aggressive bully—amounts to very little. Typically, there is no effective criminal remedy to complement civil redress in such cases. Although an occasional criminal prosecution for assault and battery may occur, most tortious intentional harms involve conduct that is emotionally or physically bruising to the unfortunate victim, but of little consequence to society at large. Hence, punitive damages traditionally have served the important function of ensuring a measure of punishment for essentially private unlawful conduct that is commensurate with the antisocial nature of the act.

The present unrest about punitive damages in tort is wholly unrelated to the traditional cases of intentional harm in which the remedy was fashioned. In recent years, many jurisdictions have allowed punitive damages to be awarded in situations where the defendant's conduct falls short of intentional wrongdoing. When it appears that the defendant has engaged in "willful and wanton" misbehavior, even though less than intended misconduct, a consensus would probably still exist in favor of allowing punitive damages—and there would be no chilling effect on patterns of everyday behavior. But concepts such as "willful misconduct" and the lesser standard of "gross negligence" have no easily identifiable referents in the real world of careless behavior. As a consequence, the judicial willingness to allow punitive damage awards in cases involving egregious conduct falling short of intentional wrongdoing has increasingly fostered a sense of concern that the limited function of such awards—to punish misconduct that is either clearly malicious or at least borders on intentional wrongdoing—might be exceeded in some cases.

The problem is well-illustrated by the case of *Taylor v. Superior Court*, 24 Cal. 3d 890 (1979), in which the California Supreme Court engaged in a wide-ranging dialogue, involving separate concurring and dissenting opinions, on the issue whether punitive damages are appropriate in a case of injuries caused by an intoxicated driver. The majority answered in the affirmative, adopting a standard of whether the defendant's behavior manifested "such a conscious and deliberate disregard of the interests of others that his conduct may be called willful or wanton." But a consensus could not be reached. The court divided both on whether this standard was an appropriately narrow expression of the limited scope of punitive damages in civil cases and on whether driving under the influence of alcohol typically involves conduct that in fact meets such a standard.

For many observers of the tort scene, the key question underlying any such debate would be who decides. Even if a "conscious disregard" standard is viewed as appropriately narrow language, it leaves considerable room for jury discretion in determining the propriety of punitive damages—unless additional controls are placed on the finder of fact. Critics of the present day operation of punitive damage awards would place special emphasis on the leeway given to juries and argue for judges to exercise greater control.

Critics also argue that the magnitude of punitive damage awards—both in number and size of awards—has reached intolerable proportions for businesses and professionals. This contention is usually an aspect of the more general charge that non-economic loss awards are out of control and wreaking havoc in the tort system.... [C]ritics frequently propose a ceiling on punitive damages or controls on jury discretion.

A balanced assessment of whether punitive damages are a major problem clearly requires an evaluation of whatever empirical data are available. Preliminary studies by the American Bar Foundation and Rand provide some assistance. These studies suggest that punitive damage awards continue to be most common in traditional areas such as personal violence, fraud, false arrest and defamation. The ABF study found that punitive damages continue to be very infrequently awarded in accidental injury cases in any of the thirty jurisdictions studied.

Critics of punitive damages argue that even if the incidence of awards remains relatively stable in unintentional injury cases, an occasional large award introduces an element of unpredictability that undermines the stability of the tort system, and distorts the settlement process. Moreover, they argue that the major strategic import of punitive damages is the introduction of evidence of the defendant's wealth to influence the size of *compensatory* awards. This consequence, it is asserted, is masked by the focus on rates of growth in the number and size of recorded punitive damages judgments.

In response, defenders of punitive damage awards argue that ceilings would preclude the multimillion dollar "sting" that is the only effective safeguard against serious corporate misconduct. As to the concern about jury prejudice (through evidence of defendant's wealth), some observers would respond by proposing bifurcation of the trial process.

The principal reason for the Commission's opposition to a ceiling on punitive damages is the deterrence concern. Although it cannot be conclusively demonstrated that the prospect of punitive damages serves as an effective deterrent in cases of catastrophic widespread harm, it does serve as a complementary strategy to criminal sanctions, which are typically minimal or non-existent in such cases, administrative remedies, which may be prospective only, and civil compensatory damages, which are sometimes disproportionately less than the magnitude of the defendant's wrongdoing.

But the Commission is not insensitive to the fairness concern about random cases of burdensome awards. Nor do we dismiss the boundaries problem—the possibility of abuses in the stringent limitation of punitive awards to cases of truly outrageous indifference to the safety of others. In our judgment, however, the most effective means of addressing these issues is through a rigorous set of procedures for determining punitive damages....

D. Joint-and-Several Liability

Under the doctrine of joint-and-several liability, every defendant who is found to be legally responsible for a tortious injury may be held responsible for the plaintiff's entire damages in the event that other defendants cannot be joined or are incapable of contributing their equitable share of the plaintiff's loss. Although this rule is not of recent origin, its earlier applications typically involved a relatively uncontroversial set of circumstances. An illustrative case would be the situation where a passenger in a car is injured in an accident caused by negligent driving of his driver and the driver of another car. Even though the two were not acting jointly, each would be liable for the entire loss, and if one were insolvent the other might in fact bear the total cost of the harm done.

This classic application of joint-and-several liability was uncontroversial for two distinct reasons. To begin with, the common law of negligence, as it has evolved from the beginning of the Industrial Revolution, has been characterized by an all-or-nothing approach. The defendant who was at fault was liable for all harm done. As the negligence system developed, the question whether the defendant was seriously or slightly at fault was simply irrelevant as a prerequisite to establishing responsibility. Similarly, as far as defenses were concerned, the contributory negligence doctrine was an absolute bar to plaintiff's recovery in cases where *any* degree of negligence could be established on the victim's part. Indeed, the doctrines that were developed to counter the harshness of the contributory negligence defense, such as last clear chance, had precisely the same all-or-nothing effect. If the plaintiff could establish that the defendant had the last clear chance to avoid the injury, the bar to recovery was lifted *in its entirety,* and the defendant was, once again, held fully responsible. Joint and-several liability must be understood in this context of all-or-nothing thinking.

In addition, the early cases were probably uncontroversial because defendants who were held jointly-and-severally liable typically were engaged *in like activities:* two drivers carelessly injured plaintiff pedestrian, two hunters carelessly shot in the direction of plaintiff bystander, and so on. Undoubtedly, if one looked beyond the activity itself to the manner in which it was being conducted (e.g., the precise allegations of faulty driving on the part of drivers A and B respectively), varying degrees of carelessness would have been apparent. But once again, it was outside the common law tradition to think in terms of degrees of wrongdoing, and the circumstance that jointly liable defendants tended to be engaged in common activities was consonant with this approach.

The current dissatisfaction with joint and several liability appears to be an outgrowth of a series of related departures from the common law tradition. First, the all-or-nothing approach has been seriously compromised by the recent development of comparative negligence, and its corollary, comparative contribution among defendants. The tort system is now committed to thinking in terms of degrees of fault. Second, in a superficially distinct area, the long-standing tort immunity that shielded municipal entities from liability has been substantially reduced in recent years. This change, in turn, has created the prospect of suits against municipalities for creating dangerous conditions or failing to provide services which, in conjunction with the negligent acts of others, cause harm to innocent parties. As a consequence of the expansion of municipal liability, a joint-and-several liability scenario developed in which defendants engaged in *distinct activities—e.g.*, a negligent driver and a careless roadway maintenance department—rather than like courses of conduct, harm the plaintiff.

The argument for changing the doctrine of joint-and-several liability proceeds from these premises. To put an extreme case, consider a scenario in which a city is found to be 5% at fault for failure to trim a hedge that slightly impedes the view at an intersection where a reckless driver (95% at fault) runs a stop sign and seriously injures plaintiff pedestrian. If the driver is insolvent, the city ends up footing the entire bill for the plaintiff's injuries. There is a perceived sense of unfairness in cases where the blameworthiness of the defendant's conduct contributing to the plaintiff's harm is so dramatically out of line with the ultimate burden of damages borne by the defendant.

There are counter-arguments, however. The principal argument in favor of the doctrine of joint-and-several liability is that it promotes the fundamental goal of making innocent plaintiffs whole when they have been wrongfully injured. To the extent that we recognize the inequity of taking a defendant beyond proportionate responsibility for the plaintiff's harm, we do so in some cases at the cost of full recovery for the plaintiff's injuries. Moreover, the sense of inequity engendered by the doctrine of joint-and-several liability arguably loses some of its force as the defendant's proportionate blameworthiness increases. Thus, some observers would undoubtedly feel far less concern about making the plaintiff whole through assigning full loss responsibility to a defendant who was 50% responsible for the plaintiff's injury (i.e., as responsible as the insolvent defendant) in contrast to a defendant who was only 5% responsible for the plaintiff's injury.

To complicate matters, there are no informative data sources on the extent to which "extreme" cases of joint-and-several liability arise. It is conceivable that municipalities and insurers have been reacting to a handful of horror stories in their recently expressed concern about the imposition of grossly disproportionate liability. Perhaps, instead, such cases arise infrequently, juries are largely unsympathetic to claims based on *de minimis* carelessness, and as a consequence, the number of these cases is not likely to rise dramatically in the future. On the other hand, it may be that the temptation to find the solvent "deep-pocket" defendant liable in cases of grievous loss, particularly in auto accident situations where hit-and-run and uninsured motorists abound, is sufficiently widespread to constitute a real and growing problem.

To round out the picture, it should be emphasized that the deep-pocket concern is generally triggered by the underinsurance or insolvency of the primarily responsible party. If adequate insurance or no-fault compensation arrangements existed to backstop the responsibility of the impecunious or absent defendant, by definition there would be no need for recourse to deep-pocket, joint-and-several liability.

What, then, are the options? It would be possible to retain the *status quo,* re-affirming the long-standing rule of joint-and-several liability as a means of ensuring adequate compensation to injury victims. At the other extreme, it would be feasible to abolish joint-and-several liability altogether on the ground that a defendant should never be liable for more than a proportionate share of responsibility for an accident situation. Between these polar positions, there is an array of possibilities for "compromise" solutions (recognizing the equitable claims of both plaintiffs and defendants) based on partial limitations of joint-and-several recovery. . . .

LIFTING OF TRADE SANCTIONS AGAINST POLAND

February 19, 1987

The United States February 19 lifted economic sanctions it had imposed on Poland five years earlier. In a statement explaining the new action, President Ronald Reagan acknowledged that in Poland "thousands of political prisoners have been released in a series of amnesties." He promised "the continuation of better relations between our countries only if we see maintained the spirit and principle of the amnesty and a reliance on dialog and respect for human rights."

A simultaneous presidential proclamation restored most-favored-nation tariff treatment and guaranteed credits to Poland. Most-favored-nation status grants exporting countries low tariffs on goods imported into the United States. Guaranteed credits allow countries to seek loans from U.S. banks.

Solidarity and Sanctions

The events that led the United States to invoke sanctions against Poland in 1981 and to rescind them in 1987 began in the early 1980s when Polish workers, exerting power gained through a series of strikes, demanded and won freedoms unusual in a communist-bloc country. The Soviet Union, uneasy that such activities might spread to other countries in communist-dominated Eastern Europe, stood ready to intervene. The United States, encouraged by the workers' success, was hopeful that progressive granting of human rights might eventually result in a more democratic Poland.

Poland's failing economy as well as its form of government influenced the turn of events. The strikes that led to the Polish workers' 1980 demands had been brought on by increases in food prices. That same year the communist government had permitted formation of the new Solidarity trade union, led by electrician Lech Walesa. Government censorship was eased, and dissidents jailed during the strikes were released. But the Polish economy grew worse, and the trade unions were demanding a five-day work week.

When the Soviets threatened to move in and put down the workers' rebellion, U.S. president Jimmy Carter warned against intervention and rallied the support of the North Atlantic Treaty Organization (NATO). (Historic Documents of 1980, p. 793)

The world watched the power struggle in Poland continue through 1981 until on December 13 the government imposed martial law. Solidarity union operations were suspended and Walesa was arrested. The United States retaliated by cutting off economic aid, including food, to Poland, withdrawing the rights of Poland's fishing fleet to operate in U.S. waters, canceling Export-Import Bank credit insurance, and rescinding the right of Polish aircraft to land in the United States. President Reagan, placing most of the blame for the Polish situation on the Soviet government, extended similar sanctions to the Soviet Union. (Historic Documents of 1981, p. 947)

During 1982 the United States persuaded the NATO allies to avoid high-level contacts with Polish officials. In 1983 Poland refused to accept the U.S. ambassador named by Reagan. Poland had lost both economic and diplomatic contact with the Western democracies.

Reactions to 1981 Sanctions

Even though U.S. economic aid to Poland had been requested by the Solidarity movement in the spring of 1981, the Reagan government had refused to supply it. Critics of the decision contended later that granting aid at that crucial time might have prevented both the collapse of the Polish economy and the imposition of martial law.

Pope John Paul II, himself Polish, criticized the economic sanctions imposed on Poland by Western nations, saying they caused more economic hardships to the people than to the government.

The political sanctions were partially relaxed over the years as the Polish government restored some freedoms to its people. In 1986 Poland was allowed to join the International Monetary Fund. But Reagan never wavered in his condemnation of the repressive regime, nor did he consider removing trade sanctions when Polish leader General Wojciech Jaruzelski lifted the basic restrictions of martial law in December 1982. Reagan said more "meaningful liberalizing measures" would have to be taken before the United States would consider "equally significant and concrete actions of our own." (Historic Documents of 1982, p. 947)

Restrictions Eased

It was, however, the existence of a well-organized underground in Poland that was thought to have been a moving force behind the decision to end martial law and to grant the people of Poland other freedoms, such as the right to disagree openly with the government. To fill the communication vacuum that existed under martial law, the Poles gradually built an efficient underground information system. Faced with an increasingly well-informed populace, the government was forced to become more open.

General Jaruzelski began actively seeking improved relations with France, West Germany, and Japan in 1986. In early 1987 he traveled to Italy, where he had a lengthy audience with the pope and meetings with Italian prime minister Bettino Craxi and business and labor leaders.

In September 1986 U.S. secretary of state George P. Shultz announced that the Reagan government was "actively examining" the possibility of lifting Polish trade sanctions. The Polish government chose this time to release 225 political prisoners, thereby meeting one of Reagan's original conditions for removing sanctions.

Following the first high-level contact between the Polish and U.S. governments since martial law was declared—a January 1987 visit to Poland by John C. Whitehead, U.S. deputy secretary of state—the remaining economic sanctions were lifted.

President Reagan remained cautious, saying, "The threat of arrest still hangs over those who seek their freedom. . . . The right to genuinely independent trade unions is still stifled. . . . National reconciliation remains a dream, a goal for the future, rather than a reality of today." As the months passed, however, the Polish government seemed to be holding to its pledge not to reimprison dissidents or to deny them jobs. And, following the lead of Soviet general secretary Mikhail Gorbachev, the Polish government was reported ready to make even more reforms, such as putting ownership of farms as well as manufacturing in private hands. (Gorbachev on democratic reforms, p. 79)

By September, the promise of better U.S.-Poland relations seemed to be bearing fruit. U.S. vice president George Bush made a four-day trip to Poland, during which he met with General Jaruzelski, Lech Walesa, and leaders of the Catholic church in Poland. About the same time, Poland and the United States named new ambassadors to each other's capitals in a restoration of full diplomatic relations after a four-year hiatus.

Following are President Ronald Reagan's statement on the lifting of economic sanctions against Poland on February 19, 1987, and Proclamation 5610, which lifted the sanctions:

STATEMENT BY THE PRESIDENT

Five years ago I asked all Americans to light a candle in support of freedom in Poland. During that Christmas season of 1981 candles were lit in millions of American homes. We had confidence that the spirit of freedom would continue to shine in the darkness that martial law had brought to that brave country. As Americans, we were showing solidarity with Solidarity.

Symbolic gestures were not enough. Economic and other sanctions were imposed on Poland in response to the repression that descended on the Polish people as a result of martial law. Our message was that America would not passively stand by while a grand experiment in freedom was brutally smashed in Poland. If the Polish Government wanted a decent relationship with the United States, we made it clear they would have to lift martial law, release the political prisoners, and enter into a real political dialog with Polish society.

Today, more than 5 years later, the light of freedom continues to shine in Poland. The commitment and sacrifice of hundreds of thousands of Polish men and women have kept the flame alive, even amid the gloom.

In 1983 martial law was lifted and thousands of political prisoners have been freed in a series of amnesties. Since the final amnesty last September, no one has been arrested on political charges in Poland. Yet there is still far to go. The threat of arrest still hangs over those who seek their freedom.

The right to genuinely independent trade unions is still stifled. Independent political activity continues to be repressed by various governmental measures. National reconciliation remains a dream, a goal for the future, rather than a reality of today.

I continue to believe, as do the Polish people, that it is a possible dream. The Church in Poland has greeted the major amnesty of political prisoners last September as a significant step by the Polish Government. In response to that amnesty, we initiated a step-by-step process of expanding our dialog with the Government of Poland. In our dealings with Polish authorities, we have made one point clear: The continuation of better relations between our countries, and their further improvement, will be possible only if we see maintained the spirit and principle of the amnesty and a reliance on dialog and respect for human rights. Only through genuine and meaningful reconciliation can the plight of the Polish people be alleviated. We will be watching to see that further steps are taken toward national reconciliation in Poland and that the progress made is not reversed.

Significantly, the leaders of Solidarity and of the Catholic Church in Poland agree that this is the right course for us to take. They have now urged us to lift our remaining economic sanctions in order to encourage further movement in the right direction. In considering this question, I have drawn on a broad cross section of views. We have been in touch at the highest levels with the Polish Government, with the Church, and with Solidarity. We have also consulted with our allies.

After careful review, I have decided that the economic sanctions imposed in December 1981 and October 1982 should be rescinded, and I am accordingly restoring most-favored-nation tariff treatment for Poland and lifting the ban on Poland's eligibility for official U.S. credits and credit guarantees. We have always worked closely with our allies on issues concerning Poland, and they have sent messages of support for this step forward.

I am honored by the expression of concern from distinguished Members of Congress, leaders of the Polish-American community in this country, and Solidarity. Together we underscore the heartfelt concern of our citizens about Poland. Let no one doubt our brothers and sisters who struggle to build a freer and more humane Poland, or our resolve to stand by them.

As it was in 1981, freedom is precious to us. The slogan of the Polish independence struggle of the last century was: "For Your Freedom And Ours." That is our slogan, too. And it is more than a slogan; it is a program of action.

Today is a first step, a big step. Our relations with Poland can only develop in ways that encourage genuine progress toward national reconciliation in that country. We will be steady. We will be committed. The flame that burns in the hearts of the Polish people, a flame represented by the candles we lit in 1981, that flame of justice and liberty will never be extinguished.

RESTORATION OF THE APPLICATION OF COLUMN 1 RATES OF DUTY OF THE TARIFF SCHEDULES OF THE UNITED STATES TO THE PRODUCTS OF POLAND

By the President of the United States of America

A Proclamation

1. On October 27, 1982, by Proclamation No. 4991, I suspended the application of column 1 rates of duty of the Tariff Schedules of the United States (TSUS) to the products of Poland. This followed from my determination that the Government of the Polish People's Republic had failed to meet certain import commitments under its Protocol of Accession to the General Agreement on Tariffs and Trade (19 UST 4331), and that the Polish martial law government had increased its repression of the Polish people, leaving the United States without any reason to continue withholding action on its trade complaints against Poland.

2. Since issuance of that Proclamation, the Polish Government has taken steps that lead me to believe that Poland should be given a renewed opportunity to address its trade obligations with the benefit of most-favored-nation tariff treatment.

3. The President may, pursuant to his constitutional and statutory authority, including Section 125(b) of the Trade Act of 1974, as amended, terminate in whole or in part Proclamation No. 4991.

4. I have determined in this case that the national interest requires expeditious action.

Now, Therefore, I, Ronald Reagan, President of the United States of America, by the authority vested in me by the Constitution and the statutes of the United States, including, but not limited to, the Trade Expansion Act of 1962, as amended, and the Trade Act of 1974, as amended, do hereby proclaim as follows:

1. Proclamation No. 4991 of October 27, 1982, is hereby revoked.

2. General Headnote 3(d) of the TSUS is modified:

(a) by deleting "or pursuant to Presidential Proclamation No. 4991, dated October 27, 1982" and

(b) by deleting "Polish People's Republic" from the list of countries therein.

3. This Proclamation shall take effect with respect to articles entered, or withdrawn from warehouse for consumption, on or after the date of publication of this Proclamation in the *Federal Register*.

In Witness Whereof, I have hereunto set my hand this 19th day of February, in the year of our Lord nineteen hundred and eighty-seven, and of the Independence of the United States of America the two hundred and eleventh.

STATE DEPARTMENT REPORT ON HUMAN RIGHTS PRACTICES

February 19, 1987

The State Department February 19 released to Congress its Country Reports on Human Rights Practices for 1986. *The report detailed the human rights practices of 167 nations on the freedoms of speech, assembly, and religion, as well as the rights of citizens to replace their leaders. It was one in a series of annual reviews required since 1961 on nations receiving U.S. foreign aid and since 1979 on all members of the United Nations.*

As in past reports, the Reagan administration continued to note that communist countries were serious offenders of human rights and democratic nations were most responsive to the rights of their citizens. "As we again survey human rights conditions in the world, we are once more struck by the close correlation between the existence of a democratic form of government and respect for the integrity of the person."

Throughout most of the 1980s the Reagan administration opted for quiet diplomacy on the human rights front. That policy changed, however, in 1986 as administration officials stepped up criticism of the political situation in South Africa and pushed for the removal of repressive dictators in the Philippines and Haiti. Although the administration frequently refrained from public rebuke of South Africa, the State Department report proved an effective vehicle to increase criticism. The administration in early 1987 also pressed more actively for human rights reform in the Philippines and Haiti, seeking to build on recent gains in those two countries. (Historic Documents of 1986, pp. 97, 307, 1037)

The Soviet Union

The report also continued sharp criticism of the Soviet Union. Despite the Soviets' recently declared policy of glasnost, *or openness, and the release of several prominent dissidents, the administration offered few encouraging words about the Soviets' human rights record. The report praised the release of Andrei Sakharov and Yelena Bonner from internal exile and others from labor camps as "positive developments." "But," the report asserted, "the deaths of human rights advocates Anatoliy Marchenko and Mark Morozov in Chistopol' prison underscored the continuing perilous position of thousands of Soviet prisoners of conscience."* (Gorbachev on democratic reforms, p. 79)

The report also chastised the Soviets for limiting Jewish emigration, which during 1986 was the second lowest in twenty years. The report said that, by stipulating that family reunification was the only legitimate ground for emigration, the Soviets were acting in violation of the Helsinki declaration on human rights.

South Africa

Responding to pressure from Congress, President Reagan in 1985 signed an executive order imposing economic sanctions against the South African government. Despite such action, the administration often held back on its public criticism of apartheid, the country's system of racial separation. But the 1986 human rights report noted a "major deterioration of human rights in South Africa." (Historic Documents of 1986, p. 369)

Under a state of emergency that ran through March 1986 and another that began in June 1986, South African "police and military exercised extraordinary arrest and detention powers," the report said. An estimated 1,263 people died as a result of political unrest and 20,000 people were detained by the government. The State Department document also contained detailed reports of beatings and torture by security forces and asserted that government agents helped instigate incidents of "black-on-black" violence.

The human rights report also noted that the South African government had placed tougher curbs on freedom of the press and had extended "little or no cooperation" to United Nations or private organizations attempting to investigate the country's human rights record. "The country's black majority (72 percent of its population) continues to suffer from pervasive, legally sanctioned discrimination based on race in political, economic, and social aspects of life."

The Philippines

The Reagan administration reported some encouraging news on the Philippines, where long-time ruler Ferdinand Marcos was ousted in 1986. Marcos's successor, Corazon Aquino, "has moved to restore the rule of law and respect for human rights," the report said. Aquino had released some 600 political detainees, including communist insurgents, laid the foundation for a new constitution, and allowed for a rebirth of political activity despite a communist insurgency, according to the report. Although reports of human rights abuses by Philippine police emerged, the report found no evidence that such practice was "widespread, systematic or condoned at senior military levels." Paramilitary forces, armed religious cults, and private armies continued in 1986 to commit political killings, especially where insurgents were active.

Under Aquino's leadership, the government created the Presidential Commission on Human Rights and designed a new constitution, which was adopted February 2, 1987, in a popular referendum. Elections for the new bicameral congress were held May 11. "Freedom of peaceful assembly and association was widely observed in 1986," the report said. Restrictions on freedom of the press were lifted in 1986 for the first time in fourteen years. (Aquino speech, p. 843)

Haiti and Central America

In Haiti, another closely watched country, where the National Governing Council (CNG) replaced President-for-Life Jean-Claude "Baby Doc" Duvalier, the human rights situation also had improved in 1986, according to the report. "The CNG committed itself to the protection of human rights and the end of the systemic repression of the Duvalier regime." The document went on to detail the new government's efforts to hold elections, release political prisoners, and dissolve Duvalier's secret police.

Although nearly all Haitians welcomed Duvalier's ouster, reforms seemed to progress too slowly, the report said. Haitians occasionally had shown their "impatience" with the pace of reform, confronting police and security forces. Given the extreme poverty of the country, the CNG faced a tough task ahead, according to the report. (Haiti elections, p. 939)

With the end of the Haitian dictatorship and the beginning of a new democratic government in Guatemala, the Reagan administration said there was further proof of a "spectacular shift" to democracy throughout Latin America. The report also contended that death squads in El Salvador had ceased operating, but that human rights violations by the Sandinistas in Nicaragua were still rampant, including mass arrests of civilians, mysterious disappearances, and summary executions.

Following are excerpts from the U.S. State Department's Country Reports on Human Rights Practices for 1986, *released February 19, 1987:*

Ethiopia

Ethiopia is ruled by Chairman Mengistu Haile-Mariam who exercises absolute power over the majority of Ethiopians. The ability of the

Mengistu regime to maintain itself in power is based on the conviction of most Ethiopians that it is prepared to take whatever steps are necessary to continue in power....

Ethiopia deploys the largest standing army in Africa south of the Sahara, numbering over 250,000 soldiers. It uses this power to pursue military solutions to the armed insurgencies of varying intensities directed against the Government.... The Government has an extensive security apparatus which uses a comprehensive system of surveillance and informers to strengthen its control over the population....

Ethiopia's record on human rights remains deplorable. Ethiopians have no civil or political freedoms and no institutions or laws to protect their human rights. Over 1 million Ethiopians have fled the country, many preferring life in refugee camps....

...There were reliable reports in 1986 of the execution of approximately 60 political prisoners in October 1985. None of the executed is known to have been granted a trial, much less an appeal, and the Government has never acknowledged the executions nor attempted to justify them....

Methods of torture, including severe beatings, crushing of bones of the hand, and the use of electric shocks, although technically illegal, are practiced by Ethiopian officials in cases involving insurgent combatants and those believed to be engaged in political activities against the Government. Amnesty International states that reports indicate torture is often practiced on Ethiopian prisoners interrogated at the Central Revolutionary Investigation Department ("Third Police Station") in the capital and is routinely used in other parts of the country to interrogate prisoners about opposition organizations....

In November 1984, the Government began a massive and forced resettlement of famine victims, especially from the northern regions to western parts of the country. To date this program has involved the forcible removal, transport, and resettlement of over 500,000 persons, and eventual resettlement of up to 1 million more is projected. The program, as conducted in 1984-85, was rife with abuses, including the wholesale separation of families and inhumane conditions of transport to resettlement sites up to 700 kilometers distant. Following an international outcry, the resettlement program was suspended in December 1985. Efforts were made to improve the conditions in the resettlement areas, but people already moved were not officially permitted to return to their homes, although some have left on their own. Several thousand reportedly attempted to flee towards Sudan. Suffering from hunger, exposure, and attacks by Sudanese rebels, fewer than a thousand reached Sudanese relief centers. The Ethiopian Government has publicly stated its intention to resume the program on a "voluntary" basis in the near future....

South Africa

...In 1986 there was a major deterioration of human rights in South Africa. Throughout the year, political discontent and violence persisted in the nation's black and colored townships. Following the July 1985-March 1986 State of Emergency, the Government imposed a new State of Emergency on June 12, 1986, which remained in effect at the end of the year. Under both States of Emergency, police and military exercised extraordinary arrest and detention powers. . . .

The South African Institute of Race Relations (SAIRR) reported that 1,263 people had died as the result of political unrest from January to November. Most of the deaths occurred in the first half of the year, prior to the imposition of the second State of Emergency. By the end of 1986, human rights groups estimated more than 20,000 people had been detained under this second State of Emergency. An estimated 10,000 remained in detention at the end of the year. The Black Sash, an antiapartheid organization, estimated up to 1,800 of these detainees were under the age of 18, including many children 15 years of age or younger. . . .

In the first half of 1986, Parliament enacted some changes in the apartheid system. These changes included abolition of influx control or "pass" laws, which for years extensively regulated the right of South African blacks to be present in urban areas. Parliament passed legislation permitting some blacks to regain the South African citizenship they had lost involuntarily in previous years when some homelands were given '"independence." The Government also introduced a freehold system of land ownership for blacks, permitting them to own residences in urban areas designated for blacks under the Group Areas Act. Notwithstanding the reforms, race still remains the fundamental basis for the organization of South African society. Discriminatory laws and practices remain woven throughout the fabric of South African life. . . .

While many unrest-related deaths occurred as a result of police action, a sizable number of killings resulted from internecine political strife within the black community. In August the Government Bureau of Information said that there were more than 300 deaths by burning alone as a result of "black-on-black" violence from January through mid-June of 1986. . . .

Some critics of the Government have claimed that much black-on-black violence was instigated by covert government agents. In some instances, most notably in fighting in May and June in the '"Crossroads" squatter camps in Cape Town, there was ample evidence to support this charge. Early in the year, residents of the black township of Alexandra (near Johannesburg) furnished affidavits in which they said that known police officers had participated in fire bomb incidents that ostensibly ensure neighborhood safety, and, in some cases of unrest, the police have stood aside to let armed vigilante groups subdue dissidents. . . .

Chile

Chile is ruled by a military government which took power in a 1973 coup. . . . The military junta exercises the legislative function, and a separate judicial branch carries out judicial duties, but primary authority resides with the . . . President, Augusto Pinochet. . . .

Many fundamental political freedoms in Chile during 1986 were severely restricted. Rights of private property, freedom of religion, and minority rights are respected, but freedom of association and assembly, freedom from arbitrary arrest and exile, and freedom of speech and of the press are limited....

Reliable and documented reports of torture and mistreatment of those detained by Chilean security forces continue to be received by human rights organizations. In addition, members of the security and military forces are widely believed to be responsible for the many kidnapings, beatings, torture, and in a few cases, murders, carried out against human rights, Catholic Church and opposition figures, for which no suspects have been identified or apprehended....

The number of people killed or injured in acts of violence with apparent political motives continued at a high level. According to the Vicariate of Solidarity, the human rights organization of the Catholic Church, 72 persons died and 490 were wounded in acts of political violence during 1986. The deaths and injuries resulted from both deliberate and random actions by security and military forces and by left-and right-wing terrorists. The Vicariate said half the deaths were caused by government forces....

Arbitrary arrests and dententions showed a marked increase in 1986. Before the state of siege was invoked in September, the Government had conducted massive sweeps, or police roundups, in the poorer areas in and around large urban centers. These sweeps involved brief detentions of thousands of persons, although only eight persons were eventually charged with violations of law....

El Salvador

El Salvador is a recently established and developing democracy....

For 7 years, El Salvador has fought a Marxist insurgency supported by the Soviet Union and Cuba through Nicaragua. The Farabundo Marti National Liberation Front (FMLN), whose numbers have been halved to under 6,000 combatants, has increasingly resorted to indiscriminate use of land mines, machine-gunning and burning of vehicles on the nation's roads, and generalized economic sabotage. The conflict is a major cause of the displacement of approximately 400,000 Salvadorans from their homes....

Despite the internal conflict and the resulting state of emergency which nominally restricts a number of civil liberties, the rights of free speech, press, association, and assembly are respected by the Government....

The infamous death squads, which used to advertise their murders, made no claims of any killings during 1986, and there was no indication they are still operating. Some unexplained deaths may still be the work of extreme rightist elements, but there is no evidence that the Government is linked to or condones these killings....

A third round of dialog to end the war was proposed by President

Duarte and scheduled for September, but the guerrillas failed to attend after unilaterally imposing conditions the Government felt were unacceptable. The Government continues to seek productive discussions with the FMLN. In his October 1986 report, the United Nations Special Rapporteur for Human Rights stated that dialog "should not be converted into a means of gaining tactical political advantages, but should be considered as a means of obtaining peace, or, at a minimum, humanization of the conflict." . . .

Guatemala

In 1986 Guatemala completed an orderly and open transition from a military regime to a democratically elected, civilian government. On January 14, the President, 100 deputies, and 300 mayors chosen in the 1985 general and presidential runoff elections took office, the first civilian government to assume power in Guatemala since 1966.

The new government, headed by President Marco Vinicio Cerezo Arevalo, inherited a deeply divided country which for more than 20 years has suffered a Marxist-led guerrilla insurgency as well as political violence carried out by rightist death squads and government security forces. . . .

Upon coming to power, the new Government announced that ending political violence and establishing the rule of law would be its top priorities. To that end, President Cerezo undertook a reorganization of the security forces and disbanded the Department of Technical Investigations, the plainclothes arm of the national police widely acknowledged to have engaged in extortion, robbery, and political kidnapings and assassinations. A new Supreme Court also embarked on a series of reforms designed to end corruption and improve the efficiency of the legal system. New laws are designed to give citizens legal recourse when they believe their rights threatened by the authorities. The Congress, in accordance with the Constitution, has established a Human Rights Committee. It recently approved legislation covering the duties of a human rights ombudsman.

In 1986 political killings and kidnapings dropped to the lowest level in this decade. Human rights groups blame the security forces for the abuses that remain, but they have not produced evidence linking the new Government to these crimes. In 1986 the United Nations rescinded the mandate of its Special Rapporteur for Guatemala, noting the return to civilian government and the Government's commitment to end political violence.

The decline in political violence has helped focus attention on the issue of accounting for past human rights abuses. Amnesty, available to insurgents since 1982, was expanded by decree by the outgoing military government to include anyone guilty of common crimes committed with political motivation. This applies to members of the security forces guilty of kidnaping and assassination. The Mutual Support Group (GAM), an organization of relatives of disappeared persons, has called on the Government to rescind the decree and set up a special presidential commission to investigate past abuses. President Cerezo told GAM members that only the judiciary is constitutionally competent to conduct such an investigation. He has urged GAM to bring charges in the courts against alleged violators of human rights, something which GAM so far has refused to do. This impasse has bred ill will between the Government and GAM and has contributed to the politicization of human rights issues in Guatemala....

Haiti

After months of mounting unrest, President-for-Life Jean-Claude Duvalier fled Haiti on February 7, 1986. This ended the hereditary dictatorship begun by his father, Francois Duvalier, in 1957. The National Governing Council (CNG) replaced Duvalier and is presently composed of three members: Lieutenant General Henri Namphy, President, Colonel Williams Regala, and Jacques Francois. On assuming office, the CNG suspended Duvalier's 1983 constitution and currently rules by decree. It has largely retained the inherited government structure while replacing most senior officials. The CNG at its inception stated that its primary goal was to oversee a transition to a freely elected government. To this end, it announced on June 7 a comprehensive program for building democratic institutions, to culminate in the inauguration of an elected president and legislature on February 7, 1988.

The CNG committed itself to the protection of human rights and the end of the systemic repression of the Duvalier regime. In one of its first acts, it freed all political prisoners. It also dissolved the Volunteers for National Security (VSN) or "Tontons Macoute," Duvalier's secret police. All defense and police functions are now performed by the Haitian armed forces, an integrated organization composed of army, navy, air force, and police elements.

The CNG has instituted basic freedoms of expression and association. The press now functions without restraint. Dozens of political parties have emerged, and Haitian politicians are attempting to build electoral support. The CNG has issued two decrees governing the press and political parties, respectively. Both decrees have been criticized as unduly restrictive, but in practice, press and political activity have flourished without hindrance by the Government....

Virtually all Haitians welcomed Duvalier's ouster and the new opportunities it provided. However, the CNG has moved only gradually to make changes many Haitians and other observers expected. Haitians have manifested their impatience in several periods of unrest since Duvalier's departure. Often stimulated by agitators, they have marched and demonstrated during these periods. There have been about a dozen deaths at government hands, generally during confrontations with police and military forces; approximately three soldiers and police also have died. While the Government has implemented positive human rights measures, incidents contrary to CNG policy demonstrate that further progress remains to be made, especially in the professionalization of the security forces....

The CNG's stated purpose is to provide a transition to a democratic government. On June 7 it announced a calendar for political reform that will culminate in 1988. Intermediate steps include election of rural councils, an advisory "consultative council," and a constituent assembly to draft and present a new constitution for approval in a referendum; enactment of press and political parties laws; and municipal, local, legislative, and presidential elections, the last two in November 1987. The CNG completed all steps on schedule, with no evident fraud or deception. . . .

These elections did not arouse a great deal of public interest or participation. Observers attributed this to Haitians' inexperience with free elections, mass illiteracy, uncertainty about procedures, distrust of the CNG, and a lack of civic responsibility and participation by political parties and pressure groups. The Government did not provide clear instructions well enough in advance to give voters a good idea of the significance of and procedures involved in each election. Rudimentary voting procedures were employed. For the constituent assembly election, voting assistants helped illiterate voters indicate their choices, and marked their hands with indelible ink to prevent multiple voting. Observers estimate that only 5 to 10 percent of eligible voters actually cast ballots. Nevertheless, the Government, operating with little experience, few technical resources, and a cramped timetable, met its electoral commitments. That it did so in the face of multiple handicaps impressed many observers. . . .

Nicaragua

The Government expanded its drive to immobilize the opposition during 1986 with official attacks on political parties previously spared more threatening forms of intimidation, such as detention or arrest. It increasingly circumscribed the legal activities of political, labor, private sector, and religious organizations. . . .

Major human rights abuses in 1986 included mass arrests of civilians on vague charges of counterrevolutionary activity; torture and abuse of prisoners; disappearances; summary executions of civilians and prisoners of war; the continuing involuntary relocation of rural residents; civilian deaths resulting from the Sandinista military's indiscriminate use of artillery and air bombardment; the closure of the opposition newspaper La Prensa and Radio Catolica, operated by the Catholic Archdiocese of Managua—the last vestiges of the independent, nongovernment-controlled mass media; and the forced exile of a leading bishop, the Curia's spokesman, and a priest.

There were also continuing unconfirmed claims of the murder of civilians in the Atlantic coast region during 1986. These reports came from refugees entering Costa Rican camps who allege that the Sandinistas have begun using "death squads" for the execution of rural inhabitants, mostly young males, considered sympathetic to the resistance.

The armed resistance similarly has been charged with numerous violations of human rights, including forced recruitment, use of pressure-sensitive mines, summary executions of prisoners and regime officials, torture, kidnapings of noncombatants, and attacks on civilians....

As of September 1986, the Government had announced the detention of over 3,000 people on suspicion of involvement in "counterrevolution." It is unknown how many of those detained remain in Sandinista custody. Another 2,300 people were detained and then released and granted amnesty for similar crimes. In early 1986, over 200 Catholic "Delegates of the Word" were arrested in the Nueva Guinea area. Almost 100 members of the Autonomous Nicaraguan Workers Confederation (CTN-A) were arrested at the same time. In the largest single operation announced by the Government, 1,500 persons were reported arrested during a 2-week period in March in the Rio Coco de Matagalpa area. The Government press reported 518 people arrested in February, 250 arrested in the Rama-Nueva Guinea area in March, and another 328 detained in May. On at least one occasion, in March in El Jicote, the entire male population of a village was detained on suspicion of counterrevolutionary involvement....

Democratic People's Republic of Korea*

The Democratic People's Republic of Korea, formed in 1948 during the Soviet administration of the northern half of the Korean peninsula, is a rigid Communist dictatorship maintained by the ruling Korean Workers' (Communist) Party (KWP), with its overriding aim of imposing a social revolution and enforcing unanimous popular support for the country's governing system and its leader, Kim Il Sung. Individual rights are entirely subordinated to the KWP. Although there were pro forma elections to the Supreme People's Assembly in November, free elections do not exist since citizens have no choice among candidates.

The North Korean people are subject to rigid controls. The State establishes security ratings for each person, and these ratings determine access to jobs, schools, medical facilities, and stores as well as admission to the KWP, the route to the highest levels and privileges of the society. The party, government, and military elite enjoy significant economic privileges such as access to special stores and medical facilities, better housing, and better education, which are not available to ordinary citizens.

Persons who fail to conform to the rigid dictates of the State face imprisonment or, more often, enforced removal to remote villages. Surveillance by informers is prevalent. Punishment for "political crimes" against

---

*The United States does not have diplomatic relations with the Democratic People's Republic of Korea. Representatives of governments that do have relations with the DPRK, as well as journalists and other invited visitors to North Korea, are not permitted the freedom of movement that would enable them to assess effectively human rights conditions there. Most of this report, therefore, is a repeat of previous human rights reports based on information obtained over a period of time extending from well before 1986. While limited in scope and detail, the information is indicative of the human rights situation in North Korea today.

the State is severe. No outside information other than that approved and disseminated by the North Korean authorities is allowed to reach the general public, although senior government officials are somewhat better informed.

President Kim Il Sung's 13-year effort to groom his son, Kim Chong Il, as his successor is testimony to the enormous power the elder Kim has amassed during 38 years of rule. The younger Kim has been elevated to several senior party positions during the last few years. The absence of any evidence of public debate about the succession is also indicative of the lack of real popular participation in the political process. . . .

The populace is subjected to regular indoctrination, designed to shape individual consciousness. Preschool children are drilled in homage to Kim Il Sung and his family, while youths and adults are required to participate in daily ideological training conducted during school or at places of employment. Approximately half the school day is devoted to indoctrination. Neighborhood units have been organized to provide indoctrination for persons who neither work nor go to school. The daily indoctrination requires rote recitation of party maxims and policies and strives for ideological purity. Multiple North Korean security organizations enforce these controls. . . .

. . In school, children are encouraged to discuss what their parents have said at home. The Government conducts monthly "sanitation" inspections to check on household activities. Each house is required to have portraits of Kim Il Sung and Kim Chong Il, his son and expected successor. . . .

Republic of Korea

President Chun Doo Hwan dominates the political scene in the Republic of Korea. The elected legislature has limited power but considerable influence on public opinion. . . . The Constitution was adopted by referendum in October 1980 under strict martial law conditions, leading many Koreans to question the referendum's fairness. President Chun has promised to step down in early 1988, when his term of office ends, to provide for a peaceful and constitutional change of power. . . .

The issue of constitutional reform dominated Korean politics in 1986. In February the opposition launched a petition campaign in support of its demand that the Constitution be amended to provide for direct popular election of the next President. The Government initially declared the campaign illegal and sought to block it, placing some opposition leaders under house arrest. The Government subsequently moderated its position, but the opposition party continued to apply pressure by staging a series of large public rallies throughout the nation. In late spring President Chun responded by agreeing to negotiations between the political parties in the National Assembly to amend the Constitution. The government party proposed creating a parliamentary system of government while the main opposition party insists on a directly elected President. At the end of the year the debate remained stalemated with both sides seeking to bolster popular support for their positions.

The Government continued to take a hard line towards dissident, particularly student dissident, political activism in 1986, citing increasing radicalism and violence. As the year progressed, student protest slogans became increasingly revolutionary and in some instances closely paralleled North Korean propaganda. Approximately 3,400 persons were jailed in connection with political activities, some of them violent. In December well over 1,000 persons remained in custody for politically related offenses. For the first time under the present Government, an opposition Assemblyman was indicted and jailed in connection with the distribution of the text of an Assembly speech the Government claimed violated the National Security Law in its criticism of the Government's unification and anti-Communist policies. In 1986 there continued to be numerous charges of police mistreatment of prisoners including credible allegations of torture in some cases....

There were unconfirmed reports that the deaths of several persons said to be critical of the Government or engaged in opposition political activity may have been at the hands of the police or other government security agencies. In one case, involving the death of a military reservist in police custody, there were charges that he died as a result of beatings by police or military officials after making remarks critical of the Government. The Minister of Home Affairs told the National Assembly that the reservist died of acute renal paralysis while in police custody on charges of violating the law on assembly and demonstrations. In the other cases, including the deaths of a university student and a worker, which the police announced were suicides, some opposition and human rights groups expressed suspicions of official culpability....

While continuing to deny that it holds any "political prisoners," the Government did make public several times during the year the number of persons being held in connection with the "political situation." In December, government prosecutors announced that 3,405 persons had been arrested in 1986 in connection with political activities, including campus demonstrations such as the seizure of buildings at Konkuk University in October. The total included 2,919 students, 919 workers, 146 "dissidents," and 240 "ordinary citizens." Prosecution sources said that as of mid-December, 1,480 persons, including students, remained under arrest, and police were searching for another 150 persons suspected of politically related offenses. The release of political prisoners was the subject of debate and negotiation in the National Assembly. According to the Government, 26 persons convicted of politically related offenses were released in a special clemency in August, and indictments against a number of others were suspended over the course of the year....

As part of the overall crackdown on dissident activities in late 1986, the Minister of Labor in November ordered the "voluntary" disbandment of fourteen "leftist-oriented" labor organizations, including the Chonggye Garment Workers Union, which the Minister claimed was responsible for many labor problems. Government authorities also announced that they had uncovered several "clandestine" labor networks that were purportedly engaged in attempts to indoctrinate workers with leftist ideology. Human rights groups estimated that as many as 150 people, including some students, were in prison in late 1986 because of involvement in various labor-related activities. This in part reflects continuing efforts by student dissidents to contact and influence labor groups. . . .

The Philippines

Tumultuous events in February 1986 led to a peaceful transfer of power from the authoritarian regime of former President Marcos to a new democratic Government dedicated to political and economic reform. Assuming office in the aftermath of elections marked by widespread fraud and intimidation, President Corazon Aquino has moved to restore the rule of law and respect for human rights. . . .

During 1986 the Aquino Government promulgated executive orders recognizing key civil rights, including the restoration of the writ of habeas corpus and reinstatement of protections against unreasonable search and siezure. Its commitment to human rights was dramatically demonstrated by the release of over 600 political detainees and the establishment of a Presidential Commission on Human Rights. Freedom of speech and association were reaffirmed as an uncensored press contributed to revitalized political activity.

Restoration of civil rights occurred in the shadow of an armed Communist insurgency active in most of the country's 73 provinces. . . .

Political killings are alleged to occur regularly in areas where the Communist New People's Army (NPA) is actively engaged in combat with government forces. Confrontations between armed forces occur frequently and an accurate estimate of fatalities is difficult. The gathering of reliable statistics on the incidence of politically motivated killing is further complicated by the common use of violence for both personal and political purposes. Distinctions between common criminal activity, personal vendettas, unauthorized reprisals, and legitimate counterinsurgency operations are often blurred. . . .

Philippine human rights groups . . . continue to allege that torture and related abuses by the military are prevalent in areas where government forces are actively engaged in counterinsurgency operations. They claim that innocent farmers in insurgent-influenced areas are detained and tortured by military officials seeking information on rebel activity.

Such claims notwithstanding, there is no evidence to suggest that such occurrences are presently widespread, systematic, or condoned at senior military levels. While abuses may still occur sporadically in the field, the MND [Ministry of National Defense] is engaged in an educational campaign to improve military treatment of civilians. . . .

Restrictions on freedom of expression in the Philippines were lifted in 1986 for the first time in nearly 14 years. The Aquino Government tolerates criticism of its policies, permitting the expression of dissent on government-owned television and radio stations. While allowing their continued operation, the Government has sequestered the assets of several newspapers, radio and television stations directly or indirectly owned by relatives and close associates of former President Marcos....

Freedom of peaceful assembly and association was widely observed in 1986. A broad range of private, professional, religious, social, charitable, and political organizations flourish in the Philippines. Countless popular and civic organizations exist and meet regularly....

Union of Soviet Socialist Republics

...Those who attempt to exercise their rights face arrest, trial, and imprisonment, or internment in a psychiatric hospital. Human rights monitors, religious believers, peace activists, and proponents of greater cultural and political rights for ethnic minorities were all subjected to arrest and imprisonment in 1986.

The December release of Andrey Sakharov and Yelena Bonner from internal exile and the early releases from labor camp of several other prominent dissidents were positive developments. But the deaths of human rights advocates Anatoliy Marchenko and Mark Morozov in Chistopol' prison underscored the continuing perilous position of thousands of Soviet prisoners of conscience.

Jewish, ethnic German, and Armenian emigration remained at severely restricted levels, despite the desire of many thousands to emigrate. Jewish emigration was the second lowest in 20 years. Those few who were allowed to emigrate during 1986 included a number of prominent "refuseniks" whose applications had been pending for more than 10 years.

In early November, the Soviet authorities made public regulations controlling the granting of exit permission to Soviet citizens. In singling out family reunification as the only legitimate ground for emigration, the regulations violated the Soviet commitment to the Universal Declaration of Human Rights, which was incorporated into the Helsinki Final Act....

So many Soviet political prisoners suffer both mental and physical abuse and mistreatment during interrogation, trial, and confinement, according to a wide variety of sources, that such treatment must be regarded as a systematic policy and practice. Sources indicate that before trial, some defendants have been threatened, humiliated, and beaten to force confessions. Once convicted, prisoners find that the limited rights guaranteed them by prison or camp regulations—the ability to receive packages, send letters, and see family—are frequently and arbitrarily withdrawn. Life in prison is marked by isolation, poor diet and malnutrition, compulsory hard labor, beatings, frequent illness, and inadequate medical care....

In 1986 human rights activist Naum Yefremov was beaten systematically by other prisoners in a labor camp near the Tyumen region, according to reliable sources. In late 1985, the psychiatrist and Helsinki psychiatric abuse monitor Dr. Anatoliy Koryagin, now serving a 12-year sentence in

Chistopol' Prison for "anti-Soviet agitation and propaganda," was placed in self-tightening handcuffs. He subsequently spent large portions of December, January, February, and April in a punishment cell for refusing to acknowledge his "guilt." ...

Provisions in Soviet law for early release from prison for the very ill are seldom used. At the time of release, many prisoners have tuberculosis, heart disease, ulcers, arthritis, pneumonia, meningitis, and vision and hearing problems. The 32-year old poetess Irina Ratushinskaya emerged from prison in October weak from several hunger strikes and a beating.

The Government continues to place selected political and religious activists in psychiatric hospitals where they are often subjected to the painful, forced administration of sedatives, antipsychotics, and other drugs. . . .

Many Jews have waited in vain for more than 10 years for permission to emigrate. Official Israeli sources estimate that there are approximately 370,000 Soviet Jews who have requested the letters of invitation (vyzovs) necessary to apply to emigrate, and that many more Jews would eventually leave if emigration restrictions were lifted. However, a variety of administrative and extralegal sanctions, including loss of employment, harassment, social ostracism, and long delays, dissuade many Jews from even attempting to submit an emigration application. Jewish emigration in 1986 totaled 914, down from 1140 in 1985, and only marginally higher than the 20-year low figure of 896 in 1984. . . .

Libya

The disregard of human rights traditionally displayed by the Libyan regime of Colonel Qadhafi became even more apparent in 1986 with the evidence of Libyan support for, or direction of, attacks or attempted attacks on civilian targets in Austria, Italy, the Federal Republic of Germany, France, Sudan, Tunisia, North Yemen, United Kingdom, Togo, Lebanon, Turkey, Cyprus, and Chad. As a result of these terrorist activities, all members of the European Community and the Tokyo Economic Summit declared that they could not have normal relations with the Libyan regime and would take measures to isolate it until it altered its behavior. . . .

The governing principles of the society are expressed in Qadhafi's "Green Book" rather than in the Constitution. Qadhafi has created a political system borrowing from pan-Islamic and pan-Arab sources and purporting to establish a "third way" superior to both capitalism and communism. His philosophy on human rights is summed up in his statement that "it is an honor to jail or liquidate the enemies of the authorities." Indeed, he has instigated the assassination of his enemies abroad, and he controls enemies at home in a variety of summary and judicial proceedings which are employed wherever popular resistance exists. While ethnic minorities are allegedly allowed full exercise of their human rights, in practice such groups as the Berber population are tightly and systematically controlled.

Libya's security apparatus operates at multiple levels, involving not only Qadhafi's personal bodyguards and the official police and security establishment, but also the Revolutionary Committees and People's Committees which act independently of other authorities, sometimes encouraged directly by Qadhafi. The result is a complex of multilayered, tight controls over individual activities and freedoms....

Legal freedoms and rights are generally lacking inside Libya except for minimal guarantees for minorities and women. There is no right of peaceful association and assembly, no freedom of speech, no right to express opposition to the Government in any form, to form trade unions, or to strike. There are no legal or judicial rights such as the right to be considered innocent until proved guilty, the right to a public or speedy trial, to be secure in one's home or person, or even to hold property.

Libya's human rights record worsened in 1986. There were continued reports of torture and abuse. Although Qadhafi has urged a reduction in the number of offenses subject to capital punishment, he made it clear that such sentences would continue to apply to political acts against the regime, and he also reiterated his call for the searching out and "physical liquidation" of the regime's "enemies abroad." In statements made in the autumn of 1986, Revolutionary Committees urged, and carried out in some cases, the total expropriation and burning of the homes of "enemies of the revolution."...

TOWER COMMISSION REPORT

February 26, 1987

A three-member special review commission appointed by President Ronald Reagan to investigate the National Security Council (NSC) reported February 26 that Reagan had lost control of his staff, which mismanaged a policy of arms sales to Iran and apparently allowed funds from those sales to be diverted to the contra rebels in Nicaragua. (Historic Documents of 1986, p. 1013)

"I believe that the president was poorly advised and poorly served," said John Tower, chairman of the review board. "I think that he should have followed up more and monitored this operation more closely. I think he was not aware of a lot of the things that were going on and the way the operation was structured and who was involved in it."

Reagan had appointed the board November 26, 1986, the day after his administration announced that funds from the arms sales had been diverted. The purpose of the board was to conduct a "comprehensive review" of NSC operations. Tower, a former senator, was joined on the commission by former senator and secretary of state Edmund S. Muskie and retired lieutenant general Brent Scowcroft, a former national security adviser.

Without subpoena power, the commission was unable to interview principal players in the arms deal and contra support operations. The Israeli government declined to respond to questions. The board also worked without the assistance of the independent counsel, Lawrence E. Walsh, and the FBI. However, the commission did interview eighty people, including the president, and executive departments and agencies required that their employees cooperate with the investigation. Others heard from were former presidents and vice presidents, secretaries of state, NSC advisers and members, and officials of the Central Intelligence Agency (CIA) and Joint Chiefs of Staff.

Commission Findings

The Tower report described three foundations for the policy disaster known as the Iran-contra affair: Reagan's hands-off management style, the failure of his aides to compensate for the president's lack of attention to detail, and the willingness of White House staffers to sidestep the institutional process for making and carrying out decisions.

The panel placed much of the blame squarely on Reagan, saying he made little effort to find out what his staff was doing and allowed his compassion for the American hostages in Lebanon—believed held by Shi'ite Moslems with ties to Iran—to override his stated policy of not dealing with terrorists. Reagan's principal failure, the board said, was that he did not demand that his staff—especially aides to the National Security Council—follow normal procedures.

The Arms Sale and the Diversion

On the Iranian arms sales issue, the report found that a policy originally intended to improve relations with the radical government in Tehran (by supplying Iran with arms badly needed in its war with Iraq) quickly evolved into a series of arms swaps for hostages, largely because of Reagan's concern for the hostages. Opening ties to Iran "may have been in the national interest," the panel said, but the United States "should never have become a party to the arms transfers" that were first suggested by Israel. The board did not blame Israel for inducing the United States into dealing with Iran, but it did note that Israeli officials repeatedly provided rationales and encouragement.

The panel was unable to resolve fully one of the major mysteries of the entire affair: when did Reagan first approve an Israeli shipment of U.S.-made arms to Iran? The president's aides disagreed about whether he gave the legally required approval before or after the first shipments in August and September 1985—or whether he had approved only replenishment of Israel's stocks of the weapons shipped to Iran. In his February 27, 1987, letter to the board, Reagan said he simply could not remember. The board concluded that Reagan probably approved the shipment in advance. The report did not find any evidence that Reagan himself knew of the diversion of funds to the Nicaraguan contras.

Key Recommendations

The Tower panel produced no major recommendations for legal or institutional changes, but its members said Reagan's administration and future ones should adhere to existing structures and procedures instead of creating ad hoc means of carrying out foreign policy.

The panel opposed several often-recommended changes, such as requiring Senate confirmation of the national security adviser and barring the NSC staff from engaging in operations. Instead, it said the White House staff should be more responsive to congressional concerns, and the president should assign operational duties to his NSC staff only in highly unusual cases. The administration should carefully consider policies and their consequences before implementing them, involve all the relevant agencies and experts in the government, review policies periodically to make sure they are working as intended, and limit the use of private individuals to carry out government policy.

The board also recommended that House and Senate Intelligence committees be merged, thereby reducing the number of leaks of classified information and "curing" the executive branch's obsession with secrecy. Supporters of the existing two-committee system countered that it worked well and that the administration was responsible for more leaks than Congress. They also argued that the Iran-contra affair demonstrated that intelligence agencies needed more—not less—supervision from Congress.

Hill, White House Reaction

Congressional reaction to the report broke predictably along partisan lines. Most Republicans praised Reagan for having the "courage" to appoint the review board in the first place. Senate minority leader Robert Dole, R-Kan., said the report indicated that "blunders were made of colossal proportions, and the president didn't adopt a hands-on approach toward the National Security Council." Democrats used the report to bolster their claim that the president was dangerously "disengaged" from the making of policy. "This report shows that the president has been asleep at the switch," said Representative Norman Y. Mineta, D-Calif.

As his first act in reaction to the report, Reagan on February 27 replaced Chief of Staff Donald T. Regan, who had been sharply criticized by the Tower panel, with former Senate majority leader Howard H. Baker, Jr. A widely respected moderate and a popular choice, Baker was expected to shore up Reagan's sagging relations with Capitol Hill.

Reagan also responded to the Tower report's findings in a nationally televised address on March 4. At the heart of his twelve-minute speech were two statements: that he accepted "full responsibility" for his administration's actions, and that the United States did in fact trade arms to Iran for hostages. "As angry as I may be about activities undertaken without my knowledge, I am still accountable for those activities," the president said.

The indirect references to mistakes were not clear-cut admissions of presidential error. As in the past, Reagan seemed to blame unnamed aides for most of the lapses in the Iran-contra affair. For example, he said inaccurate recordkeeping was at fault for his inability to remember just when he approved the first Israeli shipment of U.S.-made arms to Iran. Acknowledging that the United States did swap arms for hostages, the president recalled his earlier denials, saying, "My heart and my best intentions still tell me that is true, but the facts and the evidence tell me it is not." The Tower report showed, he said, that "what began as a strategic opening to Iran deteriorated in its implementation into trading arms for hostages." Reagan said he had no excuses: "It was a mistake." Referring to the Tower board's criticism of his management style, he said his methods had worked in the past but "when it came to managing the NSC staff, let's face it, my style didn't match its previous track record." He guaranteed "no more freelancing by individuals when it comes to our national security." (Historic Documents of 1986, p. 1049)

In addition to naming Baker chief of staff, Reagan had taken decisive action in December 1986, by appointing Frank C. Carlucci as national security adviser to replace Vice Admiral John M. Poindexter and instructing Carlucci to revamp NSC procedures. The appointment of former FBI director William H. Webster to head the CIA was another visible step toward gaining firmer control of the national security apparatus.

Following are excerpts from the "Report of the President's Special Review Board," investigating National Security Council operations in the Iran-contra affair, released February 26, 1987:

Part I. Introduction

In November, 1986, it was disclosed that the United States had, in August, 1985, and subsequently, participated in secret dealings with Iran involving the sale of military equipment. There appeared to be a linkage between these dealings and efforts to obtain the release of U.S. citizens held hostage in Lebanon by terrorists believed to be closely associated with the Iranian regime. After the initial story broke, the Attorney General announced that proceeds from the arms transfers may have been diverted to assist U.S.-backed rebel forces in Nicaragua, known as Contras. This possibility enlarged the controversy and added questions not only of policy and propriety but also violations of law.

These disclosures became the focus of substantial public attention. The secret arms transfers appeared to run directly counter to declared U.S. policies. The United States had announced a policy of neutrality in the six-year old Iran/Iraq war and had proclaimed an embargo on arms sales to Iran. It had worked actively to isolate Iran and other regimes known to give aid and comfort to terrorists. It had declared that it would not pay ransom to hostage-takers.

Public concern was not limited to the issues of policy, however. Questions arose as to the propriety of certain actions taken by the National Security Council [NSC] staff and the manner in which the decision to transfer arms to Iran had been made. Congress was never informed. A variety of intermediaries, both private and governmental, some with motives open to question, had central roles. The NSC staff rather than the CIA seemed to be running the operation. The President appeared to be unaware of key elements of the operation. The controversy threatened a crisis of confidence in the manner in which national security decisions are made and the role played by the NSC staff.

It was this latter set of concerns that prompted the President to establish this Special Review Board on December 1, 1986. The President directed the Board to examine the proper role of the National Security Council staff in national security operations, including the arms transfers to Iran. The President made clear that he wanted "all the facts to come out."

The Board was not, however, called upon to assess individual culpability or be the final arbiter of the facts. These tasks have been properly left to others. Indeed, the short deadline set by the President for completion of the Board's work and its limited resources precluded a separate and thorough field investigation. Instead, the Board has examined the events surrounding the transfer of arms to Iran as a principal case study in evaluating the operation of the National Security Council in general and the role of the NSC staff in particular.

The President gave the Board a broad charter. It was directed to conduct "a comprehensive study of the future role and procedures of the National Security Council (NSC) staff in the development, coordination, oversight, and conduct of foreign and national security policy."

It has been forty years since the enactment of the National Security Act of 1947 and the creation of the National Security Council. Since that time the NSC staff has grown in importance and the Assistant to the President for National Security Affairs has emerged as a key player in national security decision-making. This is the first Presidential Commission to have as its sole responsibility a comprehensive review of how these institutions have performed. We believe that, quite aside from the circumstances which brought about the Board's creation, such a review was overdue.

The Board divided its work into three major inquiries: the circumstances surrounding the Iran/Contra matter, other case studies that might reveal strengths and weaknesses in the operation of the National Security Council system under stress, and the manner in which that system has served eight different Presidents since its inception in 1947. . . .

. . . [I]t is important to emphasize that the President is responsible for the national security policy of the United States. In the development and execution of that policy, the President is the decision-maker. He is not obliged to consult with or seek approval from anyone in the Executive Branch. The structure and procedures of the National Security Council system should be designed to give the President every assistance in discharging these heavy responsibilities. It is not possible to make a system immune from error without paralyzing its capacity to act.

At its senior levels, the National Security Council is primarily the interaction of people. We have examined with care its operation in the Iran/Contra matter and have set out in considerable detail mistakes of omission, commission, judgment, and perspective. We believe that this record and analysis can warn future Presidents, members of the National Security Council, and National Security Advisors of the potential pitfalls they face even when they are operating with what they consider the best of motives. We would hope that this record would be carefully read and its lessons fully absorbed by all aspirants to senior positions in the National Security Council system....

Our review validates the current National Security Council system. That system has been utilized by different Presidents in very different ways, in accordance with their individual work habits and philosophical predilections. On occasion over the years it has functioned with real brilliance; at other times serious mistakes have been made. The problems we examined in the case of Iran/Contra caused us deep concern. But their solution does not lie in revamping the National Security Council system.

That system is properly the President's creature. It must be left flexible to be molded by the President into the form most useful to him. Otherwise it will become either an obstacle to the President, and a source of frustration; or an institutional irrelevance, as the President fashions informal structures more to his liking.

Having said that, there are certain functions which need to be performed in some way for any President. What we have tried to do is to distill from the wisdom of those who have participated in the National Security Council system over the past forty years the essence of these functions and the manner in which that system can be operated so as to minimize the likelihood of major error without destroying the creative impulses of the President.

Part II. Organizing for National Security

Ours is a government of checks and balances, of shared power and responsibility. The Constitution places the President and the Congress in dynamic tension. They both cooperate and compete in the making of national policy.

National security is no exception. The Constitution gives both the President and the Congress an important role. The Congress is critical in formulating national policies and in marshalling the resources to carry them out. But those resources—the nation's military personnel, its diplomats, its intelligence capability—are lodged in the Executive Branch. As Chief Executive and Commander-in-Chief, and with broad authority in the area of foreign affairs, it is the President who is empowered to act for the nation and protect its interests.

A. The National Security Council

The present organization of the Executive Branch for national security matters was established by the National Security Act of 1947. That Act created the National Security Council. As now constituted, its statutory members are the President, Vice President, Secretary of State, and Secretary of Defense. The President is the head of the National Security Council.

Presidents have from time to time invited the heads of other departments or agencies to attend National Security Council meetings or to participate as de facto members. These have included the Director of Central Intelligence (the "DCI") and the Chairman of the Joint Chiefs of Staff (the "CJCS"). The President (or, in his absence, his designee) presides.

The National Security Council deals with the most vital issues in the nation's national security policy. It is this body that discusses recent developments in arms control and the Strategic Defense Initiative; that discussed whether or not to bomb the Cambodia mainland after the *Mayaguez* was captured; that debated the timetable for the U.S. withdrawal from Vietnam; and that considered the risky and daring attempt to rescue U.S. hostages in Iran in 1980. The National Security Council deals with issues that are difficult, complex, and often secret. Decisions are often required in hours rather than weeks. Advice must be given under great stress and with imperfect information.

The National Security Council is not a decision-making body. Although its other members hold official positions in the Government, when meeting as the National Security Council they sit as advisors to the President. This is clear from the language of the 1947 Act:

> "The function of the Council shall be to advise the President with respect to the integration of domestic, foreign, and military policies relating to the national security so as to enable the military services and the other departments and agencies of the Government to cooperate more effectively in matters involving the national security."

The National Security Council has from its inception been a highly personal instrument. Every President has turned for advice to those individuals and institutions whose judgment he has valued and trusted. For some Presidents, such as President Eisenhower, the National Security Council served as a primary forum for obtaining advice on national security matters. Other Presidents, such as President Kennedy, relied on more informal groupings of advisors, often including some but not all of the Council members. . . .

Regardless of the frequency of its use, the NSC has remained a strictly advisory body. Each President has kept the burden of decision for himself, in accordance with his Constitutional responsibilities.

B. The Assistant to the President for National Security Affairs

Although closely associated with the National Security Council in the public mind, the Assistant to the President for National Security Affairs is not one of its members. Indeed, no mention of this position is made in the National Security Act of 1947.

The position was created by President Eisenhower in 1953. Although its precise title has varied, the position has come to be known (somewhat misleadingly) as the National Security Advisor.

Under President Eisenhower, the holder of this position served as the principal executive officer of the Council, setting the agenda, briefing the President on Council matters, and supervising the staff. He was not a policy advocate.

It was not until President Kennedy, with McGeorge Bundy in the role, that the position took on its current form. Bundy emerged as an important personal advisor to the President on national security affairs. This introduced an element of direct competition into Bundy's relationship with the members of the National Security Council. Although President Johnson changed the title of the position to simply "Special Assistant," in the hands of Walt Rostow it continued to play an important role.

President Nixon relied heavily on his National Security Advisor, maintaining and even enhancing its prominence. In that position, Henry Kissinger became a key spokesman for the President's national security policies both to the U.S. press and to foreign governments. President Nixon used him to negotiate on behalf of the United States with Vietnam, China, the Soviet Union, and other countries. The roles of spokesman and negotiator had traditionally been the province of the Secretary of State, not of the National Security Advisor. The emerging tension between the two positions was only resolved when Kissinger assumed them both.

Under President Ford, Lt Gen Brent Scowcroft became National Security Advisor, with Henry Kissinger remaining as Secretary of State. The National Security Advisor exercised major responsibility for coordinating for the President the advice of his NSC principals and overseeing the process of policy development and implementation within the Executive Branch.

President Carter returned in large part to the early Kissinger model, with a resulting increase in tensions with the Secretary of State. President Carter wanted to take the lead in matters of foreign policy, and used his National Security Advisor as a source of information, ideas, and new initiatives.

The role of the National Security Advisor, like the role of the NSC itself, has in large measure been a function of the operating style of the President. Notwithstanding, the National Security Advisor has come to perform, to a greater or lesser extent, certain functions which appear essential to the effective discharge of the President's responsibilities in national security affairs.

• He is an "honest broker" for the NSC process. He assures that issues are clearly presented to the President; that all reasonable options, together with an analysis of their disadvantages and risks, are brought to his attention; and that the views of the President's other principal advisors are accurately conveyed.

• He provides advice from the President's vantage point, unalloyed by institutional responsibilities and biases. Unlike the Secretaries of State or Defense, who have substantial organizations for which they are responsible, the President is the National Security Advisor's only constituency.

• He monitors the actions taken by the executive departments in implementing the President's national security policies. He asks the question whether these actions are consistent with Presidential decisions and whether, over time, the underlying policies continue to serve U.S. interests.

• He has a special role in crisis management. This has resulted from the need for prompt and coordinated action under Presidential control, often with secrecy being esssential.

• He reaches out for new ideas and initiatives that will give substance to broad Presidential objectives for national security.

• He keeps the President informed about international developments and developments in the Congress and the Executive Branch that affect the President's policies and priorities.

But the National Security Advisor remains the creature of the President. The position will be largely what he wants it to be. This presents any President with a series of dilemmas.

• The President must surround himself with people he trusts and to whom he can speak in confidence. To this end, the National Security Advisor, unlike the Secretaries of State and Defense, is not subject to confirmation by the Senate and does not testify before Congress. But the more the President relies on the National Security Advisor for advice, especially to the exclusion of his Cabinet officials, the greater will be the unease with this arrangement.

• As the "honest broker" of the NSC process, the National Security Advisor must ensure that the different and often conflicting views of the NSC principals are presented fairly to the President. But as an independent advisor to the President, he must provide his own judgment. To the extent that the National Security Advisor becomes a strong advocate for a particular point of view, his role as "honest broker" may be compromised and the President's access to the unedited views of the NSC principals may be impaired.

• The Secretaries of State and Defense, and the Director of Central Intelligence, head agencies of government that have specific statutory responsibilities and are subject to Congressional oversight for the implementation of U.S. national security policy. To the extent that the National Security Advisor assumes operational responsibilities, whether by negotiating with foreign governments or becoming heavily involved in military or intelligence operations, the legitimacy of that role and his authority to perform it may be challenged.

- The more the National Security Advisor becomes an "operator" in implementing policy, the less will he be able objectively to review that implementation—and whether the underlying policy continues to serve the interests of the President and the nation.
- The Secretary of State has traditionally been the President's spokesman on matters of national security and foreign affairs. To the extent that the National Security Advisor speaks publicly on these matters or meets with representatives of foreign governments, the result may be confusion as to what is the President's policy.

C. The NSC Staff

At the time it established the National Security Council, Congress authorized a staff headed by an Executive Secretary appointed by the President. Initially quite small, the NSC staff expanded substantially under President Eisenhower.

During the Eisenhower Administration, the NSC staff assumed two important functions: coordinating the executive departments in the development of national policy (through the NSC Planning Board) and overseeing the implementation of that policy (through the Operations Coordination Board). A systematic effort was made to coordinate policy development and its implementation by the various agencies through an elaborate set of committees. The system worked fairly well in bringing together for the President the views of the other NSC principals. But it has been criticized as biased toward reaching consensus among these principals rather than developing options for Presidential decision. By the end of his second term, President Eisenhower himself had reached the conclusion that a highly competent individual and a small staff could perform the needed functions in a better way. Such a change was made by President Kennedy.

Under President Kennedy, a number of the functions of the NSC staff were eliminated and its size was sharply reduced. The Planning and Operations Coordinating Boards were abolished. Policy development and policy implementation were assigned to individual Cabinet officers, responsible directly to the President. By late 1962 the staff was only 12 professionals, serving largely as an independent source of ideas and information to the President. The system was lean and responsive, but frequently suffered from a lack of coordination. The Johnson Administration followed much the same pattern.

The Nixon Administration returned to a model more like Eisenhower's but with something of the informality of the Kennedy/Johnson staffs. The Eisenhower system had emphasized coordination; the Kennedy-Johnson system tilted to innovation and the generation of new ideas. The Nixon system emphasized both. The objective was not inter-departmental consensus but the generation of policy options for Presidential decision, and then ensuring that those decisions were carried out. The staff grew to 50 professionals in 1970 and became a major factor in the national security decision-making process. This approach was largely continued under President Ford.

The NSC staff retained an important role under President Carter. While continuing to have responsibility for coordinating policy among the various executive agencies, President Carter particularly looked to the NSC staff as a personal source of independent advice. President Carter felt the need to have a group loyal only to him from which to launch his own initiatives and to move a vast and lethargic government. During his time in office, President Carter reduced the size of the professional staff to 35, feeling that a smaller group could do the job and would have a closer relationship to him.

... [The NSC staff] has remained the President's creature, molded as he sees fit, to serve as his personal staff for national security affairs. For this reason, it has generally operated out of the public view and has not been subject to direct oversight by the Congress.

D. The Interagency Committee System

The National Security Council has frequently been supported by committees made up of representatives of the relevant national security departments and agencies. These committees analyze issues prior to consideration by the Council. There are generally several levels of committees. At the top level, officials from each agency (at the Deputy Secretary or Under Secretary level) meet to provide a senior level policy review. These senior-level committees are in turn supported by more junior interagency groups (usually at the Assistant Secretary level). These in turn may oversee staff level working groups that prepare detailed analysis of important issues....

E. The Reagan Model

President Reagan entered office with a strong commitment to cabinet government. His principal advisors on national security affairs were to be the Secretaries of State and Defense, and to a lesser extent the Director of Central Intelligence. The position of the National Security Advisor was initially downgraded in both status and access to the President. Over the next six years, five different people held that position.

The Administration's first National Security Advisor, Richard [V.] Allen, reported to the President through the senior White House staff. Consequently, the NSC staff assumed a reduced role. Mr. Allen believed that the Secretary of State had primacy in the field of foreign policy. He viewed the job of the National Security Advisor as that of a policy coordinator.

President Reagan initially declared that the National Security Council would be the principal forum for consideration of national security issues.

To support the work of the Council, President Reagan established an interagency committee system headed by three Senior Interagency Groups (or "SIGs"), one each for foreign policy, defense policy, and intelligence. They were chaired by the Secretary of State, the Secretary of Defense, and the Director of Central Intelligence, respectively.

Over time, the Administration's original conception of the role of the National Security Advisor changed. William [P.] Clark, who succeeded Richard Allen in 1982, was a long-time associate of the President and dealt directly with him. Robert [C.] McFarlane, who replaced Judge Clark in 1983, although personally less close to the President, continued to have direct access to him. The same was true for VADM [Vice Admiral] John [M.] Poindexter, who was appointed to the position in December, 1985.

President Reagan appointed several additional members to his National Security Council and allowed staff attendance at meetings. The resultant size of the meetings led the President to turn increasingly to a smaller group (called the National Security Planning Group or "NSPG"). Attendance at its meetings was more restricted but included the statutory principals of the NSC. The NSPG was supported by the SIGs, and new SIGs were occasionally created to deal with particular issues. These were frequently chaired by the National Security Advisor. But generally the SIGs and many of their subsidiary groups (called Interagency Groups or "IGs") fell into disuse.

As a supplement to the normal NSC process, the Reagan Administration adopted comprehensive procedures for covert actions. These are contained in a classified document, NSDD-159, establishing the process for deciding, implementing, monitoring, and reviewing covert activities.

F. The Problem of Covert Operations

Covert activities place a great strain on the process of decision in a free society. Disclosure of even the existence of the operation could threaten its effectiveness and risk embarrassment to the Government. As a result, there is strong pressure to withhold information, to limit knowledge of the operation to a minimum number of people.

These pressures come into play with great force when covert activities are undertaken in an effort to obtain the release of U.S. citizens held hostage abroad. Because of the legitimate human concern all Presidents have felt over the fate of such hostages, our national pride as a powerful country with a tradition of protecting its citizens abroad, and the great attention paid by the news media to hostage situations, the pressures on any President to take action to free hostages are enormous. Frequently to be effective, this action must necessarily be covert. Disclosure would directly threaten the lives of the hostages as well as those willing to contemplate their release.

Since covert arms sales to Iran played such a central role in the creation of this Board, it has focused its attention in large measure on the role of the NSC staff where covert activity is involved.... [I]n many respects the best test of a system is its performance under stress. The conditions of greatest stress are often found in the crucible of covert activities.

Part III. Arms Transfers to Iran, Diversion, and Support for the Contras

The Iran/Contra matter has been and, in some respects, still is an enigma. For three months the Board sought to learn the facts, and still the whole matter cannot be fully explained. The general outlines of the story are clear....

Section A: The Arms Transfers to Iran

Two persistent concerns lay behind U.S. participation in arms transfers to Iran.

First, the U.S. government anxiously sought the release of seven U.S. citizens abducted in Beirut, Lebanon, in seven separate incidents between March 7, 1984, and June 9, 1985. One of those abducted was William Buckley, CIA station chief in Beirut, seized on March 16, 1984. Available intelligence suggested that most, if not all, of the Americans were held hostage by members of Hizballah, a fundamentalist Shiite terrorist group with links to the regime of the Ayatollah Khomeini.

Second, the U.S. government had a latent and unresolved interest in establishing ties to Iran. Few in the U.S. government doubted Iran's strategic importance or the risk of Soviet meddling in the succession crisis that might follow the death of Khomeini. For this reason, some in the U.S. government were convinced that efforts should be made to open potential channels to Iran.

Arms transfers ultimately appeared to offer a means to achieve both the release of the hostages and a strategic opening to Iran....

Section C: The NSC Staff and Support for the Contras

Inquiry into the arms sale to Iran and the possible diversion of funds to the Contras disclosed evidence of substantial NSC staff involvement in a related area; private support for the Contras during the period that support from the U.S. Government was either banned or restricted by Congress.

There are similarities in the two cases. Indeed, the NSC staff's role in support for the Contras set the stage for its subsequent role in the Iran initiative. In both, LtCol [Oliver L.] North, with the acquiescence of the National Security Advisor, was deeply involved in the operational details of a covert program. He relied heavily on private U.S. citizens and foreigners to carry out key operational tasks. Some of the same individuals were involved in both. When Israeli plans for the November HAWK shipment began to unravel, LtCol North turned to the private network that was already in place to run the Contra support operation. This network, under the direction of Mr. [Richard] Secord, undertook increasing responsibility for the Iran initiative. Neither program was subjected to rigorous and periodic inter-agency overview. In neither case was Congress informed. In the case of Contra support, Congress may have been actively misled.

These two operations also differ in several key aspects. While Iran policy was the subject of strong disagreement within the Executive Branch, the President's emphatic support for the Contras provoked an often bitter debate with the Congress. The result was an intense political struggle between the President and the Congress over how to define U.S. policy toward Nicaragua. Congress sought to restrict the President's ability to implement his policy. What emerged was a highly ambiguous legal environment.

On December 21, 1982, Congress passed the first "Boland amendment" prohibiting the Department of Defense and the Central Intelligence Agency from spending funds to overthrow Nicaragua or provoke conflict between Nicaragua and Honduras. The following year, $24 million was authorized for the Contras. On October 3, 1984, Congress cut off all funding for the Contras and prohibited DoD, CIA, and any other agency or entity "involved in intelligence activities" from directly or indirectly supporting military operations in Nicaragua.

The 1984 prohibition was subject to conflicting interpretation. On the one hand, several of its Congressional supporters believed that the legislation covered the activities of the NSC staff. On the other hand, it appears that LtCol North and VADM Poindexter received legal advice from the President's Intelligence Oversight Board that the restrictions on lethal assistance to the Contras did not cover the NSC staff.

Confusion only increased. In December 1985 Congress approved classified amounts of funds to the Contras for "communications" and "advice." The authorization was subject, however, to a classified annex negotiated by the Senate and House intelligence committees. An exchange of letters, initiated the day the law passed, evidences the extreme difficulty even the Chairmen of the two committees had in deciding what the annex permitted or proscribed.

The support for the Contras differs from the Iranian initiative in some other important respects. First, the activities undertaken by LtCol North with respect to the Contras, unlike in the Iranian case, were in support of the declared policy of at least the Executive. Second, the President may never have authorized or, indeed, even been apprised of what the NSC staff was doing. The President never issued a Covert Action Finding or any other formal decision authorizing NSC staff activities in support of the Contras. Third, the NSC staff's role in support of the Contras was not in derogation of the CIA's role because, CIA involvement was expressly barred by statute....

Part IV. What Was Wrong

The arms transfers to Iran and the activities of the NSC staff in support of the Contras are case studies in the perils of policy pursued outside the constraints of orderly process.

The Iran initiative ran directly counter to the Administration's own policies on terrorism, the Iran/Iraq war, and military support to Iran. This inconsistency was never resolved, nor were the consequences of this inconsistency fully considered and provided for. The result taken as a whole was a U.S. policy that worked against itself.

The Board believes that failure to deal adequately with these contradictions resulted in large part from the flaws in the manner in which decisions were made. Established procedures for making national security decisions were ignored. Reviews of the initiative by all the NSC principals were too infrequent. The initiatives were not adequately vetted below the cabinet level. Intelligence resources were underutilized. Applicable legal constraints were not adequately addressed. The whole matter was handled too informally, without adequate written records of what had been considered, discussed, and decided.

This pattern persisted in the implementation of the Iran initiative. The NSC staff assumed direct operational control. The initiative fell within the traditional jurisdictions of the Departments of State, Defense, and CIA. Yet these agencies were largely ignored. Great reliance was placed on a network of private operators and intermediaries. How the initiative was to be carried out never received adequate attention from the NSC principals or a tough working-level review. No periodic evaluation of the progress of the initiative was ever conducted. The result was an unprofessional and, in substantial part, unsatisfactory operation.

In all of this process, Congress was never notified.

. . . [T]he record of the role of the NSC staff in support of the Contras is much less complete. Nonetheless, what is known suggests that many of the same problems plagued that effort as well. . . .

A. A Flawed Process

1. Contradictory Policies Were Pursued

The arms sales to Iran and the NSC support for the Contras demonstrate the risks involved when highly controversial initiatives are pursued covertly.

Arms Transfers to Iran. The initiative to Iran was a covert operation directly at odds with important and well-publicized policies of the Executive Branch. But the initiative itself embodied a fundamental contradiction. Two objectives were apparent from the outset: a strategic opening to Iran, and release of the U.S. citizens held hostage in Lebanon. The sale of arms to Iran appeared to provide a means to achieve both these objectives. It also played into the hands of those who had other interests—some of them personal financial gain—in engaging the United States in an arms deal with Iran.

In fact, the sale of arms was not equally appropriate for achieving both these objectives. Arms were what Iran wanted. If all the United States sought was to free the hostages, then an arms-for-hostages deal could achieve the immediate objectives of both sides. But if the U.S. objective was a broader strategic relationship, then the sale of arms should have been contingent upon first putting into place the elements of that relationship. An arms-for-hostages deal in this context could become counter-productive to achieving this broader strategic objective. In addition, release of the hostages would require exerting influence with Hizballah, which could involve the most radical elements of the Iranian regime. The kind of strategic opening sought by the United States, however, involved what were regarded as more moderate elements.

The U.S. officials involved in the initiative appeared to have held three distinct views. For some, the principal motivation seemed consistently a strategic opening to Iran. For others, the strategic opening became a rationale for using arms sales to obtain the release of the hostages. For still others, the initiative appeared clearly as an arms-for-hostages deal from first to last.

Whatever the intent, almost from the beginning the initiative became in fact a series of arms-for-hostages deals. The shipment of arms in November, 1985, was directly tied to a hostage release. Indeed, the August/September transfer may have been nothing more than an arms-for-hostages trade. By July 14, 1985, a specific proposal for the sale of 100 TOWs to Iran in exchange for Iranian efforts to secure the release of all the hostages had been transmitted to the White House and discussed with the President. What actually occurred, at least so far as the September shipment was concerned, involved a direct link of arms and a hostage.

The initiative continued to be described in terms of its broader strategic relationship. But those elements never really materialized.... Even if one accepts the explanation that arms and hostages represented only "bona fides" of seriousness of purpose for each side, that had clearly been established, one way or another, by the September exchange.

It is true that, strictly speaking, arms were not exchanged for the hostages. The arms were sold for cash; and to Iran, rather than the terrorists holding the hostages. Iran clearly wanted to buy the arms, however, and time and time again U.S. willingness to sell was directly conditioned upon the release of hostages. Although Iran might claim that it did not itself hold the hostages, the whole arrangement was premised on Iran's ability to secure their release.

While the United States was seeking the release of the hostages in this way, it was vigorously pursuing policies that were dramatically opposed to such efforts. The Reagan Administration in particular had come into office declaring a firm stand against terrorism, which it continued to maintain. In December of 1985, the Administration completed a major study under the chairmanship of the Vice President. It resulted in a vigorous reaffirmation of U.S. opposition to terrorism in all its forms and a vow of total war on terrorism whatever its source. The Administration continued to pressure

U.S. allies not to sell arms to Iran and not to make concessions to terrorists.

No serious effort was made to reconcile the inconsistency between these policies and the Iran initiative. No effort was made systematically to address the consequences of this inconsistency—the effect on U.S. policy when, as it inevitably would, the Iran initiative became known.

The Board believes that a strategic opening to Iran may have been in the national interest but that the United States never should have been a party to the arms transfers. As arms-for-hostages trades, they could not help but create an incentive for further hostage-taking. As a violation of the U.S. arms embargo, they could only remove inhibitions on other nations from selling arms to Iran. This threatened to upset the military balance between Iran and Iraq, with consequent jeopardy to the Gulf States and the interests of the West in that region. The arms-for-hostages trades rewarded a regime that clearly supported terrorism and hostage-taking. They increased the risk that the United States would be perceived, especially in the Arab world, as a creature of Israel. They suggested to other U.S. allies and friends in the region that the United States had shifted its policy in favor of Iran. They raised questions as to whether U.S. policy statements could be relied upon.

As the arms-for-hostages proposal first came to the United States, it clearly was tempting. The sale of just 100 TOWs was to produce the release of all seven Americans held in Lebanon. Even had the offer been genuine, it would have been unsound. But it was not genuine. The 100 TOWs did not produce seven hostages. Very quickly the price went up, and the arrangements became protracted. A pattern of successive bargained exchanges of arms and hostages was quickly established. While release of all the hostages continued to be promised, in fact the hostages came out singly if at all. This sad history is powerful evidence of why the United States should never have become involved in the arms transfers.

NSC Staff Support for the Contras. The activities of the NSC staff in support of the Contras sought to achieve an important objective of the Administration's foreign policy. The President had publicly and emphatically declared his support for the Nicaragua resistance. That brought his policy in direct conflict with that of the Congress, at least during the period that direct or indirect support of military operations in Nicaragua was barred.

. . .[N]o serious effort appears to have been made to come to grips with the risks to the President of direct NSC support for the Contras in the face of these Congressional restrictions. Even if it could be argued that these restrictions did not technically apply to the NSC staff, these activities presented great political risk to the President. The appearance of the President's personal staff doing what Congress had forbade other agencies to do could, once disclosed, only touch off a firestorm in the Congress and threaten the Administration's whole policy on the Contras.

2. The Decision-making Process Was Flawed

Because the arms sales to Iran and the NSC support for the Contras occurred in settings of such controversy, one would expect that the decisions to undertake these activities would have been made only after intense and thorough consideration. In fact, a far different picture emerges.

Arms Transfers to Iran. The Iran initiative was handled almost casually and through informal channels, always apparently with an expectation that the process would end with the next arms-for-hostages exchange. It was subjected neither to the general procedures for interagency consideration and review of policy issues nor the more restrictive procedures set out in NSDD 159 for handling covert operations. This had a number of consequences.

(i) The Opportunity for a Full Hearing before the President Was Inadequate. In the last half of 1985, the Israelis made three separate proposals to the United States with respect to the Iran initiative (two in July and one in August). In addition, Israel made three separate deliveries of arms to Iran, one each in August, September, and November. Yet prior to December 7, 1985, there was at most one meeting of the NSC principals, a meeting which several participants recall taking place on August 6. There is no dispute that full meetings of the principals did occur on December 7, 1985, and on January 7, 1986. But the proposal to shift to direct U.S. arms sales to Iran appears not to have been discussed until later. It was considered by the President at a meeting on January 17 which only the Vice President, Mr. Regan, Mr. Fortier, and VADM Poindexter attended. Thereafter, the only senior-level review the Iran initiative received was during one or another of the President's daily national security briefings. These were routinely attended only by the President, the Vice President, Mr. Regan, and VADM Poindexter. There was no subsequent collective consideration of the Iran initiative by the NSC principals before it became public 11 months later.

This was not sufficient for a matter as important and consequential as the Iran initiative. Two or three cabinet-level reviews in a period of 17 months was not enough. The meeting on December 7 came late in the day, after the pattern of arms-for-hostages exchanges had become well established. The January 7 meeting had earmarks of a meeting held after a decision had already been made. Indeed, a draft Covert Action Finding authorizing the initiative had been signed by the President, though perhaps inadvertently, the previous day.

At each significant step in the Iran initiative, deliberations among the NSC principals in the presence of the President should have been virtually automatic. This was not and should not have been a formal requirement, something prescribed by statute. Rather, it should have been something the NSC principals desired as a means of ensuring an optimal environment for Presidential judgment. The meetings should have been preceded by consideration by the NSC principals of staff papers prepared according to the procedures applicable to covert actions. These should have reviewed the history of the initiative, analyzed the issues then presented, developed a range of realistic options, presented the odds of success and the costs of failure, and addressed questions of implementation and execution. Had this been done, the objectives of the Iran initiative might have been clarified and alternatives to the sale of arms might have been identified.

(ii) The Initiative Was Never Subjected to a Rigorous Review below the Cabinet Level. Because of the obsession with secrecy, interagency consideration of the initiative was limited to the cabinet level. With the exception of the NSC staff and, after January 17, 1986, a handful of CIA officials, the rest of the executive departments and agencies were largely excluded.

As a consequence, the initiative was never vetted at the staff level. This deprived those responsible for the initiative of considerable expertise—on the situation in Iran; on the difficulties of dealing with terrorists; on the mechanics of conducting a diplomatic opening. It also kept the plan from receiving a tough, critical review.

Moreover, the initiative did not receive a policy review below cabinet level. Careful consideration at the Deputy/Under Secretary level might have exposed the confusion in U.S. objectives and clarified the risks of using arms as an instrument of policy in this instance.

The vetting process would also have ensured better use of U.S. intelligence. As it was, the intelligence input into the decision process was clearly inadequate. First, no independent evaluation of the Israeli proposals offered in July and August appears to have been sought or offered by U.S. intelligence agencies. The Israelis represented that they for some time had had contacts with elements in Iran. The prospects for an opening to Iran depended heavily on these contacts, yet no systematic assessment appears to have been made by U.S. intelligence agencies of the reliability and motivations of these contacts, and the identity and objectives of the elements in Iran that the opening was supposed to reach. Neither was any systematic assessment made of the motivation of the Israelis.

Second, neither Mr. [Manucher] Ghorbanifar nor the second channel seem to have been subjected to a systematic intelligence vetting before they were engaged as intermediaries. Mr. Ghorbanifar had been known to the CIA for some time and the agency had substantial doubts as to his reliability and truthfulness. Yet the agency did not volunteer that information or inquire about the identity of the intermediary if his name was unknown. Conversely, no early request for a name check was made of the CIA, and it was not until January 11, 1986, that the agency gave Mr. Ghorbanifar a new polygraph, which he failed. Notwithstanding this situation, with the signing of the January 17 Finding, the United States took control of the initiative and became even more directly involved with Mr. Ghorbanifar.... [N]o prior intelligence check appears to have been made on the second channel.

Third, although the President recalled being assured that the arms sales to Iran would not alter the military balance with Iran, the Board could find no evidence that the President was ever briefed on this subject. The question of the impact of any intelligence shared with the Iranians does not appear to have been brought to the President's attention.

A thorough vetting would have included consideration of the legal implications of the initiative. There appeared little effort to face squarely the legal restrictions and notification requirements applicable to the operation. At several points, other agencies raised questions about violations of law or regulations. These concerns were dismissed without, it appears, investigating them with the benefit of legal counsel.

Finally, insufficient attention was given to the implications of implementation. The implementation of the initiative raised a number of issues: should the NSC staff rather than the CIA have had operational control; what were the implications of Israeli involvement; how reliable were the Iranian and various other private intermediaries; what were the implications of the use of Mr. Secord's private network of operatives; what were the implications for the military balance in the region; was operational security adequate. Nowhere do these issues appear to have been sufficiently addressed.

The concern for preserving the secrecy of the initiative provided an excuse for abandoning sound process. Yet the initiative was known to a variety of persons with diverse interests and ambitions—Israelis, Iranians, various arms dealers and business intermediaries, and LtCol North's network of private operatives. While concern for secrecy would have justified limiting the circle of persons knowledgeable about the initiative, in this case it was drawn too tightly. As a consequence, important advice and counsel were lost.

In January of 1985, the President had adopted procedures for striking the proper balance between secrecy and the need for consultation on sensitive programs. These covered the institution, implementation, and review of covert operations. In the case of the Iran initiative, these procedures were almost totally ignored.

The only staff work the President apparently reviewed in connection with the Iran initiative was prepared by NSC staff members, under the direction of the National Security Advisor. These were, of course, the principal proponents of the initiative. A portion of this staff work was reviewed by the Board. It was frequently striking in its failure to present the record of past efforts—particularly past failures. Alternative ways of achieving U.S. objectives—other than yet another arms-for-hostages deal—were not discussed. Frequently it neither adequately presented the risks involved in pursuing the initiative nor the full force of the dissenting views of other NSC principals. On balance, it did not serve the President well.

(iii) The Process Was Too Informal. The whole decision process was too informal. Even when meetings among NSC principals did occur, often there was no prior notice of the agenda. No formal written minutes seem to have been kept. Decisions subsequently taken by the President were not formally recorded. An exception was the January 17 Finding, but even this was apparently not circulated or shown to key U.S. officials.

The effect of this informality was that the initiative lacked a formal institutional record. This precluded the participants from undertaking the more informed analysis and reflection that is afforded by a written record, as opposed to mere recollection. It made it difficult to determine where the initiative stood, and to learn lessons from the record that could guide future action. This lack of an institutional record permitted specific proposals for arms-for-hostages exchanges to be presented in a vacuum, without reference to the results of past proposals. Had a searching and thorough review of the Iran initiative been undertaken at any stage in the process, it would have been extremely difficult to conduct. The Board can attest first hand to the problem of conducting a review in the absence of such records. Indeed, the exposition in the wake of public revelation suffered the most.

NSC Staff Support for the Contras. It is not clear how LtCol North first became involved in activities in direct support of the Contras during the period of the Congressional ban. . . . In the evidence that the Board did have, there is no suggestion at any point of any discussion of LtCol North's activities with the President in any forum. There also does not appear to have been any interagency review of LtCol North's activities at any level.

This latter point is not surprising given the Congressional restrictions under which the other relevant agencies were operating. But the NSC staff apparently did not compensate for the lack of any interagency review with its own internal vetting of these activities. LtCol North apparently worked largely in isolation, keeping first Mr. McFarlane and then VADM Poindexter informed.

The lack of adequate vetting is particularly evident on the question of the legality of LtCol North's activities. . . .

If these activities were illegal, obviously they should not have been conducted. If there was any doubt on the matter, systematic legal advice should have been obtained. The political cost to the President of illegal action by the NSC staff was particularly high, both because the NSC staff is the personal staff of the President and because of the history of serious conflict with the Congress over the issue of Contra support. For these reasons, the President should have been kept apprised of any review of the legality of LtCol North's activities.

Legal advice was apparently obtained from the President's Intelligence Oversight Board. Without passing on the quality of that advice, it is an odd source. It would be one thing for the Intelligence Oversight Board to review the legal advice provided by some other agency. It is another for the Intelligence Oversight Board to be originating legal advice of its own. That is a function more appropriate for the NSC staff's own legal counsel.

3. Implementation Was Unprofessional

The manner in which the Iran initiative was implemented and LtCol North undertook to support the Contras are very similar. This is in large part because the same cast of characters was involved. In both cases the operations were unprofessional, although the Board has much less evidence with respect to LtCol North's Contra activities.

Arms Transfers to Iran. With the signing of the January 17 Finding, the Iran initiative became a U.S. operation run by the NSC staff. LtCol North made most of the significant operational decisions. He conducted the operation through Mr. Secord and his associates, a network of private individuals already involved in the Contra resupply operation. To this was added a handful of selected individuals from the CIA....

Because so few people from the departments and agencies were told of the initiative, LtCol North cut himself off from resources and expertise from within the government. He relied instead on a number of private intermediaries, businessmen and other financial brokers, private operators, and Iranians hostile to the United States. Some of these were individuals with questionable credentials and potentially large personal financial interests in the transactions. This made the transactions unnecessarily complicated and invited kick-backs and payoffs. This arrangement also dramatically increased the risks that the initiative would leak. Yet no provision was made for such an eventuality. Further, the use of Mr. Secord's private network in the Iran initiative linked those operators with the resupply of the Contras, threatening exposure of both operations if either became public.

The result was a very unprofessional operation....

The conduct of the negotiators with Mr. Ghorbanifar and the second channel were handled in a way that revealed obvious inexperience. The discussions were too casual for dealings with intermediaries to a regime so hostile to U.S. interests. The U.S. hand was repeatedly tipped and unskillfully played. The arrangements failed to guarantee that the U.S. obtained its hostages in exchange for the arms. Repeatedly, LtCol North permitted arms to be delivered without the release of a single captive.

The implementation of the initiative was never subjected to a rigorous review. LtCol North appears to have kept VADM Poindexter fully informed of his activities. In addition, VADM Poindexter, LtCol North, and the CIA officials involved apparently apprised Director Casey of many of the operational details. But LtCol North and his operation functioned largely outside the orbit of the U.S. Government. Their activities were not subject to critical reviews of any kind.

After the initial hostage release in September, 1985, it was over 10 months before another hostage was released. This despite recurring promises of the release of all the hostages and four intervening arms shipments. Beginning with the November shipment, the United States increasingly took over the operation of the initiative. In January, 1986, it decided to transfer arms directly to Iran.

Any of these developments could have served as a useful occasion for a systematic reconsideration of the initiative. Indeed, at least one of the schemes contained a provision for reconsideration if the initial assumptions proved to be invalid. They did, but the reconsideration never took place. It was the responsibility of the National Security Advisor and the responsible officers on the NSC staff to call for such a review. But they were too involved in the initiative both as advocates and as implementors. . . .

iv. Congress Was Never Notified. Congress was not apprised either of the Iran initiative or of the NSC staff's activities in support of the Contras.

In the case of Iran, because release of the hostages was expected within a short time after the delivery of equipment, and because public disclosure could have destroyed the operation and perhaps endangered the hostages, it could be argued that it was justifiable to defer notification of Congress prior to the first shipment of arms to Iran. The plan apparently was to inform Congress immediately after the hostages were safely in U.S. hands. But after the first delivery failed to release all the hostages, and as one hostage release plan was replaced by another, Congress certainly should have been informed. This could have been done during a period when no specific hostage release plan was in execution. Consultation with Congress could have been useful to the President, for it might have given him some sense of how the public would react to the initiative. It also might have influenced his decision to continue to pursue it.

v. Legal Issues. In addition to conflicting with several fundamental U.S. policies, selling arms to Iran raised far-reaching legal questions. How it dealt with these is important to an evaluation of the Iran initiative.

Arms Transfers to Iran. . . . The Arms Export Control Act, the principal U.S. statute governing arms sales abroad, makes it unlawful to export arms without a license. Exports of arms by U.S. government agencies, however, do not require a license if they are otherwise authorized by law. Criminal penalties—fines and imprisonment—are provided for willful violations.

The initial arms transfers in the Iran initiative involved the sale and shipment by Israel of U.S.-origin missiles. The usual way for such international retransfer of arms to be authorized under U.S. law is pursuant to the Arms Export Control Act. This Act requires that the President consent to any transfers by another country of arms exported under the Act and imposes three conditions before such Presidential consent may be given:

(a) the United States would itself transfer the arms in question to the recipient country;
(b) a commitment in writing has been obtained from the recipient country against unauthorized retransfer of significant arms, such as missiles; and
(c) a prior written certification regarding the retransfer is submitted to the Congress if the defense equipment, such as missiles, has an acquisition cost of 14 million dollars or more. 22 U.S.C. 2753 (a), (d).

In addition, the Act generally imposes restrictions on which countries are eligible to receive U.S. arms and on the purposes for which arms may be sold.

The other possible avenue whereby government arms transfers to Iran may be authorized by law would be in connection with intelligence operations conducted under the National Security Act. This Act requires that the Director of Central Intelligence and the heads of other intelligence agencies keep the two Congressional intelligence committees "fully and currently informed" of all intelligence activities under their responsibility. 50 U.S.C. 413. Where prior notice of significant intelligence activities is not given, the intelligence committees are to be informed "in a timely fashion." In addition, the so called Hughes-Ryan Amendment to the Foreign Assistance Act requires that "significant anticipated intelligence activities" may not be conducted by the CIA unless and until the President finds that "each such operation is important to the national security of the United States." 22 U.S.C. 2422.

When the Israelis began transfering arms to Iran in August, 1985, they were not acting on their own. U.S. officials had knowledge about the essential elements of the proposed shipments. The United States shared some common purpose in the transfers and received a benefit from them—the release of a hostage. More importantly, Mr. McFarlane communicated prior U.S. approval to the Israelis for the shipments, including an undertaking for replenishment. But for this U.S. approval, the transactions may not have gone forward. In short, the United States was an essential participant in the arms transfers to Iran that occurred in 1985.

Whether this U.S. involvement in the arms transfers by the Israelis was lawful depends fundamentally upon whether the President approved the transactions before they occurred. In the absence of Presidential approval, there does not appear to be any authority in this case for the United States to engage in the transfer of arms or consent to the transfer by another country. The arms transfers to Iran in 1985 and hence the Iran initiative itself would have proceeded contrary to U.S. law....

The Board was unable to reach a conclusive judgment about whether the 1985 shipments of arms to Iran were approved in advance by the President. On balance the Board believes that it is plausible to conclude that he did approve them in advance.

Yet even if the President in some sense consented to or approved the transactions, a serious question of law remains. It is not clear that the form of the approval was sufficient for purposes of either the Arms Export Control Act or the Hughes-Ryan Amendment. The consent did not meet the conditions of the Arms Export Control Act, especially in the absence of a prior written commitment from the Iranians regarding unauthorized retransfer.

Under the National Security Act, it is not clear that mere oral approval by the President would qualify as a Presidential finding that the initiative was vital to the national security interests of the United States. The approval was never reduced to writing. It appears to have been conveyed to only one person. The President himself has no memory of it. And there is contradictory evidence from the President's advisors about how the President responded when he learned of the arms shipments which the approval was to support. In addition, the requirement for Congressional notification was ignored. In these circumstances, even if the President approved of the transactions, it is difficult to conclude that his actions constituted adequate legal authority.

The legal requirements pertaining to the sale of arms to Iran are complex; the availability of legal authority, including that which may flow from the President's constitutional powers, is difficult to delineate.... Nevertheless, [the evidence] was sufficient for the Board's purposes to conclude that the legal underpinning of the Iran initiative during 1985 was at best highly questionable.

The Presidential Finding of January 17, 1986, formally approved the Iran initiative as a covert intelligence operation under the National Security Act. This ended the uncertainty about the legal status of the initiative and provided legal authority for the United States to transfer arms directly to Iran.

The National Security Act also requires notification of Congress of covert intelligence activities. If not done in advance, notification must be "in a timely fashion." The Presidential finding of January 17 directed that Congressional notification be withheld, and this decision appears to have never been reconsidered. While there was surely justification to suspend Congressional notification in advance of a particular transaction relating to a hostage release, the law would seem to require disclosure where, as in the Iran case, a pattern of relative inactivity occurs over an extended period. To do otherwise prevents the Congress from fulfilling its proper oversight responsibilities.

Throughout the Iran initiative, significant questions of law do not appear to have been adequately addressed. In the face of a sweeping statutory prohibition and explicit requirements relating to Presidential consent to arms transfers by third countries, there appears to have been at the outset in 1985 little attention, let alone systematic analysis, devoted to how Presidential actions would comply with U.S. law. The Board has found no evidence that an evaluation was ever done during the life of the operation to determine whether it continued to comply with the terms of the January 17 Presidential Finding. Similarly, when a new prohibition was added to the Arms Export Control Act in August of 1986 to prohibit exports to countries on the terrorism list (a list which contained Iran), no evaluation was made to determine whether this law affected authority to transfer arms to Iran in connection with intelligence operations under the National Security Act. This lack of legal vigilance markedly increased the chances that the initiative would proceed contrary to law.

NSC Staff Support for the Contras

The NSC staff activities in support of the Contras were marked by the same uncertainty as to legal authority and insensitivity to legal issues as were present in the Iran initiative. The ambiguity of the law governing activities in support of the Contras presented a greater challenge than even the considerable complexity of laws governing arms transfers. Intense Congressional scrutiny with respect to the NSC staff activities relating to the Contras added to the potential costs of actions that pushed the limits of the law.

In this context, the NSC staff should have been particularly cautious, avoiding operational activity in this area and seeking legal counsel. The Board saw no signs of such restraint.

B. Failure of Responsibility

The NSC system will not work unless the President makes it work. After all, this system was created to serve the President of the United States in ways of his choosing. By his actions, by his leadership, the President therefore determines the quality of its performance.

By his own account, as evidenced in his diary notes, and as conveyed to the Board by his principal advisors, President Reagan was deeply committed to securing the release of the hostages. It was this intense compassion for the hostages that appeared to motivate his steadfast support of the Iran initiative, even in the face of opposition from his Secretaries of State and Defense.

In his obvious commitment, the President appears to have proceeded with a concept of the initiative that was not accurately reflected in the reality of the operation. The President did not seem to be aware of the way in which the operation was implemented and the full consequences of U.S. participation.

The President's expressed concern for the safety of both the hostages and the Iranians who could have been at risk may have been conveyed in a manner so as to inhibit the full functioning of the system.

The President's management style is to put the principal responsibility for policy review and implementation on the shoulders of his advisors. Nevertheless, with such a complex, high-risk operation and so much at stake, the President should have ensured that the NSC system did not fail him. He did not force his policy to undergo the most critical review of which the NSC participants and the process were capable. At no time did he insist upon accountability and performance review. Had the President chosen to drive the NSC system, the outcome could well have been different. As it was, the most powerful features of the NSC system—providing comprehensive analysis, alternatives and follow-up—were not utilized.

The Board found a strong consensus among NSC participants that the President's priority in the Iran initiative was the release of U.S. hostages. But setting priorities is not enough when it comes to sensitive and risky initiatives that directly affect U.S. national security. He must ensure that the content and tactics of an initiative match his priorities and objectives. He must insist upon accountability. For it is the President who must take responsibility for the NSC system and deal with the consequences.

Beyond the President, the other NSC principals and the National Security Advisor must share in the responsibility for the NSC system.

President Reagan's personal management style places an especially heavy responsibility on his key advisors. Knowing his style, they should have been particularly mindful of the need for special attention to the manner in which this arms sale initiative developed and proceeded. On this score, neither the National Security Advisor nor the other NSC principals deserve high marks.

It is their obligation as members and advisors to the Council to ensure that the President is adequately served. The principal subordinates to the President must not be deterred from urging the President not to proceed on a highly questionable course of action even in the face of his strong conviction to the contrary.

In the case of the Iran initiative, the NSC process did not fail, it simply was largely ignored. The National Security Advisor and the NSC principals all had a duty to raise this issue and insist that orderly process [b]e imposed. None of them did so.

All had the opportunity. While the National Security Advisor had the responsibility to see that an orderly process was observed, his failure to do so does not excuse the other NSC principals. It does not appear that any of the NSC principals called for more frequent consideration of the Iran initiative by the NSC principals in the presence of the President. None of the principals called for a serious vetting of the initiative by even a restricted group of disinterested individuals. The intelligence questions do not appear to have been raised, and legal considerations, while raised, were not pressed. No one seemed to have complained about the informality of the process. No one called for a thorough reexamination once the initiative did not meet expectations or the manner of execution changed. While one or another of the NSC principals suspected that something was amiss, none vigorously pursued the issue.

Mr. Regan also shares in this responsibility. More than almost any Chief of Staff of recent memory, he asserted personal control over the White House staff and sought to extend this control to the National Security Advisor. He was personally active in national security affairs and attended almost all of the relevant meetings regarding the Iran initiative. He, as much as anyone, should have insisted that an orderly process be observed. In addition, he especially should have ensured that plans were made for handling any public disclosure of the initiative. He must bear primary responsibility for the chaos that descended upon the White House when such disclosure did occur.

Mr. McFarlane appeared caught between a President who supported the initiative and the cabinet officers who strongly opposed it. While he made efforts to keep these cabinet officers informed, the Board heard complaints from some that he was not always successful. VADM Poindexter on several occasions apparently sought to exclude NSC principals other than the President from knowledge of the initiative. Indeed, on one or more occasions Secretary Shultz may have been actively misled by VADM Poindexter.

VADM Poindexter also failed grievously on the matter of Contra diversion. Evidence indicates that VADM Poindexter knew that a diversion occurred, yet he did not take the steps that were required given the gravity of that prospect. He apparently failed to appreciate or ignored the serious legal and political risks presented. His clear obligation was either to investigate the matter or take it to the President—or both. He did neither. Director Casey shared a similar responsibility. Evidence suggests that he received information about the possible diversion of funds to the Contras almost a month before the story broke. He, too, did not move promptly to raise the matter with the President. Yet his responsibility to do so was clear.

The NSC principals other than the President may be somewhat excused by the insufficient attention on the part of the National Security Advisor to the need to keep all the principals fully informed. Given the importance of the issue and the sharp policy divergences involved, however, Secretary Shultz and Secretary Weinberger in particular distanced themselves from the march of events. Secretary Shultz specifically requested to be informed only as necessary to perform his job. Secretary Weinberger had access through intelligence to details about the operation. Their obligation was to give the President their full support and continued advice with respect to the program or, if they could not in conscience do that, to so inform the President. Instead, they simply distanced themselves from the program. They protected the record as to their own positions on this issue. They were not energetic in attempting to protect the President from the consequences of his personal commitment to freeing the hostages.

Director Casey appears to have been informed in considerable detail about the specifics of the Iranian operation. He appears to have acquiesced in and to have encouraged North's exercise of direct operational control over the operation. Because of the NSC staff's proximity to and close identification with the President, this increased the risks to the President if the initiative became public or the operation failed.

There is no evidence, however, that Director Casey explained this risk to the President or made clear to the President that LtCol North, rather than the CIA, was running the operation. The President does not recall ever being informed of this fact. Indeed, Director Casey should have gone further and pressed for operational responsibility to be transferred to the CIA.

Director Casey should have taken the lead in vetting the assumptions presented by the Israelis on which the program was based and in pressing for an early examination of the reliance upon Mr. Ghorbanifar and the second channel as intermediaries. He should also have assumed responsibility for checking out the other intermediaries involved in the operation. Finally, because Congressional restrictions on covert actions are both largely directed at and familiar to the CIA, Director Casey should have taken the lead in keeping the question of Congressional notification active.

Finally, Director Casey, and, to a lesser extent, Secretary Weinberger, should have taken it upon themselves to assess the effect of the transfer of arms and intelligence to Iran on the Iran/Iraq military balance, and to transmit that information to the President.

C. The Role of the Israelis

Conversations with emissaries from the Government of Israel took place prior to the commencement of the initiative. It remains unclear whether the initial proposal to open the Ghorbanifar channel was an Israeli initiative, was brought on by the avarice of arms dealers, or came as a result of an American request for assistance. There is no doubt, however, that it was Israel that pressed Mr. Ghorbanifar on the United States. U.S. officials accepted Israeli assurances that they had had for some time an extensive dialogue that involved high-level Iranians, as well as their assurances of Mr. Ghorbanifar's bona fides. Thereafter, at critical points in the initiative, when doubts were expressed by critical U.S. participants, an Israeli emissary would arrive with encouragement, often a specific proposal, and pressure to stay with the Ghorbanifar channel. . . .

It is clear, however, that Israel had its own interests, some in direct conflict with those of the United States, in having the United States pursue the initiative. For this reason, it had an incentive to keep the initiative alive. It sought to do this by interventions with the NSC staff, the National Security Advisor, and the President. Although it may have received suggestions from LtCol North, Mr. [Michael] Ledeen, and others, it responded affirmatively to these suggestions by reason of its own interests.

Even if the Government of Israel actively worked to begin the initiative and to keep it going, the U.S. Government is responsible for its own decisions. Key participants in U.S. deliberations made the point that Israel's objectives and interests in this initiative were different from, and in some respects in conflict with, those of the United States. Although Israel dealt with those portions of the U.S. Government that it deemed were sympathetic to the initiative, there is nothing improper *per se* about this fact. U.S. decision-makers made their own decisions and must bear responsibility for the consequences....

Part V. Recommendations

... Whereas the ultimate power to formulate domestic policy resides in the Congress, the primary responsibility for the formulation and implementation of national security policy falls on the President.

It is the President who is the usual source of innovation and responsiveness in this field. The departments and agencies—the Defense Department, State Department, and CIA bureaucracies—tend to resist policy change. Each has its own perspective based on long experience. The challenge for the President is to bring his perspective to bear on these bureaucracies for they are his instruments for executing national security policy, and he must work through them. His task is to provide them leadership and direction.

The National Security Act of 1947 and the system that has grown up under it affords the President special tools for carrying out this important role. These tools are the National Security Council, the National Security Advisor, and the NSC Staff. These are the means through which the creative impulses of the President are brought to bear on the permanent government. The National Security Act, and custom and practice, rightly give the President wide latitude in fashioning exactly how these means are used.

There is no magic formula which can be applied to the NSC structure and process to produce an optimal system. Because the system is the vehicle through which the President formulates and implements his national security policy, it must adapt to each individual President's style and management philosophy. This means that NSC structures and processes must be flexible, not rigid. Overprescription would ... either destroy the system or render it ineffective.

Nevertheless, this does not mean there can be no guidelines or recommendations that might improve the operation of the system, whatever the particular style of the incumbent President. We have reviewed the operation of the system over the past 40 years, through good times and bad.... With the strong caveat that flexibility and adaptability must be at the core, it is our judgment that the national security system seems to have worked best when it has in general operated along the lines set forth below.

Organizing for National Security

Because of the wide latitude in the National Security Act, the President bears a special responsibility for the effective performance of the NSC system. A President must at the outset provide guidelines to the members of the National Security Council, his National Security Advisor, and the National Security Council staff. These guidelines, to be effective, must include how they will relate to one another, what procedures will be followed, what the President expects of them. If his advisors are not performing as he likes, only the President can intervene.

The National Security Council principals other than the President participate on the Council in a unique capacity. Although holding a seat by virtue of their official positions in the Administration, when they sit as members of the Council they sit not as cabinet secretaries or department heads but as advisors to the President. They are there not simply to advance or defend the particular positions of the departments or agencies they head but to give their best advice to the President. Their job—and their challenge—is to see the issue from this perspective, not from the narrower interests of their respective bureaucracies.

The National Security Council is only advisory. It is the President alone who decides. When the NSC principals receive those decisions, they do so as heads of the appropriate departments or agencies. They are then responsible to see that the President's decisions are carried out by those organizations accurately and effectively.

This is an important point. The policy innovation and creativity of the President encounters a natural resistance from the executing departments. While this resistance is a source of frustration to every President, it is inherent in the design of the government. It is up to the politically appointed agency heads to ensure that the President's goals, designs, and policies are brought to bear on this permanent structure. Circumventing the departments, perhaps by using the National Security Advisor or the NSC Staff to execute policy, robs the President of the experience and capacity resident in the departments. The President must act largely through them, but the agency heads must ensure that they execute the President's policies in an expeditious and effective manner. It is not just the obligation of the National Security Advisor to see that the national security process is used. All of the NSC principals—and particularly the President—have that obligation.

This tension between the President and the Executive Departments is worked out through the national security process described in the opening sections of this report. It is through this process that the nation obtains both the best of the creativity of the President and the learning and expertise of the national security departments and agencies. . . .

The National Security Advisor

It is the National Security Advisor who is primarily responsible for managing this process on a daily basis. The job requires skill, sensitivity, and integrity. It is his responsibility to ensure that matters submitted for consideration by the Council cover the full range of issues on which review is required; that those issues are fully analyzed; that a full range of options is considered; that the prospects and risks of each are examined; that all relevant intelligence and other information is available to the principals; that legal considerations are addressed; that difficulties in implementation are confronted. Usually, this can best be accomplished through inter-agency participation in the analysis of the issue and a preparatory policy review at the Deputy or Under Secretary level.

The National Security Advisor assumes these responsibilities not only with respect to the President but with respect to all the NSC principals. He must keep them informed of the President's thinking and decisions. They should have adequate notice and an agenda for all meetings. Decision papers should, if at all possible, be provided in advance.

The National Security Advisor must also ensure that adequate records are kept of NSC consultations and Presidential decisions. This is essential to avoid confusion among Presidential advisors and departmental staffs about what was actually decided and what is wanted. Those records are also essential for conducting a periodic review of a policy or initiative, and to learn from the past.

It is the responsibility of the National Security Advisor to monitor policy implementation and to ensure that policies are executed in conformity with the intent of the President's decision. Monitoring includes initiating periodic reassessments of a policy or operation, especially when changed circumstances suggest that the policy or operation no longer serves U.S. interests.

But the National Security Advisor does not simply manage the national security process. He is himself an important source of advice on national security matters to the President. He is . . . perhaps the one most able to see things from the President's perspective. He is unburdened by departmental responsibilities. The President is his only master. His advice is confidential. He is not subject to Senate confirmation and traditionally does not formally appear before Congressional committees.

To serve the President well, the National Security Advisor should present his own views, but he must at the same time represent the views of others fully and faithfully to the President. The system will not work well if the National Security Advisor does not have the trust of the NSC principals. He, therefore, must not use his proximity to the President to manipulate the process so as to produce his own position. He should not interpose himself between the President and the NSC principals. He should not seek to exclude the NSC principals from the decision process. Performing both these roles well is an essential, if not easy, task.

In order for the National Security Advisor to serve the President adequately, he must have direct access to the President. Unless he knows first hand the views of the President and is known to reflect them in his management of the NSC system, he will be ineffective. He should not report to the President through some other official. While the Chief of Staff or others can usefully interject domestic political considerations into national security deliberations, they should do so as additional advisors to the President.

Ideally, the National Security Advisor should not have a high public profile. He should not try to compete with the Secretary of State or the Secretary of Defense as the articulator of public policy. They, along with the President, should be the spokesmen for the policies of the Administration. . .

The NSC principals of course must have direct access to the President, with whatever frequency the President feels is appropriate. But these individual meetings should not be used by the principal to seek decisions or otherwise circumvent the system in the absence of the other principals. In the same way, the National Security Advisor should not use his scheduled intelligence or other daily briefings of the President as an opportunity to seek Presidential decision on significant issues.

If the system is to operate well, the National Security Advisor must promote cooperation rather than competition among himself and the other NSC principals. But the President is ultimately responsible for the operation of this system. If rancorous infighting develops among his principal national security functionaries, only he can deal with them. Public dispute over external policy by senior officials undermines the process of decision-making and narrows his options. It is the President's responsibility to ensure that it does not take place.

Finally, the National Security Advisor should focus on advice and management, not implementation and execution. Implementation is the responsibility and the strength of the departments and agencies. The National Security Advisor and the NSC Staff generally do not have the depth of resources for the conduct of operations. In addition, when they take on implementation responsibilities, they risk compromising their objectivity. They can no longer act as impartial overseers of the implementation, ensuring that Presidential guidance is followed, that policies are kept under review, and that the results are serving the President's policy and the national interest.

The NSC Staff

The NSC staff should be small, highly competent, and experienced in the making of public policy. Staff members should be drawn both from within and from outside government. Those from within government should come from the several departments and agencies concerned with national security matters. No particular department or agency should have a predominate role. A proper balance must be maintained between people from within and outside the government. Staff members should generally rotate with a stay of more than four years viewed as the exception.

A large number of staff action officers organized along essentially horizontal lines enhances the possibilities for poorly supervised and monitored activities by individual staff members. Such a system is made to order for energetic self-starters to take unauthorized initiatives. Clear vertical lines of control and authority, responsibility and accountability, are essential to good management.

One problem affecting the NSC staff is lack of institutional memory. This results from the understandable desire of a President to replace the staff in order to be sure it is responsive to him. Departments provide continuity that can help the Council, but the Council as an institution also needs some means to assure adequate records and memory. . . .

We recognize the problem and have identified a range of possibilities that a President might consider on this subject. One would be to create a small permanent executive secretariat. Another would be to have one person, the Executive Secretary, as a permanent position. Finally, a pattern of limited tenure and overlapping rotation could be used. Any of these would help reduce the problem of loss of institutional memory; none would be practical unless each succeeding President subscribed to it.

The guidelines for the role of the National Security Advisor also apply generally to the NSC staff. They should protect the process and thereby the President. Departments and agencies should not be excluded from participation in that process. The staff should not be implementors or operators and staff should keep a low profile with the press.

Principal Recommendation

The model we have outlined above for the National Security Council system constitutes our first and most important recommendation. It includes guidelines that address virtually all of the deficiencies in procedure and practice that the Board encountered in the Iran/Contra affair as well as in other case studies of this and previous administrations....

The Board recommends that the proposed model be used by Presidents in their management of the national security system.

Specific Recommendations

In addition to its principal recommendation regarding the organization and functioning of the NSC system and roles to be played by the participants, the Board has a number of specific recommendations.

1. The National Security Act of 1947. The flaws of procedure and failures of responsibility revealed by our study do not suggest any inadequacies in the provisions of the National Security Act of 1947 that deal with the structure and operation of the NSC system. Forty years of experience under that Act demonstrate to the Board that it remains a fundamentally sound framework for national security decision-making. It strikes a balance between formal structure and flexibility adequate to permit each President to tailor the system to fit his needs.

As a general matter, the NSC Staff should not engage in the implementation of policy or the conduct of operations. This compromises their oversight role and usurps the responsibilities of the departments and agencies. But the inflexibility of a legislative restriction should be avoided. Terms such as "operation" and "implementation" are difficult to define, and a legislative proscription might preclude some future President from making a very constructive use of the NSC Staff.

Predisposition on sizing of the staff should be toward fewer rather than more. But a legislative restriction cannot forsee [*sic*] the requirements of future Presidents. Size is best left to the discretion of the President, with the admonition that the role of the NSC staff is to review, not to duplicate or replace, the work of the departments and agencies.

We recommend that no substantive change be made in the provisions of the National Security Act dealing with the structure and operation of the NSC system.

2. Senate Confirmation of the National Security Advisor. It has been suggested that the job of the National Security Advisor has become so important that its holder should be screened by the process of confirmation, and that once confirmed he should return frequently for questioning by the Congress. It is argued that this would improve the accountability of the National Security Advisor.

We hold a different view. The National Security Advisor does, and should continue, to serve only one master, and that is the President. Further, confirmation is inconsistent with the role the National Security Advisor should play. He should not decide, only advise. He should not engage in policy implementation or operations. He should serve the President, with no collateral and potentially diverting loyalties.

Confirmation would tend to institutionalize the natural tension that exists between the Secretary of State and the National Security Advisor. Questions would increasingly arise about who really speaks for the President in national security matters. Foreign governments could be confused or would be encouraged to engage in "forum shopping."

Only one of the former government officials interviewed favored Senate confirmation of the National Security Advisor. While consultation with Congress received wide support, confirmation and formal questioning were opposed. Several suggested that if the National Security Advisor were to become a position subject to confirmation, it could induce the President to turn to other internal staff or to people outside government to play that role.

We urge the Congress not to require Senate confirmation of the National Security Advisor.

3. The Interagency Process. It is the National Security Advisor who has the greatest interest in making the national security process work, for it is this process by which the President obtains the information, background, and analysis he requires to make decisions and build support for his program. Most Presidents have set up interagency committees at both a staff and policy level to surface issues, develop options, and clarify choices. There has typically been a struggle for the chairmanships of these groups between the National Security Advisor and the NSC staff on the one hand, and the cabinet secretaries and department officials on the other.

Our review of the operation of the present system and that of other administrations where committee chairmen came from the departments has led us to the conclusion that the system generally operates better when the committees are chaired by the individual with the greatest stake in making the NSC system work.

We recommend that the National Security Advisor chair the senior-level committees of the NSC system.

4. Covert Actions. Policy formulation and implementation are usually managed by a team of experts led by policymaking generalists. Covert action requirements are no different, but there is a need to limit, sometimes severely, the number of individuals involved. The lives of many people may be at stake, as was the case in the attempt to rescue the hostages in Tehran. Premature disclosure might kill the idea in embryo, as could have been the case in the opening of relations with China. In such cases, there is a tendency to limit those involved to a small number of top officials. This practice tends to limit severely the expertise brought to bear on the problem and should be used very sparingly indeed.

The obsession with secrecy and preoccupation with leaks threaten to paralyze the government in its handling of covert operations. Unfortunately, the concern is not misplaced. The selective leak has become a principal means of waging bureaucratic warfare. Opponents of an operation kill it with a leak; supporters seek to build support through the same means.

We have witnessed over the past years a significant deterioration in the integrity of process. Rather than a means to obtain results more satisfactory than the position of any of the individual departments, it has frequently become something to be manipulated to reach a specific outcome. The leak becomes a primary instrument in that process.

This practice is destructive of orderly governance. It can only be reversed if the most senior officials take the lead. If senior decision-makers set a clear example and demand compliance, subordinates are more likely to conform.

Most recent administrations have had carefully drawn procedures for the consideration of covert activities. The Reagan Administration established such procedures in January, 1985, then promptly ignored them in their consideration of the Iran initiative.

We recommend that each administration formulate precise procedures for restricted consideration of covert action and that, once formulated, those procedures be strictly adhered to.

5. The Role of the CIA. Some aspects of the Iran arms sales raised broader questions in the minds of members of the Board regarding the role of CIA. The first deals with intelligence.

The NSC staff was actively involved in the preparation of the May 20, 1985, update to the Special National Intelligence Estimate on Iran. It is a matter for concern if this involvement and the strong views of NSC staff members were allowed to influence the intelligence judgments contained in the update. It is also of concern that the update contained the hint that the United States should change its existing policy and encourage its allies to provide arms to Iran. It is critical that the line between intelligence and advocacy of a particular policy be preserved if intelligence is to retain its integrity and perform its proper function. In this instance, the CIA came close enough to the line to warrant concern.

We emphasize to both the intelligence community and policy-makers the importance of maintaining the integrity and objectivity of the intelligence process.

6. Legal Counsel. From time to time issues with important legal ramifications will come before the National Security Council. The Attorney General is currently a member of the Council by invitation and should be in a position to provide legal advice to the Council and the President. It is important that the Attorney General and his department be available to interagency deliberations.

The Justice Department, however, should not replace the role of counsel in the other departments. As the principal counsel on foreign affairs, the Legal Adviser to the Secretary of State should also be available to all the NSC participants.

Of all the NSC participants, it is the Assistant for National Security Affairs who seems to have had the least access to expert counsel familiar with his activities.

The Board recommends that the position of Legal Adviser to the NSC be enhanced in stature and in its role within the NSC staff.

7. Secrecy and Congress. There is a natural tension between the desire for secrecy and the need to consult Congress on covert operations. Presidents seem to become increasingly concerned about leaks of classified information as their administrations progress. They blame Congress disproportionately. Various cabinet officials from prior administrations indicated to the Board that they believe Congress bears no more blame than the Executive Branch. However, the number of Members and staff involved in reviewing covert activities is large; it provides cause for concern and a convenient excuse for Presidents to avoid Congressional consultation.

We recommend that Congress consider replacing the existing Intelligence Committees of the respective Houses with a new joint committee with a restricted staff to oversee the intelligence community, patterned after the Joint Committee on Atomic Energy that existed until the mid-1970s.

8. Privatizing National Security Policy. Careful and limited use of people outside the U.S. Government may be very helpful in some unique cases. But this practice raises substantial questions. It can create conflict of interest problems. Private or foreign sources may have different policy interests or personal motives and may exploit their association with a U.S.

government effort. Such involvement gives private and foreign sources potentially powerful leverage in the form of demands for return favors or even blackmail.

The U.S. has enormous resources invested in agencies and departments in order to conduct the government's business. In all but a very few cases, these can perform the functions needed. If not, then inquiry is required to find out why.

We recommend against having implementation and policy oversight dominated by intermediaries. We do not recommend barring limited use of private individuals to assist in United States diplomatic initiatives or in covert activities. We caution against use of such people except in very limited ways and under close observation and supervision....

March

COURT ON VICTIMS OF CONTAGIOUS DISEASES

March 3, 1987

The Supreme Court ruled 7-2 that Section 504 of the Rehabilitation Act of 1973 barred federally funded employers from discriminating against persons suffering from contagious diseases. The March 3 decision affected most public schools, hospitals, many state and local agencies, and all federal agencies and contractors. The ruling was a defeat for the Reagan administration, which had argued that persons with contagious diseases were not "handicapped" within the meaning of the law.

The Rehabilitation Act prohibited discrimination against any "otherwise qualified handicapped individual" participating in a federally funded program. In School Board of Nassau County, Florida v. Arline *the Court held that the law applied to a person "with a record of impairment [who] is also contagious." The Court also endorsed a friend-of-the-court brief filed by the American Medical Association that outlined the chief considerations in determining whether a person with a contagious disease is "otherwise qualified."*

Background

Gene Arline, a third grade teacher, contracted tuberculosis when she was fourteen years old. Told by her doctor that she was cured, she later considered it unnecessary to indicate her history of the disease on her application for employment by the public schools.

Arline taught from 1966 until she was discharged in 1979. Her dismissal came at the end of a two-year period during which she suffered three relapses of her disease. From 1977 to 1979 she was suspended with pay for some months but was allowed to return to her job when her doctor determined that she was not contagious. Arline was dismissed on the basis of testimony by the superintendent of schools that her presence in the school community threatened the health of her pupils and colleagues.

Decision and Dissent

The Court's ruling notified employers receiving federal funds that "persons with actual or perceived contagious diseases" could be considered "handicapped" under the law. These employees were therefore due the same job protection as those with more obvious physical handicaps such as blindness.

Writing for the majority, Justice William J. Brennan, Jr., emphasized that the "basic purpose" of Section 504 "is to ensure that handicapped individuals are not denied jobs or other benefits because of the prejudiced attitudes or the ignorance of others," and referred specifically to "society's accumulated myths and fears about disability and disease."

The Court then considered whether Arline was "otherwise qualified" under the law for her post and remanded the case to the district court. The opinion stated that employees were entitled to a hearing to make findings of facts, based on reasonable medical judgments of public health officials on the severity of the disease and the probability that it could be transmitted to others.

Chief Justice William H. Rehnquist, joined in dissent by Justice Antonin Scalia, defined the key issue as "whether discrimination on the basis of contagiousness" is covered under the act's definition of "handicapped." He argued that "the language of the Act ... and legislative history are silent on this issue," and therefore that the Court's "own sense of fairness and implied support for the Act" did not provide sufficient grounds to support the conclusion of the majority.

Application to Carriers of AIDS Virus

Although the case pertained specifically to an employee with a recurrent case of tuberculosis, the ruling applied generally to people with any contagious disease. The decision was widely regarded as signaling the Court's thinking on AIDS. Civil liberties and homosexual rights groups praised the decision as an important victory, and noted in particular that the decision repudiated a 1986 Justice Department memorandum that sanctioned federal contractors to dismiss an employee solely because they feared that the employee might be contagious.

Spokespersons for these groups expressed disappointment, however, that the Court left open the question of "whether a carrier of a contagious disease such as AIDS" qualified as a "handicapped" person under the act. The status of persons dismissed from their jobs because they tested positive to exposure to the AIDS virus, even if they showed no obvious physical impairment, was left undetermined.

The Court stated that persons who posed "a significant risk of communicating an infectious disease to others in the workplace" might not be considered "otherwise qualified" for employment. The ruling held that "the Act would not require a school board to place a teacher with active, contagious tuberculosis in a classroom."

Following are excerpts from the Supreme Court's March 3, 1987, decision in School Board of Nassau County, Florida v. Arline, *that barred federally funded employers from discriminating against "otherwise qualified" individuals suffering from contagious diseases; and from the dissent of Chief Justice William H. Rehnquist:*

No. 85-1277

School Board of Nassau County, Florida and Craig Marsh, Individually and as Superintendent of Schools of Nassau County, Florida *v.* Gene H. Arline	On writ of certiorari to the United States Court of Appeals for the Eleventh Circuit

[March 3, 1987]

JUSTICE BRENNAN delivered the opinion of the Court.

Section 504 of the Rehabilitation Act of 1973, 87 Stat. 394, as amended, 29 U.S.C. § 794 (Act), prohibits a federally funded state program from discriminating against a handicapped individual solely by reason of his or her handicap. This case presents the questions whether a person afflicted with tuberculosis, a contagious disease, may be considered a "handicapped individual" within the meaning of § 504 of the Act, and, if so, whether such an individual is "otherwise qualified" to teach elementary school.

I

From 1966 until 1979, respondent Gene Arline taught elementary school in Nassau County, Florida. She was discharged in 1979 after suffering a third relapse of tuberculosis within two years. After she was denied relief in state administrative proceedings, she brought suit in federal court, alleging that the School Board's decision to dismiss her because of her tuberculosis violated § 504 of the Act....

In her trial memorandum, Arline argued that it was "not disputed that the [School Board dismissed her] solely on the basis of her illness. Since the illness in this case qualifies the Plaintiff as a 'handicapped person' it is clear that she was dismissed solely as a result of her handicap in violation of Section 504." The District Court held, however, that although there was "[n]o question that she suffers a handicap," Arline was nevertheless not "a handicapped person under the terms of that statute." The court found it "difficult . . . to conceive that Congress intended contagious diseases to be included within the definition of a handicapped person." The court then went on to state that, "even assuming" that a person with a contagious disease could be deemed a handicapped person, Arline was not "qualified" to teach elementary school.

The Court of Appeals reversed, holding that "persons with contagious diseases are within the coverage of section 504," and that Arline's condition "falls . . . neatly within the statutory and regulatory framework" of the Act. . . .

II

. . . Section 504 of the Rehabilitation Act reads in pertinent part:

> "No otherwise qualified handicapped individual in the United States, as defined in section 706(7) of this title, shall, solely by reason of his handicap, be excluded from participation in, be denied the benefits of, or be subjected to discrimination under any program or activity receiving Federal financial assistance. . . ." 29 U.S.C. § 794.

In 1974 Congress expanded the definition of "handicapped individuals" for use in § 504 to read as follows:

> "[A]ny person who (i) has a physical or mental impairment which substantially limits one or more of such person's major life activities, (ii) has a record of such an impairment, or (iii) is regarded as having such an impairment." 29 U.S.C. § 706(7)(B).

The amended definition reflected Congress' concern with protecting the handicapped against discrimination stemming not only from simple prejudice, but from "archaic attitudes and laws" and from "the fact that the American people are simply unfamiliar with and insensitive to the difficulties confront[ing] individuals with handicaps.". . .

III

Within this statutory and regulatory framework, then, we must consider whether Arline can be considered a handicapped individual. According to the testimony of Dr. McEuen, Arline suffered tuberculosis "in an acute form in such a degree that it affected her respiratory system," and was hospitalized for this condition. Arline thus had a physical impairment as that term is defined by the regulations. . . . This impairment was serious enough to require hospitalization, a fact more than sufficient to establish that one or more of her major life activities were substantially limited by her impairment. . . . Arline's hospitalization for tuberculosis in 1957 suffices to establish that she . . . is therefore a handicapped individual. . . .

We do not agree with petitioners that, in defining a handicapped individual under § 504, the contagious effects of a disease can be meaningfully distinguished from the disease's physical effects on a claimant in a case such as this. Arline's contagiousness and her physical impairment each resulted from the same underlying condition, tuberculosis. It would be unfair to allow an employer to seize upon the distinction between the effects of a disease on others and the effects of a disease on a patient and use that distinction to justify discriminatory treatment.[1] . . .

Allowing discrimination based on the contagious effects of a physical impairment would be inconsistent with the basic purpose of § 504, which is to ensure that handicapped individuals are not denied jobs or other benefits because of the prejudiced attitudes or the ignorance of others. By amending the definition of "handicapped individual" to include not only those who are actually physically impaired, but also those who are regarded as impaired and who, as a result, are substantially limited in a major life activity, Congress acknowledged that society's accumulated myths and fears about disability and disease are as handicapping as are the physical limitations that flow from actual impairment. Few aspects of a handicap give rise to the same level of public fear and misapprehension as contagiousness. Even those who suffer or have recovered from such noninfectious diseases as epilepsy or cancer have faced discrimination based on the irrational fear that they might be contagious. The Act is carefully structured to replace such reflexive reactions to actual or perceived handicaps with actions based on reasoned and medically sound judgments: the definition of "handicapped individual" is broad, but only those individuals who are both handicapped *and* otherwise qualified are eligible for relief. The fact that *some* persons who have contagious diseases may pose a serious health threat to others under certain circumstances does not justify excluding from the coverage of the Act *all* persons with actual or perceived contagious diseases. . . . We conclude that the fact that a person with a record of a physical impairment is also contagious does not suffice to remove that person from coverage under § 504.

IV

The remaining question is whether Arline is otherwise qualified for the job of elementary school teacher. To answer this question in most cases, the District Court will need to conduct an individualized inquiry and make appropriate findings of fact. Such an inquiry is essential if § 504 is to

[1] The United States argues that it is possible for a person to be simply a carrier of a disease, that is, to be capable of spreading a disease without having a "physical impairment" or suffering from any other symptoms associated with the disease. The United States contends that this [is] true in the case of some carriers of the Acquired Immune Deficiency Syndrome (AIDS) virus. From this premise the United States concludes that discrimination solely on the basis of contagiousness is never discrimination on the basis of a handicap. The argument is misplaced in this case, because the handicap here, tuberculosis, gave rise both to a physical impairment *and* to contagiousness. This case does not present, and we therefore do not reach, the questions whether a carrier of a contagious disease such as AIDS could be considered to have a physical impairment, or whether such a person could be considered, solely on the basis of contagiousness, a handicapped person as defined by the Act.

achieve its goal of protecting handicapped individuals from deprivations based on prejudice, stereotypes, or unfounded fear, while giving appropriate weight to such legitimate concerns of grantees as avoiding exposing others to significant health and safety risks.[2] The basic factors to be considered in conducting this inquiry are well established. In the context of the employment of a person handicapped with a contagious disease, we agree with *amicus* American Medical Association that this inquiry should include:

> "[findings of] facts, based on reasonable medical judgments given the state of medical knowledge, about (a) the nature of the risk (how the disease is transmitted), (b) the duration of the risk (how long is the carrier infectious), (c) the severity of the risk (what is the potential harm to third parties) and (d) the probabilities the disease will be transmitted and will cause varying degrees of harm."

In making these findings, courts normally should defer to the reasonable medical judgments of public health officials.[3] The next step in the "otherwise-qualified" inquiry is for the court to evaluate, in light of these medical findings, whether the employer could reasonably accommodate the employee under the established standards for that inquiry....

V

We hold that a person suffering from the contagious disease of tuberculosis can be a handicapped person within the meaning of the § 504 of the Rehabilitation Act of 1973, and that respondent Arline is such a person. We remand the case to the District Court to determine whether Arline is otherwise qualified for her position. The judgment of the Court of Appeals is

Affirmed.

CHIEF JUSTICE REHNQUIST, with whom JUSTICE SCALIA joins, dissenting.

In *Pennhurst State School and Hospital* v. *Halderman* (1981), this Court made clear that, where Congress intends to impose a condition on the grant of federal funds, "it must do so unambiguously." This principle applies with full force to § 504 of the Rehabilitation Act, which Congress limited in scope to "those who actually 'receive' federal financial assistance." *United States Department of Transportation* v. *Paralyzed Veterans* (1986). Yet, the Court today ignores this principle, resting its holding on its own sense of fairness and implied support from the Act. Such an ap-

---

[2] A person who poses a significant risk of communicating an infectious disease to others in the workplace will not be otherwise qualified for his or her job if reasonable accommodation will not eliminate that risk. The Act would not require a school board to place a teacher with active, contagious tuberculosis in a classroom with elementary school children. Respondent conceded as much at oral argument. Tr. of Oral Arg. 45.

[3] This case does not present, and we do not address, the question whether courts should also defer to the reasonable medical judgments of private physicians on which an employer has relied.

proach, I believe, is foreclosed not only by *Pennhurst,* but also by our prior decisions interpreting the Rehabilitation Act.

Our decision in *Pennhurst* was premised on the view that federal legislation imposing obligations only on recipients of federal funds is "much in the nature of a contract." See also *Board of Education of Hendrick Hudson Central School District* v. *Rowley* (1982). As we have stated in the context of the Rehabilitation Act, " 'Congress apparently determined it would require . . . grantees to bear the costs of providing employment for the handicapped as a *quid pro quo* for the receipt of federal funds.' " *United States Department of Transportation* v. *Paralyzed Veterans,* quoting *Consolidated Rail Corporation* v. *Darrone* (1984). The legitimacy of this *quid pro quo* rests on whether recipients of federal funds voluntarily and knowingly accept the terms of the exchange. *Pennhurst.* There can be no knowing acceptance unless Congress speaks "with a clear voice" in identifying the conditions attached to the receipt of funds.

The requirement that Congress unambiguously express conditions imposed on federal moneys is particularly compelling in cases such as this where there exists long-standing state and federal regulation of the subject matter. From as early as 1796, Congress has legislated directly in the area of contagious diseases. Congress has also, however, left significant leeway to the States, which have enacted a myriad of public health statutes designed to protect against the introduction and spread of contagious diseases. When faced with such extensive regulation, this Court has declined to read the Rehabilitation Act expansively. See *Bowen* v. *American Hospital Assn.* (1986); *Alexander* v. *Choate* (1985). Absent an expression of intent to the contrary, "Congress . . . 'will not be deemed to have significantly changed the federal state balance.' " *Bowen* v. *American Hospital Assn.,* quoting *United States* v. *Bass* (1971).

Applying these principles, I conclude that the Rehabilitation Act cannot be read to support the result reached by the Court. The record in this case leaves no doubt that Arline was discharged because of the contagious nature of tuberculosis, and not because of any diminished physical or mental capabilities resulting from her condition. Thus, in the language of § 504, the central question here is whether discrimination on the basis of contagiousness constitutes discrimination "by reason of . . . handicap." Because the language of the Act, regulations, and legislative history are silent on this issue, the principles outlined above compel the conclusion that contagiousness is not a handicap within the meaning of § 504. It is therefore clear that the protections of the Act do not extend to individuals such as Arline.

In reaching a contrary conclusion, the Court never questions that Arline was discharged because of the threat her condition posed to others. Instead, it posits that the contagious effects of a disease cannot be "meaningfully" distinguished from the disease's effect on a claimant under the Act. To support this position, the Court observes that Congress intended to extend the Act's protections to individuals who have a condition that does not impair their mental and physical capabilities, but limits their major life activities because of the adverse reactions of others. This congressional recognition of a handicap resulting from the reactions of others, we are told, reveals that Congress intended the Rehabilitation Act to regulate discrimination on the basis of contagiousness.

This analysis misses the mark in several respects. To begin with, Congress' recognition that an individual may be handicapped under the Act solely by reason of the reactions of others in no way demonstrates that, for the purposes of interpreting the Act, the reactions of others to the condition cannot be considered separately from the effects of the condition on the claimant. In addition, the Court provides no basis for extending the Act's generalized coverage of individuals suffering discrimination as a result of the reactions of others to coverage of individuals with contagious diseases. Although citing examples of handicapped individuals described in the regulations and legislative history, the Court points to nothing in these materials suggesting that Congress contemplated that a person with a condition posing a threat to the health of others may be considered handicapped under the Act. Even in an ordinary case of statutory construction, such meager proof of congressional intent would not be determinative. The Court's evidence, therefore, could not possibly provide the basis for "knowing acceptance" by such entities as the Nassau County School Board that their receipt of federal funds is conditioned on Rehabilitation Act regulation of public health issues. *Pennhurst.*

In *Alexander* v. *Choate* this Court stated that "[a]ny interpretation of § 504 must . . . be responsive to two powerful but countervailing considerations—the need to give effect to the statutory objectives and the desire to keep § 504 within manageable bounds." The Court has wholly disregarded this admonition here.

COURT ON POLITICAL ASYLUM

March 9, 1987

In a ruling that nearly coincided with the enactment of sweeping changes in the nation's immigration laws, the Supreme Court March 9 made it easier for aliens who feared prosecution in their homeland to receive political asylum in the United States. The 6-3 decision, which was opposed by the Reagan administration, stated that an alien who demonstrated a "well-founded fear" of persecution on return to his native land could be eligible for asylum in the United States. The ruling cut down the administration's argument that such asylum could be granted only upon proof of a "clear probability" that an alien would face torture, death, or other severe persecution if he returned home.

Justice John Paul Stevens, writing for the Court, commented that the test for asylum applicants was too stiff. "In enacting the Refugee Act of 1980, Congress sought to give the United States sufficient flexibility to respond to situations involving political or religious dissidents and detainees throughout the world. Our holding today increases that flexibility." Stevens continued: "Whether or not a 'refugee' is eventually granted asylum is a matter which Congress has left for the attorney general to decide. But it is clear that Congress did not intend to restrict eligibility for that relief to those who could prove that it is more likely than not that they will be persecuted if deported." Stevens was joined by Justices William J. Brennan, Jr., Thurgood Marshall, Harry A. Blackmun, Sandra Day O'Connor, and—with a separate opinion—Antonin Scalia.

Justice Lewis F. Powell, Jr., dissented from the majority; he was joined by Chief Justice William H. Rehnquist and Justice Byron R. White. They agreed with the administration's argument that the "clear probability" standard that was used in deportation cases was equally applicable in asylum cases—thereby contradicting the majority view that Congress intended a less restrictive standard in asylum cases.

Facts of the Case

The case before the Court, Immigration and Naturalization Service v. Luz Marina Cardoza-Fonseca, *involved a larger issue—the plight of thousands of Central Americans who had sought refuge in the United States from political wars and unrest in El Salvador and Nicaragua. The administration had granted legal permission to stay to only a small percentage of applicants. Many others stayed illegally, harbored in some cases by U.S. churches and citizens active in the "sanctuary" movement.*

Luz Marina Cardoza-Fonseca, a Nicaraguan citizen, had come to the United States in 1979 as a visitor. She overstayed her visa, and when the Immigration and Naturalization Service (INS) moved to deport her, she invoked two provisions of the 1980 Refugee Act. The first required the attorney general to withhold deportation of an alien who demonstrated that his or her life or freedom would be threatened by deportation. The second permitted the attorney general to grant asylum to a refugee who did not wish to return home because of a "well-founded fear" of persecution. A similar provision had been added to the immigration reform bill by the House in 1986, but had been dropped from the final version of the bill. (Historic Documents of 1986, p. 963)

In presenting her case, Cardoza-Fonseca argued that because her brother, an opponent of the Sandinista government, had been imprisoned and tortured before they left Nicaragua, she would be interrogated and persecuted about his whereabouts if she returned. At her hearing, the immigration judge applied the standard for withholding deportation—a clear probability of persecution—to her request for asylum and denied her application. The Board of Immigration Appeals upheld that decision, but the U.S. Court of Appeals for the Ninth Circuit reversed it.

Decision and Dissent

The appeals court held that two different standards governed decisions under the two provisions of the law, and the Supreme Court agreed. "Congress did not intend the two standards to be identical," wrote Stevens. "Congress never intended to restrict eligibility for asylum to aliens who can satisfy" the stiffer standard for avoiding deportation. The Court also dismissed the government's contention that it should defer to the INS interpretation of the matter. Such deference was not appropriate, wrote Stevens, when the wording of the law was so clear. Stevens suggested that a person with "a 10 percent chance of being shot, tortured or otherwise persecuted" might qualify for asylum. Because the statutory test was "a well-founded fear of persecution," the alien's "subjective mental state" was important, but only as determined by individual cases. Thus, determinations by the attorney general still would be decisive in grants of asylum. Blackmun, in a concurring opinion, criticized the INS for "years of seemingly purposeful blindness" to the meaning of the law.

Dissenting, Powell said the government's interpretation of the law was "reasonable" and should have been upheld, thereby supporting the government's position that the legal standard for determining eligibility for asylum was the same as that used to determine an alien's right not to be deported to a particular country. In 1984 the Court had held that the "clear probability" standard should apply in such deportation cases.

Reaction, Outlook, and the Law

Assessments of the impact of the Court ruling were mixed. A General Accounting Office (GAO) study found that only 2 percent of aliens denied asylum actually were deported from the United States. In 1986 the government received 18,889 applications for asylum, granted 3,359 and denied 7,822, with the rest pending. The GAO noted that the government generally did not give reason for approval or denial of applications.

Although its effect was limited by the fact that the attorney general still would retain authority to rule on individual cases, the decision was termed "tremendously significant" by Ira J. Kurban, an immigration lawyer who was president-elect of the American Immigration Lawyers' Association, in a March 10 New York Times *article. "It recognizes at least implicitly the difficulty that asylum applicants have in proving their claims, so more people will be eligible for asylum who should be eligible."*

Gilbert Paul Carrasco, associate director of migration and refugee services for the U.S. Catholic Conference, concurred that it would be "easier for aliens to prove their eligibility for asylum," and predicted an increase in the number of applicants. Noting that, "from a symbolic point of view, the decision is a significant victory for human rights advocates, civil libertarians and workers in the [refugee] sanctuary movement," Wade J. Henderson of the American Civil Liberties Union cautioned: "[I]t will not be a panacea because the attorney general retains discretion to decide when asylum should be granted." Henderson, among others, recommended that Congress pass legislation temporarily suspending the deportation of persons from El Salvador and Nicaragua until conditions in those countries were further studied. But the administration opposed the idea on grounds that many refugees from those nations were seeking better economic opportunities rather than escaping political persecution.

The Court's decision was handed down two months before a major revision in the nation's immigration law took effect May 5. The legislation, drafted after years of controversy that cut across party and regional lines, was extremely complex, with undetermined consequences. Basically, it had three major parts: new penalties—fines and, in extreme cases, prison terms—against employers who knowingly hired illegal aliens; legal status for aliens in the United States who could meet specified criteria; and legal status for thousands of foreign farm workers who had worked at least 90 days in American agriculture between May 1985 and May 1986. Even before the legislation went into effect, numerous lawsuits had been filed challenging parts of it.

Following are excerpts from the Supreme Court's March 9, 1987, decision in Immigration and Naturalization Service v. Luz Marina Cardoza-Fonseca, *with excerpts from the dissent of Justice Lewis F. Powell, Jr.:*

No. 85-782

Immigration and Naturalization Service, Petitioner *v.* Luz Marina Cardoza-Fonseca	On writ of certiorari to the United States Court of Appeals for the Ninth Circuit

[March 9, 1987]

JUSTICE STEVENS delivered the opinion of the Court.

Since 1980, the Immigration and Nationality Act has provided two methods through which an otherwise deportable alien who claims that he will be persecuted if deported can seek relief. Section 243(h) of the Act, 8 U.S.C. §1253(h), requires the Attorney General to withhold deportation of an alien who demonstrates that his "life or freedom would be threatened" on account of one of the listed factors if he is deported. In *INS* v. *Stevic* (1984), we held that to qualify for this entitlement to withholding of deportation, an alien must demonstrate that "it is more likely than not that the alien would be subject to persecution" in the country to which he would be returned. The Refugee Act of 1980, 94 Stat. 102, also established a second type of broader relief. Section 208(a) of the Act, 8 U.S.C. §1158(a), authorizes the Attorney General, in his discretion, to grant asylum to an alien who is unable or unwilling to return to his home country "because of persecution or a well-founded fear of persecution on account of race, religion, nationality, membership in a particular social group, or political opinion."

In *Stevic,* we rejected an alien's contention that the §208(a) "well-founded fear" standard governs applications for withholding of deportation under §243(h). Similarly, today we reject the Government's contention that the §243(h) standard, which requires an alien to show that he is more likely than not to be subject to persecution, governs applications for asylum under §208(a). Congress used different, broader language to define the term "refugee" as used in §208(a) than it used to describe the class of aliens who have a right to withholding of deportation under §243(h). The Act's establishment of a broad class of refugees who are eligible for a discretionary grant of asylum, and a narrower class of aliens who are given a statutory right not to be deported to the country where they are in danger, mirrors the provisions of the United Nations Protocol Relating to the Status of Refugees, which provided the motivation for the enactment of the Refugee Act of 1980. In addition, the legislative history of the 1980 Act makes it perfectly clear that Congress did not intend the class of aliens who qualify as refugees to be coextensive with the class who qualify for §243(h) relief.

I

Respondent is a 38-year-old Nicaraguan citizen who entered the United States in 1979 as a visitor. After she remained in the United States longer than permitted, and failed to take advantage of the Immigration and Naturalization Service's (INS) offer of voluntary departure, the INS commenced deportation proceedings against her. Respondent conceded that she was in the country illegally, but requested withholding of deportation pursuant to §243(h), and asylum as a refugee pursuant to §208(a).

To support her request under §243(h), respondent attempted to show that if she were returned to Nicaragua her "life or freedom would be threatened" on account of her political views; to support her request under §208(a), she attempted to show that she had a "well-founded fear of persecution" upon her return. The evidence supporting both claims related primarily to the activities of respondent's brother who had been tortured and imprisoned because of his political activities in Nicaragua. Both respondent and her brother testified that they believed the Sandinistas knew that the two of them had fled Nicaragua together and that even though she had not been active politically herself, she would be interrogated about her brother's whereabouts and activities. Respondent also testified that because of her brother's status, her own political opposition to the Sandinistas would be brought to that government's attention. Based on these facts, respondent claimed that she would be tortured if forced to return.

The Immigration Judge applied the same standard in evaluating respondent's claim for withholding of deportation under §243(h) as he did in evaluating her application for asylum under §208(a). He found that she had not established "a clear probability of persecution" and therefore was not entitled to either form of relief. On appeal, the Board of Immigration Appeals (BIA) agreed that the respondent had "failed to establish that she would suffer persecution within the meaning of section 208(a) or 243(h) of the Immigration and Nationality Act."

In the Court of Appeals for the Ninth Circuit, respondent did not challenge the BIA's decision that she was not entitled to withholding of deportation under §243(h), but argued that she was eligible for asylum under §208(a), and contended that the Immigration Judge and BIA erred in applying the "more likely than not" standard of proof from §243(h) to her §208(a) asylum claim. Instead, she asserted, they should have applied the "well-founded fear" standard, which she considered to be more generous. The court agreed. Relying on both the text and the structure of the Act, the court held that the "well-founded fear" standard which governs asylum proceedings is different, and in fact more generous, than the "clear probability" standard which governs withholding of deportation proceedings. Agreeing with the Court of Appeals for the Seventh Circuit, the court interpreted the standard to require asylum applicants to present " 'specific facts' through objective evidence to prove either past persecution or 'good reason' to fear future persecution."... The court remanded respondent's asylum claim to the BIA to evaluate under the proper legal standard. We granted certiorari to resolve a circuit conflict on this important question.

II

The Refugee Act of 1980 established a new statutory procedure for granting asylum to refugees. The 1980 Act added a new §208(a) to the Immigration and Naturalization Act of 1952, reading as follows:

> "The Attorney General shall establish a procedure for an alien physically present in the United States or at a land border or port of entry, irrespective of such alien's status, to apply for asylum, and the alien may be granted asylum in the discretion of the Attorney General if the Attorney General determines that such alien is a refugee within the meaning of section 1101(a)(42)(A) of this title."

Under this section, eligibility for asylum depends entirely on the Attorney General's determination that an alien is a "refugee," as that term is defined in §101(a)(42), which was also added to the Act in 1980. That section provides:

> "The term 'refugee' means (A) any person who is outside any country of such person's nationality or, in the case of a person having no nationality, is outside any country in which such person last habitually resided, and who is unable or unwilling to return to, and is unable or unwilling to avail himself or herself of the protection of, that country because of persecution or a well-founded fear of persecution on account of race, religion, nationality, membership in a particular social group, or political opinion...."

Thus, the "persecution or well-founded fear of persecution" standard governs the Attorney General's determination whether an alien is eligible for asylum.

In addition to establishing a statutory asylum process, the 1980 Act amended the withholding of deportation provision, §243(h).... Prior to 1968, the Attorney General had discretion whether to grant withholding of deportation to aliens under §243(h). In 1968, however, the United States agreed to comply with the substantive provisions of Articles 2 thru 34 of the 1951 United Nations Convention Relating to the Status of Refugees. . . . Article 33.1 of the Convention, which is the counterpart of §243(h) of our statute, imposed a mandatory duty on contracting States not to return an alien to a country where his "life or freedom would be threatened" on account of one of the enumerated reasons. Thus, although §243(h) itself did not constrain the Attorney General's discretion after 1968, presumably he honored the dictates of the United Nations Convention. In any event, the 1980 Act removed the Attorney General's discretion in §243(h) proceedings.

In *Stevic* we considered it significant that in enacting the 1980 Act Congress did not amend the standard of eligibility for relief under §243(h). While the terms "refugee" and hence "well-founded fear" were made an integral part of the §208(a) procedure, they continued to play no part in §243(h). Thus we held that the prior consistent construction of §243(h) that required an applicant for withholding of deportation to demonstrate a "clear probability of persecution" upon deportation remained in force. Of course, this reasoning, based in large part on the plain language of §243(h), is of no avail here since §208(a) expressly provides that the "well founded fear" standard governs eligibility for asylum.

The Government argues, however, that even though the "well-founded fear" standard is applicable, there is no difference between it and the "would be threatened" test of §243(h). It asks us to hold that the only way an applicant can demonstrate a "well founded fear of persecution" is to prove a "clear probability of persecution." The statutory language does not lend itself to this reading.

To begin with, the language Congress used to describe the two standards conveys very different meanings. The "would be threatened" language of §243(h) has no subjective component, but instead requires the alien to establish by objective evidence that it is more likely than not that he or she will be subject to persecution upon deportation. . . . In contrast, the reference to "fear" in the §208(a) standard obviously makes the eligibility determination turn to some extent on the subjective mental state of the alien. "The linguistic difference between the words 'well-founded fear' and 'clear probability' may be as striking as that between a subjective and an objective frame of reference. . . . We simply cannot conclude that the standards are identical.". . . *Guevara Flores* v. *INS* (CA5 1986).

That the fear must be "well-founded" does not alter the obvious focus on the individual's subjective beliefs, nor does it transform the standard into a "more likely than not" one. One can certainly have a well-founded fear of an event happening when there is less than a 50% chance of the occurrence taking place. . . .

The different emphasis of the two standards which is so clear on the face of the statute is significantly highlighted by the fact that the same Congress simultaneously drafted §208(a) and amended §243(h). . . . Congress chose to maintain the old standard in §243(h), but to incorporate a different standard in §208(a). "Where Congress includes particular language in one section of a statute but omits it in another section of the same Act, it is generally presumed that Congress acts intentionally and purposely in the disparate inclusion or exclusion." *Russello* v. *United States* (1983). The contrast between the language used in the two standards, and the fact that Congress used a new standard to define the term "refugee," certainly indicate that Congress intended the two standards to differ.

III

The message conveyed by the plain language of the Act is confirmed by an examination of its history. Three aspects of that history are particularly compelling: The pre-1980 experience under §203(a)(7), the only prior statute dealing with asylum; the abundant evidence of an intent to conform the definition of "refugee" and our asylum law to the United Nations Protocol to which the United States has been bound since 1968; and the fact that Congress declined to enact the Senate version of the bill that would have made a refugee ineligible for asylum unless "his deportation or return would be prohibited by §243(h)."...

IV

The Government makes two major arguments to support its contention that we should reverse the Court of Appeals and hold that an applicant can only show a "well-founded fear of persecution" by proving that it is more likely than not that he or she will be persecuted. We reject both of these arguments: the first ignores the structure of the Act; the second misconstrues the federal court's role in reviewing an agency's statutory construction.

First, the Government repeatedly argues that the structure of the Act dictates a decision in its favor, since it is anomalous for §208(a), which affords greater benefits than §243(h), to have a less stringent standard of eligibility. This argument sorely fails because it does not take into account the fact that an alien who satisfies the applicable standard under §208(a) does not have a *right* to remain in the United States; he or she is simply *eligible* for asylum, if the Attorney General, in his discretion, chooses to grant it. An alien satisfying §243(h)'s stricter standard, in contrast, is automatically entitled to withholding of deportation. In *Matter of Salim* (1982), for example, the [Immigration] Board held that the alien was eligible for both asylum and withholding of deportation, but granted him the more limited remedy only, exercising its discretion to deny him asylum.... We do not consider it at all anomalous that out of the entire class of "refugees," those who can show a clear probability of persecution are *entitled* to mandatory suspension of deportation and *eligible* for discretionary asylum, while those who can only show a well-founded fear of persecution are not *entitled* to anything, but are *eligible* for the discretionary relief of asylum.

There is no basis for the Government's assertion that the

discretionary/mandatory distinction has no practical significance.... Moreover, the 1980 Act amended §243(h) for the very purpose of changing it from a discretionary to a mandatory provision. Congress surely considered the discretionary/mandatory distinction important then, as it did with respect to the very definition of "refugee" involved here. The House Report provides:

> The Committee carefully considered arguments that the new definition might expand the numbers of refugees eligible to come to the United States and force substantially greater refugee admissions than the country could absorb. However, merely because an individual or group comes within the definition will not guarantee resettlement in the United States." H. R. Rep. 10 (1979).

This vesting of discretion in the Attorney General is quite typical in the immigration area.... If anything is anomalous, it is that the Government now asks us to restrict its discretion to a narrow class of aliens. Congress has assigned to the Attorney General and his delegates the task of making these hard individualized decisions; although Congress could have crafted a narrower definition, it chose to authorize the Attorney General to determine which, if any, eligible refugees should be denied asylum.

The Government's second principal argument in support of the proposition that the "well founded fear" and "clear probability" standard are equivalent is that the BIA so construes the two standards. The Government argues that the BIA's construction of the Refugee Act of 1980 is entitled to substantial deference, even if we conclude that the Court of Appeals' reading of the statutes is more in keeping with Congress' intent. This argument is unpersuasive.

The question whether Congress intended the two standards to be identical is a pure question of statutory construction for the courts to decide. Employing traditional tools of statutory construction, we have concluded that Congress did not intend the two standards to be identical....

The narrow legal question whether the two standards are the same is, of course, quite different from the question of interpretation that arises in each case in which the agency is required to apply either or both standards to a particular set of facts. There is obviously some ambiguity in a term like "well-founded fear" which can only be given concrete meaning through a process of case-by-case adjudication. In that process of filling " 'any gap left, implicitly or explicitly, by Congress,' " the courts must respect the interpretation of the agency to which Congress has delegated the responsibility for administering the statutory program. But our task today is much narrower, and is well within the province of the judiciary. We do not attempt to set forth a detailed description of how the well-founded fear test should be applied. Instead, we merely hold that the Immigration Judge and the BIA were incorrect in holding that the two standards are identical.

Our analysis of the plain language of the Act, its symmetry with the United Nations Protocol, and its legislative history, lead inexorably to the conclusion that to show a "well-founded fear of persecution," an alien need not prove that it is more likely than not that he or she will be persecuted in his or her home country....

Deportation is always a harsh measure; it is all the more replete with danger when the alien makes a claim that he or she will be subject to death or persecution if forced to return to his or her home country. In enacting the Refugee Act of 1980 Congress sought to "give the United States sufficient flexibility to respond to situations involving political or religious dissidents and detainees throughout the world." Our holding today increases the flexibility by rejecting the Government's contention that the Attorney General may not even consider granting asylum to one who fails to satisfy the strict §243(h) standard. Whether or not a "refugee" is eventually granted asylum is a matter which Congress has left for the Attorney General to decide. But it is clear that Congress did not intend to restrict eligibility for that relief to those who could prove that it is more likely than not that they will be persecuted if deported.

The judgment of the Court of Appeals is

Affirmed.

JUSTICE POWELL, with whom THE CHIEF JUSTICE and JUSTICE WHITE join, dissenting.

Many people come to our country because they fear persecution in their homeland. Congress has provided two forms of relief for such people: asylum, see Immigration and Nationality Act of 1952, §208(a), and withholding of deportation, see §243(h).... The Board of Immigration Appeals (BIA) has concluded that there is no practical distinction between the objective proofs an alien must submit to be eligible for these two forms of relief. The Court rejects this conclusion. Because I believe the BIA's interpretation of the statute is reasonable, I dissent.

I

The Court's opinion seems to assume that the BIA has adopted a rigorous mathematical approach to asylum cases, requiring aliens to demonstrate an objectively quantifiable risk of persecution in their homeland that is more than 50%. The Court then argues that such a position is inconsistent with the language and history of the Act. But this has never been the BIA's position....

...[C]ontrary to the Court's apparent conclusion, the BIA does not contend that both the "well-founded fear" standard and the "clear probability" standard require proof of a 51% chance that the alien will suffer persecution if he is returned to his homeland. The BIA plainly eschews analysis resting on mathematical probabilities. Rather, the BIA has adopted a four-part test requiring proof of facts that demonstrate a realistic likelihood of persecution actually occurring.... [T]he BIA's empirical conclusion, based on its experience in adjudicating asylum applications, [is] that if the facts establish such a basis for an alien's fear, it rarely will make a difference whether the judge asks if persecution is "likely" to occur or "more likely than not" to occur. If the alien can establish such a basis, he normally will be eligible for relief under either standard.

II

In Part II of its opinion, the Court examines the language of the Act. Section 243(h) provides that the Attorney General shall grant withholding of deportation to any country where "such alien's life or freedom would be threatened." Section 208(a) provides that the Attorney General has discretion to grant asylum "if the Attorney General determines that such alien is a refugee." The crucial language of §101(a)(42)(A) of the Act, as added by 94 Stat. 102, defines a refugee as a person who has "a well-founded fear of persecution."...

With respect to the issue presented by this case, I find the language far more ambiguous than the Court does. Respondent contends that the BIA has fallen into error by equating the objective showings required under §§208(a) and 243(h). The Court notes that the language of §208(a) differs from the language of §243(h) in that it contemplates a partially subjective inquiry. From this premise, the Court moves with little explanation to the conclusion that the objective inquiries under the two sections necessarily are different.

In reaching this conclusion, the Court gives short shrift to the words "well-founded," that clearly require some objective basis for the alien's fear. The critical question presented by this case is whether the objective basis required for a fear of persecution to be "well-founded" differs *in practice* from the objective basis required for there to be a "clear probability" of persecution. Because both standards necessarily contemplate some objective basis, I cannot agree with the Court's implicit conclusion that the statute resolves this question on its face. In my view, the character of evidence sufficent to meet these two standards is a question best answered by an entity familiar with the types of evidence and issues that arise in such cases. Congress limited eligibility for asylum to those persons whom "the Attorney General determines" to be refugees. The Attorney General has delegated the responsibility for making these determinations to the BIA. That Board has examined more of these cases than any court ever has or ever can. It has made a considered judgment that the difference between the "well-founded" and the "clear probability" standards is of no practical import: that is, the evidence presented in asylum and withholding of deportation cases rarely, if ever, will meet one of these standards without meeting both. This is just the type of expert judgment—formed by the entity to whom Congress has committed the question—to which we should defer.

The Court ignores the practical realities recognized by the expert agency and instead concentrates on semantic niceties....

Common sense and human experience support the BIA's conclusion. Governments rarely persecute people by the numbers. It is highly unlikely that the evidence presented at an asylum or withholding of deportation hearing will demonstrate the mathematically specific risk of persecution posited by the Court's hypothetical. Taking account of the types of evidence normally available in asylum cases, the BIA has chosen to make a *qualitative* evaluation of "realistic likelihoods." As I read the *Acosta* opinion, an individual who fled his country to avoid mass executions might be eligible for both withholding of deportation *and* asylum, whether or not he presented evidence of the numerical reach of the persecution. [*Matter of Acosta,* Interim Decision #2986 (BIA Mar. 1 1985)]....

In sum, the words Congress has chosen—"well-founded" fear—are ambiguous. They contemplate some objective basis without specifying a particular evidentiary threshold.... The BIA has concluded that a fear is not "well-founded" unless the fear has an objective basis indicating that there is a "realistic likelihood" that persecution would occur. Based on the text of the Act alone, I can not conclude that this conclusion is unreasonable.

III

The Court bolsters its interpretation of the language of the Act by reference to three parts of the legislative history. A closer examination of these materials demonstrates that each of them is ambiguous. Nothing the Court relies on provides a positive basis for arguing that there is a material difference between the two standards....

IV

Even if I agreed with the Court's conclusion that there is a significant difference between the standards for asylum and withholding of deportation, I would reverse the decision of the Court of Appeals and uphold the decision of the BIA *in this case.* A careful reading of the decisions of the BIA and the Immigration Judge demonstrates that the BIA applied the lower asylum standard to this case.

Respondent's claim for asylum rested solely on testimony that her brother had experienced difficulties with the authorities in Nicaragua. The Immigration Judge rejected respondent's claim because he found "no evidence of any substance in the record other than her brother's claim to asylum." He further found:

> "None of the evidence indicates that the respondent would be persecuted for political beliefs, whatever they may be, or because she belongs to a particular social group. She has not proven that she or any other members of her family, other than her brother, has [sic] been detained, interrogated, arrested and imprisoned, tortured and convicted and sentenced by the regime presently in power in Nicaragua."

The absence of such evidence was particularly probative, because many of the other members of respondent's family—her parents, two sisters, her brother's wife, and her brother's two children—were still in Nicaragua and thus presumably subject to the persecution respondent feared.

On appeal, the BIA affirmed. . . . Reviewing the evidence respondent had submitted to the Immigration Judge, the BIA concluded that respondent could not obtain relief under any of the standards. The BIA focused especially on the fact that respondent

> "has openly admitted that she herself has taken no actions against the Nicaraguan government. She admits that she has never been politically active. She testified that she never assisted her brother in any of his political activities. Moreover, she admits that she has never been singled out for persecution by the present government."

Respondent filed a petition for review with the Court of Appeals for the Ninth Circuit. Without examining either the factual or legal basis for the BIA's decision, the court granted the petition, reversed the BIA's decision, and remanded the application to the BIA for further consideration. . . .

. . . As I have explained, the BIA acknowledged the conflicting decisions of the various Courts of Appeals and explicitly tested the application under three different standards. The least burdensome of these—the "good reason" standard—is identical to the court's statement quoted *supra*. The Court of Appeals completely ignored the words in which the BIA framed its decision. It failed to examine the factual findings on which the decision rested. At least in this case, it appears that the Court of Appeals, and not the BIA, has misunderstood the proper relation between courts and agencies. That court properly could have considered whether substantial evidence supported the BIA's conclusion that respondent failed to demonstrate a "good reason" to fear persecution, but it should not have assumed that the BIA tested respondent's application by a higher standard than the BIA's own opinion reflects.

V

In my view, the Court misconstrues the Act and misreads its legislative history. Moreover, neither this Court nor the Court of Appeals has identified an error in the decision of the BIA in *this* case. Neither court has examined the factual findings on which the decision rested, or the legal standard the BIA applied to these facts. I would reverse the decision of the Court of Appeals.

VATICAN STATEMENT ON BIOETHICS

March 10, 1987

The Vatican issued a statement March 10 that clarified the Roman Catholic church's views on bioethical issues. It condemned many of the recently developed reproductive technologies, including in vitro fertilization, embryo banks, donor insemination, and surrogate motherhood. The document, "Instruction on Respect for Human Life in Its Origin and on the Dignity of Procreation," also called on civic authorities to outlaw the condemned technologies, restating the church's long-held positions that the sexual union of a married couple is the only way to create human life and that all life is sacred from the moment of conception. Although not as morally binding for Catholics as a papal edict, the document broadened the debate over questions of sexual and reproductive ethics in the Catholic community.

Guidance to Catholics

In 1978 Louise Brown, the first child conceived in vitro, or in a laboratory dish, was born in England. Albino Cardinal Luciani, who became Pope John Paul I, sent her family a telegram of good wishes but expressed reservations about the method of her birth. By 1987 an estimated one thousand babies had been born in the United States as a result of in vitro fertilization, according to the Congressional Biomedical Ethics Board. When the Vatican document was issued, a New Jersey judge was deciding the outcome of the emotional battle for custody of "Baby M," born to a "surrogate" mother who after the birth had changed her mind about relinquishing the infant. (New Jersey court on rights of surrogates, p. 373)

Issued by the Congregation for the Doctrine of the Faith, and signed by Joseph Cardinal Ratzinger, a close adviser of Pope John Paul II, the document was intended to provide guidance to Catholics about the morality of new reproductive technologies. At a news conference Cardinal Ratzinger said the Catholic church welcomed scientific research but stressed that "science is not absolute, to which everything must be subordinated and eventually sacrificed, including the dignity of man."

The paper was approved by the pope, who restated its basic premise in his Easter message: "[G]rant that . . . man . . . may not reduce himself to a mere object, but may respect from its first beginning the unrenounceable dignity that is proper to him."

Church's Traditional Teachings

Despite the scientific advances making conception outside a woman's body possible, the church's teachings, the document stated, remained firm. If an embryo has the potential for becoming a complete human being, the Vatican reasoned, it must already indeed be a person, deserving of an inviolable right to life and respect for its "physical integrity."

Prenatal diagnostic testing and research on embryos were termed improper unless done solely to detect or treat fetal abnormalities. Because many in vitro programs destroyed some of the embryos obtained through their efforts, the Vatican condemned the role of researchers involved, saying they made unacceptable decisions about who should live and who should die. The paper went on to disallow in vitro fertilization because it produced life "without any connection to sexuality." Embryo freezing, which is undertaken by some in vitro programs if too many embryos are produced to be implanted at one time, and genetic manipulation for sex selection were condemned as being contrary to the personal dignity of the human being.

The document judged donor insemination and donor ovum programs morally illicit for violating the unity of marriage and the child's right to a biological link to his or her parents. For the same reason, artificial insemination of a widow, even with the sperm of her late husband, was disapproved. Surrogate motherhood came under harsh attack for failing "to meet the obligations of maternal love, of conjugal fidelity and of responsible motherhood."

On the question of artificial insemination of a woman by her husband's sperm, and in vitro procedures using the egg and sperm of husband and wife, the document reasoned that because the sexual act does not occur, the procedures are not morally perfect. They reduce a child who should be "the fruit of his parents' love" to "an object of scientific technology."

The document appealed to Catholic medical institutions and medical workers to heed its guidelines concerning respect due to the embryo and the dignity of procreation, and went on to urge civic authorities to enact its principles into law by banning donor sperm and ovum programs, surrogate motherhood, embryo banks, and other technologies not considered moral.

While acknowledging the valid desire of infertile couples to have children, the Vatican stressed that having a baby is not a right, but a gift. If no morally justifiable technologies can help a couple conceive, the document suggested adoption or "various forms of education work and assistance to other families and to poor or handicapped children" as ways to find fulfillment.

Document Rejected by Some

Conservative Catholics and moderate or liberal Catholics differed in their reactions to the instruction. Most of the church's hierarchy welcomed the document. Archbishop James Hickey of Washington, D.C., said it was a "much needed statement." Joseph Cardinal Bernardin of Chicago also praised the instruction, saying, "It will provide Catholics and other people of good will with criteria for making moral judgments." In a speech in April, however, Bernardin indicated that some Catholic couples might choose to ignore the document's teachings. He said, "[I]n the end after prayer and careful reflection on this teaching, they must make their own decision."

University of Notre Dame professor Rev. Richard McCormick termed the document unpersuasive and differed sharply with the insistence that children be conceived only as the result of a sexual act. He stated that parents "can be just as moral and loving as they go about overcoming obstacles to fertility through technology."

> *Following are excerpts from the Congregation for the Doctrine of the Faith's "Instruction on Respect for Human Life in Its Origin and on the Dignity of Procreation: Replies to Certain Questions of the Day," issued in Rome March 10, 1987:*

Foreword

The Congregation for the Doctrine of the Faith has been approached by various episcopal conferences of individual bishops, by theologians, doctors and scientists, concerning biomedical techniques which make it possible to intervene in the initial phase of the life of a human being and in the very processes of procreation and their conformity with the principles of Catholic morality. The present instruction, which is the result of wide consultation and in particular of a careful evaluation of the declarations made by episcopates, does not intend to repeat all the church's teaching on the dignity of human life as it originates and on procreation, but to offer, in the light of the previous teaching of the magisterium, some specific replies to the main questions being asked in this regard....

Introduction

1. Biomedical Research and the Teaching of the Church

The gift of life which God the Creator and Father has entrusted to man calls him to appreciate the inestimable value of what he has been given and to take responsibility for it: This fundamental principle must be placed at the center of one's reflection in order to clarify and solve the moral problems raised by artificial interventions on life as it originates and on the processes of procreation.

Thanks to the progress of the biological and medical sciences, man has at his disposal ever more effective therapeutic resources; but he can also acquire new powers, with unforeseeable consequences, over human life at its very beginning and in its first stages. Various procedures now make it possible to intervene not only in order to assist, but also to dominate the processes of procreation. These techniques can enable man to "take in hand his own destiny," but they also expose him "to the temptation to go beyond the limits of a reasonable domination over nature." They might constitute progress in the service of man, but they also involve serious risks. Many people are therefore expressing an urgent appeal that in interventions on procreation the values and rights of the human person be safeguarded. Requests for clarification and guidance are coming not only from the faithful, but also from those who recognize the church as "an expert in humanity" with a mission to serve the "civilization of love" and of life.

The church's magisterium does not intervene on the basis of a particular competence in the area of the experimental sciences; but having taken account of the data of research and technology, it intends to put forward, by virtue of its evangelical mission and apostolic duty, the moral teaching corresponding to the dignity of the person and to his or her integral vocation. It intends to do so by expounding the criteria of moral judgment as regards the applications of scientific research and technology, especially in relation to human life and its beginnings. These criteria are the respect, defense and promotion of man, his "primary and fundamental right" to life, his dignity as a person who is endowed with a spiritual soul and with moral responsibility and who is called to beatific communion with God....

2. Science and Technology at the Service of the Human Person

God created man in his own image and likeness: "Male and female he created them" (Gn. 1:27), entrusting to them the task of "having dominion over the earth" (Gn. 1:28). Basic scientific research and applied research constitute a significant expression of this dominion of man over creation. Science and technology are valuable resources for man when placed at his service and when they promote his integral development for the benefit of all; but they cannot of themselves show the meaning of existence and of human progress. Being ordered to man, who initiates and develops them, they draw from the person and his moral values the indication of their purpose and the awareness of their limits.

It would on the one hand be illusory to claim that scientific research and its applications are morally neutral; on the other hand one cannot derive criteria for guidance from mere technical efficiency, from research's possible usefulness to some at the expense of others or, worse still, from prevailing ideologies. Thus science and technology require for their own intrinsic meaning an unconditional respect for . . . the moral law: . . . they must be at the service of the human person, of his inalienable rights and his true and integral good according to the design and will of God.

The rapid development of technological discoveries gives greater urgency to this need to respect the criteria just mentioned: Science without conscience can only lead to man's ruin. "Our era needs such wisdom more than bygone ages if the discoveries made by man are to be further humanized. For the future of the world stands in peril unless wiser people are forthcoming."

3. Anthropology and Procedures in the Biomedical Field

Which moral criteria must be applied in order to clarify the problems posed today in the field of biomedicine? The answer to this question presupposes a proper idea of the nature of the human person in his bodily dimension.

For it is only in keeping with his true nature that the human person can achieve self-realization as a "unified totality"; and this nature is at the same time corporal and spiritual. By virtue of its substantial union with a spiritual soul, the human body cannot be considered as a mere complex of tissues, organs and functions, nor can it be evaluated in the same way as the body of animals; rather it is a constitutive part of the person who manifests and expresses himself through it. . . .

. . . No biologist or doctor can reasonably claim, by virtue of scientific competence, to be able to decide on people's origin and destiny. . . .

God, who is love and life, has inscribed in man and woman the vocation to share in a special way in his mystery of personal communion and in his work as Creator and Father. For this reason marriage possesses specific goods and values in its union and in procreation which cannot be likened to those existing in lower forms of life. Such values and meanings are of the personal order and determine from the moral point of view the meaning and limits of artificial interventions on procreation and on the origin of human life. These interventions are not to be rejected on the grounds that they are artificial. As such, they bear witness to the possibilities of the art of medicine. But they must be given a moral evaluation in reference to the dignity of the human person, who is called to realize his vocation from God to the gift of love and the gift of life.

4. Fundamental Criteria for a Moral Judgment

The fundamental values connected with the techniques of artificial human procreation are two: the life of the human being called into existence and the special nature of the transmission of human life in marriage. The moral judgment on such methods of artificial procreation must therefore be formulated in reference to these values.

Physical life, with which the course of human life in the world begins, certainly does not itself contain the whole of a person's value nor does it represent the supreme good of man, who is called to eternal life. However it does constitute in a certain way the "fundamental" value of life precisely because upon this physical life all the other values of the person are based and developed. The inviolability of the innocent human being's right to life "from the moment of conception until death" is a sign and requirement of the very inviolability of the person to whom the Creator has given the gift of life. . . .

I
Respect for Human Embryos

Careful reflection on this teaching of the magisterium and on the evidence of reason, as mentioned above, enables us to respond to the numerous moral problems posed by technical interventions upon the human being in the first phases of his life and upon the processes of his conception.

1. What respect is due to the human embryo, taking into account his nature and identity?

The human being must be respected—as a person—from the very first instant of his existence.

The implementation of procedures of artificial fertilization has made possible various interventions upon embryos and human fetuses. The aims pursued are of various kinds: diagnostic and therapeutic, scientific and commercial. From all of this, serious problems arise. Can one speak of a right to experimentation upon human embryos for the purpose of scientific research? What norms or laws should be worked out with regard to this matter? The response to these problems presupposes a detailed reflection on the nature and specific identity—the word *status* is used—of the human embryo itself.

At the Second Vatican Council, the church for her part presented once again to modern man her constant and certain doctrine according to which: "Life once conceived, must be protected with the utmost care; abortion and infanticide are abominable crimes." More recently, the Charter of the Rights of the Family, published by the Holy See, confirmed that "human life must be absolutely respected and protected from the moment of conception."

This congregation is aware of the current debates concerning the beginning of human life, concerning the individuality of the human being and concerning the identity of the human person. The congregation recalls the teachings found in the Declaration on Procured Abortion:

> "From the time that the ovum is fertilized, a new life is begun which is neither that of the father nor of the mother; it is rather the life of a new human being with his own growth. It would never be made human if it were not human already. To this perpetual evidence . . . modern genetic science brings valuable confirmation. It has demonstrated that, from the first instant, the program is fixed as to what this living being will be: a man, this individual man with his characteristic aspects already well determined. Right from fertilization is begun the adventure of a human life, and each of its great capacities requires time . . . to find its place and to be in a position to act."

This teaching remains valid and is further confirmed, if confirmation were needed, by recent findings of human biological science which recognize that in the zygote (the cell produced when the nuclei of the two gametes have fused) resulting from fertilization the biological identity of a new human individual is already constituted.

Certainly no experimental datum can be in itself sufficient to bring us to the recognition of a spiritual soul; nevertheless, the conclusions of science regarding the human embryo provide a valuable indication for discerning by the use of reason a personal presence at the moment of this first appearance of a human life: How could a human individual not be a human person? The magisterium has not expressly committed itself to an affirmation of a philosophical nature, but it constantly reaffirms the moral condemnation of any kind of procured abortion. This teaching has not been changed and is unchangeable. . . .

This doctrinal reminder provides the fundamental criterion for the solution of the various problems posed by the development of the biomedical sciences in this field: Since the embryo must be treated as a person, it must also be defended in its integrity, tended and cared for, to the extent possible, in the same way as any other human being as far as medical assistance is concerned.

2. Is prenatal diagnosis morally licit?

If prenatal diagnosis respects the life and integrity of the embryo and the human fetus and is directed toward its safeguarding or healing as an individual, then the answer is affirmative.

For prenatal diagnosis makes it possible to know the condition of the embryo and of the fetus when still in the mother's womb. It permits or makes it possible to anticipate earlier and more effectively, certain therapeutic, medical or surgical procedures.

Such diagnosis is permissible, with the consent of the parents after they have been adequately informed, if the methods employed safeguard the life and integrity of the embryo and the mother, without subjecting them to disproportionate risks. But this diagnosis is gravely opposed to the moral law when it is done with the thought of possibly inducing an abortion depending upon the results: A diagnosis which shows the existence of a malformation or a hereditary illness must not be the equivalent of a death sentence. Thus a woman would be committing a gravely illicit act if she were to request such a diagnosis with the deliberate intention of having an abortion should the results confirm the existence of a malformation or abnormality. The spouse or relatives or anyone else would similarly be acting in a manner contrary to the moral law if they were to counsel or impose such a diagnostic procedure on the expectant mother with the same intention of possibly proceeding to an abortion. So too the specialist would be guilty of illicit collaboration if, in conducting the diagnosis and in communicating its results, he were deliberately to contribute to establishing or favoring a link between prenatal diagnosis and abortion.

In conclusion, any directive or program of the civil and health authorities or of scientific organizations which in any way were to favor a link between prenatal diagnosis and abortion, or which were to go as far as directly to induce expectant mothers to submit to prenatal diagnosis planned for the purpose of eliminating fetuses which are affected by malformations or which are carriers of hereditary illness, is to be condemned as a violation of the unborn child's right to life and as an abuse of the prior rights and duties of the spouses.

3. Are therapeutic procedures carried out on the human embryo licit?

As with all medical interventions on patients, *one must uphold as licit procedures carried out on the human embryo which respect the life and integrity of the embryo and do not involve disproportionate risks for it, but are directed toward its healing, the improvement of its condition of health or its individual survival.*

Whatever the type of medical, surgical or other therapy, the free and informed consent of the parents is required, according to the deontological rules followed in the case of children. The application of this moral principle may call for delicate and particular precautions in the case of embryonic or fetal life.

The legitimacy and criteria of such procedures have been clearly stated by Pope John Paul II: "A strictly therapeutic intervention whose explicit objective is the healing of various maladies such as those stemming from chromosomal defects will, in principle, be considered desirable, provided it is directed to the true promotion of the personal well-being of the individual without doing harm to his integrity or worsening his conditions of life. Such an intervention would indeed fall within the logic of the Christian moral tradition."

4. How is one to evaluate morally research and experimentation on human embryos and fetuses?

Medical research must refrain from operations on live embryos, unless there is a moral certainty of not causing harm to the life or integrity of the unborn child and the mother, and on condition that the parents have given their free and informed consent to the procedure. It follows that all research, even when limited to the simple observation of the embryo, would become illicit were it to involve risk to the embryo's physical integrity or life by reason of the methods used or the effects induced.

As regards experimentation, and presupposing the general distinction between experimentation for purposes which are not directly therapeutic and experimentation which is clearly therapeutic for the subject himself, in the case in point one must also distingush between experimentation carried out on embryos which are still alive and experimentation carried out on embryos which are dead. *If the embryos are living, whether viable or not they must be respected just like any other human person; experimentation on embryos which is not directly therapeutic is illicit.*

No objective, even though noble in itself such as a foreseeable advantage to science, to other human beings or to society, can in any way justify experimentation on living human embryos or fetuses, whether viable or not, either inside or outside the mother's womb. The informed consent ordinarily required for clinical experimentation on adults cannot be granted by the parents, who may not freely dispose of the physical integrity or life of the unborn child. Moreover, experimentation on embyros and fetuses always involves risk, and indeed in most cases it involves the certain expectation of harm to their physical integrity or even their death.

To use human embryos or fetuses as the object or instrument of experimentation constitutes a crime against their dignity as human beings having a right to the same respect that is due to the child already born and to every human person.

The Charter of the Rights of the Family published by the Holy See affirms: "Respect for the dignity of the human being excludes all experimental manipulation or exploitation of the human embryo." The practice of keeping alive human embryos *in vivo* or *in vitro* for experimental or commercial purposes is totally opposed to human dignity.

In the case of experimentation that is clearly therapeutic, namely, when it is a matter of experimental forms of therapy used for the benefit of the embryo itself in a final attempt to save its life and in the absence of other reliable forms of therapy, recourse to drugs or procedures not yet fully tested can be licit.

The corpses of human embryos and fetuses, whether they have been deliberately aborted or not, must be respected just as the remains of other human beings. In particular, they cannot be subjected to mutilation or to autopsies if their death has not yet been verified and without the consent of the parents or of the mother. Furthermore, the moral requirements must be safeguarded that there be no complicity in deliberate abortion and that the risk of scandal be avoided. Also, in the case of dead fetuses, as for the corpses of adult persons, all commercial trafficking must be considered illicit and should be prohibited.

5. How is one to evaluate morally the use for research purposes of embryos obtained by fertilization "in vitro"?

Human embryos obtained *in vitro* are human beings and subjects with rights: Their dignity and right to life must be respected from the first moment of their existence. *It is immoral to produce human embryos destined to be exploited as disposable "biological material."*

In the usual practice of *in vitro* fertilization, not all of the embryos are transferred to the woman's body; some are destroyed. Just as the church condemns induced abortion, so she also forbids acts against the life of these human beings. *It is a duty to condemn the particular gravity of the voluntary destruction of human embryos obtained "in vitro" for the sole purpose of research, either by means of artificial insemination or by means of "twin fission."* By acting in this way the researcher usurps the place of God; and, even though he may be unaware of this, he sets himself up as the master of the destiny of others inasmuch as he arbitrarily chooses whom he will allow to live and whom he will send to death and kills defenseless human beings.

Methods of observation or experimentation which damage or impose grave and disproportionate risks upon embryos obtained *in vitro* are morally illicit for the same reasons. Every human being is to be respected for himself and cannot be reduced in worth to a pure and simple instrument for the advantage of others. *It is therefore not in conformity with the moral law deliberately to expose to death human embryos obtained "in vitro."* In consequence of the fact that they have been produced *in vitro,* those embryos which are not transferred into the body of the mother and are called "spare" are exposed to an absurd fate, with no possibility of their being offered safe means of survival which can be licitly pursued.

6. What judgment should be made on other procedures of manipulating embryos connected with the "techniques of human reproduction"?

Techniques of fertilization *in vitro* can open the way to other forms of biological and genetic manipulation of human embryos, such as attempts or plans for fertilization between human and animal gametes and the gestation of human embryos in the uterus of animals, or the hypothesis or project of constructing artificial uteruses for the human embryo. *These procedures are contrary to the human dignity proper to the embryo, and at the same time they are contrary to the right of every person to be conceived and to be born within marriage and from marriage. Also, attempts or hypotheses for obtaining a human being without any connection with sexuality through "twin fission," cloning or parthenogenesis are to be considered contrary to the moral law, since they are in opposition to the dignity both of human procreation and of the conjugal union.*

The freezing of embryos, even when carried out in order to preserve the life of an embryo—cryopreservation—*constitutes an offense against the respect due to human beings* by exposing them to grave risks of death or harm to their physical integrity and depriving them, at least temporarily, of maternal shelter and gestation, thus placing them in a situation in which further offenses and manipulation are possible.

Certain attempts to influence chromosomic or genetic inheritance are not therapeutic, but are aimed at producing human beings selected according to sex or other predetermined qualities. These manipulations are contrary to the personal dignity of the human being and his or her integrity and identity. Therefore in no way can they be justified on the grounds of possible beneficial consequences for future humanity. Every person must be respected for himself: In this consists the dignity and right of every human being from his or her beginning.

II
Interventions upon Human Procreation

By *artificial procreation* or *artificial fertilization* are understood here the different technical procedures directed toward obtaining a human conception in a manner other than the sexual union of man and woman. This instruction deals with fertilization of an ovum in a test tube (*in vitro* fertilization) and artificial insemination through transfer into the woman's genital tracts of previously collected sperm.

A preliminary point for the moral evaluation of such technical procedures is constituted by the consideration of the circumstances and consequences which those procedures involve in relation to the respect due the human embryo. Development of the practice of *in vitro* fertilization has required innumerable fertilizations and destructions of human embryos. Even today, the usual practice presupposes a hyperovulation on the part of the woman: A number of ova are withdrawn, fertilized and then cultivated *in vitro* for some days. Usually not all are transferred into the genital tracts of the woman; some embryos, generally called "spare," are destroyed or frozen. On occasion, some of the implanted embryos are sacrificed for various eugenic, economic or psychological reasons. Such deliberate destruction of human beings or their utilization for different purposes to the detriment of their integrity and life is contrary to the doctrine on procured abortion already recalled.

The connection between *in vitro* fertilization and the voluntary destruction of human embryos occurs too often. This is significant: Through these procedures, with apparently contrary purposes, life and death are subjected to the decision of man, who thus sets himself up as the giver of life and death by decree. This dynamic of violence and domination may remain unnoticed by those very individuals who, in wishing to utilize this procedure, become subject to it themselves. The facts recorded and the cold logic which links them must be taken into consideration for a moral judgment on *in vitro* fertilization and embryo transfer: The abortion mentality which had made this procedure possible thus leads, whether one wants it or not, to man's domination over the life and death of his fellow human beings and can lead to a system of radical eugenics.

Nevertheless, such abuses do not exempt one from a further and thorough ethical study of the techniques of artificial procreation considered in themselves, abstracting as far as possible from the destruction of embryos produced *in vitro*....

A. Heterologous Artificial Fertilization

1. Why must human procreation take place in marriage?

Every human being is always to be accepted as a gift and blessing of God. However, from the moral point of view a truly responsible procreation vis-a-vis the unborn child must be the fruit of marriage.

For human procreation has specific characteristics by virtue of the personal dignity of the parents and of the children: The procreation of a new person, whereby the man and the woman collaborate with the power of the Creator, must be the fruit and the sign of the mutual self-giving of the spouses, of their love and of their fidelity. *The fidelity of the spouses in the unity of marriage involves reciprocal respect of their right to become a father and mother only through each other.*

The child has the right to be conceived, carried in the womb, brought into the world and brought up within marriage: It is through the secure and recognized relationship to his own parents that the child can discover his own identity and achieve his own proper human development.

The parents find in their child a confirmation and completion of their reciprocal self-giving: The child is the living image of their love, the permanent sign of their conjugal union, the living and indissoluble concrete expression of their paternity and maternity.

By reason of the vocation and social responsibilities of the person, the good of the children and of the parents contributes to the good of civil society; the vitality and stability of society require that children come into the world within a family and that the family be firmly based on marriage.

The tradition of the church and anthropological reflection recognize in marriage and in its indissoluble unity the only setting worthy of truly responsible procreation.

2. Does heterologous artificial fertilization conform to the dignity of the couple and to the truth of marriage?

Through *in vitro* fertilization and embryo transfer and heterologous artificial insemination, human conception is achieved through the fusion of gametes of at least one donor other than the spouses who are united in marriage. *Heterologous artificial fertilization is contrary to the unity of marriage, to the dignity of the spouses, to the vocation proper to parents, and to the child's right to be conceived and brought into the world in marriage and from marriage.*

Respect for the unity of marriage and for conjugal fidelity demands that the child be conceived in marriage; the bond existing between husband and wife accords the spouses, in an objective and inalienable manner, the exclusive right to become father and mother solely through each other. Recourse to the gametes of a third person in order to have sperm or ovum available constitutes a violation of the reciprocal commitment of the spouses and a grave lack in regard to that essential property of marriage which is its unity.

Heterologous artificial fertilization violates the rights of the child; it deprives him of his filial relationship with his parental origins and can hinder the maturing of his personal identity. Furthermore, it offends the common vocation of the spouses who are called to fatherhood and motherhood: It objectively deprives conjugal fruitfulness of its unity and integrity; it brings about and manifests a rupture between genetic parenthood, gestational parenthood and responsibility for upbringing. Such damage to the personal relationships within the family has repercussions on civil society: What threatens the unity and stability of the family is a source of dissension, disorder and injustice in the whole of social life.

These reasons lead to a negative moral judgment concerning heterologous artificial fertilization: Consequently, fertilization of a married woman with the sperm of a donor different from her husband and fertilization with the husband's sperm of an ovum not coming from his wife are morally illicit. Furthermore, the artificial fertilization of a woman who is unmarried or a widow, whoever the donor may be, cannot be morally justified.

The desire to have a child and the love between spouses who long to obviate a sterility which cannot be overcome in any other way constitute understandable motivations; but subjectively good intentions do not render heterologous artificial fertilization conformable to the objective and inalienable properties of marriage or respectful of the rights of the child and of the spouses.

3. Is "surrogate" motherhood morally licit?

No, for the same reasons which lead one to reject heterologous artificial fertilization: For it is contrary to the unity of marriage and to the dignity of the procreation of the human person.

Surrogate motherhood represents an objective failure to meet the obligations of maternal love, of conjugal fidelity and of responsible motherhood; it offends the dignity and the right of the child to be conceived, carried in the womb, brought into the world and brought up by his own parents; it sets up, to the detriment of families, a division between the physical, psychological and moral elements which constitute those families.

B. Homologous Artificial Fertilization

Since heterologous artificial fertilization has been declared unacceptable, the question arises of how to evaluate morally the process of homologous artificial fertilization: *in vitro* fertilization and embryo transfer and artificial insemination between husband and wife. First a question of principle must be clarified.

4. What connection is required from the moral point of view between procreation and the conjugal act?

a) The church's teaching on marriage and human procreation affirms the "inseparable connection, willed by God and unable to be broken by man on his own initiative, between the two meanings of the conjugal act: the unitive meaning and the procreative meaning. Indeed by its intimate structure the conjugal act, while most closely uniting husband and wife, capacitates them for the generation of new lives according to laws inscribed in the very being of man and of woman." This principle, which is based upon the nature of marriage and the intimate connection of the goods of marriage, has well-known consequences on the level of responsible fatherhood and motherhood. "By safeguarding both these essential aspects, the unitive and the procreative, the conjugal act preserves in its fullness the sense of true mutual love and its ordination toward man's exalted vocation to parenthood...."

Contraception deliberately deprives the conjugal act of its openness to procreation and in this way brings about a voluntary dissociation of the ends of marriage. Homologous artificial fertilization, in seeking a procreation which is not the fruit of a specific act of conjugal union, objectively effects an analogous separation between the goods and the meanings of marriage.

Thus *fertilization is licitly sought when it is the result of a "conjugal act which is per se suitable for the generation of children, to which marriage is ordered by its nature and by which the spouses become one flesh." But from the moral point of view procreation is deprived of its proper perfection when it is not desired as the fruit of the conjugal act, that is to say, of the specific act of the spouses' union.*

b) The moral value of the intimate link between the goods of marriage and between the meanings of the conjugal act is based upon the unity of the human being, a unity involving body and spiritual soul. Spouses mutually express their personal love in the "language of the body," which clearly involves both "spousal meanings" and parental ones. The conjugal act by which the couple mutually express their self-gift at the same time expresses openness to the gift of life. It is an act that is inseparably corporal and spiritual. It is in their bodies and through their bodies that the spouses consummate their marriage and are able to become father and mother. In order to respect the language of their bodies and their natural generosity, the conjugal union must take place with respect for its openness to procreation; and the procreation of a person must be the fruit and the result of married love. The origin of the human being thus follows from a procreation that is "linked to the union, not only biological but also spiritual, of the parents, made one by the bond of marriage." Fertilization achieved outside the bodies of the couple remains by this very fact deprived of the meanings and values which are expressed in the language of the body and in the union of human persons.

c) Only respect for the link betwen the meanings of the conjugal act and respect for the unity of the human being make possible procreation in conformity with the dignity of the person. In his unique and irrepeatable origin, the child must be respected and recognized as equal in personal dignity to those who give him life. The human person must be accepted in his parents' act of union and love; the generation of a child must therefore be the fruit of that mutual giving which is realized in the conjugal act wherein the spouses cooperate as servants and not as masters in the work of the Creator, who is love.

In reality, the origin of a human person is the result of an act of giving. The one conceived must be the fruit of his parents' love. He cannot be desired or conceived as the product of an intervention of medical or biological techniques; that would be equivalent to reducing him to an object of scientific technology. No one may subject the coming of a child into the world to conditions of technical efficiency which are to be evaluated according to standards of control and dominion.

The moral relevance of the link between the meanings of the conjugal act and between the goods of marriage, as well as the unity of the human being and the dignity of his origin, demand that the procreation of a human person be brought about as the fruit of the conjugal act specific to the love between the spouses. The link between procreation and the conjugal act is thus shown to be of great importance on the anthropological and moral planes, and it throws light on the positions of the magisterium with regard to homologous artificial fertilization.

5. Is homologous "in vitro" fertilization morally licit?

The answer to this question is strictly dependent on the principles just mentioned. Certainly one cannot ignore the legitimate aspirations of sterile couples. For some, recourse to homologous *in vitro* fertilization and embryo transfer appears to be the only way of fulfilling their sincere desire for a child. The question is asked whether the totality of conjugal life in such situations is not sufficient to ensure the dignity proper to human procreation. It is acknowledged that *in vitro* fertilization and embryo transfer certainly cannot supply for the absence of sexual relations and cannot be preferred to the specific acts of conjugal union, given the risks involved for the child and the difficulties of the procedure. But it is asked whether, when there is no other way of overcoming the sterility which is a source of suffering, homologous *in vitro* fertilization may not constitute an aid, if not a form of therapy, whereby its moral licitness could be admitted.

The desire for a child—or at the very least an openness to the transmission of life—is a necessary prerequisite from the moral point of view for responsible human procreation. But this good intention is not sufficient for making a positive moral evaluation of *in vitro* fertilization between spouses. The process of *in vitro* fertilization and embryo transfer must be judged in itself and cannot borrow its definitive moral quality from the totality of conjugal life of which it becomes part nor from the conjugal acts which may precede or follow it.

... [E]ven in a situation in which every precaution were taken to avoid the death of human embryos, homologous *in vitro* fertilization and embryo transfer dissociates from the conjugal act the actions which are directed to human fertilization. For this reason the very nature of homologous *in vitro* fertilization and embryo transfer also must be taken into account, even abstracting from the link with procured abortion.

Homologous *in vitro* fertilization and embryo transfer is brought about outside the bodies of the couple through actions of third parties whose competence and technical activity determine the success of the procedure. Such fertilization entrusts the life and identity of the embryo into the power of doctors and biologists and establishes the domination of technology over the origin and destiny of the human person. Such a relationship of domination is in itself contrary to the dignity and equality that must be common to parents and children.

Conception *in vitro* is the result of the technical action which presides over fertilization. *Such fertilization is neither in fact achieved nor positively willed as the expression and fruit of a specific act of the conjugal union. In homologous "in vitro" fertilization and embryo transfer, therefore, even if it is considered in the context of de facto existing sexual relations, the generation of the human person is objectively deprived of its proper perfection: namely, that of being the result and fruit of a conjugal act* in which the spouses can become "cooperators with God for giving life to a new person."

These reasons enable us to understand why the act of conjugal love is considered in the teaching of the church as the only setting worthy of human procreation. For the same reasons the so-called "simple case," i.e., a homologous *in vitro* fertilization and embryo transfer procedure that is free of any compromise with the abortive practice of destroying embryos and with masturbation, remains a technique which is morally illicit because it deprives human procreation of the dignity which is proper and connatural to it.

Certainly, homologous *in vitro* fertilization and embryo transfer fertilization is not marked by all that ethical negativity found in extraconjugal procreation; the family and marriage continue to constitute the setting for the birth and upbringing of the children. Nevertheless, in conformity with the traditional doctrine relating to the goods of marriage and the dignity of the person, *the church remains opposed from the moral point of view to homologous "in vitro" fertilization. Such fertilization is in itself illicit and in opposition to the dignity of procreation and of the conjugal union, even when everything is done to avoid the death of the human embryo.*

Although the manner in which human conception is achieved with *in vitro* fertilization and embryo transfer cannot be approved, every child which comes into the world must in any case be accepted as a living gift of the divine Goodness and must be brought up with love.

6. How is homologous artificial insemination to be evaluated from the moral point of view?

Homologous artificial insemination within marriage cannot be admitted except for those cases in which the technical means is not a substitute for the conjugal act but serves to facilitate and to help so that the act attains its natural purpose. . . .

Artificial insemination as a substitute for the conjugal act is prohibited by reason of the voluntarily achieved dissociation of the two meanings of the conjugal act. Masturbation, through which the sperm is normally obtained, is another sign of this dissociation: Even when it is done for the purpose of procreation the act remains deprived of its unitive meaning: "It lacks the sexual relationship called for by the moral order, namely the relationship which realizes 'the full sense of mutual self-giving and human procreation in the context of true love.' "

7. What moral criterion can be proposed with regard to medical intervention in human procreation?

The medical act must be evaluated not only with reference to its technical dimension, but also and above all in relation to its goal, which is the good of persons and their bodily and psychological health. The moral criteria for medical intervention in procreation are deduced from the dignity of human persons, of their sexuality and of their origin.

Medicine which seeks to be ordered to the integral good of the person must respect the specifically human values of sexuality. The doctor is at the service of persons and of human procreation. He does not have the authority to dispose of them or to decide their fate. A medical intervention respects the dignity of persons when it seeks to assist the conjugal act either in order to facilitate its performance or in order to enable it to achieve its objective once it has been normally performed.

On the other hand, it sometimes happens that a medical procedure technologically replaces the conjugal act in order to obtain a procreation which is neither its result nor its fruit. In this case the medical act is not, as it should be, at the service of conjugal union, but rather appropriates to itself the procreative function and thus contradicts the dignity and the inalienable rights of the spouses and of the child to be born.

The humanization of medicine, which is insisted upon today by everyone, requires respect for the integral dignity of the human person first of all in the act and at the moment in which the spouses transmit life to a new person. It is only logical therefore to address an urgent appeal to Catholic doctors and scientists that they bear exemplary witness to the respect due to the human embryo and to the dignity of procreation. The medical and nursing staff of Catholic hospitals and clinics are in a special way urged to do justice to the moral obligations which they have assumed, frequently also, as part of their contract. Those who are in charge of Catholic hospitals and clinics and who are often religious will take special care to safeguard and promote a diligent observance of the moral norms recalled in the present instruction.

8. The suffering caused by infertility in marriage.

The suffering of spouses who cannot have children or who are afraid of bringing a handicapped child into the world is a suffering that everyone must understand and properly evaluate.

On the part of the spouses, the desire for a child is natural: It expresses the vocation to fatherhood and motherhood inscribed in conjugal love. This desire can be even stronger if the couple is affected by sterility which appears incurable. Nevertheless, marriage does not confer upon the spouses the right to have a child, but only the right to perform those natural acts which are per se ordered to procreation.

A true and proper right to a child would be contrary to the child's dignity and nature. The child is not an object to which one has a right nor can he be considered as an object of ownership: Rather, a child is a gift, "the supreme gift" and the most gratuitous gift of marriage, and is a living testimony of the mutual giving of his parents. For this reason, the child has the right as already mentioned, to be the fruit of the specific act of the conjugal love of his parents; and he also has the right to be respected as a person from the moment of his conception.

Nevertheless, whatever its cause or prognosis, sterility is certainly a difficult trial. The community of believers is called to shed light upon and support the suffering of those who are unable to fulfill their legitimate aspiration to motherhood and fatherhood. Spouses who find themselves in this sad situation are called to find in it an opportunity for sharing in a particular way the Lord's cross, the source of spiritual fruitfulness. Sterile couples must not forget that "even when procreation is not possible, conjugal life does not for this reason lose its value. Physical sterility in fact can be for spouses the occasion for other important services to the life of the human person, for example, adoption, various forms of educational work and assistance to other families and to poor or handicapped children."

Many researchers are engaged in the fight against sterility. While fully safeguarding the dignity of human procreation, some have achieved results which previously seemed unattainable. Scientists therefore are to be encouraged to continue their research with the aim of preventing the causes of sterility and of being able to remedy them so that sterile couples will be able to procreate in full respect for their own personal dignity and that of the child to be born.

III
Moral and Civil Law

The Values and Moral Obligations That Civil Legislation Must Respect and Sanction in This Matter

The inviolable right to life of every innocent human individual and the rights of the family and of the institution of marriage constitute fundamental moral values because they concern the natural condition and integral vocation of the human person; at the same time they are constitutive elements of civil society and its order.

For this reason the new technological possibilities which have opened up in the field of biomedicine require the intervention of the political authorities and of the legislator, since an uncontrolled application of such techniques could lead to unforeseeable and damaging consequences for civil society. Recourse to the conscience of each individual and to the self-regulation of researchers cannot be sufficient for ensuring respect for personal rights and public order. If the legislator responsible for the common good were not watchful, he could be deprived of his prerogatives by researchers claiming to govern humanity in the name of the biological discoveries and the alleged "improvement" processes which they would draw from those discoveries. "Eugenism" and forms of discrimination between human beings could come to be legitimized: This would constitute an act of violence and a serious offense to the equality, dignity and fundamental rights of the human person.

The intervention of the public authority must be inspired by the rational principles which regulate the relationships between civil law and moral law. The task of the civil law is to ensure the common good of people through the recognition of and the defense of fundamental rights and through the promotion of peace and of public morality. In no sphere of life can the civil law take the place of conscience or dictate norms concerning things which are outside its competence. It must sometimes tolerate, for the sake of public order, things which it cannot forbid without a greater evil resulting. However, the inalienable rights of the person must be recognized and respected by civil society and the political authority. These human rights depend neither on single individuals nor on parents; nor do they represent a concession made by society and the state: They pertain to human nature and are inherent in the person by virtue of the creative act from which the person took his or her origin.

Among such fundamental rights one should mention in this regard a) every human being's right to life and physical integrity from the moment of conception until death; b) the rights of the family and of marriage as an institution and, in this area, the child's right to be conceived, brought into the world and brought up by his parents. To each of these two themes it is necessary here to give some further consideration.

In various states certain laws have authorized the direct suppression of innocents: The moment a positive law deprives a category of human beings of the protection which civil legislation must accord them, the state is denying the equality of all before the law. When the state does not place its power at the service of the rights of each citizen, and in particular of the more vulnerable, the very foundations of a state based on law are undermined. The political authority consequently cannot give approval to the calling of human beings into existence through procedures which would expose them to those very grave risks noted previously. The possible recognition by positive law and the political authorities of techniques of artificial transmission of life and the experimentation connected with it would widen the breach already opened by the legalization of abortion.

As a consequence of the respect and protection which must be ensured for the unborn child from the moment of his conception, the law must provide appropriate penal sanctions for every deliberate violation of the child's rights. The law cannot tolerate—indeed it must expressly forbid—that human beings, even at the embryonic stage, should be treated as objects of experimentation, be mutilated or destroyed with the excuse that they are superfluous or incapable of developing normally.

The political authority is bound to guarantee to the institution of the family, upon which society is based, the juridical protection to which it has a right. From the very fact that it is at the service of people, the political authority must also be at the service of the family. Civil law cannot grant approval to techniques of artificial procreation which, for the benefit of third parties (doctors, biologists, economic or governmental powers), take away what is a right inherent in the relationship between spouses; and therefore civil law cannot legalize the donation of gametes between persons who are not legitimately united in marriage.

Legislation must also prohibit, by virtue of the support which is due to the family, embryo banks, post-mortem insemination and "surrogate motherhood." ...

The civil legislation of many states confers an undue legitimation upon certain practices in the eyes of many today; it is seen to be incapable of guaranteeing that morality which is in conformity with the natural exigencies of the human person and with the "unwritten laws" etched by the Creator upon the human heart. All men of good will must commit themselves, particularly within their professional field and in the exercise of their civil rights, to ensuring the reform of morally unacceptable civil laws and the correction of illicit practices. In addition, "conscientious objection" vis-a-vis such laws must be supported and recognized. A movement of passive resistance to the legitimation of practices contrary to human life and dignity is beginning to make an ever sharper impression upon the moral conscience of many, especially among specialists in the biomedical sciences.

Conclusion

The spread of technologies of intervention in the processes of human procreation raises very serious moral problems in relation to the respect due to the human being from the moment of conception, to the dignity of the person, of his or her sexuality and of the transmission of life.

With this instruction the Congregation for the Doctrine of the Faith, in fulfilling its responsibility to promote and defend the church's teaching in so serious a matter, addresses a new and heartfelt invitation to all those who, by reason of their role and their commitment, can exercise a positive influence and ensure that in the family and in society due respect is accorded to life and love. It addresses this invitation to those responsible for the formation of consciences and of public opinion, to scientists and medical professionals, to jurists and politicians. It hopes that all will understand the incompatibility between recognition of the dignity of the human person and contempt for life and love, between faith in the living God and the claim to decide arbitrarily the origin and fate of a human being.

In particular, the Congregation for the Doctrine of the Faith addresses an invitation with confidence and encouragement to theologians, and above all to moralists, that they study more deeply and make ever more accessible to the faithful the contents of the teaching of the church's magisterium in the light of a valid anthropology in the matter of sexuality and marriage and in the context of the necessary interdisciplinary approach. Thus they will make it possible to understand ever more clearly the reasons for and the validity of this teaching. By defending man against the excesses of his own power, the church of God reminds him of the reasons for his true nobility; only in this way can the possibility of living and loving with that dignity and liberty which derive from respect for the truth be ensured for the men and women of tomorrow. The precise indications which are offered in the present instruction therefore are not meant to halt the effort of reflection, but rather to give it a renewed impulse in unrenounceable fidelity to the teaching of the church. . . .

SENATOR NUNN ON ABM TREATY INTERPRETATION

March 11-13, 1987

The already uncertain political outlook for President Ronald Reagan's effort to develop a nationwide antimissile defense program—officially called the Strategic Defense Initiative (SDI), but more widely referred to as Star Wars—took a serious turn for the worse early in March 1987. Senate Armed Services Committee Chairman Sam Nunn, D-Ga., widely regarded as one of Capitol Hill's most influential voices on defense issues, launched a scathing attack on a key policy in Reagan's political strategy for promoting the costly program.

At issue was whether the 1972 U.S.-Soviet treaty limiting antiballistic missile (ABM) weapons would allow tests of certain antimissile weapons and detection devices that were based in space or aboard aircraft. Contrary to the opinion generally held by U.S. observers since the treaty was signed, Abraham Sofaer, the State Department legal adviser, declared in October 1985 that such tests were allowed. This view would shield the SDI program for several years from the politically damaging charge that it would require U.S. abrogation of the ABM pact.

But after reviewing for months the secret record of the negotiations that produced the treaty, Nunn came down hard on the other side. In three lengthy, footnote-laden speeches delivered to the Senate on March 11, 12, and 13, Nunn rejected the administration's case with an uncustomary asperity. No relevant body of evidence supported the administration view, Nunn maintained—neither the negotiating record, nor the record of what the Senate was told the treaty meant when it debated ratification in 1972, nor the subsequent track record of the two parties to the pact.

Not only did the administration position misrepresent the negotiations, Nunn argued, but it would impair the Senate's constitutional role in approving the ratification of treaties. Since the Senate had held the traditional, restrictive view of the treaty's effect when it approved ratification, he maintained, the Reagan administration could not start basing U.S. policy on a different interpretation without Senate approval.

The SDI Debate

Nunn's position moved the treaty interpretation issue to the center of the 1987 congressional battles over SDI.

The size of the SDI budget seemed to have been settled, with all indications suggesting that Congress would approve for the fiscal 1988 budget slightly more than the $3.5 billion appropriated in fiscal 1987, which ended September 30, 1987. Reagan had requested $5.8 billion for fiscal 1988.

There was little public scrapping during the year over Reagan's general goal of exploring large-scale antimissile defenses, though there clearly was no consensus about the scope and purpose of the system being sought. Many liberal arms control advocates feared that antimissile programs would add a new dimension to the arms race, but they had abandoned as politically impractical efforts to block SDI outright.

The politically active front in the SDI debate through 1987 was the ABM treaty issue, and Nunn's unusually vigorous repudiation of the administration's position put Reagan on the defensive. After lengthy negotiations in October and November between top White House aides and leaders of the Senate and House Armed Services committees—including Nunn—the administration backed away from a showdown with Nunn and his allies, at least for this year: during fiscal 1988, the administration would conduct no tests inconsistent with the traditional, restrictive interpretation of the ABM treaty.

ABM Treaty Provisions

The fundamental and immediate impact of the 1972 treaty was to permit the deployment of an ABM system on two sites in each country, with no more than 100 missile launchers at each site and additional limits on the number and location of associated radars.

The 1987 debate focused on four provisions that had been relatively uncontroversial for more than a dozen years after the treaty was signed:

- *Article 1 declared that neither of the two countries would deploy ABM systems "for a defense of the territory of its country."*
- *Article 2 defined an ABM system as "a system to counter ballistic*

missiles or their elements in flight trajectory, currently consisting of" radars, interceptor missiles, and missile launchers.

- *Article 5 committed the two countries "not to develop, test or deploy ABM systems or components which are sea-based, air-based, space-based or mobile land-based."*
- *Agreed Statement D—one of several explanatory appendixes—read: "In order to assure fulfillment of the obligation not to deploy ABM systems and their components," except for the limited deployments allowed by the treaty, "specific limitations on such systems and their components would be subject to discussion" if "ABM systems based on other physical principles . . . are created in the future."*

The traditional interpretation had been that Article 2 covered all current and future antimissile systems. The references to the particular kinds of components of which the systems "currently" consisted was only illustrative. Accordingly, Article 5's ban on space-based and air-based components was deemed all-inclusive, and the only "new technology" systems allowed would be fixed, ground-based systems. From this viewpoint, Agreed Statement D served only to make explicit the right of the parties to work out the details of how to apply to new-technology ABM systems the treaty's limits, which were worded in terms of 1970s technology.

The administration's case for its new, less restrictive reading of the treaty emphasized that Soviet negotiators repeatedly had rejected U.S. efforts to include language that would have explicitly banned futuristic, space-based ABM weapons. As ratified, officials argued, the treaty used terms such as "ABM system" and "ABM component" in contexts that clearly referred only to 1972-style ABM systems.

Accordingly, they maintained, Article 5's ban on development of space-based weapons covered only 1972-style systems—that is, those comprising radars, interceptor missiles, and missile launchers. Actual deployment of a novel, space-based system would require amendment or abrogation of the treaty, they conceded. If the prohibitions in Article 5 had been intended to bar new-technology, space-based systems as well, they argued, there would have been no need to attach Agreed Statement D to the treaty.

Treaty Interpretation Issue

From the time Reagan inaugurated SDI early in 1983, the program was fundamentally at odds with the ABM treaty's basic purpose: to prevent efforts to deploy a nationwide antimissile defense, in the belief that each side's vulnerability to the other's retaliation would deter it from starting a nuclear war.

By its own terms, the treaty could be abrogated on six months' notice, a course long advocated by antimissile defense advocates. But the Reagan administration evidently wanted to defer a political battle over a decision to nullify the most politically visible U.S.-Soviet arms control treaty. To the contrary, Reagan and his aides emphasized repeatedly that SDI research would be in line with the treaty for years to come. That was consistent with the fact that early discussion of the program focused on the development of laser-armed satellites. Since these could not be tested for a decade or more, the issue of SDI's relationship to the ABM treaty was not immediately joined.

When the administration announced its revised interpretation of the treaty in 1985, a storm of protest arose in Congress and among U.S. allies. The Reagan team defused the objections by announcing that, while it stood by its position on the treaty, as a matter of policy SDI tests would continue to be governed by the traditional, more restrictive interpretation of the pact.

The treaty interpretation issue came to a head late in 1986. Some administration officials, led by Defense Secretary Caspar W. Weinberger, urged Reagan to shift the SDI emphasis to less exotic weapons that could be deployed as early as 1994 but that would require before 1990 some tests prohibited under the traditional interpretation. Late in January 1987, Nunn, who had begun reviewing the ABM negotiating record, charged that the White House was risking a "constitutional crisis" by pushing its new interpretation without consulting the Senate. Reagan promised early in February that he would consult the Senate and U.S. allies before making any final decision. A month later, Nunn weighed in with his own judgment of the matter.

Following are excerpts from Senator Sam Nunn's speeches before the Senate March 11, 12, and 13, 1987, concerning the Reagan administration's interpretation of the 1972 antiballistic missile treaty between the United States and the Soviet Union:

Part One: The Senate Ratification Proceedings

... [T]he Reagan administration's unilateral interpretation of the ABM Treaty constitutes a fundamental constitutional challenge to the Senate as a whole with respect to its powers and prerogatives in this area. The seriousness of this challenge has been further underscored in recent weeks by the administration's new claim that testimony during Senate treaty ratification proceedings "has absolutely no standing" in terms of establishing other parties' obligations under these treaties. In effect, the Reagan administration is telling the Senate not only that the executive branch is free to ignore the meaning of the treaty as originally described in the Senate of the United States, but also that other nations who are party to such treaties can disregard what the executive branch told the Senate at the time of ratification.

I am certain that this novel doctrine will receive close scrutiny during the hearings before the Foreign Relations Committee and the Judiciary Committee.

. . . [B]efore I present the results of my review of 1972 Senate ABM Treaty ratification proceedings, I believe that a few comments are in order about the overall context in which the Senate must consider the ABM reinterpretation issue.

First, I do not believe that the reinterpretation debate should be cast in terms of whether one is for or against the ABM Treaty. The treaty was accepted in 1972 by the Nixon administration and the United States Senate on the assumption, first, that the Soviet Union would strictly observe its terms, and second, that significant reductions in strategic offensive arms would be accomplished within 5 years.

Neither expectation has been fulfilled. The Soviets have not restrained the relentless expansion of their strategic offensive forces. Their massive investment in strategic defenses, primarily air defenses—while not a violation of the ABM Treaty—does contradict the spirit of the agreement; that is, that both sides recognized and accepted in 1972 that there can be no shield against retaliation. And violations such as the strategic Krasnoyarsk radar undermine the integrity of the agreement.

In the light of these circumstances . . . the Soviet Union must recognize that the United States commitment to the ABM Treaty cannot be deemed unalterable or open-ended—whether or not the traditional interpretation of the treaty is upheld. If arms control or unilateral strategic modernization efforts—such as moving to mobile ICBM's—fail to restore stability to the strategic balance in the future, the United States may well have to deploy strategic defenses designed to protect its retaliatory forces and command, control and communications. Unless the ABM Treaty could be amended by mutual agreement to permit such deployments, which would require approval of both parties, this action would necessarily require the United States to exercise its right under the supreme national interest clause of the treaty to withdraw on 6 months notice.

Certainly a U.S. decision to withdraw from the ABM Treaty would be enormously controversial at home and abroad. I am not counseling this course at this time. Nonetheless, the American public and our allies need to understand that if we cannot solve current strategic vulnerabilities through arms control or our own strategic programs, we may have no recourse but to consider deploying some form of strategic defense, in the future.

Second, those who support the reinterpretation of the ABM Treaty in the name of accelerating the SDI may be laboring under a fundamental and erroneous misimpression. There is a strong case that the specific SDI early deployment system now favored by Secretary [Caspar] Weinberger cannot be developed or tested under either interpretation.

This requires a rather complicated explanation which I will not go into at this time, but it is not at all certain, in fact I would say the evidence is leaning against it, that even the broad interpretation of the treaty would permit the testing and development of the so-called space-based kinetic-kill system that is now apparently favored for early deployment.

Finally, those who would cast this issue as a question of whether one is for or against Soviet violations of arms control agreements miss the point: there are other, more honorable responses available to the United States. These include, first, insisting that the Soviets correct the violations; second, proportional U.S. responses; and third and last, abrogation of the agreement.

For 200 years, the United States has stood for the rule of law as embodied in our Constitution. The reinterpretation issue must be approached not with an eye toward near-term gains, but rather with a decent respect for the long-term interests of the rule of law and the continued integrity of this Constitution—that magnificent document whose 200th birthday we celebrate this year.

... [T]he record of the ratification proceedings before the U.S. Senate in 1972 supports ... the following conclusions about the scope of the treaty.

First, executive branch witnesses clearly stated that development and testing of mobile space-based exotics was banned while development and testing of fixed land-based exotics was permitted. Key Members of the Senate, including Senators Henry Jackson, Barry Goldwater, John Sparkman, and James Buckley, were directly involved in the dialog and debate concerning the implications of the treaty which the record indicates they clearly understood to ban testing and development of mobile space-based exotics....

The question of exotics was raised in the first Senate hearing that considered the treaty. Senator Goldwater, in a question for the record to Secretary of Defense [Melvin R.] Laird, noted that he had "long favored" moving ahead with space-based ABM's capable of conducting boost-phase intercepts using "shot, nuces (sic.), or lasers," and asked whether it was correct that nothing in the treaty "prevents development to proceed in that direction."

The written reply from DOD distinguishes between development of fixed, land-based ABM's—which is permitted by the treaty—and this is extremely important, very complicated, but it is the key to this overall consideration—and development of mobile/space-based ABM's, which is prohibited. The reply from Secretary Laird expressly related these provisions to lasers, which in our terms today would be considered an "exotic" ABM component:

> With reference to development of a boost-phase intercept capability or lasers, there is no specific provision in the ABM Treaty which prohibits development of such systems. There is, however, a prohibition on the development, testing, or deployment of ABM systems which are space-based, as well as sea-based, air-based, or mobile land-based. The U.S. side under-

> stands this prohibition not to apply to basic and advanced research and exploratory development of technology which could be associated with such systems, or their components. There are no restrictions on the development of lasers for fixed, land-based ABM systems. The sides have agreed, however, that deployment of such systems which would be capable of substituting for current ABM components, that is, ABM launchers, ABM interceptor missiles, and ABM radars, shall be subject to discussion in accordance with Article XIII (Standing Consultative Commission) and agreement in accordance with Article XIV (amendments to the treaty).

This statement is particularly significant because it embodies a formal, written executive branch response. It clearly sets forth the traditional interpretation of the treaty with respect to exotics, permitting development, and testing only in a fixed, land-based mode. The reply makes it clear that mobile/space exotics are subject to the comprehensive ban on development, testing, and deployment, with the understanding . . . that the treaty only permits "basic and advanced research and exploratory development."

. . . [T]he reply clearly links the ban on development of mobile/space-based ABM laser systems to article V of the treaty. Article V contains a comprehensive ban on mobile/space-based, ABM systems. Secretary Laird's express linkage between mobile/space-based exotics and article V directly refutes the reinterpretation's analysis of the treaty's text, which asserts that article V applies only to components existing in 1972; that is, missiles, launchers, and radars.

The detailed executive branch reply was omitted from an October 30, 1985, analysis of the ratification debate submitted to the Senate Armed Services Committee by [State Department Legal Adviser Abraham D.] Sofaer on November 21, 1985. This omission was brought to the attention of the committee on January 6, 1986, in a letter from John Rhinelander, the legal adviser to the U.S. SALT I delegation. In a subsequent analysis of the ratification debate published in the June 1986 Harvard Law Review, Sofaer conceded in a footnote that the DOD [Department of Defense] reply to Goldwater supports the traditional interpretation.

The second example is an exchange between Senator Henry Jackson and DOD's Director of Research and Engineering which confirmed the treaty's ban on testing and development of mobile/space-based exotics. During the Senate debate on the SALT I accords, which included the ABM Treaty, the late Senator Henry Jackson, a senior member of the Armed Services Committee, conducted a rigorous inquiry into the agreements, with a profound impact on the conditions of Senate acceptance. From the outset, he exhibited a keen sensitivity to the issue of exotics by focusing on laser ABM's. For example, just 5 days after the treaty's signing, he made a statement sharply critical of the Army's reputed cancellation of a research contract involving laser ABM's.

When Secretary Laird came before the committee on June 6, 1972, he quickly assured Senator Jackson that no such contract had been canceled. When Senator Jackson asked about ABM Treaty limits in this area,

Secretary Laird gave a general reply—noting only that "research and development can continue, but certain components and systems are not to be developed"—without getting into the distinction between fixed, land-based systems and mobile/space-based systems.

Senator Jackson pursued that distinction in [a] June 22, 1972, hearing during testimony by Dr. John Foster, Director of Defense Research and Engineering, and Lt. Gen. Walter Leber, the program manager of the Army's Safeguard ABM system. This hearing involved a careful discussion of treaty's limits regarding development of ABM's using exotics, with a specific focus on the distinction between fixed, land-based systems and mobile/space based systems.

Senator Jackson began by noting that there were limitations in the treaty on lasers and then asked whether the agreement prohibited land-based laser development[.] Dr. Foster replied, "No sir; it does not." The text of the printed hearing reads as follows:

> Senator JACKSON. Article V says each party undertakes not to develop and test or deploy ABM systems or components which are sea based, air based, space based or mobile land based.
>
> Dr. FOSTER. Yes sir, I understand. We do not have a program to develop a laser ABM system.
>
> Senator JACKSON. If it is sea based, air based, spaced based or mobile land based. If it is a fixed, land-based ABM system, it is permitted; am I not correct?
>
> Dr. FOSTER. That is right.
>
> Senator JACKSON. What does this do to our research—I will read it to you; section 1 of article 5—this is the treaty: "each party undertakes to develop"—it hits all of these things—"not to develop, test or deploy ABM systems." You can't do anything; you can't develop; you can't test and finally, you can't deploy. It is not "or".
>
> Dr. FOSTER. One cannot deploy a fixed, land-based laser ABM system which is capable of substituting for an ABM radar, ABM launcher, or ABM interceptor missile.
>
> Senator JACKSON. You can't even test; you can't develop.
>
> Dr. FOSTER. You can develop and test up to the deployment phase of future ABM system components which are fixed and land based. My understanding is that you can develop and test but you cannot deploy. You can use lasers in connection with our present land-based Safeguard system provided that such lasers augment, or are an addendum to, current ABM components. Or, in other words, you could use lasers as an ancillary piece of equipment but not as one of the prime components either as a radar or as an interceptor to destroy the vehicle.

When Senator Jackson suggested that even research on ABM lasers might be prohibited, Dr. Foster said, "No." Interposed between Senator Jackson's question and Dr. Foster's answer is the following insert for the [Congressional] RECORD:

> Article V prohibits the development and testing of ABM systems or components that are sea-based, air-based, space-based, or mobile land-based. Constraints imposed by the phrase "development and testing" would be applicable only to that portion of the "advanced development stage" following laboratory testing, i.e., that stage which is verifiable by national means.

> Therefore, a prohibition on development—the Russian word is "creation"—would begin only at the stage where laboratory testing ended on ABM components, on either a prototype or bread-board model.

. . . This transcript reveals two key points. First, Dr. Foster pledged to submit the insert after Senator Jackson had declared that "we had better find out" exactly how the treaty applied to research and development in this area. Second, the transcript reveals that Dr. Foster declared that in order to clarify this issue, the submission would reflect a detailed review of the negotiating record. . . .

Several observations about the extensive exchange between Senator Jackson and Dr. Foster deserve emphasis. First, this exchange in the record includes a formal, written submission, which provided the executive branch with an opportunity to prepare an official coordinated statement after review of the negotiating record. As such, it clearly represents an authoritative statement of the administration's position. Second, the fact that the statement refers to article V—the treaty's ban on testing, development, and deployment of mobile/space-based ABM's—in the context of lasers again refutes the reinterpretation's premise that article V does not apply to ABM's using exotics.

The Jackson-Foster exchange directly contradicts the reinterpretation of the treaty. . . .

Dr. Foster, a Presidential appointee, was the highest ranking technical official, and third-ranking civilian in the Defense Department. He had served in his position since 1965. Nonetheless, the Sofaer analysis tries to disparage his testimony by stating Foster was "not involved in the drafting or negotiation of the treaty." The suggestion that the Director of Defense Research and Engineering would not have acquainted himself thoroughly with the treaty's effect on programs under his supervision prior to representing the administration before the Armed Services Committee is absurd. . . .

Sofaer's account of the exchange excises Senator Jackson's half of this dialog in its entirety. As a result, anyone reading this analysis would not know that Senator Jackson had acquired a detailed understanding of the treaty limits in this area or, indeed, that the Senator took the lead in drawing out of the witness explicit confirmation of these restrictions.

As a result of this omission, the only mention of Senator Jackson in Sofaer's October 1985 analysis of all of the Armed Services Committee's ratification hearings is in a discussion of a hearing on July 19, 1972. In a summary comment on Senator Jackson's July 19 statements, the reinterpretation concludes: "Fairly read, Senator Jackson's comments do not address future systems."

Mr. President, this is perhaps the most egregious omission and misinterpretation that I have come across in the entire record.

By omitting the extensive June 22 Jackson/Foster exchange on laser ABM's—as well as other instances when Senator Jackson queried witnesses on the question of laser ABM's, including a highly classified session on June 26 with CIA Director Richard Helms—the reinterpretation is then able to claim in a paragraph summarizing all congressional hearings during the ratification proceedings that "Senator Jackson's comments do not appear to address future systems." Sofaer's assertion that Senator Jackson never addressed the question of limits on laser ABM's during the entire Senate debate on the ABM Treaty is flatly and unequivocally contradicted by the record of the debate.

In the third example is a July 19 exchange with Senator Jackson, in which General Palmer confirmed that the JCS supported the limitation under which testing and development of exotics was restricted to fixed, land-based systems. The record of this Armed Services Committee hearing not only repudiates the claim that Senator Jackson did not address future systems, it also contains a crucial passage confirming the Joint Chiefs' understanding of the difference between fixed, land-based and mobile/space-based exotics in terms of the restrictions on development and testing.

This hearing involved an extensive exploration of treaty's limits on exotics, focusing on laser ABM's. The key exchange occurred between three Senators: Goldwater, Jackson, and [Peter] Dominick, and three executive branch witnesses: General Ryan, Chief of Staff of the Air Force, General Palmer, Acting Chief of Staff of the Army, and Lieutenant General Leber, project manager of the Safeguard ABM Program. This exchange covers seven pages of the printed hearing. During this exchange, the word "laser" was used 13 times, descriptions of or references to lasers were made 6 other times, and the phrase "futuristic systems" was mentioned 3 times.

During the same hearing, Senator Jackson also questioned the witness about General Palmer's broad statement that the treaty "does not limit R&D on futuristic systems." Senator Jackson, expressing concern about the generality of this response, drew the witnesses' attention to article V's prohibition on development of mobile ABM systems. General Ryan noted the distinction between permissible development of fixed, land-based systems and the prohibited development of mobile/space-based systems. Finally, General Palmer provided an authoritative statement on the prohibition on development of mobile/space-based exotics....

Sofaer's analysis of this discussion omits Palmer's crucial closing comment that the JCS were aware of the limits on development and testing of laser ABM's, had agreed to them, and recognized that this was a fundamental part of the final agreement. Thus, the record demonstrates that Sofaer's assertion that Senator Jackson did not address the question of exotics during the ratification debate is a complete and total misrepresentation. It also underscores the inadequacy of its analysis by its omission of this additional, and authoritative, confirmation that the treaty banned the development and testing of all but fixed, land-based exotics.

... Senator Jackson and the executive branch witnesses clearly cited the prohibition on testing and development of mobile/space-based systems in article V of the treaty as the authority for the prohibition on testing and development of missile/space based ABM using exotics. This further undermines the reinterpretation's analysis ... in which it asserts that article V should not be read as applying to mobile/space-based exotics.

... [T]he reinterpretation is based on two categories of incomplete, imprecise, or general statements—those which indicate that exotics cannot be deployed and those which indicate that R&D on lasers is permitted. However, each of these statements can be read as consistent with either the traditional interpretation or the reinterpretation. This is ... the heart of the case for reinterpretation so far as the Senate record is concerned. . . .

The record of the Senate proceedings does not support Sofaer's assertion that the record of the Senate ratification proceedings on the ABM Treaty and statements made at or near the ratification period "can be fairly read to support the so-called broader interpretation." On the contrary, the record of these proceedings makes a compelling case for the opposite conclusion: that the Senate was presented with a treaty that prohibited testing or development of mobile/space-based exotics; both the proponents and opponents of the treaty understood the agreement to have this effect; and there was no challenge to this understanding in the course of the Senate's approval of the treaty.

In summary, I have examined the reinterpretation's analysis of the Senate ratification proceedings and found its conclusions with respect to this record not to be credible. I have concluded that the Nixon administration presented the Senate with the traditional interpretation of the treaty's limits on mobile/space-based exotics. I have also concluded that the Senate clearly understood this to be the case at the time it gave its advice and consent to the ratification of the treaty. In my judgment, this conclusion is compelling beyond a reasonable doubt.

This finding at this juncture does not address all issues raised by the reinterpretation. In the two succeeding reports, I will examine the issues of subsequent practice and the negotiating record, and any final judgments must incorporate those assessments. Nonetheless, the findings that the Senate approved the ABM Treaty on the basis of its clear understanding, the acceptance of the traditional interpretation has serious ramifications for executive branch conduct. I would like to address these implications in closing my remarks.

... [I]n recent weeks, the State Department has raised a new theory, apparently pleading its case in the alternative; that is, the first part of the case is "the Senate was given the broad interpretation;" the second part of the case is, "just in case it was not given the broad interpretation here is the way we view it."

The State Department has argued that regardless of whether the ratification proceedings support the reinterpretation or broad interpretation, executive branch testimony presented to the Senate during the treaty-making process can be disregarded because it "has absolutely no standing" with the Soviets. In my opinion, this argument is incorrect in the context of the ABM Treaty, and is squarely in conflict with the constitutional role of the Senate.

Recent Soviet statements indicate that they now consider themselves bound by the traditional interpretation. For example, in an October 19, 1985, article in Pravda, Marshall Sergei Akhromeyev, the Chief of the Soviet General Staff, stated: "Article V of the Treaty absolutely unambiguously bans the development, testing, and deployment of ABM systems or components of space or mobile ground basing, and, moreover, regardless of whether these systems are based on existing or 'future' technologies."

The Reagan administration has not argued that the Soviets do not now claim to be bound by the traditional interpretation. Rather, the administration's position—as stated by Judge Sofaer—is that, "Only after the United States announcement of its support for the broader interpretation in October 1986 did the Soviet Union begin explicitly to articulate the restrictive interpretation."

Since the Soviets clearly agree with the traditional interpretation, the State Department's suggestion that statements made by U.S. officials during ratification proceedings have no standing with the Soviets is a rather curious, if not bizarre, argument. Let us look ... at the flip side of this interesting legal question. Let us assume for the purpose of this discussion that the Soviets were now taking the opposite postion.

Let us assume that they were asserting now that U.S. statements during the ratification proceedings had "no standing" with them.

In other words, if hypothetically the Soviets took the position the State Department is taking, would the United States have any basis in international law for relying on the statements to the Senate if we were insisting that the Soviets comply with the traditional view?

As a matter of international law, the actions of the parties, including their statements, provide an important guide to the meaning of a treaty. As Lord McNair notes in his classic treatise, The Law of Treaties, "when there is a doubt as to the meaning of a provision or an expression contained in a treaty, the relevant conduct of the parties after conclusion of the treaty (sometimes called the 'practical construction') has a high probative value as to the intention of the parties at the time of its conclusion."

Furthermore, he goes on to state, ... "[w]hen one party to a treaty discovers that other parties to a treaty are placing upon it an interpretation which in the opinion of the former it cannot bear, and it is not practical to secure agreement upon the matter, the former party should at once notify its dissent to the other parties and publish a reasoned explanation of the interpretation which it places upon the term in dispute." This is similar to the proposition under U.S. domestic law, that "if one party knows or has reason to know that the other party interprets language in a particular way, his failure to speak will bind him to the other party's understanding." Although not necessarily binding as a matter of international law, the failure to object to a publicly announced interpretation by another party to a treaty is clearly relevant to interpreting the treaty and to the treaty's meaning.

In the case of the ABM Treaty, these principles take on even greater significance in view of attendance by Soviet officials at the Senate hearings on the agreement. It is very interesting that Senators Goldwater and Jackson noted the presence of one such Soviet official—who was apparently a regular attendee—during an extensive discussion with Nixon administration officials during a July 19 Armed Services Committee hearing that dealt at length and in great detail with the specific question of the treaty's limitations in the area of laser ABM's, exactly the point we are debating now. . . . [I]t is obvious that the Soviets, who understand how our treaty-making process works, monitored the proceedings and reviewed the public records. Based on their clear awareness of the interpretation being presented to the Senate, if the Soviets chose to enter into the treaty and have the treaty go into force without raising an objection, the United States would have had a very strong basis in law for insisting on the original meaning as presented to the Senate—particularly if the Soviets waited until 15 years later to undertake a different view of the treaty.

Aside from the immediate issue of the ABM Treaty, it is contrary to the long-term interests of the United States to assert that statements made to the Senate have no standing with other parties to a treaty. The international community is well aware of the constitutional role of the Senate in the treatymaking process, and they are on notice that the executive branch explains treaties to the Senate during the ratification proceedings. It is to our national advantage to ensure that such authoritative explanations remain available as powerful evidence of a treaty's meaning in the event of an interpretative dispute among nations.

By asserting that the executive branch may now disregard the views of those who spoke for the Nixon administration and those who debated the issue in the Senate, the State Department is arguing, in effect, that administration witnesses need not accurately reflect the executive's understanding of a treaty; instead, they are free to keep that understanding a secret and may indeed mislead the Senate into consenting to a treaty which has a secret interpretation different from the meaning presented to the Senate. This line of argument has profound implications for the legislative process in general and the constitutional role of the Senate in particular.

Executive branch statements to the Senate during hearings on a proposed treaty may provide important evidence on issues of treaty interpretation in the international arena. They fill an even more important role, however, in our constitutional system, and this should not be overlooked. Such statements are an integral part of the making of a treaty, often shaping its content, and well-known to all parties to the proposal.

Under article II, section 2, clause 2 of the United States Constitution, the Presidential power to make treaties is subject to the requirement for advice and consent by two-thirds of the Senators present. Article VI, paragraph 2 of our Constitution provides that treaties are the supreme law of the land, which results in giving treaties the same force and effect as legislation enacted after action by both Houses of Congress.

Louis Henkin, one of the leading constitutional authorities in this field, ... has noted that "although treaty making has often been characterized as an executive function (in that special sense in which the conduct of foreign relations is executive), constitutional writers have considered the making of treaties to be different from other exercises of Presidential power, principally because of the Senate's role in the process, perhaps too because treaties have particular legal and political qualities and consequences."

Hamilton, in The Federalist (No. 75), clearly illustrated the intent of the Framers that treaty making be a shared power between Congress and the President, based on mutual trust.

Madison also took the position that "there are sufficient indications that the power of treaties is regarded by the Constitution as materially different from mere executive power, and as having more affinity to the legislative than to the executive character."

The Senate has played a vital role in numerous treaty negotiations, through means such as the process of confirming negotiators, statutory requirements for congressional consultation during the negotiations process, and informal discussions. Under current practice, when a proposed treaty is submitted, the Senate may consent to the treaty, withhold its consent—either expressly or through inaction—or approve it with conditions.

Because the Senate is an active participant in the making of the treaty, the hearings and debates are a vital source of information as to what the treaty means. The nature of the issue and the testimony of executive branch witnesses may lead the Senate to attach conditions or forego conditions, if there is an authoritative statement as to the meaning of a provision.

The position of the State Department I hope would be reexamined, because this position sends a clear message to the Senate: you cannot rely on our representations as to the meaning of a treaty. The adverse consequences of this proposition extend far beyond the issues at hand regarding the ABM Treaty. Our treaty relationships involve not only arms control matters, but also trade and business matters affecting the economic well-being of our Nation. We cannot ask the public to support proposed treaties if the executive takes the position that uncontradicted formal representations by senior officials are irrelevant as to the meaning of a treaty.

Because treaties are the supreme law of the land, the position of the State Department, if accepted by the executive branch, would compel the Senate to incorporate into its resolution of consent an "amendment" or "understanding" for every explanation given by an executive branch witness lest it be disavowed as "unilateral" after ratification. We would have to have so many understandings and conditions that the treaty would have to be negotiated all over again between the parties. Treaties so laden would eventually sink under their own weight. It would be extremely difficult to achieve bilateral agreements, and virtually impossible for the United States to participate in multilateral treaties. In addition, the Senate would feel compelled to request in each case a complete record of the negotiating history in order to ensure that no secret understandings would emerge contrary to assurances given to the Senate.

In short, in an effort to save the reinterpretation by asserting that executive branch statements to the Senate in 1972 are essentially meaningless, the State Department is risking a serious constitutional confrontation involving the executive branch and Congress that would go far beyond this matter. It would be a mistake for the executive branch to compound the problem further by asserting that the Senate has no role to play with respect to the meaning of treaties.

As a general proposition, the views of the executive on the interpretation of a treaty normally receive great deference[,] as well they should, from the Congress. Application of that principle in terms of the meaning presented to the Senate by the executive branch at the time of ratification leads to an interpretation that mobile/space-based exotics may not be developed or tested. Under the reinterpretation, such testing and development is permitted. In this situation, many in the Senate may be inclined to apply that classic line of cross-examination to the executive branch: "Should we believe what you are telling us now or should we believe what you were telling us back then?"

The Senate has the right to presume that executive branch witnesses are informed and truthful in their testimony, particularly when it comes to the Senate's constitutional role as a participant in the treaty-making process. The State Department's assertion that the executive, in effect, may mislead the Senate as to the meaning of a treaty has the unfortunate effect of directly challenging the Senate's constitutional role. This effect could carry over and may well produce a congressional backlash through its exercise of the power of the purse and the power to raise and support armies in a manner that would give effect to the original meaning of the treaty as presented to the Senate.

In conclusion, ... the Senate was clearly informed by the executive branch that the ABM Treaty prohibits testing and development of mobile/space-based ABM's using exotics. This was an issue which key Senators viewed as a matter of significance, and which was directly addressed by the executive branch during the treaty-making process in statements to the Senate. These circumstances raise a number of possibilities with respect to the significance of other evidence as to the meaning of the treaty. There are three distinct possibilities here.

First, if the negotiating record and evidence of subsequent practice by the parties supports the traditional interpretation, the issue would be beyond question. The traditional interpretation would apply....

Second, if the negotiating record and evidence of subsequent practice is ambiguous or inconclusive, there would be no basis for abandoning the traditional interpretation as clearly understood by the Senate at the time it gave its advice and consent on the basis of this understanding. Absent compelling evidence that the Senate was misinformed as to the agreement between the United States and the Soviet Union, the compact reached between the Senate and the executive branch at the time of ratification[,] in my view, should be upheld.

The third possibility, and perhaps the most disturbing possibility: If the negotiating record and evidence of the subsequent practices of the United States and Soviet Union establish a conclusive basis for the reinterpretation—in other words, if Judge Sofaer is right on the negotiating record—this would mean that the Nixon administration signed one contract with the Soviets and the Senate ratified a different contract. Such a conclusion would have profoundly disturbing constitutional implications—to say the least. In effect, the President would have to choose between the executive branch's obligations to the Senate and its contract with the Soviet Union. If the President did not choose to honor the commitments to the Senate, the Senate will then be faced with developing an appropriate response or risk having its role in the treaty-making process become meaningless....

Part Two: Subsequent Practice Under the ABM Treaty

...In my speech yesterday, I stated that I have concluded that the Nixon administration presented the Senate with the so-called "Traditional Interpretation" of the treaty's limits on the development or testing of mobile/space-based exotics—that is, that such activities were banned. I stated that I have also concluded that the Senate clearly understood this to be the case at the time it gave its advice and consent to the ratification of the treaty....

...I also took sharp exception to the administration's recent claim that statements made by the executive branch to the Senate at the time of treaty ratification proceedings have "absolutely no standing" with other states party to such treaties. In my opinion, this claim is incorrect in the specific case of the ABM Treaty and is squarely in conflict with the constitutional role of the Senate....

The report that I am delivering today addresses the available record of United States and Soviet practices since 1972. I stress the words, "available record," because we do not have the entire record. No one should be under a misimpression here. The record we have now is comprised of a 1985 analysis that was submitted by the Department of State to the U.S. Senate and several other documents.

This report addresses the available record of United States and Soviet practices—including their public statement—since the treaty was signed in May 1972. As I noted yesterday, both international law and U.S. domestic law recognize that the practices of the parties, including their statements, provide evidence of their intent with regard to the meaning of a treaty.

The record of United States and Soviet subsequent practice now available to the Senate is far from comprehensive. For example, the Senate has no access to statements made by American and Soviet officials in the 1972-85 timeframe in the course of negotiations in SALT II, START, INF, or the Standing Consultative Commission, known as the SCC. Nor does the Senate have access to statements made by United States or Soviet officials during summit meetings, foreign minister-level discussions, or routine diplomatic contacts.

So my statement today is based on what we now have available. There may be more information forthcoming.

I also stress, though, that this is the record that was examined by Judge Sofaer in arriving at his opinion. So to the best of my knowledge, what we have is what he had, and his opinion was derived therefrom.

President Reagan recently directed the State Department to conduct a thorough review of this issue. It is unfortunate that a rigorous administration study of subsequent practice—which has an important bearing on the whole question of treaty interpretation—was not conducted prior to such a major shift in U.S. policy. The administration has indicated that this study will be completed by April 30 and has promised that it will be submitted to the Senate for its review. Once the Senate has had an opportunity to review this second, or subsequent study, consultations will be—we hope—conducted on its conclusions. . . .

In an analysis submitted to the Armed Services Committee in a 1985 hearing, the State Department Legal Adviser, Abraham Sofaer, examined the record of subsequent practices. These conclusions were reiterated in an article which he published in the June, 1986, Harvard Law Review.

In both of these analyses, Sofaer claims that prior to the Reagan administration's announcement of the reinterpretation in October, 1985, the U.S. Government had not held a consistent position on the correct interpretation of the treaty provisions governing mobile/space-based exotics. In short, Sofaer denies that the traditional interpretation is in fact "traditional." Rather, Sofaer insists that the version of the treaty originally presented to the Senate was more consistent with the reinterpretation than the traditional interpretation and that successive administrations fluctuated back and forth between the broader and the more restrictive positions:

> Statements made during the post-ratification period have been mixed. Early statements tended to support the broader interpretation; several later ones presented a more restrictive view, some explicitly. At no time, however, was one interpretation universally accepted.

In support of the reinterpretation, Reagan administration officials have made other claims about subsequent practice. For example, in an appearance before the Senate Armed Services Committee on February 17 of this year, Secretary Weinberger was asked about the treaty's effect on the development and testing of mobile/space-based exotics. The Secretary replied that "you have a situation in which this point was never either specifically considered in the ratification process, nor has it been seriously considered in the years between, because the issue itself never had any importance since no one was on our side working on strategic defense." In short, Secretary Weinberger claims that not only did the issue of restrictions on exotics under the treaty never come up during the 1972 Senate ratification debate, but also that the issue never came up in the intervening years prior to the initiation of the strategic defense initiative [SDI].

The report which I released yesterday totally contradicts the first of Secretary Weinberger's assertions—that is, that the question of the treaty's applicability to the development, testing, or deployment of laser and other exotic ABM systems or components was never addressed during the 1972 Senate ratification proceedings. Today, I will discuss Secretary Weinberger's assertion that the question never arose until work began on SDI, as well as Sofaer's claim that there has been no consistent U.S. view since 1972.

First, let me address U.S. behavior under the treaty. The United States has not tested or developed a mobile/space-based ABM system or component of an exotic design. As late as 1985, the executive branch, in a Department of Defense report to Congress on the SDI Program, expressly endorsed the traditional view of the treaty as the basis for structuring its activities. This pattern of behavior is fully consistent with the traditional view of the treaty.

What about Soviet behavior under the treaty? Neither the Reagan administration nor any of its predecessors has asserted that the Soviet Union has developed or tested a mobile/space-based ABM system or component in contravention of the traditional view of the treaty....

I have examined the 13-year period from May 26, 1972, until October 6, 1985, with a view toward developing three categories of statements, and this goes to the question of U.S. statements about limitations on so-called exotics. The first category: Those which explicitly support the reinterpretation. The second category: Those which explicitly support the traditional view. The third category: Those which generally address the subject of [testing], development, or deployment of exotics but which do not explicitly support either interpretation.

The first category I will address is those which explicitly support the reinterpretation.

Judge Sofaer has not identified any official statements prior to October 1985 in which the U.S. Government expressly took the position that the treaty permitted testing and development of mobile/space-based exotics....

The second category is U.S. statements that expressly support the traditional view—and there are many such statements. I will name a few of them today.

... [T]he Nixon administration clearly took the position in its testimony to the Senate that the treaty banned mobile/space-based ABM's using exotics. This position was announced in public subsequent to the signing of the agreement by the heads of state, but prior to when the treaty entered into force.

With respect to statements made after the treaty entered into force, the available record of both official and unofficial U.S. statements directly contradicts both Secretary Weinberger's assertion that this issue never came up prior to the initiation of SDI and Judge Sofaer's claim that the U.S. position on the issue has not been consistent. . . .

In 1975, Congress amended the Arms Control and Disarmament Act to require the executive branch to prepare an arms control impact statement for submission with requests for authorization and appropriation of defense and nuclear programs. The first two such submissions, for fiscal year 1977 and fiscal year 1978, were criticized as too general by the chairmen of the Senate Foreign Relations Committee and House Foreign Affairs Committee. A more detailed report was prepared for fiscal year 1979, involving an intensive interagency review process, including final review and approval by the National Security Council. As such, it represented the formal, coordinated views of the executive branch.

The fiscal year 1979 ACIS, which was the first arms control impact statement to address the issue of testing and development of mobile/space-based ABM's using exotics under the ABM treaty, contained the following key passage:

> PBWs [particle beam weapons] used for BMD [ballistic missile defense] which are fixed, land-based could be developed and tested but not deployed without amendment of the ABM Treaty, and the development, testing, and deployment of such systems which are other than fixed, land-based is prohibited by Article V of the treaty.

This clear statement by the executive branch severely undermines the reinterpretation because it confirms the traditional meaning of the treaty as provided to the Senate in 1972. . . ,

The arms control impact statements submitted by the executive branch for fiscal year 1980 through fiscal year 1986, including those submitted by the Reagan administration, consistently took the position that mobile/space-based ABM's using exotics could not be tested and developed under the ABM treaty. I want to emphasize that these statements include express reaffirmation by the Reagan administration of the traditional interpretation. These statements were coordinated between the various departments of government.

The 1985 SDI report, submitted to the Congress in March 1985, contained an appendix on "The Strategic Defense Initiative [SDI] and the ABM treaty." As Sofaer has noted, this document "expressly embraced the restrictive interpretation." This one has been acknowledged by the administration.

It is further confirmation of the traditional view by the Reagan administration.

Let me now discuss several unofficial statements concerning negotiations. In the years after the ABM Treaty entered into force, several books were published which provided unofficial accounts of the negotiations and descriptions of the meaning of the treaty's provisions. "Cold Dawn: The Story of SALT," published in 1973, was written by John Newhouse, a former Senate Foreign Relations Committee staff member, based on interviews with the participants. It has also been reported that Newhouse had direct access to classified Nixon administration documents. "Cold Dawn," which was widely regarded as the first comprehensive account of the negotiations, contains the following passages concerning exotics:

> NSDM 127 [the instructions to the negotiators] banned everything other than research and development of fixed, land-based exotics. There remained to convince Moscow that the great powers should remove exotics future threats to stability, as well as the immediate ones.
>
> Although the basic ABM agreement would be left for an eleventh-hour White House decision, the delegation managed a major breakthrough toward the end of January when the Soviets accepted the U.S. position on exotic systems. Back in the summer, Moscow's attitude, as reflected by its delegation, had been sympathetic. Then, in the autumn, it hardened, probably under pressure from the military bureaucracy. Washington was accused of injecting an entirely new issue. Moscow would not agree to a ban on future defensive systems, except for those that might be space-based, sea-based, air-based, or mobile land-based. The U.S. Delegation persisted and was rewarded. Land-based exotics would also be banned. The front channel had produced an achievement of incalculable value.

In 1974, John Rhinelander, legal adviser to the U.S. delegation, coauthored a book on the SALT accords which contains the following passages relevant to the exotics issue:

> ... The future systems ban applies to devices which would be capable of substituting for one or more of the three basic ABM components, such as "killer" laser or particle accelerator. Article III of the Treaty does not preclude either development or testing of fixed, land-based devices which could substitute for ABM components, but does prohibit their deployment. Article V, on the other hand, prohibits development and testing, as well as deployment, of air-based, sea-based, space-based, or mobile land-based ABM systems or components, which includes "future systems" for those kinds of environments. The overall effect of the treaty is, therefore, to prohibit any deployment of future systems and to limit their development and testing to those in a fixed, land-based mode.

... The third category is comprised of U.S. statements supportive of either interpretation.

Let me first mention testimony to the House in 1972. During the House of Representatives' review of the SALT I accords, the question of the applicability of the ABM Treaty to lasers or other exotic ABM's was only raised on a few occasions and never in any detail. In general, statements by executive branch officials that did touch on this issue in the course of House testimony fell into one or the other of the two categories of imprecise or incomplete comments which I discussed yesterday in my report on the Senate ratification proceedings. These two categories are, first, a general statement to the effect that exotics cannot be deployed unless the treaty is amended but which provided no elaboration as to the limits on development or testing; and second, a general assurance that R&D on laser ABM's could continue, but which did not distinguish between fixed, land-based systems and mobile/space-based systems.

For example, on July 25, 1972, Ambassador Smith [head of the U.S. negotiating delegation] told the House Armed Services Committee:

> An additional important qualitative limitation is the prohibition on the development and testing, as well as deployment, of sea, air, space-based and land-mobile ABM systems and components. Of perhaps even greater importance as a qualitative limitation is the prohibition on the deployment of future types of ABM systems that are based on physical principles different from present technology.

As I discussed yesterday, the reinterpretation presumes that if Smith had believed that the traditional interpretation had been agreed to, he would not have said only that futures were not deployable, he would have said that the development, testing, or deployment of futures was banned.

There are three major problems with the logic on which this analysis is based. First, the Smith statement is true and accurate on its face because under either interpretation deployment of exotics is banned. Second, it attempts to build a major case on what was not said. Third, if Smith had said what the reinterpretation postulates he should have said, he would have been wrong. Why? Because under either interpretation the development or testing of fixed, land-based exotics is permitted. Development or testing of mobile/space-based exotics is, of course, banned under the traditional interpretation.

... Secretary [of State William] Rogers made a similar statement to the House Foreign Affairs Committee on July 20, 1972.

An example of the second category of statement, including a discussion of research and development, was a July 27, 1972, response by Admiral [Thomas] Moorer, Chairman of the Joint Chiefs of Staff, to a question from Congressman [George] Whitehurst about the treaty's effect on "some kind of technological breakthrough, perhaps something beyond Spartan or Sprint in the state of the art." Admiral Moorer read agreed statement D and then said "there is no restraint on research and development."

Several comments about this reply are in order. First, Admiral Moorer did not differentiate between basing modes, that is, fixed, land based versus mobile/space-based. Thus under the traditional interpretation, Admiral Moorer's statement is correct as it applies to fixed, land-based laser ABM's. Second, as I mentioned yesterday, the administration, which had been stung by Senator Jackson's criticism of an alleged canceled laser contract, was going to lengths to assure Congress that the then-current U.S. laser ABM Program—which was fixed, land-based—could go forward through the research and development stages. In sum, the statement does not contradict either interpretation; nor does it provide explicit support for this view. Finally, as I noted yesterday, Congress was expressly advised that the Chiefs were aware that the treaty permitted testing and development of exotics only in a fixed, land-based mode, they concurred in that view, and they understood it to be a fundamental part of the treaty.

Turning to postratification statements, in his 1985 submission to the Armed Services Committee, Judge Sofaer identified three cases in which official U.S. reports or statements noted that under the treaty, new ABM systems based on "other physical principles" could not be deployed. The three cases are: An October 23, 1972, speech at the United Nations by Ambassador [George] Bush; the ACDA [Arms Control and Disarmament Agency] annual report for 1972; and Secretary Rogers' foreign policy report of April 19, 1973. Judge Sofaer does not identify any aspect of these statements that directly addresses testing and development. . . .[B]rief statements to the effect that "exotics can not be deployed," but which are silent on the question of limits on development and testing, cannot be read as compelling any particular interpretation of the treaty.

These statements are totally consistent with ... either the broad interpretation or the narrow interpretation. . . .

Since 1972, the Arms Control and Disarmament Agency has prepared five editions of a publication containing the texts of the principal arms control agreements to which the United States is a party, accompanied by brief narrative descriptions of the texts and the history of the negotiations which led to the agreements.

Each edition, including the most recent—1982—contains a paragraph relevant to the issue of exotics. In his 1985 submission to the committee, Judge Sofaer quotes the following excerpt from the 1982 ACDA compilation report:

> Should future technology bring forth new ABM systems "based on other physical principles" than those employed in current systems, it was agreed that limiting such systems would be discussed, in accordance with the treaty's provisions for consultation and amendment.

Judge Sofaer cites this in his review of subsequent practice for the proposition that: "ACDA's periodic compilation of arms control agreements has consistently supported the 'broad' view of the Treaty." He maintains that although the record of U.S. statements between 1972 and 1985 is "mixed," "the one document that tracks the issue over the 1972-1982 period—the ACDA publication [']Arms Control and Disarmament Agreements[']—appears to reflect that future systems are regulated only by Agreed Statement D."

There are a number of problems with Judge Sofaer's effort to represent this ACDA publication as a definitive interpretation. As with similar statements made during the ratification hearings, the ACDA report does not compel any particular interpretation of the treaty. It is entirely consistent with either the traditional view—under which exotics may be tested or developed in a fixed, land-based mode, which was then the focus of U.S. research—or the reinterpretation permitting testing and development of all exotics. The preface to the ACDA publication underscores the generality of its content, specifically noting that this material provides a "brief narrative discussion" of the treaties contained therein. Another difficulty—and I would say this is a key difficulty—is that in his 1985 submission to the Senate Armed Services Committee, Judge Sofaer omitted the crucial first sentence of this paragraph which is being heavily relied on in his analysis as a statement which consistently supports the broad view. I would like to share with my colleagues that particular sentence. . . .

> Further, to decrease the pressures of technological change and its unsettling impact on the strategic balance, both sides agree to prohibit development, testing, or deployment of sea-based, air-based, or space-based ABM systems and their components, along with mobile land-based ABM systems.

This sentence clearly ties to prohibitions in article V of the treaty against testing and development of mobile systems to the goal of decreasing "the pressures of technological change," thereby implying strongly that the treaty prohibits testing and development of mobile ABM systems which would incorporate future technologies. Judge Sofaer reinserted this sentence in his June 1986 article in the Harvard Law Review, but he fails in any way to deal with its implications for his analysis.

I do not cite this sentence as proving the traditional view. But what is amazing about this dialog . . . is that the heart of what Judge Sofaer is relying on to support the broader view contains a sentence which he originally left out, and which implicitly supports the traditional view. So what we have here is that the heart of the case for the reinterpretation as it concerns subsequent practice has an omitted sentence which supports the traditional view, and the sentence which is quoted does not support either view. . . .

A more serious problem for the Sofaer analysis is its failure to reconcile the brief, narrative statement in ACDA's compilation of treaties with the executive branch's express treatment of the prohibition on testing and development of mobile exotics in the fiscal year 1979-86 arms control impact statements [ACIS]. . . .

In summary, there are three main problems with Judge Sofaer's reliance on the ACDA compilation. First, the statement which he cites does not support the reinterpretation. . . . It does not go to the question one way or the other. Second, the compilation does not purport to be a comprehensive statement of U.S. Government policy. Third, a far more authoritative and comprehensive statement is contained in the arms control impact statements, which were submitted to the Congress on behalf of the President for the express purpose of assisting the Congress in making policy decisions concerning the funding of U.S. defense programs.

Turning to the question of Soviet statements, Judge Sofaer does not rely on any Soviet statements in the case for reinterpretation, but notes that the few remarks by the Soviets on the subject are illuminating. He quotes only one Soviet statement, a 1972 speech by Marshall Grechko generally noting that the "Treaty imposes no limitations on the performance of research and experimental work aimed at resolving the problem of defending the country against nuclear missile attack."

Several comments about this statement are in order. First, Marshall Grechko does not define "experimental work." He did not use the word "development," nor did he refer to "exotics" in that statement.

But even if he had said those words, and to get much out of his statement you have to assume he said those words—which he did not[—] even if he had said "development," and even if he had linked it specifically to "exotics," that statement would have still been entirely consistent with the traditional view because the traditional view permits the testing and development of fixed, land-based ABM's using exotics. Because this statement makes no reference to mobile/space-based exotics, it is simply another general statement consistent with either view of the treaty. It does not reflect on one view or the other.

Judge Sofaer also states that the Soviets did not "begin explicitly to articulate the restrictive interpretation" until the new United States position was announced in October, 1985.

Now, that is an interesting bit of information, but it is not particularly helpful to the case for reinterpretation. The Soviets were on notice of United States adherence to the traditional view not only from the ratification debate, but also from the official arms control impact statements noted above, and as far as available information shows, they made no objection to the traditional view of the treaty.

In other words, why should the Soviet Union have, prior to 1985, protested and said that we were, in effect, implementing the broad view when we were not and when during that whole period our own official publications said we were adhering to the traditional view.

So I do not think there would really have been a burden on them to comment during that time frame.

Finally, the administration has not provided any information to date demonstrating Soviet practices or statements expressly embracing the reinterpretation. Given the Reagan administration's repeated endorsement of the traditional interpretation in the annual Arms Control Impact Statements it submitted prior to October 1985, any violations of that view presumably would have been brought to the public's attention.

It is possible, of course, that the new administration review which is now under way will uncover some heretofore unknown Soviet activities or statements....

...It must be remembered, however, that subsequent statements and practices constitute evidence to be used on treaty interpretation but the context of the practices or statements is crucial. So we will not really be able to examine any statements we may be presented unless we see the overall context....

Part [Three]: The ABM Negotiating Record

...Today I will address the record of the ABM Treaty negotiations in 1971 and 1972 as provided to the Senate by the Department of State....

Yesterday, I reviewed the available record of the United States and Soviet practices and statements during the 13-year period between the signing of the treaty and the announcement of the reinterpretation which occurred in October of 1985.

Under both international and domestic law, such evidence may be considered in determining the meaning of the treaty.

Based on the information provided to the Senate to date by the State Department, I found no evidence which contradicted the Senate's original understanding of the meaning of the treaty. On the contrary, I noted that successive administrations, including the Reagan administration, had prior to 1985 consistently indicated that the treaty banned the development and testing of mobile/space-based ABM's using exotics.

Summarizing then, where the situation now stands after the first two reports: First, the Reagan administration made a case for a broader reading of the treaty based, in part, on an analysis of the Senate ratification proceedings, arguing that the record of this debate supported the reinterpretation. I found this case not to be credible. Second, the Reagan administration made a case for a broader reading of the treaty based, in part, on subsequent practice, arguing that the record of the United States and Soviet statements and practices supported the reinterpretation. I also found this case not to be persuasive.

Some advocates of the broader reading—including its principal author, Judge Sofaer—now appear to be hanging their hats on the negotiating record, arguing that this negotiating record provides persuasive or compelling support for their case. As I noted on Wednesday, the administration's focus on the negotiating record as a primary source of treaty interpretation confronts us with three separate possibilities:

The first possibility: If the negotiating record is consistent with the original meaning of the treaty as provided to the Senate by the executive branch, the traditional interpretation would prevail beyond question.

The second possibility: If the negotiating record is ambiguous or inconclusive, there would be no basis for abandoning the traditional interpretation. Absent compelling evidence that the contract consented to by the U.S. Senate was not the same contract entered into between the Nixon administration and the Soviet Union—and we do not have that kind of evidence—the treaty presented to the Senate at the time of ratification should be upheld.

There is a third possibility: If the negotiating record clearly establishes a conclusive basis for the reinterpretation, this would mean that the President at that time signed one contract with the Soviets and the Senate ratified a different contract. Such a conclusion would have profoundly disturbing constitutional implications and as far as I know would be a case of first impression. . . .

It is important to note that the material presented in terms of the negotiating record consists of a disjointed collection of cables and memoranda.

This is not unusual. A lot of people really do not understand what a negotiating record is. It is not a clear transcript of a dialog between the two superpowers as they negotiate around the table—far from that.... There is no single document or even set of documents that constitutes an official negotiating history. There is no transcript of the proceedings. Instead, what we have is a variety of documents of uneven quality—some of them precise, some of them well structured, some of them done hastily, some of them simply notes in the margin. Some involve detailed recollections of conversations, others contain nothing more than cryptic comments.

Nonetheless, this is the record on which the Reagan administration's decision was based. If the State Department identifies and submits other relevant documents, I shall be prepared to review them as well....

Having been through the material, I will understand why, as a matter of international law, the negotiating record is the least persuasive evidence of a treaty's meaning. It does not have the same standing, of course, as the treaty itself under international law; it does not have the same standing as the conduct of the parties subsequent to entering into the agreement; it does not have the same standing as the ratification proceedings whereby the Senate takes formal testimony and has formal debate and has formal presentation of matter by administration witnesses. To put this in the right international legal framework Lord McNair, who is an expert on treaties and interpretations thereof, states as follows:

> The preceding reveiw of the practice indicates that no litigant before an international tribunal can afford to ignore the preparatory work of a treaty, but that he would probably err in making it the main plank of his argument. Subject to the limitations indicated in this chapter, it is a useful makeweight but in our submission it would be unfortunate if preparatory work ever became a main basis of interpretation. In particular, it should only be admitted when it affords evidence of the common intention of both or all parties.

This same general view is set forth in the commentary on the second restatement of the foreign relations law of the United States, which notes that "conference records kept by delegations for their own uses * * * will usually be excluded" from consideration under international law, although they may be considered by national courts for domestic purposes....

Based on my review, I believe that Judge Sofaer has identified some ambiguities in this record. One cannot help but wish that the United States and Soviet negotiators had achieved a higher level of clarity and precision in their drafting of this accord. Of course, as we in the Senate well know, writing clear law is a worthy goal but one which is not easily attained. These ambiguities are not, however, of sufficient magnitude to demonstrate that the Nixon administration reached one agreement with the Soviets and then presented a different one to the Senate....

Notwithstanding the ambiguities, the negotiating record contains substantial and credible information which indicates that the Soviet Union did agree that the development and testing of mobile/space-based exotics was banned. I have concluded that the preponderance of evidence in the negotiating record supports the Senate's original understanding of the treaty—that is, the traditional interpretation.

I have drafted a detailed classified analysis which examines Sofaer's arguments about the negotiating record at great length. Over the next few days, I intend to consult with the distinguished majority leader, Senator [Robert C.] BYRD, about submitting this report for the review of Senators in room S-407. I will also work with the State Department to see how much of this analysis can be declassified and released for public review.

I would, of course, like for all of it to be released.

. . . I believe it is appropriate at this juncture to pause for a moment and reflect on how the administration could be in such serious error on its position on this very important issue. First, the administration, in my view, is wrong in its analysis of the Senate ratification debate. I think I have set that forth in great detail.

Second, I think the Reagan administration is wrong in its analysis of the record of subsequent practice, at least insofar as we have been given information on that subject.

Third, I believe the administration is wrong in its analysis of the negotiating record itself. I believe that we need to take a look at the procedure by which the administration arrived at its position. I think the procedure itself, as people find out more about it, will reveal itself as having been fundamentally flawed.

At the time the decision was announced by the Reagan administration in 1985, the administration was divided as to the correct reading of the negotiating record, with lawyers at the Arms Control and Disarmament Agency, the Defense Department, and even within Judge Sofaer's own office holding conflicting views. By his own admission, Judge Sofaer had not conducted a rigorous study of the Senate ratification proceedings or the record of United States and Soviet practice, even though these are critical—indeed crucial—elements of the overall process by which one interprets treaties. Judge Sofaer made no effort to interview any principal ABM negotiator except Ambassador [Paul] Nitze—even though most of these gentlemen were still active professionally and living in or near Washington, DC. Finally, there was no discussion with the Senate, despite the Senate's constitutional responsibilities as a conguarantor of treaties.

Mr. President, to say that this is a woefully inadequate foundation for a major policy and legal change is a vast understatement. I hope that we can now . . . begin to address the real problems that confront our Nation in the areas of strategic balance and arms control.

There are a number of specific steps which I believe our Government should take in trying to bring a final resolution to this legal controversy. . . . First, I believe the State Department should declassify the ABM Treaty negotiating record after consulting with and informing the Soviet Union of our intentions. The only downside I can see to declassification, since this record is at least 15 years old, is the diplomatic precedent, and that is to be considered. However, if the Soviet Union is informed and consulted in advance of declassification, it seems to me that there would be no adverse precedent.

Second, we must recognize that by upholding the traditional interpretation of the treaty we certainly will not eliminate all the ambiguities with respect to the effect of the treaty. Some ambiguities remain. The United States and the Soviet Union have not reached a meeting of the minds on the precise meaning of such important words as "development," "component," "testing in an ABM mode," and "other physical principles." The appropriate forum for attempting to remove these ambiguities is the Standing Consultative Commission [SCC], as specified in the treaty. I strongly recommend that the SCC be tasked with the very important job of discussing these terms with the Soviet representatives and trying to come to mutual agreement.

Third and most important, we should continue to negotiate toward agreement in Geneva on a new accord limiting offensive as well as defensive systems, which would supersede the ABM Treaty as well as SALT II, and that would, of course, render moot this whole debate about narrow versus broad interpretation. Nothing would be better than to render this argument moot by entering into a comprehensive agreement on offense and defense and to have the terms defined with precision, clear up these ambiguities, and move on into the new arms control era.

Finally, we must develop an objective analysis of what tests are necessary under the strategic defense initiative which cannot be conducted under the traditional interpretation. We were told last year by General Abramson, the head of this project, that there were no tests which would be adversely impacted by the traditional interpretation before the early 1990's. If that has changed, we need to know what changes have taken place and what has driven those changes. I want to emphasize that our Armed Services Committee needs this analysis and we need it before we begin the markup of our committee bill, because any discussion of what this SDI money is going to be used for has to have as a foundation the overall interpretation and the tests that will be conducted thereunder.

I emphasize also that the determination should be based on a sound technological assessment and not on an ideologically driven kind of judgment. It is important for us to know that we are getting an analysis of scientists and not ideologs who have some agenda that has nothing to do with the technology and the tests at hand....

Mr. President, I should like to read for the RECORD what I think is a very important statement by six former Secretaries of Defense of our country on the ABM Treaty. The statement, dated March 9, 1987, is signed by ... three Republicans and three Democrats who served under different administrations.

Statement by Former Secretaries of
Defense on the ABM Treaty

March 9, 1987.

We reaffirm our view that the ABM Treaty makes an important contribution to American security and to reducing the risk of nuclear war. By prohibiting nationwide deployment of strategic defenses, the Treaty plays an important role in guaranteeing the effectiveness of our strategic deterrent and makes possible the negotiation of substantial reductions in strategic offensive forces. The prospect of such reductions makes it more important than ever that the U.S. and Soviet governments both avoid actions that erode the ABM Treaty and bring to an end any prior departures from the terms of the Treaty, such as the Krasnoyarsk radar. To this end, we believe that the United States and the Soviet Union should continue to adhere to the traditional interpretation of Article V of the Treaty as it was presented to the Senate for advice and consent and as it has been observed by both sides since the Treaty was signed in 1972.

Harold Brown.
Melvin R. Laird.
Elliot L. Richardson.
Clark M. Clifford.
Robert S. McNamara.
James R. Schlesinger.

I thank the Chair, and again I thank the majority leader for giving me the opportunity to make this series of presentations before the Senate.

PUBLIC HEALTH SERVICE ON AIDS EDUCATION

March 16, 1987

The Public Health Service (PHS) estimated that by March 1987 1.5 million Americans had been infected with the acquired immune deficiency syndrome (AIDS) virus. Nearly 32,000 had developed the disease; more than 16,000 had died. Although research efforts were under way across the country, no cure for the disease or vaccine against it was yet available. The PHS saw stopping high-risk behavior as its only weapon against the spread of the AIDS epidemic.

But the Reagan administration was split by a bitter debate about the government's proper role in AIDS education. How explicit should educational materials be about routes of transmission and control strategies? Should schools be required to give AIDS instruction to all students? Should information about safe sexual practices be included in the curriculum or should students be told that refraining from intravenous drug use and extramarital sex was the only way to avoid AIDS infection? Against this backdrop, Health and Human Services Secretary Otis R. Bowen March 16 released what he termed "a comprehensive plan for informing and educating the American people about AIDS."

Conservative Approach Highlighted

The report embraced the views of administration officials led by Education Secretary William J. Bennett that state and local officials should make the decisions on AIDS education for students and that the material developed by the PHS, while factual, would teach "that children should not engage in sex," and would encourage "responsible sexual behavior, ... placing sexuality within the context of marriage." The report did not mention Surgeon General C. Everett Koop's controversial October 1986 recommendations that, for AIDS to be effectively controlled, frank education about sexual practices must begin in elementary school. (Historic Documents of 1986, p. 887)

President Reagan endorsed the report's community value-centered approach, telling the College of Physicians of Philadelphia that, while AIDS education in the schools was appropriate, he agreed with Bennett that "abstinence has been lacking in much of education.... [N]o kind of values of right and wrong are being taught." A congressional critic of the administration's approach to the AIDS epidemic, Rep. Henry Waxman, D-Calif., disagreed: "The administration is confusing the handling of a public health epidemic with their social agenda." (AMA report on AIDS prevention and control, p. 817)

Four Audiences Targeted

Saying that AIDS "clearly represents a national and international emergency," Bowen made the PHS's highest priority an educational effort aimed at persons already known to be infected with AIDS or those in high-risk groups, such as intravenous drug users and homosexuals. That program, the report said, should be aimed at halting behavior that could spread the virus further. For the general public, the report proposed an advertising campaign spelling out what actions could put people at risk of contracting AIDS. For students, Bowen said, "up-to-date, factual AIDS information" would be provided to educators around the country, but, "State and local school boards, along with families, community, and parent groups have the primary responsibility for educating the young." Finally, increased educational efforts for health care workers were proposed, including training on new laboratory procedures and counseling techniques for professionals who worked with AIDS victims. Bowen said the education plan would require $80 million in fiscal year 1987 and $104 million in fiscal 1988. Reagan pledged to his Philadelphia audience in April that the government would spend $766 million in 1987 and $1 billion in 1988.

Both the Senate and House had legislation pending at the end of 1987 to address the AIDS epidemic, but because of the complexity of the problem neither chamber was able to agree on a program. Sen. Edward M. Kennedy, D-Mass., sponsored an uncontroversial AIDS research, treatment, and education bill that was stymied by a series of amendments proposed by Sen. Jesse Helms, R-N.C., concerning issues such as mandatory testing of certain populations. Stalled in the House were Waxman's proposals authorizing funds for voluntary AIDS testing, seeking to ensure confidentiality of test results, and extending antidiscrimination protections to AIDS carriers. Despite these setbacks, funding for AIDS research and prevention was likely to approach $1 billion for fiscal 1988.

Following are excerpts from the U.S. Public Health Service's "Information/Education Plan to Prevent and Control AIDS in the United States," released March 16, 1987:

Overview

Introduction

Deaths due to acquired immunodeficiency syndrome (AIDS) became the 11th leading cause of years of potential life lost in 1985. In 1986, AIDS was one of the first 10 causes. The report of the Public Health Service (PHS) Coolfont Conference in June 1986 projected that by the end of 1991 the cumulative total of AIDS cases would exceed 270,000, with more than 179,000 deaths. Most of these projected future AIDS cases will be among persons who in 1986 are already infected. Current estimates of infected persons in the United States range from 1 million to 1.5 million. AIDS will remain a serious problem for the nation for some time to come.

The current data indicate that ninety-seven percent of AIDS patients in the United States can be placed in groups related to possible means of disease acquisition: men with homosexual or bisexual orientation who have histories of using intravenous (IV) drugs (8% of cases); homosexual or bisexual men who are not known IV drug users (65%); heterosexual IV drug users (17%); persons with hemophilia (1%); heterosexual sex partners of persons with AIDS or at risk for AIDS (4%); and recipients of transfused blood or blood components (2%). Insufficient information is available to classify the remaining 3% by the above recognized risk factors for AIDS.

In Africa over 90% of cases have occurred through heterosexual transmission, equally divided among men and women.

The World Health Organization estimates that 50 to 100 million persons worldwide may be infected with the AIDS virus by 1991. Based on current information, 20-30% will progress to AIDS within 5 years of initial infection. This percentage is likely to increase beyond 5 years. Thus, AIDS represents a health disaster of pandemic proportions.

The best hopes at this time for prevention rest on a strategy based on information and education. Knowledge about AIDS has already proved to be effective in changing behavior among gay men. The effectiveness of information/education programs, however, remains to be demonstrated in populations whose members have not been as personally touched by AIDS and who do not perceive themselves to be at risk. The fact that the AIDS virus can be spread by sexual contact with persons who may otherwise appear healthy adds to the complexity of the task.

Key to changing attitudes and behaviors is the provision of factual, consistent, and understandable information about AIDS by persons and organizations in whom the recipient has confidence. Thus, multiple channels must be used, including the Federal, State, and local governments, medical professionals, teachers, parents, religious leaders, voluntary organizations, employee organizations, State and local departments of health and education, business, commercial organizations, and public figures held in high esteen.

Information/education efforts will be designed for the general public and for specific groups based on the risks of AIDS, the messages to be provided, and the channels for delivering those messages. The use of multiple channels will reinforce the basic messages and increase the opportunities to inform and educate the U.S. population about AIDS.

Planning

In order to meet its responsibility in controlling the spread of AIDS, the Public Health Service created the Executive Task Force on AIDS in 1984. The Task Force, chaired by the Assistant Secretary for Health, serves as the mechanism by which AIDS related issues are identified and addressed in a coordinated fashion by the PHS constituent agencies: Alcohol, Drug Abuse and Mental Health Administration (ADAMHA), Centers for Disease Control (CDC), Food and Drug Administration (FDA), Health Resources and Services Administration (HRSA), and the National Institutes of Health (NIH). Within the Task Force, CDC has been designated as the lead agency in the area of AIDS information, education, and risk reduction....

From 1983 through 1986 the Public Health Service spent $40 million in direct expenditures to inform and educate the public and groups at high risk of acquiring infection. In 1987, PHS will spend $79.5 million for AIDS education; the President's FY 1988 budget requests $103.9 million for this activity. States, local governments, voluntary organizations, and community service organizations have also contributed significantly in information/education efforts.

This plan draws on the knowledge and experience gained since the recognition of the AIDS epidemic in 1981. Each of the PHS member agencies has contributed to the plan. The plan will be reassessed and revised on an annual basis....

Implementing

...Successful implementation of this plan depends upon action from and cooperation among State, county, and municipal governments, professional and service organizations, the private sector, and the Federal government. It is expected that funds appropriated by Congress in any given year for information/education will be multiplied many fold by the efforts and resources of others....

The information/education plan addresses the following:

1. The Public

In order to control transmission of the AIDS virus, everyone must be aware of behavior that puts them at risk of infection. They must learn how the virus is and is not spread.

2. School and College Aged

Schools, colleges, and family institutions provide an effective channel for appropriately instructing the young people of our nation about AIDS before, and as, they reach the ages when they might practice behaviors that place them at risk of infection.

School and college aged populations who do not attend schools or colleges will be informed/educated about AIDS through other agencies that serve youth.

3. Persons at Increased Risk or Infected

The highest priority for AIDS information and education efforts are those groups at increased risk of acquiring or transmitting the AIDS virus because of certain behaviors or circumstances: gay and bisexual men, IV drug abusers, hemophiliacs, female sex partners of those at risk (because of potential pregnancy), and prostitutes and their clients. Persons known to be infected must receive information to prevent their transmission of the virus to others.

4. Health Workers

Members of this group have direct responsibility for patient care, for counseling persons with laboratory evidence of infection or AIDS patients, and for providing leadership in informing and educating the public. By virtue of their occupations, there is some risk, albeit small, of infection. . . .

Basic Elements of AIDS Information

The elements described below will need to be adapted to varying degrees of specificity for different subgroups within the four major groups: the public, the school and college-aged, persons at increased risk or infected, and health workers.

Communities and their important institutions, such as churches, families, and voluntary organizations, will need to adapt the presentation of this information to fit within their value systems. Within this framework, individuals will be able to determine responsible behavior, thereby avoiding adverse health consequences to themselves and others.

The specific wording and style of presentation, once developed, should be pretested on representative samples of the intended audiences to ensure effectiveness. Expert advice, consultation, and creative assistance can be provided by public and private health education and communication experts.

Individuals in All Groups Need to Know:

1. Current Information on the Seriousness of the Disease
2. How the Virus Is Spread

- The AIDS virus has been shown to be spread from an infected person to an uninfected person by:

  sexual contact (penis / vagina, penis / rectum, mouth / rectum, mouth / genital),

  sharing needles or "works" used in injecting drugs,

an infected woman to her fetus or newly born baby, and
transfusion or injection of infectious blood or blood fractions.

- An individual can be infected with the virus that causes AIDS without having symptoms of AIDS or appearing ill. Infected individuals without symptoms can transmit the infection to others. Once infected, a person is presumed infected for life, but actual symptoms may not develop for many years.

- A single exposure to the AIDS virus may result in infection.

3. How the Virus Is NOT Known to Be Spread

- There is no evidence that the virus is spread through casual social contact (shaking hands, social kissing, coughing, sneezing, sharing swimming pools, bed linens, eating utensils, office equipment, being next to or served by an infected person). There is no reason to avoid an infected person in ordinary social contact.

- It is not spread by the process of *giving* blood; new transfusion equipment is used for each donor.

- It is *not* spread by sexual intercourse between individuals who have maintained a sexual relationship exclusively with each other assuming that they have not been infected through contaminated blood, blood factors, IV drug abuse, or a previous sexual partner.

4. How to Prevent Infection in Yourself and Others

- Infection through sexual contact can be avoided by practicing abstinence or having a mutually monogamous marriage/relationship with an uninfected person.

- If you suspect you or your sex partner is or may be infected,

  the only certain way to protect yourself or your partner is to abstain from sexual intercourse with him or her. If it is not possible to practice abstinence until infection status can be determined, always use condoms during sex because use of condoms can reduce the risk of transmission of the AIDS virus.

  avoid sexual activity that may damage the condom or body tissues. A condom is effective only if it is used properly; it *must* remain intact and in place from start to finish of sexual activity to ensure that semen and blood are not avoidably exchanged. Be aware that condoms sometimes fail. The failure rate may be ten percent when used as a contraceptive.

  seek counseling and AIDS virus antibody testing to be sure of your own infection status. Be aware that weeks to months may elapse from the time of infection to the time that antibodies to the AIDS virus appear in the blood. During this time persons may be infectious but the test may be negative.

  encourage your partner to obtain counseling and testing.

- Be aware that multiple sex partners increase your risk of acquiring the AIDS virus unless you can be certain that each is uninfected. If you have more than one sex partner or your partner has more than one partner, always use condoms because use of condoms can reduce the risk of transmission of the AIDS virus.

Avoid prostitutes; engaging in sexual activity with those who have multiple sex partners increases the risk. . . .

- Do not use IV drugs; do not share needles or "works."

5. How to Get More Information About AIDS

- Call an AIDS Hotline number. . . .
- Call your personal physician, health department, or an AIDS community service organization.

6. Information Which Will Emphasize the Seriousness of the Problem, Yet Reduce Inappropriate Fear

- AIDS is a national emergency requiring attention from all citizens.
- If people change their behaviors, the spread of AIDS virus can be reduced.
- Blood for transfusion in the United States is screened for antibody to the AIDS virus and is now essentially safe, but some risks cannot be eliminated.
- Everyone who engages in high risk behavior is at risk for AIDS, regardless of age, race, or socioeconomic status.

Additional Information Needed by the School and College Aged

- Saying no to sex and drugs *can* virtually eliminate the risk of AIDS.
- Instructions on how the virus is known to be transmitted and how transmission may be prevented.
- Sexual transmission of the AIDS virus is not a threat to those uninfected individuals who practice responsible sexual behavior, based on fidelity, commitment and maturity, placing human sexuality within the context of marriage and family life.

Additional Information Needed by Persons at Increased Risk or Infected

- Know where to get more information and help.
- Where to seek counseling and voluntary testing.
- Do not donate blood, semen, tissues, or organs.
- Know the signs and symptoms of AIDS infection. . . .
- Infected women must know that the AIDS virus can be transmitted to unborn babies and to newborns. Female partners of those at increased risk or infected must be aware of the need to be tested to assist in family planning.

• For those infected, inform past and present sexual partners. Avoid sexual contact that may transmit the virus to others. The only certain way to ensure that others will not be infected is to abstain from sex.

Additional Information Needed by Health Workers (as Appropriate)

• The basic facts about AIDS (transmission, diagnosis, signs and symptoms, high risk behavior).

• Current public health recommendations.

• How to interpret the test.

• The need to hold test results and diagnosis confidential in accordance with relevant laws.

• How best to cooperate with local public health authorities in surveillance and prevention of AIDS virus infections.

• How to manage AIDS patients clinically.

• How to counsel persons about infection and where to refer high risk individuals and people with AIDS virus infections.

• Current research findings.

• Appropriate infection control measures, including risks of needle stick injuries which present a small but serious risk of virus transmission.

• Which isolation procedures or restrictions of visitors are or are not necessary.

• Where to get additional information for medical professionals, patients and persons caring for the AIDS patients at home....

FDA APPROVAL OF AZT

March 20, 1987

In 1981 medical researchers recognized the first cases of acquired immune deficiency syndrome (AIDS), and the search for effective ways to combat the disease began. By March 1987 AIDS had killed some 18,000 Americans, and the Public Health Service (PHS) estimated that 1.5 million others were infected with the virus. Yet despite a $417 million research budget in fiscal 1987 and what the New York Times *called "probably the greatest concentrated effort ever made to find therapies for a single virus disease," the scientific community remained baffled by the complexities of AIDS. Hundreds of drugs had been tested, but most proved ineffective or otherwise disappointing. On March 20 the Food and Drug Administration (FDA) announced the first success: approval of the drug azidothymidine (AZT) for certain AIDS and AIDS-related complex (ARC) patients.* (Public Health Service on AIDS education, p. 319)

The announcement by Assistant Secretary Robert E. Windom of the Department of Health and Human Services (HHS) stressed the new drug's limitations. Manufactured by Burroughs Wellcome Company of North Carolina under the brand name Retrovir, it was initially available in limited quantities at an extremely high cost. Windom said that while AZT was "not a cure" for AIDS, it had "a demonstrated ability to improve the short-term survival" of AIDS patients suffering from a certain type of AIDS-related pneumonia and some patients with severe ARC. Windom termed it a chance for "significant medical relief" for thousands of AIDS victims.

Speedy Approval

AZT works by preventing the AIDS virus from duplicating itself inside body cells. It does not help all patients, however, and is known to cause serious side effects, including severe anemia in some people. Nevertheless, the drug made a speedy trip through the approval process. Burroughs began development of AZT in 1984. By mid-1986 the company suspended a clinical trial when it recognized that patients receiving AZT were doing so much better than those on a placebo that the company felt that to continue to administer the placebo would have been unethical. FDA approval came less than four months after application was made, one of the fastest cases on record, as Windom noted.

Despite the drug's speedy course of approval, its development had been an expensive gamble. Burroughs told Congress it spent $80 million developing AZT, with no guarantee it would be approved, a fact the company used to justify the drug's stiff price tag of $8,000 to $10,000 a year per patient. Even when Burroughs cut AZT's price by 20 percent in December 1987, patient advocates such as Jeffrey Levi of the National Gay Rights Task Force charged that the manufacturer was trying to make a quick profit before the drug was surpassed by a newer product.

By the end of the year, 20,000 patients were receiving AZT, and no other anti-AIDS drug seemed close to receiving approval. According to a New York Times *report, doctors began prescribing the drug for healthy AIDS virus carriers, in spite of the FDA's recommendation that the drug be given only to certain patients with AIDS or ARC. The prescribing doctors believed that AZT's side effects might be less severe in healthy patients. Some asserted that they prescribed for patients who did not show symptoms but whose immune system cells were dangerously low.*

Vaccine and Other Drug Prospects

Limited human trials were approved in August for the first potential AIDS vaccine, a drug manufactured by the Connecticut firm, MicroGeneSys. But vaccine researchers who gathered for a Washington conference the following month remained pessimistic about final approval of an AIDS vaccine before the mid-1990s. They said the AIDS virus and its actions were extremely complex. They cited as serious research challenges the virus's ability to immobilize the immune system and to lie dormant for years in the victim's body.

In early 1987 the research community had high hopes for the drug dideoxycytidine (DDC), which worked on the same principle as AZT. But human testing revealed that DDC had extremely toxic side effects. Other drug research focused on finding a combination of drugs that together could knock out the AIDS virus.

Following are excerpts from the U.S. Food and Drug Administra-

tion's announcement of approval of the drug AZT, released March 20, 1987:

Robert E. Windom, M.D., assistant secretary for health, today announced that the Food and Drug Administration has approved the drug zidovudine, commonly known as azidothymidine, or AZT, to help certain patients with Acquired Immunodeficiency Syndrome (AIDS) and advanced AIDS-related Complex (ARC).

The drug will be marketed by Burroughs Wellcome Company of Research Triangle Park, N.C., under the trade name Retrovir.

Retrovir is the first approved treatment of AIDS. Because of a limited supply of the drug, distribution will be restricted initially by the company to those patients for whom it is indicated under the approved labeling, including AIDS and ARC patients with specific laboratory evidence of severely depressed immunity or a history of Pneumocystis carinii pneumonia (PCP).

"Today's approval marks an important step, but by no means a final victory, in our ongoing war against AIDS," Dr. Windom said. "Retrovir is not a cure for AIDS, but it has a demonstrated ability to improve the short-term survival of AIDS patients with recently diagnosed PCP and certain patients with advanced ARC."

He noted that available clinical data were sufficient for approving the use of Retrovir only for certain indications, and not for all AIDS-associated conditions. "Nevertheless," Dr. Windom said, "today's action means that significant medical relief will be available to thousands of those afflicted with this dreaded disease."

"Current data," Dr. Windom said, "indicate that about 32,000 persons have been afflicted with AIDS in the United States, with about 14,000 of them still living. Most of them, particularly those who have had a serious opportunistic infection associated with AIDS, are expected to qualify for Retrovir treatment under the approved indications. Certain patients with advanced ARC, a condition that frequently precedes and develops into AIDS within a short period of time, have also been shown to benefit from therapy with Retrovir."

Advanced ARC patients have symptoms that include weight loss, persistent fever and diarrhea, and less severe opportunistic infections such as oral candida and herpes infections. They also have a markedly reduced number of T-helper lymphocytes, critical elements of the immune system which are destroyed by the AIDS virus. It is estimated that about two to three times as many Americans may suffer from advanced ARC as suffer from AIDS.

Retrovir was originally developed in 1964 by Dr. Jerome Horowitz of the Michigan Cancer Foundation as a possible treatment for cancer. In February 1985, the National Cancer Institute, under the direction of Dr. Samuel Broder, tested AZT and found that it was a potent inhibitor of AIDS. . . .

Dr. Windom noted that under FDA's 1-AA priority review designation for AIDS drugs, the agency's review and approval of the new drug application for Retrovir was accomplished within less than four months—one of the shortest approval actions on record. The 1-AA designation, which gives AIDS drug[s] top priority for review within the agency, is an extension of the official 1-A, 1-B, 1-C classification system FDA uses to prioritize the review of drugs within the review process and exemplifies FDA's effort to produce more timely and efficient reviews for all break-through drugs.

"Today's action is an important demonstration of FDA's ability to move swiftly, with impressive scientific precision, to review and approve promising treatments for AIDS, when such action is justified by sound and convincing clinical evidence," Dr. Windom concluded.

COURT ON AFFIRMATIVE ACTION

March 25, 1987

In a landmark decision, the Supreme Court March 25 in Johnson v. Transportation Agency, Santa Clara, California, *upheld regulations to make certain that women and minority groups were given the same access to job opportunities as that afforded white males. The 6-3 decision reinforced a number of previous cases in which the Court sustained affirmative action enforcement. In those rulings the Court had repeatedly upheld both voluntary and court-ordered affirmative action programs, provided they did not unduly harm innocent white males.*

The majority held in Johnson *that actions upholding affirmative action legislation, when properly applied, did not violate the Constitution or Title VII of the 1964 Civil Rights Act, which banned bias in employment decisions that were based on race, sex, religion, or national origin.*

A Question of Reverse Discrimination?

The 1987 case concerned the promotion of a woman to road dispatcher for the Santa Clara, California, County Transportation Agency (no women had ever held that position in the county), instead of a male who had scored two points higher on a qualifying interview. Both the woman, Diane Joyce, and the man, Paul Johnson, were among seven fully qualified applicants for the position. Johnson tied for second on his interview score, while Joyce was third. Johnson claimed that he had been denied the promotion that went to Joyce solely because of his sex. The district court ruled in his favor, but the Court of Appeals for the Ninth

Circuit reversed. Johnson appealed, supported in his claim by the Reagan administration.

The decision marked the fourth time in nine months that the Court had rejected the Reagan administration's policy denouncing affirmative action as in fact "reverse discrimination against white males that was inappropriate unless used to compensate specific victims of prior racial discrimination."

Between 1978, when the issue received its first thorough Supreme Court review, and 1987, the Court had struck down as many affirmative action plans as it upheld. A majority of justices approved some use of affirmative action in school admissions, hiring, training programs, contract set-asides, admission to union membership, and promotions, but it ruled against affirmative action in cases of layoffs to preserve the jobs of blacks at the expense of more senior white employees. (Supreme Court decisions, Historic Documents of 1979, p. 493; Historic Documents of 1980, p. 539; Historic Documents of 1984, p. 365; Historic Documents of 1986, p. 651)

Some of the plans considered by the Court had been challenged as inconsistent with the nondiscrimination guarantees of federal law—particularly Title VII of the 1964 Civil Rights Act, which barred employment discrimination based on race, sex, religion, and national origin. Other plans had been attacked as unconstitutional violations of the guarantees of equal protection and due process.

Beyond those considerations, the Court's decisions were influenced by a number of other variables, among them the identity and track record of the employer, whether there had been judicial findings of prior discrimination, and the extent to which the affirmative action plan operated to injure individuals who were innocent of any wrongdoing. One month before the Johnson *ruling, on February 25, the Supreme Court had upheld a court-ordered one-black-for-one-white promotion plan imposed on the Alabama state police, which had never hired a black trooper before being sued for discrimination in 1972.*

The Court tended to examine the particular facts of each case closely to see if use of affirmative action was appropriate. And the justices generally emerged from that scrutiny sharply divided. Six of the seven cases decided during the 1978-1987 period resulted in votes of of 5-4 or 6-3. The seventh was decided by 5-2; two justices did not participate.

Solidly in favor of affirmative action were Justices William J. Brennan, Jr., Thurgood Marshall, Harry A. Blackmun, and—since 1983—John Paul Stevens. Chief Justice William H. Rehnquist and Justice Byron R. White were opposed; they usually were joined by Justice Sandra Day O'Connor. The newest member of the Court, Justice Antonin Scalia, was outspoken in his criticism of affirmative action. The balance of power, therefore, lay in the hands of Justice Lewis F. Powell, Jr.

Arguments for Quotas

That division was somewhat altered by the Johnson *ruling. Writing for the majority, Brennan was joined by Powell, Blackmun, and Stevens. O'Connor concurred in the outcome. Rehnquist and White joined Scalia in his scathing dissent. Scalia, whom Reagan appointed to the Court in 1986, wrote, "The Court today completes the process of converting [Title VII] from a guarantee that race or sex will* not *be the basis for employment determinations to a guarantee that it often* will."

Brennan, however, concluded that the decision of the California transportation agency to hire Joyce was "appropriately [based] . . . on the sex of Diana Joyce in determining that she should be promoted to the road dispatcher position." Brennan continued, "The decision to do so was made pursuant to an affirmative action plan that represents a moderate, flexible, case-by-case approach to effecting a gradual improvement in the representation of minorities and women in the work force." Citing a previous case, United Steelworkers of America v. Weber *(1979), Brennan noted that the Court had upheld a private employer's voluntary adoption of a quota that guaranteed black workers—who had previously been under-represented in skilled jobs in the employer's plant—half of the positions in a job training program.*

"Our decision was grounded in the recognition that voluntary employer action can play a crucial role in furthering Title VII's purpose of eliminating the effects of discrimination in the work place, and that Title VII should not be read to thwart such efforts," wrote Brennan. He noted further that "Congress has not amended the statute to reject our construction, nor have any amendments even been proposed, and we may therefore assume that our interpretation was correct." He also pointed out that there need not be a finding that an agency had previously discriminated against women; there was only a need to point to a "conspicuous imbalance in traditionally segregated job categories" to warrant affirmative action remedies.

The majority extended the scope of its finding to public as well as private employers, but noted that the decision did not imply an absolute bar to the advancement of white males; nor did it mean that they should be replaced in their positions by women or blacks. In a concurring opinion, O'Connor said that there were solid grounds for an affirmative action ruling, but added that she felt the Court had taken "an expansive and ill-defined approach to voluntary affirmative action."

Dissent: Biased Against the 'Politically Impotent'?

"Ever so subtly, without even alluding to the last obstacles preserved by earlier opinions that we now push out of our path, we effectively replace the goal of a discrimination-free society with the quite incompatible goal of proportionate representation by race and by sex in the

workplace," wrote Scalia in his dissent. "The most significant proposition of law established by today's decision is that racial or sexual discrimination is permitted under Title VII when it is intended to overcome the effect not of the employer's own discrimination, but of societal attitudes that have limited the entry of certain races, or of a particular sex, into certain jobs."

Scalia further commented that women had not in fact desired work as "road crews." The "only losers" in the decision, he concluded, "are the Johnsons of the country, for whom Title VII has been not merely repealed but actually inverted. The irony is that these individuals—predominantly unknown, unaffluent, unorganized—suffer this injustice at the hands of a Court fond of thinking itself the champion of the politically impotent."

Reaction: Future Implications

Reaction to the Court's opinion was decidedly mixed. A number of civil rights advocates, who basically applauded the ruling, were apprehensive that the decision might have over-extended affirmative action. The interpretation was varied. Said Barry L. Goldstein, of the National Association for the Advancement of Colored People (NAACP): "This is the most important affirmative action decision because it applies to the most typical situation. It allows employers to join in the national purpose to remove the consequences of discrimination in the marketplace, regardless of whether it is the employer's discrimination."

Agreeing with Goldstein about the significance of the case, Bruce E. Fein of the Heritage Foundation, a conservative research organization, questioned the wisdom of the Court's decision to require strict quotas. A number of those opposing the decision did not question the merits of affirmative action, but said that employers might be led to disregard merit in the hiring or promotion of employees.

Following are excerpts from the Supreme Court's March 25, 1987, decision in Johnson v. Transportation Agency, Santa Clara County, California, *affirming that nothing in the Constitution or Title VII of the 1964 Civil Rights Act disallowed affirmative action; from the concurrences of Justices John Paul Stevens and Sandra Day O'Connor; and from the dissenting opinion of Justice Antonin Scalia.*

No. 85-1129

Paul C. Johnson, Petitioner *v.* Transportation Agency, Santa Clara County, California, et al.	On writ of certiorari to the United States Court of Appeals for the Ninth Circuit

[March 25, 1987]

JUSTICE BRENNAN delivered the opinion of the Court.

Respondent, Transportation Agency of Santa Clara County, California, unilaterally promulgated an Affirmative Action Plan applicable, *inter alia,* to promotions of employees. In selecting applicants for the promotional position of road dispatcher, the Agency, pursuant to the Plan, passed over petitioner Paul Johnson, a male employee, and promoted a female employee applicant, Diane Joyce. The question for decision is whether in making the promotion the Agency impermissibly took into account the sex of the applicants in violation of Title VII of the Civil Rights Act of 1964, 42 U.S.C. § 2000e *et seq.* The District Court for the Northern District of California, in an action filed by petitioner following receipt of a right-to-sue letter from the Equal Employment Opportunity Commission (EEOC), held that respondent had violated Title VII. The Court of Appeals for the Ninth Circuit reversed. We granted certiorari (1986). We affirm.

I

A

In December 1978, the Santa Clara County Transit District Board of Supervisors adopted an Affirmative Action Plan (Plan) for the County Transportation Agency. The Plan implemented a County Affirmative Action Plan, which had been adopted, declared the County, because "mere prohibition of discriminatory practices is not enough to remedy the effects of past practices and to permit attainment of an equitable representation of minorities, women and handicapped persons." Relevant to this case, the Agency Plan provides that, in making promotions to positions within a traditionally segregated job classification in which women have been significantly underrepresented, the Agency is authorized to consider as one factor the sex of a qualified applicant.

In reviewing the composition of its work force, the Agency noted in its Plan that women were represented in numbers far less than their proportion of the county labor force in both the Agency as a whole and in five of seven job categories. Specifically, while women constituted 36.4% of the area labor market, they composed only 22.4% of Agency employees. Furthermore, women working at the Agency were concentrated largely in EEOC job categories traditionally held by women: women made up 76% of Office and Clerical Workers, but only 7.1% of Agency Officials and Administrators, 8.6% of Professionals, 9.7% of Technicians, and 22% of Service and Maintenance workers. As for the job classification relevant to this case, none of the 238 Skilled Craft Worker positions was held by a woman. The Plan noted that this underrepresentation of women in part reflected the fact that women had not traditionally been employed in these positions, and that they had not been strongly motivated to seek training or employment in them "because of the limited opportunities that have existed in the past for them to work in such classifications." The Plan also observed that, while the proportion of ethnic minorities in the Agency as a whole exceeded the proportion of such minorities in the county work force, a smaller percentage of minority employees held management, professional, and technical positions.

The Agency stated that its Plan was intended to achieve "a statistically measurable yearly improvement in hiring, training and promotion of minorities and women throughout the Agency in all major job classifications where they are under represented." As a benchmark by which to evaluate progress, the Agency stated that its long-term goal was to attain a work force whose composition reflected the proportion of minorities and women in the area labor force. Thus, for the Skilled Craft category in which the road dispatcher position at issue here was classified, the Agency's aspiration was that eventually about 36% of the jobs would be occupied by women.

The Plan acknowledged that a number of factors might make it unrealistic to rely on the Agency's long-term goals in evaluating the Agency's progress in expanding job opportunities for minorities and women. Among the factors identified were low turnover rates in some classifications, the fact that some jobs involved heavy labor, the small number of positions within some job categories, the limited number of entry positions leading to the Technical and Skilled Craft classifications, and the limited number of minorities and women qualified for positions requiring specialized training and experience. As a result, the Plan counselled that short-range goals be established and annually adjusted to serve as the most realistic guide for actual employment decisions. Among the tasks identified as important in establishing such short-term goals was the acquisition of data "reflecting the ratio of minorities, women and handicapped persons who are working in the local area in major job classifications relating to those utilized by the County Administration," so as to determine the availability of members of such groups who "possess the desired qualifications or potential for placement." These data on qualified group members, along with predictions of position vacancies, were to serve as the basis for "realistic yearly employment goals for women, minorities and handicapped persons in each EEOC job category and major job classification."

The Agency's Plan thus set aside no specific number of positions for minorities or women, but authorized the consideration of ethnicity or sex as a factor when evaluating qualified candidates for jobs in which members of such groups were poorly represented. One such job was the road dispatcher position that is the subject of the dispute in this case.

B

On December 12, 1979, the Agency announced a vacancy for the promotional position of road dispatcher in the Agency's Roads Division. Dispatchers assign road crews, equipment, and materials, and maintain records pertaining to road maintenance jobs. The position requires at minimum four years of dispatch or road maintenance work experience for Santa Clara County. . . .

Twelve County employees applied for the promotion, including Joyce and Johnson. Joyce had worked for the County since 1970, serving as an account clerk until 1975. She had applied for a road dispatcher position in 1974, but was deemed ineligible because she had not served as a road maintenance worker. In 1975, Joyce transferred from a senior account clerk position to a road maintenance worker position, becoming the first woman to fill such a job. During her four years in that position, she occasionally worked out of class as a road dispatcher.

Petitioner Johnson began with the county in 1967 as a road yard clerk, after private employment that included working as a supervisor and dispatcher. He had also unsuccessfully applied for the road dispatcher opening in 1974. In 1977, his clerical position was downgraded, and he sought and received a transfer to the position of road maintenance worker. He also occasionally worked out of class as a dispatcher while performing that job.

Nine of the applicants, including Joyce and Johnson, were deemed qualified for the job, and were interviewed by a two-person board. Seven of the applicants scored above 70 on this interview, which meant that they were certified as eligible for selection by the appointing authority. The scores awarded ranged from 70 to 80. Johnson was tied for second with score of 75, while Joyce ranked next with a score of 73. A second interview was conducted by three Agency supervisors, who ultimately recommended that Johnson be promoted. Prior to the second interview, Joyce had contacted the County's Affirmative Action Office because she feared that her application might not receive disinterested review. The Office in turn contacted the Agency's Affirmative Action Coordinator, whom the Agency's Plan makes responsible for, *inter alia,* keeping the Director informed of opportunities for the Agency to accomplish its objectives under the Plan. At the time, the Agency employed no women in any Skilled Craft position, and had never employed a woman as a road dispatcher. The Coordinator recommended to the Director of the Agency, James Graebner, that Joyce be promoted.

Graebner, authorized to choose any of the seven persons deemed eligible, thus had the benefit of suggestions by the second interview panel and by the Agency Coordinator in arriving at his decision. After deliberation, Graebner concluded that the promotion should be given to Joyce. As he testified: "I tried to look at the whole picture, the combination of her qualifications and Mr. Johnson's qualifications, their test scores, their expertise, their background, affirmative action matters, things like that . . . I believe it was a combination of all those."

The certification form naming Joyce as the person promoted to the dispatcher position stated that both she and Johnson were rated as well-qualified for the job. The evaluation of Joyce read: "Well qualified by virtue of 18 years of past clerical experience including 3½ years at West

Yard plus almost 5 years as a [road maintenance worker]." The evaluation of Johnson was as follows: "Well qualified applicant; two years of [road maintenance worker] experience plus 11 years of Road Yard Clerk. Has had previous outside Dispatch experience but was 13 years ago." Graebner testified that he did not regard as significant the fact that Johnson scored 75 and Joyce 73 when interviewed by the two-person board.

Petitioner Johnson filed a complaint with the EEOC alleging that he had been denied promotion on the basis of sex in violation of Title VII. He received a right-to-sue letter from the agency on March 10, 1981, and on March 20, 1981, filed suit in the United States District Court for the Northern District of California. The District Court found that Johnson was more qualified for the dispatcher position than Joyce, and that the sex of Joyce was the "*determining factor* in her selection." App. to Pet. for Cert. 4a (emphasis in original). The court acknowledged that, since the Agency justified its decision on the basis of its Affirmative Action Plan, the criteria announced in *Steelworkers* v. *Weber* (1979), should be applied in evaluating the validity of the plan. It then found the Agency's Plan invalid on the ground that the evidence did not satisfy *Weber*'s criterion that the Plan be temporary. The Court of Appeals for the Ninth Circuit reversed, holding that the absence of an express termination date in the Plan was not dispositive, since the Plan repeatedly expressed its objective as the attainment, rather than the maintenance, of a work force mirroring the labor force in the county. The Court of Appeals added that the fact that the Plan established no fixed percentage of positions for minorities or women made it less essential that the Plan contain a relatively explicit deadline. The Court held further that the Agency's consideration of Joyce's sex in filling the road dispatcher position was lawful. The Agency Plan had been adopted, the court said, to address a conspicuous imbalance in the Agency's work force, and neither unnecessarily trammeled the rights of other employees, nor created an absolute bar to their advancement.

II

As a preliminary matter, we note that petitioner bears the burden of establishing the invalidity of the Agency's Plan. Only last term in *Wygant* v. *Jackson Board of Education* (1986), we held that "[t]he ultimate burden remains with the employees to demonstrate the unconstitutionality of an affirmative-action program," and we see no basis for a different rule regarding a plan's alleged violation of Title VII. This case also fits readily within the analytical framework set forth in *McDonnell Douglas Corp.* v. *Green* (1973). Once a plaintiff establishes a prima facie case that race or sex has been taken into account in an employer's employment decision, the burden shifts to the employer to articulate a nondiscriminatory rationale for its decision. The existence of an affirmative action plan provides such a rationale. If such a plan is articulated as the basis for the employer's decision, the burden shifts to the plaintiff to prove that the employer's justification is pretextual and the plan is invalid. As a practical matter, of course, an employer will generally seek to avoid a charge of pretext by presenting evidence in support of its plan. That does not mean, however, as petitioner suggests, that reliance on an affirmative action plan is to be treated as an affirmative defense requiring the employer to carry the burden of proving the validity of the plan. The burden of proving its invalidity remains on the plaintiff.

The assessment of the legality of the Agency Plan must be guided by our decision in *Weber*. In that case, the Court addressed the question whether the employer violated Title VII by adopting a voluntary affirmative action plan designed to "eliminate manifest racial imbalances in traditionally segregated job categories." The respondent employee in that case challenged the employer's denial of his application for a position in a newly established craft training program, contending that the employer's selection process impermissibly took into account the race of the applicants. The selection process was guided by an affirmative action plan, which provided that 50% of the new trainees were to be black until the percentage of black skilled craftworkers in the employer's plant approximated the percentage of blacks in the local labor force. Adoption of the plan had been prompted by the fact that only 5 of 273, or 1.83%, of skilled craftworkers at the plant were black, even though the workforce in the area was approximately 39% black. Because of the historical exclusion of blacks from craft positions, the employer regarded its former policy of hiring trained outsiders as inadequate to redress the imbalance in its work force.

We upheld the employer's decision to select less senior black applicants over the white respondent, for we found that taking race into account was consistent with Title VII's objective of "break[ing] down old patterns of racial segregation and hierarchy." As we stated:

> "It would be ironic indeed if a law triggered by a Nation's concern over centuries of racial injustice and intended to improve the lot of those who had 'been excluded from the American dream for so long' constituted the first legislative prohibition of all voluntary, private, race-conscious efforts to abolish traditional patterns of racial segregation and hierarchy." ([Q]uoting remarks of Sen. Humphrey, 110 Cong. Rec. 6552 (1964)).

We noted that the plan did not "unnecessarily trammel the interests of the white employees," since it did not require "the discharge of white workers and their replacement with new black hirees." Nor did the plan create "an absolute bar to the advancement of white employees," since half of those trained in the new program were to be white. Finally, we observed that the plan was a temporary measure, not designed to maintain racial balance, but to "eliminate a manifest racial imbalance." As JUSTICE BLACKMUN's concurrence made clear, *Weber* held that an employer seeking to justify the adoption of a plan need not point to its own prior discriminatory practices, nor even to evidence of an "arguable violation" on its part. Rather, it need point only to a "conspicuous ... imbalance in traditionally segregated job categories." Our decision was grounded in the recognition that voluntary employer action can play a crucial role in furthering Title VII's purpose of eliminating the effects of discrimination in the workplace, and that Title VII should not be read to thwart such efforts.

In reviewing the employment decision at issue in this case, we must first examine whether that decision was made pursuant to a plan prompted by concerns similar to those of the employer in *Weber*. Next, we must determine whether the effect of the plan on males and non-minorities is comparable to the effect of the plan in that case.

The first issue is therefore whether consideration of the sex of applicants for skilled craft jobs was justified by the existence of a "manifest imbalance" that reflected underrepresentation of women in "traditionally segregated job categories." In determining whether an imbalance exists that would justify taking sex or race into account, a comparison of the percentage of minorities or women in the employer's work force with the percentage in the area labor market or general population is appropriate in analyzing jobs that require no special expertise, see *Teamsters* v. *United States* (1977) (comparison between percentage of blacks in employer's work force and in general population proper in determining extent of imbalance in truck driving positions), or training programs designed to provide expertise, see *Weber* (comparison between proportion of blacks working at plant and proportion of blacks in area labor force appropriate in calculating imbalance for purpose of establishing preferential admission to craft training program). Where a job requires special training, however, the comparison should be with those in the labor force who possess the relevant qualifications. See *Hazelwood School District* v. *United States* (1977) (must compare percentage of blacks in employer's work ranks with percentage of qualified black teachers in area labor force in determining underrepresentation in teaching positions). The requirement that the "manifest imbalance" relates to a "traditionally segregated job category" provides assurance both that sex or race will be taken into account in a manner consistent with Title VII's purpose of eliminating the effects of employment discrimination, and that the interests of those employees not benefitting from the plan will not be unduly infringed.

A manifest imbalance need not be such that it would support a prima facie case against the employer, as suggested in JUSTICE O'CONNOR's concurrence, *post,* since we do not regard as identical the constraints of Title VII and the federal constitution on voluntarily adopted affirmative action plans. Application of the "prima facie" standard in Title VII cases would be inconsistent with *Weber*'s focus on statistical imbalance, and could inappropriately create a significant disincentive for employers to adopt an affirmative action plan. See *Weber* (Title VII intended as a "catalyst" for employer efforts to eliminate vestiges of discrimination). A corporation concerned with maximizing return on investment, for instance, is hardly likely to adopt a plan if in order to do so it must compile evidence that could be used to subject it to a colorable Title VII suit.

It is clear that the decision to hire Joyce was made pursuant to an

Agency plan that directed that sex or race be taken into account for the purpose of remedying underrepresentation. The Agency Plan acknowledged the "limited opportunities that have existed in the past" for women to find employment in certain job classifications "where women have not been traditionally employed in significant numbers." As a result, observed the Plan, women were concentrated in traditionally female jobs in the Agency, and represented a lower percentage in other job classifications than would be expected if such traditional segregation had not occurred. Specifically, 9 of the 10 Para-Professionals and 110 of the 145 Office and Clerical Workers were women. By contrast, women were only 2 of the 28 Officials and Administrators, 5 of the 58 Professionals, 12 of the 124 Technicians, none of the Skilled Craft Workers, and 1—who was Joyce—of the 110 Road Maintenance Workers. The Plan sought to remedy these imbalances through "hiring, training and promotion of . . . women throughout the Agency in all major job classifications where they are underrepresented."

As an initial matter, the Agency adopted as a benchmark for measuring progress in eliminating underrepresentation the long-term goal of a work force that mirrored in its major job classifications the percentage of women in the area labor market. Even as it did so, however, the Agency acknowledged that such a figure could not by itself necessarily justify taking into account the sex of applicants for positions in all job categories. For positions requiring specialized training and experience, the Plan observed that the number of minorities and women "who possess the qualifications required for entry into such job classifications is limited." The Plan therefore directed that annual short-term goals be formulated that would provide a more realistic indication of the degree to which sex should be taken into account in filling particular positions. The Plan stressed that such goals "should not be construed as 'quotas' that must be met," but as reasonable aspirations in correcting the imbalance in the Agency's work force. These goals were to take into account factors such as "turnover, layoffs, lateral transfers, new job openings, retirements and availability of minorities, women and handicapped persons in the area work force who possess the desired qualifications or potential for placement." The Plan specifically directed that, in establishing such goals, the Agency work with the County Planning Department and other sources in attempting to compile data on the percentage of minorities and women in the local labor force that were actually working in the job classifications comprising the Agency work force. From the outset, therefore, the Plan sought annually to develop even more refined measures of the underrepresentation in each job category that required attention.

As the Agency Plan recognized, women were most egregiously underrepresented in the Skilled Craft job category, since *none* of the 238 positions was occupied by a woman. In mid-1980, when Joyce was selected for the road dispatcher position, the Agency was still in the process of refining its short-term goals for Skilled Craft Workers in accordance with the directive of the Plan. This process did not reach fruition until 1982, when the Agency established a short-term goal for that year of three women for the 55 expected openings in that job category—a modest goal of about 6% for that category.

We reject petitioner's argument that, since only the long-term goal was in place for Skilled Craft positions at the time of Joyce's promotion, it was inappropriate for the Director to take into account affirmative action considerations in filling the road dispatcher position. The Agency's Plan emphasized that the long-term goals were not to be taken as guides for actual hiring decisions, but that supervisors were to consider a host of practical factors in seeking to meet affirmative action objectives, including the fact that in some job categories women were not qualified in numbers comparable to their representation in the labor force.

By contrast, had the Plan simply calculated imbalances in all categories according to the proportion of women in the area labor pool, and then directed that hiring be governed solely by those figures, its validity fairly could be called into question. This is because analysis of a more specialized labor pool normally is necessary in determining underrepresentation in some positions. If a plan failed to take distinctions in qualifications into account in providing guidance for actual employment decisions, it would dictate mere blind hiring by the numbers, for it would hold supervisors to "achievement of a particular percentage of minority employment or membership ... regardless of circumstances such as economic conditions or the number of qualified minority applicants" ... *Sheet Metal Workers' v. EEOC* (1986)....

The Agency's Plan emphatically did *not* authorize such blind hiring. It expressly directed that numerous factors be taken into account in making hiring decisions, including specifically the qualifications of female applicants for particular jobs. Thus, despite the fact that no precise short-term goal was yet in place for the Skilled Craft category in mid-1980, the Agency's management nevertheless had been clearly instructed that they were not to hire solely by reference to statistics. The fact that only the long-term goal had been established for this category posed no danger that personnel decisions would be made by reflexive adherence to a numerical standard.

Furthermore, in considering the candidates for the road dispatcher position in 1980, the Agency hardly needed to rely on a refined short-term goal to realize that it had a significant problem of underrepresentation that required attention. Given the obvious imbalance in the Skilled Craft category, and given the Agency's commitment to eliminating such imbalances, it was plainly not unreasonable for the Agency to determine that it was appropriate to consider as one factor the sex of Ms. Joyce in making its decision. The promotion of Joyce thus satisfies the first requirement enunciated in *Weber,* since it was undertaken to further an affirmative action plan designed to eliminate Agency work force imbalances in traditionally segregated job categories.

We next consider whether the Agency Plan unnecessarily trammeled the rights of male employees or created an absolute bar to their advancement. In contrast to the plan in *Weber,* which provided that 50% of the positions in the craft training program were exclusively for blacks, and to the consent decree upheld last term in *Firefighters* v. *Cleveland* (1986), which required the promotion of specific numbers of minorities, the Plan sets aside no positions for women. The Plan expressly states that "[t]he 'goals' established for each Division should not be construed as 'quotas' that must be met." Rather, the Plan merely authorized that consideration be given to affirmative action concerns when evaluating qualified applicants. As the Agency Director testified, the sex of Joyce was but one of numerous factors he took into account in arriving at his decision. The Plan thus resembles the "Harvard Plan" approvingly noted by JUSTICE POWELL in *University of California Regents* v. *Bakke* (1978), which considers race along with other criteria in determining admission to the college. As JUSTICE POWELL observed, "In such an admissions program, race or ethnic background may be deemed a 'plus' in a particular applicant's file, yet it does not insulate the individual from comparison with all other candidates for the available seats." Similarly, the Agency Plan requires women to compete with all other qualified applicants. *No* persons are automatically excluded from consideration; *all* are able to have their qualifications weighed against those of other applicants.

In addition, petitioner had no absolute entitlement to the road dispatcher position. Seven of the applicants were classified as qualified and eligible, and the Agency Director was authorized to promote any of the seven. Thus, denial of the promotion unsettled no legitimate firmly rooted expectation on the part of the petitioner. Furthermore, while the petitioner in this case was denied a promotion, he retained his employment with the Agency, at the same salary and with the same seniority, and remained eligible for other promotions.

Finally, the Agency's Plan was intended to *attain* a balanced work force, not to maintain one. The Plan contains ten references to the Agency's desire to "attain" such a balance, but no reference whatsoever to a goal of maintaining it. The Director testified that, while the "broader goal" of affirmative action, defined as "the desire to hire, to promote, to give opportunity and training on an equitable, non-discriminatory basis," is something that is "a permanent part" of "the Agency's operating philosophy," that broader goal "is divorced, if you will, from specific numbers or percentages."

The Agency acknowledged the difficulties that it would confront in remedying the imbalance in its work force, and it anticipated only gradual increases in the representation of minorities and women. It is thus unsurprising that the Plan contains no explicit end date, for the Agency's flexible, case-by-case approach was not expected to yield success in a brief period of time. Express assurance that a program is only temporary may be necessary if the program actually sets aside positions according to specific numbers. See, e.g., *Firefighters* (four-year duration for consent decree providing for promotion of particular number of minorities); *Weber* (plan requiring that blacks constitute 50% of new trainees in effect until percentage of employer work force equal to percentage in local labor force). This is necessary both to minimize the effect of the program on other employees, and to ensure that the plan's goals "[are] not being used simply to achieve and maintain ... balance, but rather as a benchmark against which" the employer may measure its progress in eliminating the underrepresentation of minorities and women. *Sheet Metal Workers*. In this case, however, substantial evidence shows that the Agency has sought to take a moderate, gradual approach to eliminating the imbalance in its work force, one which establishes realistic guidance for employment decisions, and which visits minimal intrusion on the legitimate expectations of other employees. Given this fact, as well as the Agency's express commitment to "attain" a balanced work force, there is ample assurance that the Agency does not seek to use its Plan to maintain a permanent racial and sexual balance.

III

In evaluating the compliance of an affirmative action plan with Title VII's prohibition on discrimination, we must be mindful of "this Court's and Congress' consistent emphasis on 'the value of voluntary efforts to further the objectives of the law.' "... The Agency in the case before us has undertaken such a voluntary effort, and has done so in full recognition of both the difficulties and the potential for intrusion on males and nonminorities. The Agency has identified a conspicuous imbalance in job categories traditionally segregated by race and sex. It has made clear from the outset, however, that employment decisions may not be justified solely by reference to this imbalance, but must rest on a multitude of practical, realistic factors. It has therefore committed itself to annual adjustment of goals so as to provide a reasonable guide for actual hiring and promotion decisions. The Agency earmarks no positions for anyone; sex is but one of several factors that may be taken into account in evaluating qualified applicants for a position. As both the Plan's language and its manner of operation attest, the Agency has no intention of establishing a work force whose permanent composition is dictated by rigid numerical standards.

We therefore hold that the Agency appropriately took into account as one factor the sex of Diane Joyce in determining that she should be promoted to the road dispatcher position. The decision to do so was made pursuant to an affirmative action plan that represents a moderate, flexible, case-by-case approach to effecting a gradual improvement in the representation of minorities and women.... Such a plan is fully consistent with Title VII, for it embodies the contribution that voluntary employer action can make in eliminating the vestiges of discrimination in the workplace. Accordingly, the judgment of the Court of Appeals is

Affirmed.

JUSTICE STEVENS, concurring.

While I join the Court's opinion, I write separately to explain my view of this case's position in our evolving antidiscrimination law and to emphasize that the opinion does not establish the permissible outer limit of voluntary programs undertaken by employers to benefit disadvantaged groups.

I

Antidiscrimination measures may benefit protected groups in two distinct ways. As a sword, such measures may confer benefits by specifying that a person's membership in a disadvantaged group must be a neutral, irrelevant factor in governmental or private decisionmaking or, alternatively, by compelling decisionmakers to give favorable consideration to disadvantaged group status. As a shield, an antidiscrimination statute can also help a member of a protected class by assuring decisionmakers in some instances that, when they elect for good reasons of their own to grant a preference of some sort to a minority citizen, they will not violate the law. The Court properly holds that the statutory shield allowed respondent to take Diane Joyce's sex into account in promoting her to the road dispatcher position.

Prior to 1978 the Court construed the Civil Rights Act of 1964 as an absolute blanket prohibition against discrimination which neither required nor permitted discriminatory preferences for any group, minority or majority. . . .

In the *Bakke* case in 1978 and again in *Steelworkers* v. *Weber* (1979), a majority of the Court interpreted the antidiscriminatory strategy of the statute in a fundamentally different way. The Court held in the *Weber* case that an employer's program designed to increase the number of black craftworkers in an aluminum plant did not violate Title VII. It remains clear that the Act does not *require* any employer to grant preferential treatment on the basis of race or gender, but since 1978 the Court has unambiguously interpreted the statute to *permit* the voluntary adoption of special programs to benefit members of the minority groups for whose protection the statute was enacted. . . .

The logic of antidiscrimination legislation requires that judicial constructions of Title VII leave "breathing room" for employer initiatives to benefit members of minority groups. . . .

II

Whether a voluntary decision of the kind made by respondent would ever be prohibited by Title VII is a question we need not answer until it is squarely presented. Given the interpretation of the statute the Court adopted in *Weber*, I see no reason why the employer has any duty, prior to granting a preference to a qualified minority employee, to determine whether his past conduct might constitute an arguable violation of Title VII. Indeed, in some instances the employer may find it more helpful to focus on the future. Instead of retroactively scrutinizing his own or society's possible exclusions of minorities in the past to determine the outer limits of a valid affirmative-action program—or indeed, any particular affirmative-action decision—in many cases the employer will find it more appropriate to consider other legitimate reasons to give preferences to members of under-represented groups. Statutes enacted for the benefit of minority groups should not block these forward-looking considerations....

The Court today does not foreclose other voluntary decisions based in part on a qualified employee's membership in a disadvantaged group. Accordingly, I concur.

JUSTICE O'CONNOR, concurring in the judgment.

... I concur in the judgment of the Court in light of our precedents. I write separately, however, because the Court has chosen to follow an expansive and ill-defined approach to voluntary affirmative action by public employers despite the limitations imposed by the Constitution and by the provisions of Title VII, and because the dissent rejects the Court's precedents and addresses the question of how Title VII should be interpreted as if the Court were writing on a clean slate. The former course of action gives insufficient guidance to courts and litigants; the latter course of action ... fails to reckon with the reality of the course that the majority of the Court has determined to follow.

In my view, the proper initial inquiry in evaluating the legality of an affirmative action plan by a public employer under Title VII is no different from that required by the Equal Protection Clause. In either case, consistent with the congressional intent to provide some measure of protection to the interests of the employer's nonminority employees, the employer must have had a firm basis for believing that remedial action was required. An employer would have such a firm basis if it can point to a statistical disparity sufficient to support a prima facie claim under Title VII by the employee beneficiaries of the affirmative action plan of a pattern or practice claim of discrimination....

Unfortunately, the Court today gives little guidance for what statistical imbalance is sufficient to support an affirmative action plan. Although the Court denies that the statistical imbalance need be sufficient to make out a prima facie case of discrimination against women, the Court fails to suggest an alternative standard. Because both *Wygant* (1986) and *Weber* (1979) attempt to reconcile the same competing concerns, I see little justification for the adoption of different standards for affirmative action under Title VII and the Equal Protection Clause....

JUSTICE SCALIA, with whom THE CHIEF JUSTICE joins, and with whom JUSTICE WHITE joins in Parts I and II, dissenting.

With a clarity which, had it not proven so unavailing, one might well recommend as a model of statutory draftsmanship, Title VII of the Civil Rights Act of 1964 declares:

"It shall be an unlawful employment practice for an employer—

"(1) to fail or refuse to hire or to discharge any individual, or otherwise to discriminate against any individual with respect to his compensation, terms, conditions, or privileges of employment, because of such individual's race, color, religion, sex, or national origin; or

"(2) to limit, segregate, or classify his employees or applicants for employment in any way which would deprive or tend to deprive any individual of employment opportunities or otherwise adversely affect his status as an employee, because of such individual's race, color, religion, sex, or national origin."

The Court today completes the process of converting this from a guarantee that race or sex will *not* be the basis for employment determinations, to a guarantee that it often *will*. Ever so subtly, without even alluding to the last obstacles preserved by earlier opinions that we now push out of our path, we effectively replace the goal of a discrimination-free society with the quite incompatible goal of proportionate representation by race and by sex in the workplace. . . .

I

. . . Several salient features of the [Santa Clara County affirmative action] plan should be noted. Most importantly, the plan's purpose was assuredly not to remedy prior sex discrimination by the Agency. It could not have been, because there was no prior sex discrimination to remedy. The majority, in cataloguing the Agency's alleged misdeeds, neglects to mention the District Court's finding that the Agency "has not discriminated in the past, and does not discriminate in the present against women in regard to employment opportunities in general and promotions in particular." This finding was not disturbed by the Ninth Circuit.

Not only was the plan not directed at the results of past sex discrimination by the Agency, but its objective was not to achieve the state of affairs that this Court has dubiously assumed would result from an absence of discrimination—an overall work force "more or less representative of the racial and ethnic composition of the population in the community." *Teamsters* v. *United States* (1977). Rather, the oft-stated goal was to mirror the racial and sexual composition of the entire county labor force, not merely in the Agency work force as a whole, but in each and every individual job category at the Agency. In a discrimination-free world, it would obviously be a statistical oddity for every job category to match the racial and sexual composition of even that portion of the county work force *qualified* for that job; it would be utterly miraculous for each of them to match, as the plan expected, the composition of the *entire* work force. Quite obviously, the plan did not seek to replicate what a lack of discrimination would produce, but rather imposed racial and sexual tailoring that would, in defiance of normal expectations and laws of probability, give each protected racial and sexual group a governmentally determined "proper" proportion of each job category. . . .

II

The most significant proposition of law established by today's decision is that racial or sexual discrimination is permitted under Title VII when it is intended to overcome the effect, not of the employer's own discrimination, but of societal attitudes that have limited the entry of certain races, or of a particular sex, into certain jobs. Even if the societal attitudes in question consisted exclusively of conscious discrimination by other employers, this holding would contradict a decision of this Court rendered only last Term. *Wygant* v. *Jackson Board of Education* (1986), held that the objective of remedying societal discrimination cannot prevent remedial affirmative action from violating the Equal Protection Clause....

...There is no sensible basis for construing Title VII to permit employers to engage in race- or sex-conscious employment practices that courts would be forbidden from ordering them to engage in following a judicial finding of discrimination....

In fact, however, today's decision goes well beyond merely allowing racial or sexual discrimination in order to eliminate the effects of prior societal *discrimination.* The majority opinion often uses the phrase "traditionally segregated job category" to describe the evil against which the plan is legitimately (according to the majority) directed. As originally used in *Steelworkers* v. *Weber* (1979), that phrase described skilled jobs from which employers and unions had systematically and intentionally excluded black workers—traditionally segregated jobs, that is, in the sense of conscious, exclusionary discrimination. But that is assuredly not the sense in which the phrase is used here. It is absurd to think that the nationwide failure of road maintenance crews, for example, to achieve the Agency's ambition of 36.4% female representation is attributable primarily, if even substantially, to systematic exclusion of women eager to shoulder pick and shovel. It is a "traditionally segregated job category" *not* in the *Weber* sense, but in the sense that, because of longstanding social attitudes, it has not been regarded *by women themselves* as desirable work.... And it is the alteration of social attitudes, rather than the elimination of discrimination, which today's decision approves as justification for state-enforced discrimination. This is an enormous expansion, undertaken without the slightest justification or analysis.

III

...The majority's response to this criticism ... asserts that, since "Congress has not amended the statute to reject our construction, ... we ... may assume that our interpretation was correct." This assumption, which frequently haunts our opinions, should be put to rest. It is based, to begin with, on the patently false premise that the correctness of statutory construction is to be measured by what the current Congress desires, rather than by what the law as enacted meant. To make matters worse, it assays the current Congress' desires *with respect to the particular provision in isolation,* rather than (the way the provision was originally enacted) as part of a total legislative package containing many *quids pro quo*. . . .

It is unlikely that today's result will be displeasing to politically elected officials, to whom it provides the means of quickly accommodating the demands of organized groups to achieve concrete, numerical improvement in the economic status of particular constituencies. Nor will it displease the world of corporate and governmental employers (many of whom have filed briefs as *amici* in the present case, all on the side of Santa Clara) for whom the cost of hiring less qualified workers is often substantially less—and infinitely more predictable—than the cost of litigating Title VII cases and of seeking to convince federal agencies by nonnumerical means that no discrimination exists. In fact, the only losers in the process are the Johnsons of the country, for whom Title VII has been not merely repealed but actually inverted. The irony is that these individuals—predominantly unknown, unaffluent, unorganized—suffer this injustice at the hands of a Court fond of thinking itself the champion of the politically impotent. I dissent.

OTA REPORT ON OWNERSHIP OF HUMAN TISSUES AND CELLS

March 25, 1987

The Office of Technology Assessment (OTA) March 25 released the first in a series of reports dealing with recent developments in biotechnology. The report concerned the ownership and use of human tissues and cells in research and development. Prepared at the request of the House Committee on Science and Technology and the House Committee on Energy and Commerce, the 167-page report addressed the economic, legal, and ethical rights of human donors of tissues and cells and also those of doctors and researchers who obtained and developed biological materials. The study described new techniques to manipulate human tissues and cells to yield commercially valuable products. Finally, it discussed options for congressional action on the issues of commercialization of human biological materials, regulation of research with human subjects, and disclosure of physicians' commercial interests in patient treatment.

Growth of the Biotechnology Industry

In the 1960s the term "biotechnology" did not exist. But the discovery in the 1970s of techniques for splicing genetic information of one organism into that of another and fusing cells to produce large quantities of valuable proteins made it clear that a revolution in biological technology—the science of applied biology to study or modify the genetic code of organisms—was in the offing. By the beginning of the 1980s, predictions abounded that breakthroughs in biotechnology would have a profound impact on health care. It was envisioned that the new industry would produce a wealth of drugs and vaccines to treat a variety of diseases, including cancer. But scientists encountered technical problems, ranging from bulk production to purification of their biologically engineered products, and progress was slower than expected.

Beginning in the mid-1980s, however, a number of discoveries hastened the growth of the industry, which by 1987 included some three hundred companies. Examples of such innovations included:

- *The pinpointing among the genes that make up the hundreds of thousands in the human genetic code of certain ones linked with several inherited defects, among them manic depressive illness and Alzheimer's.*
- *The availability in reliable supply and purer form of a genetically engineered human growth hormone used to treat dwarfism in children.*
- *The development of a protein (alpha interferon) used to treat certain types of cancer; a protein that induced blood clotting (Factor VIIIC, particularly applicable to hemophiliacs); a substance that dissolved blood clotting (for treating heart disease); and a substance called Interleukin-2 for treatment of certain types of cancer.*

Questions Raised

But these and numerous other developments raised troubling questions. In the cases of human treatment, should individuals automatically be informed of test results that indicated they were carriers of a disease like Alzheimer's? Should insurance companies be informed of test results? Who should be permitted to use a substance, such as a human growth hormone? Should treatment be available to any child to boost height for social or athletic reasons?

Similar questions were raised by the research on AIDS (acquired immune deficiency syndrome) by several biotech groups trying to genetically engineer a vaccine against the generally fatal disease, using recombinant DNA technology to isolate the virus. But what if the vaccine failed and the person being tested contracted AIDS? How should a study demonstrate that the vaccine was effective if all the individuals in the test were warned to avoid exposure to AIDS? Because the disease develops many years after exposure, could the effectiveness of an AIDS vaccine be reliably judged?

Another pressing issue was the ownership and commercialization of biotech products. In 1980 the Supreme Court ruled in Diamond v. Chakrabarty *that new life forms created by DNA recombinations could be patented. And in April 1987 the U.S. Patent and Trademark Office went a step further, holding that researchers who added genes to animal embryos by gene splicing in an effort to improve animal strains (cows who gave more milk, leaner hogs, and so forth) could apply for a patent.*

The patentability of genetically engineered organisms raised a host of new issues, resulting in a rapid increase in the number of court cases over ownership. Among the questions was how to compensate a scientist whose work had been taken a step further by another scientist (a common problem in the fast-growing biotech industry).

To critics of such "commercialization" of human life forms, representatives of the industry responded that research and development of new products involved staggering costs and that investments would be drastically reduced if companies could not hold onto the fruits of their labor. As of early 1987 more than six thousand patent applications were pending for biotech-related products.

Human Tissues and Cells

It was the ethical issues, property rights, and commercialization that the OTA addressed in its report on the use of human tissues and cells. Whereas twenty years ago, such questions would seldom have been raised, the OTA noted that the formulation of answers and policies had become increasingly urgent. As posed by the OTA, the major questions included: "Who owns a cell line—the human source of the original tissues and cells or the scientist who developed the cell line? Should biological materials be sold, and if so, what are the implications for equity of distribution? Should disclosure, informed consent, and regulatory requirements be modified to cope with the new questions raised by the increased importance and value of human biological materials?"

The uncertainty that surrounded those issues in 1987 might have adverse affects on potentially valuable research, particularly if the donor could claim ownership long after the specimen was obtained. The scientists could be sued; researchers could find it difficult to obtain title insurance; and commercialization could be thwarted as a result.

Heretofore, most human biological material had been donated under the spirit of regulations such as the 1984 National Organ Transplant Act, whereby tissues had been given free of charge in a cooperative relation between patient and researcher or physician. But the growing commercialization of the use of new life forms created by DNA recombinants, including those in humans, gave rise to legal questions of ownership.

The extent to which a donor's consent was required also was raised. Although federal regulations existed to cover some measure of consent and disclosure of what was to be done with the material, the commercial use of tissue raised questions as to whether the potential monetary gain should be disclosed to the donor. At the heart of that controversy lay the question: Should human tissue be voluntarily provided, or should it be the source of financial reward? And with the commercialization of those human biotech products came the question of their equitable production and distribution, among other economic issues. Like the protest over patenting other life forms—animals and plants—ethical considerations also played a role. Was life simply a commodity—"patentable subject matter?" Should living human materials be bought and sold in the marketplace?

Like a number of other observers of and participants in the biotechnology field, the OTA concluded that the answer could not come from legal solutions or patent office regulation but should come from congressional consideration of the new guidelines.

Following are excerpts from the March 25, 1987, Office of Technology Assessment report, "Ownership of Human Tissues and Cells," the first in a series of OTA reports on new developments in biotechnology:

Human Biological Materials: Questions for the Future

New developments in biotechnology hold great promise for advancing knowledge about various life forms and improving human health. But with this promise come greater responsibilities for scientists and policymakers. Human biological materials—tissues and cells—can be used to develop commercial products (e.g., hybridomas and cultured cell lines[1]), and for diagnostic and therapeutic purposes. The use of human biological materials for therapy, research, and profit raises important legal, ethical, and economic issues (see table 1).

Many of these issues are similar to those that have been raised concerning human organ donation, which is currently regulated as a result of the Uniform Anatomical Gift Act (National Conference of Commissioners on Uniform State Laws, 1968) and the 1984 National Organ Transplant Act (Public Law 98-507).

But the use of human tissues and cells in biotechnology raises questions that have not been answered in previous public policy deliberations concerning the acquisition of human organs. *Who owns a cell line—the human source of the original tissues and cells or the scientist who developed the cell line? Should biological materials be sold, and if so, what are the implications for equity of distribution? Should disclosure, informed consent, and regulatory requirements be modified to cope with the new questions raised by the increased importance and value of human biological materials?*

There are no easy answers. These issues are novel and complex, and no single body of law, policy, or ethics applies directly.

[1] A *hybridoma* is a hybrid cell resulting from the fusion of a particular type of immortal tumor cell line, a myeloma, with an antibody producing B lymphocyte. Cultures of such cells are capable of continuous growth and specific, monoclonal antibody production. A *cell line* is a sample of cells, having undergone the process of adaptation to artificial laboratory cultivation, that is now capable of sustaining continuous, long-term growth in culture.

Table 1.—Human Biological Materials: Many Questions, Few Definitive Answers

- Are bodily substances "property" to be disposed of by any means one chooses, including donation or sale?
- Do property rights to their genetic identity adhere to individuals or to the species?
- Who should make the basic decisions affecting the acquisition of tissues and cells, and under what circumstances should such acquisition be permitted or denied?
- What are patients and research subjects entitled to know about the potential for commercial exploitation of an invention that uses their bodily materials? And what is the probability that an individual's tissues and cells will end up in a commercial product?
- How is it that inventions incorporating human cells are patentable in the first place? How similar is the invention to the original biological material?
- What is the nature of the researcher's contribution versus the source's contribution to the invention?
- Who should profit from federally funded research using human tissue? To what extent are the issues raised by ownership of human biological materials related to commercial relationships between universities and companies?
- What are the implications of these issues for scientists, physicians, patients, volunteer research subjects, universities, and the biomedical product industry?

SOURCE: Office of Technology Assessment, 1987.

Definitions

Human bodies contain a number of elements that are useful in biomedical research. Healthy people continually produce a variety of replenishable substances, including blood, skin, bone marrow, hair, urine, perspiration, saliva, milk, semen, and tears. Human bodies also contain nonreplenishing parts, such as organs or oocytes. Organs may be either vital (e.g., heart) or to some extent expendable (e.g., lymph nodes or a second kidney). Finally, the body can also have diseased parts. *While this report refers to all human parts—replenishing and nonreplenishing, living and nonliving, beneficial and detrimental—collectively as human biological materials, it focuses primarily on those biological materials most frequently used in biotechnology: tissues and cells.* The terms specimens, body parts, human tissue, fluids, bodily substances, and biologicals are also used. *OTA distinguishes these undeveloped human biological materials from the biological inventions developed from them (and in some cases patented) such as cell lines, hybridomas, and cloned genes.*

The Problem of Uncertainty

At present, there is great uncertainty about how courts will resolve disputes between the human sources of specimens and specimen users. This could be detrimental to both academic researchers and the nascent biotechnology industry, particularly if the rights of a human source are asserted long after the specimen was obtained. The assertion of rights by human sources would affect not only the researcher who obtained the original specimen, but other researchers as well because biological materials are routinely distributed to other researchers for experimental purposes. Thus, scientists who obtain cell lines or other specimen-derivative products (e.g., gene clones) from the original researcher might also be sued. Furthermore, because inventions containing biological materials can be patented and licensed for commercial use, companies are unlikely to invest in developing, manufacturing, or marketing a product when uncertainty about clear title exists.

This uncertainty about the rights of specimen sources and specimen users could have far-reaching implications as research and development progresses. Research using human biological materials could be thwarted if universities and companies have difficulty obtaining title insurance covering ownership of cell lines or gene clones, or liability insurance. Insurers would be concerned not only with suits by individuals who can be identified as the sources of specimens, but also by the potential for class action lawsuits on behalf of all those who contributed specimens to a particular research project. Researchers generally claim that the pervasive use of human cells and tissues in biomedical research makes it impractical and inefficient to try to identify the sources of various specimens or to try to value their contributions. Regardless of the merit of these claims, however, resolving the current uncertainty may be more important to the future of biotechnology than resolving it in any particular way.

The Technologies

Three broad classes of basic biological techniques are of particular relevance to this report. They are *tissue and cell culture technology, hybridoma technology, and recombinant DNA technology.*

Tissue and Cell Culture Technology

Cells are the basic structural unit of living organisms. A single cell is a complex collection of molecules with integrated functions forming a self-assembling, self-regulating entity. There are two broad classes of cells: prokaryotic and eukaryotic. Prokaryotes, generally considered to be the simpler of the two classes, include bacteria. Their genetic material is not housed in a separate structure (a nucleus) and the majority of prokaryotic organisms are unicelluar. Eukaryotes are usually multicellular organisms; they contain a nucleus and other specialized structures to coordinate different cell functions. Human beings are eukaryotes.

Because eukaryotes are complex, scientists often study these organisms by examining isolated cells independent of the whole organism. This reductionist approach, called tissue and cell culture, is an essential technique for the study of human biological materials and the development of related biotechnologies. *Establishing human cell culture directly from human tissue is a relatively difficult enterprise and the probability of establishing a cell line from a given sample varies, ranging from 0.01 percent for some liver cells to nearly 100 percent for some human skin cells.*

Cell cultures isolated from nontumor tissue have a finite lifespan in the laboratory and most will die after a limited number of population doublings. These cultures will age (called senescence) unless pushed into immortality by outside interventions involving viruses or chemicals. The type of donor tissue involved and culture conditions are important variables of cell lifespan. Long-term growth of human cells and tissues is difficult, often an art. Most established cell cultures have been derived from malignant tissue samples. Tissue and cell culture techniques have greatly increased knowledge about cell biology and set the stage for the development of hybridoma technology.

Hybridoma Technology

In response to foreign substances, the body produces a constellation of different substances. Antibodies are one component of the immune response and they have a unique ability to identify specific molecules. Lymphokines, sometimes called bioregulators, are also produced during an immune response.

Cell culture technology provides the tools scientists need to produce pure, highly specific antibodies. By fusing two types of cells—an antibody-producing B lymphocyte with a certain tumor cell line (a myeloma)—scientists found that the resulting immortal hybrid cells, called hybridomas, secrete large amounts of homogeneous (or monoclonal) antibodies. Monoclonal antibodies have led to a greater understanding of the intricacies of the immune response and they have become powerful and widely used laboratory tools. They also have been approved for use as therapeutic agents. *Although the production of human monoclonal antibodies has proved much more difficult than the production of rodent monoclonal antibodies, the increasing availability of large supplies of monoclonal antibodies is revolutionizing research, commerce, and medicine.*

Lymphokines (e.g., interferon) were previously available in minute and usually impure amounts—if at all. Hybridoma, cell culture, and recombinant DNA technologies now permit lymphokines to be isolated in pure form and in quantities facilitating further analysis and use. The increased production and availability of these molecules has significant therapeutic promise in the treatment of a spectrum of diseases because of their exquisite specificity and reduced toxicity.

Recombinant DNA Technology

Recombinant DNA technology, also referred to as genetic engineering, involves the direct manipulation of the genetic material (the DNA) of a cell. Using this technique, it is now possible to speed the isolation, examination, and development of a wide range of biological compounds. Like the use of cell culture, the use of recombinant DNA techniques has shed further light on the details of many important biological processes.

Gene cloning is a process that uses a variety of recombinant DNA procedures to produce multiple copies of a particular piece of genetic information. It is an important tool that accelerates the study or production of genes. All recombinant DNA methods require the following:

- a suitable vector to move DNA into the host cell,
- an appropriate host,
- a system to select and cull host cells that have received recombinant DNA, and,
- a probe to detect the particular recombinant organisms of interest.

Recombinant DNA techniques have done much to illuminate the regulation and control of important human processes. In addition, advances in this technology underlie many commercial ventures to isolate or manufacture large quantities of scarce biological commodities.

The Interested Parties

Although tissues and cells can be used for diagnostic, therapeutic, research, and commercial purposes, in fact the various uses of biological materials are usually intertwined, sometimes inextricably. This means that *a variety of people, including scientists in the research community (universities and industry), plus physicians, and patient and nonpatient sources, share an interest in the acquisition and use of human tissues and cells.* All would likely benefit from a resolution of the uncertainty surrounding the uses of biotechnology.

Commercial Interest in Human Biological Research and Inventions

The government has always maintained an interest in the legal, ethical, and economic implications of the research it is funding, and this interest is magnified when such research might result in inventions that are patentable under Federal law. In addition to advances in technology, *two events occurred in 1980 to precipitate the increasing research and commercial interest in human biological materials. First, the U.S. Supreme Court held for the first time that Federal patent law applies to new life forms created by DNA recombinations—opening up the possibility that products containing altered human cells and genes might also be patentable. Second, Congress amended the patent statute to encourage patenting and licensing of inventions resulting from government-sponsored research (Public Law 96-517).*

Even though the government is the primary source of funding for basic biomedical research, no single patent policy existed for government-supported research until 1980. Instead, each agency developed its own rules, resulting in 26 different patent policies. Under this system, only about 4 percent of some 30,000 government-owned patents were licensed. Furthermore, the government policy of granting nonexclusive licenses discouraged private investment, since a company lacking an exclusive license is reluctant to pay the cost of developing, producing, and marketing a product. Thus, potentially valuable research remained unexploited. To resolve this problem, Congress passed the Patent and Trademark Amendment Act in 1980 to prompt efforts to develop a uniform patent policy that would encourage cooperative relationships between universities and industry, and ultimately take government-sponsored inventions off the shelf and into the marketplace.

The changing legal climate has provided a fertile medium for the growth of university biomedical research and development using novel biotechnologies. *From 1980 through 1984, patent applications by universities and hospitals for inventions containing human biologicals increased more than 300 percent (compared to the preceding 5-year period). The extent to which these and forthcoming patents will be of commercial value is difficult to assess.*

Sources of Human Tissue

There are three major sources of specimens: patients, healthy research subjects, and cadavers.

- Patients are a source of both normal and atypical specimens and these individuals may or may not be research subjects. Patient-derived specimens may be "leftovers" obtained from diagnostic or therapeutic procedures and most human tissues or cells that find their way into research protocols are of this type. Patient-derived samples can also be provided as part of a research protocol.
- Healthy volunteer research subjects may donate replenishing biologicals if specimen removal involves little or no risk of harm, according to generally accepted principles of human subject research.
- Cadavers are the only permissible source of normal and atypical vital organs (including the brain, heart, and liver, but excluding kidneys and corneas.) They are also the only permissible source of healthy benign organs (e.g., corneas) destined for research rather than transplantation.

While these donor classifications may seem fairly straightfoward, the human relationships involved are more dynamic than these categories suggest. In particular, the physician-patient relationship may change over the course of time into a researcher-subject relationship.

The Research Community

Research uses of human tissue are diverse and difficult to categorize. Generally, researchers are studying the characteristics and functions of healthy and diseased organs, tissues, and cells. Commercial products developed from human specimens are usually related to medical or research uses. The use of human biologicals is widespread; a recent survey conducted by the House Committee on Science and Technology found that 49 percent of the researchers at the medical institutions surveyed used patients' tissues or fluid in their research.

The revolutionizing effect of biotechnology on the use of human specimens is principally due to three factors:

- isolation of increasingly smaller amounts of important naturally occurring human biological factors (also known as biopharmaceuticals, bioresponse modulators, or biological mediators);
- production of virtually unlimited quantities of these factors (usually found in the body in only small amounts) using recombinant DNA methods; and
- discovery of techniques to create hybridomas, making it possible to generate large, pure supplies of specific antibodies.

At the most fundamental scientific level, human material is a source for studies designed to understand basic biological processes. From this basic research, commercial development may follow. However, *the probability that any one person's biological materials will be developed into a valuable product is exceedingly small. Thus, the issue of great potential commercial gain from donated materials is relevant to a small minority of sources.* However, in the future—as biotechnology progresses—the importance of the issue and the number of people involved could increase. The potential for commercial gain, while to date mostly a speculative consideration, could quickly become a reality. It is appropriate to consider these issues and the possible roles of the interested parties now, in advance of their becoming highly visible, so that public policy perspectives can be developed with wisdom and foresight.

Industry

The biotechnology industry is a major interested party in the controversy surrounding the use of human tissues and cells for financial gain. It is comprised of a variety of different types of organizations including the established pharmaceutical companies, oil and chemical companies, agricultural product manufacturers, and the new biotechnology companies. Of the nearly 350 commercial biotechnology firms in the United States actively engaged in biotechnology research and commercial product development, approximately 25 to 30 percent are engaged in research to develop a human therapeutic or diagnostic reagent. There is a strong international component to the biotechnology industry, with numerous research and development arrangements and partnerships between American firms and firms in Japan and Europe.

Legal Considerations

United States law has long protected people from injury and damages. Much of this protection is afforded by the common law, the body of judge-made law built on judicial precedents. This body of legal principles has evolved over centuries as judges are called on to resolve disputes that have not been addressed by statute. Congress and State legislatures, however, have enacted numerous statutes to codify, modify, or overrule the common law, or to address larger societal issues that are inaccessible through the use of common law.

The common law does not provide any definitive answer to the questions of rights that arise when a patient or nonpatient source supplies biological materials to an academic or commercial researcher. Because neither judicial precedents nor statutes directly address this question, the court must do what common law judges have done for centuries: reason by analogy, using legal principles and precedent developed for other circumstances.

Three large collections of legal principles could prove relevant to the use of human tissues and cells: property law, tort law, and contract law. These three areas include a broad variety of statutes and precedents that might be relevant and thus this issue could arguably touch almost all facets of U.S. law. . . . *Overall, however, there is no discrete body of law that deals specifically with these human biological materials.* Because common law reacts to damages only after they have occurred, it does not anticipate possible interests that have not existed previously. In the area of the use of human tissues and cells, technology in fact has advanced beyond existing law. It is not possible to predict what principles and arguments of law might actually be used as cases of this sort come before the courts.

Can Human Biological Materials Be Sold Like Property?

No area of law clearly provides ownership rights with respect to human tissues and cells. Nor does any law prohibit the use or sale of human bodily substances by the living person who generates them or one who acquires them from such a person, except under certain circumstances unrelated to biotechnology research. *In the absence of clear legal restrictions, the sale of tissues and cells is generally permissible unless the circumstances surrounding the sale suggest a significant threat to individual or public health, or strong offense to public sensibility.* To date, neither deleterious health effects nor public moral outrage have occurred even though occasional reports of sales of replenishing cells have been publicized. But while the law permits the sale of such replenishing cells as blood and semen, it does not endorse such transactions and does not characterize such transactions as involving property. In this sense, *either permitting or forbidding the sale of human specimens by patients and research subjects can be claimed to be consistent with existing law.*

Informed Consent and Disclosure

Every human being of adult years and sound mind has a right to determine what shall be done with his own body. . . .

—*Scholendorff v. Society of New York Hospital, 1914*

The fundamental principle underlying the need for consent for medical or research purposes is respect for personal autonomy. Consent is a process of communication, a two-way flow of information between caregiver/researcher and the patient/subject about the risks and benefits of the treatment or research.

For consent to be valid, the patient or research subject must be given an adequate amount of information with which to reach a reasoned choice. Although there are differences from State to State, the information that generally needs to be disclosed to obtain consent focuses on the nature and purpose of the treatment or research, risk-benefit information, and the availability of beneficial, alternative procedures or treatment. Consent in a research setting ... must be obtained in circumstances free from the prospect of coercion or undue influence.

There are two main sources of Federal regulations governing human research. The Department of Health and Human Services (DHHS) and the Food and Drug Administration (FDA) have promulgated regulations that delineate the elements necessary for informed consent to research. DHHS regulations govern research conducted or funded by DHHS, including the National Institutes of Health. FDA regulations govern clinical investigations that support applications for research or marketing permits for products such as drugs, food additives, medical devices, and biological products. Where these Federal regulations apply, disclosure requirements go beyond the accepted norms and include disclosure regarding confidentiality, compensation for research-related injuries, and the right to withdraw from research without incurring a penalty or loss of rights.

These Federal regulations are a deliberate attempt to set ethical and legal constraints on human research. A balance has been struck between the needs of researchers and the rights and safety of human subjects. The success of these regulations in achieving this balance is in no small measure a function of the integrity of investigators and the diligence of institutional review boards, which review proposed research projects for compliance with human subject research regulations.

Consent and the Prospect of Commercial Gain

The traditional view has been that in therapeutic settings, information disclosed to patients should be related to the risks and benefits of diagnostic tests or treatment, and that it should include alternative procedures. Similarly, in the research setting the disclosure of information has focused on the nature of the study and its effects on subjects. *Until recently, little thought had been given to disclosing information about the prospect for commercial gain, but with the advent of biotechnology and its potential use of human tissues and cells in valuable products, this issue merits consideration.*

Arguments can be made both for and against the idea of including information about potential financial gain in the required disclosure of information to patients and research subjects.

Arguments Favoring Disclosure of Potential Commercial Gain

If the notion of personal autonomy and the right to decide what will be done with one's body is to be given full legal recognition, then the prospect of commercial gain should be disclosed because this information may help a person decide whether or not to take part in research. Indeed, the overall trend has been toward greater disclosure of information—details about the probable impact of a procedure on lifestyle, the financial costs of one procedure over another, even the length of disability. Requiring disclosure about commercial gain can be viewed as a logical extension of the consent process.

In fact, it can be argued that the Federal regulations should explicitly require disclosure of potential commercial gain because they require disclosure of "significant new findings developed during the course of the research that may relate to the subject's willingness to continue participation." Discovery of a commercially significant tissue or cell in a subject's body may constitute a "significant new finding."

Arguments Against Disclosure of Potential Commercial Gain

The primary argument against disclosing the prospect of commercial gain concerns the impact such information might have on the subject's ability to reach an informed choice free of undue influence. The prospect of financial gain stemming from marketable discoveries could hamper subjects from reaching informed decisions because attention to this highly speculative topic could distract attention from other important aspects of the consent process.

Disclosing information about commercial gain could sometimes jeopardize the health and safety of subjects, as well as the validity of the research itself. The hope of gain, for example, might lead subjects to give less than candid answers to questions about medical or personal history that might otherwise disqualify them from the study. It might encourage them to expose themselves to risks they would otherwise consider unacceptable. In addition, because disclosure of potential gain is so speculative, such disclosure could generate unreasonable expectations or be considered misinformation.

It can also be argued that Federal human research regulations embody a philosophy that bans participation for inappropriate reasons. DHHS regulations, for example, make it clear that parole boards should not consider participation when making prisoners' parole decisions. DHHS might consider it improper for subjects to participate in research specifically because they might profit financially. Some people thus might argue that banning reference to the prospect of financial gain is necessary to safeguard subjects from undue influence on their decisions.

Are Changes Needed in the Consent Process?

The question of disclosing potential commercial gain related to diagnostic tests or treatment is one the courts or State legislatures will need to address. However, the Federal Government funds substantial amounts of human research and will also need to consider its regulations in light of this debate. *Policymakers, institutional review boards, and researchers face these questions related to disclosure: Should potential commercial gain be disclosed? If so, what pertinent information is necessary? When is such disclosure best made? What safeguards need to be developed to minimize any detrimental impacts resulting from disclosure of probable commercial gain?*

The prospect of financial gain is a troublesome issue in terms of voluntary consent and the use of human biological materials. *It can be argued that to assure truly voluntary consent, research subjects should not be offered compensation for their time and inconvenience, let alone substantial financial gain. The counter argument is that the sources of human tissues and cells have rights or interests in marketable substances taken or developed from their bodies and so have a right to know about potential profits or to be paid outright for their tissues and cells.* Regardless of what decision is reached, care must be taken so research is not adversely affected because it becomes too complicated to get specimens.

Economic Considerations

The traditional relationships between donors and researchers, and among researchers at different institutions, have been informal; both information and biological materials have been exchanged freely. Today, however, the techniques of biotechnology and the potential for profits and scientific recognition have introduced new concerns. At present, there is no widespread sentiment favoring a move toward a market system for the exchange of human tissues and cells. However, a few types of materials, such as plasma and some patented cell lines, are currently transferred within a market system. Future changes in the extent of profits generated . . . could force some changes in the current, primarily nonmarket system.

Two key factors probably will determine whether a change occurs in the current system of free donation of human biological materials for use in biotechnology research and commerce. First, a change could arise from judicial decisions in present or future cases under litigation. Second, a change could be initiated through greater public interest as the commercial applications of biotechnology increase and profits begin to be realized.

There are arguments both for and against payments for donations of human biological materials. Arguments over payments for human tissues and cells used in biotechnological research echo similar debates about markets in human organs. There are five principal issues in the debate:

- the equity of production and distribution,
- the added costs of payments to sources and costs associated with that process,
- social goals (the merits of an altruistic system of donations versus a market system),

- safety and quality (both of the source and the biological materials), and
- potential shortages or inefficiencies resulting from a nonmarket system or from changing from a nonmarket system to a market system.

The factors related to social goals, safety and quality, and shortages do not now offer compelling support either for or against paying the sources of human tissues and cells. But two of the issues are central to the debate, and they seem to argue in favor of opposing approaches. *Issues of equity argue in favor of a payment system to human sources. On the other hand, the added costs of payments to sources argue against such a payment system. . . .*

From the point of view of equity, a market structure is favored because it eliminates the potential windfall realized by those who would otherwise receive free tissues and cells. On the other hand, the magnitude of the transaction costs associated with payment to human sources may be sufficient to deter any forays into a market structure. Nonprofit organizations can play an important role in the procurement and distribution of human biological materials, just as they have played a key role in marketing blood and organs. *At present, there does not appear to be movement toward a change in the existing system of free donations of human biological materials for use in research and commerce in biotechnology.*

Ethical Considerations

Are the human body and its parts fit objects for commerce, things that may properly be bought and sold? *There are three broad ethical grounds for objecting to or supporting commercial activities in human biological materials: respect for persons, concern for beneficence, and concern for justice.*

First, the ethical principle of respect for persons relates to the idea that trade in human tissues and cells ought to be limited if the body is considered part of the basic dignity of human beings. To the extent that the body is indivisible from that which makes up personhood, the same respect is due the body as is due persons. If the body is incidental to the essence of personhood, however, then trade in the body is not protected by the ethical principle of respect for persons.

The second ethical principle relevant to the acceptability of trade in human materials is beneficence—who would benefit. The basic question could be stated this way: would commercialization of human materials be more beneficial than a ban on such commercialization? Marketing human tissues and cells might be justified if that would lead to only good results or to a preponderance of good results over bad. Those who hold differing ethical perspectives might consider different outcomes as beneficent.

A third relevant principle is justice. Would a market setting be equitable to all members of society, including those who are financially disadvantaged? Part of the public ambivalence about a market in human tissues stems from a sense that such a market would foster inequities.

The Moral Status of Bodies and Their Parts

Ethical and religious traditions do not provide clear guidelines about the ways in which human biological materials should be developed or exchanged. The absence of established customs regarding these materials is due to the relatively new potential for conducting and profiting from the development of human cells into cell lines. *The debate about whether or not it is ethical for bodily materials to be bought and sold underlies all discussions about the commercialization of human biological materials.* In addition, there are important questions about how justice should be preserved in the distribution of profits accruing from developed human biological materials.

Decisions about the commercialization of human biological materials depend in part on the ways in which human tissues are regarded or valued. Selected Western religious traditions offer some insights about the significance of the human body. *Although there are significant variations among them, Jewish, Catholic, and Protestant traditions generally favor the transfer of human biological materials as gifts.*

There are two main reasons why it is important to examine religious perspectives when the goal is to develop public policies in a pluralistic society. One reason is historical: many of the laws regarding bodies and their parts have been influenced by religious sources. A second reason is that religious traditions still shape the ethical values of many people and hence they influence whether some uses of bodily parts or materials will be viewed as ethically acceptable or unacceptable. A related reason is that religious organizations have to be considered when policymakers try to develop policies that are politically feasible.

Two major variables are present in these Western religious traditions that affect the use of human tissues and cells: the type of materials and the mode of transfer. The significance of different modes of transfer (or acquisition, if viewed from the viewpoint of the user) and different materials hinges on various ethical principles, such as:

- respect for persons;
- benefits to others;
- not harming others; and
- justice, or treating others fairly and distributing benefits and burdens equitably.

There is a distinction between ethically acceptable and ethically preferable policies and practices. Some modes of transfer and some uses may be ethically preferred—for example, tradition prefers explicit gifts and donations without necessarily excluding sales, abandonment, and appropriation in all cases. Western religious tradition prefers transfer methods that depend on voluntary, knowledgeable consent. Thus, preferred methods recognize some kind of property right by the original possessor of the biological materials.

Tomorrow's Choices

Choices about how to handle transfers of tissues and cells from patients and research subjects to doctors, teachers, and researchers are important ethical decisions in two respects. First, these choices will characterize how individuals regard the human body. If certain human parts are "dignified," then social traditions suggest that they may be given, but not sold. Second, like the choice of how to obtain blood for transfusions, the system that is chosen for obtaining human tissues and cells will convey a sense of the symbolic weight modern society places on the human body and the use of human biological materials in order to relieve suffering and enhance human health.

The dispute between those who believe that commercialization of the human body is justified and those who think it is not is in part an argument between people who accept a philosophical view that separates the body (a material, physiological being) from personhood, identity, or mind (an immaterial, rational being) and those who do not.

Policy Issues and Options for Congressional Action

Four policy issues related to the use of human tissues and cells in biotechnology were identified [in] this study. The first concerns actions that Congress might take to regulate the commercialization of human tissues and cells. The second involves the adequacy of existing regulations covering commercialization of cell lines, gene probes, and other products developed from human biological materials. The third concerns the adequacy of existing regulations covering research with human subjects. The fourth centers on whether present practice is adequate to ensure that health care providers disclose their potential research and commercial interests in the care of a specific patient or group of patients.

Associated with each policy issue are several options for congressional action, ranging in each case from taking no specific steps to making major changes. Some of the options involve direct legislative action. Others are oriented to the actions of the executive branch but involve congressional oversight or direction. The order in which the options are presented should not imply their priority. Furthermore, the options are not, for the most part, mutually exclusive: adopting one does not necessarily disqualify others in the same category or within another category. A careful combination of options might produce the most desirable effects. In some cases, an option may suggest alterations in more than one aspect of using human tissues and cells in biotechnology. It is important to keep in mind that changes in one area have repercussions in others.

ISSUE 1: Should the commercialization of human tissues and cells be permitted by the Federal Government?

Option 1.1: Take no action. Congress may conclude that at present, the largely nonmarket basis for the transfer of human tissues and cells is appropriate. If a commercial market in human biological materials should arise, the lack of Federal regulation might result in great variability in the amounts of money paid to the sources of the original tissues and cells. If no action is taken, it is unlikely that human patients or research subjects will be routinely compensated for their tissues or cells in the near future.

Option 1.2: Mandate that donors of human tissues and cells are compensated for their donations. Some people argue that in the interest of equity, the sources of human tissues and cells should be compensated. Congress could decide that human biological materials have a monetary value, even in their unimproved state, and that the sources of these materials have a right to this value. The amount and form of such compensation could vary. Sources could be paid for their time and trouble or paid for the actual specimen. Payment for service as opposed to substance is now standard practice in the case of sperm donation....

Option 1.3: Enact a statute modeled after the National Organ Transplant Act that prohibits the buying and selling of human tissues and cells. Congress may conclude that at present, the existing situation in which human tissues and cells are largely either donated or abandoned for research purposes is satisfactory. If Congress concludes that any for-profit market in human tissues and cells should be stifled or avoided, it could prohibit the sale of these biological materials. Such a statute would prevent patients, research subjects, or other sources from making money from providing their tissues and cells. If Congress enacted a statute modeled after the National Organ Transplant Act in particular, there would be a consistent line of Federal reasoning concerning the transfer of human organs, tissues, and cells.

ISSUE 2: Should the commercialization of cell lines, gene probes, and other products developed from human tissues and cells be modified by the Federal Government?

Option 2.1: Take no action. At present, cell lines, gene probes, and other products developed from human tissues and cells are exchanged informally among researchers as well as by means of a market system. For the most part, profits are accrued in the form of royalties paid by those who want access to the developed products. If Congress takes no action, the use of patented inventions based on human biological materials will continue to be restricted to those who engage in licensing agreements for access to the patented products.

Option 2.2: Amend current patent law so parties other than inventors (e.g., patients, research subjects, or the Federal Government) have protected interests and access to any commercial products developed from their tissues and cells. Within the context of current patent law, the inventor has exclusive rights to patented material and this effectively bars access by the sources to their original biological material. Some argue, however, that the patients or research subjects, particularly if they suffer from a disease, should have access to or some say in the use of patented products derived from their tissues and cells. At present, licensing agreements for the use of these patented materials do not commonly stipulate any protected interest for the original source.

Option 2.3: Enact a statute protecting the rights of patients or research subjects to share in profits accruing from licensing agreements for the use of cell lines or gene probes developed from their original human biological material. The profitable features of patented cell lines and gene probes are the royalties that accrue from licensing agreements for access to these products. Congress may conclude that it is fair and equitable for the original sources of human biological materials to share in the derived profits. Such a profit sharing could be in addition to or instead of a flat fee for the original unimproved tissues and cells. Some researchers argue, however, that it is often impossible to identify the source of the original material as cell lines and gene probes are developed. Many laboratory transformations over a long period of time separate the original sample from the patented invention. If Congress enacts a statute ensuring that the sources of human tissues and cells share in the profits accruing from licensing agreements, then an extensive and costly system of recordkeeping will be necessary. . . .

Option 2.4: Mandate that any cell line be presumed to be in the public domain unless it has been formally registered at the time the tissue was extracted or placed into culture. The presumption that cell lines are in the public domain would bar anyone from claiming property rights to these products. While this would not directly compensate the donor or source of the unimproved tissues and cells or the researcher, it might relieve any sense of exploitation that someone else has taken over that original property right. The patent and similar systems could still apply for further inventions made in developing applications of the cell line.

Option 2.5: Enact a statute prohibiting parties other than inventors from sharing in any reimbursement for, or any profits derived from, the use of products developed from human tissues or cells. Under the present market system, only those who have patent law protection or enter into a contractual relationship (e.g., licensing agreement) realize commercial gain from developed tissues and cells. Congress may conclude that the sources should be barred from obtaining any reimbursement for products developed from their tissues and cells. Such action would affirm that commercialization of products developed through the use of human biological materials should be limited to the patent holder and licensees, and that patients and research subjects have no right to the value of their tissues and cells in their altered forms. While such an action might serve as an economic inducement for those who would obtain human tissues and cells for the purposes of developing new inventions, it is arguably contrary to current patent and contract law (which encourages commercial negotiation between willing parties) as well as the concept of a person's autonomy over the use of bodily materials.

ISSUE 3: Are guidelines on the Protection of Human Subjects (45 CFR Part 46) issued by the Department of Health and Human Services adequate for the use of human tissues and cells in biotechnology?

Option 3.1: Take no action. If no action is taken by the Department of Health and Human Services to alter the guidelines on the Protection of Human Subjects, it will remain unnecessary for researchers to inform subjects about possible uses of pathological or diagnostic specimens. As a result, researchers can continue to use these materials as they choose without informing the patient (see option 3.2). In addition, if the guidelines are not altered, it will not be possible for subjects to specifically waive their interests in the uses of their tissues and cells when giving informed consent because of the existing ban on the use of exculpatory language (see option 3.4).

Option 3.2: Direct the Secretary of Health and Human Services to modify or remove the exemption regarding the collection or study of existing pathological or diagnostic specimens from the regulatory requirements (§46.101(b)(5)). Current DHHS guidelines exempt research involving the collection or study of existing data, documents, or pathological or diagnostic specimens if these are publicly available or if the donor is otherwise unidentifiable. Researchers are therefore not obliged to disclose their research interests to sources of specimens when this exemption applies.

Congress could modify or remove this section of the regulations so that it becomes necessary for research subjects covered by this exemption to be informed about and have some say in the use of their tissues and cells. This option would assure that additional research subjects would be informed of the possible uses of biological specimens and related data and may be consistent with the general spirit of the guidelines to protect the interests of the research subject. Removal of the exemption, however, could restrict research on a wide variety of currently available data, documents, records, and pathological or diagnostic specimens when a researcher cannot: 1) determine the identity of the subject, and 2) assure that the subject provided an informed consent as required by the DHHS regulations. Modifying the exemption by removing only pathological specimens or diagnostic specimens could likewise curb research using currently available unidentified specimens, but would continue the exclusion for other existing data, documents, and records.

Option 3.3: Direct the Secretary of Health and Human Services to amend the general requirements for informed consent (§46.116) to include potential commercial gain as a basic element of informed consent. Under current DHHS regulations, certain information must be provided to each subject during the informed consent process. It could be decided to add a provision requiring that in seeking informed consent, a disclosure be made regarding the potential for commercial gain resulting from data, documents, records, or pathological or diagnostic specimens obtained during the research. Such a requirement could be codified as a basic element of informed consent that shall be provided to each subject (§46.116(a)), or as an additional element of informed consent to be provided to each subject when appropriate (§46.116(b)). Such a requirement would make clear that potential commercial gain is an issue that would be reviewed by the Institutional Review Board.

Option 3.4: Direct the Secretary of Health and Human Services to remove the ban on exculpatory language as it pertains to commercial gain (§46.116). Under the current DHHS regulations, informed consent documents may not include exculpatory language which is used to make research subjects or their representatives waive or appear to waive any of the subject's legal rights. The intent of this provision is to safeguard subjects and to make certain that they do not relinquish any legal rights. Some subjects may not want to reap financial benefits as the result of or as a byproduct of their participation in research, and some researchers and their sponsors may be deterred from conducting important research if they must share possible financial gain with research subjects. A change in the regulations could be made to modify the prohibition on the use of exculpatory language to permit research subjects to waive any rights to commercial gain. Such a provision would need to be clearly worded. Research subjects should understand exactly what rights are being waived and that they will not be denied treatment to which they are otherwise entitled even if they decide not to waive their rights. If the regulations are amended to permit the use of exculpatory language as it relates to potential commercial gain, the Institutional Review Board will have a greater role.

Option 3.5: Under its power to regulate interstate commerce, Congress could enact a statute to permit and regulate the buying and selling of human tissues and cells. The advantage of such a statute is that it would offer the possibility of financial compensation to the sources of human tissues and cells. In addition, such a statute would apply to the interstate transfer of these materials from all sources and therefore go far beyond any alteration in guidelines for the protection of human subjects involved in federally funded research. The disadvantage of such a statute is that it would permit commercialization of all human tissues and cells transferred interstate and extend Federal regulation into a previously unregulated area.

ISSUE 4: Is present practice adequate to ensure that health care providers disclose their potential research and commercial interests in the care of a specific patient or group of patients?

Option 4.1: Take no action. Congress may decide that existing or altered DHHS guidelines concerning the protection of human subjects provide sufficient safeguards to ensure that individuals are aware of the purposes and methods of the research in which they are involved. At the present time, however, these guidelines only extend to research subjects participating in federally funded research. There are no protections for research subjects in privately funded research.

There are no guidelines to ensure that health care providers disclose their commercial interests in caring for a particular patient or group of patients. If Congress takes no action, physician/researchers will not be obliged to tell a patient about their intention to develop commercially valuable products from the patient's tissues and cells. Congress may decide that the commercial interests of health care providers do not necessitate new forms of disclosure in order for patients to be adequately informed.

Option 4.2: Direct the Secretary of Health and Human Services to promulgate guidelines that require health care providers receiving any Federal reimbursement to disclose any research or commercial interests they may have in the care of a specific patient or group of patients. If Congress acts to ensure that health care providers disclose their research and commercial interests in caring for particular patients, it will be necessary to discern what sort of commercial interests in particular merit disclosure. Physicians in private practice obviously have commercial interests in treating patients so their practice remains economically viable. It comes as a surprise to many people, however, to learn that their physician might also engage in research using a patient's tissues and cells and subsequently develop a profitable product based on these donated or abandoned materials. The relationship between physician and patient may be compromised if patients suspect that their caregivers may profit in unanticipated ways. The development of guidelines concerning this type of disclosure could promote greater trust between physicians and patients in the delivery of health care.

NEW JERSEY COURT ON RIGHTS OF SURROGATES

March 31, 1987

In a decision that produced as much controversy as it addressed, the Superior Court of New Jersey March 31 ruled that a "surrogate mother," a woman who agreed under contract to carry a baby produced by her egg and the sperm of a man who was not her husband, could not thereafter petition for custody of the child. Under the contract, according to the decision, the surrogate had abandoned parental rights to the infant.

That ruling, handed down by Judge Harvey R. Sorkow of the family court, dealt with the highly publicized case of the infant known as "Baby M." In the first case testing the legality of such contracts, the judge concluded that the agreement between the surrogate mother and biological father was "constitutionally protected" as binding and that, therefore, custody was awarded to the father. At the same time, he denied all visitation rights to the biological mother.

The verdict came after seven weeks of hearings, which captured headlines and sparked debates throughout the nation. The case involved the surrogate mother, Mary Beth Whitehead, and the biological father, William Stern. Whitehead had contracted with Stern to be impregnated with his sperm and carry the child to term, after which Stern and his wife would obtain sole custody of the child. Soon after the birth of the infant girl, Whitehead decided that she could not give up the child and renounced the money the Sterns had agreed to pay her.

The case—and the decision—raised a number of troubling moral and legal issues. Several state legislatures moved to enact laws that would clarify the conditions of surrogate parenthood. An estimated five hundred babies had been born under such arrangements in the preceding decade.

Contract, Abduction, Custody Trial

Stern was a biochemist who had been born in Berlin near the end of World War II. All of his blood relatives were dead; many had been killed by the Nazis. His wife, Elizabeth, a pediatrician, had postponed bearing children until her medical studies were completed. Subsequently, she developed a mild case of multiple sclerosis that could possibly endanger her life if she became pregnant (although not impeding her ability to care for a child). Because of that fear, the Sterns decided to contract for a surrogate mother to be implanted with his sperm and carry the child to term.

In February 1985 Whitehead signed a contract with Stern, agreeing to bear his child in return for payment of $10,000. In addition to the $10,000, Stern agreed to pay all medical expenses for the surrogate. Whitehead was given physical and psychological examinations, and she agreed to follow certain proscriptions during pregnancy and to relinquish parental rights after she gave birth. Whitehead had two children, both born before she was nineteen.

Baby M was born on March 27, 1986. Whitehead gave the infant to the Sterns, but a few days later asked to take her back for a week. On April 12 Whitehead told the Sterns she could not relinquish the baby. The Sterns sued for custody, and on May 5 police officers arrived at the Whitehead home, armed with a court order granting temporary custody of Baby M—called Melissa Elizabeth by the Sterns and Sara by the Whiteheads—to the Sterns. Mary Beth Whitehead passed the baby through a window to her husband Richard, a sanitation worker who initially had opposed the surrogate agreement. The Whitehead family fled to Florida, where they stayed at the home of Mary Beth Whitehead's mother.

On July 31 private detectives hired by the Sterns located the baby and turned her over to them. A New Jersey judge ruled September 10 that Baby M would remain with them until a final ruling was issued on the surrogacy contract's validity and on permanent custody. In the meantime, Whitehead was granted rights to supervised visitation twice a week. The New Jersey Supreme Court November 21 denied her petition to receive temporary custody of the child, and on January 5, 1987, the custody/surrogate contract trial opened in the Bergen County Superior Court.

Sorkow awarded custody to the Sterns March 31 and terminated Whitehead's parental rights. (The court-appointed guardian and attorney, Lorraine Abraham, had testified that custody should be awarded to the Sterns, but that visitation rights should be allowed for Whitehead.) Immediately after the three-hour reading of his 121-page decision,

Sorkow summoned the Sterns into his chambers and presented Elizabeth Stern with papers allowing her to adopt the infant.

Whitehead's lawyer appealed the decision, and on April 10, 1987, justices on the New Jersey Supreme Court ruled 6-1 to restore Whitehead's visitation rights to two supervised hours once a week, pending appeal of the case.

Sorkow's Decision: Untested Legal Ground

Although he termed it a "routine custody case," Judge Sorkow acknowledged that he was entering untested legal ground. He, and other legal experts, made clear that the case was unique and should not be seen as setting a precedent. Noting that there were no previous court rulings dealing with surrogacy in New Jersey, Sorkow said, "It is held that the only concept of law that can presently attach to surrogacy arrangements are contract law principles and parens patriae *concepts for the benefit of the child." (The* parens patriae *concept gives courts broad power and discretion to serve the interests of those unable to protect themselves, including children.)*

The judge cast his arguments primarily in terms of those two principles. Concerning the contractual agreement, Sorkow concluded, "The male gave his sperm; the female gave her egg in their pre-planned effort to create a child—thus a valid contract." Moreover, he held that procedures applying to adoption did not apply in the case of surrogates. While a woman already pregnant "may want to keep the child but cannot do so for financial reasons," he said, the surrogate "has an opportunity to consult, take advice and consider her act and is not forced into the relationship."

Constitutional considerations—based on the rights of privacy guaranteed by the Fourteenth Amendment—also guaranteed the validity of the agreement. According to the judge, "if one has a right to procreate coitally, then one has the right to reproduce noncoitally. If it is the reproduction that is protected, then the means of reproduction are also to be protected. . . . This court holds that the protected means extends to the use of surrogates."

In addition to the contractual considerations, Sorkow emphasized the parens patriae *concept that the decision should be based on the baby's best interests. "We find by clear and convincing evidence," he concluded, "that Melissa's [Baby M's] best interest will be served by being placed in her father's sole custody." The judge ruled that the $10,000 surrogacy fee, which had been placed in escrow, be given to Whitehead.*

Reaction: The Pros and Cons

Throughout the trial, questions were raised not only about the legality of surrogate arrangements, but about the character of the parents.

Supporters of the Whiteheads argued that surrogacy not only took advantage of financially less well-off women who agreed to bear the children, but that any resulting custody battles would be decided in favor of the more affluent couple. However, supporters of and attorneys for the Sterns, as well as Sorkow, countered that the family life and financial circumstances of Richard and Mary Beth Whitehead had been filled with upheavals that made them less able to provide a secure home for Baby M. Cited in the testimony was a tape-recorded conversation Whitehead had with William Stern during the abduction period, in which Whitehead threatened to kill herself and the baby if he tried to take the baby back; she also accused Stern of sexually molesting her nine-year-old daughter. In his decision, Sorkow described Whitehead as "manipulative, impulsive, and exploitative." While some "expert witness" psychiatrists had characterized Whitehead as unstable, others had said that, under the very trying circumstances, she had acted in an understandable manner.

Numerous friend-of-the-court briefs were filed. The principal focus of the concern was not related to the personalities and parental "fitness" of the Whiteheads or Sterns; rather, it zeroed in on the question of whether surrogate parenthood should be permitted, and if so, how it should be regulated. Those opposed to surrogacy included the Roman Catholic church; profamily organizations such as the Eagle Forum, headed by Phyllis Schlafly; and feminists, including Gloria Steinem and Betty Friedan. "It is a terrifying denial of what should be basic rights for women, an utter denial of the personhood of women," said Friedan. "It is an important human rights case. To put it at the level of contract law is to dehumanize women and the human bond between mother and child."

"Surrogate parenting is here to stay," said William Handel, director of the Center for Surrogate Parenting in Los Angeles. "It simply makes too much sense for too many infertile couples who have no other alternative."

Although legal scholars differed over whether custody should have been granted to the Sterns, many of them opposed the decision to uphold the original surrogate contract. And a brief submitted July 17, 1987, by the fourteen Roman Catholic bishops of New Jersey argued that surrogate motherhood "promotes the exploitation of women and infertile couples and the dehumanization of babies." The brief stated that Britain had banned commercial surrogacy and that government studies in eight countries had concluded that the practice was ethically unacceptable.

Following are excerpts from the March 31, 1987, decision by the Superior Court of New Jersey, Judge Harvey R. Sorkow, presiding, "In the Matter of Baby M, a pseudonym for an actual person," holding that a contract entered into for surrogate motherhood was valid and that the biological father should have custody:

The Issue

The primary issue to be determined by this litigation is what are the best interests of a child until now called "Baby M." All other concerns raised by counsel constitute commentary.

That commentary includes the need to determine if a unique arrangement between a man and a woman, unmarried to each other, creates a contract. If so, is the contract enforceable; and if so, by what criteria, means and manner. If not, what are the rights and duties of the parties with regard to custody, visitation and support.

Jurisdiction

There can be no solution satisfactory to all in this kind of case. Justice, our desired objective, to the child and the mother, to the child and the father, cannot be obtained for both parents. The court will seek to achieve justice for the child. This court's fact finding and application of relevant law must mitigate against the heartfelt desires of one or the other of the natural parents.

Where courts are forced to choose between a parent's rights and a child's welfare, the choice is and must be the child's welfare and best interest by virtue of the court's responsibility as *parens patriae*. . . .

Probably the most important authority of the court is the exercise of its *parens patriae* jurisdiction. Jurisdiction is a word of broad and comprehensive impact. It means the authority by which courts and judicial officers take cognizance of and decide cases. It means the authority to act, to find, define and apply the law.

Parens patriae is that power of the sovereign (in this case the State of New Jersey by its judicial branch) to watch over the interests of those who are incapable of protecting themselves. . . .

Thus, . . . this court . . . applies . . . jurisdiction to . . . the best interest of a child and contractual rights, if any, of the litigating parties. . . .

[Findings]

It took years of legislative debate and judicial inquiry to define and develop today's laws of abortion and artificial insemination. The issues and dimensions of surrogacy are still evolving but it is necessary that laws be adopted to give our society a sense of definition and direction if the concept is to be allowed to further develop. With an increasing number of surrogate births, legislation can avoid harm to society, the family and the child. Some of the issues that need legislation are: establishing standards for sperm donors, legitimacy of the child, rights of the biological father's spouse, rights of the biological mother's spouse, rights of the two biological actors as to each other and to the child, qualifications for the surrogate, is compensation to the surrogate to be allowed, concerns regarding the imperfect child. Many questions must be answered; answers must come from legislation. If there is no law then society will suffer the negative aspects of this alternative reproduction vehicle that appears to hold out so much hope to the childless who make up a substantial segment of our society.

Today, however, this court can only decide what is before it.... It will decide on legal principles alone. This court must not manage morality or temper theology. Its charge is to examine what law there is and apply it to the facts proven in this cause [*sic*]....

[Terms of Contract]

On February 6, 1986, Mr. Stern and Mr. and Mrs. Whitehead signed the Surrogate Parenting Agreement. It was in all material respects the same contract that Mrs. Whitehead signed the spring of 1984. At that time, Mr. and Mrs. Whitehead had consulted with an attorney. As already noted, he read and explained the contract to them. Several minor changes were negotiated. Mrs. Whitehead believed the second contract to be as the first and thus, although able to do so, chose not to seek legal advice prior to signing the subject agreement. It is noted with more than passing importance that Mrs. Stern was not a signatory to the agreement. Mrs. Whitehead testified that her obligation was to attempt conception by artificial insemination, upon conception to carry the child to term, deliver the child and surrender the child to Mr. Stern renouncing at that time all of her parental rights and acknowledging that doing so is in the child's best interest. It was also agreed that Mr. Stern's name would appear on the child's birth certificate.

In addition, the contract provided the following: Mrs. Whitehead would assume the risks of the pregnancy and child birth. She would submit to a psychiatric evaluation for which Mr. Stern would pay. Mr. Stern had the right to name the child. That in the event of the death of Mr. Stern, the child would be placed in the custody of Mr. Stern's wife. Mrs. Whitehead would not abort the child. In addition, she would undergo amniocentesis; and if the child was found to have a genetic or congenital abnormality, it would be aborted *if* Mr. Stern requested it.

That in the event the child possessed genetic or congenital abnormalities William Stern would assume legal responsibility for the child once it was born. The agreement also contained a severability clause.

The Whiteheads and the Sterns clearly understood the terms of the agreement and their obligations....

Mrs. Whitehead was to be paid $10,000.00 and all medical expenses including dental expenses for performing her contractual obligations....

Under the present medical definition, Mrs. Whitehead had informed consent as to the procedure, if indeed, such consent was required. She was competent at the time of entering into the contract and was aware of its terms.

Subsequent to entering into the Surrogate Parenting Agreement of February 6, 1985, Mrs. Whitehead was inseminated with the semenal [*sic*] fluid of Mr. Stern 9 times. Finally, in July, 1985, she conceived.

Mr. and Mrs. Stern were overjoyed with Mrs. Whitehead's pregnancy.

They met with Mr. and Mrs. Whitehead and took them to dinner to celebrate. . . .

Approximately one month prior to the birth of the child, in February, 1986, Mr. and Mrs. Stern learned that Mrs. Whitehead had delayed signing the papers acknowledging Mr. Stern's paternity of the child. Mrs. Whitehead, nevertheless, indicated that she had no intention of repudiating her contract with Mr. Stern. Eventually, Mr. and Mrs. Whitehead signed the acknowledgment of paternity.

"Baby M" was born on March 27, 1986, at Monmouth Medical Center, Long Branch, New Jersey. Mr. and Mrs. Whitehead never told anyone at the hospital that Mrs. Whitehead was a surrogate mother. They prevailed on Mr. and Mrs. Stern not to reveal their relationship to the child. On March 27, 1986, Mr. and Mrs. Stern went to the hospital to see the infant and Mr. and Mrs. Whitehead. Because he was not identified as the child's father, Mr. Stern could not hold his newborn daughter. He could only view the infant through the nursery window. Mr. Whitehead's name appeared on the Birth Certificate as the child's father as did the name Sara Elizabeth Whitehead. This information was given to the hospital by either or both of the Whiteheads. Their unilateral action without consulting Mr. Stern was a violation of their understanding with Mr. and Mrs. Stern.

Mrs. Whitehead testified that throughout her pregnancy, she recognized the child being carried was not to be hers but was Mr. Stern's. This view was maintained throughout the pregnancy. . . .

On March 31, 1986, Mrs. Whitehead telephoned Mr. and Mrs. Stern and requested permission to visit the child. . . . She told Mr. and Mrs. Stern that she did not want to live and that she had considered taking the entire bottle of valium pills the night before. Mrs. Whitehead said she wanted to take "Baby M" home with her for a one week visit. Residence for the one week was offered by the Sterns but was rejected. Out of concern for Mrs. Whitehead's mental health, Mr. and Mrs. Stern acquiesced.

After listening to and observing Mr. Stern who testified about this wrenching moment, this court had no doubt that he fully expected to have his daughter returned to him after the week. His immense concern for Mrs. Whitehead and an almost naive belief in her good will was soon to be destroyed.

On April 1, 1986, Mrs. Whitehead telephoned Mr. and Mrs. Stern and indicated that she was going to be visiting with an aunt. She indicated that she would be unreachable. In fact, Mrs. Whitehead left the State of New Jersey on April 3, 1986, with the 5 day old child and traveled to Florida to visit her parents. . . .

On May 5, 1986, this court signed an order to show cause directing Mrs. Whitehead to deliver the infant to Mr. Stern. . . .

On that same day, Mr. and Mrs. Stern accompanied the Bricktown Police to the Whitehead residence. They brought with them the court order giving temporary custody of the child to Mr. and Mrs. Stern. . . . Although Mr. and Mrs. Whitehead understood that they were being ordered by a court to return the child to Mr. and Mrs. Stern, during ensuing confusion Mrs. Whitehead took the child into a bedroom at the rear of the house and passed the child out the window to her waiting husband.... The following morning, the Whitehead family: Mary Beth Whitehead, Richard Whitehead, their ten year old daughter and the baby disappeared. Their whereabouts remained unknown to Mr. and Mrs. Stern for 87 days.

On May 6, 1986, Mr. and Mrs. Whitehead, their daughter and the infant child flew to the State of Florida....

On or about July 15, 1986, Mr. Stern received a telephone call at this [*sic*] place of employment from Mrs. Whitehead. In addition to making demands for relief on Mr. Stern, Mrs. Whitehead threatened to kill herself and to take the life of the child, stating, "I'd rather see me and her (the infant child) dead before you get her," and "I gave her life. I can take her life away," in addition to numerous other threats to the child's well-being. Another telephone call was received by Mr. Stern from Mrs. Whitehead on the following day, July 16, 1986. At that time, Mrs. Whitehead threatened to accuse Mr. Stern of sexually molesting her 10 year old daughter. No evidence of any abuse was offered by this threat by Mr. and Mrs. Whitehead and Mrs. Whitehead admitted her threat and accusations were false and without the slightest measure of foundation....

On July 31, 1986, the child was taken into the care of Florida authorities....

All of the parties ultimately returned to New Jersey and Mr. and Mrs. Whitehead began to defend against the complaint of Mr. and Mrs. Stern....

A total of 38 witnesses testified at this trial, 23 fact witnesses and 15 experts. Four of the experts dealt with Mrs. Stern's multiple sclerosis and 11 dealt with the issue of best interests of the child....

The testimony of the parties indicates conflict on whether they are capable of being joint custodians of "Baby M." They have different life styles, different social values and standards. Mrs. Whitehead has complained, without basis, of Mrs. Stern's care in the several months that Mr. Stern has had custody.

Each parent here is not willing to share custody. While Mrs. Whitehead claims to be willing, Mr. Stern is not. His belief is that shared custody will create conflict presently and in the future for the child.

... [T]he hurt perceived by these litigants, at the hands of the other, is too great to premise a joint custody award. The rancor is too great. This court doubts that they can isolate their personal animosity and "all of a sudden" cooperate for the child's benefit....

[Arguments]

Concerns have been expressed about the efficacy of surrogate arrangements. They are: 1) that the child will not be protected; 2) ... the potential for exploitation of the surrogate mother; 3) the alleged denigration of human dignity by recognizing any agreement in which a child is produced for money; 4) surrogacy is invalid because it is contrary to adoption statutes and other child benefit laws such as statutes establishing standards for termination of parental rights; 5) it will undermine traditional notions of family; and 6) surrogacy allows an elite economic group to use a poorer group of people to achieve their purposes.

It is argued that the child will not be protected. So long as there is no legislation and some court action in surrogacy arrangements is required, the child born of surrogacy will be protected in New Jersey. If there is compliance with the contract terms, adoption will be necessary; hence, court inquiry about best interests must take place. If there is non-compliance with the contract, as in this case, best interest is still litigated with protection to the child, with its own guardian and experts retained to aid the court in its best interest determination.

The second argument against surrogacy is that the surrogate mother will be exploited. To the contrary. It is the private adoption that has that great potential, if not fact, for the exploitation of the mother. In the private adoption, the woman is already pregnant. The biological father may be unknown or at best uninterested in his obligations. The woman may want to keep the child but cannot do so for financial reasons. There is the risk of illegal consideration being paid to the mother. In surrogacy, none of these "downside" elements appear. The arrangement is made when the desire and intention to have a family exist on the couple's part. The surrogate has an opportunity to consult, take advice and consider her act and is not forced into the relationship. She is not yet pregnant.

The third argument is that to produce or deal with a child for money denigrates human dignity. To that premise, this court urgently agrees. The 13th Amendment to the United States Constitution is still valid law. The law of adoption in New Jersey does prohibit the exchange of any consideration for obtaining a child. The fact is, however, that the money to be paid to the surrogate is not being paid for the surrender of the child to the father. And that is just the point—at birth, mother and father have equal rights to the child absent any other agreement. The biological father pays the surrogate for her willingness to be impregnated and carry his child to term. At birth, the father does not purchase the child. It is his own biological genetically related child. He cannot purchase what is already his.

The fourth argument against surrogacy is that it is a concept running contrary to the laws of adoption in New Jersey. It is in this court's view that the laws of adoption in this state do not apply to surrogacy contracts. . . .

The fifth argument against surrogacy is that it will undermine the traditional notions of family. How can that be when the childless husband and wife so very much want a child? They seek to make a family. They intend to have a family. The surrogate mother could not make a valid contract without her husband's consent to her act. This statement should not be construed anti-feminist. It means that if the surrogate is married, her husband will, in all probability, have to sign the contract to establish his non-paternity pursuant to the New Jersey Parentage Law. Both sides of the equation must agree.

The final and sixth argument suggests an elite upper economic group of people will use the lower economic group of woman to "make their babies". This argument is insensitive and offensive to the intense drive to procreate naturally and when that is impossible, to use what lawful means [are] ... possible to gain a child. This intense desire to propagate the species is fundamental. It is within the soul of all men regardless of economic status....

For the past year, there has been a child in being. She is alive and well. She is tangible proof of that which the Whiteheads and Mr. Stern in concert agreed to do. The child was conceived with a mutual understanding by the parties of her future life. Except that now, Mrs. Whitehead has failed to perform one of her last promises which was to surrender the child and renounce parental rights. She has otherwise performed the personal service that she had undertaken—the conception and carrying the child to term. The terms of the contract have been executed but for the surrender.

It is argued that Mrs. Whitehead should have a time period after delivery to determine if she wants to surrender the child. Such a rule has been developed in Kentucky by the use of Kentucky's private placement adoption statute. Use of laws not intended for their intended purpose creates forced and confusing results. There should be no use of the New Jersey adoption statutes to accommodate or deny surrogacy contracts. Indeed, again it is held that there is no law governing surrogacy contracts in New Jersey and that the laws of adoption do not apply to surrogacy contracts. The sole legal concepts that control are *parens patriae* and best interests of the child. To wait for birth, to plan, pray and dream of the joy it will bring and then be told that the child will not come home, that a new set of rules applies and to ask a court to approve such a result deeply offends the conscience of this court. A person who has promised is entitled to rely on the concomitant promise of the other promisor. This court holds therefore that in New Jersey, although the surrogacy contract is signed, the surrogate may nevertheless renounce and terminate the contract until the time of conception. She may be subject then for such monetary damages as may be proven. Specific performance to compel the promised conception, gestation, and birth shall not be available to the male promisor. However, once conception has occurred the parties' rights are fixed, the terms of the contract are firm and performance will be anticipated with the joy that only a newborn can bring.

Having defined a new rule of law, this court hastens to add an exception. After conception, only the surrogate shall have the right, to the exclusion of the sperm donor, to decide whether to abort the fetus....

It is argued by amicus that the $10,000.00 to be paid Mrs. Whitehead is so low as to be unconscionable. In counterpoint, it is stated that not all services can be compensated by money. Millions of men and women work for each other in their marital relationship. There may even be mutual inequality in the value of the work performed but the benefits obtained from the relationship serve to reject the concept of equating societal acts to a monetary balancing. Perhaps the risk was great for the money to be paid but the risk was what Mrs. Whitehead chose to assume and at the agreed upon fee. And it is assumed she received other intangible benefits and satisfaction from doing what she did. Her original application set forth her highly altruistic purpose. Notwithstanding amicus position, all in this world cannot be equated to money.

It is defendants' claim of unconscionability. They must show the unfairness, the overreaching, the bargaining disparity or the patent unfairness that no reasonable person acting without duress would accept them.... This, the defendants have failed to do.

The defendants next claim relief from the contract because the Whiteheads had no attorney at the time they entered the contract. It is hornbook law that any person who possesses legal capacity may be bound by a contract even when it is entered without representation unless there is fraud, overreaching or undue influence which caused the party to enter the contract.

... [O]ne of the defendants' own psychiatrists ... testified unequivocally that the Whiteheads had legal capacity to contract. There were no mental disabilities. They understood what they were doing. They understood the contract terms. That there was capacity to contract is proven by preponderance of credible evidence....

... [I]t must be reasoned that if one has a right to procreate coitally, then one has the right to reproduce non-coitally. If it is the reproduction that is protected, then the means of reproduction are also to be protected. The value and interests underlying the creation of family are the same by whatever means obtained. This court holds that the protected means extends to the use of surrogates. The contract cannot fall because of the use of a third party. It is reasoned that the donor or surrogate aids the childless couple by contributing a factor of conception and for gestation that the couple lacks. The third party is essential if the couple is to rear a genetically related child. While a state could regulate, indeed should and must regulate the circumstances under which parties enter into reproductive contracts, it could not ban or refuse to enforce such transactions altogether without compelling reason. It might even be argued that refusal to enforce these contracts and prohibition of money payments would constitute an unconstitutional interference with procreative liberty since it would prevent childless couples from obtaining the means with which to have families....

... Legislation or court action that denies the surrogate contract impedes a couple's liberty that is otherwise constitutionally protected. The surrogate who voluntarily chooses to enter such a contract is deprived of a constitutionally protected right to perform services....

A final constitutional premise requires scrutiny and that is the equal protection clause of the United States Constitution's 14th Amendment.

Classifications of persons to be sustained for equal protection purposes "must be reasonable, not arbitrary and must rest upon some ground of difference having a fair and substantial relation to the object of the legislation so that all persons similarly circumstanced shall be treated alike." *Reed v. Reed* (1976). This is the test to be applied to classifications dealing with gender and legitimacy. Currently, males may sell their sperm. The "surrogate father" sperm donor is legally recognized in all states. The surrogate mother is not. If a man may offer the means for procreation then a woman must equally be allowed to do so. To rule otherwise denies equal protection of the law to the childless couple, the surrogate whether male or female and the unborn child....

For the foregoing reasons, this court concludes and holds that the surrogate parenting agreement is a valid and enforceable contract pursuant to the Laws of New Jersey. The rights of the parties to contract are constitutionally protected under the 14th Amendment of the United States Constitution. This court further finds that Mrs. Whitehead has breached her contract in two ways: 1) by failing to surrender to Mr. Stern the child born to her and Mr. Stern and 2) by failing to renounce her parental rights to that child....

[Considerations]

1) Was the child wanted and planned for? We now know the Sterns desperately wanted a child. They intended by the contract to have a child.... Mrs. Whitehead wanted to carry a child for a childless couple. It is clear that the Sterns planned for and wanted the child. Mrs. Whitehead did not. Her testimony is quite to that effect.

2) What is the emotional stability of the people in the child's home environment? The Sterns are found to have a strong and mutually supportive relationship....

The Whiteheads appear to have a stable marriage now. It was earlier plagued with separations, domestic violence and severe financial difficulties requiring numerous house moves.... Mrs. Whitehead dominates the family. Mr. Whitehead is clearly in a subordinate role. He has little to do with the subject child. Mrs. Whitehead is found to be thoroughly enmeshed with Baby M, unable to separate out her own needs from the baby's. This overbearing could inhibit the child's development of independence.... Mrs. Whitehead has been shown, by clear and convincing proof to this court's satisfaction, to be impulsive.... She has been shown, by clear and convincing proof to this court's satisfaction, to be manipulative.... She has been shown by clear and convincing proof to this court's satisfaction that she is also exploitive. She uses her children for her own ends: witness the bringing of her older daughter to court where the child was terrorized by the crush of media, by her fawning use of the media to her own narcissistic ends. It appears she totally failed to consider the impact of the false sex abuse charge on her daughter....

3) What is the stability and peacefulness of the families? Again, the Sterns are found to be living private unremarkable lives. The Whiteheads have known marital discord, domestic violence and many residential moves, although things are tranquil now.

4) What is the ability of the subject adults to recognize and respond to the child's physical and emotional needs? This court finds from clear and convincing proofs presented to it that Mrs. Whitehead has been shown to impose herself on her children. Her emphasis with the infant may impair the parenting of her other two children for whom she has been, with limited exception until now, a good mother. She exhibits an emotional over-investment. . . .

The Sterns show sensitivity to the child's needs but at the same time allow her to develop independently. Both families recognize and satisfy the infant's physical needs.

5) What are the family attitudes towards education and their motivation to encourage curiosity and learning? The Sterns have demonstrated the strong role that education has played in their lives. They both hold doctoral degrees in the sciences. Mrs. Stern is a medical doctor. Mrs. Whitehead dropped out of the 10th grade in high school. Mr. Whitehead graduated high school doing enough, as he said, "to get by.". . .

6) What is the ability of the adults to make rational judgments? Mr. Whitehead permits his wife to make most of the important decisions in their family. His active participation in the May 5, 1986 elopement is hardly evidence of cogent thought. Mrs. Whitehead is found to be impulsive especially in crisis circumstances or moments of heightened concern. . . . She impulsively, not to say maliciously, makes an untruthful allegation about Mr. Stern. Mr. & Mrs. Stern have shown a capability to make logical reasoned decisions in all circumstances. . . .

9) Which adults would better help the child cope with her own life? It has been shown that Mrs. Whitehead has trouble coping in crisis. She can manage the routine. The Sterns have shown no aberration in either circumstance.

The court also evaluates the climate to which the child may be exposed with the Whiteheads. In addition to a history of economic and domestic instability with another house move imminent, in addition to the reduced level of importance given to education in the Whitehead home and in addition to the character trait problems defined by almost all the mental health professionals including Mrs. Whitehead's own chosen experts, Mrs. Whitehead has a genuine problem in recognizing and reporting the truth. . . .

. . . This court is satisfied by clear and convincing proofs that Mrs. Whitehead is unreliable insofar as her promise is concerned. She breached her contract without regard to her legal obligations. There has been domestic violence in her household that she could not recall until the court documents refreshed her recollection. She should have known of these facts as she is the one who called the police. There were many house moves in the earlier years of marriage and another move appears imminent. The Whiteheads have had severe economic difficulties including a bankruptcy. In those court papers there appears to be a flawed statement of assets in that the Whiteheads omitted two assets thus misleading the court and their creditors. Mrs. Whitehead has been found too enmeshed with this infant child and unable to separate her own needs from those of the child. She tends to smother the child with her presence even to the exclusion of access by her other two children. She does not have the ability to subordinate herself to the needs of this child. The court is satisfied that based on the details above, Mrs. Whitehead is manipulative, impulsive and exploitive. She is also for the most part, untruthful choosing only to remember what may enhance her position, or altering the facts about which she is testifying or intentionally not remembering. . . .

Her lack of candor makers her a poor candidate to report to the child in an age-appropriate manner and time, the facts of the child's origins. She is a woman without empathy. She expresses none for her husband's problems with alcohol and her infusion of her other children into this process exposing them rather than protecting them from the searing scrutiny of the media mitigates against her claim for custody. She is a good mother for and to her older children. She would not be a good custodian for Baby M.

This court is satisfied by clear and convincing proof that Mr. and Mrs. Stern wanted and planned for this child. They intended to be parents of the child. They have a strong and mutually supportive relationship wherein each respects the other and there is a balancing of obligations. There is proof of a successful cooperative parenting effort. The Sterns have a private, quiet and unremarkable life which augers well for a stable household environment. Mr. and Mrs. Stern show sensitivity to the child's physical and emotional needs. They would be supportive of education and have shown, at least in their own lives, a motivation for learning. It can be concluded that they would initiate and encourage intellectual curiosity and learning for the child. They have shown an ability to make rational judgments in the face of most trying emotional circumstances. They have obeyed the law. With the health and medical education of Mrs. Stern and the scientific training of Mr. Stern, the child's health will not be jeopardized. Mr. & Mrs. Stern have presented as credible, sincere and truthful people. They have expressed a willingness and a history of obtaining professional help to address the child's unique problems. Finally, they have shown no difficulty in coping with crisis. It may be anticipated that because the child is unique and at risk, crisis for the next several years will be part of their lives. Mr. & Mrs. Stern have shown an ability to deal with such exigencies. It is for all these reasons, it is because of all of the facts found by this court as the trier of fact that we find by clear and convincing evidence, indeed by a measure of evidence reaching beyond reasonable doubt that Melissa's best interest will be served by being placed in her father's sole custody.

Now having found that the best interest of the child will be enhanced and served in paternal custody, that there is no evidence of fraud overreaching or violation of any other principle of equity by Mr. Stern, this court having evaluated the equities finds them weighted in favor of Mr. Stern. Enforcing the contract will leave Mr. & Mrs. Whitehead in the same position that they were in when the contract was made. To not enforce the contract will give them the child and deprive Mr. Stern of his promised benefits. This court therefore will specifically enforce the surrogate parenting agreement to compel delivery of the child to the father and to terminate the mother's parental rights....

Specifically enforcing the contract ... will automatically sever and terminate all parental rights of Mrs. Whitehead. By definition, termination of parental rights is an extraordinary judicial remedy which is to be granted only after intensive consideration of parental conduct and the needs of the child....

Premised on the historic equitable principle of *parens patriae,* this court invokes the maxim of treating done that which ought to have been done and this court, as noted above, orders specific performance of the surrogate parenting agreement. The result of these conclusions is to terminate all parental rights that Mary Beth Whitehead has or had in the child to be known as Melissa Stern. She agreed to terminate. This court gives effect to her agreement....

The application of the maternal grandparents for visitation is next addressed....

Both Mr. & Mrs. Messer [Mrs. Whitehead's parents] have exhibited something less than candor in their testimony to the court. Furthermore, by doing nothing, by seeing nothing, by seeking to know nothing about their daughter's activities with the child, they became participants in efforts to thwart this court's orders and by their acts or failure to act, they have proven themselves unworthy of the benefit and relief [visitation rights] they seek from this court....

Accordingly, for the facts found and reasons stated herein, this court denies grandparental visitation as being contrary to Melissa's best interest.

This court enters judgment in favor of plaintiffs as follows:

1) The surrogate parenting agreement of February 6, 1985, will be specifically enforced.

2) The prior order of the court giving temporary custody to Mr. Stern is herewith made permanent. Prior orders of visitation are vacated.

3) The parental rights of the defendant Mary Beth Whitehead are terminated.

4) Mr. Stern is formally adjudged the father of Melissa Stern....

11) The $10,000.00 being held by the Clerk of the Superior Court shall be the property of Mary Beth Whitehead....

Melissa needs stability and peace, so that she can be nurtured in a loving environment free from chaos and sheltered from the public eye.

This court says that Melissa deserved nothing less—stability and peace.

April

OTA REPORT ON ALZHEIMER'S DISEASE

April 7, 1987

A picture of cruel, widespread, and growing suffering emerged from Losing a Million Minds, *a 539-page report on Alzheimer's disease and other dementias published April 7 by the Office of Technology Assessment (OTA). The report estimated that 1.5 million Americans suffered from severe dementia—the loss of mental functions in an alert and awake individual. The report predicted that, unless cures or preventatives were discovered for the common causes of dementia, the number of victims would reach 7.4 million Americans by the year 2040. These figures did not account for the family members, providers of most of the demanding care of those afflicted with dementia, who are the indirect victims of these diseases.*

The OTA study, undertaken at the request of seven congressional committees, found that medical and social services for victims of dementia were inadequate and poorly organized. A statement accompanying the report observed that "federal policies have not been designed to reinforce family and community supports."

The number of victims of dementia had increased tenfold since the turn of the century, but the affliction had attracted little notice until the late 1970s. A 1976 article in Archives of Neurology *served as a catalyst for heightened medical attention to Alzheimer's disease, which accounted for two-thirds of dementia cases. First recognized in 1906 by Dr. Alois Alzheimer in Germany, the disease became a household word in the mid-1980s after attention in the mass media and publicity from organizations such as the Alzheimer's Disease and Related Disorders Association*

(ADRDA), established in 1979. Federally funded research on dementia increased from $3.9 million in 1976 to an estimated $67 million in 1987.

Medical Puzzle

The causes of Alzheimer's disease (which may in fact be a group of diseases) were unknown, and no preventive measure or cure had been found. Research disclosed changes in, and loss of, nerve cells in brain tissue in Alzheimer's patients, but had not found the source of these changes. Scientists also pursued genetic factors. For example, an article published February 20, 1987, in Science *reported evidence of a defective gene in chromosome 21 in families with a high incidence of Alzheimer's disease.*

However, as the OTA report observed, scientific discoveries may not lead to a means of prevention or cure or even effective treatments. Their consequences may not be known for several decades, and "may only much later improve clinical care." The report warned that "public policy that presumes a revolution in care methods—based on discoveries not yet made—is not advisable."

The character of Alzheimer's disease and other dementias raised multiple problems. All but 2 percent to 3 percent of dementia cases were considered irreversible. The progressive mental deterioration of Alzheimer's victims, which typically began with loss of short-term memory and gradually advanced to loss of speech and physical incapacity—took years to develop. One study found an average duration of 8.1 years from onset of symptoms until death. The difficulty of care and length of care placed severe strains on both family caregivers and long-term care institutions.

Family Burden

The OTA report noted that most dementia victims were cared for by their families and that "the tasks of caring for a person with dementia are constant." A significant number of caregivers spent more than forty hours per week in direct personal care. Behavioral problems frequently cited by families included memory loss, emotional outbursts, demanding and critical behavior, night walking, hiding things, communication difficulties, suspiciousness, accusations, wandering, violence, and incontinence. Moreover, the OTA observed, the financial costs of care "can have a catastrophic impact on family caregivers, not just the ill person." According to a 1984 article quoted by the OTA, "In the overwhelming majority of cases, nursing home placement occurs only after responsible family caregivers have endured prolonged, unrelenting strain (often for years), and no longer have the capacity to continue their caregiving efforts."

A wide variety of programs assisted families with home care, but often the services most needed—paid companion, homemaker, personal care, and twenty-four-hour supervision—were not available. Home care services that gave a family temporary respite from caregiving were especially difficult to find. Moreover, home care personnel often were not trained to work with dementia victims, and their roles were often ill defined. "They may create more problems for the patient and the primary caregiver than they solve," the OTA noted. Few standards or procedures existed for monitoring home care services.

Nursing homes were the most frequently used institutional setting (others included state mental hospitals, board and care facilities, adult day care centers, and community mental health centers) for care of dementia victims. The deficiencies often noted in nursing homes were compounded for persons with dementia for many reasons, ranging from lack of staff training for dementia care to routines that confused demented patients. The difficult behavior of these patients also created problems for other residents.

Estimates of dementia's total costs to society ranged from $24 billion to $48 billion. Because of lack of agreement on proper distribution of this cost burden, the OTA report observed, "programs for persons with dementia have been shaped by historical accident rather than considered principles." The resulting confusion in existing programs, combined with the size of the problems and the recentness of public attention, placed heavy demands on policy makers.

> *Following are excerpts from "Policy Issues," in Chapter 1 of* Losing a Million Minds: Confronting the Tragedy of Alzheimer's Disease and Other Dementias, *published April 7, 1987, by the Office of Technology Assessment:*

Policy Issues

The problems faced by persons with dementia and their families impinge on public policy in many ways. There is no cure, no means of prevention, and no fully effective treatment for most dementias. The government strategies for addressing this public health problem are: 1) to support research in hopes of discovering a cure or means of prevention, and 2) to deliver or facilitate delivery of services for those who develop dementia. The roles played by the Federal Government that are relevant to the problems of dementia include:

- supporting research, including basic science, clinical research, and the study of health care delivery;
- directly providing health care to special populations;
- paying for care through Medicaid, Medicare, Mental Health Block Grants, and tax subsidies;
- training and educating health professionals and caregivers;
- assuring the quality of acute and long-term care;

- planning health and social services; and
- disseminating information on care, research, and services. . . .

Should There Be Special Programs for Dementia?

Any discussion of the government's role in this field must consider whether there should be special programs for individuals with dementia. Furthermore, judgments about the fairness and effectiveness of different policies require a clear distinction between special services, entitlements, and research.

Specialized Services

Specialized services for those with dementia include support groups, day care centers, nursing home units, and in-home respite care programs designed specifically to aid those with mental impairment. Such specialized emphasis helps in the training of caregivers and focuses attention on the special problems of delivering services to those with dementia. The existence of specialized services for one group of diseases need not discourage developing specialized services for others. Patients with cancer, for example, do not receive the same treatment as those with heart disease, and yet may be covered under the same medical program (e.g., Medicare).

There is no consensus that persons with dementia should receive specialized services. Yet special care units at nursing homes, special day care centers, special board and care facilities, and even special hospitals for patients with Alzheimer's disease are proliferating. The rationales for such units are the opportunity to improve the care of persons with dementia by having better trained staff and adaptive environments, reduced interference with residents without dementing disorders, and the need for activities that specifically take account of diminished intellectual and communicative skills. Many worry, however, that such facilities will become the repository for neglected individuals. At present, no separate guidelines are available for special care units and programs, and philosophies and methods for administering them differ markedly. The ferment of activity in special care is generally improving care for those with dementia, however, and is generating innovative care techniques.

Special Entitlements

Special entitlements for individuals with dementia would make eligibility for services contingent on a particular diagnosis or type of disability. A special Medicare or Medicaid entitlement for dementia could be created, analogous to the special Medicare eligibility reserved for those with end-stage renal disease (although a special dementia entitlement would be primarily for long-term personal, rather than medical, care). Those favoring special entitlements contend that the problems of patients with dementia are so severe and different from those with other disorders that they deserve special eligibility. Others contend that those with dementia are merely one group among many vying for services in a fragmented health care market. They point to other groups with similar problems in obtaining needed services, particularly long-term care. Other groups also have limited access to long-term care (e.g., adults with mental retardation or adults with spinal injury) and difficulty finding adequate mental health or social services (e.g., schizophrenics or the homeless). Still others may need health services from public programs with limited budgets (e.g., maternal and child health for the indigent under Medicaid).

Some of the consequences of developing special entitlements for dementia can be predicted. A special long-term care program for those with Alzheimer's disease would face several problems. If based on diagnosis, it would be unduly restrictive (eliminating services for those with multi-infarct [caused by faulty blood circulation in the brain] or other dementias) or it would be vulnerable to inappropriate utilization because of vague definitions of the conditions covered. Making services contingent on diagnosis or a restricted list of conditions would put severe strain on the accuracy of diagnosis. While special diagnostic centers report 90 percent diagnostic accuracy, that proportion would likely drop if there were incentives favoring one diagnosis over another. Physicians wishing to aid their patients would likely list the diagnosis of Alzheimer's disease in preference to other dementing conditions if there were any room for doubt, thereby increasing the number of persons reported to have Alzheimer's disease even if the true prevalence did not change. If services were triggered by severity of disability, then a method to screen out those with lesser disability would have to be in place. That would likely entail mandatory assessment for eligibility, and would necessitate a measure of mental disability that is quick, accurate, reliable, and auditable.

A special entitlement for dementia, or specifically for Alzheimer's disease, also raises a question of fairness. An adult with spina bifida, Huntington's disease, or multiple sclerosis needs many of the same services as an individual with dementia. A special entitlement restricted to persons with Alzheimer's disease would likely promote conflict among interest groups for different diseases. A broader definition encompassing "related disorders" will be vague and difficult to implement. The prudent course appears to involve providing the services most needed but not restricting their use to *only* those with dementia.

Specialized Research

Although no consensus exists about the risks and benefits of special care or special entitlements, it is generally agreed that specialized *research* on relevant science, clinical care, and service use is essential. Serious study of the large group of people with severe functional disabilities due to dementia has only begun in the past few years, and much more information is necessary before public policies, medical practices, and service use can be rationally assessed. Such information can come only from research that focuses on individuals with dementia. Studies need not deal exclusively with persons with dementia to yield useful information. Those that survey long-term care or mental health in elderly people could shed light on the problems of someone with dementia if they include sufficient information to evaluate cognitive function (measured by a standard scale), service use, diagnosis, assessment of lost functions, efficacy of special care, and costs.

Diagnosis and Treatment

The main policy concern about diagnosis and treatment is rapid dissemination of knowledge to permit accurate diagnosis and appropriate treatment. The primary mechanisms for improving diagnosis and treatment are research and education.

Also of concern is how to link medical evaluation to long-term care service planning, patient assessment, and social services. Creating new entitlements restricted to those with dementia would, for example, provide strong incentives to widen diagnostic criteria for those conditions, in order for more patients to qualify for public programs. The fragmented nature, complex organization, limited access, and uncertain eligibility criteria for long-term care services cause problems for individuals with dementia and their families. The physician is commonly responsible for coordinating medical services, but there is no analogous person to coordinate long-term care, mental health, social, and aging services. The concern here is for clients to have a person to turn to for information, and to begin planning service needs as soon as possible so that long-term care decisions are not made in a crisis atmosphere.

One mechanism to begin service planning would be to refer persons who receive the diagnosis of a disorder causing dementia to another professional or organization that can deal with the family and client in planning and coordinating services. This role is variously referred to by such terms as case management, case coordination, or linkage. Having such a professional available for referral from physicians would greatly improve the rational provision of services, but the costs are uncertain....

A third issue related to diagnosis and treatment concerns methods of diagnosis. The National Institute of Neurological and Communicative Disorders and Stroke (NINCDS), NIA, ADRDA, and the American Psychiatric Association each have published general criteria for diagnosis of dementing conditions, but none is specific as to which tests should be ordered and how they should be interpreted. Consensus may not be possible or advisable, but current criteria are not useful for the general practitioner trying to determine the diagnosis of a patient....

One recent bill passed by Congress and signed by the President (Public Law 99-509) will establish up to 10 centers for diagnosis and treatment of dementing disorders. These would be distinct in function from the existing biomedical *research* centers, although they might be related geographically and administratively. The State of California has established six such centers, and reports that, even without publicity, the centers cannot meet demand for service. The centers are intended to diagnose and treat local cases of dementia, foster research, provide training for health professionals, aid families, and collect and analyze standardized information of use in planning services.

California reports that budget cutbacks at the State level have seriously impaired delivery of the expected services at the State-supported centers.

Diagnosis and treatment centers could be useful in training, setting standards for care, and focusing clinical research, but they should not be expected to make the diagnosis and treat all cases of dementia in the United States. The cutbacks California has reported could also occur at the national level.

Legal and Ethical Concerns

Decisions about medical care, family finances, and other important topics are often difficult. . . . They become even more difficult when someone has dementia. Eventually decisions must be made on behalf of the individuals—decisions about driving an automobile, working, controlling financial assets, or participating in research that may not be of direct benefit. Such decisions are particularly difficult when someone's employment involves professional work that is not closely supervised, such as medicine or law, . . . in which good judgment is essential.

State and Federal laws include several ways to appoint someone to make decisions for another person. Guardians and conservators can be appointed by a court following a procedure to decide that an individual is indeed incapable of autonomous choice. Durable powers of attorney allow a person to set certain constraints on finances or medical care and to appoint someone to make decisions *before* becoming mentally incompetent. Living wills can indicate what types of medical care an individual would wish to receive or refuse.

Each of these mechanisms for making decisions raises difficult questions. At what point is someone mentally incompetent? That is not a purely medical or purely legal question, and competence (legally defined) depends not only on the individual's mental ability, but also on the type of decision being made. Other questions include who is to oversee the decisions made by an appointed surrogate and how someone can be protected from conflicts of interest. Few of these questions can be directly addressed by Federal legislation. Most are now being decided through the judicial system at both the State and Federal levels. Many States have also passed or considered laws about living wills, powers of attorney, guardianship, and conservatorship.

Legal issues related to Federal programs such as Medicare and Medicaid are also important. . . .

Education and Training

Providing high-quality services for those with dementia presumes the availability of trained people to deliver them. The sudden increase in awareness about dementia has meant that few centers are expert in care and research on this topic. Efforts to correct that deficiency have begun in the last 5 years, but most of those who care for individuals with dementia have never had special training.

Family members and other informal caregivers need information about the nature of the diseases and how their daily lives might change. That knowledge can improve their ability to plan and anticipate problems. They also need information about how to provide care. Persons with dementia are increasingly receiving special care, yet the results of innovations are not widely disseminated. When they are published, it is frequently in professional journals not readily available to family members. Health professionals can assist by preparing books, pamphlets, videotapes, and other educational materials intended for family caregivers. A few such materials are available: a guide to home care has been prepared, and several books have been published in recent years.

The care of someone with dementia, as with other chronic illnesses, demands a range of skills and duration of service that no individual can fully supply. That realization has led to the development of interdisciplinary teams consisting of physicians, nurses, psychologists, social workers, and others. Multidisciplinary teams can better coordinate different services and bring their various areas of expertise to bear on the problems of someone with dementia.

Physicians now in general practice have had little formal training in geriatrics, although those who graduated from medical schools recently are likely to have had some courses. Attention to dementia has increased dramatically in some specialties, particularly neurology and psychiatry. Other specialties, such as family practice and internal medicine, are also publishing more articles, developing continuing education courses, and modifying medical school and residency curricula to include more material about dementing illness. Physician training in geriatrics should be improved by supportive provisions in the Omnibus Health Act of 1986 (Public Law 99-660). The results of such efforts should be felt over the next decade.

The physician's role in dementing illness extends well beyond making a diagnosis and rendering medical treatment. It also involves interacting with the care team and referring patients and their families to support groups, social services, and long-term care agencies.

Nurses are the backbone of long-term care, but long-term care is a low prestige and low paying specialty among these professionals. A shortfall of 75,000 nurses in long-term care is projected by 1990. The medical training that nurses receive may not prepare them for the predominantly administrative and supervisory roles they perform in long-term care settings, and coverage of dementia varies among nursing schools even more than among medical schools.

Geriatric nurse practitioners, who receive special training in geriatrics, typically learn about the medical needs of older people, including coverage of dementia, and can perform many of the diagnostic, assessment, and treatment functions of physicians. They also generally learn about the service delivery system and how to coordinate services. They can form a bridge between the medical and social service systems, and are less costly to use than physicians.

Nurse's aides provide an estimated 80 to 90 percent of direct patient contact hours in long-term care. Yet they are poorly paid (usually minimum wage), have low educational levels, and have high turnover rates. Nurse's aides frequently have different socioeconomic and cultural backgrounds than those of their clients. The responsibility to train nurse's aides falls to long-term care facilities. Administrators are reluctant to invest heavily in training because aides are unlikely to remain long at the facility, but patient care depends on such training. Even those facilities that do wish to train aides have been hampered by lack of materials on dementia. Materials for training have recently become available through a cooperative effort of ADRDA and the American Health Care Association, and through the Hillhaven Corp.

Other professionals are also involved in the care of those with dementia. Complete care frequently involves social workers, psychologists, physical and occupational therapists, speech therapists, and administrators who are familiar with the problems faced by individuals with dementia and knowledgeable about available services.

The Federal Government could play a critical role in ensuring that health and social service personnel working with persons with dementia receive the education and training necessary to deliver high-quality care. This role extends to educational institutions, programs that train professionals, and facilities that provide care.

Disseminating information about care to professional networks, family support groups, and the lay press can be an important function. The role of the Federal Government in providing information is most important in those areas in which it predominates (e.g., biomedical research, health services research, and how to use government programs). One example is the Alzheimer's Resource Center of New York City, which is preparing a book on nationwide resources about dementia available through the network of Area Agencies on Aging and State Units on Aging. The effort is the result of cooperation between a local chapter of ADRDA, the New York State Department for the Aging, and the Administration on Aging.

Accreditation of educational programs that train health and social service professionals is generally performed at the State level, but it is subject to Federal guidelines for those services reimbursed by Federal monies (e.g., Medicare and Medicaid). Licensure of professionals is also largely a State function, subject to Federal standards. Training and staffing requirements for acute, mental health, and long-term care facilities are written by States subject to Federal regulations. Requiring training about the care needs of those with dementia could be incorporated into certification guidelines. Although certification is a State function, the

Federal Government could make receipt of Federal funds conditional on certain certification requirements.

Direct funding of training programs for physicians, nurses, and other health professionals is supported by the Department of Health and Human Services and the Veterans Administration. Continued support, with increased emphasis on geriatrics and particularly dementia, is likely to result in faculty whose talents are multiplied by teaching others to tackle the problems related to dementia.

Delivery of Long-Term Care

Formal long-term care services for persons with dementia are provided in nursing homes, board and care facilities, day care centers, mental health facilities, or individuals' homes. Until recently, there has been little study of which services are used or needed by persons with dementia and by their caregivers. Equally little is known about which settings are best suited to deliver many of the needed services. Some studies suggest that 40 to 75 percent of those in nursing homes have dementia; data on prevalence of dementia in other settings are unavailable.

Individuals with dementia often need personal care, chore, and homemaker services in addition to—and often more than—medical care. Personal and social services are less widely available and less likely than medical care to be covered by government programs. Families may need temporary respite from continual supervision and care, but few agencies deliver care that is intended to relieve the burden of caregivers rather than patients (although most services do both).

Who Delivers Care?

Several factors determine who delivers long-term care for persons with dementia. For any one person, care may come from family at home, day care centers, home care providers, or a nursing home. Which provider is most appropriate depends on the extent of family and community informal supports, the quality and range of available services, the individual's symptoms, and the cost of the various options.

Families play a predominant role in providing long-term care for older Americans. A General Accounting Office study of the elderly population in Cleveland conducted in 1975 concluded that families were providing more than 50 percent of all long-term care services received, and that as the impairment of the patient increased, so did the proportion of services provided by the family. For the extremely impaired group, families provided 80 percent of needed services.

The degree of informal support may diminish in coming decades, however, for several reasons. Those most at risk of developing dementia are people in their eighties, and the children and spouses of such individuals are also likely to be older and themselves at risk of disability. At the same time, the declining birth rate in the United States has reduced the proportion of those who will be available to care for tomorrow's older people. The rapid influx of women into the work force also portends reduced availability of family caregivers; although women today report that work is important, one study found that they act as though they give caregiving priority over employment in most cases. Rising divorce rates and remarriage rates also complicate determining who will render care to an older relative; a person newly married into a family may feel less obliged to care for the new spouse's parent with dementia. Finally, the growing mobility of families increases geographic dispersion, and may make family caregiving less likely. Each of these trends weakens the informal care system, and may increase dependence on government services.

Caregiver Support

The primary needs of informal caregivers are respite care, information about the diseases and care methods, information about services, and a broadened range of services. Family members' efforts can be aided by the Federal Government by giving them optimal information (especially that arising from federally supported research), assisting them in finding out about or obtaining services, and extending some benefits to caregivers and the person needing care as a unit, rather than restricting them to the individual with dementia.

Range of Services

Caregivers believe that more services should be available to care for individuals with dementia. The caregiver survey conducted for OTA [Office of Technology Assessment] found that the majority of those who listed respite care, adult day care, board and care, and nursing home care as "essential" either knew these services were not available or did not know if they were available. That finding suggests that there is an unmet need both for services and for information about them.

Increasing the number of choices for care of persons with dementia will not necessarily diminish demand for nursing home care or reduce institutional care costs borne by government. Day and home care is much more widely available in the United Kingdom, for example, but rates of nursing home residency are not significantly lower. Community-based care has not led to cost savings over nursing home care according to many recent studies. Some studies, however, report better patient outcomes with home care, and—of particular importance for persons with dementia who tend to reside for long periods in nursing homes once admitted—studies have not predicted what "the benefits of coordinated, expanded home care services might be for older, chronically impaired individuals who do not meet the skilled care requirement but, rather, need ongoing maintenance care."

Patient Assessment and Eligibility for Services

Assessment is the process of identifying, describing, and evaluating patient characteristics associated with illness. While diagnosis of a dementing illness identifies the disease, assessment describes its impact on the individual, quantifies its severity, and is therefore essential in determining long-term care needs.

Eligibility for Medicare and Medicaid long-term care services and reimbursement levels for covered services are based primarily on the medical and nursing care needs of the individual. Some States are now using assessment instruments that measure cognitive and behavioral deficits and limitations in activities of daily living to determine Medicaid eligibility or reimbursement levels. These case mix assessments can reduce incentives to discriminate against heavy care patients, but have not been rigorously studied to ascertain their impact on persons with dementia. . . .

Special Services for Individuals with Dementia

An increasing number of long-term care facilities and agencies are developing special services for persons with dementia, but these services are not yet widely available and most such individuals are treated elsewhere. Preliminary data suggest that 1 to 2 percent of nursing home residents with dementia are in special care units. These facilities appear to be raising the standard of care, and are focusing attention on the large subpopulation of nursing home residents who suffer from dementia. Special care involves training of nurses and aides, redesign of rooms and common areas, and activities intended to take advantage of spared mental functions. Adapting the environment to altered needs of those with dementia appears to be useful, but the optimal way to do so is a topic of debate. The number of special care units has increased dramatically in recent years, yet no national body is responsible for identifying them, coordinating studies (to reduce duplication and disseminate results rapidly), or evaluating their efficacy.

Several policy issues are raised by special care units and programs. First, there is an apparent shortage of people highly knowledgeable about dementia available to staff such units or evaluate them. Second, evaluation and coordination of different units is currently haphazard. Third, standards for quality are unclear. Fourth, the type of individual eligible for care on special units is not uniform among different units, and optimal care methods may differ according to severity, type of symptoms, or disease. Finally, the costs and fair reimbursement rates for special units merit further inquiry. Do special care units cost more? Should they be paid more to care for those with dementia? Will special reimbursement lead to inequitable treatment of other types of patients, or will failure to pay more for those with dementia diminish their care?

Quality Assurance

Persons with dementia are at particular risk of receiving substandard care. They cannot communicate effectively, and their complaints may be discounted or ascribed to mental instability or misunderstanding. Reduced intellectual abilities interfere with rational consumer choice, an important component of quality assurance. Family members can act on behalf of individuals with dementia to assess and ensure the quality of care. If they are not available or the family is not cohesive, then ombudsmen, case managers, or designated surrogates must do so.

Quality of care in hospitals paid by Medicare is subject to the review of Professional Review Organizations. Outpatient and ambulatory acute care are less subject to direct inspection. The threat of malpractice is a strong incentive for providing adequate care in most acute care settings, but it has not been widely applied in long-term care settings.

The quality of care in nursing homes is regulated by States, subject to certification standards for Medicare and Medicaid. The system for assessing quality under Medicaid and Medicare is changing from a focus on inspection of facilities and physical plant to one that adds a client-centered assessment. Residents with dementia, however, are unlikely to be able to answer many of the questions about quality; inspection of their physical condition will yield clues as to their physical care, but will not assess overall quality of staff interactions or the resident's emotional satisfaction and staff regard for the person's dignity. These concerns are difficult to solve through purely regulatory means. Family assessment of a relative's health and happiness is another means of quality assurance. It is not available to residents without families, however, and its efficacy hinges on facilities' willingness to attend to suggestions or the availability of alternative care settings if they do not.

For Medicare and Medicaid administrators, only limited options exist to ensure compliance with care standards. In many areas, the scarcity of nursing home beds makes moving out of a poorly managed facility an unattractive option for the resident because an alternative one may not be available; that same scarcity makes State agencies reluctant to close down facilities. Less stringent enforcement actions have been successful in some States, and legislation permitting more use of them might be useful. Professional organizations (e.g., American Health Care Association and the American Association of Homes for the Aging), proprietary and nonprofit nursing home chains, and new programs in teaching nursing homes can also promote higher standards and adherence to existing standards.

Day care, home care, board and care, and other community-based settings are licensed and regulated much less than nursing homes. Information about quality in such settings is sparse and much less thoroughly analyzed than information regarding quality of care in hospitals or nursing homes. Payment levels are generally lower and tend to be direct rather than through public subsidy, making any government regulation beyond licensing unlikely. Family or case manager assessment of quality is thus the main assurance of quality, perhaps supplemented by final resort to the legal system. Organizations . . . can help develop guidelines for care and suggest means of quality assurance. Federal and State Governments could also choose to have a direct role. If the range of services is expanded, examination of the quality of care in day care, home care, and board and care settings would be an important topic for health services research—to identify innovative ways to ensure that individuals have quality care that respects their rights and preserves their dignity.

Financing Long-Term Care

Financing long-term care for persons with dementia is one of the policy issues of greatest concern to caregivers and policymakers, and about which there is the least consensus. Policy options fall into several groups, according to the range of services reimbursed; the source of payment (individual, Medicaid, Medicare, insurance); and the relative responsibility of individuals and government.

These factors are woven together in a confusingly complex fabric of existing policies and priorities. Caregivers would prefer to see an expanded range of services available, whatever the source of payment. Government program administrators, legislators, and insurers also wish to fund the broadest number of options, but they do not want to leave commitments open-ended or to pay for services used by those who do not need them. The extremely complex set of laws, regulations, and contract arrangements for long-term care services reflects that concern for overutilization. Restricting payment to institutional settings has been one way to discourage illegitimate use and to attempt to concentrate resources on those who most obviously need them.

The source of payment determines not only who pays but also which services are covered and how those services are regulated and financed. Acute care under Medicare, for example, is paid under the diagnosis-related group payment system in most States, covers only some medically necessary services, and is relatively uniform—from the point of view of the individual—throughout the United States. Medicaid, in contrast, varies tremendously among the States in its eligibility criteria, funding levels, extent of coverage of nonmedical services, access to home services, method of payment, and enforcement of quality standards—for both acute and long-term care.

Options for financing long-term care also differ in degree of public subsidy, ranging from complete private financing to heavy public subsidy....

Financing of long-term care is one of the issues affecting individuals with dementia (and their families) that is most sensitive to public policies. Through Medicaid, Federal and State Governments are important payers of long-term care, covering the majority of those in nursing homes. The amounts paid by State and Federal Governments for nursing home care are roughly equal to total payments by individuals. The American Health Care Association estimates that 70 percent of nursing home residents are covered by Medicaid, and the figure is well over 80 percent for some States. The proportion of patients covered by Medicaid is higher than its fraction of payments for two reasons:

1. some patients on Medicaid also receive some income (from social

security or other sources) that is paid to the facility to reduce Medicaid payments, and

2. levels of reimbursement per person are generally lower through Medicaid than other sources of payments.

The dominance of Medicaid means that decisions about the Medicaid program have a great effect on how nursing homes operate. Policies affecting nursing home coverage under Medicare affect a smaller, but still significant, fraction of nursing homes. Because of the absence of private insurers in long-term care, Federal and State Government decisions about financing are pivotal in determining access to and availability of day care, home care, respite care, and other services outside nursing homes.

Biomedical Research

Biomedical research includes basic biological, clinical, and public health research. It roughly corresponds to the type of research conducted under the auspices of the National Institutes of Health (either directly or through universities and medical centers). Basic research is conducted in the pursuit of scientific knowledge without primary regard for the applications of such knowledge. Clinical research applies basic knowledge in the search for preventive measures, treatments, and methods of diagnosis. Public health research builds on both basic and clinical research and applies it to population aggregates. The most common type of dementia, Alzheimer's disease, cannot be prevented or its symptoms reversed with current knowledge and techniques. The severity of future medical and social problems could be dramatically reduced if an effective drug or surgical treatment were found to significantly reduce symptoms or arrest the disease. Only a small proportion of those expected to develop dementia now have it, so finding a means of prevention could drastically reduce the projected number of people affected. . . .

Federal support for biomedical research . . . has gone from less than $4 million in 1976 to over $65 million estimated for 1987. The number of publications on "Alzheimer's disease," "dementia," and "senility" leapt from 30 in 1972 to 87 in 1976, and then to 548 in 1985, reflecting the importance of increased Federal support. Nongovernment organizations such as ADRDA, the John Douglas French Foundation on Alzheimer's Disease, the American Federation for Aging Research, and the Howard Hughes Medical Institute are also contributing research funds, at levels corresponding to 5 to 10 percent of Federal funding. Private pharmaceutical and medical products companies are supporting applied research to find effective drugs and diagnostic devices, but their work builds on the basic research supported by the Federal Government.

Biomedical research on dementing conditions is likely to yield benefits in addition to its clinical applications. Knowledge of the brain is still scant in comparison to the size of the task, and the study of the nervous system—neuroscience—is one of the most exciting areas in biology today. Support for research on dementing conditions will likely support work that will increase such knowledge in these disciplines. Research on dementia could, in fact, become a focus for neuroscience, just as cancer research led to many important advances in molecular biology and the spawning of biotechnology.

Major successes in biomedical research could also substantially reduce the costs and projected social and personal burdens of dementia....

An exclusive focus on biomedical research is unwise, however. Although increased funding makes scientific discoveries more likely, such discoveries will not necessarily lead to a means of prevention or cure, diagnostic tests, or even effective treatments. The consequences of new scientific findings may not be known for several decades, and may only much later improve clinical care. Scientific problems posed by disorders causing dementia are likely to yield to scientific inquiry, but public policy that presumes a revolution in care methods—based on discoveries not yet made—is not advisable.

Health Services Research

Health services research, as it applies to the subject of this report, is the multidisciplinary study of those with dementia and of the systems that serve them. It includes the community and family, but excludes biomedical research. Some types of research, such as epidemiology and patient assessment, bridge the gap between health services and biomedical research. Study of how to care for individuals, especially evaluation of methods that do not employ drugs or medical devices, is included in health services research, although some elements are also clinical. Topics range from studying how best to care for persons with dementia (at home, in nursing homes, or in day care centers) to evaluating different methods of paying for long-term care services....

The type of information derived from health services research is crucial to rational planning of public policy and informed consumer choice. One analyst has observed, however, that "public policy is hampered by the woeful state of information about almost all social aspects of senile dementia and the deplorable quality of studies of intervention effects"....

SENTENCING COMMISSION REPORT

April 13, 1987

The U.S. Sentencing Commission proposed major changes in sentencing procedures for federal criminals in a report to Congress dated April 13. New guidelines classified each federal offense to one of forty-three levels of punishment that would set upper and lower bounds for the amount of time to be served by a convicted offender. The guidelines reduced judicial leeway in deciding whether a given offender should be sentenced to prison and for how long. They also established which factors would be taken into consideration during sentencing and when departures from these factors were permissible.

The commission, created by the Comprehensive Crime Control Act of 1984, was charged by Congress to develop a more rational sentencing system in which defendants found guilty of similar crimes would receive similar punishments. The intent of Congress was to limit the discretion of federal judges to set punishment based on subjective factors and to regularize the equally subjective decision of granting parole. In place of the current system in which a bank robber, for instance, might be given an indeterminate sentence of eight to twenty-five years, with the prisoner's actual release date determined by parole officials, Congress wished to establish a system of determinate sentences without possibility of parole. It was hoped that uniform guidelines would end the wide disparity in sentences handed down by different judges in different jurisdictions. Rather than legislate the factors that judges must consider and the associated sentence, Congress deferred to the experts and established a commission. The legislation provided that the commission's guidelines would enter into force six months after adoption unless Congress passed, and the president signed, a bill disapproving them.

The Time for Each Crime

Although the work of the commission was marked by controversy at each stage of its deliberations, there was no disagreement that sentencing in the federal system had become haphazard. A 1974 study found the average sentence served for bank robbery was eleven years nationwide, but only five and a half years for convicts sentenced by the federal courts of northern Illinois. Another study showed that when a sample of fifty federal judges were given identical files in an extortion case, they recommended sentences varying from twenty years in prison and a $65,000 fine to three years and no fine. On the other hand, there was general agreement that there were many factors to be taken into consideration when imposing sentence, such as previous criminal record or whether a weapon was used, that precluded a purely mechanical approach.

The commission issued a draft report in September 1986 that proposed guidelines based on a complex array of 360 different factors. This attempt received widespread criticism as unworkable, and the April 13 report represented a second effort. Even then, the seven-member commission asked Congress for more time before the guidelines took effect, so that the impact of the guidelines could be assessed and federal judges could play a greater role in fine-tuning them.

The April report narrowed the range of sentences to forty-three levels, with the most severe penalties reserved for the crimes of first degree murder, aircraft hijacking resulting in death, and treason. Each of these crimes ranked level forty-three, which called for a life sentence without parole. Lesser crimes were assigned a base level corresponding to the commission's view of their severity, to which additional levels could be added or subtracted for aggravating or mitigating circumstances. For example, under the guidelines envisioned by the commission a defendant convicted of carrying a dangerous weapon on board an aircraft would have committed an offense with a base level of nine. The defendant would be eligible for a sentence of four to ten months in prison for a first offense. But actual prison time could be reduced to probation plus some form of community service because the minimum possible sentence was less than six months. However, if the conviction was for a third or greater offense, the minimum term under the guidelines would be from eight to twenty-one months, and probation would no longer be possible. Even if the defendant had no previous criminal history, a finding that he had acted willfully and without regard for human safety would increase the severity of the sentence by fifteen levels to the equivalent of fifty-one, which called for sixty-three months in jail. Conversely, if the defendant's possession of the weapon was otherwise lawful, and he acted only negligently rather than willfully, the sentence would be decreased three levels, so that even a third offender acting negligently might be eligible for probation.

For crimes such as embezzlement or fraud, in which the amount taken provided an indication of how serious an offense was, the base level of the offense was determined by the amount taken and a proportionately stiffer sentence was given for a greater amount taken. The commission allowed federal judges to depart from the guidelines when a plea bargain between the defendant and the state had been reached.

Is Fish Smuggling as Serious as Assault?

The report proved highly controversial. In a sharply worded dissenting view, Commissioner Paul H. Robinson attacked the majority report for failing to provide a rational sentencing policy, failing to accord proper weight to aggravating or mitigating factors during the crime, failing to rank offenses according to their true seriousness, allowing plea bargaining to subvert the goals of the reform, and several other shortcomings. He argued that the guidelines often ignored the difference between a completed offense and an unsuccessful attempt or a mere threat. According to Robinson, "the offender who telephones a witness in a trial and threatens to throw eggs at her car is treated the same as he would be if he had firebombed her car, seriously burning her."

He also criticized the guidelines for failing to account sufficiently for aggravating circumstances, allowing a burglar who beats a homeowner to receive the same sentence as a burglar who does not. A second illustration used by Robinson concerned the father who returns from a hunting trip and sees his child run over and killed by a drunk driver and who immediately shoots and kills the driver with his hunting gun. Under the guideline the father would receive the same sentence as an offender who repeatedly stabs and kills a person who punched him in a barroom brawl. Similarly, the guidelines assigned the same offense level to aggravated assault as to smuggling $11,000 worth of fish.

Robinson also pointed out that the guidelines would not apply in situations where the prosecution and the defense have reached a plea bargain with a recommended sentence. He believed this to be contrary to the intent of Congress in the authorizing legislation and likely to be a factor in continuing sentencing disparity, because 87 percent of federal criminal cases are disposed of by plea bargaining.

A second type of criticism came from Alan Morrison, director of the Public Citizen Litigation Group. He argued that the commission guidelines were unconstitutional because the commission's structure and the way its members were chosen violated the separation of powers clause. Under the law, the president was granted authority to select all seven commission members. According to Morrison, this allowed the executive branch to control the judicial branch to an unacceptable extent. He believed that there was a strong potential for chaos if the guidelines were ruled unconstitutional after several years of use. A consultant to the commission who had helped draft the original statute conceded in retrospect that the commission should have been structured differently.

The New York Times *strongly criticized the commission, calling the guidelines half-baked, and rejected the commission's contention that any problems could be rectified later. The* Times *argued that by ending parole, the commission would have removed one of the safety valves needed to handle prison overcrowding. With serious questions being raised about the legality of the guidelines,* The Times *felt that it would be irresponsible to implement them without being certain that intolerable crowding could be avoided.*

The House Judiciary Subcommittee on Criminal Justice approved legislation September 23 to delay implementing the guidelines for nine months. The commission and the subcommittee chairman contended that judges, prosecutors, and defense lawyers needed more time to learn new procedures. Critics hoped the delay would give them time to kill the guidelines.

> *Following are excerpts from the U.S. Sentencing Commission's "Sentencing Guidelines and Policy Statements," issued April 13, 1987, and from the dissenting view of Commissioner Paul H. Robinson, issued May 1, 1987:*

SENTENCING GUIDELINES

... The guidelines and policy statements promulgated by the Commission are issued pursuant to Section 994(a) of Title 28, United States Code.

The Statutory Mission

The Comprehensive Crime Control Act of 1984 foresees guidelines that will further the basic purposes of criminal punishment, *i.e.*, deterring crime, incapacitating the offender, providing just punishment, and rehabilitating the offender. It delegates to the Commission broad authority to review and rationalize the federal sentencing process.

The statute contains many detailed instructions as to how this determination should be made, but the most important of them instructs the Commission to create categories of offense behavior and offender characteristics. An offense behavior category might consist, for example, of "bank robbery/committed with a gun/$2500 taken." An offender characteristic category might be "offender with one prior conviction who was not sentenced to imprisonment." The Commission is required to prescribe guidelines ranges that specify an appropriate sentence for each class of convicted persons, to be determined by coordinating the offense behavior categories with the offender characteristic categories. The statute contemplates the guidelines will establish a range of sentences for every coordination of categories. Where the guidelines call for imprisonment, the range must be narrow: the maximum imprisonment cannot exceed the minimum by more than the greater of 25 percent or 6 months.

The sentencing judge must select a sentence from within the guideline range. If, however, a particular case presents atypical features, the Act allows the judge to depart from the guidelines and sentence outside the range. In that case, the judge must specify reasons for departure. If the court sentences within the guideline range, an appellate court may review the sentence to see if the guideline was correctly applied. If the judge departs from the guideline range, an appellate court may review the reasonableness of the departure. The Act requires the offender to serve virtually all of any prison sentence imposed, for it abolishes parole and substantially restructures good behavior adjustments.

The law requires the Commission to send its initial guidelines to Congress by April 13, 1987, and under the present statute they take effect automatically on November 1, 1987. The Commission may submit guideline amendments each year to Congress between the beginning of a regular session and May 1. The amendments will take effect automatically 180 days after submission unless a law is enacted to the contrary.

The Commission, with the aid of its legal and research staff, considerable public testimony and written commentary, has developed an initial set of guidelines which it now transmits to Congress. The Commission emphasizes, however, that it views the guideline-writing process as evolutionary. It expects, and the governing statute anticipates, that continuing research, experience, and analysis will result in modifications and revisions to the guidelines by submission of amendments to Congress. To this end, the Commission is established as a permanent agency to monitor sentencing practices in the federal courts throughout the nation.

The Basic Approach

To understand these guidelines and the rationale that underlies them, one must begin with the three objectives that Congress, in enacting the new sentencing law, sought to achieve. Its basic objective was to enhance the ability of the criminal justice system to reduce crime through an effective, fair sentencing system. To achieve this objective, Congress first sought *honesty* in sentencing. It sought to avoid the confusion and implicit deception that arises out of the present sentencing system which requires a judge to impose an indeterminate sentence that is automatically reduced in most cases by "good time" credits. In addition, the parole commission is permitted to determine how much of the remainder of any prison sentence an offender actually will serve. This usually results in a substantial reduction in the effective length of the sentence imposed, with defendants often serving only about one-third of the sentence handed down by the court.

Second, Congress sought *uniformity* in sentencing by narrowing the wide disparity in sentences imposed by different federal courts for similar criminal conduct by similar offenders. Third, Congress sought *proportionality* in sentencing through a system that imposes appropriately different sentences for criminal conduct of different severity.

Honesty is easy to achieve: The abolition of parole makes the sentence imposed by the court the sentence the offender will serve. There is a tension, however, between the mandate of uniformity (treat similar cases alike) and the mandate of proportionality (treat different cases differently) which, like the historical tension between law and equity, makes it difficult to achieve both goals simultaneously. Perfect uniformity — sentencing every offender to five years — destroys proportionality. Having only a few simple categories of crimes would make the guidelines uniform and easy to administer, but might lump together offenses that are different in important respects. . . .

At the same time, a sentencing system tailored to fit every conceivable wrinkle of each case can become unworkable and seriously compromise the certainty of punishment and its deterrent effect. . . .

The list of potentially relevant features of criminal behavior is long; the fact that they can occur in multiple combinations means that the list of possible permutations of factors is virtually endless. The appropriate relationships among these different factors are exceedingly difficult to establish, for they are often context specific. Sentencing courts do not treat the occurrence of a simple bruise identically in all cases, irrespective of whether that bruise occurred in the context of a bank robbery or in the context of a breach of peace. This is so, in part, because the risk that such a harm will occur differs depending on the underlying offense with which it is connected (and therefore may already be counted, to a different degree, in the punishment for the underlying offense); and also because, in part, the relationship between punishment and multiple harms is not simply additive. The relation varies, depending on how much other harm has occurred. (Thus, one cannot easily assign points for each kind of harm and simply add them up, irrespective of context and total amounts).

The larger the number of subcategories, the greater the complexity that is created and the less workable the system. Moreover, the subcategories themselves, sometimes too broad and sometimes too narrow, will apply and interact in unforeseen ways to unforeseen situations, thus failing to cure the unfairness of a simple, broad category system. Finally, and perhaps most importantly, probation officers and courts, in applying a complex system of subcategories, would have to make a host of decisions about whether the underlying facts are sufficient to bring the case within a particular subcategory. The greater the number of decisions required and the greater their complexity, the greater the risk that different judges will apply the guidelines differently to situations that, in fact, are similar, thereby reintroducing the very disparity that the guidelines were designed to eliminate.

In view of the arguments, it is tempting to retreat to the simple, broad-category approach and to grant judges the discretion to select the proper point along a broad sentencing range. Obviously, however, granting such broad discretion risks correspondingly broad disparity in sentencing, for different courts may exercise their discretionary powers in different ways. That is to say, such an approach risks a return to the wide disparity that Congress established the Commission to limit.

In the end, there is no completely satisfying solution to this practical stalemate. The Commission has had to simply balance the comparative virtues and vices of broad, simple categorization and detailed, complex subcategorization, and within the constraints established by that balance, minimize the discretionary powers of the sentencing court. Any ultimate system will, to a degree, enjoy the benefits and suffer from the drawbacks of each approach.

A philosophical problem arose when the Commission attempted to reconcile the differing perceptions of the purposes of criminal punishment. Most observers of the criminal law agree that the ultimate aim of the law itself, and of punishment in particular, is the control of crime. Beyond this point, however, the consensus seems to break down. Some argue that appropriate punishment should be defined primarily on the basis of the moral principle of "just deserts." Under this principle, punishment should be scaled to the offender's culpability and the resulting harms. Thus, if a defendant is less culpable, the defendant deserves less punishment. Others argue that punishment should be imposed primarily on the basis of practical "crime control" considerations. Defendants sentenced under this scheme should receive the punishment that most effectively lessens the likelihood of future crime, either by deterring others or incapacitating the defendant.

Adherents of these points of view have urged the Commission to choose between them, to accord one primacy over the other. Such a choice would be profoundly difficult. . . . A clear-cut Commission decision in favor of one of these approaches would diminish the chance that the guidelines would find the widespread acceptance they need for effective implementation. As a practical matter, in most sentencing decisions both philosophies may prove consistent with the same result.

For now, the Commission has sought to solve both the practical and philosophical problems of developing a coherent sentencing system by taking an empirical approach that uses data estimating the existing sentencing system as a starting point. It has analyzed data drawn from 10,000 presentence investigations, crimes as distinguished in substantive criminal statutes, the United States Parole Commission's guidelines and resulting statistics, and data from other relevant sources, in order to determine which distinctions are important in present practice. . . .

This empirical approach has helped the Commission resolve its practical problem by defining a list of relevant distinctions that, although of considerable length, is short enough to create a manageable set of guidelines. Existing categories are relatively broad and omit many distinctions that some may believe important, yet they include most of the major distinctions that statutes and presentence data suggest make a significant difference in sentencing decisions. Important distinctions that are ignored in existing practice probably occur rarely. A sentencing judge may take this unusual case into account by departing from the guidelines.

The Commission's empirical approach has also helped resolve its philosophical dilemma. Those who adhere to a just deserts philosophy may concede that the lack of moral consensus might make it difficult to say exactly what punishment is deserved for a particular crime, specified in minute detail. Likewise, those who subscribe to a philosophy of crime control may acknowledge that the lack of sufficient, readily available data might make it difficult to say exactly what punishment will best prevent that crime. Both groups might therefore recognize the wisdom of looking to those distinctions that judges and legislators have in fact made over the course of time. These established distinctions are ones that the community believes, or has found over time, to be important from either a moral or crime-control perspective.

The Commission has not simply copied estimates of existing practice as revealed by the data (even though establishing offense values on this basis would help eliminate disparity, for the data represent averages). Rather, it has departed from the data at different points for various important reasons. Congressional statutes, for example, may suggest or require departure, as in the case of the new drug law that imposes increased and mandatory minimum sentences. In addition, the data may reveal inconsistencies in treatment, such as punishing economic crime less severely than other apparently equivalent behavior.

Despite these policy-oriented departures from present practice, the guidelines represent an approach that begins with, and builds upon, empirical data. The guidelines will not please those who wish the Commission to adopt a single philosophical theory and then work deductively to establish a simple and perfect set of categorizations and distinctions. The guidelines may prove acceptable, however, to those who seek more modest, incremental improvements in the status quo, who believe the best is often the enemy of the good, and who recognize that these initial guidelines are but the first step in an evolutionary process. After spending considerable time and resources exploring alternative approaches, the Commission has developed these guidelines as a practical effort toward the achievement of a more honest, uniform, equitable, and therefore effective, sentencing system.

The Guidelines' Resolution of Major Issues

The guideline-writing process has required the Commission to resolve a host of important policy questions, typically involving rather evenly balanced sets of competing considerations. As an aid to understanding the guidelines, this introduction will briefly discuss several of those issues.

Commentary in the guidelines explains others.

Real Offense vs. Charge Offense Sentencing

One of the most important questions for the Commission to decide was whether to base sentences upon the actual conduct in which the defendant engaged regardless of the charges for which he was indicted or convicted ("real offense" sentencing), or upon the conduct that constitutes the elements of the offense with which the defendant was charged and of which he was convicted ("charge offense" sentencing). A bank robber, for example, might have used a gun, frightened bystanders, taken $50,000, injured a teller, refused to stop when ordered, and raced away damaging property during escape. A pure real offense system would sentence on the basis of all identifiable conduct. A pure charge offense system would overlook some of the harms that did not constitute statutory elements of the offenses of which the defendant was convicted.

The Commission initially sought to develop a real offense system. After all, the present sentencing system is, in a sense, a real offense system. The sentencing court (and the parole commission) take account of the conduct in which the defendant actually engaged, as determined in a presentence report, at the sentencing hearing, or before a parole commission hearing officer. The Commission's initial efforts in this direction . . . proved unproductive mostly for practical reasons. To make such a system work, even to formalize and rationalize the status quo, would have required the Commission to decide precisely which harms to take into account, how to add them up, and what kinds of procedures the courts should use to determine the presence or absence of disputed factual elements. The Commission found no practical way to combine and account for the large number of diverse harms arising in different circumstances; nor did it find a practical way to reconcile the need for a fair adjudicatory procedure with the need for a speedy sentencing process, given the potential existence of hosts of adjudicated "real harm" facts in many typical cases. The effort proposed as a solution to these problems required the use of, for example, quadratic roots and other mathematical operations that the Commission considered too complex to be workable, and, in the Commission's view, risked return to wide disparity in practice.

The Commission therefore abandoned the effort to devise a "pure" real offense system and instead experimented with a "modified real offense system." . . .

This version also foundered in several major respects on the rock of practicality. It was highly complex and its mechanical rules for adding harms (*e.g.*, bodily injury added the same punishment irrespective of context) threatened to work considerable unfairness. Ultimately, the Commission decided that it could not find a practical or fair and efficient way to implement either a pure or modified real offense system of the sort it originally wanted, and it abandoned that approach.

The Commission . . . moved closer to a "charge offense" system. The system is not, however, pure; it has a number of real elements. For one thing, the hundreds of overlapping and duplicative statutory provisions that make up the federal criminal law have forced the Commission to write guidelines that are descriptive of generic conduct rather than tracking purely statutory language. For another, the guidelines, both through specific offense characteristics and adjustments, take account of a number of important, commonly occurring real offense elements such as role in the offense, the presence of a gun, or the amount of money actually taken.

Finally, it is important not to overstate the difference in practice between a real and a charge offense system. The federal criminal system, in practice, deals mostly with drug offenses, bank robberies and white collar crimes (such as fraud, embezzlement, and bribery). For the most part, the conduct that an indictment charges approximates the real and relevant conduct in which the offender actually engaged.

The Commission recognizes its system will not completely cure the problems of a real offense system. It may still be necessary, for example, for a court to determine some particular real facts that will make a difference to the sentence. Yet, the Commission believes that the instances of controversial facts will be far fewer; indeed, there will be few enough that the court system will be able to devise fair procedures for their determination. . . .

The Commission also recognizes that a charge offense system has drawbacks of its own. One of the most important is its potential to turn over to the prosecutor the power to determine the sentence by increasing or decreasing the number (or content) of the counts in an indictment. Of course, the defendant's actual conduct (that which the prosecutor can prove in court) imposes a natural limit upon the prosecutor's ability to increase a defendant's sentence. Moreover, the Commission has written its rules for the treatment of multicount convictions with an eye toward eliminating unfair treatment that might flow from count manipulation. . . . [T]he Commission will closely monitor problems arising out of count manipulation and will make appropriate adjustments should they become necessary.

Departures

The new sentencing statute permits a court to depart from a guideline-specified sentence only when it finds "an aggravating or mitigating circumstance . . . that was not adequately taken into consideration by the Sentencing Commission. . . ." Thus, in principle, the Commission, by specifying that it had adequately considered a particular factor, could prevent a court from using it as grounds for departure. In this initial set of guidelines, however, the Commission does not so limit the courts' departure powers. The Commission intends the sentencing courts to treat each guideline as carving out a "heartland," a set of typical cases embodying the conduct that each guideline describes. When a court finds an atypical case, one to which a particular guideline linguistically applies but where conduct significantly differs from the norm, the court may consider whether a departure is warranted....

The Commission has adopted this departure policy for two basic reasons. First is the difficulty of foreseeing and capturing a single set of guidelines that encompasses the vast range of human conduct potentially relevant to a sentencing decision. The Commission also recognizes that in the initial set of guidelines it need not do so. The Commission is a permanent body, empowered by law to write and rewrite guidelines, with progressive changes, over many years. By monitoring when courts depart from the guidelines and by analyzing their stated reasons for doing so, the Commission, over time, will be able to create more accurate guidelines that specify precisely where departures should and should not be permitted.

Second, the Commission believes that despite the courts' legal freedom to depart from the guidelines, they will not do so very often. This is because the guidelines, offense by offense, seek to take account of those factors that the Commission's sentencing data indicate make a significant difference in sentencing at the present time. Thus, for example, where the presence of actual physical injury currently makes an important difference in final sentences, as in the case of robbery, assault, or arson, the guidelines specifically instruct the judge to use this factor to augment the sentence. Where the guidelines do not specify an augmentation or diminution, this is generally because the sentencing data do not permit the Commission, at this time, to conclude that the factor is empirically important in relation to the particular offense.... [T]he Commission recognizes that even its collection and analysis of 10,000 presentence reports are an imperfect source of data sentencing estimates. Rather than rely heavily at this time upon impressionistic accounts, however, the Commission believes it wiser to wait and collect additional data from our continuing monitoring process that may demonstrate how the guidelines work in practice before further modification.

It is important to note that the guidelines refer to three different kinds of departure. The first kind, which will most frequently be used, is in effect an interpolation between two adjacent, numerically oriented guideline rules. A specific offense characteristic, for example, might require an increase of four levels for serious bodily injury but two levels for bodily injury. Rather than requiring a court to force middle instances into either the "serious" or the "simple" category, the guideline commentary suggests that the court may interpolate and select a midpoint increase of three levels. The Commission has decided to call such an interpolation a "departure" in light of the legal views that a guideline providing for a range of increases in offense levels may violate the statute's 25 percent rule (though others have presented contrary legal arguments). Since interpolations are technically departures, the courts will have to provide reasons for their selection, and it will be subject to review for "reasonableness" on appeal. The Commission believes, however, that a simple reference by the court to the "mid-category" nature of the facts will typically provide sufficient reason. It does not foresee serious practical problems arising out of the application of the appeal provisions to this form of departure.

The second kind involves instances in which the guidelines provide specific guidance for departure, by analogy or by other numerical or non-numerical suggestions.... The Commission intends such suggestions as policy guidance for the courts. The Commission expects that most departures will reflect the suggestions, and that the courts of appeals may prove more likely to find departures "unreasonable" where they fall outside suggested levels.

A third kind of departure will remain unguided.... The Commission recognizes that there may be other grounds for departure;... it also believes there may be cases in which a departure outside suggested levels is warranted. In its view, however, such cases will be highly unusual.

Plea Agreements

Nearly ninety percent of all federal criminal cases involve guilty pleas, and many of these cases involve some form of plea agreement. Some commentators on early Commission guideline drafts have urged the Commission not to attempt any major reforms of the agreement process, on the grounds that any set of guidelines that threatens to radically change present practice also threatens to make the federal system unmanageable. Others, starting with the same facts, have argued that guidelines which fail to control and limit plea agreements would leave untouched a "loophole" large enough to undo the good that sentencing guidelines may bring....

The Commission has decided that these initial guidelines will not, in general, make significant changes in current plea agreement practices. The court will accept or reject any such agreements primarily in accordance with the rules set forth in Fed.R.Crim.P. 11(e). The Commission will collect data on the courts' plea practices and will analyze this information to determine when and why the courts accept or reject plea agreements. In light of this information and analysis, the Commission will seek to further regulate the plea agreement process as appropriate.

The Commission nonetheless expects the initial set of guidelines to have a positive, rationalizing impact upon plea agreements for two reasons. First, the guidelines create a clear, definite expectation in respect to the sentence that a court will impose if a trial takes place. Insofar as a prosecutor and defense attorney seek to agree about a likely sentence or range of sentences, they will no longer work in the dark. This fact alone should help to reduce irrationality in respect to actual sentencing outcomes. Second, the guidelines create a norm to which judges will likely refer when they decide whether ... to accept or to reject a plea agreement or recommendation. Since they will have before them the norm, the relevant factors (as disclosed in the plea agreement), and the reason for the agreement, they will find it easier than at present to determine whether there is sufficient reason to accept a plea agreement that departs from the norm....

Multi-Count Convictions

The Commission, like other sentencing commissions, has found it particularly difficult to develop rules for sentencing defendants convicted of multiple violations of law, each of which makes up a separate count in an indictment. The reason it is difficult is that when a defendant engages in conduct that causes several harms, each additional harm, even if it increases the extent to which punishment is warranted, does not necessarily warrant a proportionate increase in punishment. A defendant who assaults others during a fight, for example, may warrant more punishment if he injures ten people than if he injures one, but his conduct does not necessarily warrant ten times the punishment. If it did, many of the simplest offenses, for reasons that are often fortuitous, would lead to life sentences of imprisonment—sentences that neither "just deserts" nor "crime control" theories of punishment would find justified.

Several individual guidelines provide special instructions for increasing punishment when the conduct that is the subject of that count involves multiple occurrences or has caused several harms. The guidelines also provide general rules for aggravating punishment in light of multiple harms charged separately in separate counts. These rules may produce occasional anomalies, but normally they will permit an appropriate degree of aggravation of punishment when multiple offenses that are the subjects of separate counts take place.

These rules ... essentially provide: (1) When the conduct involves fungible items, *e.g.*, separate drug transactions or thefts of money, the amounts are added and the guidelines apply to the total amount. (2) When nonfungible harms are involved, the offense level for the most serious count is increased (according to a somewhat diminishing scale) to reflect the existence of other counts of conviction.

The rules have been written in order to minimize the possibility that an arbitrary casting of a single transaction into several counts will produce a longer sentence. In addition, the sentencing court will have adequate power to prevent such a result through departures where necessary to produce a mitigated sentence.

Regulatory Offenses

Regulatory statutes, though primarily civil in nature, sometimes contain criminal provisions in respect to particularly harmful activity. Such criminal provisions often describe not only substantive offenses, but also more technical, administratively-related offenses such as failure to keep accurate records or to provide requested information. These criminal statutes pose two problems. First, which criminal regulatory provisions should the Commission initially consider, and second, how should it treat technical or administratively-related criminal violations?

In respect to the first problem, the Commission found that it cannot comprehensively treat all regulatory violations in the initial set of guidelines.... Because of this practical difficulty, the Commission has sought to determine, with the assistance of the Department of Justice and several regulatory agencies, which criminal regulatory offenses are particularly important in light of the need for enforcement of the general regulatory scheme....

In respect to the second problem, the Commission has developed a system for treating technical recordkeeping and reporting offenses, dividing them into four categories.

First, in the simplest of cases, the offender may have failed to fill out a form intentionally, but without knowledge or intent that substantive harm would likely follow. He might fail, for example, to keep an accurate record of toxic substance transport, but that failure may not lead, nor be likely to lead, to the release or improper treatment of any toxic substance. Second, the same failure may be accompanied by a significant likelihood that substantive harm will occur; it may make a release of a toxic substance more likely. Third, the same failure may have led to substantive harm. Fourth, the failure may represent an effort to conceal a substantive harm that has occurred.

The structure of a typical guideline for a regulatory offense is as follows:

(1) The guideline provides a low base offense level (6) aimed at the first type of recordkeeping or reporting offense. It gives the court the legal authority to impose a punishment ranging from probation up to six months of imprisonment.

(2) Specific offense characteristics designed to reflect substantive offenses that do occur (in respect to some regulatory offenses), or that are likely to occur, increase the offense level.

(3) A specific offense characteristic also provides that a recordkeeping or reporting offense that conceals a substantive offense will be treated like the substantive offense.

The Commission views this structure as an initial effort. It may revise its approach in light of further experience and analysis of regulatory crimes.

Sentencing Ranges

In determining the appropriate sentencing ranges for each offense, the Commission began by estimating the average sentences now being served within each category. It also examined the sentence specified in congressional statutes, in the parole guidelines, and in other relevant, analogous sources....

While the Commission has not considered itself bound by existing sentencing practice, it has not tried to develop an entirely new system of sentencing on the basis of theory alone. Guideline sentences in many instances will approximate existing practice, but adherence to the guidelines will help to eliminate wide disparity. For example, where a high percentage of persons now receive probation, a guideline may include one or more specific offense characteristics in an effort to distinguish those types of defendants who now receive probation from those who receive more severe sentences. In some instances, short sentences of incarceration for all offenders in a category have been substituted for a current sentencing practice of very wide variability in which some defendants receive probation while others receive several years in prison for the same offense. Moreover, inasmuch as those who currently plead guilty often receive lesser sentences, the guidelines also permit the court to impose lesser sentences on those defendants who accept responsibility and those who cooperate with the government.

The Commission has also examined its sentencing ranges in light of their likely impact upon prison population. Specific legislation, such as the new drug law and the career offender provisions of the sentencing law, require the Commission to promulgate rules that will lead to substantial prison population increases. These increases will occur irrespective of any guidelines. The guidelines themselves, insofar as they reflect policy decisions made by the Commission (rather than legislated mandatory minimum, or career offender, sentences), will lead to an increase in prison population that computer models, produced by the Commission and the Bureau of Prisons, estimate at approximately 10 percent, over a period of ten years.

The Sentencing Table

The Commission has established a sentencing table. For technical and practical reasons it has 43 levels. Each row in the table contains levels that overlap with the levels in the preceding and succeeding rows. By overlapping the levels, the table should discourage unnecessary litigation. Both prosecutor and defendant will realize that the difference between one level and another will not necessarily make a difference in the sentence that the judge imposes. Thus, little purpose will be served in protracted litigation trying to determine, for example, whether $10,000 or $11,000 was obtained as a result of a fraud. At the same time, the rows work to increase a sentence proportionately. A change of 6 levels roughly doubles the sentence irrespective of the level at which one starts. The Commission, aware of the legal requirement that the maximum of any range cannot exceed the minimum by more than the greater of 25 percent or six months, also wishes to permit courts the greatest possible range for exercising discretion. The table overlaps offense levels meaningfully, works proportionately, and at the same time preserves the maximum degree of allowable discretion for the judge within each level. . . .

A Concluding Note

The Commission emphasizes that its approach in this initial set of guidelines is one of caution. It has examined the many hundreds of criminal statutes in the United States Code. It has begun with those that are the basis for a significant number of prosecutions. It has sought to place them in a rational order. It has developed additional distinctions relevant to the application of these provisions, and it has applied sentencing ranges to each resulting category. In doing so, it has relied upon estimates of existing sentencing practices as revealed by its own statistical analyses, based on summary reports of some 40,000 convictions, a sample of 10,000 augmented presentence reports, the parole guidelines and policy judgments.

The Commission recognizes that some will criticize this approach as overly cautious, as representing too little a departure from existing practice. Yet, it will cure wide disparity. The Commission is a permanent body that can amend the guidelines each year. Although the data available to it, like all data, are imperfect, experience with these guidelines will lead to additional information and provide a firm empirical basis for revision.

Finally, the guidelines will apply to approximately 90 percent of all cases in the federal courts. Because of time constraints and the nonexistence of statistical information, some offenses that occur infrequently are not considered in this initial set of guidelines. They will, however, be addressed in the near future. Their exclusion from this initial submission does not reflect any judgment about their seriousness....

[ROBINSON'S DISSENTING VIEW]

When it passed the Sentencing Reform Act of 1984, by a vote of 91 to 1 in the Senate and 316 to 91 in the House, the United States Congress committed the federal system to rationality and consistency in criminal sentencing. The Act built upon a decade of state experience in sentencing reform, but devoted resources on a greater scale and called for sentencing guidelines of a higher order of sophistication than any existing system. With that Act, Congress announced its inspired vision for modern American sentencing.

The vision was rationality in criminal sentencing. Rather than simply continuing past practices, the newly-created United States Sentencing Commission was directed to devise and articulate a sentencing policy. That sentencing policy was, in turn, to direct the decisions necessary for guidelines that would further the statutorily-defined purposes of sentencing—the imposition of just punishment, the deterrence of potential offenders, the incapacitation of dangerous offenders, and, where possible, rehabilitation. The ultimate goal was a rational sentencing system and a system that would be perceived as rational.

The vision was consistency in criminal sentencing. Instead of 1,042 federal judges and magistrates imposing discretionary sentences in more than 102,000 cases annually, the new Commission was to devise comprehensive and binding sentencing guidelines. Judges were to be bound by the guidelines unless there existed in a case an unusual factor that "was not adequately taken into consideration" by the Commission in drafting the guidelines. This would be a rare case because the guidelines were to take account of "every important factor relevant to sentencing." The guideline imprisonment range for each combination of offense and offender characteristic was to be narrow—not more than 25%.

The Congressional vision of sentencing reform also showed wisdom and self-restraint; Congress chose to forego the opportunities for posturing that come with crime and punishment issues. It took the high road, delegating the task of rational sentencing reform to what was to be an independent, nonpolitical Commission of experts, giving the Commission the power to promulgate the new sentencing system without further action by Congress.

Such invitations to visionary reform are the sort of rare events that inspire men and women to their greatest accomplishments. With the guidelines promulgated today, however, the vision dims.

[The Failure to Provide a Rational and Coherent System]

Of all of the goals of the Sentencing Reform Act, it is most unfortunate that the goal of rationality has been abandoned and even frustrated by these guidelines.

The Failure to Define a Rational and Coherent Policy and to Provide Sentences Calculated to Achieve the Statutory Purposes of Sentencing. The Act requires the Commission to establish guidelines designed to "assure the meeting of the purposes of sentencing [i.e., just punishment, deterrence, incapacitation of the dangerous, and rehabilitation]." Instead of calculating sentences to achieve such statutory purposes, however, the guidelines simply mimic the mathematical averages of past sentences.

To improve its ability to further the statutory purposes, the Commission was expected to "develo[p] and coordinat[e] research studies (including, for example, basic research on sentencing theories as well as applied research on the effectiveness of certain policies)." In contrast, the Commission neither undertook studies nor gave serious consideration to existing studies on the means of achieving deterrence and incapacitation. Nor did the Commission undertake studies or systematically consider existing studies on public perceptions of relevant sentencing factors and their appropriate weight for punitive purposes. While the guidelines' commentary sometimes gives reasons for the adoption of a particular policy, neither the guidelines nor the commentary cite a single empirical research study.

Rather than being guided by the statutory purposes of sentencing, the guideline drafting reflected simply a haphazard "fiddling with the numbers" that established the guideline sentences. The lack of a credible basis for the numbers became painfully obvious, however, and in the last few weeks, the intuitive approach was abandoned in favor of "past sentencing averages" as the primary basis for establishing guideline sentences. Because they simply continue what judges do, some will argue, the effects of these guidelines need not be explained or defended.

In addition to the criticisms that are detailed below, the guideline's claimed past-practice "principle" of drafting may be challenged on the grounds that it is not followed. Offenders under current practice receive sanctions other than imprisonment (e.g., fines, conditions of probation) in approximately 50% of the cases, yet the guidelines provide for imprisonment in all but the most minor cases. If the "theory" of the guidelines is that they simply follow past practices, how can the effect of the guidelines so dramatically deviate from past practice? My own view is that, in many cases, reducing the availability of probation or, at very least, making probation more punitive, would further the statutory purposes of sentencing. But the guideline drafters have rejected this sort of principled approach—i.e., devising sentences to meet the statutory goals....

The Failure to Rank Systematically Offenses According to Seriousness. Perhaps the most basic and the most obvious initial step in constructing rational guidelines is to systematically rank offenses according to their relative seriousness. Deterrence and just punishment both call for more serious offenses to be sanctioned more seriously, as does the Sentencing Reform Act. Unfortunately, the guidelines do not reflect a systematic ranking of offenses determined after analysis of existing research studies on relative societal harm and on public perceptions of relative seriousness.

As one might predict, the guidelines create significant anomalies. Under the guidelines, the judge could give the same sentence for abusive sexual contact that puts the child in fear as for unlawfully entering or remaining in the United States. Similarly, the guidelines permit equivalent sentences for the following pairs of offenses: drug trafficking and a violation of the Wild Free-Roaming Horses and Burros Act; arson with a destructive device and failure to surrender a cancelled naturalization certificate; operation of a common carrier under the influence of drugs that causes injury and alteration of one motor vehicle identification number; illegal trafficking in explosives and trespass; interference with a flight attendant and unlawful conduct relating to contraband cigarettes; aggravated assault and smuggling $11,000 worth of fish.

The Failure to Provide Different Sentences for Cases That Are Very Different in Seriousness: Promoting "Free" Harms and Ignoring Relevant Mitigations. The most basic function of any rational sentencing system is to provide appropriately different sentences for cases that are meaningfully different. Taking account of relevant aggravating and mitigating factors assures that additional harms will not go unpunished—that there are no "free" harms—and that significant mitigations will be reflected in an appropriately reduced sanction. These guidelines, however, systematically promote "free" harms and ignore relevant mitigations.

First, despite a "Relevant Conduct" provision that seems to suggest that the guidelines take account of most aspects of the offender's conduct, the only conduct or factors that the judge is permitted to take into account under the guidelines are those specifically listed in the applicable guideline section. For example, because the burglary guideline does not specifically aggravate the guideline sentence where the offender causes physical injury, the burglar who beats a homeowner will be treated the same as the burglar who does not. That is, the beating of the homeowner is "free" in burglary, as it is in a host of other offenses. . . .

The guidelines routinely ignore the difference between a completed offense and an unsuccessful attempt or a mere threat. Thus, the offender who telephones a witness in a trial and threatens to throw eggs at her car is treated the same as he would be if he had firebombed her car, seriously burning her. Indeed, under the guidelines, one judge can frequently give a *higher* sentence to an offender who unsuccessfully attempts or threatens an offense than another judge gives to an offender who successfully completes the same offense under the same circumstances.

The guidelines' treatment of multiple offenses is yet another source of systematically ignoring additional factors and additional offenses. The guidelines provide no additional sanction for additional offenses against the same victim during the same "transaction." Thus, upon convictions for transportation for the purposes of prostitution and for aggravated assault of one of the prostitutes, the court can only sanction the offender for the more serious offense; the other is "free." Nor is there additional sanction where multiple offenses are part of the same "common scheme or plan" against the same victim. Thus, after robbing the local postmaster once, all subsequent robberies of the postmaster as part of the same scheme are "free."

Even where offenses are unrelated and against different victims, frequently only the most serious offense is punished; the others are "free." Thus, if one assault victim suffers serious bodily injury, the wounding of two other victims on two other occasions will go unsanctioned under the guidelines. Still further, because amounts are often accumulated, multiple offenses of a similar nature are often treated as a single offense. Thus, an offender who defrauds two widows of $100,000 is treated the same as he would be if he had defrauded 40 widows of $5,000 each.

The guidelines' multiple-offenses provision appears to be in direct violation of the Sentencing Reform Act's requirement that the guidelines provide "an incremental penalty for each offense in a case in which a defendant is convicted of (A) multiple offenses committed in the same course of conduct that result in the exercise of ancillary jurisdiction over one or more of the offenses; and (B) multiple offenses committed at different times. . . ." . . .

[The Failure to Prevent Plea-Bargaining from Subverting the Goals of the System]

In addition to the guidelines' numerous directions to depart and the broad categories of departures, the judges are told that they need not follow the guidelines whenever the sentence is pursuant to a plea bargain, not an uncommon occurrence. This single invitation to depart, as a practical matter, may swallow the entire guidelines. It gives the judge and the counsel a ready means to routinely avoid the guideline sentences. Because 87% of all criminal cases in the federal system last year were disposed of through a plea bargain, it is likely that this provision will be the only "guideline" applicable to the overwhelming majority of sentences.

But this departure provision, like many of the invitations to depart in the guidelines, may be illegal. The statute simply does not permit judges to depart from the guidelines for "justifiable reasons" if the sentence is pursuant to a plea-bargain. The Act is explicit on this point:

> The court *shall* impose a sentence of the kind, and within the range, referred to in [the guidelines] *unless the court finds that an aggravating or mitigating circumstance exists that was not adequately taken into consideration by the Sentencing Commission in formulating the guidelines....*

It is not enough that the court feels that there are "justifiable reasons" to depart....

U.S.-JAPAN TRADE DISPUTE

April 17, 30, and May 1, 1987

Rising economic tensions between the United States and Japan came to a climax April 17 when the Reagan administration imposed sanctions on $300 million worth of Japanese exports to the United States. The action was in response to the alleged Japanese violation of an agreement to import more semiconductors and to stop "dumping" its own products on world markets. A visit by Japanese prime minister Yasuhiro Nakasone to Washington, where he met with President Ronald Reagan April 30 and May 1, and a number of conciliatory moves by Japan eased the deep-seated dispute, and a possible trade war was averted.

Although irritation with Japan over what many members of Congress and administration officials thought was its use of unfair trade practices precipitated the crisis, simmering resentment over Japan's huge trade surplus with the United States lay at the bottom of the dispute. The sanctions Reagan imposed represented the strongest economic action the United States had taken against Japan since World War II. At about the same time, both the U.S. Senate and House were preparing broad trade legislation designed to confront the myriad problems created by the burgeoning U.S. trade deficit.

Reagan lifted most of the sanctions during the economic summit of leaders of the seven industrialized nations in Venice, Italy, on July 8. (Venice economic summit, p. 525) *But feelings against Japan again ran high in July when it was discovered that the Toshiba Machine Company, a subsidiary of the giant Toshiba Corporation, had sold militarily sensitive technology to the Soviet Union.*

U.S.-Japanese Relations

Although tensions between the United States and Japan over trade reached a peak in 1987, other aspects of the relationship were widely viewed as good. Writing from Tokyo in the Washington Post, *correspondent John Burgess called the United States and Japan "the great 'odd couple' of the Western alliance." Burgess suggested that the closer the two countries moved together the "more unhappy" each became with the other.*

Military cooperation between the United States and Japan was close. Despite restrictions springing from pacifist and antinuclear sentiments, Japan was seen as the cornerstone of the U.S. strategic position in the Western Pacific.

U.S. Trade Deficit

Many members of Congress, administration officials, and others believed that Japan's large trade surpluses were in part a consequence of that country's unfair trading tactics in selling its products in world markets and of doors in Japan closed to imports from the United States and other countries. Indeed, a Japanese trade official had recently asserted that the United States could never sell a supercomputer to an agency of the Japanese government. In 1986 the U.S. trade deficit with Japan was a record $58.6 billion, representing more than a third of the U.S. worldwide deficit of $170 billion.

However, it was clear that many of the problems with regard to foreign trade lay in the United States. Writing in the New York Times, *Gerald M. Marks, director of the Chicago office of the Commerce Department, said that America must return "to the basics of product development, increased productivity, aggressive selling, and international marketing."*

Many economists believed that the trade deficit was directly linked to the large U.S. budget deficit, which equaled 5.3 percent of the gross national product (GNP) in 1986. In his economic message accompanying the 1987 Annual Report of the Council of Economic Advisers, Reagan had said that "a vote for more government spending is a vote against correcting our trade deficit." (Economic report, p. 117)

Reagan Administration Sanctions

Although a strong believer in free trade, Reagan March 27 announced that he planned to impose stiff tariffs on a wide array of Japanese electronic products. His announcement set off sharp drops in stock and bond markets and a further decline in the U.S. dollar.

The tariffs went into effect April 17. The action was in retaliation for what U.S. government officials regarded as Japan's failure to comply with a 1985 agreement to open its markets to American semiconductors and to stop selling Japanese semiconductors at prices below fair market value. For the most part, the semiconductors in question were the memory chips used in computers and other types of electronic gear. Some observers believed that the administration imposed the sanctions to avert passage by Congress of a stronger measure that might restrict the president in his dealings with Japan.

Nakasone Visit

Nakasone arrived in Washington April 29. Although warmly greeted by Reagan, he was pointedly not invited to address a joint session of Congress. Nakasone, whose popularity in Japan had recently plummeted, was known as an internationalist who had aligned Japan closely with U.S. military strategy.

During his meetings with Reagan April 30 and May 1, he pressed the president to lift the trade sanctions. He disclosed that he had called on the Bank of Japan to lower its rates on short-term money market instruments. Coupled with action by the Federal Reserve Board to raise rates in the United States, the move was seen as an attempt to strengthen the dollar in relation to the Japanese yen.

He also asserted that foreign contractors would be able to bid on the huge Kansai International Airport project and that a Japanese government agency would purchase a $20 million supercomputer manufactured in the United States. After Nakasone returned home, on July 21, Japan formally joined the U.S. Strategic Defense Initiative, known as the Star Wars program. Under the agreement, Japanese companies would not work on nuclear aspects of the project.

Trade Legislation

Members of the Senate and the House sought to address, in separate bills, an array of issues growing out of concern over U.S. trading problems. The House April 30 passed, 290-137, a package of measures to improve competitiveness and to strengthen the U.S. response to unfair trading practices abroad. By a far closer vote, 218-214, the House adopted an amendment that would force the president to reduce the huge bilateral trade surpluses of Japan and other countries. The amendment was offered by Rep. Richard A. Gephardt, D-Mo., who had made the trade issue the centerpiece of his campaign for his party's nomination for president in 1988. The Senate July 21 passed its own, less stringent trade legislation, 71-27. Reagan threatened to veto any trade legislation that included Gephardt's amendment.

A provision in the Senate bill would ban sales in the United States for two to five years of all Toshiba products and those of a Norwegian firm, Kongsberg Vaapenfabrikk. The two firms had been involved in the sale of sensitive metal-milling equipment and software to the Soviet Union. U.S. officials said there was a link between the sale of the equipment and quieter Soviet submarines.

Following are the texts of President Ronald Reagan's Proclamation 5631, his statement, and the memorandum for the United States Trade Representative, all concerning the imposition of tariffs on certain Japanese goods and issued on April 17, 1987; the remarks of President Reagan and Prime Minister Yasuhiro Nakasone on Nakasone's arrival in the United States on April 30, 1987; and the joint statement of the two heads of state on May 1, 1987:

PROCLAMATION 5631

INCREASE IN THE RATES OF DUTY FOR CERTAIN ARTICLES FROM JAPAN

By the President of the United States of America

A Proclamation

1. On April 17, 1987, I determined pursuant to section 301 of the Trade Act of 1974, as amended ("the Act") (19 U.S.C. 2411), that the Government of Japan has not implemented or enforced major provisions of the Arrangement concerning Trade in Semiconductor Products, signed on September 2, 1986, and that this is inconsistent with the provisions of, or otherwise denies benefits to the United States under, a trade agreement; and is unjustifiable and unreasonable and constitutes a burden or restriction on United States commerce. Specifically, the Government of Japan has not met its commitments to increase market access opportunities in Japan for foreign-based semiconductor producers or to prevent "dumping" through monitoring of costs and export prices of exports from Japan of semiconductor products. I have further determined, pursuant to section 301(b) of the Act (19 U.S.C. 2411(b)), that the appropriate and feasible action in response to such failure is to impose increased duties on certain imported articles that are the products of Japan.

2. Section 301(a) of the Act (19 U.S.C. 2411(a)) authorizes the President to take all appropriate and feasible action within his power to obtain the elimination of an act, policy, or practice of a foreign government or instrumentality that (1) is inconsistent with the provisions of, or otherwise denies benefits to the United States under, a trade agreement; or (2) is unjustifiable, unreasonable, or discriminatory and burdens or restricts United States commerce. Section 301(b) of the Act authorizes the President to suspend, withdraw, or prevent the application of benefits of trade agreement concessions with respect to, and to impose duties or other import restrictions on the products of, such foreign government or instrumentality for such time as he determines appropriate. Pursuant to section 301(a) of the Act, such actions can be taken on a nondiscriminatory basis or solely against the products of the foreign government or instrumentality involved. Section 301(d)(1) of the Act (19 U.S.C. 2411(d)(1))

authorizes the President to take action on his own motion.

3. I have decided, pursuant to section 301(a), (b), and (d)(1) of the Act, to increase U.S. import duties on the articles provided for in the Annex to this Proclamation that are the products of Japan.

Now, Therefore, I, Ronald Reagan, President of the United States of America, acting under the authority vested in me by the Constitution and the statutes of the United States, including but not limited to sections 301(a), (b), and (d)(1) and section 604 of the Act (19 U.S.C. 2483), do proclaim that:

1. Subpart B of part 2 of the Appendix to the Tariff Schedules of the United States (19 U.S.C. 1202) is modified as set forth in the Annex to this Proclamation.

2. The United States Trade Representative is authorized to suspend, modify, or terminate the increased duties imposed by this Proclamation upon publication in the *Federal Register* of his determination that such action is in the interest of the United States.

3. This Proclamation shall be effective with respect to articles entered, or withdrawn from warehouse for consumption, on or after April 17, 1987, except that it shall not apply with respect to articles that were admitted into a U.S. foreign trade zone on or before March 31, 1987.

In Witness Whereof, I have hereunto set my hand this seventeenth day of April, in the year of our Lord nineteen hundred and eighty-seven, and of the Independence of the United States of America the two hundred and eleventh.

[TARIFF INCREASES FOR CERTAIN JAPANESE EXPORTS]

I am today releasing the list of Japanese exports to the United States upon which tariffs are being raised, effective today, in response to Japan's inability to enforce our September 1986 agreement on semiconductor trade.

I announced my intent to take these actions on March 27 after it became apparent that Japan has not enforced major provisions of the agreement aimed at preventing dumping of semiconductor chips in third-country markets and improving U.S. producers access to the Japanese market. The health and vitality of the U.S. semiconductor industry are essential to America's future competitiveness. We cannot allow it to be jeopardized by unfair trading practices.

In my March 27 announcement, I said we would impose tariffs on $300 million in Japanese exports to the United States to offset losses suffered by American semiconductor producers as a result of the agreement not being fully implemented. The products upon which the tariffs are being raised were chosen to minimize the impact on American consumers and businesses. All these products are available from domestic or other foreign producers.

These actions are being taken to enforce the principles of free and fair trade. I regret that these actions were necessary. We will eliminate them as soon as we have firm and continuing evidence that the dumping in third-country markets has stopped and that access to the Japanese market has improved.

I am encouraged by recent actions taken by the Government of Japan to improve their compliance with the U.S.-Japan semiconductor agreement. I believe the agreement is in the best interests of both Japan and the United States, and I look forward to the day when it is working as effectively as it should.

[MEMORANDUM]

Memorandum for the United States Trade Representative

Subject: Determination Under Section 301 of the Trade Act of 1974

Pursuant to section 301 of the Trade Act of 1974, as amended (19 U.S.C. 2411), I have determined that the Government of Japan has not implemented or enforced major provisions of the Arrangement concerning Trade in Semiconductor Products ("the Arrangement"), signed on September 2, 1986, and that this is inconsistent with the provisions of, or otherwise denies benefits to the United States under, the Arrangment; and is unjustifiable and unreasonable, and constitutes a burden or restriction on U.S. commerce. I also have determined, pursuant to section 301 of the Act, to proclaim increases in customs duties to a level of 100 percent *ad valorem* on certain products of Japan in response. The tariff increases I am proclaiming shall be effective with respect to the covered products of Japan which are entered on and after April 17, 1987. I am taking this action to enforce U.S. rights under a trade agreement and to respond to the acts, policies and practices of the Government of Japan with respect to the Arrangement.

Reasons for Determination

In the Arrangement, the Government of Japan joined the Government of the United States in declaring its desire to enhance free trade in semiconductors on the basis of market principles and the competitive positions of the semiconductor industries in the two countries. The Government of Japan committed: (1) to impress upon Japanese semiconductor producers and users the need aggressively to take advantage of increased market access opportunities in Japan for foreign-based semiconductor firms; and (2) to provide further support for expanded sales of foreign-produced semiconductors in Japan through establishment of a sales assistance organization and promotion of stable long-term relationships between Japanese purchasers and foreign-based semiconductor producers. Finally, both Governments agreed that the expected improvement in access to foreign-based semiconductor producers should be gradual and steady over the period of the Arrangement.

Although the Government of Japan has taken some steps toward satisfying these obligations, they have been inadequate; foreign-based semiconductor producers still do not have access in that market equivalent to that enjoyed by Japanese firms.

In the Arrangement, the Government of Japan also committed: (1) to prevent "dumping" through monitoring of costs and export prices of semiconductor products exported from Japan; and (2) to encourage Japanese semiconductor producers to conform to antidumping principles. Again, the Government of Japan has taken steps toward satisfying these obligations, but they have been inadequate.

Consultations were held with the Government of Japan on numerous occasions between September 1986 and April 1987 in order to enforce U.S. rights under the Arrangement and to ensure that the Government of Japan undertake concerted efforts to fulfill its obligations under the Arrangement. To date these obligations have not been met.

On March 27, 1987, I announced my intention to raise customs duties to a level of 100 percent *ad valorem* on as much as $300 million in Japanese exports to the United States in response to the lack of implementation or enforcement by the Government of Japan of major provisions of the Arrangement. I also announced that the products against which retaliatory action would be taken would be selected after a comment period ending April 14, 1987. Finally, I announced that sanctions would remain in effect until there is firm and continuing evidence that indicates that the Government of Japan is fully implementing and enforcing the Arrangement.

This determination shall be published in the *Federal Register*.

[REMARKS AT NAKASONE'S ARRIVAL]

The President. It's a pleasure today to welcome again Prime Minister Nakasone, Mrs. Nakasone, trusted friends, and he is the elected leader of a valued ally, which is also one of the world's great democracies.

The good will and cooperation between Japan and the United States has been a tremendous boon to both our peoples. Such relationships as our countries enjoy and benefit from are an historical rarity. Great care has been taken over four decades by political leaders on both sides of the Pacific to mold and create this gem of friendship which is of such immense value.

This hasn't been easy; it has taken effort on both sides. Ours, after all, is a dynamic and changing friendship, filled with all the energy and spirit which one would expect between two robust peoples. Today our governments must meet the great responsibility of overseeing a continued, positive evolution between the United States and Japan. I have confidence in your judgment, and by working together, any problem we face can be solved.

Even the closest of friends have differences. Ours is the challenge of keeping trade and commerce, the lifeblood of prosperity, flowing equitably between our peoples. To do that, we must address the current unsustainable trade balance. It has spawned calls for protectionism that would undo the shining economic accomplishments we've achieved together. If history tells us anything, it is that great advances in the human condition occur during times of increasing trade. Conversely, it is also clear that interruptions in international commerce result in stagnation and decline.

We recognize the domestic political pressures that play a part in the decision-making processes of our respective countries, but we also know that it is the long-term well-being of our societies that must govern. Today the trade system is in need of adjustment, yet the answer is not in restrictions, but in increased opportunities. So together, let us seek positive solutions.

As we've learned, progress will not happen on its own; tangible actions must be taken by us both. Mr. Prime Minister, I have heard outlines of new measures that you are considering, and I'm most encouraged by what appears to be a commitment to policies of domestic growth and the expansion of consumer demand in Japan—something we strongly believe will have a positive effect on the trade balance. I look forward to exploring these new approaches with you in our meetings today.

Americans firmly believe that the free flow of goods and services, accentuated with head-on and above-board competition, benefits everyone. We would like to see Japan, for example, open its markets more fully to trade and commerce. Many of our companies in manufacturing, agriculture, construction, and the financial and high technology industries want to fully participate in the Japanese market. This, too, would also provide the benefits of lower prices in Japan.

Mr. Prime Minister, there's an unseen bridge that spans the vast Pacific, a bridge built by the hard work, commercial genius, and productive powers of our two peoples. We must strive to see that it is maintained in good order and is traveled with equal intensity in both directions, carrying the goods and services that improve lives and increase happiness.

The bridge to which I refer rests on the firm bedrock of democracy. Today free government and free economics complement one another and are the basis of our Pacific partnership. Today Japan and the United States, with two of the world's most powerful economies, share heavy global responsibilities. Your country's skillful leadership at last year's Tokyo summit demonstrated the role Japan now plays. As we prepare for the upcoming summit in Venice, our two governments will continue working closely together, fully appreciating that our cooperation has much to do with prosperity enjoyed throughout the world. The summit is an opportunity to look to the future, to ensure the peace and prosperity of the last 40 years is maintained and strengthened as we approach the new century.

Similarly, our mutual dedication to the cause of peace and security has had vast implications, especially on the Pacific rim, where the upward thrust of human progress is so apparent. We're well into the third decade of the 1960 U.S.-Japan mutual security treaty, and we look forward, Mr. Prime Minister, to continuing and expanding upon our security cooperation.

I am pleased to have this opportunity to speak directly with Prime Minister Nakasone on the bilateral and international issues. It was a hundred and twenty years ago since Commodore Perry first arrived on the shores of Japan. Commodore Perry sent a message, explaining his purpose to be "a mutual interchange of those acts of kindness and good will which will serve to cement the friendship happily commenced and to endure, I trust, for many years."

Mr. Prime Minister, in coming to our shores, we welcome you in that spirit. Let us, too, cement the friendship happily commenced so that it will endure for many years.

Prime Minister Nakasone, Mrs. Nakasone, we most sincerely welcome you.

The Prime Minister. Mr. President, ladies and gentlemen, thank you very much for your warm words of welcome. It gives me great pleasure to make an official visit to the United States at your invitation and to have this opportunity, together with my family, to meet again with you and Mrs. Reagan.

Since I assumed the Office of the Prime Minister of Japan, I have consistently made my utmost efforts to strengthen further the friendly and cooperative relations between our two countries. Today the relations are basically strong and sound. In addition to our bilateral cooperation in many areas, the two countries are working closely together to solve the political and economic problems facing the world.

Mr. President, the United States is continuing a genuine effort to build upon the potential agreements reached in Reykjavik on arms control, to lay a solid foundation for world peace. For the success of such efforts, it is now more important than ever to strengthen solidarity among the Western nations.

Looking towards the upcoming summit meeting in Venice, I strongly hope that my visit will prove to be constructive from this global perspective, as well. If our two countries are to fully discharge our global responsibilities, it is essential that our bilateral relations develop on an unshakable foundation.

I am deeply concerned that serious frictions on the trade and economic issues are on the rise between our two countries. We should not allow such a situation to undermine the friendship and mutual trust between our two countries. Throughout my visit, I intend to state clearly the policy measures Japan has taken so far and will take in the future for overcoming these problems. At the same time, I will listen carefully to the views of the administration, the Congress, and the people of the United States.

I have journeyed across the Pacific Ocean knowing that at times one must sail on high waves. But I hope that my visit, with everyone's assistance, will offer maximum beneficial results for our two countries.

Mr. President, in your Inaugural Address in 1981, you said, "We have every right to dream historic dreams." With energetic leadership, the American people have built this great nation constantly moving forward and aspiring to seek out new frontiers. This pursuit of heroic dreams forms the driving spirit of your nation. We, the Japanese people, have built our present nation desiring to occupy an honored place in the international society and determined to contribute to world peace and prosperity. I am determined to exert all my efforts, too, so that our two peoples can dream heroic dreams together, looking towards a bright future for all mankind.

Thank you.

JOINT STATEMENT

President Reagan and Prime Minister Nakasone reaffirmed their commitment made at the 1986 Tokyo Summit to strengthen international economic policy coordination. They welcomed the progress that has been made toward this end, including the commitments and action embodied in the Louvre Accord, and in the recent statement of the G-7 [1] in Washington. They agreed that reducing the large trade imbalances of the U.S. and Japan—which they view as politically unsustainable—is a key objective of their policy efforts.

In this regard, the President emphasized his determination to reduce the U.S. budget deficit. He also pledged to pursue vigorously policies designed to improve the competitiveness of American industry, and to resist firmly protectionist pressures. Prime Minister Nakasone outlined his plan to take vigorous action to stimulate domestic growth in Japan. This action includes the step just taken by the Bank of Japan to begin operations to lower short-term interest rates. The Ministry of Finance supports this action. Other short and medium-term policy actions to stimulate growth will include: support for the governing Liberal Democratic Party's proposals for near-term enactment of a comprehensive economic package, including unprecedented front-loading of public works expenditures and fiscal

[1] G-7, or the Group of Seven, is a reference to the seven countries that participate in the annual economic summits.

stimulus measures amounting to more than 5 trillion yen; further measures to liberalize Japanese financial markets; and redoubled efforts to implement the recommendations for structural reform in the Maekawa Report.

The President and Prime Minister agreed that outstanding trade issues between the two countries need to be resolved expeditiously. In this connection, they referred to the specific discussion of trade policy matters in their respective departure statements.

The President and Prime Minister agreed that a further decline of the dollar could be counterproductive to their mutual efforts for stronger growth in their economies and for reduced imbalances. In that connection, they reaffirmed the commitment of their governments to continue to cooperate closely to foster stability of exchange rates.

POPULATION INSTITUTE REPORT

April 19, 1987

Without conscientious control measures the world's population could double to 10 billion in forty-one years, according to a report issued by the Population Institute April 19. The report, Gaining People, Losing Ground: A Blueprint for World Population Stabilization, *recommended a worldwide program of contraception, counseling, and education to help stem the rising population tide. The report, written by Werner Fornos, president of the institute, described the population control efforts and prospects for twenty developing countries.*

The report warned that unchecked population growth could continue to deplete ecological resources, place unbearable strains on developing economies, and contribute to social unrest. It criticized the U.S. decision to cut funding to groups advocating population control by nearly $70 million since 1984. "To many nations in the developing world, for whom mounting population pressures are not abstract policy issues but are a matter of life and death, the U.S. retreat from international cooperative efforts seems capricious and even mean-spirited."

The report recommended action, stressing that population control was a viable social issue that could be addressed with the support of the industrialized countries of the world: "[T]he world today possesses all the tools it needs to bring population growth into a more stable pattern. In this sense, world population growth is not a problem, but a challenge."

Characteristics of Growth

The catalyst for population growth, according to the report, was the imbalance between birth rates and death rates: birth rates had fallen in recent years, but death rates had declined more rapidly. As a result, the world's population now increased at a rate of 80 million per year. Ninety percent of this increase occurred in less-developed countries. The report listed several countries—Kenya, Jordan, Iran, Honduras, Haiti, and Vietnam among others—whose populations would double within twenty years at present growth rates.

The report also made clear that rapid urbanization, already rampant in the developing world, would continue if present demographic trends held true. By the year 2000, forty-six cities would have populations of more than 5 million, and twenty-one cities would have populations of 10 million. (By comparison, only three cities had populations of more than 10 million in 1975.) Mexico City, the most heavily populated city in the world, would be inhabited by 26 million people.

Another characteristic revealed by the report was the "phenomenon of younger and younger populations." This swelling number of youth would place enormous demands on already strained educational systems, job markets, housing, transportation, and basic governmental services. These trends could result in huge urban centers filled with youth who were idle, uneducated, and poor—a condition likely to exacerbate social tensions.

The report stated that unchecked population growth often led to increases in the risk of child mortality and in the number of unwanted pregnancies. The United States had cited opposition to abortion among its reasons for cutting support to population control groups, but the decline in aid had the opposite effect, according to the report. Inadequate population control methods had led to a worldwide increase in the number of abortions and the number of unsafe abortions. In Brazil, for example, 40 percent of the public health budget for obstetrical and gynecological services was used caring for women injured in self-inflicted or "back alley" abortions. A more indirect effect of population growth was the strain on public health services, particularly in rural areas. In urban areas, crowded housing conditions made adequate sanitation more difficult to provide, thus producing areas ripe for disease.

Ecologies and Economies

Perhaps the most alarming impact of population growth on the environment, according to the report, was the depletion of fixed natural resources such as oil and coal. But the effect on renewable resources, such as forests, water, and soil, was equally devastating. Growing populations in many parts of the developing world were beginning to exceed the carrying capacities of their environments and to affect the cycle of rain and water recovery. Ecologists found that in parts of Asia, Latin America, and Africa rapid deforestation was followed by a decline in rainfall. This, in turn, affected the capacity to grow new vegetation cover and encouraged erosion.

These factors—reduction of soil fertility, loss of ground cover, reduction in precipitation, and soil erosion—combined to produce a proliferation of desert land. The report cited Ethiopia as an example of this desertification. Only 4 percent of the country had forest cover—down from 40 percent in 1900—and the encroachment of deserts was currently measured in miles each year. The destruction of rainforests, at a rate of 27 million acres lost a year, represented a serious threat to the world's biological diversity. As a result of these ecological changes, agricultural productivity declined in a number of Third World nations. In virtually every African nation, per capita agricultural productivity and per capita income had fallen consistently since the late 1970s. And while Africa's population has grown by 3 percent each year, its food supply has increased by only 1 percent a year.

Countries unable to produce enough food were forced to depend on foreign sources. The report cited Nigeria, which resisted family planning efforts when its economy skyrocketed as a result of increased oil prices in the 1970s. Faced with a drop in oil prices, the country in March 1987 began an ambitious program to stem population growth.

Recommendations

Despite the good intentions of many nations in the developing world, the report claimed that recent advances in growth control could not be maintained without substantial monetary support from the United States. It recommended that the United States return to its advocacy role in helping to curb the world's population by restoring full funding to international groups that support such policies.

The status of women, infant mortality, age at marriage, and breastfeeding practices were found to affect fertility and population growth. Educational efforts needed to be focused on these areas as well as on the direct dissemination of information on family planning. In addition the report called for increased government funding of research on contraception methods.

Finally, the report urged the U.S. Congress to reassess its funding commitment to population control. "[T]he Congress must ask not only how much it will cost to fund population programs," the report said, "but also what will be the costs of not *funding them. . . . [I]f our actions are inadequate, no amount of U.S. dollars later will be able to break the powerful cycle of overpopulation, economic and environmental deterioration, and human despair."*

Following are excerpts from Gaining People, Losing Ground: A Blueprint for World Population Stabilization, *released April 19, 1987, by the Population Institute:*

Gaining People, Losing Ground

When the world's population soared past the five-billion mark recently, the public announcement merited a five-inch mention on the bottom of page B-8 of the New York Times. There were public expressions of concern, calls for action, and a brief flurry of newspaper editorials. But the attention soon faded and the world returned to what some say the world does best—reproducing itself.

In 1986 alone, the world has added another 87 million people to its numbers. By the time this day is out, still another 345,600 human beings will have been born onto this planet....

For more than 20 years the demographic trends of world population and its likely impact on the world's economy, environment, and human community have been clear. And yet public understanding of these issues remains limited.

Chief among the reasons why Americans tend to avoid confronting the issues related to world population growth is the intimidating scope of the problem. Like the number of dollars in the national debt, the issues of population are defined in billions and multiple millions, and their sheer size can blur comprehension and inspire avoidance.

And yet if we permit the six-billion mark or the eight-billion mark to pass casually as we have the fifth, our children will pay the price. For the world they inherit from us will be one in which the nations of the developing world will have lost the struggle for economic self-sufficiency. Staggering under the weight of huge and impoverished populations, having overtaxed and depleted their once-renewable natural resources, many of these nations would descend into a fierce cycle of economic deterioration and political and social instability.

This bleak scenario does not arise from any defeatism or cynicism. Rather, it is founded on the most objective and realistic demographic data available and on science's best knowledge of the relationships between population and world environment. And it is offered in stark contrast to the striking opportunities and possibilities we now have for a far brighter international future. For the fate of the world is not sealed; it is being determined by the choices and decisions we are now making....

World population actually should be some cause for optimism, because it is one social issue that we can really do something about.... [T]he world today possesses all the tools it needs to bring population growth into a more stable pattern. In this sense, world population growth is not so much a problem as it is a challenge.

We are today at a critical juncture. The Free World still stands as a positive example of prosperity and opportunity to much of the developing world. And, just as important, the nations of the Third World can still reasonably expect to follow that example of economic development. Although their success in reaching economic self-sufficiency has been slower in coming than some imagined 20 or 30 years ago—hampered in part by booming population growth—the economies and often-rich natural resources of many of these developing nations remain strong and plentiful enough to propel their populations toward greater prosperity.

That goal is clearly essential to a stable, democratic world. Achieving that end, however, will require sustained assistance from industrialized Western nations, wise economic planning, and, not least of all, responsible strategies for limiting population expansion....

Where We Stand Now: Recent Population Trends

The "population crisis" is of very recent origin.... The number of people inhabiting the earth remained quite stable from earliest recorded history through the Renaissance.... Throughout that long period, the world's birth rate remained very high, but was necessarily so because the death rate was equally high. Despite occasional surges in births or deaths with the occurrence of good harvests or epidemics, the net result over time was very slow and steady population growth.

The picture began to change, however, in the 1800s, when industrialization and improvements in nutrition, agriculture, sanitation and medicine began to lower the death rate dramatically. Death rates fell first in the industrialized nations of Europe and North America, and because birth rates were slower to adjust, population then began to grow markedly.... Eventually, however, these nations reduced their birth rates in concert with rising standards of living, and population growth slowed so that today it is negligible across Europe and only slightly greater in North America.

This movement—starting with high but balanced birth and death rates, followed by imbalance as deaths decline, and completed when birth rates fall to restore balance at a lower level—is known as "the demographic transition." In the 1950s, academicians believed that Third World nations would follow the industrialized world in making this transition to economic development and stable population. These observers did not anticipate, however, that as many as 100 developing countries would become lodged in a "holding pattern" in the middle stage, with still-high birth rates and lowered death rates.... The longer these countries remain in this stage, and the more their populations swell as a result, the more difficult it becomes for them to achieve economic development and complete "the demographic transition" to industrialized economies and stable populations.

The doubling time for many of these countries—that is, the number of years required for a given population to double its size—is less than a single generation. The populations of Kenya, Jordan, Iran, Honduras, Haiti, and Vietnam, as only a few examples, will require no more than 20 years to double their populations at the present growth rates. The total population of the entire African continent will double in just 24 years....

Those statistics are in stark contrast to demographic trends in the industrialized Northern Hemisphere. Population growth in Europe leveled off after World War II. In recent years, a handful of European nations, namely West Germany, Denmark, and Hungary, have actually experienced small reductions in their populations. And virtually every other European nation has achieved or approaches zero population growth. Although the United States and Canada have been somewhat slower to scale back their growth rates, and although the United States is presently experiencing something of a "baby boomlet," North America's population growth rate too has slowed to a modest 0.7 percent....

Decline and Destabilization: Characteristics of Present Growth

The result of this discrepancy between booming Third World population growth and rather stable industrialized populations can be seen in a current worldwide demographic snapshot. The world's population of 5 billion will double itself in 40 years if current growth rates continue. A full 91 percent of that growth will occur in the developing world—in precisely the nations that can least afford to support that kind of expansion.

And as the size of world population increases, the time required to add the next billion people decreases. For world population to grow from 1 billion to 2 billion people, for example, took a century (1830 to 1930). From 2 billion to 3 billion took 30 years (1930 to 1960), despite the fact that the world fought the most destructive war in human history during this interval. The fourth billion arrived in only 15 years (1975). The fifth in 11 years (1986). And the sixth billion may take as little as nine years (1995)....

This accelerating growth is the inevitable result of "population momentum." Once a pattern of rapid growth is established, causing the number of young people to balloon, then even if fertility is radically curbed, it will require several generations for that "bulge"—all of whom are potential parents themselves to yet more children—to work its way through the population cycle. Consequently, even if recent gains can be extended throughout the Third World, an ambitious and uncertain goal, world population would continue to grow and would not peak until at least the year 2050. And then the stabilized population could be anywhere from a low of 7.4 billion to an incredible 12.4 billion, depending on how successful we are in the immediate future in changing present growth patterns.

A great deal of that population growth will take place in the Third World's congested urban centers.... Many Third World cities are already clogged by people who migrated from depressed rural areas in search of job opportunities. Unskilled and finding few jobs once they arrived, these rural migrants often have ended up settling in squalid shantytowns surrounding the cities. As these urban centers have swelled with the unemployed and the homeless, their populations have stretched fragile local economies in which food, shelter, drinking water, and fuel are already in short supply.

Urban congestion and unemployment has pushed a number of developing nations to launch relocation programs (some of which are more voluntary than others) designed to encourage the resettlement of urban dwellers to sparsely populated and undeveloped rural areas. Indonesia, Egypt, Tanzania, Ethiopia, and Brazil, among others, have initiated resettlement programs. Each such program, however, has met with only limited success, in some cases because of resistance in the target population and in some cases because the lands chosen for settlement were unproductive or non-arable areas. . . .

. . . If present demographic trends are not altered, the populations of most major African cities, already wracked by poverty, will double in a single decade. . . .

This urbanization is by no means limited to Africa. In 1950, in the entire developing world, only three cities had populations greater than 5 million; by the year 2000, there will be 46 such cities. While only three of those cities had populations greater than 10 million in 1975; by 2000, there will be 21. Most of these cities are today already clogged with the poor, and unemployment rates higher than 25 percent are common.

The population of Dhaka, Bangladesh, for example, already suffers from 30 percent unemployment and one of the highest population density rates in the world. Yet, its population, 4.9 million in 1985, will swell to perhaps 11.2 million by the year 2000. Even then, there would be 15 other Third World megacities with even larger populations. Mexico City, the largest, would be inhabited by an incredible 26 million people! . . .

Pressures on Societies

Related to the trend toward Third World urbanization is the phenomenon of younger and younger populations. With family size averaging seven or eight children in many parts of the developing world, the Third World is increasingly populated by the young. In Latin America and Asia, nearly 40 percent of the population is under 15 years old; in Africa a full 45 percent is under age 15. This compares with a steady 22 percent in Europe, the United States and Canada.

Furthermore, the proportion of youth in Third World populations will continue to grow larger as the 40 percent now under age 15 reach their prime reproductive years. . . . Even if programs are successful in persuading these groups to have smaller families than their parents had, simple arithmetic dictates that the proportion of populations under age 15 may grow much larger. . . .

As population growth overwhelms the capacity of developing economies to provide jobs and services, these trends will result in huge urban centers filled with youth who are idle, uneducated and poor, with little reasonable hope for the future. That would certainly exacerbate social splintering and ethnic tensions that already exist in many Third World nations, and would contribute to increased political instability. . . .

Pressures on Human Health

Family planning has clearly demonstrated benefits for human health, just as excessive population growth has the indisputable effect of undermining public health.... Studies have documented the link between birth spacing and a decline in infant and maternal mortality. When couples can be educated about how to allow more time between the birth of each child, the chances of survival for each child and for the mother are dramatically improved.

In Tunisia, Syria, Jordan, and Yemen, as examples, infants born less than two years apart are about two and a half times more likely to die in their first year than children born two years apart. The odds of survival improve even more if there is a four-year interval between births. This pattern was present in all 41 developing countries included in the World Fertility Survey, a massive social research project conducted by the International Statistical Institute.... That consistency suggests that as many as half of the 15 million infants who die each year in the Third World could be saved through better child-spacing....

In addition, by enabling couples to prevent unwanted pregnancies, family planning also helps to prevent abortions and all of their associated health risks. A Columbia University study has estimated that nearly 1,400 women die every day because of complications from pregnancy and abortion, many of which might not have been necessary had family planning been successfully employed.

The example of Brazil is illustrative. Until relatively recently, the Brazilian government did not promote family planning because of the opposition of the Catholic Church and the military. Not coincidentally, the number of unwanted pregnancies was high and many women turned to the prospect of illegal abortions. Consequently, fully 40 percent of the government's public health budget for obstetrical and gynecological services went toward caring for women injured in self-inflicted or "back-alley" abortion procedures.

Overpopulation has a less direct impact on public health as well. By undermining economic development and helping to keep large populations in poverty, overpopulation impedes the delivery of health care in developing nations, particularly to rural areas. In crowded urban centers, public sanitation efforts are undercut by the proliferation of shantytowns.... With poor sanitation, these areas breed disease and early death for many.

Pressures on Ecologies

Perhaps the most obvious impact that growing population has on the environment is in the depletion of fixed natural resources. When population increases significantly in a given area, there will naturally be greater demand on fixed natural resources, such as oil, coal, and certain minerals. This also, of course, results in greater pollution and destruction of other fixed and atmospheric resources, such as the ozone layer.

...[E]qually certain is the impact of overpopulation on renewable resource systems, such as forests, water, and soil. All such resources have "carrying capacities"—that is, the level at which they can provide maximum yields without injuring their ability to repeat that yield. Just as one can only withdraw so much money from an interest-bearing fund without dipping into the capital, so can one only chop down a certain number of trees in a forest each year without injuring its ability to replace those trees. Carrying capacities can sometimes be enlarged through technological advances, but when population advances faster than technology, carrying capacities are eroded.

Populations in many parts of the developing world have grown so large that they are beginning to exceed the "carrying capacities" of their environments. This is of crucial concern because the economic development of these nations depends largely upon the integrity of their natural resources. If the damage to local environments which results from over-population becomes too great, it will jeopardize that population's chances of ever achieving economic self-sufficiency. . . .

The loss of tree and vegetation cover, when it occurs on a grand enough scale, can affect the cycle of rain and water recovery. Without the vegetation to help absorb and retain moisture, the eventual recycling of water through transpiration, evaporation and new precipitation is crippled. Thus, ecologists have found that in parts of Asia, Latin America, and Africa where there has been rapid deforestation, there has also followed a decline in rainfall. This, in turn, affects the capacity to grow new vegetation cover.

The sandy and unstable soil of the African Sahel, for instance, once deprived of vegetation cover, is particularly vulnerable to erosion. Consequently, in an area where agricultural fertility is already weak, thousands of tons of topsoil and nutrients are washed away each year into the sea. On the global scale, 25 billion tons of arable topsoil vanish from the world's cropland every year.

These factors—the reduction of soil fertility, the loss of ground cover, reduction in precipitation, and soil erosion—have combined to cause the expansion of the vast deserts of the Sahel. The great deserts there have been slowly expanding in recent years, converting what were once acres of arable land into desert. A vivid example of this impact can be seen in Ethiopia. In 1900, 40 percent of Ethiopia was covered by trees and brush. The loss of this tree cover for fuelwood, however, has been so widespread that less than 4 percent of the country now has forest cover. The resulting encroachment of deserts—called desertification—is measured each year in miles. . . .

Population growth has upset the environmental balance of other parts of the world as well. In Indonesia, the government's population relocation program promoted the rapid settlement of formerly unpopulated parts of Borneo. As the new population cleared large areas of Borneo's rainforests for settlement and fuel, there followed a decline in rainfall and an eventual drying-up of swampland in the region. In early 1983, a subsequent fire, perhaps started when lightning struck dried timber, raged for several months destroying 3.5 million hectares of forest, and causing vast ecological destruction. Ecologists have estimated that it could take 700 years to restore the area's indigenous rainforests, if indeed they can ever be replaced.

Worldwide, the destruction of rainforests represents a serious threat to the world's biological diversity and the stability of the carbon cycle. Twenty-seven million acres of rainforests (about the same size as would cover the entire state of Pennsylvania) are lost each year, spurred by disruptions to ecological cycles, by the search for new farmland and fuelwood, and by the temptation to harvest the forests' timber as a quick, but not readily replaceable cash crop....

Pressures on Economies

...The related developments of declining soil fertility, desertification, and changes in rainfall have caused agricultural productivity to decline in a number of Third World nations. Africa used to be an exporter of grain to the rest of the globe. Now, in virtually every African nation, per capita agricultural productivity and per capita income have fallen consistently over the past 10 years....

And while African population grows by 3 percent each year, the continent's food supply increases by only 1 percent. The obvious result of that difference is that each African's share of the continent's food supply is getting smaller and smaller.... The Worldwatch Institute has charted the divergence in grain production per capita in Western Europe and Africa. The contrast is vivid. In 1950, the Western Europeans produced 234 kilograms of grain per capita, while Africans produced 157 kilograms per person. After 35 years, as Europe's population stabilized and Africa's ballooned, production diverged dramatically; Africa's grain production had lost ground to 150 kilograms per capita, while Western Europe's had soared to 501 kilograms per person....

When prolonged declines in agricultural productivity coincide with consistent increases in population, the unavoidable consequence is increased dependence on foreign sources of food.... Concerns over "food security" have helped to convince some reticent Third World governments of the need to control population growth.

Oil-producing Nigeria is a timely example. In the 1970s boom years of the Organization of Petroleum Exporting Countries (OPEC), when skyrocketing oil prices were raising Nigeria's per capita income, the government believed it could provide for any sized population and resisted family planning efforts. More recently, however, as oil prices have plunged, taking Nigeria's wealth down with them, the Nigerian government has rethought its policy. Faced with an increasingly enormous population and a seriously weakened economy, Nigeria in March 1987 embraced one of the continent's most comprehensive and ambitious policies to tame population growth....

Fertility—defined as the number of children an average woman will have in her lifetime—and standards of living are inextricably linked. The desire for large families is evident in many parts of the Third World. In

Mauritania and Senegal, for example, married women report desiring an average of about nine children. . . . When childhood mortality is high and living standards are low, there is an apparent incentive to have more children under the assumption that increasing the number of offspring will increase the chances of financial security in older age.

In this way, rising fertility and declining living standards reinforce each other. With greater numbers of children, per capita income declines. As poverty increases, along with a related increase in infant mortality, it fuels the desire to have more children. In precisely the same way, declining fertility and improving standards of living reinforce each other. Higher living standards diminish the need for parents to have large families. As family size declines, per capita income rises and living standards improve.

These two cycles operate on the family level and on the national level—the first characterized by rapidly increasing population and poverty (as in Africa), and the reverse cycle by stable population and rising economic well-being (as in South Korea and Taiwan). The challenge is how nations can break out of the first cycle and into the second. . . .

Recent Progress

There have been some encouraging developments in the past two decades. Fertility and population growth rates in a number of countries have declined. In the industrialized world, they have nearly leveled off.

In the developing world, there have also been a few success stories. Thailand, South Korea, Taiwan, and Colombia have all had remarkable success in curbing population growth through committed and well-managed programs to promote voluntary family planning. China's well-publicized program to encourage the one-child family norm has also led to a sharp decline in population expansion. And in a country that accounts for more than 20 percent of total world population, such a decline can have a very important impact. . . . Even so, however, there is a long way to go, and there is no assurance that the recent positive trends will continue in the absence of sustained assistance from the industrial world. . . .

A growing number of Third World governments have arrived at the realization that economic development is not possible without more stable population growth. Some of these governments, like Bangladesh, have declared the reduction of population expansion to be the nation's first priority. The importance of this transformation in outlook for the Third World toward population planning cannot be overestimated. In Bucharest in 1974, at the first major international conference held to discuss rapid world population growth, it was the nations of the industrialized world that sounded the alarm that overpopulation threatened economic development. Delegates from North America and Europe pressed for the recognition of the relationship between population and development, while most Third World delegates reacted with skepticism. Some suspected racist motivations for American and European calls for limits to African and Asian fertility.

Ten years later, however, when the nations reconvened in Mexico City for the second U.N. International Conference on Population, it was the nations of the Third World that sounded the alarm. Having seen the increasingly vivid impact of rapid population growth in their countries, the Third World delegates led the conference in pressing for a more coherent international response.

The emergence in the Third World of a recognition of the problem and a commitment to work toward solutions has made possible the recent progress that some developing nations have made in curbing fertility. Now one of the greatest uncertainties is whether the United States and other industrialized nations will stand by their original commitments to help.

Factors Affecting Fertility

There are a great many ways to reduce fertility and population growth. ... [F]amily planning can directly reduce a nation's birth rate. Extending the availability of contraceptives is the single most effective way of reducing fertility. In addition, research and development of more convenient, cheaper, and more effective contraceptives can make a difference.

In less direct ways, an elevation in the status of women, delaying age at marriage, wider practice of breastfeeding, reductions in infant mortality, and government social security programs can each contribute to slower population growth.... [A] significant reduction in population expansion will require the successful employment of several of these approaches....

... [T]he most easily accomplished and effective among these options—the extension of family planning programs—really works. Financial investments in programs that encourage the use and increase the availability of family planning services yield direct positive results....

In developing countries with effective family planning programs, fertility declined an average of 30 percent between 1965 and 1975—compared with roughly 4 percent in countries with weak or ineffective family planning efforts and 2 percent in countries without any program.

Successful family planning programs consist of two basic elements: first, efforts to encourage couples to desire smaller families, and second, efforts to increase the availability and effectiveness of contraceptive methods. At bottom, no progress in reducing population growth can be made without three fundamental ingredients: the availability of contraceptives, motivation to use them, and the political will to encourage both.

While it is very true that 400 million people in the developing world want to limit the size of their families but lack the birth control or knowledge of family planning to do so, it is also true that some Third World couples continue to desire large families.

Those couples have desired large families for several reasons. First, in societies in which the status of women is not considered equal to men's, women are often denied options other than bearing and raising children. Second, and perhaps most important, a concern is shared by some Third World couples for raising a sufficient number of children who can later support them in their old age. In the largely agrarian societies of the developing world, there can be an additional motivation because children can double as farm laborers. And, finally, there are sometimes cultural factors that create a sort of peer pressure to bear more children. . . .

Education About Family Planning

The most effective strategy for overcoming these sorts of problems is education. It must be demonstrated to couples that having very large families diminishes the income available for each child. And that must be backed up by programs that provide couples with some assurance of financial security in their old age. . . .

The full range of family planning options—from abstinence and rhythm to the pill and sterilization—must be explained to prospective users. Successful government programs in Thailand, Indonesia, and other parts of the world have found that once couples understand exactly how contraception works, its benefits, and its potential drawbacks, their initial suspicions are dispelled and they can make informed choices to suit their situations. In fact, they often become enthusiastic about the promise family planning holds for a smaller, healthier, and more financially secure family. . . .

Age at Marriage

. . . A number of Third World nations in recent years have enacted their first laws setting a minimum age for marriage. In doing so, these countries have somewhat reduced early teenage fertility and, by postponing the birth of a woman's first child, have led to smaller average family sizes.

Beyond legislative efforts, however, the World Fertility Survey found that the two greatest factors influencing age at first marriage were employment and educational opportunities for young women.

The Survey found that in developing nations that had extended primary education for teenage girls, the average age at first marriage increased. . . . [S]ocieties expanding employment opportunities for young women also experienced rising ages at first marriage. Conversely, the Survey found that in societies without enlarged educational and employment opportunities for girls and women, females continued to marry at very young ages.

Overall, countries with high population growth rates continued to have low average ages at marriage, whereas countries with more successful population programs had experienced significant increases in such averages. . . .

Promoting Opportunities for Women

In societies in which women are confined to the roles of wife and mother, there is also typically high fertility. The nations of Africa and the Middle East stand out as examples.

On the other hand, in societies in which women are accepted in the work-force and there are alternatives to child-bearing, fertility usually declines. This has been the case with the industrialized nations of the Northern Hemisphere, and in developing countries such as Brazil, Mexico, Thailand, and South Korea....

The relationship between the status of women and fertility is much like that between population growth and impaired economic development: It is not always clear which phenomenon causes the other, nor can it usually be scientifically documented, but the two are almost always seen as a pair. Progress or decline in one category almost universally is seen in concert, respectively, with progress or decline in the other....

... [M]any nations have integrated into their population-control efforts programs to promote education and employment opportunities for women. Current statistics, however, demonstrate how far we have to go: women still do two-thirds of the world's work, but earn only 10 percent of its income and own less than one percent of its property.

Infant Mortality

Some couples in the Third World's impoverished countries feel pressure to have a sufficient number of children to help provide family income and security in the parents' old age. In many of these countries, medical and social conditions are such that many children will die before reaching their first birthdays....

It has been argued by some that if parents can be given a satisfactory assurance that all of their children will survive and reach adulthood, they will be more inclined to limit the number of their pregnancies....

Breastfeeding

Programs promoting breastfeeding also help to reduce fertility in two ways. The first and most direct way is that when a woman breastfeeds her child, it delays the return of ovulation, in some cases for as long as a year. While breastfeeding is an unreliable contraceptive method for an individual, it can prevent or delay a successive pregnancy for some months following a birth and can reduce overall fertility.

As a secondary impact, breastfeeding also can influence fertility by reducing infant mortality. By delaying second pregnancies, breastfeeding contributes to better child-spacing, which, in turn, greatly improves each child's life-chances. Also, breastfeeding often improves a newborn's nutritional intake over alternative methods of feeding....

A Closer Look at 20 Nations

The experiences of ... 20 developing nations ... suggest that over the past two decades many have heeded the message traditionally pressed by the United States and other industrialized nations that controlling population growth is an essential prerequisite to economic development. Some who learned that lesson early, like the nations of East Asia, have made substantial progress. Some others, like Mexico and Brazil, reached that conclusion somewhat later but have begun making up for lost time.

Still others, like many of the African nations, have only very recently demonstrated a willingness to tackle the problem, if necessary foreign assistance can be found. Finally, there remain a dwindling handful of Third World nations that cling to the belief that population pressures will be solved naturally through economic development. These nations, which include some of the developing world's poorest (such as Burma, Mongolia, Mauritania, and Mozambique), consider independent efforts to curb fertility to be unnecessary or even undesirable. . . .

There have been a few observers who have mistakenly assumed that because population growth rates have declined in all of the industrialized world and much of the developing world, there is no longer a "crisis" in world population. This is a dangerously misguided conclusion.

It is true that the world's "developed" nations have generally achieved very low population growth, but these nations account for only 25 percent of the world's population. It is also true that many developing nations have slowed their rates of population growth, but even the most successful among them are still growing quickly.

Any temptation toward complacency should be dispelled by noting that barely 20 percent of Third World couples now use family planning. If the world is to reach replacement fertility by 2000, that use must increase very soon to 80 percent, a level not often seen even in developed Western societies. . . .

Recent Setbacks in U.S. Assistance

The industrialized nations . . . spent much of the 1960s and 1970s engaged in a determined and sometimes arduous effort to persuade the governments of the developing world that they should act to control their population growth. Although some developing nations . . . required no persuasion, the majority of the Third World still viewed their booming populations as a stimulant, and not a hindrance, to their economic development. . . . Slowly, however—thanks in part to unwavering counsel from the United States and other industrialized countries, and in part to the increasingly unmistakable damage caused by unchecked growth—most Third World countries now seek slower growth. . . .

This policy of counsel and assistance has already yielded tangible gains. Lowered fertility and growth rates virtually the world over are due in no small part to external assistance. The happy progress seen in Thailand, Tunisia, Colombia, and elsewhere is the early fruit of this investment. Furthermore, across Africa, where high fertility has been the least receptive to change, there is now an emerging commitment to action on the population issue—a commitment which can be credited in good part to an intelligent and consistent donor country partnership. By all evidence, the international donor community is on the verge of reaping the returns on its investment in this continent so crucial to world progress.

That international partnership, and the progress it is beginning to produce, is now threatened, however, by faltering U.S. policy. After two decades of telling the developing world that it is not sufficient to wait for economic progress to "solve" the problem of rapid population growth, the U.S. government abruptly reversed this position at the 1984 United Nations Conference on World Population in Mexico City. America spent 20 years preaching independent efforts to moderate rapid population growth as a necessary component of any economic development plan. And just as the developing world was beginning to agree, the United States changed its mind. This view left the United States virtually alone among the 148 countries represented at the conference....

What damage this confusing policy reversal caused to the American (and international) objective of a more stable world population has been seriously compounded by steadily declining U.S. financial commitments to international population assistance.

U.S. Withdrawal from International Efforts

Traditionally, the channel through which the United States made its most significant contribution to world population stabilization was not direct, bilateral aid, but U.S. financial support for two international family planning programs, as well as a host of non-governmental organizations. The two major programs—the United Nations Fund for Population Activities (UNFPA) and the International Planned Parenthood Federation (IPPF)—as well as their non-governmental colleagues, had several distinct advantages over direct "government-to-government" aid.

For one thing, the U.S. government is reluctant to enter, or is not always welcome in some Third World countries with sensitive political situations. Using multi-lateral, umbrella organizations such as UNFPA and IPPF provides the United States with a vehicle for accomplishing its population policy objectives without upsetting delicate relationships with these foreign governments. A second advantage is that U.S. contributions to international agencies can encourage other donor nations to increase their contributions as well....

In the past three years, however, in a sharp departure from traditional, bipartisan U.S. population policy, the U.S. government has withdrawn its support from both IPPF and UNFPA, casting serious doubts on the futures of these and other cooperative international efforts.

The reason given by the United States for cutting off its support in both cases was the same—opposition to abortion. And yet in both cases, the withdrawal of support has not caused a decline in abortions and may well have caused an increase.

The first to lose U.S. aid was IPPF, the global arm of the respected American family planning organization. The program was a casualty of the new U.S. population policy unveiled at the Mexico City conference. Part of that policy forbids U.S. financial support to any private organization that counsels, refers, or provides abortion services to women, even if those services are paid for entirely by private contributions.

It should be noted that an amendment to the Foreign Assistance Act, ...

passed by Congress in 1973, already prohibited any U.S. tax dollars from being used to "pay for the performance of abortions as a method of family planning or to motivate or coerce any person to practice abortions." The new "Mexico City Policy" essentially extended that prohibition to cover not only tax dollars, but even private dollars spent by a tax-supported institution. As with the 1973 law, the new policy prohibited support for abotions of any kind, including the strictly voluntary abortions provided by IPPF and other family planning organizations.

In IPPF's case, U.S. government aid, in accordance with the 1973 law, did not go toward abortion-related services. Furthermore, of IPPF's private, non-restricted budget, less than one half of one percent actually went toward providing voluntary abortions. Nonetheless, the new U.S. regulation was pressed by some activists as grounds for cutting off U.S. support for IPPF, which remains by far the most effective and accomplished private family planning organization active in the Third World.

Efforts to correct this policy are already underway in Congress. The U.S. Senate Committee on Foreign Relations, in its 1988 authorizing legislation, has sought to bring administration policy back into line with the laws established by Congress. The Committee has adopted an amendment offered by Kansas Republican Senator Nancy Kassebaum that would prevent the administration from penalizing multi-lateral or non-governmental organizations from carrying out lawful activities with private funds. In its report on the amendment, the Committee stressed that its action is specifically intended to overturn the administration's policy. . .

The second international organization to lose U.S. aid was the UNFPA. The UNFPA is the largest multi-lateral, international organization working to promote family planning and population stabilization in the developing world and it derives most of its annual budget from support from industrialized Western member states.

U.S. aid to UNFPA was reduced by $10 million in fiscal year 1985 and was eliminated entirely in 1986 and 1987. The impact on UNFPA's budget is substantial because the United States had originally pledged to contribute $46 million in 1985. That pledge had already been incorporated into UNFPA's extended budget for program planning. Thus, the elimination of all U.S. aid meant a long-range disruption to UNFPA's efforts. The U.S. actions to cut off aid were taken to protest what the administration believes is a coercive abortion policy in China. In choking off funds to UNFPA in August 1986, the administration cited a provision in the 1985 Foreign Assistance Act that prohibits U.S. aid to any organization which "participates in the management" of a program of coerced abortions and involuntary sterilizations. The administration argued that because UNFPA contributions make up one percent of China's population program budget, the United States cannot legally support UNFPA.

Declining U.S. Aid

. . . Programs to promote family planning and stable population growth around the world make up only 4 percent of U.S. humanitarian assistance. The portion allocated for population programs is further restricted because foreign aid dollars go first to the State Department's priority clients: Israel, Egypt, Pakistan, and now Ireland. Only after priority programs in those nations have been funded, and after money is set aside for programs to curb terrorism and narcotics traffic, are the remaining programs—including all other foreign development aid and, finally, population assistance—permitted to compete for the funds left over.

In recent years, those leftover funds have dwindled. The U.S. government's commitment to international population assistance (which is part of the budget of the U.S. Agency for International Development) has dropped from $290 million in FY84 to $250 million in FY85, to $235 million in FY86. The FY87 allocation of $236.5 million was later reduced by 15 percent to create an emergency relief set-aside fund. For FY88, the Reagan administration has sought to erode the population assistance budget further, to $207 million, although the House Foreign Affairs Committee has moved to increase that to $222 million (still nearly $15 million less than was budgeted in the last fiscal year).

The sudden reversal of long-standing U.S. policy encouraging wise population strategies and the controversial withdrawal of U.S. support from UNFPA and IPPF have deeply concerned our Western allies and our friends in the Third World....

They do not understand why the United States, which for so long was leading forward-looking nations in the search for solutions, has now decided, in effect, to sit on its hands with regard to world population.

To many nations in the developing world, for whom mounting population pressures are not abstract policy issues but are a matter of life and death, the U.S. retreat from international cooperative efforts seems capricious and even mean-spirited.

This perception of the United States is too costly in the strategically important Third World. The stakes are too high, and the immediate opportunities for political, social, and economic progress are too great to shrug off....

A Blueprint for Survival: Recommendations

The nations of the world have made real and measurable progress in the past 20 years toward controlling the growth of their populations. The efforts made over two decades by the United States and other nations to build a consensus for action in the developing world are now paying off. Population growth rates have subsided in much of Asia and Latin America. In Africa, the final holdout in population planning, five major nations have or are presently announcing comprehensive national policies to curb future growth. Ten more are in the process of drawing up such policies.

These gains, made possible by outside financial and technical assistance, will be erased without it. For anyone who doubts that fact, the experience of Pakistan is edifying. There, the dramatic advances of an early national family planning effort, were all but wiped away by just a three-year suspension of government population programs in the 1970s. In 1975, just before the government suspended its efforts, fully three-quarters of Pakistani women reported knowledge of at least one method of family planning. When the next survey was taken in 1980, after the three-year lapse of efforts, that number had plunged to 25 percent.

The nations of the Third World, for all their charged commitment to curbing population growth, will fail without U.S. support. It costs money to educate far-flung, disparate rural peoples about family planning and it costs more money to then provide them access to contraceptives and essential services. . . .

Neither can America's industrialized allies be expected to bear the burden alone. The United States, by virtue of its history and place in the world economy, must share in the task, and it must share not only its wealth but also its knowledge and technical expertise.

For Americans prepared to take responsibility for the future world our children will inhabit, a number of steps that can and should be taken immediately. Most, though not all, of them cost money, but they are all cost-effective and, in combination, they extend hope to the developing world for a better, healthier, and more stable future:

- **Restore U.S. Population Policy:** The United States should recommit itself to the population policy it advocated for 20 years until its reversal in Mexico City in 1984. That policy acknowledges that rapid population growth can present a significant obstacle to economic development in the Third World. It also urges developing nations to set goals for future population growth and to help families who want to limit their numbers of children to do so through voluntary family planning. . . .

- **Restore U.S. Support For UNFPA:** The United States, for better or worse, has made its views clear in the international community about China's population program. Without entering the fray over whether the Chinese policy is sufficiently voluntary or whether the U.S. withdrawal was justified, it is enough to say that the United States has made its point.

  . . . Because no U.S. funds channelled through UNFPA were used in China, the withdrawal of these funds has not stopped a single Chinese abortion. What it has done is undercut UNFPA family planning programs in more than 120 other developing nations and denied many impoverished couples the birth control they have sought. In so doing, it is almost certain that the withdrawal of U.S. funds has resulted in more unwanted pregnancies and more abortions—not in China, but in countless anonymous cities and villages around the globe. Worse yet, many of those abortions will have been dangerous self-inflicted or illegal procedures that contribute greatly to maternal mortality. . . .

- **Restore U.S. Support for IPPF:** For the same reasons outlined above, the United States should restore its long-standing support for the International Planned Parenthood Federation. . . .

- **Restore U.S. Direct Aid For Population Programs:** Aside from

U.S. assistance to international cooperative efforts like UNFPA and IPPF, the United States has also backed away from its commitment to bilateral and direct population assistance. This retreat is reflected in the consistent declines in the population budget of the U.S. Agency for International Development, which offers bilateral population assistance in 30 Third World nations. These reductions have undercut long-established U.S. and international population programs and threaten to chip away at the fragile progress made in the recent past toward controlling population growth.

The Congress should turn aside future administration efforts to reduce population assistance funds and should restore these budgets at least to their 1984 levels.

• **Promote Comprehensive Population Policies Abroad:** In aiding and counseling developing countries seeking to curb population growth, the United States should continue to encourage governments to adopt a comprehensive approach. Such an approach, of course, promotes the acceptance and availability of family planning, but also includes programs to advance the status of women, encourage breastfeeding, delay age at marriage, and reduce infant mortality. Such a program, of course, also emphasizes that all efforts to limit family size must be strictly voluntary.

• **Spur R & D in New Contraceptives:** For some years, the federal government has been the primary financial supporter of research and development of new contraceptives. This research is important because it could well lead to safer, cheaper, more convenient, and more effective methods of birth control.... [P]rivate contraceptive manufacturers would not undertake much of [the research] without government incentives. The long-term investments required, the length of protracted government safety reviews, and the increasing difficulty of obtaining affordable liability insurance all deter companies from pressing ahead with contraceptive research and development....

Government-supported contraceptive research, in the United States and abroad, has yielded several promising products. Although each requires further testing for effectiveness and safety, each has fared quite well in preliminary tests....

The Cost and Benefit of Providing Services: Some New Projections

All research into world fertility agrees on at least one conclusion: There are over 400 million people in the developing world who want to limit the size of their families, but who do not have the knowledge or the means to do so.

Perhaps the most comprehensive of this research, the World Fertility Survey and the Contraceptive Prevalence Survey, conducted in 61 nations between 1972 and 1984, found that about half of those interviewed did not want a future pregnancy. Another 25 percent said they wanted to wait for at least two years before becoming pregnant. Therefore, all told, 75 percent wanted to avoid pregnancy, at least for the time being.

Yet, when these same individuals were asked about their knowledge of family planning and where to obtain it, only 40 percent said they knew where to get safe and effective contraceptives. Sixty percent did not know of any family planning source.

Even the 40 percent who reported knowledge of a family planning outlet often did not have effective access. Too often, prospective family planning clients must travel long distances, not infrequently to find the outlet closed or out of supplies or too busy to see them.

Or, they may find that contraceptives are priced beyond their means. Third World couples may earn a dollar a day or less—and then only when they can find work. A month's supply of contraceptives may be too costly for them. The immediate need for food usually wins out.

The fact that more than 400 million people in the developing world want family planning services but lack the access or money to secure them is encouraging to the extent that it suggests a receptivity to reducing average family size and population growth. But it is also intimidating because it gives us some idea of the financial commitment that will be required to provide them with the services they need. . . .

Currently, the international donor community spends approximately $500 million annually on population programs in the developing world, and Third World governments are spending three dollars for every one donated. The amount of money spent by the private sector—including employer contributions to family planning services, private foundations in the respective countries, and the individual couples themselves—is harder to fix, but probably totals another $200 million. . . .

. . . .[W]e estimate that roughly a billion dollars of new funds must be raised if the family planning and population goals of these nations are to be realized. . . . [T]he majority of the new money needed simply must come from the international donor community. For the approximate U.S. share of that total, that would require an increase in population spending of $600 million or about twice the fiscal year 1984 appropriation for such programs.

That is a substantial amount of money. . . . Actions to expand family planning services now may actually save the United States money in the future by making emergency relief efforts less costly.

To demonstrate that point, the Population Institute constructed a model in 1984 to determine what might have happened had Ethiopia launched a family planning program in 1970, at the same time certain other developing nations were taking such action. The model showed that a family planning program even half as effective as those in Thailand, Indonesia, or Mexico would have reduced the size of Ethiopia's 1985 population by 1.7 million—a number roughly equal to the people forced to rely on emergency food aid during that year's famine. . . .

An additional reason for making the investment in family planning services is the effect population growth has on economic development. It is imprudent to spend large sums of U.S. aid on economic development abroad without also working to control population growth....

The Tangible Results

...[T]he goals we have assumed are not exceedingly ambitious. They call for the roughly 100 developing nations with average family sizes now higher than four children to bring that average down to just four children....

If the developing nations with family averages of more than four children successfully reduce that average to four children per family by the year 2000 ... there would then be approximately 200 million fewer people in the world. By 2010, there would be almost 750 million fewer people, and by 2030, the world would be fully 3.2 billion smaller than if these nations maintained current family sizes averaging larger than four children....

The projections contained here for population growth based on extension of family planning services over the next several decades to all those who want them are truly encouraging. They depend, of course, upon the willingness of the United States and other donor nations to increase their financial commitments as outlined earlier. These data suggest that with sufficient international support world population can be brought into a more liveable pattern within a relatively short period of time.

A Call to Action: Conclusions

...Moreover, the United States can certainly not solve the problem by any unilateral effort. Ultimately, it is up to the developing world to win the fight for stable population growth. And, to that end, 45 heads of state from the developing world have demonstrated their willingness and commitment to a solution by signing the Statement on Population Stabilization....

In it, the leaders of some of the largest and most populous Third World nations agreed:

> Degradation of the world's environment, income inequality, and the potential for conflict exist today because of over-consumption and over-population. If this unprecedented population growth continues, future generations of children will not have adequate food, housing, medical care, education, earth resources, and employment opportunities. We believe the time has come now to recognize the world-wide necessity to stop population growth within the near future and for each country to adopt the necessary policies and programs to do so.

This agreement is vitally important because it represents one of the three basic ingredients required for progress toward an end to the world's population crisis: political leadership. Given sufficient political leadership, the other two ingredients—the availability of contraceptives and the motivation to use them—will follow. But the above declaration represents only one half of the political leadership necessary: that from the developing world. The other half—sustained and far-sighted political leadership in the industrialized world and the international donor community—must be proven anew.

. . . The United States can make a pivotal contribution toward an eventual solution by rejoining the international partnership it once had led.

It is true that responsible action, as outlined in the previous recommendations, will require more money than has been committed in recent years by the United States. And, in an era of fiscal restraint and painful budget cutbacks, it is fair to seek a rigorous justification for such spending. The Congress must ask hard questions about U.S. population policy and spending, because effective progress depends not only on the size of budgets, but also on how wisely those budgets are spent.

The status of women, infant mortality, age at marriage, breastfeeding and other factors all play important roles in influencing fertility and population growth. But the most effective way to reduce population growth is to do it directly: to extend to couples the information and access to family planning so that they may decide for themselves the number of their children.

Unlike building a new interstate highway or a new weapons system, spending on population programs cannot be successfully deferred. We have very real opportunities before us to wrestle population growth into a more stable pattern. The solution, built upon 20 years of international cooperation and investment, is within reach. But these opportunities exist now, in our world of 5 billion people and still-plentiful natural resources. If we choose not to grasp these opportunities, they will slip away. If we decide to wait until the world swells to 6 billion or 8 billion people (we will reach the former in less than 9 years) and until overpopulation and poverty have ravaged the natural and economic resources of the Third World, it will be too late.

If Americans now feel anguish over witnessing the recent human suffering and needless deaths in Ethiopia, just imagine a world in which virtually the entire Third World will be wracked by vast poverty and human misery. If Americans now think they have a problem with illegal immigration, imagine a world in which spreading despair will create tremendous new pressures on U.S. borders, especially from Latin America and the Caribbean.

And if Americans are now troubled by the specter of instability, revolution, and authoritarianism in the Third World, they have only to imagine the consequences of inaction, because the fragile seed of democracy cannot survive long in societies with escalating misery, crippled economies, and dying environments.

In shaping federal budgets, the U.S. Congress must ask not only how much it will cost to fund population programs, but also what will be the costs of *not* funding them. The investment required now is modest by any standard. And the returns will be great because in helping developing nations to control their population growth, the United States will also build stronger economies and friendships in the strategically important Third World. . . .

COURT ON DEATH PENALTY AND RACE

April 22, 1987

By a 5-4 vote the Supreme Court April 22 upheld Georgia's death penalty, despite statistical evidence that it was applied unevenly between the races. The data, which was accepted by both the majority and the minority, showed clearly that killers of white people were far more likely to receive the death penalty than killers of blacks. Nevertheless, the majority found that this evidence by itself was not enough to establish unconstitutional discrimination in McCleskey v. Kemp.

Justice Lewis F. Powell, Jr., wrote the Court's opinion, which was joined by Chief Justice William H. Rehnquist and Justices Byron R. White, Sandra Day O'Connor, and Antonin Scalia. Justice William J. Brennan, Jr., filed a dissent, which was joined by Justice Thurgood Marshall and in part by Justices Harry A. Blackmun and John Paul Stevens. Blackmun also filed a dissent, joined by Marshall and Stevens and in part by Brennan. Stevens filed a dissent in which Blackmun joined.

The ruling was seen as a major setback to opponents of the death penalty, prompting the head of the American Civil Liberties Union to predict that a greater percentage of the nearly two thousand death row inmates eventually would be executed. When considered with a companion case decided the day before (Tison v. Arizona), *which held that accomplices to a crime also could be executed, even though they were not directly responsible for murder, if they acted with reckless disregard of human life, it appeared that the way had been cleared for many more executions.*

The Executioner Need Not Be Colorblind

Warren McCleskey, a black man, was convicted of murder for shooting a white police officer during the armed robbery of a Georgia furniture store. He admitted being present at the scene of the crime and taking part but denied shooting the officer. However, independent testimony revealed that he had carried the murder weapon. At the penalty phase of his trial, the jury determined that the statutory requirements for imposing the death penalty existed and recommended that it be imposed. McCleskey offered no evidence in mitigation.

After making various unsuccessful appeals, his lawyers eventually entered federal court to allege, among other claims, that the Georgia capital sentencing process was administered in a racially discriminatory way in violation of the Fourteenth Amendment right to equal protection of the laws and the Eighth Amendment prohibition of cruel and unusual punishments. In support they offered a statistical study performed by several professors headed by David C. Baldus.

The Baldus study examined more than two thousand Georgia murder cases from the 1970s. The study showed that defendants charged with killing white persons received the death penalty 11 percent of the time, but defendants charged with killing black persons received the death penalty in only 1 percent of the cases. There was also a reverse racial disparity in that 4 percent of black murder defendants and 7 percent of white murder defendants were sentenced to death. When these numbers were further broken down they showed that the death penalty was assessed in 22 percent of the cases involving a black defendant and a white victim but in 3 percent of the cases of a white murderer and a black victim. The study showed that defendants of either race charged with killing whites were 4.3 times more likely to be sentenced to death as defendants who had killed blacks.

Powell noted that McCleskey had not offered any evidence specific to his own case showing racial bias in the imposition of the death penalty, and was therefore bound by the limited use courts make of statistical studies to prove racial discrimination. He established that the application of statistical studies to death penalty cases was even more limited than similar studies used to examine the racial trends in juror selection or civil rights cases because there was necessarily a wide discretion that had to be granted to judges when deciding whether to impose the ultimate penalty. Such a study could not by itself show that those responsible for the sentence had acted with discriminatory purpose. To meet the necessary standard of proof, "McCleskey would have to prove that the Georgia Legislature enacted or maintained the death penalty because of *an anticipated racially discriminatory effect."*

On the claim that the racial imbalance in death sentences violated the rule against cruel and unusual punishments, the Court rejected the charge that the Georgia death penalty process was applied in an arbitrary and capricious fashion. Powell reasoned that because there was never a perfect procedure for deciding when to impose the death penalty, and all that could be done was to keep the proceeding as fair as possible, there was no reason to assume that the racial discrimination in sentencing was necessarily invidious. "The Constitution does not require that a State eliminate any demonstrable disparity that correlates with a potentially irrelevant factor in order to operate a criminal justice system that includes capital punishment." The statistics cited by Baldus, while indicating a discrepancy in sentencing that appears to correlate with race, did not prove an unacceptable risk of racial prejudice, since that must also be shown by the particular facts of this case.

Intolerable by Any Standard

In his dissent Brennan wrote that the Baldus study indicated that "the risk that race influenced McCleskey's sentence is intolerable by any standard." Because the study showed that it was more likely than not that the jury would have spared McCleskey's life had his victim been black, the dissent pointed out that it was also likely that the death sentence had been irrationally imposed, and therefore amounted to a cruel and unusual punishment.

Brennan also based part of his analysis on the history of the death penalty in Georgia. He noted the progress of the past few decades, but denied they had yet overcome the historical legacy of centuries. He concluded, "Warren McCleskey's evidence confronts us with the subtle and persistent influence of the past. His message is a disturbing one to a society that has formally repudiated racism, and a frustrating one to a Nation accustomed to regarding its destiny as the product of its own will. Nonetheless, we ignore him at our peril, for we remain imprisoned by the past as long as we deny its influence in the present."

Following are excerpts from the Supreme Court's decision in McCleskey v. Kemp, *decided April 22, 1987, and from the dissent by Justice William J. Brennan, Jr.:*

No. 84-6811

Warren McCleskey, Petitioner *v.* Ralph Kemp, Superintendent, Georgia Diagnostic and Classification Center	On writ of certiorari to the United States Court of Appeals for the Eleventh Circuit

[April 22, 1987]

JUSTICE POWELL delivered the opinion of the Court.

This case presents the question whether a complex statistical study that indicates a risk that racial considerations enter into capital sentencing determinations proves that petitioner McCleskey's capital sentence is unconstitutional under the Eighth or Fourteenth Amendment.

I

McCleskey, a black man, was convicted of two counts of armed robbery and one count of murder in the Superior Court of Fulton County, Georgia, on October 12, 1978. McCleskey's convictions arose out of the robbery of a furniture store and the killing of a white police officer during the course of the robbery. The evidence at trial indicated that McCleskey and three accomplices planned and carried out the robbery. All four were armed. McCleskey entered the front of the store while the other three entered the rear. McCleskey secured the front of the store by rounding up the customers and forcing them to lie face down on the floor. The other three rounded up the employees in the rear and tied them up with tape. The manager was forced at gunpoint to turn over the store receipts, his watch, and $6.00. During the course of the robbery, a police officer, answering a silent alarm, entered the store through the front door. As he was walking down the center aisle of the store, two shots were fired. Both struck the officer. One hit him in the face and killed him.

Several weeks later, McCleskey was arrested in connection with an unrelated offense. He confessed that he had participated in the furniture store robbery, but denied that he had shot the police officer. At trial, the State introduced evidence that at least one of the bullets that struck the officer was fired from a .38 caliber Rossi revolver. This description matched the description of the gun that McCleskey had carried during the robbery. The State also introduced the testimony of two witnesses who had heard McCleskey admit to the shooting.

The jury convicted McCleskey of murder. At the penalty hearing, the jury heard arguments as to the appropriate sentence. Under Georgia law, the jury could not consider imposing the death penalty unless it found beyond a reasonable doubt that the murder was accompanied by one of the statutory aggravating circumstances. The jury in this case found two aggravating circumstances to exist beyond a reasonable doubt: the murder was committed during the course of an armed robbery, and the murder was committed upon a peace officer engaged in the performance of his duties. In making its decision whether to impose the death sentence, the jury considered the mitigating and aggravating circumstances of McCleskey's conduct. McCleskey offered no mitigating evidence. The jury recommended that he be sentenced to death on the murder charge and to consecutive life sentences on the armed robbery charges. The court followed the jury's recommendation and sentenced McCleskey to death.

On appeal, the Supreme Court of Georgia affirmed the convictions and the sentences. This Court denied a petition for a writ of certiorari. *McCleskey* v. *Georgia* (1980). The Superior Court of Fulton County denied McCleskey's extraordinary motion for a new trial. McCleskey then filed a petition for a writ of habeas corpus in the Superior Court of Butts County. After holding an evidentiary hearing, the Superior Court denied relief. The Supreme Court of Georgia denied McCleskey's application for a certificate of probable cause to appeal the Superior Court's denial of his petition, and this Court again denied certiorari. *McCleskey* v. *Zant* (1981).

McCleskey next filed a petition for a writ of habeas corpus in the federal District Court for the Northern District of Georgia. His petition raised 18 claims, one of which was that the Georgia capital sentencing process is administered in a racially discriminatory manner in violation of the Eighth and Fourteenth Amendments to the United States Constitution. In support of his claim, McCleskey proffered a statistical study performed by Professors David C. Baldus, George Woodworth, and Charles Pulanski, (the Baldus study) that purports to show a disparity in the imposition of the death sentence in Georgia based on the race of the murder victim and, to a lesser extent, the race of the defendant....

[T]he Baldus study indicates that black defendants, such as McCleskey, who kill white victims have the greatest likelihood of receiving the death penalty....

II

McCleskey's first claim is that the Georgia capital punishment statute violates the Equal Protection Clause of the Fourteenth Amendment. He argues that race has infected the administration of Georgia's statute in two ways: persons who murder whites are more likely to be sentenced to death than persons who murder blacks, and black murderers are more likely to be sentenced to death than white murderers. As a black defendant who killed a white victim, McCleskey claims that the Baldus study demonstrates that he was discriminated against because of his race and because of the race of his victim. In its broadest form, McCleskey's claim of discrimination extends to every actor in the Georgia capital sentencing process, from the prosecutor who sought the death penalty and the jury that imposed the sentence, to the State itself that enacted the capital punishment statute and allows it to remain in effect despite its allegedly discriminatory application. We agree with the Court of Appeals, and every other court that has considered such a challenge, that this claim must fail.

A

Our analysis begins with the basic principle that a defendant who alleges an equal protection violation has the burden of proving "the existence of purposeful discrimination." *Whitus* v. *Georgia* (1967). A corollary to this principle is that a criminal defendant must prove that the purposeful discrimination "had a discriminatory effect" on him. *Wayte* v. *United*

States (1985). Thus, to prevail under the Equal Protection Clause, McCleskey must prove that the decisionmakers in *his* case acted with discriminatory purpose. He offers no evidence specific to his own case that would support an inference that racial considerations played a part in his sentence. Instead, he relies solely on the Baldus study. McCleskey argues that the Baldus study compels an inference that his sentence rests on purposeful discrimination. McCleskey's claim that these statistics are sufficient proof of discrimination, without regard to the facts of a particular case, would extend to all capital cases in Georgia, at least where the victim was white and the defendant is black.

The Court has accepted statistics as proof of intent to discriminate in certain limited contexts. First, this Court has accepted statistical disparities as proof of an equal protection violation in the selection of the jury venire in a particular district. Although statistical proof normally must present a "stark" pattern to be accepted as the sole proof of discriminatory intent under the Constitution, *Arlington Heights* v. *Metropolitan Housing Dev. Corp.* (1977), "[b]ecause of the nature of the jury-selection task, ... we have permitted a finding of constitutional violation even when the statistical pattern does not approach [such] extremes." Second, this Court has accepted statistics in the form of multiple regression analysis to prove statutory violations under Title VII. *Bazemore* v. *Friday* (1986) (opinion of BRENNAN, J., concurring in part).

But the nature of the capital sentencing decision, and the relationship of the statistics to that decision, are fundamentally different from the corresponding elements in the venire-selection or Title VII cases. Most importantly, each particular decision to impose the death penalty is made by a petit jury selected from a properly constituted venire. Each jury is unique in its composition, and the Constitution requires that its decision rest on consideration of innumerable factors that vary according to the characteristics of the individual defendant and the facts of the particular capital offense. See ... *Lockett* v. *Ohio* (1978) (plurality opinion of Burger, C. J.). Thus, the application of an inference drawn from the general statistics to a specific decision in a trial and sentencing simply is not comparable to the application of an inference drawn from general statistics to a specific venire-selection or Title VII case. In those cases, the statistics relate to fewer entities, and fewer variables are relevant to the challenged decisions.

Another important difference between the cases in which we have accepted statistics as proof of discriminatory intent and this case is that, in the venire-selection and Title VII contexts, the decisionmaker has an opportunity to explain the statistical disparity. See *Whitus* v. *Georgia; Texas Dept. of Community Affairs* v. *Burdine* (1981); *McDonnell Douglas Corp.* v. *Green* (1973). Here, the State has no practical opportunity to rebut the Baldus study. "[C]ontrolling considerations of ... public policy," *McDonald* v. *Pless* (1915), dictate that jurors "cannot be called ... to testify to the motives and influences that led to their verdict." *Chicago,*

B. & Q. R. Co. v. *Babcock* (1907). Similarly, the policy considerations behind a prosecutor's traditionally "wide discretion" suggest the impropriety of our requiring prosecutors to defend their decisions to seek death penalties, "often years after they were made." See *Imbler* v. *Pachtman* (1976). Moreover, absent far stronger proof, it is unnecessary to seek such a rebuttal, because a legitimate and unchallenged explanation for the decision is apparent from the record: McCleskey committed an act for which the United States Constitution and Georgia laws permit imposition of the death penalty.

Finally, McCleskey's statistical proffer must be viewed in the context of his challenge. McCleskey challenges decisions at the heart of the State's criminal justice system. "[O]ne of society's most basic tasks is that of protecting the lives of its citizens and one of the most basic ways in which it achieves the task is through criminal laws against murder." *Gregg* v. *Georgia* (1976) (WHITE, J., concurring). Implementation of these laws necessarily requires discretionary judgments. Because discretion is essential to the criminal justice process, we would demand exceptionally clear proof before we would infer that the discretion has been abused. The unique nature of the decisions at issue in the case also counsel against adopting such an inference from the disparities indicated by the Baldus study. Accordingly, we hold that the Baldus study is clearly insufficient to support an inference that any of the decisionmakers in McCleskey's case acted with discriminatory purpose.

B

McCleskey also suggests that the Baldus study proves that the State as a whole has acted with a discriminatory purpose. He appears to argue that the State has violated the Equal Protection Clause by adopting the capital punishment statute and allowing it to remain in force despite its allegedly discriminatory application. But "'[d]iscriminatory purpose' . . . implies more than intent as volition or intent as awareness of consequences. It implies that the decisionmaker, in this case a state legislature, selected or reaffirmed a particular course of action at least in part 'because of,' not merely 'in spite of,' its adverse effects upon an identifiable group," *Personnel Administrator of Massachusetts* v. *Feeney* (1979). See *Wayte* v. *United States* (1985). For this claim to prevail, McCleskey would have to prove that the Georgia Legislature enacted or maintained the death penalty statute *because of* an anticipated racially discriminatory effect. In *Gregg* v. *Georgia* (1976), this Court found that the Georgia capital sentencing system could operate in a fair and neutral manner. There was no evidence then, and there is none now, that the Georgia Legislature enacted the capital punishment statute to further a racially discriminatory purpose.

Nor has McCleskey demonstrated that the legislature maintains the capital punishment statute because of the racially disproportionate impact suggested by the Baldus study. As legislatures necessarily have wide discretion in the choice of criminal laws and penalties, and as there were legitimate reasons for the Georgia Legislature to adopt and maintain capital punishment, see *Gregg* v. *Georgia* (joint opinion of Stewart, POWELL, and STEVENS, JJ.), we will not infer a discriminatory purpose on the part of the State of Georgia. Accordingly, we reject McCleskey's equal protection claims.

[Part III omitted]

IV

B

... [McCleskey] further contends that the Georgia capital punishment system is arbitrary and capricious in *application,* and therefore his sentence is excessive, because racial considerations may influence capital sentencing decisions in Georgia. We now address this claim.

To evaluate McCleskey's challenge, we must examine exactly what the Baldus study may show. Even Professor Baldus does not contend that his statistics *prove* that race enters into any capital sentencing decisions or that race was a factor in McCleskey's particular case. Statistics at most may show only a likelihood that a particular factor entered into some decisions. There is, of course, some risk of racial prejudice influencing a jury's decision in a criminal case. There are similar risks that other kinds of prejudice will influence other criminal trials. The question "is at what point that risk becomes constitutionally unacceptable," *Turner* v. *Murray* (1986). McCleskey asks us to accept the likelihood allegedly shown by the Baldus study as the constitutional measure of an unacceptable risk of racial prejudice influencing capital sentencing decisions. This we decline to do.

Because of the risk that the factor of race may enter the criminal justice process, we have engaged in "unceasing efforts" to eradicate racial prejudice from our criminal justice system. *Batson* v. *Kentucky* (1986). Our efforts have been guided by our recognition that "the inestimable privilege of trial by jury ... is a vital principle, underlying the whole administration of criminal justice," *Ex parte Milligan* (1866). See *Duncan* v. *Louisiana* (1968). Thus, it is the jury that is a criminal defendant's fundamental "protection of life and liberty against race or color prejudice." *Strauder* v. *West Virginia* (1880). Specifically, a capital sentencing jury representative of a criminal defendant's community assures a " 'diffused impartiality,' " *Taylor* v. *Louisiana* (1975) (quoting *Thiel* v. *Southern Pacific Co.* (1946) (Frankfurter, J., dissenting)), in the jury's task of "express[ing] the conscience of the community on the ultimate question of life or death," *Witherspoon* v. *Illinois* (1968).

Individual jurors bring to their deliberations "qualities of human nature and varieties of human experience, the range of which is unknown and perhaps unknowable." *Peters* v. *Kiff* (1972) (opinion of MARSHALL, J.). The capital sentencing decision requires the individual jurors to focus their collective judgment on the unique characteristics of a particular criminal defendant. It is not surprising that such collective judgments often are difficult to explain. But the inherent lack of predictability of jury decisions does not justify their condemnation. On the contrary, it is the jury's function to make the difficult and uniquely human judgments that defy codification and that "buil[d] discretion, equity, and flexibility into a legal system." H. Kalven & H. Zeisel, The American Jury (1966).

McCleskey's argument that the Constitution condemns the discretion allowed decisionmakers in the Georgia capital sentencing system is antithetical to the fundamental role of discretion in our criminal justice system. Discretion in the criminal justice system offers substantial benefits to the criminal defendant. Not only can a jury decline to impose the death sentence, it can decline to convict, or choose to convict of a lesser offense. Whereas decisions against a defendant's interest may be reversed by the trial judge or on appeal, these discretionary exercises of leniency are final and unreviewable. Similarly, the capacity of prosecutorial discretion to provide individualized justice is "firmly entrenched in American law." 2 W. LaFave & D. Israel, Criminal Procedure § 13.2(a) (1984). As we have noted, a prosecutor can decline to charge, offer a plea bargain, or decline to seek a death sentence in any particular case. Of course, "the power to be lenient [also] is the power to discriminate," K. Davis, Discretionary Justice (1973), but a capital-punishment system that did not allow for discretionary acts of leniency "would be totally alien to our notions of criminal justice." *Gregg* v. *Georgia*.

C

At most, the Baldus study indicates a discrepancy that appears to correlate with race. Apparent disparities in sentencing are an inevitable part of our criminal justice system. The discrepancy indicated by the Baldus study is "a far cry from the major systemic defects identified in *Furman*," *Pulley* v. *Harris* [1984]. As this Court has recognized, any mode for determining guilt or punishment "has its weaknesses and the potential for misuse." *Singer* v. *United States* (1965).... Specifically, "there can be 'no perfect procedure for deciding in which cases governmental authority should be used to impose death.'" *Zant* v. *Stephens* (1983).... Despite these imperfections, our consistent rule has been that constitutional guarantees are met when "the mode [for determining guilt or punishment] itself has been surrounded with safeguards to make it as fair as possible." *Singer* v. *United States*. Where the discretion that is fundamental to our criminal process is involved, we decline to assume that what is unexplained is invidious. In light of the safeguards designed to minimize racial bias in the process, the fundamental value of jury trial in our criminal justice system, and the benefits that discretion provides to criminal defendants, we hold that the Baldus study does not demonstrate a constitutionally significant risk of racial bias affecting the Georgia capital-sentencing process.

V

Two additional concerns inform our decision in this case. First, McCleskey's claim, taken to its logical conclusion, throws into serious question the principles that underlie our entire criminal justice system. The Eighth Amendment is not limited in application to capital punishment, but applies to all penalties. *Solem* v. *Helm* (1983); see *Rummel* v. *Estelle* (1980) (POWELL, J., dissenting). Thus, if we accepted McCleskey's claim that racial bias has impermissibly tainted the capital sentencing decision, we could soon be faced with similar claims as to other types of penalty. Moreover, the claim that his sentence rests on the irrelevant factor of race easily could be extended to apply to claims based on unexplained discrepancies that correlate to membership in other minority groups, and even to gender. Similarly, since McCleskey's claim relates to the race of his victim, other claims could apply with equally logical force to statistical disparities that correlate with the race or sex of other actors in the criminal justice system, such as defense attorneys, or judges. Also, there is no logical reason that such a claim need be limited to racial or sexual bias. If arbitrary and capricious punishment is the touchstone under the Eighth Amendment, such a claim could—at least in theory—be based upon any arbitrary variable, such as the defendant's facial characteristics, or the physical attractiveness of the defendant or the victim, that some statistical study indicates may be influential in jury decisionmaking. As these examples illustrate, there is no limiting principle to the type of challenge brought by McCleskey. The Constitution does not require that a State eliminate any demonstrable disparity that correlates with a potentially irrelevant factor in order to operate a criminal justice system that includes capital punishment. As we have stated specifically in the context of capital punishment, the Constitution does not "plac[e] totally unrealistic conditions on its use." *Gregg* v. *Georgia.*

Second, McCleskey's arguments are best presented to the legislative bodies. It is not the responsibility—or indeed even the right—of this Court to determine the appropriate punishment for particular crimes. It is the legislatures, the elected representatives of the people, that are "constituted to respond to the will and consequently the moral values of the people." *Furman* v. *Georgia* (1972) (Burger, C. J., dissenting). Legislatures also are better qualified to weigh and "evaluate the results of statistical studies in terms of their own local conditions and with a flexibility of approach that is not available to the courts," *Gregg* v. *Georgia.* Capital punishment is now the law in more than two thirds of our States. It is the ultimate duty of courts to determine on a case-by-case basis whether these laws are applied consistently with the Constitution. Despite McCleskey's wide ranging arguments that basically challenge the validity of capital punishment in our multi-racial society, the only question before us is whether in his case ... the law of Georgia was properly applied. We agree with the District Court and the Court of Appeals for the Eleventh Circuit that this was carefully and correctly done in this case.

VI

Accordingly, we affirm the judgment of the Court of Appeals for the Eleventh Circuit.

It is so ordered.

JUSTICE BRENNAN, with whom JUSTICE MARSHALL joins, and with whom JUSTICE BLACKMUN and JUSTICE STEVENS join in all but Part I, dissenting.

[Part I omitted]

II

At some point in this case, Warren McCleskey doubtless asked his lawyer whether a jury was likely to sentence him to die. A candid reply to this question would have been disturbing. First, counsel would have to tell McCleskey that few of the details of the crime or of McCleskey's past criminal conduct were more important than the fact that his victim was white. Furthermore, counsel would feel bound to tell McCleskey that defendants charged with killing white victims in Georgia are 4.3 times as likely to be sentenced to death as defendants charged with killing blacks. In addition, frankness would compel the disclosure that it was more likely than not that the race of McCleskey's victim would determine whether he received a death sentence: 6 of every 11 defendants convicted of killing a white person would not have received the death penalty if their victims had been black, while, among defendants with aggravating and mitigating factors comparable to McCleskey, 20 of every 34 would not have been sentenced to die if their victims had been black. Finally, the assessment would not be complete without the information that cases involving black defendants and white victims are more likely to result in a death sentence than cases featuring any other racial combination of defendant and victim. The story could be told in a variety of ways, but McCleskey could not fail to grasp its essential narrative line: there was a significant chance that race would play a prominent role in determining if he lived or died.

The Court today holds that Warren McCleskey's sentence was constitutionally imposed. It finds no fault in a system in which lawyers must tell their clients that race casts a large shadow on the capital sentencing process. The Court arrives at this conclusion by stating that the Baldus Study cannot "*prove* that race enters into any capital sentencing decisions or that race was a factor in McCleskey's particular case." Since, according to Professor Baldus, we cannot say "to a moral certainty" that race influenced a decision, we can identify only "a likelihood that a particular factor entered into some decisions," and "a discrepancy that appears to correlate with race." This "likelihood" and "discrepancy," holds the Court, is insufficient to establish a constitutional violation. The Court reaches this conclusion by placing four factors on the scales opposite McCleskey's evidence: the desire to encourage sentencing discretion, the existence of "statutory safeguards" in the Georgia scheme, the fear of encouraging widespread challenges to other sentencing decisions, and the limits of the judicial role. The Court's evaluation of the significance of petitioner's evidence is fundamentally at odds with our consistent concern for rationality in capital sentencing, and the considerations that the majority invokes to discount that evidence cannot justify ignoring its force....

III

B

The Baldus study indicates that, after taking into account some 230 nonracial factors that might legitimately influence a sentencer, the jury *more likely than not* would have spared McCleskey's life had his victim been black. The study distinguishes between those cases in which (1) the jury exercises virtually no discretion because the strength or weakness of aggravating factors usually suggests that only one outcome is appropriate; and (2) cases reflecting an "intermediate" level of aggravation, in which the jury has considerable discretion in choosing a sentence. McCleskey's case falls into the intermediate range. In such cases, death is imposed in 34% of white-victim crimes and 14% of black-victim crimes, a difference of 139% in the rate of imposition of the death penalty. In other words, just under 59%—almost 6 in 10—defendants comparable to McCleskey would not have received the death penalty if their victims had been black.

Furthermore, even examination of the sentencing system as a whole, factoring in those cases in which the jury exercises little discretion, indicates the influence of race on capital sentencing. For the Georgia system as a whole, race accounts for a six percentage point difference in the rate at which capital punishment is imposed. Since death is imposed in 11% of all white-victim cases, the rate in comparably aggravated black-victim cases is 5%. The rate of capital sentencing in a white-victim case is thus 120% greater than the rate in a black-victim case. Put another way, over half—55%—of defendants in white-victim crimes in Georgia would not have been sentenced to die if their victims had been black. Of the more than 200 variables potentially relevant to a sentencing decision, race of the victim is a powerful explanation for variation in death sentence rates—as powerful as nonracial aggravating factors such as a prior murder conviction or acting as the principal planner of the homicide.

These adjusted figures are only the most conservative indication of the risk that race will influence the death sentences of defendants in Georgia. Data unadjusted for the mitigating or aggravating effect of other factors show an even more pronounced disparity by race. The capital sentencing rate for all white-victim cases was almost *11 times* greater than the rate for black-victim cases. Furthermore, blacks who kill whites are sentenced to death at nearly *22 times* the rate of blacks who kill blacks, and more than *7 times* the rate of whites who kill blacks. In addition, prosecutors seek the death penalty for 70% of black defendants with white victims, but for only 15% of black defendants with black victims, and only 19% of white defendants with black victims. Since our decision upholding the Georgia capital-sentencing system in *Gregg,* the State has executed 7 persons. All of the 7 were convicted of killing whites, and 6 of the 7 executed were black. Such execution figures are especially striking in light of the fact that, during the period encompassed by the Baldus study, only 9.2% of Georgia homicides involved black defendants and white victims, while 60.7% involved black victims. . . .

The statistical evidence in this case thus relentlessly documents the risk that McCleskey's sentence was influenced by racial considerations. This evidence shows that there is a better than even chance in Georgia that race will influence the decision to impose the death penalty: a majority of defendants in white-victim crimes would not have been sentenced to die if their victims had been black. In determining whether this risk is acceptable, our judgment must be shaped by the awareness that "[t]he risk of racial prejudice infecting a capital sentencing proceeding is especially serious in light of the complete finality of the death sentence." *Turner* v. *Murray* (1986), and that "[i]t is of vital importance to the defendant and to the community that any decision to impose the death sentence be, and appear to be, based on reason rather than caprice or emotion." *Gardner* v. *Florida* (1977). In determining the guilt of a defendant, a state must prove its case beyond a reasonable doubt. That is, we refuse to convict if the chance of error is simply less likely than not. Surely, we should not be willing to take a person's life if the chance that his death sentence was irrationally imposed is *more* likely than not. In light of the gravity of the interest at stake, petitioner's statistics on their face are a powerful demonstration of the type of risk that our Eighth Amendment jurisprudence has consistently condemned. . . .

[Part IV omitted]

V

At the time our Constitution was framed 200 years ago this year, blacks "had for more than a century before been regarded as beings of an inferior order, and altogether unfit to associate with the white race, either in social or political relations; and so far inferior, that they had no rights which the white man was bound to respect." *Dred Scott* v. *Sandford* (1857). Only 130 years ago, this Court relied on these observations to deny American citizenship to blacks. A mere three generations ago, this Court sanctioned racial segregation, stating that "[i]f one race be inferior to the other socially, the Constitution of the United States cannot put them upon the same plane." *Plessy* v. *Ferguson* (1896).

In more recent times, we have sought to free ourselves from the burden of this history. Yet it has been scarcely a generation since this Court's first decision striking down racial segregation, and barely two decades since the legislative prohibition of racial discrimination in major domains of national life. These have been honorable steps, but we cannot pretend that in three decades we have completely escaped the grip of an historical legacy spanning centuries. Warren McCleskey's evidence confronts us with the subtle and persistent influence of the past. His message is a disturbing one to a society that has formally repudiated racism, and a frustrating one to a Nation accustomed to regarding its destiny as the product of its own will. Nonetheless, we ignore him at our peril, for we remain imprisoned by the past as long as we deny its influence in the present.

It is tempting to pretend that minorities on death row share a fate in no way connected to our own, that our treatment of them sounds no echoes beyond the chambers in which they die. Such an illusion is ultimately corrosive, for the reverberations of injustice are not so easily confined. "The destinies of the two races in this country are indissolubly linked together," ... and the way in which we choose those who will die reveals the depth of moral commitment among the living.

The Court's decision today will not change what attorneys in Georgia tell other Warren McCleskeys about their chances of execution. Nothing will soften the harsh message they must convey, nor alter the prospect that race undoubtedly will continue to be a topic of discussion. McCleskey's evidence will not have obtained judicial acceptance, but that will not affect what is said on death row. However many criticisms of today's decision may be rendered, these painful conversations will serve as the most eloquent dissents of all....

May

COURT ON OBSCENITY

May 4, 1987

The Supreme Court May 4 provided further clarification to the legal test for determining when a given book, magazine, or movie is obscene. By a 6-3 vote the Court decided that a jury may not be instructed by a judge to apply contemporary community standards when considering whether the work lacks social value. Instead, the majority of the Court opted for a test based on whether a reasonable person would find social value in the work. The effect of the decision was to guarantee that somewhat more objective, and somewhat less parochial, standards were applied by the jury when evaluating the facts applying to one element of the crime of obscenity.

Justice Byron R. White wrote the Court's opinion, in which he was joined by Chief Justice William H. Rehnquist and Justices Lewis F. Powell, Jr., Sandra Day O'Connor, and Antonin Scalia, and in part by Justice Harry A. Blackmun. Scalia filed a concurring opinion, and Blackmun filed an opinion concurring in part and dissenting in part. Justice William J. Brennan, Jr., filed a dissenting opinion. Justice John Paul Stevens also filed a dissenting opinion, in which Brennan and Justice Thurgood Marshall joined, and in Part I of which Blackmun joined.

The decision also involved an important second question, as the Court was required to decide whether an error in instructing the trial jury should be sufficient to overturn the conviction of defendants tried under the erroneous instruction. On this issue the Court decided that the error had been harmless and let the conviction stand.

Local Acceptance of Artistic Content

Since 1973 it had been established that the test of whether a work was obscene, and therefore not entitled to First Amendment protections, had three parts. The first test was whether the work appealed to prurient interests; that is, whether it was solely intended to be sexually arousing to an obsessive extent. The second was whether the content of the material in question was patently offensive. The third was "whether the work, taken as a whole, lacks serious literary, artistic, political or scientific value." These tripartite criteria had been established in the landmark case of Miller v. California *(1973).*

That decision also made clear how the first two parts of the test were to be applied. Using the prevailing community standards, juries were to decide whether a work appealed to prurient interests and was patently offensive. This meant that a work acceptable to juries in New York or Los Angeles might not be acceptable elsewhere. Therefore, the constitutional protections enjoyed by a publisher could vary, depending on where works were sold. Although the publisher might not be subject to prosecution, the owners and employees of the retail outlets where the works were sold were liable to arrest if what they sold was not acceptable locally.

In the case before the Court, two employees of an "adult" bookstore were arrested for selling magazines the police in Rockford, Illinois, believed to be obscene. The defendants argued at trial and at each intermediate appellate stage that the Constitution required use of an objective standard when deciding whether the work had literary, artistic, or social value, and not a standard linked to contemporary community standards. The jury that convicted them was instructed by the judge to decide whether "ordinary adults in the whole State of Illinois" would consider the magazines to have literary or artistic value. The defendants' argument was rejected by the lower courts but accepted with little debate by the Supreme Court.

White disposed of the issue in a few sentences: "Just as the ideas a work represents need not obtain majority approval to merit protection, neither, insofar as the First Amendment is concerned, does the value of the work vary from community to community based on the degree of local acceptance it has won. The proper inquiry is not whether an ordinary member of any given community would find serious literary, artistic, political, or scientific value in the allegedly obscene material, but whether a reasonable person would find such value in the material, taken as a whole."

Scalia's concurring opinion indicated how slippery either standard could be. Denying that there was any possibility of coming to an objective assessment of a work's value, since what was at issue was more a matter of taste than a subject open to rational decision, he suggested, dryly, that the "reasonable man" standard would seemingly have to give way to the "man of tolerably good taste" standard. This latter standard, whatever its potential merit as an idea, could never be a useful legal standard without ascertainable criteria capable of uniform application. He suggested that the issue of what was obscene was not really a proper subject for judicial inquiry and called for a reexamination of Miller.

Harmless Error

There was no question that the trial court had erred by instructing the jury to decide the value issue under local standards. But was this error serious enough to require that the convictions be reversed? For the majority of justices, the error was not so serious that the convictions should be reversed at the Supreme Court level. This troubled Stevens, who argued in dissent that the majority view "would not only violate petitioners' constitutional right to trial by jury, but would also pervert the notion of harmless error. . . . It is fundamental that an appellate court (and for that matter, a trial court) is not free to decide in a criminal case that, if asked, a jury would *have found something that it did not find."*

The majority was not willing to take this view of harmless error, requiring instead that if a reviewing court concludes that no rational juror, if properly instructed, could find value in the magazines, the conviction should stand. The majority did not find the trial court's error harmless, and it remanded the case to the Illinois Court of Appeal.

Following are excerpts from the Supreme Court's opinion in Pope v. Illinois, *ruling that a jury may not be instructed to apply community standards in deciding whether obscene material has serious value; the concurring opinion of Justice Antonin Scalia; and excerpts from the dissent of Justice John Paul Stevens, issued May 4, 1987:*

No. 85-1973

Richard Pope and Charles G. Morrison, Petitioners *v.* Illinois	On writ of certiorari to the Appellate Court of Illinois, Second District

[May 4, 1987]

JUSTICE WHITE delivered the opinion of the Court.

In *Miller* v. *California* (1973), the Court set out a tripartite test for judging whether material is obscene. The third prong of the *Miller* test requires the trier of fact to determine "whether the work, taken as a whole, lacks serious literary, artistic, political, or scientific value." The issue in these cases is whether, in a prosecution for the sale of allegedly obscene materials, the jury may be instructed to apply community standards in deciding the value question.

I

On July 21, 1983, Rockford, Illinois police detectives purchased certain magazines from the two petitioners, each of whom was an attendant at an adult bookstore. Petitioners were subsequently charged separately with the offense of "obscenity" for the sale of these magazines. Each petitioner moved to dismiss the charges against him on the ground that the then-current version of the Illinois obscenity statute violated the First and Fourteenth Amendments to the United States Constitution. Both petitioners argued, among other things, that the statute was unconstitutional in failing to require that the value question be judged "solely on an objective basis as opposed to reference [*sic*] to contemporary community standards." Both trial courts rejected this contention and instructed the respective juries to judge whether the material was obscene by determining how it would be viewed by ordinary adults in the whole State of Illinois. Both petitioners were found guilty, and both appealed to the Illinois Court of Appeals, Second District. That court also rejected petitioners' contention that the issue of value must be determined on an objective basis and not by reference to contemporary community standards. The Illinois Supreme Court denied review, and we granted certiorari (1986).

II

There is no suggestion in our cases that the question of the value of an allegedly obscene work is to be determined by reference to community standards. Indeed, our cases are to the contrary. *Smith* v. *United States* (1977), held that, in a federal prosecution for mailing obscene materials, the first and second prongs of the *Miller* test—appeal to prurient interest and patent offensiveness—are issues of fact for the jury to determine applying contemporary community standards. The Court then observed that unlike prurient appeal and patent offensiveness, "[l]iterary, artistic, political, or scientific value ... is not discussed in *Miller* in terms of contemporary community standards." This comment was not meant to point out an oversight in the *Miller* opinion, but to call attention to and approve a deliberate choice.

In *Miller* itself, the Court was careful to point out that "[t]he First Amendment protects works which, taken as a whole, have serious literary, artistic, political, or scientific value, regardless of whether the government or a majority of the people approve of the ideas these works represent." Just as the ideas a work represents need not obtain majority approval to merit protection, neither, insofar as the First Amendment is concerned, does the value of the work vary from community to community based on the degree of local acceptance it has won. The proper inquiry is not whether an ordinary member of any given community would find serious literary, artistic, political, or scientific value in allegedly obscene material, but whether a reasonable person would find such value in the material, taken as a whole. The instruction at issue in this case was therefore unconstitutional.

III

The question remains whether the convictions should be reversed outright or are subject to salvage if the erroneous instruction is found to be harmless error. Petitioners contend that the statute is invalid on its face and that the convictions must necessarily be reversed because, as we understand it, the State should not be allowed to preserve any conviction under a law that poses a threat to First Amendment values. But the statute under which petitioners were convicted is no longer on the books; it has been repealed and replaced by a statute that does not call for the application of community standards to the value question. Facial invalidation of the repealed statute would not serve the purpose of preventing future prosecutions under a constitutionally defective standard. Cf., *e.g.*, *Secretary of State of Maryland* v. *Joseph H. Munson Co.* (1984). And if we did facially invalidate the repealed statute and reverse petitioners' convictions, petitioners could still be retried under that statute, provided that the erroneous instruction was not repeated, because petitioners could not plausibly claim that the repealed statute failed to give them notice that the sale of obscene materials would be prosecuted. See *Dombrowski* v. *Pfister* (1965); *United States* v. *Thirty-Seven Photographs* (1971). Under these circumstances, we see no reason to require a retrial if it can be said beyond a reasonable doubt that the jury's verdict in this case was not affected by the erroneous instruction.

The situation here is comparable to that in *Rose* v. *Clark* (1986). In *Rose*, the jury in a murder trial was incorrectly instructed on the element of malice, yet the Court held that a harmless error inquiry was appropriate. The Court explained that in the absence of error that renders a trial fundamentally unfair, such as denial of the right to counsel or trial before a finanically interested judge, a conviction should be affirmed "where a reviewing court can find that the record developed at trial established guilt beyond a reasonable doubt. . . . " The error in *Rose* did not entirely preclude the jury from considering the element of malice, and the fact that the jury could conceivably have had the impermissible presumption in mind when it considered the element of malice was not a reason to retry the defendant if the facts that the jury necessarily found established guilt beyond a reasonable doubt. The Court said, "When a jury is instructed to presume malice from predicate facts, it still must find the existence of those facts beyond reasonable doubt. *Connecticut* v. *Johnson* (1983) (Powell, J., dissenting). In many cases, the predicate facts conclusively establish intent, so that no rational jury could find that the defendant committed the relevant criminal act but did not *intend* to cause injury."

Similarly, in the present cases the jurors were not precluded from considering the question of value: they were informed that to convict they must find, among other things, that the magazines petitioners sold were utterly without redeeming social value. While it was error to instruct the juries to use a state community standard in considering the value question, if a reviewing court concludes that no rational juror, if properly instructed, could find value in the magazines, the convictions should stand.

Although we plainly have the authority to decide whether, on the facts of a given case, a constitutional error was harmless under the standard of *Chapman* v. *California* (1967), we do so sparingly.... In this case the Illinois Court of Appeals has not considered the harmless-error issue. We therefore vacate its judgment and remand so that it may do so.

It is so ordered.

JUSTICE SCALIA, concurring.

I join the Court's opinion with regard to harmless error because I think it implausible that a community standard embracing the entire State of Illinois would cause any jury to convict where a "reasonable person" standard would not. At least in these circumstances, if a reviewing court concludes that no rational juror, properly instructed, could find value in the magazines, the Constitution is not offended by letting the convictions stand.

I join the Court's opinion with regard to an "objective" or "reasonable person" test of "serious literary, artistic, political, or scientific value," *Miller* v. *California* (1973), because I think that the most faithful assessment of what *Miller* intended, and because we have not been asked to reconsider *Miller* in the present case. I must note, however, that in my view it is quite impossible to come to an objective assessment of (at least) literary or artistic value, there being many accomplished people who have found literature in Dada, and art in the replication of a soup can. Since ratiocination has little to do with esthetics, the fabled "reasonable man" is of little help in the inquiry, and would have to be replaced with, perhaps, the "man of tolerably good taste"—a description that betrays the lack of an ascertainable standard. If evenhanded and accurate decisionmaking is not always impossible under such a regime, it is at least impossible in the cases that matter. I think we would be better advised to adopt as a legal maxim what has long been the wisdom of mankind: *De gustibus non est disputandum.* Just as there is no use arguing about taste, there is no use litigating about it. For the law courts to decide "What is Beauty" is a novelty even by today's standards.

The approach proposed by Part II of JUSTICE STEVENS' dissent does not eliminate this difficulty, but arguably aggravates it. It is a refined enough judgment to estimate whether a reasonable person *would* find literary or artistic value in a particular publication; it carries refinement to the point of meaninglessness to ask whether he *could* do so. Taste being, as I have said, unpredictable, the answer to the question must always be "yes"—so that there is little practical difference between that proposal and Part III of JUSTICE STEVENS' dissent, which asserts more forthrightly that "government may not constitutionally criminalize mere possession or sale of obscene literature, absent some connection to minors, or obtrusive display to unconsenting adults."

All of today's opinions, I suggest, display the need for reexamination of *Miller*.

JUSTICE STEVENS, with whom JUSTICE MARSHALL joins, dissenting.

The Court correctly holds that the juries that convicted petitioners were given erroneous instructions on one of the three essential elements of an obscenity conviction. Nevertheless, I disagree with its disposition of the case for three separate reasons: (1) the error in the instructions was not harmless; (2) the Court's attempt to clarify the constitutional definition of obscenity is not faithful to the First Amendment; and (3) I do not believe Illinois may criminalize the sale of magazines to consenting adults who enjoy the constitutional right to read and possess them.

I

The distribution of magazines is presumptively protected by the First Amendment. The Court has held, however, that the constitutional protection does not apply to obscene literature. If a state prosecutor can convince the trier of fact that the three components of the obscenity standard set forth in *Miller* v. *California* (1973), are satisfied, it may, in the Court's view, prohibit the sale of sexually-explicit magazines. In a criminal prosecution, the prosecutor must prove each of these three elements beyond a reasonable doubt. Thus, in these cases, in addition to the first two elements of the *Miller* standard, the juries were required to find, on the basis of proof beyond a reasonable doubt, that each of the magazines "lacks serious literary, artistic, political, or scientific value."

The required finding is fundamentally different from a conclusion that a majority of the populace considers the magazines offensive or worthless. As the court correctly holds, the juries in these cases were not instructed to make the required finding; instead, they were asked to decide whether "ordinary adults in the whole State of Illinois" would view the magazines that petitioners sold as having value. Because of these erroneous instructions, the juries that found petitioners guilty of obscenity did not find one of the essential elements of that crime. This type of omission can never constitute harmless error.

Just as the constitutional right to trial by jury forbids a judge from directing a verdict for the prosecution, *United States* v. *Martin Linen Supply Co.* (1977), so too, "a jury's verdict cannot stand if the instructions provided the jury do not require it to find each element of the crime under the proper standard of proof." *Cabana* v. *Bullock* (1986). As JUSTICE WHITE has explained:

> "It should hardly need saying that a judgment or conviction cannot be entered against a defendant no matter how strong the evidence is against him, unless that evidence has been presented to a jury (or a judge, if a jury is waived) and unless the jury (or judge) finds from that evidence that the defendant's guilt has been proved beyond a reasonable doubt. It cannot be 'harmless error' wholly to deny a defendant a jury trial *on one or all elements of the offense* with which he is charged." *Henderson* v. *Morgan* (1976) (WHITE, J. concurring) (emphasis added).

Yet, this is exactly what happened in these cases. Because of the constitutionally erroneous instructions, petitioners were denied a jury determination on one of the critical elements of an obscenity prosecution.

An application of the harmless error doctrine under these circumstances would not only violate petitioners' constitutional right to trial by jury, but would also pervert the notion of harmless error. When a court is asked to hold that an error that occurred did not interfere with the jury's ability to legitimately reach the verdict that it reached, harmless-error analysis may often be appropriate. But this principle cannot apply unless the jury found all of the elements required to support a conviction. The harmless-error doctrine may enable a court to remove a taint from proceedings in order to *preserve* a jury's findings, but it cannot constitutionally *supplement* those findings. It is fundamental that an appellate court (and for that matter, a trial court) is not free to decide in a criminal case that, if asked, a jury *would* have found something that it did not find. We have consistently rejected the possibility of harmless error in these circumstances. See *Jackson* v. *Virginia* (1979); *Carpenters* v. *United States* (1947); *Bollenbach* v. *United States* (1946); *Marks* v. *United States* (1977).

The Court suggests that these cases "are no longer good authority" in light of the decision last term in *Rose* v. *Clark*. I emphatically disagree. In *Rose* v. *Clark* the Court held that harmless-error analysis is applicable to instructions that informed the jury of the proper elements of the crime and the proper standard of proof, but impermissibly gave the jury the option of finding one of the elements through a presumption, in violation of *Sandstrom* v. *Montana* (1979), and *Francis* v. *Franklin* (1985). In holding harmless-error analysis applicable, the Court explained that because the presumption in question " 'does not remove the issue of intent from the jury's consideration, *it is distinguishable from other instructional errors that prevent a jury from considering an issue.*' " ([E]mphasis added, quoting *Connecticut* v. *Johnson* (1983) (POWELL, J., dissenting). The Court reasoned that when the evidence is overwhelming on intent, the instruction allowing the jury to use a presumption can be deemed "simply superfluous," for as JUSTICE POWELL had earlier stated, in some cases the evidence may be so "dispositive of intent that a reviewing court can say beyond a reasonable doubt that the jury would have found it unnecessary to rely on the presumption." *Connecticut* v. *Johnson* (1983) (POWELL, J., dissenting). This case is, of course, far different. No court could ever determine that the instructions on the element were superfluous, since the error in the instructions went to the ultimate fact that the juries were required to find. *Rose* v. *Clark* did not modify the precedents requiring that a jury find all of the elements of a crime under the proper standard, any more than it modified the Sixth Amendment's provision that "[i]n all criminal prosecutions, the accused shall enjoy the right to a . . . trial by an impartial jury."

II

Aside from its error in remanding convictions which must clearly be reversed, the Court announces an obscenity standard that fails to accomplish the goal that the Court ascribes to it. After stressing the need to avoid a mere majoritarian inquiry, the Court states:

> "The proper inquiry is not whether an ordinary member of any given community would find serious literary, artistic, political, or scientific value in allegedly obscene material, but whether a reasonable person could find such value in the material, taken as a whole."

The problem with this formulation is that it assumes that all reasonable persons would resolve the value inquiry in the same way. In fact, there are many cases in which *some* reasonable people would find that specific sexually oriented materials have serious artistic, political, literary, or scientific value, while *other* reasonable people would conclude that they have no such value. The Court's formulation does not tell the jury how to decide such cases.

In my judgment, communicative material of this sort is entitled to the protection of the First Amendment if *some reasonable persons* could consider it as having serious literary artistic, political, or scientific value. Over 40 years ago, the Court recognized that

> "Under our system of government there is an accommodation for the widest varieties of tastes and ideas. What is good literature, what has educational value, what is refined public information, what is good art, varies with individuals as it does from one generation to another. . . . From the multitude of competing offerings the public will pick and choose. What seems to one to be trash may have for others fleeting or even enduring values." *Hannegan* v. *Esquire* (1946).

The purpose of the third element of the *Miller* test is to ensure that the obscenity laws not be allowed to " 'level' the available reading matter to the majority or lowest common denominator of the population. . . . It is obvious that neither *Ulysses* nor *Lady Chatterley's Lover* would have literary appeal to the majority of the population." F. Schauer, The Law of Obscenity 144 (1976). A juror asked to create "a reasonable person" in order to apply the standard that the Court announces today, might well believe that the majority of the population who find no value in such a book are more reasonable than the minority who do find value. First Amendment protection surely must not be contingent on this type of subjective determination.

III

There is an even more basic reason why I believe these convictions must be reversed. The difficulties inherent in the Court's "reasonable person" standard reaffirm my conviction that government may not constitutionally criminalize mere possession or sale of obscene literature, absent some connection to minors, or obtrusive display to unconsenting adults. During the recent years in which the court has struggled with the proper definition of obscenity, six Members of the Court have expressed the opinion that the First Amendment, at the very least, precludes criminal prosecutions for sales such as those involved in this case. Dissenting in *Smith* v. *United States* (1977) I explained my view:

> "The question of offensiveness to community standards, whether national or local, is not one that the average juror can be expected to answer with evenhanded consistency. The average juror may well have one reaction to sexually oriented materials in a completely private setting and an entirely different reaction in a social context. Studies have shown that an opinion held by a large majority of a group concerning a neutral and objective subject has a significant impact in distorting the perceptions of group members who would normally take a different position. Since obscenity is by no means a neutral subject, and since the ascertainment of a community standard is such a subjective task, the expression of individual jurors' sentiments will inevitably influence the perceptions of other jurors, particularly those who would normally be in the minority. Moreover, because the record never discloses the obscenity standards which the jurors actually apply, their decisions in these cases are effectively unreviewable by an appellate court. In the final analysis, the guilt or innocence of a criminal defendant in an obscenity trial is determined primarily by individual jurors' subjective reactions to the materials in question rather than by the predictable application of rules of law.
>
> "This conclusion is especially troubling because the same image—whether created by words, sounds, or pictures—may produce such a wide variety of reactions.... In my judgment, the line between communications which 'offend' and those which do not is too blurred to identify criminal conduct. It is also too blurred to delimit the protections of the First Amendment."

The Court has repeatedly recognized that the Constitution "requires that a penal statute define the criminal offense with sufficient definiteness that ordinary people can understand what conduct is prohibited and in a manner that does not encourage arbitrary and discriminatory enforcement." *Kolender* v. *Lawson* (1983). These two requirements serve overlapping functions. Not only do vague statutes tend to give rise to selective and arbitrary prosecution, but selective and arbitrary prosecution often lessens the degree to which an actor is on notice that his or her conduct is illegal.

When petitioners Pope and Morrison accepted part-time employment as clerks in the bookstores, they could hardly have been expected to examine the stores' entire inventories, and even if they had, they would have had no way of knowing which, if any, of the magazines being sold were legally "obscene." Perhaps if the enterprise were being carried out in a clandestine manner, it might be fair to impute to them knowledge that something illegal was going on. But these stores both had large signs indicating the nature of the enterprise, one claiming that the store had "The Largest Selection of Adult Merchandise in Northern Illinois". The Illinois appellate court found that Pope had the necessary scienter because it was "difficult to believe that [he] would not be fully apprised of the type and character of the three magazines simply by looking at them." It is obvious that Pope knew that the magazines were "pornographic," but that does not mean he knew, or should have known, that they were legally "obscene" under the Illinois statute, and our precedents. It would have been quite reasonable for him to conclude that if sale of the magazines were indeed against the law, then the police would never allow the store to remain in operation, much less publicly advertise its goods. Nor would an examination of the statute have given him much guidance.

Under ordinary circumstances, ignorance of the law is no excuse for committing a crime. But the principle presupposes a penal statute that adequately puts citizens on notice of what is illegal. The Constitution cannot tolerate schemes that criminalize categories of speech that the Court has conceded to be so vague and uncertain that they cannot "be defined legislatively." *Smith* v. *United States*. If a legislature cannot define the crime, . . . Pope and . . . Morrison should not be expected to. . . .

Concern with the vagueness inherent in criminal obscenity statutes is not the only constitutional objection to the criminalization of the sale of sexually-explicit material (not involving children) to consenting adults. In *Stanley* v. *Georgia* (1969), the Court held that Georgia could not criminalize the mere possession of obscene matter. The decision was grounded upon a recognition that "[o]ur whole constitutional heritage rebels at the thought of giving government the power to control men's minds." The only justification we could find for the law there was Georgia's desire to "protect the individual's mind from the effects of obscenity," and we concluded that such a desire to "control the moral content of a person's thoughts . . . is wholly inconsistent with the philosophy of the First Amendment."

The Court has adopted a restrictive reading of *Stanley*, opining that it has no implications to the criminalization of the sale or distribution of obscenity. See *United States* v. *Reidel* (1971); *United States* v. *12 200-Ft. Reels of Super 8mm. Film* (1973). But such a crabbed approach offends the overarching First Amendment principles discussed in *Stanley*, almost as much as it insults the citizenry by declaring its right to read and possess material which it may not legally obtain. In *Stanley*, the Court recognized that there are legitimate reasons for the state to regulate obscenity: protecting children and protecting the sensibilities of unwilling viewers. But surely a broad criminal prohibition on all sale of obscene material cannot survive simply because the state may constitutionally restrict public display or prohibit sale of the material to minors.

As was the case in *Smith*, "I do not know whether the ugly pictures in this record have any beneficial value." (STEVENS, J., dissenting). I do know though that

> "[t]he fact that there is a large demand for comparable materials indicates that they do provide amusement or information, or at least satisfy the curiosity of interested persons. Moreover, there are serious well-intentioned people who are persuaded that they serve a worthwhile purpose. Others believe they arouse passions that lead to the commission of crimes; if that be true, surely there is a mountain of material just within the protected zone that is equally capable of motivating comparable conduct. Moreover, the baneful effects of these materials are disturbingly reminiscent of arguments formerly made about what are now valued as works of art. In the end, I believe we must rely on the capacity of the free marketplace of ideas to distinguish that which is useful or beautiful from that which is ugly or worthless."

I respectfully dissent.

COURT ON PREVENTIVE DETENTION

May 26, 1987

The Supreme Court May 26 upheld, 6-3, the constitutionality of pretrial detention of felony suspects deemed to be dangerous to the community. The decision in United States v. Salerno *proved highly controversial and provoked a quick reaction from those opposed to jailing suspects without trial. It was condemned by the* Washington Post, *the* New York Times, *the American Civil Liberties Union, and various legal scholars. And yet the Court affirmed a provision of the 1984 federal anticrime statute that had passed by overwhelming bipartisan majorities in the House and Senate and appeared to have widespread public support. The decision was seen as a victory for those advocating tougher measures against crime, and represented a triumph for the Reagan administration.*

Chief Justice William H. Rehnquist wrote the Court's opinion, in which Justices Byron R. White, Harry A. Blackmun, Lewis F. Powell, Jr., Sandra Day O'Connor, and Antonin Scalia joined. Justice Thurgood Marshall filed a dissenting opinion, which was joined by Justice William J. Brennan, Jr. Justice John Paul Stevens also filed a dissenting opinion.

At issue was the very heart of due process: does preventive detention constitute punishment without trial? The Court issued a qualified endorsement that the type of pretrial detention contemplated by the Bail Reform Act of 1984 does not violate due process. In doing so, it upheld a law that had been used fairly frequently since its passage. In the twelve months following July 1, 1985, federal judges reported presiding at 9,440 hearings on requests for preventive detention. But the greatest effect of the ruling was at the state level, where most criminal trials take place. Twenty-four states and the District of Columbia allowed preventive detention.

The Dangers of Tough Talk

The case had all the ingredients for a lively novel. The defendants had already achieved notoriety as the alleged head and principal deputy of the Genovese crime family based in New York City. Anthony (Fat Tony) Salerno and Vincent (Fish) Cafaro were arrested March 21, 1986, and charged with a twenty-nine count indictment under the Racketeer Influenced and Corrupt Organizations Act (RICO), as well as statutes outlawing mail and wire fraud, extortion, gambling, and conspiracy to commit murder. (Historic Documents of 1986, p. 215)

Federal prosecutors sought pretrial detention on the ground that the two Mafia bosses were dangerous. At a hearing the government introduced wiretap evidence and the testimony of informants to show that the two had participated in conspiracies to pursue family business through violent means. Salerno formally opposed the government's request, but Cafaro did not, dismissing the evidence as mere "tough talk." The district court granted the request and ordered both defendants detained.

Salerno and Cafaro appealed on the ground that if the Bail Reform Act of 1984 permitted detention because the person arrested was likely to commit future crimes, it was unconstitutional on its face. This type of challenge was known as a facial challenge and required a showing that there were no circumstances under which the acts authorized by the statute would be constitutional. They also argued that the act imposed excessive bail in violation of the Eighth Amendment. The appeals court agreed with the defendants' first ground, causing the government to appeal the matter to the Supreme Court.

Test Case or Moot

Before the case could reach the Supreme Court, defendant Salerno was convicted on unrelated charges and sentenced to one hundred years in prison. As this conviction, rather than the pretrial order, was the basis for keeping him in jail, it appeared to Marshall, Brennan, and Stevens that the case had become moot and should not have been decided.

Also before the Supreme Court could act and unknown to his codefendant, Cafaro decided to cooperate with the government and was released, ostensibly for medical reasons. The medical release was conditioned upon a $1 million general bond, to which the government consented. Therefore, he was not detained under the Bail Reform Act of 1984 at the time the case came before the Supreme Court. For the minority of the Court, these facts again meant no justiciable issue because Cafaro had been released under different statutory authority with government consent.

According to a footnote in Marshall's dissent, the government's brief did not disclose these facts. Instead, the government contended that Cafaro was "still subject to the pretrial detention order." The majority dealt with these matters in a short footnote: "Salerno was subsequently sentenced in unrelated proceedings before a different judge. To this date, however, Salerno has not confined pursuant to that sentence. The authority for Salerno's present incarceration remains the District Court's pretrial detention order. The case is therefore very much alive and is properly presented for our resolution." The majority made no reference to Cafaro's status.

Due Process

Writing for the majority, Rehnquist reasoned that pretrial detention would be a violation of substantive due process if it were punishment. However, because it was not punishment but regulation intended to secure community safety, pretrial detention was legitimate. As examples of societal interests that outweighed the individual's interest in freedom, Rehnquist cited the government's rights to detain individuals believed to be dangerous in times of war or insurrection, and to restrain mental patients who present a danger to the community. He reasoned that the government's interest in preventing crime was no less legitimate and compelling than the interest that permitted detention under other circumstances. Provided that preventive detention was accompanied by a showing of probable cause for making the arrest in the first place and a showing of clear and convincing evidence that no conditions of release would reasonably assure the safety of the community or any person (such as adverse witnesses), it could be used to further that interest.

For Marshall the majority's decision disregarded basic legal principles central to the Bill of Rights and previously honored for hundreds of years. There was more than a touch of bitterness in his assessment. "This case brings before the Court for the first time a statute in which Congress declares that a person innocent of any crime may be jailed indefinitely, pending the trial of allegations which are legally presumed to be untrue, if the Government shows to the satisfaction of a judge that the accused is likely to commit crimes, unrelated to the pending charges, at any time in the future. Such statutes, consistent with the usages of tyranny and the excesses of what bitter experience teaches us to call the police state, have long been thought incompatible with the fundamental human rights protected by our Constitution." He claimed that "the majority's technique for infringing on [the right to be free from punishment before conviction] is simple: merely redefine any measure which is claimed to be punishment as 'regulation,' and, magically, the Constitution no longer prohibits its imposition."

Following are excerpts from the Supreme Court's decision in United States v. Salerno, *issued May 26, 1987, upholding the constitutionality of pretrial detention of felony suspects deemed dangerous to the community; and from the dissent of Justice Thurgood Marshall:*

No. 86-87

United States, Petitioner v. Anthony Salerno and Vincent Cafaro	On writ of certiorari to the United States Court of Appeals for the Second Circuit

[May 26, 1987]

CHIEF JUSTICE REHNQUIST delivered the opinion of the Court.

The Bail Reform Act of 1984 allows a federal court to detain an arrestee pending trial if the government demonstrates by clear and convincing evidence after an adversary hearing that no release conditions "will reasonably assure . . . the safety of any other person and the community." The United States Court of Appeals for the Second Circuit struck down this provision of the Act as facially unconstitutional, because, in that court's words, this type of pretrial detention violates "substantive due process." We granted certiorari because of a conflict among the Courts of Appeals regarding the validity of the Act. We hold that, as against the facial attack mounted by these respondents, the Act fully comports with constitutional requirements. We therefore reverse.

I

Responding to "the alarming problem of crimes committed by persons on release," Congress formulated the Bail Reform Act of 1984 as the solution to a bail crisis in the federal courts. The Act represents the National Legislature's considered response to numerous perceived deficiencies in the federal bail process. By providing for sweeping changes in both the way federal courts consider bail applications and the circumstances under which bail is granted, Congress hoped to "give the courts adequate authority to make release decisions that give appropriate recognition to the danger a person may pose to others if released."

To this end, § 3141(a) of the Act requires a judicial officer to determine whether an arrestee shall be detained. Section 3142(e) provides that "[i]f, after a hearing pursuant to the provisions of subsection (f), the judicial officer finds that no condition or combination of conditions will reasonably assure the appearance of the person as required and the safety of any other person and the community, he shall order the detention of the person prior to trial." Section 3142(f) provides the arrestee with a number of procedural safeguards. He may request the presence of counsel at the detention hearings, he may testify and present witnesses in his behalf, as well as proffer evidence, and he may cross-examine other witnesses appearing at the hearing. If the judicial officer finds that no conditions of pretrial release can reasonably assure the safety of other persons and the community, he must state his findings of fact in writing, § 3142(i), and support his conclusion with "clear and convincing evidence," § 3142(f).

The judicial officer is not given unbridled discretion in making the detention determination. Congress has specified the considerations relevant to that decision. These factors include the nature and seriousness of the charges, the substantiality of the government's evidence against the arrestee, the arrestee's background and characteristics, and the nature and seriousness of the danger posed by the suspect's release. § 3142(g). Should a judicial officer order detention, the detainee is entitled to expedited appellate review of the detention order. § 3145(b), (c).

Respondents Anthony Salerno and Vincent Cafaro were arrested on March 21, 1986, after being charged in a 29-count indictment alleging various Racketeer Influenced and Corrupt Organizations Act (RICO) violations, mail and wire fraud offenses, extortion, and various criminal gambling violations. The RICO counts alleged 35 acts of racketeering activity, including fraud, extortion, gambling, and conspiracy to commit murder. At respondents' arraignment, the Government moved to have Salerno and Cafaro detained pursuant to § 3142(e), on the ground that no condition of release would assure the safety of the community or any person. The District Court held a hearing at which the Government made a detailed proffer of evidence. The Government's case showed that Salerno was the "boss" of the Genovese Crime Family of La Cosa Nostra and that Cafaro was a "captain" in the Genovese Family. According to the Government's proffer, based in large part on conversations intercepted by a court-ordered wiretap, the two respondents had participated in wide-ranging conspiracies to aid their illegitimate enterprises through violent means. The Government also offered the testimony of two of its trial witnesses, who would assert that Salerno personally participated in two murder conspiracies. Salerno opposed the motion for detention, challenging the credibility of the Government's witnesses. He offered the testimony of several character witnesses as well as a letter from his doctor stating that he was suffering from a serious medical condition. Cafaro presented no evidence at the hearing, but instead characterized the wiretap conversations as merely "tough talk."

The District Court granted the Government's detention motion, concluding that the Government had established by clear and convincing evidence that no condition or combination of conditions of release would ensure the safety of the community or any person:

> "The activities of a criminal organization such as the Genovese Family do not cease with the arrest of its principals and their release on even the most stringent of bail conditions. The illegal businesses, in place for many years, require constant attention and protection, or they will fail.... [T]his court recognizes a strong incentive ... to continue business as usual. When business as usual involves threats, beatings, and murder, the present danger such people pose in the community is self-evident."

Respondents appealed, contending that to the extent that the Bail Reform Act permits pretrial detention on the ground that the arrestee is likely to commit future crimes, it is unconstitutional on its face. Over a dissent, the United States Court of Appeals for the Second Circuit agreed. (1986). Although the court agreed that pretrial detention could be imposed if the defendants were likely to intimidate witnesses or otherwise jeopardize the trial process, it found "§ 3142(e)'s authorization of pretrial detention [on the ground of future dangerousness] repugnant to the concept of substantive due process, which we believe prohibits the total deprivation of liberty simply as a means of preventing future crimes." The court concluded that the Government could not, consistent with due process, detain persons who had not been accused of any crime merely because they were thought to present a danger to the community. It reasoned that our criminal law system holds persons accountable for past actions, not anticipated future actions. Although a court could detain an arrestee who threatened to flee before trial, such detention would be permissible because it would serve the basic objective of a criminal system—bringing the accused to trial. The court distinguished our decision in *Gerstein* v. *Pugh* (1975), in which we upheld police detention pursuant to arrest. The court construed *Gerstein* as limiting such detention to the " 'administrative steps incident to arrest.' " The Court of Appeals also found our decision in *Schall* v. *Martin* (1984), upholding postarrest pretrial detention of juveniles, inapposite because juveniles have a lesser interest in liberty than do adults. The dissenting judge concluded that on its face, the Bail Reform Act adequately balanced the Federal Government's compelling interests in public safety against the detainee's liberty interests.

II

A facial challenge to a legislative Act is, of course, the most difficult challenge to mount successfully, since the challenger must establish that no set of circumstances exists under which the Act would be valid. The fact that the Bail Reform Act might operate unconstitutionally under some conceivable set of circumstances is insufficient to render it wholly invalid, since we have not recognized an "overbreadth" doctrine outside the limited context of the First Amendment. *Schall* v. *Martin*. We think respondents have failed to shoulder their heavy burden to demonstrate that the Act is "facially" unconstitutional.

Respondents present two grounds for invalidating the Bail Reform Act's provisions permitting pretrial detention on the basis of future dangerousness. First, they rely upon the Court of Appeals' conclusion that the Act exceeds the limitations placed upon the Federal Government by the Due Process Clause of the Fifth Amendment. Second, they contend that the Act contravenes the Eighth Amendment's proscription against excessive bail. We treat these contentions in turn.

A

The Due Process Clause of the Fifth Amendment provides that "No person shall ... be deprived of life, liberty, or property, without due process of law. . . ." This Court has held that the Due Process Clause protects individuals against two types of government action. So-called "substantive due process" prevents the government from engaging in conduct that "shocks the conscience," *Rochin* v. *California* (1952), or interferes with rights "implicit in the concept of ordered liberty," *Palko* v. *Connecticut* (1937). When government action depriving a person of life, liberty, or property survives substantive due process scrutiny, it must still be implemented in a fair manner. *Mathews* v. *Eldridge* (1976). This requirement has traditionally been referred to as "procedural" due process.

Respondents first argue that the Act violates substantive due process because the pretrial detention it authorizes constitutes impermissible punishment before trial. See *Bell* v. *Wolfish* (1979). The Government, however, has never argued that pretrial detention could be upheld if it were "punishment." The Court of Appeals assumed that pretrial detention under the Bail Reform Act is regulatory, not penal, and we agree that it is.

As an initial matter, the mere fact that a person is detained does not inexorably lead to the conclusion that the government has imposed punishment. *Bell* v. *Wolfish.* To determine whether a restriction on liberty constitutes impermissible punishment or permissible regulation, we first look to legislative intent. *Schall* v. *Martin.* Unless Congress expressly intended to impose punitive restrictions, the punitive/regulatory distinction turns on " 'whether an alternative purpose to which [the restriction] may rationally be connected is assignable for it, and whether it appears excessive in relation to the alternative purpose assigned [to it].' " *Ibid.*, quoting *Kennedy* v. *Mendoża-Martinez* (1963).

We conclude that the detention imposed by the Act falls on the regulatory side of the dichotomy. The legislative history of the Bail Reform Act clearly indicates that Congress did not formulate the pretrial detention provisions as punishment for dangerous individuals. Congress instead perceived pretrial detention as a potential solution to a pressing societal problem. There is no doubt that preventing danger to the community is a legitimate regulatory goal. *Schall* v. *Martin.*

Nor are the incidents of pretrial detention excessive in relation to the regulatory goal Congress sought to achieve. The Bail Reform Act carefully limits the circumstances under which detention may be sought to the most serious of crimes. See 18 U.S.C. § 3142(f) (detention hearings available if case involves crimes of violence, offenses for which the sentence is life imprisonment or death, serious drug offenses, or certain repeat offenders). The arrestee is entitled to a prompt detention hearing, and the maximum length of pretrial detention is limited by the stringent time limitations of the Speedy Trial Act. See 18 U.S.C. § 3161 *et seq.* Moreover, as in *Schall* v. *Martin,* the conditions of confinement envisioned by the Act "appear to reflect the regulatory purposes relied upon by the" government. As in *Schall,* the statute at issue here requires that detainees be housed in a "facility separate, to the extent practicable, from persons awaiting or serving sentences or being held in custody pending appeal." We conclude, therefore, that the pretrial detention contemplated by the Bail Reform Act is regulatory in nature, and does not constitute punishment before trial in violation of the Due Process Clause.

The Court of Appeals nevertheless concluded that "the Due Process Clause prohibits pretrial detention on the ground of danger to the community as a regulatory measure, without regard to the duration of the detention." Respondents characterize the Due Process Clause as erecting an impenetrable "wall" in this area that "no governmental interest—rational, important, compelling or otherwise—may surmount."

We do not think the Clause lays down any such categorical imperative. We have repeatedly held that the government's regulatory interest in community safety can, in appropriate circumstances, outweigh an individual's liberty interest. For example, in times of war or insurrection, when society's interest is at its peak, the government may detain individuals whom the government believes to be dangerous. See *Ludecke* v. *Watkins* (1948) (approving unreviewable Executive power to detain enemy aliens in time of war); *Moyer* v. *Peabody* (1909) (rejecting due process claim of individual jailed without probable cause by Governor in time of insurrection). Even outside the exigencies of war, we have found that sufficiently compelling governmental interests can justify detention of dangerous persons. Thus, we have found no absolute constitutional barrier to detention of potentially dangerous resident aliens pending deportation proceedings. *Carlson* v. *Landon* (1952); *Wong Wing* v. *United States* (1896). We have also held that the government may detain mentally unstable individuals who present a danger to the public, *Addington* v. *Texas* (1979), and dangerous defendants who become incompetent to stand trial, *Jackson* v. *Indiana* (1972); *Greenwood* v. *United States* (1956)....

Respondents characterize all of these cases as exceptions to the "general rule" of substantive due process that the government may not detain a person prior to a judgment of guilt in a criminal trial. Such a "general rule" may freely be conceded, but we think that these cases show a sufficient number of exceptions to the rule that the congressional action challenged here can hardly be characterized as totally novel. Given the well-established authority of the government, in special circumstances, to restrain individuals' liberty prior to or even without criminal trial and conviction, we think that the present statute providing for pretrial detention on the basis of dangerousness must be evaluated in precisely the same manner that we evaluated the laws in the cases discussed above.

The government's interest in preventing crime by arrestees is both legitimate and compelling. *De Veau* v. *Braisted* (1960). In *Schall,* we recognized the strength of the State's interest in preventing juvenile crime. This general concern with crime prevention is no less compelling when the suspects are adults. . . . The Bail Reform Act of 1984 responds to an even more particularized governmental interest than the interest we sustained in *Schall.* The statute we upheld in *Schall* permitted pretrial detention of any juvenile arrested on any charge after a showing that the individual might commit some undefined further crimes. The Bail Reform Act, in contrast, narrowly focuses on a particularly acute problem in which the government interests are overwhelming. The Act operates only on individuals who have been arrested for a specific category of extremely serious offenses. Congress specifically found that these individuals are far more likely to be responsible for dangerous acts in the community after arrest. Nor is the Act by any means a scattershot attempt to incapacitate those who are merely suspected of these serious crimes. The government must first of all demonstrate probable cause to believe that the charged crime has been committed by the arrestee, but that is not enough. In a full-blown adversary hearing, the government must convince a neutral decisionmaker by clear and convincing evidence that no conditions of release can reasonably assure the safety of the community or any person. While the government's general interest in preventing crime is compelling, even this interest is heightened when the government musters convincing proof that the arrestee, already indicted or held to answer for a serious crime, presents a demonstrable danger to the community. Under these narrow circumstances, society's interest in crime prevention is at its greatest.

On the other side of the scale, of course, is the individual's strong interest in liberty. We do not minimize the importance and fundamental nature of this right. But, as our cases hold, this right may, in circumstances where the government's interest is sufficiently weighty, be subordinated to the greater needs of society. We think that Congress' careful delineation of the circumstances under which detention will be permitted satisfies this standard. When the government proves by clear and convincing evidence that an arrestee presents an identified and articulable threat to an individual or the community, we believe that, consistent with the Due Process Clause, a court may disable the arrestee from executing that threat. Under these circumstances, we cannot categorically state that pretrial detention "offends some principle of justice so rooted in the traditions and conscience of our people as to be ranked as fundamental." *Snyder* v. *Massachusetts* (1934).

Finally, we may dispose briefly of respondents' facial challenge to the procedures of the Bail Reform Act. To sustain them against such a challenge, we need only find them "adequate to authorize the pretrial detention of at least some [persons] charged with crimes," *Schall,* whether or not they might be insufficient in some particular circumstances. We think they pass that test. As we stated in *Schall,* "there is nothing inherently unattainable about a prediction of future criminal conduct." Under the Bail Reform Act, the procedures by which a judicial officer evaluates the likelihood of future dangerousness are specifically designed to further the accuracy of that determination. Detainees have a right to counsel at the detention hearing. They may testify in their own behalf, present information by proffer or otherwise, and cross-examine witnesses who appear at the hearing. The judicial officer charged with the responsibility of determining the appropriateness of detention is guided by statutorily enumerated factors, which include the nature and the circumstances of the charges, the weight of the evidence, the history and characteristics of the putative offender, and the danger to the community. The government must prove its case by clear and convincing evidence. Finally, the judicial officer must include written findings of fact and a written statement of reasons for a decision to detain. The Act's review provisions, § 3145(c), provide for immediate appellate review of the detention decision.

We think these extensive safeguards suffice to repel a facial challenge. The protections are more exacting than those we found sufficient in the juvenile context, and they far exceed what we found necessary to effect limited postarrest detention in *Gerstein* v. *Pugh* (1975). Given the legitimate and compelling regulatory purpose of the Act and the procedural protections it offers, we conclude that the Act is not facially invalid under the Due Process Clause of the Fifth Amendment.

B

Respondents also contend that the Bail Reform Act violates the Excessive Bail Clause of the Eighth Amendment. The Court of Appeals did not address this issue because it found that the Act violates the Due Process Clause. We think that the Act survives a challenge founded upon the Eighth Amendment.

The Eighth Amendment addresses pretrial release by providing merely that "Excessive bail shall not be required." This Clause, of course, says nothing about whether bail shall be available at all. Respondents nevertheless contend that this Clause grants them a right to bail calculated solely upon considerations of flight. They rely on *Stack* v. *Boyle* (1951), in which the Court stated that "Bail set at a figure higher than an amount reasonably calculated [to ensure the defendant's presence at trial] is 'excessive' under the Eighth Amendment." In respondents' view, since the Bail Reform Act allows a court essentially to set bail at an infinite amount for reasons not related to the risk of flight, it violates the Excessive Bail Clause. Respondents concede that the right to bail they have discovered in the Eighth Amendment is not absolute. A court may, for example, refuse bail in capital cases. And, as the Court of Appeals noted and respondents admit, a court may refuse bail when the defendant presents a threat to the judicial process by intimidating witnesses. Respondents characterize these exceptions as consistent with what they claim to be the sole purpose of bail—to ensure integrity of the judicial process.

While we agree that a primary function of bail is to safeguard the courts' role in adjudicating the guilt or innocence of defendants, we reject the proposition that the Eighth Amendment categorically prohibits the government from pursuing other admittedly compelling interests through regulation of pretrial release. The above-quoted *dicta* in *Stack* v. *Boyle* is far too slender a reed on which to rest this argument. The Court in *Stack* had no occasion to consider whether the Excessive Bail Clause requires courts to admit all defendants to bail, because the statute before the Court in that case in fact allowed the defendants to be bailed. Thus, the Court had to determine only whether bail, admittedly available in that case, was excessive if set at a sum greater than that necessary to ensure the arrestees' presence at trial.

The holding of *Stack* is illuminated by the Court's holding just four months later in *Carlson* v. *Landon* (1952). In that case, remarkably similar to the present action, the detainees had been arrested and held without bail pending a determination of deportability. The Attorney General refused to release the individuals, "on the ground that there was reasonable cause to believe that [their] release would be prejudicial to the public interest and *would endanger the welfare and safety of the United States.*" ([E]mphasis added). The detainees brought the same challenge that respondents bring to us today: the Eighth Amendment required them to be admitted to bail. The Court squarely rejected this proposition:

> "The bail clause was lifted with slight changes from the English Bill of Rights Act. In England that clause has never been thought to accord a right to bail in all cases, but merely to provide that bail shall not be excessive in those cases where it is proper to grant bail. When this clause was carried over into our Bill of Rights, nothing was said that indicated any different concept. The Eighth Amendment has not prevented Congress from defining the classes of cases in which bail shall be allowed in this country. Thus, in criminal cases bail is not compulsory where the punishment may be death. Indeed, the very language of the Amendment fails to say all arrests must be bailable."

Carlson v. *Landon* was a civil case, and we need not decide today whether the Excessive Bail Clause speaks at all to Congress' power to define the classes of criminal arrestees who shall be admitted to bail. For even if we were to conclude that the Eighth Amendment imposes some substantive limitations on the National Legislature's powers in this area, we would still hold that the Bail Reform Act is valid. Nothing in the text of the Bail Clause limits permissible government considerations solely to questions of flight. The only arguable substantive limitation of the Bail Clause is that the government's proposed conditions of release or detention not be "excessive" in light of the perceived evil. Of course, to determine whether the government's response is excessive, we must compare that response against the interest the government seeks to protect by means of that response. Thus, when the government has admitted that its only interest is in preventing flight, bail must be set by a court at a sum designed to ensure that goal, and no more. *Stack* v. *Boyle*. We believe that when Congress has mandated detention on the basis of a compelling interest other than prevention of flight, as it has here, the Eighth Amendment does not require release on bail.

III

In our society liberty is the norm, and detention prior to trial or without trial is the carefully limited exception. We hold that the provisions for pretrial detention in the Bail Reform Act of 1984 fall within that carefully limited exception. The Act authorizes the detention prior to trial of arrestees charged with serious felonies who are found after an adversary hearing to pose a threat to the safety of individuals or to the community which no condition of release can dispel. The numerous procedural safeguards detailed above must attend this adversary hearing. We are unwilling to say that this congressional determination, based as it is upon that primary concern of every government—a concern for the safety and indeed the lives of its citizens—on its face violates either the Due Process Clause of the Fifth Amendment or the Excessive Bail Clause of the Eighth Amendment.

The judgment of the Court of Appeals is therefore

Reversed.

JUSTICE MARSHALL, with whom JUSTICE BRENNAN joins, dissenting.

This case brings before the Court for the first time a statute in which Congress delcares that a person innocent of any crime may be jailed indefinitely, pending the trial of allegations which are legally presumed to be untrue, if the Government shows to the satisfaction of a judge that the accused is likely to commit crimes, unrelated to the pending charges, at any time in the future. Such statutes, consistent with the usages of tyranny and the excesses of what bitter experience teaches us to call the police state, have long been thought incompatible with the fundamental human rights protected by our Constitution. Today a majority of this Court holds otherwise. Its decision disregards basic principles of justice established centuries ago and enshrined beyond the reach of governmental interference in the Bill of Rights.

I

A few preliminary words are necessary with respect to the majority's treatment of the facts in this case. The two paragraphs which the majority devotes to the procedural posture are essentially correct, but they omit certain matters which are of substantial legal relevance.

The Solicitor General's petition for certiorari was filed on July 21, 1986. On October 9, 1986, respondent Salerno filed a response to the petition. No response or appearance of counsel was filed on behalf of respondent Cafaro. The petition for certiorari was granted on November 3, 1986.

On November 19, 1986, respondent Salerno was convicted after a jury trial on charges unrelated to those alleged in the indictment in this case. On January 13, 1987, Salerno was sentenced on those charges to 100 years' imprisonment. As of that date, the Government no longer required a pretrial detention order for the purpose of keeping Salerno incarcerated; it could simply take him into custody on the judgment and commitment order. The present case thus became moot as to respondent Salerno.

The situation with respect to respondent Cafaro is still more disturbing. In early October 1986, before the Solicitor General's petition for certiorari was granted, respondent Cafaro became a cooperating witness, assisting the Government's investigation "by working in a covert capacity." The information that Cafaro was cooperating with the Government was not revealed to his co-defendants, including respondent Salerno. On October 9, 1986, respondent Cafaro was released, ostensibly "temporarily for medical care and treatment," with the Government's consent. This release was conditioned upon execution of a personal recognizance bond in the sum of $1,000,000, under the general pretrial release provisions of 18 U.S.C. § 3141. In short, respondent Cafaro became an informant and the Government agreed to his release on bail in order that he might better serve the Government's purposes. As to Cafaro, this case was no longer justiciable even before certiorari was granted, but the information bearing upon the essential issue of the Court's jurisdiction was not made available to us.

The Government thus invites the Court to address the facial constitutionality of the pretrial detention statute in a case involving two respondents, one of whom has been sentenced to a century of jail time in another case and released pending appeal with the Government's consent, while the other was released on bail *in this case,* with the Government's consent, because he had become an informant. These facts raise, at the very least, a substantial question as to the Court's jurisdiction, for it is far from clear that there is now an actual controversy between these parties. As we have recently said, "Article III of the Constitution requires that there be a live case or controversy at the time that a federal court decides the case; it is not enough that there may have been a live case or controversy when the case was decided by the court whose judgment we are reviewing." *Burke* v. *Barnes* (1987).... Only by flatly ignoring these matters is the majority able to maintain the pretense that it has jurisdiction to decide the question which it is in such a hurry to reach.

II

The majority approaches respondents' challenge to the Act by dividing the discussion into two sections, one concerned with the substantive guarantees implicit in the Due Process Clause, and the other concerned with the protection afforded by the Excessive Bail Clause of the Eighth Amendment. This is a sterile formalism, which divides a unitary argument into two independent parts and then professes to demonstrate that the parts are individually inadequate.

On the due process side of this false dichotomy appears an argument concerning the distinction between regulatory and punitive legislation. The majority concludes that the Act is a regulatory rather than a punitive measure. The ease with which the conclusion is reached suggests the worthlessness of the achievement. The major premise is that "[u]nless

Congress expressly intended to impose punitive restrictions, the punitive/regulatory distinction turns on ' "whether an alternative purpose to which [the restriction] may rationally be connected is assignable for it, and whether it appears excessive in relation to the alternative purpose assigned [to it]." ' " The majority finds that "Congress did not formulate the pretrial detention provisions as punishment for dangerous individuals," but instead was pursuing the "legitimate regulatory goal" of "preventing danger to the community." Concluding that pretrial detention is not an excessive solution to the problem of preventing danger to the community, the majority thus finds that no substantive element of the guarantee of due process invalidates the statute.

This argument does not demonstrate the conclusion it purports to justify. Let us apply the majority's reasoning to a similar, hypothetical case. After investigation, Congress determines (not unrealistically) that a large proportion of violent crime is perpetrated by persons who are unemployed. It also determines, equally reasonably, that much violent crime is committed at night. From amongst the panoply of "potential solutions," Congress chooses a statute which permits, after judicial proceedings, the imposition of a dusk-to-dawn curfew on anyone who is unemployed. Since this is not a measure enacted for the purpose of punishing the unemployed, and since the majority finds that preventing danger to the community is a legitimate regulatory goal, the curfew statute would, according to the majority's analysis, be a mere "regulatory" detention statute, entirely compatible with the substantive components of the Due Process Clause.

The absurdity of this conclusion arises, of course, from the majority's cramped concept of substantive due process. The majority proceeds as though the only substantive right protected by the Due Process Clause is a right to be free from punishment before conviction. The majority's technique for infringing this right is simple: merely redefine any measure which is claimed to be punishment as "regulation," and, magically, the Constitution no longer prohibits its imposition. Because ... the Due Process Clause protects other substantive rights which are infringed by this legislation, the majority's argument is merely an exercise in obfuscation.

The logic of the majority's Eighth Amendment analysis is equally unsatisfactory. The Eighth Amendment, as the majority notes, states that "[e]xcessive bail shall not be required." The majority then declares, as if it were undeniable, that: "[t]his Clause, of course, says nothing about whether bail shall be available at all." If excessive bail is imposed the defendant stays in jail. The same result is achieved if bail is denied altogether. Whether the magistrate sets bail at $1 billion or refuses to set bail at all, the consequences are indistinguishable. It would be mere sophistry to suggest that the Eighth Amendment protects against the former decision, and not the latter. Indeed, such a result would lead to the conclusion that there was no need for Congress to pass a preventive detention measure of any kind; every federal magistrate and district judge could simply refuse, despite the absence of any evidence of risk of flight or danger to the community, to set bail. This would be entirely constitutional, since, according to the majority, the Eighth Amendment "says nothing about whether bail shall be available at all."

But perhaps, the majority says, this manifest absurdity can be avoided. Perhaps the Bail Clause is addressed only to the judiciary. "[W]e need not decide today," the majority says, "whether the Excessive Bail Clause speaks at all to Congress' power to define the classes of criminal arrestees who shall be admitted to bail." The majority is correct that this question need not be decided today; it was decided long ago. Federal and state statutes which purport to accomplish what the Eighth Amendment forbids, such as imposing cruel and unusual punishments, may not stand. See, e.g., *Trop* v. *Dulles* (1958); *Furman* v. *Georgia* (1972). The text of the Amendment, which provides simply that "[e]xcessive bail shall not be required, nor excessive fines imposed, nor cruel and unusual punishments inflicted," provides absolutely no support for the majority's speculation that both courts and Congress are forbidden to inflict cruel and unusual punishments, while only the courts are forbidden to require excessive bail.

The majority's attempts to deny the relevance of the Bail Clause to this case are unavailing, but the majority is nonetheless correct that the prohibition of excessive bail means that in order "to determine whether the government's response is excessive, we must compare that response against the interest the government seeks to protect by means of that response." The majority concedes, as it must, that "when the government has admitted that its only interest is in preventing flight, bail must be set by a court at a sum designed to ensure that goal, and no more." But, the majority says, "when Congress has mandated detention on the basis of a compelling interest other than prevention of flight, as it has here, the Eighth Amendment does not require release on bail." This conclusion follows only if the "compelling" interest upon which Congress acted is an interest which the Constitution permits Congress to further through the denial of bail. The majority does not ask, as a result of its disingenuous division of the analysis, if there are any substantive limits contained in both the Eighth Amendment and the Due Process Clause which render this system of preventive detention unconstitutional. The majority does not ask because the answer is apparent and, to the majority, inconvenient.

III

The essence of this case may be found, ironically enough, in a provision of the Act to which the majority does not refer. Title 18 U.S.C. § 3142(j) provides that "[n]othing in this section shall be construed as modifying or limiting the presumption of innocence." But the very pith and purpose of this statute is an abhorrent limitation of the presumption of innocence. The majority's untenable conclusion that the present Act is constitutional arises from a specious denial of the role of the Bail Clause and the Due

Process Clause in protecting the invaluable guarantee afforded by the presumption of innocence.

"The principle that there is a presumption of innocence in favor of the accused is the undoubted law, axiomatic and elementary, and its enforcement lies at the foundation of the administration of our criminal law." *Coffin* v. *United States* (1895). Our society's belief, reinforced over the centuries, that all are innocent until the state has proved them to be guilty, like the companion principle that guilt must be proved beyond a reasonable doubt, is "implicit in the concept of ordered liberty," *Palko* v. *Connecticut* (1937), and is established beyond legislative contravention in the Due Process Clause....

The statute now before us declares that persons who have been indicted may be detained if a judicial officer finds clear and convincing evidence that they pose a danger to individuals or to the community. The statute does not authorize the government to imprison anyone it has evidence is dangerous; indictment is necessary. But let us suppose that a defendant is indicted and the government shows by clear and convincing evidence that he is dangerous and should be detained pending a trial, at which trial the defendant is acquitted. May the government continue to hold the defendant in detention based upon its showing that he is dangerous? The answer cannot be yes, for that would allow the government to imprison someone for uncommitted crimes based upon "proof" not beyond a reasonable doubt. The result must therefore be that once the indictment has failed, detention cannot continue. But our fundamental principles of justice declare that the defendant is as innocent on the day before his trial as he is on the morning after his acquittal. Under this statute an untried indictment somehow acts to permit a detention, based on other charges, which after an acquittal would be unconstitutional. The conclusion is inescapable that the indictment has been turned into evidence, if not that the defendant is guilty of the crime charged, then that left to his own devices he will soon be guilty of something else. " 'If it suffices to accuse, what will become of the innocent?' " *Coffin* v. *United States*.

To be sure, an indictment is not without legal consequences. It establishes that there is probable cause to believe that an offense was committed, and that the defendant committed it. Upon probable cause a warrant for the defendant's arrest may issue; a period of administrative detention may occur before the evidence of probable cause is presented to a neutral magistrate. See *Gerstein* v. *Pugh* (1975). Once a defendant has been committed for trial he may be detained in custody if the magistrate finds that no conditions of release will prevent him from becoming a fugitive. But in this connection the charging instrument is evidence of nothing more than the fact that there will be a trial, and

> "release before trial is conditioned upon the accused's giving adequate assurance that he will stand trial and submit to sentence if found guilty.... *Stack* v. *Boyle* (1951).

The finding of probable cause conveys power to try, and the power to try imports of necessity the power to assure that the processes of justice will not be evaded or obstructed.... The detention purportedly authorized by this statute bears no relation to the government's power to try charges supported by a finding of probable cause, and thus the interests it serves are outside the scope of interests which may be considered in weighing the excessiveness of bail under the Eighth Amendment.

It is not a novel proposition that the Bail Clause plays a vital role in protecting the presumption of innocence. Reviewing the application for bail pending appeal by members of the American Communist Party convicted under the Smith Act, 18 U.S.C. § 2385, Justice Jackson wrote:

> "Grave public danger is said to result from what [the defendants] may be expected to do, in addition to what they have done since their conviction. If I assume that defendants are disposed to commit every opportune disloyal act helpful to Communist countries, it is still difficult to reconcile with traditional American law the jailing of persons by the courts because of anticipated but as yet uncommitted crimes. Imprisonment to protect society from predicted but unconsummated offenses is . . . unprecedented in this country and . . . fraught with danger of excesses and injustice...." *Williamson* v. *United States* (1950) (Jackson, J., in chambers).

As Chief Justice Vinson wrote for the Court in *Stack* v. *Boyle*, "Unless th[e] right to bail before trial is preserved, the presumption of innocence, secured only after centuries of struggle, would lose its meaning."

IV

There is a connection between the peculiar facts of this case and the evident constitutional defects in the statute which the Court upholds today. Respondent Cafaro was originally incarcerated for an indeterminate period at the request of the Government, which believed (or professed to believe) that his release imminently threatened the safety of the community. That threat apparently vanished, from the Government's point of view, when Cafaro agreed to act as a covert agent of the Government. There could be no more eloquent demonstration of the coercive power of authority to imprison upon prediction, or of the dangers which the almost inevitable abuses pose to the cherished liberties of a free society.

"It is a fair summary of history to say that the safeguards of liberty have frequently been forged in controversies involving not very nice people." *United States* v. *Rabinowitz* (1950) (Frankfurter, J., dissenting). Honoring the presumption of innocence is often difficult; sometimes we must pay substantial social costs as a result of our commitment to the values we espouse. But at the end of the day the presumption of innocence protects the innocent; the shortcuts we take with those whom we believe to be guilty injure only those wrongfully accused and, ultimately, ourselves.

Throughout the world today there are men, women, and children interned indefinitely, awaiting trials which may never come or which may be a mockery of the word, because their governments believe them to be "dangerous." Our Constitution, whose construction began two centuries ago, can shelter us forever from the evils of such unchecked power. Over two hundred years it has slowly, through our efforts, grown more durable, more expansive, and more just. But it cannot protect us if we lack the courage, and the self-restraint, to protect ourselves. Today a majority of the Court applies itself to an ominous exercise in demolition. Theirs is truly a decision which will go forth without authority, and come back without respect.

I dissent.

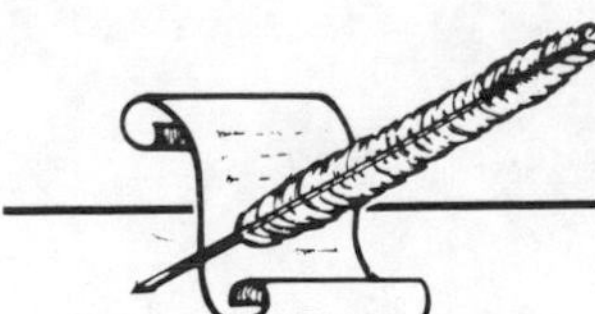

June

VOLCKER RESIGNATION AND GREENSPAN APPOINTMENT

June 2, 1987

President Ronald Reagan surprised most observers June 2 with the announcement that Paul A. Volcker, the nation's top banker and inflation fighter, was stepping down as chairman of the Federal Reserve Board. Alan Greenspan, who had advised President Richard Nixon on economic matters and served for two years as chairman of President Gerald Ford's Council of Economic Advisers, was tapped to succeed Volcker. The Senate August 3 confirmed the nomination, by a vote of 91-2. That made Reagan the first president since Franklin D. Roosevelt to have appointed all seven members of the Fed's Board of Governors.

The announcement—the day before Reagan departed for an economic summit in Venice with six other Western leaders—came amid speculation that Volcker might be reappointed to a third four-year term as chairman. Reaction on Capitol Hill, where Volcker's stature was virtually unassailable, was predictable. Members at both ends of the political spectrum expressed admiration for his single-minded approach to monetary policy and the Fed's success at controlling inflation, despite the recession of 1981-1982.

Reactions to Greenspan's appointment, while fewer and more restrained, were uncritical. Greenspan, a private economic consultant, was expected to be a like-minded advocate of tight reins on the money supply, allowing interest rates to rise if necessary to keep inflation under control. Greenspan said June 2, "It will be up to those of us who follow [Volcker] to be certain that those very hard-won gains are not lost. Assuring that will be one of my primary goals."

Volcker, whose term expired August 6, was a Democrat. He was appointed by President Jimmy Carter in 1979 and reappointed by Reagan in 1983. Greenspan, a Republican, served as an honorary official of Reagan's 1980 presidential campaign. (Volcker reappointment, Historic Documents of 1983, p. 595)

Timing of Announcement

Some observers speculated that the president's announcement of Greenspan's appointment might have been timed to coincide with Reagan's meeting June 8-10 with government leaders from Britain, Canada, France, Italy, Japan, and West Germany. Although Volcker had not been scheduled to attend the conference, the Federal Reserve Board, which regulates America's twelve federally chartered banks and controls the nation's flow of money, was one of the world's most influential economic forces. Among the issues on the summit table were key monetary and fiscal questions, including the stability of the dollar against other currencies and economic growth abroad, particularly in Japan and Germany. Volcker had been a key player in international economics, working to halt the dollar's fall and predicting worldwide calamity if the dollar did not stabilize. (Venice economic summit, p. 525)

The Senate Banking Committee July 28 unanimously recommended confirmation of Greenspan. During floor debate August 3, senators mixed approval of Greenspan with praise for his predecessor and awestruck bows to the power of the position. "I am confident that Alan Greenspan is up to the heavy responsibility that faces the chairman, and that he will measure up to the very high standards of his predecessor," said Christopher S. "Kit" Bond, R-Mo.

A Difficult Challenge

In office just over a month, Greenspan had to face a tumultuous economic scene that included a rapid drop in the dollar's value, rising interest rates, and the largest stock market plunge in history, which occurred on "Black Monday," October 19. (Stock market crash, p. 833) *Volcker, too, had faced a major financial crisis when he assumed the Fed chairmanship in 1979. At that time, the dollar was weak, inflation was rising, and the nation was suffering from a second round of oil price hikes.*

But Greenspan confronted a different combination of problems: an alarming trade imbalance and a budget deficit that was growing out of hand. (The latter led—partly because of international pressures—to an unprecedented budget-cutting negotiation between Congress and the executive branch.) While Volcker "inherited a situation he was able to move and address," according to Roger Guffey, president of the Kansas City Federal Reserve Bank, Greenspan "inherited a situation but had no time to address it."

To strengthen his hand in dealing with those problems, the new Fed chairman tried to involve his staff and board members in the decision-making process. "I think it has been great," said H. Robert Heller, a member of the board. "He has been open and communicative. . . . Now he has been tested by fire." Guffey said, "Greenspan has demonstrated an understanding of the institution, the strengths and the barriers in it. To me, he has shown a quick read of the Federal Reserve and what makes it strong."

Following is the text of President Ronald Reagan's June 2, 1987, statement on the retirement of Paul Volcker as chairman of the Federal Reserve Board and the nomination of Alan Greenspan to succeed him, and excerpts from the news conference following the announcement:

PRESIDENT REAGAN'S ANNOUNCEMENT

I have a statement for you: Paul Volcker has advised me of his decision not to accept a third term as a member and Chairman of the Federal Reserve Board.

I accepted Mr. Volcker's decision with great reluctance and regret. He has served with distinction on the Board of Governors and has been an historic chairman during this time of economic recovery and expansion. Therefore, it's my intention to nominate Dr. Alan Greenspan to a 4-year term as Chairman of the Federal Reserve. Mr. Volcker has indicated his strong support for Dr. Greenspan.

And let me add, my dedication to our fight to hold down the forces of inflation remains as strong as ever. And I know that Dr. Greenspan shares that same commitment.

Now, let me explain that because of my schedule and an appointment waiting for me, I am going to leave you and these three gentlemen here—Chairman Volcker and Secretary of the Treasury [James A.] Baker [III] and Dr. Greenspan all will have statements for you and take your questions.

PRESS BRIEFING

CHAIRMAN VOLCKER: If I could just say one word or two. I've known Alan Greenspan for a good many years. We were reminiscing earlier that it goes back about 30 years. And I know something of his talents, I know of his experience, his capacity, I know his dedication. And I'm delighted that the President asked him to serve and that he agreed. I have a certain interest in the Federal Reserve and I—

Q: Why are you leaving?

CHAIRMAN VOLCKER: —I feel very happy that Alan's going to take over that institution and—

Q: Why are you leaving?

CHAIRMAN VOLCKER: —and I'm sure maintain it.

Q: Why did you decline to take a third term?

CHAIRMAN VOLCKER: Well, you know, there's a time to come and a time to leave and there were a variety of considerations and I thought this was—

Q: Were you asked to stay?

CHAIRMAN VOLCKER: I had no feeling I was being pushed....

DR. GREENSPAN: I just wanted to say that I'm deeply grateful to the President for this opportunity to serve my country in one of its most sensitive economic posts.

Filling Paul Volcker's shoes will be a major challenge. As Paul has pointed out, we've known each other for a very long time, and I've followed him very closely, and there are very few people in this profession that are more impressive than he and who seem to do the right thing at the right time almost every time.

During the 1970's there was increasing fear that inflation was destined to ratchet ever-upward with ultimately disastrous effects and consequences to economic growth and employment. Under Paul's chairmanship, inflation has been effectively subdued. It will be up to those of us who follow him to be certain that those very hard-won gains are not lost. Assuring that will be one of my primary goals.

Paul, you have served as the model of the ideal chairman of the Federal Reserve. If the Senate confirms me, I intend to follow that model. Thank you.

SECRETARY BAKER: Ladies and gentlemen, I simply want to say that I think it goes without saying that the United States has been extremely fortunate to have had a man of Paul Volcker's extraordinary ability and commitment serve in this sensitive position for two full terms. I happen to think that the United States is also extremely fortunate to have a man of Alan Greenspan's outstanding capacity and ability willing to serve as his successor.

I have enjoyed an effective working relationship with the former, and I look forward to an effective working relationship with the latter....

Q: Mr. Greenspan, was there any discussion with the administration over what your policy on interest rates might be if you're confirmed by the Senate?

DR. GREENSPAN: No, there was not.

Q: When did you accept the job, Mr. Greenspan?

DR. GREENSPAN: Late yesterday....

Q: Did it take you a long time to decide?

DR. GREENSPAN: Milliseconds, probably, is the most appropriate. Had it taken longer, I probably would have declined.

Q: Well, serious question, though. Why are you so anxious to accept such a difficult job?

DR. GREENSPAN: It's not that I'm anxious to, it's the type of job which for an economist is clearly the most difficult challenge that one can imagine. And, having been back in the private sector for a long time and done well, it came time to basically look to something like this, and trying to fill Paul Volcker's shoes is going to be an extraordinary challenge for me.

Q: Dr. Greenspan, do you feel that the inflation monster has effectively been tamed over these last years, or do you see current trends leading toward a more upward pressure on inflation?

DR. GREENSPAN: Inflation is never ultimately tamed. It only becomes subdued in our type of societies. And that's what Paul's contribution has been and why it's so extraordinary. I think that one must be vigilant against inflation at all times.

Q: Do you see current trends indicating greater inflationary pressures than in the recent past?

DR. GREENSPAN: I'm going to hold off on substantive comments of that type until I appear before the Senate Banking Committee.

Q: Dr. Greenspan, a couple of years ago you raised the question of returning to a gold standard in a public appearance. Are you still interested in moving in that direction?

DR. GREENSPAN: I think what I said was that the gold standard would be one of a number of ways of getting a stable, international economic system. I said further that under current and foreseeable circumstances, it's very difficult for me to envisage our being able to do that. So, it's a theoretical—it's not a practical alternative.

Q: Dr. Greenspan, you talked about trying to follow Mr. Volcker's model in every way. In the past, he has shown historically that when it came down to a question of inflation or growth, he was willing to raise interest rates, to cut inflation even if that might also cut into growth. Are you willing to do that as well? Is that part of the model you're willing to follow?

DR. GREENSPAN: The model is the intellectual approach to individual problems, not specific solutions to hypothetical questions.

Q: Mr. Volcker, can you confirm for us that there were not policy issues that caused you to decline a third term, but rather personal considerations?

CHAIRMAN VOLCKER: I'm not aware of any issue on monetary policy at the moment, and I think the White House has made that quite clear in some of their recent statements. I'm not saying we never have differences. At the moment, there is not an issue of monetary policy.

Q: And so your decision was personal and not policy-related?

CHAIRMAN VOLCKER: Well, personal—I don't know what you mean by personal. It was a personal decision taking account of a lot of things, including purely personal considerations and others.

Q: When did you reach it and when did you inform the White House? . . .

CHAIRMAN VOLCKER: Look, I told the President, and this is all public—at the time I accepted re-appointment last time, that I did not accept a commitment to serve a full other term. I, in fact, have served, for all practical purposes, a full other term. And I think the time has now come to return to private life.

Q: When did you tell him that, Mr. Volcker?

CHAIRMAN VOLCKER: I told him that with considerable definitiveness yesterday.

Q: Mr. Greenspan, a lot of economists think we're walking very close to a recession. How big a risk do you see that?

DR. GREENSPAN: At the moment I must say to you I don't see the evidence of that. The economy, at the moment, looks reasonably strong and hopefully will continue so for the indefinite future.

Q: Mr. Volcker, did the President ask you for your recommendation on a successor, or did you volunteer one?

CHAIRMAN VOLCKER: Well, we—I don't remember how it arose. We certainly discussed it, and I expressed my happiness and delight of his intention to appoint Alan....

WIESEL TESTIMONY AT KLAUS BARBIE TRIAL

June 2, 1987

In an eloquent statement before a court in Lyon, France, Elie Wiesel June 2 described the horrors and memories of the World War II Holocaust during which at least 6 million Jews were exterminated in prison camps by Adolf Hitler's German Nazi regime. Wiesel, a survivor of one of the most infamous camps, Auschwitz, later became a U.S. citizen, noted author, and champion of the Jewish cause. He was awarded the 1986 Nobel Peace Prize. (Historic Documents of 1986, p. 1075) *In his testimony Wiesel urged that one of the perpetrators of Nazi war crimes be brought to justice.*

That perpetrator was Klaus Barbie, an officer of Hitler's feared Gestapo police force. Although many Nazi agents had been confronted in Nuremburg during dramatic trials held in 1947, Barbie had escaped detection and lived for thirty-two years under the assumed name of Klaus Altmann. The French government had spent years tracking down the "butcher of Lyon," as Barbie was called for his alleged role in the deaths of 4,000 people and the deportation of 7,500 others during his service as a Gestapo officer in Lyon from 1941 to 1944.

French courts in 1952 and 1954 had convicted Barbie of war crimes and sentenced him to death in absentia. In 1972 he was discovered to be living in Bolivia. After a number of difficulties had been surmounted—among them a change of government in Bolivia and accounts that Barbie had been employed as an intelligence source by the United States after the war—Barbie was extradited and returned to France in 1983 to await trial. Judicial proceedings began in May 1987. (Background and report on

Barbie, Historic Documents of 1983, p. 738)

On July 4 the French court convicted Barbie, aged 73, on all 341 charges brought against him. It sentenced him to life imprisonment for the deportation, unlawful imprisonment, and torture of Jews and members of the French Resistance during the German occupation of Lyon between 1942 and 1944.

The eight-week trial was the first held by a French court to deal with charges of crimes against humanity. The trial was controversial for the French, many of whom still felt the humiliation of German occupation during 1940-1944 under the Vichy government, a puppet regime installed by the Germans. Barbie's lawyer, Jacques Vergès, attempted to use that sentiment in his plea for leniency. On the one hand, he tried to portray his client as simply doing was was expected of him and as a lone victim of injustice. At the same time, he blasted the West for its commission of what he termed "colonialist" crimes, which, Vergès asserted, equaled in scope those of the Nazis. But the jury did not agree with his final argument that the charges against Barbie had been fabricated.

Wiesel Testimony, Lawyers' Response

After fifteen days of emotional appearances by witnesses who testified to Barbie's atrocities, Wiesel appeared before the jury to say "there is no hatred in me." But he went on to question: "How was this possible? ... Why was there so much hatred in the enemy toward Jewish children and old people? Why this relentlessness against a people whose memory of suffering is the oldest in the world? At the time, it seemed to me that the enemy's aim was to attack God himself.... As a Jew, I insist on this: Not all of Hitler's victims were Jews; but all Jews were victims."

When Vergès angrily responded that the French had fought a bloody war in Algeria, the United States had massacred Vietnamese at My Lai, and Jews had committed atrocities against Arabs, specifically the massacre of Arab civilians in the village of Deir Yassin in 1948, Wiesel responded that he was "against all brutality, no matter where it comes from." But at the same time, he found it "regrettable, deplorable, that the lawyer of the defense, who defends a man accused of crimes against humanity, dares to accuse the Jewish people."

In summation, Vergès charged that much of the testimony of witnesses who had been in Lyon—including Barbie's alleged victims—was "an evolution of phantasms," concluding that "we have to accept a difficult truth," that "Nazism was not an absolute evil, but only one of its modern manifestations."

In response, Serge Klarsfeld, who was instrumental in locating Barbie, replied, "It would have been a beautiful trial if he [Barbie] had the courage to recognize that he hated Jews, that he hated the Resistance. But you never encounter one of these people who says, 'I am a Nazi and I am happy about what I did.' They always say, 'My ideals were betrayed by Auschwitz. I didn't know anything. I didn't have anything to do with the Jews. Whenever there was an excess, I had nothing to do with it. I was not responsible.' "

Sentencing, Future Action

Barbie's sentence was handed down after the jury of nine civilians and three judges deliberated for six and a half hours. Barbie, who had not appeared to testify since the third day, stated, "I did not commit the roundup of Izieu [which involved the deportation to Auchwitz of forty-four Jewish children and seven teachers in April 1944]. I fought the Resistance, which I respect, with severity. But that was war, and now the war is over."

Remembrance of the war, however, was not finished. A number of alleged Nazi persecutors still remained at large, and the government of Israel was seeking to open the United Nations files on Nazi war criminals that had been compiled between 1943 and 1947 by seventeen nations comprising the UN War Crimes Commission. The commission had investigated alleged war crimes committed by the Axis powers (Germany, Italy, and Japan) during World War II and had assembled more than 38,000 files on suspects. When the files were turned over to the United Nations, the commission stipulated that they be available only "for official United Nations purposes." The Israelis initially were denied the request in March 1987 because sixteen of the seventeen member nations of the commission—including the United States—had vetoed it. The Israeli government, however, vowed to pursue the matter.

> *Following is the text of Elie Wiesel's June 2, 1987, testimony on the war crimes of Klaus Barbie, as it appeared in* Newsday, *translated from the French by Lydia Davis:*

Mr. President, gentlemen of the bench, gentlemen of the jury, I thank you for inviting me to appear before you today. I will try to speak about some of the nameless absent—but not for them. No one has a right to speak in their name. If the dead have something to say, they will say it in their own way. Perhaps they are already saying it. Are we capable, are we worthy, of hearing them?

May I say immediately that I feel no hatred toward the accused? I have never met him; our paths never crossed. But I have met killers who, like him, along with him, chose to be enemies of my people and of humanity. I may have known one or another of his victims. I resembled them, just as they resembled me: Within the kingdom of malediction created by the accused and his comrades, all Jewish prisoners, all Jews, had the same face, the same eyes; all shared the same fate. Sometimes one has the impression the same Jew was being killed by the enemy everywhere 6 million times over.

No, there is no hatred in me: there never was any. There is no question of hatred here—only justice. And memory. We are trying to do justice to our memory.

Here is one memory: the spring of 1944. A few days before the Jewish Pentecostal holiday—Shavuot. This was 43 years ago, almost to the day. I was 15½ years old—my own son will turn 15 in three days. I lived in a small Jewish town hidden away in the Carpathian Mountains. A profoundly religious child, I was moved by messianic dreams and prayers. Far from Jerusalem, I lived for Jerusalem, and Jerusalem lived in me.

Though subjected to a fascist regime, the Jews of Hungary did not suffer too much. My parents ran a business, my three sisters went to school, the Sabbath enveloped us in its peace . . . The war? It was nearing its end. The Allies were going to land in a day, in a week. The Red Army was 20 or 30 kilometers away. But then. . .

The Germans invaded Hungary on March 19, 1944. Starting then, events moved at a headlong pace that gave us no respite. A succession of anti-Semitic decrees and measures were passed: the prohibition of travel, confiscation of goods, wearing of yellow stars, ghettoes, transports.

We watched as our world was systematically narrowed. For the Jews, the country was limited to one town, the town to one neighborhood, the neighborhood to one street, the street to one room, the room to a sealed boxcar crossing the Polish countryside at night.

Like the Jewish children of Izieu, the Jewish adolescents from my town arrived at the Auschwitz station one afternoon. What is this? we wondered. No one knew. The name did not evoke any memory in us. Shortly before midnight, the train began to move. A woman in our car began shouting: "I see a fire, I see a fire!" They made her be quiet. I remember the silence in the car. As I remember the rest. The barbed wire fences stretching away to infinity. The yelling of the prisoners whose duty it was to "welcome" us, the gunshots fired by the SS, the barking of their dogs. And up above us all, above the planet itself, immense flames rising toward the sky as though to consume it.

Since that night, I often look at the sky and see it in flames . . . But that night, I could not look at the sky for long. I was too busy clinging to my family. An order rang out: "Line up by family." That's good, I thought, we will stay together. Only for a few minutes, however: "Men to the right, women to the left." The blows rained down on all sides. I was not able to say goodbye to my mother. Nor to my grandmother. I could not kiss my little sister . . . With my two older sisters, she was moving away, borne by the crazed, black tide . . .

This was a separation that cut my life in half. I rarely speak of it, almost never. I cannot recall my mother or my little sister . . . With my eyes, I still look for them, I will always look for them . . . And yet, I know . . . I know everything . . . No, not everything. . . . One cannot know everything . . . I could imagine it, but I do not allow myself to . . . One must know when to stop . . . My gaze stops at the threshold of the gas chambers: Even in thought, I refuse to violate the privacy of the victims at the moment of their death.

What I saw is enough for me. In a small woods somewhere in Birkenau I saw children being thrown into the flames alive by the SS. . . . Sometimes I curse my ability to see . . . It should have left me without ever returning . . . I should have remained with those little charred bodies . . . Since that night, I have felt a profound, immense love for old people and children. Every old person recalls my grandfather, my grandmother, every child brings me close to my little sister, the sister of the Jewish children of Izieu . . .

Night after night, I kept asking myself: What does all this mean? What is the sense of this murderous enterprise? It functioned perfectly. The killers killed, the victims died, the fire burned and an entire people thirsting for eternity turned to ash, annihilated by a nation which, until then, was considered to be the best educated, the most cultivated in the world . . . Graduates from the great universities, lovers of music and painting, doctors, lawyers, and philosophers participated in the Final Solution and became accomplices of Death . . . Scholars and engineers invented more efficient methods for exterminating denser and denser masses in record time . . . How was this possible?

I do not know the answer. In its scope, its ontological aspect, and its eschatological ambitions, this tragedy defies and exceeds all answers. If anyone claims to have found an answer, it can only be a false one. So much mourning, so much agony, so many deaths on one side, and a single answer on the other? One cannot understand Auschwitz either without God or with God. One cannot conceive of it in terms of man or of heaven. Why was there so much hatred in the enemy toward Jewish children and old people? Why this relentlessness against a people whose memory of suffering is the oldest in the world?

At the time, it seemed to me that the enemy's aim was to attack God himself in order to drive him from his celestial throne. Thus, the enemy was creating a society parallel to our society, a world opposed to ours, with its own madmen and princes, laws and customs, prophets and judges.

Yes, a cursed, enchanted world, where another language was spoken, where a new religion was proclaimed: one of cruelty, dominated by the inhuman; a society that had evolved from the other side of society, from the other side of life, from the other side of death, perhaps; a world where one small piece of bread was worth all theories, where an adolescent in uniform had absolute power over thousands of prisoners, where human beings seemed to belong to a different species, trembling before death, which had all the attributes of God . . .

As a Jew, it is impossible for me not to stress the affliction of my people during their torment. Do not see this as an attempt to deny or minimize the sufferings of the populations of the occupied countries or the torture undergone by our comrades, our Christian or non-religious friends whom the common enemy punished with unpardonable brutality. We feel affection and admiration for them. As though they were our brothers? They are our brothers.

As a Jew, I insist on this: Not all of Hitler's victims were Jews; but all Jews were victims. For the first time, an entire people—from the smallest to the largest, from the richest to the most destitute—were condemned to annihilation. To uproot it, to extract it from history, to kill it in memory by killing all memory of it: Such was the enemy's plan. At Izieu, the Jewish children were playing and singing, as the Jewish children in my town played and sang: they were already dead—in Berlin they were seen as dead—but they did not know it. Because to be Jewish was a crime that required capital punishment.

Marked, isolated, humiliated, beaten, starved, tortured, the Jew was handed over to the executioner, not for having proclaimed some truth, nor for having possessed envied riches and treasures, nor for having adopted a certain forbidden behavior. The Jew was condemned to death because he was born Jewish, because he carried in him a Jewish memory.

Declared to be less than a man, and therefore deserving neither compassion nor pity, the Jew was only born to die—just as the killer was only born to kill. Consequently, the killer did not feel in any way guilty. One American investigator formulated it this way: The killer had not lost his sense of morality, but his sense of reality. He thought he was doing good by ridding the earth of its Jewish "parasites."

Is this the reason Klaus Barbie, like Adolph Eichmann before him, does not feel guilty? Except for Hoss, the commander of Auschwitz, condemned and hanged in Poland, no killer has repented—and yet, there were killers. There had to be executioners to eliminate a million-and-a-half Jewish children; killers were needed to annihilate four-and-a-half million Jewish adults . . .

Auschwitz and Treblinka, Majdanek and Ponar, Belzec and Mathausen, and so many others, so many other names: The apocalypse was everywhere. Everywhere, mute processions headed toward pits filled with dead bodies. Very few tears, very little crying. From their appearance, resigned, thoughtful, the victims seemed to be leaving the world without regret. It was as though these men and women were choosing not to live in a society disfigured, denatured by hatred and violence.

After the war, the survivor tried to tell about it, bear witness . . . But who could find words to speak of the unspeakable?

The contemplative silence of old people who knew, of children who were afraid of knowing . . . The horror of mothers who had gone mad, the terrifying lucidity of mad people in a delirious world . . . The grave chant of a rabbi reciting the Kaddish, the murmur of his followers going after him to the very end, to heaven . . . The good little girl undressing her younger brother . . . Telling him not to be afraid; no, one must not be afraid of death . . . Perhaps she said: One must not be afraid of dead people . . .

And in the city, the grand, ancient city of Kiev, that mother and her two children in front of some German soldiers who are laughing . . . They take one child from her and kill it before her eyes ... Then, they seize the second and kill it too ... She wants to die, but the killers prefer her to remain alive but inhabited by death ... Then, she takes the two little bodies, hugs them against her chest and begins to dance ... How can one describe that mother? How can one tell of her dance? In this tragedy, there is something that hurts beyond hurting—and I do not know what it is.

I know we must speak, I do not know how. Since this crime is absolute, no language can be more than imperfect. Which is why there is such a feeling of powerlessness in the survivor. It was easier for him to imagine himself free in Auschwitz than it would be for a free man to imagine himself a prisoner in Auschwitz. That is the problem: No one who has not experienced the event will ever be able to understand it. And yet, the survivor is conscious of his duty to bear witness. To tell. To protest every time any investigator, morally perverse as he may be, dares to deny the death of deaths. And the truthfulness of the memory transmitted by the survivors.

For the survivors, however, it is getting late. Their number is diminishing. There are not many of them, there are fewer and fewer of them. They meet one another more and more often at funerals. Can one die more than once? Yes, one can. The survivor dies every time he rejoins, in his thoughts, the nightly procession he has never really left. How can he detach himself from them without betraying them? For a long time he talked to them—as I talk to my mother and my little sister: I still see them moving away under the fiery sky ... I ask them to forgive me for not following them ...

It is for the dead, but also for the survivors, and even more for their children—and yours—that this trial is important: It will weigh on the future. In the name of justice? In the name of memory. Justice without memory is an incomplete justice, false and unjust. To forget would be an absolute injustice in the same way that Auschwitz was the absolute crime. To forget would be the enemy's final triumph.

The fact is that the enemy kills twice, the second time in trying to obliterate the traces of his crime. This is why he pushed his outrageous, terrifying plan to the limits of language, and well beyond: to situate it too far, out of reach, out of our range of perception. "Even if you survive, even if you tell, no one will believe you," an SS told a young Jew somewhere in Galicia.

This trial has already contradicted that killer. The witnesses have spoken; their truth has entered the awareness of humanity. Thanks to them, the Jewish children of Izieu will never be forgotten.

As guardians of their invisible graves, graves of ash encrusted in a sky of eternal night and fog, we must remain faithful to them. It is difficult, even impossible, to recall them in words? We must try. To refuse to speak, when speech is awaited, would be to acknowledge the ultimate triumph of despair.

"Do you seek fire?" said a great Hassidic rabbi. "Seek it in the ash."

This is what you have been doing here since the beginning of this trial, this is what we have attempted to do since the Liberation. We have sought, in the ash, a truth to affirm—despite everything—man's dignity; it exists only in memory.

Thanks to this trial, the survivors have a justification for their survival. Their testimony counts, their memories will be part of the collective memory. Of course, nothing could bring the dead back to life. But because of the meetings that have taken place within these precincts, because of the words spoken, the accused will not be able to kill the dead again. If he had succeeded it would not have been his fault, but ours.

Though it takes place under the sign of justice, this trial must also honor memory.

VENICE ECONOMIC SUMMIT

June 8-10, 1987

Leaders of the seven largest industrialized democracies met in Venice, Italy, June 8-10, for the thirteenth annual economic summit. While the leaders discussed some economic matters, their communiqués dealt with pressing political issues: East-West relations, terrorism, the Iran-Iraq war, and freedom of navigation in the Persian Gulf.

Most observers felt that the Venice summit accomplished substantially less than a number of earlier economic summits and that the United States had fallen well short of achieving its goals. But President Ronald Reagan staunchly defended the summit's achievements. "The truth is," he said in a televised address June 15, "we came home with everything we'd hoped to accomplish."

It seemed clear, however, that this meeting was not the right time for bold initiatives. Political uncertainties plagued several of the participants. Italy was in a campaign for parliamentary elections, leaving that country with a seventy-nine-year-old caretaker prime minister, Amintore Fanfani. Prime Minister Yasuhiro Nakasone of Japan was a lame duck, expected to leave office in the near future. Margaret Thatcher, the British prime minister, stayed at the summit only eighteen hours, returning home to finish her successful campaign for a third term. And Reagan was seen by many at Venice as weakened at home by the Iran-contra scandal. "Reagan Diminished," read a headline in the widely respected Economist *of London, England, after the summit.*

Reagan's trip lasted nine days. In an address June 5, televised throughout Western Europe, the president attempted to soothe European anxieties over a pending accord with the Soviet Union that would eliminate European-based medium-range missiles. His most dramatic appearance came in West Berlin, where June 12 he spoke while standing less than one hundred yards from the Berlin Wall and within sight of the Brandenburg Gate in East Berlin. In a rhetorical appeal to Mikhail S. Gorbachev, the Soviet leader, Reagan said, "Mr. Gorbachev, open this gate! Mr. Gorbachev, tear down this wall!" The Berlin Wall had been hastily erected in 1961. (Historic Documents of 1986, p. 791)

Economic Package

The United States pressed for measures to sustain world economic growth, to reduce agricultural subsidies, and to establish a process for coordinating economic policy among the seven summit countries. A lack of any coordination of economic policy among the Western nations during the 1920s was widely seen by economists as contributing to the severity of the Great Depression.

Press reports said that Helmut Kohl, the West German chancellor, joined by François Mitterand, the French president, singled out the budget deficit in the United States as the most critical economic problem facing the seven industrialized countries. As he often had before, Reagan responded by saying that the U.S. deficit was going down.

Reagan urged the other leaders to eliminate farm subsidies by the year 2000, a proposal that adhered closely to Reagan's strong belief in a market economy. In his June 15 televised speech to the nation, he said that "it was really a step forward to get this issue on the summit agenda, and I think the fact our urgings were heeded indicates the kind of responsiveness our summit partners showed towards American concerns."

During the summit, the United States partially lifted economic sanctions earlier imposed on Japan, which had been accused of dumping semiconductors at less than cost on the world market. (U.S.-Japan trade dispute, p. 427)

Terrorism

The seven leaders reaffirmed their determination to cooperate in antiterrorist efforts. But the statement disappointed many observers by omitting a passage in a similar statement issued at the Tokyo economic summit in 1986. That passage had pledged "refusal to export arms to states which sponsor or support terrorism." It was widely believed that the United States did not want to draw attention to the Reagan administration's clandestine arms sales to Iran.

In a strong action, the leaders pledged to "take immediate action to cease flights" if a country "refuses extradition or prosecution" in the wake of a hijacking. In an editorial headed "A Hijacking Sanction That Works," the Washington Post *praised the promised air embargo as "a penalty that fits the crime."*

Other Statements

A statement on the Persian Gulf was seen as falling short of language the United States wanted. However, the leaders did affirm support for the principle of free navigation in the gulf. "The free flow of oil and other traffic through the Strait of Hormuz must continue unimpeded," the statement said. Reagan told reporters that he was "delighted with the support we are getting . . . with regard to the gulf." The United States was making plans to escort oil tankers in the Persian Gulf.

A statement on the Iran-Iraq war, which had raged since 1980, also appeared to have been watered down. The Americans had hoped for an endorsement of a United Nations Security Council ban on arms sales to Iran and Iraq if they refused to negotiate a cease-fire. But in the communiqué, an "enforceable" Security Council resolution became a "just and effective" one. Reagan tried to minimize the difference in tone. (UN resolution, p. 609)

In the area of East-West relations, the seven leaders reaffirmed their commitment to arms control, but their statement did not mention specifically the pending U.S.-Soviet accord.

Following are texts of statements on East-West relations, terrorism, and the Iran-Iraq war and freedom of navigation in the Persian Gulf, all issued June 9, 1987, at the Venice Economic Summit:

STATEMENT ON EAST-WEST RELATIONS

1. We, the Heads of State or Government of seven major industrial nations and the Representatives of the European Community, have discussed East-West relations. We reaffirm our shared principles and objectives, and our common dedication to preserving and strengthening peace.

2. We recognize with pride that our shared values of freedom, democracy and respect for human rights are the source of the dynamism and prosperity of our societies. We renew our commitment to the search for a freer, more democratic and more humane world.

3. Within existing alliances each of us is resolved to maintain a strong and credible defence which threatens the security of no-one, protects freedom, deters aggression and maintains peace. We shall continue to consult closely on all matters affecting our common interest. We will not be separated from the principles that guide us all.

4. Since we last met, new opportunities have opened for progress in East-West relations. We are encouraged by these developments. They

confirm the soundness of the policies we have each pursued in our determination to achieve a freer and safer world.

5. We are following with close interest recent developments in the internal and external policies of the Soviet Union. It is our hope that they will prove to be of great significance for the improvement of political, economic and security relations between the countries of East and West. At the same time, profound differences persist; each of us must remain vigilantly alert in responding to all aspects of Soviet policy.

6. We reaffirm our commitment to peace and increased security at lower levels of arms. We seek a comprehensive effort to lower tensions and to achieve verifiable arms reductions. While reaffirming the continuing importance of nuclear deterrence in preserving peace, we note with satisfaction that dialogue on arms control has intensified and that more favourable prospects have emerged for the reduction of nuclear forces. We appreciate US efforts to negotiate balanced, substantial and verifiable reductions in nuclear weapons. We emphasize our determination to enhance conventional stability at a lower level of forces and achieve the total elimination of chemical weapons. We believe that these goals should be actively pursued and translated into concrete agreements. We urge the Soviet Union to negotiate in a positive and constructive manner. An effective resolution of these issues is an essential requirement for real and enduring stability in the world.

7. We will be paying close attention not only to Soviet statements but also to Soviet actions on issues of common concern to us. In particular:

—We call for significant and lasting progress in human rights, which is essential to building trust between our societies. Much still remains to be done to meet the principles agreed and commitments undertaken in the Helsinki Final Act and confirmed since.

—We look for an early and peaceful resolution of regional conflicts, and especially for a rapid and total withdrawal of Soviet forces from Afghanistan so that the people of Afghanistan may freely determine their own future.

—We encourage greater contacts, freer interchange of ideas and more extensive dialogue between our people and the people of the Soviet Union and Eastern Europe.

8. Thus, we each seek to stabilize military competition between East and West at lower levels of arms; to encourage stable political solutions to regional conflicts; to secure lasting improvements in human rights; and to build contacts, confidence and trust between governments and peoples in a more humane world. Progress across the board is necessary to establish a durable foundation for stable and constructive relationships between the countries of East and West.

STATEMENT ON TERRORISM

We, the Heads of State or Government of seven major democracies and the Representatives of the European Community assembled here in

Venice, profoundly aware of our peoples' concern at the threat posed by terrorism;

—reaffirm our commitment to the statements on terrorism made at previous Summits, in Bonn, Venice, Ottawa, London and Tokyo;

—resolutely condemn all forms of terrorism, including aircraft hijackings and hostage-taking, and reiterate our belief that whatever its motives, terrorism has no justification;

—confirm the commitment of each of us to the principle of making no concessions to terrorists or their sponsors;

—remain resolved to apply, in respect of any State clearly involved in sponsoring or supporting international terrorism, effective measures within the framework of international law and in our own jurisdictions;

—welcome the progress made in international cooperation against terrorism since we last met in Tokyo in May 1986, and in particular the initiative taken by France and Germany to convene in May in Paris a meeting of Ministers of nine countries, who are responsible for counter-terrorism;

—reaffirm our determination to combat terrorism both through national measures and through international cooperation among ourselves and with others, when appropriate, and therefore renew our appeal to all like-minded countries to consolidate and extend international cooperation in all appropriate fora;

—will continue our efforts to improve the safety of travellers. We welcome improvements in airport and maritime security, and encourage the work of ICAO [International Civil Aviation Organization] and IMO [International Maritime Organization] in this regard. Each of us will continue to monitor closely the activities of airlines which raise security problems. The Heads of State or government have decided on measures, annexed to this statement, to make the 1978 Bonn Declaration more effective in dealing with all forms of terrorism affecting civil aviation;

—commit ourselves to support the rule of law in bringing terrorists to justice. Each of us pledges increased cooperation in the relevant fora and within the framework of domestic and international law on the investigation, apprehension and prosecution of terrorists. In particular we reaffirm the principle established by relevant international conventions of trying or extraditing, according to national laws and those international conventions, those who have perpetrated acts of terrorism.

Annex

The Heads of State or Government recall that in their Tokyo Statement on international terrorism they agreed to make the 1978 Bonn Declaration more effective in dealing with all forms of terrorism affecting civil aviation. To this end, in cases where a country refuses extradition or prosecution of those who have committed offences described in the Montreal Convention for the Suppression of Unlawful Acts against the Safety of Civil Aviation and/or does not return the aircraft involved, the Heads of State or Government are jointly resolved that their Governments shall take immediate action to cease flights to that country as stated in the Bonn Declaration.

At the same time, their Governments will initiate action to halt incoming flights from that country or from any country by the airlines of the country concerned as stated in the Bonn Declaration.

The Heads of State or Government intend also to extend the Bonn Declaration in due time to cover any future relevant amendment to the above Convention or any other aviation conventions relating to the extradition or prosecution of the offenders.

The Heads of State or Government urge other governments to join them in this commitment.

STATEMENT ON IRAQ-IRAN WAR AND FREEDOM OF NAVIGATION IN THE GULF

We agree that new and concerted international efforts are urgently required to help bring the Iraq-Iran war to an end. We favour the earliest possible negotiated end to the war with the territorial integrity and independence of both Iraq and Iran intact. Both countries have suffered grievously from this long and tragic war. Neighbouring countries are threatened with the possible spread of the conflict. We call once more upon both parties to negotiate an immediate end of the war. We strongly support the mediation efforts of the United Nations Secretary-General and urge the adoption of just and effective measures by the UN Security Council. With these objectives in mind, we reaffirm that the principle of freedom of navigation in the Gulf is of paramount importance for us and for others and must be upheld. The free flow of oil and other traffic through the Strait of Hormuz must continue unimpeded.

We pledge to continue to consult on ways to pursue these important goals effectively.

COURT ON UNCOMPENSATED TAKINGS AND LAND USE

June 9 and 26, 1987

The Supreme Court issued two important decisions in June on the rights of private property owners facing restrictive land-use regulations. The first case, First English Evangelical Lutheran Church of Glendale v. County of Los Angeles, *which was decided June 9 by a 6-3 vote, held that when the government effectively forbids all use of private property by regulatory restrictions, it must compensate the owner even if the taking proved only temporary. The case concerned a church-owned campground, Lutherglen, located in a flood plain, and the restrictions imposed by Los Angeles County officials to prevent reconstruction of buildings washed away by a major flood.*

The second decision, in Nollan v. California Coastal Commission, *decided June 26 by a 5-4 majority, concerned an attempt by land-use officials to condition the granting of a building permit upon the owner's willingness to give a public easement through his private beach front. In both cases the Court found that the actions were actually uncompensated takings of property and were therefore in violation of the Fifth Amendment, made applicable to the states through the Fourteenth Amendment. The decisions were viewed as a warning to land-use officials that unless there was a direct relationship between the public interest they sought to advance and the regulatory action taken, compensation would be due to property owners hurt by the regulations.*

Rebuilding Lutherglen

For more than twenty years the First English church had operated a small retreat center and camp for handicapped children on a twenty-one-acre parcel of land in Los Angeles County. The land was located in a canyon by the banks of the drainage channel of a large forest. In 1977 forest fires burnt the upstream land cover, creating the potential for severe erosion and floods. The following year flooding from an eleven-inch rain destroyed all of the buildings in Lutherglen, causing loss of life. Los Angeles County responded by enacting an interim ordinance that prohibited reconstruction of buildings in the flood plain to prevent recurrence of the problem. The church then sued the county, alleging that it was entitled to compensation on a theory of "inverse condemnation." In inverse condemnation, the government, instead of exercising its power of eminent domain by condemning a property and paying the owner the value of what was taken, regulates what can be done with the property so that for all practical purposes it has been "taken" without compensation.

Since the line between permissible and prohibited land-use regulation was hard to draw, the state courts of California fashioned a rule that prohibited litigants from trying to collect damages for inverse condemnation. They were instead limited to bringing actions to have a court invalidate the regulations. If the regulations were declared invalid and rescinded, the taking had been temporary and there was no right to compensation. Only when the state persisted in keeping the regulations despite the judicial declaration to the contrary were litigants allowed to seek compensation. Accordingly, under these rules the California state courts dismissed the church's action and the church eventually took the matter to the Supreme Court.

The majority opinion by Chief Justice William H. Rehnquist stated that the issue was whether, once the government had taken use of a property, any subsequent government action could relieve it of the duty of paying compensation for the entire effective period of the taking. Justice Rehnquist found that there was no action, including a subsequent invalidation and withdrawal of the regulation, that would relieve the government of its duty to compensate the landowner for loss.

The dissent by Justice John Paul Stevens questioned whether this issue need be reached, since the church had not alleged that the taking had been unconstitutional. Justice Rehnquist noted that although the church had claimed only that it had been denied use of Lutherglen, the California courts had considered the taking issue on appeal, and, secondly, though the courts had thrown out the complaint on other grounds, the allegation that the church had been denied all use had never been shown to be false. For Justice Stevens, even if these allegations were assumed to be true, the fact that only a regulatory and temporary taking was involved, rather than a physical taking, meant that the church had to show that this second less invasive taking rose to the level requiring constitutional protection by showing that the property had lost substantial value through government action. Justice Stevens thought the majority opinion might lead to a flood of litigation as developers tried to recover compensation for regulatory delays and would cause land-use planning officials to grow more cautious in case some new program, if later invalidated, would force them to pay damages from the date the program began.

Seeing the Sea

The second case involved beach-front property owned by James and Marilyn Nollan in Ventura County, California. A small outbuilding on the property had fallen into disrepair, and the Nollans wanted to replace it with a larger modern house. However, the California Coastal Commission would grant permission for the building permit only if the Nollans promised to record an easement allowing the public to walk along the beach between their sea wall and the high-tide level. The easement would facilitate public access to a nearby county park. The Nollans protested that replacing an old house with a new one in no way affected public access to the sea. They lost in the California courts and took the case to the Supreme Court.

The law had long been that no taking existed when authorities issued regulations that advanced state interests and did not deny an owner economic use of his land. For Justice Antonin Scalia, author of the majority opinion, the issue in the Nollan case was the logical connection between the state interest and the action taken. He granted that the state might well have a legitimate interest in allowing the public to see the ocean, which might be advanced by special conditions requiring the Nollans to respect height limitations or provide special places for the public to view the sea. But Justice Scalia saw no logical connection between legitimate state interests and a requirement that the Nollans grant a lateral easement along the beach. The restriction, according to Scalia, was little more than a plan of extortion.

The majority's reasoning drew three separate dissents. In one, Justice William J. Brennan, Jr., found the California Coastal Commission's action to be well within its power and a flexible response to encroachment upon protected lands. He found the majority "insensitive to the fact that increasing intensity of development in many areas calls for far-sighted, comprehensive planning that takes into account both the interdependence of land uses and the cumulative impact of development" and hoped that "today's decision is an aberration, and that a broader vision ultimately prevails."

> *Following are excerpts from the Court's opinion and the dissent of Justice John Paul Stevens in* First English Evangelical Lutheran Church of Glendale v. County of Los Angeles, California, *decided on June 9, 1987; and from the Court's opinion and the dissent by Justice William J.*

Brennan, Jr., in Nollan v. California Coastal Commission, *decided June 26, 1987:*

No. 85-1199

First English Evangelical Lutheran Church of Glendale, Appellant *v.* County of Los Angeles, California	On appeal from the Court of Appeal of California, Second Appellate District

[June 9, 1987]

CHIEF JUSTICE REHNQUIST delivered the opinion of the Court.

In this case the California Court of Appeal held that a landowner who claims that his property has been "taken" by a land-use regulation may not recover damages for the time before it is finally determined that the regulation constitutes a "taking" of his property. We disagree, and conclude that in these circumstances the Fifth and Fourteenth Amendments to the United States Constitution would require compensation for that period.

In 1957, appellant First English Evangelical Lutheran Church purchased a 21-acre parcel of land in a canyon along the banks of the Middle Fork of Mill Creek in the Angeles National Forest. The Middle Fork is a natural drainage channel for a watershed area owned by the National Forest Service. Twelve of the acres owned by the church are flat land, and contained a dining hall, two bunkhouses, a caretaker's lodge, an outdoor chapel, and a footbridge acress the creek. The church operated on the site a campground, known as "Lutherglen," as a retreat center and a recreational area for handicapped children.

In July 1977, a forest fire denuded the hills upstream from Lutherglen, destroying approximately 3,860 acres of the watershed area and creating a serious flood hazard. Such flooding occurred on February 9 and 10, 1978, when a storm dropped 11 inches of rain in the watershed. The runoff from the storm overflowed the banks of the Mill Creek, flooding Lutherglen and destroying its buildings.

In response to the flooding of the canyon, appellee County of Los Angeles adopted Interim Ordinance No. 11,855 in January 1979. The ordinance provided that "[a] person shall not construct, reconstruct, place or enlarge any building or structure, any portion of which is, or will be, located within the outer boundary lines of the interim flood protection area located in Mill Creek Canyon...." The ordinance was effective immediately because the county determined that it was "required for the immediate preservation of the public health and safety...." The interim flood protection area described by the ordinance included the flat areas on either side of Mill Creek on which Lutherglen had stood.

The church filed a complaint in the Superior Court of California a little more than a month after the ordinance was adopted. As subsequently amended, the complaint alleged two claims against the county and the Los Angeles County Flood Control District. The first alleged that the defendants were liable under Cal. Gov't. Code Ann. §835 (West 1980) for dangerous conditions on their upstream properties that contributed to the flooding of Lutherglen. As a part of this claim, appellant also alleged that "Ordinance No. 11,855 denies [appellant] all use of Lutherglen." The second claim sought to recover from the Flood District in inverse condemnation and in tort for engaging in cloud seeding during the storm that flooded Lutherglen. Appellant sought damages under each count for loss of use of Lutherglen. The defendants moved to strike the portions of the complaint alleging that the county's ordinance denied all use of Lutherglen, on the view that the California Supreme Court's decision in *Agins* v. *Tiburon* (1979), aff'd on other grounds (1980), rendered the allegation "entirely immaterial and irrelevant[, with] no bearing upon any conceivable cause of action herein." ("The court may . . . strike out any irrelevant, false, or improper matter inserted in any pleading").

In *Agins* v. *Tiburon* the Supreme Court of California decided that a landowner may not maintain an inverse condemnation suit in the courts of that State based upon a "regulatory" taking. In the court's view, maintenance of such a suit would allow a landowner to force the legislature to exercise its power of eminent domain. Under this decision, then, compensation is not required until the challenged regulation or ordinance has been held excessive in an action for declaratory relief or a writ of mandamus and the government has nevertheless decided to continue the regulation in effect. Based on this decision, the trial court in the present case granted the motion to strike the allegation that the church had been denied all use of Lutherglen. It explained that "a careful rereading of the *Agins* case persuades the Court that when an ordinance, even a non-zoning ordinance, deprives a person of the total use of his lands, his challenge to the ordinance is by way of declaratory relief or possibly mandamus." App. 26. Because the appellant alleged a regulatory taking and sought only damages, the allegation that the ordinance denied all use of Lutherglen was deemed irrelevant.

On appeal, the California Court of Appeal read the complaint as one seeking "damages for the uncompensated taking of all use of Lutherglen by County Ordinance No. 11,855. . . ." It too relied on the California Supreme Court's decision in *Agins* in rejecting the cause of action, declining appellant's invitation to reevaluate *Agins* in light of this Court's opinions in *San Diego Gas & Electric Co.* v. *San Diego* (1981). The court found itself obligated to follow *Agins* "because the United States Supreme Court has not yet ruled on the question of whether a state may constitutionally limit the remedy for a taking to nonmonetary relief. . . ." It accordingly affirmed the trial court's decision to strike the allegations concerning appellee's ordinance. The Supreme Court of California denied review.

This appeal followed, and we noted probable jurisdiction. Appellant asks us to hold that the Supreme Court of California erred in *Agins* v. *Tiburon* in determining that the Fifth Amendment, as made applicable to the States through the Fourteenth Amendment, does not require compensation as a remedy for "temporary" regulatory takings—those regulatory takings which are ultimately invalidated by the courts. Four times this decade, we have considered similar claims and have found ourselves for one reason or another unable to consider the merits of the *Agins* rule. See *MacDonald, Sommer & Frates* v. *Yolo County* (1986); *Willamson County Regional Planning Comm'n* v. *Hamilton Bank* (1985); *San Diego Gas & Electric Co.; Agins* v. *Tiburon.* For the reasons explained below, however, we find the constitutional claim properly presented in this case, and hold that on these facts the California courts have decided the compensation question inconsistently with the requirements of the Fifth Amendment.

I

Concerns with finality left us unable to reach the remedial question in the earlier cases where we have been asked to consider the rule of *Agins.* See *MacDonald, Sommer & Frates.* In each of these cases, we concluded either that regulations considered to be in issue by the state court did not effect a taking, *Agins* v. *Tiburon,* or that the factual disputes yet to be resolved by state authorities might still lead to the conclusion that no taking had occurred. *MacDonald, Sommer & Frates; Williamson County; San Diego Gas & Electric Co.* Consideration of the remedial question in those circumstances, we concluded, would be premature.

The posture of the present case is quite different. Appellant's complaint alleged that "Ordinance No. 11,855 denies [it] all use of Lutherglen," and sought damages for this deprivation. In affirming the decision to strike this allegation, the Court of Appeal assumed that the complaint sought "damages for the uncompensated *taking* of all use of Lutherglen by County Ordinance No. 11,855." App. to Juris. Statement A13-A14 (emphasis added). It relied on the California Supreme Court's *Agins* decision for the conclusion that "the remedy for a *taking* [is limited] to nonmonetary relief...." (emphasis added). The disposition of the case on these grounds isolates the remedial question for our consideration. The rejection of appellant's allegations did not rest on the view that they were false. Cf. *MacDonald, Sommer & Frates* (California court rejected allegation in the complaint that the appellant was deprived of all beneficial use of its property); *Agins* v. *Tiburon.* Nor did the court rely on the theory that regulatory measures such as Ordinance No. 11,855 may never constitute a taking in the constitutional sense. Instead, the claims were deemed irrelevant solely because of the California Supreme Court's decision in *Agins* that damages are unavailable to redress a "temporary" regulatory taking. The California Court of Appeal has thus held that regardless of the correctness of appellant's claim that the challenged ordinance denies it "all use of Lutherglen" appellant may not recover damages until the ordinance is finally declared unconstitutional, and then only for any period after that declaration for which the county seeks to enforce it. The constitutional question pretermitted in our earlier cases is therefore squarely presented here.

We reject appellee's suggestion that, regardless of the state court's treatment of the question, we must independently evaluate the adequacy of the complaint and resolve the takings claim on the merits before we can reach the remedial question. However "cryptic"—to use appellee's description—the allegations with respect to the taking were, the California courts deemed them sufficient to present the issue. We accordingly have no occasion to decide whether the ordinance at issue actually denied appellant all use of its property or whether the county might avoid the conclusion that a compensable taking had occurred by establishing that the denial of all use was insulated as a part of the State's authority to enact safety regulations. See *e.g., Goldblatt* v. *Hampstead* (1962); *Hadacheck* v. *Sebastian* (1915); *Mugler* v. *Kansas* (1887). These questions, of course, remain open for decision on the remand we direct today. We now turn to the question of whether the Just Compensation Clause requires the government to pay for "temporary" regulatory takings.

II

Consideration of the compensation question must begin with direct reference to the language of the Fifth Amendment, which provides in relevant part that "private property [shall not] be taken for public use, without just compensation." ... [T]his provision does not prohibit the taking of private property, but instead places a condition on the exercise of that power. See *Williamson County; Hodel* v. *Virginia Surface Mining & Reclamation Assn., Inc.* (1981); *Hurley* v. *Kincaid* (1932); *Monongahela Navigation Co.* v. *United States* (1893); *United States* v. *Jones* (1883). This basic understanding of the Amendment makes clear that it is designed not to limit the governmental interference with property rights *per se,* but rather to secure *compensation* in the event of otherwise proper interference amounting to a taking. Thus, government action that works a taking of property rights necessarily implicates the "constitutional obligation to pay just compensation." *Armstrong* v. *United States* (1960).

We have recognized that a landowner is entitled to bring an action in inverse condemnation as a result of " 'the self-executing character of the constitutional provision with respect to compensation. . . .' " *United States* v. *Clarke* (1980), quoting 6 P. Nichols, Eminent Domain §25.41 (3d rev. ed. 1972). As noted in JUSTICE BRENNAN's dissent in *San Diego Gas & Electric Co.,* it has been established at least since *Jacobs* v. *United States* (1933), that claims for just compensation are grounded in the Constitution itself:

> "The suits were based on the right to recover just compensation for property taken by the United States for public use in the exercise of its power of eminent domain. *That right was guaranteed by the Constitution.* The fact that condemnation proceedings were not instituted and that the right was asserted in suits by the owners did not change the essential nature of the claim. The form of the remedy did not qualify the right. It rested upon the Fifth Amendment. Statutory recognition was not necessary. A promise to pay was not necessary. Such a promise was implied because of the duty imposed by the Amendment. *The suits were thus founded upon the Constitution of the United States.*" (Emphasis added.)

Jacobs, moveover, does not stand alone, for the Court has frequently repeated the view that, in the event of a taking, the compensation remedy is required by the Constitution. See *e.g., Kirby Forest Industries, Inc.* v. *United States* (1984); *United States* v. *Causby* (1946); *Seaboard Air Line R. Co.* v. *United States* (1923); *Monongahela Navigation.*

It has also been established doctrine at least since Justice Holmes' opinion for the Court in *Pennsylvania Coal Co.* v. *Mahon* (1922) that "[t]he general rule at least is, that while property may be regulated to a certain extent, if regulation goes too far it will be recognized as a taking." While the typical taking occurs when the government acts to condemn property in the exercise of its power of eminent domain, the entire doctrine of inverse condemnation is predicated on the proposition that a taking may occur without such formal proceedings. In *Pumpelly* v. *Green Bay Co.* (1872), construing a provision in the Wisconsin constitution identical to the Just Compensation Clause, this Court said:

> "It would be a very curious and unsatisfactory result if ... it shall be held that if the government refrains from the absolute conversion of real property to the uses of the public it can destroy its value entirely, can inflict irreparable and permanent injury to any extent, can, in effect, subject it to total destruction without making any compensation, because, in the narrowest sense of that word, it is not *taken* for the public use."

Later cases have unhesitatingly applied this principle. See, *e.g., Kaiser Aetna* v. *United States* (1979); *United States* v. *Dickinson* (1947); *United States* v. *Causby* (1946).

While the Supreme Court of California may not have actually disavowed this general rule in *Agins,* we believe that it has truncated the rule by disallowing damages that occurred prior to the ultimate invalidation of the challenged regulation. The Supreme Court of California justified its conclusion at length in the *Agins* opinion, concluding that:

> "In combination, the need for preserving a degree of freedom in the land-use planning function, and the inhibiting financial force which inheres in the inverse condemnation remedy, persuade us that on balance mandamus or declaratory relief rather than inverse condemnation is the appropriate relief under the circumstances." *Agins* v. *Tiburon.*

We, of course, are not unmindful of these considerations, but they must be evaluated in the light of the command of the Just Compensation Clause of the Fifth Amendment. The Court has recognized in more than one case that the government may elect to abandon its intrusion or discontinue regulations. See *e.g., Kirby Forest Industries, Inc.* v. *United States* (1984); *United States* v. *Dow* (1958). Similarly, a governmental body may acquiesce in a judicial declaration that one of its ordinances has effected an unconstitutional taking of property; the landowner has no right under the Just Compensation Clause to insist that a "temporary" taking be deemed a permanent taking. But we have not resolved whether abandonment by the government requires payment of compensation for the period of time during which regulations deny a landowner all use of his land.

In considering this question, we find substantial guidance in cases where the government has only temporarily exercised its right to use private property. In *United States* v. *Dow,* though rejecting a claim that the Government may not abandon condemnation proceedings, the Court observed that abandonment "results in an alteration in the property interest taken—from [one of] full ownership to one of temporary use and occupation. . . . In such cases compensation would be measured by the principles normally governing the taking of a right to use property temporarily. See *Kimball Laundry Co.* v. *United States* [1949]; *United States* v. *Petty Motor Co.* [1946]; *United States* v. *General Motors Corp.* [1945]." Each of the cases cited by the *Dow* Court involved appropriation of private property by the United States for use during World War II. Though the takings were in fact "temporary," see *Petty Motor Co.,* there was no question that compensation would be required for the Government's interference with the use of the property; the Court was concerned in each case with determining the proper measure of the monetary relief to which the property holders were entitled. See *Kimball Laundry Co., Petty Motor Co.; General Motors.*

These cases reflect the fact that "temporary" takings which, as here, deny a landowner all use of his property, are not different in kind from permanent takings, for which the Constitution clearly requires compensation. Cf. *San Diego Gas & Electric Co.* (BRENNAN J., dissenting) ("Nothing in the Just Compensation Clause suggests that 'takings' must be permanent and irrevocable"). It is axiomatic that the Fifth Amendment's just compensation provision is "designed to bar Government from forcing some people alone to bear public burdens which, in all fairness and justice, should be borne by the public as a whole." *Armstrong* v. *United States.* See also *Penn Central Transportation Co.* v. *New York City; Monongahela Navigation Co.* v. *United States.* In the present case the interim ordinance was adopted by the county of Los Angeles in January 1979, and became effective immediately. Appellant filed suit within a month after the effective date of the ordinance and yet when the Supreme Court of California denied a hearing in the case on October 17, 1985, the merits of appellant's claim had yet to be determined. The United States has been required to pay compensation for leasehold interests of shorter duration than this. The value of a leasehold interest in property for a period of years may be substantial, and the burden on the property owner in extinguishing such an interest for a period of years may be great indeed. See, *e.g., United States* v. *General Motors.* Where this burden results from governmental action that amounted to a taking, the Just Compensation Clause of the Fifth Amendment requires that the government pay the landowner for the value of the use of the land during this period. Cf. *United States* v. *Causby* ("It is the owner's loss, not the taker's gain, which is the measure of the value of the property taken"). Invalidation of the ordinance or its successor ordinance after this period of time, though converting the taking into a "temporary" one, is not a sufficient remedy to meet the demands of the Just Compensation Clause.

Appellee argues that requiring compensation for denial of all use of land prior to invalidation is inconsistent with this Court's decisions in *Danforth* v. *United States* (1939) and *Agins* v. *Tiburon* (1980). In *Danforth,* the landowner contended that the "taking" of his property had occurred prior to the institution of condemnation proceedings, by reason of the enactment of the Flood Control Act itself. He claimed that the passage of that Act had diminished the value of his property because the plan embodied in the Act required condemnation of a flowage easement across his property. The Court held that in the context of condemnation proceedings a taking does not occur until compensation is determined and paid, and went on to say that "[a] reduction or increase in the value of property may occur by reason of legislation for or the beginning or completion of a project," but "[s]uch changes in value are incidents of ownership. They cannot be considered as a 'taking' in the constitutional sense." *Danforth. Agins* likewise rejected a claim that the city's preliminary activities constituted a taking, saying that "[m]ere fluctuations in value during the process of governmental decisionmaking, absent extraordinary delay, are 'incidents of ownership.' "

But these cases merely stand for the unexceptional proposition that the valuation of property which has been taken must be calculated as of the time of the taking, and that depreciation in value of the property by reason of preliminary activity is not chargeable to the government. Thus, in *Agins,* we concluded that the preliminary activity did not work a taking. It would require a considerable extension of these decisions to say that no compensable regulatory taking may occur until a challenged ordinance has ultimately been held invalid.

Nothing we say today is intended to abrogate the principle that the decision to exercise the power of eminent domain is a legislative function, " 'for Congress and Congress alone to determine.' " *Hawaii Housing Authority* v. *Midkiff* (1984), quoting *Berman* v. *Parker* (1954). Once a court determines that a taking has occurred, the government retains the whole range of options already available—amendment of the regulation, withdrawal of the invalidated regulation, or exercise of eminent domain. Thus we do not, as the Solicitor General suggests, "permit a court, at the behest of a private person, to require the ... Government to exercise the power of eminent domain...." Brief for United States as *Amicus Curiae*

22. We merely hold that where the government's activities have already worked a taking of all use of property, no subsequent action by the government can relieve it of the duty to provide compensation for the period during which the taking was effective.

We also point out that the allegation of the complaint which we treat as true for purposes of our decision was that the ordinance in question denied appellant all use of the property. We limit our holding to the facts presented, and of course do not deal with the quite different questions that would arise in the case of normal delays in obtaining building permits, changes in zoning ordinances, variances, and the like which are not before us. We realize that even our present holding will undoubtedly lessen to some extent the freedom and flexibility of land-use planners and governing bodies of municipal corporations when enacting land-use regulations. But such consequences necessarily flow from any decision upholding a claim of constitutional right; many of the provisions of the Constitution are designed to limit the flexibility and freedom of governmental authorities and the Just Compensation Clause is one of them. As Justice Holmes aptly noted more than 50 years ago, "a strong public desire to improve the public condition is not enough to warrant achieving the desire by a shorter cut than the constitutional way of paying for the change." *Pennsylvania Coal Co.* v. *Mahon.*

Here we must assume that the Los Angeles County ordinances have denied appellant all use of its property for a considerable period of years, and we hold that invalidation of the ordinance without payment of fair value for the use of the property during this period of time would be a constitutionally insufficient remedy. The judgment of the California Court of Appeals is therefore reversed, and the case is remanded for further proceedings not inconsistent with this opinion.

It is so ordered.

JUSTICE STEVENS, with whom JUSTICE BLACKMUN and JUSTICE O'CONNOR join as to Parts I and III, dissenting.

One thing is certain. The Court's decision today will generate a great deal of litigation. Most of it, I believe, will be unproductive. But the mere duty to defend the actions that today's decision will spawn will undoubtedly have a significant adverse impact on the land-use regulatory process. The Court has reached out to address an issue not actually presented in this case, and has then answered that self-imposed question in a superficial and, I believe, dangerous way.

Four flaws in the Court's analysis merit special comment. First, the Court unnecessarily and imprudently assumes that appellant's complaint alleges an unconstitutional taking of Lutherglen. Second, the Court distorts our precedents in the area of regulatory takings when it concludes that all ordinances which would constitute takings if allowed to remain in effect permanently, necessarily also constitute takings if they are in effect for only a limited period of time. Third, the Court incorrectly assumes that the California Supreme Court has already decided that it will never allow a state court to grant monetary relief for a temporary regulatory taking, and then uses that conclusion to reverse a judgment which is correct under the Court's own theories. Finally, the Court errs in concluding that it is the Takings Clause, rather than the Due Process Clause, which is the primary constraint on the use of unfair and dilatory procedures in the land-use area.

I

In the relevant portion of its complaint for inverse condemnation, appellant alleged:

> "16
>
> "On January 11, 1979, the County adopted Ordinance No. 11,855, which provides:
>
> " 'Section 1. A person shall not construct, reconstruct, place or enlarge any building or structure, any portion of which is, or will be, located within the outer boundary lines of the interim flood protection area located in Mill Creek Canyon, vicinity of Hidden Springs, as shown on Map No. 63 ML 52, attached hereto and incorporated herein by reference as though fully set forth.' "
>
> "17
>
> "Lutherglen is within the flood protection area created by Ordinance No. 11,855.
>
> "18
>
> "Ordinance No. 11,855 denies First Church all use of Lutherglen." App. 49.

Because the Church sought only compensation, and did not request invalidation of the ordinance, the Superior Court granted a motion to strike those three paragraphs, and consequently never decided whether they alleged a "taking." The Superior Court granted the motion to strike on the basis of the rule announced in *Agins* v. *Tiburon* (1979). Under the rule of that case a property owner who claims that a land-use restriction has taken property for public use without compensation, must file an action seeking invalidation of the regulation, and may not simply demand compensation. The Court of Appeal affirmed on the authority of *Agins* alone, also without holding that the complaint had alleged a violation of either the California Constitution or the Federal Constitution. At most, it assumed, *arguendo,* that a constitutional violation had been alleged.

This Court clearly has the authority to decide this case by ruling that the complaint did not allege a taking under the Federal Constitution, and therefore to avoid the novel constitutional issue that it addresses. Even though I believe the Court's lack of self-restraint is imprudent, it is imperative to stress that the Court does not hold that appellant is entitled to compensation as a result of the flood protection regulation that the County enacted. No matter whether the regulation is treated as one that deprives appellant of its property on a permanent or temporary basis, this Court's precedents demonstrate that the type of regulatory program at issue here cannot constitute a taking....

II

There is no dispute about the proposition that a regulation which goes "too far" must be deemed a taking. See *Pennsylvania Coal Co.* v. *Mahon* (1922). When that happens, the Government has a choice: it may abandon the regulation or it may continue to regulate and compensate those whose property it takes. In the usual case, either of these options is wholly satisfactory. Paying compensation for the property is, of course, a constitutional prerogative of the sovereign. Alternatively, if the sovereign chooses not to retain the regulation, repeal will, in virtually all cases, mitigate the overall effect of the regulation so substantially that the slight diminution in value that the regulation caused while in effect cannot be classified as a taking of property. We may assume, however, that this may not always be the case. There may be some situations in which even the temporary existence of a regulation has such severe consequences that invalidation or repeal will not mitigate the damage enough to remove the "taking" label. This hypothetical situation is what the Court calls a "temporary taking." But, contrary to the Court's implications, the fact that a regulation would constitute a taking if allowed to remain in effect permanently is by no means dispositive of the question whether the effect that the regulation has already had on the property is so severe that a taking occurred during the period before the regulation was invalidated.

A temporary interference with an owner's use of his property may constitute a taking for which the Constitution requires that compensation be paid. At least with respect to physical takings, the Court has so held. Thus, if the Government appropriates a leasehold interest and uses it for a public purpose, the return of the premises at the expiration of the lease would obviously not erase the fact of the Government's temporary occupation. Or if the Government destroys a chicken farm by building a road through it or flying planes over it, removing the road or terminating the flights would not palliate the physical damage that had already occurred. These examples are consistent with the rule that even minimal physical occupations constitute takings which give rise to a duty to compensate. See *Loretto* v. *Teleprompter Manhattan CATV Corp.* (1982).

But our cases also make it clear that regulatory takings and physical takings are very different in this, as well as other, respects. While virtually all physical invasions are deemed takings, see, *e.g., Loretto; United States* v. *Causby* (1946), a regulatory program that adversely affects property values does not constitute a taking, unless it destroys a major portion of the property's value. See *Keystone Bituminous* (1987); *Hodel* v. *Virginia Surface Mining & Reclamation Assn.* (1981); *Agins* v. *Tiburon* (1980). This diminution of value inquiry is unique to regulatory takings. Unlike physical invasions, which are relatively rare and easily identifiable without making any economic analysis, regulatory programs constantly affect property values in countless ways, and only the most extreme regulations can constitute takings. Some dividing line must be established between everyday regulatory inconveniences and those so severe that they constitute takings. The diminution of value inquiry has long been used in identifying that line. As Justice Holmes put it: "Government hardly could go on if to some extent values incident to property could not be diminished without paying for every such change in the general law." *Pennsylvania Coal.* It is this basic distinction between regulatory and physical takings that the Court ignores today.

Regulations are three dimensional; they have depth, width, and length. As for depth, regulations define the extent to which the owner may not use the property in question. With respect to width, regulations define the amount of property encompassed by the restrictions. Finally, and for purposes of this case, essentially, regulations set forth the duration of the restrictions. It is obvious that no one of these elements can be analyzed alone to evaluate the impact of a regulation, and hence to determine whether a taking has occurred. For example, in *Keystone Bituminous* we declined to focus in on any discrete segment of the coal in the petitioners' mines, but rather looked to the effect that the restriction had on their entire mining project. [S]ee also *Penn Central* [*Transportation Co.* v. *New York City* (1978)] (looking at owner's other buildings). Similarly, in *Penn Central,* the Court concluded that it was error to focus on the nature of the uses which were prohibited without also examining the many profitable uses to which the property could still be put. [S]ee also *Agins; Andrus* v. *Allard* (1979). Both of these factors are essential to a meaningful analysis of the economic effect that regulations have on the value of property and on an owner's reasonable investment-based expectations with respect to the property.

Just as it would be senseless to ignore these first two factors in assessing the economic effect of a regulation, one cannot conduct the inquiry without considering the duration of the restriction. See generally, Williams, Smith, Siemon, Mandelker, & Babcock, The White River Junction Manifesto, Vt. L. Rev. (Fall 1984). For example, while I agreed with the Chief Justice's view that the permanent restriction on building involved in *Penn Central* constituted a taking, I assume that no one would have suggested that a temporary freeze on building would have also constituted a taking. Similarly, I am confident that even the dissenters in *Keystone Bituminous* would not have concluded that the restriction on bituminous coal mining would have constituted a taking had it simply required the mining companies to delay their operations until an appropriate safety inspection could be made.

On the other hand, I am willing to assume that some cases may arise in which a property owner can show that prospective invalidation of the regulation cannot cure the taking—that the temporary operation of a regulation has caused such a significant diminution in the property's value that compensation must be afforded for the taking that has already occurred. For this ever to happen, the restriction on the use of the property would not only have to be a substantial one, but it would have to remain in effect for a significant percentage of the property's useful life. In such a case an application of our test for regulatory takings would obviously require an inquiry into the duration of the restriction, as well as its scope and severity. See *Williamson Planning Comm'n* v. *Hamilton Bank* (1985) (refusing to evaluate taking claim when the long-term economic effects were uncertain because it was not clear that restrictions would remain in effect permanently).

The cases that the Court relies upon for the proposition that there is no distinction between temporary and permanent takings are inapposite, for they all deal with physical takings—where the diminution of value test is inapplicable. None of those cases is controversial; the state certainly may not occupy an individual's home for a month and then escape compensation by leaving and declaring the occupation "temporary." But what does that have to do with the proper inquiry for regulatory takings? Why should there be a constitutional distinction between a permanent restriction that only reduces the economic value of the property by a fraction—perhaps one-third—and a restriction that merely postpones the development of a property for a fraction of its useful life—presumably far less than a third? In the former instance, no taking has occurred; in the latter case, the Court now proclaims that compensation for a taking must be provided. The Court makes no effort to explain these irreconcilable results. Instead, without any attempt to fit its proclamation into our regulatory takings cases, the Court boldly announces that once a property owner makes out a claim that a regulation would constitute a taking if allowed to stand, then he or she is entitled to damages for the period of time between its enactment and its invalidation.

Until today, we have repeatedly rejected the notion that all temporary diminutions in the value of property automatically activate the compensation requirement of the Takings Clause. In *Agins*, we held:

> "The State Supreme Court correctly rejected the contention that the municipality's good-faith planning activities, which did not result in successful prosecution of an eminent domain claim, so burdened the appellants' enjoyment of their property as to constitute a taking. . . . Even if the appellants' ability to sell their property was limited during the pendency of the condemnation proceeding, the appellants were free to sell or develop their property when the proceedings ended. Mere fluctuations in value during the process of governmental decisionmaking, absent extraordinary delay, are 'incidents of ownership. They cannot be considered as a "taking" in the constitutional sense.'" [Q]uoting *Danforth* v. *United States* (1939).

Our more recent takings cases also cut against the approach the Court now takes. In *Williamson*, and *MacDonald, Sommer & Frates* v. *County of Yolo* (1986), we held that we could not review a taking claim as long as the property owner had an opportunity to obtain a variance or some other form of relief from the zoning authorities that would permit the development of the property to go forward. See *Williamson; County of Yolo*. Implicit in those holdings was the assumption that the temporary deprivation of all use of the property would not constitute a taking if it would be adequately remedied by a belated grant of approval of the developer's plans. See Sallet, Regulatory "Takings" and Just Compensation: The Supreme Court's Search for a Solution Continues, Urb. Law. (1986).

The Court's reasoning also suffers from severe internal inconsistency. Although it purports to put to one side "normal delays in obtaining building permits, changes in zoning ordinances, variances and the like," the Court does not explain why there is a constitutional distinction between a total denial of all use of property during such "normal delays" and an equally total denial for the same length of time in order to determine whether a regulation has "gone too far" to be sustained unless the Government is prepared to condemn the property. Precisely the same interference with a real estate developer's plans may be occasioned by protracted proceedings which terminate with a zoning board's decision that the public interest would be served by modification of its regulation and equally protracted litigation which ends with a judicial determination that the existing zoning restraint has "gone too far," and that the board must therefore grant the developer a variance. The Court's analysis takes no cognizance of these realities. Instead, it appears to erect an artificial distinction between "normal delays" and the delays involved in obtaining a court declaration that the regulation constitutes a taking.

In my opinion, the question whether a "temporary taking" has occurred should not be answered by simply looking at the reason a temporary interference with an owner's use of his property is terminated. Litigation challenging the validity of a land-use restriction gives rise to a delay that is just as "normal" as an administrative procedure seeking a variance or an approval of a controversial plan. Just because a plaintiff can prove that a land-use restriction would constitute a taking if allowed to remain in effect permanently does not mean that he or she can also prove that its temporary application rose to the level of a constitutional taking. . . .

[Part III omitted]

IV

. . . The policy implications of today's decision are obvious and, I fear, far reaching. Cautious local officials and land-use planners may avoid taking any action that might later be challenged and thus give rise to a damage action. Much important regulation will never be enacted, even perhaps in the health and safety area. Were this result mandated by the Constitution, these serious implications would have to be ignored. But the loose cannon the Court fires today is not only unattached to the Constitution, but it also takes aim at a long line of precedents in the regulatory takings area. It would be the better part of valor simply to decide the case at hand instead of igniting the kind of litigation explosion that this decision will undoubtedly touch off.

I respectfully dissent.

No. 86-133

James Patrick Nollan, et ux., Appellant *v.* California Coastal Commission	On appeal from the Court of Appeal of California, Second Appellate District

[June 26, 1987]

JUSTICE SCALIA delivered the opinion of the Court.

James and Marilyn Nollan appeal from a decision of the California Court of Appeal ruling that the California Coastal Commission could condition its grant of permission to rebuild their house on their transfer to the public of an easement across their beachfront property. 177 Cal. App. 3d 719, 223 Cal. Rptr. 28 (1986). The California Court rejected their claim that imposition of that condition violates the Takings Clause of the Fifth Amendment, as incorporated against the States by the Fourteenth Amendment. We noted probable jurisdiction. (1986). . . .

II

Had California simply required the Nollans to make an easement across their beachfront available to the public on a permanent basis in order to increase the public access to the beach, rather than conditioning their permit to rebuild their house on their agreeing to do so, we have no doubt there would have been a taking. To say that the appropriation of a public easement across a landowner's premises does not constitute the taking of a property interest but rather, (as JUSTICE BRENNAN contends) "a mere restriction on its use," is to use words in a manner that deprives them of all their ordinary meaning. Indeed, one of the principal uses of the eminent domain power is to assure that the government be able to require conveyance of just such interests, so long as it pays for them. J. Sackman, 1 Nichols on Eminent Domain § 2.1[1] (Rev. 3d ed. 1985), 2 *id.*, § 5.01[5]; see 1 *id.*, § 1.42[9], 2 *id.*, § 6.14. Perhaps because the point is so obvious, we have never been confronted with a controversy that required us to rule upon it, but our cases' analysis of the effect of other governmental action leads to the same conclusion. We have repeatedly held that, as to property reserved by its owner for private use, "the right to exclude [others is] 'one of the most essential sticks in the bundle of rights that are commonly characterized as property.'" *Loretto* v. *Teleprompter Manhattan CATV Corp.* (1982), quoting *Kaiser Aetna* v. *United States* (1979). In *Loretto* we observed that where governmental action results in "[a] permanent physical occupation" of the property, by the government itself or by others, "our cases uniformly have found a taking to the extent of the occupation, without regard to whether the action achieves an important public benefit or has only minimal economic impact on the owner." We think a "permanent physical occupation" has occurred, for purposes of that rule, where individuals are given a permanent and continuous right to pass to and fro, so that the real property may continuously be traversed, even though no particular individual is permitted to station himself permanently upon the premises. . . .

Given, then, that requiring uncompensated conveyance of the easement outright would violate the Fourteenth Amendment, the question becomes whether requiring it to be conveyed as a condition for issuing a land use permit alters the outcome. We have long recognized that land use regulation does not effect a taking if it "substantially advance[s] legitimate state interests" and does not "den[y] an owner economically viable use of his land," *Agins* v. *Tiburon* (1980). See also *Penn Central Transportation Co.* v. *New York City* (1978) ("a use restriction may constitute a 'taking' if not reasonably necessary to the effectuation of a substantial government purpose"). Our cases have not elaborated on the standards for determining what constitutes a "legitimate state interest" or what type of connection between the regulation and the state interest satisfies the requirement that the former "substantially advance" the latter. They have made clear, however, that a broad range of governmental purposes and regulations satisfies these requirements. See *Agins* v. *Tiburon* (scenic zoning); *Penn Central Transportation Co.* v. *New York City* (landmark preservation); *Euclid* v. *Ambler Realty Co.* (1926) (residential zoning); Laitos and Westfall, Government Interference with Private Interests in Public Resources, Harv. Envtl. L. Rev. (1987). The Commission argues that among these permissible purposes are protecting the public's ability to see the beach, assisting the public in overcoming the "psychological barrier" to using the beach created by a developed shorefront, and preventing congestion on the public beaches. We assume, without deciding, that this is so—in which case the Commission unquestionably would be able to deny the Nollans their permit outright if their new house (alone, or by reason of the cumulative impact produced in conjunction with other construction) would substantially impede these purposes, unless the denial would interfere so drastically with the Nollans' use of their property as to constitute a taking. See *Penn Central Transportation Co.* v. *New York City*.

The Commission argues that a permit condition that serves the same legitimate police-power purpose as a refusal to issue the permit should not be found to be a taking if the refusal to issue the permit would not constitute a taking. We agree. Thus, if the Commission attached to the permit some condition that would have protected the public's ability to see the beach notwithstanding construction of the new house—for example, a height limitation, a width restriction, or a ban on fences—so long as the Commission could have exercised its police power (as we have assumed it could) to forbid construction of the house altogether, imposition of the condition would also be constitutional. Moreover (and here we come closer to the facts of the present case), the condition would be constitutional even if it consisted of the requirement that the Nollans provide a viewing spot on their property for passersby with whose sighting of the ocean their new house would interfere. Although such a requirement, constituting a permanent grant of continuous access to the property, would have to be considered a taking if it were not attached to a development permit, the Commission's assumed power to forbid construction of the house in order to protect the public's view of the beach must surely include the power to condition construction upon some concession by the owner, even a concession of property rights, that serves the same end. If a prohibition designed to accomplish that purpose would be a legitimate exercise of the police power rather than a taking, it would be strange to conclude that providing the owner an alternative to that prohibition which accomplishes the same purpose is not.

The evident constitutional propriety disappears, however, if the condition substituted for the prohibition utterly fails to further the end advanced as the justification for the prohibition. When that essential nexus is eliminated, the situation becomes the same as if California law forbade shouting fire in a crowded theater, but granted dispensations to those willing to contribute $100 to the state treasury. While a ban on shouting fire can be a core exercise of the State's police power to protect the public safety, and can thus meet even our stringent standards for regulation of speech, adding the unrelated condition alters the purpose to one which, while it may be legitimate, is inadequate to sustain the ban. Therefore, even though, in a sense, requiring a $100 tax contribution in order to shout fire is a lesser restriction on speech than an outright ban, it would not pass constitutional muster. Similarly here, the lack of nexus between the condition and the original purpose of the building restriction converts that purpose to something other than what it was. The purpose then becomes, quite simply, the obtaining of an easement to serve some valid governmental purpose, but without payment of compensation. Whatever may be the outer limits of "legitimate state interests" in the takings and land use context, this is not one of them. In short, unless the permit condition serves the same governmental purpose as the development ban, the building restriction is not a valid regulation of land use but "an out-and-out plan of extortion." *J.E.D. Associates, Inc.* v. *Atkinson* 121 N.H.; 432 A.2d (1981); see Brief for United States as *Amicus Curiae* 22. . . .

JUSTICE BRENNAN, with whom JUSTICE MARSHALL joins, dissenting.

Appellants in this case sought to construct a new dwelling on their beach lot that would both diminish visual access to the beach and move private development closer to the public tidelands. The Commission reasonably concluded that such "buildout," both individually and cumulatively, threatens public access to the shore. It sought to offset this encroachment by obtaining assurance that the public may walk along the shoreline in order to gain access to the ocean. The Court finds this an illegitimate exercise of the police power, because it maintains that there is no reasonable relationship between the effect of the development and the condition imposed.

The first problem with this conclusion is that the Court imposes a standard of precision for the exercise of a State's police power that has been discredited for the better part of this century. Furthermore, even under the Court's cramped standard, the permit condition imposed in this case directly responds to the specific type of burden on access created by appellants' development. Finally, a review of those factors deemed most significant in takings analysis makes clear that the Commission's action implicates none of the concerns underlying the Takings Clause. The Court has thus struck down the Commission's reasonable effort to respond to intensified development along the California coast, on behalf of landowners who can make no claim that their reasonable expectations have been disrupted. The Court has, in short, given appellants a windfall at the expense of the public....

I

[Part A omitted]

B

Even if we accept the Court's unusual demand for a precise match between the condition imposed and the specific type of burden on access created by the appellants, the State's action easily satisfies this requirement. First, the lateral access condition serves to dissipate the impression that the beach that lies behind the wall of homes along the shore is for private use only. It requires no exceptional imaginative powers to find plausible the Commission's point that the average person passing along the road in front of a phalanx of imposing permanent residences, including the appellants' new home, is likely to conclude that this particular portion of the shore is not open to the public. If, however, that person can see that numerous people are passing and repassing along the dry sand, this conveys the message that the beach is in fact open for use by the public. Furthermore, those persons who go down to the public beach a quarter-mile away will be able to look down the coastline and see that persons have continuous access to the tidelands, and will observe signs that proclaim the public's right of access over the dry sand. The burden produced by the diminution in visual access—the impression that the beach is not open to the public—is thus directly alleviated by the provision for public access over the dry sand. The Court therefore has an unrealistically limited conception of what measures could reasonably be chosen to mitigate the burden produced by a diminution of visual access.

The second flaw in the Court's analysis of the fit between burden and exaction is more fundamental. The Court assumes that the only burden with which the Coastal Commission was concerned was blockage of visual access to the beach. This is incorrect. The Commission specifically stated in its report in support of the permit condition that "[t]he Commission finds that the applicants' proposed development would present an increase in view blockage, *an increase in private use of the shorefront,* and that this impact would burden the public's ability to traverse to and along the shorefront." ([E]mphasis added). It declared that the possibility that "the public may get the impression that the beachfront is no longer available for public use" would be "due to *the encroaching nature of private use immediately adjacent to the public use, as well as* the visual 'block' of increased residential build-out impacting the visual quality of the beachfront." ([E]mphasis added).

The record prepared by the Commission is replete with references to the threat to public access along the coastline resulting from the seaward encroachment of private development along a beach whose mean high tide line is constantly shifting. As the Commission observed in its report, "The Faria Beach shoreline fluctuates during the year depending on the seasons and accompanying storms, and the public is not always able to traverse the shoreline below the mean high tide line." As a result, the boundary between publicly owned tidelands and privately owned beach is not a stable one, and "[t]he existing seawall is located very near to the mean high water line." When the beach is at its largest, the seawall is about 10 feet from the mean high tide mark; "[d]uring the period of the year when the beach suffers erosion, the mean high water line appears to be located either on or beyond the existing seawall." *Ibid.* Expansion of private development on appellants' lot toward the seawall would thus "increase private use immediately adjacent to public tidelands, which has the potential of causing adverse impacts on the public's ability to traverse the shoreline." As the Commission explained:

> "The placement of more private use adjacent to public tidelands has the potential of creating conflicts between the applicants and the public. The results of new private use encroachment into boundary/buffer areas between private and public property can create situations in which landowners intimidate the public and seek to prevent them from using public tidelands because of disputes between the two parties over where the exact boundary between private and public ownership is located. If the applicants' project would result in further seaward encroachment of private use into an area of clouded title, new private use in the subject encroachment area could result in use conflict between private and public entities on the subject shorefront."

The deed restriction on which permit approval was conditioned would directly address this threat to the public's access to the tidelands. It would provide a formal declaration of the public's right of access, thereby ensuring that the shifting character of the tidelands, and the presence of private development immediately adjacent to it, would not jeopardize enjoyment of that right. The imposition of the permit condition was therefore directly related to the fact that appellant's development would be "located along a unique stretch of coast where lateral access is inadequate due to the construction of private residential structures and shoreline protective devices along a fluctuating shoreline." The deed restriction was crafted to deal with the particular character of the beach along which appellants sought to build, and with the specific problems created by expansion of development toward the public tidelands. In imposing the restriction, the State sought to ensure that such development would not disrupt the historical expectation of the public regarding access to the sea.

The Court is therefore simply wrong that there is no reasonable relationship between the permit condition and the specific type of burden on public access created by the appellants' proposed development. Even were the Court desirous of assuming the added responsibility of closely monitoring the regulation of development along the California coast, this record reveals rational public action by any conceivable standard....

[Part II omitted]

III

...With respect to the permit condition program in general, the Commission should have little difficulty in the future in utilizing its expertise to demonstrate a specific connection between provisions for access and burdens on access produced by new development. Neither the Commission in its report nor the State in its briefs and at argument highlighted the particular threat to lateral access created by appellants' development project. In defending its action, the State emphasized the general point that *overall* access to the beach had been preserved, since the diminution of access created by the project had been offset by the gain in lateral access. This approach is understandable, given that the State relied on the reasonable assumption that its action was justified under the normal standard of review for determining legitimate exercises of a State's police power. In the future, alerted to the Court's apparently more demanding requirement, it need only make clear that a provision for public access directly responds to a particular type of burden on access created by a new development. Even if I did not believe that the record in this case satisfies this requirement, I would have to acknowledge that the record's documentation of the impact of coastal development indicates that the Commission should have little problem presenting its findings in a way that avoids a takings problem.

Nonetheless it is important to point out that the Court's insistence on a precise accounting system in this case is insensitive to the fact that increasing intensity of development in many areas calls for far-sighted, comprehensive planning that takes into account both the interdependence of land uses and the cumulative impact of development. As one scholar has noted:

> "Property does not exist in isolation. Particular parcels are tied to one another in complex ways, and property is more accurately described as being inextricably part of a network of relationships that is neither limited to, nor usefully defined by, the property boundaries with which the legal system is accustomed to dealing. Frequently, use of any given parcel of property is at the same time ef-

fectively a use of, or a demand upon, property beyond the border of the user." Sax, Takings, Private Property, and Public Rights, Yale L.J. (1971).

As Congress has declared, "The key to more effective protection and use of the land and water resources of the coastal zone [is for the states to] develo[p] land and water use programs for the coastal zone, including unified policies, criteria, standards, methods, and processes for dealing with land and water use decisions of more than local significance." This is clearly a call for a focus on the overall impact of development on coastal areas. State agencies therefore require considerable flexibility in responding to private desires for development in a way that guarantees the preservation of public access to the coast. They should be encouraged to regulate development in the context of the overall balance of competing uses of the shoreline. The Court today does precisely the opposite, overruling an eminently reasonable exercise of an expert state agency's judgment, substituting its own narrow view of how this balance should be struck. Its reasoning is hardly suited to the complex reality of natural resource protection in the twentieth century. I can only hope that today's decision is an aberration, and that a broader vision ultimately prevails.

I dissent.

POPE'S TRIP TO POLAND

June 12 and 13, 1987

Pope John Paul II toured nine cities and nearby rural areas during his third visit as pope to his native Poland. He had traveled to Poland in 1979, not long after his 1978 election, and again in 1983, when the country was under martial law. The pope's speeches and informal remarks in June 1987 focused worldwide attention on conflicts between the policies of the communist Polish government and the political and national aspirations of the Polish people.

Polish leader General Wojciech Jaruzelski, who had conferred with the pope during a Vatican visit in January, hoped that John Paul's interest in creating full diplomatic relations between the Vatican and the Polish People's Republic would be the main focus of the visit. This hope was echoed by Polish primate Jozef Cardinal Glemp and others in the church hierarchy. They anticipated that the papal visit to Warsaw might pave the way for a similar pilgrimage to Moscow and to Lithuania, home of the largest number of Roman Catholics in the Soviet Union.

Although the Vatican had also stressed its desire to inaugurate formal relations with Poland, it became clear during the course of his seven-day stay that John Paul considered this a secondary goal. He indicated that any upgrading of relations would depend on reforms implemented by the Jaruzelski government.

Major Themes

On the day of his arrival the pope made a strong appeal for a widening of civil liberties in Poland, specifically citing the UN Universal Declara-

tion on Human Rights. In a speech to government leaders, televised live to Polish audiences, the pontiff admonished his listeners to remember each person's "right to religious freedom, his right to form associations and to express his own opinions."

The following day in Lublin, forty miles from the Soviet border, the pope urged a rethinking of the communist system. "As a son of this homeland," he said, "I risk expressing the view that it is necessary to think over many questions of social life, structures, organization of labor, all the way to the very premises of the contemporary state organism from the point of view of the future of the young generation on Polish soil."

In his home city of Krakow on June 10 the pope addressed economic reform—another major theme of his visit. Speaking at an open-air mass to 2 million people, many of them farmers, the pope denounced government agricultural policies and called for a reinstatement of Rural Solidarity, the outlawed farmers' union. Agreements concluded by the government granting rights to private farmers "should not be passed over in silence, but should be fully realized," he said.

The pope made his strongest attack on Poland's economic policies during a tour of a Lodz textile mill. He declared that working conditions at the mill, operated almost exclusively by women, were unsafe, and that all working women should be covered by health benefits. In his speech to the workers the pope stated that society has "the duty" to develop "conditions of life in which married women and mothers are not forced to undertake work outside the home."

Solidarity, Religious Freedom

The pope made his most forceful and emotional statements during his visit to Gdansk, home of the banned Solidarity trade union, where he had been forbidden to travel in 1983. Avoiding reference to specific economic problems, he praised Solidarity's aims of unity and nonviolence and endorsed each individual's "right to self-determination as an employee—which is expressed in, among other forms, trade unions."

The government allowed Solidarity leader Lech Walesa to meet with the pope, but refused to place the meeting on the official calendar or to allow journalists to interview Walesa. This signal of official disapproval was dramatically reinforced by the presence of large numbers of government troops, riot squads, and armored vans at every stop made by the papal entourage. These forces easily contained pro-Solidarity demonstrations during the first few days of the visit. After the pope firmly endorsed Solidarity in a speech to thousands of shipworkers, security forces blocked downtown Gdansk, preventing citizens and foreign journalists from seeing the pontiff as he placed a wreath on a Solidarity monument.

Even though forty leading activists had been detained before the pope's visit, more than 10,000 residents of Gdansk joined together after an outdoor mass to march under Solidarity banners. Thousands of police halted the mile-long column, using sticks and truncheons to force marchers to disperse.

John Paul II was officially in Poland to lead a eucharist congress celebrating the "moral renewal of man and the nation." In this context he emphasized the rights of Poles to practice their religion publicly, praising the work and sacrifice of the Reverend Jerzy Popieluszko, a pro-Solidarity priest murdered by the secret police in 1984. Although his visit to the priest's grave was not announced, 5,000 people waited outside the churchyard for the pontiff. More than 1 million Poles attended an outdoor mass in Warsaw on the last day of the visit—an unprecedented event in a communist country. (Sentencing of Popieluszko's slayers, Historic Documents of 1985, p. 119)

Following are excerpts from Pope John Paul II's addresses in Gdansk, Poland, June 12, 1987, and in Lodz June 13, 1987:

ADDRESS IN GDANSK

. . . 2. Today, on the path of my pilgrimage throughout the homeland, which is also the route of the eucharistic congress, I welcome and greet Gdansk. I express my joy at being here together with you.

Gdansk, a thousand-year-old town where St. Wojciech arrived in the spring of 997 on his way to Prussia and where "groups of people accepted baptism." Gdansk, which through the ups and downs of history cleaved to the mouth of the Vistula, the river of Polish rivers. The perspectives which the sea opens to a man on land have always been open here in Gdansk on the Baltic coast. The perspectives of boundless distance, the perspective of the depth of its waters, the perspective of freedom. A man at sea feels free, free from those conditions which are created by life on the shore, and at the same time subjected to the requirements of the new element. He is inspired for new responsibility.

. . . I greet in this town all that was so important for us in the different periods of our past and all that it has become in recent years. . . . I greet the town and the environment in which was reborn the need for man's renewal through work. The liberation of man through work. . . .

3. Today's liturgy tells us about this renewal and liberation when it refers to the biblical beginning of man on earth. Here is man, whom God created in his image and likeness, created as a man and woman, created in the center of the visible universe. Here is man, to whom the Creator says: "Be fertile and multiply; fill the earth and subdue it."

God gives man the earth and involves him in it. So in this way he involves man in work: work in any possible form it takes in the course of the history of mankind, together with the progress and development of his knowledge about the world and himself....

5. Human work. Once again I express my joy that at this stage of the eucharistic congress I can be with you in Gdansk. For in this town and simultaneously on the whole Baltic coast and in other workplaces in Poland were undertaken enormous efforts aimed at restoring the full personal and social dimensions of human work.

This effort institutes in the history of "working on work," as somebody in this country has rightly said, a momentous phase. And not only from the Polish point of view. This is an important phase for different places, for different regions of the contemporary world.

Perhaps this matter is less understood in prosperous countries where prosperity borders on consumeristic abuse. But it is understood everywhere that the problem of work lies at the base of the authentic progress and liberation of man. For work has exactly this dimension, as indicated in church teaching....

6. The Gospel in today's liturgy introduces us in a way to the heart of this problem. Here is a landlord who (at different times of the day) hires laborers for work in a vineyard.... Even if this field of activity may rightly seem very modest in comparison with contemporary fields of industrial activity such as, for instance, the Gdansk shipyards, we are still talking about the same eternal analogy.

The landlord says to the laborers: "Go into my vineyard, and I will give you what is just." Consequently he draws up a contract for work and at the same time for just payment, for just remuneration of work.

The history of justice and injustice has developed around this eternal issue from one generation to another in the mutual relations between employer and employee....

It is true that work needs to be paid for, but this is not all. Work means man. Working man. As far as just relations between work and pay are concerned, they never can be adequately described if one does not start from man—the subject of labor.

Labor cannot be treated—at any time or place—as a commodity, because man cannot be a commodity for another man but must be a subject. He participates in labor through his entire humanity and all his subjectivity. Labor opens the entire dimension of human subjectivity in social life and also the subjectivity of society composed of working men. Thus all human rights should be perceived in connection with man's work, and all of them should be fulfilled.

Human labor has to be paid for, and at the same time it is impossible to respond to human work with only payment. After all, man is not only an "executor" but a co-creator of the work which develops in his workshop. He has the right to self-determination as an employee—which is expressed in, among other forms, trade unions: "independent and self-governing" as it was underlined here in Gdansk.

In turn, human labor—through hundreds and thousands (if not millions) of workshops—contributes to the common good of society. Working people in their labor find an entitlement . . . to determine matters in all of society, which lives and develops from their work.

The Gdansk Agreements will remain in the history of Poland an expression of this growing consciousness of the working man, of the entire social and moral harmony on Polish soil. The genesis of those agreements stemmed from that tragic December 1970. And the agreements remain a task to be fulfilled.

7. Let us move to the second reading of today's liturgy.

"Bear one another's burdens" writes St. Paul to the Galatians, and those words bear great power. "One another's." A man is not alone, he lives with others, through others and for others. A communal and social dimension is appropriate to the entire human experience, appropriate for itself. This dimension can mean the diminution of the human person, his talents, his possibilities, his tasks. Just from the point of view of the social community there must be enough space for everybody. One of the important tasks of the state is to create this space in such way that everybody can develop himself, his personality and vocation through work. This personal development, this space of the person in social life, is at the same time a condition for the common good. If the possibilities are taken away from a man, if the organization of social life establishes parameters too narrow for human abilities and human initiatives—even if it follows in the name of some "social" motivation—it is, unfortunately, against the common good.

"Bear one another's burdens"—this concise sentence of the apostle is an inspiration for solidarity between people and in society. Solidarity—it means one and another, and if there is a burden, a burden carried together, in community. Thus never one against another. Others against others. And never a "burden" carried by a man alone, without help from others. The struggle cannot be stronger than solidarity. The program of struggle cannot be above the program of solidarity. Otherwise the burdens grow too heavy and the spread of these burdens increases disproportionately. Even worse, when struggle is put first (especially in the meaning of the struggle between classes), it can easily happen that some of the others remain on the "social field" as enemies, . . . rather than as those with whom should be conducted a search for agreement or thought of as jointly "bearing burdens.". . .

8. Dear brothers and sisters from the shipyards, from the harbors and from all the workplaces in Gdansk! Workplaces all over the world thank you, working people, that you have taken up this struggle and difficult "work on work." The church thanks you for taking it up in the presence of Christ and his mother.

People in different places wonder how this can be, that there can be a link between the working world and Christ's cross, between human labor and the holy Mass, the sacrifice of Christ. The sight of Polish workers confessing and going to holy communion in their place of work prompts admiration and respect. . . .

In every holy Mass, the sacrifice of our redemption enters the fruit of "human labor," every human work. Bread is a "synthetic" example of this and wine as well. Everyday human work inscribes itself in the eucharist: in the sacrament of our redemption and the "great mystery of our faith." Every day, in so many places on the earth, God's perspectives are revealed in human labor.

"May this bread become for us the food of redemption ... This wine our spiritual drink."

But "one does not live by bread alone." His existence and his work must have meaning—and not only immediate and passing meaning. It must have an ultimate meaning. By the measure of who man is....

God says to man, in the vineyard of his eternal and ultimate destinies, why do you want to limit me to the measure of your justice alone? The order of justice is basic, but not ultimate. In God's kingdom justice is accomplished. It is "exceeded" by love. This is the love which adopts man, elevates him, even he who was a prodigal son. There is no complete justice without love....

Draw from this love the spiritual strength for work. For "work on work." For solidarity ...

Your adoration and glory, our eternal Lord, for all the centuries.... Amen.

ADDRESS IN LODZ

1. "Blessed are you, Lord, God of all creation. Through your goodness we have this bread to offer, which earth has given and human hands have made."...

... These words accompany me during the whole course of my pilgrimage in my native land, right from the first moment. And they are bound up in a particular manner with the eucharist—in fact, my stay in Poland this time has a close connection with the national eucharistic congress.

The eucharist is organically bound up with the work of human hands, and the words of the sacrifice bear witness to this. We bring to the altar bread, and this bread—fruit of the earth—is at the same time the fruit of the work of human hands. Man works for bread. Therefore bread at the same time represents and symbolizes man's work as a whole, wherever and in whatsoever manner it is executed.

2. Bread, as an expression and a symbol of human work, assumes a particular eloquence here in Polish Lodz, which developed in a short time from a formerly small settlement into a city of almost 1 million inhabitants, the center of the Polish textile industry.

The life of this industrial center and of its inhabitants meant numerous social and economic conflicts right from the outset. Despite various efforts and initiatives undertaken by the community of Lodz—for a duration of almost 200 years—now there are deeply felt problems connected with industry, which are nowadays not just those of the textile industry: with the natural and town environment, ecology, living and sanitary conditions, employment and social matters, with the development of spiritual and material needs in this great collection of different kinds of physical and mental work, characterized also by difficult processes of contemporary social changes.

I wish to express my joy that today, in this city of yours, I can meet the Polish world of work, which is represented—particularly here in Lodz—in the majority by women. With all my heart and with deep respect of which women are worthy, I greet and salute all the women workers of the textile industry gathered here—and through you all the professional working women throughout the land of Poland who are in different situations of life. I am doing this at the beginning of the Marian year, when the church all over the world is looking up with particular hope to the bride chosen by God, who was to be the mother of the Redeemer of the world.

3. . . . Already in the Old Testament we find the description—what's more, the praise—of a woman's work, of a "worthy wife," as the author of the Book of Proverbs expresses himself. This work is above all within the precincts of the family home, which was closely linked during the stage of the material civilization of that time to the family workshop of work.

Modern civilization has brought with it the separation of this erstwhile connection between the home and the workshop of work. Great workshops of industrial labor make it necessary for a man, and so likewise for a woman, to leave home in order to seek the means to support his family as well as himself—sometimes near home and at times far away—in factories and other establishments which are sometimes tens of kilometers away from home.

To this are added the hardships of the work itself, deriving either from uncongenial living conditions or from difficult conditions in which women carry out professional work, such as moisture, heat and noise, which does not take place without a negative influence on the state of health and the health of their progeny. In this city—as I know—not all industrial establishments belong yet to the category of "protected work establishment." Also not all working women are under the protection of an "industrial health service." Therefore one would wish for you women and for all those responsible for the organization of professional work that these positive initiatives might soon become a part of the whole working world.

4. . . . One cannot forejudge from the outset that the situation of moving away from home and family during the course of many hours of the day entails more losses than gains from the point of view of the good of the family union and especially of the upbringing of children. . . . For here come into play the fundamental hierarchy of values and commandments; but they are bound up in an inseparable manner with the good of man. If therefore the premise is "not, above all, man for work, but work for man," then that humanist axiom must be particularly taken into consideration when one is dealing with the professional work of women.

Because a woman, as we know from experience, is above all the heart of family unity. She gives life, and she is also the first to do the bringing up although obviously she is helped by the husband and shares systematically with him the whole round of the responsibilities for the family and the upbringing. Nevertheless, it is known that the human organism stops living when the work of the heart is wanting. The analogy is fairly clear. She who is the heart of the family cannot be missing from the family.

5. Does this mean that women should not work professionally? The social teaching of the church puts forward first and foremost the requirement that everything that a woman does at home should be fully appreciated, the whole activity of a mother and educator. This great work cannot be socially belittled; it must be constantly more valued, if society is not to act to its own detriment.

After all, however, the professional work of women must be treated everywhere and always with an explicit regard for what results from a woman's vocation as a wife and a mother in a family.

6. This vocation—the essential link with God's gift of motherhood—also finds expression in the mission as wife and mother and as a custodian of the truths of faith and ethnic values....

... The woman-mother on an equal basis with the man-father, in asking baptism for the child, consciously takes upon herself the hardship of bringing up the child in the faith. With her whole love and responsibility for the new human being she is carefully watchful so that evil does not change his mind and heart. She tries with all her strength toward the aim that the child should reach a many-sided development both physical and spiritual. Above all, however, with the personal example of her life she leads her child to a mature Christian life—toward the fullness of humanity.

7. This natural mission of the woman-mother often happens to be subjected to the doubts of those who emphasize the social equality of women. Sometimes they look at her professional work as a social advance, and a total dedication to family affairs and the upbringing of children comes to be considered a resignation of the development of one's personality.

It is true that an equal esteem and responsibility of men and women justifies the full access of women to public functions. On the other hand, the true advancement of women requires that clear recognition be given to the value of their maternal and family role, by comparison with all other public roles and with all other professions. Furthermore, these roles and professions should be harmoniously combined if we wish the evolution of society and culture to be truly and fully human.... The right of access to various public functions—the recognition of women on an equal basis with men—lays at the same time on society the duty to care about the development of such structures of work and conditions of life in which married women and mothers are not forced to undertake work outside the home, and so that their work at home might ensure for the family also a many-sided development. Children are in particular need of maternal care so that they can develop as responsible persons, religiously and morally mature, as well as psychologically balanced. The good of the family is so great that it rightly demands from contemporary society a greater appreciation of maternal tasks in those structures which advocate the social advance of women and establish the necessity of undertaking paid work outside the home.

This reminder of the principles expressed in Christian social ethics at today's meeting with the women textile workers is justified by the perturbing phenomenon making its appearance in your professional work. Many women are now beginning to work in three shifts and also during the night, and this contributes to the multiplication of occupational illnesses. But this also has an influence on the rise in the number of broken marriages. The result of this is that many women are forced to bring up their children alone and to care for their material existence.

8. During recent years there ran through the whole of Poland a great call of solidarity—to which women, including the female textile workers of Lodz, made their great contribution—for respect of human dignity, so each one might decide about himself, about his work according to his capabilities and abilities; so that each one might choose his moral ideal, to live according to his own convictions and publicly proclaim, profess and practice his religious faith.

In this calling there was no lack of references to the ultimate values shown in the Gospel. The conviction has matured that it is not just a matter of living better and more comfortably or possessing more. But it is a matter of creating a situation of greater social respect for man, for each one to be able to develop his personal worth and to better fulfill his calling as received by him from God.

It is very important that the conscience of the working woman should always form itself in this way. Then will she perceive in its entirety the value of her vocation as a mother and wife and will discover the full meaning of the hardship of professional work. . . .

9. . . . Human work serves transient purposes. Man works for his daily bread. Christ—redeemer of the world—made this bread at the same time with a visible sign, namely the sacrament of eternal life.

And it is through this sacrament that Christ became for us in a special manner "the way and the truth and the life." Consequently, we work for our daily bread. At the same time let us not lose sight of what is the ultimate destiny of each human being, of man and of woman.

"What profit is there for one to gain the whole world and forfeit his life?"

10. My dear countrywomen and sisters! Do not lose sight of this! Polish women have frankly incalculable merits in our history, especially during the most difficult periods. And unmeasurable are—during the space of this history—the whole nation's debts toward Polish women: mothers, educators, workers . . . heroines. . . .

11. Remember that it is through the deeds of people and nations that God writes at the same time the deeds of salvation of mankind. And in his plan of salvation, he called from the beginning of the earth the "Virgin." She likewise—as the mother of the Redeemer—illuminates all of God's people on their pilgrimage through faith, hope and love toward man's ultimate destiny in God himself.

Look at this "Virgin"! Learn from her, from Mary, truths about your dignity, about your calling. So much depends on each one of you women in the life of man, the family, the native land.

On the path of the eucharistic congress in Poland I pray today for each one of you women. And at the same time I ask God's mother that there may not be missing from Polish life that which is rightly called the "genius of woman," which each one of you and each woman, thanks to the gift of the Creator and Redeemer, can and should put to the common good and to the common heritage of all Poles.

COURT ON CREATION SCIENCE

June 19, 1987

In a 7-2 ruling the Supreme Court June 19 struck down a Louisiana statute that required public schools to teach "creation-science" theory whenever the theory of evolution was taught. In one of its most significant church-state decisions in recent years, the majority held that the law did not promote its asserted purpose of protecting academic freedom; rather, the legislative history of the act indicated that it was designed to advance the religious belief that a supernatural or divine being created man. As such, the Court ruled in Edwards v. Aguillard, *the law violated the First Amendment stricture that "Congress shall make no law respecting an establishment of religion, or prohibiting the free exercise thereof."*

Development of Louisiana Case

In 1985 a federal district judge in New Orleans ruled that the 1981 Louisiana law, the Balanced Treatment for Creation-Science and Evolution-Science in Public School Instruction Act, which had passed by large majorities in the state legislature after a vigorous lobbying campaign by Christian fundamentalists and others, violated the First Amendment. The judge held that the law's purpose was to promote a religious belief—the scriptural account of the creation. The U.S. Circuit Court of Appeals for the Fifth Circuit upheld the ruling, rejecting the argument of the statute's sponsors that it promoted academic freedom. Academic freedom meant that teachers, not the state, made decisions on what to teach, the circuit court concluded. A similar ruling had struck down Arkansas' "balanced treatment" law in 1982. That case was not appealed. (Historic Documents of 1982, p. 3)

The Supreme Court agreed in May 1986 to review the constitutionality of the law and heard arguments in December. In August 1986, seventy-two Nobel Prize-winning scientists and twenty-four scientific organizations—including the National Academy of Sciences—issued a legal brief urging the Supreme Court to strike down the Louisiana law, saying that it threatened "the future of scientific education in this nation" by attempting to discredit proven scientific facts in order to promote fundamentalist beliefs. They were joined by the American Civil Liberties Union and representatives of several "mainstream" religious groups.

Creation science held that life appeared suddenly in complex form, rather than evolving slowly over eons. Lawyers for Louisiana argued that the state law was intended to foster free inquiry by promoting consideration of alternative theories of creation. Moreover, they contended that creation theory was a "science" and was therefore "nonreligious." Attorneys representing a group of Louisiana educators, religious leaders, and parents of school children challenged that view, arguing that creationism was in fact a religion.

The issue had its judicial roots in the famous 1925 "monkey trial" in Tennessee, when John Scopes was convicted for teaching evolution in public schools. In 1968 the Supreme Court struck down laws banning the teaching of evolution. "The First Amendment mandates governmental neutrality between religion and religion, and between religion and nonreligion," the Court held in Epperson v. Arkansas.

The Majority Decision

Justice William J. Brennan, Jr., said the Court "need not be blind" to the Louisiana legislature's true purpose, as revealed by the law's legislative history and the comments of its sponsors. "The pre-eminent purpose of the Louisiana Legislature was clearly to advance the religious viewpoint that a supernatural being created humankind," Brennan said. Emphasizing a point made by the appeals court, Brennan said the law "does not serve to protect academic freedom, but has the distinctly different purpose of discrediting 'evolution by counterbalancing its teaching at every turn with the teaching of creation science.'"

Joining Brennan were Justices Byron R. White, Thurgood Marshall, Harry A. Blackmun, Lewis F. Powell, Jr., John Paul Stevens, and Sandra Day O'Connor. White, who often disagreed with the Court's demands for a wall between church and state, declared that the Edwards *case was "not a difficult" one. He emphasized that both the U.S. District Court and the Fifth U.S. Circuit Court of Appeals had found "creation science" to be a religious belief, which the law required to be taught if evolution was taught. "In other words," White said, "the teaching of evolution was conditioned on the teaching of a religious belief," a clearly unconstitutional demand.*

As it had done in previous church-state cases, the Court tested Louisiana's law against a standard it first devised in the 1971 case of Lemon v. Kurtzman. *To comply with that standard and to be found constitutional in the face of a challenge, a law must have a secular purpose. Its primary effect must neither advance nor inhibit religion, and it must not result in an excessive entanglement of government with religion. The Louisiana law failed the first test, Brennan said, because its defenders had not adequately identified any genuine secular purpose for the law. "While the Court is normally deferential to a state's articulation of a secular purpose, it is required that the statement of such purpose be sincere and not a sham," he said.*

Scalia's Dissent

Justice Antonin Scalia, joined by Chief Justice William H. Rehnquist, dissented. Scalia criticized the Court for disposing of the constitutional question "on the gallop, by impugning the motives" of the law's supporters. He argued that the law should be struck down "only if the record indicated that the Louisiana Legislature had no secular purpose" in passing it. Accepting the academic freedom rationale offered by the state, Scalia rebuked the Court for presuming "that the sole purpose of a law is to advance religion merely because it was supported strongly by organized religions or by adherents of particular faiths."

"Political activism by the religiously motivated is part of our heritage," Scalia said. "Today's religious activism may give us the Balanced Treatment Act, but yesterday's resulted in the abolition of slavery, and tomorrow's may bring relief for famine victims."

> *Following are excerpts from the majority, concurring, and dissenting opinions in the Supreme Court's June 19, 1987, decision in* Edwards v. Aguillard, *ruling unconstitutional a Louisiana law that forbade the teaching of evolution in public schools unless it was accompanied by instruction in "creation science":*

No. 85-1513

Edwards W. Edwards, etc., et al. Appellants *v.* Don Aguillard et al.	On appeal from the United States Court of Appeals for the Fifth Circuit

[June 19, 1987]

JUSTICE BRENNAN delivered the opinion of the Court.

The question for decision is whether Louisiana's "Balanced Treatment for Creation-Science and Evolution-Science in Public School Instruction"

Act (Creationism Act) is facially invalid as violative of the Establishment Clause of the First Amendment.

I

The Creationism Act forbids the teaching of the theory of evolution in public schools unless accompanied by instruction in "creation science." No school is required to teach evolution or creation science. If either is taught, however, the other must also be taught. The theories of evolution and creation science are statutorily defined as "the scientific evidences for [creation or evolution] and inferences from those scientific evidences."

Appellees, who include parents of children attending Louisiana public schools, Louisiana teachers, and religious leaders, challenged the constitutionality of the Act in District Court, seeking an injunction and declaratory relief. Appellants, Louisiana officials charged with implementing the Act, defended on the ground that the purpose of the Act is to protect a legitimate secular interest, namely, academic freedom. Appellees attacked the Act as facially invalid because it violated the Establishment Clause and made a motion for summary judgment. The District Court granted the motion.... The court held that there can be no valid secular reason for prohibiting the teaching of evolution, a theory historically opposed by some religious denominations. The court further concluded that "the teaching of 'creation-science' and 'creationism,' as contemplated by the statute, involves teaching 'tailored to the principles' of a particular religious sect or group of sects."... The District Court therefore held that the Creationism Act violated the Establishment Clause either because it prohibited the teaching of evolution or because it required the teaching of creation science with the purpose of advancing a particular religious doctrine.

The Court of Appeals affirmed. The court observed that the statute's avowed purpose of protecting academic freedom was inconsistent with requiring, upon risk of sanction, the teaching of creation science whenever evolution is taught. The court found that the Louisiana legislature's actual intent was "to discredit evolution by counterbalancing its teaching at every turn with the teaching of creationism, a religious belief." Because the Creationism Act was thus a law furthering a particular religious belief, the Court of Appeals held that the Act violated the Establishment Clause. A suggestion for rehearing en banc was denied over a dissent. We noted probable jurisdiction and now affirm.

II

The Establishment Clause forbids the enactment of any law "respecting an establishment of religion." The Court has applied a three-pronged test to determine whether legislation comports with the Establishment Clause. First, the legislature must have adopted the law with a secular purpose. Second, the statute's principal or primary effect must be one that neither advances nor inhibits religion. Third, the statute must not result in an excessive entanglement of government with religion. *Lemon* v. *Kurtzman* (1971). State action violates the Establishment Clause if it fails to satisfy any of these prongs.

In this case, the Court must determine whether the Establishment Clause was violated in the special context of the public elementary and secondary school system. States and local school boards are generally afforded considerable discretion in operating public schools.... "At the same time ... we have necessarily recognized that the discretion of the States and local school boards in matters of education must be exercised in a manner that comports with the transcendent imperatives of the First Amendment." *Board of Education* v. *Pico* (1982).

The Court has been particularly vigilant in monitoring compliance with the Establishment Clause in elementary and secondary schools. Families entrust public schools with the education of their children, but condition their trust on the understanding that the classroom will not purposely be used to advance religious views that may conflict with the private beliefs of the student and his or her family. Students in such institutions are impressionable and their attendance is involuntary.... The State exerts great authority and coercive power through mandatory attendance requirements, and because of the students' emulation of teachers as role models and the children's susceptibility to peer pressure.... Furthermore, "[t]he public school is at once the symbol of our democracy and the most pervasive means for promoting our common destiny. In no activity of the State is it more vital to keep out divisive forces than in its schools...." *Illinois ex rel. McCollum* v. *Board of Education* (1948)....

Consequently, the Court has been required often to invalidate statutes which advance religion in public elementary and secondary schools....

Therefore, in employing the three-pronged *Lemon* test, we must do so mindful of the particular concerns that arise in the context of public elementary and secondary schools. We now turn to the evaluation of the Act under the *Lemon* test.

III

Lemon's first prong focuses on the purpose that animated adoption of the Act. "The purpose prong of the *Lemon* test asks whether government's actual purpose is to endorse or disapprove of religion." *Lynch* v. *Donnelly* (1984).... In this case, the petitioners have identified no clear secular purpose for the Louisiana Act.

True, the Act's stated purpose is to protect academic freedom. This phrase might, in common parlance, be understood as referring to enhancing the freedom of teachers to teach what they will. The Court of Appeals, however, correctly concluded that the Act was not designed to further that goal. We find no merit in the State's argument that the "legislature may not [have] use[d] the terms 'academic freedom' in the correct legal sense. They might have [had] in mind, instead, a basic concept of fairness; teaching all of the evidence." Even if "academic freedom" is read to mean "teaching all of the evidence" with respect to the origin of human beings, the Act does not further this purpose. The goal of providing a more comprehensive science curriculum is not furthered either by outlawing the teaching of evolution or by requiring the teaching of creation science.

A

... It is clear from the legislative history that the purpose of the legislative sponsor, [state] Senator Bill Keith, was to narrow the science curriculum. During the legislative hearings, Senator Keith stated: "My preference would be that neither [creationism nor evolution] be taught." Such a ban on teaching does not promote—indeed, it undermines—the provision of a comprehensive scientific education.

It is equally clear that requiring schools to teach creation science with evolution does not advance academic freedom. The Act does not grant teachers a flexibility that they did not already possess to supplant the present science curriculum with the presentation of theories, besides evolution, about the origin of life. Indeed, the Court of Appeals found that no law prohibited Louisiana public schoolteachers from teaching any scientific theory.... The Act provides Louisiana schoolteachers with no new authority. Thus the stated purpose is not furthered by it.

The Alabama statute held unconstitutional in *Wallace* v. *Jaffree* [1985] is analogous. In *Wallace,* the State characterized its new law as one designed to provide a one-minute period for meditation. We rejected that stated purpose as insufficient, because a previously adopted Alabama law already provided for such a one-minute period. Thus, in this case, as in *Wallace,* "[a]ppellants have not identified any secular purpose that was not fully served by [existing state law] before the enactment of [the statute in question]."

Furthermore, the goal of basic "fairness" is hardly furthered by the Act's discriminatory preference for the teaching of creation science and against the teaching of evolution. While requiring that curriculum guides be developed for creation science, the Act says nothing of comparable guides for evolution. Similarly, research services are supplied for creation science but not for evolution. Only "creation scientists" can serve on the panel that supplies the resource services. The Act forbids school boards to discriminate against anyone who "chooses to be a creation-scientist" or to teach "creationism," but fails to protect those who choose to teach evolution or any other non-creation science theory, or who refuse to teach creation science.

If the Louisiana legislature's purpose was solely to maximize the comprehensiveness and effectiveness of science instruction, it would have encouraged the teaching of all scientific theories about the origins of humankind. But under the Act's requirements, teachers who were once free to teach any and all facets of this subject are now unable to do so. Moreover, the Act fails even to ensure that creation science will be taught, but instead requires the teaching of this theory only when the theory of evolution is taught. Thus we agree with the Court of Appeals' conclusion that the Act does not serve to protect academic freedom, but has the distinctly different purpose of discrediting "evolution by counterbalancing its teaching at every turn with the teaching of creation science. . . ."

B

. . . [W]e need not be blind in this case to the legislature's preeminent religious purpose in enacting this statute. There is a historic and contemporaneous link between the teachings of certain religious denominations and the teaching of evolution. It was this link that concerned the Court in *Epperson* v. *Arkansas* (1968), which also involved a facial challenge to a statute regulating the teaching of evolution. In that case, the Court reviewed an Arkansas statute that made it unlawful for an instructor to teach evolution or to use a textbook that referred to this scientific theory. Although the . . . law did not explicitly state its predominate religious purpose, the Court could not ignore that "[t]he statute was a product of the upsurge of 'fundamentalist' religious fervor" that has long viewed this particular scientific theory as contradicting the literal interpretation of the Bible. After reviewing the history of anti-evolution statutes, the Court determined that "there can be no doubt that the motivation for the [Arkansas] law was the same [as other anti-evolution statutes]: to suppress the teaching of a theory which, it was thought, 'denied' the divine creation of man." The Court found that there can be no legitimate state interest in protecting particular religions from scientific views "distasteful to them," and concluded "that the First Amendment does not permit the State to require that teaching and learning must be tailored to the principles or prohibitions of any religious sect or dogma."

These same historic and contemporaneous antagonisms between the teachings of certain religious denominations and the teaching of evolution are present in this case. The preeminent purpose of the Louisiana legislature was clearly to advance the religious viewpoint that a supernatural being created humankind. . . .

Furthermore, it is not happenstance that the legislature required the teaching of a theory that coincided with this religious view. The legislative history documents that the Act's primary purpose was to change the science curriculum of public schools in order to provide persuasive advantage to a particular religious doctrine that rejects the factual basis of evolution in its entirety. . . .

. . . [T]he Creationism Act is designed *either* to promote the theory of creation science which embodies a particular religious tenet by requiring that creation science be taught whenever evolution is taught *or* to prohibit the teaching of a scientific theory disfavored by certain religious sects by forbidding the teaching of evolution when creation science is not also taught. The Establishment Clause, however, "forbids *alike* the preference of a religious doctrine *or* the prohibition of theory which is deemed antagonistic to a particular dogma." Because the primary purpose of the

Creationism Act is to advance a particular religious belief, the Act endorses religion in violation of the First Amendment.

We do not imply that a legislature could never require that scientific critiques of prevailing scientific theories be taught.... [T]eaching a variety of scientific theories about the origins of humankind to schoolchildren might be validly done with the clear secular intent of enhancing the effectiveness of science instruction. But because the primary purpose of the Creationism Act is to endorse a particular religious doctrine, the Act furthers religion in violation of the Establishment Clause....

[Part IV omitted]

V

The Louisiana Creationism Act advances a religious doctrine by requiring either the banishment of the theory of evolution from public school classrooms or the presentation of a religious viewpoint that rejects evolution in its entirety. The Act violates the Establishment Clause of the First Amendment because it seeks to employ the symbolic and financial support of government to achieve a religious purpose. The judgment of the Court of Appeals therefore is

Affirmed.

JUSTICE POWELL, with whom JUSTICE O'CONNOR joins, concurring.

I write separately to note certain aspects of the legislative history, and to emphasize that nothing in the Court's opinion diminishes the traditionally broad discretion accorded state and local school officials in the selection of the public school curriculum.

I

This Court consistently has applied the three-pronged test of *Lemon* v. *Kurtzman* (1971), to determine whether a particular state action violates the Establishment Clause of the Constitution.... If no valid secular purpose can be identified, then the statute violates the Establishment Clause.

A

...The Balanced Treatment for Creation-Science and Evolution-Science Act (Act or Balanced Treatment Act) provides in part:

> "[P]ublic schools within [the] state shall give balanced treatment to creation-science and to evolution-science. Balanced treatment of these two models shall be given in classroom lectures taken as a whole for each course, in textbook materials taken as a whole for each course, in library materials taken as a whole for the sciences and taken as a whole for the humanities, and in other educational programs in public schools, to the extent that such lectures, textbooks, library materials, or educational programs deal in any way with the subject of the origin of man, life, the earth, or the universe. When creation or evolution is taught, each shall be taught as a theory, rather than as proven scientific fact."

. . . Although the Act requires the teaching of the scientific evidences of both creation and evolution whenever either is taught, it does not define either term. "A fundamental canon of statutory construction is that, unless otherwise defined, words will be interpreted as taking their ordinary, contemporary, common meaning." *Perrin* v. *United States* (1979). The "doctrine or theory of creation" is commonly defined as "holding that matter, the various forms of life, and the world were created by a transcendent God out of nothing." Webster's Third New International Dictionary 532 (unabridged 1981). "Evolution" is defined as "the theory that the various types of animals and plants have their origin in other preexisting types, the distinguishable differences being due to modifications in successive generations." Thus, the Balanced Treatment Act mandates that public schools present the scientific evidence to support a theory of divine creation whenever they present the scientific evidence to support the theory of evolution. "[C]oncepts concerning God or a supreme being of some sort are manifestly religious. . . . These concepts do not shed that religiosity merely because they are presented as a philosophy or as a science." *Malnak* v. *Yogi* (NJ 1977). From the face of the statute, a purpose to advance a religious belief is apparent. . . .

C

When, as here, "both [lower] courts below are unable to discern an arguably valid secular purpose, this Court normally should hesitate to find one." *Wallace* v. *Jaffree* [1985]. My examination of the language and the legislative history of the Balanced Treatment Act confirms that the intent of the Louisiana legislature was to promote a particular religious belief. The legislative history of the Arkansas statute prohibiting the teaching of evolution examined in *Epperson* v. *Arkansas* (1968), was strikingly similar to the legislative history of the Balanced Treatment Act. In *Epperson*, the Court found:

> "It is clear that fundamentalist sectarian conviction was and is the law's reason for existence. Its antecedent, Tennessee's 'monkey law,' candidly stated its purpose: to make it unlawful 'to teach any theory that denies the story of the Divine Creation of man as taught in the Bible, and to teach instead that man has descended from a lower order of animals.' Perhaps the sensational publicity attendant upon the *Scopes* trial induced Arkansas to adopt less explicit language. It eliminated Tennessee's reference to 'the story of the Divine creation of man' as taught in the Bible, but there is no doubt that the motivation for the law was the same: to suppress the teaching of a theory which, it was thought, 'denied' the divine creation of man."

Here, it is clear that religious belief is the Balanced Treatment Act's "reason for existence." The tenets of creation-science parallel the Genesis story of creation, and this is a religious belief. . . .

II

Even though I find Louisiana's Balanced Treatment Act unconstitutional, I adhere to the view "that the States and locally elected school boards should have the responsibility for determining the educational policy of the public schools." *Board of Education* v. *Pico* (1982)....

As a matter of history, school children can and should properly be informed of all aspects of this Nation's religious heritage. I would see no constitutional problem if school children were taught the nature of the Founding Fathers' religious beliefs and how these beliefs affected the attitudes of the times and the structure of our government. Courses in comparative religion of course are customary and constitutionally appropriate. In fact, since religion permeates our history, a familiarity with the nature of religious beliefs is necessary to understand many historical as well as contemporary events.... [T]he Establishment Clause does not prohibit *per se* the educational use of religious documents.... The Establishment Clause is properly understood to prohibit the use of the Bible and other religious documents in public school education only when the purpose of the use is to advance a particular religious belief.

III

In sum, I find that the language and the legislative history of the Balanced Treatment Act unquestionably demonstrate that its purpose is to advance a particular religious belief.... Accordingly, I concur in the opinion of the Court and its judgment that the Balanced Treatment Act violates the Establishment Clause of the Constitution.

JUSTICE SCALIA, with whom THE CHIEF JUSTICE joins, dissenting.

Even if I agreed with the questionable premise that legislation can be invalidated under the Establishment Clause on the basis of its motivation alone, without regard to its effects, I would still find no justification for today's decision. The Louisiana legislators who passed the "Balanced Treatment for Creation-Science and Evolution-Science Act" (Balanced Treatment Act), each of whom had sworn to support the Constitution, were well aware of the potential Establishment Clause problems and considered that aspect of the legislation with great care. After seven hearings and several months of study, resulting in substantial revision of the original proposal, they approved the Act overwhelmingly and specifically articulated the secular purpose they meant it to serve. Although the record contains abundant evidence of the sincerity of that purpose (the only issue pertinent to this case), the Court today holds, essentially on the basis of "its visceral knowledge regarding what *must* have motivated the legislators," that the members of the Louisiana Legislature knowingly violated their oaths and then lied about it. I dissent. Had requirements of the Balanced Treatment Act that are not apparent on its face been clarified by an interpretation of the Louisiana Supreme Court, or by the manner of its implementation, the Act might well be found unconstitutional; but the question of its constitutionality cannot rightly be disposed of on the gallop, by impugning the motives of its supporters....

I

... [T]he majority's invalidation of the Balanced Treatment Act is defensible only if the record indicates that the Louisiana Legislature had *no* secular purpose....

It is important to stress that the purpose forbidden by [*Lemon* v. *Kurtzman,* 1971] is the purpose to "advance religion." ... Our cases in no way imply that the Establishment Clause forbids legislators merely to act upon their religious convictions. We surely would not strike down a law providing money to feed the hungry or shelter the homeless if it could be demonstrated that, but for the religious beliefs of the legislators, the funds would not have been approved. Also, political activism by the religiously motivated is part of our heritage. Notwithstanding the majority's implication to the contrary, we do not presume that the sole purpose of a law is to advance religion merely because it was supported strongly by organized religions or by adherents of particular faiths.... To do so would deprive religious men and women of their right to participate in the political process. Today's religious activism may give us the Balanced Treatment Act, but yesterday's resulted in the abolition of slavery, and tomorrow's may bring relief for famine victims.

Similarly, we will not presume that a law's purpose is to advance religion merely because it " 'happens to coincide or harmonize with the tenets of some or all religions,' " *Harris* v. *McRae* (1961), or because it benefits religion, even substantially....

II

[Section A omitted]

B

Even with nothing more than this legislative history to go on, I think it would be extraordinary to invalidate the Balanced Treatment Act for lack of a valid secular pupose. Striking down a law approved by the democratically elected representatives of the people is no minor matter. "The cardinal principle of statutory construction is to save and not to destroy. We have repeatedly held that as between two possible interpretations of a statute, by one of which it would be unconstitutional and by the other valid, our plain duty is to adopt that which will save the act." *NLRB* v. *Jones & Laughlin Steel Corp.* (1937). So, too, it seems to me, with discerning statutory purpose....

In sum, even if one concedes, for the sake of argument, that a majority of the Louisiana Legislature voted for the Balanced Treatment Act partly in order to foster (rather than merely eliminate discrimination against) Christian fundamentalist beliefs, our cases establish that that alone would not suffice to invalidate the Act, so long as there was a genuine secular purpose as well. We have, moreover, no adequate basis for disbelieving the secular purpose set forth in the Act itself, or for concluding that it is a sham enacted to conceal the legislators' violation of their oaths of office. I am astonished by the Court's unprecedented readiness to reach such a conclusion, which I can only attribute to an intellectual predisposition created by the facts and the legend of *Scopes* v. *State* (1927)—an instinctive reaction that any governmentally imposed requirements bearing upon the teaching of evolution must be a manifestation of Christian fundamentalist repression. In this case, however, it seems to me the Court's position is the repressive one....

Because I believe that the Balanced Treatment Act had a secular purpose, which is all the first component of the *Lemon* test requires, I would reverse the judgment of the Court of Appeals and remand for further consideration....

JUSTICE POWELL'S RETIREMENT

June 26, 1987

Supreme Court Associate Justice Lewis F. Powell, Jr., announced his retirement June 26 after fifteen years of service. The unexpected announcement came on the last day of the Court's 1986-1987 term. The vacancy gave President Ronald Reagan an opportunity to put a more conservative stamp on a Court that generally had been more liberal than his administration had wanted.

For years Powell had been one of the most influential justices on the precariously balanced nine-member Court. His was the deciding vote on a number of highly significant cases. For example, Powell had cast the pivotal fifth vote to uphold a woman's right to an abortion and to support the use of affirmative action to remedy past discrimination against blacks and women. The president vehemently opposed both rulings, and Powell's retirement gave Reagan a chance to tip the balance on highly charged social issues.

Powell informed Chief Justice William H. Rehnquist earlier in the week that he was considering retirement; he told his colleagues only ten minutes before the announcement. Rehnquist then notified Howard H. Baker, Jr., Reagan's chief of staff. Powell said he was retiring because of his age, because he had already served well beyond the ten years he had originally planned to stay, and because past illnesses had made him aware that the prolonged absence of a member imposed a severe handicap on the Court. Rehnquist, announcing Powell's retirement, said the justices "shall miss his wise counsel in our deliberations, but we look forward to being the continuing beneficiaries of his friendship." Reagan telephoned Powell, telling him the nation owed him "a great debt" for his service on the bench.

Powell: Man in the Middle

Already a well-respected member of the nation's legal establishment who had served as president of the American Bar Association and head of the Virginia Board of Education, Powell was sixty-four years old when he was nominated in 1971 by President Richard Nixon. A native Virginian who spent most of his life in his home state, Powell was a moderate man who in recent years generally voted with Rehnquist and Sandra Day O'Connor on questions of criminal law and government power. But from his wide experience in law and community service, he brought to the Court a clear concern for the individual, which at critical times outweighed his commitment to judicial restraint.

Powell's remarkable ability to stay in step with the zigzag dance of the Court led some observers to wonder if he was calling the tune. At a press conference following his retirement announcement, Powell with characteristic modesty disclaimed any "swing" role on the Court. But the record spoke for itself.

Early in his career on the Court, Powell sounded the conservatives' traditional theme of judicial deference to political policy making, emphasizing how important it was to avoid "repeated and essentially head-on confrontations" with "the representative branches of the government." By the 1980s, however, he was notably more willing to exercise judicial power when political solutions fell short.

In his last term, Powell joined the Court's liberal members—William J. Brennan, Jr., Thurgood Marshall, Harry A. Blackmun, and John Paul Stevens—in the majority in Local 28 of the Sheet Metal Workers v. Equal Employment Opportunity Commission, *which reiterated the Court's continuing commitment to affirmative action that initially had been handed down in the 1978 decision,* University of California Regents v. Bakke. *But he joined the more conservative members—Rehnquist, O'Connor, Antonin Scalia, and Byron R. White—in upholding the death penalty against one last sweeping legal challenge.* (*McKleskey v. Kemp,* p. 463; *Sheet Metal Workers,* Historic Documents of 1986, p. 651; *Bakke,* Historic Documents of 1978, p. 467)

Sensitive to the dangers of combining religion and politics, Powell sided with Court liberals in 1985 to strike down Alabama's moment-of-silence law (Wallace v. Jaffree). *Just a week before his retirement, he joined six other justices in holding that Louisiana violated the First Amendment's "establishment clause" when it required the teaching of evolution in public schools to be accompanied by instruction in "creation science"* (Edwards v. Aguillard). *With the conservatives, he voted to permit death sentences for accomplices in murder cases* (Tison v.

Arizona). *With the liberals, he cast the decisive vote against use of victim-impact statements at the sentencing phase of capital cases* (Booth v. Maryland). (*Edwards,* p. 565; *Wallace,* Historic Documents of 1985, p. 379)

Powell's was a key vote on abortion, one of the most explosive issues ever before the Court. A member of the majority that declared in Roe v. Wade *(1973) that states could not ban abortion altogether, Powell spoke for the Court ten years later when it reaffirmed that ruling in the face of intense political pressure to abandon it.* (*Akron v. Akron Center for Reproductive Health,* Historic Documents of 1983, p. 546; *Roe,* Historic Documents of 1973, p. 101)

The balance of power between federal and state governments was the single major issue on which Powell consistently was in the minority, opting for state and local authority. (*National League of Cities v. Usery,* Historic Documents of 1976, p. 377)

Assessing Powell's Record

Powell's service on the Court generally won high marks. "Powell was extraordinarily important in keeping the Court down the middle of the road, which was probably appropriate, given the era," said his former law clerk, Ben W. Heineman. "He displayed caution, moderation. He ... didn't have an agenda, but he ... cared an awful lot about the law," commented Michigan Law School professor Yale Kamisar. "It will be difficult to find a man to replace him," said A. E. Dick Howard, law professor at the University of Virginia. "One needs an ideologue or two like a Brennan or a Rehnquist to stake out the positions for argument. But then one needs a man of moderate instinct and craftsmanlike ability. One hopes Powell's replacement will have those qualities."

Appointing a Successor

Reaction to Powell's departure was divided along ideological lines. Conservatives, who had been disappointed by a number of liberal victories in the 1986-1987 term, hoped that Powell's successor would more consistently adhere to their positions. Liberals expressed dismay at the prospect that Reagan's appointee would reverse controversial decisions on social issues on which Powell had voted with the majority. (Bork confirmation fight, p. 717)

Reagan had already made two appointments to the Court—Sandra Day O'Connor in 1981 and Antonin Scalia in 1986. In addition, he had promoted William Rehnquist from associate justice to chief justice after the 1986 retirement of Warren E. Burger. (Historic Documents of 1981, p. 575; Historic Documents of 1986, p. 591)

The major question facing Reagan and his aides as they pondered the choice of a successor to Powell was how to find a conservative acceptable to the Democratic-controlled Senate, which would confirm the new justice. Throughout history, presidents had found it difficult to win approval for Court nominations submitted late in their terms. They had to overcome a "save-the-seat" syndrome, in which senators of the party not represented in the White House worked to block confirmation of a Court nominee, hoping that their party would take the White House in the next election and, with it, the chance to fill the vacancy. The most recent example of this situation occurred in 1968, when Senate Republicans, although in the minority, managed to block confirmation of Associate Justice Abe Fortas as chief justice. Fortas was the choice of retiring president Lyndon B. Johnson to succeed Earl Warren.

The longest vacancy on the Court lasted two years, three months, and twenty-three days—from April 21, 1844, to August 4, 1846—when the Senate rejected four nominations by two presidents. The second longest was two years, one month, and sixteen days, from May 31, 1860, to July 16, 1862. The longest recent vacancy—a result of the Fortas fight—was just thirteen months. It ended with the confirmation of Harry A. Blackmun in 1970.

Following is the June 26, 1987, statement by Associate Justice Lewis F. Powell, Jr., announcing his retirement from the Supreme Court:

I have advised the Chief Justice and Associate Justices that I have elected to retire as an Associate Justice. The President will be advised today.

This is a decision I have made quite recently, but after careful thought. Although I was reluctant to come to the Court at age 64, this institution—apart from family—has been my life now for 15½ years. My respect for it as a unique institution has been enhanced by the privilege of serving here. I will miss being an active Justice more than I can say. I summarize briefly, in no particular order, my reasons for retiring at this time:

(i) On September 19, I will be 80 years of age. I believe I said some years ago that it would have been wise for the Founding Fathers to have required retirement of federal judges at a specified age, perhaps at seventy-five. Of course, such a limitation would have deprived the Court of the service after that age by a number of the most distinguished Justices ever to sit on this Court. I specifically include present Brothers among this group. But for me, age 80 suggests retirement.

(ii) When President Nixon requested that I accept appointment to the Court, in addition to expressing my reservation about appointing anyone to this Court at age 64, I stated that if I were confirmed I would not expect to remain on the Court for more than ten years. As former Chief Justice Burger will confirm, I seriously considered—and discussed with him—retirement at the end of June 1982. Our children, two of whom are lawyers, persuaded me not to retire. In retrospect, I am glad I remained an additional five years.

(iii) My health has not been "robust." I have undergone major surgery three times since coming to the Court, including prostate cancer surgery at Mayo in 1985. I have had regular semiannual checkups at Mayo, and underwent the full range of tests there earlier this month. Happily, all tests were favorable, and both of the physicians in charge concluded that I am presently in good health. But my past illnesses have created problems for the Court and for litigants.

In sum, I am motivated by (i) the imminence of my 80th birthday, (ii) by having served 15½ years when I contemplated no more than ten years of service, and (iii) by concern—based on past experience—that I could handicap the Court in the event of reoccurrences of serious health problems.

I have no specific plans for the future. As the record makes clear, I carried my full load on the Court during the Term now ending. This required long working hours including Saturdays, and a large part of Sundays. I am tired, but no more so than I have been at the end of recent Terms.

I therefore expect to continue to be active in appropriate public service when this is available. As other retired Justices have done, I also will consider sitting on Courts of Appeals—though I would not expect to do this on a regular basis. Other possibilities could include some association with a law school. We do look forward to spending more time with our children and grandchildren.

This has been a difficult decision. It was finally made by Mrs. Powell and me only this week, and after consulting with each of our children. I leave the Court to become a retired Justice with a considerable measure of sadness. I have mentioned my respect and admiration for the Court as a unique institution essential to the preservation of Equal Justice Under Law in our country.

It is with special personal regret that I will not have—in full measure—the close association that I have shared with the other members of this Court. I count all eight of them as friends. As I said last summer in a talk at the ABA [American Bar Association], I have the highest respect and admiration for the legal ability, devotion to duty, and—of course—the integrity of each of them.

SOUTH KOREAN LEADERS ON DEMOCRATIC REFORMS

June 29 and July 1, 1987

The nationwide demonstrations that led the Republic of Korea to the brink of internal collapse in June 1987 were suddenly brought to an end by proposals made by Roh Tae Woo on national television June 29. Roh, the long-time right-hand man of President Chun Doo Hwan and his personal choice for the presidency in the 1988 elections, surprised the nation by accepting virtually all of the opposition's demands.

The most important of these was the amendment of the constitution, drawn up by Chun following his accession to the presidency in 1980, to permit direct presidential elections. Although Roh cited his party's preference for a parliamentary system, he acknowledged that "the people are the masters of the country" and that "if the majority of the people do not want it, even the best-conceived system will alienate the public."

Roh advocated a number of other reforms as well, including restoring the political rights of Kim Dae Jung, the opposition leader most disliked by Chun's government and its military backers. He also favored increasing freedom of the press and giving more autonomy to colleges and universities—an implicit acknowledgment of the significance of the student riots that had precipitated the national crisis. Although it was assumed that he had consulted Chun prior to his statement, Roh put his political future on the line by vowing he would resign his candidacy and the chairmanship of the Democratic Justice Party if his suggestions were not accepted.

In his national address two days later, President Chun acknowledged that this was a "crucial moment in the destiny of the nation" and that after consulting with national leaders, he had decided to accept Roh's recommendations. Chun's speech was less devoted to specifics, however, than was Roh's. Instead he concentrated on his "sense of responsibility" and defended his April 13, 1987, decision to suspend constitutional dialogue with the opposition, an act that was to ignite demonstrations throughout the country. He spoke of what he considered his administration's three major achievements: "sustained economic success, a peaceful change of administrations and the '88 Olympics."

But he also sounded a cautionary note about electoral reforms and the dangers of direct elections, warning the nation about "social chaos" and the violence that could "destroy the free and democratic system."

Events Leading to Statements

The legislative elections of February 1985 had brought together South Korea's two most prominent opposition politicians, Kim Young Sam and Kim Dae Jung, the latter having only recently returned from exile in the United States. Their relative success, despite obstacles put in their path by the government, gave rise to hopes for political change. At the same time, Chun eased restrictions placed on some 800 political figures, permitting a level of political dissent previously unknown under his rule. Demonstrating students, the most radical element in South Korean politics, were by then already a familiar part of the political landscape. Strongly backed by the military and facing a continuing threat from hostile North Korea, however, Chun retained a firm hold on the country. His position was further strengthened by South Korea's continuing economic growth.

In September 1985 the two Kims issued an ultimatum for Chun to meet with them and to amend the constitution to permit direct elections. Chun responded that he would voluntarily step down when his seven-year term ended in February 1988, something no president in South Korea's forty-year history had ever done. He insisted that constitutional reform be put off until that time.

In February 1986, a new series of student demonstrations began as the two opposition leaders launched a drive to garner millions of signatures demanding direct elections. The government in turn deployed thousands of policemen to put down the demonstrations, and it placed under house arrest some 270 opposition figures, but the uproar continued unabated.

Many Koreans saw in the demonstrations parallels with the situation in the Philippines, where Ferdinand Marcos had just fallen. Although he maintained his policies, Chun paid close attention to the attitude of the United States as well as the international community. The 1988 Summer Olympics were a major priority for the government, and the choice of Seoul as a site for the games was perceived throughout the nation as a sign that the country had come of age. The fear of losing the games was to temper Chun's reaction to the continuing social chaos throughout 1986 and 1987.

In March 1986 the head of the country's small but influential Roman Catholic community, Stephen Cardinal Kim Sou Hwan, came out in support of the opposition's petition drive. Although some dialogue was being conducted in the National Assembly, student demonstrations continued throughout the spring, driving events and punctuating them with occasional outbursts of violence. In January 1987 Park Chong Chol, a student held by the police, died from a beating, sparking a further round of demonstrations when classes resumed in February.

The constitutional dialogue remained deadlocked: the opposition continued to press for direct elections, while Chun (whose party held a clear majority in the Assembly) advocated a parliamentary/prime ministerial system. Chun issued an "irreversible" decision on April 13 to close off the constitutional debate, initiating a hardening of positions on both sides. The police immediately began breaking up demonstrations more forcefully than before as a warning that there were limits to the military's tolerance. The use of tear gas was widespread. Although the United States had previously signaled that it would not interfere in South Korea's internal affairs, American pressures gradually began to be exerted on Chun to moderate his position. The riots continued throughout the school year, straining the government's ability to control the nation.

Late in May, Chun reshuffled his cabinet, dismissing the prime minister and the head of the National Security Planning Agency. This removed two major opponents within the ruling party to the nomination of Roh Tae Woo. Roh, like Chun, was a former general who had played an important role in the 1979 coup. Roh was formally accepted by the party on June 14, the same day that a series of major demonstrations against the government began. South Korea was brought to a standstill. Most of the country's major cities soon were enveloped in clouds of tear gas. More and more middle-class Koreans, traditionally the backbone of the government's civilian support, joined the demonstrators. Seoul's National Cathedral was opened as a sanctuary for demonstrators, becoming a rallying point for many previously unconcerned citizens. The police, prohibited from using weapons, frequently were stretched beyond their limits, as demonstrators continually broke through their ranks.

There was evidence that Chun had begun to mobilize the army during the night of June 19, following the death of a policeman, but he soon reversed himself. U.S. officials were thought to have played a role in convincing Chun to call the army off. The fear of losing the Olympic Games was surely a factor in that decision as well. Almost no one was prepared for Roh's speech on June 29.

Impact of the Speeches

The first effect of Roh's speech was to raise him significantly in the public's estimation, for by now the military was held in low regard by the vast majority of Korean citizens. By agreeing to the opposition's demands, he managed to steal a good deal of their thunder. The riots calmed down and the debate once again returned to the floor of the National Assembly, where the constitutional amendment was soon written.

Another unforeseen result was an explosion of labor unrest, as millions of workers began to agitate for their long-frozen rights. Although it was still illegal to strike, the government had little choice but to tolerate the many hundreds of strikes that erupted over the summer. In fact, some business leaders would complain that the government had pressured them to give in to the workers' demands, marking a clear change in the policy of a government now intent on improving its chances in an open election.

The rise in Roh's popularity corresponded to an increasing split between the two opposition leaders, culminating in the decision in early October by first Kim Young Sam and then Kim Dae Jung to declare themselves presidential candidates. Their inability to agree on a single candidate divided the opposition and gave Roh a victory in the December 16 election, South Korea's first since 1970.

Roh received 36.6 percent of the 22.6 million votes, Kim Young Sam 28 percent, and Kim Dae Jung 27 percent. The remainder was divided among two other candidates. Because most Koreans had voted for one of the two principal opposition candidates, Roh, who was scheduled to take office February 25, 1988, offered to submit to a plebiscite on his performance his first year in office. The United States accepted the results of the election and congratulated Roh the following day. Though both the government and opposition candidates had accused the other of election fraud, independent observers from the United States found no evidence of widespread cheating.

Following are the speech of Roh Tae Woo, chairman of the Democratic Justice Party, on June 29, 1987, and excerpts from the speech of South Korean president Chun Doo Hwan, on July 1, 1987:

STATEMENT BY CHAIRMAN OF THE DEMOCRATIC JUSTICE PARTY ROH TAE WOO

My dear fellow citizens,
I have now come to a firm conviction about the future of our nation. I

have anguished long and hard over the genuine mission of politicians at this historic time when deep-seated conflicts and antagonisms have so accumulated among our citizens that they have erupted into a national crisis. I have also solicited the wisdom of people from various walks of life—academicians, journalists, businessmen, religious leaders, workers, and young people, including students, and have thus ascertained the will of the people.

Today, I stand before history and the nation with an extraordinary determination to help build a great homeland in which there is love and harmony among all segments and strata of the population, in which all are proud of being citizens and in which the government can acquire wisdom, courage and genuine strength from the people.

I will hereby forthrightly present my ideas. I intend to recommend them to President Chun Doo Hwan and am resolved to translate them into concrete action with the enthusiastic support of my party colleagues and the general public.

First, the Constitution should be expeditiously amended, through agreement between the government party and the opposition, to adopt a direct presidential election system, and presidential elections should be held under a new Constitution to realize a peaceful change of government in February 1988. This does not mean a change in my belief that a parliamentary cabinet system, under which the majority of the cabinet members are National Assemblymen directly elected by the people and under which the principles of democratic and responsible politics can be most faithfully realized through free and open dialogue and compromise, is the form of government best suited to enabling democracy to take hold in our country. However, if the majority of the people do not want it, even the best-conceived system will alienate the public, and the government which is born under it will not be able to dream and suffer together with the people. Accordingly, I have come to the conclusion that a presidential election system must be adopted at this juncture in order to overcome social confusion and achieve national reconciliation. The people are the masters of the country and the people's will must come before everything else.

Second, in addition to switching to a direct presidential election system through constitutional revision, I think that to carry out elections democratically, it is necessary to also revise the Presidential Election Law so that freedom of candidacy and fair competition are guaranteed and so that the genuine verdict of the people can be given. A revised election law should also ensure maximum fairness and justness in election management, from the campaigns to the casting, opening and counting of ballots.

Even under a direct election system, there should not be groundless character smearing and demagoguery to incite hostility, confusion, disorder and regional antagonisms, thereby undermining national stability and impeding genuine democratic development. There must be a solid framework to ensure that elections are *bona fide* competitions in policies and ideas.

Third, antagonisms and confrontations must be resolutely eradicated not only from our political community but also from all other sectors to achieve grand national reconciliation and unity. In this connection, I believe that Mr. Kim Dae-jung also should be amnestied and his civil rights restored, no matter what he has done in the past. At the same time, all those who are being detained in connection with the political situation should also be set free, except for those who have committed treason by repudiating the basic free and democratic order on which our survival and posterity hinges and a small number of people who have shaken the national foundation by committing homicide, bodily injury, arson and vandalism. I ardently hope that all those people will thus be able to return to society as democratic citizens.

There can be no present without a past. However, I believe it is important at this divide in our history to create an occasion for all to rejoice heartily. In such an event, the next presidential elections will be elevated into a national festival, and the new government thus elected with solid and broad public support will be able to work even more effectively to build a great nation.

Fourth, human dignity must be respected even more greatly and the basic rights of citizens should be promoted and protected to the maximum. I hope that the forthcoming constitutional amendments will include all the strengthened basic rights clauses being proposed by the Democratic Justice Party, including a drastic extension of *habeas corpus*.

The government should take utmost care not to let human rights abuses occur. The Democratic Justice Party should make greater efforts to effectively promote human rights. For example, it should hold periodical meetings with the lawyers associations and other human rights groups to promptly learn of and redress human rights violations.

Fifth, to promote the freedom of the press, the relevant systems and practices must be drastically improved. The Basic Press Law, which may have been well-meant but has nonetheless been criticized by most journalists, should promptly be either extensively revised or abolished and replaced by a different law. Newspapers should again be permitted to station their correspondents in the provinces, the press card system should be abolished and newspapers should be allowed to increase the number of their pages as they see fit. These and other necessary steps must be taken to guarantee the freedom of the press to the maximum.

The government cannot control the press nor should it attempt to do so. No restrictions should be imposed on the press except when national security is at risk. It must be remembered that the press can be tried only by an independent judiciary or by individual citizens.

Sixth, freedom and self-regulation must be guaranteed to the maximum in all other sectors also, because private initiative is the driving force behind diverse and balanced social development which in turn fuels national progress. In spite of the forthcoming processes of amending the Constitution, local councils should be elected and organized without any hitch according to schedule. The establishment of municipal and provincial councils should also be studied in concrete terms and carried out soon thereafter.

Colleges and universities—the institutions of higher learning—must be made self-governing and educational autonomy in general must be expeditiously put into practice. To that end, the personnel and budgetary policies and general administration of universities and colleges should be free of outside intervention. Enrollment and graduation systems should also be improved to allow them greater autonomy. Scholarship systems should be improved with sufficient budgetary provisions made so that good students need not be frustrated by financial difficulties.

Seventh, a political climate conducive to dialogue and compromise must be created expeditiously, with healthy activities of political parties guaranteed. A political party should be a democratic organization that presents responsible demands and policies to mold and crystalize [*sic*] the political opinion of the people. The state should exert utmost efforts to protect and nurture political parties, so long as they engage in sound activities and do not contravene such objectives. Within such a framework, political parties should abide by the laws of the nation and exercise their political capabilities to resolve social conflicts and contradictions through dialogue and compromise in an amicable and harmonious manner to forge and maintain national coherence. As long as there exists an opposition party which is intent on pressing its unilateral demands by all means, even through violence, the governing party cannot always make concession after concession.

Eighth, bold social reforms must be carried out to build a clean and honest society. In order that all citizens can lead a secure and happy life, crime against life and property, such as hooliganism, robbery and theft, must be stamped out, and deep-seated corruption and improprieties that still linger in our society must be eradicated. Groundless rumors, along with regional antagonism and black-and-white attitudes, should be banished forever to build a society in which mutual trust and love prevail. In that way, we must ensure that all citizens can live an active life in a stable social environment, free of anxiety and with pride and confidence. I believe that these are the immediate tasks which must be accomplished if we are to resolve the current difficult situation and project the nation forward.

My fellow countrymen,

On the strength of your expectations that there will be continued development rather than disruptions, I dare to make this proposal today in humble veneration of history and the people. These ideas stem from my genuine patriotism, and I am confident that they will blossom with support from all the people, and not only President Chun and members of the Democratic Justice Party.

When these basic ideas have been accepted, additional details can be worked out. If they fail to be accepted, however, I want to make it very clear that I will resign from all public duties, including the presidential candidacy and the chairmanship of the Democratic Justice Party.

My fellow countrymen,

The shining achievements of the government of the Fifth Republic should at no time be underestimated. We have begun to root democracy deep into the soil of our nation's constitutional history by implementing a single term presidency. We have realized a trade surplus by stabilizing prices and improving our international competitiveness. We have drastically bolstered national security and obtained the right to host the Olympic Games.

Under no circumstances must we neglect to safeguard and promote the liberal democratic system. The task of peacefully changing administrations is the immediate task at hand. Furthermore, now that the Olympics are approaching, all of us are responsible for avoiding the national disgrace of dividing ourselves and thus causing the world to ridicule us.

With the sacred right to vote at hand, let us all work together to create a society where young people develop their capabilities to realize their ideas, where workers and farmers can work free of anxiety, where businessmen exert even greater creative efforts and where politicians exercise the art of debate and compromise to work out the nation's future. I pledge my utmost efforts to help create a dynamic, developing and genuinely democratic society where law and order prevail.

This country belongs to us. It is our historic duty to both exert our efforts and exercise restraint and wisdom to more successfully develop the country which was founded and nurtured with the blood of our forefathers and the lives of the patriots and to proudly hand it over to the next generation. I sincerely hope that national wisdom will be pooled to demonstrate to the world that the Korean people will not go backward but will go forward to make a contribution to world history.

My fellow countrymen, my party colleagues and opposition politicians,

I earnestly pray that my genuinely well-meant proposals will be accepted and will solve our current problems, that it will be a breakthrough in the effort to create a great nation where all our people can live stable and happy lives.

Thank you.

STATEMENT BY PRESIDENT CHUN DOO HWAN

Fellow citizens,

With an acute sense of responsibility for the recent political situation that has greatly troubled you, I want today to expound the way for us all to shape together the future of the nation in this period of historic transition. Because social stability and national harmony were being undermined by the recent continuing demonstrations and strife over the constitutional issue, I believe that you, my fellow countrymen, not only experienced serious inconvenience and anxiety but were also worried that catastrophe might befall the nation if that state of affairs continued. Under such circumstances, I spent many sleepless nights thinking long and hard about what should be done for the sake of the present and future of the Republic and its people and how.

Now is a crucial moment in the destiny of the nation. The time has come to think about today and tomorrow in the light of the best interest of the country and the people, transcending any and all personal interests, factional advantages and partisan strategies.

Accordingly, I have been meeting recently with elder statesmen including the former Presidents, representatives of political parties and religious, journalistic and other leaders to exchange frank views with them and was thus able to ascertain well the popular will.

As you know well, I was, at the same time briefed by Mr. Roh Tae Woo, chairman of the Democratic Justice Party, about his recommendations on how to resolve the current situation. I keenly sensed the strong determination and profound thoughts about the country and the people reflected in his proposals. Furthermore, I was convinced that the substance of his proposals was not only in full accord with my own thinking but would certainly open the way for a grand national compromise and reconciliation. I thus decided to fully accept Mr. Roh's recommendations and take measures to promote epochal democratic development and national harmony.

I hereby make it clear that the 13th presidential elections will be held under a new Constitution if the basic law is expeditiously revised and enacted following an agreement between the government party and the opposition on a direct presidential election system and that on February 25, 1988, I will transfer the reins of government to the president thus elected. In order to resolve antagonisms and confrontations among citizens and to promote national reconciliation and unity, amnesties and the restoration of civil rights will be extensively granted, while all those detained in connection with the political situation, except for a very small number of felonious offenders, will be set free.

In addition, I make it clear that I have instructed the Cabinet to take the necessary measures, including all recommendations by Mr. Roh, to further democratic development and national cohesion and to stabilize the life of all citizens, including farmers and workers.

Fellow citizens,

As I have repeatedly emphasized, the key to democratic development in our country lies in establishing a tradition of the president peacefully handing over the reins of government to a successor at the end of his term of office and then retiring with the blessing of the public. I have always maintained an unwavering resolve to set such an example to ensure that a tradition of peaceful changes of administrations, which is the long-cherished goal of the 40-year political history of the Republic, will evolve and take hold in this land. In fact, I have always run the affairs of state with that goal in mind.

On the other hand, in the course of fulfilling my ardent desire and that of my fellow countrymen to attain that goal, we have experienced conflicts and tribulations, as attested to by the recent political situation. I know well that when I announced on April 13 a decision to suspend counterproductive debate on constitutional reform and to pursue a peaceful transition of power under the present Constitution, my true intention was misunderstood and opposed by many.

At that time, only about 10 months remained in my presidency. And yet, efforts of the government party and the opposition to amend the Constitution by consensus were not making any progress at all and there were no prospects for resolving the deadlock through compromise. Thereupon, I made the April 13 decision because I had to hurry with preparations to fulfill my promise to step down at the end of my single-term presidency.

As I made clear in my New Year Policy Statement early this year, neither the form of government nor the method of electing the president prescribed in the Constitution of and by itself determines the substance of democracy. Until now, I could not readily accept a direct presidential election system on account of my concern about various ills that such a system may entail. My judgment was not based on any partisan consideration that a specific election system would be advantageous to one political party and disadvantageous to another. It was based solely on my earnest thinking about which system is in the best interest of the country and the people.

The direct presidential election system that we had in the past led to protracted one-man rule. Moreover, direct elections fanned regional antagonisms, causing serious confrontation among citizens from different districts, as well as general social confusion. Campaigns were overzealous and demagoguery rampant. Those who lost elections refused to accept the results as fair. Thus a vicious political cycle was perpetuated.

However, I clearly recognize the fact that regardless of the possible merits and demerits of a particular system, and irrespective of the preferences of any specific political party, the general public has an ardent desire to choose the president directly. No matter how good a system may be, it is of no use if the people do not want it. I believe that the intrinsic function of politics is to carry out the public will, if only on a probational basis, and to make sure that it works well. Especially since there are no prospects for even an iota of concession from the opposition, I have determined that the government camp, which must take responsibility for the future, ought to be sufficiently liberal to unravel the tough political knot, if we are to ensure genuine democratic development and national harmony and thus save the nation.

Fellow citizens,

We must all realize that both the fruit of the growth that we have achieved thus far and the opportunity at hand to make a big leap forward are too precious to spoil. Not only I but all citizens deeply desire to successfully carry out sustained economic development, a peaceful change of administrations, and the '88 Olympics that will be a catalyst for national prosperity.

At the same time, however, many of my fellow citizens who remember our political past must be worried whether or not a direct presidential election system will function without a major hitch. And yet, I am confident that if you, my fellow citizens, watchfully prod the politicians in the right direction with such an anxious concern, things will really work out all right.

Democracy is a process of progressive reform on the strength of reason and restraint; it is not a *coup de main* or a revolution intended to solve everything in one stroke. Democracy is implemented not by word but by action. We can no longer ignore the fact that the only means democracy has are dialogue and compromise within the framework of law and order. To trigger social chaos through illegal activities and violence under any name now would be to destroy the free and democratic system. My fellow citizens will never tolerate such acts. Our politics must now develop into competition in harmony to promote the national interest and public welfare.

With the decision I have made today, I join you in looking forward to a new era of democratic development and mature politics. Our politics must now cast aside its old shabby ways that are incongruous with our level of economic development and thus achieve an advanced form of democracy that we can proudly show to the world.

The legacy of mistrust, antagonism, arbitrary rule and extreme confrontation that persisted over the past four decades must now be committed to the dust bin of history. Let us now take the lead in spurring social development by virtue of mutual concession, compromise, trust and harmony.

To develop such advanced politics, I solicit my fellow countrymen not only to serve as wise judges in your capacity as mature democratic citizens but also to alertly guard against and sternly condemn undemocratic acts that undermine stability and harmony, as well as dialogue and fair play. Let us work another miracle by developing Korea into a model of political development deserving to be so recorded in world history; we must not be content with having merely become a model of economic development.

We must now discard all past misunderstandings, mistrust and mutual hatred and build up trust and goodwill as members of one ethnic family and as democratic citizens of one nation. On the thrust of my decision today, let us renew our determination to eradicate irregularities and contradictions and to build an honest and vibrant society characterized by a refreshing atmosphere and constant renewal in all sectors. In that way, the great Korean people who have achieved miraculous growth and development after overcoming backwardness and poverty will be able to build a great nation. All its citizens will thus experience the joy of triumphing together.

My dear fellow countrymen,

I have truly no other personal ambition than to be appreciated by posterity as the pioneer who opened a new era of genuine democracy in Korean history by setting an example of a peaceful transfer of power and by thus solidifying the foundation of democracy. My desire is to put a period to the vicious cycle of conflict, confusion, resentment and retaliation while I am serving as the chief executive in this decade of the '80s so that democracy characterized by accommodation and harmony will take root.

I believe that my fellow citizens understand that my decision today is grounded in a genuine intention to translate such convictions into reality. During the remainder of my presidency, I will do my utmost to fairly administer the affairs of state from a strictly impartial standpoint and to stringently maintain law and order so that liberal democracy can develop without disruptions.

In seven months, I am due to leave Chong Wa Dae (the presidential office and residence) and return to the life of an ordinary citizen. Whoever may become the next president, I just pray from the bottom of my heart that he will bring genuine democracy into blossom, successfully stage the Olympics, build a rich and strong country, and accomplish the sacred task of unification on the strength of expanded national power and the abundant inner resources of the Korean people.

I believe that everyone—the students who participated in demonstrations, the policemen who have labored to quell them, the citizens who have been tormented by the clouds of tear gas—has the same desire to defend and promote freedom and democracy. I think all the rest of my fellow countrymen who have been greatly inconvenienced by the turbulence are equally worried about the future of the nation and equally eager to build a better country.

I solicit you, my fellow citizens, to continue to support and encourage me in keeping with the ardent desire and enthusiasm for democratic development so that a political miracle can be brought off. I also hope that all politicians, in and out of power, will now make concerted efforts to prevent the recurrence of a state of affairs that causes trouble and inconvenience to innocent citizens. We must never discontinue our endeavors to ensure national security and prosperity.

At this divide of history, let us mobilize our great inner resources to take advantage of this excellent opportunity without fail. We have nothing to fear, as long as the Korean people who have weathered numerous crises and have achieved illustrious growth and development that will be proudly recorded in national history exist with their experience and potential and as long as the people have the strong determination to promote democratic development and national prosperity.

If we march forward with renewed harmony and unity from this turning point, I am confident that we will be able to create without fail a great homeland featuring democracy, an advanced economy, prosperity and unification. . . .

July

CURRICULUM GROUP ON RELIGION IN SCHOOLS

July 1, 1987

"References to religion have all but been excised from the public school curriculum," concluded the Association for Supervision and Curriculum Development (ASCD) in a report entitled "Religion in the Curriculum" and released July 1. ASCD is an 80,000-member national organization of professors, principals, teachers, and administrators whose mission is developing leadership in quality education for all students. While the gradual disappearance of religious references from texts and teaching had been the subject of other reports, the ASCD report documented the reasons for the disappearance, its effect on public education, and the difference between teaching about *religion and promoting a specific religion.*

A broadly based nine-member panel considered three basic questions: "How can schools walk the fine line between teaching about religion and unconstitutionally promoting one or more specific religions? In a pluralistic society, what is the legitimate place of religion in the curriculum? How can educators avoid litigation while discharging their obligation to educate?"

While the panel chosen by ASCD deliberated, criticism of the public schools' handling of religion and religious observance continued to come from those who wanted religion taught as a subject and those who wanted religious ritual restored to the classroom. President Ronald Reagan favored a return to school prayer and Bible reading, practices the Supreme Court had held unconstitutional. (Historic Documents of 1985, p. 379)

There was both hope and fear that conservatives newly appointed to the Supreme Court by Reagan would, in the future, overturn the school prayer decisions. But liberal and conservative groups echoed ASCD's finding that "the quest for religious freedom that fueled the establishment of this nation receives scant treatment at best in many of the textbooks currently in use" and that more needed to be taught about "the profound part religious belief has played in ... the abolitionist and temperance movements of the nineteenth century or the civil rights movement of the twentieth." (Humanities in education, p. 681)

Educators Fear Controversy

Excision of religion from the public school curriculum stemmed from an "exaggerated fear of controversy," the ASCD found. The report sought to clarify the distinction between teaching about *religion and teaching the tenets of a particular religion. Bombarded by school prayer cases and (sometimes successful) attempts to ban books and censor teaching materials, educators had overreacted, according to the report, gradually dropping courses about the Bible and references to the influence of religion on U.S. and world history. Quotations from the Bible, such as the Psalms, had been removed from literature texts and reading lists.*

Secular Humanism Decisions

Even as ASCD was preparing its report, fundamentalist Christian parents were fighting, in the courts, schools they claimed were promoting "secular humanism" as a religion. First, in October 1986, a federal district court allowed some East Tennessee children to be excused from a reading class because their parents found evidence of "secular humanism" in the books being used. Secular humanism, they charged, denies God as the creator and holds that man is the center of all things. The school board argued that if parents were allowed to withhold their children from any part of the curriculum that offended them, schools would settle for the least common denominator—education that was objectionable to no one. The ASCD report agreed with the school board, saying the Tennessee decision "invites educational anarchy and the disintegration of common schooling in America." A federal appeals court reversed the ruling in August 1987, having found no proof "that any plaintiff student was ever called upon to affirm or deny a religious belief."

In March 1987 a federal judge in Alabama found evidence of secular humanism in forty-four textbooks, which he summarily banned. The Alabama public school system, said Judge Brevard Hand, had violated the First Amendment to the Constitution in promoting secular humanism as a religion. Judge Hand expressed this view of the banned texts: "The texts reviewed are not merely bad history, but lack so many facts as to equal ideological promotion. Omission, if sufficient, does affect a person's ability to develop religious beliefs and exercise that religious freedom guaranteed by the Constitution."

It was hard to find an expert in constitutional law or education who did not deplore the Hand decision for its potential to inspire more textbook challenges. (The Hand decision was in fact overturned by a federal district court in August 1987.) The critics agreed too that the outcome of the two cases would figure in the debate over what American public schools should teach children about religion and moral values. (Court on creation science, p. 565)

Teaching Moral Values

Addressing the question of teaching values, the ASCD report said, "Whatever one's views of moral education, it is undeniable that religious events and commitments have influenced history and culture at moments of crisis. But here the textbooks have let us down."

Writing in the Washington Post, *Diane Ravitch, professor of history at Teachers College, Columbia University, commented, "The only way out of this morass . . . is to derive values from the content of the curriculum by examining the consequences of major decisions that shaped history, by discussing great stories in literature that show how others have found meaning in life, by considering the moral teachings of different religious traditions in our own and other cultures."*

ASCD usually counted on its members to disseminate the information it provided to school districts, but because of the significance of this particular report, 6,500 extra copies were distributed. One was sent to every governor and every state commissioner of education, and ASCD officials discussed with the Textbook Publishers' Association particular religious events that might be restored to the public school curriculum.

Following are excerpts from "Religion in the Curriculum," released by the Association for Supervision and Curriculum Development July 1, 1987:

Introduction

"It was religion that gave birth to the English colonies in America. One must never forget that," wrote Alexis de Tocqueville in *Democracy in America*. Yet, more than a century later, the quest for religious freedom that fueled the establishment of this nation receives scant treatment at best in many of the textbooks currently in use. The texts have even less to say about the profound part religious belief has played in more recent U.S. history. Students probably won't find out from their textbooks that religious groups were a vital force in the abolitionist and temperance movements of the nineteenth century or the civil-rights movement of the twentieth.

Nor is it only texts in American history that are affected. The critical influence of religion on world history and culture is similarly slighted in texts on political science, sociology, literature, and world history. An elementary student can come away from a textbook account of the Crusades, for example, with the notion that these wars to win the Holy Land for Christendom were little more than exotic shopping expeditions. So, too, in discussions of current events, students study the situations in Northern Ireland and Lebanon or the war between Iran and Iraq without benefit of information that would help them understand the role of religion in these conflicts. Moreover, discussion of religious allusions and themes necessary for understanding many great works of literature are not found in the textbooks.

As these few examples suggest, references to religion have been all but excised from the public school curriculum. Their absence has been documented in various recent studies. This filtering of religious influences—intended as such or not, that is what it amounts to—is the result, in part, of a concern that the constitutional wall separating church and state might be breached. It also reflects an exaggerated fear of controversy—as if blandness begets self-preservation. Despite the absence of teaching about religion in our schools—or perhaps because of it—some parents charge that school officials are scaling that wall by promoting "secular humanism" as a religion in itself. Others demand that schools shield their children from ideas that conflict with the family's religious beliefs.

These challenges, and the growing realization that schools are failing to teach the profound part religion plays in human history and culture, pose a dilemma for educators. How can schools walk the fine line between teaching about religion and unconstitutionally promoting one or more specific religions? In a pluralistic society, what is the legitimate place of religion in the curriculum? And how can educators avoid litigation while discharging their obligation to educate? ...

The Flight from Controversy

The increasing politicization of religious fervor in the United States has caught many administrators and teachers unprepared to face the explosive forces that now surround teaching about religion in the public schools. Because religion is so controversial a subject, many educators have opted for benign neglect in their classrooms and accepted textbooks that virtually ignore religion. The outcome has been massive ignorance of any faith beside one's own (and sometimes even of one's own)—an ignorance compounded by the scarcity of information about traditional religions in elementary and secondary school textbooks, college courses, and the mass media.

The distinction between morality and religious dogma, so painfully established and so long revered in the American system of "common" or public schools, has shattered under the hammer blows of sectarians on both the ideological right and left. Some social scientists, realizing that moral convictions are central to systems of popular faith, appear to have concluded that to teach morality is to promote the establishment of religion. Some church leaders, on the other hand, have renewed the longstanding but shallow argument that ethical behavior will disappear if their particular religious dogma is not taught to all young people. . . .

Unfortunately, this confusion about moral education has contributed to the decline of curricular integrity. Whatever one's views of moral education, it is undeniable that religious events and commitments have influenced history and culture at moments of crisis. But here the textbooks have let us down. . . . Students cannot fully understand the successful outcome of the long crusade against slavery (either in the United States or in the West Indies), for example, without knowing the part that Christian abolitionists played. Nor can they comprehend the vibrant black culture that sprang to life in the South following the Civil War without reference to the role of black churches. Likewise, students cannot evaluate the career of Martin Luther King, Jr., without knowing his profound religious convictions about racism and war. . . .

Not only do students need to understand the influence religion has exerted in history, but they also need to know the basic tenets of the world's major religions, most of which are represented in America's diverse student population. To be thoughtful citizens, to vote intelligently, to relate constructively to one another in schools and colleges, students need to understand as much as possible of the diverse religions of the world in which they live.

Combating Ignorance

A major obstacle to reversing the prevailing ignorance about religion is the lack of adequate instructional materials. Textbooks—especially those dealing with the social sciences, history, and literature—typically exclude almost all significant treatment of traditional religions. Students occasionally find mentions of Jews and Catholics in high school American history texts, for example, but never any discussion of Judaism or Roman Catholicism or Eastern Orthodoxy. The economic and political activity of Mormons receives some treatment, but never Mormon religious doctrine. All the textbooks ignore Pennsylvania German churches and sects of the colonial period, as well as German and Scandinavian Lutheran immigrants who later settled in America. Fundamentalists might turn up in accounts of the Scopes trial, but they and the twentieth-century evangelicals, white and black, to whom they are related, appear nowhere else in the texts.

Nor are textbooks the only problem. . . . Supplementary classroom materials on religion also only rarely find their way into teachers' hands. Moreover, many university courses in the liberal arts, social sciences, and education have for decades neglected to focus on historical or contemporary expressions of religion in American and world cultures or on the influence of religious texts in world literature. Clearly, a major overhaul of the resources for teaching and learning about religion must be high priority in primary and secondary education and in university courses taken by teacher candidates.

De Facto Policy

School policies concerning religion generally address noncurricular issues, such as the observance of religious holidays. Many of these policies, which vary widely from school district to school district, were adopted in response to legal challenges to such practices as displaying religious symbols in classrooms, observing religious holidays, or performing religious music at school concerts. But policies addressing the place of religion in the curriculum are less common; in practice, decisions concerning the study of religions or of religious literature frequently are a matter of de facto, rather than explicit, policy. A brief sketch of how public schools have treated the study of the Bible in recent decades suggests the evolution of that de facto policy.

Public school courses called "The Bible" or "The Bible as Literature" were offered in the 1930s through the 1950s. These courses took two different approaches. The first presented the Bible as religion, and students studied the word of God as it was thought to be presented in the Bible. Under the second approach, which focused on the Bible as literature, students read and analyzed stories and poems from a variety of books, primarily from the Old Testament.

Most of the Bible-as-religion courses disappeared shortly after the U.S. Supreme Court's decisions on prayer and Bible reading in the schools, but some Bible-as-literature courses flourished in the 1960s and early 1970s as electives in the high school English program. Because these courses were not required, they came in for relatively little criticism. Objections arose primarily from a few members of the clergy who thought students should study the Bible primarily as a source of religious doctrine, rather than as literature.

In the late 1970s, however, elective courses began to be curtailed as the back-to-basics movement gained momentum. Separate courses in the Bible as literature either became units in regular English courses or, more likely, vanished from the curriculum altogether.

During this same period, attempts to censor school materials increased dramatically, and many educators and publishers were confused by the contradictory challenges of the protesters. On the one hand, critics (including President Ronald Reagan) denounced the courts for removing prayer and Bible reading from the public schools and criticized the schools for not advancing certain moral precepts. On the other hand, some sociologists and spokesmen for traditional religions condemned schools and publishers alike for presenting ideas in an open-ended way that allowed students to develop their own individual moral codes. Some conservative Protestants also criticized them for referring to religions in other cultures, promoting the beliefs of "secular humanism," and—picking up an old concern—advancing the theory of evolution.

In response to these conflicting pressures and as a result of specifications from certain adoption committees, some textbook publishers removed any mention of evolution from biology texts. Similarly, because some adoption committees objected to texts that might be charged with advancing a particular religion, the publishers de-emphasized or ignored the role of religion in the founding and development of this nation. Some even edited works of literature to remove references to God or any other words or phrases that might offend anyone on religious grounds.

The overreaction trickled down to the classroom, where teachers often ignored religious references in English or history classes for fear of violating what they mistakenly thought the Supreme Court had ruled. One school librarian even asked her principal what she should do with a copy of the Bible that she found tucked away in the stacks! . . .

. . . [T]he fact that no uniform policy exists is of less importance than the fact that most schools have no written policies at all concerning the study of the Bible or of religion. Instead, classroom practice often is based on a series of de facto policies, which encourage educators to avoid explicit references to religion altogether or at least to tread gently around the subject and, if it is necessary to mention religion at all, to treat all religions "objectively." These de facto policies flourish in an atmosphere of assumptions that, while commonly held, are not necessarily correct.

Underlying Assumptions

Religious Assumptions

. . . [P]ublic schools are cautious to avoid even the possibility of invading individuals' belief systems—a caution that honors the abiding American assumption of religion as private as much as it skirts constitutional issues of church and state. Moreover, distinctions among dogmas, practices, and observances in different religions are not easily drawn. This difficulty leads many schools to back away from teaching *about* religion to escape the charge that they are teaching the dogma of a particular religion.

In addition, widespread confusion about the relationship of religion and morality makes shaping school policy more difficult. . . . Faced with the prospect of picking their way through a minefield of conflicting opinions, educators generally assert that adherence to moral precepts is essential to society and then leave it to individuals to decide, in the light of their own religious beliefs, what these precepts are.

Historical and Social Assumptions

Elements of religion as belief and practice, such as prayer and Bible reading, were present in many American public schools for generations. In our century, however, increasing secularization and pluralism made such practices unsustainable, and landmark Supreme Court decisions of the early 1960s struck them down. Nevertheless, the persistence of religious convictions, however pluralistic, requires educators to face up to the question of diverse religious beliefs in the schools.

The central purposes of public schools are intellectual and civic, however, not religious. Religious education, or teaching *of* religion, is the job of parents and religious institutions, but teaching *about* religion is a legitimate purpose of public schools. Thus, the roles of religion in society, particularly in American society, should receive renewed emphasis in schools, as should the comparative study of religions....

Psychological and Educational Assumptions

... Educators must reexamine the assumption that any particular area of knowledge is too risky for the classroom. This assumption is subversive to the purpose of schooling and threatening to the growth of the intellect.

A companion assumption holds that teachers are uncomfortable dealing with the subject of religion. To the extent that this is true, it might be because they feel threatened; remove the threat, and teachers might be more inclined to engage their students in the study of religion and its roles in society. Teachers want to do the best job they can, and many realize they need to know more about the different religions in order to handle the subject without putting themselves on the razor's edge. This assumption, in short, is only partially valid.

Current administrative procedures are not adequate to deal with the complexities of the problem. Simply to label religious matters "controversial" is too limiting; assuming there is "one best way" to treat such matters is too rigid and, commonly, simply wrongheaded. "Opt-out" plans, which allow students to absent themselves from classroom discussions of topics they and their parents find offensive, may defuse inflamed sentiment on such sensitive issues as drug or sex education. But when opting out reaches core curriculum areas, such as reading—as was mandated in the mischievous judicial decision in *Mozert v. Hawkins County* [Tennessee] *Public Schools*—the practice invites educational anarchy and the disintegration of common schooling in America. Deliberations about school policies and procedures must seek an agenda for invention so that the schools' treatment of religion in the curriculum may rest on sounder assumptions.

Legal and Political Assumptions

... Americans who want good schools must realize that political activity is necessary to support them. The assumption that education is "above" politics was always a contrivance; it has become a liability.... [G]ood schools can become better; appropriate attention to the varied roles of religions constitutes one avenue to school improvement. For guidance along the way, educators should look to the political process, to common sense (even when uncommonly applied), and to constitutional law.

What the Courts Say

... For almost 25 years, the law of the land, as articulated in the school prayer cases, has been that ritual prayer and Bible reading in the public schools violate the Establishment Clause of the First Amendment of the U.S. Constitution. More recently, in *Wallace v. Jaffree* and *Edwards v. Aguillard,* the Supreme Court held unconstitutional laws requiring moments of silence and the teaching of alternative theories of the origin of man in public schools because their purpose was to promote prayer and religious doctrine. Such cases have occasioned a great national debate, which focuses on the historical meaning of the Establishment Clause, the role of the Supreme Court, and the wisdom and need for a constitutional amendment to allow voluntary prayer in public schools.

The metaphor of the wall of separation between church and state is so alluring, the hydraulic pressure of Establishment Clause litigation so powerful, and the compulsion to embrace simplistic solutions so irresistible, that many people appear convinced that all historical and other contextual references to religion must be eradicated from public education.... But "purification" of public education from all nonsecular influences is not the law of the land, nor has it ever been....

... [C]onsider the words of Justice Blackmun [in the 1971 case, *Lemon v. Kurtzman:*] "Our precedents command the conclusion that the State may not act to deny access to an idea simply because state officials disapprove of that idea for partisan or political reasons."...

Religion in the Curriculum

The schools' silence on religion results in failure to tell students the whole story of human civilization....

The Unstated Curriculum

Certain religious assumptions and practices are subtly fostered in most public schools. This hidden curriculum is apparent in the school calendar, which generally follows the Christian liturgical calendar by tying vacations to Christmas and Easter observances.... Thus, while schools seem to be sanitized and devoid of teaching about religion, deference to certain aspects of faith intrudes into the classroom through such practices as these....

Suggestions for Schools

Including religion in the curriculum for its educational value requires informed, honest, and sensitive teachers. It also requires the cooperation of administrators, students, parents, and religious and community leaders with those teachers. The following suggestions can help schools get started:

1. Teachers, administrators, and members of the community must be committed to the concept of a pluralistic and democratic society that accepts diversity of religious belief and practice as the norm.

2. Teachers must understand that although religion is a sensitive issue, it is not too hot for them to handle in an informed, descriptive, and impartial way.

3. All educators must be committed to keeping individual religious beliefs and practices inviolate. Children's religious beliefs are nurtured by their families and religious institutions, not by the public schools, and schools must respect those beliefs.

4. Teachers and administrators must be open and honest with each

other—and with parents and religious leaders—concerning what, where, and when the school teaches about religion.

5. Teachers need to be objectively informed about different religions and how they function in the lives of their adherents. They need to be skilled and respectful in helping students identify the functions of religion. They need to help students understand that the ideals of religion direct people toward worthy goals. Finally, they need to help students learn that religions have been both a force for conserving culture and a motivation for changing it.

6. Although teachers must play the major role in including religion in the curriculum, they will have little success without the support of colleagues, administrators, parents (at least, the great majority of them), and community and religious leaders.

7. Teaching about religion requires textbooks and other instructional materials that are accurate, objective, honest, fair, and interesting. Educators and members of the public must push for the creation of well-researched print and audiovisual materials.

8. School systems and universities (particularly schools of education) should work together to provide both preservice and inservice programs that help teachers develop the knowledge, skills, attitudes, and confidence they need for the effective inclusion of religion in the curriculum.

9. On a broader scale, a massive research and development effort is necessary in order to produce effective curriculum models to aid teachers, school systems, and teacher educators. This might well be a national effort in order to avoid multiple reinventions of the wheel.

10. Finally, educators must exert extreme care to avoid assuming the role of the family and the religious institution in youngsters' religious, spiritual, and moral education and development. The teacher's chief task in teaching about religion is to help students better understand faiths other than their own and the roles of religions in the life of their nation and that of other cultures.

Religion in the Context of School Goals

The issue of religion in the curriculum should be considered within the larger context of what we expect education to accomplish. In local school systems and individual schools, these tacit expectations often take the form of stated goals. Questions deriving from these goals direct what we do in schools and help us understand why we do it. Although goal statements vary widely, John Goodlad and his colleagues have found many commonalities among them. Three of the goals listed by Goodlad, and guiding questions that might be derived from them, are as follows:

1. *Enculturation*.... [T]he schools' purpose is to develop an understanding of the ways in which the heritage and traditions of the past influence the present directions and values of society.... What experiences can we provide students that will promote their understanding of

how the past continues to influence the present? For example, how did the religious beliefs of early immigrants to the United States influence the formation and persistence of solidarity among modern ethnic groups?

2. *Interpersonal relations.* The schools' role here is to develop a knowledge of diverse values and their influence on individuals and society.... How can we help students learn about diverse value systems and their influence on individuals and society?

3. *Citizenship.* Here, a goal is to develop an attitude of inquiry in order to examine social values.... What classroom experiences will promote inquiry into such values as racial tolerance, civic honesty, regard for law, and opposition to cruelty or violence?

These questions lead to another inescapable one: How can we respond to any of these goal statements without teaching about religion? By basing their inquiry on statements of purpose in this way, educators have a means by which to exercise their professional judgment responsibly. Teachers, administrators, and citizens should be involved in such inquiry and in decisions arising from it.

Furthermore, these goal statements and the questions that derive from them have implications not only for curriculum and teacher preparation,... but also for instructional materials. Textbooks and other classroom materials must be responsive to the same reasoning. Publishers must ask themselves, "How does this material help students develop insight into the shaping values of their civilization? What information does it provide about opposing value systems? How does it demonstrate the enduring influence of religion in society?"...

Recommendations

Clearly, decisive action is needed to end the current curricular silence on religion.... Our recommendations for ending the silence are embedded throughout the text of this report, but some bear reiterating briefly here:

1. Local decision making on the role of religion in the curriculum should be exercised within the context of religious diversity at the local, state, national, and international levels.

2. Religious professionals and other community leaders should contribute, along with educators, to discussions of the role of religion in the curriculum, but the results of these deliberations should not be allowed to be shaped by particular ideological views.

3. Educators at all levels should be committed to the concept of a pluralistic and democratic society that accepts diversity of religious belief and practice as the norm.

4. State departments of education should address the issue of fair and factual treatment of religion in the curriculum by all local education agencies.

5. Textbook selection committees at the state, district, and local school levels should require such treatment of religion in all curricular materials. To aid these committees in their selections, education agencies and

professional associations like ASCD should conduct staff development sessions on religion in the curriculum and issue specific guidelines concerning the treatment of religion in textbooks.

6. Publishers should revise textbooks and other instructional materials to provide adequate treatment of diverse religions and their roles in American and world culture and to include appropriate religious and moral themes in literary and art history anthologies.

7. A major research and development effort should be undertaken to develop new curricular materials and instructional designs for teaching about religion within the various subject areas. Scholars and educators should work together to identify significant ideas, events, people, and literature to be considered for inclusion in the curriculum.

8. Teacher educators, both preservice and inservice, should ensure that teachers acquire not only the substantive knowledge required to teach about religion in society but also the attitudes and understanding necessary to treat the subject with sensitivity in the classroom.

9. Teachers, administrators, and members of the public should be aware of the impact of court decisions on the curriculum and should recognize that teaching about religion is not unconstitutional.

10. Teachers and administrators should analyze both the hidden and the explicit curriculums regularly to ensure sensitive concern for teaching about religion in society and for the faiths of individual students.

11. Educators should study federal court decisions regarding opting-out before developing their own policies, which should be applied strictly on a case-by-case basis. The option should be limited to those cases in which the material or content of instruction can be shown to significantly or substantially assault an individual's religious beliefs.

12. Local educators and their national organizations, including ASCD, should explore ways to foster public support for the teaching of rigorous, intellectually demanding accounts of religion in society, particularly in American society.

13. ASCD and other national education groups should aid educators in their deliberations on this matter by providing clear and accurate information on relevant court decisions, on curriculum development, on state and local textbook adoption criteria, and on policy issues affecting the role of religion in the curriculum (with representative policy statements).

These recommendations, and the report that precedes them, in no way advocate the teaching of religious belief or the sponsorship of religious practice in the public schools. To do so would be to trample what Charles Haynes has called "humanity's boldest and most successful experiment in religious freedom." But to understand America's bold experiment—and to understand the driving force of many historical and cultural movements worldwide—requires an understanding of the role religion has played, and continues to play, in human civilization.

UN RESOLUTION ON IRAN-IRAQ WAR

July 20, 1987

In a rare show of unanimity, the five permanent members of the United Nations Security Council, joined by the ten nonpermanent members, July 20 adopted Resolution 598, which called for an end to the seven-year war between Iran and Iraq. In so doing, the United Nations joined several regional organizations and a number of individual countries that had offered to mediate a settlement of the conflict—one of the longest and bloodiest of modern times. Though no precise body count was available from either combatant, the U.S. State Department estimated total casualties on both sides at 700,000, as of September 1987. That was slightly more than the combined U.S. casualty toll in World War I, Korea, and Vietnam.

Although the resolution did not provide for enforcement, it was adopted under a section of the UN Charter authorizing sanctions in the event of noncompliance. The sanctions, if put into effect, most likely would take the form of an arms embargo, which the Reagan administration advocated, but which other nations were reluctant to impose.

Secretary of State George P. Shultz July 20 said the United States would support "the decisive application of enforcement measures" against either nation if it rejected the UN resolution. Although Shultz said there was "grave concern" about terrorist activities condoned, if not fomented by, the militant fundamentalist Moslem regime of Ayatollah Ruhollah Khomeini, Shultz added that the administration was "ready and willing" to discuss "the serious problems which continue to divide us." The secretary also said that "a positive Iranian response to this resolution and an end to aggressive actions against other states and their citizens would do much to make possible a mutually beneficial bilateral relationship in the future."

Iraq Accepts, Iran Rejects Resolution

The resolution was a milestone: it marked the first time in UN history that the council's five permanent members—Britain, China, France, the Soviet Union, and the United States—had acted in concert to end an active conflict without the prior agreements of the combatants. The resolution called for an immediate and total cease-fire, mutual withdrawal of forces to internationally recognized boundaries, and prompt exchange of war prisoners. In language designed to appease Iran, the measure also called for a halt to chemical warfare (reportedly waged by Iraq) and the establishment of a panel to fix responsibility for starting the war (generally considered to be Iraq's).

Iraq quickly announced its acceptance of the resolution, but Iraq's ambassador in London, Abdul Amir al-Anbar, suggested that his country could not adhere to it without Iran's compliance. "It is possible for one to make war, but for peace, it takes two parties to cooperate," he said. Iran, however, denounced the resolution and insisted that it would not comply until an international tribunal determined the aggressor, and Iran achieved its war aim of toppling the Iraqi government of President Saddam Hussein and his ruling Ba'ath party. Iranian UN delegate Said Rajaie-Khorassani termed the resolution July 21 a "vicious American diplomatic maneuver."

Secretary General's Efforts

Adoption of the resolution capped months of effort by the Reagan administration and UN Secretary General Javier Pérez de Cuéllar, who was mandated by the resolution to undertake consultations with Iran and Iraq. The secretary general met with Iran's deputy foreign minister, Mohammed Jiwad Larinjani, in late August.

Meanwhile, frustrated by Iran's refusal to agree to UN Resolution 598, Iraq August 29 broke its forty-five-day informal cease-fire by bombing offshore Iranian oil installations, stating that similar attacks would be conducted until Iran accepted the resolution. For its part, the Iranian government warned of a "crushing response" to the raids, raising apprehensions—subsequently borne out—of retaliation against merchant shipping in the Persian Gulf. The "tanker war" had been relatively quiet since mid-July, but by early September it had stepped up considerably, with attacks by both nations on merchant ships. (Iraqi attack on USS *Stark*, p. 791)

As tensions heightened, the fifteen members of the Security Council agreed to send the secretary general back to the gulf and appealed to Iran and Iraq to suspend hostilities during Pérez de Cuéllar's mission.

Initially, the situation appeared promising. "The Iranians have told me they are prepared to discuss implementation of the resolution," the secretary general said September 4.

Extensive discussions between Pérez de Cuéllar and high Iranian officials September 12 were described by a UN spokesman as "cordial and very detailed." The secretary general then traveled to Baghdad where, on arrival, he said he was "neither optimistic nor pessimistic" about the prospects for a cease-fire. In fact, the talks bore little fruit; both warring nations continued their artillery barrages against cities and towns, Iraqi planes struck at an Iranian oil terminal, and the secretary general's trip ended in apparent failure.

Throughout August and September, the Reagan administration moved to tighten trade restrictions against Iran and lobbied the UN Security Council to support an arms embargo. U.S. intelligence officials estimated that Iran had purchased about $1 billion in arms during 1987, including a number of Chinese-made Silkworm antiship missiles. However, the administration was unable to persuade Security Council members—particularly the Soviet Union and China—to impose sanctions. Speaking to the opening session of the Forty-second UN General Assembly in New York on September 21, President Ronald Reagan urged the Security Council to "rapidly adopt enforcement measures" against Iran if the government did not "clearly and unequivocally state" that it accepted the cease-fire resolution.

Although cool to suggestions of an arms embargo, the five permanent Security Council members September 25 issued a joint statement giving "full support" to the secretary general's "efforts to implement" Resolution 598. Shortly thereafter, the council drafted new guidelines for Pérez de Cuéllar's negotiating instructions. In a concession to Iran, the more detailed guidelines suggested that "the observance of a cease-fire" should proceed simultaneously with the "setting into motion" of an international commission to determine which nation instigated the conflict.

The search for peace continued, but at year's end tensions remained high in the gulf. Iran was mobilizing for an offensive on the ground, while Iraq continued to dominate the air war. Fleets and minesweepers from a number of nations continued to patrol the waters, and attacks on ships of many different registries occurred.

Following is the text of Resolution 598, adopted July 20, 1987, by the UN Security Council, calling for a cease-fire in the Iran-Iraq war:

The Security Council,

Reaffirming its resolution 582 (1986),

Deeply concerned that, despite its calls for a cease-fire, the conflict between Iran and Iraq continues unabated, with further heavy loss of human life and material destruction,

Deploring the initiation and continuation of the conflict,

Deploring also the bombing of purely civilian population centres, attacks on neutral shipping or civilian aircraft, the violation of international humanitarian law and other laws of armed conflict, and, in particular, the use of chemical weapons contrary to obligations under the 1925 Geneva Protocol,

Deeply concerned that further escalation and widening of the conflict may take place,

Determined to bring to an end all military actions between Iran and Iraq,

Convinced that a comprehensive, just, honourable and durable settlement should be achieved between Iran and Iraq,

Recalling the provisions of the Charter of the United Nations, and in particular the obligation of all Member States to settle their international disputes by peaceful means in such a manner that international peace and security and justice are not endangered,

Determining that there exists a breach of the peace as regards the conflict between Iran and Iraq,

Acting under Articles 39 and 40 of the Charter of the United Nations,

1. *Demands* that, as a first step towards a negotiated settlement, Iran and Iraq observe an immediate cease-fire, discontinue all military actions on land, at sea and in the air, and withdraw all forces to the internationally recognized boundaries without delay;

2. *Requests* the Secretary-General to dispatch a team of United Nations Observers to verify, confirm and supervise the cease-fire and withdrawal and further requests the Secretary-General to make the necessary arrangements in consultation with the Parties and to submit a report thereon to the Security Council;

3. *Urges* that prisoners-of-war be released and repatriated without delay after the cessation of active hostilities in accordance with the Third Geneva Convention of 12 August 1949;

4. *Calls upon* Iran and Iraq to co-operate with the Secretary-General in implementing this resolution and in mediation efforts to achieve a comprehensive, just and honourable settlement, acceptable to both sides, of all outstanding issues, in accordance with the principles contained in the Charter of the United Nations;

5. *Calls upon* all other States to exercise the utmost restraint and to refrain from any act which may lead to further escalation and widening of the conflict, and thus to facilitate the implementation of the present resolution;

6. *Requests* the Secretary-General to explore, in consultation with Iran and Iraq, the question of entrusting an impartial body with inquiring into responsibility for the conflict and to report to the Security Council as soon as possible;

7. *Recognizes* the magnitude of the damage inflicted during the

conflict and the need for reconstruction efforts, with appropriate international assistance, once the conflict is ended and, in this regard, requests the Secretary-General to assign a team of experts to study the question of reconstruction and to report to the Security Council;

8. *Further requests* the Secretary-General to examine, in consultation with Iran and Iraq and with other States of the region, measures to enhance the security and stability of the region;

9. *Requests* the Secretary-General to keep the Security Council informed on the implementation of this resolution;

10. *Decides* to meet again as necessary to consider further steps to ensure compliance with this resolution.

INDO-SRI LANKAN ACCORD

July 29, 1987

Sri Lanka's president, Junius Jayewardene, and the prime minister of India, Rajiv Gandhi, in Colombo, Sri Lanka, July 29 formally agreed to try to halt Sri Lanka's bitter ethnic conflict, which had already resulted in over 6,000 deaths. India would guarantee the accord, if necessary, through the use of military force.

The government of Sri Lanka agreed to permit its north and east provinces—regions where the Tamils' separatist insurgency was the strongest—to form a single "administrative unit." In the east, where Tamils constituted less than a clear majority, a referendum to decide whether the eastern province should "remain linked with the northern province" or form a separate unit was to take place by the end of 1988. Those displaced during the previous years of the conflict would have the right to vote on the referendum.

The agreement called for a cease-fire within forty-eight hours. The Sri Lankan military forces were to return to their barracks, "militant groups" were to surrender their arms, and a general amnesty was to follow.

In addition to guaranteeing the resolutions militarily, India would not permit its territory to be used for "activities prejudicial" to Sri Lanka. The countries would conduct joint naval operations to prevent military supplies from reaching the island from southern India. Many of the 52 million Tamils residing in India's southernmost state, Tamil Nadu, openly sided with Sri Lanka's Tamil rebels. In addition, all rebel organizations maintained offices in Madras, Tamil Nudu's capital.

Another provision of the accord recognized English and Tamil as official languages along with Sinhalese.

Origins of the Sri Lankan Conflict

There had long been ethnic tensions between Sri Lanka's largely Buddhist Sinhalese, who made up approximately 70 percent of the country, and the mostly Hindu Tamils. In the 1950s the policies of S. W. Bandaranaike, a Sinhalese nationalist, exacerbated these tensions and led to sporadic violence. Among his acts was to make Sinhalese the national language. Throughout most of the 1970s and 1980s, the country had been under some form of martial law, as various revolutionary Tamil separatist groups continued to provoke unrest. The current president, Jayewardene, was elected in 1977; a constitutional revision the following year increased his power.

India, with its large Tamil population and its proximity to Sri Lanka—only six miles across the Palk Strait—probably could not have avoided becoming involved in the island's troubled affairs. For years India had tried to ignore the support southern India's Tamils were giving to their Sri Lankan counterparts. India's growing sense of itself as a political and military power in South Asia had also been a factor in Indian involvement, particularly under Rajiv Gandhi, who actively sought to mediate between the conflicting parties in Sri Lanka. Not everyone in Sri Lanka was pleased by the participation of a largely Hindu country, however, as many felt New Delhi was primarily interested in bringing Sri Lanka under its domination.

Most accounts date the current phase of the Sri Lankan conflict from an attack on Tamil prisoners by Sinhalese troops in July 1983. In the ensuing violence, hundreds of Tamils were killed, and some 50,000 fled to Tamil-dominated centers in the north. Despite a number of attempts by the government to negotiate with Tamil leaders, notably during the 1985 meetings at Thimphu, Bhutan, the question of a separate Tamil state always prevented agreement. When talks invariably ended in failure, the Jayewardene government responded by increasing the resources it devoted to the military.

With his forces numbering 20,000, Jayewardene ordered "Operation Liberation" against the insurgents' positions in the Jaffna Peninsula on the northernmost coast of Sri Lanka. A June 3 massacre of a busload of Buddhist monks escalated the fighting's intensity. Hundreds of Tamils, many of them civilians, died in the violence. A relief convoy en route to Jaffna from Tamil Nadu was stopped by the Sri Lankan navy. On June 4 New Delhi air-dropped supplies, using Mirage fighter aircraft to fly close-in support. Having made his point, Prime Minister Gandhi turned again to cooperating with Jayewardene. India began pressing the Tamil leadership, including the leader of the strongest Tamil group, the Liberation Tigers, Velupillai Prabakaran, who flew to meet with Gandhi in July. By July 24 both nations were ready to announce an agreement in principle to end the four-year conflict.

As word of the agreement leaked out, however, opposition to it grew, especially in Sri Lanka, where many Sinhalese accused Jayewardene of "selling out" to India and the Hindus. Jayewardene's own prime minister, Ranasinghe Premadasa, openly opposed him. A series of national strikes was organized by Buddhist monks. Although many Tamil leaders appeared to accept the cease-fire, others would not commit themselves to surrendering their weapons.

By July 29 the Sri Lankan military had defeated the Tamils in the Vadamarachi Peninsula, just east of Jaffna, and forts were being constructed in the region. Reassuring Jayewardene that India would handle those elements who refused to honor the agreement, Gandhi arrived in Colombo, the capital, to sign the accord.

Indian Forces Counter Tamil Resistance

The pact did little to soothe feelings in southern Sri Lanka. Colombo soon erupted in violent demonstrations. On July 30 the first 3,000 Indian troops arrived in the north and began ferrying Sri Lankan soldiers to the south where they would be used to try to control the Sinhalese demonstrations. The deadline for the rebels to surrender their arms passed without any noticeable results. On August 2 Prabakaran returned to Sri Lanka, ostensibly to urge his followers to lay down their arms; instead, he demanded that he be made the head of the interim government to be set up in the north and east, a move that the Sri Lankan government could not accept. By then much of the country was under round-the-clock curfew. Criticism of Gandhi began to surface in India; some analysts suggested his interest in Sri Lanka was designed to draw the country's attention away from his mounting political problems at home.

India continued sending in forces; in the north the cease-fire held. Indian frigates put in at Colombo in a show of force in support of Jayewardene, and by mid-August the joint naval patrols began. On August 18, however, a grenade and rifle attack killed one member of the Sri Lankan parliament and wounded six cabinet officers. The attack had apparently been directed at Jayewardene.

Having profited from the cease-fire to eliminate well over a hundred Tamil rivals, the Liberation Tigers had effectively broken the cease-fire by mid-September. In reaction, India imposed a curfew on the eastern port of Trincomalee, where Tamils complained that the government was sending in Sinhalese, with an obvious view toward the upcoming referendum. Tamils attacked several police stations in the Jaffna region.

India strengthened its forces and in October decided to go on the attack; however, to avoid endangering civilians, the Indian army proceeded cautiously. The Liberation Tigers proved masters of guerrilla warfare; they were very well entrenched and the entrance to Jaffna was treacherous. On October 15, a mine was detonated beneath an Indian army bus, killing twenty. The army already had taken its heaviest casualties since the 1971 war with Pakistan. For the assault on Jaffna's narrow streets and alleys, India used its Gurkhas and other elite forces, amid allegations that the rebels were using the city's civilians as human shields. As the fighting intensified the rebels called for a cease-fire, but the Indian army by then insisted on an unconditional surrender. In late October India launched air strikes against Tamil rebels in the north.

Sinhalese guerrilla activity also escalated, partly in response to the efforts of Jayewardene's government to ease the conflict by giving Tamils more local autonomy. During the November debates in parliament on setting up provincial councils, measures specified in the accord, thirty-two people died in a bomb blast in downtown Colombo. Six months after the accord was signed, more than 150 policemen, government officials, and ruling party members had been killed by those who feared the Tamils would be given too much power.

Following is the text of the Indo-Sri Lankan peace accord and the annexure to the agreement, signed by J. R. Jayewardene, president of Sri Lanka, and Rajiv Gandhi, prime minister of India, in Colombo, Sri Lanka, July 29, 1987:

INDO-SRI LANKA AGREEMENT TO ESTABLISH PEACE AND NORMALCY IN SRI LANKA

The President of the Democratic Socialist Republic of Sri Lanka, His Excellency Mr. J. R. Jayewardene, and the Prime Minister of the Republic of India, His Excellency Mr. Rajiv Gandhi, having met at Colombo on July 29, 1987

Attaching utmost importance to nurturing, intensifying and strengthening the traditional friendship of Sri Lanka and India, and acknowledging the imperative need of resolving the ethnic problem of Sri Lanka, and the consequent violence, and for the safety, well-being and prosperity of people belonging to all communities in Sir Lanka

Have this day entered into the following agreement to fulfill this objective.

In this context,

1.1 Desiring to preserve the unity, sovereignty and territorial integrity of Sri Lanka:

1.2 Acknowledging that Sri Lanka is a multi-ethnic and a multi-lingual plural society consisting, inter alia, of Sinhalese, Tamils, Muslims (Moors), and Burghers:

1.3 Recognising that each ethnic group has a distinct cultural and linguistic identity which has to be carefully nurtured:

1.4 Also recognising that the northern and the eastern provinces have been areas of historical habitation of Sri Lankan Tamil speaking peoples, who have at all times hitherto lived together in this territory with other ethnic groups:

1.5 Conscious of the necessity of strengthening the forces contributing to the unity, sovereignty and territorial integrity of Sri Lanka, and preserving its character as a multi-ethnic, multi-lingual and multi-religious plural society in which all citizens can live in equality, safety and harmony, and prosper and fulfill their aspirations:

2. Resolve that:

2.1 Since the government of Sri Lanka proposes to permit adjoining provinces to join to form one administrative unit and also by a referendum to separate as may be permitted to the northern and eastern provinces as outlined below:

2.2 During the period, which shall be considered an interim period, (i.e. from the date of the elections to the provincial council, as specified in para 2.8 to the date of the referendum as specified in para 2.3, the northern and eastern provinces as now constituted, will form one administrative unit, having one elected provincial council. Such a unit will have one governor, one chief minister and one board of ministers.

2.3 There will be a referendum on or before 31st December 1988 to enable the people of the eastern province to decide whether:

(A) The eastern province should remain linked with the northern province as one administrative unit, and continue to be governed together with the northern province as specified in para 2.2 or

(B) The eastern province should constitute a separate administrative unit having its own distinct provincial council with a separate governor, chief minister and board of ministers.

The president may, at his discretion, decide to postpone such a referendum.

2.4 All persons who have been displaced due to ethnic violence, or other reasons, will have the right to vote in such a referendum. Necessary conditions to enable them to return to areas from where they were displaced will be created.

2.5 The referendum, when held, will be monitored by a committee headed by the chief justice, a member appointed by the president, nominated by the government of Sri Lanka, and a member appointed by the president, nominated by the representatives of the Tamil speaking people of the eastern province.

2.6 A simple majority will be sufficient to determine the result of the referendum.

2.7 Meetings and other forms of propaganda, permissible within the laws of the country, will be allowed before the referendum.

2.8 Elections to provincial councils will be held within the next three months, in any event before 31st December 1987. Indian observers will be invited for elections to the provincial council of the north and east.

2.9 The emergency will be lifted in the eastern and northern provinces by August 15, 1987. A cessation of hostilities will come into effect all over the island within 48 hours of the signing of this agreement. All arms presently held by militant groups will be surrendered in accordance with an agreed procedure to authorities to be designated by the government of Sri Lanka.

Consequent to the cessation of hostilities and the surrender of arms by militant groups, the army and other security personnel will be confined to barracks in camps as on 25 May 1987. The process of surrendering of arms and the confining of security personnel moving back to barracks shall be completed within 72 hours of the cessation of hostilities coming into effect.

2.10 The government of Sri Lanka will utilise for the purpose of law enforcement and maintenance of security in the northern and eastern provinces same organisations and mechanisms of government as are used in the rest of the country.

2.11 The president of Sri Lanka will grant a general amnesty to political and other prisoners now held in custody under the prevention of terrorism act and other emergency laws, and to combatants, as well as to those persons accused, charged and/or convicted under these laws. The government of Sri Lanka will make special efforts to rehabilitate militant youth with a view to bringing them back into the mainstream of national life. India will co-operate in the process.

2.12 The government of Sri Lanka will accept and abide by the above provisions and expect all others to do likewise.

2.13 If the framework for the resolutions is accepted, the government of Sri Lanka will implement the relevant proposals forthwith.

2.14 The government of India will underwrite and guarantee the resolutions, and co-operate in the implementation of these proposals.

2.15 These proposals are conditional to an acceptance of the proposals negotiated from 4.5.1986 to 19.12.1986. Residual matters not finalised during the above negotiations shall be resolved between India and Sri Lanka within a period of six weeks of signing this agreement. These proposals are also conditional to the government of India co-operating directly with the government of Sri Lanka in their implementation.

2.16 These proposals are also conditional to the government of India taking the following actions if any militant groups operating in Sri Lanka do not accept this framework of proposals for a settlement, namely,

(A) India will take all necessary steps to ensure that Indian territory is not used for activities prejudicial to the unity, integrity and security of Sri Lanka.

(B) The Indian navy/coast guard will co-operate with the Sri Lanka navy in preventing Tamil militant activities from affecting Sri Lanka.

(C) In the event that the government of Sri Lanka requests the government of India to afford military assistance to implement these proposals the government of India will co-operate by giving to the government of Sri Lanka such military assistance as and when requested.

(D) The government of India will expedite repatriation from Sri Lanka of Indian citizens to India who are resident here, concurrently with the repatriation of Sri Lankan refugees from Tamil Nadu.

(E) The governments of Sri Lanka and India will co-operate in ensuring the physical security and safety of all communities inhabiting the northern and eastern provinces.

2.17 The government of Sri Lanka shall ensure free, full and fair participation of voters from all communities in the northern and eastern provinces in electoral processes envisaged in this agreement. The government of India will extend full co-operation to the government of Sri Lanka in this regard.

2.18 The official language of Sri Lanka shall be Sinhala. Tamil and English will also be official languages.

3. This agreement and the annexure thereto shall come into force upon signature.

In witness whereof we have set our hands and seals hereunto.

Done in Colombo, Sri Lanka, on this the twenty ninth day of July of the year one thousand nine hundred and eighty seven, in duplicate, both texts being equally authentic.

ANNEXURE TO THE AGREEMENT

1. His Excellency the President of Sri Lanka and the Prime Minister of India agree that the referendum mentioned in paragraph 2 and its sub-paragraphs of the agreement will be observed by a representative of the election commission of India to be invited by His Excellency the President of Sri Lanka.

2. Similarly, both heads of government agree that the elections to the provincial council mentioned in paragraph 2.8 of the agreement will be observed by a representative of the government of India to be invited by the President of Sri Lanka.

3. His Excellency the President of Sri Lanka agrees that the home guards would be disbanded and all para-military personnel will be withdrawn from the eastern and northern provinces with a view to creating conditions conducive to fair elections to the council.

The president, in his discretion, shall absorb such para-military forces, which came into being due to ethnic violence, into the regular security forces of Sri Lanka.

4. The President of Sri Lanka and the Prime Minister of India agree that the Tamil militants shall surrender their arms to authorities agreed upon to be designated by the President of Sri Lanka. The surrender shall take place in the presence of one senior representative each of the Sri Lanka Red Cross and the Indian Red Cross.

5. The President of Sri Lanka and the Prime Minister of India agree that a joint Indo-Sri Lankan observer group consisting of qualified representatives of the government of Sri Lanka and the government of India would monitor the cessation of hostilities from 31 July 1987.

6. The President of Sri Lanka and the Prime Minister of India also agree that in terms of paragraph 2.14 and paragraph 2.16 (C) of the agreement, an Indian peace keeping contingent may be invited by the President of Sri Lanka to guarantee and enforce the cessation of hostilities, if so required.

August

FCC ON FAIRNESS DOCTRINE

August 4, 1987

The Federal Communications Commission (FCC) voted August 4 to abolish the fairness doctrine on the grounds that it violated the First Amendment rights of broadcasters. Formalized by the FCC in 1949, the fairness doctrine required broadcasters to provide coverage of controversial issues of public importance and to provide a reasonable opportunity for the presentation of contrasting viewpoints on those issues. The agency's ruling did not affect the "equal time" rule, sometimes confused with the fairness doctrine, which required a station that sold advertising time to one political candidate to provide a similar opportunity to competing candidates.

The commission in recent years had expressed doubts about the fairness doctrine's efficacy. In August 1985 the FCC released a comprehensive report on the public policy and constitutional implications of the doctrine. The agency concluded then that the doctrine no longer served the public interest. The commission maintained that the doctrine chilled free speech, impeded the broadcast of controversial issues, and placed the government in an intrusive role of scrutinizing broadcast content. The FCC also questioned whether the doctrine was consistent with First Amendment guarantees. However, in the face of intense congressional interest and uncertainty over whether the doctrine had been codified, the commission did not eliminate or restrict the scope of the doctrine. The FCC forwarded its 1985 report to Congress and stated that the question of the doctrine's constitutionality was better left to Congress and the courts.

Meredith Corporation v. FCC

Syracuse Peace Council filed a complaint with the FCC alleging that in 1982 radio station WTVH in Syracuse, New York, had violated the fairness doctrine by broadcasting editorial advertisements favoring construction of a local nuclear power plant without presenting contrasting points of view. The FCC agreed that the station had violated the doctrine. Meredith Corporation, the licensee of the station, petitioned the FCC to reconsider. Meredith argued in part that the doctrine violated the First Amendment rights of broadcasters and that the FCC's enforcement of the doctrine was unconstitutional.

The FCC declined to consider Meredith's constitutional argument, citing its 1985 decision to leave this question to Congress and the courts. Meredith then sought judicial review of the FCC's order in the U.S. Court of Appeals for the District of Columbia Circuit. The court in January 1987 agreed with the FCC's finding that the station had violated the fairness doctrine, but ordered the agency to consider Meredith's constitutional challenge.

FCC Ruling

The FCC began its review. Interested groups and individuals, including broadcasters, advertisers, trade associations, and government entities, submitted comments. The comments were almost equally divided between those supporting and those opposing the fairness doctrine. Some supporters maintained that the right to broadcast was a position of public trust. Government regulation, they said, assured the public's access to diverse views on controversial issues. Opponents argued in part that market forces were sufficient to steer the industry. Ratings of viewer and listener support, they maintained, best reflected the public interest. Some opponents argued also that the regulation of broadcast content violated the First Amendment guarantee of freedom of speech.

On August 4 the FCC ruled that the fairness doctrine had violated the First Amendment rights of broadcasters. "In sum," the commission report stated, "the fairness doctrine in operation disserves both the public's right to diverse sources of information and the broadcaster's interest in free expression. Its chilling effect thwarts its intended purpose, and it results in excessive and unnecessary government intervention into the editorial processes of broadcast journalists."

The commission suggested that with the dramatic technological and economic changes in the broadcast industry the time had come for the Supreme Court "to reconsider First Amendment principles that were developed for another market."

In 1984 the Court in FCC v. League of Women Voters of California *justified the regulation of broadcasters' speech based on the limited number of broadcast frequencies. The government could regulate the broadcast content to ensure that the frequencies were used in the public interest.* (Historic Documents of 1984, p. 449) *The Court indicated in that decision, however, that, given a signal from the Congress or the FCC, it would reconsider its application of diminished First Amendment protection to the electronic media. The Court noted that the growth of cable and satellite television systems vastly increased the number of broadcast stations and threw the scarcity rationale into question. The FCC stated that this ruling on the fairness doctrine, along with its 1985 report, provided just such a signal.*

Reactions

The repeal of the fairness doctrine had no dramatic immediate effect on television or radio broadcast content. FCC Chairman Dennis R. Patrick warned that increased instances of slanted coverage could result. He pointed out, however, that "the First Amendment does not guarantee a fair press, only a free press."

Broadcast groups applauded the FCC's action, but some public interest groups decried the move as a setback to the presentation of minority views.

Congress, long interested in the fairness doctrine, went into a flurry of activity following the FCC order. Earlier in the year, Congress had passed a measure to write the fairness doctrine into law. President Ronald Reagan vetoed the bill in June, calling the doctrine "antagonistic to the freedom of expression guaranteed by the First Amendment."

In keeping with a congressional directive, the FCC sent to Capitol Hill an eighty-five-page report outlining alternatives, including limiting enforcement of the fairness doctrine to areas with few broadcast sources and limiting the doctrine's application to television.

After the FCC ruling, some members of Congress vowed to revive legislation to codify the doctrine. In fact, the issue surfaced again as Congress wrestled with catch-all budget bills at the end of the year. Rep. John D. Dingell, D-Mich., attached a provision in the conference committee that would renew the fairness doctrine, but President Reagan said he would veto the entire appropriations bill if that provision were included. When it became clear that Republicans—even those who supported the doctrine—would back the president, the provision was dropped.

> *Following are excerpts from the August 4, 1987, Federal Communications Commission memorandum opinion and order abolishing the fairness doctrine on the grounds that it violated the First Amendment rights of broadcasters:*

FCC 87-266

In re Complaint of Syracuse Peace Council against Television Station WTVH Syracuse, New York	Memorandum Opinion and Order

[August 4, 1987]

[Parts I and II omitted]

III. Discussion

Scope of This Proceeding—Procedural Issues

Discussion of Policy and Constitutional Issues

... 19. [I]n this *Memorandum Opinion and Order,* we consider whether the fairness doctrine is consistent with the guarantees of the First Amendment and whether it comports with the public interest. ... [T]he court ordered the Commission to consider Meredith's constitutional arguments unless it decided, on policy grounds, not to enforce the fairness doctrine. As we began to examine the policy issues, however, it became evident to us that ... it would be difficult, if not impossible, to isolate the policy considerations from the constitutional aspects underlying the doctrine.[1] We believe, as a result, that it is appropriate and necessary to address the policy and constitutional issues together....

32. ... [B]roadcasters are faced daily with editorial decisions concerning what types of commercial or noncommercial material on controversial public issues to present to their listeners and viewers. The fundamental issue embodied in this fairness doctrine litigation is the same as that presented in all other fairness doctrine cases: whether it is constitutional and thereby sound public policy for a government agency to oversee

[1] Our decision to analyze the constitutional and policy issues separately in the *1985 Fairness Report* was out of an abundance of caution not to overstep our appropriate role in this matter. At that time, the uncertainty as to the fairness doctrine's codification, together with Congress' intense interest in the issue, led us to question the propriety of reaching a conclusion on the constitutionality of the doctrine.... Furthermore, ... we believed that the resolution of the constitutional issues was better left to Congress and the courts.... Consequently, our analysis in the *1985 Fairness Report* focused on a policy perspective so as not to run afoul of these concerns. We believe, however, as we reiterate today, that our analysis of the fairness doctrine in 1985 was in fact informed and driven by First Amendment principles, and with the uncertainty of the doctrine's codification removed and the *Meredith* court's directive to consider the constitutional issues, we believe that it is now incumbent upon us to consider the doctrine in terms of the inextricable constitutional issues on which the policy rests.

editorial decisions of broadcast journalists concerning the broadcast of controversial issues of public importance. Because the case before us is a product of the fairness doctrine itself, and because it raises important policy and constitutional issues common to all fairness doctrine litigation, we do not believe that the resolution of this proceeding turns on any specific facts that are unique to this adjudication.

33. Nor do we believe that it would be appropriate, in passing on the constitutional and policy issues raised by our enforcement of the fairness doctrine, to limit our consideration of such issues to the one part of the fairness doctrine that we determined had been violated in this case. The fairness doctrine, although consisting of two parts, is a unified doctrine; without both parts, the doctrine loses its identity. . . . Consequently, if the constitutional infirmity of the doctrine arises from the enforcement of one of its parts, we do not believe it appropriate to sever that part of the doctrine and to continue enforcing only the other part. . . .

Constitutional Considerations Under Red Lion

36. . . . [T]he extraordinary technological advances that have been made in the electronic media since the 1969 *Red Lion* [*Broadcasting v. FCC*] decision, together with a consideration of fundamental First Amendment principles, provide an ample basis for the Supreme Court to reconsider the premise or approach of its decision in *Red Lion*. Nevertheless, while we believe that the Court, after reexamining the issue, may well be persuaded that the transformation in the communications marketplace justifies alteration of the *Red Lion* approach to broadcast regulation, we recognize that to date the Court has determined that governmental regulation of broadcast speech is subject to a standard of review under the First Amendment that is more lenient than the standard generally applicable to the print media. Until the Supreme Court reevaluates that determination, therefore, we shall evaluate the constitutionality of the fairness doctrine under the standard enunciated in *Red Lion* and its progeny.[2]

Red Lion Broadcasting Co. v. FCC

37. Eighteen years ago, the Supreme Court, in *Red Lion Broadcasting*

---

[2] Some commenters, however, contend that the fact that the Supreme Court in *Red Lion* determined that the fairness doctrine was constitutional almost two decades ago mandates a finding by this Commission that the doctrine is constitutional today. We disagree. If this were so, the Court of Appeals would not have remanded this case for us to consider Meredith's constitutional arguments, because our initial failure to consider them would not have been reversible error. Indeed, for the reasons set forth below, we believe the rationale employed by the Court in *Red Lion* compels the conclusion that the fairness doctrine contravenes the First Amendment today, when evaluated consistent with the principles of *Red Lion*. Furthermore, the relationship between the application of constitutional principles in this area and the advances in technology are such, as the Supreme Court has indicated, that it is necessary to review past decisions to ensure their consistency with current technology.

Co. v. FCC, upheld the constitutionality of the fairness doctrine because it believed, at that time, that the doctrine promoted "the paramount [F]irst [A]mendment rights of viewers and listeners to receive 'suitable access to . . . ideas and experiences.' " In that decision, the Court clearly articulated a First Amendment standard for evaluating broadcast regulation which provided less protection to the speech of broadcast journalists than that accorded to journalists in other media. The Court held that, "[i]n view of the scarcity of broadcasting frequencies, the Government's role in allocating those frequencies, and the legitimate claims of those unable without government assistance to gain access to those frequencies for expression of their views," the government could require persons who were granted a license to operate "as a proxy or fiduciary with obligations to present those views and voices which are representative of his community." The Court thus described what it subsequently characterized as "an unusual order of First Amendment values;" it determined that governmental restrictions on the speech of broadcasters could be justified if they furthered the interests of listeners and viewers. . . .

The Court in *Red Lion* expressly stated that it would reconsider its holding "if experience with the administration of [the fairness doctrine] indicates that [it] ha[s] the net effect of reducing rather than enhancing the volume and quality of coverage [of controversial issues of public importance]." . . .

Application of the Red Lion Standard

Chilling Effect of the Doctrine

42. In the *1985 Fairness Report,* the Commission evaluated the efficacy of the fairness doctrine in achieving its regulatory objective. Based upon the compelling evidence of record, the Commission determined that the fairness doctrine, in operation, thwarts the purpose that it is designed to promote. Instead of enhancing the discussion of controversial issues of public importance, the Commission found that the fairness doctrine, in operation, "chills" speech.

43. The Commission documented that the fairness doctrine provides broadcasters with a powerful incentive not to air controversial issue programming above that minimal amount required by the first part of the doctrine. Each time a broadcaster presents what may be construed as a controversial issue of public importance, it runs the risk of a complaint being filed, resulting in litigation and penalties, including loss of license. This risk still exists even if a broadcaster has met its obligations by airing contrasting viewpoints, because the process necessarily involves a vague standard, the application and meaning of which is hard to predict. Therefore, by limiting the amount of controversial issue programming to that required by the first prong (*i.e.*, its obligation to cover controversial issues of vital importance to the community), a licensee is able to lessen the substantial burdens associated with the second prong of the doctrine (*i.e.*,

its obligation to present contrasting viewpoints) while conforming to the strict letter of its regulatory obligations. The licensee, consistent with its fairness doctrine obligations, may forego coverage of other issues that, although important, do not rise to the level of being vital.

44. As the Commission demonstrated, the incentives involved in limiting the amount of controversial issue programming are substantial. A broadcaster may seek to lessen the possibility that an opponent may challenge the method in which it provided "balance" in a renewal proceeding. If it provides one side of a controversial issue, it may wish to avoid either a formal Commission determination that it violated agency policy or the financial costs of providing responsive programming. More important, however, even if it intends to or believes that it has presented balanced coverage of a controversial issue, it may be inhibited by the expenses of being second-guessed by the government in defending a fairness doctrine complaint at the Commission, and if the case is litigated in court, the costs of an appeal. Further, in view of its dependence upon the goodwill of its audience, a licensee may seek to avoid the possible tarnish to its reputation that even an allegation that it violated the governmental policy of "balanced" programming could entail.

45. Furthermore, the Commission determined that the doctrine inherently provides incentives that are more favorable to the expression of orthodox and well-established opinion with respect to controversial issues than to less established viewpoints. The Commission pointed out that a number of broadcasters who were denied or threatened with the denial of renewal of their licenses on fairness grounds had provided controversial issue programming far in excess of the typical broadcaster. Yet these broadcasters espoused provocative opinions that many found to be abhorrent and extreme, thereby increasing the probability that these broadcasters would be subject to fairness doctrine challenges. The Commission consequently expressed concern that the doctrine, in operation, may have penalized or impeded the expression of unorthodox or unpopular opinion, depriving the public of debates on issues of public opinion that are "uninhibited, robust, and wide-open." The doctrine's encouragement to cover only major or significant viewpoints, with which much of the public will be familiar, inhibits First Amendment goals of ensuring that the public has access to innovative and less popular viewpoints. . . .

47. The Commission demonstrated in the *1985 Fairness Report* that broadcasters—from network television anchors to those in the smallest radio stations—recounted that the fear of governmental sanction resulting from the doctrine creates a climate of timidity and fear, which deters the coverage of controversial issue programming. The record contained numerous instances in which the broadcasters decided that it was "safer" to avoid broadcasting specific controversial issue programming, such as series prepared for local news programs, than to incur the potentially burdensome administrative, legal, personnel, and reputational costs of either complying with the doctrine or defending

their editorial decisions to governmental authorities....

48. The record in the fairness inquiry demonstrated that this self-censorship is not limited to individual programs. In order to avoid fairness doctrine burdens, the Commission found that stations have adopted company "policies" which have the direct effect of diminishing the amount of controversial material that is presented to the public on broadcast stations. For example, some stations refuse to present editorials; other stations will not accept political advertisements; still others decline to air public issue (or editorial) advertising; and others have policies to decline acceptance of nationally produced programming that discusses controversial subjects or to have their news staffs avoid controversial issues as a matter of routine. The Commission concluded, therefore, that the doctrine "inhibits the presentation of controversial issues of public importance to the detriment of the public and in degradation of the editorial prerogatives of broadcast journalists."...

The Extent and Necessity of Government Intervention into Editorial Discretion

52. ... The Commission found that the enforcement of the doctrine requires the "minute and subjective scrutiny of program content," which perilously treads upon the editorial prerogatives of broadcast journalists. The Commission further found that in administering the doctrine it is forced to undertake the dangerous task of evaluating particular viewpoints. The fairness doctrine thus indisputably represents an intrusion into a broadcaster's editorial discretion, both in its enforcement and in the threat of enforcement. It requires the government to second-guess broadcasters' judgment on the issues they cover, as well as on the manner and balance of coverage....

54. In addition, the Commission expressed concern that the fairness doctrine provides a dangerous vehicle—which had been exercised in the past by unscrupulous officials—for the intimidation of broadcasters who criticize governmental policy. It concluded that the inherently subjective evaluation of program content by the Commission in administering the doctrine contravenes fundamental First Amendment principles. We reaffirm these determinations and find that enforcement of the fairness doctrine necessarily injects the government into the editorial process of broadcast journalists.

55. In further analyzing whether the fairness doctrine is narrowly tailored to achieve a substantial government interest, we look again to our evaluation in the *1985 Fairness Report* of whether this type of government regulation is in fact necessary to ensure the availability of diverse sources of information and viewpoints to the public. In that *Report,* the Commission undertook a comprehensive review of the information outlets currently available to the public. This review ... revealed an explosive growth in both the number and types of such outlets in every market since the 1969 *Red Lion* decision. And this trend has continued unabated since 1985.

For example, 96% of the public now has access to five or more television stations. Currently, listeners in the top 25 markets have access to an average of 59 radio stations, while those in even the smallest markets have access to an average of six radio stations. In contrast to that, only 125 cities have two or more daily newspapers published locally. Nationwide, there are 1,315 television and 10,128 radio stations, while recent evidence indicates that there are 1,657 daily newspapers. The number of television stations represents a 54% increase since the *Red Lion* decision, while the number of radio stations represents a 57% increase. Not only has the number of television and radio stations increased the public's access to a multiplicity of media outlets since 1969, but the advent and increased availability of such other technologies as cable and satellite television services have dramatically enhanced that access. As a result of its 1985 review, the Commission determined that "the interest of the public in viewpoint diversity is fully served by the multiplicity of voices in the marketplace today" and that the growth in both radio and television broadcasting alone provided "a reasonable assurance that a sufficient diversity of opinion on controversial issues of public importance [would] be provided in each broadcast market." It concluded, therefore, and we continue to believe, that government regulation such as the fairness doctrine is not necessary to ensure that the public has access to the marketplace of ideas. . . .

Conclusion

. . . 61. In sum, the fairness doctrine in operation disserves both the public's right to diverse sources of information and the broadcaster's interest in free expression. Its chilling effect thwarts its intended purpose, and it results in excessive and unnecessary government intervention into the editorial processes of broadcast journalists. We hold, therefore, that under the constitutional standard established by *Red Lion* and its progeny, the fairness doctrine contravenes the First Amendment and its enforcement is no longer in the public interest.

Preferred Constitutional Approach

62. Our review of the Supreme Court precedent in the application of First Amendment principles to the electronic media leads to an inescapable conclusion: throughout the development of these principles, the Supreme Court has repeatedly emphasized that its constitutional determinations in this area of the law are closely related to the technological changes in the telecommunications marketplace. For example, in the *Red Lion* decision itself, the Court indicated that advances in technology could have an effect on its analysis of the constitutional principles applicable to the electronic media. . . .

63. The Court's most recent statement on this issue came in its decision in *FCC v. League of Women Voters of California*. Acknowledging that certain persons, including former Chairman Mark Fowler, "charge that

with the advent of cable and satellite television technology, communities now have access to such a wide variety of stations that the scarcity doctrine is obsolete," the Court indicated that it may be willing to reassess its traditional reliance upon spectrum scarcity upon a "signal" from the Congress or this Commission "that technological developments have advanced so far that some revision of the system of broadcast regulation may be required." ...

72. We believe that the dramatic changes in the electronic media, together with the unacceptable chilling effect resulting from the implementation of such regulations as the fairness doctrine, form a compelling and convincing basis on which to reconsider First Amendment principles that were developed for another market. Today's telecommunications market offers individuals a plethora of information outlets to which they have access on a daily basis. Indeed, this market is strikingly different from even that offered by the daily print media. While there are 11,443 broadcast stations nationwide, recent evidence indicates that there are only 1,657 daily newspapers overall. On a local level, 96% of the public has access to five or more television stations, while only 125 cities have two or more local newspapers. The one-newspaper town is becoming an increasing phenomenon. Our review of the Supreme Court's statements on the relationship between constitutional principles and technological developments leads us to conclude that it would now be appropriate for the Supreme Court to reassess its *Red Lion* decision....

The Scarcity Rationale

... 75. Because there is no longer a scarcity in the number of broadcast outlets, proponents of a scarcity rationale for the justification of diminished First Amendment rights applicable to the broadcast medium must rely on the concept of spectrum (or allocational) scarcity. This concept is based upon the physical limitations of the electromagnetic spectrum. Because only a limited number of persons can utilize broadcast frequencies at any particular point in time, spectrum scarcity is said to be present when the number of persons desiring to disseminate information on broadcast frequencies exceeds the number of available frequencies. Consequently, these frequencies, like all scarce resources, must be allocated among those who wish to use them.

76. In fact, spectrum scarcity was one of the bases articulated by the Court in *Red Lion* for the disparate treatment of the broadcast and the print media. Reliance on spectrum scarcity, however, "has come under increasing criticism in recent years." For example, the Court of Appeals has recently questioned the rationality of spectrum scarcity as the basis for differentiating between the print and broadcast media....

82. ... As Judge [Robert] Bork stated in *TRAC v. FCC,* "Since scarcity is a universal fact, it can hardly explain regulation in one context and not another. The attempt to use a universal fact as a distinguishing principle necessarily leads to analytical confusion." Consequently, we believe that

an evaluation of First Amendment standards should not focus on the *physical differences* between the electronic press and the printed press, but on the *functional similarities* between these two media and upon the underlying values and goals of the First Amendment. We believe that the function of the electronic press in a free society is identical to that of the printed press and that, therefore, the constitutional analysis of government control of content should be no different. . . .

First Amendment Standard Applicable to the Press

95. Under a traditional First Amendment analysis, the type of governmental intrusion inherent in the fairness doctrine would not be tolerated if it were applied to the print media. Indeed, in *Miami Herald Publishing Co. v. Tornillo,* the Supreme Court struck down, on First Amendment grounds, a Florida statute that compelled a newspaper to print the response of a political candidate that it had criticized. . . .

97. We believe that the role of electronic press in our society is the same as that of the printed press. Both are sources of information and viewpoint. Accordingly, the reasons for proscribing government intrusion into the editorial discretion of print journalists provide the same basis for proscribing such interference into the editorial discretion of broadcast journalists. The First Amendment was adopted to protect the people *not from journalists, but from government.* It gives the people the right to receive ideas that are unfettered by government interference. We fail to see how that right changes when individuals choose to receive ideas from the electronic media instead of the print media. There is no doubt that the electronic media is powerful and that broadcasters can abuse their freedom of speech. But the framers of the Constitution believed that the potential for abuse of private freedoms posed far less a threat to democracy than the potential for abuse by a government given the power to control the press. We concur. We therefore believe that First Amendment protections against content regulation should apply equally to the electronic and the printed press.

IV. Conclusion

98. The court in *Meredith Corp. v. FCC* "remand[ed] the case to the FCC with instructions to consider [Meredith's] constitutional arguments." In response to the court's directive, we find that the fairness doctrine chills speech and is not narrowly tailored to achieve a substantial government interest. We therefore conclude, under existing Supreme Court precedent, as set forth in *Red Lion* and its progeny, that the fairness doctrine contravenes the First Amendment and thereby disserves the public interest. We have reached these determinations only after the most careful and searching deliberation. We believe, however, that the evidence presented in the recent fairness inquiry and the record in this proceeding leads inescapably to these conclusions. Each member of this Commission has taken an oath to support and defend the United States Constitution

and, as the court in *Meredith v. FCC* stated, "to enforce a Commission-generated policy that the Commission itself believes is unconstitutional may well constitute a violation of that oath." As a consequence, we determine that the editorial decision of station WTVH to broadcast the editorial advertisements at issue in this adjudication is an action protected by the First Amendment from government interference. Accordingly, we reconsider our prior determinations in this matter and conclude that the Constitution bars us from enforcing the fairness doctrine against station WTVH.

99. We further believe, as the Supreme Court indicated in *FCC v. League of Women Voters of California,* that the dramatic transformation in the telecommunications marketplace provides a basis for the Court to reconsider its application of diminished First Amendment protection to the electronic media. Despite the physical differences between the electronic and print media, their roles in our society are identical, and we believe that the same First Amendment principles should be equally applicable to both. This is the method set forth in our Constitution for maximizing the public interest; and furthering the public interest is likewise our mandate under the Communications Act. It is, therefore, to advance the public interest that we advocate these rights for broadcasters. . . .

CENTRAL AMERICAN PEACE AGREEMENT

August 7, 1987

On August 7 the presidents of Costa Rica, Nicaragua, Honduras, El Salvador, and Guatemala met in Guatemala City to sign a comprehensive peace plan proposed by Costa Rican president Oscar Arias Sánchez. The announcement in October 1987 that Arias had won the Nobel Peace Prize added significantly to his prestige and that of the plan. Whether the agreement could actually bring "a stable and lasting peace" to the region, however, remained a question. (Arias Nobel Peace Prize, p. 1007)

The Arias plan set up goals for each signatory: domestic reconciliation; democratization; free elections; and the cessation of hostilities, of aid to insurgent movements, and of use of territory to attack other states. The plan called for simultaneous "commitments" to begin ninety days after the document was signed and an analysis of progress by an international committee thirty days after that. A month later the five presidents would meet again and "make pertinent decisions" based on the verification committee's report.

The ambitious agreement represented the first defined by Central American governments themselves. The troubled region traditionally had been overshadowed by larger powers, particularly the United States. The primary focus of the plan was Nicaragua, but compliance entailed substantial difficulties for all five countries, each saddled with its own particular social, economic, political, and military problems.

Contadora and the Wright Plan

The earliest multinational effort to come to terms with Central

American problems was initiated by the Contadora Group—Mexico, Panama, Colombia, and Venezuela—later joined by the Support Group countries—Brazil, Uruguay, Argentina, and Peru. Purposely remaining a Latin effort, the Contadora Group proposed several documents to the five Central American countries between 1983 and 1986. None was ever signed, largely because of the differences between Nicaragua on the one hand and U.S. allies Honduras and El Salvador on the other.

Just before the Guatemala City meeting, the Reagan administration and Speaker of the U.S. House of Representatives Jim Wright, D-Texas, outlined a peace proposal. This bipartisan effort seemed to add resolve to the Central Americans' work. When the Arias plan was signed a few days later, Wright dropped his own plan in favor of Arias's. Democrats in the U.S. Congress continued to follow Wright's lead and focus their attention on the progress made since August, thus thwarting President Ronald Reagan's hopes to continue funding the contras.

Costa Rica

Since its 1948 civil war, Costa Rica had been a pluralistic democracy with no armed services, yet its proximity to Nicaragua inevitably drew it into the latter's conflicts. Before the 1979 ouster of Nicaraguan president Anastasio Somoza, Costa Rica had been an important transshipment base for Cuban arms for the Sandinistas and had sheltered other Nicaraguans opposed to Somoza's regime. As the Sandinistas' Marxist tendencies became more apparent, Costa Rican support for the Sandinistas gradually eroded. But mistrust of the Sandinistas did not always translate into broad support for the contras. Rather, Costa Ricans tended to back certain individuals such as Edén Pastora (Commandante Zero), Alfonso Robelo, and Alfredo César, all of whom were once part of the Sandinista cause but later joined contra organizations.

In spite of Costa Rica's relatively high standard of living, it remained one of the most heavily indebted countries per capita in the world. Thus it was particularly vulnerable to U.S. economic pressure. By 1984, when the contra movement was operating out of Honduras, Pastora and Robelo's forces were permitted to establish bases in northern Costa Rica along the Nicaraguan border. Adding to Costa Rica's concerns in 1987 was the presence of more than 100,000 Nicaraguan refugees.

Guatemala

Separated geographically from involvement with the Nicaraguan conflict, Guatemala portrayed itself as "neutral," although the country's military governments traditionally had been anticommunist. Cut off from U.S. aid during the Carter administration because of human rights abuses, Guatemala's military focused on eradication of the insurgency in the countryside. Brutal and efficient, their efforts were largely successful. Despite receiving aid from Cuba and the Sandinistas, the guerrillas had been capable of only sporadic raids since the early 1980s.

Following a series of military coups, the first open elections in a generation were held in late 1985. Christian Democrat Vinicio Cerezo Arévalo came to office with a plan for a Central American parliament and called for a meeting of the five Central American presidents at Esquipulas in mid-1986. Arias's initiative built upon the groundwork laid at Esquipulas.

In compliance with the Arias plan, the first direct discussions between the Guatemalan government and insurgent leaders took place in Madrid in September 1987. Although the talks were unproductive, they marked Cerezo's progress in curbing the power of the Guatemalan military, which had always opposed negotiations. (Historic Documents of 1986, p. 104)

Honduras

Although civilian government had been restored in 1981, political power in Honduras had long been in the hands of a conservative military establishment. The country was relatively free of internal insurrection, but guerrilla wars in El Salvador and Nicaragua left Honduras with thousands of refugees on its borders. A staunch ally of the United States, Honduras served as a base for U.S. operations in both conflicts.

With the overthrow of Somoza in 1979, many Somoza supporters and national guardsmen fled to Honduras. Within a year sporadic raids against Nicaraguan installations had begun, supported by Argentina. In 1981 President Reagan authorized the Central Intelligence Agency to organize and train these groups, later known collectively as the contras. By 1983 they were formally organized with Adolfo Calero and Enrique Bermúdez as their leaders.

Given the importance of U.S. aid and influence in Honduras and the anticommunist views of the military and government, it was not surprising that southern Honduras became a base for contra operations. The region had also sheltered César Sandino during the late 1920s and many of the Sandinistas during the 1960s and 1970s. As U.S. involvement with the contras grew, American military facilities began to sprout up in Honduras. Tegucigalpa consistently denied the contras were in Honduras, but at times as many as 10,000 were located at bases there.

The Arias plan's reference to the "non-use of territory to attack other states," clearly directed at Honduras, was put in the agreement to help bring Nicaragua to the table. Compliance with this provision would be difficult, however, because Honduras did not control its southern border. President José Azcona Hoyo feared that if the United States halted all aid to the contra movement an estimated 10,000 contra fighters could be forced back into Honduran territory. The Honduran military would find it difficult to contain such a well-armed and politicized force and to avoid a war with the sizable Nicaraguan army. Honduras was, however, protected by the Rio Pact, whereby American forces could be called in if needed.

El Salvador

The origins of the Salvadoran civil war lay in the historic domination of the country's wealth and political power by the "fourteen families." A peasant uprising in 1932 called "the Matanza" or Massacre—in which an estimated 30,000 were killed within the space of a few weeks—remained a brutal reminder of the Salvadoran military response toward organized agitation. The country's conservative military and landowning families retained great power despite a popularly elected government.

In the early 1970s a group of Salvadoran moderate and leftist political leaders joined the revolutionary organizations that later formed the Farabundo Marti Liberation Front (FMLN) under the guidance of Cuba's Fidel Castro. After the Sandinistas triumphed in July 1979, they furnished military equipment to the FMLN, and the Salvadoran civil war began in earnest, with the United States providing military assistance to the Salvadoran government. The early years of the civil war were marked by hundreds of "death squad" murders by members of the Salvadoran military and their right-wing supporters. Death squad activity declined in the mid-1980s.

José Napoleon Duarte, a civilian elected president in 1983, had only limited success in controlling the country's powerful military leaders, who opposed all efforts at reconciliation with the FMLN. Since 1984 Duarte had tried to discuss with FMLN leaders ways to resolve the civil conflict. Talks were held after the Arias agreement was signed, but the rebels broke off the talks following the murder of a human rights activist. An amnesty for political crimes was proposed by Duarte and approved by the National Assembly, liberating death squad participants as well as nearly 1,000 leftist activists. The Arias plan seemed unlikely to lead El Salvador toward reconciliation, partly because the rebels were far from unified themselves. The unarmed political exiles' group, although allied with the FMLN, contained many moderates who might be willing to accept a compromise unacceptable to the FMLN.

In many ways, El Salvador and Nicaragua mirrored the Cental American conflict, with the government of each offering assistance to the rebels trying to overthrow the other. (Historic Documents of 1986, p. 103)

Nicaragua

For fifty years Nicaragua was dominated by the Somoza family, which was supported by the United States. The true base of the Somozas' power was the national guard, set up in the 1920s by the U.S. Marines. Largely to counter the Marines, César Sandino raised a peasant army against the regime. Sandino was assassinated by Somoza henchmen in 1934.

Founded in the early 1960s by Tomás Borge and others, the FSLN (Sandinista National Liberation Front) was little more than a nuisance to the national guard until the mid-1970s. The movement picked up adherents after the 1972 earthquake in Managua, when President "Tacho" Somoza pocketed most of the relief aid. The FSLN carried out a few spectacular actions, such as Edén Pastora's raid on the National Congress. Although there had already been a number of national strikes, the murder of La Prensa *editor Pedro Joaquín Chamorro in 1978 galvanized widespread opposition to Somoza. As the government began to dissolve, a number of opposition leaders formed alliances with the Sandinistas, whose organization and ideology were still largely unknown. With the national guard disintegrating, and the Carter administration pressuring him, Somoza fled in 1979.*

The defeat of Somoza was hailed as a national victory, but those who did not belong to the Sandinistas were forced out or resigned from the government. In the two years after the revolution, the United States voted Nicaragua more than $160 million in aid. Donations from Western Europe poured into the country as well. It was not until Ronald Reagan became president, and the Marxist leanings of the Sandinista regime became clear, that U.S. policy changed to one of active hostility, a policy opposed by many sectors within the United States. Cuba and the Soviet Union provided extensive military aid to the Nicaraguan government.

The Sandinistas' need for a 70,000-member army—not counting reserves—was debated: was the army's main purpose to fight the contras, ensure control over population centers, or take over new territory? A similar debate revolved around the Nicaraguan state of emergency that had suspended many constitutional rights since 1982. Arias said the contras provided the Sandinistas with justification for these measures. Internal opposition to the Sandinistas remained significant, partly because of Nicaragua's acute economic difficulties.

The Sandinistas' most prominent opponent was Managua's cardinal Miguel Obando y Bravo, who also had been a forceful critic of Somoza. Although the Sandinistas appeared to moderate their opposition to the church in the late 1980s, many of Nicaragua's faithful were the regime's strongest opponents. Although other adversaries were from the country's middle class, which suffered from Managua's central planning directives, the bulk of the contra fighters were peasants. (Historic Documents of 1985, pp. 153 and 255; Historic Documents of 1986, p. 107)

The Arias plan's calls for reconciliation, democratization, free elections, and free media were a direct challenge to the Sandinistas' authority. But Nicaraguan leaders—especially President Daniel Ortega Saavedra and his brother Humberto, the defense minister—were pragmatists and skilled political players. They followed the debate in the United States closely and recognized Congress's reluctance to fund the contras;

they also knew that implementation of the peace agreement would prevent an outright U.S. invasion.

After signing the Arias plan in August, the Sandinistas made a number of gestures toward compliance with the plan: allowing La Prensa *to publish, initiating limited cease-fires, appointing Cardinal Obando y Bravo to head the Nicaraguan Reconciliation Committee, and asking him to serve as intermediary for indirect talks with the contra leadership. Nicaragua's concessions were seen by some as merely cosmetic gestures.*

Late in 1987 the prospects for the contras' reintegration into a Sandinista-controlled Nicaragua—essentially what the Arias plan called for—seemed remote. But then, few thought that the plan could accomplish as much as it already had.

Following is the text of the Central American peace agreement signed by five governments in Guatemala City, Guatemala, August 7, 1987:

Voices calling out and hopeful
winds seeking a joyous peace for all.
Arturo Echeverría Loria

Preamble

The Presidents of the Republics of Guatemala, El Salvador, Honduras, Nicaragua, and Costa Rica, meeting in Guatemala City on August 6 and 7, 1987, encouraged by the vision and continuing desire of Contadora and the Support Group in favor of peace, strengthened by the constant support of all the governments and peoples of the world, their principal international organizations and, especially by the European Economic Community and His Holiness John Paul II, inspired by Esquipulas I, and having gathered together in Guatemala in order to discuss the peace plan presented by the Government of Costa Rica, have agreed to:

- Assume fully the historic challenge to forge a destiny of peace for Central America,
- Undertake to fight for peace and eliminate war,
- Make dialogue prevail over violence, and reason over rancor,
- Dedicate these peace efforts to the youth of Central America, whose legitimate aspirations for peace and social justice, for freedom and reconciliation, have been frustrated for many generations.
- Establish the Central American Parliament as a symbol of freedom and independence of the reconciliation to which we in Central America aspire.

We ask for the respect and assistance of the international community in our efforts. Central America has its own pathways to peace and development, but we need help to make them a reality. We ask for an international agreement that would ensure development so that the peace we seek may be a lasting one. We firmly reiterate that peace and development are inseparable.

We express our appreciation to President Vinicio Cerezo Arévalo and to the noble people of Guatemala for having served as the host for this meeting. The generosity of the Guatemalan people and their leader has been vital in creating the climate in which the peace agreements were adopted.

Procedure for Establishing a Stable and Lasting Peace in Central America

The Governments of the Republics of Costa Rica, El Salvador, Guatemala, Honduras, and Nicaragua, having undertaken to achieve the objectives and develop the principles established in the United Nations Charter, the Charter of the Organization of American States, the Document of Objectives, the Caraballeda Message for Peace, Security, and Democracy in Central America, the Guatemala Declaration, the Punta del Este Communiqué, the Panama Message, the Esquipulas Declaration, and the draft Contadora Act for Peace and Cooperation in Central America of June 6, 1986, have agreed upon the following procedure for establishing a stable and lasting peace in Central America.

1. National reconciliation

(a) Dialogue. To carry out urgently, in those cases in which deep divisions have occurred within a society, actions of national reconciliation to allow the people to participate, with full guaranties, in authentic political processes of a democratic nature, on the basis of justice, freedom, and democracy and, for that purpose, to establish mechanisms for dialogue with opposition groups, in accordance with the law.

To that end, the respective Governments shall initiate dialogue with all domestic political opposition groups that have laid down their arms and with those that have accepted the Amnesty.

(b) Amnesty. In each Central American country, except in those where the International Evaluation and Follow-up Committee determines that it is not necessary, decrees of amnesty shall be issued which shall establish all the provisions to guarantee the inviolability of life, freedom in all its forms, property, and the security of the persons to whom such decrees apply. Simultaneously with the issue of the amnesty decrees, the irregular forces in the respective country shall release any persons they may be holding.

(c) National Reconciliation Committee. In order to verify the fulfillment of the commitments undertaken by the five Central American Governments upon signing this document, with regard to amnesty, ceasefire, democratization, and free elections, a National Reconciliation Committee shall be created. Its function shall be to determine whether the process of national reconciliation is actually underway, and whether there is absolute respect for all the civil and political rights of Central American citizens guaranteed herein.

The National Reconciliation Committee shall be composed of one regular delegate and one alternate from the Executive Branch, and one regular member and one alternate suggested by the Episcopal Conference and selected by the Government from a slate of three Bishops to be submitted within fifteen days of receipt of the formal invitation. This invitation shall be extended by the governments within five working days of the signing of this document. The same nomination procedure shall be used to select one regular member and one alternate from the legally-registered opposition political parties. The three-person slate shall be submitted in the same time period as mentioned above. Each Central American Government shall also select to serve on the committee one outstanding citizen who is not part of the government and does not belong to the government party, as well as one alternate. Copies of the agreements or decrees creating each National Committee shall be transmitted immediately to the other Central American governments.

2. Urging a cessation of hostilities

The governments vehemently urge that a cessation of hostilities be arranged in those States in the area presently experiencing the action of irregular or insurgent groups. The governments of such States undertake to carry out all actions necessary to achieve an effective ceasefire within a constitutional framework.

3. Democratization

The governments undertake to provide the impetus for an authentic democratic process, both pluralistic and participatory, which entails the promotion of social justice, respect for human rights, sovereignty, territorial integrity of the States, and the right of all nations to choose, freely and without any outside interference whatsoever, their economic, political, and social system. Furthermore, the governments shall adopt in a verifiable manner measures conducive to the establishment and, where appropriate, improvement of democratic, representative, and pluralistic systems that will guarantee the organization of political parties and effective participation by the people in the decision-making process and ensure that the various currents of opinion have free access to fair and regular elections based on the full observance of citizens' rights. To ensure good faith in the development of this process of democratization, it shall be understood that:

(a) There must be complete freedom for television, radio, and the press which shall encompass the freedom for all ideological groups to open and maintain in operation communications media, and the freedom to operate such media without prior censorship.

(b) There shall be complete pluralism of political parties. In this respect, political groups shall have broad access to the communications media and full enjoyment of the rights of association and the ability to hold public demonstrations in the unrestricted exercise of the right to publicize their ideas orally, in writing, and on television, as well as freedom of mobility for the members of the political parties in their campaign activities.

(c) Similarly, the Central American Governments which are maintaining in effect a state of siege or emergency shall abolish it and bring about the rule of law in which all constitutional guarantees are in effect.

4. Free elections

Once the conditions inherent in any democracy have been created, free, pluralistic, and fair elections shall be held.

As a joint gesture of the Central American States toward reconciliation and lasting peace for their peoples, elections shall be held for the Central American Parliament, which was proposed in the Esquipulas Declaration of May 25, 1986.

To that end, the Presidents have expressed their wish to move forward with the organization of the Parliament. The Preparatory Committee of the Central American Parliament shall therefore conclude its deliberations and deliver the respective draft treaty to the Central American Presidents within 150 days.

These elections shall be held simultaneously in all the countries of Central America during the first six months of 1988 on a date to be agreed upon in due course by the Presidents of these States. They shall be subject to monitoring by the appropriate electoral bodies, and the respective governments agree to extend an invitation to the Organization of American States and to the United Nations, as well as to governments of third States, to send observers to attest to the fact that the electoral procedures have been governed by the strictest rules of equal access for all political parties to the communications media, as well as extensive opportunities for holding public demonstrations and engaging in any other type of campaign propaganda.

In order that the elections for membership in the Central American Parliament may be held within the time period indicated in this section, the treaty establishing that body shall be submitted for approval or ratification in the five countries.

As soon as elections for membership in the Central American Parliament have been held, equally free and democratic elections shall be held in each country, with international observers and the same guarantees and within the established intervals and the timetables to be proposed under the present political constitutions, to select the people's representatives in the municipalities, congresses and legislative assemblies, as well as the Presidents of the Republics.

5. Cessation of aid to irregular forces and insurgent movements

The Governments of the five Central American States shall request governments in the region or those outside it that are providing, either overtly or covertly, military, logistic, financial or propagandistic aid, or assistance in the form of troops, weapons, munitions and equipment to irregular forces or insurgent movements to cease such aid, as an essential requirement for achieving a stable and lasting peace in the region.

The foregoing does not include assistance used for repatriation, or, if that does not occur, relocation, and assistance needed to accomplish the reintegration into normal life of those persons who have belonged to the above-mentioned groups or forces. Similarly, the irregular forces and insurgent groups active in Central America shall be asked to refrain from receiving such aid for the sake of a genuine Latin Americanist spirit. These requests shall be made in fulfillment of the provisions of the Document of Objectives as regards elimination of the traffic in weapons within the region or from outside sources to persons, organizations, or groups attempting to destabilize the Central American Governments.

6. Non-use of territory to attack other States

The five countries signing this document reiterate their commitment to prevent the use of their own territory and to neither furnish nor allow logistical military support for persons, organizations, or groups seeking to destabilize the Governments of the Central American countries.

7. Negotiations on security, verification, control, and limitation of weapons

The Governments of the five Central American States, with participation by the Contadora Group in the exercise of its function as mediator, shall proceed with negotiations on the points on which agreement is pending in matters of security, verification, and control under the draft Contadora Act for Peace and Cooperation in Central America.

These negotiations shall also cover measures for the disarmament of those irregular forces that are willing to accept the amnesty decrees.

8. Refugees and displaced persons

The Central American Governments undertake to address, with a sense of urgency, [the problem of] the flow of refugees and displaced persons caused by the regional crisis, by means of protection and assistance, especially with regard to health, education, employment, and security and, furthermore, to facilitate their repatriation, resettlement, or relocation, provided that it is of a voluntary nature and takes the form of individual cases.

They also undertake to arrange for aid from the international community for the Central American refugees and displaced persons, whether such assistance is direct under bilateral or multilateral agreements or obtained through the United Nations High Commissioner for Refugees

(UNHCR) or other organizations and agencies.

9. Cooperation, democracy, and freedom for peace and development

In the climate of freedom guaranteed by democracy, the Central American countries shall adopt such agreements as will permit them to accelerate their development in order to achieve societies that are more egalitarian and free from misery.

The consolidation of democracy entails the creation of an economy of well-being and economic and social democracy. In order to attain those objectives the governments shall jointly seek special economic assistance from the international community.

10. International verification and follow-up

(a) International Verification and Follow-up Committee. An International Verification and Follow-up Committee shall be created, composed of the Secretaries General of the Organization of American States and the United Nations, or their representatives, as well as by the foreign ministers of Central America, the Contadora Group, and the Support Group. The functions of this committee shall be to verify and follow-up on the fulfillment of the commitments contained herein.

(b) Support and facilities for the mechanisms of reconciliation and of verification and follow-up. In order to reinforce the efforts of the International Verification and Follow-up Committee, the Governments of the five Central American states shall issue statements of support for its work. All nations interested in promoting the cause of freedom, democracy, and peace in Central America may adhere to these statements.

The five governments shall provide all necessary facilities for the proper conduct of the verification and follow-up functions of the National Reconciliation Committee in each country, and of the International Verification and Follow-up Committee.

11. Timetable for implementing the commitments

Within 15 days of the signing of this document, the Central American foreign ministers shall meet as an Executive Committee to regulate and promote the agreements contained herein and to make their application feasible. They shall also organize the working committees so that, as from this date, the processes leading to the fulfillment of the commitments entered into within the intervals stipulated may begin through consultations, negotiations, and any other mechanisms deemed necessary.

When 90 days have elapsed from the date of the signature of this document, the commitments with regard to amnesty, ceasefire, democratization, cessation of aid to irregular forces or insurgent movements, and the non-use of territory to attack other States, as defined in this document, shall simultaneously begin to govern publicly.

When 120 days have elapsed from the date of the signature of this document, the International Verification and Follow-up Committee shall analyze the progress made in the fulfillment of the agreements provided for herein.

When 150 days have elapsed, the five Central American Presidents shall meet and receive a report from the International Verification and Follow-up Committee and shall make pertinent decisions.

Final Provisions

The points included in this document form a harmonious and indivisible whole. Signing it entails the obligation, accepted in good faith, to comply simultaneously and within the established time limits with the provisions agreed upon.

The Presidents of the five Central American States, with the political will to respond to our peoples' yearnings for Peace, hereby sign this document in Guatemala City on August 7, 1987.

RIDE REPORT TO NASA

August 17, 1987

Reeling in the aftermath of the space shuttle Challenger*'s explosion in January 1986, administrators at the National Aeronautics and Space Administration (NASA) appointed astronaut Sally K. Ride to help put the U.S. space program back on track. After eleven months of study, a panel chaired by Ride released a sixty-three-page report August 17, warning that America might lose its preeminence in space unless the agency changed course. The report called on NASA to eschew its traditional practice of spectacular one-goal ventures and instead undertake an orderly, "evolutionary" program of expansion. Opposing some enthusiasts' call for a manned mission to Mars in the near future, the Ride group suggested an approach designed to move gradually from low-orbit earth studies and a bigger shuttle fleet to a fully operative space station and a functional lunar outpost.*

"Settling Mars should be our eventual goal," wrote Ride, "but it should not be our only goal." Such a narrow focus, she concluded, would threaten NASA's plans for reviving the shuttle fleet or building a new space station. A "race to Mars" would require tripling the agency's budget at a time when public and political support were expected to be tenuous. "It would not be good strategy, good science or good policy," according to the report, "for the U.S. to select a single initiative, then pursue it single-mindedly."

The Ride report also concluded that the U.S. space program already had ceded much of its leadership to the Soviet Union. Panel members warned that the USSR had outpaced America in the unmanned explora-

tion of Mars and the use of space stations in low-earth orbit. They said that the U.S. was "in danger of being surpassed" in other areas as well.

A Loss of Leadership

For the quarter of a century after it was spurred by the Soviet launch in 1957 of the Sputnik *satellite, the U.S. space program enjoyed virtual hegemony in the trailblazing of space. NASA landed the first human beings on the Moon and pioneered robotic exploration of Venus and Mars. Then came the controlled crash of the Skylab space station in 1978 and the* Challenger *accident on January 28, 1986. The space agency's prestige waned considerably.*

A special commission appointed by President Ronald Reagan to investigate the Challenger *accident was headed by former secretary of state William P. Rogers and included Sally Ride. That panel faulted both NASA's particular handling of the* Challenger *launch and its general management of programs and contractors. The study was followed by a report from the House Science and Technology Committee, which questioned whether NASA was equipped with "the technical and scientific expertise to conduct the space shuttle program properly."* (Historic Documents of 1986, p. 515)

Meanwhile, the agency suffered a series of unsuccessful launchings that included the loss of an Atlas-Centaur rocket fired into a lightning storm in March 1987. Increasingly, both NASA and the Reagan administration came under attack from critics who complained that U.S. space policy was rudderless. Donald E. Fink, editor of the influential trade magazine Aviation Week and Space Technology, *published an unusually virulent editorial just before the Ride report's release. Fink asserted that NASA was "foundering under the worst management crisis in its history." Other industry experts and some political observers asserted that the space agency was crippled by bureaucratic infighting and budgetary constraints. Almost all cited a lack of long-term planning.*

By the time the Ride report was released, NASA's rocket fleet effectively had been grounded. The already troubled satellite network had been further atrophied by battles between NASA regulars and advocates of a stepped-up military presence in the civilian agency. The space sciences program had withered from neglect. In addition, cost estimates for the proposed U.S. space station had been growing wildly. In his 1984 State of the Union message, President Reagan mentioned the figure of $8 billion. But a 1987 report from the National Research Council said $32 billion was a more realistic estimate.

Summarizing the troubled status quo, Ride's panel focused on the need for new, coherent direction that could survive in both "political and fiscal arenas." Ride quoted NASA's own administrator, Dr. James Fletcher, who eleven months earlier implicitly had conceded NASA's decline when he commissioned the panel: "It is our intent," he had said, "that this process produce a blueprint to guide the United States to a position of leadership among the spacefaring nations of the Earth."

Recommendations

Ride wrote in the preface to the report that the state of modern space exploration precluded one nation's preeminence in all areas and disciplines: "Being an effective leader does mandate, however, that this country have capabilities to act independently and impressively when and where it chooses, and that its goals be capable of inspiring others—at home and abroad—to support them," she wrote.

Interviewed by Aviation Week *just prior to her report's release, Ride explained that the panel had responded to this "leadership challenge" by focusing on two areas—human exploration and the pursuit of science. Conceding that the shuttle fleet and space station did offer opportunities for manned space travel, Ride said that they nevertheless constituted merely ad hoc operations. At the same time, she warned, both low-Earth orbit and unmanned exploration of Mars had been largely lost to the Soviets. Ride argued that manned and unmanned efforts alike would require a fully renovated strategy—if they were to garner public support and counter the Soviet challenge.*

Reactions

While the Ride panel's study represented the most comprehensive recent effort to develop long-term direction for the beleaguered space agency, some critics feared that the report would be ignored. They noted that agency head James Fletcher, who had assigned Ride to the study, commended the study but stopped short of endorsing its recommendations. Among other problems, NASA's own advisory council previously had recommended the manned Mars goal without a lunar base. Some saw a Mars mission as the only effort capable of rekindling public support.

Following are excerpts from "NASA Leadership and America's Future in Space," a NASA task force report by Sally K. Ride, released August 17, 1987:

Leadership in Space

For two decades, the United States was the undisputed leader in nearly all civilian space endeavors. However, over the last decade the United States has relinquished, or is relinquishing, its leadership in certain critical areas; one such area is the exploration of Mars. With the *Mariner* and *Viking* missions in the 1960s and 1970s, this country pioneered exploration of Mars—but no American spacecraft has visited that planet since 1976. Our current plans for future exploration of Mars include only the *Mars Observer* mission, to be launched in 1992. In contrast, the Soviets have announced a program of extensive robotic exploration of the Martian surface, beginning in 1988 and extending through the 1990s.

The Soviets are now the sole long-term inhabitants of low-Earth orbit. The first, and only, U.S. space station, *Skylab,* was visited by three crews of astronauts before it was vacated in 1974; the U.S. has had no space station since. The Soviets have had eight space stations in orbit since the mid-1970s. The latest, *Mir,* was launched in 1986 and could accommodate cosmonauts and scientific experiments for nearly a decade before the U.S. Space Station can accommodate astronauts in 1995.

The United States has clearly lost leadership in these two areas, and is in danger of being surpassed in many others during the next several years.

The National Space Policy of 1982, which "establishes the basic goals of United States Policy," incudes the directive to "maintain United States space leadership." It further specifies that "the United States is fully committed to maintaining world leadership in space transportation," and that the civilian space program "shall be conducted ... to preserve the United States leadership in critical aspects of space science, applications, and technology." ...

Leadership does not require that the U.S. be preeminent in all areas and disciplines of space enterprise. In fact, the broad spectrum of space activities and the increasing number of spacefaring nations make it virtually impossible for any nation to dominate in this way. Being an effective leader does mandate, however, that this country have capabilities which enable it to act independently and impressively when and where it chooses, and that its goals be capable of inspiring others—at home and abroad—to support them. It is essential for this country to move promptly to determine its priorities and to make conscious choices to pursue a set of objectives which will restore its leadership status....

A U.S. space leadership program must have two distinct attributes. First, it must contain a sound program of scientific research and technology development—a program that builds the nation's understanding of space and the space environment, and that builds its capabilities to explore and operate in that environment. The United States will not be a leader in the 21st Century if it is dependent on other countries for access to space or for the technologies required to explore the space frontier. Second, the program must incorporate visible and significant accomplishments; the United States will not be perceived as a leader unless it accomplishes feats which demonstrate prowess, inspire national pride, and engender international respect and a worldwide desire to associate with U.S. space activities....

Perhaps most significant, leadership is also a process. That process involves selecting and enunciating priorities for the civilian space program and then building and maintaining the resources required to accomplish the objectives.... NASA can contribute to this process by: (1) establishing a vision and goals consistent with national space interests; (2) developing and recommending objectives and programs that support those goals; (3) articulating, promoting, and defending them in the political and fiscal arenas; and (4) effectively executing approved programs.

To this end, NASA embarked last fall on a review of its goals and objectives. As NASA Administrator Dr. James Fletcher stated, "It is our intent that this process produce a blueprint to guide the United States to a position of leadership among the spacefaring nations of Earth."

The first step in this necessarily lengthy process was taken by NASA Senior Management's Strategic Planning Council when it adopted the [following] statement. . . .

Meeting the Challenge in Aeronautics and Space

NASA's vision is to be at the forefront of advancements in aeronautics, space science, and exploration. To set our course into the 21st Century and bring this vision to reality, NASA will pursue major goals which represent its aspirations in aviation and space. These goals are:

- Advance scientific knowledge of the planet Earth, the solar system, and the universe beyond.
- Expand human presence beyond the Earth into the solar system.
- Strengthen aeronautics research and develop technology toward promoting U.S. leadership in civil and military aviation.

Successful pursuit of these major goals requires commitment to the following supporting goals:

- Return the Space Shuttle to flight status and develop advanced space transportation capabilities.
- Develop facilities and pursue science and technology needed for the Nation's space program.

As NASA pursues these goals, we will:

- Promote domestic application of aerospace technologies to improve the quality of life on Earth and to extend human enterprise beyond Earth.
- Conduct cooperative activities with other countries when such cooperation is consistent with our national space goals.

This statement reflects the belief that NASA embodies the human spirit's desire to discover, to explore, and to understand. It should be noted that the Space Shuttle and Space Station are not viewed as ends in themselves, but as the means toward achieving the broader goals of the nation's space program. Transportation and orbital facilities support and enable our efforts in science, exploration, and enterprise.

The next step in this process should be to articulate specific objectives and to identify the programs required to achieve these objectives. Of course, in some areas of study the programs have already been identified and are well under way. For example, the Hubble Space Telescope, a general-purpose astronomical observatory in space, is an element of NASA's program to increase our understanding of the universe in which we live; the redesign and requalification of the Space Shuttle's solid rocket booster joint is part of NASA's program to return the Space Shuttle to flight status. However, in other areas, such as piloted exploration, our objectives have not been clearly identified. Does this country intend to establish a lunar outpost? To send an expedition to Mars? What are NASA's major objectives for the late 20th and early 21st Centuries? The Space Shuttle and Space Station will clearly support the objectives, but what will they be supporting?

These questions cannot, of course, be answered by NASA alone. But NASA should lead the discussion, propose technically feasible options, and make thoughtful recommendations....

Strategic Option Development

... NASA is currently developing a process to systematically assess the posture of our space program and to refine and assess candidate strategies to direct its future. This process, strategic option development, is still in its early stages; nevertheless, the development of the process has yielded some interesting insights into existing and potential space strategies.

The application of strategic option development to charting the future of the U.S. space program initially evolved from analogies drawn from relevant aspects of business theory. Although it is unconventional to think of space endeavors in terms of a business, many concepts from the business world are applicable and quite useful.

Leadership in business is possible at any time during a product's life cycle. When a new product is introduced (the innovator stage) there is no competition. If the product is successful, the firm becomes the market leader by default. The drawback, of course, is that innovators must accept the high cost and high risk associated with being first. The space program in the early 1960s was an innovator's market. Nearly every successful effort produced a "first," but the risks, as well as the number of failures, were very high.

In a mature business market (the late majority stage) there exists a balance, as many firms compete for some share of the market. At this stage, it is still possible to be a market leader by carving out a particular niche of that market or by delivering the highest quality or best value. The launch vehicle market, for example, is approaching a more mature stage, and many countries will be vying for leadership in the 1990s.

A firm engaged in more than one market must develop an integrated strategy which provides the flexibility to be both an innovator in a new market and the leading competitor in a mature market....

The business of space has expanded considerably since the 1960s. The areas of scientific research, space technology, space exploration, and space services are still open to leadership through innovation, but some are also now open to leadership in more mature markets. In fact, national space programs must now look at four stages of space leadership: (1) the *pioneer* stage, innovation in some particular area of research, technology, or exploration; (2) the *complex second* stage, a continuation of a pioneering effort, but with broader, more complex objectives; (3) the *operational* stage, with relatively mature and routine capabilities; and (4) the *commercially viable* stage, with the potential for profit-making.

The activities of a space program can be characterized by physical regions of space: (1) deep space, (2) the outer solar system (the planets beyond the asteroid belt), (3) the inner solar system (the inner planets, the Moon, and the Sun), (4) high-Earth orbit, and (5) low-Earth orbit. Supporting technologies, such as launch capabilities and orbital facilities, are required to undertake all programs. . . .

Being a leader in one area no longer results in overall space leadership. In the early 1960s, the United States and the Soviet Union were the only competitors. . . . As technology advanced and nations gained experience in space, the opportunities began to expand. In the 1960s, the U.S. learned to send satellites to geosynchronous orbit, scientific experiments to low-Earth orbit, spacecraft to Mars, and even astronauts to the Moon. America was undeniably the leader in space exploration, but the range of space activities was (by today's standards) relatively limited. In the 1980s, not only has the number of spacefaring nations increased, but so has the range of activities that an interested nation might undertake.

The business of space has expanded and branched, and now encompasses such diverse and mature fields as remote sensing, microgravity materials research, commercial communications, and interplanetary exploration. . . . Since the U.S. can no longer reasonably expect to lead the way in all activities, it is now important to adopt a strategy to strive for leadership in carefully chosen areas. . . .

Examining the programs of the spacefaring nations shows the basic character of each. The U.S. space program has historically been composed of pioneering efforts—significant firsts and complex second efforts, which emphasized advanced research, technology, and exploration. The general trend can be characterized as revolutionary, producing spectacular events, rather than moderate, evolutionary advances. Even the United States Space Shuttle, though designed to be operational, was a revolutionary concept—it did not evolve from existing launch vehicles.

The Soviet space program, which is radically different from the American program, can be characterized as systematic and evolutionary. The primary focus is not on advanced research and technology, but on incrementally developed operational capabilities, achieved through a strong commitment to a robust infrastructure. The Soviets have steadily evolved toward this operational state and they are now beginning to build on that operational base to move slowly into the commercial arena.

The Europeans and the Japanese appear to be pursuing strategies that combine desires to pursue science in selected areas and to achieve commercial viability in others. . . .

These observations suggest that there is no one "correct" strategy.... Clearly, each nation should choose and pursue a strategy which is consistent with its own national objectives.

What should our choice be? Do we want to mature our operational Earth-orbiting capabilities to a viable commercial enterprise? Should we continue our leadership role in solar system and deep-space exploration? Or should we focus on venturing ever further outward from Earth with human expeditions to the planets?

Leadership Initiatives

To energize a discussion of long-range goals and strategies for the civilian space program, four bold initiatives were selected for definition, study, and evaluation:

1. **Mission to Planet Earth:** a program that would use the perspective afforded from space to study and characterize our home planet on a global scale.
2. **Exploration of the Solar System:** a program to retain U.S. leadership in exploration of the outer solar system, and regain U.S. leadership in exploration of comets, asteroids, and Mars.
3. **Outpost on the Moon:** a program that would build on and extend the legacy of the Apollo Program, returning Americans to the Moon to continue exploration, to establish a permanent scientific outpost, and to begin prospecting the Moon's resources.
4. **Humans to Mars:** a program to send astronauts on a series of round trips to land on the surface of Mars, leading to the eventual establishment of a permanent base.

The intent is not to choose one initiative and discard the other three, but rather to use the four candidate initiatives as a basis for discussion....

... The ground rules, set forward at the outset of this study, were:

- The initiatives should be considered *in addition* to currently planned NASA programs. They were not judged against, nor would they supplant, existing programs.
- Each initiative should be developed independently....
- The initiatives should achieve major milestones within two decades.
- The Humans to Mars initiative should be assumed to be an American venture. It was beyond the scope of this work to consider joint U.S./Soviet human exploration....

Mission to Planet Earth

Mission to Planet Earth is an initiative to understand our home planet, how forces shape and affect its environment, how that environment is changing, and how those changes will affect us. The goal of this initiative is to obtain a comprehensive scientific understanding of the entire Earth System, by describing how its various components function, how they interact, and how they may be expected to evolve on all time scales.

The challenge is to develop a fundamental understanding of the Earth

System, and of the consequences of changes to that system, in order to eventually develop the capability to predict changes that might occur—either naturally, or as a result of human activity.

Background

With the launch of the first experimental satellites in the 1960s, NASA pioneered the remote sensing of Earth from space. Over the past two decades, the scientific community has concluded that Earth is in a process of global change, and scientists now believe that it is necessary to study Earth as a synergistic system.... Interactive physical, chemical, and biological processes connect the oceans, continents, atmosphere, and biosphere of Earth in a complex way. Oceans, ice-covered regions, and the atmosphere are closely linked and shape Earth's climate; volcanism links inner Earth with the atmosphere; and biological activity significantly contributes to the cycling of chemicals (e.g., carbon, oxygen, and carbon dioxide) important to life. And now it is clear that human activity also has a major impact on the evolution of the Earth System.

Global-scale changes of uncertain impact, ranging from an increase in the atmospheric warming gases, carbon dioxide and methane, to a hole in the ozone layer over the Antarctic, to important variations in vegetation covers and in coastlines, have already been observed with existing measurement capabilities. The potentially major consequences, either detrimental or beneficial, suggest an urgent need to understand these variations.

We currently lack the ability to foresee changes in the Earth System, and their subsequent effects on the planet's physical, economic, and social climate....

Strategy and Scenario

The guiding principle behind this initiative is to adopt an integrated approach to observing Earth....

Mission to Planet Earth proposes:

1. To establish and maintain a global observational system in space, which would include experiments and free-flying platforms, in polar, low-inclination, and geostationary orbits, and which would perform integrated, long-term measurements.
2. To use the data from these satellites along with *in-situ* information and numerical modeling to document, understand, and eventually predict global change.

... [T]he global observational system would include a suite of nine orbiting platforms.... Low-inclination, low-altitude payloads would also be included in the system....

The integrated system would measure the full complement of the planet's characteristics, including: global cloud cover, vegetation cover, and ice cover; global rainfall and moisture; ocean chlorophyll content and ocean topography; motions and deformations of Earth's tectonic plates; and atmospheric concentration of gases such as carbon dioxide, methane, and ozone.

Space-based observations would also be coordinated with ground-based experiments and the data from all observations would be integrated by an essential component of this initiative: a versatile, state-of-the-art information management system....

Because of its international and interdisciplinary nature, the Mission to Planet Earth requires the strong support and involvement of other U.S. government agencies (particularly the National Science Foundation and the National Oceanic and Atmospheric Administration) and of our international partners.... NASA's responsibilities would include the information management system and platforms and experiments described previously. Most important, NASA would also provide the supporting technology, space transportation, space support services, and much of the scientific leadership.

Technology, Transportation, and Orbital Facilities

... Sophisticated sensors and information systems must be designed and developed, and advances must be made in automation and robotics (whether platform servicing is performed by astronauts or robotic systems).

To achieve its full scope, this initiative requires the operational support of Earth-to-orbit and space transportation systems to accommodate the launching of polar and geostationary platforms. This does not represent a large number of additional launches, but it does require the capability to launch large payloads to polar orbit; Titan IVs would be used to accomplish this. Since the envisioned geostationary platforms would be lifted to low-Earth orbit, assembled at the Space Station, and then lifted to geosynchronous orbit with a space transfer vehicle, well-developed orbital facilities are essential. By the late 1990s, the Space Station must be able to support on-orbit assembly, and a space transfer vehicle must exist....

Exploration of the Solar System

This initiative would build on NASA's long-standing tradition of solar system exploration and would continue the quest to understand our planetary system, its origin, and its evolution. Solar system bodies are divided into three distinct classes: the primitive bodies (comets and asteroids), the outer (gas giant) planets, and the inner (terrestrial) planets. Each class occupies a unique position in the history of the solar system, and each is the target of a major mission in this initiative, which includes a comet rendezvous (the *Comet Rendezvous Asteroid Flyby* mission), and mission to Saturn *(Cassini)*, and three sample return missions to Mars. The centerpiece of the initiative is the robotic exploration of Mars; the first of these three automated missions would bring a handful of Mars back to Earth before the year 2000.

Background

In the 1960s and 1970s, exploration of the solar system was an important and visible component of the U.S. space program. Highly successful missions such as *Pioneer, Viking,* and *Voyager* made the United States the unchallenged leader in the exploration of the planets. Our spacecraft were consistently both the first and the best. While the Soviet Union concentrated most of its efforts on the exploration of Venus, the rest of the solar system was left to the United States.

But now almost a decade has elapsed between U.S. planetary missions—the last was *Pioneer Venus,* launched in 1978. *Galileo* (to Jupiter), *Magellan* (to Venus), and the *Mars Observer* are in line for launch between 1989 and 1992, but no other planetary missions have been approved. Although the successful *Voyager* missions to the outer planets clearly established U.S. leadership in exploration of the outer solar system, plans for the future beyond the *Galileo* mission are uncertain.

Other nations have recently begun to undertake innovative and challenging programs (the recent international flotilla to Halley's Comet is an excellent example). The Soviets have announced an ambitious program for the exploration of Mars which will culminate in a sample return mission, and the Europeans have set a long-term goal of returning a sample from a comet. Although currently scheduled U.S. missions will ensure [U.S. leadership] in certain areas of solar system exploration through 1995, the position of the United States beyond 1995 is in question. . . .

Strategy and Scenario

This initiative is based on the balanced strategy developed by the Solar System Exploration Committee of the NASA Advisory Council and elucidated in its two reports. . . .

1. The *Comet Rendezvous Asteroid Flyby* (CRAF) mission would investigate the beginnings of our solar system, studying a Main Belt asteroid and a comet. . . .
2. The *Cassini* mission would explore Saturn and its largest moon, Titan. The giant outer planets offer us an opportunity to address key questions about their internal structures and compositions through detailed studies of their atmospheres. Titan is an especially interesting target for exploration because the organic chemistry now taking place there provides the only planetary-scale laboratory for studying processes that may have been important in the prebiotic terrestrial atmosphere. . . .
3. The *Mars Rover/Sample Return* missions would, in journeys covering hundreds of millions of miles, gather samples of Mars and bring them back to Earth. Because of its relevance to understanding Earth and other terrestrial planets, and because it is the only other potentially habitable planet in our solar system, Mars is an intriguing target for exploration. . . .

Technology, Transportation, and Orbital Facilities

As it is defined, this initiative places a premium on advanced technology and enhanced launch capabilities to maximize the scientific return. It requires aerobraking technology for aerocapture and aeromaneuvering at Mars, and a high level of sophistication in automation, robotics, and sampling techniques. Advanced sampling methods are necessary to ensure that geologically and chemically varied and interesting samples are collected for analysis.

The Solar System Exploration initiative significantly benefits from improved launch capability in terms of the science returned from both the Mars and the *Cassini* missions. In fact, it is a heavy-lift launch vehicle that enables the full complement of three different probes to be carried in the expanded *Cassini* mission.

The Space Shuttle is not required for any of the missions in the initiative. The Space Station would not be needed until 1999, when an isolation module may be used to receive the Martian samples....

Outpost on the Moon

This initiative builds on the legacy of *Apollo* and envisions a new phase of lunar exploration and development—a phase leading to a human outpost on another world. That outpost would support scientific research and exploration of the Moon's resource potential, and would represent a significant extraterrestrial step toward learning to live and work in the hostile environments of other worlds.

Beginning with robotic exploration in the 1990s, this initiative would land astronauts on the lunar surface in the year 2000, to construct an outpost that would evolve in size and capability....

Background

The Apollo Program was a great national adventure. We sent explorers to scout the cratered highlands and smooth maria of the Moon, and to bring samples collected on their trips back to laboratories on Earth. The world was fascinated by the *Apollo* missions and the information they obtained, and the samples provided scientists many exciting clues about the Moon's origin and chemical composition.

The *Apollo* era ended 15 years ago, before we could fully explore the promise of lunar science and lunar resources. But we learned that human beings can work on the surface of the Moon, and we laid the technical foundation to develop the scientific and engineering tasks for the next stages of exploration. This initiative would send the next generation of pioneers—to pitch their tents, establish supply lines, and gradually build a scientifically and technically productive outpost suitable for long-term habitation.

... As our experience and capabilities on the lunar surface grow, this extraterrestrial outpost will gradually become less and less dependent on the supply line to Earth. The first steps toward "living off the lunar land" will be learning to extract oxygen from the lunar soil, where it is plentiful, and learning to make construction materials. The lunar soil would eventually be a source of oxygen for propellant and life-support systems, and a source of material for shelters and facilities.

... [S]ince the Moon is seismically stable and has no atmosphere, and since its far side is shielded from the radio noise from Earth, it is a very attractive spot for experiments and observations in astrophysics, gravity wave physics, and neutrino physics, to name a few. It is also an excellent location for materials science and life science research because of its low gravitational field (one-sixth of Earth's).

Strategy and Scenario

This initiative proposes the gradual, three-phase evolution of our ability to live and work on the lunar surface.

Phase I: Search for a Site (1990s). The initial phase would focus on robotic exploration of the Moon.... The discovery of water or other volatiles would be extremely significant, and would have important implications for the location of a habitable outpost.

Phase II: Return to the Moon (2000-2005). Phase II begins with the return of astronauts to the lunar surface....

Over the first few flights, the early outpost would grow to include a habitation area, a research facility, a rover, some small machinery to move lunar soil, and a pilot plant to demonstrate the extraction of lunar oxygen. By 2001, a crew could stay the entire lunar night (14 Earth days), and by 2005 the outpost would support five people for several weeks at a time.

Phase III: At Home on the Moon (2005-2010). Phase III evolves ... as scientific and technological capabilities allow the outpost to expand to a permanently occupied base. The base would have closed-loop life-support systems and an operational lunar oxygen plant, and would be involved in frontline scientific research and technology development. The program also requires the mobilization of disciplines not previously required in the space program: surface construction and transportation, mining, and materials processing.

By 2010, up to 30 people would be productively living and working on the lunar surface for months at a time. Lunar oxygen will be available for use at the outpost and possibly for propellant for further exploration.

Technology, Transportation, and Orbital Facilities

This initiative envisions frequent trips to the Moon after the year 2000—trips that would require a significant investment in technology and in transportation and orbital facilities in the early 1990s.

The critical technologies for this initiative are those which would make human presence on the Moon meaningful and productive. They include life-support system technologies to create a habitable outpost; automation and expert systems and surface power technologies to make the outpost functional and its inhabitants productive; and lunar mining and processing technologies to enable the prospecting for lunar resources.

The transportation system must be capable of regularly transporting the elements of the lunar outpost, the fuel for the voyage, and the lunar crew to low-Earth orbit. This requires a heavy-lift launch vehicle and a healthy Space Shuttle fleet. The transfer of both cargo and crew from the Space Station to lunar orbit requires the development of a reusable space transfer vehicle. This and a heavy-lift launch vehicle will be the work-horses of the Lunar initiative.

The Space Station is an essential part of this initiative. As the lunar outpost evolves, the Space Station would become its operational hub in low-Earth orbit. Supplies, equipment, and propellants would be marshalled at the Station for transit to the Moon. It is therefore required that the Space Station evolve to include spaceport facilities.

In the 1990s, the Phase I Space Station would be used as a technology and systems test bed for developing closed-loop life-support systems, automation and robotics, and the expert systems required for the lunar outpost. The outpost would, in fact, rely on the Space Station for many of its systems and subsystems, including lunar habitation modules which would be derivatives of the Space Station habitation/laboratory modules....

Humans to Mars

This bold initiative is committed to the human exploration, and eventual habitation, of Mars. Robotic exploration of the planet would be the first phase and would include the return of samples of Martian rocks and soil. Early in the 21st Century, Americans would land on the surface of Mars; within a decade of these first piloted landings, this initiative would advance human presence to an outpost on Mars.

Background

The Red Planet has piqued our curiosity and stimulated our imaginations for decades. Our previous exploration of Mars has revealed a fascinating world of enormous mountains and deep canyons, and a surface etched by erosion during ancient floods. Mars may once have supported life; in any case, it is the only potentially habitable planet in our solar system besides Earth....

The United States has ... led the way in the robotic exploration of Mars. The last visitor to that planet was the extremely successful *Viking* spacecraft, which landed on the Martian surface in 1976, and transmitted data to Earth until late in 1982. During the coming decade, humanity will learn more about Mars, but it will largely be the result of ambitious Soviet, not American, programs. Our single mission to Mars, the *Mars Observer,* to be launched in 1992, is a small spacecraft which will perform an important geochemical characterization of Mars while in orbit around the planet. Meanwhile, the Soviets have announced three separate missions to Mars before 1995. . . .

Strategy and Scenario

This initiative would:

1. Carry out comprehensive robotic exploration of Mars in the 1990s. . . . These missions would perform geochemical characterization of the planet, and complete global mapping and support landing site selection and certification.
2. Establish an aggressive Space Station life sciences research program to validate the feasibility of long-duration spaceflight. This program would develop an understanding of the physiological effects of long-duration flights, of measures to counteract those effects, and of medical techniques and equipment for use on such flights. An important result would be the determination of whether eventual Mars transport vehicles must provide artificial gravity.
3. Design, prepare for, and perform three fast piloted round-trip missions to Mars. These flights would enable the commitment, by 2010, to an outpost on Mars.

The Mars missions described in this initiative are one-year, round-trip "sprints," with astronauts exploring the Martian surface for two weeks before returning to Earth. The chosen scenario significantly reduces the amount of mass which must be launched into low-Earth orbit, and by doing so brings a one-year round trip into the realm of feasibility. . . .

Technology, Transportation, and Orbital Facilities

. . . The Mars expeditions require the development of a number of technologies, including aerobraking (which significantly reduces the amount of mass which must be lifted to low-Earth orbit), efficient interplanetary propulsion, automation and robotics, storage and transfer of cryogenics in space, fault-tolerant systems, and advanced medical technology. Technology development must be initiated immediately. . . .

Even with separate cargo and personnel vehicles, and technological advances such as aerobraking, each of these sprint missions requires that approximately 2.5 million pounds be lifted to low-Earth orbit. (In comparison, the Phase I Space Station is projected to weigh approximately 0.5 million pounds.) It is clear that a robust, efficient transportation system, including a heavy-lift launch vehicle, is required. The complement of launch vehicles must be able to lift the cargo and personnel required by the sprint missions to the Space Station in a reasonable period of time. Like the outpost on the Moon, this initiative requires a substantial investment in launch systems, for transport of both cargo and crew.

The Phase I Space Station is a crucial part of this initiative. In the 1990s, it must support the critical life sciences research and medical technique development. It will also be the technology test bed for life-support systems, automation and robotics, and expert systems.

Furthermore, we must develop facilities in low-Earth orbit to store large quantities of propellant, and to assemble large vehicles. The Space Station would have to evolve in a way that would meet these needs....

Programmatic Assessment

... Although each [program] has something different to offer, each falls within the framework of NASA's vision, each builds on and extends existing capabilities, and each elicits the reaction, "America ought to be doing this." In the absence of fiscal and resource constraints, the United States would undoubtedly adopt all four. [With] those very real constraints, and the additional constraints imposed by the current state of our civilian space program, this course of action is not possible....

To establish a realistic level of expectation, NASA must consider the current condition of the space program, its strengths and limitations, and its capabilities for growth. Any bold initiative has to begin with and then build on today's space program, which unfortunately lacks some fundamental capabilities. For example, our most critical commodity, Earth-to-orbit transportation, is essential to each of the initiatives. But the Space Shuttle is grounded until at least June of 1988, and when it does return to flight status, the flight rate will be considerably lower than that projected before the *Challenger* accident (a four-Shuttle fleet is estimated to be capable of 12 to 14 flights per year).

In hindsight, it is easy to recognize that it was a crippling mistake to decree that the Space Shuttle would be this country's only launch vehicle. Several studies since the *Challenger* accident have recommended that the civilian space program include expendables in its fleet of launch vehicles. This strategy relieves some of the burden from the Shuttle, gives the country a broader, more flexible launch capability, and makes the space program less vulnerable in the event of an accident.

The problem of limited launch capability or availability will be magnified during the assembly and operation of the Space Station. Currently, NASA plans to use only the Space Shuttle to transport cargo and people to and from the Space Station. This places a heavy demand on the Shuttle (six to eight flights per year), but more important, it makes the Space Station absolutely dependent on the Shuttle. If Shuttle launches should be interrupted again in the mid-1990s, this nation must still have access to space and the means to transport cargo and people to and from the Space Station. The importance of this capability was emphasized by the National Commission on Space in its report, *Pioneering the Space Frontier:* "Above all, it is imperative that the U.S. maintain a continuous ability to put both humans and cargo into orbit."

From now until the mid-1990s, Earth-to-orbit transportation is NASA's most pressing problem. A space program that can't get to orbit has all the effectiveness of a navy that can't get to the sea. America must develop a cadre of launch vehicles that can first meet the near-term commitments of the civilian space program and then grow to support projected programs or initiatives.

Expendable launch vehicles should be provided for payloads which are not unique to the Space Shuttle—this is required just to implement current plans and to satisfy fundamental requirements.

A Shuttle-derived cargo vehicle should be developed immediately. A Shuttle-derived vehicle is attractive because of its lift capacity, its synergism with the Space Transportation System, and its potential to be available for service in the early 1990s. This cargo vehicle would reduce the payload requirements on the Shuttle for Space Station support and would accelerate the Space Station assembly sequence.

The United States should also seriously consider the advisability of a crew-rated expendable to lift a crew capsule or a logistics capsule to the Space Station. The logistics vehicle, for Space Station resupply and/or instrument return, would be developed with autodocking and precision reentry capabilities. The crew capsule would carry only crew members and supplies, would launch (with or without a crew) on the expendable vehicle, would have autodocking capability, and might also be used for crew rescue.

These transportation capabilities are required just to launch, assemble, operate, and safely inhabit the Space Station, and to have some prospect of being able to support future initiatives.

. . . We have stated that transportation is not our goal—but it is essential to the successful pursuit of whatever goals we choose. If we do not make a commitment now to rebuild and broaden our launch capability, we will not have the option of pursuing any of the four initiatives described in the previous section.

The same can be said for advanced technology. The National Commission on Space observed that "NASA is still living on the investment made [during the *Apollo* era], but cannot continue to do so if we are to maintain United States leadership in space." Several recent studies concur, concluding that our technology base has eroded and technological research and development are underfunded. The technology required for bold ventures beyond Earth's orbit has not yet been developed, and until it is, human exploration of the inner solar system will have to wait.

Project Pathfinder . . . would provide the technologies to enable bold missions beyond Earth's orbit: technology for autonomous systems and robotics, for lunar and planetary advanced propulsion systems, and for extraction of useful materials from lunar or planetary sources. It also deals in a significant way with the human ability to live and work in space, by developing technologies for life-support systems and the human/machine interface. Until advanced technology programs like Project Pathfinder are initiated, the exciting goals of human exploration will always remain 10 to 20 years in the future.

Life sciences research is also critical to any programs involving relatively long periods of human habitation in space....

Before astronauts are sent into space for long periods, research must be done to understand the physiological effects of the microgravity and radiation environments, to develop measures to counteract any adverse effects, and to develop medical techniques to perform routine and emergency health care aboard spacecraft.

Project Pacer, developed by NASA's Office of Space Science and Applications, is a focused program designed to develop that understanding and provide the physiological and medical foundation for extended spaceflight. This research would be conducted in laboratories and on Space Shuttle missions in preparation for the critical long-term experiments to be conducted on the Space Station....

Although the Mars initiative offers the greatest amount of human and technological drama, it also demands the greatest investment. The Mars initiative definition included only those elements required for the three sprint missions, the last in 2010, so the level of investment shown is artificially low between 2005 and 2010. The magnitude of the initiative indicates a large commitment of resources, and the timescale dictates that the investment peak in about 2000. It is possible to reduce the early investment to a level comparable to that of the other three initiatives by allowing the first human landing to occur in 2010, rather than in 2005....

Evaluation of Initiatives

To this point, we have been considering four specific initiatives, each of which would, if adopted, provide leadership in a particular area of space endeavor. Now it is important to differentiate between an initiative and a strategy. A strategy provides an overall framework and direction; it identifies and prioritizes goals, and defines a course to attain them. An initiative should be an element of a strategy; a part, but only a part, of the larger picture....

While stressing the need for a comprehensive strategy, we can nevertheless conduct a preliminary assessment of the initiatives, recognizing that the important considerations are the quality of the program, NASA's ability to carry it out, and the public's willingness to support it. In the process of this evaluation, we can see the elements of a potential strategy begin to emerge.

Exploration of the Solar System

...While other nations are now vigorously pursuing solar system exploration, the U.S. has launched no planetary missions since 1978.

What does the next decade hold in store? The Soviets have announced their intent to launch three ambitious flights to Mars by 1995, and a Mars sample return mission by 2000. If they are successful with their new-generation spacecraft, and can continue to forge cooperative agreements with European nations, they will clearly have the greater momentum in the exploration of Mars by the mid-1990s....

The Solar System Exploration Committee has devised a strategy for planetary exploration through the year 2000, which presented "the minimum-level program that could be carried out in a cost-effective manner, and would yield continuing return of scientific results." NASA should embrace this Core Program.

The *Mars Rover/Sample Return* mission is the centerpiece of the Solar System Exploration Committee's recommended augmentation to its Core Program. . . .

Although the *Mars Rover/Sample Return* was presented as a U.S. mission in this initiative, it could be performed in cooperation with our allies and/or in coordination with the Soviet Union. In fact, planetary exploration is well suited to international cooperation. . . .

Robotic planetary exploration should be actively supported and nurtured within NASA. Although it does not have the immediate relevance of the Mission to Planet Earth, or the excitement of human exploration, it is fundamental science that challenges our technology, extends our presence, and gives us a glimpse of other worlds. . . . Although not necessarily at the pace suggested in this initiative, planetary exploration must be solidly supported through the 1990s.

Mission to Planet Earth

. . . This initiative directly addresses the problems that will be facing humanity in the coming decades, and its continuous scientific return will produce results which are of major significance to all the residents of the planet. The benefits are clear to a public that is increasingly concerned about global environmental problems like ozone depletion, buildup of greenhouse gases, and acidification of lakes and forests. . . .

For this reason [the initiative] should enjoy sustained public and Congressional support and interest. The U.S. is the only country currently capable of leading a Mission to Planet Earth, but the program is designed around, and requires, international cooperation. Admittedly, the initiative's international scope could complicate its coordination and implementation, but the concept embodied in the initiative enjoys widespread international support. As more and more countries are facing ecological problems, there is increasing interest in a global approach. In fact, this concept is supported by several international organizations, and may emerge as a theme for the International Space Year, 1992. This initiative represents an important opportunity for the United States to exercise leadership in an increasingly significant area. . . .

NASA should embrace Mission to Planet Earth. This initiative is responsive, time-critical, and shows a recognition of our responsibility to our home planet. . . .

Humans to Mars

Exploring, prospecting, and settling Mars are clearly the ultimate goals of the next several decades of human exploration. But what strategy should be followed to attain those goals? ...

... NASA would be hard pressed to carry the weight of this ambitious initiative in the 1990s without severely taxing existing programs. NASA's available resources were strained to the limit flying nine Shuttle flights in one year.... It would not be wise to embark on an ambitious program whose requirements could overwhelm those of the Shuttle and Space Station during the critical next decade....

One alternative is to retain the scenario developed here, but to proceed at a more deliberate (but still aggressive) pace, and allow the first human landing to occur in 2010....

We must pursue a more deliberate program; this implies that we should avoid a "race to Mars." There is the very real danger that if the U.S. announces a human Mars initiative at this time, it could escalate into another space race. Whether such a race was real or perceived, there would be constant pressure to set a timetable, to accelerate it if possible, and to avoid falling behind. Schedule pressures, as the Rogers Commission noted [in its report on the *Challenger* accident], can have a very real, adverse effect. The pressure could make it difficult to design and implement a program which would have a strong foundation and adequate momentum to sustain itself beyond the first few piloted missions. This could turn an initiative that envisions the eventual development of a habitable outpost into another one-shot spectacular. Such a dead-end venture does *not* have the support of most NASA personnel. Neither, according to the National Commission on Space, does it have the support of the public....

Settling Mars should be our eventual goal, but it should not be our next goal. Sending people to and from Mars is not the only issue involved. Understanding the requirements and implications of building and sustaining a permanent base on another world is equally important. We should adopt a strategy of natural progression which leads, step by step, in an orderly, unhurried way, inexorably toward Mars.

Outpost on the Moon

The Lunar initiative is a logical part of a long-range strategy for human exploration.... Exploring and prospecting the Moon, learning to use lunar resources and work within lunar constraints, would provide the experience and expertise necessary for further human exploration of the solar system.

The Lunar initiative is a major undertaking. Like the Mars initiative, it requires a national commitment that spans decades. It, too, demands an early investment in advanced technology, Earth-to-orbit transportation, and a plan for Space Station evolution. Even considering its gradual evolution over the first five years, the ambitious buildup of the lunar outpost envisioned in this scenario would require a high level of effort in the mid-to-late 1990s, and would place substantial demands on transportation and orbital facilities. This is a period when resources may be scarce.

However, this initiative is quite flexible. Its pace can be controlled, and more important, adapted to capability. It is possible to lay the foundation of the outpost in the year 2000, then build it gradually, to ease the burden on transportation and Space Station at the turn of the century. . . .

Conclusion

. . . In today's world, America clearly cannot be the leader in all space endeavors. But we will be the leader in very few unless we move promptly to develop a strategy to regain and retain leadership in those areas we deem important. . . .

It would not be good strategy, good science, or good policy for the U.S. to select a single initiative, then pursue it single-mindedly. The pursuit of a single initiative to the exclusion of all others results in leadership in only a limited range of space endeavor. . . .

It is in this spirit that we suggest the outline of one strategy—a strategy of evolution and natural progression. The strategy would begin by increasing our capabilities in transportation and technology—not as goals in themselves, but as the necessary means to achieve our goals in science and exploration. The most critical and immediate needs are related to advanced transportation systems to supplement and complement the Space Shuttle, and advanced technology to enable the bold missions of the next century. Until we can get people and cargo to and from orbit reliably and efficiently, our reach will exceed our grasp; until we begin the technologies proposed by Project Pathfinder, the realization of our aspirations will remain over a decade away.

The strategy emphasizes evolving our capabilities in low-Earth orbit, and using those capabilities to study our own world and explore others. With these capabilities, we would position ourselves to lead in characterizing and understanding planet Earth; we would also position ourselves to continue leading the way in human exploration. . . .

We should explore the Moon for what it can tell us, and what it can give us—as a scientific laboratory and observing platform, as a research and technology test bed, and as a potential source of important resources. While exploring the Moon, we would learn to live and work on a hostile world beyond Earth. This should be done in an evolutionary manner, and on a time scale that is consistent with our developing capabilities.

The natural progression of human exploration then leads to Mars. There is no doubt that exploring, prospecting, and settling Mars should be the ultimate objectives of human exploration. But America should not rush headlong toward Mars; we should adopt a strategy to continue an orderly expansion outward from Earth. . . .

PENTAGON REPORT ON SEXUAL HARASSMENT

August 26, 1987

An August 26 report by the Defense Advisory Committee on Women in the Services (DACOWITS) found evidence of bias against military women posted outside the continental United States. The seven-member team of advisers had been commissioned by the Pentagon to visit Navy and Marine Corps bases in Hawaii, the Philippines, and Japan. This series of visits had been preceded by 1986 visits to Army and Air Force bases in Western Europe. An October 1986 report had reached similar conclusions on the status of women in the armed forces overseas.

Consultant Jacquelyn K. Davis, author of both reports, concluded that "there is a widespread perception among female officers and enlisted personnel that the institutional hierarchy and Command Structure of each of the Services are biased against women." Large numbers of women in both services, but particularly in the Navy, felt that their "professional competence" was doubted by male team members and officers and that the "Command leadership is seeking 'to force women out of the Armed Forces' by making promotional opportunities for women difficult."

The report charged that "abusive behavior" against women occurred in both the Navy and the Marine Corps, again noting the "more serious" situation in the Navy. Specific allegations of sexual harassment and misconduct made against Lt. Comdr. Kenneth D. Harvey, senior officer of the USS Safeguard, *were cited as extreme examples from "an environment in which all females are regarded with little or no respect and abusive behavior toward all women is not only passively accepted and condoned but encouraged." Commander Harvey was removed from his command, fined, and reprimanded following a September 1987 hearing.*

Impact of Treatment of Women

The 1987 report warned that the Navy's lack of concern for the needs of enlisted women and their poor opportunities for promotion had led to job dissatisfaction and a drop in reenlistment. Unhealthy and unpleasant housing and inadequate recreational facilities were documented. The report also charged that poor medical care and "misperceptions which persist among the male leadership in the Services" have made the "pregnancy issue" a serious problem that should be studied.

Both the 1986 and the 1987 reports indicated that female military personnel had expressed strong interest in a reassessment by Congress of policies that prohibit combat-related assignments. The 1987 report specifically charged that the Navy had been even more restrictive than Congress had intended in refusing to allow women in certain combat-related posts. Because they were not being assigned to jobs for which they had been trained, women did not have opportunities to advance.

Reaction from Defense Department, Congress

In response, then defense secretary Caspar W. Weinberger reminded all services of policies forbidding sexual harassment, and Pentagon personnel chief David J. Armor formed a commission to review policies related to military women and to study laws and regulations excluding them from combat-related positions. Secretary of the Navy James H. Webb, Jr., in December 1987 opened up to women more assignments closer to combat, and the Marine Corps and the Air Force announced new studies of *the situations of military women and spouses of servicemen.*

On September 1987, in a speech on the Senate floor, William Proxmire, D-Wis., demanded "strong action" by the Defense Department to halt sexual harassment and ensure professional treatment. Legislation designed to "increase the combat support assignments open to women in the Armed Forces" (S581) had been introduced in February by Proxmire and Sen. William Cohen, R-Maine. Rep. Beverly Byron, D-Md., also introduced a bill intended to expand opportunities for military women.

> *Following are excerpts from the August 26, 1987, report of the Defense Advisory Committee on Women in the Services on sexual harassment and sex bias in U.S. Navy and Marine Corps installations overseas:*

. . . I. With respect to both Services, but especially the Navy, there is a widespread perception among female officers and enlisted personnel that the institutional hierarchy and Command Structure of each of the Services are biased against women. Navy women, in particular, complain of low self-esteem due to the lack of professionalism with which they perceive they are regarded by their male peers and leaders. Even more serious is the view, held widely among Navy women—officer and enlisted personnel—that their professional competence is constantly in question, demeaning any contribution that they make to the mission objectives of the Service. To be sure, not all women in the Navy feel this way and for some this is not an issue at all. Nevertheless we heard enough of these types of comments to conclude . . . that women in the Navy continue to experience a lack of acceptance as part of the team, and like other minorities have been subject to frequent abuses (mental/verbal) that unfortunately often characterize relationships between dominant and minority groups.

To a lesser degree we heard similar comments from Marine Corps women, many of whom resent being referred to as "WMs" (i.e. Women Marines). To them this appellation implies an entity separate from the whole (i.e. the U.S. Marine Corps). . . . Related to this complaint is the feeling, widespread among women Marines, that they are not part of the "first team." In part, this may be explained as a result of the Corps' mystique as the nation's elite fighting force. (In this regard, it is interesting to note that this was cited most often by women in the Marine Corps as the reason they chose the Corps over the other Services.) However, for a number of reasons, the combat restriction policy being but one, women Marines by and large are made to feel as if they belong to an auxiliary organization, the "second team" whose contribution to the Corps' mission objectives is not as significant as that of their male peers.

II. In both Services, but again more so in the Navy than the Marine Corps, there is a widely held perception that the Command leadership is seeking "to force women out of the Armed Forces" by making promotional opportunities for women difficult . . . and, at the same time, restricting through policy (and not law, Title 10, section 6015) opportunities for women to serve in ratings that would make them more competitive with their male counterparts. . . . The extent to which this perception exists among Navy women was illustrated time and again in the discussions the DACOWITS members had with Navy women at each of the facilities we visited. In my view certain recent personnel policy planning decisions have exacerbated these adverse perceptions (of current Navy leadership) of Navy women, especially those dealing with the sea-shore rotation issue.

Related to the negative perceptions many Navy women have of the Service's leadership is the view that women are discriminated against in their job performance. It is widely felt that leadership attitudes condone such discriminatory behavior, especially as males are perceived as "failing to set the same standards" for women as men in such diverse areas as comportment (weight standards) and absenteeism (due to alcohol or drug abuse). The use by male leadership of diminutive terms like "my girls," "honey," or the "Navy gals" further exacerbates perceptions of women as less than the professionals that most of them are. Similar complaints were aired by many of the female Marines with whom we spoke.

III. Related to the attitudinal issue is my impression that abusive behavior (manifested in a variety of forms, from verbal abuse to overt and blatant sexual harassment) continues to exist in both the Navy and Marine Corps, although again the problem appears to be more serious in the Navy than the Marine Corps. However, in both services the encouragement of a "macho" male image contributes to behavior that is at best inappropriate and at worst morally repugnant. Such behavior was encountered by the DACOWITS at each installation we visited. Clearly the most serious incidence of this behavior surfaced during our visit to the *U.S.S. Safeguard* (ARS-50) where allegations of sexual harassment and misconduct were cited (repeatedly by a majority of the 94 females aboard) against the ship's senior officer, Lt. Commander Harvey, (who has since been relieved and whose future status is pending the results of a Navy investigation which was initiated as a result of the DACOWITS' complaint) and its leadership authorities, including the complicity of officers involved in the "cover-up" of the Commander's shipboard activities which allegedly included public sex, attempts to "sell" female sailors to the Koreans (during a recent WestPac Tour) and "fraternization" with enlisted female sailors. From our discussion with Navy women elsewhere during our trip such behavior should not be considered surprising given the Service's support for such on-base activities as "peso-parties" (Subic/Cubi terminology for the liberal and routine public "use" of Philippine females at places such as the enlisted, NCO and Officer's Clubs), noon-time burlesque shows and "dining-ins" that emphasize sexually-oriented entertainment, with the alleged participation of audience members. The issue of moral acceptability aside, on-base activities such as these contribute to creating an environment in which all females are regarded with little or no respect and abusive behavior toward all women is not only passively accepted and condoned but encouraged. For women in the U.S. Armed Services the situation is worsened by the absence of any refuge (on-base) except their barracks (or housing off-base) where they can gather without being humiliated and feeling denigrated as human beings. To suggest, as we heard, that because Subic, for example, exists only to serve the Fleet without regard for those men and women who are deployed in shore billets outside of the United States bespeaks the kind of attitude that fosters behavior that is inappropriate ... at U.S. government installations.

IV. Communication between the Navy leadership and enlisted personnel, in particular, appears to be a significant problem.... [S]uch an apparent lack of communication both facilitates and fosters the perception that "the Chain of Command" does not work, either with regard to filing complaints of sexual harassment or on issues pertaining to job performance. In this context I wonder if the creation of a DACOWITS newsletter to Service Women is feasible. It could provide one means of communication with service personnel on issues that pertain directly to them.

V. Over and over we heard that the Navy "lacks concern for the needs of the people." This is why, increasingly, retention will loom as an even more important issue in the future. The retention of U.S. Naval personnel will be critical in coming years if we are "to man" a 600 ship Navy using an "all volunteer force concept." The retention issue will be exacerbated by the lack of job satisfaction that is widespread among enlisted personnel in the Navy. . . .

Related to the issue of the Navy's perceived lack of management of its female sailors, there is a concern, expressed by female officers that to meet recruitment quotas, etc., and to "man the 600 ship fleet," the Navy is accepting large numbers of enlisted women, without looking ahead as to their deployment possibilities beyond the E-3 level. Currently, we were told that in the non-traditional job ratings, there is nothing to strike for (AE's are now closed to females; AK ratings above E-5 are also closed to women).

A major issue that was raised during this trip related to that of women in the Navy not working in their ratings and the problem this creates for promotion opportunities. I believe that Navy promotion boards should be given specific direction regarding males and females not working in their ratings.

VI. For both Navy and Marine Corps women the Services' narrow definition of "combat" and their interpretations of U.S.C. Title 10, 6015 continue to be central to the concerns of female officers. We heard much discussion, in particular from Navy women who resent the deployment of civilian females on platforms that they themselves are restricted from deploying on. We heard Marine Corps women complain of not being able to deploy with their units (and thus being singled out and not able to enjoy the benefits of the group bonding process) because of Navy policy restricting the deployment of women on Navy platforms. As a result of this trip and based on other primary data (conversations) obtained during previous DACOWITS visits I really believe that Navy policy is too restrictive (i.e. that the Service's interpretation of Title 10, 6015 goes beyond the intent of Congress) and that in two specific areas (i.e. CLF deployments and P-3 squadrons and air crew) the country and the Service will benefit more from a change in policy than they will from the continuation of the current restrictions. Thanks to Secretary [James H.] Webb, the Executive Committee of the DACOWITS had occasion, on this trip, to sail on the *U.S.S. Wichita* (AOR-1), a ship that is classified as part of the Combat Logistics Force. From that experience we observed that the mission of that particular vessel was not to seek out and engage enemy forces, but rather to supply and support the combatants of the carrier battle group. The *Wichita* deploys only four 20mm MK67 (single) guns for self-defense purposes, (in the future the AOR will be fitted with one Sea Sparrow missile system) and in no way can be construed as a combatant vessel. This is not to say that in a conflict contingency it would not be subject to hostile fire because of its physical proximity to the carrier battle group. However, I believe that in a future global conflict or one in which

U.S. Naval assets were threatened in a regional scenario, geographical factors would play less a factor in enemy strike calculations than would the mission-orientation of enemy forces, together with its specific politico-strategic objectives. Moreover, I believe that the benefits to be derived in peacetime from the deployment of women on CLF vessels would by far outweigh the perceived danger (arising in a potential conflict contingency). In this context it is important to note that American females (on hospital ships, critical base installations, and in forward areas, as in Europe) will be involved in combat, even if they do not themselves have a combat mission. However, as with the CLF, the potential benefits to be derived from the deployment of women in these mission areas is critical to the successful realization of U.S. national security objectives....

Women in the Marine Corps also expressed concern over the Corps' interpretation of the Congressional imposition of combat restrictions for females. Marine Corps women complained that their training in "Boot Camp" was not rigorous enough, including their weapons training. The central issue around which Marine Corps women coalesced in this regard was that of embassy security guards. Since the MOS [military occupation specialty] had once been open to Marine Corps women, its current status (closed to women) is a source of particular frustration. I recommend that the Marine Corps reconsider its position on this issue, perhaps adopting a compromise formula in which larger embassies in major cities could be classified in such a way as to permit the utilization of Marine Corps women as embassy guards. Marine Corps women also complained of the closing of air crew MOSes related to the C-130 which they allege is not listed as a "tactical combat" airlifter. Helicopter (Huey and Cobra) aircrews are eliminating females, although women Marines can serve in the squadron. Like the ratings for the T-39 (which on Okinawa are apparently closed to women Marines) the helicopter crew issue is of growing interest and obviously needs to be examined closely by the Corps' leadership.

VII. For both the Navy and Marine Corps females the environment of the Philippines and Okinawa poses hardships that are not appreciated by male Service members. Beyond the issue of availability of inexpensive female companionship from the local population and its adverse consequences for legitimate social opportunities of Service women, there is the question of the environment in which these women live and are expected to perform their duties. This relates specifically to the environment outside of the workplace, where females go for relaxation and in most instances to live. In both Japan and the Philippines the women complain of inadequate recreational facilities. In this regard it was interesting to note that most women would be satisfied to have a kitchen-like facility where they can cook and congregate in a relaxed and homelike atmosphere and/or adequate and clean Health Center facilities.

The problem of providing for women a "place" where they can go to unwind is exacerbated, I think, in both Services, by their segregation within the Service Communities. Both in Subic and on Okinawa female housing units are separated from male facilities, presumably for security reasons. However, most of the women with whom we talked felt that this situation only aggravated their "separateness" and the perception of women as "second team" members. More serious, at least as we heard in Okinawa, were allegations that this "living" situation contributes to conditions in which extremist behavior (lesbianism) is fostered and, in some cases, supported by the chain of command (particularly among the Non-Commissioned Officers) who are supposed to be supervising the barracks. . . .

The female barracks situation is created in part by the lack of available and affordable off-base housing in Japan. Due to cost and priority waiting-list considerations (such as those persons on accompanied vs. unaccompanied tours; and the E-5/E-6 and below situation relative to base housing availability and the lack thereof) single women and/or females on an unaccompanied tour appear to have very little in the way of options and are dependent on the Service for providing a reasonable and comfortable living environment. . . .

At Subic/Cubi there is a great deal of resentment among female officers and enlisted personnel at the BAQ. For officers at the O-3 level and above we were told that approximately $400.00/month for a space (cubicle) of 450 square feet was automatically deducted from their take-home pay as BAQ. This, allegedly, is below OpNav standards (set for base housing). . . . On Okinawa the barracks living conditions, especially at Camps Hansen and Foster, are less than acceptable for persons who are in the Service of their country. Particularly at Camp Hansen, the female barracks were hot (no airconditioning or adequate ventilation, allegedly due to security considerations), overcrowded in terms of bathroom facilities, and conferred no privacy upon its occupants given the absence of doors (in the case of the Transient barracks) and the utilization of "swingdoors" which, needless to say, cannot be secured. As a result of this latter situation, women Marines report a high incidence of theft as well as malicious behavior (i.e. destruction of personal property). Such activity, together with the widespread reports of sexual approaches, especially to new, young Marines, suggests the need for better supervision beyond the NCO level. Current policy provides for a rotating position of barracks supervision. Perhaps this job assignment can be made longer term (it is currently for a six month period we were told), so as to instill greater confidence in new recruits and to give them a sense of security (to the extent that they feel that they can identify and perhaps confide in an individual with whom they interact on a daily basis in their respective living situations).

The housing situation is so bad in some locations that we were told of a growing number of situations in which female sailors and marines married just to get out of the barracks. In this same vein we heard at Subic and Cubi of a growing number of women who opt to become pregnant to ease the loneliness of their situations. Here, too, we also heard of women becoming pregnant to avoid deployment aboard ship (not realizing, of course, that pregnancy provides only a temporary "reprieve" to the deployment requirements).

VIII. The pregnancy issue remains a serious problem for both Services, although male perceptions of female lost time due to pregnancy are exaggerated, I believe, in relation to the objective reality and certainly when compared to male absenteeism due to alcohol and drug-related abuses. (It was interesting to note that during our visit to Cubi Naval Air Station on August 10, 1987, there was a board notice in the VRC-50 hanger which informed us that there had been no accidents due to drug-related incidents (for the last 163 days), alcoholism (last 23 days), and work-related (for the last 15 days). Clearly, as has been pointed out previously in DACOWITS' installation reports, the misperceptions which persist among the male leadership in the Services over the pregnancy issue need to be addressed by each of the Services. Certainly it is true that some women abuse the condition (of pregnancy) and seek special allowances (with regard to job obligations). Most do not, however; and they work in their ratings or MOSes up to the time of delivery (depending, of course, on their medical condition and the nature of their occupation specialty). For those women who are professionals and regard their Service obligation with a seriousness of purpose, the others (women service members) who seek to use their pregnancy as a condition for work referral and to avoid duty assignments create perception problems as well as difficulties in the daily working relationships between males and female Service members and between "single" female Service members and pregnant women.... I do think that the entire question needs to be explored, perhaps through the convening of a blue-ribbon panel, ... to look at all aspects of this particularly difficult issue....

IX. The pregnancy issue has a lot to do with how women in the Services are regarded professionally. What is less apparent, perhaps, are the implications of male attitudes (of working with women, including those who are pregnant) for cohort bonding and unit cohesiveness. We heard much discussion of these issues during our Westpac visit. Some of us had hoped that the attitudinal problems associated with the integration of women (in large numbers) in the Services would be alleviated when older generation leaders (particularly NCOs) retire from the Services. Many younger males who have undergone a very different socialization experience (from their Chiefs etc.) appear to be more receptive to working constructively with women in the Services. However, it has been alleged that the hierarchies of the Navy and Marine Corps, in particular, continue to project attitudes that are biased against women, in part as a means of fostering the macho mystique that is intrinsic to military service. Some women even suggested that "reasonable males" change their views (of women) to accommodate prevailing attitudes and to enhance their prospects for career advancement....

X. Beyond the esoteric issue of attitudes, perceptions and behaviors, this trip revealed once again the pervasive problem that the Services have in managing their people. Not just with regard to personnel assignments and matching ratings and MOSes with a qualified "manpower" pool, but with regard to ensuring unit readiness and the deployability of military personnel. I am convinced that the dependent child issue is a "ticking time-bomb" for all the Services. This issue which affects an increasing pool of single males as much as it does females in the military has potential implications for contingency planning that goes far beyond the purview of any one of the Services. Day Care centers at most installations are inadequate (i.e. understaffed, inflexible operating hours, too small for base population) and, in any case, are not designed to deal with long term dependent care (as may be necessary in a crisis or deployment situation).

The joint spouse issue will also be of increasing concern to the Services. It was suggested that for both the Marine Corps and the Navy, the option of deploying military couples (together on overseas assignments) on joint tours for a one year period would be a great morale builder.

XI. Quality of life considerations are a major concern of women deployed out of CONUS [Continental United States]. We heard many complaints about the quality of medical care and in particular of OB/GYN professionals. At Camp Hansen, for example, enlisted women Marines claimed that "at the clinic" Corpsmen were performing OB/GYN functions and that referrals to Camp Lester (where the large Navy Hospital is located) were difficult to get and even harder to accomplish (given its distance from Camp and "the hastle" [*sic*] to get an appointment). There is in both the Navy and Marine Corps the perception that dependents are favored (in appointments) over active duty females. Marine Corps women at Kaneohe also complained of their treatment at Tripler, stating that the Army doctors were abusive to them and that the quality of medical care at the base clinic was poor.

The Medical Command of the Navy is apparently experiencing real problems due to a shortage of qualified personnel, fiscal constraints, and low morale. . . .

XII. Uniform issues continue to be of concern to Marine and Navy women, particularly their availability and sizing. As you may know the DACOWITS has long been concerned about these uniform-related issues and over the years has placed specific proposals on its agenda. During our trip specific requests were aired by Marine and Navy women. They include: (1) retaining the Navy beret (which is scheduled to be eliminated in September 1987); (2) greater availability (especially in the Philippines where the women are allocated one small corner of the uniform shop); and [(3)] developing a cotton skirt for the Summer whites.

NATIONAL ENDOWMENT REPORT ON HUMANITIES EDUCATION

August 30, 1987

Concern about the state of the nation's educational system figured prominently during Ronald Reagan's presidency. This concern was somewhat reminiscent of reaction in the wake of the 1957 Soviet launch of the Sputnik satellite, which awakened Americans to the fact that they no longer had a distinct advantage in scientific achievement. The results were a new emphasis on science and mathematics, the establishment of the National Aeronautics and Space Administration (NASA), and the triumphant U.S. landing of men on the moon.

By the 1980s, however, there was a growing awareness, perhaps engendered by the challenge to America's technological supremacy by nations in Europe and Asia, that again all was not well with public education. This time, however, much of the concern was focused on the state of the humanities. Secondary students' alarming lack of knowledge about history and literature was vividly demonstrated by a study sponsored by the National Endowment for the Humanities (NEH), chaired by Lynne V. Cheney, and issued August 30 in a report called "American Memory."

The report concluded that American schools were graduating students with "startling gaps in knowledge" about the facts and substance of history and literature, because instruction concentrated more on the procedures of reasoning than on the content of the ideas discussed. The two-year study by the NEH and the National Endowment for the Arts (NEA)—independent federal grant-making agencies established to assist artists, educators, and programs dealing with the arts—painted a grim picture of humanities education in the nation's public schools.

Previous Studies

The NEH report was one of several issued during the Reagan presidency that were critical of the U.S. education system and its curricula. Many of those reports had been undertaken by government or government-supported organizations. Among the most prominent was an April 1983 report entitled "A Nation At Risk," which warned of a "tide of mediocrity [threatening] our very future as a Nation and a people" unless the public schools began to raise academic standards generally and to emphasize English, math, science, social studies, and computer science. (Historic Documents of 1983, p. 416)

In 1984 William Bennett, then chairman of the NEH (who became education secretary in 1986), issued a report on the state of humanities education in colleges. His report, "To Reclaim a Legacy," concluded that the nation's college students lacked "even the most rudimentary knowledge about the history, literature, art, and philosophical foundations of their nation and civilization." (Historic Documents of 1984, p. 998)

A blunt message on the state of the U.S. educational system was delivered by the Carnegie Corporation's Forum on Education and the Economy in May 1986. "A Nation Prepared: Teachers in the 21st Century" warned that the quality and type of education provided in the United States was inadequate to meet the nation's economic needs. The focus of the panel's proposed reforms was on teacher education and incentives, as well as the restructuring of elementary and secondary administrative procedures. (Historic Documents of 1986, p. 457)

NEH Findings, Recommendations

The NEH study, "American Memory," was inaugurated by Bennett in 1984. Cheney wrote the final report, with contributions from numerous experts, including Daniel J. Boorstin, then Librarian of Congress. Under a $370,000 NEH grant, the research was conducted by Chester E. Finn, Jr., assistant secretary of education for research and improvement, and Diane Ravitch, a historian at Teachers College of Columbia University. The study was based on multiple choice tests and a background questionnaire administered to 7,812 high school juniors, four-fifths of whom were enrolled in an American history course. The surprising results were that only slightly more than half of the students correctly answered 141 history and 121 literature questions (the number of correct answers was slightly lower for literature). If measured against public secondary school standards, 50 percent "correct" would mean a failing grade.

The survey further revealed that 43 percent of the seventeen-year-olds could not place World War I in the correct half-century, and 39 percent of them could not place within a half-century the writing of the

Constitution. Thirty-six percent believed that the Watergate crisis, which led to President Richard Nixon's resignation in 1974, occurred before 1950; and more than 20 percent answered that the radio and phonograph were invented after 1960.

In literature, the survey students registered high recognition of passages from Shakespeare and the Bible, but a disturbing two-thirds could not name the author of Canterbury Tales *(Geoffrey Chaucer), and most were not familiar with works by Dante, Nathaniel Hawthorne, Herman Melville, Jane Austen, Feodor Dostoevsky, and James Joyce.*

In releasing the report, Cheney noted that despite previous studies on the state of education, "history and literature were not emerging as central concerns in the various state, regional, and national commissions looking at education. Educational reform was in the air, but the humanities were seldom a part of it."

To redress the imbalance in public elementary and secondary school education, the NEH basically recommended a three-pronged approach: more time devoted to, and more concern with, the substance of history, literature, and foreign languages; and more emphasis on teachers' knowledge of the subjects they teach, "freed from excessive study of pedagogy."

> *Following are excerpts from "American Memory: A Report on the Humanities in the Nation's Public Schools," issued by Lynne V. Cheney, chairman of the National Endowment for the Humanities, on August 30, 1987:*

The Humanities and the Nation

"A refusal to remember," according to Nobel Prize poet Czeslaw Milosz, is a primary characteristic of our age. Certainly there is abundant evidence that it is a primary characteristic of our nation. Teachers tell of students who do not know that George Washington led American forces in the Revolutionary War; that there was a World War I; that Spanish, not Latin, is the principal language in Latin America. Nationwide polls show startling gaps in knowledge. In a recent survey done for the Hearst Corporation, 45 percent of those polled thought that Karl Marx's phrase "from each according to his ability, to each according to his need" is in the U.S. Constitution.

Cultural memory flourishes or declines for many reasons, but among the most important is what happens in our schools. Long relied upon to transmit knowledge of the past to upcoming generations, our schools today appear to be about a different task. Instead of preserving the past, they more often disregard it, sometimes in the name of "progress"—the idea that today has little to learn from yesterday. But usually the culprit is "process"—the belief that we can teach our children *how* to think without troubling them to learn anything worth thinking about, the belief that we can teach them *how* to understand the world in which they live without conveying to them the events and ideas that have brought it into existence.

To be sure, countless people within our schools resist this approach. I have met school administrators who are convinced that education should be about mastery of knowledge. I have met teachers who, deeply knowledgeable themselves about the roots of our culture, are passionate about wanting their students to be. In Little Rock, Arkansas, for example, I encountered a classics teacher who is determined to teach Greek. For bureaucratic reasons, she has to offer it outside regular school hours; and so she comes early each day to teach a class before school and stays late to teach another after—even though this means she teaches eight classes a day.

Among good teachers, the idea persists that teaching is about transmitting culture. What I heard from them again and again, however, is how many obstacles stand in the way of doing the kind of teaching they think is important.

An educational system that devalues knowledge of the past produces students who do not firmly grasp the facts of history and literature. A 1987 study, based on a survey funded by the National Endowment for the Humanities and conducted by the National Assessment of Educational Progress, reports that more than two-thirds of the nation's seventeen-year-olds are unable to locate the Civil War within the correct half century. More than two-thirds cannot identify the Reformation or *Magna Carta*. By vast majorities, students demonstrate unfamiliarity with writers whose works are regarded as classics: Dante, Chaucer, Dostoevsky, Austen, Whitman, Hawthorne, Melville, and Cather.

Dates and names are not all that students should know, but such facts are a beginning, an initial connection to the sweep of human experience....

By reaching into the past, we affirm our humanity. And we inevitably come to the essence of it. Because we cannot encompass the totality of other lives and times, we strip away the thousand details of existence and come to its heart. We come to the age-old questions, to the enduring subjects of both historian and poet. How do we know our duty? How do we deal with our fate? How do we give our lives meaning and dignity? Pondering these questions, we realize others have pondered them. We realize that we are not the first to know joy and sadness, not the first to set out on the human journey.

The past also offers lessons, and although we shall surely dispute what they are, even as we do so we enlarge our perspectives on the present. What does it mean that Rome fell? And Athens? What does it mean for us? The Framers of the Constitution debated such questions two hundred years ago in Philadelphia. Their achievement is a reminder that history is not merely what has happened: it is a way of finding paths into the future.

A system of education that fails to nurture memory of the past denies its students a great deal: the satisfactions of mature thought, an attachment to avoiding concerns, a perspective on human existence. As advisory group member Linda Miller observed, "We take a tremendous risk of national character by failing to ground our students in history and literature."

Indeed, we put our sense of nationhood at risk by failing to familiarize our young people with the story of how the society in which they live came to be. Knowledge of the ideas that have molded us and the ideas that have mattered to us functions as a kind of civic glue. Our history and literature give us symbols to share; they help us all, no matter how diverse our backgrounds, feel part of a common undertaking. . . .

In our schools today we run the danger of unwittingly proscribing our own heritage. The purpose of this report is to describe how this has happened and to suggest ways it can be remedied.

History and Literature

In 1892, a school reform commission met that was distinguished in its membership and decided in its views. Known as the Committee of Ten, the panel called together scholars from universities—a young Princeton professor named Woodrow Wilson was among them—and representatives from the schools. As participants saw it, cultural content should be central to what was taught and learned. The Committee emphasized the importance of literature (as well as "training in expression") and recommended an eight-year course of history. This plan of study . . . was for *all* students, not just for those who would be attending college.

For a time a curriculum of the kind the Committee of Ten endorsed prevailed. Gradually, however, an opposing view came to dominate: Schools should concern themselves not with intellectual life, but with practical life. As millions of children who would once have been outside the educational system enrolled in the schools, progressive educators argued that what most students needed was not study in history and literature, but preparation for homemaking and for work in trades.

"Skill" training began to drive more traditional offerings, like ancient history, out of the curriculum. Indeed, the very concept of history became submerged in "social studies," a term that emphasizes the present rather than the past; English courses, transformed into "language arts," stressed communication rather than literature; and as the schools adopted a fundamentally different orientation from colleges and universities, humanities scholars turned away from precollegiate education. Curricula, textbooks, and teacher training became the domain of professional educationists.

Under their guidance, schools began to emphasize the process of learning rather than its content. Both are important, extremely important in the teaching of history and literature. But so much emphasis has been placed on process that content has been seriously neglected. One can see the imbalance in the opening pages of a teacher's guide to a widely used textbook series. Scores of skills to be taught are set forth: everything from drawing conclusions and predicting outcomes to filling in forms and compiling recipes. The cultural content of learning, on the other hand, is given only brief mention....

Perhaps the most obvious indicator of how process-driven our schools have become is the dominant role played by the Scholastic Aptitude Test (SAT). In the 1985-86 school year, almost 1.7 million students took the two-and-a-half-hour examination; and many of them, and many of their parents and teachers as well, regarded it as the single most crucial experience of their academic lives. Looming over our educational landscape is an examination that, in its verbal component, carefully avoids assessing substantive knowledge gained from course work. Whether test-takers have studied the Civil War, learned about *Magna Carta,* or read *Macbeth* are matters to which the SAT is studiously indifferent.

Skills—such as reading comprehension, which the SAT assesses—are crucial, I repeat. But the content of education also deserves close attention. Indeed, common sense argues that the two are connected. How can mental skills be developed except through exercise on materials that are challenging and substantial?...

Current reformers have emphasized the necessity of paying close attention to *what* our children learn as well as to *how* they learn, but their message has proved difficult to translate into the classroom....

Recent attempts to improve our schools have also stumbled over organizational structures previously set in place by those who wanted the system to take a less academic direction. Across the nation, graduation requirements have been tightened for social studies and English/language arts: In 1981-82, the average number of credits required was 2.6 for social studies and 3.6 for English/language arts; in 1984-85, the figures were 2.8 and 3.8 respectively. One assumes that policy makers increased requirements so that students would take a greater number of academic courses; but that is not necessarily the effect since "social studies" and "English/language arts" often describe courses that are decidedly unacademic. In Maine, for example, "Introductions to Careers" and "Business Communications" can partially satisfy graduation requirements in social studies and English/language arts.

Words have consequences. Broad terms like "social studies" make it difficult to raise standards concerned with content. For years courses in everything from driver education to "values clarification" have been making their way into curricula under the "social studies" umbrella. "Language arts" has been somewhat less a cover for non-academic courses, but that term too complicates the task of restoring study of the humanities to a central role. Indeed, such terminology makes it difficult even to assess accurately whether progress is being made.

The problem extends far beyond vocabulary into matters of equity. Not all students are fulfilling graduation requirements with courses like "Introductions to Careers" and "Business Communications." Only certain groups are: those in "general education" and "vocational education" programs. For these students—more than 60 percent of those enrolled in our schools—the core of education thus becomes different from that studied by their peers in academic programs. In history and literature, it inevitably becomes diminished. . . .

The educational reform movement of the 1980s has rightfully espoused the cause of educational equity. It has, in general, raised the expectations we have for our schools. Perhaps most important, it has kept the subject of education in the forefront of national attention by making a pragmatic and important case: Our country's economic role in the world will surely decline unless we improve American education.

One effect of this approach, however, has been to concentrate reform effort on basic skills, mathematics, and science. While these aspects of schooling assuredly deserve close attention, it is now time to elaborate the argument; to be clear that world competition is not just about dollars but about ideas. Our students need to know what those ideas are, need to understand our democratic institutions, to know their origins in Western thought, to be familiar with how and why other cultures have evolved differently from our own. They need to read great works of literature, thus confronting questions of good and evil, freedom and responsibility that have determined the character of people and nations. These needs cannot be met in an elementary and secondary curriculum that typically devotes no more than three or four years to history in a twelve-year sequence. They cannot be met in a curriculum that takes a hit or miss—and mostly miss—approach to literature.

It is sometimes argued that the story of our nation's past and the Western tradition that forms our heritage is irrelevant to a population that increasingly comes from other traditions, but I would argue that the opposite is true. . . .

. . . [S]tudents want to understand the society in which they live—a society which they, repeating a pattern basic to the American story, will shape for generations to follow.

Foreign Languages

. . . Self-knowledge requires that we understand other cultures. Daily life increasingly demands it. The world our children live and work in will seem even smaller than the one we know now. Its parts will be even more tightly linked by technology; its citizens more interdependent.

Nothing has greater potential for giving young people the expanded awareness they need than foreign language study—an area that was once considered an important part of education. In 1915, for example, 37 percent of this country's high school students were studying Latin, and 36 percent were studyng a modern foreign language. As the population of the schools expanded and curricula became less academic, these percentages plummeted. There was a reversal when the launching of Sputnik made foreign language knowledge seem useful for a time, but generally the trend has been downward. In 1978, only 21 percent of high school students were enrolled in either a classical or modern foreign language.

The last few years have seen a substantial revival: . . .

- Nationwide, 29 percent of high school students were enrolled in foreign language classes in 1985-86. This represents a 38 percent increase since 1978.
- Severe shortages of foreign language teachers are occurring and threaten to become worse, particularly in parts of the country where expanded programs are under way.

Characteristic of the current revival is a practical, often vocational approach to foreign language education. Students take Latin to improve SAT scores. They see modern foreign languages as a key to employment opportunities. Schools and colleges that once concentrated on literature now offer such courses as "Spanish for Hotel Management."

At all educational levels, oral proficiency is being emphasized. To aid in the tasks of producing speakers of other languages, foreign language educators are concentrating on examinations that assess a student's oral command.

Laudable as the goal of producing proficient speakers is, the concentration on it does raise concerns. Shouldn't reading also be stressed? Shouldn't cultural study? Indeed, without cultural awareness, can a person become an effective speaker? ...

Just as there are teachers of history and literature committed to teaching culturally significant materials, so there are foreign language teachers determined to make culture the content of foreign language education. As their students begin to explore the rich storehouse a second language unlocks, they also acquire the facts, myths, metaphors, and allusions that make them effective speakers.

... Studying a second language gives us greater mastery over our own speech, helps us shape our thoughts with greater precision and our expressions with greater eloquence. Studying a foreign language also provides insight into the nature of language itself, into its power to shape ideas and experience.

A broad vision of foreign language study also includes the great texts of other cultures. The ability to read them with understanding requires years of studying both language and culture, but starting foreign language education in elementary school, as many localities are beginning to do, will allow students time to become sufficiently knowledgeable....

Even at beginning levels, students should be made aware that foreign language study provides more than practical skills. It can be a way of understanding ourselves and others. It can be, as Jefferson put it, "a rich source of delight."

Textbooks

"It has been the object to obtain as wide a range of leading authors as possible, to present the best specimens of style," begins the *McGuffey's Fifth Eclectic Reader* used around the turn of this century. In books like McGuffey's, children encountered Longfellow, Hawthorne, Alcott, Dickens, and Shakespeare. They read stirring speeches, stories about heroes, and selections from the Bible. To be sure, the reading books of the late nineteenth and early twentieth century also contained stories and essays that have since, deservedly, faded into oblivion; but at least half the content of these readers was composed of enduring literature. . . .

Not so today. In the basal readers most widely used now, 10 percent or less of the content is classic children's literature. The emphasis in current readers is overwhelmingly on contemporary writing, generally by writers whose names are unknown outside the textbook industry. They produce a variety of materials, mostly aimed at developing skills, everything from how to recognize cause and effect to how to make grocery lists and use the telephone book.

Far from providing "the best specimens of style," modern readers usually offer prose that satisfies "readability formulas." These calculations, which dictate sentence length, word length, and the number of new words that can be introduced, can lay waste to even the best of stories. . . .

Most elementary reading books contain little literature; most social studies texts in the early grades contain little history. Dominated by a concept called "expanding environments," they report on such matters as where cars come from and where letters go; and they do so in ways meant to develop "human-relations skills" (like "recognizing interdependence among people") or "life skills" (like "addressing an envelope"). These textbooks belabor what is obvious even to six-, seven-, and eight-year-olds: that people live in families, for example, or that children go to school.

. . . In the early decades of this century, [grade-schoolers] read myths, fables, stories from the distant past, and tales of heroes. They learned about Daedalus and King Arthur, George Washington and Joan of Arc, exercising their imaginations and beginning to develop a sense of life in other times.

Textbooks used to teach American history are also disappointing. The advisory group on history and literature looked at samples used in high schools. They were large, . . . heavy with facts, but seldom were those facts made part of a compelling narrative, part of a drama with individuals at center stage. The human ambitions and aspirations that are both the motivating force of history and its fascination were largely absent. One textbook's account of the Constitutional Convention, for example, mentioned only James Madison's age and the fact that he took notes. A second recognized him as a "profound student of government," credited him with being "the Father of the Constitution," but provided no further explanation. A third set forth his contributions to the Convention in some detail, but beyond describing him as "the most astute political thinker of his day" gave little sense of the character of this shy and driven man.

Missing also was a sense of the significance of the historical record. A reader was left with little notion of the ideas that inform our institutions, the arguments and debates that helped shape the kind of nation we are, the reasons behind the choices we have made or why those choices are important. . . .

Good, even excellent textbooks do exist, but they are the exception rather than the rule. For the most part, textbooks used in U.S. schools are poor in content, and what content they do contain is not presented in a way to make anyone care to remember it. Thought by many to be the primary determinant of what is taught in U.S. classrooms, textbooks are tangible evidence of how little we are doing to make our children shareholders in their cultural heritage.

How Do Textbooks Come About?

Publishers are frequently blamed for textbooks. It should be noted, however, that when they decide to put out new books or new series, they first consider what various states and localities say they want.... Curriculum guides, thick manuals full of lists and charts produced by education specialists, set forth what students are to know—skills for the most part, though in the case of history there will often be many pages of topics to be covered. Checklists detail what adoption committees look for, including whether or not textbooks fulfill the requirements of the curriculum guides.

Many checklists specify reading levels, thus bringing readability formulas into play. Checklists also provide a way for various interest groups to make their influence felt. Feminists, environmentalists, ethnic minorities, nutritionists—all have concerns, often important ones. But adding them to the checklist of textbook requirements frequently results in what critics call the "mentioning" problem. A native American will be mentioned or a suffragist pictured, but no full account given of his or her contributions. Name will be heaped upon name, cause upon cause, until the textbook becomes an overcrowded flea market of disconnected facts.

Many checklists have an entry about whether the textbook is likely to engage students; but as one item among many, it is of no more consequence than whether the textbook has a recent copyright date (the most common question on checklists) or whether it will withstand wear and tear. Even if adoption committees were to focus more on content and quality of writing, one has to wonder how textbook editors and writers could meet their expectations. They have dozens of curriculum guides and adoption checklists to try to satisfy as they work....

Fearful that controversy will keep them out of important markets, publishers have tried to avoid controversial subjects like religion....

Literature has also felt the effect of publishers' desire to avoid controversy....

The committees who gather to make centralized textbook adoptions have a complicated task and insufficient time to complete it properly. Matching a single book against an elaborate curriculum guide might take months. Adoption committees seldom have months, at least not of full-time work; and they have many books to consider. And so committee members find themselves running down checklists and flipping through pages. Are women and blacks included? A picture of Susie King Taylor will satisfy—no matter that her contributions as a Civil War nurse are inadequately explained. Is this textbook up to date? A recent copyright will satisfy—no matter that the book has been changed only superficially since the last edition.

Even if textbook committees had time to do their assignments thoroughly, good textbooks would not likely be the result. Curriculum guides that emphasize skills at the expense of content are not a proper matrix for producing textbooks that will teach either skills or content well. Nor can checklists that fail to set priorities produce textbooks in which essential matters receive proper attention. The "great textbook machine," . . . is not geared to produce textbooks that are rich in intellectual content and interesting to read. It functions to perpetuate an idea of education that concentrates on skills. It grinds away, trying to satisfy almost every interest group imaginable—except our children.

What Can Be Done?

One possibility is to move away from centralized adoptions. Let teachers and faculties decide what textbooks they will use and hope that when individuals and small groups choose, they will do so by asking a few important questions: Is this a book a child might love? Does it tell him or her about things that really matter?

But so long as there is centralized adoption anywhere, all textbooks will feel the effect. And it is hard to imagine adoption states, which gain power from the practice, all deciding simultaneously to give it up.

Another possible remedy is for that power to be used in a good cause. With the development of a new history curriculum, California is sending a powerful and simple message to textbook publishers: Give us books that engage students; . . . books that put the facts of the past into compelling narratives and stimulating intellectual form; . . . books that take religion into account and that make the problems and accomplishments of this country clear. Whether California's clout will be sufficient to get the machine to produce a largely unfamiliar product remains to be seen.

One step that should be taken is to assign textbooks a less important role. Let teachers enlighten their students with real books—real works by real authors in the same form in which they are read by the rest of us. Many teachers do this now, often paying for real books out of their own pockets since their schools' book budgets are consumed by textbooks.

Teachers who have tried it testify that students at all levels benefit when challenged by texts that are not only real but great. . . .

History is full of stories of young people learning from great works. One thinks of Lincoln working his way through the Bible. Or one thinks of Frederick Douglass struggling through *The Columbian Orator*, a collection of classic orations used as a schoolbook in the nineteenth century. For both Lincoln and Douglass, these works were more than intellectual training ground. They were entrances to the past, doorways to memory. Through them lay worlds of parable and myth, warning and aspiration that neither man would ever forget.

Teachers

Miss Julia Mortimer, in Eudora Welty's novel *Losing Battles,* knew what teaching was about: "She didn't ever doubt but that all worth preserving is going to be preserved, and all we had to do was keep it going, right from where we are, one teacher on down to the next."

The idea of being transmitters of culture is difficult for today's humanities teachers to hold in mind. They are besieged by educational theorists, administrators, and bureaucrats, all determined that daily classroom activity take another direction. They are beset by curriculum guides that set forth behavioral objectives; by required textbooks that follow the curriculum guides; by teachers' guides to the textbooks that tell them what questions to ask, what answers to give, what skills to emphasize.

Good teachers tend to become subversives in such a system....

... All too often, ... good teachers—the ones who know and love their subjects and want above all else to teach them—have to endure distractions they regard as meaningless.

To find and bring into the classroom literature that is not in the textbooks takes time; to draw up plans for introducing students to original historical documents takes time; and time is the commodity teachers have least of. Even those who ignore official curriculum guides when they teach often have to file lesson plans that pay homage to them. And there are meetings to attend; parents to see; report cards, library fines, permission slips, and bus passes to worry about; lunchrooms to supervise....

How much easier, then, to use the textbook, to follow the teacher's guide, to go with the curriculum chart that says students should practice "finding the main idea"—and never mind if the main idea is worth finding.

How Are Teachers Trained and Sustained?

Some teachers are glad to follow the guides and textbooks since their college years have left them unprepared to do otherwise. They have come through teacher preparation programs in which they have taken courses of dubious intellectual quality. Sometimes the subject matter is trivial, at least to judge from course titles like "Lettering, Posters, and Displays in the School Program." Usually the approach is at fault: Courses treat teaching and learning in abstraction, elevating process to dogma and elaborating it in scientific-sounding language. Those future teachers who assume there is significance here go forth armed with jargon and convinced that what matters is what students can *do* after a lesson rather than what they know....

Most teachers I talked with, however, regarded most education courses as a waste of time.... To be sure, there is one education course teachers almost always said was valuable: practice teaching. Occasionally teachers cited methods courses as worthwhile—if they were taught by someone with classroom experience and directed toward practical rather than theoretical ends.

An elementary school teacher, expected to teach everything from history to mathematics, will typically have spent 41 percent of his or her time as an undergraduate taking courses in education. Many states require fewer education courses for secondary teachers than for elementary teachers, but in others the requirement is the same. Of concern for all levels of teaching is that requirements for education courses have increased in recent years. Colleges and universities in 1983 required their teacher candidates to have, on the average, four more hours in education courses than they did a decade earlier. They also required five more hours of practice teaching.

Time spent taking education courses is time that cannot be spent studying in content areas. . . .

Whether teachers have strong majors is only one consideration in judging how well they know what they teach, because they can also be certified in other subjects. State requirements differ drastically, but in some localities, a few courses in a subject are considered sufficient qualification. School districts can demand more, but too often they do not. And too often, factors other than preparation in subject area are given consideration in hiring. Of particular concern to the history profession is the value placed on coaching ability when history teachers are hired. In a 1979 survey, 58 percent of the school superintendents in Iowa reported that the need to fill coaching positions sometimes (and some superintendents said frequently) led to the hiring of history teachers less competent in the subject than other candidates. One of every five history teachers in Iowa, the survey reported, had majored in physical education.

Teacher preparation requirements can leave teachers knowing less than they should about the subjects they teach; and, once on the job, they have insufficient encouragement to become more knowledgeable. Recertification requirements direct teachers toward courses in education rather than in history, literature, and foreign languages. Heavy classloads and an extraordinary number of paraprofessional demands often make the rigors of content-area study seem impossible in any case. . . .

What Can Be Done?

College and university programs for preparing teachers usually give them too little time to study the subjects they will teach. These programs are also one factor discouraging bright people from entering the profession.

A number of colleges and universities have recently begun programs that try to solve this problem by improving the quality of education courses. A few also offer financial incentives to good students who intend to become teachers. . . .

Various localities and states . . . have also begun alternative certification programs. Designed for those who have already completed a bachelor's degree, these programs allow a person to earn a teaching certificate without going through a traditional teacher education program. Alternative certification plans typically provide more experience in the classroom and fewer hours of education course work than do regular programs. A 1986 study reported that the alternative programs are producing competent and well-trained teachers with above average preparation in subject areas.

Positive as these results are, there was strong feeling in the advisory group on history and literature that finding ways to circumvent regular certification is a limited solution to the problem of attracting bright and knowledgeable teachers. The issue of certification must be faced head on, the group felt, if good teaching in the humanities, as well as other disciplines, is to thrive. As it is now, colleges of education and state education agencies are the strongest forces in determining who gets to teach in public schools. Horror stories growing out of this situation abound, and they almost always play on a single theme: that knowledgeable people with teaching skill cannot teach because they have not taken certain education courses—even when those courses are of no demonstrable use in making better teachers.

We should do more than find alternative ways to get bright and knowledgeable people into classrooms. We should be sure that regular paths to certification are fashioned with but a single interest in mind: securing good teachers. This cannot be accomplished until the process of certifying teachers becomes independent of the colleges that prepare them.

The Carnegie Forum on Education and the Economy has funded a project to create tests that will serve as the basis for certification from a national board. This effort holds promise as a way of separating teacher training from teacher certification. Recent suggestions that only those who have completed approved education programs be allowed to take the tests are of concern, however, since such a requirement would allow colleges of education to continue in their role of not only training teachers but also recommending them for credentialing.

The Holmes Group, a consortium of education deans and chief academic officers from major research universities, has rightly stressed the importance of strong undergraduate education in academic disciplines for future teachers. But that group's emphasis on graduate study in education as the path to advancement in teaching is troubling. Surely the career path upward for teachers ought to lie at least as much in study of what is to be taught as in study of how to teach.

Securing and sustaining good teachers will require commitment from humanities faculties at colleges and universities. Future teachers must be of concern to them in a way they have not always been in the past....

The ongoing intellectual lives of teachers must also be of concern to institutions of higher education....

...If the humanities are not taught well in our schools, students will continue to arrive on campuses without knowledge and appreciation of them; and if they have not begun to see the value of the humanities by the time they enter college, they may well be uninterested in further study. The sharp decline in humanities enrollments and majors on the nation's campuses over the last twenty years should demonstrate that humanities faculties in colleges and universities have a stake in helping to improve humanities teaching in our [elementary and secondary] schools.

Teachers must be relieved of too-heavy classloads and of the many non-teaching duties that clutter their days. They need "time to get ideas from each other, to learn what works and what doesn't," said Brooklyn elementary school principal Jo Bruno, an advisory group member....

Giving teachers more time need not mean spending more on education since what is already being spent is so clearly in need of reallocation. Between 1960 and 1984, while the number of teachers grew by 57 percent and the number of principals and supervisors by 79 percent, the number of other staffers, from curriculum specialists to supervisors of instruction, was up by almost 500 percent. Resources are increasingly being drawn into salaries for people who are not in the classroom but who attempt to direct the activity going on there. Specialists in education for the most part, they inevitably steer in the direction of process rather than content, toward skills rather than substance. How much better to spend this money giving teachers time and resources so they can work out teaching methods and gain greater command of the subjects they teach....

There has been debate in recent years about whether teacher shortages lie ahead. In states where foreign language instruction has drastically expanded, there are already shortages that will undoubtedly become worse unless specific steps are taken to recruit and train a sufficient number of teachers. But for the humanities generally, the challenge is not quantity, but quality....

Recommendations

In *Life on the Mississippi*, Mr. Bixby advises young Sam Clemens, "My boy, you've got to know the *shape* of the river perfectly. It's all there is to steer by on a very dark night. Everything else is blotted out and gone."...

...We would wish for our children that their decisions be informed not by the wisdom of the moment, but by the wisdom of the ages; and that is what we give them when we give them knowledge of culture. The story of past lives and triumphs and failures, the great texts with their enduring themes—these do not necessarily provide *the* answers, but they are a rich context out of which our children's answers can come.

It is in this spirit that the following recommendations are made:

I. More time should be devoted to the study of history, literature, and foreign languages.

- Much that is in school curricula now under the guise of "social studies" should be discarded and replaced with systematic study of history. What goes under the name of "social studies" in the early grades should be replaced with activities that involve imaginative thought and introduce children to great figures of the past.

- Both history and enduring works of literature should be a part of every school year and a part of every student's academic life.

- Foreign language study should start in grade school and continue through high school. From the beginning, it should teach students the history, literature, and thought of other nations.

II. Textbooks should be made more substantive.

- Reading textbooks should contain more recognizably good literature and less formulaic writing.

- History textbooks should present the events of the past so that their significance is clear. This means providing more sophisticated information than dates, names, and places. Textbooks should inform students about ideas and their consequences; about the effect of human personality; about what it is possible for men and women to accomplish.

- In literature, history, and foreign language classes, original works and original documents should be central to classroom instruction.

III. Teachers should be given opportunities to become more knowledgeable about the subjects that they teach.

- In their college years, future teachers should be freed from excessive study of pedagogy so that they can take more courses in subject areas like history, literature, French, and Spanish.

- Teacher preparation and teacher certification must be independent activities. This will help ensure that education courses taken by prospective teachers are of value to effective teaching.

- Higher education liberal arts faculties must recognize their responsibility for the humanities education of future teachers....

- School districts should invest less in curriculum supervisors, instructional overseers, and other mid-level administrators and more in paraprofessionals and aides who can relieve teachers of time-consuming custodial and secretarial duties. This will help accomplish two important goals: It will give teachers time to study and think; and it will put them, rather than outside education specialists, in charge of what goes on in the classroom.

Because American education is—and should be—a local responsibility, implementation of these recommendations will fall largely to policy makers in the states, educators in the schools, and scholars in colleges and universities. Implementation will fall above all to local school boards, parents, and other concerned citizens....

We all have a stake in seeing to it that the humanities are properly taught and thoroughly learned in our schools. We all have a stake in making sure our children know the shape of the river they are traveling....

September

POPE'S SECOND VISIT TO THE UNITED STATES

September 10-19, 1987

Pope John Paul II made his second trip to the United States September 10-19, visiting nine cities and speaking out on a number of social issues. His last U.S. visit had taken place in 1979. (Historic Documents of 1979, p. 725)

President and Mrs. Ronald Reagan greeted the pontiff upon his arrival in Miami September 10. The next day the pope held a key meeting with Jewish leaders. From Miami John Paul II traveled to Columbia, South Carolina; New Orleans; San Antonio; Phoenix; Los Angeles; Monterey; San Francisco; and Detroit. In many of these cities lived large numbers of immigrants and refugees; repeatedly the pope spoke of America's responsibility to these and other needy people. He also recognized the contributions of Hispanic, black, and Native American Catholics to the U.S. church. The trip gave the pope an opportunity to address the dissatisfaction of some American Catholics with Vatican teachings on a number of controversial issues. Dissent, he made clear, was unacceptable. Other issues receiving papal attention on the trip included ecumenism, Catholic education, health care, and acquired immune deficiency syndrome (AIDS).

Jewish Leaders

One key event of the papal visit was a meeting between John Paul II and Jewish leaders in Miami September 11, culminating several months of tense relations arising from the pontiff's decision to receive Austrian president Kurt Waldheim in Rome in June. The Vatican meeting dismayed and angered Jews around the world because Waldheim in 1986 had been accused of knowledge of or participation in Nazi war crimes during World War II. The Vatican explained that allowing Waldheim's visit was necessary "to show the same appreciation, the same esteem for every people." In response, Jewish leaders threatened to boycott the long-planned Miami meeting with the pope.

Publication of an emotional papal letter on the horrors of the Holocaust in late August helped somewhat to defuse Jewish anger over the Waldheim visit. In a further effort to amend relations, the pope invited an international Jewish delegation to a meeting at his summer palace in Castel Gondolfo outside Rome September 1. As a result, the Miami meeting was salvaged.

In his Miami address, the pope spoke out against anti-Semitism, expressed support for a joint Jewish-Catholic study of the Nazi Holocaust, and defended Israel as a Jewish homeland. He also asserted the right of Palestinians to a homeland. The pope did not refer to the Waldheim meeting, nor did he address the Jewish desire for establishment of full diplomatic ties between Israel and the Holy See.

From Miami, John Paul II traveled to Columbia, South Carolina, the heart of the Protestant Bible belt. Here he met with Protestant leaders and participated in ecumenical events. At his next stop, New Orleans, the pope met with 1,800 black Catholic leaders, supporting the cultural contributions of black Catholics to the church. He also praised the nonviolent approach of the U.S. civil rights movement and indicated the church's commitment to help end the enduring "economic deprivation" of many American blacks.

Hispanic Focus

In San Antonio, where 75 percent of the Catholics were of Hispanic descent, the pope's presence gave official recognition to the growing importance of Hispanics in the American church. Nationally, 35 percent of American Catholics were Hispanic; that number was expected to increase to 50 percent by the end of the century. Hispanic Catholics brought to the American church their cultural traditions and spiritual vitality. Also, in places like San Antonio, many Hispanic parishes were actively concerned about social issues such as immigration. Speaking in both English and Spanish to a crowd of 300,000 worshippers September 13, the pope acknowledged the active role the Catholic church in the Southwest had played in aiding Latin American immigrants. He praised those "people of great courage and generosity who have been doing much on behalf of suffering brothers and sisters arriving from the south."

American Catholic Dissent

In recent years many American Catholics had questioned or disagreed with the Vatican's conservative stands on a number of important issues, including abortion, birth control, divorce, ordination of women, and the celibacy of priests.

In his address to U.S. bishops in Los Angeles on September 16, the pope took a strong stand against dissent. He listened as four American bishops painted a picture of American Catholics who, determined to think for themselves, questioned and criticized church teachings. The pontiff responded that dissent was not acceptable. The church, he stated, must be compassionate but not adaptable. He defended the church's right to withhold Holy Communion and other sacraments from those who defy church doctrine. While the pope's message was uncompromising, the tone of his meeting with the bishops was warm.

Other Issues

The primary theme to which the pontiff returned throughout the trip was America's responsibility as a free, wealthy, and technologically advanced country to provide for the poor at home and abroad. In his departure speech September 19 in Detroit, the pope left Americans with this message: "[T]he ultimate test of your greatness is the way you treat every human being, but especially the weakest and most defenseless." His words referred to the unborn, to the immigrants and refugees he had seen in American cities, and to poor people around the world.

Throughout his trip the pope repeated the Vatican's position on a number of controversial issues. The church rejects abortion, euthanasia, and the use of reproductive technologies, he told health care workers in Phoenix. Women are not called to the priesthood, he asserted in San Francisco. To a group of entertainment and communications leaders in Los Angeles he denounced sex and violence in the mass media. The pontiff made his first public allusion to AIDS on this trip, terming the illness "a crisis of immense proportions." He urged compassion for AIDS victims, but did not discuss the Vatican's opposition to homosexuality. (Vatican on bioethics, p. 267)

The pope made a brief stop in northern Canada after leaving the United States. Celebrating Mass with north Canadian Indians and Eskimos at Fort Simpson, he endorsed their fight for aboriginal rights, especially land control.

Reactions

Crowds throughout the pope's trip were smaller than expected. A few demonstrations occurred—the largest by a group of homosexuals in San Francisco—but no major incidents marred the visit. The messages the pope delivered were not always what people wanted to hear, but his personal appeal was undeniable. The trip was a costly one, with security measures accounting for the greatest expense. Three months after the pope's visit, localities and Roman Catholic dioceses were working to pay off debts from the trip, which cost an estimated $32 million.

Following are excerpts from the speech of Pope John Paul II to Jewish leaders in Miami September 11, 1987; from a homily in San Antonio September 13; from an address to U.S. bishops in Los Angeles September 16; and from remarks in Detroit September 19:

ADDRESS TO JEWISH LEADERS

... It is fitting at the beginning of our meeting to emphasize our faith in the one God, who chose Abraham, Isaac and Jacob, and made with them a covenant of eternal love which was never revoked. It was rather confirmed by the gift of the Torah to Moses, opened by the prophets to the hope of eternal redemption and to the universal commitment for justice and peace. The Jewish people, the church and all believers in the merciful God—who is invoked in the Jewish prayers as *'Av Ha-Rakhamim*—can find in this fundamental covenant with the patriarchs a very substantial starting point for our dialogue and our common witness in the world.

It is also fitting to recall God's promise to Abraham and the spiritual fraternity which it established: "In your descendants all the nations shall find blessing—all this because you obeyed my command." This spiritual fraternity, linked to obedience to God, requires a great mutual respect in humility and confidence. An objective consideration of our relations during the centuries must take into account this great need.

2. It is indeed worthy of note that the United States was founded by people who came to these shores, often as religious refugees. They aspired to being treated justly and to being accorded hospitality according to the word of God, as we read in Leviticus: "You shall treat the alien who resides with you no differently than the natives born among you; have the same love for him as for yourself; for you too were once aliens in the land of Egypt. I, the Lord, am your God" (19:34). Among these millions of immigrants there was a large number of Catholics and Jews. The same basic religious principles of freedom and justice, of equality and moral solidarity, affirmed in the Torah as well as in the Gospel, were in fact reflected in the high human ideals and in the protection of universal rights found in the United States. These in turn exercised a strong positive influence on the history of Europe and other parts of the world. But the paths of the immigrants in their new land were not always easy. Sadly enough, prejudice and discrimination were also known in the New World as well as in the Old. Nevertheless, together, Jews and Catholics have contributed to the success of the American experiment in religious freedom and, in this unique context, have given to the world a vigorous form of interreligious dialogue between our two ancient traditions....

3. At the same time, our common heritage, task and hope do not eliminate our distinctive identities. Because of her specific Christian witness, "the church must preach Jesus Christ to the world." In so doing we proclaim that "Christ is our peace." As the apostle Paul said: "All this

is from God, who through Christ reconciled us to himself and gave us the ministry of reconciliation." At the same time, we recognize and appreciate the spiritual treasures of the Jewish people and their religious witness to God. A fraternal theological dialogue will try to understand, in the light of the mystery of redemption, how differences in faith should not cause enmity but open up the way of "reconciliation," so that in the end "God may be all in all."

In this regard I am pleased that the National Conference of Catholic Bishops and the Synagogue Council of America are initiating a consultation between Jewish leaders and bishops which should carry forward a dialogue on issues of the greatest interest to the two faith communities.

4. Considering history in the light of the principles of faith in God, we must also reflect on the catastrophic event of the Shoah, that ruthless and inhuman attempt to exterminate the Jewish people in Europe, an attempt that resulted in millions of victims—including women and children, the elderly and the sick—exterminated only because they were Jews. . . .

It is also fitting to recall the strong, unequivocal efforts of the popes against anti-Semitism and Nazism at the height of the persecution against the Jews. Back in 1938, Pius XI declared that "anti-Semitism cannot be admitted," and he declared the total opposition between Christianity and Nazism by stating that the Nazi cross is an "enemy of the cross of Christ." And I am convinced that history will reveal ever more clearly and convincingly how deeply Pius XII felt the tragedy of the Jewish people and how hard and effectively he worked to assist them during the Second World War.

Speaking in the name of humanity and Christian principles, the bishops conference of the United States denounced the atrocities with a clear statement: "Since the murderous assault on Poland, utterly devoid of every semblance of humanity, there has been a premeditated and systematic extermination of the people of this nation. The same satanic technique is being applied to many other peoples. We feel a deep sense of revulsion against the cruel indignities heaped upon the Jews in conquered countries and upon defenseless peoples not of our faith."

We also remember many others who, at risk of their own lives, helped persecuted Jews and are honored by the Jews with the title of *Tzaddiqe 'ummot ha-'olam* (righteous of the nations).

5. The terrible tragedy of your people has led many Jewish thinkers to reflect on the human condition with acute insights. Their vision of man and the roots of this vision in the teachings of the Bible, which we share in our common heritage of the Hebrew Scriptures, offer Jewish and Catholic scholars much useful material for reflection and dialogue.

In order to understand even more deeply the meaning of the Shoah and the historical roots of anti-Semitism that are related to it, joint collaboration and studies by Catholics and Jews on the Shoah should be continued. Such studies have already taken place through many conferences in your country, such as the national workshops on Christian-Jewish relations.

The religious and historical implications of the Shoah for Christians and Jews will now be taken up formally by the International Catholic-Jewish Liaison Committee, meeting later this year in the United States for the first time. And as was affirmed in the important and very cordial meeting I had with Jewish leaders in Castel Gandolfo on Sept. 1, a Catholic document on the Shoah and anti-Semitism will be forthcoming, resulting from such serious studies.

Similarly, it is to be hoped that common educational programs on our historical and religious relations, which are well developed in your country, will truly promote mutual respect and teach future generations about the Holocaust so that never again will such a horror be possible. Never again!

When meeting the leaders of the Polish Jewish community in Warsaw in June of this year, I underscored the fact that through the terrible experience of the Shoah, your people have become "a loud warning voice for all of humanity, for all nations, for all the powers of this world, for every system and every individual.... A saving warning."

6. It is also desirable that in every diocese Catholics should implement, under the direction of the bishops, the statement of the Second Vatican Council and the subsequent instructions issued by the Holy See regarding the correct way to preach and teach about Jews and Judaism. I know that a great many efforts in this direction have already been made by Catholics, and I wish to express my gratitude to all those who have worked so diligently for this aim.

7. Necessary for any sincere dialogue is the intention of each partner to allow others to define themselves "in the light of their own religious experience." In fidelity to this affirmation, Catholics recognize among the elements of the Jewish experience that Jews have a religious attachment to the land, which finds its roots in biblical tradition.

After the tragic extermination of the Shoah, the Jewish people began a new period in their history. They have a right to a homeland, as does any civil nation, according to international law. "For the Jewish people who live in the State of Israel and who preserve in that land such precious testimonies to their history and their faith, we must ask for the desired security and the due tranquility that is the prerogative of every nation and condition of life and of progress for every society."

What has been said about the right to a homeland also applies to the Palestinian people, so many of whom remain homeless and refugees. While all concerned must honestly reflect on the past—Moslems no less than Jews and Christians—it is time to forge those solutions which will lead to a just, complete and lasting peace in that area....

8. Finally, as I thank you once again for the warmth of your greeting to me, I give praise and thanks to the Lord for this fraternal meeting, for the gift of dialogue between our peoples and for the new and deeper understanding between us. As our long relationship moves toward its third millennium, it is our great privilege in this generation to be witnesses to this progress.

It is my sincere hope that, as partners in dialogue, as fellow believers in the God who revealed himself, as children of Abraham, we will strive to render a common service to humanity, which is so much needed in this our day. We are called to collaborate in service and to unite in a common cause wherever a brother or sister is unattended, forgotten, neglected or suffering in any way; wherever human rights are endangered or human dignity offended; wherever the rights of God are violated or ignored. . . .

ADDRESS IN SAN ANTONIO

. . . 1. It gives me an immense joy to be with you on this Sunday morning and to invoke God's blessings upon this vast state and upon the whole church in this region.

Texas! The name immediately brings to mind the rich history and cultural development of this part of the United States. In this marvelous setting overlooking the city of San Antonio, I cannot but reverently evoke the memory of the Franciscan Father Massanet who, on the feast of St. Anthony of Padua, June 13, 1691, celebrated Mass along the banks of the San Antonio River for the members of an early Spanish expedition and a group of local Indian people.

Since then, people of many different origins have come here, so that today yours is a multicultural society, striving for the fullness of harmony and collaboration among all. . . .

3. What is the message of today's liturgy? To us gathered here in San Antonio in the state of Texas and taking part in the eucharistic sacrifice of our Lord and Savior Jesus Christ, St. Paul addresses these words: "None of us lives as his own master, and none of us dies as his own master. While we live we are responsible to the Lord and when we die we die as his servants. Both in life and death we are the Lord's."

These words are concise, but filled with a moving message. "We live" and "we die." We live in this material world that surrounds us, limited by the horizons of our earthly journey through time. We live in this world, with the inevitable prospect of death, right from the moment of conception and of birth. And yet, we must look beyond the material aspect of our earthly existence. Certainly bodily death is a necessary passage for us all; but it is also true that what from its very beginning has borne in itself the image and likeness of God cannot be completely given back to the corruptible matter of the universe. This is a fundamental truth and attitude of our Christian faith. . . .

"Never forget!" Today's reading from the gospel according to St. Matthew gives us an example of a man who has forgotten. He has forgotten the favors given by his lord—and consequently he has shown himself to be cruel and heartless in regard to his fellow human being. In this way the liturgy introduces us to the experience of sin as it has developed from the beginning of the history of man alongside the experience of death.

We die in the physical body when all the energies of life are extinguished. We die through sin when love dies in us. Outside of love there is no life. If man opposes love and lives without love, death takes root in his soul and grows. For this reason Christ cries out: "I give you a new commandment: Love one another. Such as my love has been for you, so must your love be for each other." The cry for love is the cry for life, for the victory of the soul over sin and death. The source of this victory is the cross of Jesus Christ: his death and his resurrection....

5... The ministry of reconciliation is a fundamental part of the church's life and mission. Without overlooking any of the many ways in which Christ's victory over sin becomes a reality in the life of the church and of the world, it is important for me to emphasize that it is above all in the sacrament of forgiveness and reconciliation that the power of the redeeming blood of Christ is made effective in our personal lives....

7. In Jesus Christ the world has truly known the mystery of forgiveness mercy and reconciliation, which is proclaimed by God's word this day. At the same time, God's inexhaustible mercy to us obliges us to be reconciled among ourselves. This makes practical demands on the church in Texas and the Southwest of the United States. It means bringing hope and love wherever there is division and alienation.

Your history registers a meeting of cultures, indigenous and immigrant, sometimes marked by tensions and conflicts, yet constantly moving toward reconciliation and harmony. People of different races and languages, colors and customs, have come to this land to make it their home. Together with the indigenous peoples of these territories, there are the descendants of those who came from almost every country in Europe: from Spain and France, from Germany and Belgium, from Italy, Hungary and Czechoslovakia, from Ireland, England and Scotland. And even from my own native Poland—for it was to Texas, and Panna Maria, that the first Polish immigrants came to the United States. There are descendants of those who came in chains from Africa; those from Lebanon, the Philippines and Vietnam, and from every Latin American country, especially from Mexico.

This land is a crossroads, standing at the border of two great nations and experiencing both the enrichment and the complications which arise from this circumstance. You are thus a symbol and a kind of laboratory testing America's commitment to her founding moral principles and human values. These principles and values are now being reaffirmed by America, as she celebrates the bicentennial of her Constitution and speaks once more about justice and freedom, and about the acceptance of diversity within a fundamental unity—a unity arising from a shared vision of the dignity of every human person, and a shared responsibility for the welfare of all, especially of the needy and the persecuted.

8. Against this background one may speak of a current phenomenon here and elsewhere—the movement of people northward, not only from Mexico but from other southern neighbors of the United States. On this

matter also there is work of reconciliation to be done. Among you there are people of great courage and generosity who have been doing much on behalf of suffering brothers and sisters arriving from the south. They have sought to show compassion in the face of complex human, social and political realities. Here human needs, both spiritual and material, continue to call out to the church with thousands of voices, and the whole church must respond by the proclamation of God's word and by selfless deeds of service. Here too there is ample space for continuing and growing collaboration among members of the various Christian communions.

In all of this the Hispanic community itself faces the greatest challenge. Those of you of Hispanic descent—so numerous, so long present in this land, so well-equipped to respond—are called to hear the word of Christ and take it to heart: "I give you a new commandment: Love one another. Such as my love has been for you, so must your love be for each other." And Jesus specified that this love embraces the entire range of human needs from the least to the greatest: "I promise you that whoever gives a cup of cold water to one of these lowly ones . . . will not want for his reward." The Hispanic community also needs to respond to its own needs and to show generous and effective solidarity among its own members. I urge you to hold fast to your Christian faith and traditions, especially in defense of the family. And I pray that the Lord may provide many more vocations to the priesthood and to the religious life among your young people.

May you who have received so much from God hear the call to a renewal of your Christian life and to fidelity to the faith of your fathers. May you respond in the spirit of Mary, the virgin mother whom the church sees "maternally present and sharing in the many complicated problems which today beset the lives of individuals, families and nations . . . helping the Christian people in the constant struggle between good and evil, to ensure that it 'does not fall,' or if it has fallen, that it 'rises again.' ". . .

ADDRESS TO U.S. BISHOPS

. . . At the heart of the church's self-understanding is the notion of *communio:* primarily, a sharing through grace in the life of the Father given us through Christ and in the Holy Spirit. . . . This communion has its origin in a divine call, the eternal decree which predestined us to share the image of the Son. It is realized through sacramental union with Christ and through organic participation in all that constitutes the divine and human reality of the church, the body of Christ, which spans the centuries and is sent into the world to embrace all people without distinction.

2. It is clear that in the decades since the [Second Vatican C]ouncil this "vertical dimension" of ecclesial communion has been less deeply experienced by many who, on the other hand, have a vivid sense of its

"horizontal dimension." Unless, however, the entire Christian community has a keen awareness of the marvelous and utterly gratuitous outpouring of "the kindness and love of God, our Savior" which saved us "not because of any righteous deeds we had done, but because of his mercy," the whole ordering of the church's life and the exercise of her mission of service to the human family will be radically weakened and never reach the level intended by the council.

...Our pastoral efforts are fruitful, in the last analysis, when the people of God—we bishops with the clergy, religious and laity—are led to Christ, grow in faith, hope and charity, and become authentic witnesses of God's love in a world in need of transfiguration.

Cardinal [Joseph] Bernardin has stated very well that just as there is but one faith, one Lord, one baptism, so there can be but one loyalty—to the word of God perennially proclaimed in the church entrusted to the episcopal college, with the Roman pontiff as its visible head and perpetual source of unity....

3. The "vertical dimension" of ecclesial communion is of profound significance in understanding the relationship of the particular churches to the universal church. It is important to avoid a merely sociological view of this relationship. "In and from such individual churches there comes into being the one and only Catholic Church," but this universal church cannot be conceived as the sum of the particular churches or as a federation of particular churches.

In the celebration of the eucharist these principles come fully to the fore.... Wherever a community gathers around the altar under the ministry of a bishop, there Christ is present and there, because of Christ, the one, holy, catholic and apostolic church gathers together....

"... It is precisely because you are pastors of particular churches in which there subsists the fullness of the universal church that you are, and must always be, in full communion with the successor of Peter. To recognize your ministry as 'vicars and delegates of Christ' for your particular churches is to understand all the more clearly the ministry of the Chair of Peter, which 'presides over the whole assembly of charity, protects legitimate variety and at the same time sees to it that differences do not hinder unity but rather contribute to it.' "

4. In this perspective too we must see the ministry of the successor of Peter not only as a "global" service, reaching each particular church from "outside" as it were, but as belonging already to the essence of each particular church from "within." Precisely because this relationship of ecclesial communion—our *collegialitas effectiva et affectiva*—is such an intimate part of the structure of the church's life, its exercise calls for each and every one of us to be completely one in mind and heart with the will of Christ regarding our different roles in the college of bishops. The council took pains not only to formulate these roles but also to place the exercise of authority in the church in its proper perspective, which is precisely the perspective of *communio*. In this respect also the council was—in the

words of the extraordinary synod—"a legitimate and valid expression and interpretation of the deposit of faith as it is found in Sacred Scripture and in the living tradition of the church."

. . . It is sometimes reported that a large number of Catholics today do not adhere to the teaching of the church on a number of questions, notably sexual and conjugal morality, divorce and remarriage. Some are reported as not accepting the church's clear position on abortion. It has also been noted that there is a tendency on the part of some Catholics to be selective in their adherence to the church's moral teachings. It is sometimes claimed that dissent from the magisterium is totally compatible with being a "good Catholic" and poses no obstacle to the reception of the sacraments. This is a grave error that challenges the teaching office of the bishops of the United States and elsewhere. I wish to encourage you in the love of Christ to address this situation courageously in your pastoral ministry, relying on the power of God's truth to attract assent and on the grace of the Holy Spirit, which is given both to those who proclaim the message and to those to whom it is addressed.

We must also constantly recall that the teaching of Christ's church—like Christ himself—is a "sign of contradiction." It has never been easy to accept the gospel teaching in its entirety, and it never will be. The church is committed, both in faith and morals, to make her teaching as clear and understandable as possible, presenting it in all the attractiveness of divine truth. And yet the challenge of the Gospel remains inherent in the Christian message transmitted to each generation. Archbishop [John] Quinn has made reference to a principle with extremely important consequences for every area of the church's life: "(T)he revelation of God par excellence is found in the cross of Christ, which makes God's folly wiser than human wisdom. Often human wisdom in a given age appears to have the last word. But the cross brings a perspective that changes judgments radically." . . .

6. A number of other general points may be made. First, the church is a community of faith. To accept faith is to give assent to the word of God as transmitted by the church's authentic magisterium. Such assent constitutes the basic attitude of the believer and is an act of the will as well as of the mind. It would be altogether out of place to try to model this act of religion on attitudes drawn from secular culture.

Within the ecclesial community, theological discussion takes place within the framework of faith. Dissent from church doctrine remains what it is, dissent; as such it may not be proposed or received on an equal footing with the church's authentic teaching.

Moreover, as bishops we must be especially responsive to our role as authentic teachers of the faith when opinions at variance with the church's teaching are proposed as a basis for pastoral practice.

I wish to support you as you continue to engage in fruitful dialogue with theologians regarding the legitimate freedom of inquiry, which is their right. . . . They, on their part, will recognize that the title *Catholic* theologian expresses a vocation and a responsibility at the service of the community of faith and subject to the authority of the pastors of the church. In particular, your dialogue will seek to show the inacceptability of dissent and confrontation as a policy and method in the area of church teaching.

7. Speaking on your behalf, Archbishop Quinn has shown full awareness of the seriousness of the challenge facing your teaching ministry. He has spoken of the dual task of the conversion of the mind and the conversion of the heart. The way to the heart very often passes through the mind, and throughout the length and breadth of the church there is need today for a new effort of evangelization and catechesis directed to the mind....

Catholic children and young people need to be given an effective opportunity to learn the truths of the faith in such a way that they become capable of formulating their Catholic identity in terms of doctrine and thought. Here the Catholic press can make a magnificent contribution to raising the general level of Catholic thought and culture. Seminaries, especially, have the responsibility of ensuring that future priests should acquire a high level of intellectual preparation and competence. Continuing education programs for priests, religious and laity play an important part in stimulating a necessary and serious intellectual approach to the multitude of questions confronting faith in our contemporary world.

A crucial aspect of this "apostolate of the mind" concerns the duty and right of bishops to be present in an effective way in Catholic colleges and universities and institutes of higher studies in order to safeguard and promote their Catholic character, especially in what affects the transmission of Catholic doctrine.... The intellectual approach that is needed, however, is one intimately linked to faith and prayer. Our people must be aware of their dependence on Christ's grace and on the great need to open themselves ever more to its action....

8... Primarily through her laity, the church is in a position to exercise great influence upon American culture.... And culture, while having a certain dynamic endurance, is always changing and developing as a way of life. Thus the American culture of today stands in continuity with your culture of 50 years ago. Yet it has changed; it has been greatly influenced by attitudes and currents of thought.

But how is the American culture evolving today? Is this evolution being influenced by the Gospel? Does it clearly reflect Christian inspiration? Your music, your poetry and art, your drama, your painting and sculpture, the literature that you are producing—are all those things which reflect the soul of the nation being influenced by the spirit of Christ for the perfection of humanity?

I realize these are difficult questions to answer, given the complexity and diversity of your culture. But they are relevant to any consideration of the role of the Catholic laity, "the largest number of educated faithful in the world." And it is above all the laity, once they have themselves been inspired by the Gospel, who bring the Gospel's uplifting and purifying influence to the world of culture, to the whole realm of thought and artistic creativity, to the various professions and places of work, to family life and to society in general. As bishops, with the task of leading the laity and of encouraging them to fulfill their ecclesial mission in the world, we must continue to support them as they endeavor to make their specific contribution to the evolution and development of culture and to its impact on society.

9. With reference to this question, and in such areas as politics, economics, mass media and international life, the service we bring is primarily a priestly service: the service of preaching and teaching the word of God with fidelity to the truth, and of drawing the laity ever more into the dialogue of salvation. We are charged to lead our people to holiness, especially through the grace of the eucharist and the whole sacramental life. The service of our pastoral leadership, purified in personal prayer and penance, far from bearing an authoritarian style in any way, must listen and encourage, challenge and at times correct. Certainly, there is no question of condemning the technological world, but rather of urging the laity to transform it from within so that it may receive the imprint of the Gospel.

10. We serve our laity best when we make every effort to provide for them, and in collaboration with them, a comprehensive and solid program of catechesis with the aim of "maturing the initial faith and of educating the true disciple of Christ by means of a deeper and more systematic knowledge of the person and the message of our Lord Jesus Christ." Such a program will also assist them in developing that habit of discernment which can distinguish the spirit of the world from the Spirit of God and which can distinguish authentic culture from elements that degrade human dignity. It can provide them a solid basis for growing in their knowledge and love of Jesus Christ through continual conversion and personal commitment to the demands of the Gospel.

11. In speaking of the laity, I feel a particular desire to support you in all you are doing on behalf of family life. Archbishop [Rembert] Weakland has mentioned "the large number of divorces and the breakup of so many families" as a special pastoral problem. I know that all of us feel great sadness and deep pastoral concern for all those whose lives are affected in this way. . . .

The faithful teaching of the intrinsic relationship between the unitive and procreative dimensions of the marriage act is, of course, only a part of our pastoral responsibility. With pastoral solicitude for couples *Familiaris Consortio* pointed out that "the ecclesial community at the present time must take on the task of instilling conviction and offering practical help to those who wish to live out their parenthood in a truly responsible way. . . . This implies a broader, more decisive and more systematic effort to make the natural methods of regulating fertility known, respected and applied." . . .

12. My profound gratitude to you extends to the many other areas in

which, with generous dedication, you have worked for and with the laity. These include your persevering efforts at promoting peace, fostering justice and supporting the missions. In the area of the defense of human life, you have worked with exceptional commitment and constancy. Already during the *ad limina* visits of 1978, Paul VI drew attention to this activity of yours, assuring you of the appreciation of the Holy See. Because of their exceptional importance, I wish to quote at some length his words of strong support for you and make them my own:...

"With the enlightenment of faith, the incentive of love and an awareness of your pastoral accountability, you have worked to oppose whatever wounds, weakens or dishonors human life....

"In this regard, your efforts have been directed to the eradication of hunger, the elimination of subhuman living conditions and the promotion of programs on behalf of the poor, the elderly and minorities. You have worked for the improvement of the social order itself. At the same time, we know that you have held up to your people the goal to which God calls them: the life above, in Christ Jesus.

"Among your many activities at the service of life there is one which, especially at this juncture of history, deserves our strongest commendation and our firmest support: It is the continuing struggle against what the Second Vatican Council calls the 'abominable crime' of abortion. Disregard for the sacred character of life in the womb weakens the very fabric of civilization: It prepares a mentality and even a public attitude that can lead to the acceptance of other practices that are against the fundamental rights of the individual. This mentality can, for example, completely undermine concern for those in want, manifesting itself in insensitivity to social needs; it can produce contempt for the elderly to the point of advocating euthanasia; it can prepare the way for those forms of genetic engineering that go against life, the dangers of which are not yet fully known to the general public.

"It is therefore very encouraging to see the great service you render to humanity by constantly holding up to your people the value of human life."...

Nine years have passed since these words were spoken and yet they are still relevant today—relevant in their prophetic vision, relevant in the needs they express, relevant in the defense of life.

13. In his encyclical *Pacem in Terris,* Pope John XXIII placed the question of the advancement of women in the context of the characteristics of the present day, "the signs of the times." He made it clear that the cause in question was one of human dignity....

There are many other aspects involved in the question of women's equal dignity and responsibility, which will undoubtedly be properly dealt with in the forthcoming Synod of Bishops. At the basis of all considerations are two firm principles: the equal human dignity of women and their true feminine humanity.... As I have stated and as Archbishop Weakland has pointed out, women are not called to the priesthood. Although the teaching of the church on this point is quite clear, it in no way alters the fact that women are indeed an essential part of the gospel plan to spread the good news of the kingdom. And the church is irrevocably committed to this truth.

14. My interest in the question of vocations is well known to all of you.... Therefore, I am very pleased that you have chosen this topic as one of those to be emphasized today.

Archbishop [Daniel] Pilarczyk has presented an "overview of the ministerial realities of the church in this country," mentioning aspects that offer much consolation to you as bishops and aspects which are cause for pastoral concern. He mentioned that it was important "to speak of some of the very positive implications of lay, religious and clerical vocations in America." In doing this, he rightly drew attention to the way that the Holy Spirit is at work in your midst, something that we must indeed be ever attentive to and grateful for....

It is indeed encouraging to note how lay people in ever-increasing numbers have become involved in the life of the church and how this has led to "a depth and variety of ministry far greater than ever before."...

It is important for our people to see clearly that the ministry of the ordained priest and the involvement of the laity in the church's mission are not at all opposed to one another. On the contrary, the one complements the other. Just as the priestly ministry is not an end in and of itself, but serves to awaken and unify the various charisms within the church, so too the involvement of the laity does not replace the priesthood, but supports it, promotes it and offers it space for its own specific service....

The insufficient number of seminarians and candidates for religious life is indeed a cause of pastoral concern for all of us, for we know that their public witness to the Gospel and their specific roles in the church are irreplaceable. In many parts of the world the church is experiencing, as Archbishop Pilarczyk observed, that "society is becoming increasingly secular and therefore increasingly inhospitable to Christian belief." It is especially difficult today for young people to make the generous sacrifices entailed in accepting God's call....

Prayer for vocations remains the primary way to success, since Jesus himself left us the commandment: "Beg the harvest master to send out laborers to gather his harvest." I ask you therefore to encourage prayer for vocations among all the people, particularly among priests and religious themselves but also in families, where the first seeds of vocations are usually planted, and in schools and religious education programs. The prayers of the elderly and the sick have an efficacy that must not be forgotten.

In addition to prayer, young people must be invited. It was Andrew who brought his brother Peter to the Lord. It was Philip who brought Nathanael. And how many of us and of our priests and religious came to hear the Lord's call through the invitation of someone else? Your own presence among the youth is a blessing and an opportune time to extend this invitation to them and to ask young people themselves to pray for vocations....

18. I wish to encourage you also in the pastoral care that you give to homosexual persons. This includes a clear explanation of the church's teaching, which by its nature is unpopular. Nevertheless, your own pastoral experience confirms the fact that the truth, howsoever difficult to accept, brings grace and often leads to a deep inner conversion. No matter what problem individual Christians have, and no matter what degree of response to grace they make, they are always worthy of the church's love and Christ's truth. All homosexual and other persons striving to fulfill the Gospel precept of chastity are worthy of special encouragement and esteem.

19. From time to time the question of sex education, especially as regards programs being used in schools, becomes a matter of concern to Catholic parents. The principles governing this area have been succinctly but clearly enunciated in *Familiaris Consortio.* First among these principles is the need to recognize that sex education is a basic right and duty of parents themselves. They have to be helped to become increasingly more effective in fulfilling this task. Other educational agencies have an important role, but always in a subsidiary manner, with due subordination to the rights of parents.

Many parents will undoubtedly be heartened by the reference in the pastoral letter of the bishops of California, "A Call to Compassion," to an absolutely essential aspect of this whole question: "The recovery of the virtue of chastity," they wrote, "may be one of the most urgent needs of contemporary society." We cannot doubt that the Catholic Church in the United States, as elsewhere, is called to make great efforts to assist parents in teaching their children the sublime value of self-giving love; young people need great support in living this fundamental aspect of their human and Christian vocation....

21. I wish at this time to offer you my encouragement as you seek to guide the church of God in so many areas: as you seek to lead your people in fulfilling their mission within the United States and well beyond her boundaries. Everything you do to help your people to look outside themselves to Christ in need is a great ecclesial and apostolic service....

DEPARTURE ADDRESS

Mr. Vice President, dear friends, dear people of America,

1. Once again God has given me the joy of making a pastoral visit to your country—the United States of America. I am filled with gratitude to him and to you....

I cannot leave without expressing my thanks to all those who worked so hard to make this visit possible....

As I leave, I express my gratitude to God also for what he is accomplishing in your midst. With the words of St. Paul, I too can say with confident assurance "that he who has begun the good work in you will carry it through to completion, right up to the day of Christ Jesus." And so I am confident too that America will be ever more conscious of her responsibility for justice and peace in the world. As a nation that has received so much, she is called to continued generosity and service toward others.

2. As I go, I take with me vivid memories of a dynamic nation, a warm and welcoming people, a church abundantly blessed with a rich blend of cultural traditions. I depart with admiration for the ecumenical spirit that breathes strongly throughout this land, for the genuine enthusiasm of your young people and for the hopeful aspirations of your most recent immigrants. I take with me an unforgettable memory of a country that God has richly blessed from the beginning until now.

America the beautiful! So you sing in one of your national songs. Yes, America, you are beautiful indeed and blessed in so many ways:

—In your majestic mountains and fertile plains.

—In the goodness and sacrifice hidden in your teeming cities and expanding suburbs.

—In your genius for invention and for splendid progress.

—In the power that you use for service and in the wealth that you share with others.

—In what you give to your own and in what you do for others beyond your borders.

—In how you serve and in how you keep alive the flame of hope in many hearts.

—In your quest for excellence and in your desire to right all wrongs.

Yes, America, all this belongs to you. But your greatest beauty and your richest blessing is found in the human person: in each man, woman and child, in every immigrant, in every native-born son and daughter.

3. For this reason, America, your deepest identity and truest character as a nation is revealed in the position you take toward the human person. The ultimate test of your greatness is the way you treat every human being, but especially the weakest and most defenseless ones.

The best traditions of your land presume respect for those who cannot defend themselves. If you want equal justice for all and true freedom and lasting peace, then, America, defend life! All the great causes that are yours today will have meaning only to the extent that you guarantee the right to life and protect the human person.

—Feeding the poor and welcoming refugees.

—Reinforcing the social fabric of this nation.

—Promoting the true advancement of women.

—Securing the rights of minorities.

—Pursuing disarmament, while guaranteeing legitimate defense.

All this will succeed only if respect for life and its protection by the law are granted to every human being from conception until natural death.

Every human person—no matter how vulnerable or helpless, no matter how young or how old, no matter how healthy, handicapped or sick, no matter how useful or productive for society—is a being of inestimable worth created in the image and likeness of God. This is the dignity of America, the reason she exists, the condition for her survival—yes, the ultimate test of her greatness: to respect every human person, especially the weakest and most defenseless ones, those as yet unborn.

With these sentiments of love and hope for America, I now say goodbye in words that I spoke once before: "Today, therefore, my final prayer is this: that God will bless America, so that she may increasingly become—and truly be—and long remain—'one nation, under God, indivisible. With liberty and justice for all.' "

May God bless you all.

God bless America!

BORK CONFIRMATION BATTLE

September 15, October 9 and 13, 1987

The resignation of Supreme Court Justice Lewis F. Powell, Jr., on June 26 gave President Ronald Reagan an opportunity to stamp his conservative agenda on the nation's highest judicial body and to have an impact long after his presidency ended. But Reagan's first choice to fill the vacancy, Robert H. Bork, was rejected 42-58 by the Senate October 23. (Powell resignation, p. 577)

The president announced the nomination of Bork, a judge on the U.S. Court of Appeals for the District of Columbia, on July 1. The Senate immediately began preparing for what was to become the most vigorous and lengthy Court nomination fight since President Richard Nixon nominated Clement F. Haynsworth, Jr., and G. Harrold Carswell to the Court in 1969 and 1970 (both were rejected).

In an opening statement before the Senate Judiciary Committee September 15, Bork summarized his "philosophy of judging" as "neither liberal nor conservative." But as the hearings progressed it appeared that confirmation of Reagan's nominee was in jeopardy. The Judiciary Committee October 6 voted 9-5 to send Bork's name to the floor with a recommendation that it be rejected. Three days later, a defiant Bork announced that he would not withdraw from the fight and asked for a Senate floor vote, although he said he had "no illusions" about the outcome. Charging that events had transformed the process of confirming judges into a political campaign that "should not occur again," he said, "Federal judges are not appointed to decide cases according to the latest opinion polls." When judicial nominees "are treated as political candi-

dates . . . the effect will be to erode public confidence and endanger the independence of the judiciary."

On October 13, the committee issued its final report recommending 9-5 against the nomination.

Bork's Record

The Supreme Court for a number of years had been equally divided among justices who supported an activist role in matters of social policy—such as affirmative action and women's rights—and those who preferred to interpret the Constitution strictly, basing many of their decisions on arguments that the Court should not step into legislative and political affairs, which rested with the two other branches of government. Powell had been widely considered the pivotal justice in decisions affecting those considerations, siding frequently with the "activists." Bork, in contrast, was a conservative. His statements on abortion and the role of the federal courts and his decisions on the appeals court suggested he would have tilted the Supreme Court to the right.

Bork's four years as U.S. solicitor general had thrust him into the spotlight. Following President Nixon's order, Bork fired special Watergate prosecutor Archibald Cox in 1973, after Attorney General Elliot L. Richardson and Deputy Attorney General William D. Ruckelshaus resigned their offices rather than fire Cox. The incident quickly became known as the "Saturday night massacre" and prompted the introduction of impeachment resolutions against Nixon.

Bork left the Justice Department in 1977 to teach at Yale University. In 1981 he returned to Washington, where he practiced law until Reagan appointed him to the appeals court in 1982. Bork remained in the public eye through provocative interviews, extensive legal writings, and congressional testimony. In a 1981 appearance before a Senate Judiciary subcommittee, for example, Bork said that the high Court's 1973 Roe v. Wade *decision, which established a constitutional right to abortion, was "an unconstitutional decision, a serious and wholly unjustifiable usurpation of state legislative authority. [The decision] is by no means the only example of such unconstitutional behavior by the Supreme Court."*

The Court majority had premised the Roe *decision on a right of privacy, a doctrine Bork rejected in a 1984 decision upholding a Navy policy prohibiting homosexual activity. Dissenters on the appeals court challenged his conclusion, contending that Bork was substituting his "preferences for the constitutional principles established by the Supreme Court."*

Earlier in his career, Bork had criticized the Supreme Court under Chief Justice Earl Warren, a Court that was responsible for historic civil rights advances and new protections for the rights of criminal defendants. Chastising the Court for "judicial activism," Bork wrote in 1977 that "We have also damaged law, and created disrespect for it, through our failure to observe the distinction, essential to democracy, between judges and legislators." Bork continued, "The era of the Warren Court was, in my opinion, deeply harmful to the prestige of law."

The Confirmation Battle

Well before the Judiciary Committee began its hearings, civil rights groups launched a campaign to frame the nomination as one of the most important decisions senators would face in their careers. At stake, they believed, were decades of rulings that broke down the barriers of racial discrimination in schools, housing, and employment, and that gave women the right to an abortion.

The Bork nomination fueled an unprecedented lobbying effort by both liberal and conservative groups. His views on topics from antitrust to free speech to privacy rights, and his often pungent manner of expressing them, prompted the most vigorous opposition to a judicial nomination in nearly two decades. A panoply of civil rights and civil liberties groups, including the American Civil Liberties Union, Common Cause, the AFL-CIO, and the Leadership Conference (an umbrella group of some 180 organizations) joined forces to keep Bork off the Court. Active Bork supporters, led by Reagan and the White House staff, included conservative organizations such as the Free Congress Foundation and Phyllis Schlafly's Eagle Forum.

"Everybody has made this [nomination] priority No. 1," said Art Kropp, executive director of People for the American Way, an organization concerned with civil liberties. "Nobody's holding anything back on this one," said a lobbyist active in the conservative community. "It's high stakes for all sides."

Within the Senate, the debate over the nomination took on harsh political overtones when Senate Minority Leader Robert Dole, R-Kan.—a candidate for the Republican presidential nomination—July 27 accused Judiciary Chairman Joseph R. Biden, Jr., D-Del.—then a Democratic presidential aspirant—of stalling the nomination. The next day, Senate Majority Leader Robert C. Byrd, D-W.Va., cautioned colleagues not to turn the Bork nomination into a partisan matter. Meanwhile, Reagan used an August 12 nationally televised address to declare that winning confirmation for Bork was a major priority of his administration.

Philosophical Debate in Hearings

The confirmation hearings gave the Senate and the public an opportunity to witness an unusually rich debate over legal philosophy. The dialogue in the Senate Judiciary Committee as Bork sparred with opposing senators and amiably answered the gentler questions of supporters was based on the bedrock concepts that governed American society, among them the right to privacy, equal protection, freedom of speech, and due process of law.

Bork asserted that his judicial philosophy was "simply a philosophy of judging which gives the Constitution a full and fair interpretation." Bork said he believed in a right to privacy but disliked the way the Supreme Court had developed it; that he believed the equal protection clause of the Constitution protected blacks, other minorities, and women but felt the Court's reasoning in this area was suspect; that he supported broad protections for speech but continued to have theoretical problems with an important Supreme Court decision defining that right; and that he had acted appropriately in firing Watergate special prosecutor Cox.

However, Bork's critics continued to assert that he was a radical theorist who was outside the mainstream of American legal thought. They professed doubts about some of the positions he expressed during the hearings because, they claimed, they were at such variance with his past positions.

Although the administration launched an intense lobbying campaign on behalf of its nominee, observers agreed that there were several reasons for the failure: underestimating the intensity and breadth of the opposition; failing to energize Reagan's traditional supporters; and adopting a strategy that was essentially defensive.

When debate began on the Senate floor, fifty-four senators had already declared their opposition to Reagan's appointment. Thirty-nine had expressed support and only seven were officially uncommitted. Four of the uncommitted voted against Bork, while three decided in favor of confirmation. After the October 23 vote, Byrd said it was time to "start the healing, to lower our voices." Bork's supporters said they were pleased that the debate had been held. "It was the correct thing," said Orrin G. Hatch, R-Utah, a member of the Judiciary Committee and one of Bork's strongest supporters. "There was a record made."

New Nominees: Ginsburg, Kennedy

On October 29, Reagan announced the nomination of Douglas H. Ginsburg, a relatively unknown and young (forty-one years old) federal appeals court judge. The Ginsburg nomination surprised many in the Senate who had expected Reagan to select a more moderate conservative who would have had an easier time winning confirmation. Again, the nomination ran into trouble, even before hearings began. Ginsburg November 7 withdrew his name from consideration after confirming news reports that he had smoked marijuana in college and as a law professor, that there might have been a conflict of interest in his participation in certain cases while on the bench, and that he had misrepresented his courtroom experience. Four days later, Reagan announced his third choice, Anthony M. Kennedy, who had been a judge on the U.S. Ninth Circuit Court of Appeals for twelve years. The nomination of an experi-

enced judge and "mainstream conservative" was well received on Capitol Hill, where other pressing problems were looming and members were weary of nomination battles.

Following are excerpts from the texts of Robert H. Bork's September 15, 1987, statement before the Senate Judiciary Committee in its opening day of hearings on his nomination to be an associate justice of the Supreme Court; his October 9 statement refusing to withdraw his name before the Senate floor vote; and excerpts from the October 13 committee report recommending against confirmation.

BORK'S OPENING STATEMENT

. . . The judge's authority derives entirely from the fact that he is applying the law and not his personal values. That is why the American public accepts the decisions of its courts, accepts even decisions that nullify the laws a majority of the electorate or of their representatives voted for.

The judge, to deserve that trust and that authority, must be every bit as governed by law as is the Congress, the President, the state governors and legislatures, and the American people. No one, including a judge, can be above the law. Only in that way will justice be done and the freedom of Americans assured.

How should a judge go about finding the law? The only legitimate way, in my opinion, is by attempting to discern what those who made the law intended. The intentions of the lawmakers govern whether the lawmakers are the Congress of the United States enacting a statute or whether they are those who ratified our Constitution and its various amendments.

Where the words are precise and the facts simple, that is a relatively easy task. Where the words are general, as is the case with some of the most profound protections of our liberties—in the Bill of Rights and in the Civil War Amendments—the task is far more complex. It is to find the principle or value that was intended to be protected and to see that it is protected.

As I wrote in an opinion for our court, the judge's responsibility "is to discern how the Framers' values, defined in the context of the world they knew, apply in the world we know."

If a judge abandons intention as his guide, there is no law available to him and he begins to legislate a social agenda for the American people. That goes well beyond his legitimate power.

He or she then diminishes liberty instead of enhancing it. That is why I agree with Judge Learned Hand, one of the great jurists in our history, when he wrote that the judge's "authority and his immunity depend upon the assumption that he speaks with the mouths of others: The momentum of his utterances must be greater than any which his personal reputation and character can command if it is to do the work assigned to it—if it is to stand against the passionate resentments arising out of the interests he must frustrate." To state that another way, the judge must speak with the authority of the past to the present.

The past, however, includes not only the intentions of those who first made the law, it also includes those past judges who interpreted it and applied it in prior cases. That is why a judge must have great respect for precedence. It is one thing as a legal theorist to criticize the reasoning of a prior decision, even to criticize it severely, as I have done. It is another and more serious thing altogether for a judge to ignore or overturn a prior decision. That requires much careful thought.

Times come, of course, when even a venerable precedent can and should be overruled. The primary example of a proper overruling is Brown against the Board of Education, the case which outlawed racial segregation accomplished by government action. Brown overturned the rule of separate but equal laid down 58 years before in Plessy against Ferguson. Yet Brown, delivered with the authority of a unanimous Court, was clearly correct and represents perhaps the greatest moral achievement of our constitutional law.

Nevertheless, overruling should be done sparingly and cautiously. Respect for precedent is a part of the great tradition of our law, just as is fidelity to the intent of those who ratified the Constitution and enacted our statutes. That does not mean that constitutional law is static. It will evolve as judges modify doctrine to meet new circumstances and new technologies. Thus, today we apply the First Amendment's guarantee of the freedom of the press to radio and television, and we apply to electronic surveillance the Fourth Amendment's guarantee of privacy for the individual against unreasonable searches of his or her home.

I can put the matter no better than I did in an opinion on my present court. Speaking of the judge's duty, I wrote: "The important thing, the ultimate consideration, is the constitutional freedom that is given into our keeping. A judge who refuses to see new threats to an established constitutional value and hence provides a crabbed interpretation that robs a provision of its full, fair and reasonable meaning, fails in his judicial duty. That duty, I repeat, is to ensure that the powers and freedoms the Framers specified are made effective in today's circumstances."

But I should add to that passage that when a judge goes beyond this and reads entirely new values into the Constitution, values the Framers and the ratifiers did not put there, he deprives the people of their liberty. That liberty, which the Constitution clearly envisions, is the liberty of the people to set their own social agenda through the processes of democracy.

Conservative judges frustrated that process in the mid-1930s by using the concept they had invented, the Fourteenth Amendment's supposed guarantee of a liberty of contract, to strike down laws designed to protect workers and labor unions. That was wrong then and it would be wrong now.

My philosophy of judging, Mr. Chairman, as you pointed out, is neither liberal nor conservative. It is simply a philosophy of judging which gives the Constitution a full and fair interpretation but, where the Constitution is silent, leaves the policy struggles to the Congress, the President, the legislatures and executives of the 50 states, and to the American people.

I welcome this opportunity to come before the Committee and answer whatever questions the members may have. I am quite willing to discuss with you my judicial philosophy and the approach I take to deciding cases. I cannot, of course, commit myself as to how I might vote on any particular case and I know you would not wish me to do that. . . .

BORK'S OCTOBER 9 STATEMENT

Good afternoon, ladies and gentlemen. More than three months ago, I was deeply honored to be nominated by the President for the position of Associate Justice of the Supreme Court of the United States.

In the 100 days since then, the country has witnessed an unprecedented event. The process of confirming justices for our nation's highest Court has been transformed in a way that should not and, indeed, must not be permitted to occur again. The tactics and techniques of national political campaigns have been unleashed on the process of confirming judges. That is not simply disturbing, it is dangerous.

Federal judges are not appointed to decide cases according to the latest opinion polls. They are appointed to decide cases impartially, according to law. But when judicial nominees are assessed and treated like political candidates, the effect will be to chill the climate in which judicial deliberations take place, to erode public confidence in the impartiality of courts, and to endanger the independence of the judiciary.

In politics, the opposing candidates exchange contentions in their efforts to sway voters. In the give and take of political debate, the choice will, in the end, be clear. A judge, however, cannot engage—political campaigning and the judge's functions are flatly incompatible.

In 200 years, no nominee for justice has ever campaigned for that high office. None ever should, and I will not. This is not to say that my public life, the decisions I have rendered, the articles I have written should be immune from consideration. They should not. Honorable persons can disagree about those matters. But the manner in which the debate is conducted makes all the difference. Far too often, the ethics that should prevail have been violated, and the facts of my professional life have been misrepresented.

It is, to say no more, unsatisfying to be the target of a campaign that must, of necessity, be one-sided; a campaign in which the candidate, a sitting federal judge, is prevented by the plain standards of his profession from becoming an energetic participant.

Were the fate of Robert Bork the only matter at stake, I would ask the President to withdraw my nomination. The most serious and lasting injury in all of this is not to me, nor is it to all of those who have steadfastly supported my nomination and to whom I am deeply grateful. Rather the damage is to the dignity and integrity of law and of public service in this country. I therefore wish to end this speculation—there should be a full debate and a final Senate decision.

In deciding on this course, I harbor no illusions. But a crucial principle is at stake. That principle is the way in which we select the men and women who guard the liberties of all the American people. That should not be done through public campaigns of distortion.

If I withdraw now, that campaign would be seen as a success, and it would be mounted against future nominees. For the sake of the federal judiciary and the American people, that must not happen. The deliberative process must be restored.

In the days remaining, I ask only that voices be lowered, the facts respected, and the deliberations conducted in a manner that will be fair to me and to the infinitely larger and more important cause of justice in America.

Thank you.

JUDICIARY COMMITTEE REPORT

The Committee on the Judiciary, to which was referred the nomination of Judge Robert H. Bork to be an Associate Justice of the United States Supreme Court, having considered the same reports unfavorably thereon, a quorum being present, by a vote of nine yeas and five nays, with the recommendation that the nomination be rejected.

Background and Qualifications

... The committee received the President's nomination of Judge Robert H. Bork to be an Associate Justice of the United States Supreme Court on July 7, 1987. The hearings on Judge Bork's nomination were held on September 15, 16, 17, 18, 19, 21, 22, 23, 25, 28, 29, and 30. The nominee completed 30 hours of testimony, extending over four-and-a-half days, before the committee. The 12 days of hearings lasted approximately 87 hours, and during that time the committee heard from 112 witnesses.

The testimony of public witnesses was organized so as to encourage as full and complete a discussion as possible of the various subjects relevant to this nomination. An effort was made to bring before the committee some of this nation's most eminent legal scholars and most distinguished lawyers and public servants to testify both in favor of and against the nominee. Where appropriate, witnesses testified in panels organized by subject matter, facilitating thorough questioning and debate of each issue. The committee was particularly privileged to receive testimony from President Gerald Ford, former Chief Justice Warren Burger and five former Attorneys General of the United States....

For the first time since the American Bar Association's (ABA) Standing Committee on Federal Judiciary began evaluating Supreme Court nominees, a substantial minority of the Standing Committee found a Supreme Court nominee to be "not qualified" to serve on the nation's highest court. In evaluating the nomination of Judge Bork, Harold R. Tyler, Jr., Chairman of the Standing Committee (and a former federal district court judge), testified that "ten members voted well-qualified; one, not opposed, and four, not qualified." . . .

No Supreme Court nominee who has received even a single "Not Qualified" vote from the Standing Committee has ever been confirmed by the Senate. . . .

The 15 members of the ABA Standing Committee conducted an extensive investigation of Judge Bork, including interviews with five members of the Supreme Court, with many of his colleagues on the D.C. Circuit Court of Appeals, and with approximately 170 other federal and state court judges, including female and minority members of the bench, throughout the United States. The ABA Committee also interviewed approximately 150 practicing attorneys, 79 law school deans and professors, 11 of Judge Bork's former law clerks and a number of present or former lawyers who served under Judge Bork in the office of the Solicitor General when he headed that office.

Judge Bork's opinions were examined by the dean and 10 professors at the University of Michigan Law School. The Standing Committee reviewed and considered written submissions from a number of institutions and groups, including the White House, the Lawyers Committee for Civil Rights Under Law, the past chairmen of the Antitrust Section of the ABA, the NAACP Legal Defense and Education Fund, Inc., the American Civil Liberties Union, the National Women's Law Center, Public Citizen Litigation Group and People for the American Way.

Finally, Judge Bork was personally interviewed on two separate occasions, for a total of about six hours, by three members of the ABA Standing Committee. A second interview was unprecedented for a Supreme Court nominee, but was considered necessary because of "some additional questions" that arose from discussion among members of the ABA Committee and submissions of various groups. . . .

Based on the criteria identified above, a majority of the ABA Committee concluded that Judge Bork is "well qualified" for appointment to the Supreme Court. Five members of the committee concluded that Judge Bork did not merit such a rating because of their concerns about his judicial temperament. Such concerns were related to Judge Bork's "compassion, open-mindedness, his sensitivity to the rights of women and minority persons or groups and comparatively extreme views respecting constitutional principles or their application, particularly within the ambit of the Fourteenth Amendment." In addition, one dissenting member also expressed reservations about what that member termed inconsistent and possibly misleading recollections by Judge Bork of the events surrounding the resignations of Attorney General Elliot Richardson and Deputy Attorney General William Ruckelshaus during the Watergate episode. . . .

The committee has received letters from approximately 2,000 members of the legal academic community in opposition to Judge Bork's confirmation. Simply put, the extent of this opposition is unprecedented. Prior to this nomination, the maximum number of law professors voicing their disapproval of a judicial nominee had been 300, in connection with the nomination of Judge [G. Harrold] Carswell. . . .

The committee also received a letter signed by 32 law school deans. This letter stated:

> Judge Bork has developed and repeatedly expressed a comprehensive and fixed view of the Constitution that is at odds with most of the pivotal decisions protecting civil rights and liberties that the Supreme Court has rendered over the past four decades. . . . If Judge Bork were to be confirmed, his vote could prove determinative in turning the clock back to an era when constitutional rights and liberties, and the role of the judiciary in protecting them, were viewed in a much more restrictive way. . . .

The Constitution's Unenumerated Rights

I. Judge Bork's View of the Constitution Disregards This Country's Tradition of Human Dignity, Liberty and Unenumerated Rights

The Bork hearings opened on the eve of the celebration of the 200th anniversary of our Constitution. The hearings proved to be about that Constitution, not just about a Supreme Court nominee.

The hearings reaffirmed what many understand to be a core principle upon which this nation was founded: Our Constitution recognizes inalienable rights and is not simply a grant of rights by the majority. . . .

Against this understanding of the Constitution, and of human dignity, Judge Bork offers an alternative vision—that Americans have no rights against government, except those specifically enumerated in the Constitution. . . .

A. Judge Bork's Judicial Philosophy Does Not Recognize the Concept of Unenumerated Rights and Liberties

1. Judge Bork's Core Theory. Judge Bork has consistently described his constitutional theory as "intentionalist," meaning that he considers it the function of a judge to determine the intentions of the body that wrote the laws and to apply those intentions to the case brought before the court. Interpreting law is thus a matter of discerning the original intent of those responsible for making it.

Judge Bork reaffirmed this view in his opening statement. . . .

> The judge's authority derives entirely from the fact that he is applying the law and not his own personal values. . . . How should a judge go about finding the law? The only legitimate way is by attempting to discern what those who made the law intended. The intentions of the lawmakers govern, whether the

> lawmakers are the Congress of the United States enacting a statute or those who ratified our Constitution and its various amendments.

At the end of four and one-half days of testimony, Judge Bork confirmed that he had not altered his basic philosophy....

2. Judge Bork's Judicial Philosophy Leads Him to Conclude that the Constitution "Specified Certain Liberties and Allocates All Else to Democratic Processes." The implications of Judge Bork's theory of original intent are quite clear from his writings, speeches and testimony. The most dramatic consequence of his theory is the rejection of the concept of unenumerated rights and liberties. He has consistently held to the view, both before and during the hearings, that the Constitution should not be read as recognizing an individual right unless that right can be specifically found in a particular provision of the document.

In particular, Judge Bork has repeatedly rejected the well-established line of Supreme Court decisions holding that the "liberty" clauses of the Fifth and Fourteenth Amendments protect against governmental invasion of a person's substantive personal liberty and privacy. He has said, for example, that:

> [T]he choice of "fundamental values" by the Court cannot be justified. Where constitutional materials do not clearly specify the value to be preferred, there is no principled way to prefer any claimed human value to any other. The judge must stick close to the text and the history, and their fair implications, and not construct new rights. ("Neutral Principles and Some First Amendment Problems," 47 *Indiana Law Journal* (1971).)

Judge Bork has also disregarded the text of the Ninth Amendment, which provides that "[t]he enumeration in the Constitution, of certain rights, shall not be construed to deny or disparage others retained by the people." In Judge Bork's view, while there are alternative explanations for the Amendment,

> if it ultimately turns out that no plausible interpretation can be given, the only recourse for a judge is to refrain from inventing meanings and ignore the provision, as was the practice until recently. ("Interpretation of the Constitution," 1984 Justice Lester W. Roth Lecture, University of So. California, October 25, 1984.)

This suggested disregard for the Amendment is consistent with Judge Bork's general recommendation about a judge's role "when his studies leave him unpersuaded that he understands the core of what the Framers intended" with respect to a particular constitutional provision....

... [T]he history surrounding the drafting and ratification of the Bill of Rights indicates that there had to be an express guarantee that unenumerated rights would be fully protected. The Ninth Amendment is at the core of both the Constitution and the ratification debates. The concept of unenumerated rights illustrates the depth of the tradition that the Founders meant to protect by the Ninth Amendment....

C. Judge Bork's Approach to Liberty and Unenumerated Rights Is Outside the Tradition of Supreme Court Jurisprudence

Judge Bork's approach to liberty and unenumerated rights sets him apart from every other Supreme Court Justice. Indeed, not one of the 105 past and present Justices of the Supreme Court has ever taken a view of liberty as narrow as that of Judge Bork. As Professor [Laurence] Tribe testified:

> If [Judge Bork] is confirmed as the 106th Justice, [he] would be the first to read liberty as though it were exhausted by the rights ... the majority expressly conceded individuals in the Bill of Rights. He would be the first to reject an evolving concept of liberty and to replace it with a fixed set of liberties protected at best from an evolving set of threats.

In particular, Judge Bork's philosophy is outside the mainstream of such great judicial conservatives as Justices [John Marshall] Harlan, [Felix] Frankfurter and [Hugo] Black, as well as such recent conservatives as Justices [Potter] Stewart, [Lewis F.] Powell [Jr.], [Sandra Day] O'Connor and Chief Justice [Warren E.] Burger. Each of these members of the court accepted and applied some concept of liberty, substantive due process and unenumerated rights.

As summarized by former Secretary of Transportation William T. Coleman, Jr.:

> There can be no question that privacy and substantive individual liberty interests are clearly within the Constitution as written. Moreover, for more than half a century, the Supreme Court, by recognizing the constitutional basis for the protection of such fundamental liberties, has been able to respond in a principled fashion to the ... problems and abuses which the framers could not have foreseen and thus cannot plausibly be said to have intended to immunize from constitutional protection.... Judge Bork ... simply refuses to use the specific text "liberty" and over sixty years of Supreme Court jurisprudence or, if necessary (which it is not), the open-textured language of the Due Process Clause, to afford them constitutional protection from any intrusion in addition to mere physical restraint....

Judge Bork's narrow definition of liberty sets him apart from the tradition and history from which this nation was conceived. As Professor [Philip] Kurland testified:

> Judge Bork's judicial philosophy ... reveals an unwillingness to recognize that the principal objective of the framers of our Constitution two hundred years ago was the preservation and advancement of individual liberty. Liberty was indeed the watchword of the national convention and of the state ratifying conventions as well. The Constitution did not create individual rights; the people brought them to the Convention with them and left the Convention with them, some enhanced by constitutional guarantees. The Bill of Rights in guaranteeing more, made sure that none was adversely affected.

Judge Bork's definition of liberty also sets him apart from every Justice who has ever sat on the Supreme Court. Indeed, it is because of the Court that "an established part of our legal tradition [is] to view the Constitution as forbidding government abuses which, in the words of Justice Frankfurter, 'offend those canons of decency and fairness which express the notions of justice of English-speaking peoples.' "

II. The Theory of Precedent or "Settled Law" Held by Judge Bork Cannot Transform His Judicial Philosophy into an Acceptable One for the Supreme Court

... Judge Bork has applied his theory of the Constitution to attack a large number of Supreme Court decisions, including many landmark cases. Reconsidering these cases would reopen debate on many significant issues. Perhaps this is why Judge Bork said in response to a question by Senator [Strom] Thurmond, "anybody with a philosophy of original intent requires a theory of precedent." While a theory of precedent appears to lessen the friction between Judge Bork's philosophy and accepted Supreme Court decisions, it creates in the end many uncertainties and concerns of its own.

Prior to the hearings, Judge Bork had occasionally expressed the view that some decisions ought now to be upheld, even though wrong under his theory of original intent. . . .

Under questioning by Senator Thurmond ... Judge Bork said:

> What would I look at [before overruling a prior decision]? Well, I think I would look and be absolutely sure that the prior decision was incorrectly decided. That is necessary. And if it is wrongly decided—and you have to give respect to your predecessors' judgment on these matters—the presumption against overruling remains, because it may be that there are private expectations built up on the basis of the prior decision. It may be that governmental and private institutions have grown up around that prior decision. There is a need for stability and continuity in the law. There is a need for predictability in legal doctrine. . . .

The committee finds that Judge Bork's ideas concerning precedent or settled law, in both their general terms as well as the manner in which Judge Bork applies them to particular cases, raise a number of serious concerns. . . .

... Judge Bork's embrace of precedent sets up a sharp tension with his often repeated proclamations of the ease with which a judge with his views can overrule erroneous decisions. Judge Bork's record, in fact, strongly suggests a willingness to "reformulate" "broad areas of constitutional law." ...

Prior to the hearings, Judge Bork seemed to elevate his views of original intent over respect for precedent: "Supreme Court justice[s] can always say ... their first obligation is to the Constitution, not to what their colleagues said 10 years before." ("Justice Robert H. Bork: Judicial Restraint Personified," *California Lawyer,* May 1985, at 25.) During the hearings, Senator [Edward M.] Kennedy played an audio tape of the question and answer period following a 1985 speech in which Judge Bork made perhaps his clearest declaration to that effect:

> I don't think that in the field of constitutional law precedent is all that important. I say that for two reasons. One is historical and traditional. The court has never thought constitutional precedent was all that important. The reason being that if you construe a statute incorrectly, the Congress can pass a

law and correct it. If you construe the Constitution incorrectly Congress is helpless. Everybody is helpless. *If you become convinced that a prior court has misread the Constitution I think it's your duty to go back and correct it.* Moreover, you will from time to time get willful courts who take an area of law and create precedents that have nothing to do with the name of the Constitution. And if a new court comes in and says, 'Well, I respect precedent,' what you have is a ratchet effect, with the Constitution getting further and further away from its original meaning, because some judges feel free to make up new constitutional law and other judges in the name of judicial restraint follow precedent. *I don't think precedent is all that important. I think the importance is what the Framers were driving at, and to go back to that.* (*Canisius College Speech,* October 8, 1985, emphasis added.) . . .

The committee finds that ... Judge Bork's views pose a serious dilemma. Judge Bork has strongly suggested a reformation in constitutional law, one that will bring a "second wave in constitutional theory." Although perhaps open to differing interpretations, the committee is concerned that the "second wave" is aimed at reform in the courts—in the decisions courts reach, not just in the classroom as some academic exercise. Against this drive to pursue his views on original intent, and to "sweep the elegant, erudite, pretentious, and toxic detritus of non-originalism out to sea," Judge Bork has erected the breakwater of his theory of precedent. The question is: How much will it hold back?

At the very least, Judge Bork's opposing forces pose a dilemma for litigants. As Robert Bennett, Dean of the Northwestern University School of Law, testified:

A moment's reflection will show that it will not do to say that a case was wrong but I will not vote to overrule it. What are lawyers and litigants to do with that case when the next one arises that is a little bit different? Are they to appeal to what the judge says is constitutionally right or to the precedent he says he will tolerate, even though it is wrong?

To be sure all judges suffer from this dilemma to a degree, but few insist that they know the route to constitutional truths with the vehemence that Judge Bork does. For that reason, I remain baffled and concerned about Judge Bork's likely approach to the use of precedent, despite the assurances he has offered.

The committee believes there is a substantial risk that Judge Bork would resolve this dilemma by reading a prior decision very narrowly, so that it had little, if any, substantial effect on future decisions, notwithstanding that it is never overruled. In Judge Bork's terms, a prior decision can lose its "dynamic" or "generative" force through another kind of barren reading, this time of the past decision itself. . . .

The committee finds that there are substantial uncertainties in the extent to which Judge Bork's respect for settled law would operate as a serious curb on his pursuit of his idea of original intent. All that is necessary is to understand what one witness called the "lens effect:" Judge Bork would simply see future cases through a lens that embodied his own strong views about original intent and would thereby be highly likely to see the erroneous, but settled decisions, as inapplicable to new situations. . . .

Judge Bork has said that "the Court's treatment of the Bill of Rights is theoretically the easiest to reform." Decisions involving the Bill of Rights largely involve the expansion of individual rights. As such, complex social institutions and economic structures do not usually build up around them. They are thus typically different from cases like those expanding the power of Congress to regulate commerce or the power of the U.S. government to issue paper money as legal tender. These latter cases have become, in Judge Bork's words, "the basis for a large array of social and economic institutions, [therefore] overruling them would be disastrous." . . .

The Supreme Court's prior decisions, whether settled or not, cannot cover all new situations, under even the broadest reading of those cases. . . .

In the committee's view, respect for precedent, as Judge Bork expressed it, does not alleviate the concern that the nominee would pursue his particular theory of original intent. It does not remove the risk that important precedents preserving individual liberties and human dignity would be robbed of their generative force. And it in no way compensates for his rejection of the tradition of unenumerated rights, a tradition that must be maintained to deal with new issues as they arise in the future.

A Critical Analysis of Judge Bork's Positions on Leading Matters

I. The Right to Privacy—The Right to Be Let Alone

. . . The constitutional right to privacy . . . has been a major part of Judge Bork's attack on the jurisprudence of the Supreme Court. In 1971, for example, he denounced the first modern privacy decision, *Griswold* v. *Connecticut* (1965), as "unprincipled" and "intellectually empty." *Griswold* concerned a law making it a crime for anyone to use birth control. Judge Bork said that the desire of a "husband and wife to have sexual relations without unwanted children" was indistinguishable, for constitutional purposes, from the desire of an electric utility company to "void a smoke pollution ordinance." "The cases," he said, "are identical."

Judge Bork reiterated his attack on *Griswold* after becoming a federal court judge. . . .

Judge Bork's attacks on the privacy right have extended to the principal cases upon which *Griswold* relied, and would extend, presumably, to all the cases subsequent to *Griswold,* although Judge Bork has identified only *Roe* v. *Wade* by name. . . .

As a lower court judge, . . . Judge Bork acknowledged . . . that his arguments against . . . privacy cases were "completely irrelevant to the function of a circuit judge. The Supreme Court has decided that it may create new constitutional rights and, as judges of constitutionally inferior courts, we are bound absolutely by that determination." . . .

At the hearings, Judge Bork repeated in various ways the claim that although "[t]here is a lot of privacy in the Constitution," there is no "generalized" right to privacy of the kind necessary to support *Griswold* and its progeny. He testified that in the Constitution there is no "unstructured, undefined right of privacy [such as the right] that Justice Douglas elaborated [in Griswold]."...

It became clear ... that Judge Bork also believes that there is no constitutional right extending privacy protections beyond those provided by specific amendments....

... Given Judge Bork's extensive experience in analyzing these matters, his steadfast rejection of the tradition of unenumerated rights and his professed inability thus far to find any constitutional warrant for such a right, there is little, if any, prospect that a new argument will be presented that is both unique and convincing to him.

As Chairman [Joseph P.] Biden concluded after two-and-a-half weeks of hearings:

> Will [Judge Bork] be part of the progression of 200 years of history of every generation enhancing the right to privacy and reading more firmly into the Constitution protection for individual privacy? Or will he come down on the side of government intrusion? I am left without any doubt in my mind that he intellectually must come down for government intrusion and against expansion of individual rights....

During the hearings, Judge Bork expounded on his theory of "settled law"—of accepting past cases even though they were wrong. He offered to the committee new examples of cases with which he still disagreed, but which he would not overrule because they had become, in his view, settled law. Judge Bork did not include within his examples any of the privacy decisions. Accordingly, Judge Bork left the committee with the clear impression that he feels free to overrule any or all of the privacy decisions. And given his conclusion that the doctrine of substantive due process is "pernicious," there is a substantial risk of overruling....

II. Civil Rights

Throughout his career, Judge Bork has consistently expressed harsh criticism of, and opposition to, Supreme Court decisions and legislation securing civil rights for all Americans. The committee believes that Judge Bork's unfailing criticism of landmark developments advancing civil rights, and his marked failure in numerous writings and speeches to suggest alternative methods of securing those advances, reflect a pronounced hostility to the fundamental role of the Supreme Court in guarding our civil rights.

... The struggle to end race discrimination in America was one of the greatest moral tests faced by our Nation. In the 1960's, thoughtful men and women of all races and from all parts of the country came to realize that legislation was urgently needed to put an end to segregated lunch counters and "whites only" want ads.

In 1963 and 1964, while an associate professor at Yale Law School, Judge Bork vigorously and publicly opposed the legislation banning discrimination in employment and public accommodations that ultimately became

Titles II and VII of the Civil Rights Act of 1964. In August 1963—the same month that Dr. Martin Luther King, Jr. lead [*sic*] the March on Washington to secure the passage of the Civil Rights Act—Judge Bork wrote in *The New Republic* that the principle underlying the proposed ban on discrimination in public accommodations was one of "unsurpassed ugliness." (*Civil Rights—A Challenge,* August 31, 1963.) And in a March 1, 1964 article in the *Chicago Tribune,* Judge Bork opposed both the public accommodations and the employment provisions of the bill because they would—in his words—"compel association even where it is not desired." (*Against the Bill.*) Judge Bork also asserted that there were "serious constitutional problems" with the public accommodations provision of the bill, a position unanimously rejected by the Supreme Court in *Heart of Atlanta Motel, Inc.* v. *United States* (1964).

At the time that Judge Bork's article in *The New Republic* was published, Nicholas deB. Katzenbach was Deputy Attorney General of the United States. Mr. Katzenbach later served as Attorney General from 1964-1966. During his testimony, Mr. Katzenbach eloquently described the impact of that article:

> His 1963 article in *The New Republic* . . . is one that I remember very well. It was then, and is now, absolutely inconceivable to me that a man of intelligence and perception and feeling could have opposed that legislation on the grounds that it deprived people of freedom of association.
>
> It meant, and it could only have meant, that he valued the right of people in public situations to discriminate against blacks if that is what they chose to do. What kind of judgment does that demonstrate?

As Judge Bork admitted during the hearings, he did not publicly modify his views about the Civil Rights Act until his 1973 confirmation hearings to be Solicitor General. While the Committee does not question the sincerity of Judge Bork's recantation, we believe that his earlier strident and outspoken opposition to the public accommodations and employment provisions of the Civil Rights Act of 1964 may properly be taken into account in reaching our conclusion that the nominee lacks the sensitivity and commitment to assuring equal justice under law for all Americans that any Supreme Court Justice should possess. . . .

Americans are rightly proud of the great strides our country has made in the past 40 years toward achieving our constitutional commitment to equal justice under law. The dramatic progress was eloquently described at the hearings by the Mayor of Atlanta, Andrew Young:

> The success we enjoy—the cooperation between the races, the economic prosperity—has been built upon the foundation of civil rights and equal opportunity which the United States Supreme Court has fostered for three decades. Today, I can be Mayor of Atlanta. Yet just a few decades ago, as a college student, I could not stop for gas at many service stations, was told to use "separate" rest rooms and could not stay or be served in downtown hotels and restaurants. Just 25 years ago, black Americans were second-class citizens in the City of Atlanta. And white citizens were struggling with a stagnant economy.

> But today, many people recognize our city as "the city too busy to hate." We are a city busy providing jobs, developing and protecting the environment, expanding our economy, educating our youth and opening the doors of opportunity for all our citizens.

After reviewing the totality of Judge Bork's record on civil rights, former Secretary of Transportation William T. Coleman, Jr. summarized the nominee's views as follows:

> At almost every critical turning point in the civil rights movement as exemplified in these cases, Judge Bork has, as a public speaker and scholar, turned the wrong way....

In short, Judge Bork has consistently criticized legislation and Supreme Court decisions advancing civil rights for all Americans.

To be sure, Judge Bork was not the only opponent of the Civil Rights Act of 1964, and some of the decisions he criticized were not unanimous. But Judge Bork's criticism of and opposition to the broad number and variety of civil rights achievements discloses a troubling pattern. In the committee's view, this persistent pattern of criticism of civil rights advances, coupled with a conspicuous failure to suggest alternative methods for achieving these critical objectives, reflects a certain hostility on Judge Bork's part to the role of the courts in ensuring our civil rights....

In light of Judge Bork's demonstrated hostility to the fundamental role of the courts in protecting civil rights, the committee strongly believes that confirming Judge Bork would create an unacceptable risk that as a Supreme Court Justice, he would reopen debate on the country's proudest achievements in the area of civil rights and return our country to more troubled times.

III. The Equal Protection Clause and Gender Discrimination

The words of the Equal Protection Clause are grand but general: "nor shall any state ... deny to any person within its jurisdiction the equal protection of the laws." One of the more troubling aspects of Judge Bork's philosophy of equality under the Constitution is his application of the general language of the Clause to discrimination on the basis of gender.

The committee explored two principal questions with Judge Bork on this issue. First, does he believe that the Equal Protection Clause applies to women? Second, by what standard should a court evaluate a challenge to a law that discriminates between men and women? The committee finds that Judge Bork's philosophy—as expressed both before and during the hearings—raises very serious concerns....

Prior to the hearings, Judge Bork engaged in a sustained critique of applying the Equal Protection Clause to women. He argued that to extend the Clause to women departs from the original intent of the Fourteenth Amendment, produces unprincipled and subjective decision-making and involves the courts in "enormously sensitive" and "highly political" matters.

In 1971, for example, then-Professor Bork said that "cases of race discrimination aside, it is always a mistake for the court to try to construct substantive individual rights under the . . . equal protection clause" and that "[t]he Supreme Court has no principled way of saying which non-racial inequalities are impermissible." . . .

. . . Judge Bork insisted that the courts were not competent to decide which legislative attitudes toward women were legitimate judgments, and which were outmoded stereotypes:

> There being no criteria available to the court, the identification of favored minorities will proceed according to *current fads in sentimentality*. . . . This involves the judge in deciding which motives for legislation are respectable and which are not, a denial of the majority's right to choose its own rationales. (Emphasis added.)

. . . During his testimony, Judge Bork publicly stated for the first time that he now believes that the Equal Protection Clause should be extended beyond race and ethnicity, and should apply to classifications based on gender. According to Judge Bork, "[e]verybody is covered—men, women, everybody." Judge Bork explained that all forms of governmental classifications were unconstitutional unless they had a "reasonable basis." He also said that he would reach the same results that the Supreme Court had reached in virtually all of its recent sex discrimination cases. . . .

Judge Bork's rationale for his change in position was that the Equal Protection Clause should be interpreted according to evolving standards and social mores about the role of women:

> As the culture changes and as the position of women in society changes, those distinctions which seemed reasonable now seemed outmoded stereotypes and they seem unreasonable and they get struck down. That is the way a reasonable basis test should be applied.

. . . The central debate concerns the *standard* of equal protection that should apply in such cases. Importantly, that standard is a presumptive guide to courts to use in evaluating claims of gender-based discrimination. The pertinent question is thus whether Judge Bork's currently expressed position would adequately protect women from such discrimination. For several reasons, the committee believes that it would not. . . .

Judge Bork's testimony on the Court's decision in *Craig* v. *Boren* (1976) provides particular insight into the weakness of his standard. In *Craig,* the Court struck down an Oklahoma statute that allowed women to obtain beer at age 18 but did not allow men to do so until they were 21. During his testimony, Judge Bork explained why he thought that the classification would be upheld using a reasonable basis test: The law, he said, "[p]robably is justified *because they have statistics*. . . . [T]hey had evidence that there was a problem with young men drinking more than there was with young women drinking." (Emphasis added.) According to Judge Bork, therefore, sex-based treatment should have been allowed because it rested upon a generalization supported by statistics.

Several witnesses testified about the serious problems associated with relying on statistical generalizations....

Prior to the hearings, Judge Bork said on several occasions—most recently, less than one month before his nomination—that the Equal Protection Clause of the Fourteenth Amendment should not be applied to women. At the hearings, Judge Bork announced for the first time that he would apply the Clause to women pursuant to a "reasonable basis" standard. The Committee agrees with Senator [Arlen] Specter's statement that there is

> substantial doubt about Judge Bork's application of this fundamental legal principle where he has over the years disagreed with the scope of coverage and has a settled philosophy that constitutional rights do not exist unless specified or are within original intent....

IV. First Amendment

In 1971, while a Professor at Yale Law School, Judge Bork wrote his now famous *Indiana Law Journal* article entitled "Neutral Principles and Some First Amendment Problems." In his analysis of the First Amendment, Judge Bork reached the following rather striking conclusion:

> Constitutional protection should be accorded only to speech that is explicitly political. There is no basis for judicial intervention to protect any other forum of expression, be it scientific, literary or that variety of expression we call obscene or pornographic. Moreover, within that category of speech we ordinarily call political, these should be no constitutional obstruction to laws making criminal any speech that advocates forcible overthrow of the government or the violation of any law.

The committee explored each of the First Amendment issues raised by this statement and the manner in which Judge Bork has modified his First Amendment views....

During World War I and the Red Scare period that followed, the Supreme Court began to consider the conditions under which political speech that calls for law-breaking or violence could be prohibited. Although a majority of the Court at that time held that such speech could be suppressed even though there was no immediate threat of law-breaking or violence (*see Abrams* v. *United States* (1919) and *Gitlow* v. *New York* (1925)), Justices Holmes and Brandeis wrote stirring and historic dissents.

Their dissenting view—that the Constitution allows political speech to be stopped only when there is a "clear and present danger" of violence or law-breaking—began to be adopted by the Supreme Court in the 1950s, and a similar but somewhat more stringent test eventually was accepted by a unanimous Supreme Court in *Brandenburg* v. *Ohio* (1969). The Court held in *Brandenburg* that speech calling for violence or law-breaking could be forbidden only if such speech called for, and would probably produce, "imminent lawless action." This standard, therefore, addresses the nature of the speech itself and the chance that, realistically, it will lead to any harm under the circumstances in which it was uttered. Prior to the hearings, Judge Bork made three separate attacks on the *Brandenburg* decision and its underlying doctrine.

First, in his 1971 *Indiana Law Journal* article, then-Professor Bork removed from the protection of the First Amendment "any speech advocating the violation of law," even if it presents no danger of violence or law-breaking.

Second, in a 1979 speech at the University of Michigan, he repeated that view and called *Brandenburg* a "fundamentally wrong interpretation of the First Amendment." . . .

Third, in a speech delivered to the Judge Advocate General's School two years after he became a judge, the nominee expressed his continuing displeasure with *Brandenburg,* which he defined as holding that "catatonic sentiments . . . could not be inhibited or punished in any way."

. . . [I]n his testimony Judge Bork reiterated a distinction that he had suggested for the first time in an interview published immediately before the hearings (*U.S. News and World Report,* Sept. 14, 1987 at 22): "It seems to me that if the attempt [to advocate law violation] is by a person or a group to challenge the constitutionality of a law, then I do not see how it can be made illegal to advocate that attempt." . . .

. . . Judge Bork's "test of constitutionality" exception is of more academic interest than real-world use. Dr. Martin Luther King, for example, did not advocate illegal sit-ins and other forms of civil disobedience in order to stimulate court tests. He advocated them to prick the conscience of the nation—to dramatize the injustice of segregation laws that were immoral but not necessarily unconstitutional. In sum, Judge Bork's newly formulated exception is not simply new and uncertain, but is also a technical distinction with little concrete application. . . .

A major concern voiced by several members of the committee (particularly by Senator Specter)—and voiced generally about those issues that Judge Bork accepted as "settled law"—was how he would apply doctrines of which he expressly disapproved in new cases with new facts. . . .

. . . [T]here is great concern that in new cases, Judge Bork would find reasons not to apply the rules from decisions he dislikes but says are too "settled" to overturn completely. In other words, while he might not try to reverse those decisions, he could find them irrelevant or apply them in such a narrow way that their importance and effect would be greatly diminished.

Political dissidents who make statements that flirt with the edges of the law rarely make very appealing parties in a lawsuit. It is for precisely that reason that the basic values of our political system are seriously threatened in cases that involve the sometimes incendiary and generally unpopular speech of such dissidents. Our system is built upon the precept that any political speech, short of that which will produce imminent violence, furthers public understanding and national progress—sometimes, by showing the virtues of the existing system.

And sometimes dissident speech becomes the precursor of political change and ultimately, a new national consensus. . . .

At the hearings, Judge Bork drew back substantially from his 1985 remarks. He explained that "if I was starting over again, I might sit down and draw a line that did not cover some things that are now covered," but stated that he would "gladly" accept the Supreme Court's First Amendment decisions protecting non-political expression. Referring to the well-established principle that speech is protected regardless of its lack of relationship to the political process, Judge Bork said: "That is what the law is, and I accept that law."

The committee finds that Judge Bork's testimony was somewhat reassuring on the question of First Amendment protection for non-political speech. While his testimony was welcome, however, it "still must be read," in Senator [Patrick J.] Leahy's words, "against the background of Judge Bork's prior statements on the issue."...

V. Executive Power

The Framers clearly recognized that unchecked power in the Executive Branch represents the greatest threat to individual liberty. The genius of the Constitution is perhaps most apparent in the separation of powers among the branches of government and in the system of checks and balances, carefully designed to ensure that no single branch would possess unlimited authority in any area.

In extensive writings and congressional testimony over the course of his professional career, Judge Bork has expressed a broad, almost limitless, view of presidential power, particularly with respect to the conduct of foreign affairs, and a correspondingly narrow view of Congress's ability to restrict abuses of that power. The committee believes that, when viewed as a whole, Judge Bork's views on the scope of executive power place him well outside of the mainstream of legal thought, and run directly contrary to the limits on executive power intended by the Framers.

...The War Powers Act places certain limitations on the President's authority to send and maintain American military forces in hostile circumstances without congressional approval. In an article in the *Wall Street Journal,* Judge Bork stated that the War Powers Act "is probably unconstitutional and certainly unworkable." ("Reforming Foreign Intelligence," March 9, 1978, at 24.) During his appearance before the committee, Judge Bork adhered to this view, suggesting that both the Act's legislative veto provision, and its provisions limiting the time during which troops may be introduced into a hostile situation without congressional approval, may be unconstitutional....

Judge Bork has also taken the position that when the United States is engaged in an undeclared conflict against one nation, Congress cannot constitutionally prohibit a President from expanding that conflict by commencing hostilities against another country....

Judge Bork's suggestion that the President has the inherent power to ignore such limitations is profoundly troubling....

Judge Bork has expressed an exceedingly narrow view of Congress's right to participate in or restrict intelligence activities, even when such activities are conducted in the United States against U.S. residents....

Reasonable people may differ about whether particular intelligence activities are appropriate or inappropriate. But under our constitutional system of checks and balances, Congress simply must have the power to oversee and ultimately to control the ability of the Executive Branch to conduct intelligence operations. In light of the Framers' great concern about the risks presented by concentrated power in the Executive Branch, the committee finds Judge Bork's rejection of congressional limitations on such power particularly disturbing....

In November 1973, in the aftermath of the firing of Watergate Special Prosecutor Archibald Cox, a number of measures were introduced in Congress to provide for establishment of an independent special prosecutor when allegations were made of wrongdoing by high-level Administration officials. Judge Bork testified [at the time] that that legislation was unconstitutional....

Judge Bork's view that court-appointed independent counsels are unconstitutional is troubling because of his adherence to a rigid version of the separation of powers, without any regard for the practical accommodations that are inherent in our system of checks and balances. At rare times, the appearance of possible corruption within the upper levels of the executive branch threatens public confidence in government itself. In some instances, the impartial investigation by government officials of the executive branch, especially of those individuals who are politically or personally close to the President, seems impossible. Following the national trauma of Watergate, Congress faced up to that problem and devised a balanced legislative solution—which has twice been reauthorized—that has significantly helped to restore public confidence. The series of constitutional arguments devised by Judge Bork against such incipient special prosecutor statutes is consistent with his willingness in other contexts to restrict Congressional power, and to enhance and protect the autonomy of the President....

The committee believes that Judge Bork's views on the scope of presidential authority are troubling, not merely because those views would impose unprecedented limitations on Congress's ability to curb abuses of presidential power, but because his views in this area are the antithesis of judicial restraint. In the area of executive power, Judge Bork shows little deference to duly enacted legislation and little regard for either the text of the Constitution itself or for the principle of checks and balances that resonates throughout the document.

VI. Watergate

...In the committee's view, perhaps the most significant aspect regarding the firing of the Watergate Special Prosecutor is Judge Bork's immediate and continuing perception that an effective Watergate investigation could be run out of the same Department of Justice that had just carried out the task of firing Mr. Cox for seeking to run such an investigation. The degree of deference to executive authority and executive representations required to hold that perception is astonishing in the face of the abuses of executive authority represented by President Nixon's actions at the time.

Institutionalized checks on unrestrained power constitute the very life of our Constitution and are an indispensable ingredient of our freedom. The great deference to executive power shown by the nominee in the actions related here, as well as in many of his other statements and judicial opinions, seems inappropriate for a member of a Supreme Court, which is responsible for preserving the constitutional system of checks and balances.

VII. Antitrust

Judge Bork has called antitrust "a particularly instructive microcosm" of his over-all judicial, social and political philosophy. Despite his reputation as a practitioner of judicial restraint, he is, in the words of Robert Pitofsky, a respected antitrust scholar and Dean of the Georgetown University Law Center, "an activist of the right" in the antitrust field, "ready and willing to substitute his views for legislative history and precedent in order to achieve his ideological goals; and ... even when examined by comparison to other conservative critics of antitrust enforcement, his views are extreme." Judge Bork's appointment to the Supreme Court is likely to result in "antitrust changes of truly tidal proportions" that, in the words of the editor of the *Antitrust Law and Economics Review* (a professional journal for antitrust economists), "are likely to do great damage to the country's domestic and thus its international competitiveness well into the 21st century." (Letter to Hon. Edward Kennedy, August 13, 1987.)

... Judge Bork made his early reputation as an antitrust scholar. He first attracted attention in the 1960s with several important articles arguing that there was too much antitrust enforcement. (*See, e.g.,* "The Crisis in Antitrust," *Fortune,* December, 1963.) He expanded his analysis into an influential book, *The Antitrust Paradox,* published in 1978, and he has continued to write and lecture on the subject while serving on the D.C. Circuit Court of Appeals. While Judge Bork has, over the past few years, tried to distance himself from earlier views in several other areas of the law, he still is closely associated with his long-held views on antitrust.

The central premise of Judge Bork's antitrust philosophy is that in enacting the federal antitrust laws, Congress sought to promote only one purpose—industrial or "allocation" efficiency, which he has labeled "consumer welfare." In fact, he has repeatedly called the promotion of economic efficiency the only legitimate goal of antitrust....

Judge Bork has criticized most of the landmark antitrust Supreme Court decisions, including *Brown Shoe* v. *United States* (1962) (horizontal and vertical mergers); *FTC* v. *Procter & Gamble* (1967) (conglomerate mergers); *Dr. Miles Medical Co.* v. *John D. Park & Sons Co.* (1911) (per se illegality of resale price maintenance); and *Standard Oil Co. of California* v.

United States (1949) (illegality of exclusive dealing arrangements). In fact, he has called the entire body of Supreme Court precedent in the antitrust field "mindless law." . . .

In the antitrust arena, Judge Bork has called for unprecedented judicial activism, proposing that the courts ignore almost 100 years of judicial precedents and congressional enactments. His views are particularly relevant to his constitutional jurisprudence because he has analogized the basic antitrust statutes to the Constitution: "[T]he antitrust laws are so open-textured, leave so much to be filled in by the judiciary, that the Court plays in antitrust almost as unconstrained a role as it does in constitutional law." (*The Antitrust Paradox* at 409.) Judge Bork uses the failure of the courts and the Congress to consider or understand economics to reject as "mindless law" cases and statutes that expand application of the antitrust laws beyond the narrow range of practices that he believes should be prohibited. His undisguised distrust of and disregard for congressional enactments cannot be reconciled with his professed philosophy of judicial deference to the will of Congress. This inconsistency is what Chairman Biden labeled "the Bork paradox." . . .

In the antitrust field, Judge Bork interprets congressional will selectively to suit his own agenda. He not only considers his interpretation of the original intent of the antitrust laws to be the only "correct" one, but he also denounces as unconstitutionally vague any conclusions to the contrary. . . .

Judge Bork's antitrust views, together with the "Bork Paradox"—the willingness of Judge Bork to engage in judicial activism despite his supposed adherence to a philosophy of judicial restraint—are yet further reasons why the committee concludes that his nomination to the Supreme Court should be rejected. . . .

X. Judge Bork's So-Called "Confirmation Conversion:" The Weight the Senate Must Give to Newly Announced Positions

As Senator Leahy has said, Judge Bork throughout the hearings told the committee many things "that he has never told anyone else before—at least not in public—about his approach to fundamental constitutional issues." Much has been made of this so-called "confirmation conversion."

In the committee's view, the issue is not whether Judge Bork was candid in those aspects of his sworn testimony that seem to contradict many of his previously announced positions. In Senator Specter's words, "it is not a matter of questioning his credibility or integrity, or his sincerity in insisting that he will not be disgraced in history by acting contrary to his sworn testimony. . . ." Rather, "the real issue is what weight the Senate should give to these newly expressed views," in light of Judge Bork's "judicial disposition in applying principles of law which he has so long decried."

The Committee has concluded that Judge Bork's newly announced positions are not likely fully to outweigh his deeply considered and long-held views. The novelist William Styron cut to the heart of this matter when he said that the Senate must decide whether Judge Bork's new positions reflect "a matter not of passing opinion but of conviction and faith." "Measured against this standard, Judge Bork's testimony ... mitigates some of his previous statements, but does not erase them from the record which the Senate must consider."...

There were three principal changes in positions that Judge Bork announced for the first time, at least publicly, at the hearings. These related to: (1) the Equal Protection Clause of the Fourteenth Amendment and gender discrimination, (2) dissident political speech under the First Amendment; and (3) First Amendment protection for artistic expression.

At his confirmation hearings, Judge Bork for the first time said that he would apply the Equal Protection Clause to women pursuant to a "reasonable basis" standard. As discussed in Part Three, Section III, this position contrasts markedly with Judge Bork's historical approach to this issue. The committee agrees with Senator Specter's statement that there is

> substantial doubt about Judge Bork's application of this fundamental legal principle where he has over the years disagreed with the scope of coverage and has a settled philosophy that constitutional rights do not exist unless specified or are within original intent....

On the question of dissident political speech—that is, speech that advocates the violation of law—Judge Bork also announced a dramatic change in position. As discussed in Part Three, ... Judge Bork had, prior to the hearings, consistently rejected the "clear and present danger" test even though a unanimous Supreme Court had accepted it for years. During the hearings, Judge Bork took inconsistent positions on this issue, but ultimately said that he accepted the Supreme Court's formulation as "settled law." Again, the statements of Senators Specter and Leahy are particularly cogent. Said Senator Specter:

> I have substantial doubt about Judge Bork's application of [the clear and present danger] standard to future cases involving different fact situations where he retains his deep-seated philosophical objections.

Senator Leahy observed:

> [I]n the end, I am not persuaded that Justice Bork would be an energetic and effective guardian of this most basic of our constitutional freedoms. Belated acceptance of these well-established principles does not match what we expect of a Supreme Court Justice.

The third principal area in which Judge Bork modified his views is the area of artistic expression. Prior to the hearings, Judge Bork had expanded his concept of protected speech under the First Amendment from his original and somewhat radical position set forth in his *Indiana Law Journal* article. He had still seemed to maintain, however, that speech must relate in some way to the political process. By the time of his testimony, Judge Bork accepted the proposition that speech should be protected regardless of its lack of relationship to the political process. He accepted, in other words, "a consensus that has existed for decades." As Senator Leahy concluded:

> While this testimony was welcome, it still must be read against the background of Judge Bork's prior statements on the issue.... The over-all picture presented by Judge Bork's free speech decisions and his writings on the subject belies the extravagant claim made by some of the proponents of this nomination that he is 'at the forefront' of modern free speech jurisprudence. At best he is somewhere in the pack and running to catch up.

Any discussion of the so-called "confirmation conversion" would not be complete without mention of the principal area in which Judge Bork did not change his views. On the related questions of liberty, unenumerated rights and the right to privacy, Judge Bork's views have not changed in any substantial degree. He still challenges the role of the Supreme Court in defining liberty; he still challenges the legitimacy of *Griswold* and its progeny; and he still maintains that the people of the nation have only those rights that are specified in the text of the Constitution....

Conclusion

The hearings before this committee on the nomination of Robert H. Bork have been about what the Framers called "free government." And free government, as one witness put it, "is a complicated blend of principle and preference." Through these hearings millions of Americans have been reminded that free government "empowers the majority and makes it the touchstone of legitimacy, but at the same time it protects individuals, minorities, and powerless groups in our society against laws and practices that are sometimes demanded by a majority but which might be deeply regretted by the people at more reflective moments."

Two hundred years ago, the founders of this great nation created a Constitution for their heirs and descendants, enabling them continually to refine the balance between principle and preference. Our Constitution has scarcely more than 5,000 words. But those words have enabled this Nation to flourish for two centuries, and they now lead us into a third.

At the same time, the Constitution's words alone have never been deemed sufficient to gain its ends. As John Randolph reminded the new nation, "[y]ou may cover whole skins of parchment with limitations, but power alone can limit power." Faithful to this mandate, the Supreme Court has been the ultimate bulwark of protection when the majority has attempted to impose its preference upon the fundamental principles of the Constitution—when it has attempted, in other words, to channel the force of government to override the rights of the individual. In the words of former Congresswoman Barbara Jordan, "[t]he Supreme Court will throw out a lifeline when the legislators and the governors and everybody else refuse[s] to do so."...

Judge Bork's constitutional philosophy places him at odds with this history and tradition....

It is often stated that America's strength lies in being a government of laws and not of men. For such a government to endure, interpretation of our most fundamental law must comprehend the lives of the people and accord with their deepest values. The Supreme Court sets the terms of that interpretation, and its members must view the forum as far more than what the nominee has termed an "intellectual feast." Justices of the Supreme Court hold the solemn charge to embody justice, and to unleash or resolve the aspirations and grievances of a nation. Nor can constitutional interpretation be based simply on an "understand[ing of] constitutional governance," as Judge Bork also has suggested. To update Justice Holmes' reminder many decades ago, the words of the Constitution

> have called into being a life the development of which could not have been foreseen completely by the most gifted of its begetters. It was enough for them to realize or to hope that they had created an organism; it has taken [two] centur[ies] and cost their successors much sweat and blood to prove that they created a nation. The case[s] before us must be considered in the light of our whole experience and not merely in that of what was said [two] hundred years ago. (*Missouri* v. *Holland*, 1920.)

This broad context for the justices' role frames, in turn, the question for this committee. That question was put well by Secretary Coleman:

> In this day and age, can we really take the risk of nominating to the Supreme Court a man who fails to recognize the fundamental rights of privacy and substantive liberty . . . which are already imbedded in the very fiber of our Constitution . . . [?]

The nation cannot take this risk. The positions adopted by Judge Bork at critical moments of decision bespeak a perilous inclination for one who would guide our nation's future. The constitutional problems of the next generation will take new and unexpected forms, but they will juxtapose the same values of liberty and sovereignty, of preference and principle, that antedate the birth of our Constitution. Judge Bork's confined vision of the Constitution and of the task of judging itself carries too great a risk of disservice to future national needs and distortion of age-old constitutional commitments to permit his confirmation. . . .

. . . [T]he Supreme Court acts to define our lasting values as a people. In exercising powers of advice and consent for Justices of the Supreme Court, the Senate must speak for generations yet unborn, whose lives will be shaped by the fundamental principles that those Justices enunciate. As we face that task here today, we keep faith with our forefathers' bold experiment by reaffirming for *our* time their promise that liberty would be the American birthright for *all* time.

OZONE TREATY AND SCIENTIFIC STUDY

September 16 and 30, 1987

Capping nine months of effort initiated and propelled by the Reagan administration, delegates from forty-five nations met in Montreal September 14-15 to negotiate a treaty designed to stem the damage caused by the release of chemical substances in the earth's protective ozone layer. The pact was signed September 16.

An American research team September 30 released preliminary findings that resulted from aerial investigations over Antarctica. This expedition, which included the first known flight directly over the South Pole, was another of several that had taken place since the seasonal thinning of the ozone layer was first discovered by British researchers in the late 1970s.

The study was coordinated by the National Aeronautics and Space Administration (NASA) and cosponsored by NASA, the National Oceanic and Atmospheric Administration (NOAA), the National Science Foundation (NSF), and the Chemical Manufacturers Association (CMA). The British Meteorological Office also participated, as did scientists and engineers from a number of universities and research centers.

The subject of the investigation was a mysterious doughnut-shaped hole that had been observed in the ozone over Antarctica each polar spring (which occurs in October) since 1977. The ozone over the South Pole had decreased in a stepwise fashion, showing a big drop one year and a slight recovery the next. What surprised scientists about the Antarctic hole was its size (as large as North America) and the magni-

tude of the ozone loss. (Ozone levels in 1987 were about half those recorded from the 1950s through the early 1970s.)

Explanations for the phenomenon have included meteorological theories attributing ozone depletion to natural causes and a chemical theory blaming man-made products. The NASA-coordinated study concluded that both meteorological and chemical factors contributed to the ozone hole and that the problem was linked specifically to a group of man-made chemicals called chlorofluorocarbons (CFCs).

Both the treaty and the latest scientific study indicated that concern was growing over the apparent loss of ozone and that the search had intensified to identify the causes. There was general agreement that more effort was needed to investigate and protect what NOAA termed, in an August 18, 1987, report, "the single most important chemically active trace gas in the earth's atmosphere."

Dangers from Ozone Loss

Ozone is created through the action of ultraviolet radiation on oxygen. Ultraviolet rays break up the two-atom oxygen molecules to form ozone, which is composed of three oxygen atoms. The earth relies on the ozone shield in the stratosphere, located ten to thirty-five miles above the ground, to limit the destructive effects of the sun's ultraviolet rays. For humans, overexposure to these rays could produce skin cancer (which increased 83 percent between 1980 and 1987 in the United States), weakened immunities, and damage to the eye's retina. For crops and forests, the effects could be stunted growth and lower yields. The threat to ocean life was destruction of plankton, the microscopic organisms that form the basis of the ocean food chain. Overall, decreasing ozone could contribute to the gradual elevation of the earth's temperature—the so-called "greenhouse effect."

In 1974 two chemists at the University of California at Irvine hypothesized that man-made CFCs—a type of gas foam—could be depleting the stratospheric ozone layer. According to current theory, CFCs rise to the ozone layer and are decomposed by sunlight, releasing their chlorine. The chlorine acts as a catalyst, breaking apart ozone molecules. So powerful is this reaction that one chlorine molecule can destroy about 100,000 ozone molecules before drifting out of the stratosphere.

CFCs are used in air conditioners, refrigerators, foam insulation, and electronics. CFCs are discharged when air conditioners and refrigerators are junked or serviced or when coolant is replaced. In automobile air conditioners, about 30 percent of the CFCs used are emitted during routine leakage. During the manufacture of rigid foam insulation, which contains air bubbles with CFCs trapped inside, the chemicals are released into the atmosphere; they are also released if the foam is crushed when discarded. CFC solvents are used in production to wash the microchips that run digital televisions, videocassette recorders, and other electronic consumer products. Halons, chemicals used in fire extinguishers, cause more ozone depletion per pound than CFCs, and their use has been growing as rapidly as that of chlorofluorocarbons.

Debate over Causes, Solutions

Regulations to control emissions of CFCs at 1986 levels were proposed by the U.S. Environmental Protection Agency (EPA), which in 1978 banned their use in aerosol spray cans, as did Canada, Sweden, and Norway. U.S. producers and users of CFCs stated they could tolerate a production freeze if foreign competitors would abide by it as well. However, some of America's leading trade partners—including the twelve-member European Community (EC) and Japan—initially resisted the U.S.-proposed phase-out, arguing that it would penalize some of their most competitive export industries.

Debate in the scientific community pointed to questions about the reliability of information on the extent of ozone reduction, the cause-and-effect relationship between chemicals and ozone, the potential degree of future ozone depletion, and, finally, the amount of data needed by policy makers.

Diplomatic Steps

The international movement to control the problem began in March 1985, when twenty-eight nations signed the Vienna Convention for the Protection of the Ozone Layer. Meeting in Geneva in November 1986 under the auspices of the UN Environment Programme, representatives of forty-five governments agreed to discuss measures to control emissions of CFCs and other gases. The United States and the Soviet Union agreed in December 1986 to extend their 1972 agreement to cooperate on a wide range of environmental issues, including support of a treaty to reduce ozone depletion.

At a February 25, 1987, meeting of legal experts from thirty nations in Vienna, the United States, Canada, Sweden, Norway, and Finland proposed a freeze on existing production of CFCs and halons and a gradual reduction in their use, culminating in an effective ban. But Japan and the EC objected to the last stage until further research had provided definitive evidence that the chemicals were the cause of the problem.

Accord was finally reached on September 15. The protocol would freeze all use of CFCs at 1986 levels, effective January 1, 1990. An exception was allowed for the Soviet Union, which could freeze at levels prevailing in 1990, when its five-year plan for CFC development expired. CFC use would be reduced another 20 percent by 1994 and an additional 30 percent by 1999. However, global CFC production was allowed to rise as much as 10 percent over ten years to meet the needs of developing countries for industrial growth. Consumption of halon also would be frozen by 1994.

"This is perhaps the most historically significant international environment agreement," said Richard E. Benedick, the chief negotiator for the United States. "For the first time the international community has initiated controls on production of an economically valuable commodity before there was tangible evidence of damage." Environmentalist groups generally praised the agreement, and Kevin Fay, executive director of the Alliance for Responsible CFC Policy (a U.S. industry group), said it was a "significant step." But he added that the timetable for compliance might be "too tight." Industry spokesmen said it would take at least five years to develop alternatives to CFCs.

Following are excerpts from the Montreal Protocol on Substances that Deplete the Ozone Layer, signed September 16, 1987; and from the fact sheet on the initial findings, released September 30, 1987, of a scientific investigation of Antarctic ozone coordinated by the National Aeronautics and Space Administration:

MONTREAL PROTOCOL ON SUBSTANCES THAT DEPLETE THE OZONE LAYER

The Parties to this Protocol,

Being Parties to the Vienna Convention for the Protection of the Ozone Layer,

Mindful of their obligation under that Convention to take appropriate measures to protect human health and the environment against adverse effects resulting or likely to result from human activities which modify or are likely to modify the ozone layer,

Recognizing that world-wide emissions of certain substances can significantly deplete and otherwise modify the ozone layer in a manner that is likely to result in adverse effects on human health and the environment,

Conscious of the potential climatic effects of emissions of these substances,

Aware that measures taken to protect the ozone layer from depletion should be based on relevant scientific knowledge, taking into account technical and economic considerations,

Determined to protect the ozone layer by taking precautionary measures to control equitably total global emissions of substances that deplete it, with the ultimate objective of their elimination on the basis of developments in scientific knowledge, taking into account technical and economic considerations,

Acknowledging that special provision is required to meet the needs of developing countries for these substances,

Noting the precautionary measures for controlling emissions of certain chlorofluorocarbons that have already been taken at national and regional levels,

Considering the importance of promoting international co-operation in the research and development of science and technology relating to the control and reduction of emissions of substances that deplete the ozone layer, bearing in mind in particular the needs of developing countries,

HAVE AGREED AS FOLLOWS:

Article 1: Definitions

For the purposes of this Protocol:

1. "Convention" means the Vienna Convention for the Protection of the Ozone Layer, adopted on 22 March 1985.
2. "Parties" means, unless the text otherwise indicates, Parties to this Protocol.
3. "Secretariat" means the secretariat of the Convention.
4. "Controlled substance" means a substance listed in Annex A to this Protocol, whether existing alone or in a mixture. It excludes, however, any such substance or mixture which is in a manufactured product other than a container used for the transportation or storage of the substance listed.
5. "Production" means the amount of controlled substances produced minus the amount destroyed by technologies to be approved by the Parties.
6. "Consumption" means production plus imports minus exports of controlled substances.
7. "Calculated levels" of production, imports, exports and consumption means levels determined in accordance with Article 3.
8. "Industrial rationalization" means the transfer of all or a portion of the calculated level of production of one Party to another, for the purpose of achieving economic efficiencies or responding to anticipated shortfalls in supply as a result of plant closures.

Article 2: Control Measures

1. Each Party shall ensure that for the twelve-month period commencing on the first day of the seventh month following the date of the entry into force of this Protocol, and in each twelve-month period thereafter, its calculated level of consumption of the controlled substances in Group I of Annex A does not exceed its calculated level of consumption in 1986. By the end of the same period, each Party producing one or more of these substances shall ensure that its calculated level of production of the substances does not exceed its calculated level of production in 1986, except that such level may have increased by no more than ten percent based on the 1986 level. Such increase shall be permitted only so as to satisfy the basic domestic needs of the Parties operating under Article 5 and for the purpose of industrial rationalization between Parties.

2. Each Party shall ensure that for the twelve-month period commenc-

ing on the first day of the thirty-seventh month following the date of the entry into force of this Protocol, and in each twelve month period thereafter, its calculated level of consumption of the controlled substances listed in Group II of Annex A does not exceed its calculated level of consumption in 1986. Each Party producing one or more of these substances shall ensure that its calculated level of production of the substances does not exceed its calculated level of production in 1986, except that such level may have increased by no more than ten percent based on the 1986 level. Such increase shall be permitted only so as to satisfy the basic domestic needs of the Parties operating under Article 5 and for the purposes of industrial rationalization between Parties. The mechanisms for implementing these measures shall be decided by the Parties at their first meeting following the first scientific review.

3. Each Party shall ensure that for the period 1 July 1993 to 30 June 1994 and in each twelve-month period thereafter, its calculated level of consumption of the controlled substances in Group I of Annex A does not exceed, annually, eighty percent of its calculated level of consumption in 1986. Each Party producing one or more of these substances shall, for the same periods, ensure that its calculated level of production of the substances does not exceed, annually, eighty percent of its calculated level of production in 1986. However, in order to satisfy the basic domestic needs of the Parties operating under Article 5 and for the purposes of industrial rationalization between Parties, its calculated level of production may exceed that limit by up to ten percent of its calculated level of production in 1986.

4. Each Party shall ensure that for the period 1 July 1998 to 30 June 1999, and in each twelve-month period thereafter, its calculated level of consumption of the controlled substances in Group I of Annex A does not exceed, annually, fifty percent of its calculated level of consumption in 1986. Each Party producing one or more of these substances shall, for the same periods, ensure that its calculated level of production of the substances does not exceed, annually, fifty percent of its calculated level of production in 1986. However, in order to satisfy the basic domestic needs of the Parties operating under Article 5 and for the purposes of industrial rationalization between Parties, its calculated level of production may exceed that limit by up to fifteen percent of its calculated level of production in 1986. This paragraph will apply unless the Parties decide otherwise at a meeting by a two-thirds majority of Parties present and voting, representing at least two-thirds of the total calculated level of consumption of these substances of the Parties. This decision shall be considered and made in the light of the assessments referred to in Article 6.

5. Any Party whose calculated level of production in 1986 of the controlled substances in Group I of Annex A was less than twenty-five kilotonnes may, for the purpose of industrial rationalization, transfer to or receive from any other Party, production in excess of the limits set out in

paragraphs 1, 3 and 4 provided that the total combined calculated levels of production of the Parties concerned does not exceed the production limits set out in this Article. Any transfer of such production shall be notified to the secretariat, no later than the time of the transfer.

6. Any Party not operating under Article 5, that has facilities for the production of controlled substances under construction, or contracted for, prior to 16 September 1987, and provided for in national legislation prior to 1 January 1987, may add the production from such facilities to its 1986 production of such substances for the purposes of determining its calculated level of production for 1986, provided that such facilities are completed by 31 December 1990 and that such production does not raise that Party's annual calculated level of consumption of the controlled substances above 0.5 kilograms per capita.

7. Any transfer of production pursuant to paragraph 5 or any addition of production pursuant to paragraph 6 shall be notified to the secretariat, no later than the time of the transfer or addition.

8. (a) Any Parties which are Member States of a regional economic integration organization as defined in Article 1(6) of the Convention may agree that they shall jointly fulfill their obligations respecting consumption under this Article provided that their total combined calculated level of consumption does not exceed the levels required by this Article.

(b) The Parties to any such agreement shall inform the secretariat of the terms of the agreement before the date of the reduction in consumption with which the agreement is concerned.

(c) Such agreement will become operative only if all Member States of the regional economic integration organization and the organization concerned are Parties to the Protocol and have notified the secretariat of their manner of implementation.

9. (a) Based on the assessments made pursuant to Article 6, the Parties may decide whether:

(i) adjustments to the ozone depleting potentials specified in Annex A should be made and, if so, what the adjustments should be; and

(ii) further adjustments and reductions of production or consumption of the controlled substances from 1986 levels should be undertaken and, if so, what the scope, amount and timing of any such adjustments and reductions should be.

(b) Proposals for such adjustments shall be communicated to the Parties by the secretariat at least six months before the meeting of the Parties at which they are proposed for adoption.

(c) In taking such decisions, the Parties shall make every effort to reach agreement by consensus. If all efforts at consensus have been exhausted, and no agreement reached, such decisions shall, as a last resort, be adopted by a two-thirds majority vote of the Parties present and voting representing at least fifty per cent of the total consumption of the controlled substances of the Parties.

(d) The decisions, which shall be binding on all Parties, shall forthwith be communicated to the Parties by the Depositary. Unless otherwise provided in the decisions, they shall enter into force on the expiry of six months from the date of the circulation of the communication by the Depositary.

10. (a) Based on the assessments made pursuant to Article 6 of this Protocol and in accordance with the procedure set out in Article 9 of the Convention, the Parties may decide:

(i) whether any substances, and if so which, should be added to or removed from any annex to this Protocol; and

(ii) the mechanism, scope and timing of the control measures that should apply to those substances;

(b) Any such decision shall become effective, provided that it has been accepted by a two-thirds majority vote of the parties present and voting.

11. Notwithstanding the provisions contained in this Article, Parties may take more stringent measures than those required by this Article.

Article 3: Calculation of Control Levels

For the purposes of Articles 2 and 5, each Party shall, for each Group of substances in Annex A, determine its calculated levels of:

(a) production by:

(i) multiplying its annual production of each controlled substance by the ozone depleting potential specified in respect of it in Annex A; and

(ii) adding together, for each such Group, the resulting figures;

(b) imports and exports, respectively, by following, *mutatis mutandis,* the procedure set out in subparagraph (a); and

(c) consumption by adding together its calculated levels of production and imports and subtracting its calculated level of exports as determined in accordance with subparagraphs (a) and (b). However, beginning on 1 January 1993, any export of controlled substances to non-Parties shall not be subtracted in calculating the consumption level of the exporting Party.

Article 4: Control of Trade with Non-Parties

1. Within one year of the entry into force of this Protocol, each Party shall ban the import of controlled substances from any State not party to this Protocol.

2. Beginning on 1 January 1993, no Party operating under paragraph 1 of Article 5 may export any controlled substance to any State not party to this Protocol.

3. Within three years of the date of the entry into force of this Protocol, the Parties shall, following the procedures in Article 10 of the Convention, elaborate in an annex a list of products containing controlled substances. Parties that have not objected to the annex in accordance with those procedures shall ban, within one year of the annex having become effective, the import of those products from any State not party to this Protocol.

4. Within five years of the entry into force of this Protocol, the Parties shall determine the feasibility of banning or restricting, from States not party to this Protocol, the import of products produced with, but not containing, controlled substances. If determined feasible, the Parties shall, following the procedures in Article 10 of the Convention, elaborate in an annex a list of such products. Parties that have not objected to it in accordance with those procedures shall ban or restrict, within one year of the annex having become effective, the import of those products from any State not party to this Protocol.

5. Each Party shall discourage the export, to any State not party to this Protocol, of technology for producing and for utilizing controlled substances.

6. Each Party shall refrain from providing new subsidies, aid, credits, guarantees or insurance programmes for the export to States not party to this Protocol of products, equipment, plants or technology that would facilitate the production of controlled substances.

7. Paragraphs 5 and 6 shall not apply to products, equipment, plants or technology that improve the containment, recovery, recycling or destruction of controlled substances, promote the development of alternative substances, or otherwise contribute to the reduction of emissions of controlled substances.

8. Notwithstanding the provisions of this Article, imports referred to in paragraphs 1, 3 and 4 may be permitted from any State not party to this Protocol if that State is determined, by a meeting of the Parties, to be in full compliance with Article 2 and this Article, and has submitted data to that effect as specified in Article 7.

Article 5: Special Situation of Developing Countries

1. Any Party that is a developing country and whose annual calculated level of consumption of the controlled substances is less than 0.3 kilograms per capita on the date of the entry into force of the Protocol for it, or any time thereafter within ten years of the date of entry into force of the Protocol shall, in order to meet its basic domestic needs, be entitled to delay its compliance with the control measures set out in paragraphs 1 to 4 of Article 2 by ten years after that specified in those paragraphs. However, such Party shall not exceed an annual calculated level of consumption of 0.3 kilograms per capita. Any such Party shall be entitled to use either the average of its annual calculated level of consumption for the period 1995 to

1997 inclusive or a calculated level of consumption of 0.3 kilograms per capita, whichever is the lower, as the basis for its compliance with the control measures.

2. The Parties undertake to facilitate access to environmentally safe alternative substances and technology for Parties that are developing countries and assist them to make expeditious use of such alternatives.

3. The Parties undertake to facilitate bilaterally or multilaterally the provision of subsidies, aid, credits, guarantees or insurance programmes to Parties that are developing countries for the use of alternative technology and for substitute products.

Article 6: Assessment and Review of Control Measures

Beginning in 1990, and at least every four years thereafter, the Parties shall assess the control measures provided for in Article 2 on the basis of available scientific, environmental, technical and economic information. At least one year before each assessment, the Parties shall convene appropriate panels of experts qualified in the fields mentioned and determine the composition and terms of reference of any such panels. Within one year of being convened, the panels will report their conclusions, through the secretariat, to the Parties.

Article 7: Reporting of Data

1. Each Party shall provide to the secretariat, within three months of becoming a Party, statistical data on its production, imports and exports of each of the controlled substances for the year 1986, or the best possible estimates of such data where actual data are not available.

2. Each Party shall provide statistical data to the secretariat on its annual production (with separate data on amounts destroyed by technologies to be approved by the Parties), imports, and exports to Parties and non-Parties, respectively, of such substances for the year during which it becomes a Party and for each year thereafter. It shall forward the data no later than nine months after the end of the year to which the data relate.

Article 8: Non-compliance

The Parties, at their first meeting, shall consider and approve procedures and institutional mechanisms for determining non-compliance with the provisions of this Protocol and for treatment of Parties found to be in non-compliance.

Article 9: Research, Development, Public Awareness and Exchange of Information

1. The Parties shall co-operate, consistent with their national laws, regulations and practices and taking into account in particular the needs of developing countries, in promoting, directly or through competent international bodies, research, development and exchange of information on:

(a) best technologies for improving the containment, recovery, recycling or destruction of controlled substances or otherwise reducing their emissions;

(b) possible alternatives to controlled substances, to products containing such substances, and to products manufactured with them; and

(c) costs and benefits of relevant control strategies.

2. The Parties, individually, jointly or through competent international bodies, shall co-operate in promoting public awareness of the environmental effects of the emissions of controlled substances and other substances that deplete the ozone layer.

3. Within two years of the entry into force of this Protocol and every two years thereafter, each Party shall submit to the secretariat a summary of the activities it has conducted pursuant to this Article.

Article 10: Technical Assistance

1. The Parties shall, in the context of the provisions of Article 4 of the Convention, and taking into account in particular the needs of developing countries, co-operate in promoting technical assistance to facilitate participation in and implementation of this Protocol.

2. Any Party or Signatory to this Protocol may submit a request to the secretariat for technical assistance for the purposes of implementing or participating in the Protocol.

3. The Parties, at their first meeting, shall begin deliberations on the means of fulfilling the obligations set out in Article 9, and paragraphs 1 and 2 of this Article, including the preparation of workplans. Such workplans shall pay special attention to the needs and circumstances of the developing countries. States and regional economic integration organizations not party to the Protocol should be encouraged to participate in activities specified in such workplans. . . .

Article 15: Signature

This Protocol shall be open for signature by States and by regional economic integration organizations in Montreal on 16 September 1987, in Ottawa from 17 September 1987 to 16 January 1988, and at United Nations Headquarters in New York from 17 January 1988 to 15 September 1988.

Article 16: Entry into Force

1. This Protocol shall enter into force on 1 January 1989, provided that at least eleven instruments of ratification, acceptance, approval of the Protocol or accession thereto have been deposited by States or regional economic integration organizations representing at least two-thirds of 1986 estimated global consumption of the controlled substances, and the provisions of paragraph 1 of Article 17 of the Convention have been fulfilled. In the event that these conditions have not been fulfilled by that

date, the Protocol shall enter into force on the ninetieth day following the date on which the conditions have been fulfilled....

ANTARCTIC OZONE: INITIAL FINDINGS FROM PUNTA ARENAS, CHILE

This statement has been prepared by the scientists who went to Punta Arenas, Chile to study the Antarctic ozone hole. This summary represents the views of the scientists themselves and not necessarily those of the cosponsoring organizations. The findings that will be presented are preliminary. Under normal circumstances, scientists studying such a complex scientific issue would take many months to years to disclose their initial findings. However, the issue of ozone perturbation is one of justifiable public concern, and hence the public should be kept abreast of the current scientific thinking. It is in this spirit that we would like to share our provisional picture of the Antarctic springtime ozone hole. Furthermore, this will help to stimulate the scientific inquiry and debate that can only lead to an improved and timely understanding of the phenomenon. A much more complete and final interpretation of our findings will be forthcoming after a planned intensive series of scientific meetings and the submittal of a group of scientific papers to the peer review process. This procedure will occur within the next six months.

Description of Goals and Objectives of the Mission

Three basic theories have been proposed to explain the observed decrease in spring-time Antarctic ozone that has been occurring since the late 1970's. One class of theories suggest[s] that the hole is caused by the human activity of loading the atmosphere with chlorinated and brominated chemicals. Chlorofluorocarbons (CFC's) and Halons are contributing increasing levels of chlorine and bromine to the atmosphere. These compounds could then efficiently destroy stratospheric ozone in the Antarctic environment because of the special geophysical conditions that exist in this region of the atmosphere, i.e. a contained polar vortex (an isolated air mass), cold temperatures, and the presence of polar stratospheric clouds. A second class of theories suggests that there have been changes in the circulation of the atmosphere, which now transports ozone-poor air into Antarctica. A third theory postulates solar and cosmic ray induced, periodically enhanced abundances of oxides of nitrogen, which can cyclically destroy ozone.

The NSF-coordinated expedition to the McMurdo station in Antarctica last year was exceptionally successful in increasing our understanding of the Antarctic ozone hole. In conjunction with other experiments, this ground based effort demonstrated the recurrence of the ozone hole, the altitude over which ozone was depleted, that chlorine and nitrogen chemistry was highly perturbed relative to that observed at mid-latitudes, and that the solar cycle theory is an unlikely explanation. However, the McMurdo data were insufficient to distinguish adequately between the relative contributions of the first two classes of theories. Therefore, the goal of the present airborne campaign is to improve our understanding of the relative contributions of these, and possibly other, mechanisms to the formation of the Antarctic ozone hole.

One of the key environmental issues is whether the ozone depletion observed in Antarctica will always be localized in and around Antarctica, or whether it is a precursor of future global changes. A longer term objective of this campaign is to be able to provide information relevant to answering this question. . . .

Description of Campaign

The Airborne Antarctic Ozone Campaign succeeded in making 12 flights of the high altitude ER-2 aircraft, and 13 flights of the DC-8 medium altitude aircraft over Antarctica. The ER-2 typically operated at geometric altitudes relative to sea level between 12.0 and 18.7 km and flew to 72 degrees South along the Palmer Peninsula. The DC-8 operated at altitudes up to about 10 km and with its long range capability was able to reach the South Pole on several occasions, and is currently returning to the United States via New Zealand after crossing the Antarctic continent. The project had available to it Total Ozone Mapping Spectrometer (TOMS) images of the total ozone column of the southern hemisphere within a day of observation and of the orbits passing over the region of the Antarctic peninsula within 2 to 4 hours of observation. Aerosol and cloud extinction data were also available from the Stratospheric Aerosol Measurement (SAM II) and Stratospheric Aerosol and Gas Experiment (SAGE II), with the latter providing ozone measurements as well. Twice daily analyses and forecasts of winds and temperatures up to 30 mb, 22 km, for three days ahead, were provided by the BMO in chart form, plus forecasts of the trajectories of air parcels on surfaces along which air masses move. Photochemical modelling along these trajectories was done using the aircraft observations. The ECMWF provided once a day analyses and forecasts up to 30 mb for 10 days ahead. A small theory team assisted the experimental scientists with the interpretation on a day to day basis. This approach was possible because of the availability of rapid data reduction facilities and an extensive, dedicated international telecommunications network. . . .

Data Obtained from the ER-2 and DC-8 Instrumentation

The spatial and temporal distribution of a large number of relatively short-lived chemical constituents that participate in chemical reactions that affect the abundance of ozone were measured from both the ER-2 and DC-8. Instruments aboard the ER-2 resulted in measurements of the distributions of ozone (O_3), chlorine monoxide radical (ClO), bromine monoxide radical (BrO), total odd nitrogen (NO_y), nitric oxide (NO), and water (H_2O) in the vicinity of the aircraft at altitudes ranging from 12 to 18 km above the Earth's surface, well into the altitude region where ozone is undergoing depletion. Instruments aboard the DC-8 measured the abundances of H_2O and O_3 in the vicinity of the aircraft, the vertical distribution of O_3 for approximately 10 km above the aircraft, and the total column amounts of O_3, hydrochloric acid (HCl), chlorine nitrate ($ClONO_2$), chlorine dioxide (OClO), BrO, hydrofluoric acid (HF), NO, nitrogen dioxide (NO_2), nitric acid (HNO_3), as well as a number of other constituents, above the aircraft altitude.

Additionally, the temporal and spatial distributions of long-lived chemical tracers and dynamical variables were measured in order to understand atmospheric motions. These included measurements of nitrous oxide (N_2O), methane (CH_4), chlorofluorocarbons 11 ($CFCl_3$) and 12 (CF_2Cl_2), carbon tetrachloride (CCl_4), and methylchloroform (CH_3CCl_3). In-situ measurements of all of these species were made from both the ER-2 and DC-8, and column measurements of most from the DC-8. The size distribution, abundance, and composition of particles was determined by instrumentation aboard the ER-2, as well as the vertical distribution of aerosols from 12 to 28 km by the DC-8 lidar, in an effort to understand the role of heterogeneous processes. Additionally, atmospheric pressure, temperature, lapse rate, and winds were measured aboard the ER-2 to determine the state variables and dynamical structure of the atmosphere.

The project had regular ozone sonde data available from the Palmer station, the Halley Bay station, the South Pole station, and McMurdo. These define the vertical distribution of ozone at points not routinely covered by the flight tracks. Ozonesondes were launched at special times from Palmer and the South Pole to coincide with aircraft overflights of those locations.

The analyses of some of these data sets have not yet been completed, either because of the lengthy data reduction procedures required or because of the sheer volume of raw data acquired. An example of the latter is the meteorological data set, whose initial analyses had the primary goal of forecasting the flight conditions. Furthermore, many of the analyses of the chemical data sets are clearly only preliminary, to be refined by recalibration checks and more sophisticated re-analyses available at the home laboratories. As a consequence, the initial picture summarized below cannot be a balanced, complete, and final one.

Results and Their Relationships to Theories

The processes controlling the abundance and distribution of ozone in Antarctica are complex and intertwined. However, given the successful nature of this campaign, we are now in a position to start to more fully appreciate the exquisite balance between the meteorological motions and the photochemistry. We will present our preliminary scientific findings as answers to a series of posed scientific questions that are relevant to public policy.

1) Did the springtime ozone hole occur over Antarctica in 1987?

Yes. TOMS satellite, balloon ozonesonde, and both ER-2 and DC-8 aircraft measurements of ozone showed that the springtime ozone decrease occurred again this year. TOMS showed the spatial extent of the phenomenon is continental or greater in scale and revealed the temporal change in the total column of ozone. The abundance of ozone in August and September of 1987 was lower than any previous year at all latitudes south of 60 degrees. In mid-September of this year column ozone was approximately 15% lower at both 70 and 80 degrees south than the values observed in the lowest previous year of 1985. The balloon-sonde data demonstrated that ozone was depleted in the altitude region between approximately 13 and 24 km at Halley Bay, and 15 and 24 km at Palmer. Ozone trends observed at Halley Bay and at Palmer are quite similar, with an approximate 50% decrease observed from mid-August to mid-September near 18 km. The upward looking lidar aboard the DC-8 observed more than a 50% decrease in O_3 at 77 to 90 degrees south between 14 and 19 km, during September, but no discernible trend between 12 and 14 km. There was also evidence from the lidar data of a decrease in O_3 up to 23 km. The in-situ ER-2 instruments observed changes consistent with this picture.

The TOMS data showed that ozone did not simply change monotonically with time, but in some instances changed dramatically over large spatial scales in the matter of only a day or so. One example of such a rapid change in ozone is demonstrated by the TOMS data for September 4-6 over the Palmer Peninsula and Weddell Sea. Changes of greater than 25 Dobson units (DU) in one day were observed over large regions (3 million square km). The ozone sonde data from Halley Bay and the DC-8 lidar data showed that, during this event, the ozone was depleted over a wide altitude range, from about 14 to 23 km.

2) Does the evidence indicate that both chemical and meteorological processes are responsible for the ozone hole?

The weight of observational evidence strongly suggests that both chemical and meteorological mechanisms perturbed the zone. Additionally, it is clear that meteorology sets up the special conditions required for the perturbed chemistry.

3) Was the chemical composition of the Antarctic stratosphere observed to be perturbed?

Yes. It is quite evident that the chemical composition of the Antarctic stratosphere is highly perturbed compared to predictions based on currently accepted chemical and dynamical theories. The present findings are consistent with the observations made last year from McMurdo. The distribution of chlorine species is significantly different from that observed at mid-latitudes, as is the abundance and distribution of nitrogen species. The amount of total water within some regions of the vortex is significantly lower than anticipated.

Since late August the abundance of the chlorine monoxide radical within the polar chemically perturbed region has been elevated by a factor of more than 100 relative to that measured at mid-latitudes at the highest altitude at which the ER-2 was flown, about 18.5 km. However, the abundance of ClO was observed to decrease rapidly towards lower altitudes. At the highest flight levels, the abundance of ClO at local solar noon ranged between 0.5 and 1 ppbv for the last month of the campaign. While we have no data at higher altitudes, the observed increase in the abundance of ClO from lower altitudes, coupled with the observed low column abundances of HCl, suggests that the ClO abundance may increase somewhat at altitudes above 18 km. In addition to the steep decrease in ClO abundance at lower altitude, the abundance of ClO was also observed to decrease dramatically outside of the chemically perturbed region.

Chlorine dioxide, OClO, which is most likely formed in a reaction sequence involving the ClO radical, was observed both day and night at highly elevated concentrations compared to those at mid-latitude. The preliminary analyses of these observations are consistent with measurements made from McMurdo last year. The column content of hydrochloric acid, HCl, which is one of the major chlorine reservoirs at mid-latitudes, is very low within the chemically perturbed region reaching column contents below 1×10^{15} molecules per cm^2. In addition, the column amount ratio of HCl/HF within the chemically perturbed region decreased significantly from a normal mid-latitude value of 4 to a value less than unity. While chlorine nitrate was observed, the data have yet to be fully analyzed thus precluding a statement at this time about its abundance.

The bromine monoxide radical has been observed at concentrations of a few pptv within the chemically perturbed region of the vortex at the flight levels of the ER-2. The abundance of BrO decreases at lower altitudes. However, because the observed concentrations are close to the detection limit of the instrument, little more can be said about the altitude dependence. The low measured abundances of BrO, coupled with our current lack of understanding of the ClO ÷ BrO reaction means that we cannot currently assess the significance of this mechanism for ozone reductions at the ER-2 flight levels.

The ER-2 observations of the abundance of odd nitrogen, which is the sum of all nitrogen-containing reservoir and radical species, show, like total water, very low values within the chemically perturbed region of the vortex, indicating that the atmosphere has been denitrified, as well as dehydrated. Abundances of NO_y of 8-12 ppbv were observed outside the chemically perturbed region, while abundances of 0.5 to 4 ppbv were observed inside the chemically perturbed region. A similar large change was observed for one of the nitrogen components, i.e. nitric oxide, NO. In addition, some of the NO_y observations suggest that NO_y component species are incorporated into polar stratospheric cloud (PSC) particles and nitrate was observed in the particle phase on some of the filter samples and on some of the wire impactor samples taken in the chemically perturbed region of the vortex. The column measurements of nitric oxide, nitrogen oxide, and nitric acid made from the DC-8 exhibit a strong decrease in the abundance of these species towards the center of the vortex. These low values of nitrogen species are contrary to all theories requiring elevated levels of nitrogen oxides, such as the proposed solar cycle theory.

4) How do the observed elevated ClO abundances support a chemical role in the formation of the ozone hole?

There is no longer debate as to whether ClO exists within the chemically perturbed region near 18 km at abundances sufficient to destroy ozone if our current understanding of the chlorine-ozone catalytic cycle is correct. The rate of decrease in ozone during the month of September at the highest altitudes at which the ER-2 was operated during this campaign is consistent with simultaneously observed concentrations of ClO. However, our present understanding of key chemical reaction rates and photodissociation products within the catalytic process is incomplete. Thus, laboratory studies are urgently needed. It is essential to define the rate of ClO dimer (Cl_2O_2) formation and the photolysis products of dimer decomposition because only one of several possible routes leads to ozone destruction. Once the results of ongoing laboratory studies become available, these in-situ ClO data will allow the chemical mechanism to be quantitatively defined and its consequences better understood.

There is another line of observational evidence consistent with ozone destruction by chlorine catalysis. In the month of August, a consistent positive correlation between ClO and O_3 was observed. By the middle of September, as the ozone concentration was dropping at ER-2 altitudes, a strong anti-correlation developed between ClO and O_3. The anti-correlation was usually present on both large and small scales within the chemically perturbed region.

There are observations that are not entirely consistent with these chemical arguments. For example, based on preliminary data from this year and data from last year from McMurdo, the observed diurnal behavior of OClO, is difficult to rationalize with the present chemical mechanisms, particularly in light of the new observations that the abundances of BrO are low at ER-2 flight altitudes.

5) Can the elevated abundances of ClO inside the chemically perturbed region of the vortex be explained?

Significant progress was made. Observational data that air within the chemically perturbed region of the vortex is dehydrated and that the NO_y

abundances are very low are consistent with theories that have been invoked whereby the chlorine reservoir species, $ClONO_2$ and HCl, can react on the surfaces of polar stratospheric clouds to enhance the abundance of active chlorine species, i.e. ClO. The observations also support the picture that the abundance of NO_y is low because odd nitrogen can be removed from the atmosphere by being tied up in ice crystals, which can then gravitationally settle to much lower altitudes. Low abundances of NO_y are needed to prevent the rapid reconversion of ClO to $ClONO_2$. This picture is further supported by the observations of low column abundances of HCl, by occasional observations of high levels of nitrate found in the ice particles, and by the visual and lidar observations of high cirrus and polar stratospheric clouds.

One observation which is currently difficult to understand is the sharp decrease in the abundance of ClO at lower altitudes. This could be due to a lack of understanding of either the abundance or partitioning of ClO_y, or to dynamical effects. Lack of observations of reactive hydrogen containing radicals, hydroxyl (OH) and hydroperoxy (HO_2) currently prevents an assessment of their role in the conversion of chlorine reservoir species to ClO.

6) How do the observations support a meteorological role in the formation of the ozone hole?

There were instances of rapid large scale changes in total ozone where meteorology appears to have been the controlling factor. One such event occurred over the Palmer Peninsula on September 5. Over a period of 24 hours total ozone as observed by TOMS decreased by 25 DU to below 200 DU over an area of about 3 million square km. Such a rapid decrease is difficult to explain chemically. The origin of that air is not known. It could be either air naturally low in ozone, tropospheric/lower stratospheric, or air in which ozone had been chemically depleted. The feature moved over the Weddell Sea and persisted until September 16, when it merged with two other regions of low total ozone. Lidar measurements from the DC-8 showed low ozone values and extensive aerosol layers between 14 and 19 km in the region of the TOMS minimum of ozone. This and other similar events evident in the TOMS ozone data and the SAM II PSC data between September 5 and 14 were spatially correlated with deepening surface pressure lows with marked meridional flow from middle to high latitudes at lower stratospheric levels. The detailed meteorological mechanism by which the surface lows produce the low column ozone remains unclear and further analysis is required.

The data offer no support for sustained large scale upwelling. In the restricted region covered by the ER-2, 54 to 72 degrees south latitude and from altitudes of 12.5 to 18.5 km, measurements of CFC-11 and N_2O which act as tracers of air motions show no evidence of a general increase in abundances above about 14 km during the mission, although there were instances of structure and elevated values.

The meteorology must play a role in the dehydration and denitrification processes. It is crucial to understand whether the necessary low temperatures are maintained radiatively or by ascent, or some combination of both.

7) Does the complexity of the situation suggest that we need to understand the interplay between meteorology and chemistry?

Yes. It is clear from our ER-2 flights that the region of dehydrated and denitrified air maintained a sharply defined latitude gradient throughout most of the campaign. On a purely meteorological definition, the vortex edge would be well outside the dehydrated, denitrified region. The meteorological flow must therefore have been such as to maintain a kind of "containment vessel," in which the perturbed chemistry could proceed without being influenced by mixing in more normal stratospheric air from outside or below.

Very low values of CFC-11, CFC-12, CH_3CCl_3, and N_2O were observed at the upper levels of the ER-2 flight track within the "containment vessel." A key question is how these low values are produced and maintained in the chemically perturbed region.

The concept of mixing at the region of sharp latitudinal gradient is important, since it has the potential to supply nitrogen oxides which would tend to decelerate the chlorine chemistry. The meteorology is thus important in the termination phase as well as in the initiation phase.

8) Can we quantitatively separate the contributions of chemistry and meteorology to the formation of the ozone hole?

No. The September 5 event illustrates the complexity of the ozone hole, and the difficulty of deriving unambiguous dynamical or chemical signatures. The magnitude and rapidity of the decrease are difficult to ascribe to a chemical cause. Air of low ozone content appears to have been transported into the region. The origin of that air is not known. It could be either air naturally low in ozone, tropospheric/lower stratospheric, or air in which ozone had been chemically depleted.

Another illustration of the difficulty of clearly establishing chemical or dynamical mechanisms is the decreasing trends in ozone in regions of low ClO outside of the vortex whose magnitudes are comparable to those within the vortex. This is evident from an examination of the ozonesonde data from the Palmer station at 64°S and comparing it to the Halley Bay data at 78°S, and the DC-8 lidar data. In addition, downward trends of ozone were observed in the lower altitude region where ClO concentrations were substantially lower than at 18 km.

9) What are the global implications of the Antarctic ozone hole?

Until we understand the cause or causes of the spring-time Antarctic hole, we will not be able to address this key question in a responsible manner. Thus, at this time, it is premature for us to speculate on this important topic. However, as we continue to analyze the data that we have acquired and further test and expand the pictures that we have developed, we will be in a better position to address this important question.

10) When will the data be in a form suitable for use in formulating national and international regulatory policies?

As noted in the opening paragraph, the schedule for the assimilation and publication of the results is brisk. Peer reviewed publications will appear in 1988. The results from the 1987 ground-based McMurdo campaign will likely appear on about the same schedule. Both sets of these completed conclusions would be the best basis for any possible policy reevaluations. The major international scientific review schedule for 1989, which will serve as input to the 1990 policy review of the Montreal Protocol, will have these conclusions available.

BICENTENNIAL OBSERVANCE OF THE U.S. CONSTITUTION

September 17 and 18, 1987

"If our Constitution has endured, through times perilous as well as prosperous, it has not been simply as a plan of government, no matter how ingenious or inspired that might be. This document that we honor today has always been something more to us, filled with a deeper feeling than one of simple admiration—a feeling, one might say, more of reverence." Those words were spoken by the thirty-ninth president of the United States, Ronald Reagan, in a speech commemorating the 200th birthday of the signing of the Constitution September 17. His remarks were delivered at a gala festival in Philadelphia, where—after months of heated debate—thirty-nine of the fifty-five delegates to the Constitutional Convention had signed a historic document on that date in 1787.

The celebration capped months of festivities and instruction to remind Americans of the Constitution's vitality as the foundation of the U.S. democratic system—the oldest constitution in existence, fashioned by one of the world's youngest nations. A prime organizer of the celebration was former chief justice of the United States Warren E. Burger (1969-1986). Speaking before a joint session of the Pennsylvania General Assembly in Philadelphia September 18, Burger noted the Constitution's commercial importance in preventing the "Balkanization" of the original thirteen states.

The 1987 Fête and Other Anniversaries

The September 1987 panoply had been preceded by two other patriotic extravangazas. One was the July 1986 unveiling of the restored Statue of

Liberty. Ten years earlier communities across America had celebrated the best-known and most frequently quoted of U.S. civic treatises, the Declaration of Independence. Although the Constitution's bicentennial was similar in many ways, its aura was somewhat different, perhaps because the document itself was not viewed as "glamorous" or vivid, as were the "spirit of '76" or "the Lady." (Historic Documents of 1976, p. 509; Historic Documents of 1986, p. 697)

Yet the September festivities recalled a similar event of July 4, 1788. Then, bells pealed from Philadelphia's Christ Church steeple and cannon discharged from the ship Rising Sun, *anchored in the Delaware River. Later that morning, the streets of Philadelphia saw a Federal Procession, complete with a herald on horseback proclaiming a new era and a float in the form of a large eagle. More than the twelve-year-old Declaration of Independence was being celebrated that day: in the preceding months the new Constitution had been ratified by Pennsylvania and nine of the other thirteen states, enough to give the document life and the fledgling nation hope. After the parade, 17,000 people—more than half the city—gathered at Union Green. That evening, in honor of the festival, the* Rising Sun *was handsomely illuminated.*

The September 1987 fifteen-hour gala provided a spectacle of floats, balloons, flags, bells, and speeches, with the Goodyear blimp providing a bird's eye view. College bands from every state in the Union played a brass fanfare written especially for the occasion, and a flag-waving drill team performed in front of Independence Hall. In all, 20,000 people marched and performed—including fifers and drummers, a colonial saluting battery, and nine bell-ringing town criers in eighteenth-century garb—before a quarter of a million spectators. At 4:00 p.m., the moment the Framers had signed the four-page Constitution, Burger rang a replica of the Liberty Bell, signaling a round of bell ringing in communities throughout the nation and at U.S. diplomatic missions and military installations abroad.

Assembly at Philadelphia

Speaking at the ceremonies, Reagan described the Constitution as having been "born in crisis" as the new nation, bound loosely under the Articles of Confederation, confronted outstanding debts from the Revolutionary War and dissension among the thirteen states. But, the president continued, "the vision of democratic government" that had inspired the revolution was the driving force enabling the delegates to the Constitutional Convention "to rise above politics and self-interest" and reach compromises on a new framework of government. "In a very real sense, it was then, in 1787, that the revolution truly began," he said.

The call for the Philadelphia convention had been agreed to by the Continental Congress in 1787. All states except Rhode Island sent delegations chosen by the respective state legislatures. The Framers, whose average age was just over forty-three, were lawyers, planters, farmers, merchants, and politicians. They were, for the most part, men of reputation and experience.

The consensus that it was necessary to establish a strong national government emerged very early on, when the delegates agreed to scrap the Articles of Confederation and write a new Constitution that would be supreme. The new government was to have three branches—legislative, executive, and judicial. The rest of the negotiations, for all the serious disagreements and famous compromises that occurred, really amounted to working out the details.

But ratification of the new Constitution was by no means assured. As the months went on and the struggle over approval proceeded, the Federalists (as proponents called themselves) began to agree to "ratification with recommendations"—that is, approval of the Constitution with the proviso that the new Congress initiate amendments, especially to guarantee individual rights and liberties. In five states ratification was obtained with "recommendations" that ultimately resulted in the Bill of Rights.

On June 21, 1788, New Hampshire became the ninth state to ratify the new document; although nine was the required number, the still-to-come verdicts in Virginia and New York were critical to the success of the Union. Virginia's approval came on June 25 and New York's on July 26, after struggles in both states. The two remaining states, North Carolina and Rhode Island, did not approve the Constitution until 1789 and 1790.

Within only a few years, men of all political views came to hold the Constitution in great respect, even if they disagreed about the meaning of some of its clauses. But respected or not, the Constitution itself was mere words on parchment. It provided for a national government, but could hardly guarantee that government's effectiveness. Moreover, the strength of the national government was tested at critical periods in the nation's history, and heated debate over interpreting the Constitution has continued.

Imperfections and Ignorance

Although Americans celebrated the 200th birthday of the federal government's charter, renewed attention pointed to what some felt were the document's flaws and demonstrated that many citizens lacked a clear perception of what the Constitution actually said.

One of the Constitution's critics was Supreme Court Justice Thurgood Marshall, the Court's only black justice. While paying tribute to the document, Marshall, in a May 6, 1987, speech, said the Constitution was "defective from the start, requiring several amendments, a civil war, and momentous social transformation to attain the system of constitutional government, and its respect for the individual freedoms and human rights, we hold as fundamental today." The credit for abolishing slavery and granting women the right to vote "does not belong to the framers," he said. "It belongs to those who refused to acquiesce in outdated notions of 'liberty,' 'justice' and 'equality' and who strived to better them." Marshall said he planned "to celebrate the bicentennial of the Constitution as a living document" that included "the Bill of Rights and other amendments protecting individual freedoms and human rights."

A fall 1986 survey conducted by the Hearst Corporation indicated that although 54 percent of those questioned knew the purpose of the Constitution was "to create a federal government and define its powers," 25 percent thought the document declared independence from England. Most seemed to confuse the Constitution with the Declaration of Independence or with President Abraham Lincoln's Gettysburg Address. Only four persons in ten knew that the Bill of Rights was the first ten amendments to the Constitution.

Following are excerpts from President Ronald Reagan's remarks at a "Celebration of Citizenship" in Philadelphia on September 17, 1987; and the text of the speech delivered by former chief justice of the United States Warren E. Burger before the Pennsylvania General Assembly in Philadelphia on September 18, 1987:

REMARKS OF PRESIDENT REAGAN

Thank you all very much. With so many distinguished guests, I hope you'll excuse me if I single out just one. He has devoted a lifetime of service to his country, and occupied one of the highest offices in our land. And recently he stepped down to lead the nation in our bicentennial celebrations. Well, by a happy coincidence, this day that marks the 200th anniversary of the signing of our Constitution, also happens to be his birthday. Today, Chief Justice Warren Burger is 80 years old. And Warren, we of the younger generation salute you. Congratulations.

As we stand here today before Independence Hall, we can easily imagine that day, September 17, 1787, when the delegates rose from their chairs and arranged themselves according to the geography of their States, beginning with New Hampshire and moving south to Georgia. They had labored for 4 months through the terrible heat of the Philadelphia summer, but they knew as they moved forward to sign their names to that new document that in many ways their work had just begun. This new Constitution, this new plan of government, faced a skeptical, even hostile reception in much of the country.

To look back on that time, at the difficulties faced and surmounted, can only give us perspective on the present. Each generation, every age, I imagine, is prone to think itself beset by unusual and particularly threatening difficulties, to look back on the past as a golden age when issues were not so complex and politics not so divisive, when problems did not seem so intractable.

Sometimes we're tempted to think of the birth of our country as one such golden age, a time characterized primarily by harmony and cooperation. In fact, the Constitution and our government were born in crisis. The years leading up to our Constitutional Convention were some of the most difficult our nation ever endured. This young nation, threatened on every side by hostile powers, was on the verge of economic collapse. In some States inflation raged out of control; debt was crushing. In Massachusetts, ruinously high taxes provided—or provoked an uprising of poor farmers led by a former Revolutionary War captain, Daniel Shays.

Trade disputes between the States were bitter and sometimes violent, threatening not only the economy but even the peace. No one thought him guilty of exaggeration when Edmund Randolph described the perilous state of the confederacy. "Look at the public countenance," he said, "from New Hampshire to Georgia! Are we not on the eve of war, which is only prevented by the hopes from this Convention?"

Yes, but these hopes were matched in many others by equally strong suspicions. Wasn't this Convention just designed to steal from the States their sovereignty, to usurp their freedoms so recently fought for? Patrick Henry, the famous orator of the Revolution, thought so. He refused to attend the Convention, saying with his usual talent for understatement, that he "smelt a rat."

The Articles of Confederation, all could see, were not strong enough to hold this new nation together. But there was no general agreement on how a stronger Federal Government should be constituted—or, indeed, whether one should be constituted at all. There were strong secessionist feelings in many parts of the country. In Boston, some were calling for a separate nation of New England. Others felt the 13 States should divide into three independent nations. And it came as a shock to George Washington, recently traveling in New England, to find that sentiment in favor of returning to a monarchy still ran strong in that region.

No, it wasn't the absence of problems that won the day in 1787. It wasn't the absence of division and difficulty; it was the presence of something higher—the vision of democratic government founded upon those self-evident truths that still resounded in Independence Hall. It was that ideal, proclaimed so proudly in this hall a decade earlier, that enabled them to rise above politics and self-interest, to transcend their differences and together create this document, this Constitution that would profoundly and forever alter not just these United States but the world.

In a very real sense, it was then, in 1787, that the Revolution truly began. For it was with the writing of our Constitution, setting down the architecture of democratic government, that the noble sentiments and brave rhetoric of 1776 took on substance, that the hopes and dreams of the revolutionists could become a living, enduring reality.

All men are created equal and endowed by their Creator with certain inalienable rights—until that moment some might have said that was just a high-blown sentiment, the dreams of a few philosophers and their hot-headed followers. But could one really construct a government, run a country, with such idealistic notions?

But once those ideals took root in living, functioning institutions, once those notions became a nation—well, then, as I said, the revolution could really begin, not just in America but around the world, a revolution to free man from tyranny of every sort and secure his freedom the only way possible in this world, through the checks and balances and institutions of limited, democratic government.

Checks and balances, limited government—the genius of our constitutional system is its recognition that no one branch of government alone could be relied on to preserve our freedoms. The great safeguard of our liberty is the totality of the constitutional system, with no one part getting the upper hand. And that's why the judiciary must be independent. And that's why it also must exercise restraint.

If our Constitution has endured, through times perilous as well as prosperous, it has not been simply as a plan of government, no matter how ingenious or inspired that might be. This document that we honor today has always been something more to us, filled with a deeper feeling than one of simple admiration—a feeling, one might say, more of reverence.

One scholar described our Constitution as a kind of covenant. It is a covenant we've made not only with ourselves but with all of mankind. As John Quincy Adams promised, "Whenever the standard of freedom and independence has been or shall be unfurled, there will be America's heart, her benedictions and her prayers." It's a human covenant; yes, and beyond that, a covenant with the Supreme Being to whom our Founding Fathers did constantly appeal for assistance.

It is an oath of allegiance to that in man that is truly universal, that core of being that exists before and beyond distinctions of class, race, or national origin. It is a dedication of faith to the humanity we all share, that part of each man and woman that most closely touches on the divine.

And it was perhaps from that divine source that the men who came together in this hall 200 years ago drew the inspiration and strength to face the crisis of their great hopes and overcome their many divisions. After all, both Madison and Washington were to refer to the outcome of the Constitutional Convention as a miracle; and miracles, of course, have only one origin.

"No people," said George Washington in his Inaugural Address, "can be bound to acknowledge and adore the Invisible Hand which conducts the affairs of men more than those of the United States. Every step by which they have advanced to the character of an independent nation seems to have been distinguished by some providential agency." No doubt he was thinking of the great and good fortune of this young land: the abundant and fertile continent given us, far from the warring powers of Europe; the successful struggle against the greatest proof—or power of that day, England; the happy outcome of the Constitutional Convention and the debate over ratification.

But he knew, too, as he also said, that there is an "indissoluble union" between duty and advantage, and that the guiding hand of providence did not create this new nation of America for ourselves alone, but for a higher cause: the preservation and extension of the sacred fire of human liberty. This is America's solemn duty.

During the summer of 1787, as the delegates clashed and debated, Washington left the heat of Philadelphia with his trout fishing companion, Gouverneur Morris of Pennsylvania, made a pilgrimage to Valley Forge. Ten years before, his Continental Army had been camped there through the winter. Food was low, medical supplies nonexistent, his soldiers had to go "half in rags in the killing cold, their torn feet leaving bloodstains as they walked shoeless on the icy ground."

Gouverneur Morris reported that the general was silent throughout the trip. He did not confide his emotions as he surveyed the scene of past hardship. One can imagine that his conversation was with someone else—that it took more the form of prayer for this new nation, that such sacrifices be not in vain, that the hope and promise that survived such a terrible winter of suffering not be allowed to wither now that it was summer.

One imagines that he also did what we do today in this gathering and celebration, what will always be America's foremost duty—to constantly renew that covenant with humanity, with a world yearning to breathe free; to complete the work begun 200 years ago, that grand, noble work that is America's particular calling—the triumph of human freedom, the triumph of human freedom under God.

I have, a number of times, said that you may call it mysticism, but I have always believed that this land was put here to be found by a special kind of people. And may I simply say also, a man wrote me a letter, and I would call to your attention what he did to mine. You could go from here to live in another country, France, but you wouldn't become a Frenchman. You could go to Japan and live there, but you wouldn't become a Japanese. But people from every corner of the world can come to this country and become an American.

I think a moment ago I was given a cue, and I can think of no more fitting tribute to the Constitution's bicentennial than ringing the Centennial Bell, and with it, will be rung bells all over the Nation. . . .

REMARKS OF FORMER CHIEF JUSTICE BURGER

In this city, in this setting, and on this day when the Constitution first became available 200 years ago for a waiting people—and for the Pennsylvania Assembly—it is a good time to turn back to those events. Probably it goes too far to suggest that the people as a whole—3 to 4 million—were "waiting." Most were going about their daily affairs, only vaguely aware that something was going on in distant Philadelphia, two weeks travel from Georgia, four days from Mount Vernon.

We remember that the resolution of the Continental Congress calling the Philadelphia meeting had given no hint of drafting a new Constitution and that it was drafted in secrecy at a time when the "leakage" malady that plagues some aspects of modern government was not a serious problem.

We remember, too, that when the Annapolis Convention in September 1786 resolved to ask for a meeting of the states to consider both commercial and political problems of the thirteen states, only five states were present. The resistance to central planning, to the idea of a central, federal government, was so strong that the Continental Congress rejected the idea of calling a "Constitutional Convention." Their resolution invited states to send delegates to Philadelphia in May, 1787, "for the sole and express purpose of revising the Articles of Confederation."

It is difficult to realize that those hardy people operating under the feeble Articles of Confederation had won a Revolution against a great world power. The Articles were hardly more than a multilateral treaty which the 13 allied states described as "a firm league of friendship." [Indeed, the Revolutionary War was carried on under a *de facto* government since the Articles of Confederation were not ratified until 1781.]

After the victory at Yorktown, many of the leaders knew that "a firm league of friendship" would not work for the future. George Washington had spent that terrible winter at Valley Forge, a few miles from where we meet today. Alexander Hamilton was one of his staff aides. They had watched their comrades die for want of needed supplies. There was no way to compel the states to pay for the armies.

Once peace had been achieved, the rivalries and tensions between the states began to surface. What happened was what has happened to every victorious alliance in history; the 13 allies began to fall out; Virginia and Maryland quarreled over boundaries and navigation, Pennsylvania and Connecticut over territory in western Pennsylvania claimed by Connecticut, New Jersey and New York over commercial matters. Since each state was free to maintain its own army and navy, there were threats—and acts—to resolve claims with force. In Massachusetts, Colonel Shays' troops engaged in a small war against state forces. For a time Shays' Rebellion closed courts in Massachusetts.

How long could a "firm league of friendship" secure that "domestic tranquillity" so essential to unity—and progress?

The spirit of the New Jersey troops who resisted taking an oath to the United States saying, "Our country is New Jersey," was pervasive throughout the 13 states.

In the Virginia Declaration of Rights George Mason had written that if a free people do not, from time to time, look back at their freedoms and how they got them, they risk losing those freedoms. In looking back the wonder of what happened can be seen. When we do that it becomes clear that it was not all predestined, foreordained or easy to make a nation out of 13 independent "sovereigns."

Sometimes I find it useful to compare several episodes of history that help me to understand the significance of what happened in Philadelphia.

We remember that these 13 states were independent and sovereign in 1787 and some of the leading figures, like Patrick Henry and New York's Governor Clinton, missed no opportunity to press that point. Henry refused to be a delegate to Philadelphia; he wanted no part of a strong federal union. In 1787 each state could issue its own currency, each could raise protectionist tariffs against other states' products, whether anvils, rifles, horse harness or carrots.

No one had combined the words, "common" and "market," but Hamilton and Madison and some of the great Pennsylvania delegates like Franklin and the Morrises knew there must be a "common market" if manufacture and trade—and the new nation—were to develop. Sixteen words in Article I of the Constitution—the Commerce Clause—gave us the reality of a common market from the beginning. Few parts of the new Constitution had more impact on our moving from a cluster of independent states on the edge of a wilderness to a great world power.

Had it not been for the wisdom of those extraordinary men who sat here 200 years ago, our thirteen independent states would have been Balkanized from the beginning. If we had not created a "more perfect union," to provide for the common defense, it would have been easy for the Great Powers of that day to pick off our "sovereign" and "independent" states one by one. One great power might say to another, "let us have Massachusetts and New Hampshire and we won't bother you about the Carolinas and Georgia."

That is what those Founding Fathers meant when they made a national policy out of John Dickinson's slogan, "United We Stand, Divided We Fall."

It was not until the Treaty of Rome, 170 years after the delegates sat down for dinner at Philadelphia's City Tavern, that Europe began to reach for a common market—and its objectives are not yet fully realized.

Speculate with me, if you will, what would have been the history of Europe—and of the world—if something like the 1957 Treaty of Rome had opened the doors of Europe to the Common Market in 1789. Would it not have encouraged commercial competition in place of cartels? Would a common market for Europe in 1789 have led to swift development of a common second language to expedite trade—as has developed in the 30 years since the Treaty of Rome?

We know, too, that the Common Market of the 13 states lessened the tensions and parochial attitudes just as modern travel has opened doors and borders for us over the years.

Would a common market for Europe in 1789 have tolerated Napoleon, Kaiser Wilhelm, Mussolini, Hitler, Stalin? If business leaders in Berlin, Paris, Brussels, Rome and Madrid had shared an interest in manufacture and open trade—and peace—is it possible that they would have insisted on policies and leadership that would have avoided the Napoleonic Wars, World Wars I and II?

It is 70 years since the ideas of Karl Marx brought a revolution in Russia under the guiding hand of Lenin. These revolutionists knew, as our leaders of 1776 knew, how to plan and fight a revolution, but there was an important difference. Our leaders also knew how to govern. The Communists imposed—and still to this day impose—their will by fear and force. Our leaders charted a course of rule by the consent of the governed. Today, seventy years after the Red Revolution, Mr. Gorbachev seems to be drawing away from the policy of maintaining a state of constant fear of attack from the Western World.

Of course, we have social and economic problems here at home, but our domestic problems are chiefly the expansion and enforcement of individual rights and opportunities.

History tells us that dreams and hopes can lead to change because of the power of an idea in a free society. And this is what happened with those who came here more than three centuries ago—at Plymouth and in Jamestown—who came here seeking freedom and opportunity. Those who met in Philadelphia had a dream of a strong union that would provide the freedoms and opportunities they sought.

In recent days we have read and heard much of the hopes and aspiration of our neighbors in the five Central American countries. The people and leaders of those countries are no less concerned with liberty than we are.

The delegates at Philadelphia, 200 years ago, saw the need to forge a union to preserve their independence and security. They knew that a union of the 13 states was imperative to insure the domestic tranquillity essential to growth and development—and to protect their new freedoms.

In many respects the search of our Central American neighbors for independence and individual freedom parallels our search that began so long ago. Their proposed plan to foreclose outside influences and interference with their affairs and their desire to terminate military activities that have interfered with development of much of Central America for years. Some of those leaders recognize that if a third country can divide them, that third country can conquer them.

Our 13 states had some advantages 200 years ago; they shared a common language and a common tradition. They knew that England, Spain and other powers had designs on North America. Even after our independence the great powers still had designs on the rich lands South and West of our 13 states. And France, our recent ally, could not stand by and allow other great powers to enlarge their footholds on this continent.

Just as the Communist world seeks to enlarge its influence and control in the Caribbean Basin our risk 200 years ago was that unless we united our states—each with its own currency, each controlling its borders, each carrying on small commercial wars with the others—we would have been easy victims of the Great Powers in the decades following the end of the Revolution.

I have speculated with you on what would have been the impact of a Common Market for Europe beginning in 1789; it may be useful to speculate on the problems of the five Central American states today.

Would it not stabilize this hemisphere as a whole if the five Central American states had a long period of domestic tranquillity and freedom from outside interference or subversion? Could that come about if a James Madison of Costa Rica, an Alexander Hamilton of Honduras joined in, calling for a meeting like our Annapolis Convention of 1786, followed by a call for a meeting like ours here in Philadelphia, to "form a more perfect union"?

Is it fanciful to think that leaders of those five states, all of whom want greater freedom and greater economic opportunity for their people, might see, as our Founding Fathers saw, that there is strength in unity and that only the strong can be free? Such a gathering should be as free as our 13 states were to shape their own future. When they look at today's world with so many millions ruled by dictatorships—of the Right or the Left—surely they will see that their people should be guaranteed a third alternative, as the delegates did in Philadelphia.

The five Central American states have, in many respects, an even more favorable setting than did our 13 states two hundred years ago. Then we had a common language, common borders, and a common tradition, but marked diversity in religion. The five Central American states have geographic unity, a common tradition, a common language *and* largely a common religion. And surely they share hopes for the kind of domestic tranquillity that will assure freedom and greater individual opportunity. The urge to be free is not confined within any political borders or Berlin Walls.

Of course, the resolution of their problems and their future is exclusively a matter for the people of those five states for each is wholly sovereign and independent, as were our states. We share with them the urge for the domestic tranquillity essential to freedom under the rule of law. And, as we drew on the wisdom of France, England and Scotland, they can draw on our experience if they choose.

Here, as the nation joins Philadelphia in this celebration, we must remember that 200 years ago our people faced great perils. A wilderness and great social and economic problems were there to conquer. Risks and challenges are present today. But, if we remain on course, keeping faith with the vision of the Founders, with freedom under ordered liberty, we will have done our part to see that the great new idea of government by consent—by We the People—remains in place.

October

REPORT ON CHOLESTEROL

October 5, 1987

The federal government October 5 issued the first detailed guidelines for identifying and treating adults whose cholesterol levels put them at risk. The report, entitled "So You Have High Blood Cholesterol," was produced by the National Cholesterol Education Program, a project of the National Heart, Lung, and Blood Institute, which is a division of the National Institutes of Health (NIH).

Cooperating in the program were twenty-three major medical associations and health organizations, including the American Medical Association, the American Heart Association, and the American College of Cardiology. The group's twenty-five-page pamphlet, designed for use by physicians and the general public, called for all Americans, starting at age twenty, to have cholesterol tests as part of their regular physical examinations.

Cholesterol Levels

The report discussed four cholesterol levels: "desirable" (less than 200 milligrams per deciliter of blood), "borderline high" (a count of 200 to 239), "borderline high with risk factors" (such as cigarette smoking, high blood pressure, obesity, family history of premature heart disease, and being male), and "high" (a count of 240 or higher). For each level, the report suggested steps physicians should recommend to their patients. Those with desirable levels should be rechecked every five years; borderline cases should restrict their intake of total fats, saturated fats, and foods with high cholesterol content (such as meat and some dairy products), and should be checked annually. Doctors treating cases of borderline/risk and high level should first analyze the composition of the patient's cholesterol (which is contained in "bad," or low density lipoproteins—LDLs—and "good," or high density lipoproteins—HDLs). An LDL level of 130 to 159 was classified as "borderline high risk." The follow-up regimen should include a stringent dietary program and, if necessary, further treatment with drugs.

The report stated that about one-quarter of all Americans between ages twenty and seventy-four had high blood cholesterol, a major factor in coronary disease. Of the 500,000 Americans who died of heart attacks each year, an estimated 300,000 could be saved if they adhered to the guidelines rigorously, according to NIH officials. "If doctors follow the guidelines, medical practice will undergo a major change as a result of this report," said Dr. DeWitt S. Goodman, professor of medicine at Columbia University and chairman of the panel. "It will have a lasting impact on coronary heart disease and public health in the United States."

Treatment

The panel emphasized diet, rather than drugs, as a means to lower cholesterol levels, and suggested a two-stage approach to regulation through diet. Initially, no more than 30 percent of total caloric intake should consist of fat, of which no more than 10 percent should be saturated fat. If cholesterol levels remained high, further dietary restrictions should be effected and drugs used as a last resort.

Several drugs currently available were effective in lowering cholesterol levels. Among the "drugs of first choice" were cholestyramine, colestipol, and nicotinic acid or niacin, a type of vitamin B. In August the Food and Drug Administration (FDA) approved a new drug, lovastatin, which the panel called "a major advance." At the same time, however, the report noted that drug therapy required an extended commitment, perhaps for life. Because its long-term safety had not been documented, lovastatin was categorized a "second-choice drug." (FDA approval of TPA, p. 875)

Although the participating organizations said they would immediately launch a nationwide effort to inform doctors and patients about the new guidelines, critics charged that the dangers of cholesterol had been exaggerated and that the panel's findings were based on incomplete documentation. In an October 5 interview with the New York Times, *Dr. Eliot Corday, a member of the official advisory council to the National Heart, Lung, and Blood Institute, said that it had "stampeded the country into a hysterical situation" about the perils of a high cholesterol count.*

The report did not address the controversial issue of limiting cholesterol intake for children and adolescents, thereby reducing fats needed for growth. Other panels were scheduled to study that issue.

Following are excerpts from the October 5, 1987, report, "So You Have High Blood Cholesterol," prepared by the National Cholesterol Education Program sponsored by the National Heart, Lung, and Blood Institute of the National Institutes of Health:

Anyone can develop high blood cholesterol regardless of age, sex, race, or ethnic background. But, because there are no warning symptoms or signs, you are likely to be surprised at such a diagnosis. Don't be alarmed, but do take it seriously. Like high blood pressure, most people are unaware that their blood cholesterol levels are high until they learn it from their doctor. And, like high blood pressure, it is a potential threat to your health that you can do something about.

If you have just learned that you have high blood cholesterol, there are some important facts you need to know to protect your health. First, you need to find out what high blood cholesterol is, how high your level is, and what you can do to lower it. Then prepare to make some changes. Although these changes will depend on many factors considered by your doctor, modifying your diet is the preferred way to lower blood cholesterol. . . .

High Blood Cholesterol: What It Means

High blood cholesterol is one of the three major risk factors for coronary heart disease (cigarette smoking and high blood pressure are the other two). In other words, high blood cholesterol can significantly increase your risk of developing heart disease. Fortunately all three risk factors are "modifiable"; that is, you can do something about them. You can take steps to lower your cholesterol level and thus lower your risk for coronary heart disease.

High blood cholesterol occurs when there is too much cholesterol in your blood. Your cholesterol level is determined partly by your genetic makeup and the saturated fat and cholesterol in the foods you eat. Even if you didn't eat any cholesterol, your body would manufacture enough for its needs.

How High Does Your Blood Cholesterol Level Have to Be to Affect Your Health?

The risk of developing coronary heart disease increases as your blood cholesterol level rises. This is why it is so important that you have your blood cholesterol level measured. Currently, more than half of all adult Americans have blood cholesterol levels of 200 mg/dl or greater, which places them at an increased risk for coronary heart disease. Approximately 25 percent of the adult population 20 years of age or older has blood cholesterol levels that are considered "high," that is, 240 mg/dl or greater.

Your doctor will measure your level with a blood sample taken from your finger or your arm and will confirm this result with a second test if it is greater than 200 mg/dl....

A blood cholesterol level of 240 mg/dl or greater is considered "high" blood cholesterol. But any level above 200 mg/dl, even in the "borderline-high" category, increases your risk for heart disease. If your blood cholesterol is 240 mg/dl or greater, you have more than twice the risk of someone whose cholesterol is 200 mg/dl, and you need medical attention and further testing.

When your high blood cholesterol level is combined with another major risk factor (either high blood pressure or cigarette smoking), your risk for coronary heart disease increases even further. For example, if your cholesterol level is in the "high"category and you have high blood pressure, your risk for coronary heart disease increases six times. If you also smoke, your risk increases more than 20-fold. Other factors that increase your risk for coronary heart disease include a family history of coronary heart disease before the age of 55, diabetes, vascular (blood vessel) disease, obesity, and being male. Whether your total blood cholesterol is in the "borderline-high" category or "high" category, you should make some changes in your diet to lower your level. More specifically, if your level is in the "borderline-high" category and you have coronary heart disease or two other risk factors for coronary heart disease or is in the "high" category, your physician will prescribe more aggressive treatment and follow your cholesterol levels more closely. If your cholesterol level is desirable, you should have your level checked again in 5 years and take steps to prevent it from rising.

How Does High Blood Cholesterol Lead to Coronary Heart Disease?

Most coronary heart disease is caused by atherosclerosis, which occurs when cholesterol, fat, and other substances build up in the walls of the arteries that supply blood to the heart. These deposits narrow the arteries and can slow or block the flow of blood.... [B]lood carries a constant supply of oxygen to the heart. Without oxygen, heart muscle weakens, resulting in chest pain (angina), a heart attack (myocardial infarction), or even death. Atherosclerosis is a slow progressive disease that may start very early in life yet might not produce symptoms for many years.

What Will Lowering Your High Blood Cholesterol Level Do?

Lowering your high blood cholesterol level will slow fatty buildup in the walls of the arteries and reduce your risk of a heart attack and death caused by a heart attack. In fact, some studies have shown that, in adults with "high" blood cholesterol levels, for each 1 percent reduction in total cholesterol levels, there is a 2 percent reduction in the number of heart attacks. In other words, if you reduce your cholesterol level 15 percent, your risk of coronary heart disease could drop by 30 percent.

What Factors Influence Your Blood Cholesterol Level?

- **Diet.** Among the factors you can do something about, diet has the largest effect on your blood cholesterol level. Saturated fat raises your blood cholesterol level more than anything else you eat. Dietary cholesterol also increases your blood cholesterol level. If you have high blood cholesterol, changing your diet will be a very important step to lower it.
- **Weight.** Being overweight may also increase your blood cholesterol level. Most overweight patients with high levels of cholesterol can help lower their levels by weight reduction.
- **Physical activity/exercise.** Although it is not clear whether physical activity can prevent atherosclerosis, regular exercise may help you control weight, lower your blood pressure, and increase your level of HDL-cholesterol, the "good" type of blood cholesterol. . . .
- **Genetic factors.** Genetic factors play a major role in determining your blood cholesterol level and can determine your ability to lower your level by diet. A small number of people have an inherited tendency to have a high blood cholesterol level. If you have a genetic disorder contributing to a high blood cholesterol level, then your parents, children, brothers, and sisters should also have their blood cholesterol levels measured.
- **Sex/age.** Coronary heart disease is the leading cause of death and disability for both men and women in the United States. Estimates are that 1 out of 5 men and 1 out of 17 women will have symptoms of heart disease before the age of 60. This means that men have two to three times the risk of developing heart disease as women. However, in women as in men, cholesterol levels are predictive of coronary heart disease.

  In the United States, blood cholesterol levels in men and women start to rise at about age 20. Women's blood cholesterol levels prior to menopause (45-60 years) are lower than those of men of the same age. After menopause, however, the cholesterol level of women usually increases to a level higher than that of men. In men, blood cholesterol levels off around age 50 and the average blood cholesterol level declines slightly after age 50. Since the risk of coronary heart disease is especially high in the later decades of life, reducing blood cholesterol levels may be important in the elderly.

  In addition, oral contraceptives and pregnancy can increase blood cholesterol levels in some women. For pregnant women, blood cholesterol levels should return to normal 20 weeks after delivery.
- **Alcohol.** You may have heard that modest amounts of alcohol can improve your cholesterol profile by increasing your HDL-cholesterol

level. However, it is not known whether the higher level produced by alcohol protects against coronary heart disease. With this in mind and because drinking can have serious adverse effects, alcohol is not recommended in the prevention of coronary heart disease.

- **Stress.** Although stress has been reported to raise blood cholesterol levels, there may be other explanations for this effect. For example, during periods of stress, people may eat more foods that are high in saturated fat and cholesterol, which may increase their blood cholesterol levels—rather than the stress itself.

While all of these factors can influence your blood cholesterol level, clearly you can do something about a number of them. In fact, most people are able to lower their blood cholesterol levels with diet alone.

Blood Cholesterol and Lipoproteins: What They Are

Cholesterol is an odorless, soft, waxy substance. Your body needs cholesterol to function normally (for example, as a component of cell membranes and for the production of many hormones, vitamin D, and bile acids—which are important for the absorption of fat). Cholesterol is present in all parts of the body, including the brain and nervous system, muscle, skin, liver, intestines, heart, skeleton, etc.

Your blood cholesterol level is affected not only by the saturated fat and cholesterol in your diet, but also by the cholesterol your body produces. As a matter of fact, your body produces all the cholesterol it needs, and the saturated fat and cholesterol in your diet only serve to increase your blood cholesterol level.

Is There "Good" and "Bad" Blood Cholesterol?

Cholesterol travels in the blood in packages called lipoproteins. All lipoproteins are formed in the liver and carry cholesterol through the body.

Blood cholesterol packaged in low density lipoproteins (LDLs) is transported from the liver to other parts of the body where it can be used. LDLs carry most of the cholesterol in the blood, and if not removed from the blood, cholesterol and fat can build up in the arteries contributing to atherosclerosis. This is why LDL-cholesterol is often called "bad cholesterol."

Cholesterol is also packaged in high density lipoproteins (HDLs). HDLs carry cholesterol back to the liver for processing or removal from the body. HDLs therefore help remove cholesterol from the blood, preventing the accumulation of cholesterol in the walls of the arteries. Thus they are often referred to as "good cholesterol."

How Are LDL and HDL Levels Determined?

If your total cholesterol level is either in the "high" category or in the "borderline-high" category and you have coronary heart disease or two other risk factors for coronary heart disease, your doctor will want a more complete "cholesterol profile" that includes LDL-cholesterol, HDL-cholesterol levels, and triglyceride levels. A blood test provides this information: you will have to fast for 12 hours prior to the test. (You may notice that your LDL- and HDL-cholesterol values do not add up to your total blood cholesterol level. LDLs usually carry about 60-70 percent and HDLs about 25 percent of the total cholesterol in your blood. Other lipoproteins carry the rest.)

Some laboratories may calculate your cholesterol ratio. This measurement is actually just your total cholesterol or LDL-cholesterol divided by your HDL-cholesterol. For example, if your LDL-cholesterol level is 140 mg/dl and your HDL-cholesterol level is 35 mg/dl, your cholesterol ratio is 140/35, or 4. However, HDL-, LDL-, and total cholesterol levels are independent predictors of your risk for coronary heart disease. Because combining these values into a ratio can conceal information useful to you and your physician, it is more important to know each value separately.

What Do Your LDL and HDL Levels Mean?

Along with your total blood cholesterol level, your LDL and HDL levels provide more information on your risk of developing coronary heart disease. A high LDL-cholesterol level or a low HDL-cholesterol level puts you at increased risk. LDL- and HDL-cholesterol levels more accurately predict your risk for coronary heart disease than a total cholesterol level alone. . . .

If your LDL-cholesterol level is in the "desirable" category, you are at an acceptable level of risk. If your LDL level is in the "borderline-high risk" category, you could benefit from lowering your blood cholesterol level by making some dietary changes. If your LDL level is in the "borderline-high risk" category and you have coronary heart disease or two risk factors for coronary heart disease, you should begin diet treatment under your physician's supervision, as should a person in the "high risk" category. In general, this means you will be paying closer attention to your cholesterol level and making more dietary changes than a person at lower risk.

HDL-cholesterol will also be measured if your total blood cholesterol puts you in a high risk category. The lower your HDL-cholesterol level, the greater your risk for coronary heart disease. *Any HDL-cholesterol level lower than 35 mg/dl is considered too low.* Quitting smoking, losing weight, and becoming physically active may help raise your HDL-cholesterol level. Although it is not known for certain that raising HDL levels in this way will reduce the risk of coronary heart disease, these measures are likely to be good for your heart in any case.

How to Lower Your High Blood Cholesterol

The primary treatment for high blood cholesterol is a diet that is low in saturated fat and low in cholesterol. This new way of eating is also nutritious, with all the protein, carbohydrate, fat, vitamins, and minerals your body needs. To lower your blood cholesterol, you will:

- Eat less high-fat food (especially those high in saturated fat);
- Replace part of the saturated fat in your diet with unsaturated fat;
- Eat less high-cholesterol food;
- Choose foods high in complex carbohydrates (starch and fiber); and
- Reduce your weight, if you are overweight.

Saturated fats raise your cholesterol level more than anything else in your diet. Dietary cholesterol also raises blood cholesterol levels. Instead of eating foods rich in saturated fat and cholesterol, try more breads, cereals, and other foods high in complex carbohydrates as well as more fruits and vegetables. Using unsaturated fats in place of saturated fats can also help lower your blood cholesterol.

Fortunately, these dietary changes work together. For example, eating less saturated fat may also help you decrease the amount of cholesterol you eat and may help you lose weight. This is because foods high in saturated fat are often high in cholesterol as well and are high in calories. In fact, all fats have more than twice as many calories as either carbohydrates or protein. And, by losing weight if you are overweight, you can help lower your LDL-cholesterol level and increase your HDL-cholesterol level.

What Foods Contain Fat and Cholesterol?

- Saturated fats are found primarily in animal products, particularly fatty meats and many dairy products.
- Coconut oil, palm kernel oil, and palm oil are also very saturated.
- Some of the unsaturated fats in vegetable oils are also made more saturated by a process called hydrogenation.
- Commercially prepared and processed foods made with these vegetable oils or with saturated fats like butter and lard can also be high in saturated fat.

There are two kinds of unsaturated fat: polyunsaturated and monounsaturated. You should substitute both of these for saturated fat in your diet. Polyunsaturated fats are found primarily in plant products—including safflower, sunflower, corn, soybean, and cottonseed oils; nuts; and seeds—and in fatty fish. Major vegetable oil sources of monounsaturated fats are primarily olive oil and canola oil.

Cholesterol is found only in foods of animal origin, both high-fat foods (like hotdogs and cheddar cheese) and low-fat foods (like liver and other organ meats). And the amount of cholesterol in these foods varies. A daily intake of less than 300 mg is recommended. A 3-ounce piece of meat, fish, or poultry has 60-90 mg of cholesterol; one egg yolk contains about 270 mg; and a 3-ounce serving of liver has about 390 mg of cholesterol. . . .

What You Can Expect

Remember, by closely following your diet and monitoring your progress with regular checkups, you can lower your blood cholesterol level and greatly reduce your risk of developing coronary heart disease.

How Soon and How Much Can You Expect Your Blood Cholesterol Levels to Change?

Generally, both your total and LDL-cholesterol levels will begin to drop 2-3 weeks after you begin your cholesterol-lowering diet. Over time, you may reduce your cholesterol levels by 30-55 mg/dl or even more. The more you reduce your level, the more you will reduce your risk of developing coronary heart disease.

How much you reduce your blood cholesterol levels depends on how much fat, specifically saturated fat, and how much cholesterol you were eating before starting your cholesterol-lowering diet; how well you follow your new diet; and how responsive your body is to the diet. Also, the higher your blood cholesterol level is to begin with, the greater or more dramatic reduction you can expect with your new diet.

How Long Do You Need to Follow This Diet?

Your new cholesterol-lowering diet should be continued for life. While eating some foods high in saturated fat and cholesterol for one day or at one meal will not raise blood cholesterol levels, resuming old eating patterns will. Surprisingly, after a while your new way of eating won't seem like a "diet" at all, but simply like your regular routine—full of appealing and appetizing foods.

What Should Your Blood Cholesterol Goal Be?

Before starting your cholesterol-lowering diet, your physician will determine your blood cholesterol goal, specifically the LDL-cholesterol level, that is right for you. This goal will vary depending on whether you have coronary heart disease or any of the other risk factors for coronary heart disease. Even though achieving your LDL-cholesterol goal is more important than the total cholesterol goal, your physician can check your progress by measuring your total cholesterol level because it is a good deal simpler and because you do not have to fast before its measurement. Remember, a total cholesterol level below 200 mg/dl and an LDL-cholesterol below 130 mg/dl are desirable.

How Do You Check Your Progress?

To get your blood cholesterol measured, see your doctor or local clinic. They will take a blood sample and send it to a laboratory. There may be differences in your blood cholesterol level from day to day. Cholesterol measurements may also differ somewhat from one laboratory to the next. Your doctor will consider these factors when you return to check your progress. It is important that you have your cholesterol level measured at the same place each time.

How Often Should You Have Your Blood Cholesterol Levels Checked?

Your physician will probably want to measure your cholesterol level after you have been on the diet for 4 to 6 weeks and again after 3 months. If the total cholesterol goal is met after 3 months, measuring your LDL-cholesterol level will confirm that the LDL-cholesterol goal has been met. If your response to the diet has been satisfactory (both total cholesterol and LDL-cholesterol goals have been met), you will enter a phase of long-term monitoring. Long-term monitoring may involve remeasuring total cholesterol twice a year and LDL-cholesterol once a year.

If you have not met your blood cholesterol goal in 3 months, your doctor may further restrict the saturated fat and cholesterol in your diet and enlist the help of a dietitian. Then, after 4-6 weeks more and again after 3 months, your doctor may measure your cholesterol level. If you have attained your goal, long-term monitoring can begin. If not, your doctor may decide you need medication along with your dietary changes.

Can You Eat Before Your Test?

Since total cholesterol levels do not change much after a meal, total cholesterol can be measured at any time of day, whether or not you have just eaten. Therefore, you do not need to fast. However, you should not eat or drink anything except water or black coffee for at least 12 hours before having your lipoprotein levels determined (LDL, HDL, triglycerides). Therefore, it may be convenient to eat your last meal at about 9 p.m. and have your test the next day before breakfast.

Other Steps You Can Take

While dietary change is the first and most important action you will be taking to lower your blood cholesterol level, your doctor may suggest other steps.... These will depend on how well the diet lowers your blood cholesterol level and whether or not you have any other risk factors for coronary heart disease.

Do You Need to Take Special Medications Along with Your Diet?

In most cases, a blood cholesterol-lowering diet is the only step necessary to lower blood cholesterol levels. However, if your LDL-cholesterol level is still too high after you've been on your diet for 6 months, your doctor may decide to include medication as part of your treatment. In addition, if your cholesterol level is unusually high or if you have other major risk factors for coronary heart disease, your doctor may prescribe medications to lower blood cholesterol even sooner.

If your doctor does prescribe medications, you must continue your cholesterol-lowering diet since the combination may allow you to take less medication.... And, because diet is still the safest treatment, you should always try to lower your levels with diet alone before adding medication.

What Are These Medications?

There are several medications your physician can prescribe to help you lower your blood cholesterol levels. The recommended medications for lowering blood cholesterol in most instances are bile acid sequestrants (either cholestyramine or colestipol) and niacin. Although our bodies need a small amount of the vitamin niacin, the amount used to lower blood cholesterol is so large that it cannot be taken safely without close medical supervision. All cholesterol-lowering medications should be taken only with the advice and under the supervision of your physician.

Currently, many new medications are being developed to help treat high blood cholesterol levels, but most of these are still in the experimental stages. A new class of cholesterol-lowering drugs, the "HMG-CoA reductase inhibitors," seems to be quite promising. One drug of this class, lovastatin, has recently been approved by the Food and Drug Administration and other drugs of this class are likely to follow as well. Although such drugs seem to be extremely effective in lowering cholesterol levels, long-term safety information is limited. . . .

What Else Can You Do to Lower Your Risk for Coronary Heart Disease?

. . . [Y]ou can do something about all three of the major risk factors for coronary heart disease—high blood cholesterol, cigarette smoking, and high blood pressure. Thus, in addition to lowering your blood cholesterol level, it's a good idea to quit smoking and control your blood pressure. Maintaining your desirable weight will also help you lower your risk for coronary heart disease. And all of these steps will help you to feel better.

Where You Can Go for Help

Need more help? Want to know more? There are many places you can go to get information about your new diet, your diagnosis, and the latest findings about treatment and medications for high blood cholesterol.

What Other Health Professionals, in Addition to Your Doctor, Can Give You Help?

If you want some help following your recommended diet, talk to a registered dietitian or qualified nutritionist. They can explain the diet to you in greater detail and show you ways to follow it. They can give you advice on shopping and preparing foods, eating away from home, and changing your eating habits to help you stay on your new diet. They will also help you set goals for dietary change so that you can successfully lower your high blood cholesterol levels without drastically changing your eating pattern and overall lifestyle all at one time. The Division of Practice of the American Dietetic Association [(312) 899-0040] can help you find a registered dietitian in your area. State and local branches of the American Dietetic Association, your local hospital, or your doctor can recommend a dietitian for you.

There are also other resources. The nurse in your doctor's office can answer questions you may have about your high blood cholesterol or your new diet. If your blood cholesterol level is not lowered by diet and medication, your doctor may refer you to a physician who is a lipid specialist. Lipid specialists are experts in the management of high blood cholesterol and other lipid disorders. If you have questions about drug therapy or the medication your doctor is prescribing, ask your doctor.... [P]harmacists are also aware of the best ways to take medication, of ways to minimize side effects, and of the latest research about specific drugs....

NAVY REPORTS ON ATTACK ON USS STARK

October 15, 1987

After months of scrutiny, a naval investigating team and a blue ribbon panel concluded that some of the damages resulting from the May 17 Iraqi attack on the USS Stark *could have been averted had those in command taken steps to ensure that the ship was on full alert. However, both reports praised quick action taken by the crew and rescue teams from nearby ships to control the damage and to save as many lives as possible. The panels also recommended a number of changes to upgrade equipment on* Stark*-class frigates (FFG 7). Both the report of the seven-member blue ribbon panel and a declassified version of the Navy's formal investigation were made public October 15.*

Failure to Act on Warnings

While the Stark *was cruising in international waters on May 17, an Iraqi Mirage F1 fighter approached and fired two Exocet missiles. Both hit the ship; the first was a dud, but the second exploded in one of the crew's sleeping compartments, setting off an inferno that killed amost forty men and seriously damaged the ship before being brought under control. According to the Navy report, the crew members waged a "heroic battle" to save the ship in the face of 1,400-degree Fahrenheit temperatures, insufficient oxygen and water supplies, white hot decks, a severely listing ship, smoke, and melting polyester clothing.*

Chronologies indicated that the officers had only seconds to respond to the attack, but that they were remiss in failing to have the Stark's *defenses on alert. Investigators concluded that the commanding officer,*

Capt. Glenn R. Brindel, had been warned that Iraqi planes might attack randomly but had not made that clear to his officers. (Brindel and the chief weapons officer were allowed to resign in lieu of facing court-martial.)

The Iraqi plane had been tracked by an AWACS (a highly sophisticated radar-equipped plane) more than an hour and a quarter before the attack—beginning when the fighter was well over 200 miles from the Stark. *The ship's search radar detected the plane when it was about seventy miles away, more than ten minutes before the ship was struck. Although the ship had been informed that the Iraqi fighter was in the area, the weapons control officer left his station, and the weapons officer was reluctant to "lock on" to the plane with the ship's fire control radar. Shortly after 9:00 p.m., as the aircraft neared, the* Stark *radioed its first warning to the plane, allowing it to get well within the range of the plane's Exocet missiles. The Iraqi pilot fired the first Exocet three minutes later. A lookout spotted a bright light on the horizon but could not locate Brindel to inform him. Last-minute efforts to activate defensive weapons were to no avail. Moreover, the crew did not turn the ship so that the plane would come within the field of view of the ship's missile-guidance radar and its Phalanx (a radar-guided, six-barreled machine gun intended as a last defense against antiship missiles). Nor did they deploy radar decoys that might have deflected the two Iraqi missiles.*

Devastation and Aftermath

The first missile—the more damaging of the two—traveling at 600 mph, slammed through the Stark's *hull, cutting off firefighting water pipes and splitting into two. Spewing 300 pounds of flammable propellant, the pieces ripped through a sleeping area where sailors were just settling down. A few seconds later, a second missile slammed into the hull about eight feet from the first. Its warhead exploded, creating "an immediate inferno in the second deck berthing compartment." Radio communications were lost, so crew members sent distress calls with portable radios from survival kits.*

According to Pentagon reports, two Saudi Arabian F15 fighters refused a U.S. Air Force request to intercept the Iraqi plane after the attack—a refusal that brought considerable criticism from U.S. military officials and members of Congress.

In a letter to President Ronald Reagan, Iraqi President Saddam Hussein expressed "condolences and feelings of grief" for the "unintentional" attack. Eulogizing the thirty-seven sailors at a May 22 service in Mayport, Florida, the Stark's *home port, Reagan sought to justify the U.S. presence in the gulf because of its importance as a "crossroads for three continents and the starting place for the oil that is the lifeblood of much of the world economy. . . . Peace is at stake here, and so, too, is our own nation's security and our freedom."*

Debate over U.S. Presence in Gulf

The Stark *tragedy stirred apprehension among members of Congress and the public concerning the administration's plans to increase the U.S. presence in the Persian Gulf. A small U.S. naval force had been stationed at Bahrain in the gulf since 1949. But in 1979, after an anti-American Moslem regime came into power in Iran and held fifty-two Americans hostage, the United States began maintaining a large fleet of Indian Ocean ships that sailed frequently into the Gulf of Oman at the entrance to the Persian Gulf. By the time of the* Stark *bombing, more than 200 ships had been attacked by Iraqi and Iranian forces in the gulf. The U.S. force based at Bahrain had expanded to three destroyers and three frigates—all armed with antiaircraft missiles—and an unarmed flagship. As of mid-November 1987, there were more than forty U.S. warships in the area.* (UN Security Council resolution on Iran-Iraq war, p. 609; Historic Documents of 1981, p. 145)

The "tanker war" phase of the Iran-Iraq conflict dated from 1984, when Iraq began to attack vessels carrying Iranian oil through the gulf. Nearly all Iraqi oil destined for foreign consumption was sent overland via pipeline. Unable to retaliate in kind against Iraqi oil exports, Iran responded by hitting nonbelligerent shipping going to the ports of the moderate Persian Gulf states that supported Iraq. This development led the United States in March to offer to reflag eleven ships belonging to one of the targeted states, Kuwait, to protect them from Iranian attack.

Kuwait had approached the United States and Soviet Union in late 1986 in search of military protection for its fleet of tankers. The Soviets quickly agreed to lease Kuwait three of their own tankers to carry Kuwaiti oil under the Soviet flag. The prospect of an expanding Soviet presence in the gulf alarmed U.S. officials, who proposed early in 1987 to reregister Kuwaiti tankers as U.S. ships.

Many members of Congress expressed apprehension over the reflagging operation. Even supporters of reflagging concluded that the resulting risk of conflict between U.S. and Iranian forces warranted more consultation with the legislative branch. Although the Reagan administration agreed to discuss the new policy with Congress, the Pentagon announced June 2 that three more ships were being dispatched to the gulf. The announcement came as the House overwhelmingly endorsed a resolution calling on the administration to provide further details of the operation.

Escalation and Reprisals

Congressional objections reflected widespread fear that the Reagan team had undertaken the reflagging policy without having thought through its implications or alternatives. That belief was nurtured by administration justifications for the plan that seemed to minimize unduly the risk that Iranian forces would attack the reflagged tankers or their U.S. escorts. (Iran was supplying its Revolutionary Guards—militant Shi'ite Moslems—with a fleet of small high-speed attack boats and was engaged in underwater mining.)

Despite these concerns, reflagging of eleven Kuwaiti tankers began July 21. Three days later, a reflagged Kuwaiti tanker, the Bridgeton, *was damaged by a mine. On September 21, armed U.S. helicopters from the frigate* Jarrett, *using sophisticated night-viewing TV cameras, observed and captured the Iranian landing craft* Iran Ayr, *which was laying mines in the gulf. Three Iranian sailors were killed and twenty-six were captured during machine-gun and rocket fire. Reagan defended the U.S. attack as "authorized by law." On October 8, four Iranian patrol boats fired at U.S. patrol helicopters; U.S. forces returned the fire, sinking at least one boat. On October 16,* Sea Isle City, *a U.S.-flag tanker en route to Kuwait, was struck by a Chinese-built Iranian Silkworm missile in Kuwaiti waters, injuring eighteen crewmen. It was the first direct Iranian attack on a reflagged Kuwaiti ship. In retaliation, U.S. naval forces shelled two Iranian offshore drilling platforms.*

On November 11, two Iranian gunboats attacked a Japanese-owned tanker en route to the Strait of Hormuz. The attack took place within fifteen miles of a twelve-vessel U.S. convoy—the seventeenth such operation and the largest to enter the Persian Gulf to date. The attack was similar to an Iranian gunboat assault on a U.S.-owned, Panamanian-registered tanker November 6.

Those incidents were typical of Iranian military tactics of avoiding direct U.S. targets and causing incidents that were difficult to trace (such as mining shipping lanes). "The Iranians know the rules of engagement, and they have carefully tried not to step over them," noted a senior Western diplomat in the gulf region. "They know if they do, they will be blown out of the water."

Following are excerpts from the "Navy Blue Ribbon Panel Report on FFG 7 Class Design Review," and from Volume I of the Navy's "Formal Investigation into the Circumstances Surrounding the Attack on the USS Stark (FFG 31) on 17 May 1987," both issued October 15, 1987:

NAVY BLUE RIBBON PANEL REPORT

Executive Summary

... On May 17, 1987 two EXOCET missiles, fired by an Iraqi F-1 Mirage aircraft, struck USS STARK (FFG 31) while the ship was steaming independently in the Persian Gulf. (The ship's weapon systems did not engage the EXOCETs.) The first missile struck the port side of the hull forward, ruptured the firemain piping, penetrated a watertight transverse bulkhead and came to rest inside the ship, after passing through two berthing areas. This missile did not explode but started fires due to the incendiary effect of residual missile propellant. A second missile struck the ship very shortly thereafter, and detonated just forward of where the first entered the shell plating and also spread its burning residual propellant inside the ship.

Intense heat, combined with an immediate loss of firemain pressure and dense smoke, impeded initial attempts to control the fire. The heat caused an almost immediate flashover of all combustibles in the second deck berthing compartment. After the initial burning of the propellant, the fire was fed primarily by the high fuel load of the polyvinyl chloride (PVC) jacketing of electrical cables, plus normal combustibles present in the berthing compartment.

The fire affected electric power cabling in the initially inflamed compartments and then in the main deck Radar-IFF-CIC equipment room (RICER) directly above. With no installed fire pump forward of the fire, the crew used a P-250 MOD 1 portable fire/dewatering pump and fire hose deployed from fire plugs in the after part of the ship to fight the fire. The fire spread vertically, primarily by conduction, to the ricer space then subsequently to the Combat Information Center (CIC) directly above RICER, before being contained and eventually extinguished. Rescue and Assistance Teams from nearby ships and a commercial salvage tug aided the STARK crew in fighting the fire. As a result of the attack, 37 crewmen were killed or declared missing. However, none were killed or seriously injured in the ensuing valiant damage control effort that saved the ship. . . .

Background

STARK is an FFG 7 Class ship. The FFG 7 Class was designed in the early 1970s to defend non-aircraft carrier forces and to conduct ASW [anti-submarine warfare] operations in conjunction with other sea control forces. It was an austere design and the Navy's first experience in the design-to-cost acquisition concept. Other constraints imposed on the design were a 3,400-ton displacement, and a personnel accommodation ceiling of 185. Growth margins for future characteristic changes were not to be provided. While austere, the ship included a reasonably well balanced suit of then applicable survivability features. Overall, the FFG 7 Class design was thought to be good, in light of the imposed constraints.

Summary of U.S. Navy Approach to Surface Ship Survivability

U.S. Navy design practice requires certain standard survivability features common to all the Navy warships. These include watertight subdivision and fire zones to limit the spread of flooding and fire, equipment designed to withstand underwater shock, vital spaces for added protection of mission-critical systems and personnel, and separation and redundancy of vital systems, among many other standard features. STARK had all these features and more. Additional FFG 7 Class survivability features added during construction were limited-fragmentation armor (KEVLAR) and HALON firefighting systems. Because of the FFG 7 future growth margin policy, survivability and other improvements must be limited unless other items are removed as compensation.

The Navy continues to emphasize surface ship survivability strongly in its new designs and in selective backfit of improvements to the Fleet. Lessons learned from major shipboard fires, such as STARK's, are applied as they occur. In 1979, the Navy formed an Aircraft Carrier Flag Level Firefighting Steering Committee to oversee needed improvements in aircraft carrier firefighting. This committee now provides additional oversight for aviation amphibious ships and other air capable ships. In 1982, the Navy formed a Survivability Review Group (SRG) to review design practice specifications and features to enhance the resistance of surface ships to enemy weapons. The SRG selected the FFG 7 Class as a typical frigate, and developed numerous survivability design principles which are presented in its February 1987 report. These principles, many of which were confirmed by the STARK incident, are now being implemented as design requirements with completion scheduled for December 1988.

In 1983-1984, the Chief of Naval Operations (CNO) reviewed Navy programs in passive fire protection (PFP), insensitive munitions (IM), and ship survivability. The result of those reviews is a comprehensive Surface Ship Survivability Program providing survivability alterations for about 300 ships. Portable survivability equipment and PFP improvements for all Navy ships and a comprehensive R&D program for reducing the susceptibility of our own weapons to heat and shock are also included. Fleet ships are now seeing the benefits of many of these programs.

General Conclusions

1. The Navy has an effective, ongoing, and comprehensive surface ship survivability program.
2. STARK although damaged as a result of the two EXOCET hits did survive. The damage could have been worse except for crew performance and survivability features built into the ship.
3. The most significant new lessons learned were the dangers imposed by the presence of residual missile fuels and what effects were experienced by the intense heat, speed of fire growth and the resultant vertical fire spread.

Specific Recommendations

Specific recommendations that apply to STARK, other FFG 7 Class ships and other classes, as applicable, are listed below:

a. Develop improved doctrine and procedures for dealing with intense weapon-induced fires and attendant possible vertical fire spread.

b. Develop improved doctrine and procedures for topside space dewatering of firefighting water.

c. Apply current Navy policy for fire pump location and firemain arrangement/isolation capabilities to new construction ship design.

d. Require more extensive use of fire insulation on bulkheads and the underside of vital space decks.

e. Provide smoke control doctrine and improved desmoking equipment, portable and/or installed.

f. Reduce fire load (i.e., quantity of combustible material in ship), especially electrical cables, in accordance with current Navy policy in new construction and in modernization.

g. Provide improvements and additions in portable firefighting and damage control equipment in accordance with Navy ongoing action, and others cited in the report, such as:

(1) Wire-free damage control internal communications equipment

(2) Equipment for cutting access through bulkheads and decks

(3) Improved firefighter protective clothing

(4) JP-5/Navy distillate fueled portable firefighting/dewatering pump. . . .

Synopsis of the Incident

About 9:12 P.M. on 17 May 1987, two air-to-surface EXOCET missiles, launched by an Iraqi F-1 Mirage aircraft in an unprovoked attack, struck USS STARK (FFG 31) which was steaming independently in the Persian Gulf. The missiles damaged vital firefighting systems and started extremely intense fires that ultimately caused extensive damage to mission-critical command and control spaces and threatened mass detonation of the forward missile magazine. STARK's crew, through determination and, in some cases, heroic actions, combined with outside assistance, eventually extinguished the fires and saved the ship. Assistance was provided by Rescue and Assistance Teams from other U.S. Navy ships and by a commercial salvage tug. Good weather conditions with especially calm seas also aided the intensive firefighting and damage control effort.

The speed of fire growth, the thermal intensity of the fire and eventual vertical spread were unique in U.S. Navy experience for a fire starting in a crew berthing compartment. A weapons-induced fire of this nature and magnitude, emanating primarily from residual propellant fuel and spanning two watertight subdivisions, was particularly difficult for a small ship to contain and extinguish.

First Missile Impact and Immediate Damage

The first missile, arriving from about 35 degrees off the port bow, struck the port side of the ship . . . about second deck level midway between the waterline and the main deck. Upon entry, the missile severed the port firemain, failed to detonate, and separated into two pieces as it traversed diagonally across the deck. It penetrated a watertight bulkhead . . . and spread burning solid residual propellant in its wake. The missile warhead came to rest against the starboard shell of the ship.

Combined Damage of First and Second Missiles

About 20 to 30 seconds after the first hit, a second missile arrived from approximately the same relative angle off the bow and hit the ship ... approximately 8 feet forward of the first missile point of entry. The second missile detonated inside the hull and several feet below the main deck, spewing hot metal fragments throughout the area and opening a gaping hole in the port side shell plating. The residual propellant from the first (undetonated) missile and the heat of detonation and unspent propellant from the second missile combined with an unimpeded air supply to create an immediate inferno in the second deck berthing compartment. The unimpeded air supply resulted from the hole in the shell created by the detonation of the second missile.

The missile propellant burned intensely at temperatures estimated at 3,000° to 3,500°F. The extreme temperatures almost immediately ignited all combustible materials in the berthing compartment, including clothing, personal articles, bedding, and electrical cabling. Compartment overhead temperatures reached an estimated 1,400° to 1,500°F, and adjacent spaces filled quickly with acrid black smoke. The severity and intensity of the fire twisted and buckled the steel hull support structures and overhead of the second deck berthing compartment. Firemain pressure, lost after the first missile hit, was restored aft at 9:38 P.M. The fire then propagated vertically, principally by heat conduction through the main deck (steel), into the Radar-IFF-CIC-Equipment Room (RICER) directly above and spread ... into the Combat Information Center (CIC)....

STARK's crew, assisted by other Navy ships and a commercial salvage tug, fought to limit the horizontal fire spread to the original fire area. Except for a small section on the starboard side where the fire spread forward and endangered the missile magazine, firefighting efforts were successful in containing the fire fore and aft. The forward spread of the fire occurred through an open second deck watertight door on the starboard side which had been used as an escape route. Main propulsion and electrical power and firemain pressure in the after part of the ship were maintained throughout the duration of the incident. Primary fires were extinguished by 5 P.M. on 18 May and all reflashes ceased by the morning of 19 May. Propulsion and steering systems were operational but primarily due to crew fatigue STARK was towed to Bahrain by USS CONYNGHAM (DDG-17) for damage assessment and minimal repairs, arriving about 11:30 P.M. on the 19th. The ship departed the Bahrain area on July 5, 1987 and proceeded under its own power to her homeport....

Technical Assessments

...**Fire Protection Features That Worked Well.** The basic firefighting features on STARK, with the assistance of equipment provided by Rescue and Assistance Teams from other Navy ships and assistance from a commercial salvage tug, were ultimately successful in finally extinguishing the fires. Transverse fire zone bulkheads were successful in confining the major fire damage. Fire pumps provided adequate pressure to the surviving firemain segments. Good performance of the following features is particularly noteworthy:

a. Crew training was a dominant factor in averting loss of the ship.

b. The OBA [oxygen breathing apparatus] functioned properly to provide necessary breathing support for firefighters.

c. EEBDs [emergency escape breathing devices] proved effective in saving lives that otherwise would have been lost. Recent crew training in use of EEBDs was particularly effective.

d. Horizontal fire and smoke containment was effective. Standard U.S. Navy use of multiple fumetight fore and aft fire zones played a vital role in saving STARK. British ships, not having the same degree of protection, were lost in the Falklands Conflict with less initial damage.

e. The aluminum superstructure, while experiencing some local failures, remained sufficiently structurally intact to permit firefighting.

f. Multiple cable penetrators for bulkhead and deck penetrations of electrical cables performed well in limiting the spread of fire and smoke. . . .

g. Flood lanterns operated well, but were too few in number. Higher intensity lights would have been beneficial.

Recommendations. This subsection addresses recommended actions . . . to combat the type of fire experienced by STARK. Some of these actions are already underway.

a. Conflagration Control. Develop new capabilities (doctrine, procedures, and/or equipment) for controlling interior ship conflagrations such as the intensive, and perhaps multi-compartment, fires initiated by missile propellant. This effort should include an R & D program, with large-scale fire tests. . . .

b. Sprinkler Survivability. Investigate . . . possible design features to enhance the combat survivability of sprinkler systems. . . .

c. Fire and Smoke Containment. Investigate the feasibility of modifying watertight decks and bulkheads to serve as fire zone boundaries and the feasibility of subdividing superstructures into smaller fire zones. Accelerate development of lightweight fire insulation material and fire retardant surface coatings. Investigate the feasibility of installing fire insulation on fire zone boundaries, vital space boundaries, and the underside of aluminum or steel decks below vital spaces. . . .

d. Fire Threat Definition. Examine the incendiary fire threat of the arsenals of weapons held by potentially hostile countries.

e. Fire Risk and Fire Loading. Conduct fire load (i.e., quantity of combustibles per square foot of deck area) and fire risk analyses of selected high value ships and all new design combatants. Initiate development of noncombustible electrical cable and anti-sweat thermal insulation and other combustibles. Continue development of fire retardant coatings for existing ships.

f. Smoke Control. Provide improved methods for management of smoke in shipboard fires. Expedite the development and outfitting of smoke control diagrams for FFG 7 Class ships.... Smoke control diagrams are to be used by damage control personnel to rapidly identify and isolate ventilation systems involved in a fire/smoke area. Provide higher capacity portable blowers and sufficient exhaust hose and extension cords. Provide smoke curtains to cover access openings through fire zones, and airtight and watertight boundaries. Continue R&D efforts to develop a smoke ejection system for future new ship designs.

g. Water Supply. Provide on future ship designs and, where practical, backfit on existing ships, not less than one installed fire pump in each fire zone. Those in the forwardmost and aftmost fire zones should be independently powered and located as close to the ends of the ship as possible.... Provide emergency hose connections for magazines sprinkler systems.... The location of remote controls should be optimized with respect to potential damage of specified threat weapons....

h. Firefighters Apparatus. Continue development of multi-purpose JP-5/Navy distillate fueled portable power and pumping system. Continue R&D development of an improved, more durable, firefighter breathing apparatus with greater longevity....

i. Personnel Egress. Investigate feasibility of personnel escape trunks leading from berthing spaces to main deck. These trunks ... must be able to withstand debris impact and be fumetight.

Damage Control Features

Damage control, other than firefighting, also played a major role in saving STARK. Considering the magnitude of the crisis and the personnel and physical limitations of a small ship, the STARK's damage control organization and built-in features were heavily stressed in their ability to contain the damage.... Rescue and Assistance Teams from other U.S. Navy ships helped control the spread of damage....

... **Assessment of Performance of Damage Control Features.** The damage control features on STARK performed as designed and generally very well, particularly since the ship was not at battle stations, with all personnel on station, systems segregated and doors and hatches closed. Considering the scope of damage and design limitations of the ship, the ship's crew was effective in adapting the operating portions of installed systems and portable damage control equipment....

... **Recommendations.** This subsection addresses recommended actions to improve the damage control features of the FFG 7 Class and other ship classes....

a. Improve the damage control [DC] doctrine to reemphasize major conflagrations and include shipboard procedures necessary to fight residual fuel fires, which will complement firefighting doctrine.

b. Incorporate in existing DC doctrine improved guidance for draining firefighting water in superstructure spaces throughout the ship.

c. . . . [R]eview . . . ships' allowances of portable damage control equipment. . . .

d. Provide improved firefighting protective clothing to the Fleet. . . . An FFE is currently under procurement, consisting of special coveralls, anti-flash hood, gloves, helmet and boots and is to be stowed in FFE bags in or near repair stations.

e. Examine the adequacy of vital space requirements with respect to the fragmentation, ballistic and fire problems imposed by the anti-ship missile threat. . . .

f. Install larger escape scuttles in hatches of new construction ships and, space and funding permitting, backfit existing ships with 21-inch diameter scuttles to permit free passage of fully equipped firefighters.

g. Investigate alternatives for emergency egress from berthing spaces. . . .

h. Review . . . location, size, accessibility, and arrangement criteria for repair lockers.

i. Continue development of a new firefighter helmet light and portable floodlight; increase allowance of portable floodlights. . . .

j. Accelerate full Fleet introduction of an emergency portable shipboard internal communication system. . . .

k. Correct incompatibilities of portable electrical submersible pump plugs and 440 volt outlets throughout the Fleet.

l. Conduct shipboard evaluation of the lightweight steel ladder currently being developed. . . .

. . . **Assessment of the Ability of the FFG 7 Combat System to Engage the MIRAGE Aircraft and EXOCET Missile Successfully.** The panel caused a technical assessment to be made to determine the inherent capability of STARK's AAW [anti-air warfare] combat system against known characteristics of the MIRAGE aircraft and EXOCET missiles. . . . The assessment team was unaware of equipment mode settings and console manning. These factors (together with such others as "blind zones," weather, tactics, etc.) are possible degrading factors to the inherent expected performance.

The MIRAGE is a relatively large and "soft" target. The combat system has high probability of detecting the aircraft and in most situations can engage it with high confidence.

The EXOCET is a challenging threat. It is difficult to detect because of its size and profile. . . . [D]etection would be expected at short ranges from the ship, thus little time is available to engage.

Even so, this type of attack can be defeated by the FFG 7 combat system. This presumes conditions of readiness, engageable attack angles, and so forth....

Summary of Damage to the Combat System. ... The combat system spaces that were damaged or destroyed by the fire were the CIC [combat information center], SONAR, RICER, the Launcher Control Room, and the IC/GYRO [interior communication] room.... Power was lost to most combat system equipments on impact of the first EXOCET when many circuit breakers opened.

Planned Upgrades for the FFG 7 Class Combat System. ... Upgrades are planned to improve detection and identification of threats, control of weapons response, and engagement of threats. These upgrades were all planned prior to the STARK incident. Nothing that occurred on May 17, 1987 would indicate that a change should be made to any of these planned improvements.

Conclusions

The STARK incident did not measure the capability of the FFG 7 Class or similarly equipped U.S. Navy ships to respond to the F-1 MIRAGE/EXOCET threat, since STARK's weapons were not brought to bear. It did, however, demonstrate the capability of the FFG 7 and, to a degree, the capability of other modern small and mid-sized Navy ships of frigate/destroyer size to absorb an EXOCET size warhead detonation. It also provided actual lessons learned in response to a massive conflagration caused by multiple missile hits when ignited residual missile propellant, not blast damage, became the primary damage-causing agent. Major conclusions are as follows.

1. In consideration of the mission for which the ship was designed and the austere design of the ship, STARK's installed systems performed well in most areas after the damage. STARK was severely damaged but did survive. There are, however, areas for improvement in the FFG 7 Class ship's ability to combat damage.

2. This type of an attack can be defeated by the FFG combat system. Various factors will reduce performance. These range from an inability to determine inbound attackers (e.g., blockage) to factors beyond the control of ship's force or combat system design such as weather and jamming.

3. The damage experienced on STARK, the first by an anti-ship cruise missile to a U.S. Navy ship, created a fire whose speed of growth, intensity, and vertical spread were unique to Navy firefighting experience, *given its point of origin was a crew berthing compartment.* The incendiary effect from unexpended missile propellant was previously recognized from the Falklands Conflict lessons learned, but the intensity of the fire in an enclosed compartment and its resultant vertical fire spread were not fully recognized....

Lessons Learned

a. The missile propellant fire, with temperatures ranging from 3000° to 3500°F, caused rapid flashover of nearly every combustible in the compartments involved, resulting in extreme compartment temperatures that precluded normal means of firefighter entry.

b. While methods of horizontal management of the fire were generally effective, the intensity of the fire created an "oven effect" in the overhead compartments, which caused the fire to propagate vertically. The intense temperatures of decks above burning compartments, together with limited fire hose availability, preoccupation of the crew in combatting fires in initially affected spaces, blocked accesses and other factors combined to cause a vertical fire spread.

c. Fighting a large scale conflagration is an all-consuming effort for the crew of the ship affected and particularly that of a small ship.

4. A lack of firefighting water forward of the damaged area significantly reduced the effectiveness of the crew in fighting the fire. The loss of one of only two P-250 MOD-1 portable fire/dewatering pumps due to damage compounded the lack of firefighting water. The loss of all sources of installed magazine sprinkling system water to the MK 13 Guided Missile Launching System Magazine resulted from the inoperable portion of the firemain.

Lessons Learned

a. It is likely that an EXOCET or comparable missile hit can result in a loss of firemain pressure in the damaged area.

b. To combat conflagrations of the magnitude experienced by STARK, it is essential that firemain segregation and fire pump locations be such that damaged portions of the system can be rapidly and remotely isolated and the intact portion immediately reactivated.

5. The extremely high temperatures and smoke generated by burning missile propellant emphasizes the critical importance of reducing combustibles to an absolute minimum.

Lesson Learned

Every reasonable effort should be made to reduce combustibles in our ships. This is a lesson learned in World War II which the Navy continues to emphasize, but the critical importance of which is not normally relearned outside of wartime.

6. Because of the extreme temperatures likely to result from a missile fuel-induced fire, heating of decks and bulkheads of vital spaces adjacent to the fire area can easily cause the fire to propagate. . . .

Lesson Learned

Decks and bulkheads surrounding vital spaces need special protection against fire.

7. Smoke generated from such large conflagrations, principally from

electrical cables, is a major problem and requires more capable smoke control equipment and doctrine for its use....

Lesson Learned

Smoke control is critical in firefighting effectiveness.

8. The large amounts of water needed to fight the fires that spread into the superstructure resulted in a loss of stability and an adverse list that compounded firefighting efforts.

Lesson Learned

An efficient means is needed for rapid dewatering of firefighting water from superstructure spaces. Crew training is required to recognize the hazards involved.

9. Improvements and additions are needed in portable firefighting and damage control equipment to combat fires of the magnitude experienced by STARK. Examples are portable damage control internal communications equipment, exothermic and mechanical cutting tools for cutting accesses through bulkheads and decks, and improved firefighting protective clothing.

Lesson Learned

The process for development and procurement of portable equipment has been lengthy. Additionally, there is a tendency to overoptimize every development effort to the extent that delivery is frequently held up awaiting creation of a "perfect" product.

10. Despite the provision of emergency escape breathing devices (EEBDs), the magnitude and duration of the conflagration prevented escape of some personnel trapped in the berthing compartments below the fire. Both exits from the lower berthing led through the upper berthing area which was totally involved in the fire.

Lesson Learned

Secondary egress routes such as access/egress trunks, should be provided for large berthing complexes and other large occupied areas as appropriate. Primary and secondary exits should not pass through a common compartment.

11. The severe displacement limit placed on the FFG 7 Class design resulted in compromises that reduced STARK's ability to respond to a conflagration of the magnitude that incurred. A displacement limit ... can unrealistically restrict a ship's capacity to take damage and keep on fighting. It is much more cost effective to install survivability features during construction, rather than backfit. Minimal future growth weight and center of gravity margin policy, as invoked on the FFG 7 Class to reduce cost, becomes unrealistic when the ship must be upgraded to meet new threats. Increased combat system capability typically weighs more and consumes more volume than the older system it replaces. When damage experience warrants an increase in survivability features, they

cannot be accommodated without weight compensation from other critical systems.

Lesson Learned

Survivability should be included in the ship characteristics and maintained through the ship design phases. Future growth margins, by ship class, should be established in contract design and maintained in construction.

12. Several Survivability Review Group (SRG) findings from the recently completed review of FFG 7 Class survivability were substantiated in the STARK incident. The damage predicted by the study was very close to the actual resultant damage. . . .

Lesson Learned

The SRG survivability analysis process is useful in identifying design weaknesses. High-payoff survivability improvements recommended in the report should be considered for future ship designs. . . .

13. The FFG 7 TLR did not specify threats/threat characteristics the ship must be capable of meeting, and the threat weapons effects to be withstood were not definitized.

Lesson Learned

There is a need to establish minimum survivability requirements for each ship type, based upon threat weapon effects. . . .

14. While the basic aluminum superstructure did not experience massive structural failure in the extreme temperatures of the initial conflagration or in the subsequent fire in the deckhouse area, there were incidents of deck melt-through in several locations.

Lesson Learned

Continue the policy of close control of structural material which includes the use of aluminum.

15. Despite some inadequacies in the firemain systems, STARK's system redundancy was adequate for the damage that occurred.

Lesson Learned

For future ship design and modernization, maintain the policy of vital system redundancy and also provide adequate separation. . . .

FORMAL INVESTIGATION INTO THE CIRCUMSTANCES SURROUNDING THE ATTACK ON THE USS STARK (FFG 31) ON 17 MAY 1987

Executive Summary of the Attack

1. On the evening of 17 May 1987, shortly after 2100 local and while on routine patrol in the central Persian Gulf, USS STARK (FFG 31) was hit

by two Exocet anti-ship cruise missiles. The missiles were fired by a single Iraqi F-1 Mirage fighter. The attack was unprovoked and indiscriminate. STARK was—and had been—in international waters, well outside the Iraqi and Iranian declared war zones.

2. The ship's Tactical Action Officer [TAO] was aware that an Iraqi fighter was approaching. STARK had been alerted by AWACS [U.S.-controlled airborne warning and alert command systems launched from Saudi Arabia] nearly an hour prior to the attack that an Iraqi F-1 fighter, [Deleted] was proceeding southeasterly from Iraq, over water, toward the central Persian Gulf. The AWACS continued to report the Iraqi aircraft's position to STARK . . . until the attack occurred. Contact was gained by STARK's AN/SPS-49 air search radar [Deleted]. About ten minutes prior to being hit by the first Exocet, STARK detected radar emissions from a Cyrano IV radar correlating to an F-1 Mirage fighter.

3. After gaining radar contact, . . . STARK's combat information center kept a constant, real-time track of the aircraft. The Iraqi fighter changed course and speed several times. Each change brought the fighter closer to STARK. When the aircraft was thirty miles away, the fighter turned east and flew toward STARK. Less than five minutes later, the ship was hit by two Exocet cruise missiles, the second missile arriving 30 seconds after the first.

4. When the Iraqi fighter first began closing STARK's position, the Tactical Action Officer and other watch standers assumed the aircraft would fly benignly by, passing no closer than 11 nautical miles from STARK. The watch organized themselves to collect data for the Marine-Air Report they would later be required to submit. The Tactical Action Officer gave little or no credence to the possibility that the Iraqi fighter would indiscriminately attack STARK, even though it was known to be capable of firing Exocet with a nominal range of 38 nautical miles.

5. The Executive Officer entered CIC [combat information center] on routine business approximately five minutes before the attack occurred; and, he remained in CIC near the TAO station until the first missile hit. He did not inform himself of the tactical situation; and, therefore, did not feel that there was anything remiss in the way the watch was responding to the Iraqi fighter. The Executive Officer took no steps to redirect the actions of the TAO nor did he direct that the Commanding Officer be summoned to CIC.

6. In the waning minutes prior to the attack, the TAO attempted to increase STARK's combat readiness; but, it was too late. [Deleted] the positions of CIC Watch Officer (CICWO) and Weapons Control Officer (WCO) were combined and filled by a single officer. When the aircraft began its attack run, the position of Weapons Control Officer was vacant. Before the position could be properly manned, the Mirage had already fired both Exocets and the first Exocet was nearing its terminal phase. The Fire Control Technician assigned to operate the MK-92 STIR fire control radar and Close In Weapon System (CIWS) had previously left CIC on

personal business; and, at the time of the attack, that position was also vacant. [Deleted] the STIR fire control radar was in stand-by and was thought to be masked by the ship's superstructure; the MK-92 CAS fire control radar was in search mode and was never used to lock-on to the aircraft until the missiles were seconds away from impact; the Super Rapid Blooming Offboard Chaff (SRBOC) was not armed until seconds before the first missile hit; and the CIWS was still in stand-by, having not been properly brought into the AAW [anti-air warfare] manual mode.

7. At the time of missile launch, the AN/SPS-49 two dimensional air search radar and the MK-92 CAS search radar were the only radars being used to track the aircraft. No fire control radars were locked-on and tracking the aircraft; [Deleted]

9. The Commanding Officer was aware that an Iraqi fighter was flying [Deleted] southeasterly, over water, from Iraq toward the central Persian Gulf. He had visited CIC approximately 50 minutes prior to the attack and was informed about the Iraqi aircraft being reported by AWACS. About 15 minutes before the attack occurred, the Captain was on the bridge; and, he asked the JOOD [junior officer of the deck] to find out why [USS] COONTZ was reporting the Iraqi fighter's position [Deleted]. At that time, COONTZ had been reporting the aircraft's position every 3 to 5 minutes; and, according to the Commanding Officer's recollection of events that evening, his last known position of the Iraqi aircraft placed it approximately 120 miles northwest of STARK and closing the ship. The Captain was not advised when CIC gained radar contact on the Iraqi fighter. At about 2058 local, the Commanding Officer left the bridge and went to his cabin, where he remained until the first missile hit.

10. STARK never fired a weapon nor employed a countermeasure, either in self defense or in retaliation. Thirty seven members of STARK's crew died as a result of the attack.

Preliminary Statement

1. The investigation into the circumstances surrounding the attack on USS STARK (FFG 31) was conducted from two different perspectives. Rear Admiral David N. Rogers, USN, Deputy Director for Current Operations on the staff of the Joint Chiefs of Staff, headed a joint U.S.-Iraqi investigation conducted in Baghdad, Iraq, for the purpose of determining how, and under what circumstances, the Iraqi pilot executed the attack on STARK. Rear Admiral Grant Sharp, USN, Commander Cruiser Destroyer Group TWO, was appointed on 19 May 1987 by General George B. Crist, USMC, Commander in Chief, U.S. Central Command, to be the investigating officer for this formal investigation.

2. The formal investigation was conducted in port Manama, Bahrain, first, aboard USS LASALLE (AGF 3), the flagship of Commander Middle East Force [CMEF], and, later, aboard USS ACADIA (AD-42). In both cases, STARK was moored outboard the host ship.

3. Rear Admiral Sharp, and an investigating team comprised of six

officers, arrived in Bahrain on the evening of 20 May 1987. The investigation began on 21 May 1987; and, formal hearings were convened commencing 26 May 1987. STARK's Commanding Officer, Executive Officer, Tactical Action Officer and CIC Watch Officer were designated as parties to the investigation. Formal hearings were completed and the investigation was closed on the evening of 5 June 1987.

4. Concurrent with the formal hearings, a staff delegation from the U.S. Congress House Armed Services Committee came to Bahrain and conducted an informal investigation into the circumstances surrounding the attack on STARK. Their informal investigation lasted approximately three days. Parties to the formal investigation ... chose not to make statements to the staff delegation.

5. The investigation by Rear Admiral Sharp inquired into all the events which occurred prior to, during and following the attack. There were specific, technically complex issues that required the investigating officer to call upon the professional expertise of the Commander, Naval Sea Systems Command, Navy laboratories and intelligence agencies located in the United States and to also use on-scene assistance teams and technical representatives. Particular issues that fell within this category included:

a. Capability of the F-1 Mirage fighter aircraft to carry two Exocet cruise missiles....

c. Capability of the FFG-7 combat system, including the AN/SPS-49 air search radar and MK-92 Fire Control System, to detect an Exocet anti-ship cruise missile.

d. Capability of the MK-15 Close In Weapon System (CIWS) to detect, acquire and engage an Exocet anti-ship cruise missile.

e. Determination of the operational status, and operational modes employed, for each of the above systems as they existed in STARK on the night of 17 May 1987.

6. [T]he statements and testimony of the witnesses were woven together, along with transcriptions of various radio telephone transmissions, to form a chronology of the attack....

Findings of Fact

...STARK received an operations, ROE and Intel Brief from COMIDEASTFOR Staff in Djibouti 28 February 1987 prior to inchopping to Middle East Force [MEF]. The brief addressed Rules of Engagement (ROE) and the potential threat to U.S. Navy ships in the Persian Gulf....

...The ROE briefer highlighted that the probability of deliberate attack on U.S. warships was low, but that indiscriminate attack in the Persian Gulf was a significant danger....

Opinions

A. *Attack and Response:* This section incorporates the opinions concerning the mission, rules of engagement, combat systems equipment, combat systems doctrine and actions associated with the attack...

1. The damage to STARK inflicted by the Iraqi F-1 was caused by four principle [*sic*] factors:

a. Failure in general, of the Commanding Officer and watch team to appreciate and respect the hazards to STARK inherent in the Iraqi air campaign in the Persian Gulf; and failure, specifically, of the Commanding Officer and watch team to recognize the Iraqi F-1 threat and to effectively utilize the ship's combat systems to respond to that threat.

b. Improper watch manning and watch standing.

c. Failure of the Commanding Officer and watch team to institute a proper state of weapons readiness; and

d. Improper understanding by the Commanding Officer and watch team of the use of fire control radar as a measure short of deadly force in warning the threat and securing the safety of STARK.

2. The Persian Gulf was, on and prior to 17 May 87, a relatively uncomplicated air threat environment and STARK was, during the evolving action, confronted with a single air problem.

3. Contextual information, both background and current, adequate for understanding of the operating environment, was provided to STARK by CMEF; and, the prospect of indiscriminate attack was sufficiently identified and stressed.

4. Tactical information sufficient to prepare for the evolving air problem was available [Deleted] from AWACS and STARK's shipboard sensors. . . .

5. The Rules of Engagement that were in existence on 17 May 1987 were sufficient to enable STARK to properly warn the Iraqi aircraft, in a timely manner, of the presence of a U.S. warship; and, if the warning was not heeded, the Rules of Engagement were sufficient to enable STARK to defend herself against hostile intent and imminent danger without absorbing the first hit.

[Deleted]

8. If properly employed, the combat system installed in STARK had the inherent capability to enable STARK to comply with the Rules of Engagement and defend against hostile intent. . . .

9. The Commanding Officer [Capt. Glenn R. Brindel] failed to implement an effective means for supervising the readiness of his watchstanders as evidenced by the laxness that permitted the Weapons Control Console (Nr 2) operator to be absent from his watch station without proper authority and for the .50 caliber machine gun operator to be lying down at his post.

10. LT [Basil E.] Moncrief assumed that the Commanding Officer had been on the bridge earlier and had heard CIC report to the Bridge that they had detected a radar contact which correlated to the Iraqi aircraft. In making this assumption, LT Moncrief failed to comply with the Commanding Officer's oral and standing orders which

required him to inform the Captain when CIC gained radar contact on the Iraqi aircraft.

11. The Commanding Officer had an inherent responsibility to keep himself informed concerning the Iraqi Air Contact but assumed that his personal initiative was unnecessary.

12. LT Moncrief failed to consider the possibility that the Iraqi aircraft might indiscriminately attack Stark.

13. LT Moncrief did not understand what countermeasures he was required to execute, as a function of range to the Iraqi aircraft and response time required by Stark's combat system, in order to comply with the Rules of Engagement.

14. LT Moncrief was reluctant to lock-on with fire control radar to the Iraqi aircraft while the aircraft was 40 to 50 miles away from Stark because he felt that it might be interpreted by the Iraqi aircraft as a hostile act. This reluctance to use fire control radars for tracking unidentified aircraft was consistent with Stark's overall conservative command philosophy, which was typified by the practice of doing missile system DSOT's at night so that a training missile would not be seen on the launcher.

15. USS Stark did not execute adequate and timely measures [Deleted] to properly warn the Iraqi aircraft of the presence of a U.S. warship. This failure integrated into Stark's planned sequence of progressive action ultimately resulted in Stark being overcome as the action evolved into crisis.

16. The cumulative experience of the many ships that have been assigned to MIDEASTFOR [Middle East Force] since the outbreak of the tanker war indicates that, in many cases, locking-on to unidentified aircraft with fire control radars has resulted in the aircraft altering course to open its closest point of approach.

17. The uniform understanding of the principal watchstanders ... that Stark was in weapon status warning Condition "White," placed Stark's system in a condition in which quick response could not be accomplished.

18. Unused combat capabilities in Stark included the ability to: detect the Iraqi aircraft [Deleted], issue voice warnings, initialize [Deleted] in order to improve probability of detecting missile launch, initialize the AN/SLQ-32 [Deleted] and maneuver to unmask weapon systems [Deleted], lock-on and track with the MK-92 STIR fire control radar [Deleted], put a SM-1 surface to air missile on the rail, place the Close In Weapon System in AAW automatic, and arm the Super Rapid Blooming Offboard Chaff [Deleted], detect the first Exocet launch [Deleted], shoot two surface to air missiles at the aircraft [Deleted], launch SRBOC between the ship and the incoming missile, [Deleted] and engage the Exocet with SM-1 and the MK-75 gun when in range; probable shoot down of the aircraft, with the second Exocet still onboard, would occur at [Deleted] and, the CIWS

could engage the Exocet, if it was not already shot down or distracted [Deleted].

19. Stark's failure to employ the [Deleted] MK-92 STIR [separate track and illuminate radar] fire control radar, SRBOC, . . . the Close In Weapon System, along with the failure to lock-on with the MK-92 CAS [combined antenna system] fire control radar until seconds before missile impact, deprived the ship of its most capable systems to detect and destroy the first Exocet and eliminated the opportunity to shoot down the Iraqi F-1 before it launched its second missile.

20. LCDR [Ray J.] Gajan failed to inform himself of the tactical situation as it was developing after he entered CIC.

21. LCDR Gajan failed to consider the possibility that the Iraqi aircraft might indiscriminately attack STARK.

22. LCDR Gajan did not understand what countermeasures STARK was required to execute, as a function of range to the Iraqi aircraft and response time required by STARK's combat system, in order to comply with the Rules of Engagement.

23. LCDR Gajan should have directed that the Commanding Officer be called into CIC immediately when he learned that there was an Iraqi F-1 inbound with a CPA that would bring the fighter within its maximum weapons release range.

24. LCDR Gajan or LT Moncrief should have caused General Quarters [full alert] to be sounded prior to the missile impact. They knew they had been locked-on to and had sufficient reason to assume the aircraft had hostile intent.

25. LT Moncrief failed to defend STARK as his duty required.

26. The Commanding Officer failed to train his Executive Officer, Tactical Action Officers and CIC watch teams adequately to recognize specific indications of hostile intent and to execute specific and timely countermeasures to defend the ship. In particular, he failed to specify the defensive measures that must be taken, as a function of range to the threat and reaction time required by STARK's combat system, in order to defend against an Iraqi F-1 armed with Exocet anti-ship cruise missiles.

27. The Commanding Officer failed fundamentally to appreciate the significance of the intelligence information provided to him regarding the recent trend in Iraqi ship attacks occurring south of the 27-30 north parallel, into the central Persian Gulf. This error, in turn, led to a cascade of failures which included: failure to train his watch teams effectively; failure to supervise his watch teams effectively; failure to keep his CIC, at Condition III/Warning Yellow, fully manned with the watch stations required by the Type Commander's Combat Systems Doctrine; failure to keep weapons readiness at the appropriate level; failure to impress upon his Executive Officer and Tactical Action Officers to implement the Rules of Engagement properly; and, failure to maintain his awareness of the tactical

situation after being informed that an Iraqi aircraft [Deleted] was closing his ship. These cumulative failures led to the total collapse of his ship's defensive readiness posture.

28. The Commanding Officer failed to provide combat oriented leadership, allowing STARK's anti-air warfare readiness to disintegrate to the point that his CIC team was unable to defend the ship.

29. If the lookout and bridge watch had been alerted to look for possible missile launch and given the relative bearing, the missile would have been detected and identified correctly early enough to enable timely defensive action by the OOD [officer of the deck] if SRBOC was armed and the firing position for SRBOC launchers was on the bridge in accordance with the STARK's battle orders.

[Deleted]

31. In the particular case of ships assigned to MIDEASTFOR, COMIDEASTFOR must deploy his ships to widely dispersed operation areas for conducting the MEF [Deleted] mission.

32. In terms of command and control, as it relates to hostile intent, imminent danger and self-defense against indiscriminate attack, STARK held [Deleted] tactical information from her sensors and NTDS [naval tactical data system] link with AWACS [Deleted].

33. The missions and tasks of COMIDEASTFOR includes the planning and conduct of operations and training in the Persian Gulf and Red Sea in support of national interests; anti-air surveillance and early warning in support of ELF ONE; general maritime surveillance; liaison with U.S. diplomatic missions and foreign armed forces; and, other military operations as directed. It is evident that the missions assigned to COMIDEASTFOR preclude him from being able to be in close proximity with the ships in his force and his span of missions requires diverse staff efforts....

42. There were no other surface ships within 10 NM of STARK at the time of the attack.

B. *Post Attack Actions:* This section incorporates the opinions concerning post attack matters involving search and rescue (SAR), medical response, casualties, damage control [DC], damage and required repairs.

1. *SAR, Medical Response, and Casualties.*

1.1 The team which had the task of finding, identifying, and preparing the remains prior to shipment performed its task with thoroughness, accuracy and with the appropriate dignity required under the circumstances.

1.2 Bahraini Officials were extraordinarily helpful and cooperative in the effort to get the remains of the deceased to Germany for identification....

2. *Damage Control.*

2.1 In view of the heavy personnel losses and major structural and fire damage sustained as a result of the missile attack, the officers and crew of USS STARK carried out an effective, organized and heroic damage control effort.

2.2 STARK's successful damage control efforts were a direct result of an effective DC training program and a high state of DC material readiness.

2.3 Intense heat and smoke were the primary impediments to firefighting efforts.

2.4 The Commanding Officer's decision to fight fires/flooding using major conflagration method was justified in view of the locations of the missile hits.

2.5 The availability of infrared thermal heat imagers could have enabled USS STARK firefighters to pinpoint fire sources much earlier and significantly limit further damage.

2.6 Heavy personnel casualties, acid smoke, intense heat, and lack of communications contributed significantly to the confusion experienced in initial firefighting efforts.

2.7 STARK's allowance of OBA(s) [oxygen breathing apparatus] and canisters was inadequate.

2.8 STARK would have sustained significantly greater levels of personnel injury and material damage if R&A [rescue and assistance] augmentation had not been provided by area ships and helicopters.

2.9 The decision to cut holes in deck and bulkheads to fight fires and drain water was critical to the success of the damage control effort. . . .

Recommendations

A. *Attack and Response:* This section incorporates the body of recommendations concerning the mission, rules of engagement, combat systems equipment, combat systems doctrine and actions associated with the attack on STARK.

> 1.1 Require ships to develop before they deploy a set of battle orders that are tailored to the specific operating environment of the theater to which they are deploying. The battle orders must clearly address specific actions to be taken, including initiation range and closure rates, as a function of potential adversary weapons systems versus own ship's systems. . . .

B. *Post Attack Actions:* This section incorporates the recommendations concerning post attack matters involving search and rescue (SAR), medical response, casualties, damage control and required repairs.

1. *Sar, Medical Response, and Casualties.*

> 1.1 Improve training on EEBDs [emergency escape breathing devices] through out the Fleet by having shipboard personnel

rehearse the actions necessary to break open a box, rip a package, don the hood and pull the lanyard.

1.2 Develop and practice drills to teach blind escape procedures when spaces have been rearranged by explosion.

1.3 Develop techniques for avoiding electric shock when confronted with arcing cables.

1.4 Develop training for using an EEBD as a flotation device.

2. *Damage Control.*

2.1 Recommend ships set modified material condition Zebra when the threat level dictates Condition Three.

2.2 Develop waterproof, heat resistant, hand-held radios, for use during shipboard damage control efforts and distribute fleet-wide.

2.3 Backfit FFG-7 class ships with firemain jumper stations.

2.4 Distribute thermal imagers and provide necessary shipboard training.

2.5 Continue the exclusive use of low-smoke electrical cable in future ship construction and retrofit whenever feasible.

2.6 Develop quick-opening EEBD container bags that are resistant to grease, water and other friction-reducing solvents.

2.7 Increase the diameter of deck scuttles to allow easier escape and reentry by personnel with DC equipment.

2.8 Ensure everyone is trained and/or qualified for No. 1 hoseman and OBA man on minimum-manned ships.

2.9 Ensure all Air detachment personnel complete shipboard firefighting training before embarking aboard ship.

2.10 Develop portable OBA canister stowage racks to facilitate transfer of large numbers of cannisters to crucial firefighting control areas.

2.11 Develop stronger and more rip resistant OBA breathing tubes.

2.12 Prohibit the wearing of Corfam shoes and polyester clothing aboard ship.

2.13 Develop slip-on arm coverings connected by an adjustable strap across the back for firefighters who arrive wearing short-sleeved shirts.

2.14 Develop battle helmets closer in design to civilian firefighting helmets to protect the back of the neck against scalding water and falling debris.

2.15 Design boots with higher tops to keep out water and with better sole insulation against hot decks.

2.16 Install smoke curtains fleet-wide.

2.17 Develop high-capacity lightweight smoke removal equipment with long and durable extension cords.

2.18 Install deck drains in topside compartments to drain firefighting water over the side.

2.19 Install high-intensity halogen-type bulbs in DC helmet lights.

2.20 Design auxiliary DC lockers with DC plates, 2JZ and local communications for topside spaces near vital ship control areas.

2.21 Develop rubber matting for electronic spaces that is not slippery when wet.

2.22 Install high volume fire suppression systems in vital shipboard electronics spaces.

2.23 Install a dedicated firemain jumper for each ammunition magazine sprinkler system.

2.24 Increase shipboard OBA and OBA canister allowances consistent with storage constraints.

2.25 Review submersible pump electrical connections throughout the fleet and ensure total inter-operability among different ship types....

C. *Valor and Achievements:*

...3. The fact that USS Stark suffered no deaths or serious injuries in connection with their damage control efforts is directly attributable to the clear thinking, exceptional courage and extraordinary heroism displayed by many of its officers and crewmembers.

4. The men who contributed significantly to USS Stark's defense and damage control efforts should be recognized and awarded for their outstanding performance....

D. *Accountability:*

1. Detach Captain Glenn R. Brindel, USN, Commanding Officer, USS STARK for cause....

2. That the charges preferred ... against Captain Glenn R. Brindel, USN, be referred to a General Court-Martial.

3. Detach Lieutenant Commander Ray J. Gajan, USN, Executive Officer, USS STARK for cause....

4. That the charges preferred ... against Lieutenant Commander Ray J. Gajan, USN, be referred to Admiral's Mast.

5. Detach Lieutenant Basil E. Moncrief, USN, for cause....

6. That the charges preferred ... against Lieutenant Basil E. Moncrief, USN, be referred to a General Court-Martial.

7. A claim should be made against the Government of Iraq for all damages that resulted from the attack on STARK, including:

a. Personal compensation for injured and deceased service members, and;

b. The cost to restore STARK to full mission capability and to repair or replace all items damaged, including personal possessions of crew members.

AMA REPORT ON AIDS

October 16, 1987

How best to manage the acquired immune deficiency syndrome (AIDS) epidemic became the subject of increasing controversy during 1987. The Reagan administration, divided over the best approach, adopted a conservative strategy of mandatory AIDS testing for prospective immigrants, military personnel, and prisoners, combined with a call for an expanded educational effort. (Public Health Service report, p. 319) *But some White House officials pushed for an even broader mandatory testing program that would include all hospital patients and marriage license applicants. Members of Congress wrangled over how much funding should go to AIDS research and education and how federally financed educational material should handle homosexuality.*

The American Medical Association (AMA), the nation's most influential medical organization, joined the policy-making debate. In its report, "Prevention and Control of Acquired Immunodeficiency Syndrome," published October 16 in the Journal of the American Medical Association, *the AMA rejected any expansion of mandatory AIDS testing, advocated frankness in educational material, and called for legislation to protect the civil rights of AIDS victims and people being tested for exposure to the human immunodeficiency virus (HIV), which causes AIDS.*

The report was approved by the AMA's House of Delegates during its June meeting. Upon its adoption, Board of Trustees member Dr. Robert McAfee stressed the AMA's intent to help shape public policy, saying, "This is what the doctors of this country feel. . . . National policy is not just federal policy."

Education, Testing, Antidiscrimination

AIDS testing, said the document, should be mandatory for groups currently being tested: blood, organ, tissue, semen, and ova donors; immigrants; military personnel; and state and federal prison inmates. The AMA, taking issue with the Reagan administration, saw no need to test other groups for the virus. Mandatory testing would cause some homosexuals and intravenous drug users who needed medical help to stay away from the health care system, the report argued. Testing members of the general population, such as marriage license applicants or all hospital patients, might generate a high percentage of false positive results and strain the nation's already-overloaded AIDS testing and counseling facilities. The report concluded that the danger to health care workers of contracting AIDS from patients was so small that mandatory patient testing should be a last resort.

The report emphasized the need for public education about ways to modify or eliminate high-risk behavior. It called for a well-targeted campaign of public service announcements (PSAs) on television and radio. In contrast to the Reagan administration's emphasis on chastity and moral fidelity, the AMA said the PSAs must "necessarily deal with controversial subject matter." The AMA also called for a "massive education effort" for health care workers so they could better teach and counsel their clients about the AIDS epidemic.

"Testing for HIV in America will require substantially more resources than are currently being made available," the document warned. It called for a new infusion of public funding for AIDS research and the care of AIDS patients. The AMA also advocated more and better trained AIDS counselors and reliable testing facilities.

The report recommended clarifying antidiscrimination laws to protect AIDS victims: "patients with AIDS and those who test positively for the antibody to the AIDS virus should not be treated unfairly or suffer from arbitrary or irrational discrimination in their daily lives." To that end, the need for keeping AIDS test results confidential under most circumstances was stressed. However, the AMA felt that "unsuspecting sexual partners" of HIV-positive individuals should be warned of their partners' infection. It urged the Public Health Service to undertake the notification in much the same way it now handles positive venereal disease test results. The report also urged that "serious consideration" be given to establishing state penalties for knowingly refusing to inform a sexual partner of one's HIV-positive status.

Administration Reaction

While there was some applause for the report from the health care community, White House domestic policy adviser Gary Bauer criticized its conclusion that mandatory testing did not need to be expanded, saying the rights of AIDS sufferers should "take a clear back seat to the protection of those Americans who are not yet infected. . . . [I]t continues to be puzzling to me why testing for syphilis is appropriate but testing for AIDS is not."

Following are excerpts from "Prevention and Control of Acquired Immunodeficiency Syndrome," report of the American Medical Association Board of Trustees, published October 16, 1987, in the Journal of the American Medical Association:

Responding sensitively, intelligently, and effectively to the growing acquired immunodeficiency (AIDS) crisis is one of the crucial public health problems facing the nation. Prevention and control of the disease must be an essential part of that response because there is, at present, no known cure for AIDS.

Recommendations in this report have as their foundation an overriding concern for a judicious balance between the well-being of human immunodeficiency virus (HIV) positive patients and the protection of the public health. These recommendations are based upon the best information and data available. . . . The AMA will continuously monitor and analyze developments in AIDS and update AMA policy and recommendations. . . .

Education continues to be the major weapon against spread of HIV infection. Physicians should assume the leadership role in educating themselves, their patients, and the public. Individuals in society also must assume responsibility for being well informed and for actions that affect their own health and the health of others. . . . [T]he Board emphasizes the need for concerted and cooperative efforts by all members of society in the fight against AIDS. The recommendations outlined later herein are designed to help successfully confront this challenge to society's well-being.

Background

[A portion of this section omitted]

Historical Control Measures for Infectious Diseases

A primary mode of transmission of AIDS is through sexual contact, and the control efforts for sexually transmitted diseases (STDs) that have been instituted in the past are sources of analogies for prevention and control of AIDS. National programs to control STDs were established during the beginning of World War I. For the following 50 years, the focus was almost exclusively on the control of syphilis and its complications. During World War II, rapid-treatment centers for syphilis and gonorrhea were established. Public health officials instituted limited contact tracing, had the authority to close sex bars and clubs and to order tests for prostitutes, and, most important, had effective therapy to offer. Widespread availability of penicillin led to dissolution of the rapid-treatment centers and of the clinical specialty of syphilology. Every state in the Union at one time required all persons seeking marriage licenses to be tested for syphilis. During the 1950s and 1960s federal assistance programs continued to support contact tracing, serological screening, and patient education.

In the late 1960s, public health officials were concerned about the rapidly escalating cases of gonorrhea, and projects were instituted to increase case-finding and contact tracing. In 1972, financial assistance for STD control by the federal government was dramatically increased, and by 1982 gonorrhea accounted for nearly three fourths of the federal STD dollar. During the 1970s, gonorrhea control efforts evolved through overlapping phases that included objectives to lower the incidence of disease and the occurrence of drug-resistant bacteria, that focused screening on high-risk patients, that intensified follow-up of treatment failures, and that used patient counseling as a means of increasing compliance with therapy and of improving contact tracing. The latter was deemed especially important since the large numbers of patients with gonorrhea precluded the intensive follow-up of each infected person that had been characteristic of the syphilis era.

In 1982, the World Health Organization/Pan-American Health Organization identified the following key objectives for intervention to reduce STDs: (1) to minimize disease exposure by reducing sexual intercourse with persons who have a high probability of infection; (2) to prevent infection by increasing the use of condoms or other prophylactic barriers; (3) to detect and cure disease by implementing screening programs, providing effective diagnostic and treatment facilities, and promoting health-seeking behaviors; (4) to limit complications of infections by providing early treatment to symptomatic and asymptomatic infected individuals; and (5) to limit disease transmission within the community through the previously mentioned efforts.

These objectives were used as a framework for the current US program regarding STDs, which consists of the following components: health education and promotion, disease detection through testing and other means, appropriate treatment, contact tracing and patient counseling, clinical services, training, and research.

The Challenge of AIDS Control

It might seem reasonable to extend the experience in preventing the spread of other STD infections to the AIDS epidemic.... However, AIDS presents a much different social problem than other STD infections. Since there is no cure for AIDS and no protection beyond avoiding or making safer intimate contact with infected individuals, those infected with the virus must be sexually isolated from uninfected persons. A condom barrier offers some but not complete protection. Avoidance of sexual contact and use of shared needles are the only sure protections.

Further, the stigma that accompanies a diagnosis of AIDS, based on fear and society's attitude toward IV drug abusers and homosexuals, presents a factor beyond the control of the infected individual *or* medicine. An HIV-seropositive individual who might live five years or much longer with no overt health problems, once identified in a community, may be subject to many and varied discriminations—by family and loved ones, neighbors and friends, employers and fellow employees, and other providers of services.

As with prevention and control of all contagious diseases, prevention and control of AIDS involves two, sometimes competing, concerns. First, the person who is afflicted with the disease needs compassionate treatment, and both those who have the disease and those who have been infected with the virus should not be subjected to irrational discrimination based on fear, prejudice, or stereotype. Second, and of critical importance, the uninfected must be protected; those individuals who are not infected with the AIDS virus must have every opportunity to avoid transmission of the disease to them.

The Need for a National Policy on AIDS

Given the growing dimensions of the crisis and given limited national resources, it is imperative that a national policy be developed jointly by the public and private sectors. Such a policy must seek, in a cost-effective way, to achieve fundamental national goals: prevention, treatment, and cure—and adequate research in all three areas. A coherent national approach to this modern killer is needed: a comprehensive blueprint for a national response, not piecemeal solutions. Knowledge of the disease is now more than six years old, and the growing magnitude of the problem has been apparent for nearly that long.

Such a national policy must have certain characteristics:

- The policy must be comprehensive, proceeding simultaneously on the fronts of prevention, treatment, and research.
- The policy must be coordinated between public and private sectors and between the different levels of government. A national policy does not necessarily mean a federal policy: there are important roles at all levels of the health care systems and at all levels of government. Nor does it necessarily mean uniformity: on certain issues different approaches should be tried to determine efficacy.
- The policy must be carefully balanced. For example, concern for the person with the disease must be balanced with concern for those who do not have the disease but who may become infected. Similarly, careful consideration must be given to directing scarce resources toward increased prevention, even as increasingly large resources are necessarily devoted to research and treatment.
- The policy must be based on scientific information and medical judgments. Although policy choices must inevitably be made, they should be formed using the best available information and using the extensive

public health experience in dealing both with AIDS and with other contagious diseases.

- The policy should be nonpartisan. Although it may be tempting to play on fears and prejudices, public figures and officials both inside and outside the health community should avoid exploiting the crisis for partisan political advantage.
- The policy should be capable of continuous review and modification as more and more information becomes available.

Recommendation 1

A commission, modeled after the commission that made recommendations on the problems of Social Security financing in the early 1980s, should be formed with representatives from the executive branch of the federal government, the Congress, state and local governments, and the private sector and directed to develop a consensus position for consideration by the Congress, the Executive, state and local governments, and private associations and institutions. The presidential commission that has been announced, but not yet appointed, by the Administration could be broadened to implement this recommendation. A high-level body with representatives from the different branches and levels of government, but operating to the side of the more formal political processes, may have the best chance of forging the necessary national consensus which can then become the basis for concerted and coordinated action by both the public and private sectors.

The Special Role of Physicians and Other Health Care Counselors

Because there is no cure for AIDS, effective preventive techniques are vital. This involves both those who are infected and those who are not. Those who are infected must be identified so that they will not unknowingly transmit the disease to others. Many who are not infected will need to change their behavior substantially to minimize their risk of infection by the AIDS virus.

The key to changed behavior is public education coupled with counseling, which must be given by physicians and other health care counselors.

Public Awareness

The public is well aware of AIDS in a general sense. The attention of the media has been intensively focused on the disease. Translating general awareness into modifications of behavior is the challenge.

The groups that are most at risk for AIDS, eg, IV drug abusers, homosexuals, bisexuals, and prostitutes, have reason to know they are at risk. Their contacts, however, may not know they are at risk, and, hence, spouses, unborn babies, and premarital and extramarital sexual partners may become infected. Education and counseling aimed at the high-risk groups must be the first priority. The education should urge immediate counseling with a physician or other health care counselor about the risk of AIDS, the uses of antibody testing, and preventive measures.

Also, it must be recognized that persons in these groups may not respond to education and counseling; when they do not respond, more aggressive programs, such as expanded methadone maintenance programs or penalties for knowingly exposing others, must be considered.

Education aimed at the more general population is difficult for at least two reasons. First, reaching all Americans with an effective message can be expensive, and not all people respond in the same way or to the same method of learning. Messages must therefore be tailored to the target audience in question. Second, preventive messages must necessarily deal with controversial subject matter. Widespread use of the electronic media—especially television—appears to be the most effective way to reach the general public. Accordingly, public service advertising (PSA) on the electronic media must be greatly increased, and these announcements must be shown at times and in places where they will be viewed by those who need the message most.

The AMA will continue its efforts to place its own public service ads on national television. The AMA's PSA with Tony Danza directed at teenagers about abstinence and condoms, and other PSAs which the networks have agreed to use, are significant first steps. But more must be done, and it must be nationally coordinated.

Recommendation 2

The communications industry must develop voluntary guidelines for PSAs regarding AIDS in consultation with the health care community and government officials. The AMA intends to be a catalyst in this effort to immediately bring the communications and health care communities together.

Counseling and Educating Counselors

Perhaps the greatest need at the present time is effective counseling of both low-risk and high-risk populations by physicians or other health care counselors. A massive education effort for physicians and other counselors is necessary as a first step. Complete and accurate information on the disease, the modes of transmission, the appropriate application of antibody testing, and effective ways to change behavior must be understood by counselors if it is to be properly communicated to patients. In conjunction with face-to-face counseling, printed materials—like the Surgeon General's recent 36-page report on AIDS—should be widely disseminated.

Even more challenging than preparing physicians and others for generic counseling on AIDS is preparing these counselors to assist those who test positive and are infected with the virus. It is at that time that a change of behavior on the part of the person infected is most critical, and it is then that the most sophisticated counseling is required, due to the emotional impact of the test results. There is no higher prevention priority than ensuring that the community of individuals who provide health care counseling be given adequate tools to be effective....

Recommendation 3

A conference should be held immediately between the AMA, other physician organizations, and public health officials at all levels of government to determine (1) the types of education and training that are necessary for effective counseling; (2) the people in the health care community who should receive this education and training; (3) the current resources available for such education and training; (4) recommendations for providing additional resources, including consideration of the respective roles of medical associations and government at all levels; (5) recommendations on how to update information continually as new scientific data are developed; and (6) recommendations for alternative measures to prevent the spread of AIDS where education and counseling are not likely to be effective, particularly among IV drug users, through such programs as expanded methadone maintenance....

Voluntary and Mandatory Testing

Knowledge that a person is infected with the AIDS virus can be the crucial predicate to changing behavior. Thus, testing for an antibody to the AIDS virus, when used in conjunction with appropriate counseling (and when offered in the context of appropriate antidiscrimination and confidentiality protections discussed later herein), serves the important public health purpose of providing impetus for behavior changes that minimize the risk of transmitting the AIDS virus.

Clearly, the need for HIV antibody testing has expanded beyond its original purpose, the screening of blood donors. Guidelines for ... HIV antibody testing must center on the following justifications: (1) to identify infected persons and offer treatment where possible and to protect uninfected third parties, (2) to offer education and counseling that would modify high risk behavior, (3) to solicit patient cooperation for locating and referring sex partners, and (4) to obtain broadened epidemiological statistics on the prevalence of HIV infection in the population.

In addition, in considering the merits of voluntary vs mandatory testing, these facts about AIDS must be kept in mind:

1. AIDS is caused by an infectious agent, and, therefore, is an infectious disease. Appropriate precautions, procedures, and policies should be applied to protect the community from the spread of the disease.

2. The extent to which the AIDS virus already has spread into the general population is not completely understood. Current projections are based on a number of unverified assumptions.

3. The transmission of the AIDS virus does not occur through casual contacts. Sexual contact, contact with septic IV equipment, and the administration of infected blood and blood products are the main modes of transmission.

4. Heterosexual transmission of the AIDS virus, especially from men to women, does occur.

5. Seropositive pregnant women will transmit the virus to their babies in a high percentage of cases.

6. Health care workers, especially whose who perform invasive surgical procedures, and emergency department and laboratory personnel, are at some risk when caring for patients with AIDS.

7. No patient with a clinical case of AIDS has survived the disease. The disease has been uniformly fatal.

8. The disease, not its victims, is the threat from which society must be protected.

9. The confidentiality of the doctor-patient relationship is vitally important but not absolute.

10. Physicians have an ethical and professional obligation to behave in a scientifically responsible manner. . . .

General Conclusions

Except for individuals in the limited categories listed in Recommendation 5 . . . (blood, organ, and semen donors; immigrants; military personnel; and prison inmates), for whom testing serves well-established and well-accepted protection goals, mandatory national testing should not, at present, be broadly extended.

Military personnel have traditionally been subject to mandatory immunizations, and our defense forces, of course, must be as strong as possible. Prison inmates, because they are confined and have a higher incidence of high-risk individuals than the general population, require special protection. Immigrants should be tested so that we can focus on the AIDS problem already here, and the nation certainly has the right to bar entrants with communicable diseases. The need to test donors of blood, organs, and semen has never been questioned.

Public health authorities have advanced a plausible premise for their opposition to mandatory testing of homosexuals and drug abusers: such testing will only drive people underground and away from the health care system. Public health authorities also have advanced a premise for not requiring mandatory testing of large segments of the general population, such as all those seeking marriage licenses or all those admitted to hospitals: such testing in low prevalence populations would result in a high proportion of false-positive results and would not be cost-effective, given the demand for voluntary testing and the shortage of testing and counseling resources for those who voluntarily want them or who will want them following effective public awareness campaigns.

Until those premises are shown by superior studies to be incorrect, a policy regarding mandatory testing that has been rejected by the vast majority of public health officials, including the Centers for Disease Control (CDC) and the Surgeon General, cannot be recommended.

But certain high-risk groups should be regularly tested, with the right to informed consent and to refuse the test. Those groups are defined in Recommendation 6.

In addition, physicians and other hospital personnel involved in invasive surgical procedures who necessarily and unavoidably come in contact with the blood of patients, need to be aware of their risks. Limited regular testing of patients will ensure that the CDC guidelines for the protection of hospital personnel are followed rigorously and will further ensure that all patients receive prompt and full treatment. The Board emphasizes here that physicians have a long and honored tradition of tending to patients afflicted with infectious diseases with compassion and courage. That tradition must and will be continued throughout the AIDS epidemic.

Because the risk to health care personnel will be slight in most areas, any effort at mandatory testing of certain kinds of patients should be instituted after voluntary testing has failed and where a variety of factors, eg, the costs and availability of proper testing and counseling as measured against the risk presented by the relative presence of a high-risk patient population, weigh in favor of mandatory testing.

The AMA does not believe it appropriate at this time to extend regularly offered testing to persons other than those listed, eg, recommended testing should not be extended to all individuals who are considering marriage or to all persons in hospitals. Decisions about whether there should be generally recommended testing of other types of individuals should, at this time, be left to the decision of the local community, depending on its own circumstances and the judgments of its own public health officials.

At present, each case of AIDS must be reported by the individual physician to state public health authorities either by name or identifier. Anonymous or carefully implemented confidential reporting should also be extended to all confirmed instances of persons infected with AIDS virus but not afflicted with AIDS-related complex (ARC) or AIDS. Individuals who are seropositive for the HIV antibody are infected with the virus and can spread the disease as certainly as those with symptoms of AIDS. A sound epidemiologic understanding of the potential impact of AIDS on society requires the reporting of those who are confirmed as testing positive for the antibody to the AIDS virus.

Testing Recommendations

Recommendation 4

Tests for the AIDS virus should be readily available to all who wish to be tested. The tests should be routinely subsidized for individuals who cannot afford to pay the cost of their test.

Recommendation 5

Testing for the AIDS virus should be mandatory for donors of blood and blood fractions, organs, and other tissues intended for transplantation in the United States or abroad; donors of semen or ova collected for artificial insemination or in vitro fertilization; immigrants to the United States; inmates in federal and state prisons; and military personnel.

Recommendation 6

Voluntary testing should be regularly provided for the following types of individuals who give informed consent: (1) patients at STD clinics, (2) patients at drug abuse clinics, (3) pregnant women in high-risk areas in the first trimester of pregnancy; (4) individuals seeking family planning services who are from areas with a high incidence of AIDS or who engage in high-risk behavior, and (5) patients requiring surgical or other invasive procedures who are from areas with a high incidence of AIDS or who engage in high-risk behavior. If the voluntary policy is not sufficiently accepted, the hospital and medical staff should consider a mandatory program for the institution.

Recommendation 7

As a matter of medical judgment, physicians should encourage voluntary HIV testing for individuals whose history or clinical status warrant this measure.

Recommendation 8

Individuals who are seropositive for the AIDS virus should be reported to appropriate public health officials on an anonymous or confidential basis with enough information to be epidemiologically significant.

Recommendation 9

Physicians should counsel patients before tests for AIDS to educate them about effective behaviors to avoid the risk of AIDS for themselves and others. In public screening programs, counseling may be done in whatever form is appropriate given the resources and personnel available as long as effective counseling is provided.

Recommendation 10

Physicians should counsel their patients who are found to be seropositive regarding (1) responsible behavior to prevent the spread of the disease, (2) strategies for health protection with a compromised immune system, and (3) the necessity of alerting sexual contacts, past (five to ten years) and present, regarding their possible infection by the AIDS virus. Long-term emotional support should be provided or arranged for seropositive individuals.

Recommendation 11

Patients should knowingly and willingly give consent before a voluntary test is conducted.

Resources

Only recently [have] Congress and the Administration begun to seriously consider the vast resources needed to deal effectively with AIDS. Federal funding for 1988 is expected to reach $1 billion. But that amount will not be enough. The AMA endorses the bill introduced by Congressman [Henry A.] Waxman [D-Calif.] to increase resources for testing and counseling.

Testing for HIV in America will require substantially more resources than are currently being made available. Trained counselors, materials for counseling, and research on effective counseling approaches, for the variety of population groups that need these services, are urgently required. Also, dependable testing facilities with sufficient capacity to respond to the epidemic are needed now. In addition, funds for research and care must be increased to fully exploit the nation's capacity to respond effectively to this crisis.

The key premise of a prevention strategy, when there is no vaccine, is behavioral change on the part of those infected and those at risk of infection by the AIDS virus. It is therefore crucial that there be immediate and systematic studies conducted of how behavior of affected groups may have changed in recent years, and, if possible, what factors caused the changes. Most particularly, it is necessary to study and evaluate the types of counseling that have been effective so that the techniques may be replicated widely. ... [I]n a free society, suasion and voluntary change, if effective, are far preferable to compulsion.

Recommendation 12

Public funding must be provided in an amount sufficient (1) to promptly and efficiently counsel and test for AIDS, (2) to conduct the research necessary to find a cure and develop an effective vaccine, (3) to perform studies to evaluate the efficiency of counseling and education programs on changing behavior, and (4) to assist in the care of AIDS patients who cannot afford proper care or who cannot find appropriate facilities for treatment and care.

Protection Against Discrimination

Antidiscrimination

The AMA believes strongly that AIDS victims and those who test positively for the antibody to the AIDS virus should not be treated unfairly or suffer from arbitrary or irrational discrimination in their daily lives. Last year, the AMA filed a friend-of-the-court brief in *School Board of Nassau County vs Arline*, a case before the Supreme Court that addressed the question of how the federal handicapped antidiscrimination laws should apply to persons afflicted with contagious diseases. The AMA set forth a framework for the application of the law which the Supreme Court adopted, quoting verbatim from the AMA brief in its key holding.

A sound antidiscrimination approach does not allow reflexive discrimination against patients with AIDS based on fear or stereotype or prejudice. Nor does it require that all employers or other federal fund recipients automatically accommodate a person afflicted with a communicable disease. Instead, based on an individualized analysis of the nature and duration of the handicap and the nature and duration of the communicability, a federal fund recipient must make a reasonable accommodation based on reasonable medical judgments, given the state of medical knowledge at the time. This sound framework for carefully balancing the two competing concerns—the right of the afflicted to be free from irrational acts of prejudice and the right of others to be protected against an unreasonable risk of disease—should also guide state antidiscrimination efforts.

A key question left open by the Supreme Court is whether a person who is not afflicted with AIDS or ARC, but who nonetheless tests positive for the antibody, is protected by the federal antidiscrimination law.

To encourage people to seek counseling, and testing if necessary, the AMA strongly urges that antidiscrimination laws at both the federal and state levels be clarified either by regulatory interpretation or by statutory amendment to cover those who test HIV antibody positive. Allowing irrational discrimination against those who test positive . . . has the destructive effect of removing . . . otherwise productive members of society from the work force or otherwise denying them access to an important aspect of normal life. While federal law should continue to apply only to federal fund recipients, state laws should be sought to prevent irrational discrimination by entities or individuals within those jurisdictions.

Recommendation 13

Antidiscrimination laws must be clarified or amended to cover those who test positive for the antibodies to the AIDS virus.

Confidentiality

The ability of the health care community to maintain the confidentiality of patient information and restrict its use to only those purposes essential for maintenance of health is, like clarification of antidiscrimination laws, vital to an effective program of preventing and controlling AIDS. Even if antidiscrimination laws were completely effective, which unfortunately is not likely, persons who test positive (such as those with ARC or AIDS) will suffer stigma. Thus, confidentiality is crucial.

The basic principle should be that access to patient information should be limited only to health care personnel who have a legitimate need to have access to the information to assist the patient or to protect the health of others closely associated with the patient. . . .

Recommendation 14

Model confidentiality laws must be drafted that can be adopted at all levels of government to encourage as much uniformity as possible in protecting the identity of patients with AIDS and AIDS carriers, except where the public health requires otherwise.

Questions for the Future

As the national debate on prevention and control of AIDS continues, other important issues will need to be addressed.

Research and Data

There is an urgent and critical need for more scientifically sound data on the prevalence and spread of virus in the general population. At the present time, only those cases that meet the current CDC surveillance definition of AIDS are reported to that institution. Since AIDS is the terminal and fatal stage of HIV infection, it represents only the tip of the huge HIV infection iceberg. There are protean manifestations of HIV infection ranging from infected asymptomatic to full-blown AIDS. How large the base of that iceberg really is—that is, how many people are actually infected—can only be estimated from the number of reported cases of AIDS. That has been done by using a multiple (50 to 100 times the number of AIDS cases) that has been extracted largely from surveys done in high-prevalence areas. Yet, this same multiple has been used to estimate the number of current and potential HIV-infected persons in low-prevalence areas and, for that matter, in the entire country and even in the world. The CDC itself is unsure about the accuracy of its estimates. Yet, if economic and medical plans are to be made for the future, reliable projections must be available. How sufficient or exaggerated these plans may be depends on the accuracy of current and future estimates of the number of HIV-infected persons, particularly as to the extent of its spread into the low-risk heterosexual population.

Not only are accurate estimates of the number of HIV-infected persons needed, but so too are reliable data on the rate conversion of asymptomatic seropositive persons to clinical illness, including AIDS, requiring increased medical care. This information is important for the formulation of plans for the future of potentially hospitalizable patients and the economic consideration thereof. Infection with HIV has protean manifestations, and death can result not only from AIDS itself, but from severe ARC or progressive central nervous system disease as well. To obtain accurate information in HIV-infected persons on the rate of conversion from asymptomatic to clinically severe illness, baseline data on their serological status must be obtained as early as possible—not after clinically manifested disease is present. The presence of HIV antibodies indicates not only current infection with the virus, but also that the patient is potentially capable of transmitting the disease. This follows from the fact that HIV integrates its genome into the host cell genome, with the result that once infected, the patient remains infected for life and is, therefore, capable of lifelong transmission of the agent. The earlier the infected person is detected, the earlier he or she may be advised of this contagious state and counseled on how to avoid further transmission of this lethal virus.

Recommendation 15

Consistent with the proposal by the Secretary of Health and Human Services, a national study in various areas of the country must be immediately undertaken to determine the prevalence and conversion rate of the virus in the US population, and the study must be repeated at appropriate intervals to gauge the spread of the disease.

Warning to Third Parties

One of the more difficult issues for society is how to warn unsuspecting spouses or sexual partners of persons who test HIV positive. Such a warning would allow the third party to practice "safer" sex or to abstain from sexual relations with the infected person altogether. Given the life-or-death consequences, the unsuspecting third party should, as a general matter, be warned because there is no cure and because it may not be responsible to rely solely on the infected person to provide a suitable warning.

Physicians who have reason to believe that there is an unsuspecting sexual partner of an infected individual should be encouraged to inform public health authorities. The duty to warn the unsuspecting sexual partner should then reside with the public health authorities as well as the infected person and not with the physician to the infected person.

The AMA believes that mechanisms, analogous to those used by public health authorities to warn sexual partners about other STDs, should be put in place to warn unsuspecting third parties about an infected sexual partner. Such warning may be appropriate whether the infected person is bisexual, heterosexual, or homosexual.

This problem raises the general question of whether anonymous reporting should continue to be the standard for persons who test seropositive. Our recommendation at this time is limited to situations where physicians or health officials already know the identity of the AIDS carrier and have reason to believe that a risk to third parties exists.

Recommendation 16

Specific statutes must be drafted that, while protecting to the greatest extent possible the confidentiality of patient information, (1) provide a method for warning unsuspecting sexual partners, (2) protect physicians from liability for failure to warn the unsuspecting third party but (3) establish clear standards for when a physician should inform the public health authorities, and (4) provide clear guidelines for public health authorities who need to trace the unsuspecting sexual partners of the infected person.

Sanctions for Reckless Disregard for the Safety of Others

A related question which must be explored is whether an infected person, who knows he or she is infected and who knowingly fails to warn a sexual partner of the infection, should be subject not just to tort suits, but to a proceeding brought by state authorities to sanction the individual.

Recommendation 17

Given the risk of infection being transmitted sexually, and given the dire potential consequences of transmission, serious consideration should be given to sanctions, at least in circumstances where an unsuspecting sexual partner subsequently discovers a partner's infection and brings a complaint to the attention of authorities. Preemptive sanctions are not being endorsed by this recommendation....

STOCK MARKET CRASH

October 19 and 20, 1987

On October 19 Wall Street's five-year bull market disintegrated in a wave of panic selling that sent the Dow Jones Industrial Average down 508 points. The average, which is based on the performance of thirty blue-chip stocks, fell an unprecedented 22.6 percent from 2246.73 to 1738.74. The volume of trading was so great that reporting of trades on the New York Stock Exchange lagged more than two hours behind at some points during the day. Few stocks were immune to the panic. Many blue-chip issues, including IBM, General Motors, and Exxon, lost between 20 and 30 percent of their value. Virtually the only stocks to post gains were gold and silver mining issues.

Nervous investors had begun feverishly selling stocks on Friday, October 16. The market was responding in part to comments the day before by Secretary of the Treasury James A. Baker III—comments that many investors regarded as a signal that the United States would accept a further decline in the dollar. On Friday the New York Stock Exchange had its busiest day in history before Monday's collapse with 338.5 million shares traded as the Dow fell 108.35 points.

The anxiety of October 16 on Wall Street was felt in exchanges in Europe and the Far East when they opened on October 19. By the time the New York Stock Exchange began trading on Monday, foreign exchanges had already suffered staggering losses. Panic selling took over Wall Street. Rumors that the New York Stock Exchange might close and concern over hostilities in the Persian Gulf where U.S. forces had just destroyed an Iranian oil platform heightened traders' fears.

On October 20 a less-publicized crisis occurred when many banks began to tighten credit and even call in loans to securities firms because of the decrease in the value of stocks that served as collateral. Stock trading came to a virtual halt when the specialists who normally buy stocks when there are no other buyers had insufficient capital. Many investment firms were faced with catastrophic losses, creating the real possibility that financial markets would be closed. The Federal Reserve Board, recognizing the crisis, took two main actions: it pressured New York banks to extend credit to investment firms and lowered interest rates by flooding banks with capital through purchases of government securities. The stock market rebounded October 20 with a 102-point gain in the Dow average, as investors recognized that Monday's panic had driven the prices of many stocks below their true values.

Parallels to the 1929 Crash

Many commentators drew parallels between the October 19 plunge and the crash of 1929 that preceded the Great Depression. In both eras international trade relations were strained, corporations and individuals were heavily in debt, and many investors had capitalized on a prolonged bull market that had driven stock prices to artificially high levels. Charts of the Dow Jones average also displayed an ominous similarity in the movement of the market in the months before both crashes. Economists generally agreed, however, that the 1987 crash would not lead to an economic calamity of the magnitude of the Great Depression, because safeguards had been installed in the 1930s to prevent a financial disaster. Perhaps the most important of these is federal deposit insurance, which guards against a banking system collapse by protecting bank deposits of up to $100,000. The safety net also includes income-maintenance programs such as welfare, social security, and unemployment insurance.

Improved understanding of financial mechanisms and expectations of government intervention also made the situation in 1987 more stable. According to historians, the Federal Reserve Board had deepened the 1929 crisis by tightening credit, thereby slowing the growth of the money supply at a time when greater liquidity was needed.

Reagan Administration's Reaction

President Ronald Reagan tried to calm nervous investors by maintaining that the crash had been an inevitable correction of a market driven too high by speculation. The White House October 19 expressed concern but pointed to encouraging economic indicators that showed the economy was sound. Despite Reagan's optimism, he proposed on October 20 an economic summit with congressional leaders to reach agreement on deficit reductions. Reagan said he was "willing to look at whatever proposals" legislators might make. Previously the president had ruled out tax increases. Reagan the same week appointed a presidential commission headed by investment banker and former senator Nicholas F. Brady to study the causes of the crash.

The administration's depiction of a sturdy economy was not unfounded. Unemployment was 5.9 percent, corporate profits were high, and the longest peacetime economic expansion in U.S. history was ongoing. Although inflation had risen in 1987, it remained at a modest 5 percent rate, far below levels reached during the Carter administration.

Although the Dow had fallen from the August 25 peak of 2722.42 to 2246.73 before the October 19 crash, many stocks were still obviously overvalued. Few analysts believed, however, that Wall Street's freefall could be written off as a correction of an overvalued market. A 508-point drop in the Dow average had to be regarded as an indication of serious economic problems.

Causes of the Crash

Investors were reacting to the enormous federal budget deficit, rising interest rates, the falling dollar, and the trade deficit that remained despite the weakened dollar that made American goods less expensive overseas. Buoyed by speculative fever, the stock market had risen throughout 1987 as these problems became more severe. By September, however, they could no longer be ignored, and the market began a slide that culminated in the collapse.

Although the contribution of the troubled economy was undisputed, many analysts maintained that characteristics of the financial markets themselves were responsible for the unprecedented severity of the plunge. Depending on their position in the financial community, critics blamed different contributing factors: program trading in stock-index futures and options, the failure of the government to coordinate the regulation of various markets, the inadequacy of the capital reserves of some securities firms, or the inability of the markets to cope with the volume of computer trading.

A partisan debate quickly developed between the opponents and supporters of stock-index trading. Officials of the New York Stock Exchange and its overseer, the Securities and Exchange Commission, maintained that stock-index trading contributed to the market's collapse and should be curtailed or subject to tougher margin requirements. The Chicago Mercantile Exchange and the Chicago Board of Trade, the major exchanges for stock-index futures and options, along with their regulatory agency, the Commodity Futures Trading Commission, rejected these charges and attacked New York's stock trading system as outdated and in need of overhaul. Both groups commissioned studies to analyze the causes of the crash and determine measures to prevent future market instability. These reports were submitted to the president's task force, which was expected to make reform recommendations in January 1988.

Repairing the U.S. Economy

The crash sent a clear signal that the persistent problems of the U.S. economy needed to be addressed. On October 26 administration officials and congressional leaders, fired by a new sense of urgency, began meeting to plan a compromise budget aimed at reducing the 1988 budget deficit. Without a compromise, $23 billion would be cut automatically in across-the-board reductions mandated by the Gramm-Rudman-Hollings law. (Historic Documents of 1985, p. 803)

The negotiators November 20 announced an agreement on a broad framework for eliminating $30 billion from the deficit in fiscal 1988 and $46 billion the following year. Many Wall Streeters, along with political leaders of both parties, condemned the agreement as inadequate. The market posted gains in the days following the agreement, but the plan did not relieve investors' concerns about the long-term effect of the deficit.

Correcting the trade deficit and stabilizing the dollar were equally difficult problems. Trade legislation pending in Congress was designed to force U.S. trading partners to open their markets to American goods, but many economists warned that these measures were protectionist and could trigger a trade war that would lead to an international recession. If the government chose to combat the trade deficit by allowing the dollar to fall further, interest rates might need to be increased to ensure foreign investment in U.S. securities. Higher interest rates, however, would also increase the chances of a recession.

Aftermath of the Crash

Investors in Europe and Japan who had helped create the bull market of 1987 approached U.S. stocks cautiously after the crash. Some stayed away altogether. The diminished interest of foreign and domestic investors in U.S. stocks was reflected in the layoffs of over 10,000 employees of Wall Street investment and banking firms.

The market continued to vacillate in the weeks after the crash. Many stocks fell from their October 19 levels, but the Dow recovered somewhat to close the year at 1938.83, 2.26 percent higher than it opened the year. Despite this modest recovery, the market appeared unlikely to produce another bull market in the near future. The economic problems that lead to the crash could not be solved quickly. Moreover, the events of October had created an atmosphere of uncertainty that drove many small investors out of the market and turned many professional traders conservative. Fears that the crash would frighten American consumers into reducing their spending, however, appeared unwarranted at the end of the year, when retail sales rose over the levels of the previous year. As long as American consumers continued to spend as they had in 1987, the prospects for short-term economic growth seemed good.

Following are the White House statement of October 19, 1987, on the stock market crash, President Ronald Reagan's remarks of October 20, and excerpts from the front-page story in the Wall Street Journal *of October 20:*

WHITE HOUSE STATEMENT

The President has watched today with concern the continued drop in the stock market. He directed members of his administration to consult with the Chairmen of the Federal Reserve, the Securities and Exchange Commission, the New York Stock Exchange, the Chicago Commodities and Futures Exchanges, and leaders of the investment community.

Those consultations confirm our view that the underlying economy remains sound. We are in the longest peacetime expansion in history. Employment is at the highest level ever. Manufacturing output is up. The trade deficit, when adjusted for changes in currencies, is steadily improving. And as the Chairman of the Federal Reserve has recently stated, there is no evidence of a resurgence of inflation in the United States.

The President is keeping close watch on the markets here and in other countries. We will continue to closely monitor these developments.

PRESIDENT REAGAN'S REMARKS

The President. I have a statement I'd like to read here. I guess you all know now that the market closed up 102.27 points and 604 million shares traded. I've just finished a meeting with my economic advisers, and we thoroughly reviewed the developments of the financial markets of the last few days and the actions we've taken thus far and our options for additional measures.

We've been in constant contact with financial leaders of both countries, with the exchanges around the world, and with market participants. While I remain concerned, I'm pleased that the steps taken by the Federal Reserve have had a salutary effect on the markets: Interest rates are down across the spectrum. I'm also pleased with the actions by two major banks today to lower their prime interest rates. I believe that there remains room in the markets for a further decline in interest rates, and specifically I'm pleased that the bond market is strong and the foreign exchange markets are stable.

Yesterday Secretary Baker and his German counterpart reaffirmed our agreement with the Germans to coordinate our economic policies to provide for noninflationary growth and stable exchange rates. Finance Minister Miyazawa issed a similar statement reaffirming Japan's intent to cooperate with other industrial economies and and follow economic policies that will provide for a sustained growth in the Japanese economy. And in a phone conversation with Prime Minister-designate Takeshita this morning, he stated that his top priority was to maintain stable economic relations with the United States. The United States remains committed to the Louvre Agreement [an agreement signed by industrialized democracies in February 1987, calling for stabilized currencies], and today I signed the preliminary sequester order under the Gramm-Rudman-Hollings law.

However, I think it is preferable, if possible, that the executive and legislative branches reach agreement on a budget deficit reduction package. Accordingly, I am directing that discussions be undertaken with the bipartisan leadership of the Congress for that purpose. The economic fundamentals in this country remain sound, and our citizens should not panic. And I have great confidence in the future.

Q. Mr. President, how about—

Q. Are you willing to compromise on taxes, sir? Are you willing to compromise on taxes?

The President. I presented in my budget a program that provided for $22 billion in additional revenue, which was not necessarily taxes. And I am willing to look at whatever proposal they might have.

Q. Mr. President, someone described as a senior market—or economic analyst in the administration said the market might have been so weakened by this crash that there could be a recession as early as next spring.

The President. It's pretty hard for anyone to speculate on that. I would like to point out, however, that the only way that could happen would be if the people of this country ignored the economic signs. And then if you had people begin putting off purchases of automobiles, refrigerators, things of that kind because they feared hard times, yes, that could bring on a recession. But there is nothing in what has happened here that should result in a recession. We have a higher percentage of the eligible work force at work than ever in the history of our country.

... **Q.** Are you willing to personally—personally—sit down with the Democrats at an economic sumit?

The President. I don't know whether that's necessary or whether we would do it with some of our people, but certainly I'm willing to be a participant in anything that can bring us together. Let me point out—you mentioned the Democrats—for virtually a half a century or more they have controlled both Houses of the Congress, and for more than a half a century there has been, with only two single-year exceptions, a budget deficit.

Q. You never submitted a balanced budget.

The President. No, because I said from the beginning that—having predicted for 30 years that the deficit would get out of control as it did—that there was no way you could balance the budget now in 1 year, but we could set ourselves on a course that would result in that. And the end result was that I have never gotten a budget that I asked for, even though the law says I must submit it to the Congress. And the Congress is responsible for the deficit.

Q. Mr. President, is the market going to keep going down?

Q. The Democrats say you have concrete around your feet on taxes.

Concrete—

The President. If you heard that, it must have been the helicopter.

Q. Is the market going to keep going down? Will the market keep going down?

The President. It just closed at 102.27.

WALL STREET JOURNAL ARTICLE

The stock market crashed yesterday.[1]

The Dow Jones Industrial Average plummeted an astonishing 508 points, or 22.6%, to 1738.74. The drop far exceeded the 12.8% decline on the notorious day of Oct. 28, 1929, which is generally considered the start of the Great Depression.

Panic-driven trading on the New York Stock Exchange reached 604.3 million shares, nearly double the prior record volume of 338.5 million shares set last Friday when the Dow plunged a then-record 108.35 points.

Commodities prices also skidded, except for precious metals and especially gold, which surged $10.10 an ounce to $481.70, a 4½-year high. The bond market, a refuge for much of the capital being wrenched out of the stock market, recovered from steep early losses to end the day sharply higher.

Final Slide

The industrial average tumbled 130 points in the final minutes of the session. The decline yesterday and last week totaled 743.47 points, or 30%. By way of comparison, the total drop on Oct. 28 and Oct. 29, 1929, was 68.90 points, or 23.1%.

With yesterday's drop, the average has given up all its 1987 gains and now shows an 8.3% loss for the year. From its Aug. 25 high of 2722.42, it has lost 36.1%.

Virtually every other measure of market health and investor sentiment also set new lows yesterday. Standard & Poor's 500-stock index fell 57.86 to 224.84; the New York Stock Exchange index, 30.51 to 128.62; the National Association of Securities Dealers Nasdaq composite index of over-the-counter stocks, 46.12 to 360.21; and the American Stock Exchange index, 41.05 to 282.50—all record declines.

It was "the worst market I've ever seen," said John J. Phelan, the Big Board chairman, and "as close to financial meltdown as I'd ever want to see."

From the beginning yesterday, the market was clearly in for a tough day. Futures contracts on the S&P 500 index plunged to steep discounts from the value of the index itself, triggering sophisticated traders' sales of large

[1] This article was prepared by Wall Street Journal staff reporters Tim Metz, Alan Murray, Thomas E. Ricks and Beatrice E. Garcia.

baskets of blue-chip stocks. But selling by others quickly became so chaotic that this so-called program selling was sharply curtailed.

Order Imbalances

How chaotic? Because of order imbalances, 11 of the 30 stocks in the Dow Jones Industrial Average didn't open for about an hour after trading began. By late afternoon, the Big Board's transactions tape—capable of handling 900 trades a minute—was running two hours and 15 minutes late. When the dust finally settled, the ratio of Big Board stocks declining in price was an unprecedented 40 to 1 over gainers; a 3-to-1 ratio is considered a rout.

Mr. Phelan said that at least five factors contributed to the record decline: the fact that the market had gone five years without a large correction; inflation fears, whether justified or not; rising interest rates; the conflict with Iran; and the volatility caused by "derivative instruments" such as stock-index options and futures.

He declined to blame the decline on program trading alone or on reports that Securities and Exchange Commission Chairman David Ruder had said he might consider a trading halt under certain circumstances. Mr. Phelan noted that only the president and the exchange itself have the right to order a trading shutdown, but he added that if the SEC asked for one, the Big Board would give it serious consideration.

In the past, Mr. Phelan has publicly expressed his concern that options and futures could add to volatility and contribute to a cycle in which selling caused further selling. He said yesterday that such a "waterfall" effect seemed to have occurred over the past week.

Stunned Disbelief

The reaction around Wall Street, from traders, money managers and securities analysts, was mostly of stunned disbelief. "We're in the midst of a crash," said Jon Groveman, the head equity trader at Ladenburg Thalmann & Co. in New York. Added Edward Macheski, a partner with Macheski/Pappas Asset Management in Wilton, Conn.: "We are frozen. We don't want to sell what we have, and we don't want to spend the cash that we have."

In Japan and Europe, stock markets dropped precipitously overnight in a reaction to last Friday's plunge in New York, and they are expected to react further to yesterday's crash; indeed, stocks were falling as trading began in Tokyo Tuesday morning.

There was some selling by foreign investors as the U.S. market opened, but not enough to suggest that they were bailing out completely. That, coupled with the dollar's firm tone in New York trading yesterday, suggested to some observers that foreigners might not rush to liquidate their U.S. financial assets.

As stock prices collapsed, the U.S. government stood by, powerless.

President Reagan cautioned against panic "because all the economic indicators are solid," and he attributed the plunge to profit taking. "Everyone is a little puzzled," he said. "There is nothing wrong with the economy."

But as the market continued falling, government officials made a round of upbeat comments but concluded that there was little they could do other than try to stay calm in the face of Wall Street's panic. A statement from the White House acknowledged that President Reagan was concerned, and it said he had directed members of his administration to consult with the chairmen of the Federal Reserve Board, the SEC, the Big Board, and the Chicago commodities and futures exchanges, as well as other leaders of the investment community.

Merrill Lynch Statement

In an unprecedented statement to Merrill Lynch & Co.'s staff, which was released to the public shortly after the close, Chairman William O. Schreyer and President Daniel P. Tully expressed their "confidence in the financial markets and in the underlying value of financial assets in this climate." The executives added that "now is the time when it is critical that reason and objectivity prevail. America's economic system is the strongest in the world, with great inherent ability to correct itself, and it remains fundamentally sound."

But the optimistic statements rang hollow as sell orders poured in on Wall Street. "After the 1929 crash, the universal phrase was 'The economy is fundamentally sound,'" said a skeptical John Kenneth Galbraith, the Harvard economist. "Expect to hear that out of Washington over the next few days."

Early in the day, SEC Chairman Ruder suggested that he might call for a temporary suspension of trading if the market fell too rapidly. But that idea was immediately blasted by other administration officials and private analysts.

"It seems to me that's a crazy thing for the chairman of the SEC to ever talk about," one White House official said. And Sanford Grossman, a financial economist at Princeton University, called Mr. Ruder's idea "the most frightening idea I've heard in a while. Shutting the market down for a half-hour is a sure way to cause a panic."

Later, the SEC issued an unusual statement saying it "is not discussing closing the nation's securities market."

Margin Requirements

Also rejected was the idea of asking the Fed to ease or suspend margin requirements, which govern the amount of debt that an investor can use to buy stock. Easing margin requirements would reduce the need for investors to sell stock as a way to raise the cash to meet those requirements. That, in turn, would slow down stock sales triggered by such calls.

In a luncheon address, Fed Vice Chairman Manuel Johnson made it clear he saw no reason for the Fed to push interest rates higher. He said "we are satisfied" with the developments on inflation since the Fed raised the discount rate—its rate on loans to member banks—last month to 6% from 5½%.

And on Capitol Hill, legislators likewise felt powerless to act. "I don't know what kind of legislative reaction you can have to a stock-market decline," said House Majority Leader Thomas Foley.

Yesterday's thunderous collapse smashed whatever life was thought still to be in the bull market of the previous five years. Stock prices more than tripled from 776.91 on Aug. 11, 1982, to the record high of 2722.42 on Aug. 25—less than two months ago. The upward drive had been largely fueled by declining inflation and interest rates. It ended as interest rates were climbing again, raising investor jitters about prospects for renewed inflation and a recession that might come sooner rather than later....

AQUINO SPEECH FOLLOWING THWARTED COUP ATTEMPT

October 20, 1987

In her first major address following the Philippines' bloodiest military coup attempt, President Corazon Aquino told an audience of more than 1,000 Filipino businessmen October 20 that "Henceforth, I shall rule directly as president."

The forceful, forty-minute address was designed to allay growing concern both at home and abroad that Aquino was unable to control either her own military or the political factions that had divided the Philippines since the ouster of former president Ferdinand Marcos in 1986.

The audience, a joint meeting of thirteen of the Philippines' most prominent business groups, reacted positively throughout the address and roared its approval when Aquino outlined steps to combat widespread labor strikes that had plagued the country during the previous weeks. Although Aquino touched on the major concerns of the business community, the speech focused on the broader issues of her governing style and the future of her presidency.

A Tumultuous Presidency

Aquino's declaration that "the honeymoon is over" was a wistful reminder of the halcyon days of national unification immediately following the dramatic defeat of Marcos. Aquino, the widow of opposition leader Benigno S. Aquino, Jr., who was assassinated in 1983 after returning to the Philippines to challenge Marcos, had enjoyed a spectacular rise in political power and personal popularity. As head of a coalition of opposition groups that included Defense Minister Juan Ponce Enrile and armed forces chief Fidel V. Ramos, Aquino drove Marcos from power following the country's disputed 1986 elections. (Historic Documents of 1984, p. 925; Historic Documents of 1986, p. 307)

The new president initially sought to govern through consensus building among the Philippines' disparate political factions. This process included reconciliation with former Marcos allies and negotiations with the communist rebels who had been waging a seventeen-year guerrilla war against the government. However, it also led to an appearance of indecisiveness on Aquino's part and led critics to liken her governing style to "living by prayer and governing by miracle."

Negotiations with the communist rebels created tension between Aquino and the military. Enrile began attacking Aquino's policies, charging that the president was giving in to communist demands and had reneged on promises to give greater authority to the military. The split culminated in November 1986, when rumors began circulating that troops loyal to Enrile were about to launch a coup that would seize power for the military and retain President Aquino as figurehead. The attempt was blocked by General Ramos, and Enrile was fired.

Buffeted by threats from within her own armed forces and by stalled negotiations with the rebels, Aquino demanded that a cease-fire agreement be reached. That cease-fire, agreed to in November 1986, continued until February 1987, when negotiations bogged down and the rebels stepped up their attacks. (Historic Documents of 1986, p. 1037)

On January 27, 1987, rebel soldiers occupied a television and radio station, in anticipation of a takeover attempt by former president Marcos. The revolt was seen as part of a larger effort by dissident military factions to derail a special constitutional election planned for February 2.

New Constitution and Legislative Elections

Despite the threats of military uprisings and anticipated attacks by communist and Moslem rebels, the new constitution was overwhelmingly approved by the Philippine people. Written by a constitutional commission appointed by Aquino, the new document replaced a provisional constitution of March 1986 that had granted Aquino dictatorial powers similar to those wielded by Marcos. The vote was a crucial test of Aquino's personal prestige and extended her term as president until 1992.

After the constitutional referendum Aquino began to harden her policy toward the rebels and right-wing terrorists aligned with dissident troops. She called for outright military victory over the rebels and continued implementation of a controversial land-redistribution program.

On May 11 the first free legislative elections since Ferdinand Marcos declared martial law in 1972 were held in the Philippines. The elections brought victories for most candidates backed by Aquino, but the outcome also further alienated both left- and right-wing opposition groups. Leaders of the National Democratic Front, the umbrella organization of the communist rebels, vowed to step up their attacks on the government. Right-wing opposition leaders, led by Enrile, a successful senatorial candidate, charged the government with election fraud and called for a nullification of the vote.

Coup Attempt

The communist rebels took their fight to the streets of downtown Manila, where a number of military officers and government officials, including cabinet secretary Jaime Ferrer, were assassinated. The urban assassination campaign paralleled the battle in the countryside, where government troops were caught in a stalemate with the New People's Army, the military wing of the Communist party. Members of the Philippine military command, frustrated by their inability to win a decisive victory, charged the government with neglecting the plight of the military.

Aquino's announcement in August of new fuel price increases touched off the broadest public protests of her eighteen-month rule. Civil unrest erupted in urban areas. Leftist union leaders called for a nationwide general strike, crippling transport throughout much of downtown Manila as police battled demonstrators. Other protests came from more moderate labor organizations and some members of the national legislature. Although Aquino tried to defuse the protests on August 26 by partially rolling back the price increase, further strikes were scheduled by the leftist groups seeking a political victory over the president.

The capital was still under tense guard on August 28 when, shortly after midnight, several hundred rebel soldiers led by officers loyal to Enrile attacked Malacanang Palace, the seat of the Philippine presidency. In heavy fighting that lasted until morning, the invaders were repulsed by security guards and soldiers under General Ramos, who remained loyal to the president. Aquino, addressing the nation from her residence adjacent to the palace, announced that she and her family were safe, although it was later learned that her son was wounded and his three bodyguards killed.

While the fighting continued in Manila, another group of about 300 dissident troops led by Col. Gregorio Honasan, a top Enrile aide, seized part of Camp Aguinaldo in Quezon City, which housed the Philippine defense ministry and armed forces headquarters. The government television and radio were also overrun by dissident forces, cutting off all official broadcast communication. Other rebel groups attacked Villamor Air Base and a private television station in the city and began their own broad-

casts nationwide before surrendering to government forces. The rebel soldiers involved in these attacks served under Colonel Honasan at Fort Magsaysay outside Manila.

Acting simultaneously in Cebu City, the second-largest urban area in the country, rebel troops under Brig. Gen. Edgardo Abenina placed the local government under house arrest. They continued to hold out pending word of the fighting at Camp Aguinaldo where Honasan and his men were under attack from government troops sent from nearby Camp Crame. The rebels were driven from their positions in Camp Aguinaldo and eventually surrendered, although Honasan escaped. By evening of August 28 most of the mutineers had been arrested and their leaders were being sought. Enrile, who would have been in position to assume control had the coup succeeded, denied any involvement with the revolt and was not charged.

The coup attempt forced Aquino to confront the problems that had spawned it. The attempt highlighted divisions between the ruling government and the armed services concerning her policies toward the communist and Moslem rebels, as well as toward the needs of the military. The labor strikes and other economic problems that had recently plagued the country also had to be addressed. But first Aquino had to put aside questions within the military and business community about her own personal resolve and willingness to govern. Her speech before the Filipino businessmen was intended to accomplish this task.

Following is the text of the speech delivered by Philippine president Corazon Aquino to Filipino business leaders in Manila October 20, 1987:

You invited me here because you say you are concerned about the Presidency, about the way things are going—or not going—in the economy, in the labor front, in politics, in the war against the communists. Above all, I am told, you are concerned about me, and my leadership.

But first: the formalities. Let me say that it is a pleasure to meet with businessmen, "the engines of economic growth," as you are referred to in all our economic plans. In the next twenty months, I hope to see many more of you, together with those who work with you, on the shop floor and in the fields of your businesses. Because it is there, where Filipinos put their shoulders to the wheel of our national economy, that our future is made.

I have to say that at the beginning because there has been more talk than work in our country today. That is a pity. Because recovery and progress won't come through talking. At this time, when all the talk is about coups and strikes, it is worth remembering that it is work, by all of us, that is going to lift us to better times. When politics gets in the way of work, we have a problem and there's been too much politics.

Let me get down to the issues that made you invite me here.

Issue number one: Government lacks a program of economy and politics.

First, the economy. It is said that government lacks a coherent plan of economy. Wrong. We have a detailed medium term plan. We are following that plan to the letter, making adjustments here and there as need arises. A lot of spirited and intelligent debate went into the making of that plan. Some people said that the over-spirited debates proved a flaw in the government. To the contrary, I thought the debates assured a better plan. The plan sets the direction this government would like the country to take. It is not set in concrete, because we do not pretend that the plan foresees every contingency. But there is a direction. If you don't like the direction, let us know. We can reopen the debate. This is a Democracy.

The state of the economy was clearly and accurately described by me in my State of the Nation Message. I recounted the disappointments we had met in our effort to revive the economy with external assistance, but I also pointed out the healthy signs in the economy. Recession bottomed out in late 1986. We posted a modest 1.5 percent GNP growth, whereas the two previous years had been negative. The reforms we had implemented improved the situation further. First quarter GNP, 1987, posted a growth of 5.5 percent. Unemployment dropped from 12 percent to 11.2. The exchange rate remained stable, but I made no promise that it was locked there with any degree of permanence. We had $2.4 billion in reserves. For the first time in three years, investments started to grow.

These were the effects of the structural reforms we had implemented. All monopolies, from sugar to sardines are gone; more than 200 items are freed from licensing, with a further 260 items to go. Price controls, whose inefficiencies and distortions always meant they hit the poor hardest, are gone. From power costs to rural credit, we have moved to reform and clean up, so that we can put the country back to work. We shall do more to deregulate all economic activities, so that the businessman is not hostage to the bureaucrat and the politician. With due regard to public health and safety, we shall move to eliminate licenses and permits to the extent possible.

I pointed out certain weaknesses in our economy—those weaknesses have been aggravated by the public reaction to the August 28 coup attempt. The reaction. Let me emphasize. Not the coup attempt. The coup was defeated by a timely decision to use maximum force. But our victory was quickly undone by another coup: of talk about fatal weakness of the government, which had roundly defeated the coup, of divisions between military and civilians although the coup was defeated by the solidarity of the two sectors. What happened?

I am not surprised that instead of backslapping Congratulations, there was hand wringing instead. For we Filipinos did it again.

Coups, successful or unsuccessful, are usually bloodless affairs. But the last attempt was one of the bloodiest anywhere in the world. Another Filipino first. But it doesn't erase the fact that the coup was roundly defeated, the perpetrators are swaying in LST's [landing ship tanks] awaiting trial, and their leaders are in hiding.

But better than defeating coups, is deterring them, and removing, or at least reducing, the reasons they get some support. The soldiers have legitimate needs that have not been met, BUT they have never been ignored by my government. We continue to scrape the barrel of our resources to give them better conditions and better equipment for the all-important task of keeping the peace and destroying our enemies. I will go back to this later.

It is said that Government has no blueprint of political development. I had a blueprint that you helped me formulate when I challenged Marcos for the possession of state power. The blueprint called for a restoration of democracy, respect for its processes, adoption of a democratic constitution, the establishment of its necessary institutions such as an independent and honorable judiciary, an accountable Executive, and a representative legislature. I came to power with a democratic blueprint that did not sit well with those who had other ideas about how power should be shared and exercised in this country, such as by a junta. I rejected those ideas and stuck to my blueprint, and I carried it out to the letter and in record time, despite numerous attempts to sidetrack me by coups and threats, all of which I defeated.

We now have a Supreme Court and revamped judiciary that no one can take exception to, that everyone lauds for its new honesty, competence and independence.

We gave the nation a Constitution that stripped me of the vast, supreme powers I held in my single hand, and got it ratified by a sweeping majority such as this nation had never experienced in its entire history. It is truly a people's Constitution and the manner of its ratification did honor once more to the great people we are so fortunate to be part of.

Pursuant to that Constitution, I called for legislative elections. There were efforts to derail those elections. The people came through again, voting in record numbers, to give us a genuinely elected and truly representative Congress.

Early next year, we shall have local elections.

Part of the blueprint called for a reorganization of the government, to make it more efficient and responsive. And I gave you, by and large, men and women of the highest integrity and competence to administer that new government.

So did I have a blueprint? You know I did. And you helped me implement it, in record time, to the astonishment of a skeptical world. More than a blueprint, it is now an accomplished end, if I can help it, a permanent fact.

Issue number two: relations with the military. In a sound democracy, civilian government and its military arm have each others [*sic*] respective roles. One makes policy, including military policy, the other enforces it. But, obviously, we have been undergoing a period of adjustment, as all our institutions, the military included, come to terms with the new democracy. Still, the facts speak for themselves. With the military, we have crushed every challenge to the supremacy of civilian authority. There was turmoil. Naturally, because neither side would give up without a fight. They fought me, I fought back. Surrender would have been neater, but it is not in me to ever yield. I want peace as much as the next person, but not at any price. Reality is never neat or nice.

The August 28 coup attempt reveals a fissure in the military. That is true. But more importantly, the determined and forceful putting down of the attempt by the military shows the triumph of professionalism. As I said, there are groups still resisting their personal and permanent loss of power and prestige, but the military as a whole demonstrated that it is firmly with, not against, the new democracy. I retain full confidence in the professional leadership of the Armed Forces.

The period since the coup offers an even more interesting lesson. For all the threats of a further coup attempt, we have actually seen a retreat from military to political action. I suspect the coup bubble is burst. Threatened coups are used to leverage the political pressure. Somebody forgot to tell them that the place of politics is not the parade ground anymore but the halls of congress. I have every confidence that their fellow officers will finally get this message through to the dwindling band of coupmakers.

Yet I know there will always be ambition. And you should know that I will always be there to stop it from getting out of hand. Those who are desperate to retrieve their lost privileges will do what they can: I will do what I must to stop them.

The third issue is the Insurgency. There is talk again about new talks with the NDF. Let me clarify that. The truce ended last February when I ordered the AFP [Armed Forces of the Philippines] to resume operations against the communist insurgents. Talk hadn't worked, so it was time to fight. And it is still fighting time. Therefore any talk of resuming talks with the NDF is unauthorized. The insurgents are daily killing our soldiers and civilians. They are destroying bridges and power lines, burning public buildings.

They blow up bridges, we rebuild them. They take down our power lines, we put them up again. All this takes a heavy toll on our economy and meager resources, but it has not and will not in any measure reduce our resolve to fight back and defeat them. The Army has orders to hunt them down and pursue the war against the insurgents with absolute vigor.

Poor as our people are, and difficult enough as it is to recover from the ravages of dictatorship, the insurgents are determined to make life worst [*sic*] for everyone. By a twisted logic, they hope that people will invite them to power so they will stop harassing them. They forget that Marcos tried the same approach with the Filipino people and is now in Hawaii regretting it. The extreme right is using the same strategy. They think that their coups, bombings and assassinations will break the people's resistance to their brand of government and make them accept peace and quiet at any price. I invite them especially to look at their mentor in Hawaii and contemplate his fate.

The war against the communists must be waged by civilians as well as by the military, by OIC's [officers in charge, in lieu of elected mayors) and by officers. I hold both responsible for the results I'm still waiting for.

Of course, military initiative[s] are not enough. Economic improvement and expanded social services rates [*sic*] the long term and final solutions. But we need military victories to buy us the time to make our programs work: to buy us the conditions in which our services can reach the people and change their lives for the better.

One month before the August 28 coup attempt, I devoted a third of my State of the Nation message to the requirements of a better fighting force, and the congress is now acting on my specific requests.

My counterinsurgency policy has always been clear. First talk, in keeping with my pledge to negotiate a peace that have [*sic*] said clearly all that needs to be said. Am I also expected to take up an M16 myself and do it, just like I went to the Fiscal's office myself to vindicate my honor?

The fourth issue you want a straight answer to is Labor. I know you believe the strike situation has become bad, nor are you willing to accept anymore the answer that [it] is the exuberance of democracy. And I don't blame you because there is something premeditated and carefully planned about this exuberance.

I opened my remarks by saying that the future of our nation will be decided on the shop floors and fields of the economy. We have to get our labor relations right. That means tolerance, fairness, respect for the law, and a shared commitment to bring progress not chaos to our nation.

The right of collective bargaining is enshrined in the constitution but so is the duty to preserve order and respect for the law. I believe we must establish a decent daily wage for all. Our working people and, beyond that, we must have a flexible wage bargaining system that reflects productivity. But I will not tolerate the abuse of any rights. I will not allow an unruly minority to use the rights of labor to improve the conditions of labor to achieve a communist victory instead. The way to power is the ballot, not the strike.

I therefore order the police and other peacekeeping authorities to give full assistance to the Labor Department to remove all illegal blockades at the factory gates.

A special peacekeeping force has been organized and is now being trained to enforce return to work orders and injunctions issued by the department, so that a response to resistance will be calibrated and reasonable in the application of force.

The Department of National Defense and the Department of Labor will finalize and sign within this week, "The Guidelines for the Conduct of the INP/AFP [Integrated National Police/Armed Forces of the Philippines] Personnel During Strikes and Lockouts."

The Labor Department has issued the guidelines to clarify the conduct of strikes and lockouts, to clarify the rights and obligations of the parties to labor disputes.

But for all that, I ask you, the business community, to do your share. Business operates for profits, and it is hard indeed for all of us to make a go of things while the economy is still struggling to recover. Our laboring class is very poor, and their lives are truly difficult. It amazes me how they survived. I ask you to search your minds and hearts, and probe your pockets, to share with your brothers and sisters in the labor sector the gains you make. Business and labor are indispensable partners in the growth of a free economy. They should act towards each other in that light. Labor has its right as much as you have yours. But in the end, what will work is not the mutual enforcement of rights so much as a mutual commitment to grow together in prosperity. That commitment has been demonstrated by the Filipino small businessman and by the Filipino/Chinese entrepreneur who appear to have no problem about this government's alleged lack of vision, because they have a 20/20 vision for the opportunities that democracy and honest government have opened up.

They know my vision of this Nation. A Nation immersed in work, and not lost in idle talk. A Nation free and at peace with itself and its neighbors: A Nation respected in the councils of the world: A Nation strong because its people are strong, healthy, well-fed, well-housed, well-educated and firm in their commitment to the rights and freedoms that are the foundation of their dignity. It is a vision we can achieve, as surely as we achieve the first: the restoration of democracy which we now enjoy.

The fifth issue I want to raise is Foreign Debt. That debt is growing even without fresh borrowing. Servicing the debt alone takes up over 40% of the budget and over 45% of our export earnings. In the next six years we shall have to pay US$ 20 billion dollars to our official and private creditors. While we will be getting only US$ 4 billion dollars in additional loans. That means we shall pay out US$ 16 billion dollars more than we will be getting.

Our policy has been very clear from the start: *growth must take priority*, for the plain and simple reason that if we have no money to pay, we can't. And if we starve the Nation of essential services, there may be no one around willing to honor the debt.

Meanwhile, I have instructed our representatives to consolidate the rescheduling agreement by November 15th. That should end speculation and remove at least one excuse for hoarding dollars.

The sixth issue is what really brought you here. The question you all really want to ask is: Can she hack it? Isn't she weak? These are the questions that were asked by all those who have openly challenged my power, authority, and resolve, and who have suffered for it. I speak of the shamefaced officers who have abandoned their followers to await trial in LST's, and the failed politicians who made the last places in the last election and are now trying to find a backdoor to power.

Well, they can forget it. Although I am a woman and physically small, I have blocked all doors to power except election in 1992.

You invited me here on the issue of Presidential leadership. The honeymoon is over, isn't it? It didn't last very long. By mid-1986, my Cabinet was getting it. By August, the attacks were hitting closer to the Presidency. And now, it is out openly against me. The Cory who could do no wrong in those early invigorating months after February 1986, is seen as having done nothing at all. Nothing, in spite of a Constitution, a Congress, and a well-thought out body of legislation that sets the direction of this nation to progress if you have the courage to follow.

Still you ask, is she weak? Again, I say, let my scattered enemies answer that.

Still you have reason to ask. For the style of government, by consultation which I hoped would get your understanding and support, has disappointed you, has given you a sense of drift. It is time again to simplify.

Henceforth, I shall rule directly as President. To the Ad Hoc Committees and Commissions created to inform me on their special areas, I now add one more: an Action Committee with a single member: ME.

A President is supposed to be above details, but it seems I must do nearly everything myself.

For a modest start, Metro Manila Governor Jejonar Binay will now turn over the responsibility and authority for collecting the garbage in Manila to OIC Mayor Mel Lopez and the other Mayors of Metro Manila. I give Mel Lopez one week to clean up the mess that's been neglected. The public should cooperate. Let's respect ourselves by not making a garbage can of our surroundings.

The Department of Public Works is directed to cover all potholes in the First District of Manila within one week and is given one week periods to fix up all the other districts in succession.

The National Power Corporation was poised to increase its rates due to the increase in the international price of crude oil. There will be no increase in power rates this year. Instead, I have directed all concerned agencies to submit immediately the necessary measure[s] to prevent this increase, which measures I will implement this week.

The PLDT [Philippine long-distance telephone company] must attend to all complaints within 24 to 48 hours, or at least apprise the subscriber that the fault is in the cable and how long it will take to fix it.

I urge the PLDT management to come up with a comprehensive program for improving service and upgrading facilities. The Central Bank, the Department of Transportation and Communications, the NTC, and the NEDA are directed to give them the fullest assistance.

I have ordered an investigation of MERALCO on the frequent brownouts, scheduled and unscheduled, that destroy industrial machinery and cut the incomes of our workers.

There is grave doubt about the seriousness of our privatization policy. There is always an excuse for government not to sell. Fine. Therefore let me make this clear:

I want government to get out of the business sector. I want it to cash in on all the investment it should never have made.

Non-performing assets listed to be sold, WILL be sold in open bid to the highest bidder. First preference goes to the bidder with the most cash up front, using, and let me emphasize this, only fresh money. Buyers who want to use the target company's own funds are obviously going to run it to the ground. The preferred procedure is open bidding. Filipinos and foreigners will compete on the same terms, subject of course to constitutional limitations. In general, ability to pay the highest price will decide conclusively. That is how PCI Bank and Associated Bank will be sold. Combank is a negotiated deal because there is only one serious bidder. I will not tie up hundreds of millions of pesos just to keep some people in their jobs.

All our hotels are up for sale. Including Manila Hotel. Foreigners are invited to bid for the allowable equity. The sale of Philippine Airlines is under serious consideration. We can't have it landing on the South Superhighway. There's enough traffic there.

The policy, in brief, is: no funny deals. No clever schemes. No fears, no favors.

If anyone says that I have made an exception for him or her, report it to the press and to me. I got a copy of an application filed with the Central Bank for the importation of 8 million cases of apples. It is signed, "Corazon Aquino, President of the Philippines," as if the signer wasn't sure if the Central Bank knew I was President. Now that's a crook who isn't going to get far. More likely, that's a piece of black propaganda that isn't going to fly. 8 million cases means more apples than there are Filipinos.

I cannot issue a directive to all the banks on this matter, but let it be known that any application of anything, apples, castanas, oranges, and guns, alleged to be signed, endorsed, supported or whatever by me or any of my kin should be reported to me and the NBI [National Bureau of Investigation].

I have heard the talk of the coffeeshops. I am addressing your concern about graft and corruption in government. I have directed the Special Prosecutor's Office and the NBI to give first priority to the investigation and prosecution of graft and corruption cases against senior government officials, including the members of my Cabinet.

I am not sorry the honeymoon is over. The sooner we get over the fantasy of the honeymoon and face the hard work of marriage—the marriage of President and nation—the better.

I recently read a formulation of Presidential leadership by Hedley Donovan: "The honesty of Abraham Lincoln, the intelligence of Henry Kissinger and the soothing TV personality of Marcus Welby/Robert Young." He goes on to quote approvingly a former US Congressman who said: "The President should like his fellow man, and he should have read Machiavelli." Transposed to this country, you might say the ideal President would have the courage of Abad Santos, the intelligence of Diokno, the charisma of Magsaysay, and the love of country, of men and women and children who converged on EDSA [Epifanio de los Santos Avenue, the Manila street where "people power" demonstrations took place] in February '86.

That's quite a tall order, and it is no surprise that the ideal President has never lived and is defined by the traits of different leaders facing different challenges in different times.

I do just fine on the honesty and liking my fellowmen, although recently there have been exceptions. But there is no regret on my part if there is not much of Machiavelli. I don't have all those qualities. Some of my enemies, who contributed to the mess left by the previous government, claim to possess them. Maybe, but they lack the one quality I alone have: election to the Presidency and a mandate for my principles and policies that has been tested in a massive voter's registration, a plebiscite, a sweeping electoral victory for the Congress, and in five coups that were handily beaten by me and my forces. They lack the one thing the people will never give them: trust.

I do not have all the qualities of the ideal president who never existed. But I have the qualities for the leadership of our nation in these times. After years of stealing, degradation and abuse from our leaders, the Filipino people made a clear choice. They wanted a leader whose honesty and commitment to them would never be in doubt: who would not clamp down but rather open up the country so that all could be heard: and who would bind our wounds so that we could, as One Nation, work together to overcome our common crisis of economic decline.

I expect sniping from yesterday's men, passed over as they are, by the march of history. To all other Filipinos, though, I say the tide is with us. Together our future can be as bright as we choose to make it. So judge my leadership as the sum of all our strengths. What sets me apart is that I bring us together where others would divide us as a nation. Those who challenge me, challenge us.

The last time I spoke here before you, I left you with a slogan that carried us to victory. I leave you with this:

SOBRA NA ANG KOMUNISTA
TAMA NA SA KUDETA
IPAGLABAN AND DEMOKRASYA.*

* Enough of the Communists! Stop Coup d'etats [*sic*] ! Fight for Democracy!

November

GORBACHEV SPEECH ON BOLSHEVIK ANNIVERSARY

November 2, 1987

Marking the 70th anniversary of the Bolshevik revolution, Soviet Communist party leader Mikhail Gorbachev delivered a speech at the Kremlin November 2 in which he sought to bring his own interpretation to recent Soviet history. Criticizing Joseph Stalin, general secretary of the Soviet Communist party from 1922 until his death in 1953, Gorbachev said the Soviet strongman had been guilty of "enormous and unforgivable" crimes. In his speech Gorbachev revived the reputations of former Soviet leader Nikita Khrushchev and of Nikolai Bukharin, an associate of Stalin and V. I. Lenin (the father of the Soviet state).

Gorbachev's long-awaited speech was closely watched by Soviet observers for several reasons. The Soviet leader had been out of sight for a month during the summer, and some analysts suggested that his plan for economic and political restructuring, called perestroika, *might have been in jeopardy. Faced with conservative opposition, Gorbachev had shown signs of tempering his drive for change, a move greeted with alarm by some reform-minded liberals. (Gorbachev's long "vacation" had apparently been devoted to outlining his program in a book, published in the West in the fall.)*

A New Look at Soviet History

Gorbachev staked out the middle ground, urging steady but gradual change and a partial reexamination of history. While criticizing Stalin's repressive rule, Gorbachev praised Stalin's leadership during World War II. Khrushchev, the Soviet premier from 1953 until he was forced out in

1964, was singled out for his "courage" as a reformer, although Gorbachev criticized him for "capricious behavior" and failure to carry out reforms.

Gorbachev also praised Bukharin and Stalin for rebuffing outside challenges to Soviet rule during the regime's early years. Bukharin, who favored a more liberal economic policy than that of Stalin, was shot for treason in 1938. "Even now, there are still attempts to turn away from painful matters in our history, to hush them up and to make believe that nothing special happened," said Gorbachev, who urged a "moment of reflection" on past Soviet mistakes.

But in assessing the speech's revision of history, some Soviet watchers said Gorbachev did not go far enough, particularly in light of his policy of greater openness, or glasnost. *"Some expected it to be a radical review of history. Others expected he would just scratch the surface. I expected something in between, and that's about where it came out," Soviet historian Roy Medvedev told the* New York Times.

The Future of 'Perestroika' and Reform

Gorbachev's cautious tone reflected some of the turmoil in the Soviet leadership. Two weeks before the speech, Moscow party chief Boris Yeltsin had criticized the slow pace of economic reforms and blamed privileged bureaucrats, alarming high-ranking colleagues. During his speech, Gorbachev addressed this criticism, noting that the Soviets must not "succumb to the pressure of the overly zealous and impatient." The line apparently was directed at Yeltsin, who was removed from office soon after the Gorbachev speech.

*Still, Gorbachev was adamant about pursuing his agenda of change. '*Perestroika *implies not only eliminating the stagnation and conservatism of the preceding period, and correcting the mistakes committed, but also overcoming historically limited, outdated features of social organization and work methods," Gorbachev said. He praised the policy, which contained some aspects of democracy, as a natural extension of socialist ideology, a "second wind" for the Soviet system.*

He also found historical precedent for his economic reforms from Lenin. During the 1920s, Lenin's New Economic Policy provided a dose of capitalism in agriculture, offering personal incentives and some free enterprise. Gorbachev's proposed reforms had a similar objective: "loosening the creative energy of the masses, enhancing the initiative of the individual and removing the bureaucratic trammels that limited the operation of socialism's basic principle, 'From each according to his abilities, to each according to his work.'" (Gorbachev on democratic reforms, p. 79; Historic Documents of 1986, p. 145)

In the two-hour, forty-one-minute speech, Gorbachev also touched on issues in superpower relations, saying he would seek accord with President Ronald Reagan on reducing long-range nuclear weapons and ban-

ning space weapons. He also said the era of conflict between communism and capitalism was giving way to a new spirit of cooperation. Gorbachev offered these conciliatory comments as he was preparing for his December summit meeting with Reagan in Washington, D.C. (Gorbachev-Reagan summit, p. 991)

Despite the speech's balanced tone, some Soviet observers said it showed that Gorbachev maintained control of his country and his government. The last time a Soviet leader criticized Stalin and the Soviet past—Khrushchev in a 1956 speech—the talk was given in secret. In the new spirit of openness, Gorbachev's speech was given to 5,000 top Soviet officials and was nationally televised. "If, at times, we scrutinize our history with a critical eye, we do so only because we want to obtain a better and fuller idea of the ways that lead to the future," the Soviet leader explained.

> *Following are excerpts from Mikhail S. Gorbachev's November 2, 1987, speech, "The October and* Perestroika: *The Revolution Continues," delivered before the Central Committee of the Soviet Communist party, the Supreme Soviet, and the Russian Federation on the 70th anniversary of the 1917 October Revolution:*

...It is seventy years since the unforgettable days of October 1917, those legendary days that started the count of the new epoch of social progress, of the real history of humankind.

The October Revolution is truly the shining hour of humanity, its radiant dawn. The October Revolution is a revolution of the people and for the people, for every individual, for his emancipation and development.

Seventy years is not a long time in world civilization's ascent over the centuries, but history has known no other period like it for the scale of the achievements that our country has attained since the victory of the October Revolution.

There is no greater honor than to be pioneers, devoting one's strength, energy, knowledge, and ability to the triumph of the October Revolution's ideals and goals.

The jubilee moment of pride, pride in what has been achieved. Arduous trials fell to our lot. And we withstood them honorably. We did not simply withstand them, but wrested the country out of its state of dislocation and backwardness, and made it a great power, transforming life and changing man's inner world beyond recognition....

The year 1917 absorbed the energy of the people's struggle for self-sustained development and independence, of the progressive national movements, and the peasant uprisings and wars against serfdom abounding in our history.

It embodied the spirited search of the eighteenth century enlighteners, the heroes and martyrs of the Decembrist Movement, the splendid champions of revolutionary democracy, and the moral dedication of the eminent men of our culture.

Crucial for the future of our country was the time when at the dawn of the twentieth century, Vladimir Ilyich Lenin put himself at the head of a close-knit group of comrades and set out to organize a proletarian party of the new type in Russia. It was this great party of Lenin that roused the nation, its best and most devoted forces, for an assault on the old world....

Let's recall the July days of 1917. It was a painful moment when the party was compelled to give up the slogan of all power to the Soviets. But there was no other choice, because the Soviets had, for a while, fallen into the hands of Socialist-Revolutionaries and Mensheviks, and were helpless in face of the counterrevolution.

And how sensitively Lenin kept his finger on the pulse of the revolution, how brilliantly he determined the beginning of a new revival of the Soviets. They were acquiring a truly popular essence in the process of struggle, which enabled them to become the organs of a victorious armed uprising, and then also the political form of worker-peasant power.

All those are not simply pages in the chronicle of the great revolution. They are also a constant reminder to us ... of the lofty duty of communists to be always in the vanguard of events, to be able to take bold decisions to assume full responsibility for the present and future.

The October Revolution was a powerful surge of millions of people that combined the vital interests of the working class, the everlasting aspirations of the peasantry, the thirst for peace of soldiers and sailors, and the unconquerable striving of the peoples of multinational Russia for freedom and knowledge....

The main purpose of the October Revolution was to build a new life. Such building did not cease for a single day. Even the short respite was used to continue building and to look for ways leading to the socialist future.

The early 1920s were highlighted by a spectacular surge of popular initiative and creativity. They were a truly revolutionary laboratory of social innovation, of a search for the optimum forms of the workers' alliance with the working peasantry, and the shaping of a mechanism for attaining the whole spectrum of the working people's interests.

From organizing production and consumption by methods of war communism necessitated by war and dislocation, the party went over to more flexible, economically justified, "regular" instruments of influencing social reality.

The measures of the New Economic Policy were directed toward building socialism's material foundation.

These days we turn ever more often to the last works of Lenin, to Lenin's New Economic Policy, and we strive to extract from those ideas all the valuable elements that we require today.

Certainly it would be a mistake to equate the New Economic Policy and what we are doing now at a fundamentally new level of development.

Today there are none of those individual peasants in the country with whom to shape an alliance, which determined the most vital aims of the economic policy of the 1920s.

But the New Economic Policy also had a more distant target. The task had been set of building the new society "not directly relying on enthusiasm," as Lenin wrote, "but aided by the enthusiasm engendered by the Great Revolution, and on the basis of personal interests, personal incentives and business principles . . . that is what experience, the objective course of the development of the revolution, has taught us."

Speaking of the creative potential of the New Economic Policy, we should evidently refer once more to the political and methodological wealth of ideas underlying the food tax.

To be sure, we are interested not in the forms of those days that had been meant to secure a bond between workers and peasants, but the potentialities of the food tax idea in loosening the creative energy of the masses, enhancing the initiative of the individual, and removing the bureaucratic trammels that limited the operation of socialism's basic principle, "from each according to his abilities, to each according to his work." . . .

The period after Lenin—that is, the 1920s and 1930s—occupied a special place in the history of the Soviet state. Radical social changes were carried out in some fifteen years. An incredible lot was squeezed into that period—both from the point of view of search for optimum variants of socialist construction, and from the point of view of what was really achieved in building the foundations of the new society.

Those were years of hard work to the limits of human endurance, of sharp and multifarious struggle. Industrialization, collectivization, the cultural revolution, strengthening of the multinational state, consolidation of the Soviet Union's international positions, new forms of managing the economy and all social affairs—all this occurred within that period. And all of it had far-reaching consequences.

For decades, we have been returning to that time again and again. This is natural. Because that was when the world's first socialist society . . . was being built. It was an exploit on a historical scale and of historic significance. Admiration for the exploits of our fathers and grandfathers and the assessments of our real achievements will live forever. . . .

And if, at times, we scrutinize our history with a critical eye, we do so only because we want to obtain a better and fuller idea of the ways that lead to the future. . . .

There is now much discussion about the role of Stalin in our history. His was an extremely contradictory personality. To remain faithful to historical truth we have to see both Stalin's incontestable contribution to the struggle for socialism, to the defense of its gains, the gross political errors, and the abuses committed by him and by those around him, for which our people paid a heavy price and which had grave consequences for the life of our society.

It is sometimes said that Stalin did not know of many instances of lawlessness. Documents at our disposal show that this is not so. The guilt of Stalin and his immediate entourage before the party and the people for the wholesale repressive measures and acts of lawlessness is enormous and unforgiveable. This is a lesson for all generations.

Contrary to the assertions of our ideological opponents, the Stalin personality cult was certainly not inevitable. It was alien to the nature of socialism, represented a departure from its fundamental principles, and, therefore, has no justification.

At its 20th and 22nd Congresses the party severely condemned the cult itself and its consequences. We now know that the political accusations and repressive measures against a number of party leaders and statesmen, against communists and nonparty people, against economic executives and military men, against scientists and cultural personalities were a result of deliberate falsification.

Many accusations were later, especially after the 20th Party Congress, withdrawn. Thousands of innocent victims were completely exonerated.

But the process of restoring justice was not seen through to the end and was actually suspended in the middle of the sixties. Now, in line with a decision taken by the October 1987 Plenary Meeting of the Central Committee, we are having to return to this.

The Politburo of the Central Committee has set up a commission for comprehensively examining new facts and documents pertaining to these matters, and those known previously. Corresponding decisions will be taken on the basis of the commission's findings.

All this will also be reflected in a treatise on the history of the Communist Party of the Soviet Union, whose preparation is to be entrusted to a special commission of the Central Committee. This is something we have to do, the more so since even now there are still attempts to turn away from painful matters in our history, to hush them up, to make believe that nothing special happened.

We cannot agree to this. This would be disregard for the historical truth, disrespect for the memory of those who were innocent victims of lawless and arbitrary actions. Another reason why we cannot agree to this is that a truthful analysis must help us to solve today's problems of democratization, legality, openness, overcoming bureaucracy, in short, the vital problems of *perestroika,* or reorganization. . . .

An honest understanding of our enormous achievements as well as of past misfortunes, their full and true political evaluation, will provide real moral guidelines for the future. . . .

The Great Patriotic War brought out to the full the talent of outstanding military leaders who emerged from the midst of the people—Georgi Zhukov, Konstantin Rokossovsky, Alexander Vasilevsky, Ivan Konev, and other distinguished marshals, generals and officers—those who commanded fronts and armies, corps, divisions and regiments, companies and platoons.

A factor in the achievement of victory was the tremendous political will, purposefulness and persistence, ability to organize and discipline people displayed in the war years by Joseph Stalin.

But the brunt of the war was borne by the ordinary Soviet soldier—a great toiler of the people's own flesh and blood, valiant and devoted to his country. Every honor and eternal glory to him!...

When the war ended, our ill-wishers predicted an economic decline in our country and its dropping out of world politics for a long time. They considered that it would take us half a century, if not more, to cope with the aftermath of the war.

But within an extremely short period of time the Soviet people had rebuilt the war-ravaged towns and villages, and raised from their ruins factories and mills, collective and state farms, schools, and colleges, and cultural institutions.

And once again this was a manifestation of the great strength of the socialist state: the will of the party motivated by an understanding of the supreme interests of the land of the October Revolution; the staunchness and proletarian wisdom of the workers, who had shouldered the main burden of the peaceful transformation of the country's industrial might and of repairing the ravages of war, and the self-sacrifice, patience, and patriotism of the farmers, who gave up everything they had to feed the ruined country....

But during this very same time—a time of new exploits by the people in the name of socialism—a contradiction between what our society had become and the old methods of leadership was making itself felt ever more appreciably.

Abuse of power and violations of socialist legality continued. The "Leningrad case" and the "doctors' case" were fabricated. In short, there was a deficit of genuine respect for the people.

People were devotedly working, studying, seeking new knowledge, accepting difficulties and shortages, but sensing that alarm and hope were building up in society. And all this gripped the public consciousness soon after Stalin's death.

In the middle of the fifties, especially after the 20th Congress of the Communist Party, a wind of change swept the country, the people's spirits rose, they took heart, became bolder and more confident. It required no small courage of the party and its leadership, headed by Nikita Khrushchev, to criticize the personality cult and its consequences, and to re-establish socialist legality.

The old stereotypes in domestic and foreign policy began to crumble. Attempts were made to break down the command-bureaucratic methods of administration established in the thirties and the forties, to make socialism more dynamic, to emphasize humanitarian ideals and values, and to revive the creative spirit of Leninism in theory and practice.

The desire to change the priorities of economic development, to bring into play incentives related to a personal interest in work results keynoted the decisions of the September 1953 and July 1955 Plenary Meetings of the Party Central Committee.

More attention began to be devoted to the development of agriculture, housing, the light industry, the sphere of consumption, and to everything related to satisfying human needs.

In short, there were changes for the better—in Soviet society and in international relations. However, no small number of subjectivist errors were committed, and they handicapped socialism's advance to a new stage, moreover doing much to discredit progressive initiatives.

The fact is that fundamentally new problems of domestic and foreign policies, and of party development, were often being solved by voluntaristic methods, with the aid of the old political and economic mechanism.

But the failures of the reforms undertaken in that period were mainly due to the fact that they were not backed up by a broad development of democratization processes....

The March and September 1965 Plenary Meetings of the Party Central Committee formulated new approaches to economic management. An economic reform, and big programs for developing new areas and promoting the productive forces, were worked out and began to be put into effect.

In the first few years this changed the situation in the country for the better. The economic and scientific potential was increasing, the defense capacity was being strengthened, the standard of living was rising. Many foreign policy moves enhanced the international prestige of our state. Strategic parity with the USA was achieved.

The country had at its disposal extensive resources for further accelerating its development. But to utilize these resources and put them to work, cardinal new changes were needed in society and, of course, the corresponding political will. There was a shortage of the one and the other. And even much of what had been decided remained on paper.... The pace of our development was substantially retarded....

It was in response to this extremely acute social need that the April 1985 Plenary Meeting of the Central Committee put forward the concept and strategy of accelerating the country's socioeconomic development, and the course aimed at a renewal of socialism. These were given more elaborate theoretical and political formulation in the decisions of the 27th Party Congress and subsequent plenary meetings of the Central Committee, and they assumed final shape in the general policy of a revolutionary reorganization of all aspects of socialist society's life.

The idea of *perestroika* rests upon our seventy-year history, on the sound foundation of the basically new social edifice erected in the Soviet Union. It combines continuity and innovation, the historical experience of Bolshevism and the contemporaneity of socialism....

Perestroika implies not only eliminating the stagnation and conservatism of the preceding period, and correcting the mistakes committed, but overcoming historically limited, outdated features of social organization and work methods.

It implies imparting to socialism the most contemporary forms, corresponding to the conditions and needs of the scientific, technological revolution, and to the intellectual progress of Soviet society.

This is a relatively lengthy process of the revolutionary renewal of society, a process that has its logic and stages.

Lenin saw the historical mission of socialism in the need to prepare by many years of effort for the transition to communism. The leader of the Revolution spoke highly of the ability of Marx and Engels "to analyze the traditional forms with the utmost thoroughness in order to establish, in accordance with the concrete historical peculiarities of each particular case, from what and to what the given transitional form is passing."

In short, our teachers warned us repeatedly that the path of building the new society is a long series of transitions.

We have every reason to view *perestroika* as a definite historical stage in the forward movement of our society. And in reply to Lenin's question "from what and to what" we are passing, it must be said quite definitely: We have to impart to socialism a new quality or, as they say, a second wind, and this requires a profound renewal of all aspects of society's life, both material and spiritual, and the development of the humanitarian character of our system to the fullest possible extent.

The purpose of *perestroika* is the full theoretical and practical reestablishment of Lenin's conception of socialism, in which indisputable priority belongs to the working man with his ideals and interests, to humanitarian values in the economy, in social and political relations, and in culture.

Our hope of achieving revolutionary purification and renewal requires tapping the enoromous social potentialities of socialism by invigorating the individual, the human factor.

As a result of *perestroika* socialism can and must make full use of its potentialities as a truly humanitarian system, serving and elevating man. . . .

The purpose of the radical economic reform begun in the country is to assure, over the next two or three years, a transition from an overly centralized command system of management to a democratic system based mainly on economic methods and on an optimal combination of centralism and self-management.

This presupposes a sharp expansion of the autonomy of enterprises and associations, their transition to the principle of profitability and self-financing, and the investment of work collectives with all the powers necessary for this.

The economic reform is no longer just plans and intentions, still less abstract theoretical discourses. It is becoming a part of life.

Today a considerable number of enterprises and associations in industry, construction, transport, and agriculture are working on the principles of self-maintenance and self-finance.

From the beginning of next year enterprises producing 60 per cent of our industrial output will be operating on this basis. The Law on State Enterprise (association) will have become effective.

All this is already having an effect on practical economic activity. In the work collectives there is a noticeably growing interest in financial and economic performance. They are beginning to really count inputs and outputs, to save in things big and small, and to find the most effective ways of dealing with problems.

Today we must once again firmly say: The party will tolerate no departures from the adopted principles of the economic reform. All the changes planned must be and will be implemented in full....

But we can see that some cities, districts and regions, and even some republics have not yet got down to *perestroika* in earnest. This is a direct result of political and organizational inertia and lack of initiative displayed by party committees and their leaders. This must be seen as well. This is one of our realities as well.

A turn for the better is a special responsibility that now rests on the grassroots party organizations. They are in fact the terminals of all the wires of *perestroika*.

It is the initiative of the grassroots party organizations on which the progress of the transformations, the skill in mobilizing and inspiring people, and the ability to achieve tangible improvements depend above all.

To sum up, comrades, *perestroika* will not succeed without a drastic invigoration of the activities of all party organizations.

And so we must have a more businesslike and a more democratic attitude, we must improve organization and tighten discipline. Then we will be able to put *perestroika* into higher gear and impart a new impetus to socialism in its development....

The April 1985 Plenary Meeting of the CPSU Central Committee was a landmark in the development of Leninist thought along this line too. The new concept of foreign policy was presented in detail at the Twenty-seventh Congress.

As you know, this concept proceeds from the idea that for all the profound contradictions of the contemporary world, for all the radical differences among the countries that comprise it, it is interrelated, interdependent and integral.

The reasons for this include the internationalization of world economic ties, the comprehensive scope of the scientific and technological revolution, the essentially novel role played by the mass media, the state of the earth's resources, the common environmental danger, and the crying social problems of the developing world which affect us all.

The main reason, however, is the problem of human survival. This problem is now with us because the development of nuclear weapons and the threatening prospect of their use have called into question the very survival of the human race....

The October 1986 meeting in Reykjavik ranks among the events which have occurred since the new stage in international affairs began, which deserve to be mentioned on this occasion and which will go down in history.

The Reykjavik meeting gave a practical boost to the new political thinking, enabled it to gain ground in diverse social and political quarters, and made international political contacts more fruitful.

The new thinking, with its regard for universal human values and emphasis on common sense and openness, is forging ahead on the international scene, destroying the stereotypes of anti-Sovietism and dispelling distrust of our initiatives and actions.

It is true that, gauged against the scope of the tasks mankind will have to tackle to ensure its survival, very, very little has so far been accomplished. But a beginning has been made, and the first signs of change are in evidence.

This is borne out, among other things, by the understanding we have reached with the United States on concluding, in the near future, an agreement on medium- and shorter-range missiles.

The conclusion of this agreement is very important in itself: It will, for the first time, eliminate a whole class of nuclear weapons, be the first tangible step along the path of scrapping nuclear arsenals, and will show that it is in fact possible to advance in this direction without prejudice to anyone's interests.

That is obviously a major success of the new way of thinking, a result of our readiness to search for mutually acceptable solutions while strictly safeguarding the principle of equal security.

However, the question concerning this agreement was largely settled back in Reykjavik, at my second meeting with the U.S. President.

In this critical period the world expects the third and fourth Soviet-U.S. summits to produce more than merely an official acknowledgment of the decisions agreed upon a year ago, and more than merely a continuation of the discussion. The growing danger that weapons may be perfected to a point where they will become uncontrollable is urging us to waste no time.

That is why we will work unremittingly at these meetings for a palpable breakthrough, for concrete results in reducing strategic offensive armaments and barring weapons from outer space—the key to removing the nuclear threat. . . .

Slightly more than 13 years are left before the beginning of the twenty-first century. In the year 2017 the Soviet people and the whole of progressive humanity will mark the centenary of the great October Revolution.

What is the world going to be like when it reaches our revolution's centenary? What is socialism going to be like? What degree of maturity will have been attained by the world community of states and peoples? Let us not indulge in guessing. But let us remember that the foundations for the future are being laid today.

It is our duty to preserve our inimitable civilization and life on earth, to help reason win over nuclear insanity, and to create all the necessary conditions for the free and all-round development of the individual and the whole of humanity.

We are aware that there is a possibility for continuous progress. We realize that it is not easy to ensure it. But this does not frighten us. On the contrary, this inspires us, giving a lofty and humane purpose to our life and injecting it with a profound meaning.

In October 1917 we parted with the old world, rejecting it once and for all. We are moving toward a new world, the world of communism. We shall never turn off that road.

ARAB SUMMIT COMMUNIQUE

November 11, 1987

The twenty-one-member Arab League met in an emergency session in Amman, Jordan, November 8-11. The four-day summit attended by sixteen heads of state was held in response to growing Arab concern over the war between Iraq and Iran.

The league, often divided by ideological, regional, and economic differences, agreed to allow members to reestablish diplomatic relations with Egypt, which had been a pariah in the Arab world since its 1979 peace treaty with Israel. At the end of the meeting the group issued a surprisingly tough resolution attacking Iran for "occupying part of the Iraqi territory and its procrastination in accepting UN Security Council Resolution 598." The UN resolution had called for the combatants to observe a cease-fire in the seven-year-old war. (UN resolution, p. 609)

The results of the summit surprised Middle East experts and even Arab diplomats, who had expected a less unified response to the Iranian threat. The bitter feud between Syrian president Hafez Assad, a supporter of Iran, and Iraqi president Saddam Hussein appeared to rule out a consensus.

In addition, the decisions by several heads of state, most notably King Fahd of Saudi Arabia, not to attend seemed to deflate the meeting's prestige. Saudi Arabia was represented by Crown Prince Abdullah. Libyan leader Colonel Muammar al-Qaddafi also announced that he would not attend because the summit was an event "dictated by America and held specifically to combat Iran." The absence of Fahd and Qaddafi, however, may have made reaching a consensus easier. Qaddafi was a strident supporter of Iran, and King Fahd's absence enhanced the leadership role of the host, King Hussein of Jordan, a strong advocate of Arab unity and reconciliation with Egypt.

Accomplishments of the Summit

King Hussein opened the summit November 8 with a speech to a closed session of Arab leaders. He called for greater cooperation in the Arab world, the reentry of Egypt into the Arab League, and a unified response to Iran. The same day, Iran fired a missile that struck a residential section of Baghdad and killed several civilians.

Although at the outset Hafez Assad and Saddam Hussein refused to shake hands or speak to one another, they eventually settled down to the business of negotiation. They discussed their differences in the presence of other Arab leaders and by the third day began to show signs of flexibility.

On November 10 the summit agreed to open the way for individual Arab states to reestablish diplomatic relations with Egypt. The final communiqué issued on November 11 declared that "diplomatic relations between any Arab League member state and the Arab Republic of Egypt is a sovereign act decided by each state in accordance with its constitution and laws." Syria, which in the past had been able to veto any movement to rehabilitate Egypt, agreed to the decision under pressure from Saudi Arabia, Kuwait, Jordan, and other moderate Arab states. Syrian officials indicated, however, that they would block any attempt to invite Egypt to rejoin the Arab League.

The main focus of the final communiqué, however, was the Iran-Iraq war. In addition to chastising Tehran for its pursuit of the war in the face of international condemnation, the statement denounced Iran's "aggression" against Kuwait, declared the League's solidarity with Iraq, and called upon the international community to "adopt the necessary measures to make the Iranian regime respond to the peace calls."

The summit was also notable for its slight attention to the Arab-Israeli conflict. Since the establishment of Israel in 1948, Arab relations with the Jewish state and the Palestinian question had been primary issues of every Arab League summit. Iran's determination to continue its war with Iraq, its deadly attacks on shipping in the Persian Gulf, and its attempts to export its version of Moslem fundamentalism had caused moderate Arab leaders to regard Iran as the most immediate threat. The Arab-Israeli conflict was discussed, but it was clearly a secondary concern.

Motivations of Arab Leaders

The summit's decision to allow members to reestablish relations with Cairo was a recognition of Egypt's importance to the Arab world.

Following its 1979 treaty with Israel, Egypt had been expelled from the Arab League. Of the twenty-one Arab League nations, only Oman, Somalia, and the Sudan maintained full diplomatic relations. In 1985 Jordan and Djibouti reestablished diplomatic ties with Egypt. The growing threat from Iran, however, prompted Arab leaders to reconsider Egypt's role in Middle East politics. Egypt, with 50 million of the 185 million people in the Arab world, was easily the most populous Arab nation. Egypt's 500,000 troops also constituted the largest standing army of any Arab state.

Arab leaders became convinced that Egypt's military and economic strength was needed as a counterweight to Iran. Even before the Arab summit, Egypt had been contributing substantially to Iraq's war effort. It had supplied the Iraqis with about $1 billion of military hardware each year and had allowed 1 million Egyptians to move to Iraq to fill jobs left vacant by military conscription. Although an Egyptian-Iraqi alliance was unlikely, the possibility that Egyptian troops could be deployed in Iraq or elsewhere in the Persian Gulf area was seen as a check against Iranian ambitions.

Arab diplomats cited several reasons for Syria's agreeing to condemn Iran. First, moderate Arab nations had formed a strong majority in favor of the action, and President Assad did not want to become isolated and thereby lose his position as a key player in the Middle East. Second, Assad hoped to satisfy his fellow Arabs without offending Iran, which had been providing Syria with subsidized oil in return for Syrian support. His acquiescence to the anti-Iran resolution did not require his nation to take any concrete action against Iran. Third, Assad wanted to ensure the continuation of the Saudi Arabian and Kuwaiti financial aid programs that had become critical to the Syrian economy.

Aftermath of the Summit

In the days after the Arab summit, Syria and Iraq halted their propaganda war. Nevertheless, the Syrian foreign minister emphasized that his country's support of the final communiqué did not change its close relationship with Iran. He claimed that Syria was "against condemning Iran because [Iran] wasn't the beginner of the war."

Immediately after the summit the United Arab Emirates announced its intention to resume diplomatic relations with Egypt. Within a few weeks eight other nations, including Saudi Arabia, Kuwait, and Iraq, followed suit. On January 9, 1988, Egyptian president Hosni Mubarak began a tour of six Persian Gulf nations. The trip signaled the return of Egypt as an active influence in Arab diplomacy. During his trip, Mubarak conferred with Persian Gulf leaders on security issues and gathered support for his trip to the United States in late January. While in Washington, he was expected to lobby President Ronald Reagan to press Israel to move toward a solution of the Palestinian issue.

Following is the text of the final communiqué of the Arab League meeting in Amman, Jordan, issued November 11, 1987:

Pursuant to the will of the Arab countries' leaders expressed in the resolution the Arab League Council adopted in its extraordinary session which resumed in Tunis on 26 Muharram 1408 Hegira, corresponding to September 20, 1987, and in response to an invitation from His Majesty King Hussein Bin Talal, King of the Hashemite Kingdom of Jordan, the Jordanian capital of Amman hosted an extraordinary session of the Arab summit which convened from 17-20 Rabi' Al-Awwal 1408, corresponding to November 8-11, 1987.

From the premise of our historical responsibility and pan-Arab principles; based on the relations of brotherhood and the interconnection of security, political, and economic interests and the interconnection of history and civilization; out of an awareness of the sensitive and difficult stage the Arab homeland is experiencing and of the challenges against the Arab homeland's present and future which pose a threat to its existence; and realizing that the state of division and fragmentation causes a weakness that dissipates the Arab nation's resources and exhausts its potentialities, the issue of Arab solidarity has been the focus of the Arab leaders' attention. They discussed its various aspects, and pinpointed its weak and strong points. They stressed the need to support and enhance it, and allotted it priority. Their viewpoints were in agreement on this issue, and they agreed that Arab solidarity is the only means to achieve the Arab nation's dignity and pride and to ward off danger and harm from it. The leaders unanimously agreed to overcome differences and to eliminate the causes of weakness and the factors of dismemberment and division. From the premise of their loyalty to their homeland and their genuine affiliation to their nationalism, they decided to adopt Arab solidarity as a basis for a joint Arab action whose objective is to embody the unity of their stand, build the capabilities of the Arab nation, and provide it with factors of strength and impregnability.

After listening to His Majesty King Hussein's speech at the first closed session of the summit, the leaders decided to consider the speech in which His Majesty launched the slogan of reconciliation and accord as the title of the summit and an official document of the summit. They reiterated their abidance by the need to support Arab-African cooperation. They condemned the terrorism and racial discrimination which the racist regime in South Africa is carrying out. They also reiterated their support for the struggle of the people in South Africa and Namibia.

In adherence to the Arab League Charter, the Collective Arab Defense Pact, and the Arab Solidarity Charter; to emphasize the determination to protect pan-Arab security and to safeguard the Arab territory; and in an atmosphere filled with the spirit of fraternity and love which prevailed at the Amman summit, the Iraq-Iran war and the situation in the gulf region topped the summit agenda. The leaders expressed their concern over the continuation of the war and expressed their dissatisfaction with the Iranian regime's insistence on continuing it and on going too far in provoking and threatening the Arabian Gulf states. The conference condemned Iran for occupying part of the Iraqi territory and its procrastination in accepting UN Security Council Resolution Number 598. The conferees called on Iran to accept and fully implement this resolution in accordance with the sequence of its clauses. They appealed to the international community to assume its responsibilities, exert effective efforts, and adopt the necessary measures to make the Iranian regime respond to the peace calls. The conference also announced its solidarity with Iraq and its appreciation for its acceptance of Security Council Resolution Number 598 and its response to all peace initiatives. It also stressed its solidarity with and support for Iraq in protecting its territory and waters, and in defending its legitimate rights.

The leaders reviewed the developments in the gulf area and the serious consequences resulting from Iranian threats, provocations and aggressions. The conference announced its solidarity with Kuwait in confronting the Iranian regime's aggression. It also denounced the bloody criminal incidents perpetrated by Iranians in the Holy Mosque of Mecca. The conference affirmed its support for Kuwait in all of the measures it has taken to protect its territory and waters, and to guarantee its security and stability. The conference announced its support for Kuwait in confronting the Iranian regime's threats and aggressions.

The conference also affirmed its complete support for Saudi Arabia and its full support for the measures taken by Saudi Arabia to provide a suitable atmosphere so that the pilgrims can perform pilgrimage rites in peace and humility, and to prevent any encroachment on the sanctity of the Holy Mosque and Muslims' feelings. The leaders affirmed their rejection of any riotous acts in the holy places that would violate pilgrims' security and safety and encroach on the sovereignty of Saudi Arabia. The conference calls on the Islamic countries and governments to adopt this stand and to stand against the incorrect practices which contradict Islamic teachings.

The conference also discussed the Arab-Israeli conflict and reviewed its developments in the Arab and international areas. The conference reiterated that the Palestinian question is the essence and basis of the conflict, and that peace in the Middle East can only be achieved through regaining all occupied Arab territory, particularly Jerusalem; through restoring the Palestinian peoples' national, inalienable rights; and through resolving the Palestinian issue in all its aspects.

The summit announces that reinforcing the Arabs' capability, building their intrinsic strength, entrenching their solidarity, and embodying the unity of their stands are essential factors to confront the Israeli danger threatening the entire Arab nation and exposing its existence and future to harm and danger. Within the framework of supporting peaceful efforts and attempts to achieve a just, permanent peace in the Middle East within international legitimacy and UN resolutions on the basis of regaining all the occupied Arab and Palestinian territories and the Palestinian people's national inalienable rights, the leaders support the convocation of an international peace conference under UN auspices and the participation of all the concerned parties, including the PLO, the Palestinian people's sole, legitimate representative, on an equal footing, as well as the permanent Security Council members. This is because the international conference is the only appropriate means to resolve the Arab-Israeli conflict in a peaceful, just and comprehensive settlement.

The leaders express deep admiration and appreciation to the Palestinian people in the occupied Arab territories and praise their steadfastness, struggle, and their adherence to their land, and renew their commitment to support them.

The leaders discussed the Lebanese crisis and its tragic complications for the fraternal Arab Lebanese people. The leaders emphasize their concern for Lebanon's national unity, its Arabism, and unity of territory. They also affirm endeavors to help Lebanon overcome its crisis and restore its sovereignty and welfare.

The leaders discussed the issue of international terrorism. They voice condemnation of all forms of international terrorism regardless of its origin. They affirm their conviction of the justice of the peoples' struggle to achieve independence and sovereignty, and restore their freedom and legitimate rights. The leaders believe that the prerequisites, demands and conditions of pan-Arab security cannot be realized except through full solidarity that covers the entire Arab homeland and enables the mobilization of the Arab nation's capabilities and resources to achieve pan-Arab objectives. The leaders also believe in the unity of hope, aspirations and common views regarding the dangers threatening Arab existence and future in terms of evil and hostile intentions. Thus, the leaders decided that diplomatic relations between any Arab League member state and the Arab Republic of Egypt is a sovereign act decided by each state in accordance with its constitution and laws.

The summit reviewed the historical relations between the two divine religions, Islam and Christianity, embodied in Jerusalem, the symbol of peace. The summit also reviewed Israel's practices and its exposed attempts at blackmail. The summit calls on the member states to intensify dialogue with the Vatican in order to gain its support. The summit also calls on His Majesty King Hussein, the summit's chairman, to undertake contacts with the Vatican on behalf of the Arab leaders.

The leaders express their gratitude to the generous Jordanian people and their great king for their warm hospitality, reception, and perfect preparations. They also express appreciation for His Majesty's King Hussein's wise leadership, which created a clear, brotherly climate for the summit and facilitated its success. Thank you.

FDA APPROVAL OF TPA

November 13, 1987

The Food and Drug Administration (FDA) announced November 13 its approval of TPA, a genetically engineered drug that dissolves the clots responsible for most heart attacks. When TPA (tissue plasminogen activator) is administered intravenously within six hours of the onset of symptoms, the survival rate of heart attack victims increases dramatically. In clinical trials on 3,700 patients at more than 100 hospitals, TPA successfully dissolved clots more than 70 percent of the time.

In an age when heart disease was the nation's number-one killer, TPA was a particularly significant breakthrough. More than 1.25 million Americans are stricken with heart attacks each year, and half of those attacks are fatal. Seventy to 80 percent of heart attacks occur when a clot forms in one of the coronary arteries, preventing oxygen-rich blood from reaching the heart muscle. The longer the heart is deprived of oxygen, the greater the damage to the tissue. TPA rapidly breaks up the obstructing clot and restores blood flow to the heart.

Both the FDA and the manufacturers of the drug, Genentech Inc., projected that TPA would save millions of lives. In clinical trials TPA had proven to be twice as effective as the other currently available anticlotting agent, streptokinase, manufactured by Hoechst-Roussel Pharmaceuticals. A 1985 study of TPA was halted because researchers felt it was unethical to administer streptokinase to heart attack victims in the control group when TPA was clearly the faster acting of the two drugs.

Licensing History

Despite evidence of TPA's effectiveness, approval for the drug came only after months of controversy. In May the FDA's Cardiovascular and Renal Drugs Advisory Committee voted 10-1 against licensing TPA, a rejection that received an onslaught of criticism from the press, the public, and the medical community. While the committee admitted that TPA was an effective anticlotting agent, it found Genentech's reports "incomplete and confusing." Some of the problem lay with the unproven contention that TPA would actually prevent heart attacks, a well-documented effect of streptokinase.

Another concern was TPA's potential side effects. TPA, when administered in high doses, was thought early in 1987 to cause intracranial bleeding in 2 percent of cases. Studies later showed that TPA caused intracranial bleeding that resulted in severe brain damage about 0.4 percent of the time, an acceptable figure to heart specialists. TPA would not be administered to patients with severe high blood pressure or a history of stroke or hemorrhaging or to those who had recently undergone major surgery.

After the first FDA rejection, Genentech submitted further evidence that TPA lived up to company claims. The Wall Street Journal *reported that in two studies, one Australian and the other American, Genentech proved that TPA "not only dissolves clots, but is safe, improves overall heart pumping action and extends patients' lives."*

Enthusiastic Reception of TPA

The November statement issued by FDA commissioner Frank E. Young lent full support to TPA. "When used quickly, TPA is a dramatic example of the benefits of biotechnology in helping to improve medical care. I am enthusiastic about TPA in particular because in preventing damage to the heart muscle, it can save the quality of life."

Genentech, which marketed TPA under the brand name Activase, stood to gain significantly from the approval. Many analysts predicted that TPA would become the first drug to achieve $1 billion in sales, making it the most successful drug ever produced by genetic engineering. The cost, however, could prove prohibitive to many patients; TPA was estimated to cost up to ten times as much as streptokinase. In May the FDA had licensed a new form of streptokinase that could be administered intravenously rather than by cardiac catheter. As a result of these breakthroughs, the outlook for potential heart attack victims was considerably brighter.

Following is the November 13, 1987, statement by Frank E. Young, commissioner of the Food and Drug Administration, on the approval of TPA:

Heart disease, despite much progress, remains America's number one killer, responsible for about 768,000 deaths each year—or about 36 percent of all deaths.

We in the Public Health Service have tried to reduce heart disease by fighting smoking, encouraging fitness, exercise and good diet. We have tried to make Americans more knowledgeable about high blood pressure—and how it can be lowered by diet and exercise, preferably, and by drugs, such as the recently approved lovastatin. Currently, the National Heart, Lung and Blood Institute, a part of NIH, is trying to make us all aware of the need to be tested for our cholesterol levels, and what the levels mean—and how to keep them low.

These activities have had an impact: Age-adjusted death rates from heart disease are down 46 percent since 1963.

Nevertheless, there are 1.25 million heart attacks a year, 525,000[1] of them fatal. Of the total number of attacks, 800,000 are first attacks—and about 100,000 of these persons die "sudden and unexpected" deaths before they can be hospitalized. Another 150,000 die within a month, often of the damage that the heart attack caused. Unfortunately, only about a third of the survivors of initial heart attacks completely recover. The rest remain incapacitated or live lives that are limited and circumscribed by their damaged heart.

This isn't always the "other fellow," either. Probably one out of every four or five people in this room—or watching on television—will feel the pain and constriction of a heart attack sometime in their lives. (The probability, to be more precise about it, is that one in five men who are now 35 will have a heart attack by the time he is 60, and others will have heart attacks thereafter.)

But your odds of surviving a heart attack without a crippled heart can be improved.

Today, we at the Food and Drug Administration have licensed the genetically engineered blood clot dissolver alteplase, a tissue plasminogen activator commonly known as TPA—for use in decreasing permanent heart damage immediately following a heart attack.

It is a natural product—one present in our bodies in very small quantities. These amounts, however, are too small to be used to dissolve clots therapeutically. Traditional pharmaceutical methods, moreover, were not able to produce the substance.

But with the miracles of biotechnology, the gene that produces the substance was identified, and then that gene was placed into a cell it would not ordinarily be present in, a fast-reproducing cell that could then turn out TPA like a biological factory. In this way, biotechnology has produced

[1] Of 1.25 million heart attacks a year, 525,000 are fatal. About 300,000 of these are "sudden deaths"—immediate deaths before help can be obtained. Of the 1.25 million heart attacks, 800,000 are initial attacks. Of these, 250,000 are fatal within a month. Among these 250,000 are 100,000 that are "sudden and unexpected"—that is, no prior history of heart disease was known.

Among survivors of initial heart attack, about one-third are completely recovered. Many other survivors resume many activities, but some—less than 20 percent—are incapacitated.

enough TPA to be studied thoroughly, and now to be licensed as a proved therapy.

Why is it important to have an effective way to dissolve a clot quickly after a heart attack? A heart attack occurs, typically, when a blood clot occurs in one of the arteries to the heart, keeping oxygen-rich blood from reaching a part of the heart muscle. When oxygen does not reach the heart tissue, injury or death occurs. The greater the blockage and the longer it continues, the more of the heart muscle that is likely to die.

TPA has been shown to dissolve clots in about 70 percent of patients when it is injected within six hours of the onset of symptoms—with improved heart function demonstrated if administered within four hours.

Unlike previous methodologies requiring a catheterization of the coronary artery to administer a clot-dissolving drug, TPA is simply administered by intravenous drip—that is, a bag of TPA drips through a needle into a vein in an arm. The recently approved intravenous form of streptokinase is administered in the same way. These products greatly improve the outlook of heart attack victims.

But when you feel the constriction in your chest, and the pain, typically below the breastplate, or in your left arm, it is important to be prepared to act. It is only if you get help fast and not wait—if you don't waste time hoping against hope that the pain will go away—that doctors can use TPA or other methodologies to increase the chances that you will continue to live an active, productive life.

Effectiveness declines quickly, as shown with streptokinase. There are amazing results in the first hour, for example, but only half the benefit a few hours later.

You know from Red Cross first aid classes that if you are controlling bleeding with a tourniquet you can't keep it tight too long or the arm or foot affected is injured. It's the same with a clot blocking blood to the heart.

When used quickly, TPA is a dramatic example of the benefits of biotechnology in helping to improve medical care. I am enthusiastic about TPA in particular because in preventing damage to the heart muscle, it can save the quality of life. Today, only a third of initial heart attack survivors completely recover. The rest live lives limited by the damage caused to their hearts. I am hopeful that prompt treatment with TPA and other modalities will improve that situation.

Also, I am enthusiastic about the prospects for future biotech-derived products to improve the quality of life for all of us. Biotechnology, regulated carefully, has produced no freaks, no Frankenstein monsters and no runaway germs. Genetic engineering, or biotech, has instead produced human insulin (1982), human growth hormone (1985 and 1987), two alpha interferons for treating a rare form of leukemia, OKT*3 (monoclonal antibody) to reverse acute kidney transplant rejections and the first genetically engineered vaccine, for hepatitis B, (all in 1986) and, earlier this year, monoclate, a purified anhemophilic agent.

Genetically produced (recombinant) TPA is made by introducing the human gene that codes for TPA production into Chinese hamster ovary cells. These cells are thereby "programmed" to consistently produce large quantities of the drug.

Scientists in Belgium in 1979 first purified and characterized TPA and showed that it could dissolve large clots in experimental animals. Genentech Inc. of South San Francisco, Calif., in 1981 undertook development of the drug using recombinant biotechnology techniques to produce sufficient quantities of TPA to be tested therapeutically.

In all, TPA has been tested in more than 4,000 patients in the United States.

TPA will be marketed by Genentech under the brand name Activase.

COURT ON INSIDER TRADING

November 16, 1987

The Supreme Court, in an 8-0 decision on November 16, upheld the 1985 convictions of a former Wall Street Journal *reporter and two coconspirators, ruling that they had violated federal mail and wire fraud laws. The reporter, R. Foster Winans, had leaked advance information about the newspaper's "Heard on the Street" stock market column to stockbrokers who traded in the stocks mentioned in the column.*

However, the Court deadlocked 4-4 on the more sensitive issue of the convictions of Winans and his associates on a separate charge of securities fraud. While the 4-4 vote upheld the securities fraud convictions, it did not set any national precedents and left "insider trading" undefined in terms of federal securities law.

Winans's case (Carpenter v. United States) *took on added significance because of a rash of high-profile insider trading cases, some involving executives of respected Wall Street firms, that shook the U.S. financial community in 1986 and 1987. These cases raised broader questions about priorities and ethics in business and in financial companies.*

Thus, the Court's decision in the Winans case became of critical importance to enforcement officials in the Justice Department and the Securities and Exchange Commission (SEC).

Press Reaction

From the outset of the Winans case, the American press was in the position of a concerned observer. The Wall Street Journal *did not press for criminal prosecution of its reporter, Winans. The Reporters Committee for the Freedom of the Press and eight other news organizations filed briefs as friends of the court opposing Winans's conviction. After the Supreme Court decision, a* Washington Post *editorial cautioned that the decision would "bring the federal government, particularly the Securities and Exchange Commission, closer to the internal operations of the news business." While protecting the financial markets from manipulation was important, the editorial said, it was "time for Congress to strike a more durable, and more intelligible, balance."*

Supreme Court Ruling

The Supreme Court's unanimous decision upholding the wire and mail fraud convictions of Winans and his confederates was written by Associate Justice Byron R. White. The Court was short one member because Associate Justice Lewis F. Powell, Jr., had retired in June and Congress had yet to confirm the appointment of a new justice.

The scheme that led to Winans's conviction involved two stockbrokers at Kidder, Peabody & Company who bought and sold stocks on the basis of information Winans gave them about the contents and timing of the popular "Heard on the Street" column in his paper. Winans was one of two regular writers of the column.

Winans's coconspirators were David Carpenter, at the time a Wall Street Journal *news clerk and Winans's roommate, and Kenneth P. Felis, one of the stockbrokers. The other stockbroker convicted, Peter N. Brant, was a government witness against Winans. The stockbrokers made about $690,000 in illegal profits from the scheme, paying Winans and Carpenter about $31,000.*

Federal prosecutors were concerned that the Supreme Court would overturn Winans's conviction on the ground that mail and wire fraud statutes were "limited in scope to the protection of property rights," as it had held in June 1987 in McNally v. United States. *But Justice White wrote for the Court, "Here, the object of the scheme was to take the* Journal's *confidential business information—the publication and contents of the 'Heard' column—and its intangible nature does not make it any less 'property' protected by the mail and wire fraud statutes." The Court held that Winans had a fiduciary duty to his newspaper not to disclose the timing or the contents of the column before it was published.*

With the Supreme Court decision, Winans began serving an eighteen-month prison sentence. His two confederates received less severe sentences.

'Insider Trading'

The term "insider trading" was used to describe what took place when an individual in possession of secret market-sensitive information traded or helped others to trade in securities on the basis of the information. However, as the economist John Kenneth Galbraith noted in an interview in the New York Times, *there was "a very thin line between information legitimately and illegitimately conveyed."*

In most of the cases prosecuted by the federal government, such confidential information came from within a corporation. Indeed, that was true of the majority of the cases, some involving enormous sums of money, that broke on Wall Street in 1986 and 1987. In the most famous case, that of Ivan F. Boesky, a Wall Street arbitrager and speculator, some insider or confidential information concerning corporate takeover plans was conveyed to Boesky by an investment banker.

SEC Actions

The SEC had for many years declined to propose a definition of insider trading that Congress could write into law. Such a definition, it was believed, might be useful to a stock speculator attempting to evade the law. Rather, the SEC had used broad antifraud provisions of the federal securities laws to prosecute violators.

Nevertheless, the SEC, in a five-page proposal on August 7, 1987, for the first time spelled out a definition of insider trading. The commission offered the language to Congress for inclusion in a law that would plug loopholes in cases the federal government was prosecuting.

In the proposed definition, information would be "wrongfully" obtained if it were obtained through theft, bribery, misrepresentation, electronic espionage, or a breach of any "fiduciary, contractual, employment, personal or other relationship." Moreover, according to the definition, no one could trade securities while in possession of illegal information, whether or not the information was the basis of the decision to buy or sell.

Securities lawyers and scholars noted that the proposed definition did not mention the so-called misappropriation standard which the government had used in prosecuting some prominent cases. Three days after the Supreme Court's ruling in the Winans case, the SEC was joined by a group of prominent securities lawyers in presenting a new insider trading definition to Congress. The November 19, 1987, proposed definition listed misappropriation as one way information might be "wrongfully" obtained.

> *Following are excerpts from the November 16, 1987, Supreme Court opinion in* Carpenter v. United States, *ruling that federal mail and wire fraud laws had been violated by a reporter and two coconspirators in releasing inside information to stockbrokers:*

No. 86-422

David Carpenter, Kenneth P. Felis, and R. Foster Winans, Petitioners v. United States	On writ of certiorari to the United States Court of Appeals for the Second Circuit

[November 16, 1987]

JUSTICE WHITE delivered the opinion of the Court.

Petitioners Kenneth Felis and R. Foster Winans were convicted of violating § 10(b) of the Securities Exchange Act of 1934, 48 Stat. 891, 15 U.S.C. § 78j(b),[1] and Rule 10b-5, 17 CFR § 240.10b-5 (1987).[2] *United States* v. *Winans* (SDNY 1985). They were also found guilty of violating the federal mail and wire fraud statutes, 18 U.S.C. §§ 1341,[3] 1343,[4] and were convicted for conspiracy under 18 U.S.C. § 371.[5] Petitioner David Carpenter, Winans' roommate, was convicted for aiding and abetting. With a minor exception, the Court of Appeals for the Second Circuit affirmed (1986); we granted certiorari (1986).

---

[1] Section 10(b) provides: "It shall be unlawful for any person, directly or indirectly, by the use of any means or instrumentality of interstate commerce or of the mails, or of any facility of any national securities exchange —

"(b)To use or employ, in connection with the purchase or sale of any security registered on a national securities exchange or any security not so registered, any manipulative or deceptive device or contrivance in contravention of such rules and regulations as the [Securities and Exchange] Commission may prescribe as necessary or appropriate in the public interest or for the protection of investors."

[2] Rule 10b-5 provides: "It shall be unlawful for any person, directly or indirectly, by the use of any means or instrumentality of interstate commerce, or of the mails or of any national securities exchange:

"(a) To employ any device, scheme, or artifice to defraud,

"(b) To make any untrue statement of a material fact or to omit to state a material fact necessary in order to make the statements made, in the light of the circumstances under which they were made, not misleading, or

"(c) To engage in any act, practice, or course of business which operates or would operate as a fraud or deceit upon any person,

"in connection with the purchase or sale of any security."

[3] Section 1341 provides: "Whoever, having devised or intending to devise any scheme or artifice to defraud, or for obtaining money or property by means of false or fraudulent pretenses, representations, or promises, or to sell, dispose of, loan, exchange, alter, give away, distribute, supply, or furnish or procure for unlawful use any counterfeit or spurious coin, obligation, security, or other article, or anything represented to be or intimated or held out to be such counterfeit or spurious article, for the purpose of executing such scheme or artifice or attempting so to do, places in any post office or authorized depository for mail matter, any matter or thing whatever to be sent or delivered by the Postal Service, or takes or receives therefrom, any such matter or thing, or knowingly causes to be delivered by mail according to the direction thereon, or at the place at which it is directed to be delivered by the person to whom it is addressed, any such matter or thing, shall be fined not more than $1,000 or imprisoned not more than five years, or both."

[4] Section 1343 provides: "Whoever, having devised or intending to devise any scheme or

I

In 1981, Winans became a reporter for the Wall Street Journal (the Journal) and in the summer of 1982 became one of the two writers of a daily column, "Heard on the Street." That column discussed selected stocks or groups of stocks, giving positive and negative information about those stocks and taking "a point of view with respect to investment in the stocks that it reviews." Winans regularly interviewed corporate executives to put together interesting perspectives on the stocks that would be highlighted in upcoming columns, but, at least for the columns at issue here, none contained corporate inside information or any "hold for release" information. Because of the "Heard" column's perceived quality and integrity, it had the potential of affecting the price of the stocks which it examined. The District Court concluded on the basis of testimony presented at trial that the "Heard" column "does have an impact on the market, difficult though it may be to quantify in any particular case."

The official policy and practice at the Journal was that prior to publication, the contents of the column were the Journal's confidential information. Despite the rule, with which Winans was familiar, he entered into a scheme in October 1983 with Peter Brant and petitioner Felis, both connected with the Kidder Peabody brokerage firm in New York City, to give them advance information as to the timing and contents of the "Heard" column. This permitted Brant and Felis and another conspirator, David Clark, a client of Brant, to buy or sell based on the probable impact of the column on the market. Profits were to be shared. The conspirators agreed that the scheme would not affect the journalistic purity of the "Heard" column, and the District Court did not find that the contents of any of the articles were altered to further the profit potential of petitioners' stock-trading scheme. Over a four-month period, the brokers made prepublication trades on the basis of information given them by Winans about the contents of some 27 Heard columns. The net profits from these trades were about $690,000.

In November 1983, correlations between the "Heard" articles and trading in the Clark and Felis accounts were noted at Kidder Peabody and inquiries began. Brant and Felis denied knowing anyone at the Journal and took steps to conceal the trades. Later, the Securities and Exchange Commission began an investigation. Questions were met by denials both by the brokers at Kidder Peabody and by Winans at the Journal. As the

artifice to defraud, or for obtaining money or property by means of false or fraudulent pretenses, representations, or promises, transmits or causes to be transmitted by means of wire, radio, or television communication in interstate or foreign commerce, any writings, signs, signals, pictures, or sounds for the purpose of executing such scheme or artifice, shall be fined not more than $1,000 or imprisoned not more than 5 years, or both."

[5] Section 371 provides: "If two or more persons conspire either to commit any offense against the United States, or to defraud the United States, or any agency thereof in any manner or for any purpose, and one or more of such persons do any act to effect the object of the conspiracy, each shall be fined not more than $10,000 or imprisoned not more than five years, or both."

investigation progressed, the conspirators quarreled, and on March 29, 1984, Winans and Carpenter went to the SEC and revealed the entire scheme. This indictment and a bench trial followed. Brant, who had pled guilty under a plea agreement, was a witness for the Government.

The District Court found, and the Court of Appeals agreed, that Winans had knowingly breached a duty of confidentiality by misappropriating prepublication information regarding the timing and contents of the "Heard" columns, information that had been gained in the course of his employment under the understanding that it would not be revealed in advance of publication and that if it were, he would report it to his employer. It was this appropriation of confidential information that underlay both the securities laws and mail and wire fraud counts. With respect to the § 10(b) charges, the courts below held that the deliberate breach of Winans' duty of confidentiality and concealment of the scheme was a fraud and deceit on the Journal. Although the victim of the fraud, the Journal, was not a buyer or seller of the stocks traded in or otherwise a market participant, the fraud was nevertheless considered to be "in connection with" a purchase or sale of securities within the meaning of the statute and the rule. The courts reasoned that the scheme's sole purpose was to buy and sell securities at a profit based on advance information of the column's contents. The courts below rejected petitioners' submission, which is one of the two questions presented here, that criminal liability could not be imposed on petitioners under Rule 10b-5 because "the newspaper is the only alleged victim of fraud and has no interest in the securities traded."

In affirming the mail and wire fraud convictions, the Court of Appeals ruled that Winans had fraudulently misappropriated "property" within the meaning of the mail and wire fraud statutes and that its revelation had harmed the Journal. It was held as well that the use of the mail and wire services had a sufficient nexus with the scheme to satisfy §§ 1341 and 1343. The petition for certiorari challenged these conclusions.

The Court is evenly divided with respect to the convictions under the securities laws and for that reason affirms the judgment below on those counts. For the reasons that follow, we also affirm the judgment with respect to the mail and wire fraud convictions.

II

Petitioners assert that their activities were not a scheme to defraud the Journal within the meaning of the mail and wire fraud statutes; and that in any event, they did not obtain any "money or property" from the Journal, which is a necessary element of the crime under our decision last Term in *McNally* v. *United States* (1987). We are unpersuaded by either submission and address the latter first.

We held in *McNally* that the mail fraud statute does not reach "schemes to defraud citizens of their intangible rights to honest and impartial government" and that the statute is "limited in scope to the protection of property rights." Petitioners argue that the Journal's interest in prepublication confidentiality for the "Heard" columns is no more than an intangible consideration outside the reach of § 1341; nor does that law, it is urged, protect against mere injury to reputation. This is not a case like *McNally,* however. The Journal, as Winans' employer, was defrauded of much more than its contractual right to his honest and faithful service, an interest too ethereal in itself to fall within the protection of the mail fraud statute, which "had its origin in the desire to protect individual property rights." *McNally.* Here, the object of the scheme was to take the Journal's confidential business information—the publication schedule and contents of the "Heard"column—and its intangible nature does not make it any less "property" protected by the mail and wire fraud statutes. *McNally* did not limit the scope of § 1341 to tangible as distinguished from intangible property rights.

Both courts below expressly referred to the Journal's interest in the confidentiality of the contents and timing of the "Heard" column as a property right, and we agree with that conclusion. Confidential business information has long been recognized as property. See *Ruckelshaus* v. *Monsanto Co.* (1984); *Dirks* v. *SEC* (1983); *Board of Trade of Chicago* v. *Christie Grain & Stock Co.* (1905); cf. 5 U.S.C. § 552(b) (4). "Confidential information acquired or compiled by a corporation in the course and conduct of its business is a species of property to which the corporation has the exclusive right and benefit, and which a court of equity will protect through the injunctive process or other appropriate remedy." 3 W. Fletcher, Cyclopedia of Law of Private Corporations (rev. ed. 1986). The Journal had a property right in keeping confidential and making exclusive use, prior to publication, of the schedule and contents of the "Heard" columns. *Christie Grain, supra.* As the Court has observed before:

> "[N]ews matter, however little susceptible of ownership or dominion in the absolute sense, is stock in trade, to be gathered at the cost of enterprise, organization, skill, labor, and money, and to be distributed and sold to those who will pay money for it, as for any other merchandise." *International News Service* v. *Associated Press* (1918).

Petitioners' arguments that they did not interfere with the Journal's use of the information or did not publicize it and deprive the Journal of the first public use of it miss the point. The confidential information was generated from the business and the business had a right to decide how to use it prior to disclosing it to the public. Petitioners cannot successfully contend based on *Associated Press* that a scheme to defraud requires a monetary loss, such as giving the information to a competitor; it is sufficient that the Journal has been deprived of its right to exclusive use of the information, for exclusivity is an important aspect of confidential business information and most private property for that matter.

We cannot accept petitioners' further argument that Winans' conduct in revealing prepublication information was no more than a violation of workplace rules and did not amount to fraudulent activity that is proscribed by the mail fraud statute. Sections 1341 and 1343 reach any scheme to deprive another of money or property by means of false or fraudulent pretenses, representations, or promises. As we observed last Term in *McNally,* the words "to defraud" in the mail fraud statute have the "common understanding" of " 'wronging one in his property rights by dishonest methods or schemes,' and 'usually signify the deprivation of something of value by trick, deceit, chicane or overreaching.' " (quoting *Hammerschmidt* v. *United States* (1924)). The concept of "fraud" includes the act of embezzlement, which is " 'the fraudulent appropriation to one's own use of the money or goods entrusted to one's care by another.' " *Grin* v. *Shine* (1902).

The District Court found that Winans' undertaking at the Journal was not to reveal prepublication information about his column, a promise that became a sham when in violation of his duty he passed along to his co-conspirators confidential information belonging to the Journal, pursuant to an ongoing scheme to share profits from trading in anticipation of the "Heard" column's impact on the stock market. In *Snepp* v. *United States* (1980) *(per curiam),* although a decision grounded in the provisions of a written trust agreement prohibiting the unapproved use of confidential government information, we noted the similar prohibitions of the common law, that "even in the absence of a written contract, an employee has a fiduciary obligation to protect confidential information obtained during the course of his employment." As the New York courts have recognized, "It is well established, as a general proposition, that a person who acquires special knowledge or information by virtue of a confidential or fiduciary relationship with another is not free to exploit that knowledge or information for his own personal benefit but must account to his principal for any profits derived therefrom." *Diamond* v. *Oreamuno* (1969); see also Restatement (Second) of Agency §§ 388, Comment *c,* 396(c) (1958).

We have little trouble in holding that the conspiracy here to trade on the Journal's confidential information is not outside the reach of the mail and wire fraud statutes, provided the other elements of the offenses are satisfied. The Journal's business information that it intended to be kept confidential was its property; the declaration to that effect in the employee manual merely removed any doubts on that score and made the finding of specific intent to defraud that much easier. Winans continued in the employ of the Journal, appropriating its confidential business for his own use, all the while pretending to perform his duty of safeguarding it. In fact, he told his editors twice about leaks of confidential information not related to the stock-trading scheme, demonstrating both his knowledge that the Journal viewed information concerning the "Heard" column as confidential and his deceit as he played the role of loyal employee. Furthermore, the District Court's conclusion that each of the petitioners acted with the required specific intent to defraud is strongly supported by the evidence. *Id.,* at 847-850.

Lastly, we reject the submission that using the wires and the mail to print and send the Journal to its customers did not satisfy the requirement that those mediums be used to execute the scheme at issue. The courts below were quite right in observing that circulation of the "Heard" column was not only anticipated but an essential part of the scheme. Had the column not been made available to Journal customers, there would have been no effect on stock prices and no likelihood of profiting from the information leaked by Winans.

The judgment below is

Affirmed.

IRAN-CONTRA REPORTS

November 17 and 18, 1987

After ten months of interviews and eleven weeks of dramatic public hearings, the House and Senate select Iran-contra investigating committees November 17 and 18 released their reports on the affair, which had shocked the nation when the operations were first disclosed. The majority report, signed by all fifteen Democrats on the committee and three Republicans on the Senate panel, accused the Reagan administration of "secrecy, deception, and disdain for the rule of law," and faulted the president for failing to live up to his constitutional mandate to "take care that the laws be faithfully executed." The "ultimate responsibility" for the foreign policy fiasco rested with Ronald Reagan, the majority concluded. "If the President did not know what his National Security Advisers were doing, he should have."

But eight GOP members, including all House committee Republicans, took issue with the majority, asserting, "There was no constitutional crisis, no systematic disrespect for the 'rule of law,' no grand conspiracy and no Administration-wide dishonesty or cover-up." In a summary report released to the press November 16, the minority said errors made by the administration in the Iran-contra affair were "mistakes in judgment and nothing more."

A Year-long Road to Final Report

The 427-page majority report revealed few surprises because most of the evidence had been made public previously. But it painted the most complete picture to date of events surrounding the clandestine sale of

U.S.-made arms, via Israel, to the militantly anti-American Moslem regime in Iran, beginning in 1985. The arms shipments were facilitated by the Central Intelligence Agency (CIA), and subsequently some of the profits were diverted to assist the contra guerrillas fighting the leftist Sandinista government in Nicaragua. The affair was made public in November 1986, giving rise to investigations on Capitol Hill, the establishment of an independent counsel's office, and the appointment by the president of a three-member panel—the Tower commission—to undertake an initial probe. (Tower report, p. 205; Historic Documents of 1986, pp. 1013, 1049)

The arms sales and contra diversion in themselves were of questionable legality because laws—including the Boland amendments prohibiting aid to the contras and various military arms sales restrictions—barred such activities. Equally troublesome was the manner in which the policy was conducted by a handful of staffers at the National Security Council (NSC)—termed a "cabal of zealots" by the majority report—without full consultation with the president and secretaries of state and defense, who were members of the NSC. The principal actors in the affair were the president's national security advisers Robert M. McFarlane and John M. Poindexter (a vice admiral at the time); NSC aide Lt. Col. Oliver L. North; and the late director of central intelligence, William J. Casey. Under North's immediate direction, with the "express approval" of McFarlane and Poindexter, a number of private individuals were recruited to arrange the arms sales and contra diversion, reaping huge profits for themselves. Retired Air Force major general Richard V. Secord and Albert Hakim, his Iranian-born business partner, worked closely with North and were at the helm of the "Enterprise," or the web of offshore companies and secret Swiss bank accounts that controlled the logistics of the Iran deals and secret contra assistance.

North and Poindexter at first refused to testify before congressional committees, citing Fifth Amendment rights not to incriminate themselves. Subsequently, however, an arrangement between the select investigating panels and independent counsel Lawrence E. Walsh gave limited immunity to North and Poindexter as well as to other key witnesses. By the end of 1987, Walsh had handed down two indictments; Poindexter and North remained under investigation.

The Committees and Their Work

Shortly after the Iran-contra scandal broke, leaders in both chambers announced the appointment of special investigating panels. The Senate's eleven-member select committee was chaired by Daniel K. Inouye, D-Hawaii, a former Intelligence Committee chairman and member of the Senate Watergate panel that in 1973-1974 investigated activities of the Nixon White House. The other Senate Democrats were George J. Mitchell of Maine, Sam Nunn of Georgia, Paul S. Sarbanes of Maryland,

Howell Heflin of Alabama, and David L. Boren of Oklahoma. The senior Republican on the Senate panel was Warren B. Rudman of New Hampshire. His colleagues were James A. McClure of Idaho, Orrin G. Hatch of Utah, William S. Cohen of Maine, and Paul S. Trible, Jr., of Virginia.

Chairman of the House panel was Lee H. Hamilton, D-Ind., outgoing chairman of the House Intelligence Committee. Other Democrats were Dante B. Fascell, Florida; Peter W. Rodino, Jr., New Jersey; Jack Brooks, Texas; Les Aspin, Wisconsin; Louis Stokes, Ohio; Thomas S. Foley, Washington (majority leader); Edward P. Boland, Massachusetts; and Ed Jenkins, Georgia. Republicans, headed by Dick Cheney of Wyoming, were William S. Broomfield, Michigan; Henry J. Hyde, Illinois; Michael DeWine, Ohio; Bill McCollum, Florida; and Jim Courter, New Jersey.

Early in 1987 the committees agreed to consolidate their efforts in gathering evidence and receiving testimony. Both committees hired experienced investigators and lawyers who interviewed hundreds of witnesses and reviewed thousands of documents. The committees produced substantial amounts of new information, both about the use of profits from the Iran arms sales and the secret White House campaign to aid the contras.

The first public hearings, in May and June, began as an investigation into wrongdoing by White House officials and their agents, but as the hearings progressed, Reagan's Republican supporters on the committees hammered at a second theme—Congress's alleged interference in foreign policy. As committee lawyers and Democrats continued to ask detailed questions about who did what when, most Republicans made speeches defending Reagan and complaining about congressional "vacillation" on aid to the contras. During his six days in the spotlight in July, North wrested the initiative from the committees and made the Republicans' points better than they could. In uniform, with a chestful of medals symbolizing a record of service in Vietnam, North created a media sensation that lasted for a number of weeks.

The panels devoted their final public sessions to testimony by current and former officials at the top of the Reagan administration. Secretary of Defense Caspar W. Weinberger, Secretary of State George P. Shultz, and others denounced the actions of Poindexter and North and praised Reagan's leadership.

The committees spent forty days in public hearings and four days in closed sessions, handed down 311 subpoenas, heard from 250 witnesses, introduced 1,059 exhibits, and produced 9,887 pages of transcripts of public testimony.

Majority Report Findings and Recommendations

The majority report was predictably harsh in its criticism of the president. It painted a picture of a "seriously flawed" policy-making process characterized by confusion among major participants; "pervasive dishonesty," especially toward Congress but also among Reagan officials; reliance on "inordinate secrecy" out of fear of encountering opposition or jeopardizing security; the use of private individuals to conduct public policies; and a lack of accountability for the actions of individuals and organizations.

The committee depicted the president as personally involved in deciding to conceal major elements of the affair from the public and described an active administration effort to cover up possibly illegal actions.

The report found fault with the actions of Attorney General Edwin Meese III, charging that his preliminary inquiries into the arms sales were inadequate, that he did not provide sound advice to the president on whether the shipments were legal, and that he might have authorized violation of federal law by approving use of private funds by government officials in a secret operation to free Americans held hostage in Lebanon.

The report took note of Casey's role, appearing to accept North's contention that the late CIA director had approved the diversion of funds and the "full service" covert operations to help the contras and carry out other foreign policy actions. However, the panel said it had no proof to back up North's claim. The report said Casey showed "contempt for the democratic process" by withholding information from Congress and accused him of "misrepresenting" intelligence information to the president and others to bolster policies he advocated. Committee leaders said they did not expect the report to have substantial impact on public opinion or on Reagan's ability to govern during the rest of his term. The panels essentially concluded that the fault lay with the people who ran the government, not with the laws or institutions of government. Inouye said the panels could recommend only "modest" changes in law and procedure that by themselves would not prevent a future administration from making the same mistakes.

The Minority Rebuttal

The Republican minority—with the exception of Rudman, Cohen, and Trible—countered many of the points contained in the majority document. "The evidence shows that the President did not know" of the diversion of arms sales profits to the contras, said a 38-page summary report the minority released shortly before the official majority and 200-page minority reports were made public. "Any attempt to suggest otherwise can only be seen as an effort to sow meritless doubts in the hope of reaping a partisan political advantage." The minority also took issue with the majority's conclusion that Meese had mishandled his initial investigation in November 1986. The minority report further concluded that "no one in the government was acting out of corrupt motives." However, the report did fault Poindexter for his secrecy: "By keeping an important decision away from the President, Poindexter was acting to undercut one foundation for the discretionary Presidential power he was exercising."

The report reserved some of its harshest criticism for administration officials who were treated sympathetically in the majority report. For example, the report accused Shultz of a "record of disagreement" in the affair, suggesting possible disloyalty to the president. "If the appointees find the policy so repugnant that they can only distance themselves from it, then they are not doing their best to serve" the president.

The minority report was scathing in its attack on the majority report, which it described as "an advocate's legal brief that arrays and selects so-called 'facts' to fit preconceived theories." The report added, "The evidence will not support any of the more hysterical conclusions the committees' report tries to reach." The Republicans also criticized the decision to hold public hearings, "which compromised some intelligence sources and methods."

Following are excerpts from the executive summary and recommendations of the majority report of the House and Senate select Iran-contra investigating committees, released November 18, 1987; and from the minority report, released November 17.

THE REPORT

Findings and Conclusions

The common ingredients of the Iran and Contra policies were secrecy, deception, and disdain for the law. A small group of senior officials believed that they alone knew what was right. They viewed knowledge of their actions by others in the Government as a threat to their objectives. They told neither the Secretary of State, the Congress nor the American people of their actions. When exposure was threatened, they destroyed official documents and lied to Cabinet officials, to the public, and to elected representatives in Congress. They testified that they even withheld key facts from the President.

The United States Constitution specifies the process by which laws and policy are to be made and executed. Constitutional process is the essence of our democracy and our democratic form of Government is the basis of our strength. Time and again we have learned that a flawed process leads to bad results, and that a lawless process leads to worse.

Policy Contradictions and Failures

The Administration's departure from democratic processes created the conditions for policy failure, and led to contradictions which undermined the credibility of the United States.

The United States simultaneously pursued two contradictory foreign policies—a public one and a secret one:

- The public policy was not to make any concessions for the release of hostages lest such concessions encourage more hostage-taking. At the same time, the United States was secretly trading weapons to get the hostages back.
- The public policy was to ban arms shipments to Iran and to exhort other Governments to observe this embargo. At the same time, the United States was secretly selling sophisticated missiles to Iran and promising more.
- The public policy was to improve relations with Iraq. At the same time, the United States secretly shared military intelligence on Iraq with Iran and [Lt. Col. Oliver L.] North told the Iranians in contradiction to United States policy that the United States would help promote the overthrow of the Iraqi head of government.
- The public policy was to urge all Governments to punish terrorism and to support, indeed encourage, the refusal of Kuwait to free the Da'wa prisoners who were convicted of terrorist acts. At the same time, senior officials secretly endorsed a [retired Maj. Gen. Richard V.] Secord-[Albert] Hakim [Secord's business partner] plan to permit Iran to obtain the release of the Da'wa prisoners.
- The public policy was to observe the "letter and spirit" of the Boland Amendment's proscriptions against military or paramilitary assistance to the Contras. At the same time, the NSC [National Security Council] staff was secretly assuming direction and funding of the Contras' military effort.
- The public policy, embodied in agreements signed by Director [of Central Intelligence William J.] Casey, was for the Administration to consult with the Congressional oversight committees about covert activities in a "new spirit of frankness and cooperation." At the same time, the CIA and the White House were secretly withholding from those Committees all information concerning the Iran initiative and the Contra support network.
- The public policy, embodied in Executive Order 12333, was to conduct covert operations solely through the CIA or other organs of the intelligence community specifically authorized by the President. At the same time, although the NSC was not so authorized, the NSC staff secretly became operational and used private, non-accountable agents to engage in covert activities.

These contradictions in policy inevitably resulted in policy failure:

- The United States armed Iran, including its most radical elements, but attained neither a new relationship with that hostile regime nor a reduction in the number of American hostages.
- The arms sales did not lead to a moderation of Iranian policies. Moderates did not come forward, and Iran to this day sponsors actions

directed against the United States in the Persian Gulf and elsewhere.

- The United States opened itself to blackmail by adversaries who might reveal the secret arms sales and who, according to North, threatened to kill the hostages if the sales stopped.
- The United States undermined its credibility with friends and allies, including moderate Arab states, by its public stance of opposing arms sales to Iran while undertaking such arms sales in secret.
- The United States lost a $10 million contribution to the Contras from the Sultan of Brunei by directing it to the wrong bank account—the result of an improper effort to channel that humanitarian aid contribution into an account used for lethal assistance.
- The United States sought illicit funding for the Contras through profits from the secret arms sales, but a substantial portion of those profits ended up in the personal bank accounts of the private individuals executing the sales—while the exorbitant amounts charged for the weapons inflamed the Iranians with whom the United States was seeking a new relationship.

Flawed Policy Process

The record of the Iran-Contra Affair also shows a seriously flawed policy-making process.

Confusion

There was confusion and disarray at the highest levels of Government.

- [Robert C.] McFarlane embarked on a dangerous trip to Tehran under a complete misapprehension. He thought the Iranians had promised to secure the release of all hostages before he delivered arms, when in fact they had promised only to seek the hostages' release, and then only after one planeload of arms had arrived.
- The President first told the Tower Board [a special panel appointed by the president to investigate the Iran-contra affair] that he had approved the initial Israeli shipments. Then, he told the Tower Board that he had not. Finally, he told the Tower Board that he does not know whether he approved the initial Israeli arms shipments, and his top advisers disagree on the question.
- The President claims he does not recall signing a Finding approving the November 1985 HAWK [antiaircraft missile] shipment to Iran. But [Adm. John M.] Poindexter testified that the President did sign a Finding on December 5, 1985, approving the shipment retroactively. Poindexter later destroyed the Finding to save the President from embarrassment.
- That Finding was prepared without adequate discussion and stuck in Poindexter's safe for a year; Poindexter claimed he forgot about it; the White House asserts the President never signed it; and when events began to unravel, Poindexter ripped it up.
- The President and the Attorney General told the public that the President did not know about the November 1985 Israeli HAWK shipment

until February 1986—an error the White House Chief of Staff explained by saying that the preparation for the press conference "sort of confused the Presidential mind."

- Poindexter says the President would have approved the diversion, if he had been asked; and the President says he would not have.
- One National Security Adviser understood that the Boland Amendment applied to the NSC; another thought it did not. Neither sought a legal opinion on the question.
- The President incorrectly assured the American people that the NSC staff was adhering to the law and that the Government was not connected to the [Eugene] Hasenfus airplane [shot down over Nicaragua in October 1986 while transporting arms to the contras]. His staff was in fact conducting a "full service" covert operation to support the Contras which they believed he had authorized.
- North says he sent five or six completed memorandums to Poindexter seeking the President's approval for the diversion. Poindexter does not remember receiving any. Only one has been found.

Dishonesty and Secrecy

The Iran-Contra Affair was characterized by pervasive dishonesty and inordinate secrecy.

North admitted that he and other officials lied repeatedly to Congress and to the American people about the Contra covert action and Iran arms sales, and that he altered and destroyed official documents. North's testimony demonstrates that he also lied to members of the Executive branch, including the Attorney General, and officials of the State Department, CIA and NSC.

Secrecy became an obsession. Congress was never informed of the Iran or the Contra covert actions, notwithstanding the requirement in the law that Congress be notified of all covert actions in a "timely fashion."

Poindexter said that Donald Regan, the President's Chief of Staff, was not told of the NSC staff's fundraising activities because he might reveal it to the press. Secretary [of State George P.] Shultz objected to third-country solicitation in 1984 shortly before the Boland Amendment was adopted; accordingly, he was not told that, in the same time period, the National Security Adviser had accepted an $8 million contribution from Country 2 [Saudi Arabia] even though the State Department had prime responsibility for dealings with that country. Nor was the Secretary of State told by the President in February 1985 that the same country had pledged another $24 million—even though the President briefed the Secretary of State on his meeting with the head of state at which the pledge was made. Poindexter asked North to keep secrets from Casey; Casey, North and Poindexter agreed to keep secrets from Shultz.

Poindexter and North cited fear of leaks as a justification for these practices. But the need to prevent public disclosure cannot justify the deception practiced upon Members of Congress and the Executive branch officials by those who knew of the arms sale to Iran and the Contra support network. The State and Defense Departments deal each day with the most sensitive matters affecting millions of lives here and abroad. The Congressional Intelligence Committees receive only the most highly classified information, including information on covert activities. Yet, according to North and Poindexter, even the senior officials of these bodies could not be entrusted with the NSC staff's secrets because they might leak.

While Congress's record in maintaining the confidentiality of classified information is not unblemished, it is not nearly as poor or perforated as some members of the NSC staff maintained. If the Executive branch has any basis to suspect that any member of the Intelligence Committees breached security, it has the obligation to bring that breach to the attention of the House and Senate Leaders—not to make blanket accusations. Congress has the capability and responsibility of protecting secrets entrusted to it. Congress cannot fulfill its legislative responsibilities if it is denied information because members of the Executive branch, who place their faith in a band of international arms merchants and financiers, unilaterally declare Congress unworthy of trust.

In the case of the "secret" Iran arms-for-hostages deal, although the NSC staff did not inform the Secretary of State, the Chairman of the Joint Chiefs of Staff, or the leadership of the United States Congress, it was content to let the following persons know:

- Manucher Ghorbanifar [middleman in the Iranian arms deal], who flunked every polygraph test administered by the U.S. Government;
- Iranian officials, who daily denounced the United States but received an inscribed Bible from the President;
- Officials of Iran's Revolutionary Guard, who received the U.S. weapons;
- Secord and Hakim, whose personal interests could conflict with the interests of the United States;
- Israeli officials, international arms merchants, pilots and air crews, whose interests did not always coincide with ours; and
- An unknown number of shadowy intermediaries and financiers who assisted with both the First and Second Iranian Channels [contacts in the arms deal].

While sharing the secret with this disparate group, North ordered the intelligence agencies not to disseminate intelligence on the Iran initiative to the Secretaries of State and Defense. Poindexter told the Secretary of State in May 1986 that the Iran initiative was over, at the very time the McFarlane mission to Tehran was being launched. Poindexter also concealed from Cabinet officials the remarkable nine-point agreement negotiated by Hakim with the Second Channel. North assured the FBI liaison to the NSC as late as November 1986 that the United States was not bargaining for the release of hostages but seizing terrorists to exchange for hostages—a complete fabrication. The lies, omissions, shredding, attempts to rewrite history—all continued, even after the

President authorized the Attorney General to find out the facts.

It was not operational security that motivated such conduct—not when our own Government was the victim. Rather, the NSC staff feared, correctly, that any disclosure to Congress or the Cabinet of the arms-for-hostages and arms-for-profit activities would produce a storm of outrage.

As with Iran, Congress was misled about the NSC staff's support for the Contras during the period of the Boland Amendment, although the role of the NSC staff was no secret to others. North testified that his operation was well-known to the press in the Soviet Union, Cuba and Nicaragua. It was not a secret from Nicaragua's neighbors, with whom the NSC staff communicated throughout the period. It was not a secret from the third countries—including a totalitarian state—from whom the NSC staff sought arms or funds. It was not a secret from the private resupply network which North recruited and supervised. According to North, even Ghorbanifar knew.

The Administration never sought to hide its desire to assist the Contras so long as such aid was authorized by statute. On the contrary, it wanted the Sandinistas to know that the United States supported the Contras. After enactment of the Boland Amendment, the Administration repeatedly and publicly called upon Congress to resume U.S. assistance. Only the NSC staff's Contra support activities were kept under wraps. The Committees believe these actions were concealed in order to prevent Congress from learning that the Boland Amendment was being circumvented.

It was stated on several occasions that the confusion, secrecy and deception surrounding the aid program for the Nicaraguan freedom fighters was produced in part by Congress' shifting positions on Contra aid.

But Congress' inconsistency mirrored the chameleon-like nature of the rationale offered for granting assistance in the first instance. Initially, Congress was told that our purpose was simply to interdict the flow of weapons from Nicaragua into El Salvador. Then Congress was told that our purpose was to harass the Sandinistas to prevent them from consolidating their power and exporting their revolution. Eventually, Congress was told that our purpose was to eliminate all foreign forces from Nicaragua, to reduce the size of the Sandinista armed forces, and to restore the democratic reforms pledged by the Sandinistas during the overthrow of the Somoza regime.

Congress had cast a skeptical eye upon each rationale proffered by the Administration. It suspected that the Administration's true purpose was identical to that of the Contras—the overthrow of the Sandinista regime itself. Ultimately Congress yielded to domestic political pressure to discontinue assistance to the Contras, but Congress was unwilling to bear responsibility for the loss of Central America to communist military and political forces. So Congress compromised, providing in 1985 humanitarian aid to the Contras; and the NSC staff provided what Congress prohibited: lethal support for the Contras.

Compromise is no excuse for violation of law and deceiving Congress. A law is no less a law because it is passed by a slender majority, or because Congress is open-minded about its reconsideration in the future.

Privatization

The NSC staff turned to private parties and third countries to do the Government's business. Funds denied by Congress were obtained by the Administration from third countries and private citizens. Activities normally conducted by the professional intelligence services—which are accountable to Congress—were turned over to Secord and Hakim.

The solicitation of foreign funds by an Administration to pursue foreign policy goals rejected by Congress is dangerous and improper. Such solicitations, when done secretly and without Congressional authorization, create a risk that the foreign country will expect and demand something in return. . . .

Moreover, under the Constitution only Congress can provide funds for the Executive branch. The Framers intended Congress's "power of the purse" to be one of the principal checks on Executive action. It was designed, among other things, to prevent the Executive from involving this country unilaterally in a foreign conflict. The Constitutional plan does not prohibit a President from asking a foreign state, or anyone else, to contribute funds to a third party. But it does prohibit such solicitation where the United States exercises control over their receipt and expenditure. By circumventing Congress' power of the purse through third-country and private contributions to the Contras, the Administration undermined a cardinal principle of the Constitution.

Further, by turning to private citizens, the NSC staff jeopardized its own objectives. Sensitive negotiations were conducted by parties with little experience in diplomacy, and financial interests of their own. The diplomatic aspect of the mission failed—the United States today has no long-term relationship with Iran and no fewer hostages in captivity. But the private financial aspect succeeded—Secord and Hakim took $4.4 million in commissions and used $2.2 million more for their personal benefit; in addition, they set aside reserves of over $4 million in Swiss bank accounts of the Enterprise.

Covert operations of this Government should only be directed and conducted by the trained professional services that are accountable to the President and Congress. Such operations should never be delegated, as they were here, to private citizens in order to evade Governmental restrictions.

Lack of Accountability

The confusion, deception and privatization which marked the Iran-Contra Affair were the inevitable products of an attempt to avoid accountability. . . .

Officials who make public policy must be accountable to the public. But the public cannot hold officials accountable for policies of which the public is unaware. Policies that are known can be subjected to the test of reason, and mistakes can be corrected after consultation with the Congress and deliberation within the Executive branch itself. Policies that are secret become the private preserve of the few, mistakes are inevitably perpetuated, and the public loses control over Government. That is what happened in the Iran-Contra Affair:

- The President's NSC staff carried out a covert action in furtherance of his policy to sustain the Contras, but the President said he did not know about it.
- The President's NSC staff secretly diverted millions of dollars in profits from the Iran arms sales to the Contras, but the President said he did not know about it and Poindexter claimed he did not tell him.
- The Chairman of the Joint Chiefs of Staff was not informed of the Iran arms sales, nor was he ever consulted regarding the impact of such sales on the Iran-Iraq war or on U.S. military readiness.
- The Secretary of State was not informed of the millions of dollars in Contra contributions solicited by the NSC staff from foreign governments with which the State Department deals each day.
- Congress was told almost nothing—and what it was told was false.

Deniability replaced accountability. Thus, Poindexter justified his decision not to inform the President on the diversion on the ground that he wanted to give the President "deniability." Poindexter said he wanted to shield the President from political embarrassment if the diversion became public.

This kind of thinking is inconsistent with democratic governance....

The very premise of democracy is that "we the people" are entitled to make our own choices on fundamental policies. But freedom of choice is illusory if policies are kept, not only from the public, but from its elected representatives.

Intelligence Abuses

Covert Operations

...The Government cannot keep a policy secret and still secure the public support necessary to sustain it. Yet it was precisely because the public would not support the Contra policy, and was unlikely to favor arms deals with Iran, that the NSC staff went underground. This was a perversion of the proper concept of covert operations:

- Covert operations should be conducted in accordance with strict rules of accountability and oversight. In the mid-1970s, in response to disclosures of abuses within the intelligence community, the Government enacted a series of safeguards. Each covert action was to be approved personally by the President, funded by Congressional appropriations and Congress was to be informed. In the Iran-Contra Affair, these rules were violated....
- Covert actions should be consistent with publicly defined U.S. foreign

policy goals. Because covert operations are secret by definition, they are of course not openly debated or publicly approved. So long as the policies which they further are known, and so long as they are conducted in accordance with law, covert operations are acceptable. Here, however, the Contra covert operation was carried out in violation of the country's public policy as expressed in the Boland Amendment; and the Iran covert operation was carried out in violation of the country's stated policy against selling arms to Iran or making concessions to terrorists. . . .

- Finally, covert operations are intended to be kept from foreign powers, not from the Congress and responsible Executive agencies within the United States Government itself. . . .

The NSC Staff

The NSC staff was created to give the President policy advice on major national security and foreign policy issues. Here, however, it was used to gather intelligence and conduct covert operations. This departure from its proper functions contributed to policy failure. . . .

Secretary Shultz pointed out that the intelligence and policy functions do not mix, because "it is too tempting to have your analysis on the selection of information that is presented favor the policy that you are advocating." The Committees agree on the need to separate the intelligence and policy functions. Otherwise, there is too great a risk that the interpretation of intelligence will be skewed to fit predetermined policy choices.

In the Iran-Contra Affair, the NSC staff not only combined intelligence and policy functions, but it became operational and conducted covert operations. As the CIA was subjected to greater Congressional scrutiny and regulations, a few Administration officials—including even Director Casey—came to believe that the CIA could no longer be utilized for daring covert operations. So the NSC staff was enlisted to provide assistance in covert operations that the CIA could not or would not furnish.

This was a dangerous misuse of the NSC staff. When covert operations are conducted by those on whom the President relies to present policy options, there is no agency in government to objectively scrutinize, challenge and evaluate plans and activities. Checks and balances are lost. . . .

The NSC was created to provide candid and comprehensive advice to the President. It is the judgment of these Committees that the NSC staff should never again engage in covert operations.

Disdain for Law

In the Iran-Contra Affair, officials viewed the law not as setting boundaries for their actions, but raising impediments to their goals. When the goals and the law collided, the law gave way:

- The covert program of support for the Contras evaded the Constitution's most significant check on Executive power: The President can spend funds on a program only if he can convince Congress to appropriate the money.

When Congress enacted the Boland Amendment, cutting off funds for the war in Nicaragua, Administration officials raised funds for the Contras from other sources—foreign Governments, the Iran arms sales, and private individuals; and the NSC staff controlled the expenditures of these funds through power over the Enterprise. Conducting the covert program in Nicaragua with funding from the sale of U.S. Government property and contributions raised by Government officials was a flagrant violation of the Appropriations Clause of the Constitution.

- In addition, the covert program of support for the Contras was an evasion of the letter and spirit of the Boland Amendment. The President made it clear that while he opposed restrictions on military or paramilitary assistance to the Contras, he recognized that compliance with the law was not optional. "[W]hat I might personally wish or what our Government might wish still would not justify us violating the law of the land," he said in 1983.

A year later, members of the NSC staff were devising ways to continue support and direction of Contra activities during the period of the Boland Amendment. What was previously done by the CIA—and now prohibited by the Boland Amendment—would be done instead by the NSC staff.

The President set the stage by welcoming a huge donation for the Contras from a foreign Government—a contribution clearly intended to keep the Contras in the field while U.S. aid was barred. The NSC staff thereafter solicited other foreign Governments for military aid, facilitated the efforts of U.S. fundraisers to provide lethal assistance to the Contras, and ultimately developed and directed a private network that conducted, in North's words, a "full-service covert operation" in support of the Contras.

This could not have been more contrary to the intent of the Boland legislation.

Numerous other laws were disregarded:

- North's full-service covert operation was a "significant anticipated intelligence activity" required to be disclosed to the Intelligence Committees of Congress under Section 501 of the National Security Act. No such disclosure was made.
- By Executive order, a covert operation requires a personal determination by the President before it can be conducted by an agency other than the CIA. It requires a written Finding before any agency can carry it out. In the case of North's full-service covert operation in support of the Contras, there was no such personal determination and no such Finding. In fact, the President disclaims any knowledge of this covert action.
- False statements to Congress are felonies if made with knowledge and intent. Several Administration officials gave statements denying NSC staff activities in support of the Contras which North later described in his testimony as "false" and "misleading, evasive, and wrong."

- The application of proceeds from U.S. arms sales for the benefit of the Contra war effort violated the Boland Amendment's ban on U.S. military aid to the Contras, and constituted a misappropriation of Government funds derived from the transfer of U.S. property.
- The U.S. Government's approval of the pre-Finding 1985 sales by Israel of arms to the Government of Iran was inconsistent with the Government's obligations under the Arms Export Control Act.
- The testimony to Congress in November 1986 that the U.S. Government had no contemporaneous knowledge of the Israeli shipments and the shredding of documents relating to the shipments while a Congressional inquiry into those shipments was pending obstructed Congressional investigations.
- The Administration did not make, and clearly intended never to make, disclosure to the Intelligence Committees of the Finding—later destroyed—approving the November 1985 HAWK shipment, nor did it disclose the covert action to which the Finding related. . . .

Congress and the President

The Constitution of the United States gives important powers to both the President and the Congress in the making of foreign policy. The President is the principal architect of foreign policy in consultation with the Congress. The policies of the United States cannot succeed unless the President and the Congress work together.

Yet, in the Iran-Contra Affair, Administration officials holding no elected office repeatedly evidenced disrespect for Congress' efforts to perform its Constitutional oversight role in foreign policy:

- Poindexter testified, referring to his efforts to keep the covert action in support of the Contras from Congress: "I simply did not want any outside interference."
- North testified: "I didn't want to tell Congress anything" about this covert action.
- [Assistant Secretary of State Elliott] Abrams acknowledged in his testimony that, unless Members of Congressional Committees asked "exactly the right question, using exactly the right words, they weren't going to get the right answers," regarding solicitation of third countries for Contra support.
- And numerous other officials made false statements to, and misled, the Congress. . . .

Who Was Responsible?

Who was responsible for the Iran-Contra Affair? Part of our mandate was to answer that question, not in a legal sense (which is the responsibility of the Independent Counsel), but in order to reaffirm that those who serve the Government are accountable for their actions. Based on our investigation, we reach the following conclusions:

At the operational level, the central figure in the Iran-Contra Affair was

Lt. Col. North, who coordinated all of the activities and was involved in all aspects of the secret operations. North, however, did not act alone.

North's conduct had the express approval of Adm. John Poindexter, first as Deputy National Security Adviser and then as National Security Adviser. North also had at least the tacit support of Robert McFarlane, who served as National Security Adviser until December 1985.

In addition, for reasons cited earlier, we believe that the late Director of Central Intelligence, William Casey, encouraged North, gave him direction and promoted the concept of an extra-legal covert organization. Casey, for the most part, insulated CIA career employees from knowledge of what he and the NSC staff were doing. Casey's passion for covert operations ... was well known. His close relationship with North was attested to by several witnesses. Further, it was Casey who brought Richard Secord into the secret operation, and it was Secord who, with Albert Hakim, organized the Enterprise. These facts provide strong reasons to believe that Casey was involved both with the diversion and with the plans for an "off-the-shelf" covert capacity.

The Committees are mindful, however, of the fact that the evidence concerning Casey's role comes almost solely from North; that this evidence, albeit under oath, was used by North to exculpate himself; and that Casey could not respond. Although North told the Committees that Casey knew of the diversion from the start, he told a different story to the Attorney General in November 1986, as did Casey himself. Only one other witness, Lt. Col. Robert Earl, testified that he had been told by North during Casey's lifetime that Casey knew of the diversion.

The Attorney General recognized on November 31, 1986, the need for an inquiry. His staff was responsible for finding the diversion memorandum, which the Attorney General promptly made public. But as described earlier, his fact-finding inquiry departed from standard investigative techniques. The Attorney General saw Director Casey hours after the Attorney General learned of the diversion memorandum, yet he testified that he never asked Casey about the diversion. He waited two days to speak to Poindexter, North's superior, and then did not ask him what the President knew. He waited too long to seal North's offices. These lapses placed a cloud over the Attorney General's investigation.

There is no evidence that the Vice President was aware of the diversion. The Vice President attended several meetings on the Iran initiative, but none of the participants could recall his views.

The Vice President said he did not know of the Contra resupply operation. His National Security Adviser, Donald Gregg, was told in early August 1986 by a former colleague that North was running the Contra resupply operation, and that ex-associates of Edwin Wilson—a well known ex-CIA official convicted of selling arms to Libya and plotting the murder of his prosecutors—were involved in the operation. Gregg testified that he did not consider these facts worthy of the Vice President's attention and did not report them to him, even after the Hasenfus airplane was shot down and the Administration had denied any connection with it.

The central remaining question is the role of the President in the Iran-Contra Affair. On this critical point, the shredding of documents by Poindexter, North and others, and the death of Casey, leave the record incomplete.

As it stands, the President has publicly stated that he did not know of the diversion. Poindexter testified that he shielded the President from knowledge of the diversion. North said that he never told the President, but assumed that the President knew. Poindexter told North on November 21, 1986, that he had not informed the President of the diversion. Secord testified that North told him he had talked with the President about the diversion, but North testified that he had fabricated this story to bolster Secord's morale.

Nevertheless, the ultimate responsibility for the events in the Iran-Contra Affair must rest with the President. If the President did not know what his National Security Advisers were doing, he should have. It is his responsibility to communicate unambiguously to his subordinates that they must keep him advised of important actions they take for the Administration. The Constitution requires the President "to take care that the laws be faithfully executed." This charge encompasses a responsibility to leave the members of his Administration in no doubt that the rule of law governs. . . .

Several of the President's advisers pursued a covert action to support the Contras in disregard of the Boland Amendment and of several statutes and Executive orders requiring Congressional notification. Several of these same advisers lied, shredded documents, and covered up their actions. These facts have been on the public records for months. The actions of those individuals do not comport with the notion of a country guided by the rule of law. But the President has yet to condemn their conduct.

The President himself told the public that the U.S. Government had no connection to the Hasenfus airplane. He told the public that early reports of arms sales for hostages had "no foundation." He told the public the United States had not condoned the arms sales by Israel to Iran, when in fact he had approved them and signed a Finding, later destroyed by Poindexter, recording his approval. All of these statements by the President were wrong.

Thus, the question whether the President knew of the diversion is not conclusive on the issue of his responsibility. The President created or at least tolerated an environment where those who did know of the diversion believed with certainty that they were carrying out the President's policies.

This same environment enabled a secretary who shredded, smuggled, and altered documents to tell the Committees that "sometimes you have to go above the written law," and it enabled Admiral Poindexter to testify that "frankly, we were willing to take some risks with the law." It was in such an environment that former officials of the NSC staff and their private agents could lecture the Committees that a "rightful cause" justifies any means, that lying to Congress and other officials in the Executive branch itself is acceptable when the ends are just, and that Congress is to blame for passing laws that run counter to Administration policy. What may aptly be called the "cabal of the zealots" was in charge....

Fifty years ago Supreme Court Justice Louis Brandeis observed: "Our Government is the potent, the omnipresent teacher. For good or for ill, it teaches the whole people by its example. Crime is contagious. If the Government becomes a law-breaker, it breeds contempt for law, it invites every man to become a law unto himself, it invites anarchy."

The Iran-Contra Affair resulted from a failure to heed this message....

Recommendations

...Congress cannot legislate good judgment, honesty, or fidelity to law. But there are some changes in law, particularly relating to oversight of covert operations, that would make our processes function better in the future. They are set forth below:

1. Findings: Timely Notice

The Committees recommend that Section 501 of the National Security Act be amended to require that Congress be notified prior to the commencement of a covert action except in certain rare instances and in no event later than 48 hours after a Finding is approved. This recommendation is designed to assure timely notification to Congress of covert operations.

Congress was never notified of the Iranian arms sales, in spite of the existence of a statute requiring prior notice to Congress of all covert actions, or, in rare situations, notice "in a timely fashion." The Administration has reasoned that the risks of leaks justified delaying notice to Congress until after the covert action was over, and claims that notice after the action is over constitutes notice "in a timely fashion." This reasoning defeats the purpose of the law.

2. Written Findings

The Committees recommend legislation requiring that all covert action Findings be in writing and personally signed by the President. Similarly, the Committees recommend legislation that requires that the Findings be signed prior to the commencement of the covert action, unless the press of time prevents it, in which case it must be signed within 48 hours of approval by the President.

The legislation should prohibit retroactive Findings. The legal concept of ratification, which commonly arises in commercial law, is inconsistent with the rationale of Findings, which is to require Presidential approval before any covert action is initiated.

The existing law does not require explicitly that a Presidential Finding approving a covert operation be in writing, although executive orders signed by both Presidents [Jimmy] Carter and Reagan required that they be in writing. Despite this requirement, a PROF note [White House internal computer message] by McFarlane suggested that the initial arms sales to Iran were approved by a "mental finding," and there is conflicting testimony about whether certain actions were orally approved by the President. The requirement of a written Finding will remove such uncertainties in the future.

3. Disclosure of Written Findings to Congress

The Committees recommend legislation requiring that copies of all signed written Findings be sent to the Congressional Intelligence Committees. . . .

4. Findings: Agencies Covered

The Committees recommend that a Finding by the President should be required before a covert action is commenced by any department, agency or entity of the United States Government regardless of what source of funds is used.

The existing statutes require a Presidential Finding before a covert action is conducted only if the covert action uses appropriated funds and is conducted by the Central Intelligence Agency (CIA). By executive order and National Security Decision Directive (NSDD), Presidential Findings are required before covert actions may be conducted by any agency. Nonetheless, both the National Security Council (NSC) and the Drug Enforcement Administration (DEA) became engaged in covert actions without Presidential Findings fully authorizing their involvement.

The executive order requirement is sound. In the Committees' judgment, Presidential Findings for covert actions conducted by any agency should be required by law. Experience suggests that Presidential accountability, as mandated by the Finding requirement, is equally as important in the case of covert actions conducted by agencies other than the CIA. . . .

5. Findings: Identifying Participants

The Committees recommend legislation requiring that each Finding should specify each and every department, agency or entity of the United States Government authorized to fund or otherwise participate in any way in any covert action and whether any third party, including any foreign country, will be used in carrying out or providing funds for the covert action. The Congress should be informed of the identities of such third parties in an appropriate fashion.

Current law does not require a Finding to state what agencies, third parties or countries will be utilized in conducting a covert action. . . .

The record of the Iran-Contra investigation reflects repeated efforts by the executive branch to obtain funds from third countries for covert operations and for other causes the Administration supports.

These actions raise concerns of two kinds. First, there is a risk that foreign countries will expect something in return. Second, in an extreme case such as that presented by the record of these hearings, the use of third-country or private funds threatens to circumvent Congress' exclusive power of the purse.

6. Findings: The Attorney General

The Committees recommend that the Attorney General be provided with a copy of all proposed Findings for purposes of legal review.

The first Iranian arms Finding of December 5, 1985, was not reviewed by the Attorney General. The Attorney General did give oral advice on the January 17 Finding but did not do the analysis or research that a written opinion would have entailed....

7. Findings: Presidential Reporting

The Committees recommend that consistent with the concepts of accountability inherent in the Finding process, the obligation to report covert action Findings should be placed on the President.

Under current law, it is the head of the intelligence entity involved which has the obligation to report to Congress on covert action. Yet policy choices are inherently part of the Findings process and it is the President who must authorize covert operations....

8. Recertification of Findings

The Committees recommend that each Finding shall cease to be operative after one year unless the President certifies that the Finding is still in the national interest. The executive branch and the Intelligence Committees should conduct frequent periodic reviews of all covert operations.

9. Covert Actions Carried Out by Other Countries

The Committees believe that the definition of covert action should be changed so that it includes a request by an agency of the United States to a foreign country or a private citizen to conduct a covert action on behalf of the United States.

10. Reporting Covert Arms Transfers

The Committees recommend that the law regulating the reporting of covert arms transfers be changed to require notice to Congress on any covert shipment of arms where the transfer is valued at more than $1 million.

Under current law, the Administration must report covert arms transfers involving any single item valued at more than $1 million. Since a TOW [antitank] or a HAWK missile is individually worth less than $1 million, this reporting requirement did not apply to the Iranian arms sales even though two shipments involved $10 million in arms or more. It is the value of a transfer, not the value of each component of a transfer, that matters.

11. NSC Operational Activities

The Committees recommend that the members and staff of the NSC not engage in covert actions.

By statute the NSC was created to provide advice to the President on national security matters. But there is no express statutory prohibition on the NSC engaging in operational intelligence activities.

12. NSC Reporting to Congress

The Committees recommend legislation requiring that the President report to Congress periodically on the organization, size, function, and procedures of the NSC staff.

Such a report should include a list of duties for each NSC staff position from the National Security Adviser on down, and whether incumbents have been detailed from a particular department or agency. It should include a description of the President's guidelines and other instructions to the NSC, the National Security Adviser and NSC staff for their activities. Particular attention should be paid to the number and tenure of uniformed military personnel assigned to the NSC.

13. Privatization

The Committees recommend a strict accounting of all U.S. Government funds managed by private citizens during the course of a covert action.

. . . [T]he record reflects that funds generated during a covert action are subject to abuse in the hands of a private citizen involved in conducting a covert action.

14. Preservation of Presidential Documents

The Committees recommend that the Presidential Records Act be reviewed to determine how it can be made more effective. Possible improvements include the establishment of a system of consultation with the archivist of the United States to ensure complete compliance with the Act, the creation of a program of education of affected staff as to the Act's provisions and the attachment of criminal penalties for violations of the Act.

During the Iran-Contra hearings, Oliver North, John Poindexter, Fawn Hall [North's secretary], and others admitted to having altered and destroyed key documents relating to their activities. Such actions constitute violations of the Presidential Records Act, which was intended to ensure the preservation of documents of historical value that were generated by the Chief Executive and his immediate staff.

15. CIA Inspector General and General Counsel

The Committees recommend that a system be developed so that the CIA has an independent statutory Inspector General confirmed by the Senate, like the Inspectors General of other agencies, and that the General Counsel of the CIA be confirmed by the Senate.

The CIA's internal investigation of the Iran-Contra Affair—conducted by the Office of the Inspector General—paralleled those of the Intelligence Committees and then the Iran Committees. It contributed to, and cooperated with, the Tower Board. Yet, the Office of the Inspector General appears not to have had the manpower, resources or tenacity to acquire key facts uncovered by the other investigations.

The Committees also believe the General Counsel plays an important role in these matters and accordingly should be confirmed by the Senate.

16. Foreign Bank Records Treaties

The Committees recommend that treaties be negotiated with foreign countries whose banks are used to conceal financial transactions by U.S. citizens, and that these treaties covering foreign bank records specify that Congress, not just the Department of Justice, has the right to request, to receive, and to utilize such records.

Many of the important records relating to the Iran-Contra Affair were generated by foreign banks that were used by the Enterprise for the covert arms sales to Iran and the Contra supply operation. The Independent Counsel has sought access to these Swiss bank records pursuant to a treaty with Switzerland. But the Independent Counsel and the Justice Department do not believe the Congressional Committees are entitled under the terms of the treaty to receive these records. New treaties should assure Congress of access to such records and should streamline the process for obtaining them. The Independent Counsel had not received all of the Swiss bank records after 9 months of waiting. Given the use of foreign banks by drug dealers, terrorists, and others involved in unlawful activity, it is more essential than ever that binding secrecy not be a shield for serious criminal conduct.

17. National Security Council

The Committees recommend that all statutory members of the National Security Council should be informed of Findings.

18. Findings Cannot Supersede Law

The Committees recommend legislation affirming what the Committees believe to be the existing law: That a Finding cannot be used by the President or any member of the executive branch to authorize an action inconsistent with, or contrary to, any statute of the United States.

19. Improving Consistency in Dealing with Security Breaches

The Committees recommend that consistent methods of dealing with leaks of classified information by government officials be developed.

The record of these hearings is replete with expressions of concern by executive-branch officials over the problem of unauthorized handling and disclosure of classified information. The record is also replete with evidence that high NSC officials breached security regulations and disclosed classified documents to unauthorized persons when it suited their purposes. Yet no steps have been taken to withdraw or even review clearances of such people.

20. Review of Congressional Contempt Statutes

The Committees recommend that the Congressional contempt statutes be reviewed by the appropriate Committees.

There is a need, in Congressional investigations, for a swift and sure method of compelling compliance with Congressional orders for production of documents and the obtaining of testimony. These investigations raised questions about the adequacy of existing statutes.

In addition, new legislation should make clear that a Congressional deposition, including one conducted by staff, is a "proceeding" at which testimony may be compelled under the immunity statute, 18 U.S.C. Section 6001 *et seq*.

21. Review of Special Compartmented Operations Within the Department of Defense

The Committees recommend that oversight by Intelligence and Armed Services Committees of Congress of special compartmented [restricted by classification] operations within the Department of Defense be strengthened to include systematic and comprehensive review of all such programs.

22. Review of Weapons Transfers by Chairman of Joint Chiefs of Staff

The Committees recommend that the President issue an order requiring that the Chairman of the Joint Chiefs of Staff should be consulted prior to any transfer of arms by the United States for purposes of presenting his views as to the potential impact on the military balance and on the readiness of United States forces.

23. National Security Adviser

The Committees recommend that Presidents adopt as a matter of policy the principle that the National Security Adviser to the President of the United States should not be an active military officer and that there should be a limit placed on the tour of military officers assigned to the staff of the National Security Council.

24. Intelligence Oversight Board

The Committees recommend that the Intelligence Oversight Board be revitalized and strengthened.

25. Review of Other Laws

The Committees suggest that appropriate standing Committees review certain laws for possible changes:

a. Should restrictions on sales of arms to certain countries under the

Arms Export Control Act ("AECA") and other statutes governing overt sales be made applicable to covert sales?

b. Should the Hostage Act be repealed or amended?

c. Should enforcement or monitoring provisions be added to the AECA so that we better control retransfers of U.S.-manufactured arms by countries to whom we sell them?

26. Recommendations for Congress

a. The Committees recommend that the oversight capabilities of the Intelligence Committees be strengthened by acquisition of an audit staff.

b. The Committees recommend that the appropriate oversight committees conduct review of sole-source contracts for potential abuse.

c. The Committees recommend that uniform procedures be developed to ensure that classified information is handled in a secure manner and that such procedures should include clear and strengthened sanctions for unauthorized disclosure of national security secrets or classified information which shall be strictly enforced.

27. Joint Intelligence Committee

The Committees recommend against consolidating the separate House and Senate Intelligence Committees into a single joint committee. We believe that such consolidation would inevitably erode Congress' ability to perform its oversight function in connection with intelligence activities and covert operations....

THE MINORITY REPORT

President Reagan and his staff made mistakes in the Iran-Contra Affair. It is important at the outset, however, to note that the President himself has already taken the hard step of acknowledging his mistakes and reacting precisely to correct what went wrong. He has directed the National Security Council staff not to engage in covert operations. He has changed the procedures for notifying Congress when an intelligence activity does take place. Finally, he has installed people with seasoned judgment to be White House Chief of Staff, National Security Adviser and Director of Central Intelligence.

The bottom line, however, is that the mistakes of the Iran-Contra Affair were just that—mistakes in judgment, and nothing more. There was no constitutional crisis, no systematic disrespect for "the rule of law," no grand conspiracy, and no Administration-wide dishonesty or coverup. In fact, the evidence will not support any of the more hysterical conclusions the Committees' Report tries to reach....

The Committees' Report and the Ongoing Battle

The excesses of the Committees' Report are reflections of something far more profound. Deeper than the specifics of the Iran-Contra Affair lies an underlying and festering institutional wound these Committees have been unwilling to face. In order to support rhetorical overstatements about democracy and the rule of law, the Committees have rested their case upon an aggrandizing theory of Congress' foreign policy powers that is itself part of the problem. Rather than seeking to heal, the Committees' hearings and Report betray an attitude that we fear will make matters worse. The attitude is particularly regrettable in light of the unprecedented steps the President took to cooperate with the Committees and in light of the actions he already has taken to correct past errors.

A substantial number of the mistakes of the Iran-Contra Affair resulted directly from an ongoing state of political guerrilla warfare over foreign policy between the legislative and executive branches. We would include in this category the excessive secrecy of the Iran initiative that resulted from a history and legitimate fear of leaks. We also would include the approach both branches took toward the so-called Boland Amendments. Congressional Democrats tried to use vaguely worded and constantly changing laws to impose policies in Central America that went well beyond the law itself. For its own part, the Administration decided to work within the letter of the law covertly, instead of forcing a public and principled confrontation that would have been healthier in the long run.

Given these kinds of problems, a sober examination of legislative-executive branch relations in foreign policy was sorely needed. It still is. Judgments about the Iran-Contra Affair ultimately must rest upon one's views about the proper roles of Congress and the President in foreign policy. There were many statements during the public hearings, for example, about the rule of law. But the fundamental law of the land is the Constitution. Unconstitutional statutes violate the rule of law every bit as much as do willful violations of constitutional statutes. It is essential, therefore, to frame any discussion of what happened with a proper analysis of the constitutional allocation of legislative and executive power in foreign affairs.

The country's future security depends upon a modus vivendi in which each branch recognizes the other's legitimate and constitutionally sanctioned sphere of activity. Congress must recognize that an effective foreign policy requires, and the Constitution mandates, the President to be the country's foreign policy leader. At the same time, the President must recognize that his preeminence rests upon personal leadership, public education, political support, and interbranch comity. Interbranch comity does not require presidential obsequiousness, of course. Presidents are elected to lead and to persuade. But Presidents must also have Congressional support for the tools to make foreign policy effective. No President can ignore Congress and be successful over the long term. Congress must realize, however, that the power of the purse does not make it supreme. Limits must be recognized by both branches, to protect the balance that was intended by the Framers, and that is still needed today for effective policy. This mutual recognition has been sorely lacking in recent years.

Why We Reject the Committees' Report

Sadly, the Committees' Report reads as if it were a weapon in the ongoing guerrilla warfare, instead of an objective analysis. Evidence is used selectively, and unsupported inferences are drawn to support politically biased interpretations. As a result, we feel compelled to reject not only the Committees' conclusions, but the supposedly "factual" narrative as well.

We always knew, of course, that there would be differences of interpretation. We had hoped at the start of this process, however, to arrive at a mutually agreeable statement of facts. Unfortunately, that was not to be. The narrative is not a fair description of events, but an advocate's legal brief that arrays and selects so-called "facts" to fit preconceived theories. Some of the resulting narrative is accurate and supported by the evidence. A great deal is overdrawn, speculative, and built on a selective use of the Committees' documentary materials.

The tone of the Report flows naturally from the tone of the Committees' televised hearings. We feel strongly that the decision to air the hearings compromised some intelligence sources and methods by broadcasting inadvertent slips of the tongue. But one thing television did do successfully was lay bare the passions that animated too much of the Committees' work. Who can forget the massive displays of traveler's checks being shown to the country to discredit [Lt.] Col. [Oliver L.] North's character, weeks before he would be given a chance to reply? Or the "j'accuse" atmosphere with which witnesses were confronted, beginning with the first week's prosecutorial confrontation with [retired major] Gen. [Richard V.] Secord, as Members used the witnesses as objects for lecturing the cameras? These tactics had little to do with fact finding, or with a careful review of policies and institutional processes....

The President's Knowledge of the Diversion

The most politically charged example of the Committees' misuse of evidence is in the way it presents the President's lack of knowledge about the "diversion"—that is, the decision by the former national security adviser, Adm. John [M.] Poindexter, to authorize the use of some proceeds from Iran arms sales to support the Nicaraguan democratic Resistance, or Contras. This is the one case out of thousands in which the Committees—instead of going beyond the evidence as the Report usually does—refused instead to accept the overwhelming evidence with which it was presented. The Report does grudgingly acknowledge that it cannot refute the President's repeated assertion that he knew nothing about the diversion before Attorney General Edwin Meese [III] discovered it in November 1986. Instead of moving forward from this to more meaningful policy questions, however, the Report seeks, without any support, to plant doubts. We will never know what was in the documents shredded by Lt. Col. Oliver L. North in his last days on the NSC [National Security Council] staff, the

Report says. Of course we will not. That same point could have been made, however, to cast unsupported doubt upon every one of the Report's own conclusions. This one seems to be singled out because it was where the President put his own credibility squarely on the line.

The evidence shows that the President did not know about the diversion. . . . [T]his evidence includes a great deal more than just Poindexter's testimony. Poindexter was corroborated in different ways by the President's own diaries and by testimony from North, Meese, Commander Paul Thompson (formerly the NSC's General Counsel), and former White House Chief of Staff Donald Regan. The conclusion that the President did not know about the diversion, in other words, is one of the strongest of all the inferences one can make from the evidence before these Committees. Any attempt to suggest otherwise can only be seen as an effort to sow meritless doubts in the hope of reaping a partisan political advantage.

The Idea for the Diversion and the Use of Israeli Evidence

. . . [T]he lack of objectivity stems more from the way it selects, and makes questionable inferences, from a scarcity of evidence, rather than a deliberate decision to ignore what is available. This becomes most obvious when we see a witness dismissed as being not credible for one set of events, and then see the same witness' uncorroborated testimony become the basis for a major set of assertions about other events. If these flip-flops could be explained by neutral rules of evidence, or if they were random, we could treat them more lightly. But something quite different seems to be at work here. The narrative seems to make every judgment about the evidence in favor of the interpretation that puts the Administration in the worst possible light. . . .

North testified that he first got the idea for diverting some of the Iran arms sale proceeds to the Contras from Manucher Ghorbanifar [middleman in the Iranian arms deal] at a London hotel meeting in late January 1986. He acknowledged that the subject of using the residuals to replenish Israeli weapon supplies, and for related operations, came up in a discussion with Amiram Nir, an Israeli official, in late December or early January. North specifically said, however, that the Nir conversation had nothing to do with the Contras.

The Committees also received a chronology from the Israeli Government, however, that claimed North told Israeli supply officials in New York on December 6 that the Contras needed money, and that he intended to use proceeds from the Iran arms sales to get them some. When North was asked about the December 6 meeting, he reiterated that he did not recall discussing the Contras with anyone involved in the Iran initiative before the late January meeting with Ghorbanifar.

The Committees' Report has used the Israeli chronology, and the timing of North's alleged December 6 conversation, to suggest that the idea of gaining funds for the Nicaraguan Resistance was an important consideration that kept the Iran arms initiative alive, more than a month before the President signed the Finding of January 17. The problem with making this important inference is that we have no way of knowing whether the Israeli chronology is accurate. It may be, but then again it may not. The Government of Israel made its chronology available to the Committees fairly late in our investigations, and consistently refused to let key Israeli participants give depositions to the Committees' counsel.

... [W]e ... object vehemently to the idea that the Committees should use unsworn and possibly self-serving information from a foreign government to reject sworn testimony given by a U.S. official—particularly when the U.S. official's testimony was given under a grant of immunity that protected him from prosecution arising out of the testimony for any charge *except perjury*.

Even if North did mention the Contras to the Israeli supply officials in early December, however, the inference made from the timing would be unfair. The Committees have no evidence that would give them any reason to believe that anyone other than North even considered the Contras in connection with the Iran arms sales before the January finding.... [T]he diversion cannot possibly have been a consideration for people at the policy-making level when the President decided to proceed with the Iran initiative in January.

Off-the-Shelf, Privately Funded Covert Operations

Paradoxically, the Committees seem to have had no difficulty swallowing North's testimony that Director [of Central Intelligence William J.] Casey intended to create a privately funded, off-the-shelf covert operations capability for use in a variety of unforeseen circumstances. This is despite the fact that two people close to Casey at the CIA, ... John M. McMahon and ... Clair George, both denied Casey would ever have countenanced such an idea....

We have to concede the possibility, of course, that Casey might have discussed such an idea speculatively with North without mentioning it to others at the CIA. As with so many other questions, we will never know the answers with certainty. Casey's terminal illness prevented him from testifying between December 1986 and his death in May 1987. Nevertheless, it is interesting to note how much the majority is willing to make of one uncorroborated, disputed North statement that happens to suit its political purpose, in light of the way it treats others by North that are less convenient for the narrative's thesis.

The Allegation of Systematic Cover-up

The Report also tries to present the events of November 1986 as if they represent a systematic attempt by the Administration to cover up the facts of the Iran initiative. The reason for the alleged cover-up, it is suggested, was to keep the American people from learning that the 1985 arms sales were "illegal."

There can be no question that the Administration was reluctant to make all of the facts public in early November, when news of the arms sales first came out in a Lebanese weekly. It is clear from the evidence that this was a time when covert diplomatic discussions were still being conducted with Iran, and there was some basis for thinking more hostages might be released. We consider the Administration's reticence in the early part of the month to have been completely justifiable.

However, as November 1986 wore on, Poindexter and North did falsify the documentary record in a way that we find deplorable. The outstanding fact about the late November events, however, is that Attorney General Meese understood the importance of getting at the truth. Working on a very tight schedule, Meese and three others from the Department of Justice managed to uncover the so-called "diversion memorandum" and reported it to the President. The President immediately removed Poindexter and North from the NSC staff. Shortly afterwards, he asked for an Independent Counsel to be appointed, appointed the Tower Board [a special panel to investigate the Iran-contra affair], and supported the establishment of select Congressional investigative Committees, to which he has given unprecedented cooperation.

The Committees' Report criticizes Meese for not turning his fact-finding operation into a formal criminal investigation a day or two earlier than he did. In fact, the Report strongly tries to suggest that Meese either must have been incompetent or must have been trying to give Poindexter and North more time to cover their tracks. We consider the first of these charges to be untrue and the second to be outrageous. . . .

The "Rule of Law"

Finally, the Committee Report tries—almost as an overarching thesis—to portray the Administration as if it were behaving with wanton disregard for the law. In our view, *every single one* of the Committees' legal interpretations is open to serious questions. On some issues—particularly the ones involving the statutes governing covert operations—we believe the law to be clearly on the Administration's side. In every other case, the issue is at least debatable. In some, such as the Boland Amendment, we are convinced we have by far the better argument. In a few others—such as who owns the funds the Iranians paid Gen. Richard Secord and Albert Hakim [Secord's business partner]—we see the legal issue as being close. . . .

What the Committees' Report has done with the legal questions, however, is to issue a one-sided legal brief that pretends the Administration did not even have worthwhile arguments to make. As if that were not enough, the Report tries to build upon these one-sided assertions to present a politicized picture of an Administration that behaved with contempt for the law. . . .

Our View of the Iran-Contra Affair

... In our view, the Administration did proceed legally in pursuing both its Contra policy and the Iran arms initiative. We grant that the diversion does raise some legal questions, as do some technical and relatively insubstantial matters relating to the Arms Export Control Act. It is important to stress, however, that the Administration could have avoided every one of the legal problems it inadvertently encountered, while continuing to pursue the exact same policies as it did....

Nicaragua

The Nicaraguan aspect of the Iran-Contra Affair had its origins in several years of bitter political warfare over U.S. policy toward Central America between the Reagan Administration and the Democratic House of Representatives....

Actions

By the late spring of 1984, it became clear that the Resistance would need some source of money if it were to continue to survive while the Administration tried to change public and Congressional opinion. To help bridge the gap, some Administration officials began encouraging foreign governments and U.S. private citizens to support the Contras. NSC staff members played a major role in these efforts, but were specifically ordered to avoid direct solicitations. The President clearly approved of private benefactor and third-country funding, and neither he *nor his designated agents* could constitutionally be prohibited from encouraging it. To avoid political retribution, however, the Administration did not inform Congress of its actions....

Because the Boland Amendment is an appropriations rider, it is worth noting that there is no evidence that any substantial amounts of appropriated taxpayer funds were used in support of these efforts. In addition, the NSC staff believed—as we do—that the prohibition did not cover the NSC. At no time, in other words, did members of the President's staff think their activities were illegal. Nevertheless, the NSC staff did make a concerted effort to conceal its actions from Congress. There is no evidence, however, to suggest that the President or other senior Administration officials knew about this concealment.

Judgments

The effort to raise foreign government and private funds for the Resistance raised about $35 million between mid-1984 and mid-1986—virtually all of it from foreign countries. In addition, the ... unauthorized diversion orchestrated by North and Poindexter contributed about $3.8 million more. Without this support, according to uncontroverted testimony the Committees received, there can be no question that the Resistance would have been annihilated. In other words, the support clearly did make an important strategic difference in the 2 years it took the

Administration to persuade Congress to reverse its position. The short-term benefits of the effort are therefore undeniable. The long-term costs, however, seem not to have been adequately considered.

We do believe ... that virtually all of the NSC staff's activities were legal, with the possible exception of the diversion of Iran arms sale proceeds.... We concede that reasonable people may take a contrary view of what Congress intended the Boland Amendments to mean....

Notwithstanding our legal opinions, we think it was a fundamental mistake for the NSC staff to have been secretive and deceptive about what it was doing. The requirement for building long-term political support means that the Administration would have been better off if it had conducted its activities in the open. Thus, the President should simply have vetoed the strict Boland Amendment in mid-October 1984, even though the Amendment was only a few paragraphs in an approximately 1,200-page-long continuing appropriations resolution, and a veto therefore would have brought the Government to a standstill within 3 weeks of a national election. Once the President decided against a veto, it was self-defeating to think a program this important could be sustained by deceiving Congress. Whether technically illegal or not, it was politically foolish and counterproductive to mislead Congress, even if misleading took the form of artful evasion or silence instead of overt misstatement.

We do believe firmly that the NSC staff's deceits were not meant to hide illegalities. Every witness we have heard told us his concern was not over legality, but with the fear that Congress would respond to complete disclosure with political reprisals, principally by tightening the Boland Amendments. That risk should have been taken....

Iran

... The potential geopolitical importance of Iran for the United States would be obvious to anyone who looks at a map.... The United States was approached by Israel in 1985 with a proposal that the United States acquiesce in some minor Israeli arms sales to Iran. This proposal came at a time when the United States was already considering the advisability of such sales. For long term, strategic reasons, the United States had to improve relationships with at least some of the currently important factions in Iran....

Actions

To explore the chance for an opening, the President agreed first to approve Israeli sales to Iran in 1985, and then in 1986 to sell U.S. arms directly. The amounts involved were meager. The total amount, including all of the 1985 and 1986 sales combined, consisted of 2004 TOW antitank missiles, 18 Hawk antiaircraft missiles, and about 200 types of HAWK spare parts.

There was a strong division of opinion in the Administration about the advisability of these arms sales, a division that never abated. Unfortunately, this served as a pretext for Poindexter's decision not to keep the Secretaries of State or Defense informed about the detailed progress of the negotiations between the United States and Iran. One reason for the failure to inform appears to have been a past history in which some Administration officials may have leaked sensitive information as a way to halt actions with which they disagreed. Poindexter's secretive inclinations were abetted by Secretary [of State George P.] Shultz, who all but invited Poindexter not to keep him informed because he did not want to be accused of leaking. They also were abetted by Secretary [of Defense Caspar W.] Weinberger, who—like Shultz—was less than vigorous about keeping himself informed about a policy he had good reason to believe was still going forward....

As a result of factional infighting inside the Iranian Government, the initiative was exposed and substantive discussions were suspended. Not surprisingly, given the nature of Iranian politics, the Iranian Government has publicly denied that significant negotiations were under way. Congress was not informed of the Administration's dealings with Iran until after the public disclosure. The failure to disclose resembled the Carter Administration's similar decisions not to disclose in the parallel Iranian hostage crisis of 1979-81. President Reagan withheld disclosure longer than [Jimmy] Carter, however—by about 11 months to 6....

Judgments

... In retrospect, it seems clear that this initiative degenerated into a series of "arms for hostage" deals. It did not look that way to many of the U.S. participants at the time. Nevertheless, the fact that the negotiations never were able clearly to separate the long-term from the short-term issues, confirms our instinctive judgment that the United States should not have allowed arms to become the currency by which our country's bona fides were determined. There is no evidence that these relatively minor sales materially altered the military balance in the Iran-Iraq war. However, the sales damaged U.S. credibility with our allies, making it more difficult, among other things, for the Administration to enforce its pre-existing efforts to embargo arms sales to Iran.

The decision to keep Congress in the dark for 11 months disturbs all Members of these Committees. It is clear that the Reagan Administration simply did not trust the Congress to keep secrets. Based on the history of leaks, ... it unfortunately had good reason to be concerned. This observation is not offered as a justification, but as an important part of the context that must be understood....

Diversion

The lack of detailed information-sharing within the Administration was what made it possible for Poindexter to authorize the diversion and successfully keep his decision to do so from the President. We have already indicated our reasons for being convinced the President knew nothing about the diversion. The majority Report says that if the President did not know about it, he should have. We agree, and so does the President. But unlike some of the other decisions we have been discussing, the President cannot himself be faulted for this one. The decision was Admiral Poindexter's and Poindexter's alone. . . .

The diversion also differs from the basic Nicaragua and Iran policies in another important respect: We can find nothing to justify or mitigate its having occurred. We do understand the enthusiasm North displayed when he told the Committees it was a "neat idea" to use money from the Ayatollah [Ruhollah Khomeini, Iran's religious leader], who was helping the Sandinistas, to support the Contras. But enthusiasm is not a sufficient basis for important policy decisions. Even if there were nothing else wrong with the diversion, the decision to mix two intelligence operations increased the risk of pursuing either one, with predictably disastrous repercussions.

Unlike the Committees' majority, we believe there are good legal arguments on both sides of the question of whether the proceeds of the arms sales belong to the U.S. Government or to Secord and Hakim. For that reason, we think it unlikely, under the circumstances, that the funds were acquired or used with any criminal intent. Nevertheless, the fact that the ownership seems unclear under current law does not please us. We do believe that Secord and Hakim were acting as the moral equivalents of U.S. agents, even if they were not U.S. agents in law.

. . . We remain convinced that covert operations will continue to have to use private agents or contractors in the future, and that those private parties will continue to operate at least partly from profit motives. If the United States tries to limit itself to dealing only with people who act out of purely patriotic motives, it effectively will rule out any worthwhile dealing with most arms dealers and foreign agents. In the real world of international politics, it would be foolish to avoid working with people whose motives do not match our own. Nevertheless, we do feel troubled by the fact that there was not enough legal clarity, or accounting controls, placed on the Enterprise by the NSC.

The Uncovering

It is clear that officials of the National Security Council misled the Congress and other members of the Administration about their activities in support of the Nicaraguan Resistance. This occurred without authorization from outside the NSC staff. It is also clear that the NSC staff actively misled other Administration officials and Congress about the Iran initiative both before and after the first public disclosure. The shredding of documents and other efforts at covering up what had happened were also undertaken by NSC staff members acting on their own, without the knowledge, consent, or acquiescence of the President or other major Administration officials, with the possible exception of Casey.

In the week or two immediately after the Iran initiative was disclosed in a Lebanese weekly, the President did not tell the public all that he knew, because negotiations with the Second Channel [Iranian officials who became the contacts in the Iranian arms deal after the first contacts did not work out] were still going on, and there remained a good reason for hoping some more hostages might soon be released. Once the President learned that not all of the relevant facts were being brought to his attention, however, he authorized the Attorney General immediately to begin making inquiries. Attorney General Meese acted properly in his investigation, pursuing the matter as a fact-finding effort because he had no reason at the time to believe a crime had been committed. Arguments to the contrary are based strictly on hindsight. In our opinion, the Attorney General and other Justice Department officials did an impressive job with a complicated subject in a short time. After all, it was their investigation that uncovered and disclosed the diversion of funds to the Contras.

Common Threads

The different strands of the Iran-Contra Affair began coming together, in the most obvious way, on the level of personnel. Both halves of the event were run by the NSC, specifically by [Robert C.] McFarlane, Poindexter and North. With respect to Nicaragua, the Boland Amendment just about ruled all other agencies out of the picture. With respect to Iran, the other parts of the executive branch—from the State and Defense Departments to the CIA—seemed more than happy to let the NSC be in charge.

It is ironic that many have looked upon these events as signs of an excessively powerful NSC staff. In fact, the NSC's roles in the Iran and Nicaragua policies were exceptions rather than the rule. The Reagan Administration has been beleaguered from the beginning by serious policy disagreements between the Secretaries of State and Defense, among others, and the President has too often not been willing to settle those disputes definitively....

...It is not satisfactory, however, for people in the Administration simply to point the finger at him and walk away from all responsibility. For one thing, the President himself does have to bear personal responsibility for the people he picks for top office. But just as it would not be appropriate for the fingers to point only at Poindexter, neither is it right for them only to point to the top....

The discussion of personnel ultimately gets around to the importance of political judgment. We can be more precise about what that means, however, if we consider the common threads in the decisions we have already labeled as mistakes. These have included:

- The President's decision to sign the Boland Amendment of 1984, instead of vetoing it;
- The President's less-than-robust defense of his office's constitutional powers, a mistake he repeated when he acceded too readily and too completely to waive executive privilege for our Committees' investigation;

- The NSC staff's decision to deceive Congress about what it was doing in Central America;
- The decision, in Iran, to pursue a covert policy that was at odds with the Administration's public expressions, without any warning signals to Congress or our allies;
- The decision to use a necessary and constitutionally protected power of withholding information from Congress for unusually sensitive covert operations, for a length of time that stretches credulity;
- Poindexter's decision to authorize the diversion on his own; and, finally,
- Poindexter and North's apparent belief that covering up was in the President's political interest.

We emphatically reject the idea that through these mistakes, the executive branch subverted the law, undermined the Constitution, or threatened democracy. The President is every bit as much of an elected representative of the people as is a Member of Congress. In fact, he and the Vice President are the only officials elected by the whole Nation. Nevertheless, we do believe the mistakes relate in a different way to the issue of democratic accountability. They provide a good starting point for seeing what both sides of the great legislative-executive branch divide must do to improve the way the Government makes foreign policy.

Congress

Congress has a hard time even conceiving of itself as contributing to the problem of democratic accountability. But the record of ever-changing policies toward Central America that contributed to the NSC staff's behavior is symptomatic of a frequently recurring problem. When Congress is narrowly divided over highly emotional issues, it frequently ends up passing intentionally ambiguous laws or Amendments that postpone the day of decision. In foreign policy, those decisions often take the form of restrictive Amendments on money bills that are open to being amended again *every year,* with new, and equally ambiguous, language replacing the old. This matter is exacerbated by the way Congress, year after year, avoids passing appropriations bills before the fiscal year starts and then wraps them together in a governmentwide continuing resolution loaded with Amendments that cannot be vetoed without threatening the whole Government's operation.

One properly democratic way to ameliorate the problem of foreign policy inconsistency would be to give the President an opportunity to address the major differences between himself and the Congress cleanly, instead of combining them with unrelated subjects. To restore the presidency to the position it held just a few Administrations ago, Congress should exercise the self-discipline to split continuing resolutions into separate appropriations bills and present each of them individually to the President for his signature or veto. Even better would be a line-item veto that would permit the President to force Congress to an override vote without jeopardizing funding for the whole Government....

Afterword: Summary of Legal Conclusions

Nicaragua

...(1) The Constitution protects the power of the President, either acting himself or through agents of his choice, to engage in whatever diplomatic communications with other countries he may wish. It also protects the ability of the President and his agents to persuade U.S. citizens to engage voluntarily in otherwise legal activity to serve what they consider to be the national interest. That includes trying to persuade other countries to contribute their own funds for causes both countries support. To whatever extent the Boland Amendments tried to prohibit such activity, they were clearly unconstitutional.

(2) If the Constitution prohibits Congress from restricting a particular Presidential action directly, it cannot use the appropriation power to achieve the same unconstitutional effect. Congress does have the power under the Constitution, however, to use appropriations riders to prohibit the entire U.S. Government from spending any money, including salaries, to provide covert or overt military support to the Contras. Thus, the Clark Amendment prohibiting all U.S. support for the Angolan Resistance in 1976 was constitutional. Some members of Congress who supported the Boland Amendment may have thought they were enacting a prohibition as broad as the Clark Amendment. The specific language of the Boland Amendment was considerably more restricted, however, in two respects.

(a) By limiting the coverage to agencies or entities involved in intelligence activities, Congress chose to use language borrowed directly from the Intelligence Oversight Act of 1980. In the course of settling on that language in 1980, Congress deliberately decided to exclude the National Security Council from its coverage. At no time afterward did Congress indicate an intention to change the language's coverage. The NSC therefore was excluded from the Boland Amendment and its activities were therefore legal under this statute.

(b) The Boland prohibitions also were limited to spending that directly or indirectly supported military or paramilitary operations in Nicaragua. Under this language, a wide range of intelligence-gathering and political support activities were still permitted and were carried out with the full knowledge of the House and Senate Intelligence Committees.

(c) Virtually all, if not all, of the CIA's activities examined by these Committees occurred after the December 1985 law authorized intelligence sharing and communications support and were fully legal under the terms of that law.

(d) If the NSC had been covered by the Boland Amendments, most of

Oliver North's activity still would have fallen outside the prohibitions for reasons stated in (b) and (c) above.

Iran

The Administration was also in substantial compliance with the laws governing covert actions throughout the Iran arms initiative.

(1) It is possible to make a respectable legal argument to the effect that the 1985 Israeli arms transfers to Iran technically violated the terms of the Arms Export Control Act (AECA) or Foreign Assistance Act (FAA), assuming the arms Israel transferred were received from the United States under one or the other of these statutes. However:

(a) Covert transfers under the National Security Act and Economy Act were understood to be alternatives to transfers under the AECA and FAA that met both of these latter acts' essential purposes by including provisions for Presidential approval and Congressional notification.

(b) The requirement for U.S. agreement before a country can retransfer arms obtained from the United States is meant to insure that retransfers conform to U.S. national interests. In this case, the Israeli retransfers occurred with Presidential approval indicating that they did so conform.

(c) The Israeli retransfer and subsequent replenishment made the deal essentially equivalent to a direct U.S. sale, with Israel playing a role fundamentally equivalent to that of a middleman. Since the United States could obviously have engaged in a direct transfer, and did so in 1986, whatever violation may have occurred was, at most, a minor and inadvertent technicality.

(2) A verbal approval for covert transactions meets the requirements of the Hughes-Ryan Amendment [requiring the executive branch to notify certain Congressional committees of covert operations] and National Security Act. Verbal approvals ought to be reduced to writing as a matter of sound policy, but they are not illegal.

(3) Similarly, the President has the constitutional and statutory authority to withhold notifying Congress of covert activities under very rare conditions. . . . We do not agree with President Reagan's decision to withhold notification for as long as he did. The decision was legal, however, and we think the Constitution mandates that it should remain so. If a President withholds notification for too long and then cannot adequately justify the decision to Congress, that President can expect to pay a stiff political price, as President Reagan has certainly found out.

Diversion

We consider the ownership of the funds the Iranians paid to the Secord-Hakim "Enterprise" to be in legal doubt. There are respectable legal arguments to be made both for the point of view that the funds belong to the U.S. Treasury and for the contention that they do not. If the funds do not belong to the United States, then the diversion amounted to third-country or private funds being shipped to the Contras. If they did belong to the United States, there would be legal questions (although not, technically, Boland Amendment questions) about using U.S.-owned funds for purposes not specifically approved by law. The answer does not seem to us to be so obvious, however, as to warrant treating the matter as if it were criminal. . . .

U.S. AGREEMENTS WITH CUBA AND WITH CUBAN DETAINEES

November 20, 27 and December 4, 1987

On November 23 more than 1,000 Cuban detainees took control of the federal detention center in Oakdale, Louisiana, sacking the facility and taking twenty-eight hostages. Two days later 1,400 Cuban inmates at the federal detention center in Atlanta, Georgia, overpowered their guards and took ninety-four hostages.

The riots broke out following reports that the United States and Fidel Castro's Cuban government had agreed to restore an immigration pact (originally negotiated in 1984) allowing for the return to Cuba of up to 2,500 refugees classified as criminal, mentally ill, or "socially unassimilable."

Eleven days after the uprising began, the last hostages were released and the government regained control of the facilities. During that period, Department of Justice officials and the rioters with their advisers negotiated two separate agreements concerning the inmates' future status and the handling of deportation proceedings. The agreements included provisions for an "expeditious" review of individual cases, guarantees against reprisals for damage to the facilities, and prohibitions of the arbitrary canceling of paroles.

The Mariel Boatlift

The prison sieges brought into focus the plight of the Cuban detainees, many of whom had spent years in detention without representation or the prospect of release. Images of Cuban inmates, some draped in

American flags, asking to remain in prison rather than be sent back to Cuba, were prominently aired by the nation's media. The detainees' situation, called by one official a "powderkeg ready to explode," had finally come to the forefront.

The inmates at Atlanta and Oakdale constituted a fraction of the more than 125,000 Cubans who came to the United States during the 1980 Mariel boat lift. (Historic Documents of 1980, p. 337) *The dramatic "freedom flotilla," which ferried refugees from the Cuban port of Mariel to southern Florida, had been launched after a remarkable string of events on the island.*

A Cuban bus driver had rammed his bus through the gates of the Peruvian embassy compound seeking asylum. In the ensuing disturbance, a Cuban guard was killed and an angered Castro responded by withdrawing the Cuban guards from the embassy. Subsequently more than 10,000 people swarmed around the embassy, hoping to emigrate. The massive demonstration of dissent and the international media attention it attracted forced Castro to announce that anyone wishing to leave could do so. President Jimmy Carter further encouraged the mass exodus by declaring that the United States would greet the new arrivals with "open hearts and open arms." But when it was learned that Castro had increased the flood of refugees by emptying some of his prisons and mental asylums, American attitudes toward the "marielitos" hardened, and immigration officials tried to separate legitimate refugees from those set loose by Havana.

1984 Agreement

In December 1984 a migration agreement between the United States and Cuba called for Cuba to take back 2,746 refugees who were considered deportable by immigration officials. However, Castro suspended the agreement five months later when the Reagan administration's Voice of America started up Radio Marti, a Spanish-language station directed at Cuba.

The two countries were at loggerheads until November 1987, when talks were reopened in Mexico City. The restoration of the agreement provided that as many as 27,000 Cubans could emigrate legally to the United States every year. But it was Cuba's agreement to take back more than 2,500 detainees that set unprepared prison officials on alert and precipitated the uprisings.

Riots at Two Facilities

When the State Department announced the agreement November 20, U.S. prison officials were caught unaware. The news, which was broadcast over television and radio, quickly spread through the Oakdale and Atlanta facilities, prompting officials to add extra staff. However, other crisis-averting measures—such as individual counseling or identification and segregation of those eligible for deportation—were not taken.

At 7:00 p.m. the following day 300 inmates at the Oakdale detention center tried to escape by rushing the gate. Immigration officials outside the compound used tear gas to force the inmates back from the barbed-wire fences. The prisoners rushed back to their dormitories but were locked out. A stone-throwing melee ensued. More than 1,000 Cuban inmates rampaged through the prison buildings setting fires and taking guards and other prison employees hostage. As negotiations began at the Oakdale facility, prison officials in Atlanta debated whether to confine the Cuban inmates to their cells.

Two days later a scuffle in a prison factory in the Atlanta facility erupted into a full-scale uprising. The rioting Cuban inmates took seventy-five hostages and set fire to several buildings. One inmate was shot and killed by a guard and at least twenty-three others were injured.

U.S. Attorney General Edwin Meese III offered inmates at both prisons a moratorium on further deportations with assurances that cases would be reviewed individually if the uprisings ended and the hostages were released unharmed.

The offer was rejected by inmates, who charged that the government could not be trusted. On November 25 Atlanta inmates stormed the prison hospital, taking twenty-five more hostages. Army personnel were flown in to give technical support, while in Oakdale the inmates presented a list of demands to government negotiators.

Negotiations

On November 26, as respected members of the Cuban-American community entered into the Atlanta negotiations, inmates at Oakdale released one hostage, raising hopes of an agreement. However, a group of hardline inmates blocked agreement by adding demands that were unacceptable to government officials.

The inmates began to call for intervention by Auxiliary Bishop Agustin A. Roman of the Roman Catholic Archdiocese of Miami. The Cuban-born Roman had spoken out against overcrowded conditions at the facilities and the denial of detainees' constitutional rights.

On November 27, after watching a videotape in which Bishop Roman urged them to "release the prisoners" and "sign the document," the inmates at Oakdale threw down their weapons and released all their hostages. On December 4, inmates at the Atlanta center viewed a similar videotape and released the remaining hostages, ending the siege.

The provisions of the agreements were similar to the attorney general's proposal. They called for delaying the deportations until special hearings could be held on the inmates' status, but the U.S. government retained the right to repatriate "undesirables." The inmates also failed to obtain one of the most important concessions they had sought: the right to have lawyers during reviews of their cases.

Following are texts of the agreement between the United States and the Cuban government on the return of Cuban detainees, signed November 20, 1987; the statement of the same date announcing reinstatement of the Mariel agreement; and the agreements between the U.S. Justice Department and the Cuban detainees at the Oakdale, Louisiana, and Atlanta, Georgia, detention centers, signed on November 27 and December 4:

U.S.-CUBA AGREEMENT

Communiqué

Discussions between representatives of the United States of America and of the Republic of Cuba on immigration matters concluded today with the adoption of agreements for the normalization of immigration procedures between the two countries and to put an end to the abnormal situation which has existed since 1980.

The United States will resume issuance of preference immigrant visas to Cuban nationals residing in Cuba up to the number of 20,000 each year, in particular to close family relatives of United States citizens and of Cuban permanent residents in the United States.

The United States side expressed its willingness to implement—with the cooperation of the Cuban authorities—all necessary measures to ensure that Cuban nationals residing in Cuba wishing to emigrate to the United States and who qualify under United States law to receive immigrant visas, may enter the United States, taking maximum advantage of the number of up to 20,000 immigrants per year.

For its part, the United States will continue granting immigrant visas to residents of Cuba who are parents, spouses and unmarried children under 21 years of age of United States citizens. These immigrants will not be counted against the annual limit indicated above.

Cuba will accept the return of those Cuban nationals who came to the United States in 1980 via the port of Mariel and who have been declared ineligible to enter the United States legally. The number of such persons is 2,746 and their names appear on an approved list. The return of these persons will be carried out by means of an orderly program of returns with the cooperation of the immigration authorities of both countries. The returns will proceed in a phased and orderly manner until all the identified individuals who appear on the approved list have been returned. The returns will be effected at a rate of 100 each calendar month, but if the figure of 100 is not met in a given month, the remaining numbers may be used in subsequent months, provided that no more than 150 will be returned in any calendar month. The United States stated that measures were being taken so that the Cuban nationals who came to the United States in 1980 via the port of Mariel may acquire, beginning now and with retroactive effect of approximately 30 months, legal status as permanent residents of the United States.

Both delegations expressed their concern in regard to the situation of those persons who, having been released after serving sentences for acts which Cuban penal legislation defines as "Offenses against the Security of the State," wish to reside permanently in the United States. The United States will facilitate the admission of such persons and their immediate family members by means of a program to be carried out under applicable United States law. The United States delegation stated that to this end the necessary steps have been taken for admission during Fiscal Year 1985 of up to 3,000 such persons, including immediate family members. The size of the program and any possible increase in subsequent fiscal years will be determined in the light of experience with the process and the desire expressed by both parties to carry out this program in such a way as to allow its ongoing implementation until fully completed in the shortest possible time.

The representatives of the United States of America and of the Republic of Cuba decided to meet again within six months in order to analyze progress in the implementation of these agreements.

New York, December 14, 1984

Minute on Implementation

In regard to the discussions on immigration matters which concluded today, the representatives of the United States of America and of the Republic of Cuba reached the following agreements on the implementation of certain points dealt with in the Communiqué announcing the results of these talks:

Concerning the return of Cuban nationals who came to the United States in 1980 by the port of Mariel and who have been identified by the United States as persons ineligible to enter the United States legally, it was agreed that the returns would begin no earlier than 30 days from today. The United States immigration authorities will give the Cuban authorities in advance of the actual return of any person all available health information, including any available medical records, diagnoses and recommendations for treatment. Both authorities will cooperate closely to assure that appropriate measures are taken to protect both the health of the individual and the public health.

With regard to persons charged with committing crimes in the United States, the United States wil furnish a certified description, based on United States records, of the offense or offenses committed, the nature of the evidence supporting the charges, the time the person was held in detention, and the status of judicial proceedings, including the sentence imposed, if any.

Likewise, the United States will provide a certified copy of the applicable federal or state law establishing the offense. These documents will be provided as soon as possible and in no case later than 30 days prior to the date on which the person is to be returned to Cuba, allowing the Cuban authorities to analyze the criminal records of those who committed an offense during their stay in the United States and who are to be returned by the United States authorities. The United States immigration authorities will notify the Cuban immigration authorities, no less than 10 days prior to a return, of the registration number of the aircraft to be used to transport persons to Cuba, of the names of the individuals aboard such flights, and of the measures for inflight custody.

If, at the point of entry in Cuba, errors are detected which both parties agree negate the identification of a person being returned as a Cuban national who left Cuba via Mariel in 1980, that person will be returned to the United States pending further efforts to identify him.

The definition of "Offenses against the Security of the State" is understood to include former prisoners convicted of the offense of illegal departure from the country which, at the time the offense was committed, was defined by applicable criminal law as falling within that definition.

The former prisoner who emigrates to the United States may be accompanied by his parents, unmarried children under 21 years of age and spouse, and, as appropriate, other family members who live with him under his protection or custody.

In order to facilitate the ongoing and uninterrupted implementation of the program for the normal issuance of immigrant visas and the program for former prisoners, the Government of Cuba will furnish to applicants for entry into the United States the necessary documents in accordance with United States law such as certified copies of vital statistics registry extracts (birth, marriage, and death certificates), divorce decree, as well as penal records, and will facilitate to the extent possible the conduct of medical examinations including provision of chest x-rays.

The United States Interests Section will continue to employ measures which are conducive to the orderly processing of persons applying to go to the United States, including the continued use of applications by mail.

The normal processing of immigrant visas and the processing of applications for the program for former prisoners will require the assignment of 10 additional United States officials to the United States Interests Section of the Embassy of Switzerland in Havana. The Cuban Government agreed to authorize these increases, on the understanding that these officers will be assigned temporarily and will not be considered permanent staff of the United States Interests Section, and agreed to provide them with the necessary facilities for carrying out their functions.

The representatives of the United States and Cuba agreed to meet within six months to analyze progress in implementation of these steps.

New York, December 14, 1984

STATEMENT CONCERNING REINSTATEMENT OF THE MARIEL AGREEMENT

Representatives of the United States of America and the Republic of Cuba met to discuss problems of migration and radio broadcasting.

They agreed to resume implementation of the 1984 migration agreement in all of its aspects immediately.

They also agreed to continue negotiations on radio broadcasting in the medium wave band directed from one country to audiences in the other in order to find a mutually acceptable arrangement.

They further agreed that a systematic effort is required to reduce the technical interference which results from the congestion in the medium wave broadcast band and the proximity of the two nations.

The negotiations for the solution of these problems shall be conducted in strict accord with international law, including applicable international radio law and regulations.

OAKDALE AGREEMENT

Upon the release of all remaining officers being held on the compound at FDC, Oakdale, the following agreement will immediately be enforced.

1. Cuban detainees with families and/or sponsors who have already been approved for parole will not have an *arbitrary* change made in their release decision.

2. The release of the Cuban detainees with no family or sponsor, who have already been approved for parole, will be reviewed and a decision made within a reasonable time. This will permit a full, fair, and equitable review within the laws of the United States of each individual's status with respect to eligibility to remain in the United States.

   All Cuban detainees at FDC, Oakdale who have not been reviewed yet, will receive an expeditious review of their status and those eligible for release will be given the same consideration as No. 1 and No. 2, above.

3. All Cuban detainees at FDC, Oakdale with medical problems will be sent immediately to medical facilities for evaluation and treatment. Once these detainees are cleared medically, they will be given the same considerations as No. 1 and No. 2, above.

4. Cuban detainees at FDC, Oakdale will be given I-94 and other INS documents including work permit, when they are released. No Cuban detainee will be held by INS without an appropriate charge.

5. No Cuban detainees will be held liable for any damage, to this date, sustained by the institution during the hostage situation at this facility.

6. It is understood that the American Cadre at FDC, Oakdale did not have any part in this situation and can be removed immediately.
7. Those Cuban detainees who have been accepted for entrance to another country will be expeditiously reviewed.

ATLANTA AGREEMENT

Upon the release of all remaining officers being held on the compound at the USP, Atlanta, the following agreement will immediately be enforced.

1. Cuban detainees with families and/or sponsors who have already been approved for parole will not have any arbitrary change made in their release decision.
2. The release of the Cuban detainees with no family or sponsor, who have already been approved for parole, will be reviewed and a decision made within a reasonable time, the process to be completed by June 30, 1988.

   All Cuban detainees at USP, Atlanta, who have not been reviewed yet, will receive an expeditious review of their status and those eligible for release will be given the same consideration as those covered by points No. 1 and No. 2 above.
3. All Cuban detainees at USP, Atlanta, with medical problems will be sent immediately to medical facilities for evaluation and treatment. Once these detainees are cleared medically, they will be given the same consideration as those covered by points No. 1 and No. 2 above.
4. Cuban detainees at USP, Atlanta, who are approved for parole, will be given I-94 and other INS documents, including work permit, when they are released. No Cuban detainee will be held by INS without an appropriate charge.
5. No Cuban detainee will be held liable for any damage, to this date, sustained by the institution during the hostage situation at this facility. There will be no physical reprisals against the detainees. There will be no prosecution, except for specific acts of actual, assaultive violence against persons or major misconduct. This does not include mere active participation in the disturbance, failing to depart Atlanta Penitentiary during the disturbance, or acts causing property damage.
6. It is understood that the American Cadre at USP, Atlanta, did not have any part in this situation and can be removed immediately.
7. Cuban detainees who desire to go to a third country and who are accepted by a third country will be reviewed very quickly, and will be permitted to depart, with proper documentation, and barring criminal action pending. It is the option of any detainee to apply for acceptance

by a third country, and any detainee will be given the opportunity to make such an application. Such an application should be made quickly after the disturbance is resolved, if a detainee does not have such acceptance already.

8. As previously stated by the U.S. Attorney General, a moratorium has been declared on the return of the Cuban nationals to Cuba, with reference to those Cubans who came to the United States in 1980, via the Port of Mariel. This moratorium includes all Cubans detained in the U.S., and will insure a fair review of each Cuban['s] status, with respect to his eligibility to remain in the U.S.

ELECTIONS IN HAITI

November 29, 1987

Frustrated by the cancellation of presidential elections in Haiti and reported violence against civilians, the United States November 29 cut off all military assistance to the Caribbean nation in an attempt to force new, more orderly elections. The U.S. action followed a year of turmoil and upheaval as Haiti struggled to establish a democratic government after decades of dictatorial rule.

"The United States government reaffirms its support for the Haitian people in their efforts to secure a democratic political system through free and fair elections," Secretary of State George Shultz said in a cable announcing the cutoff of $101.2 million in aid. Earlier that day, the provisional government in Haiti had called off presidential elections after more than two dozen people were killed while waiting to vote. Press reports said government troops participated in or condoned some of the acts of violence.

The decision reflected U.S. bitterness at the provisional government's failure to ensure the success of the election. Presidential candidates and members of a special Haitian election council received several death threats, and the provisional government of Gen. Henri Namphy did not respond to their requests for protection. Foreign observers said Namphy did not trust a civilian democratic government and planned to stay in power. By year's end, the general had agreed to hold a new election, but opponents remained skeptical.

Violence and repression dated back several decades in Haiti. In 1986 dictator Claude "Baby Doc" Duvalier was thrown out of office, and Namphy's provisional military government pledged to hold free elections and establish a democracy. After Duvalier's ouster, human rights conditions did improve (State Department human rights report, p. 189), *and citizens approved a democratic constitution with a popularly elected president to be installed by February 1988.*

Democratic Drive Halted

But conditions deteriorated during the last half of 1987 as the country headed toward a November election. In July a weeklong national protest followed Namphy's decision to give his military-led government control of the elections. Although a civilian council eventually was assigned the task, council members faced numerous death threats and complained of not receiving the personal protection they had requested from the government.

In early November, three weeks before the election, several members of the commission went into hiding after arson attacks at their offices. Presidential candidates also received death threats, and one candidate was killed in front of the capital city's police headquarters as he demanded the release of a prisoner. The violence was attributed to former members of Duvalier's regime.

Despite warnings from some members of Congress, the Reagan administration continued to express support for the Namphy government and believed it would see that the elections were carried out fairly. But U.S. observers who went to Haiti to monitor the election were not pleased with what they saw.

Election Day Bloodbath

On election day, attacks and violence against voters began shortly after the polls opened at 6:00 a.m. Three hours later, the government suspended elections after reports of killings.

Journalists reported that former supporters of Duvalier were behind much of the violence. At one polling place, a mob armed with machetes and guns attacked 100 civilians waiting to vote, killing many of them. Some reports said that Namphy's army participated in or overlooked acts of violence.

By mid-afternoon the provisional government dismissed the civilian election commission. In response the U.S. announced it was suspending all aid to the country, except drug enforcement assistance and some humanitarian funds.

Speaking to reporters November 30, State Department spokesman Charles Redman said the next step must be Haiti's and the democratic process "must get back on the rails. The Haitian people showed very clearly that that is what they want. They were turning out in large numbers at the polls yesterday, so I think they made their desires amply evident to all concerned." To back up that position, U.S. Ambassador to Haiti Brunson McKinley visited Namphy on December 1 with a stern admonition that the government get elections moving again. But the Reagan administration was cool to a congressional proposal to send troops into Haiti to conduct the election.

By the end of the year Namphy had scheduled a new election for early 1988. He planned to name a new electoral council and play a major role in running the election. But some presidential candidates, expressing distrust for any government-run election, said they did not plan to participate.

> *Following is the text of the U.S. State Department cable announcing cutoff of aid to Haiti, sent out November 29, 1987:*

In view of the November 29 actions of the National Governing Council of Haiti (CNG) dissolving the Provisional Electoral Commission (CEP) and abrogating all electoral legislation, the USG [U.S. government] has decided to remove all U.S. military assistance personnel from Haiti and suspend all military assistance to Haiti, with the exception of anti-narcotics cooperation. In addition, all non-humanitarian economic aid programs to Haiti are being suspended, and only humanitarian assistance will continue.

The United States Government reaffirms its support for the Haitian people in their efforts to secure a democratic political system through free and fair elections.

December

U.S.-SOVIET INF TREATY

December 8, 1987

President Ronald Reagan and Soviet leader Mikhail S. Gorbachev signed December 8 a treaty scrapping intermediate-range nuclear-force (INF) missiles, amid indications that the Senate was likely to approve it in the spring of 1988 without requiring renegotiation of any points. The pact, signed at a summit meeting in Washington, D.C., would require the destruction of all missiles with ranges of between 500 and 5,500 kilometers, together with their associated launchers and support facilities. A total of 830 U.S. missiles and 1,752 Soviet weapons would be destroyed. It was the first time the two countries had agreed to get rid of an entire class of nuclear weapons.

The ratio of the number of warheads that would be removed from service was lopsidedly in the United States's favor, since a large proportion of the scrapped Soviet weapons were triple-warhead SS-20s. All of the U.S. missiles were single-warhead Pershing II and ground-launched cruise missiles (GLCMs).

The treaty signing was the highlight of the three-day meeting between the two chiefs of government. In remarks just before signing the treaty, Reagan called for the "beginning of a working relationship that will enable us to tackle other issues." (Reagan-Gorbachev summit, p. 991)

Terming the treaty "a major watershed in international development," Gorbachev said it was "only a beginning." He noted that it had been achieved through "lengthy and intense arguments" that overcame "long-held emotions and ingrained stereotypes."

Elements of the Treaty

The two leaders signed separate sets of official documents, each about four and one-half inches thick. In addition to the treaty, the documents included:

- *A memorandum listing the number of launchers and missiles, their locations, and the locations of missile production plants, test ranges, and other facilities—so-called "declared facilities"—that would be subject to on-site inspection,*
- *A protocol detailing the process by which the missiles and launchers were to be destroyed,*
- *A second protocol detailing procedures for on-site verification, including the size of the inspection teams, transportation arrangements, duration of visit, and procedures for demanding an inspection, and*
- *A document listing the rights of the inspection teams, and of the countries in which they were inspecting.*

Formal agreements would also be made between the two signatories and other countries in whose territories inspections could occur—between the Soviet Union and some European members of NATO and between the United States and Czechoslovakia and East Germany.

Missiles covered in the agreement were: U.S. Pershing IIs, 128 of which were deployed in West Germany; U.S. ground-launched cruise missiles (GLCMs), 309 of which were deployed in Britain, West Germany, and Italy; older, shorter-range Pershing IAs stored in the United States, which the Pershing IIs replaced; triple-warhead Soviet SS-20s, the only multiwarhead missiles covered; older Soviet SS-4 and SS-5 missiles; and several hundred short-range Soviet missiles designated as SS-12s (or SS-22s) and SS-23s.

Inspection Procedures

To verify compliance, the pact established an unprecedented system for each country's inspectors to visit, on very short notice, facilities in the other country. The declared facilities—those associated with manufacture, repair, deployment, or storage of banned missiles—would be subject to inspection for thirteen years after the treaty went into effect. Officials of each country would conduct a "baseline inspection" of the other country's declared sites sixty days after the treaty became effective to verify data presented by the other country about the number and location of missiles, launchers, and other equipment. From that point, each side was to begin the phased destruction of banned missiles and equipment on a three-year timetable. The items were to be destroyed or rendered useless for military purposes by verifiable methods. The nuclear warheads from the missiles would be returned to the two countries' nuclear stockpiles.

At the end of the three years, inspectors would conduct a second inventory of all designated sites to verify that all banned equipment had been removed. During the dismantling period and for a decade thereafter, each country would have the right to send an inspection team to one of the other's declared sites (the Soviet Union identified 128 sites, the United States 30). Each country was permitted to station inspectors for thirteen years at the gates of one missile-assembly plant.

Mixed Reaction

Despite the successes of the summit, a number of conservatives raised objections that the treaty

- *Could not be adequately verified, because of loopholes in the verification plan,*
- *Removed an important element of NATO's nuclear counterweight against the numerical superiority in conventional forces of the Soviet-led Warsaw Pact, and*
- *Accelerated the political momentum of the strategic arms reduction talks (START) toward another Reagan-Gorbachev agreement to be signed in 1988 in Moscow, cutting by more than one-third the number of nuclear warheads carried by longer-range, strategic bombers and missiles.*

Conservatives also feared that the INF treaty and a START agreement would hamstring development of the strategic defense initiative (SDI), Reagan's program to develop a nationwide antimissile defense system. In their joint instructions to the U.S. and Soviet START negotiators, Reagan and Gorbachev sidestepped the SDI question with deliberately ambiguous language. Reagan insisted that the compromise language meant that SDI no longer was an obstacle to a START deal. Official Soviet statements did not concede that point.

Although Senate Majority Leader Robert C. Byrd, D-W.Va., predicted that the Senate would ratify the treaty, he and others left open the possibility that the Senate might attach reservations on issues such as verification and compliance and human rights guarantees.

Following are excerpts from remarks by President Ronald Reagan and General Secretary Mikhail S. Gorbachev December 8, 1987, on signing the INF (intermediate-range nuclear-force missiles) treaty; excerpts from the two leaders' television addresses to the people of both countries; the text of the treaty; excerpts from the protocol on elimination of weapons; the text of the protocol on inspections; and the text of the annex on privileges and immunities of inspectors:

SIGNING STATEMENTS

The President: ... [S]trong and fundamental moral differences continue to exist between our nations, but today, on this vital issue, at least, we've seen what can be accomplished when we pull together.

The numbers alone demonstrate the value of this agreement. On the Soviet side, over 1,500 deployed warheads will be removed and all ground-launched intermediate-range missiles, including the SS-20s, will be destroyed. On our side, our entire complement of Pershing II and ground-launched cruise missiles, with some 400 deployed warheads, will all be destroyed. Additional backup missiles on both sides will also be destroyed.

But the importance of this treaty transcends numbers. We have listened to the wisdom in an old Russian maxim. And I'm sure you're familiar with it, Mr. General Secretary, though my pronunciation may give you difficulty. The maxim is: *Doveryai, no proveryai*—trust, but verify.

The General Secretary: You repeat that at every meeting.

The President: I like it.

This agreement contains the most stringent verification regime in history, including provisions for inspection teams actually residing in each other's territory and several other forms of on-site inspection as well. This treaty protects the interests of America's friends and allies. It also embodies another important principle, the need for *glasnost,* a greater openness—in military programs and forces.

We can only hope that this history-making agreement will not be an end in itself, but the beginning of a working relationship that will enable us to tackle the other issues—urgent issues before us—strategic offensive nuclear weapons; the balance of conventional forces in Europe; the destructive and tragic regional conflicts that beset so many parts of our globe; and respect for the human and natural rights God has granted to all men.

To all here who have worked so hard to make this vision a reality: Thank you, and congratulations. . . .

The General Secretary: Mr. President, ladies and gentlemen, comrades, succeeding generations will hand down their verdict on the importance of the event which we are about to witness. But I will venture to say that what we are going to do—the signing of the first-ever agreement eliminating nuclear weapons, has a universal significance for mankind, both from the standpoint of world politics, and from the standpoint of humanism.

For everyone, and above all, for our two great powers, the treaty whose text is on this table offers a big chance at last to get on to the road leading away from the threat of catastrophe. It is our duty to take full advantage of that chance, and move together toward a nuclear-free world which holds out for our children and grandchildren and for their children and grandchildren the promise of a fulfilling and happy life without fear and without a senseless waste of resources on weapons of destruction. . . .

May December 8, 1987, become a date that will be inscribed in the history books, a date that will mark the watershed separating the era of a mounting risk of nuclear war from the era of a demilitarization of human life.

TELEVISION ADDRESSES

The President: . . . Today, I, for the United States, and the General Secretary, for the Soviet Union, have signed the first agreement ever to eliminate an entire class of U.S. and Soviet nuclear weapons. We have made history. And yet many so-called wise men once predicted that this agreement would be impossible to achieve—too many forces and factors stood against it. Well, still we persevered. We kept at it. . . .

In the next few days we will discuss further arms reductions and other issues—and again it will take time and patience to reach agreements. But as we begin these talks, let us remember that genuine international confidence and security are inconceivable without open societies with freedom of information, freedom of conscience, the right to publish and the right to travel. So, yes, we will address human rights and regional conflicts, for surely the salvation of all mankind lies only in making everything the concern of all. With time, patience, and willpower I believe we will resolve these issues. We must if we are to achieve a true, secure, and enduring peace.

As different as our systems are, there is a great bond that draws the American and Soviet peoples together. It is the common dream of peace. . . .

Only those who don't know us believe that America is a materialistic land. But the true America is not supermarkets filled with meats, milk and goods of all descriptions. It is not highways filled with cars. No, true America is a land of faith and family. You can find it in our churches, synagogues and mosques—in our homes and schools. As one of our great writers put it: America is a willingness of the heart—the universal, human heart, for Americans come from every part of earth, including the Soviet Union. We want a peace that fulfills the dream of all peoples to raise their families in freedom and safety. And I believe that if both of our countries have courage and the patience, we will build such a peace. . . .

The General Secretary: I am addressing my fellow countrymen, the citizens of the Soviet Union. I am addressing the American people.

President Reagan and I have just signed a treaty which for the first time in history requires the most stringently verified destruction of two whole classes of nuclear arms. The treaty on the total elimination of Soviet and U.S. intermediate- and shorter-range missiles will, I am sure, become a historic milestone in the chronicle of man's eternal quest for a world without wars.

On this occasion, may I be allowed to refer for a moment to history. Not all Americans may know that at the height of a world war, the very first step taken by the Soviet Republic born in Russia in 1917, was to promulgate a decree of peace. Its author, Vladimir Lenin, the founder of our state, said, "We are willing to consider any proposal leading to peace on a just and solid basis." This has been the cornerstone of Soviet foreign policy ever since.

We also remember another concept of his—disarmament, a world without arms or violence. This is our ideal. Today, regrettably, the risk of a nuclear catastrophe persists. It is still formidable. But we believe in man's ability to get rid of the threat of self-annihilation. We are encouraged by the willing awareness in the world of the nature of the existing peril which has confronted humankind with the question of its very survival....

The treaty just signed in Washington is a major watershed in international development. Its significance and implications go far beyond what has actually been agreed upon. Our passage to this watershed was difficult. It took us lengthy and intense arguments and debate, overcoming long held emotions and ingrained stereotypes. What has been accomplished is only a beginning. That is only the start of nuclear disarmament although, as we know, even the longest journey begins with a first step.

Moving ahead from this start will require further intensive intellectual endeavour and honest effort, the abandonment of some concepts of security which seem indisputable today and of all that fuels the arms race....

Most important of all is to translate into reality as early as possible agreements on radical cuts in strategic offensive arms subject to preserving the ABM [antiballistic missile] treaty, on the elimination of chemical weapons and on reductions in conventional armament. On each of these problems, the Soviet Union has put forward specific proposals. We believe that agreements on them are within reach.

We are hopeful that during next year's return visit of the United States President to the Soviet Union, we will achieve a treaty eliminating practically one-half of all existing strategic nuclear arms. There is also a possibility of agreeing on substantial cuts in conventional forces and arms in Europe, whose buildup and upgrading causes justified concern....

TREATY BETWEEN THE UNITED STATES OF AMERICA AND THE UNION OF SOVIET SOCIALIST REPUBLICS ON THE ELIMINATION OF THEIR INTERMEDIATE-RANGE AND SHORTER-RANGE MISSILES

The United States of America and the Union of Soviet Socialist Republics, hereinafter referred to as the Parties,

Conscious that nuclear war would have devastating consequences for all mankind,

Guided by the objective of strengthening strategic stability,

Convinced that the measures set forth in this Treaty will help to reduce the risk of outbreak of war and strengthen international peace and security, and

Mindful of their obligations under Article VI of the Treaty on the Non-Proliferation of Nuclear Weapons,

Have agreed as follows:

Article I

In accordance with the provisions of this Treaty which includes the Memorandum of Understanding and Protocols which form an integral part thereof, each Party shall eliminate its intermediate-range and shorter-range missiles, not have such systems thereafter, and carry out the obligations set forth in this Treaty.

Article II

For the purposes of this Treaty:

1. The term "ballistic missile" means a missile that has a ballistic trajectory over most of its flight path. The term "ground-launched ballistic missile (GLBM)" means a ground-launched ballistic missile that is a weapon-delivery vehicle.

2. The term "cruise missile" means an unmanned, self-propelled vehicle that sustains flight through the use of aerodynamic lift over most of its flight path. The term "ground-launched cruise missile (GLCM)" means a ground-launched cruise missile that is a weapon-delivery vehicle.

3. The term "GLBM launcher" means a fixed launcher or a mobile land-based transporter-erector-launcher mechanism for launching a GLBM.

4. The term "GLCM launcher" means a fixed launcher or a mobile land-based transporter-erector-launcher mechanism for launching a GLCM.

5. The term "intermediate-range missile" means a GLBM or a GLCM having a range capability in excess of 1000 kilometers but not in excess of 5500 kilometers.

6. The term "shorter-range missile" means a GLBM or a GLCM having a range capability equal to or in excess of 500 kilometers but not in excess of 1000 kilometers.

7. The term "deployment area" means a designated area within which intermediate-range missiles and launchers of such missiles may operate and within which one or more missile operating bases are located.

8. The term "missile operating base" means:

(a) in the case of intermediate-range missiles, a complex of facilities, located within a deployment area, at which intermediate-range missiles and launchers of such missiles normally operate, in which support structures associated with such missiles and launchers are also located and in which support equipment associated with such missiles and launchers is normally located; and

(b) in the case of shorter-range missiles, a complex of facilities, located any place, at which shorter-range missiles and launchers of such missiles normally operate and in which support equipment associated with such missiles and launchers is normally located.

9. The term "missile support facility," as regards intermediate-range or

shorter-range missiles and launchers of such missiles, means a missile production facility or a launcher production facility, a missile repair facility or a launcher repair facility, a training facility, a missile storage facility or a launcher storage facility, a test range, or an elimination facility as those terms are defined in the Memorandum of Understanding.

10. The term "transit" means movement, notified in accordance with paragraph 5(f) of Article IX of this Treaty, of an intermediate-range missile or a launcher of such a misssile between missile support facilities, between such a facility and a deployment area or between deployment areas, or of a shorter-range missile or a launcher of such a missile from a missile support facility or a missile operating base to an elimination facility.

11. The term "deployed missile" means an intermediate-range missile located within a deployment area or a shorter-range missile located at a missile operating base.

12. The term "non-deployed missile" means an intermediate-range missile located outside a deployment area or a shorter-range missile located outside a missile operating base.

13. The term "deployed launcher" means a launcher of an intermediate-range missile located within a deployment area or a launcher of a shorter-range missile located at a missile operating base.

14. The term "non-deployed launcher" means a launcher of an intermediate-range missile located outside a deployment area or a launcher of a shorter-range missile located outside a missile operating base.

15. The term "basing country" means a country other than the United States of America or the Union of Soviet Socialist Republics on whose territory intermediate-range or shorter-range missiles of the Parties, launchers of such missiles or support structures associated with such missiles and launchers were located at any time after November 1, 1987. Missiles or launchers in transit are not considered to be "located."

Article III

1. For the purposes of this Treaty, existing types of intermediate-range missiles are:

(a) for the United States of America, missiles of the types designated by the United States of America as the Pershing II and the BGM-109G, which are known to the Union of Soviet Socialist Republics by the same designations; and

(b) for the Union of Soviet Socialist Republics, missiles of the types designated by the Union of Soviet Socialist Republics as the RSD-10, the R-12 and the R-14, which are known to the United States of America as the SS-20, the SS-4 and the SS-5, respectively.

2. For the purposes of this Treaty, existing types of shorter-range missiles are:

(a) for the United States of America, missiles of the type designated by the United States of America as the Pershing IA, which is known to the Union of Soviet Socialist Republics by the same designation; and

(b) for the Union of Soviet Socialist Republics, missiles of the types designated by the Union of Soviet Socialist Republics as the OTR-22 and the OTR-23, which are known to the United States of America as the SS-12 and the SS-23, respectively.

Article IV

1. Each Party shall eliminate all its intermediate-range missiles and launchers of such missiles, and all support structures and support equipment of the categories listed in the Memorandum of Understanding associated with such missiles and launchers, so that no later than three years after entry into force of this Treaty and thereafter no such missiles, launchers, support structures or support equipment shall be possessed by either Party.

2. To implement paragraph 1 of this Article, upon entry into force of this Treaty, both Parties shall begin and continue throughout the duration of each phase, the reduction of all types of their deployed and non-deployed intermediate-range missiles and deployed and non-deployed launchers of such missiles and support structures and support equipment associated with such missiles and launchers in accordance with the provisions of this Treaty. These reductions shall be implemented in two phases so that:

(a) by the end of the first phase, that is, no later than 29 months after entry into force of this Treaty:

(i) the number of deployed launchers of intermediate-range missiles for each Party shall not exceed the number of launchers that are capable of carrying or containing at one time missiles considered by the Parties to carry 171 warheads;

(ii) the number of deployed intermediate-range missiles for each Party shall not exceed the number of such missiles considered by the Parties to carry 180 warheads;

(iii) the aggregate number of deployed and non-deployed launchers of intermediate-range missiles for each Party shall not exceed the number of launchers that are capable of carrying or containing at one time missiles considered by the Parties to carry 200 warheads;

(iv) the aggregate number of deployed and non-deployed intermediate-range missiles for each Party shall not exceed the number of such missiles considered by the Parties to carry 200 warheads; and

(v) the ratio of the aggregate number of deployed and non-deployed intermediate-range GLBMs of existing types for each Party to the aggregate number of deployed and non-deployed intermediate-range missiles of existing types possessed by that Party shall not exceed the ratio of such intermediate-range GLBMs to such intermediate-range missiles for that Party as of November

1, 1987, as set forth in the Memorandum of Understanding; and

(b) by the end of the second phase, that is, no later than three years after entry into force of this Treaty, all intermediate-range missiles of each Party, launchers of such missiles and all support structures and support equipment of the categories listed in the Memorandum of Understanding associated with such missiles and launchers, shall be eliminated.

Article V

1. Each Party shall eliminate all its shorter-range missiles and launchers of such missiles, and all support equipment of the categories listed in the Memorandum of Understanding associated with such missiles and launchers, so that no later than 18 months after entry into force of this Treaty and thereafter no such missiles, launchers or support equipment shall be possessed by either Party.

2. No later than 90 days after entry into force of this Treaty, each Party shall complete the removal of all its deployed shorter-range missiles and deployed and non-deployed launchers of such missiles to elimination facilities and shall retain them at those locations until they are eliminated in accordance with the procedures set forth in the Protocol on Elimination. No later than 12 months after entry into force of this Treaty, each Party shall complete the removal of all its non-deployed shorter-range missiles to elimination facilities and shall retain them at those locations until they are eliminated in accordance with the procedures set forth in the Protocol on Elimination.

3. Shorter-range missiles and launchers of such missiles shall not be located at the same elimination facility. Such facilities shall be separated by no less than 1000 kilometers.

Article VI

1. Upon entry into force of this Treaty and thereafter, neither Party shall:

(a) produce or flight-test any intermediate-range missiles or produce any stages of such missiles or any launchers of such missiles; or

(b) produce, flight-test or launch any shorter-range missiles or produce any stages of such missiles or any launchers of such missiles.

2. Notwithstanding paragraph 1 of this Article, each party shall have the right to produce a type of GLBM not limited by this Treaty which uses a stage which is outwardly similar to, but not interchangeable with, a stage of an existing type of intermediate-range GLBM having more than one stage, providing that that Party does not produce any other stage which is outwardly similar to, but not interchangeable with, any other stage of an existing type of intermediate-range GLBM.

Article VII

For the purposes of this Treaty:

1. If a ballistic missile or a cruise missile has been flight-tested or deployed for weapon delivery, all missiles of that type shall be considered to be weapon-delivery vehicles.

2. If a GLBM or GLCM is an intermediate-range missile, all GLBMs or GLCMs of that type shall be considered to be intermediate-range missiles. If a GLBM or GLCM is a shorter-range missile, all GLBMs or GLCMs of that type shall be considered to be shorter-range missiles.

3. If a GLBM is of a type developed and tested solely to intercept and counter objects not located on the surface of the Earth, it shall not be considered to be a missile to which the limitations of this Treaty apply.

4. The range capability of the GLBM not listed in Article III of this Treaty shall be considered to be the maximum range to which it has been tested. The range capability of a GLCM not listed in Article III of this Treaty shall be considered to be the maximum distance which can be covered by the missile in its standard design mode flying until fuel exhaustion, determined by projecting its flight path onto the earth's sphere from the point of launch to the point of impact. GLBMs or GLCMs that have a range capability equal to or in excess of 500 kilometers but not in excess of 1000 kilometers shall be considered to be shorter-range missiles. GLBMs or GLCMs that have a range capability in excess of 1000 kilometers but not in excess of 5500 kilometers shall be considered to be intermediate-range missiles.

5. The maximum number of warheads an existing type of intermediate-range missile or shorter-range missile carries shall be considered to be the number listed for missiles of that type in the Memorandum of Understanding.

6. Each GLBM or GLCM shall be considered to carry the maximum number of warheads listed for a GLBM or GLCM of that type in the Memorandum of Understanding.

7. If a launcher has been tested for launching a GLBM or a GLCM, all launchers of that type shall be considered to have been tested for launching GLBMs or GLCMs.

8. If a launcher has contained or launched a particular type of GLBM or GLCM, all launchers of that type shall be considered to be launchers of that type of GLBM or GLCM.

9. The number of missiles each launcher of an existing type of intermediate-range missile or shorter-range missile shall be considered to be capable of carrying or containing at one time is the number listed for launchers of missiles of that type in the Memorandum of Understanding.

10. Except in the case of elimination in accordance with the procedures set forth in the Protocol on Elimination, the following shall apply:

(a) for GLBMs which are stored or moved in separate stages, the longest stage of an intermediate-range or shorter-range GLBM shall be counted as a complete missile;

(b) for GLBMs which are not stored or moved in separate stages, a canister of the type used in the launch of an intermediate-range

GLBM, unless a Party proves to the satisfaction of the other Party that it does not contain such a missile, or an assembled intermediate-range or shorter-range GLBM, shall be counted as a complete missile; and

(c) for GLCMs, the airframe of an intermediate-range or shorter-range GLCM shall be counted as a complete missile.

11. A ballistic missile which is not a missile to be used in a ground-based mode shall not be considered to be a GLBM if it is test-launched at a test site from a fixed land-based launcher which is used solely for test purposes and which is distinguishable from GLBM launchers. A cruise missile which is not a missile to be used in a ground-based mode shall not be considered to be a GLCM if it is test-launched at a test site from a fixed land-based launcher which is used solely for test purposes and which is distinguishable from GLCM launchers.

12. Each Party shall have the right to produce and use for booster systems, which might otherwise be considered to be intermediate-range or shorter-range missiles, only existing types of booster stages for such booster systems. Launches of such booster systems shall not be considered to be flight-testing of intermediate-range or shorter-range missiles provided that:

(a) stages used in such booster systems are different from stages used in those missiles listed as existing types of intermediate-range or shorter-range missiles in Article III of this Treaty;

(b) such booster systems are used only for research and development purposes to test objects other than the booster systems themselves;

(c) the aggregate number of launchers for such booster systems shall not exceed 35 for each Party at any one time; and

(d) the launchers for such booster systems are fixed, emplaced above ground and located only at research and development launch sites which are specified in the Memorandum of Understanding.

Research and development launch sites shall not be subject to inspection pursuant to Article XI of this Treaty.

Article VIII

1. All intermediate-range missiles and launchers of such missiles shall be located in deployment areas, at missile support facilities or shall be in transit. Intermediate-range missiles or launchers of such missiles shall not be located elsewhere.

2. Stages of intermediate-range missiles shall be located in deployment areas, at missile support facilities or moving between deployment areas, between missile support facilities or between missile support facilities and deployment areas.

3. Until their removal to elimination facilities as required by paragraph 2 of Article V of this Treaty, all shorter-range missiles and launchers of such missiles shall be located at missile operating bases, at missile support

facilities or shall be in transit. Shorter-range missiles or launchers of such missiles shall not be located elsewhere.

4. Transit of a missile or launcher subject to the provisions of this Treaty shall be completed within 25 days.

5. All deployment areas, missile operating bases and missile support facilities are specified in the Memorandum of Understanding or in subsequent updates of data pursuant to paragraphs 3, 5(a) or 5(b) of Article IX of this Treaty. Neither Party shall increase the number of, or change the location or boundaries of, deployment areas, missile operating bases or missile support facilities, except for elimination facilities, from those set forth in the Memorandum of Understanding. A missile support facility shall not be considered to be part of a deployment area even though it may be located within the geographic boundaries of a deployment area.

6. Beginning 30 days after entry into force of this Treaty, neither Party shall locate intermediate-range or shorter-range missiles, including stages of such missiles, or launchers of such missiles at missile production facilities, launcher production facilities or test ranges listed in the Memorandum of Understanding.

7. Neither Party shall locate any intermediate-range or shorter-range missiles at training facilities.

8. A non-deployed intermediate-range or shorter-range missile shall not be carried on or contained within a launcher of such a type of missile, except as required for maintenance conducted at repair facilities or for elimination by means of launching conducted at elimination facilities.

9. Training missiles and training launchers for intermediate-range or shorter-range missiles shall be subject to the same locational restrictions as are set forth for intermediate-range and shorter-range missiles and launchers of such missiles in paragraphs 1 and 3 of this Article.

Article IX

1. The Memorandum of Understanding contains categories of data relevant to obligations undertaken with regard to this Treaty and lists all intermediate-range and shorter-range missiles, launchers of such missiles, and support structures and support equipment associated with such missiles and launchers, possessed by the Parties as of November 1, 1987. Updates of that data and notifications required by this Article shall be provided according to the categories of data contained in the Memorandum of Understanding.

2. The Parties shall update that data and provide the notifications required by this Treaty through the Nuclear Risk Reduction Centers, established pursuant to the Agreement Between the United States of America and the Union of Soviet Socialist Republics on the Establishment of Nuclear Risk Reduction Centers of September 15, 1987.

3. No later than 30 days after entry into force of this Treaty, each Party shall provide the other Party with updated data, as of the date of entry

into force of this Treaty, for all categories of data contained in the Memorandum of Understanding.

4. No later than 30 days after the end of each six-month interval following the entry into force of this Treaty, each Party shall provide updated data for all categories of data contained in the Memorandum of Understanding by informing the other party of all changes, completed and in process, in that data, which have occurred during the six-month interval since the preceding data exchange, and the net effect of those changes.

5. Upon entry into force of this Treaty and thereafter, each Party shall provide the following notifications to the other Party:

(a) notification, no less than 30 days in advance, of the scheduled date of the elimination of a specific deployment area, missile operating base or missile support facility;

(b) notification, no less than 30 days in advance, of changes in the number or location of elimination facilities, including the location and scheduled date of each change;

(c) notification, except with respect to launches of intermediate-range missiles for the purpose of their elimination, no less than 30 days in advance, of the scheduled date of the initiation of the elimination of intermediate-range and shorter-range missiles, and stages of such missiles, and launchers of such missiles and support structures and support equipment associated with such missiles and launchers, including:

(i) the number and type of items of missile systems to be eliminated;

(ii) the elimination site;

(iii) for intermediate-range missiles, the location from which such missiles, launchers of such missiles and support equipment associated with such missiles and launchers are moved to the elimination facility; and

(iv) except in the case of support structures, the point of entry to be used by an inspection team conducting an inspection pursuant to paragraph 7 of Article XI of this Treaty and the estimated time of departure of an inspection team from the point of entry to the elimination facility;

(d) notification, no less than ten days in advance, of the scheduled date of the launch, or the scheduled date of the initiation of a series of launches, of intermediate-range missiles for the purpose of their elimination, including:

(i) the type of missiles to be eliminated;

(ii) the location of the launch, or, if elimination is by a series of launches, the location of such launches and the number of launches in the series;

(iii) the point of entry to be used by an inspection team conducting an inspection pursuant to paragraph 7 of Article XI of this Treaty; and

(iv) the estimated time of departure of an inspection team from the point of entry to the elimination facility;

(e) notification, no later than 48 hours after they occur, of changes in the number of intermediate-range and shorter-range missiles, launchers of such missiles and support structures and support equipment associated with such missiles and launchers resulting from elimination as described in the Protocol on Elimination, including:

(i) the number and type of items of a missile system which were eliminated; and

(ii) the date and location of such elimination; and

(f) notification of transit of intermediate-range or shorter-range missiles or launchers of such missiles, or the movement of training missiles or training launchers for such intermediate-range and shorter-range missiles, no later than 48 hours after it has been completed, including:

(i) the number of missiles or launchers;

(ii) the points, dates and times of departure and arrival;

(iii) the mode of transport; and

(iv) the location and time at that location at least once every four days during the period of transit.

6. Upon entry into force of this Treaty and thereafter, each Party shall notify the other Party, no less than ten days in advance, of the scheduled date and location of the launch of a research and development booster system as described in paragraph 12 of Article VII of this Treaty.

Article X

1. Each Party shall eliminate its intermediate-range and shorter-range missiles and launchers of such missiles and support structures and support equipment associated with such missiles and launchers in accordance with the procedures set forth in the Protocol on Elimination.

2. Verification by on-site inspection of the elimination of items of missile systems specified in the Protocol on Elimination shall be carried out in accordance with Article XI of this Treaty, the Protocol on Elimination and the Protocol on Inspection.

3. When a Party removes its intermediate-range missiles, launchers of such missiles and support equipment associated with such missiles and launchers from deployment areas to elimination facilities for the purpose of their elimination, it shall do so in complete deployed organizational units. For the United States of America, these units shall be Pershing II batteries and BGM-109G flights. For the Union of Soviet Socialist Republics, these units shall be SS-20 regiments composed of two or three battalions.

4. Elimination of intermediate-range and shorter-range missiles and launchers of such missiles and support equipment associated with such missiles and launchers shall be carried out at the facilities that are

specified in the Memorandum of Understanding or notified in accordance with paragraph 5(b) of Article IX of this Treaty, unless eliminated in accordance with Sections IV or V of the Protocol on Elimination. Support structures, associated with the missiles and launchers subject to this Treaty, that are subject to elimination shall be eliminated *in situ*.

5. Each Party shall have the right, during the first six months after entry into force of this Treaty, to eliminate by means of launching no more than 100 of its intermediate-range missiles.

6. Intermediate-range and shorter-range missiles which have been tested prior to entry into force of this Treaty, but never deployed, and which are not existing types of intermediate-range or shorter-range missiles listed in Article III of this Treaty, and launchers of such missiles, shall be eliminated within six months after entry into force of this Treaty in accordance with the procedures set forth in the Protocol on Elimination. Such missiles are:

(a) for the United States of America, missiles of the type designated by the United States of America as the Pershing IB, which is known to the Union of Soviet Socialist Republics by the same designation; and

(b) for the Union of Soviet Socialist Republics, missiles of the type designated by the Union of Soviet Socialist Republics as the RK-55, which is known to the United States of America as the SSC-X-4.

7. Intermediate-range and shorter-range missiles and launchers of such missiles and support structures and support equipment associated with such missiles and launchers shall be considered to be eliminated after completion of the procedures set forth in the Protocol on Elimination and upon the notification provided for in paragraph 5(e) of Article IX of this Treaty.

8. Each Party shall eliminate its deployment areas, missile operating bases and missile support facilities. A Party shall notify the other Party pursuant to paragraph 5(a) of Article IX of this Treaty once the conditions set forth below are fulfilled:

(a) all intermediate-range and shorter-range missiles, launchers of such missiles and support equipment associated with such missiles and launchers located there have been removed;

(b) all support structures associated with such missiles and launchers located there have been eliminated; and

(c) all activity related to production, flight-testing, training, repair, storage or deployment of such missiles and launchers has ceased there.

Such deployment areas, missile operating bases and missile support facilities shall be considered to be eliminated either when they have been inspected pursuant to paragraph 4 of Article XI of this Treaty or when 60 days have elapsed since the date of the scheduled elimination which was notified pursuant to paragraph 5(a) of Article IX of this Treaty. A deployment area, missile operating base or missile support facility listed in the Memorandum of Understanding that met the above conditions prior to entry into force of this Treaty, and is not included in the initial data exchange pursuant to paragraph 3 of Article IX of this Treaty, shall be considered to be eliminated.

9. If a Party intends to convert a missile operating base listed in the Memorandum of Understanding for use as a base associated with GLBM or GLCM systems not subject to this Treaty, then that Party shall notify the other Party, no less than 30 days in advance of the scheduled date of the initiation of the conversion, of the scheduled date and the purpose for which the base will be converted.

Article XI

1. For the purpose of ensuring verification of compliance with the provisions of this Treaty, each Party shall have the right to conduct on-site inspections. The Parties shall implement on-site inspections in accordance with this Article, the Protocol on Inspection and the Protocol on Elimination.

2. Each Party shall have the right to conduct inspections provided for by this Article both within the territory of the other Party and within the territories of basing countries.

3. Beginning 30 days after entry into force of this Treaty, each Party shall have the right to conduct inspections at all missile operating bases and missile support facilities specified in the Memorandum of Understanding other than missile production facilities, and at all elimination facilities included in the initial data update required by paragraph 3 of Article IX of this Treaty. These inspections shall be completed no later than 90 days after entry into force of this Treaty. The purpose of these inspections shall be to verify the number of missiles, launchers, support structures and support equipment and other data, as of the date of entry into force of this Treaty, provided pursuant to paragraph 3 of Article IX of this Treaty.

4. Each Party shall have the right to conduct inspections to verify the elimination, notified pursuant to paragraph 5(a) of Article IX of this Treaty, of missile operating bases and missile support facilities other than missile production facilities, which are thus no longer subject to inspections pursuant to paragraph 5(a) of this Article. Such an inspection shall be carried out within 60 days after the scheduled date of the elimination of that facility. If a Party conducts an inspection at a particular facility pursuant to paragraph 3 of this Article after the scheduled date of the elimination of that facility, then no additional inspection of that facility pursuant to this paragraph shall be permitted.

5. Each Party shall have the right to conduct inspections pursuant to this paragraph for 13 years after entry into force of this Treaty. Each Party shall have the right to conduct 20 such inspections per calendar year during the first three years after entry into force of this Treaty, 15 such inspections per calendar year during the subsequent five years, and ten such inspections per calendar year during the last five years. Neither Party shall use more than half of its total number of these inspections per calendar

year within the territory of any one basing country. Each party shall have the right to conduct:

(a) inspections, beginning 90 days after entry into force of this Treaty, of missile operating bases and missile support facilities other than elimination facilities and missile production facilities, to ascertain, according to the categories of data specified in the Memorandum of Understanding, the numbers of missiles, launchers, support structures and support equipment located at each missile operating base or missile support facility at the time of the inspection; and

(b) inspections of former missile operating bases and former missile support facilities eliminated pursuant to paragraph 8 of Article X of this Treaty other than former missile production facilities.

6. Beginning 30 days after entry into force of this Treaty, each Party shall have the right, for 13 years after entry into force of this Treaty, to inspect by means of continuous monitoring:

(a) the portals of any facility of the other Party at which the final assembly of a GLBM using stages, any of which is outwardly similar to a stage of a solid-propellant GLBM listed in Article III of this Treaty, is accomplished; or

(b) if a Party has no such facility, the portals of an agreed former missile production facility at which existing types of intermediate-range or shorter-range GLBMs were produced.

The Party whose facility is to be inspected pursuant to this paragraph shall ensure that the other Party is able to establish a permanent continuous monitoring system at that facility within six months after entry into force of this Treaty or within six months of initiation of the process of final assembly described in subparagraph (a). If, after the end of the second year after entry into force of this Treaty, neither Party conducts the process of final assembly described in subparagraph (a) for a period of 12 consecutive months, then neither Party shall have the right to inspect by means of continuous monitoring any missile production facility of the other Party unless the process of final assembly as described in this subparagraph (a) is initiated again. Upon entry into force of this Treaty, the facilities to be inspected by continuous monitoring shall be: in accordance with subparagraph (b), for the United States of America, Hercules Plant Number 1, at Magna, Utah; in accordance with subparagraph (a), for the Union of Soviet Socialist Republics, the Votkinsk Machine Building Plant, Udmurt Autonomous Soviet Socialist Republic, Russian Soviet Federative Socialist Republic.

7. Each Party shall conduct inspections of the process of elimination, including elimination of intermediate-range missiles by means of launching, of intermediate-range and shorter-range missiles and launchers of such missiles and support equipment associated with such missiles and launchers carried out at elimination facilities in accordance with Article X of this Treaty and the Protocol on Elimination. Inspectors conducting inspections provided for in this paragraph shall determine that the

processes specified for the elimination of the missiles, launchers and support equipment have been completed.

8. Each party shall have the right to conduct inspections to confirm the completion of the process of elimination of intermediate-range and shorter-range missiles and launchers of such missiles and support equipment associated with such missiles and launchers eliminated pursuant to Section V of the Protocol on Elimination, and of training missiles, training missile stages, training launch canisters and training launchers eliminated pursuant to Sections II, IV and V of the Protocol on Elimination.

Article XII

1. For the purpose of ensuring verification of compliance with the provisions of this Treaty, each Party shall use national technical means of verification at its disposal in a manner consistent with generally recognized principles of international law.

2. Neither Party shall:

(a) interfere with national technical means of verification of the other Party operating in accordance with paragraph 1 of this Article; or

(b) use concealment measures which impede verification of compliance with the provisions of this Treaty by national technical means of verification carried out in accordance with paragraph 1 of this Article. This obligation does not apply to cover or concealment practices, within a deployment area, associated with normal training, maintenance and operations, including the use of environmental shelters to protect missiles and launchers.

3. To enhance observation by national technical means of verification, each Party shall have the right until a treaty between the Parties reducing and limiting strategic offensive arms enters into force, but in any event for no more than three years after entry into force of this Treaty, to request the implementation of cooperative measures at deployment bases for road-mobile GLBMs with a range capability in excess of 5500 kilometers, which are not former missile operating bases eliminated pursuant to paragraph 8 of Article X of this Treaty. The Party making such a request shall inform the other Party of the deployment base at which cooperative measures shall be implemented. The Party whose base is to be observed shall carry out the following cooperative measures:

(a) no later than six hours after such a request, the Party shall have opened the roofs of all fixed structures for launchers located at the base, removed completely all missiles on launchers from such fixed structures for launchers and displayed such missiles on launchers in the open without using concealment measures; and

(b) the Party shall leave the roofs open and the missiles on launchers in place until twelve hours have elapsed from the time of the receipt of a request for such an observation.

Each Party shall have the right to make six such requests per calendar year. Only one deployment base shall be subject to these cooperative measures at any one time.

Article XIII

1. To promote the objectives and implementation of the provisions of this Treaty, the Parties hereby establish the Special Verification Commission. The Parties agree that, if either Party so requests, they shall meet within the framework of the Special Verification Commission to:

(a) resolve questions relating to compliance with the obligations assumed; and

(b) agree upon such measures as may be necessary to improve the viability and effectiveness of this Treaty.

2. The Parties shall use the Nuclear Risk Reduction Centers, which provide for continuous communication between the Parties, to:

(a) exchange data and provide notifications as required by paragraphs 3, 4, 5 and 6 of Article IX of this Treaty and the Protocol on Elimination;

(b) provide and receive the information required by paragraph 9 of Article X of this Treaty;

(c) provide and receive notifications of inspections as required by Article XI of this Treaty and the Protocol on Inspection; and

(d) provide and receive requests for cooperative measures as provided for in paragraph 3 of Article XII of this Treaty.

Article XIV

The Parties shall comply with this Treaty and shall not assume any international obligations or undertakings which would conflict with its provisions.

Article XV

1. This Treaty shall be of unlimited duration.

2. Each Party shall, in exercising its national sovereignty, have the right to withdraw from this Treaty if it decides that extraordinary events related to the subject matter of this Treaty have jeopardized its supreme interests. It shall give notice of its decision to withdraw to the other Party six months prior to withdrawal from this Treaty. Such notice shall include a statement of the extraordinary events the notifying Party regards as having jeopardized its supreme interests.

Article XVI

Each Party may propose amendments to this Treaty. Agreed amendments shall enter into force in accordance with the procedures set forth in Article XVII governing the entry into force of this Treaty.

Article XVII

1. This Treaty, including the Memorandum of Understanding and

Protocols, which form an integral part thereof, shall be subject to ratification in accordance with the constitutional procedures of each Party. This Treaty shall enter into force on the date of the exchange of instruments of ratification.

2. This Treaty shall be registered pursuant to Article 102 of the Charter of the United Nations.

[PROTOCOL ON PROCEDURES GOVERNING THE ELIMINATION OF THE MISSILE SYSTEMS]

Pursuant to and in implementation of the Treaty Between the United States of America and the Union of Soviet Socialist Republics on the Elimination of Their Intermediate-Range and Shorter-Range Missiles of December 8, 1987, hereinafter referred to as the Treaty, the Parties hereby agree upon procedures governing the elimination of the missile systems subject to the Treaty.

I. Items of Missile Systems Subject to Elimination

The specific items for each type of missile system to be eliminated are:

1. For the United States of America:

Pershing II: missile, launcher and launch pad shelter;
BGM-109G: missile, launch canister and launcher;
Pershing IA: missile and launcher; and
Pershing IB: missile.

2. For the Union of Soviet Socialist Republics:

SS-20: missile, launch canister, launcher, missile transporter vehicle and fixed structure for a launcher;
SS-4: missile, missile transporter vehicle, missile erector, launch stand and propellant tanks;
SS-5: missile;
SSC-X-4: missile, launch canister and launcher;
SS-12: missile, launcher and missile transporter vehicle; and
SS-23: missile, launcher and missile transporter vehicle.

3. For both Parties, all training missiles, training missile stages, training launch canisters and training launchers shall be subject to elimination.

4. For both Parties, all stages of intermediate-range and shorter-range GLBMs shall be subject to elimination.

5. For both Parties, all front sections of deployed intermediate-range and shorter-range missiles shall be subject to elimination.

II. Procedures for Elimination at Elimination Facilities

1. In order to ensure the reliable determination of the type and number of missiles, missile stages, front sections, launch canisters, launchers, missile transporter vehicles, missile erectors and launch stands, as well as training missiles, training missile stages, training launch canisters and training launchers, indicated in Section I of this Protocol, being eliminated at elimination facilities, and to preclude the possibility of restoration of such items for purposes inconsistent with the provisions of the Treaty, the Parties shall fulfill the requirements below.

2. The conduct of the elimination procedures for the items of missile systems listed in paragraph 1 of this section, except for training missiles, training missile stages, training launch canisters and training launchers, shall be subject to on-site inspection in accordance with Article XI of the Treaty and the Protocol on Inspection. The Parties shall have the right to conduct on-site inspections to confirm the completion of the elimination procedures set forth in paragraph 11 of this Section for training missiles, training missile stages, training launch canisters and training launchers. The Party possessing such a training missile, training missile stage, training launch canister or training launcher shall inform the other Party of the name and coordinates of the elimination facility at which the on-site inspection may be conducted as well as the date on which it may be conducted. Such information shall be provided no less than 30 days in advance of that date.

3. Prior to a missile's arrival at the elimination facility, its nuclear warhead device and guidance elements may be removed.

4. Each Party shall select the particular technological means necessary to implement the procedures required in paragraphs 10 and 11 of this Section and to allow for on-site inspection of the conduct of the elimination procedures required in paragraph 10 of this Section in accordance with Article XI of the Treaty, this Protocol and the Protocol on Inspection.

5. The initiation of the elimination of the items of missile systems subject to this Section shall be considered to be the commencement of the procedures set forth in paragraph 10 or 11 of this Section.

6. Immediately prior to the initiation of the elimination procedures set forth in paragraph 10 of this Section, an inspector from the Party receiving the pertinent notification required by paragraph 5(c) of Article IX of the Treaty shall confirm and record the type and number of items of missile systems, listed in paragraph 1 of this Section, which are to be eliminated. If the inspecting Party deems it necessary, this shall include a visual inspection of the contents of launch canisters.

7. A missile stage being eliminated by burning in accordance with the procedures set forth in paragraph 10 of this Section shall not be instrumented for data collection. Prior to the initiation of the elimination procedures set forth in paragraph 10 of this Section, an inspector from the

inspecting Party shall confirm that such missile stages are not instrumented for data collection. Those missile stages shall be subject to continuous observation by such an inspector from the time of that inspection until the burning is completed.

8. The completion of the elimination procedures set forth in this Section, except those for training missiles, training missile stages, training launch canisters and training launchers, along with the type and number of items of missile systems for which those procedures have been completed, shall be confirmed in writing by the representative of the Party carrying out the elimination and by the inspection team leader of the other Party. The elimination of a training missile, training missile stage, training launch canister or training launcher shall be considered to have been completed upon completion of the procedures set forth in paragraph 11 of this Section and notification as required by paragraph 5(e) of Article IX of the Treaty following the date specified pursuant to paragraph 2 of this Section.

9. The Parties agree that all United States and Soviet intermediate-range and shorter-range missiles and their associated re-entry vehicles shall be eliminated within an agreed overall period of elimination. It is further agreed that all such missiles shall, in fact, be eliminated fifteen days prior to the end of the overall period of elimination. During the last fifteen days, a Party shall withdraw to its national territory re-entry vehicles which, by unilateral decision, have been released from existing programs of cooperation and eliminate them during the same timeframe in accordance with the procedures set forth in this Section.

10. The specific procedures for the elimination of the items of missile systems listed in paragraph 1 of this Section shall be as follows, unless the Parties agree upon different procedures to achieve the same result as the procedures identified in this paragraph:

For the Pershing II:

Missile:

(a) missile stages shall be eliminated by explosive demolition or burning;

(b) solid fuel, rocket nozzles and motor cases not destroyed in this process shall be burned, crushed, flattened or destroyed by explosion; and

(c) front section, minus nuclear warhead device and guidance elements, shall be crushed or flattened.

Launcher:

(a) erector-launcher mechanism shall be removed from launcher chassis;

(b) all components of erector-launcher mechanism shall be cut at locations that are not assembly joints into two pieces of approximately equal size;

(c) missile launch support equipment, including external instrumentation compartments, shall be removed from launcher chassis; and

(d) launcher chassis shall be cut at a location that is not an assembly joint into two pieces of approximately equal size.

For the BGM-109G:

Missile:

(a) missile airframe shall be cut longitudinally into two pieces;

(b) wings and tail section shall be severed from missile airframe at locations that are not assembly joints; and

(c) front section, minus nuclear warhead device and guidance elements, shall be crushed or flattened.

Launch Canister:

launch canister shall be crushed, flattened, cut into two pieces of approximately equal size or destroyed by explosion.

Launcher:

(a) erector-launcher mechanism shall be removed from launcher chassis;

(b) all components of erector-launcher mechanism shall be cut at locations that are not assembly joints into two pieces of approximately equal size;

(c) missile launch support equipment, including external instrumentation compartments, shall be removed from launcher chassis; and

(d) launcher chassis shall be cut at a location that is not an assembly joint into two pieces of approximately equal size....

For the SS-20:

Missile:

(a) missile shall be eliminated by explosive demolition of the missile in its launch canister or by burning missile stages;

(b) solid fuel, rocket nozzles and motor cases not destroyed in this process shall be burned, crushed, flattened or destroyed by explosion;

(c) front section, including re-entry vehicles, minus nuclear warhead devices, and instrumentation compartment, minus guidance elements, shall be crushed or flattened.

Launch Canister:

launch canister shall be destroyed by explosive demolition together with a missile, or shall be destroyed separately by explosion, cut into two pieces of approximately equal size, crushed or flattened.

Launcher:

(a) erector-launcher mechanism shall be removed from launcher chassis;

(b) all components of erector-launcher mechanism shall be cut at locations that are not assembly joints into two pieces of approximately equal size;

(c) missile launch support equipment, including external instrumentation compartments, shall be removed from launcher chassis;

(d) mountings of erector-launcher mechanism and launcher leveling supports shall be cut off launcher chassis;

(e) launcher leveling supports shall be cut at locations that are not assembly joints into two pieces of approximately equal size; and

(f) a portion of the launcher chassis, at least 0.78 meters in length, shall be cut off aft of the rear axle.

Missile Transporter Vehicle:

(a) all mechanisms associated with missile loading and mounting shall be removed from transporter vehicle chassis;

(b) all mountings of such mechanisms shall be cut off transporter vehicle chassis;

(c) all components of the mechanisms associated with missile loading and mounting shall be cut at locations that are not assembly joints into two pieces of approximately equal size;

(d) external instrumentation compartments shall be removed from transporter vehicle chassis;

(e) transporter vehicle leveling supports shall be cut off transporter vehicle chassis and cut at locations that are not assembly joints into two pieces of approximately equal size; and

(f) a portion of the transporter vehicle chassis, at least 0.78 meters in length, shall be cut off aft of the rear axle.

For the SS-4:

Missile:

(a) nozzles of propulsion system shall be cut off at locations that are not assembly joints;

(b) all propellant tanks shall be cut into two pieces of approximately equal size;

(c) instrumentation compartment, minus guidance elements, shall be cut into two pieces of approximately equal size; and

(d) front section, minus nuclear warhead device, shall be crushed or flattened.

Launch Stand:

launch stand components shall be cut at locations that are not assembly joints into two pieces of approximately equal size.

Missile Erector:

(a) jib, missile erector leveling supports and missile erector mechanism shall be cut off missile erector at locations that are not assembly joints; and

(b) jib and missile erector leveling supports shall be cut into two pieces of approximately equal size.

Missile Transporter Vehicle:

mounting components for a missile and for a missile erector mechanism as well as supports for erecting a missile onto a launcher shall be cut off transporter vehicle at locations that are not assembly joints. . . .

III. Elimination of Missiles by Means of Launching

1. Elimination of missiles by means of launching pursuant to paragraph

5 of Article X of the Treaty shall be subject to on-site inspection in accordance with paragraph 7 of Article XI of the Treaty and the Protocol on Inspection. Immediately prior to each launch conducted for the purpose of elimination, an inspector from the inspecting Party shall confirm by visual observation the type of missile to be launched.

2. All missiles being eliminated by means of launching shall be launched from designated elimination facilities to existing impact areas for such missiles. No such missile shall be used as a target vehicle for a ballistic missile interceptor.

3. Missiles being eliminated by means of launching shall be launched one at a time, and no less than six hours shall elapse between such launches.

4. Such launches shall involve ignition of all missile stages. Neither Party shall transmit or recover data from missiles being eliminated by means of launching except for unencrypted data used for range safety purposes.

5. The completion of the elimination procedures set forth in this Section, and the type and number of missiles for which those procedures have been completed, shall be confirmed in writing by the representative of the Party carrying out the elimination and by the inspection team leader of the other Party.

6. A missile shall be considered to be eliminated by means of launching after completion of the procedures set forth in this Section and upon notification required by paragraph 5(e) of Article IX of the Treaty.

IV. Procedures for Elimination In Situ

1. Support Structures

(a) Support structures listed in Section I of this Protocol shall be eliminated *in situ.*

(b) The initiation of the elimination of support structures shall be considered to be the commencement of the elimination procedures required in paragraph 1(d) of this Section.

(c) The elimination of support structures shall be subject to verification by on-site inspection in accordance with paragraph 4 of Article XI of the Treaty.

(d) The specific elimination procedures for support structures shall be as follows:

(i) the superstructure of the fixed structure or shelter shall be dismantled or demolished, and removed from its base or foundation;

(ii) the base or foundation of the fixed structure or shelter shall be destroyed by excavation or explosion;

(iii) the destroyed base or foundation of a fixed structure or shelter shall remain visible to national technical means of verification for six months or until completion of an on-site inspection conducted in accordance with Article XI of the Treaty; and

(iv) upon completion of the above requirements, the elimination procedures shall be considered to have been completed.

2. *Propellant Tanks for SS-4 Missiles*

Fixed and transportable propellant tanks for SS-4 missiles shall be removed from launch sites.

3. *Training Missiles, Training Missile Stages, Training Launch Canisters and Training Launchers*

(a) Training missiles, training missile stages, training launch canisters and training launchers not eliminated at elimination facilities shall be eliminated *in situ*.

(b) Training missiles, training missile stages, training launch canisters and training launchers being eliminated *in situ* shall be eliminated in accordance with the specific procedures set forth in paragraph 11 of Section II of this Protocol.

(c) Each Party shall have the right to conduct an on-site inspection to confirm the completion of the elimination procedures for training missiles, training missile stages, training launch canisters and training launchers.

(d) The party possessing such a training missile, training missile stage, training launch canister or training launcher shall inform the other Party of the place-name and coordinates of the location at which the on-site inspection provided for in paragraph 3(c) of this Section may be conducted as well as the date on which it may be conducted. Such information shall be provided no less than 30 days in advance of that date.

(e) Elimination of a training missile, training missile stage, training launch canister or training launcher shall be considered to have been completed upon the completion of the procedures required by this paragraph and upon notification as required by paragraph 5(e) of Article IX of the Treaty following the date specified pursuant to paragraph 3(d) of this Section.

V. Other Types of Elimination

1. *Loss or Accidental Destruction*

(a) If an item listed in Section I of this Protocol is lost or destroyed as a result of an accident, the possessing Party shall notify the other Party within 48 hours, as required in paragraph 5(e) of Article IX of the Treaty, that the item has been eliminated.

(b) Such notification shall include the type of the eliminated item, its approximate or assumed location and the circumstances related to the loss or accidental destruction.

(c) In such a case, the other Party shall have the right to conduct an inspection of the specific point at which the accident occurred to provide confidence that the item has been eliminated.

2. *Static Display*

(a) The Parties shall have the right to eliminate missiles, launch canisters and launchers, as well as training missiles, training launch canisters and training launchers, listed in Section I of this Protocol by placing them on static display. Each party shall be limited to a total of 15 missiles, 15 launch canisters and 15 launchers on such static display.

(b) Prior to being placed on static display, a missile, launch canister or launcher shall be rendered unusable for purposes inconsistent with the Treaty. Missile propellant shall be removed and erector-launcher mechanisms shall be rendered inoperative.

(c) The Party possessing a missile, launch canister or launcher, as well as a training missile, training launch canister or training launcher that is to be eliminated by placing it on static display shall provide the other Party with the place-name and coordinates of the location at which such a missile, launch canister or launcher is to be on static display, as well as the location at which the on-site inspection provided for in paragraph 2(d) of this Section, may take place.

(d) Each Party shall have the right to conduct an on-site inspection of such a missile, launch canister or launcher within 60 days of receipt of the notification required in paragraph 2(c) of this Section.

(e) Elimination of a missile, launch canister or launcher, as well as a training missile, training launch canister or training launcher, by placing it on static display shall be considered to have been completed upon completion of the procedures required by this paragraph and notification as required by paragraph 5(e) of Article IX of the Treaty.

This Protocol is an integral part of the Treaty. It shall enter into force on the date of the entry into force of the Treaty and shall remain in force so long as the Treaty remains in force. As provided for in paragraph 1(b) of Article XIII of the Treaty, the Parties may agree upon such measures as may be necessary to improve the viability and effectiveness of this Protocol. Such measures shall not be deemed amendments to the Treaty.

[PROTOCOL REGARDING INSPECTIONS]

Pursuant to and in implementation of the Treaty Between the United States of America and the Union of Soviet Socialist Republics on the Elimination of Their Intermediate-Range and Shorter-Range Missiles of December 8, 1987, hereinafter referred to as the Treaty, the Parties hereby agree upon procedures governing the conduct of inspections provided for in Article XI of the Treaty.

I. Definitions

For the purposes of this Protocol, the Treaty, the Memorandum of Understanding and the Protocol on Elimination:

1. The term "inspected Party" means the Party to the Treaty whose sites are subject to inspection as provided for by Article XI of the Treaty.

2. The term "inspecting Party" means the Party to the Treaty carrying out an inspection.

3. The term "inspector" means an individual designated by one of the Parties to carry out inspections and included on that Party's list of inspectors in accordance with the provisions of Section III of this Protocol.

4. The term "inspection team" means the group of inspectors assigned by the inspecting Party to conduct a particular inspection.

5. The term "inspection site" means an area, location or facility at which an inspection is carried out.

6. The term "period of inspection" means the period of time from arrival of the inspection team at the inspection site until its departure from the inspection site, exclusive of time spent on any pre- and post-inspection procedures.

7. The term "point of entry" means: Washington, D.C., or San Francisco, California, the United States of America; Brussels (National Airport), The Kingdom of Belgium; Frankfurt (Rhein Main Airbase), The Federal Republic of Germany; Rome (Ciampino), The Republic of Italy; Schiphol, The Kingdom of the Netherlands; RAF Greenham Common, The United Kingdom of Great Britain and Northern Ireland; Moscow, or Itkutsk, the Union of Soviet Socialist Republics; Schkeuditz Airport, the German Democratic Republic; and International Airport Ruzyne, the Czechoslovak Socialist Republic.

8. The term "in-country period" means the period from the arrival of the inspection team at the point of entry until its departure from the country through the point of entry.

9. The term "in-country escort" means individuals specified by the inspected Party to accompany and assist inspectors and aircrew members as necessary throughout the in-country period.

10. The term "aircrew member" means an individual who performs duties related to the operation of an airplane and who is included on a Party's list of aircrew members in accordance with the provisions of Section III of this Protocol.

II. General Obligations

1. For the purpose of ensuring verification of compliance with the provisions of the Treaty, each Party shall facilitate inspection by the other Party pursuant to this Protocol.

2. Each Party takes note of the assurances received from the other Party regarding understandings reached between the other Party and the basing countries to the effect that the basing countries have agreed to the conduct of inspections, in accordance with the provisions of this Protocol, on their territories.

III. Pre-Inspection Requirements

1. Inspections to ensure verification of compliance by the Parties with the obligations assumed under the Treaty shall be carried out by inspec-

tors designated in accordance with paragraphs 3 and 4 of this Section.

2. No later than one day after entry into force of the Treaty, each Party shall provide to the other Party: a list of its proposed aircrew members; a list of its proposed inspectors who will carry out inspections pursuant to paragraphs 3, 4, 5, 7 and 8 of Article XI of the Treaty; and a list of its proposed inspectors who will carry out inspection activities pursuant to paragraph 6 of Article XI of the Treaty. None of these lists shall contain at any time more than 200 individuals.

3. Each Party shall review the lists of inspectors and aircrew members proposed by the other Party. With respect to an individual included on the list of proposed inspectors who will carry out inspection activities pursuant to paragraph 6 of Article XI of the Treaty, if such an individual is unacceptable to the Party reviewing the list, that Party shall, within 20 days, so inform the Party providing the list, and the individual shall be deemed not accepted and shall be deleted from the list. With respect to an individual on the list of proposed aircrew members or the list of proposed inspectors who will carry out inspections pursuant to paragraphs 3, 4, 5, 7 and 8 of Article XI of the Treaty, each Party, within 20 days after the receipt of such lists, shall inform the other Party of its agreement to the designation of each inspector and aircrew member proposed. Inspectors shall be citizens of the inspecting Party.

4. Each Party shall have the right to amend its lists of inspectors and aircrew members. New inspectors and aircrew members shall be designated in the same manner as set forth in paragraph 3 of this Section with respect to the initial lists.

5. Within 30 days of receipt of the initial lists of inspectors and aircrew members, or of subsequent changes thereto, the Party receiving such information shall provide, or shall ensure the provision of, such visas and other documents to each individual to whom it has agreed as may be required to ensure that each inspector or aircrew member may enter and remain in the territory of the Party or basing country in which an inspection site is located throughout the in-country period for the purpose of carrying out inspection activities in accordance with the provisions of this Protocol. Such visas and documents shall be valid for a period of at least 24 months.

6. To exercise their functions effectively, inspectors and aircrew members shall be accorded, throughout the in-country period, privileges and immunities in the country of the inspection site as set forth in the Annex to this Protocol.

7. Without prejudice to their privileges and immunities, inspectors and aircrew members shall be obliged to respect the laws and regulations of the State on whose territory an inspection is carried out and shall be obliged not to interfere in the internal affairs of that State. In the event the inspected Party determines that an inspector or aircrew member of the other Party has violated the conditions governing inspection activities set forth in this Protocol, or has ever committed a criminal offense on the

territory of the inspected Party or a basing country, or has ever been sentenced for committing a criminal offense or expelled by the inspected Party or a basing country, the inspected Party making such a determination shall so notify the inspecting Party, which shall immediately strike the individual from the list of inspectors or the list of aircrew members. If, at that time, the individual is on the territory of the inspected Party or a basing country, the inspecting Party shall immediately remove that individual from the country.

8. Within 30 days after entry into force of the Treaty, each Party shall inform the other Party of the standing diplomatic clearance number for airplanes of the Party transporting inspectors and equipment necessary for inspection into and out of the territory of the Party or basing country in which an inspection site is located. Aircraft routings to and from the designated point of entry shall be along established international airways that are agreed upon by the Parties as the basis for such diplomatic clearance.

IV. Notifications

1. Notification of an intention to conduct an inspection shall be made through the Nuclear Risk Reduction Centers. The receipt of this notification shall be acknowledged through the Nuclear Risk Reduction Centers by the inspected Party within one hour of its receipt.

(a) For inspections conducted pursuant to paragraphs 3, 4 or 5 of Article XI of the Treaty, such notifications shall be made no less than 16 hours in advance of the estimated time of arrival of the inspection team at the point of entry and shall include:

(i) the point of entry;

(ii) the date and estimated time of arrival at the point of entry;

(iii) the date and time when the specification of the inspection site will be provided; and

(iv) the names of inspectors and aircrew members.

(b) For inspections conducted pursuant to paragraphs 7 or 8 of Article XI of the Treaty, such notifications shall be made no less than 72 hours in advance of the estimated time of arrival of the inspection team at the point of entry and shall include:

(i) the point of entry;

(ii) the date and estimated time of arrival at the point of entry;

(iii) the site to be inspected and the type of inspection; and

(iv) the names of inspectors and aircrew members.

2. The date and time of the specification of the inspection site as notified pursuant to paragraph 1(a) of this Section shall fall within the following time intervals:

(a) for inspections conducted pursuant to paragraphs 4 or 5 of Article XI of the Treaty, neither less than four hours nor more than 24 hours after the estimated date and time of arrival at the point of entry; and

(b) for inspections conducted pursuant to paragraph 3 of Article XI of the Treaty, neither less than four hours nor more than 48 hours after the estimated date and time of arrival at the point of entry.

3. The inspecting Party shall provide the inspected Party with a flight plan, through the Nuclear Risk Reduction Centers, for its flight from the last airfield prior to entering the airspace of the country in which the inspection site is located to the point of entry, no less than six hours before the scheduled departure time from that airfield. Such a plan shall be filed in accordance with the procedures of the International Civil Aviation Organization applicable to civil aircraft. The inspecting Party shall include in the remarks section of each flight plan the standing diplomatic clearance number and the notation: "Inspection aircraft. Priority clearance processing required."

4. No less than three hours prior to the scheduled departure of the inspection team from the last airfield prior to entering the airspace of the country in which the inspection is to take place, the inspected Party shall ensure that the flight plan filed in accordance with paragraph 3 of this Section is approved so that the inspection team may arrive at the point of entry by the estimated arrival time.

5. Either Party may change the point or points of entry to the territories of the countries within which its deployment areas, missile operating bases or missile support facilities are located, by giving notice of such change to the other Party. A change in a point of entry shall become effective five months after receipt of such notification by the other Party.

V. Activities Beginning upon Arrival at the Point of Entry

1. The in-country escort and a diplomatic aircrew escort accredited to the Government of either the inspected Party or the basing country in which the inspection site is located shall meet the inspection team and aircrew members at the point of entry as soon as the airplane of the inspecting Party lands. The number of aircrew members for each airplane shall not exceed ten. The in-country escort shall expedite the entry of the inspection team and aircrew, their baggage, and equipment and supplies necessary for inspection, into the country in which the inspection site is located. A diplomatic aircrew escort shall have the right to accompany and assist aircrew members throughout the in-country period. In the case of an inspection taking place on the territory of a basing country, the in-country escort may include representatives of that basing country.

2. An inspector shall be considered to have assumed his duties upon arrival at the point of entry on the territory of the inspected Party or a basing country, and shall be considered to have ceased performing those duties when he has left the territory of the inspected Party or basing country.

3. Each Party shall ensure that equipment and supplies are exempt from all customs duties.

4. Equipment and supplies which the inspecting Party brings into the country in which an inspection site is located shall be subject to examination at the point of entry each time they are brought into that country. This examination shall be completed prior to the departure of the inspection team from the point of entry to conduct an inspection. Such equipment and supplies shall be examined by the in-country escort in the presence of the inspection team members to ascertain to the satisfaction of each Party that the equipment and supplies cannot perform functions unconnected with the inspection requirements of the Treaty. If it is established upon examination that the equipment or supplies are unconnected with these inspection requirements, then they shall not be cleared for use and shall be impounded at the point of entry until the departure of the inspection team from the country where the inspection is conducted. Storage of the inspecting Party's equipment and supplies at each point of entry shall be within tamper-proof containers within a secure facility. Access to each secure facility shall be controlled by a "dual key" system requiring the presence of both Parties to gain access to the equipment and supplies.

5. Throughout the in-country period, the inspected Party shall provide, or arrange for the provision of, meals, lodging, work space, transportation and, as necessary, medical care for the inspection team and aircrew of the inspecting Party. All the costs in connection with the stay of inspectors carrying out inspection activities pursuant to paragraph 6 of Article XI of the Treaty, on the territory of the inspected Party, including meals, services, lodging, work space, transportation and medical care, shall be borne by the inspecting Party.

6. The inspected Party shall provide parking, security protection, servicing and fuel for the airplane of the inspecting Party at the point of entry. The inspecting Party shall bear the cost of such fuel and servicing.

7. For inspections conducted on the territory of the Parties, the inspection team shall enter at the point of entry on the territory of the inspected Party that is closest to the inspection site. In the case of inspections carried out in accordance with paragraphs 3, 4 or 5 of Article XI of the Treaty, the inspection team leader shall, at or before the time notified, pursuant to paragraph 1(a)(iii) of Section IV of this Protocol, inform the inspected Party at the point of entry through the in-country escort of the type of inspection and the inspection site, by place-name and geographic coordinates.

VI. General Rules for Conducting Inspections

1. Inspectors shall discharge their functions in accordance with this Protocol.

2. Inspectors shall not disclose information received during inspections except with the express permission of the inspecting Party. They shall remain bound by this obligation after their assignment as inspectors has ended.

3. In discharging their functions, inspectors shall not interfere directly with ongoing activities at the inspection site and shall avoid unnecessarily hampering or delaying the operation of a facility or taking actions affecting its safe operation.

4. Inspections shall be conducted in accordance with the objectives set forth in Article XI of the Treaty as applicable for the type of inspection specified by the inspecting Party under paragraph 1(b) of Section IV or paragraph 7 of Section V of this Protocol.

5. The in-country escort shall have the right to accompany and assist inspectors and aircrew members as considered necessary by the inspected Party throughout the in-country period. Except as otherwise provided in this Protocol, the movement and travel of inspectors and aircrew members shall be at the discretion of the in-country escort.

6. Inspectors carrying out inspection activities pursuant to paragraph 6 of Article XI of the Treaty shall be allowed to travel within 50 kilometers from the inspection site with the permission of the in-country escort, and as considered necessary by the inspected Party, shall be accompanied by the in-country escort. Such travel shall be taken solely as a leisure activity.

7. Inspectors shall have the right throughout the period of inspection to be in communication with the embassy of the inspecting Party located within the territory of the country where the inspection is taking place using the telephone communications provided by the inspected Party.

8. At the inspection site, representatives of the inspected facility shall be included among the in-country escort.

9. The inspection team may bring onto the inspection site such documents as needed to conduct the inspection, as well as linear measurement devices; cameras; portable weighing devices; radiation detection devices; and other equipment, as agreed by the Parties. The characteristics and method of use of the equipment listed above shall also be agreed upon within 30 days after entry into force of the Treaty. During inspections conducted pursuant to paragraphs 3, 4, 5(a), 7 or 8 of Article XI of the Treaty, the inspection team may use any of the equipment listed above, except for cameras, which shall be for use only by the inspected Party at the request of the inspecting Party. During inspections conducted pursuant to paragraph 5(b) of Article XI of the Treaty, all measurements shall be made by the inspected Party at the request of the inspecting Party. At the request of inspectors, the in-country escort shall take photographs of the inspected facilities using the inspecting Party's camera systems which are capable of producing duplicate, instant-development photographic prints. Each Party shall receive one copy of every photograph.

10. For inspections conducted pursuant to paragraphs 3, 4, 5, 7 or 8 of Article XI of the Treaty, inspectors shall permit the in-country escort to observe the equipment used during the inspection by the inspection team.

11. Measurements recorded during inspections shall be certified by the signature of a member of the inspection team and a member of the in-country escort when they are taken. Such certified data shall be included

in the inspection report.

12. Inspectors shall have the right to request clarifications in connection with ambiguities that arise during an inspection. Such requests shall be made promptly through the in-country escort. The in-country escort shall provide the inspection team, during the inspection, with such clarifications as may be necessary to remove the ambiguity. In the event questions relating to an object or building located within the inspection site are not resolved, the inspected Party shall photograph the object or building as requested by the inspecting Party for the purpose of clarifying its nature and function. If the ambiguity cannot be removed during the inspection, then the question, relevant clarifications and a copy of any photographs taken shall be included in the inspection report.

13. In carrying out their activities, inspectors shall observe safety regulations established at the inspection site, including those for the protection of controlled environments within a facility and for personal safety. Individual protective clothing and equipment shall be provided by the inspected Party, as necessary.

14. For inspections pursuant to paragraphs 3, 4, 5, 7 or 8 of Article XI of the Treaty, pre-inspection procedures, including briefings and safety-related activities, shall begin upon arrival of the inspection team at the inspection site and shall be completed within one hour. The inspection team shall begin the inspection immediately upon completion of the pre-inspection procedures. The period of inspection shall not exceed 24 hours except for inspections pursuant to paragraphs 6, 7 or 8 of Article XI of the Treaty. The period of inspection may be extended, by agreement with the in-country escort, by no more than eight hours. Post-inspection procedures, which include completing the inspection report in accordance with the provisions of Section XI of this Protocol, shall begin immediately upon completion of the inspection and shall be completed at the inspection site within four hours.

15. An inspection team conducting an inspection pursuant to Article XI of the Treaty shall include no more than ten inspectors, except for an inspection team conducting an inspection pursuant to paragraphs 7 or 8 of that Article, which shall include no more than 20 inspectors, and an inspection team conducting inspection activities pursuant to paragraph 6 of that Article, which shall include no more than 30 inspectors. At least two inspectors on each team must speak the language of the inspected Party. An inspection team shall operate under the direction of the team leader and deputy team leader. Upon arrival at the inspection site, the inspection team may divide itself into subgroups consisting of no fewer than two inspectors each. There shall be no more than one inspection team at an inspection site at any one time.

16. Except in the case of inspections conducted pursuant to paragraphs 3, 4, 7 or 8 of Article XI of the Treaty, upon completion of the post-inspection procedures, the inspection team shall return promptly to the point of entry from which it commenced inspection activities and shall

then leave, within 24 hours, the territory of the country in which the inspection site is located, using its own airplane. In the case of inspections conducted pursuant to paragraphs 3, 4, 7 or 8 of Article XI of the Treaty, if the inspection team intends to conduct another inspection it shall either:

(a) notify the inspected Party of its intent upon return to the point of entry; or

(b) notify the inspected Party of the type of inspection and the inspection site upon completion of the post-inspection procedures. In this case it shall be the responsibility of the inspected Party to ensure that the inspection team reaches the next inspection site without unjustified delay. The inspected Party shall determine the means of transportation and route involved in such travel.

With respect to subparagraph (a), the procedures set forth in paragraph 7 of Section V of this Protocol and paragraphs 1 and 2 of Section VII of this Protocol shall apply.

VII. Inspections Conducted Pursuant to Paragraphs 3, 4 or 5 of Article XI of the Treaty

1. Within one hour after the time for the specification of the inspection site notified pursuant to paragraph 1(a) of Section IV of this Protocol, the inspected Party shall implement pre-inspection movement restrictions at the inspection site, which shall remain in effect until the inspection team arrives at the inspection site. During the period that pre-inspection movement restrictions are in effect, missiles, stages of such missiles, launchers or support equipment subject to the Treaty shall not be removed from the inspection site.

2. The inspected party shall transport the inspection team from the point of entry to the inspection site so that the inspection team arrives at the inspection site no later than nine hours after the time for the specification of the inspection site notified pursuant to paragraph 1(a) of Section IV of this Protocol.

3. In the event that an inspection is conducted in a basing country, the aircrew of the inspected Party may include representatives of the basing country.

4. Neither Party shall conduct more than one inspection pursuant to paragraph 5(a) of Article XI of the Treaty at any one time, more than one inspection pursuant to paragraph 5(b) of Article XI of the Treaty at any one time, or more than 10 inspections pursuant to paragraph 3 of Article XI of the Treaty at any one time.

5. The boundaries of the inspection site at the facility to be inspected shall be the boundaries of that facility set forth in the Memorandum of Understanding.

6. Except in the case of an inspection conducted pursuant to paragraphs 4 or 5(b) of Article XI of the Treaty, upon arrival of the inspection team at the inspection site, the in-country escort shall inform the inspection team leader of the number of missiles, stages of missiles, launchers, support

structures and support equipment at the site that are subject to the Treaty and provide the inspection team leader with a diagram of the inspection site indicating the location of these missiles, stages of missiles, launchers, support structures and support equipment at the inspection site.

7. Subject to the procedures of paragraphs 8 through 14 of this Section, inspectors shall have the right to inspect the entire inspection site, including the interior of structures, containers or vehicles, or including covered objects, whose dimensions are equal to or greater than the dimensions specified in Section VI of the Memorandum of Understanding for the missiles, stages of such missiles, launchers or support equipment of the inspected Party.

8. A missile, a stage of such a missile or a launcher subject to the Treaty shall be subject to inspection only by external visual observation, including measuring, as necessary, the dimensions of such a missile, stage of such a missile or launcher. A container that the inspected Party declares to contain a missile or stage of a missile subject to the Treaty, and which is not sufficiently large to be capable of containing more than one missile or stage of such a missile of the inspected Party subject to the Treaty, shall be subject to inspection only by external visual observation, including measuring, as necessary, the dimensions of such a container to confirm that it cannot contain more than one missile or stage of such a missile of the inspected Party subject to the Treaty. Except as provided for in paragraph 14 of this Section, a container that is sufficiently large to contain a missile or stage of such a missile of the inspected Party subject to the Treaty that the inspected Party declares not to contain a missile or stage of such a missile subject to the Treaty shall be subject to inspection only by means of weighing or visual observation of the interior of the container, as necessary, to confirm that it does not, in fact, contain a missile or stage of such a missile of the inspected Party subject to the Treaty. If such a container is a launch canister associated with a type of missile not subject to the Treaty, and declared by the inspected Party to contain such a missile, it shall be subject to external inspection only, including use of radiation detection devices, visual observation and linear measurement, as necessary, of the dimensions of such a canister.

9. A structure or container that is not sufficiently large to contain a missile, stage of such a missile or launcher of the inspected Party subject to the Treaty shall be subject to inspection only by external visual observation including measuring, as necessary, the dimensions of such a structure or container to confirm that it is not sufficiently large to be capable of containing a missile, stage of such a missile or launcher of the inspected Party subject to the Treaty.

10. Within a structure, a space which is sufficiently large to contain a missile, stage of such a missile or launcher of the inspected Party subject to the Treaty, but which is demonstrated to the satisfaction of the inspection team not to be accessible by the smallest missile, stage of a missile or launcher of the inspected Party subject to the Treaty, shall not be subject

to further inspection. If the inspected Party demonstrates to the satisfaction of the inspection team by means of a visual inspection of the interior of an enclosed space from its entrance that the enclosed space does not contain any missile, stage of such a missile or launcher of the inspected Party subject to the Treaty, such an enclosed space shall not be subject to further inspection.

11. The inspection team shall be permitted to patrol the perimeter of the inspection site and station inspectors at the exits of the site for the duration of the inspection.

12. The inspection team shall be permitted to inspect any vehicle capable of carrying missiles, stages of such missiles, launchers or support equipment of the inspected Party subject to the Treaty at any time during the course of an inspection and no such vehicle shall leave the inspection site during the course of the inspection until inspected at site exits by the inspection team.

13. Prior to inspection of a building within the inspection site, the inspection team may station subgroups at the exits of the building that are large enough to permit passage of any missile, stage of such a missile, launcher or support equipment of the inspected Party subject to the Treaty. During the time that the building is being inspected, no vehicle or object capable of containing any missile, stage of such a missile, launcher or support equipment of the inspected Party subject to the Treaty shall be permitted to leave the building until inspected.

14. During an inspection conducted pursuant to paragraph 5(b) of Article XI of the Treaty, it shall be the responsibility of the inspected Party to demonstrate that a shrouded or environmentally protected object which is equal to or larger than the smallest missile, stage of a missile or launcher of the inspected Party subject to the Treaty is not, in fact, a missile, stage of such a missile or launcher of the inspected Party subject to the Treaty. This may be accomplished by partial removal of the shroud or environmental protection cover, measuring, or weighing the covered object or by other methods. If the inspected Party satisfies the inspection team by its demonstration that the object is not a missile, stage of such a missile or launcher of the inspected Party subject to the Treaty, then there shall be no further inspection of that object. If the container is a launch canister associated with a type of missile not subject to the Treaty, and declared by the inspected Party to contain such a missile, then it shall be subject to external inspection only, including use of radiation detection devices, visual observation and linear measurement, as necessary, of the dimensions of such a canister.

VIII. Inspections Conducted Pursuant to Paragraphs 7 or 8 of Article XI of the Treaty

1. Inspections of the process of elimination of items of missile systems specified in the Protocol on Elimination carried out pursuant to paragraph 7 of Article XI of the Treaty shall be conducted in accordance with the

procedures set forth in this paragraph and the Protocol on Elimination.

(a) Upon arrival at the elimination facility, inspectors shall be provided with a schedule of elimination activities.

(b) Inspectors shall check the data which are specified in the notification provided by the inspected Party regarding the number and type of items of missile systems to be eliminated against the number and type of such items which are at the elimination facility prior to the initiation of the elimination procedures.

(c) Subject to paragraphs 3 and 11 of Section VI of this Protocol, inspectors shall observe the execution of the specific procedures for the elimination of the items of missile systems as provided for in the Protocol of Elimination. If any deviations from the agreed elimination procedures are found, the inspectors shall have the right to call the attention of the in-country escort to the need for strict compliance with the above-mentioned procedures. The completion of such procedures shall be confirmed in accordance with the procedures specified in the Protocol on Elimination.

(d) During the elimination of missiles by means of launching, the inspectors shall have the right to ascertain by visual observation that a missile prepared for launch is a missile of the type subject to elimination. The inspectors shall also be allowed to observe such a missile from a safe location specified by the inspected Party until the completion of its launch. During the inspection of a series of launches for the elimination of missiles by means of launching, the inspected Party shall determine the means of transport and route for the transportation of inspectors between inspection sites.

2. Inspections of the elimination of items of missile systems specified in the Protocol on Elimination carried out pursuant to paragraph 8 of Article XI of the Treaty shall be conducted in accordance with the procedures set forth in Sections II, IV or V of the Protocol on Elimination or as otherwise agreed by the Parties.

IX. Inspection Activities Conducted Pursuant to Paragraph 6 of Article XI of the Treaty

1. The inspected Party shall maintain an agreed perimeter around the periphery of the inspection site and shall designate a portal with not more than one rail line and one road which shall be within 50 meters of each other. All vehicles which can contain an intermediate-range GLBM or longest stage of such a GLBM of the inspected Party shall exit only through this portal.

2. For the purposes of this Section, the provisions of paragraph 10 of Article VII of the Treaty shall be applied to intermediate-range GLBMs of the inspected Party and the longest stage of such GLBMs.

3. There shall not be more than two other exits from the inspection site. Such exits shall be monitored by appropriate sensors. The perimeter of and exits from the inspection site may be monitored as provided for by

paragraph 11 of Section VII of this Protocol.

4. The inspecting Party shall have the right to establish continuous monitoring systems at the portal specified in paragraph 1 of this Section and appropriate sensors at the exits specified in paragraph 3 of this Section and carry out necessary engineering surveys, construction, repair and replacement of monitoring systems.

5. The inspected Party shall, at the request of and at the expense of the inspecting Party, provide the following:

(a) all necessary utilities for the construction and operation of the monitoring systems, including electrical power, water, fuel, heating and sewage;

(b) basic construction materials including concrete and lumber;

(c) the site preparation necessary to accommodate the installation of continuously operating systems for monitoring the portal specified in paragraph 1 of this Section, appropriate sensors for other exits specified in paragraph 3 of this Section and the center for collecting data obtained during inspections. Such preparation may include ground excavation, laying of concrete foundations, trenching between equipment locations and utility connections;

(d) transportation for necessary installation tools, materials and equipment from the point of entry to the inspection site; and

(e) a minimum of two telephone lines and, as necessary, high-frequency radio equipment capable of allowing direct communication with the embassy of the inspecting Party in the country in which the site is located.

6. Outside the perimeter of the inspection site, the inspecting Party shall have the right to:

(a) build no more than three buildings with a total floor space of not more than 150 square meters for a data center and inspection team headquarters, and one additional building with floor space not to exceed 500 square meters for the storage of supplies and equipment;

(b) install systems to monitor the exits to include weight sensors, vehicle sensors, surveillance systems and vehicle dimensional measuring equipment;

(c) install at the portal specified in paragraph 1 of this Section equipment for measuring the length and diameter of missile stages contained inside the launch canisters or shipping containers;

(d) install at the portal specified in paragraph 1 of this Section non-damaging image-producing equipment for imaging the contents of launch canisters or shipping containers declared to contain missiles or missile stages as provided for in paragraph 11 of this Section;

(e) install a primary and back-up power source; and

(f) use, as necessary, data authentication devices.

7. During the installation or operation of the monitoring systems, the inspecting Party shall not deny the inspected Party access to any existing structures or security systems. The inspecting Party shall not take any

actions with respect to such structures without consent of the inspected Party. If the Parties agree that such structures are to be rebuilt or demolished, either partially or completely, the inspecting Party shall provide the necessary compensation.

8. The inspected Party shall not interfere with the installed equipment or restrict the access of the inspection team to such equipment.

9. The inspecting Party shall have the right to use its own two-way systems of radio communication between inspectors patrolling the perimeter and the data collection center. Such systems shall conform to power and frequency restrictions established on the territory of the inspected Party.

10. Aircraft shall not be permitted to land within the perimeter of the monitored site except for emergencies at the site and with prior notification to the inspection team.

11. Any shipment exiting through the portal specified in paragraph 1 of this Section which is large enough and heavy enough to contain an intermediate-range GLBM or longest stage of such a GLBM of the inspected Party shall be declared by the inspected Party to the inspection team before the shipment arrives at the portal. The declaration shall state whether such a shipment contains a missile or missile stage as large or larger than and as heavy or heavier than an intermediate-range GLBM or longest stage of such a GLBM of the inspected Party.

12. The inspection team shall have the right to weigh and measure the dimensions of any vehicle, including railcars, exiting the site to ascertain whether it is large enough and heavy enough to contain an intermediate-range GLBM or longest stage of such a GLBM of the inspected Party. These measurements shall be performed so as to minimize the delay of vehicles exiting the site. Vehicles that are either not large enough or not heavy enough to contain an intermediate-range GLBM or longest stage of such a GLBM of the inspected Party shall not be subject to further inspection.

13. Vehicles exiting through the portal specified in paragraph 1 of this Section that are large enough and heavy enough to contain an intermediate-range GLBM or longest stage of such a GLBM of the inspected Party but that are declared not to contain a missile or missile stage as large or larger than and as heavy or heavier than an intermediate-range GLBM or longest stage of such a GLBM of the inspected Party shall be subject to the following procedures.

(a) The inspecting Party shall have the right to inspect the interior of all such vehicles.

(b) If the inspecting Party can determine by visual observation or dimensional measurement that, inside a particular vehicle, there are no containers or shrouded objects large enough to be or to contain an intermediate-range GLBM or longest stage of such a GLBM of the inspected Party, then that vehicle shall not be subject to further inspection.

(c) If inside a vehicle there are one or more containers or shrouded objects large enough to be or to contain an intermediate-range GLBM or longest stage of such a GLBM of the inspected Party, it shall be the responsibility of the inspected Party to demonstrate that such containers or shrouded objects are not and do not contain intermediate-range GLBMs or the longest stages of such GLBMs of the inspected Party.

14. Vehicles exiting through the portal specified in paragraph 1 of this Section that are declared to contain a missile or missile stage as large or larger than and as heavy or heavier than an intermediate-range GLBM or longest stage of such a GLBM of the inspected Party shall be subject to the following procedures.

(a) The inspecting Party shall preserve the integrity of the inspected missile or stage of a missile.

(b) Measuring equipment shall be placed only outside of the launch canister or shipping container; all measurements shall be made by the inspecting Party using the equipment provided for in paragraph 6 of this Section. Such measurements shall be observed and certified by the in-country escort.

(c) The inspecting Party shall have the right to weigh and measure the dimensions of any launch canister or of any shipping container declared to contain such a missile or missile stage and to image the contents of any launch canister or of any shipping container declared to contain such a missile or missile stage; it shall have the right to view such missiles or missile stages contained in launch canisters or shipping containers eight times per calendar year. The in-country escort shall be present during all phases of such viewing. During such interior viewing:

(i) the front end of the launch canister or the cover of the shipping container shall be opened;

(ii) the missile or missile stage shall not be removed from its launch canister or shipping container; and

(iii) the length and diameter of the stages of the missile shall be measured in accordance with the methods agreed by the Parties so as to ascertain that the missile or missile stage is not an intermediate-range GLBM of the inspected Party, or the longest stage of such a GLBM, and that the missile has no more than one stage which is outwardly similar to a stage of an existing type of intermediate-range GLBM.

(d) The inspecting Party shall also have the right to inspect any other containers or shrouded objects inside the vehicle containing such a missile or missile stage in accordance with the procedures in paragraph 13 of this Section.

X. Cancellation of Inspection

An inspection shall be canceled if, due to circumstances brought about by *force majeure,* it cannot be carried out. In the case of a delay that prevents an inspection team performing an inspection pursuant to paragraphs 3, 4 or 5 of Article XI of the Treaty from arriving at the inspection site during the time specified in paragraph 2 of Section VII of this Protocol, the inspecting Party may either cancel or carry out the inspection. If an inspection is canceled due to circumstances brought about by *force majeure* or delay, then the number of inspections to which the inspecting Party is entitled shall not be reduced.

XI. Inspection Report

1. For inspections conducted pursuant to paragraphs 3, 4, 5, 7 or 8 of Article XI of the Treaty, during post-inspection procedures, and no later than two hours after the inspection has been completed, the inspection team leader shall provide the in-country escort with a written inspection report in both the English and Russian languages. The report shall be factual. It shall include the type of inspection carried out, the inspection site, the number of missiles, stages of missiles, launchers and items of support equipment subject to the Treaty observed during the period of inspection and any measurements recorded pursuant to paragraph 10 of Section VI of this Protocol. Photographs taken during the inspection in accordance with agreed procedures, as well as the inspection site diagram provided for by paragraph 6 of Section VII of this Protocol, shall be attached to this report.

2. For inspection activities pursuant to paragraph 6 of Article XI of the Treaty, within 3 days after the end of each month, the inspection team leader shall provide the in-country escort with a written inspection report both in the English and Russian languages. The report shall be factual. It shall include the number of vehicles declared to contain a missile or stage of a missile as large or larger than and as heavy or heavier than an intermediate-range GLBM or longest stage of such a GLBM of the inspected Party that left the inspection site through the portal specified in paragraph 1 of Section IX of this Protocol during that month. The report shall also include any measurements of launch canisters or shipping containers contained in these vehicles recorded pursuant to paragraph 11 of Section VI of this Protocol. In the event the inspecting Party, under the provisions of paragraph 14(c) of Section IX of this Protocol, has viewed the interior of a launch canister or shipping container declared to contain a missile or stage of a missile as large or larger than and as heavy or heavier than an intermediate-range GLBM or longest stage of such a GLBM of the inspected Party, the report shall also include the measurements of the length and diameter of missile stages obtained during the inspection and recorded pursuant to paragraph 11 of Section VI of this Protocol. Photographs taken during the inspection in accordance with agreed procedures shall be attached to this report.

3. The inspected Party shall have the right to include written comments in the report.

4. The Parties shall, when possible, resolve ambiguities regarding factual information contained in the inspection report. Relevant clarifications shall be recorded in the report. The report shall be signed by the inspection team leader and by one of the members of the in-country escort. Each Party shall retain one copy of the report.

This Protocol is an integral part of the Treaty. It shall enter into force on the date of entry into force of the Treaty and shall remain in force as long as the Treaty remains in force. As provided for in paragraph 1(b) of Article XIII of the Treaty, the Parties may agree upon such measures as may be necessary to improve the viability and effectiveness of this Protocol. Such measures shall not be deemed amendments to the Treaty.

ANNEX PROVISIONS ON PRIVILEGES AND IMMUNITIES OF INSPECTORS AND AIRCREW MEMBERS

In order to exercise their functions effectively, for the purpose of implementing the Treaty and not for their personal benefit, the inspectors and aircrew members referred to in Section III of this Protocol shall be accorded the privileges and immunities contained in this Annex. Privileges and immunities shall be accorded for the entire in-country period in the country in which an inspection site is located, and thereafter with respect to acts previously performed in the exercise of official functions as an inspector or aircrew member.

1. Inspectors and aircrew members shall be accorded the inviolability enjoyed by diplomatic agents pursuant to Article 29 of the Vienna Convention on Diplomatic Relations of April 18, 1961.

2. The living quarters and office premises occupied by an inspector carrying out inspection activities pursuant to paragraph 6 of Article XI of the Treaty shall be accorded the inviolability and protection accorded the premises of diplomatic agents pursuant to Article 30 of the Vienna Convention on Diplomatic Relations.

3. The papers and correspondence of inspectors and aircrew members shall enjoy the inviolability accorded to the papers and correspondence of diplomatic agents pursuant to Article 30 of the Vienna Convention on Diplomatic Relations. In addition, the aircraft of the inspection team shall be inviolable.

4. Inspectors and aircrew members shall be accorded the immunities accorded diplomatic agents pursuant to paragraphs 1, 2 and 3 of Article 31 of the Vienna Convention on Diplomatic Relations. The immunity from jurisdiction of an inspector or an aircrew member may be waived by the inspecting Party in those cases when it is of the opinion that immunity would impede the course of justice and that it can be waived without prejudice to the implementation of the provisions

of the Treaty. Waiver must always be express.

5. Inspectors carrying out inspection activities pursuant to paragraph 6 of Article XI of the Treaty shall be accorded the exemption from dues and taxes accorded to diplomatic agents pursuant to Article 34 of the Vienna Convention on Diplomatic Relations.

6. Inspectors and aircrew members of a Party shall be permitted to bring into the territory of the other Party or a basing country in which an inspection site is located, without payment of any customs duties or related charges, articles for their personal use, with the exception of articles the import or export of which is prohibited by law or controlled by quarantine regulations.

7. An inspector or aircrew member shall not engage in any professional or commercial activity for personal profit on the territory of the inspected Party or that of the basing countries.

8. If the inspected Party considers that there has been an abuse of privileges and immunities specified in this Annex, consultations shall be held between the Parties to determine whether such an abuse has occurred and, if so determined, to prevent a repetition of such an abuse.

REAGAN-GORBACHEV SUMMIT

December 10, 1987

The third summit meeting between U.S. president Ronald Reagan and Soviet leader Mikhail S. Gorbachev, held in Washington, D.C., December 8-10, appeared to mark a change in the style of U.S.-Soviet relations. The long-time adversaries had come to terms with their chronic conflicts and had begun to focus on hard-nosed but practical negotiations. The arms control agreement signed on the first day was followed by glittering social functions, as well as high-level meetings of Soviet and American officials on a variety of subjects. (INF treaty, p. 945)

Yet neither the arms treaty nor the public display of friendship between the two leaders deterred either man from "plain talk" on the merits of their respective political systems. Reagan, as well as many of the American public figures Gorbachev met with during the visit, openly challenged the Soviet leader on aspects of Kremlin policy about which the Russians were very sensitive: human rights, particularly the right of emigration; and the Soviet occupation of Afghanistan.

Gorbachev flared at the persistence of the criticism and staunchly asserted the superiority of the Soviet definition of human rights. He said it included a right of economic security ignored by the capitalist West and a right of immigration that the United States itself denied by not opening its borders to all comers.

But those frank exchanges evidently did not interfere with solid progress toward a future treaty intended to reduce by half the number of long-range nuclear bombers and missiles. Officials said the new pact might be signed at a follow-up Moscow summit in the spring of 1988, but that the meeting would occur whether or not a treaty was signed. Both sides also proved sufficiently flexible to defer a showdown on the issue that had blocked agreements when the two leaders had met in Iceland in 1986: the future of the strategic defense initiative (SDI), Reagan's effort to develop a nationwide space-based antiballistic missile system.

Differences from Previous Summits

Reagan and Gorbachev had met for the first time in Geneva in 1985, when they agreed to make a "fresh start" by renewing arms control talks that had been broken off two years previously. Their second meeting, a hastily arranged conference in Reykjavik, Iceland, in October 1986, ended in an impasse after Gorbachev rejected a proposal to cut nuclear arsenals in half, citing Reagan's insistence on going ahead with SDI. In contrast to the rather chilly and formal atmosphere of the first two summits, the Washington meeting was cordial. The two leaders appeared relaxed and confident and seemed to enjoy each other's company. They were enthusiastic about the treaty and eager to conclude it. (Historic Documents of 1985, p. 749; Historic Documents of 1986, p. 875)

Both men staked a great deal on a successful summit. Reagan hoped the meeting would increase his domestic popularity, which had been adversely affected by the Iran-contra scandal and the nation's economic problems. A foreign policy victory could also strengthen Gorbachev's hand at home, as he attempted to restructure Soviet society and upgrade living standards. Since coming to power in 1985, the general secretary had portrayed himself as being in the vanguard of those seeking arms control agreements. He had been particularly well received in Western Europe, where public opinion polls gave him favorable ratings.

Originally, there had been some thought that Gorbachev might use the occasion to see more of the United States, but security considerations prevented his doing so. Indeed, security was so tight that the leader saw little of Washington, D.C. Protesters demonstrated against Gorbachev's visit and Soviet policies for a variety of reasons. The day before his arrival, an estimated 200,000 people rallied on the Mall on behalf of Soviet Jews.

Despite protests outside the White House gates, the cordial tenor of the summit was set with a colorful ceremony on the South Lawn of the White House the morning of December 8. The welcome included a twenty-one-gun salute to the Soviet leader, who arrived with his wife Raisa in a caravan of Russian-made limousines sporting Soviet and American flags. "Our peoples for too long have been both the masters and the captives of a deadly arms race," Reagan said. "This situation is not preordained and not part of some inevitable course of history." Gorbachev responded, "History has charged the governments of our countries and the two of us ... with a solemn duty to justify the hopes of Americans and Soviet people and of people the world over to undo the logic of the arms race by working together in good faith."

Reagan-Gorbachev Discussions

During the first day, the two leaders spent almost three hours in official discussions, including one-on-one morning talks in the Oval Office and an afternoon plenary session in the Cabinet room attended by senior advisers. Gorbachev later met with a group of prominent private U.S. citizens at the Soviet Embassy. A state dinner at the White House followed. In toasts, each leader expressed the hope that the INF treaty would pave the way for future cooperation and agreements.

On December 9 Gorbachev met for ninety minutes with the House and Senate leadership. (Though the possibility that Gorbachev might address a joint session of Congress had been discussed, a number of conservative members had strenuously objected and threatened to boycott such a session.) Afterwards House Majority Whip Tony Coelho, D-Calif., remarked on Gorbachev's "tremendous confidence . . . his total command of the situation." In another meeting with a group of American publishers and editors, Gorbachev defended the Soviet record on human rights and emigration. He said that, in the course of his talks with Reagan the previous day, "I told the president that you are not the prosecutor and I am not the accused. We have to strike a balance here; otherwise you will get nothing out of us."

In a private session with Reagan—with only their interpreters present—Gorbachev said that the Soviet Union was willing to withdraw its 115,000-man army from Afghanistan but refused to state when the withdrawal would begin.

With the euphoria of the treaty signing behind them, the leaders and their advisers turned to the difficult problems that lay ahead in the two nations' relations. "This was a day of heavy lifting," said White House spokesman Marlin Fitzwater. "It's in these middle chapters of the summit that the issues are joined and the plot is revealed." In an exchange of toasts December 9 at the Soviet Embassy, Reagan noted, "We've come to this summit without illusions, with no attempts to gloss over the deep differences that divide us."

The leaders began their final session on the morning of December 10. Although they concluded no major new agreements on human rights or regional issues, officials on both sides termed the talks a success. According to one Soviet official, "With the improvement in atmosphere represented at the talks, our work here is mostly completed. We have a lot of work to do, but we are prepared to move forward." Secretary of State George P. Shultz and Soviet foreign minister Eduard Shevardnadze signed three accords: one that established the first nonstop, round-trip flights between Moscow and New York, another that allowed each country to monitor some of the other's nuclear tests, and a cooperative arrangement on environmental research in the world's oceans.

Shortly before his departure, Gorbachev held a nationally televised news conference in which he said that the meeting marked "a new phase of Soviet-American bilateral relations" that saw the two powers "emerging from a long drawn-out confrontation." President Reagan went on national television that evening to recap the week's events, noting that while there was "movement—indeed dramatic movement—in the arms reduction area, much remains to be done in that area as well as in . . . other critical areas."

Following are excerpts from the text of the joint U.S.-Soviet communiqué released December 10, 1987; from the statements of President Ronald Reagan and General Secretary Mikhail S. Gorbachev during the departure ceremony the same day; and from President Reagan's televised address to the nation that evening:

JOINT COMMUNIQUE

Ronald W. Reagan, President of the United States of America, and Mikhail S. Gorbachev, General Secretary of the Central Committee of the Communist Party of the Soviet Union [CPSU], met in Washington on December 7-10, 1987. . . .

During the course of the official visit, which had been agreed during the two leaders' November 1985 meeting in Geneva, the President and the General Secretary held comprehensive and detailed discussions on the full range of issues between the two countries, including arms reductions, human rights and humanitarian issues, settlement of regional conflicts, and bilateral relations. The talks were candid and constructive, reflecting both the continuing differences between the two sides, and their understanding that these differences are not insurmountable. . . .

The President and the General Secretary affirmed the fundamental importance of their meetings in Geneva and Reykjavik, which laid the basis for concrete steps in a process intended to improve strategic stability and reduce the risk of conflict. They will continue to be guided by their solemn conviction that a nuclear war cannot be won and must never be fought. They are determined to prevent any war between the United States and the Soviet Union, whether nuclear or conventional. They will not seek to achieve military superiority.

The two leaders recognized the special responsibility of the United States and the Soviet Union to search for realistic ways to prevent confrontation and to promote a more sustainable and stable relationship between their countries. To this end, they agreed to intensify dialogue and to encourage emerging trends toward constructive cooperation in all areas of their relations. They are convinced that in so doing they will also contribute, with other nations, to the building of a safer world as humanity enters the third millennium.

I. Arms Control

The INF Treaty

The two leaders signed the Treaty between the United States of America and the Union of Soviet Socialist Republics on the Elimination of Their Intermediate-Range and Shorter-Range Missiles. This treaty is historic both for its objective—the complete elimination of an entire class of U.S. and Soviet nuclear arms—and for the innovative character and scope of its verification provisions. This mutual accomplishment makes a vital contribution to greater stability.

Nuclear and Space Talks

The President and the General Secretary discussed the negotiations on reductions in strategic offensive arms. They noted the considerable progress which has been made toward conclusion of a treaty implementing the principle of 50-percent reductions. They agreed to instruct their negotiators in Geneva to work toward the completion of the Treaty on the Reduction and Limitation of Strategic Offensive Arms and all integral documents at the earliest possible date, preferably in time for signature of the treaty during the next meeting of leaders of state in the first half of 1988. Recognizing that areas of agreement and disagreement are recorded in detail in the Joint Draft Treaty Text, they agreed to instruct their negotiators to accelerate resolution of issues within the Joint Draft Treaty Text, including early agreement on provisions for effective verification.

In so doing, the negotiators should build upon the agreements on 50-percent reductions achieved at Reykjavik as subsequently developed and now reflected in the agreed portions of the Joint Draft START [Strategic Arms Reduction Talks] Treaty Text being developed in Geneva, including agreement on ceilings of no more than 1600 strategic offensive delivery systems, 6000 warheads, 1540 warheads on 154 heavy missiles; the agreed rule of account for heavy bombers and their nuclear armament; and an agreement on ceilings of no more than 1600 strategic offensive delivery systems, 6000 warheads, 1540 warheads on 154 heavy missiles; the agreed SLBMs [submarine-launched ballistic missiles] will be reduced to a level approximately 50 percent below the existing level, and this level will not be exceeded by either side. Such an agreement will be recorded in a mutually satisfactory manner.

As priority tasks, they should focus on the following issues:

(a) The additional steps necessary to ensure that the reductions enhance strategic stability. This will include a ceiling of 4900 on the aggregate number of ICBM plus SLBM warheads within the 6000 total.

(b) The counting rules governing the number of long-range, nuclear-armed air-launched cruise missiles (ALCMs) to be attributed to each type of heavy bomber. The Delegations shall define concrete rules in this area.

(c) The counting rules with respect to existing ballistic missiles. The sides proceed from the assumption that existing types of ballistic missiles are deployed with the following numbers of warheads. In the United States: PEACEKEEPER (MX): 10, MINUTEMAN III: 3, MINUTEMAN II: 1,TRIDENT I: 8, TRIDENT II: 8, POSEIDON: 10. In the Soviet Union: SS-17: 4, SS-19: 6, SS-18: 10, SS-24: 10, SS-25: 1, SS-11: 1, SS-13: 1, SS-N-6: 1, SS-N-8: 1, SS-N-17: 1, SS-N-18: 7, SS-N-20: 10 and SS-N-23: 4. Procedures will be developed that enable verification of the number of warheads on deployed ballistic missiles of each specific type. In the event either side changes the number of warheads declared for a type of deployed ballistic missile, the sides shall notify each other in advance. There shall also be agreement on how to account for warheads on future types of ballistic missiles covered by the Treaty on the Reduction and Limitation of Strategic Offensive Arms.

(d) The sides shall find a mutually acceptable solution to the question of limiting the deployment of long-range, nuclear-armed SLCMs [submarine-launched cruise missiles]. Such limitations will not involve counting long-range, nuclear-armed SLCMs within the 6000 warhead and 1600 strategic offensive delivery systems limits. The sides committed themselves to establish ceilings on such missiles, and to seek mutually acceptable and effective methods of verification of such limitations, which could include the employment of National Technical Means, cooperative measures and on-site inspection.

(e) Building upon the provisions of the Treaty on the Elimination of Their Intermediate-Range and Shorter-Range Missiles, the measures by which the provisions of the Treaty on the Reduction and Limitation of Strategic Offensive Arms can be verified will, at a minimum, include:

1. Data exchanges, to include declarations by each side of the number and location of weapon systems limited by the Treaty and of facilities at which such systems are located and appropriate notifications. These facilities will include locations and facilities for production and final assembly, storage, testing, and deployment of systems covered by this Treaty. Such declarations will be exchanged between the sides before the Treaty is signed and updated periodically after entry into force.

2. Baseline inspection to verify the accuracy of these declarations promptly after entry into force of the Treaty.

3. On-site observation of the elimination of strategic systems necessary to achieve the agreed limits.

4. Continuous on-site monitoring of the perimeter and portals of critical production and support facilities to confirm the output of these facilities.

5. Short-notice on-site inspection of:

(i) declared locations during the process of reducing to agreed limits;

(ii) locations where systems covered by this Treaty remain after achieving the agreed limits; and

(iii) locations where such systems have been located (formerly declared facilities).

6. The right to implement, in accordance with agreed-upon procedures, short-notice inspections at locations where either side considers covert deployment, production, storage or repair of strategic offensive arms could be occurring.

7. Provisions prohibiting the use of concealment or other activities which impede verification by national technical means. Such provisions would include a ban on telemetry encryption and would allow for full access to all telemetric information broadcast during missile flight.

8. Measures designed to enhance observation of activities related to

> reduction and limitation of strategic offensive arms by National Technical Means. These would include open displays of treaty-limited items at missile bases, bomber bases, and submarine ports at locations and times chosen by the inspecting party.

Taking into account the preparation of the Treaty on Strategic Offensive Arms, the leaders of the two countries also instructed their delegations in Geneva to work out an agreement that would commit the sides to observe the ABM [Anti-Ballistic Missile] Treaty, as signed in 1972, while conducting their research, development, and testing as required, which are permitted by the ABM Treaty, and not to withdraw from the ABM Treaty, for a specified period of time. Intensive discussions of strategic stability shall begin not later than three years before the end of the specified period, after which, in the event the sides have not agreed otherwise, each side will be free to decide its course of action. Such an agreement must have the same legal status as the Treaty on Strategic Offensive Arms, the ABM Treaty, and other similar, legally binding agreements. . . . [T]hey direct their delegations to address these issues on a priority basis.

The sides shall discuss ways to ensure predictability in the development of the U.S.-Soviet strategic relationship under conditions of strategic stability, to reduce the risk of nuclear war.

Other Arms Control Issues

The President and the General Secretary reviewed a broad range of other issues concerning arms limitation and reduction. The sides emphasized the importance of productive negotiations on security matters and advancing in the main areas of arms limitation and reduction through equitable, verifiable agreements that enhance security and stability.

Nuclear Testing

The two leaders welcomed the opening on November 9, 1987, of full-scale, step-by-step negotiations, in accordance with the joint statement adopted in Washington on September 17, 1987, by the Secretary of State of the United States and the Minister of Foreign Affairs of the USSR:

> The U.S. and Soviet sides have agreed to begin before December 1, 1987, full-scale stage-by-stage negotiations which will be conducted in a single forum. In these negotiations the sides as the first step will agree upon effective verification measures which will make it possible to ratify the U.S.-USSR Threshold Test Ban Treaty of 1974 and Peaceful Nuclear Explosions Treaty of 1976, and proceed to negotiating further intermediate limitations on nuclear testing leading to the ultimate objective of the complete cessation of nuclear testing as part of an effective disarmament process. This process, among other things, would pursue, as the first priority, the goal of the reduction of nuclear weapons and, ultimately, their elimination. For the purpose of the elaboration of improved verification measures for the U.S.-USSR Treaties of 1974 and 1976 the sides intend to design and conduct joint verification experiments at each other's test sites. These verification measures will, to the extent appropriate, be used in further nuclear test limitation agreements which may subsequently be reached.

The leaders also welcomed the prompt agreement by the sides to exchange experts' visits to each other's nuclear testing sites in January 1988 and to design and subsequently to conduct a Joint Verification Experiment at each other's test site. The terms of reference for the Experiment are set forth in the statement issued on December 9, 1987, by the Foreign Ministers of the United States and the Soviet Union. The leaders noted the value of these agreements for developing more effective measures to verify compliance with the provisions of the 1974 Threshold Test Ban Treaty and the 1976 Peaceful Nuclear Explosions Treaty.

Nuclear Non-Proliferation

The President and the General Secretary reaffirmed the continued commitment of the United States and the Soviet Union to the non-proliferation of nuclear weapons, and in particular to strengthening the Treaty on the Non-Proliferation of Nuclear Weapons. The two leaders expressed satisfaction at the adherence since their last meeting of additional parties to the Treaty, and confirmed their intent to make, together with other states, additional efforts to achieve universal adherence to the Treaty.

The President and the General Secretary expressed support for international cooperation in nuclear safety and for efforts to promote the peaceful uses of nuclear energy, under further strengthened IAEA [International Atomic Energy Agency] safeguards and appropriate export controls for nuclear materials, equipment and technology. The leaders agreed that bilateral consultations on non-proliferation were constructive and useful, and should continue.

Nuclear Risk Reduction Centers

The leaders welcomed the signing on September 15, 1987, in Washington of the agreement to establish Nuclear Risk Reduction Centers in their capitals. The agreement will be implemented promptly.

Chemical Weapons

The leaders expressed their commitment to negotiation of a verifiable, comprehensive and effective international convention on the prohibition and destruction of chemical weapons. They welcomed progress to date and reaffirmed the need for intensified negotiations toward conclusion of a truly global and verifiable convention encompassing all chemical weapons-capable states. The United States and Soviet Union are in favor of greater openness and intensified confidence-building with respect to chemical weapons both on a bilateral and a multilateral basis. They agreed to continue periodic discussions by experts on the growing problem of chemical weapons proliferation and use.

Conventional Forces

The President and the General Secretary discussed the importance of the task of reducing the level of military confrontation in Europe in the area of armed forces and conventional armaments. The two leaders spoke in favor of early completion of the work in Vienna . . . on this issue, so that substantive negotiations may be started at the earliest time with a view to elaborating concrete measures. They also noted that the implementation of the provisions of the Stockholm Conference on Confidence- and Security-Building Measures and Disarmament in Europe is an important factor in strengthening mutual understanding and enhancing stability, and spoke in favor of continuing and consolidating this process. The President and the General Secretary agreed to instruct their appropriate representatives to intensify efforts to achieve solutions to outstanding issues.

They also discussed the Vienna (Mutual and Balanced Force Reduction) negotiations.

Follow-Up Meeting of the Conference on Security and Cooperation in Europe

They expressed their determination, together with the other 33 participants in the Conference on Security and Cooperation in Europe, to bring the Vienna CSCE Follow-Up Conference to a successful conclusion, based on balanced progress in all principal areas of the Helsinki Final Act and Madrid Concluding Document.

II. Human Rights and Humanitarian Concerns

The leaders held a thorough and candid discussion of human rights and humanitarian questions and their place in the U.S.-Soviet dialogue.

III. Regional Issues

The President and the General Secretary engaged in a wide-ranging, frank and businesslike discussion of regional questions, including Afghanistan, the Iran-Iraq War, the Middle East, Cambodia, southern Africa, Central America and other issues. They acknowledged serious differences but agreed on the importance of their regular exchange of views. The two leaders noted the increasing importance of settling regional conflicts to reduce international tensions and to improve East-West relations. They agreed that the goal of the dialogue between the United States and the Soviet Union on these issues should be to help the parties to regional conflicts find peaceful solutions that advance their independence, freedom and security. Both leaders emphasized the importance of enhancing the capacity of the United Nations and other international institutions to contribute to the resolution of regional conflicts.

IV. Bilateral Affairs

The President and the General Secretary reviewed in detail the state of U.S.-Soviet bilateral relations. They recognized the utility of further expanding and strengthening bilateral contacts, exchanges and coöperation.

Bilateral Negotiations

Having reviewed the state of ongoing U.S.-Soviet negotiations on a number of specific bilateral issues, the two leaders called for intensified efforts by their representatives, aimed at reaching mutually advantageous agreements on: commercial maritime issues; fishing; marine search and rescue; radio navigational systems; the U.S.-USSR maritime boundary; and cooperation in the field of transportation and other areas.

They noted with satisfaction agreement on the expansion, within the framework of the U.S.-Soviet Air Transport Agreement, of direct air passenger service, including joint operation of the New York-Moscow route by Pan American Airways and Aeroflot, and on the renewal of the U.S.-Soviet World Ocean Agreement.

People-to-People Contacts and Exchanges

The two leaders took note of progress in implementing the U.S.-Soviet General Exchanges Agreement in the areas of education, science, culture and sports, signed at their November 1985 Geneva meeting, and agreed to continue efforts to eliminate obstacles to further progress in these areas. They expressed satisfaction with plans to celebrate jointly the 30th anniversary of the first Exchanges Agreement in January 1988.

The two leaders reaffirmed the importance of contacts and exchanges in broadening understanding between their peoples. They noted with particular satisfaction the progress made in the development of people-to-people contacts under the initiative they launched at their 1985 meeting in Geneva—a process which has involved tens of thousands of U.S. and Soviet citizens over the past two years. The leaders reaffirmed their strong commitment further to expand such contacts, including among the young.

Global Climate and Environmental Change Initiative

With reference to their November 1985 agreement in Geneva to cooperate in the preservation of the environment, the two leaders approved a bilateral initiative to pursue joint studies in global climate and environmental change through cooperation in areas of mutual concern, such as protection and conservation of stratospheric ozone, and through increased data exchanges pursuant to the U.S.-Soviet Environmental Protection Agreement and the Agreement Between the United States of America and the Union of Soviet Socialist Republics Concerning Cooperation in the Exploration and Use of Outer Space for Peaceful Purposes. In this context, there will be a detailed study on the climate of the future. The two sides will continue to promote broad international and bilateral cooperation in the increasingly important area of global climate and environmental change.

Cooperative Activities

The President and the General Secretary supported further cooperation among scientists of the United States, the Soviet Union and other countries in utilizing controlled thermonuclear fusion for peaceful purposes. They affirmed the intention of the U.S. and the USSR to cooperate with the European Atomic Energy Community (EURATOM) and Japan, under the auspices of the International Atomic Energy Agency, in the quadripartite conceptual design of a fusion test reactor.

The two leaders noted with satisfaction progress under the bilateral Agreement on Peaceful Uses of Atomic Energy towards establishing a permanent working group in the field of nuclear reactor safety, and expressed their readiness to develop further cooperation in this area.

The President and the General Secretary agreed to develop bilateral cooperation in combatting international narcotics trafficking. They agreed that appropriate initial consultations would be held for these purposes in early 1988.

They also agreed to build on recent contacts to develop more effective cooperation in ensuring the security of air and maritime transportation.

The two leaders exchanged views on means of encouraging expanded contacts and cooperation on issues relating to the Arctic. They expressed support for the development of bilateral and regional cooperation among the Arctic countries on these matters, including coordination of scientific research and protection of the region's environment.

The two leaders welcomed the conclusion of negotiations to institutionalize the COSPAS/SARSAT space-based global search and rescue system, operated jointly by the United States, the Soviet Union, France and Canada.

Trade

The two sides stated their strong support for the expansion of mutually beneficial trade and economic relations. They instructed their trade ministers to convene the U.S.-USSR Joint Commercial Commission in order to develop concrete proposals to achieve that objective, including within the framework of the Long-Term Agreement between the United States of America and the Union of Soviet Socialist Republics to Facilitate Economic, Industrial, and Technical Cooperation. They agreed that commercially viable joint ventures complying with the laws and regulations of both countries could play a role in the further development of commercial relations.

Diplomatic Missions

Both sides agreed on the importance of adequate, secure facilities for their respective diplomatic and consular establishments, and emphasized the need to approach problems relating to the functioning of Embassies and Consulates General constructively and on the basis of reciprocity.

V. Further Meetings

The President and the General Secretary agreed that official contacts at all levels should be further expanded and intensified, with the goal of achieving practical and concrete results in all areas of the U.S.-Soviet relationship.

General Secretary Gorbachev renewed the invitation he extended during the Geneva summit for President Reagan to visit the Soviet Union. The President accepted with pleasure. The visit will take place in the first half of 1988.

DEPARTURE CEREMONY REMARKS

The President: Mr. General Secretary, these last few days have been exciting, indeed, for both of us and for our fellow countrymen who followed the course of our discussions. I'm pleased to report that upon the completion of our business that this summit has been a clear success. Like the star on the top of the National Christmas Tree, which was lit the evening you arrived, Mr. General Secretary, this summit has lit the sky with hope for all people of good will. And as we leave, it is up to both sides to ensure that the luster does not wear off and to follow through on our commitments as we move forward to the next steps in improving the relations between our countries and peoples.

I believe both the General Secretary and I can walk away from our meetings with a sense of accomplishment. We have proven that adversaries, even with the most basic philosophical differences, can talk candidly and respectfully with one another and, with perseverance, find common ground. We did not hide from the weighty differences that separate us; many of them, of course, remain. One of my predecessors, President Franklin Roosevelt, once said: "History cannot be rewritten by wishful thinking." Our discussions, in that spirit, were straightforward and designed to open a thoughtful communication between our governments on the critical issues that confront us.

Our exchange on the subject of human rights underscored the priority we in the Western democracies place on respect for fundamental freedoms. I'm pleased that during this summit we addressed this area of heartfelt importance and have ensured a continuing dialog on human rights at the highest levels of our governments.

Our discussions on regional conflicts were no less to the point. These conflicts continue to take a heavy toll in lives and impose a heavy burden on East-West relations. The General Secretary and I expressed different points of view—we did so bluntly—and for that reason alone, our talks have been useful in this area. Moreover, we agree that it is necessary to search for real political solutions to these conflicts. But so far, we cannot be satisfied with what has been achieved. We must now press ahead in the search for political solutions that advance the cause of peace and freedom for the people suffering in these wars. The door has been opened and it will stay open to serious discussion of ending these regional conflicts.

And as far as open doors, Mr. Gorbachev and I both agree on the desirability of freer and more extensive personal contact and the breaking down of artificial barriers between the peoples of the Soviet Union and the United States. As I said in my welcoming remarks, the fact that our governments have disagreements should not prevent our peoples from being friends.

Of course, the greatest accomplishment of these 3 days was the signing of a treaty to eliminate a whole class of U.S. and Soviet nuclear weapons. . . .

The INF [intermediate-range nuclear-force missiles] treaty, as proud of it as we are, should be viewed as a beginning, not an end. Further arms reduction is now possible. I am pleased some progress has been made toward a strategic arms reduction treaty over the last 3 days. . . .

The General Secretary: Esteemed Mr. President, esteemed Mrs. Reagan, ladies and gentlemen, in these last hours before our departure for home, we note with satisfaction that the visit to Washington has, on the whole, justified our hopes. We have had 3 days of hard work, of businesslike and frank discussions on the pivotal problems of Soviet-American relations and on important aspects of the current world situation.

A good deal has been accomplished. I would like to emphasize in particular an unprecedented step in the history of the nuclear age: the signing of the treaty under which the two militarily and strategically greatest powers have assumed an obligation to actually destroy a portion of their nuclear weapons, thus, we hope, setting in motion the process of nuclear disarmament.

In our talks with President Ronald Reagan, some headway has been made on the central issue of that process—achieving substantial reductions of strategic offensive arms, which are the most potent weapons in the world—although we still have a lot of work to do. We have had a useful exchange of views, which has clarified each other's positions concerning regional conflicts, the development of our bilateral ties, and human rights. On some of these aspects, it seems likely that we can soon identify specific solutions satisfactory both to us and to other countries. A useful result of the Washington talks is that we have been able to formulate a kind of agenda for joint efforts in the future. This puts the dialog between our two countries on a more predictable footing and is undoubtedly constructive.

While this visit has centered on our talks with the President of the United States, I have no intention of minimizing the importance of meetings with Members of Congress, with other political leaders, public figures, members of the business and academic communities, cultural figures, and media executives. Such contacts enable us to gain a better and more profound knowledge of each other, provide a wealth of opportunities for checking one's views, assessments, and even established stereotypes.

All this is important, both for policymaking and for bringing peoples and countries closer together. These meetings have confirmed the impression that there is a growing desire in American society for improved Soviet-American relations....

PRESIDENT REAGAN'S ADDRESS

Good evening. As I am speaking to you now, General Secretary [Mikhail S.] Gorbachev is leaving on his return trip to the Soviet Union. His departure marks the end of 3 historic days here in Washington in which Mr. Gorbachev and I continued to build a foundation for better relations between our governments and our peoples. During these 3 days we took a step—only a first step, but still a critical one—toward building a more durable peace; indeed, a step that may be the most important taken since World War II to slow down the arms buildup.

I'm referring to the treaty that we signed Tuesday afternoon in the East Room of the White House. I believe this treaty represents a landmark in postwar history, because it is not just an arms control but an arms reduction agreement. Unlike treaties of the past, this agreement does not simply establish ceilings for new weapons: It actually reduces the number of such weapons. In fact, it altogether abolishes an entire class of U.S. and Soviet nuclear missiles.

The verification measures in this treaty are also something new with far-reaching implications. On-site inspections and short-notice inspections will be permitted within the Soviet Union. Again, this is a first-time event, a breakthrough, and that's why I believe this treaty will not only lessen the threat of war, it can also speed along a process that may someday remove that threat entirely.

Indeed, this treaty, and all that we've achieved during this summit, signals a broader understanding between the United States and the Soviet Union. It is an understanding that will help keep the peace as we work towards the ultimate goal of our foreign policy: a world where the people of every land can decide for themselves their form of government and way of life.

Yet as important as the INF [intermediate-range nuclear force missiles] treaty is, there is a further and even more crucial point about the last 3 days and the entire summit process: Soviet-American relations are no longer focused only on arms control issues. They now cover a far broader agenda, one that has, at its root, realism and candor.

Let me explain this with a saying I've often repeated: Nations do not distrust each other because they're armed; they are armed because they distrust each other. And just as real peace means the presence of freedom and justice as well as the absence of war, so, too, summits must be discussions not just about arms but about the fundamental differences that cause nations to be armed.

Dealing then with the deeper sources of conflict between nations and systems of government is a practical and moral imperative. And that's why it was vital to establish a broader summit agenda, one that dealt not only with arms reductions but also people-to-people contacts between our nations and, most important, the issues of human rights and regional conflicts.

This is the summit agenda we've adopted. By doing so, we've dealt not just with arms control issues but also with fundamental problems such as Soviet expansionism, human rights violations, as well as our own moral opposition to the ideology that justifies such practices. In this way, we have put Soviet-American relations on a far more candid and far more realistic footing.

It also means that, while there's movement—indeed, dramatic movement—in the arms reduction area, much remains to be done in that area as well as in these other critical areas that I've mentioned, especially—and this goes without saying—in advancing our goal of a world open to the expansion of human freedom and the growth of democratic government.

So, much work lies ahead. Let me explain: On the matter of regional conflicts, I spoke candidly with Mr. Gorbachev on the issues of Afghanistan, Iran-Iraq, Cambodia, Angola, and Nicaragua. I continue to have high hopes—and he assured me that he did too—that we can have real cooperation in resolving regional conflicts on terms that promote peace and freedom. This is essential to a lasting improvement in our relations.

So, too, on human rights, there was some very limited movement: resolution of a number of individual cases in which prisoners will be released or exit visas granted. There were assurances of future, more substantial movement, which we hope to see become a reality.

And finally, with regard to the last item on our agenda—scientific, educational, cultural, and economic exchanges—we agreed to expand cooperation in ways that will break down some of the artificial barriers between our nations. For example, agreement was reached to expand and improve civil air service between our two countries.

But let me point out here that, while much work is ahead of us, the progress we've made, especially in arms reduction, does reflect a better understanding between ourselves and the Soviets. It also reflects something deeper. You see, since my first meeting with General Secretary Gorbachev in 1985, I have always regarded you, the American people, as full participants in our discussions. Though it may surprise Mr. Gorbachev to discover that all this time there has been a third party in the room with us, I do firmly believe the principal credit for the patience and persistence that brought success this year belongs to you, the American people.

Your support over these last 7 years has laid the basis for these negotiations. . . .

Now, in addition to these candid exchanges on our four-part agenda, Mr. Gorbachev and I did do some important planning for a Moscow summit next year. We agreed that we must redouble our efforts to reach agreements on reducing the levels of U.S. and Soviet long-range, or strategic, nuclear arms, as I have proposed in the START [strategic arms reduction talks] negotiations. He and I made real progress toward our goal first agreed to at Geneva: to achieve deep, 50-percent cuts in our arsenals of those powerful weapons. We agreed that we should build on our efforts to achieve agreement on a START treaty at the earliest possible date, and we've instructed our delegations in Geneva accordingly.

Now, I believe deep reduction in these offensive weapons, along with the development of SDI [strategic defense initiative], would do much to make the world safer. For that reason, I made it clear that our SDI program will continue and that when we have a defense ready to deploy we will do so.

About the future, Mr. Gorbachev and I also agreed that as nuclear weapons are reduced it becomes all the more important to redress the disparities in conventional and chemical weapons, where the Soviets now enjoy significant advantages over the United States and our allies.

I think then from all of this you can see not only the direction of Soviet-American relations but the larger framework of American foreign policy. As I told the British Parliament in 1982, we seek to rid the world of the two great nightmares of the postwar era: the threat of nuclear war and the threat of totalitarianism.

And that's why, by pursuing SDI, which is a defense against offensive missiles, and by going for arms reduction rather than just arms control, we're moving away from the so-called policy of mutual assured destruction, by which nations hold each other hostage to nuclear terror and destruction. So, too, we are saying that the postwar policy of containment is no longer enough, that the goal of American foreign policy is both world peace and world freedom, that as a people we hope and will work for a day when all of God's children will enjoy the human dignity that their creator intended. I believe we gained some ground with regard to that cause in these last few days. . . .

ARIAS NOBEL PEACE PRIZE SPEECH

December 10, 1987

Accepting the Nobel Peace Prize December 10 in Oslo, Norway, Costa Rican president Oscar Arias Sánchez urged the international community to let Central America alone. "Leave the interpretation and implementation of our peace plan to us," Arias entreated. "Support the efforts for peace instead of the forces of war in our region. Send our people plowshares instead of swords."

The award recognized Arias's contribution to a peace pact signed the previous August by the presidents of five Central American nations—Costa Rica, Nicaragua, Honduras, El Salvador, and Guatemala. The document, known as the Guatemala Accord, outlined steps for bringing an end to civil wars in three of the countries. (Central American peace agreement, p. 637)

Under the terms of the accord, the Sandinistas, the Marxist leaders of Nicaragua, pledged to try to come to terms with the contras, who had been carrying on a guerrilla war there since the early 1980s. The contras were receiving substantial aid from the United States. The presidents of El Salvador and Guatemala, countries with ties to the United States, agreed to start talks with leftist insurgents fighting their regimes.

The peace pact committed the presidents to complete a series of steps based on a definite timetable. Besides opening talks with political opponents and insurgents, the government of each country was to grant an amnesty and initiate democratic reforms, loosening constraints on the press and permitting more freedom for the political opposition. In addition, the presidents promised to halt military aid to rebels fighting in neighboring nations and to stop providing sanctuaries for insurgents.

Tentative Moves Toward Peace

When Arias spoke in Oslo, his peace plan had made little real headway. Guerrilla armies were still fighting in all three war-torn countries, although a November 7 cease-fire deadline imposed by the pact had passed.

In Nicaragua, scene of the fiercest fighting, negotiations between rebels and the Sandinistas had scarcely begun. While the Nicaraguan regime had made some moves toward compliance with the agreement, its leaders had so far refused to lift a five-year-old state of emergency curtailing civil rights or to talk face-to-face with contra political leaders. The Sandinistas said that further reform depended on an end to U.S. aid to the Nicaraguan rebels, who were unlikely to survive as a fighting force without it. Honduras had not moved to expel the contras from its southern border, nor had Nicaragua acted to cut off aid to leftist guerrillas in El Salvador and Guatemala.

Repercussions in Washington

In early November Nicaraguan president Daniel Ortega Saavedra had agreed to negotiate indirectly with contra political leaders and had asked outspoken Cardinal Obando y Bravo to serve as intermediary. The negotiations quickly became entangled in a U.S. domestic political dispute, however. Liberal Democrats in Congress saw U.S. aid to the contras as jeopardizing the peace process, while administration officials saw Nicaragua's tentative reforms as gestures designed more to placate Congress than to bring democracy to Nicaragua. President Ronald Reagan repeatedly declared that U.S. support of the contras had brought Nicaragua to the peace table. President Ortega exacerbated these differences within the U.S. government during a November trip to Washington, where he spoke to the Organization of American States (OAS) while Congress was considering an administration request for contra aid.

Ortega met with U.S. House of Representatives Speaker Jim Wright, D-Texas, who also took part in meetings with Cardinal Obando and with representatives of the contras. The Sandinistas had insisted on direct talks with the U.S. government, while the Reagan administration wanted the contra leaders to meet with the Sandinistas on an equal footing, thereby increasing the rebel group's political stature. The Ortega-Wright meetings drew immediate fire from White House spokesmen, who charged that the Speaker was meddling in foreign policy and undercutting the official U.S. position.

Ortega's plan called for insurgent troops to surrender their weapons during a month-long cease-fire to begin December 5. U.S. aid to the contras was to stop immediately. The contras' counterproposal would have allowed them to keep their weapons and control of some Nicaraguan territory. Cardinal Obando reported December 5 that talks were deadlocked and called for direct negotiations between the warring parties. Although face-to-face talks were scheduled for mid-December, the Nicaraguan government soon backed out of the arrangement. In the meantime, talks with leftist guerrilla forces in Guatemala and El Salvador had collapsed.

Aid to the Contras

While the peace talks were foundering, the contra aid question came to a head in Congress. The Democratic-controlled Senate had approved a $16 million aid package, while in the House liberal Democrats had outmaneuvered all attempts to push through aid requests. As the date for adjournment drew closer, however, the administration produced a high-ranking Sandinista defector, whose statements confirmed the administration's contention that the Sandinistas were not to be trusted. The defector, a former aide to Nicaragua's defense minister, said that while the Sandinistas pretended to comply with the peace accord, they actually planned a massive military buildup by the early 1990s that would put half a million men under arms and introduce Soviet-made attack helicopters and warplanes into the region. Nicaraguan defense minister Humberto Ortega Saavedra confirmed much of the defector's story.

With the revelations, the mood in Congress shifted. No longer certain that they had the votes to block contra aid, House leaders opted to compromise with Senate conferees. The compromise, part of a governmentwide continuing resolution, provided $14 million in additional aid for the contras to last through February 1988. House conferees managed to write conditions for contra aid into the law, however, stipulating that future aid requests must be "compatible" with the Central American peace agreement. A showdown vote on the aid issue was scheduled for February, after the Latin American presidents had met to determine whether the five nations were living up to the terms of the peace pact.

Arias's Message

In his Nobel prize address, President Arias straddled the issues that separated Nicaragua from its U.S.-backed opponents. He called for "peace and democracy, together," on the one hand, and for an end to support for the "forces of war," on the other. Arias had been an outspoken critic of U.S. aid to the contras, but he also had urged Ortega to talk face-to-face with contra leaders. The Costa Rican president had threatened to use his personal prestige to convince the OAS to impose sanctions against Nicaragua if the Sandinistas flouted the accord.

Arias had run for the Costa Rican presidency in 1986 on a peace platform. His nation was the only Latin American country with no standing army.

Following is the text of Oscar Arias Sánchez's speech accepting the 1987 Nobel Peace Prize on December 10, 1987:

When you decided to honor me with this prize, you decided to honor a country of peace, you decided to honor Costa Rica. When in this year, 1987, you carried out the will of Alfred E. Nobel to encourage peace efforts in the world, you decided to encourage the efforts to secure peace in Central America. I am very grateful for the recognition of our search for peace. We are all grateful in our Central America.

Nobody knows better than the honorable members of this committee that this prize is a sign to let the world know that you want to foster the Central American peace initiative. With your decision you are enhancing the possibilities of success.

You are declaring how well you know the search for peace can never end, and how it is a permanent cause, always in need of true support from real friends, from people with courage to promote change in favor of peace, even against all odds.

Peace is not a matter of prizes or trophies. It is not the product of a victory or command. It has no finishing line, no final deadline, no fixed definition of achievement.

Peace is a never-ending process, the work of many decisions by many people in many countries. It is an attitude, a way of life, a way of solving problems and resolving conflicts. It cannot be forced on the smallest nation or enforced by the largest. It cannot ignore our differences or overlook our common interests. It requires us to work and live together.

Peace is not only a matter of noble words and Nobel lectures. We have ample words, glorious words, inscribed in the charters of the United Nations, the World Court, the Organization of American States and a network of international treaties and laws. We need deeds that will respect those words, honor those commitments, abide by those laws. We need to strengthen our institutions of peace like the United Nations, making certain they are fully used by the weak as well as the strong.

I pay no attention to those doubters and detractors unwilling to believe that a lasting peace can be genuinely embraced by those who march under a different ideological banner or those who are more accustomed to cannons of war than to councils of peace.

We seek in Central America not peace alone, not peace to be followed someday by political progress, but peace and democracy, together, indivisible, an end to the shedding of human blood, which is inseparable from an end to the suppression of human rights.

We do not judge, much less condemn, any other nation's political or ideological systems, freely chosen and never exported. We cannot require sovereign states to conform to patterns of government not of their own choosing. But we can and do insist that every government respect those universal rights of man that have meaning beyond national boundaries and ideological labels. We believe that justice and peace can only thrive together, never apart. A nation that mistreats its own citizens is more likely to mistreat its neighbors.

To receive this Nobel Prize on the 10th of December is for me a marvelous coincidence. My son Oscar Felipe, here present, is 8 years old today. I say to him, and through him to all the children of my country, that we shall never resort to violence, we shall never support military solutions problems of Central America. It is for the new generation that we must understand more than ever that peace can only be achieved through its own instruments: dialogue and understanding, tolerance and forgiveness, freedom and democracy.

I know well you share what we say to all members of the international community, and particularly to those both in the East and the West, with far greater power and resources than my small nation could ever hope to possess. I say to them, with the utmost urgency: Let Central America decide the future of Central America. Leave the interpretation and implementation of our peace plan to us. Support the efforts for peace instead of the forces of war in our region. Send our people plowshares instead of swords, pruning hooks instead of spears. If they, for their own purposes, cannot refrain from amassing the weapons of war, then, in the name of God, at least they should leave us in peace.

I say here to his majesty and to the honorable members of the Nobel Peace Committee, to the wonderful people of Norway, that I accept this prize because I know how passionately you share our quest for peace, our eagerness for success. If, in the years to come, peace prevails, and violence and war are thus avoided, a large part of that peace will be due to the faith of the people of Norway and will be theirs forever.

CUMULATIVE INDEX, 1983-1987

A

C

D

E

F

G

H

M

N

O

P

S

T

U

V

W

Y

Z